EIGHTH EDITION

Patterns for College Writing

A RHETORICAL READER AND GUIDE

EIGHTH EDITION

Patterns for College Writing

A RHETORICAL READER AND GUIDE

LAURIE G. KIRSZNER

University of the Sciences
in Philadelphia

STEPHEN R. MANDELL

Drexel University

BEDFORD/ST. MARTIN'S

Boston ◆ New York

For Bedford/St. Martin's

Senior Developmental Editor: Talvi Laev
Production Editor: Katherine Moreau
Senior Production Supervisor: Joe Ford
Marketing Manager: Brian Wheel
Cover Design and Art Direction: Lucy Krikorian
Text Design: Anna George
Copy Editor: Pat Cabeza
Cover Art: © 2000 Succession H. Matisse, Paris/Artists Rights Society (ARS), New York
Composition: Stratford Publishing Services, Inc.
Printing and Binding: Haddon Craftsmen, an R. R. Donnelly & Sons Company

President: Charles H. Christensen
Editorial Director: Joan E. Feinberg
Editor in Chief: Nancy Perry
Director of Marketing: Karen R. Melton
Director of Editing, Design, and Production: Marcia Cohen
Managing Editor: Erica T. Appel

Library of Congress Catalog Card Number: 00-103335

For information, write: Bedford/St. Martin's, 75 Arlington Street, Boston, MA 02116 (617-399-4000)

ISBN: 0-312-24736-2

Acknowledgments

Maya Angelou, "Finishing School." Excerpt from *I Know Why the Caged Bird Sings* by Maya Angelou. Copyright © 1969 by Maya Angelou. Reprinted by permission of Random House, Inc.
Steve Bauman, "Games as a Scapegoat" from *Computer Games*, September 1999. Copyright © 1999 by Steve Bauman. Reprinted by permission.

Acknowledgments and copyrights are continued at the back of the book on pages 701–704, which constitute an extension of the copyright page.

For Peter Phelps (1936–1990), with thanks

PREFACE

Since it was first published in 1980, *Patterns for College Writing* has been adopted at close to a thousand colleges and universities across the country. We have been gratified by the overwhelmingly positive response to the first seven editions of *Patterns,* and we continue to be humbled and awed by the many instructors who find *Patterns* to be the most accessible and most pedagogically sound rhetoric-reader they have ever used. In preparing this eighth edition, we have worked hard to fine-tune — and, in some cases, to redefine — the features that have made *Patterns* the most popular composition reader available today.

WHAT STUDENTS AND INSTRUCTORS LIKE ABOUT *PATTERNS FOR COLLEGE WRITING*

An Emphasis on Critical Reading

The opening chapter, "Introduction: Reading to Write," shows students how to apply critical reading strategies to a typical selection and provides sample responses to various kinds of writing prompts. Not only does this chapter orient students to the book's features, it also prepares them to tackle reading and writing assignments in other courses.

Extensive Coverage of the Writing Process

Part One, "The Writing Process" (Chapters 1 through 3), functions as a mini-rhetoric, offering advice on planning, writing, and revising as it introduces students to activities like brainstorming, clustering, journal writing, and editing. These chapters also include some twenty writing exercises to give students opportunities for immediate practice.

Detailed Coverage of the Patterns of Development

In Part Two, "Readings for Writers," Chapters 4 through 12 explain and illustrate the patterns of development that students typically use in their college writing assignments: narration, description, exemplification, process, cause and effect, comparison and contrast, classification and division, definition, and argumentation. Each chapter begins with a comprehensive introduction that first presents a definition and a paragraph-length example of the pattern to be discussed and then explains the particular writing strategies and applications associated with it. Next, each chapter analyzes one or two annotated student papers to show how the pattern can be used in particular college writing situations. Chapter 13, "Combining the Patterns," illustrates how the various patterns of development discussed in Chapters 4 through 12 can work together in an essay.

A Diverse and Popular Selection of Readings

Varied in subject, style, and cultural perspective, the sixty-nine professional essays engage students while providing them with outstanding models for writing. We have sought a balance between classic authors (George Orwell, E. B. White, Martin Luther King Jr.) and newer voices (Alice Walker, Scott Russell Sanders, Amy Tan) so that instructors have a broad range to choose from.

More Student Essays Than Any Competing Text

To provide students with realistic models for improving their own writing, we include sixteen sample essays by actual students. These essays are also available as transparency masters so that instructors can use them more effectively in the classroom.

Apparatus Designed to Help Students Learn

To help students as they read, write, and revise, each essay is preceded by an informative headnote and followed by four types of questions. These questions are designed to help students assess their understanding of the essay's content and of the writer's purpose and audience; to recognize the stylistic and structural techniques used to shape the essay; and to become sensitive to the nuances of language. Each essay is also accompanied by a Journal Entry prompt, Writing Workshop topics (suggestions for full-length writing assignments), and Thematic Connections identifying related readings in the text. The Combining the Patterns feature highlights the ways in which different patterns are used together in the essay. Each chapter ends with a list of Writing Assignments, a Collaborative Activity, and — new to this edition — an Internet Assignment.

WHAT'S NEW IN THIS EDITION

Engaging New Readings

Eighteen new readings — more than a quarter of the selections in the text — treat topics of current interest, from the Internet to gun control to cultural identity. Some are by well-known writers such as Mary Gordon, Richard Rodriguez, and Henry Louis Gates Jr., while others introduce newer yet equally compelling voices, including those of Linda Hasselstrom, Nate Stulman, and Janet Wu.

Headnotes Situating the Readings in Time and Place

Thoroughly revised for this edition, the headnotes now provide students with a cultural and historical context for each reading, helping them make connections between the readings and the historical, social, and economic forces that shaped them.

Writing Instruction That's Easier to Use

The very popular "mini-rhetoric" in Part One, "The Writing Process," is now presented in three shorter chapters that make the material even more accessible and useful for students. Throughout Part Two, "Readings for Writers," useful checklists now reinforce each chapter's key concepts and help students plan and revise their papers.

A New Debate and a New Casebook in the Argumentation Chapter

In response to students' changing concerns, the chapter on argumentation now includes a new debate on the pros and cons of allocating separate campus housing to particular ethnic groups ("Should We Live Together or Apart?") and a new casebook of five readings on technology ("Is the Internet Good for Society?").

Guided Internet Assignments

To help students learn to use Internet sources effectively, each of the chapters in Part Two concludes with a guided assignment that asks students to write an essay incorporating information from World Wide Web sources. (The Argumentation chapter includes three Internet Assignments.)

Expanded Coverage of Writing Research Papers

The appendix "Writing a Research Paper" now takes students though the complete process of writing a research paper — from choosing a topic and doing research to avoiding plagiarism and documenting sources. The appendix also includes the most recent MLA citation guidelines as well as a fully documented student paper drawing on readings from the casebook on media violence.

MORE SUPPORT FOR INSTRUCTORS THAN ANY OTHER READER

The extensive ancillary package available to instructors who adopt *Patterns,* includes the following items:

- *An Instructor's Edition* incorporating *Resources for Instructors,* which gives instructors guidance in teaching from the text and provides sample answers to the questions following each reading. (*Resources for Instructors* is also available as a separate booklet.)
- *Transparency Masters* featuring ten peer-editing worksheets and sixteen sample student essays.
- *A Companion Web Site* <http://www.bedfordstmartins.com/patterns> offering additional argumentation support materials featuring TopLinks, a database that guides students to the best links available on the most commonly chosen writing topics.

Acknowledgments

As always, friends, colleagues, students, and family all helped this project along. Of particular value were the responses to questionnaires sent to users of the seventh edition, and we thank each of the instructors who responded so frankly and helpfully: John Michael Ames, Santa Fe Community College; Lee Barnes, Community College of Southern Nevada; Meleia Barnhill, Gadsden State Community College; Amy Barton, Mississippi State University; Guy E. Bennett III, Wayne Community College; Carl D. Brace, Daytona Beach Community College; John Brocato, Mississippi State University; Todd Bunnell, Mississippi State University; Paul N. Cahoon, Albuquerque T-VI; Donna Campbell, Gonzaga University; Carlos A. Campo, Community College of Southern Nevada; Tracy Carr, Mississippi State University; Don Chambless, Montgomery College; Michael Cochran, Santa Fe Community College; Shelby Cochran, Gadsden State Community College; Jean M. Crockett, Cleveland State Community College; Emily Dial-Driver, Rogers State University; Laura A. Eberhardt, Mississippi State University; Nancy S. Ellis, Mississippi State University; Mike Felker, South Plains College; Muriel Fuqua, Daytona Beach Community College; Loris D. Galford, McNeese State University; Iris Rose Hart, Santa Fe Community College; Ronald J. Heckelman, Montgomery College; Misty L. Hickson, Mississippi State University; Gloria B. Isles, Greenville Technical College; Jackie Jablonski, St. Clair County Community College; Karin Jackson, University Maine at Augusta; Rebecca Kamm, Northeast Iowa Community College; Stephanie H. Kauffman,

Albuquerque T-VI; Howard A. Kerner, Polk Community College; Linda Kimball, Gonzaga University; Samantha Leass, Montgomery College; Lindsay Lewan, Arapahoe Community College; Linda Lyle, Gadsden State Community College; Manuel Martinez, Santa Fe Community College; Stephen L. Mathewson, Albuquerque T-VI; Deborah McCollister, Dallas Baptist University; Deborah A. McDavis, Santa Fe Community College; Heather J. McDonald, Daytona Beach Community College; Delma McLeod-Porter, McNeese State University; Liz Meador, Wayne Community College; Barbara Muller, Albuquerque T-VI; Mary G. Newell, Santa Fe Community College; Kate Horsley Parker, Albuquerque T-VI; Andrea Porter, Mississippi State University; Ron Puckett, Polk Community College; Kyle Reynolds, Mississippi State University; Geri Rhodes, Albuquerque T-VI; Jude M. Ryan, Polk Community College; Frank Sesso, Rogers State University; Mary Pigford Smith, Gadsden State Community College; Rosie M. Soy, Hudson County Community College; Ann E. Spicer, Wayne Community College; Roberta J. Stagnaro, Southwestern College; Alison Stamps, Mississippi State University; William Stephenson, Santa Fe Community College; Phyllis M. Taufen, Gonzaga University; Nancy M. Turner, Gadsden State Community College; Chloe Warner, Polk Community College; P. K. Weston, Greenville Technical College; Hope White, Mississippi State University; and Carolyn A. Word, Santa Fe Community College.

We are also grateful to the following colleagues who provided useful commentary at various stages of the development of this new edition: J. Robert Baker, Fairmont State College; Lee Barnes, Community College of Southern Nevada; Rosemary Day, Albuquerque T-VI; Misty L. Hickson, Mississippi State University; Charles Hill, Gadsden State Community College; Jackie Jablonski, St. Clair County Community College; Martina Kusi-Mensah, Montgomery College; Susan J. Miller, Santa Fe Community College; Roxanne Munch, Joliet Junior College; Troy D. Nordman, Butler County Community College; Ron Puckett, Polk Community College; and Matt Smith, Chattanooga State Technical Community College.

Special thanks go to Mark Gallaher, a true professional and a valued friend, for revising the headnotes and the *Resources for Instructors* for this edition.

Through eight editions of *Patterns for College Writing*, we have enjoyed a wonderful working relationship with Bedford/St. Martin's. We have always found the editorial and production staff to be efficient, cooperative, and generous with their time. As always, we appreciate the encouragement and advice of our longtime friend, editor in chief Nancy Perry. In addition, we thank Chuck Christensen and Joan Feinberg, our new publishers, for their support for this project and for their trust in us. During our work on the past two editions, we have benefited from the thoughtful comments and careful attention to detail of Talvi Laev, senior development editor. We are grateful to Kathy Moreau, project editor, and to Joe Ford, senior production supervisor, for their work overseeing the production of this edition, and to Belinda Delpêche, editorial assistant, for help with tasks large and small.

We are fortunate to have enjoyed our own twenty-five-year collaboration; we know how rare a successful partnership like ours is. We also know how lucky we are to have our families — Mark, Adam, and Rebecca Kirszner and Demi, David, and Sarah Mandell — to help keep us in touch with the things that really matter.

Laurie G. Kirszner
Stephen R. Mandell

CONTENTS

    "My grandmother has bound feet. Cruelly tethered since her birth, they
    are like bonsai trees, miniature versions of what should have been. She is
    a relic even in China, where foot binding was first banned more than 80
    years ago. . . ."

    "Being only a daughter for my father meant my destiny would lead me to
    become someone's wife. That's what he believed."

    "It went without saying that all girls could iron and wash, but the fine
    touches around the home, like setting a table with real silver, baking roasts
    and cooking vegetables without meat, had to be learned elsewhere. . . . Dur-
    ing my tenth year, a white woman's kitchen became my finishing school."

7 PROCESS 217

9 COMPARISON AND CONTRAST   *321*

WILLIAM ZINSSER, *College Pressures*   390

"What I wish for all my students is some release from the clammy grip of the future. I wish them a chance to savor each segment of their education as an experience in itself and not as a grim preparation for the next step. I wish them the right to experiment, to trip and fall, to learn that defeat is as instructive as victory and is not the end of the world."

SCOTT RUSSELL SANDERS, *The Men We Carry in Our Minds*   399

"So I was baffled when the women at college accused me and my sex of having cornered the world's pleasures. I think something like my bafflement has been felt by other boys (and by girls as well) who grew up in dirt-poor farm country, in mining country, in black ghettos, in Hispanic barrios, in the shadows of factories, in Third World nations — any place where the fate of men is as grim and bleak as the fate of women."

AMY TAN, *Mother Tongue*   405

"I spend a great deal of my time thinking about the power of language — the way it can evoke an emotion, a visual image, a complex idea, or a simple truth. Language is the tool of my trade. And I use them all — all the Englishes I grew up with."

ALLEEN PACE NILSEN, *Sexism in English: Embodiment and Language*   413

"What these incidents show is that sexism is not something existing independently in American English or in the particular dictionary that I happened to read. Rather, it exists in people's minds."

STEPHANIE ERICSSON, *The Ways We Lie*   426

"We lie. We all do. We exaggerate, we minimize, we avoid confrontation, we spare people's feelings, we conveniently forget, we keep secrets, we justify lying to the big-guy institutions."

11 DEFINITION   *455*

THEMATIC GUIDE TO THE CONTENTS

READING AND WRITING

EDUCATION

BUSINESS AND WORK

SPORTS

RACE AND CULTURE

GENDER

NATURE AND THE ENVIRONMENT

MEDIA AND SOCIETY

HISTORY AND POLITICS

ETHICS

EIGHTH EDITION

Patterns for College Writing

A RHETORICAL READER AND GUIDE

INTRODUCTION: READING TO WRITE

On a purely practical level, you will read the selections in this text to answer study questions and prepare for class discussions. More significantly, however, you will also read to evaluate the ideas of others, to form judgments, and to develop original points of view. By introducing you to new ideas and new ways of thinking about familiar concepts, reading prepares you to respond critically to the ideas of others and to develop ideas of your own. When you understand what you read, you are able to form opinions, exchange ideas with others in conversation, ask and answer questions, and develop ideas that can be further explored in writing. For all of these reasons, reading is a vital part of your education.

READING CRITICALLY

Reading is a two-way street. Readers are presented with a writer's ideas, but they also bring their own responses and interpretations to what they read. After all, readers have different national, ethnic, cultural, and geographic backgrounds and different kinds of knowledge and experiences, and so they may react differently to a particular essay or story. For example, readers from an economically and ethnically homogeneous suburban neighborhood may have difficulty understanding a story about class conflict, but these readers may also be more objective than readers who are struggling with such conflict in their own lives.

These differences in reactions do not mean that every interpretation is acceptable, that an essay or story or poem may mean whatever a reader wants it to mean. Readers must make sure they are not distorting the writer's words, overlooking (or ignoring) significant details, or seeing things in an essay or story that do not exist. It is not important for all readers to agree on a particular interpretation of a work. It is important, however, for each reader to develop an interpretation that can be supported by the work itself.

1

The study questions that accompany the essays in this text encourage you to question writers' ideas. Although some of the questions — particularly those listed under *Comprehension* — call for fairly straightforward factual responses, other questions — particularly those designated *Journal Entry* — invite more complex responses, reflecting your individual reaction to the selections.

READING ACTIVELY

When you read an essay in this text, or any work that you expect to discuss in class (and perhaps to write about), you should read it carefully — and you should read it more than once.

Before You Read

Before you read, look over the essay to get an overview of its content. If the selection has a *headnote* — a paragraph or two about the author or the work — begin by reading it. Next, skim the work to get a general sense of the writer's ideas. As you read, note the title and any internal headings as well as the use of boldface type, italics, and other design elements. Also pay special attention to the introductory and concluding paragraphs, where a writer is likely to make (or reiterate) key points.

As You Read

As you read, ask yourself questions like those in the following checklist.

☑ **CHECKLIST: READING ACTIVELY**

- What is the writer's general subject?
- What is the writer's main point?
- Does the writer seem to have a particular purpose in mind?
- What kind of audience is the writer addressing?
- Are the writer's ideas consistent with your own?
- Do you have any knowledge that could challenge the writer's ideas?
- Is any information missing?
- Are any sequential or logical links missing?
- Can you identify themes or ideas that also appear in other works you have read?
- Can you identify parallels with your own experience?

HIGHLIGHTING AND ANNOTATING

As you read and reread, be sure to record your reactions in writing. These notations will help you understand the writer's ideas and your own thinking about these ideas. Every reader develops a different system of recording such responses, but many readers use a combination of *highlighting* and *annotating*.

When you **highlight,** you mark the text with symbols. You might, for example, underline important ideas, box key terms, number a series of related points, circle an unfamiliar word (or place a question mark beside it), draw vertical lines in the margin beside a particularly interesting passage, draw arrows to connect related points, or star discussions of the work's central issues or themes.

When you **annotate,** you carry on a conversation with the text in marginal notes. You might, among other things, ask questions, suggest possible parallels with other reading selections or with your own experiences, argue with the writer's points, comment on the writer's style, or define unfamiliar terms and concepts.

The following paragraph, excerpted from Maya Angelou's "Finishing School" (page 00), illustrates the method of highlighting and annotating described above.

Date written?	(Recently) a white woman from Texas, who would quickly describe herself as a (liberal,) asked me about my hometown. When I told her that in Stamps my grandmother had owned the only Negro general merchandise store since the turn of the century, she	Why does she mention this?
Serious or sarcastic?	exclaimed, "Why, you were a (debutante)." Ridiculous and even ludicrous. But Negro girls in small Southern towns, whether poverty-stricken or just munching along on a few of life's necessities, were	Also true of boys? In North as well as South?
*	given as extensive and irrelevant preparations for adulthood as rich white girls shown in magazines. Admittedly the training was not the same. While white girls learned to waltz and sit gracefully with a tea cup balanced on their knees, we were lagging	True today?
What are these values?	behind, learning the (mid-Victorian values) with very little money to indulge them. . . .	

Remember that this process of highlighting and annotating is not an end in itself but rather a step toward understanding what you have read. Annotations suggest questions; in your search for answers, you may ask your instructor for clarification, or you may raise particularly puzzling or provocative points during class discussion or in small study groups. After your questions have been answered, you will be able to discuss and write about what you have read with greater confidence, accuracy, and authority.

READING THE SELECTIONS IN THIS BOOK

The selection that follows, "'What's in a Name?'" by Henry Louis Gates Jr., is typical of the essays in this text. It is preceded by a headnote that provides information about the author's life and career and provides a social, historical, or cultural context for the essay. As you read the essay and the headnote, highlight and annotate them carefully.

HENRY LOUIS GATES JR.

Henry Louis Gates Jr. was born in 1950 in Keyser, West Virginia, and grew up in the small town of Piedmont. Currently W. E. B. Du Bois Professor of Humanities and chair of the Afro-American Studies Department at Harvard, he has edited many collections of works by African-American writers and published several volumes of literary criticism. However, he is probably best known as a social critic whose books and articles for a general audience explore a wide variety of issues and themes, often focusing on issues of race and culture.

In the following essay, which originally appeared in the journal *Dissent* in 1989, Gates recalls a childhood experience that occurred during the mid-1950s. Although the first stirrings of the civil rights movement had begun at the time, much of the country — particularly the South — was still segregated, and prejudice against blacks was the norm in many communities. The incident Gates recalls helped him understand the significance of race in his society and the extent to which even the most accommodating blacks were virtually powerless to change white people's often dehumanizing views of them.

"What's in a Name?"

The question of color takes up much space in these pages, but the question of color, especially in this country, operates to hide the graver questions of the self.
— JAMES BALDWIN, *1961*

. . . blood, darky, Tar Baby, Kaffir, shine . . . moor, blackamoor, Jim Crow, spook . . . quadroon, meriney, red bone, high yellow . . . Mammy, porch monkey, home, homeboy, George . . . spearchucker, schwarze, Leroy, Smokey . . . mouli, buck. Ethiopian, brother, sistah. . . .
— TREY ELLIS, *1989*

I had forgotten the incident completely, until I read Trey Ellis's essay "Remember My Name" in a recent issue of the *Village Voice* (June 13, 1989). But there, in the middle of an extended italicized list of the bynames of "the race" ("the race" or "our people" being the terms my parents used in polite or reverential discourse, "jigaboo" or "nigger" more commonly used in anger, jest, or pure disgust), it was: "George." Now the events of that very brief exchange return to mind so vividly that I wonder why I had forgotten it.

My father and I were walking home at dusk from his second job. He "moonlighted" as a janitor in the evenings for the telephone company. Every day but Saturday, he would come home at 3:30 from his regular job at the paper mill, wash up, eat supper, then at 4:30 head downtown to his second job. He used to make jokes frequently about a union official who moonlighted. I never got the joke, but he and his friends thought it was

5

hilarious. All I knew was that my family always ate well, that my brother and I had new clothes to wear, and that all of the white people in Piedmont, West Virginia, treated my parents with an odd mixture of resentment and respect that even we understood at the time had something directly to do with a small but certain measure of financial security.

He had left a little early that evening because I was with him and I had to be in bed early. I could not have been more than five or six, and we had stopped off at the Cut-Rate Drug Store (where no black person in town but my father could sit down to eat, and eat off real plates with real silverware) so that I could buy some caramel ice cream, two scoops in a wafer cone, please, which I was busy licking when Mr. Wilson walked by.   3

Mr. Wilson was a very quiet man, whose stony, brooding, silent manner seemed designed to scare off any overtures of friendship, even from white people. He was Irish, as was one-third of our village (another third being Italian), the more affluent among whom sent their children to "Catholic School" across the bridge in Maryland. He had white straight hair, like my Uncle Joe, whom he uncannily resembled, and he carried a black worn metal lunch pail, the kind that Riley* carried on the television show. My father always spoke to him, and for reasons that we never did understand, he always spoke to my father.   4

"Hello, Mr. Wilson," I heard my father say.   5

"Hello, George."   6

I stopped licking my ice cream cone, and asked my Dad in a loud voice why Mr. Wilson had called him "George."   7

"Doesn't he know your name, Daddy? Why don't you tell him your name? Your name isn't George."   8

For a moment I tried to think of who Mr. Wilson was mixing Pop up with. But we didn't have any Georges among the colored people in Piedmont; nor were there colored Georges living in the neighboring towns and working at the mill.   9

"Tell him your name, Daddy."   10

"He knows my name, boy," my father said after a long pause. "He calls all colored people George."   11

A long silence ensued. It was "one of those things," as my Mom would put it. Even then, that early, I knew when I was in the presence of "one of those things," one of those things that provided a glimpse, through a rent curtain, at another world that we could not affect but that affected us. There would be a painful moment of silence, and you would wait for it to give way to a discussion of a black superstar such as Sugar Ray or Jackie Robinson.   12

"Nobody hits better in a clutch than Jackie Robinson."   13

"That's right. Nobody."   14

I never again looked Mr. Wilson in the eye.   15

---

*EDS. NOTE — The lead character in a 1950s sitcom titled *The Life of Riley.*

RESPONDING TO READING SELECTIONS

Once you have read a selection carefully and recorded your initial reactions to it, you should be able to respond to specific questions about it. The study questions that follow each essay in Chapters 4 through 13 of this text will guide you through the rest of the reading process and help you think critically about what you are reading. Five types of questions follow each essay:

Comprehension questions help you to measure your understanding of what the writer is saying.

Purpose and Audience questions ask you to consider why, and for whom, each selection was written and to examine the implications of the writer's choices in view of a particular purpose or intended audience.

Style and Structure questions encourage you to examine the decisions the writer has made about elements like arrangement of ideas, paragraphing, sentence structure, diction, and imagery.

Vocabulary Projects ask you to define certain words, to consider the connotations of others, and to examine the writer's reasons for selecting particular words or word patterns.

Journal Entry questions ask you to respond informally to what you read and to speculate freely about related ideas — perhaps exploring ethical issues raised by the selection or offering your opinions about the writer's statements. Briefer, less polished, and less structured than full-length essays, journal entries not only allow you to respond critically to a reading selection but may also suggest ideas for more formal kinds of writing.

Following these sets of questions are three additional features:

Writing Workshop assignments ask you to write essays structured according to the pattern of development explained and illustrated in the chapter.

Combining the Patterns questions focus on the other patterns of development — besides the essay's dominant pattern — that the writer uses. These questions ask why a writer uses particular patterns (narration, description, exemplification, process, cause and effect, comparison and contrast, classification and division, definition), what each pattern contributes to the essay, and what other choices the writer had.

Thematic Connections identify other readings in this book that deal with the same theme or a similar one. Reading these related works will enhance your understanding and appreciation of the original work. (The Thematic Connections identify two or more works related to each reading selection; you should look for others as well.)

The final selection in each chapter, a story or poem, is followed by *Thinking about Literature* questions, a *Journal Entry,* and *Thematic Connections.* Finally, at the end of each chapter, *Writing Assignments* offer additional practice in writing essays structured according to a particular pattern of development, a *Collaborative Activity* suggests an idea for a group project, and an *Internet Assignment* suggests an additional possibility for writing about the pattern.

Following are some examples of study questions and possible responses as well as a Writing Workshop assignment and Thematic Connections for "'What's in a Name?'" (pages 5–6). The numbers in parentheses after quotations refer to the paragraphs in which the quotations appear.

• • •

COMPREHENSION

1. *In paragraph 1, Gates wonders why he forgot about the exchange between his father and Mr. Wilson. Why do you think he forgot about it?* Gates may have forgotten about the incident simply because it was something that happened a long time ago, or because such incidents were commonplace when he was a child. Alternatively, he may *not* have forgotten the exchange between his father and Mr. Wilson but rather pushed it out of his mind because he found it so painful. (After all, he says he was never again able to look Mr. Wilson in the eye.)

2. *How was the social status of Gates's family different from that of other black families in Piedmont, West Virginia? How does Gates account for this difference?* Gates's family was different from other African-American families in town in that they were treated with "an odd mixture of resentment and respect" (2) by whites. Although other blacks were not permitted to eat at the drugstore, Mr. Gates was. Gates attributes this social status to his family's "small but certain measure of financial security" (2). Even so, when Mr. Wilson insulted Mr. Gates, the privileged status of the Gates family was revealed to be false.

3. *What does Gates mean when he says, "It was 'one of those things,' as my Mom would put it" (12)?* Gates's comment indicates that the family learned to see such mistreatment as routine. In context, the word *things* in paragraph 12 refers to the kind of incident that gave Gates and his family a glimpse of the way the white world operated.

4. *Why did Gates's family turn to discussions of "black superstars" after a "painful moment of silence" (12) such as the one he describes?* Although Gates does not explain the family's behavior, we can infer that they spoke of African-American heroes like prizefighter Sugar Ray Robinson and baseball player Jackie Robinson to make themselves feel better. Such discussions were a way of balancing the negative images of African Americans created by incidents such as the one Gates describes and of bolstering the low self-esteem the family felt as a result. These heroes seemed to have won the respect denied to the Gates family; to mention them was to participate vicariously in their glory.

5. *Why do you think Gates "never again looked Mr. Wilson in the eye" (15)?* Gates may have felt that Mr. Wilson was somehow the enemy, not to be trusted, because he had insulted Gates's father. Or he may have been ashamed to look him in the eye because he believed his father should have insisted on being addressed properly.

PURPOSE AND AUDIENCE

1. *Why do you think Gates introduces his narrative with the two quotations he selects? How do you suppose he expects his audience to react to them? How do you react?* Gates begins with two quotations, both by African-American writers, written nearly thirty years apart. Baldwin's words seem to suggest that, in the United States, "the question of color" is a barrier to understanding "the graver questions of the self." That is, the labels *black* and *white* may mask more fundamental characteristics or issues. Ellis's list of names (many pejorative) for African Americans illustrates the fact that epithets can dehumanize people — they can, in effect, rob a person of his or her "self." This issue of the discrepancy between a name and what lies behind it is central to Gates's essay. In one sense, then, Gates begins with these two quotations because they are relevant to the issues he will discuss. More specifically, he is using the two quotations — particularly Ellis's string of unpleasant names — to arouse interest in his topic and provide an intellectual and emotional context for his story. He may also be intending to make his white readers uncomfortable and his black readers angry. How you react depends on your attitudes about race (and perhaps about language).

2. *What is the point of Gates's narrative? That is, why does he recount the incident?* It is difficult to isolate any one specific point this narrative makes. Certainly Gates wishes to make readers aware of the awkward, and potentially dangerous, position of his father (and, by extension, of other African Americans) in a small southern town in the 1950s. He also shows us how names help to shape people's perceptions and actions: as long as Mr. Wilson can call all black men "George," he can continue to see them as insignificant and treat them as inferiors. The title of the piece does, however, suggest that the way names shape perceptions is the writer's main point.

3. *The title of this selection, which Gates places in quotation marks, is an allusion to act 2, scene 2 of Shakespeare's* Romeo and Juliet, *where Juliet says, "What's in a name? That which we call a rose / By any other name would smell as sweet." Why do you think Gates chose this title? Does he expect his audience to recognize the quotation?* Because his work was originally published in a journal read by a well-educated audience, Gates probably expected readers to recognize the allusion (and also to be knowledgeable about 1950s race relations). Although Gates could not have been certain that all members of this audience would recognize the reference to *Romeo and Juliet,* he could have been reasonably sure that if they did, it would enhance their understanding of the selection. In Shakespeare's play the two lovers are kept apart essentially because of their names: she is a Capulet and he is a Montague, and the two families are involved in a bitter feud. In the speech from which Gates takes the title quotation, Juliet questions the logic of such a situation. In her view, what a person is called should not determine how he or she is regarded — and this, of course, is one of Gates's points as well. Even if readers are not able to recognize the allusion, however, the title still foreshadows the selection's focus on names.

STYLE AND STRUCTURE

1. *Does paragraph 1 add something vital to the narrative, or would Gates's story make sense without the introduction? Could another kind of introduction work as well?* Gates's first paragraph supplies the context in which the incident is to be read — that is, it makes clear that Mr. Wilson's calling Mr. Gates "George" was not an isolated incident but rather part of a pattern of behavior that allowed those in positions of power to mistreat those they considered inferior. For this reason, it is an effective introduction. Although the narrative would make sense without paragraph 1, the story's full impact would probably not be as great. Still, Gates could have begun differently. For example, he could have started with the incident itself (paragraph 2) and interjected his comments about the significance of names later in the piece. He could also have begun with the exchange of dialogue in paragraphs 5 through 11 and then introduced the current paragraph 1 to supply the incident's context.

2. *What does the use of dialogue contribute to the narrative? Would the selection have a different impact without dialogue? Explain.* Gates was five or six years old when the incident occurred, and the dialogue helps to establish the child's innocence as well as his father's quiet acceptance of the situation. In short, the dialogue is a valuable addition to the piece because it creates two characters, one innocent and one resigned to injustice, both of whom stand in contrast to the voice of the adult narrator: wise, worldly, but also angry and perhaps ashamed, the voice of a man who has benefited from the sacrifices of men like Gates's father.

3. *Why do you think Gates supplies the specific details he chooses in paragraphs 2 and 3? In paragraph 4? Is all this information necessary?* The details Gates provides in paragraphs 2 and 3 help to establish the status of the Gates family in Piedmont; because readers have this information, the fact that the family was ultimately disregarded and discounted by whites emerges as deeply ironic. The information in paragraph 4 also contributes to this **irony**. Here we learn that Mr. Wilson was not liked by many whites, that he looked like Gates's Uncle Joe, and that he carried a lunch box — in other words, that he had no special status in the town apart from that conferred by race.

VOCABULARY PROJECTS

1. *Define each of the following words as it is used in this selection.*

   bynames (1) — nicknames
   measure (2) — extent or degree
   uncannily (4) — strangely
   rent (12) — torn
   ensued (12) — followed

2. *Consider the connotations of the words* colored *and* black, *both of which are used by Gates to refer to African Americans. What different associations does each word have? Why does Gates use both — for example,* colored *in paragraph 9 and* black *in paragraph 12? What is your response to the father's use of the term*

boy *in paragraph 11?* In the 1950s, when the incident Gates describes took place, the term *colored* was still widely used, along with *Negro,* to designate Americans of African descent. In the 1960s the terms *Afro-American* and *black* replaced the earlier names, with *black* emerging as the preferred term and remaining dominant through the 1980s. Today, although *black* is still preferred by many, *African American* is used more and more often. Because the term *colored* is the oldest designation, it may seem old-fashioned and even racist today; *black,* which connoted a certain degree of militancy in the 1960s, is probably now considered a neutral term by most people. Gates uses both words because he is speaking from two time periods. In paragraph 9, recreating the thoughts and words of a child in a 1950s southern town, he uses the term *colored;* in paragraph 12 the adult Gates, commenting in 1989 on the incident, uses *black.* The substitution of *African American* for the older terms might give the narrative a more contemporary flavor, but it might also seem awkward or forced — and, in paragraph 9, inappropriately formal. As far as the term *boy* is concerned, different readers are apt to have different responses. Although the father's use of the term can be seen as affectionate, it can also be seen as derisive in this context since it echoes the bigot's use of *boy* for all black males, regardless of age or accomplishments.

JOURNAL ENTRY

Do you think Gates's parents should have used experiences like the one in "'What's in a Name?'" to educate him about the family's social status in the community? Why do you think they chose instead to dismiss such incidents as "one of those things" (12)? Your responses to these questions should reflect your own opinions and judgments, based on your background and experiences as well as on your interpretation of the reading selection.

WRITING WORKSHOP

Write about a time when you, like Gates's father, could have spoken out in protest but chose not to. Would you make the same decision today? By the time you approach the Writing Workshop questions, you will have read an essay, highlighted and annotated it, responded to study questions about it, discussed it in class, and perhaps considered its relationship to other essays in the text. Often your next step will be to write an essay in response to one of the Writing Workshop questions. (Chapters 1–3 follow Laura Bobnak, a first-year composition student, through the process of writing such an essay.)

COMBINING THE PATTERNS

Although **narration** *is the pattern of development that dominates "'What's in a Name?'" and gives it its structure, Gates also uses* **exemplification,** *presenting an extended example to support his thesis. What is this example? What does it illustrate? Would several brief examples have been more convincing?* The extended example is the story of the encounter between Gates's father and Mr. Wilson, which compellingly illustrates the kind of behavior African Americans were often forced to adopt in the 1950s. Because Gates's introduction focuses on "the incident" (1), one extended example is enough (although he alludes to other incidents in paragraph 12).

THEMATIC CONNECTIONS

- "Finishing School" (page 88)
- "Sexism in English: Embodiment and Language" (page 413)

As you read and think about the selections in this text, you should begin to see thematic links among them. Such parallels can add to your interest and understanding as well as give you ideas for group discussion and writing. For example, Maya Angelou's "Finishing School," another autobiographical essay by an African-American writer, has many similarities with Gates's. Both essays describe the uneasy position of a black child expected to conform to the white world's unfair code of behavior, and both deal squarely with the importance of being called by one's name. In fact, paragraph 26 of "Finishing School" offers some helpful insights into the problem Gates examines. A less obvious but equally valid thematic link exists between "'What's in a Name?'" and Alleen Pace Nilsen's "Sexism in English: Embodiment and Language," which also considers the dangers of using language to separate and demean a group of people.

In the process of thinking about Gates's narrative, discussing it in class, or preparing to write an essay on a related topic (such as those listed under Writing Workshop), you might find it useful to consider (or reconsider) Angelou's and Nilsen's essays.

Part One
THE WRITING PROCESS

Every reading selection in this book is the result of a struggle between a writer and his or her material. If a writer's struggle is successful, the finished work is welded together without a seam, and readers have no sense of the frustration the writer experienced while rearranging ideas or hunting for the right word. Writing is no easy business, even for a professional writer. Still, although no simple formula for good writing exists, some approaches are easier and more productive than others.

At this point you may be asking yourself, "So what? What has this got to do with me? I'm not a professional writer." True enough, but during the next few years you will be doing a good deal of writing. Throughout your college career, you will need to write midterms, final exams, lab reports, essays, and research papers. In your professional life, you may have to write progress reports, proposals, business correspondence, and memos. As diverse as these tasks may seem, they have something in common: they can be made easier if you are familiar with the **writing process** — the procedure experienced writers follow to produce a finished piece of writing.

The writing process has three stages:

- Invention
- Arrangement
- Drafting and revision

During *invention*, also called *prewriting*, you decide what you will write about and gather information to support or explain what you want to say. During *arrangement*, you decide how you are going to organize your ideas. Finally, during *drafting and revision*, you move through several drafts as you reconsider ideas and refine your style and structure. When you have finished revising, you move on to *editing*: correcting grammar, punctuation, and mechanics.

Although the writing process is usually presented as a series of neatly defined steps, this model does not reflect the way people actually write. For one thing, ideas do not always flow easily, and the central point you set out to develop does not always wind up in the essay you ultimately write. Writing often progresses in fits and starts, with ideas occurring sporadically or not at all. In fact, much good writing occurs when a writer gets stuck or confused but continues to work until ideas take shape on the page or on the screen.

Furthermore, because the writing process is so erratic, its three stages overlap. Most writers engage in invention, arrangement, and drafting and revision simultaneously — finding ideas, considering possible methods of organization, and looking for the right words all at the same time. In fact, writing is an idiosyncratic process: no two writers approach the writing process in exactly the same way. Some people outline; others do not. Some take elaborate notes during the prewriting stage; others keep track of everything in their heads.

The writing process discussed throughout this book illustrates the many choices writers may make at various stages of composition. But regardless of writers' different approaches, one thing is certain: the more you write, the better acquainted you will become with your personal writing process and with ways to modify it to suit various writing tasks. The three chapters that follow will help you define your needs as a writer and understand your options as you approach writing assignments both in and out of college.

1

INVENTION

Invention, or **prewriting,** is an important part of the writing process. At this stage you discover what interests you about your subject and what ideas you will develop in your essay. When you are given a writing assignment, you may be tempted to plunge into a first draft immediately. Before writing, however, you should take the time to consider the assignment, explore your subject, and decide what you wish to say about it.

UNDERSTANDING THE ASSIGNMENT

Almost everything you write in college will begin as an *assignment.* Some assignments will be direct and easy to understand:

Write about an experience that changed your life.

Discuss the procedure you used to synthesize ammonia.

Others will be more difficult and complex:

According to Wayne Booth, point of view is central to understanding modern fiction. In a short essay, discuss how Henry James uses point of view in *The Turn of the Screw.*

Before beginning to write, you need to understand what you are being asked to do. If the assignment is a written question, read it carefully several times and underline its key ideas. If the assignment is read aloud by your instructor, be sure to copy it accurately. (A missed word can make quite a difference.) If you are confused about anything, ask your instructor for clarification. Remember that no matter how well written an essay is, it will miss the mark if it does not address the assignment.

SETTING LIMITS

Once you understand the assignment, you should consider its *length, purpose, audience,* and *occasion* and your own *knowledge* of the subject. Each of these factors helps you determine what you will say about your subject and thus simplifies your writing task.

Length

Often your instructor will specify an approximate length for a paper, and this word or page limit has a direct bearing on your paper's focus. For example, you would need a narrower topic for a two-page essay than for a ten-page one. Similarly, you could not discuss a question as thoroughly during an hour-long exam as you might in a paper prepared over several days.

If your instructor sets no page limit, consider how the nature of the assignment suggests its length. A *summary* of a chapter or an article, for instance, should be much shorter than the original, whereas an *analysis* of a poem will often be longer than the poem itself. If you are uncertain about the appropriate length for your paper, consult your instructor.

Purpose

Your **purpose** also limits what you say and how you say it. For example, if you were to write to a prospective employer, you would not emphasize the same aspects of college life that you would stress in a letter to a friend. In the first case, you would want to persuade the reader to hire you, so you might include your grade-point average or a list of the relevant courses you took. In the second case, you would want to inform and perhaps entertain. To accomplish these aims, you might share anecdotes about dorm life or describe one of your favorite instructors. In each case, your purpose would help you determine what information you should include to evoke a particular response in a specific audience.

In general, you can classify your purposes for writing according to your relationship to the audience. Thus, one purpose might be to express personal feelings or impressions to your readers. *Expressive* writing includes diaries, personal letters, journals, and often narrative and descriptive essays as well. Another purpose might be to inform readers about something. *Informative* writing includes essay exams, lab reports, book reports, expository essays, and some research papers. Or your purpose might be to persuade readers to think or act in a certain way. *Persuasive* writing includes editorials, argumentative essays, and many other essays and research papers.

In addition to these general purposes, you might have a more specific purpose — to analyze, entertain, hypothesize, assess, summarize, question, report, recommend, suggest, evaluate, describe, recount, request, instruct, and so on. For example, suppose you wrote a report on the incidence of AIDS in your community. Your general purpose might be to *inform* readers of the situation, but you might also want to *assess* the progression of the disease and *instruct* readers how to avoid contracting the virus that causes it.

Audience

To be effective, your essay should be written with a particular **audience** in mind. An audience can be an *individual* — your instructor, for example — or it can be a *group,* like your classmates or coworkers. Your essay could address a *specialized* audience, such as a group of medical doctors or economists, or a *general* or *universal* audience whose members have little in common, such as the readers of a newspaper or newsmagazine.

In college, your audience is usually your instructor, and your purpose in most cases is to demonstrate your mastery of the subject matter, your reasoning ability, and your competence as a writer. Other audiences may include classmates, professional colleagues, or members of your community. Considering the age and gender of your audience, its political and religious values, its social and educational level, and its interest in your subject may help you define it. Certainly the approach you took in your report about the spread of AIDS in your community would depend on your intended audience. For example, a report written for students at a local middle school would be very different from one addressing a civic group or the city council — or the parents of those students.

Often, you will find that your audience is just too diverse to be categorized. In such cases, many writers imagine a universal audience and make points that they think will appeal to a variety of readers. Sometimes writers try to imagine one typical individual in the audience — perhaps a person they know — so that they can write to someone specific. At other times, writers identify a common denominator, a role that characterizes the entire audience. For instance, when a report on the dangers of smoking asserts, "Now is the time for health-conscious individuals to demand that cigarettes be removed from the market," it automatically casts its audience in the role of health-conscious individuals.

After you define your audience, you have to determine how much or how little its members know about your subject. This helps you decide how much background information your readers will need in order to understand the discussion. Are they highly informed? If so, you will make your points directly. Are they relatively uninformed? If this is the case, you will have to include definitions of key terms, background information, and summaries of basic research. Keep in mind that experts in one field will still need background information in other fields. If, for example, you were writing an essay analyzing the characters in Joseph Conrad's *Heart of Darkness,* you could assume that the literature instructor who assigned the novel would not need a plot summary. However, if you wrote an essay for your history instructor that used *Heart of Darkness* to illustrate the evils of European colonialism in nineteenth-century Africa, you would probably need to include a short plot summary. (Even though your history instructor would know a lot about colonialism in Africa, she might not be familiar with the details of Conrad's work.)

Occasion

In general terms, the occasion for academic writing will be either an in-class writing exercise or an at-home assignment. In addition, different subject areas create different occasions for writing. A response suitable for a psychology or history class might not be acceptable for an English class.

Although college writing situations may seem artificial, they provide valuable practice for writing you do outside of college. Like these assignments, each writing task you do outside of college requires a special approach that suits the occasion. A memo to your coworkers, for instance, will be less formal and more limited in scope than a report to your company's president. An e-mail to members of an online discussion group might be strictly informational, whereas a letter to your state senator about preserving a local historical landmark would be persuasive as well as informational.

Knowledge

Obviously, what you know (and do not know) about a subject limits what you can say about it. Before writing about any subject, ask yourself the following questions:

- What do I know about the subject?
- What do I need to find out?
- What do I think about the subject?

Different writing situations require different kinds of knowledge. A personal essay may draw on your own experiences and observations; a term paper will require you to gain new knowledge through research. Sometimes you will be able to increase your knowledge about a topic easily because you already have a strong background in the general subject. At other times, when a general subject is unfamiliar to you, you will need to select a topic particularly carefully so that you do not get out of your depth. In many cases, the amount of time you are given to do the assignment and its page limit will guide you as you consider what you know and what you need to learn before you can write knowledgeably.

EXERCISE 1

Decide whether or not each of the following topics is appropriate for the stated limits, and then write a few sentences to explain why each topic is or is not acceptable.

1. A *two-to-three-page paper:* A history of animal testing in the cosmetics industry

2. A *two-hour final exam:* The effectiveness of bilingual education programs

☑ **CHECKLIST: SETTING LIMITS**

LENGTH

- Has your instructor specified a length?
- Does the nature of your assignment suggest a length?

PURPOSE

- Is your general purpose to express personal feelings? To inform? To persuade?
- In addition to your general purpose, do you have any more specific purposes?
- Does your assignment provide any guidelines about purpose?

AUDIENCE

- Is your audience a group or an individual?
- Are you going to address a specialized or a general audience?
- Should you take into consideration the audience's age, gender, education, biases, or political or social values?
- Should you cast your audience in a particular role?
- How much can you assume your audience knows about your subject?
- How much interest does your audience have in the subject?

OCCASION

- Are you writing an in-class exercise or an at-home assignment?
- Are you addressing a situation outside the academic setting?
- What special approaches does your occasion require?

KNOWLEDGE

- What do you know about your subject?
- What do you need to find out?
- What are your opinions about your subject?

3. A *one-hour in-class essay:* An interpretation of Andy Warhol's painting of Campbell's soup cans

4. A *letter to your college newspaper:* A discussion of your school's policy on alcoholic beverages

EXERCISE 2

Make a list of the different audiences to whom you speak or write in your daily life. (Consider all the different people you see regularly, such as family members, your roommate, instructor, your boss, your friends, and so on.) Then, record your answers to the following questions.

1. Do you speak or write to each person in the same way and about the same things? If not, how do your approaches to these people differ?

2. List some subjects that would interest some of these people but not others. How do you account for these differences?

3. Choose one of the following subjects and describe how you would speak or write to each audience about it.
   - a local political issue
   - your favorite comic strip
   - curfews
   - academic cheating

MOVING FROM SUBJECT TO TOPIC

Although many essays begin as specific assignments or topics (see "A Student Writer" p. 24), some begin as broad areas of interest or concern. These general *subjects* always need to be narrowed to specific *topics* that can be reasonably discussed within the limits of the assignment. For example, a subject like DNA recombinant research should be interesting, but it is too vast to write about for any college assignment except in a general way. You need to limit such a subject to a topic that can be covered within the time and space available.

Subject	*Topic*
DNA recombinant research	Using DNA recombinant research to cure diabetes
Herman Melville's *Billy Budd*	Billy Budd as a Christ figure
Constitutional law	One result of the Miranda ruling
Personal computers	The uses of personal computers in elementary education

Two strategies can help you narrow a subject to a workable topic: *questions for probing* and **freewriting.**

Questions for Probing

One way to move from subject to topic is to examine your subject by asking a series of questions about it. These questions are useful because they reflect ways in which your mind operates: finding similarities and differences, for instance, or dividing a whole into its parts. By going through the following list of questions, you can explore your subject systematically. Of course, not all questions will work for every subject. Still, any question may elicit many different answers, and each answer is a possible topic for your essay.

When applied to a subject, some of these questions can yield many workable topics — some you might never have considered had you not

☑ **CHECKLIST: QUESTIONS FOR PROBING**

What happened?
When did it happen?
Where did it happen?
Who did it?
What does it look like?
What are its charactcristics?
What impressions does it make?
What are some typical cases or examples of it?
How did it happen?
What makes it work?
How is it made?
Why did it happen?
What caused it?
What does it cause?
What are its effects?
How is it like other things?
How is it different from other things?
What are its parts or types?
How can its parts or types be separated or grouped?
Do its parts or types fit into a logical order?
Into what categories can its parts or types be arranged?
On what basis can it be categorized?
How can it be defined?
How does it resemble other members of its class?
How does it differ from other members of its class?
What are its limits?

asked the questions. For example, by applying this approach to the general subject "the Brooklyn Bridge," you can generate more ideas and topics than you need:

What happened? A short history of the Brooklyn Bridge

What does it look like? A description of the Brooklyn Bridge

How is it made? The construction of the Brooklyn Bridge

What are its effects? The impact of the Brooklyn Bridge on American writers

How does it differ from other members of its class? Innovations in the design of the Brooklyn Bridge

At this point in the writing process, you mainly want to discover possible topics, and the more ideas you have, the wider your choice. So write down all the topics you think of. You can even repeat the process of probing several times to limit topics further. Once you have a list of topics, eliminate those that are not suitable — those that do not interest you or that are too complex or too simple to fit your assignment. When you have

---

🖵 COMPUTER STRATEGY

You can store the questions for probing listed on page 21 in a special file that you can open every time you have a new subject to probe. Make sure you also keep a record of your answers. If the topic you have chosen is too difficult or too narrow, you can return to the questions-for-probing file and select another topic.

---

discarded these less promising ideas, you should still have several left. You can then select the topic that best suits your paper's length, purpose, audience, and occasion as well as your interests and your knowledge of the subject.

EXERCISE 3

Indicate whether the following are general subjects or topics that are narrow enough for a short essay.

1. An argument against cigarette ads aimed at teenagers
2. A comparison of the salaries of professional basketball and football players
3. Children's television
4. Two creation stories in the Book of Genesis
5. Canadian and U.S. immigration law
6. The Haber process for the fixation of atmospheric nitrogen
7. The advantages of affirmative action programs
8. The advantages of term over whole life insurance
9. Managed health care
10. An analysis of a political cartoon in your local newspaper
11. Gender roles

EXERCISE 4

In preparation for writing an essay approximately 750 words long, choose two of the following subjects, and generate three or four topics from each by using as many of the questions for probing as you can.

1. Movie violence
2. Censorship and the Internet
3. Gun control
4. Animal rights
5. Substance abuse
6. Smoking

7. The minimum wage

8. Date rape

9. Women in combat

10. Welfare

11. The drinking age

12. Financial aid for college students

13. Grading

14. Television talk shows

15. The death penalty

Freewriting

Another strategy for moving from subject to topic is **freewriting**. You can use freewriting at any stage of the writing process — for example, to generate supporting information or to find a thesis. However, freewriting is a particularly useful way to narrow a general subject or assignment. When you freewrite, you write for a fixed period, perhaps five or ten minutes, without stopping and without paying attention to spelling, grammar, or punctuation. Your goal is to get your ideas down on paper so you can react to them. If you find you have nothing to say, write down anything until ideas begin to emerge — and in time they will. The secret is to *keep writing.* Try to focus on your subject, but don't worry if your ideas seem to wander off in other directions. The object of freewriting is to let your ideas flow. Often your best ideas will come to you from the unexpected connections you make as you write.

After completing your freewriting, read what you have written and look for ideas that you can write about. Some writers underline ideas they think they might explore in their essays. Any of these ideas could become essay topics, or they could become subjects for other freewriting exercises. You might want to freewrite again, using a new idea as your focus. This process of writing more and more narrowly focused freewriting exercises — called **looping** — can yield a great deal of useful information and help you decide on a workable topic.

💻 COMPUTER STRATEGY

If you do your freewriting on a computer, you may find that staring at your own words causes you to go blank or lose your spontaneity. One possible solution is to turn down the brightness until the screen becomes dark and then freewrite. This technique allows you to block out distracting elements and concentrate on your ideas. Once you finish freewriting, turn up the brightness and see what you have. If you have come up with an interesting idea, you can move it onto a new page and use it as the subject of a new freewriting exercise.

After reading Henry Louis Gates Jr.'s "'What's in a Name?'" (page 5), Laura Bobnak, a student in a composition class, chose to write an essay in response to this Writing Workshop question:

> Write about a time when you, like Gates's father, could have spoken out in protest but chose not to. Would you make the same decision today?

In an attempt to narrow this assignment to a workable topic, Laura freewrote the following:

> Write for ten minutes . . . ten minutes . . . at 9 o'clock in the morning — Just what I want to do in the morning — If you can't think of something to say, just write about anything. Right! Time to get this over with — An experience — should have talked — I can think of plenty of times I should have kept quiet! I should have brought coffee to class. I wonder what the people next to me are writing about. That reminds me. Next to me. Jeff Servin in chemistry. The time I saw him cheating. I was mad but I didn't do anything. I studied so hard and all he did was cheat. I was so mad. Nobody else seemed to care either. What's the difference between now and then? It's only a year and a half. . . . Honor code? Maturity? A lot of people cheated in high school. I bet I could write about this — Before and after, etc. My attitude then and now.

After some initial floundering, Laura discovered an idea that could be the basis for her essay. Although her discussion of the incident still had to be developed, Laura's freewriting had helped her discover a possible topic for her essay.

EXERCISE 5

Do a ten-minute freewriting exercise on one of the topics you generated in Exercise 4 (pages 22–23).

EXERCISE 6

Read what you have just written, underline the most interesting ideas, and choose one idea as a topic you might be able to write about in a short essay. Freewrite about this topic for another ten minutes to narrow it further and to generate ideas for your essay. Underline the ideas that seem most useful.

FINDING SOMETHING TO SAY

Once you have narrowed your subject to a workable topic, you need to find something to say about it. *Brainstorming* and *journal writing* are useful tools for generating ideas, and both strategies can be helpful at this stage of the writing process (and whenever you need to find additional material).

Brainstorming

Brainstorming can be a very productive way of discovering ideas about your topic. You can brainstorm in a group, exchanging ideas with several students in your composition class and writing down the useful ideas that come up. Or you can brainstorm on your own, quickly writing down every fact, idea, or association you can think of that relates to your topic. Your notes might include words, phrases, statements, questions, or even drawings or diagrams. Jot them down in whatever order you think of them, allowing your thoughts to wander freely. Some of the items may be inspired by your class notes; others may be ideas you got from reading or from talking with friends; still other items may be ideas you have begun to wonder about, points you thought of while moving from subject to topic, or thoughts that occurred to you as you brainstormed.

▶ A STUDENT WRITER: BRAINSTORMING

After she narrowed her subject by freewriting, Laura Bobnak decided to write about a time when she saw someone cheating and did not speak out. In order to limit her topic further and find something to say about it, she made the brainstorming notes on page 26. After reading these notes several times, Laura decided to concentrate on the differences between her attitude in high school and her current attitude. She knew that she could write a lot about this idea and relate it to the assignment, and she felt confident that her topic would be interesting both to her instructor and to the other students in the class.

Journal Writing

Journal writing can be a useful source of ideas at any stage of the writing process. Many writers routinely keep a journal, jotting down experiences or exploring ideas they may want to use when they write. They write journal entries even when they have no particular writing project in mind. Often these journal entries are the kernels from which longer pieces of writing develop. Your instructor may ask you to keep a writing journal, or you may decide to do so on your own. In either case, you will find that your journal entries are likely to be more narrowly focused than freewriting or brainstorming, perhaps examining a small part of a reading selection or even one particular statement. Sometimes you will write in

---

⌨ **COMPUTER STRATEGY**

If you're a good typist, brainstorming on your computer can save you time and effort. Most word-processing programs make it easy to create bulleted or numbered lists. A computer also enables you to experiment with different ways of arranging and grouping items from your brainstorming notes.

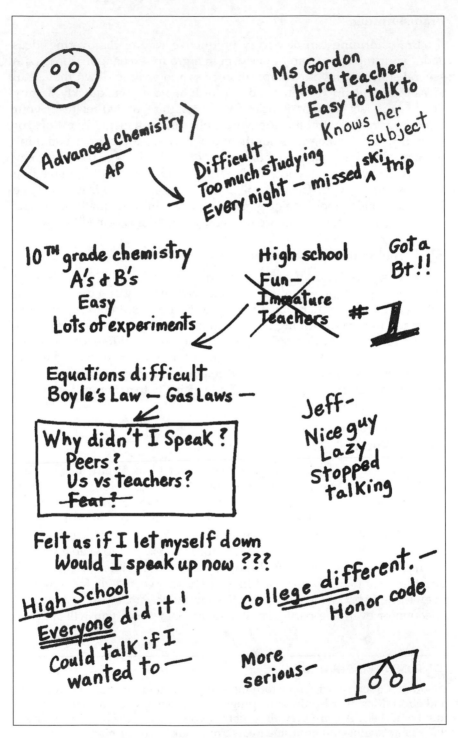

Brainstorming Notes

your journal in response to specific questions, like the Journal Entry assignments that appear throughout this book. Assignments such as these can help you start thinking about a reading selection you may later discuss in class or write about.

▶ A STUDENT WRITER: JOURNAL WRITING

In the journal entry Laura Bobnak wrote after deciding on a topic for her paper, she explores one idea from her brainstorming notes — her thoughts about her college's honor code.

> At orientation the dean of students talked about the college's honor code. She talked about how we were a community of scholars who were here for a common purpose — to take part in an intellectual dialogue. According to her, the purpose of the honor code is to make sure this dialogue continues uninterrupted. This idea sounded dumb at first, but now it makes more sense. If I saw someone cheating, I'd tell the instructor. First, though, I'd ask the *student* to go to the instructor. I don't see this as "telling" or "squealing." We're all here to get an education, and we should be able to assume everyone is being honest and fair. Besides, why should I go to all the trouble of studying while someone else does nothing and gets the same grade?

Even though Laura eventually included only a small part of this entry in her paper, writing in her journal helped her clarify her ideas about her topic.

GROUPING IDEAS

Once you have generated some material for your essay, you will want to group ideas that belong together. *Clustering* and *outlining* can help you do this.

Clustering

Clustering is a way of visually arranging your ideas so that you can tell at a glance where ideas belong and whether or not you need to generate more information. Although you can use clustering at an earlier stage of the writing process, it is especially useful now for helping you identify major points and see how ideas fit together. (Clustering can also help you

---

💻 **COMPUTER STRATEGY**

Keeping your writing journal in a computer file has some obvious advantages. Not only can you maintain a neat record of your ideas, but you can also easily move entries from your journal into an essay without retyping them.

---

narrow your paper's topic to suit its length. If you find that your cluster diagram is too detailed, you can write about just one branch of the cluster.)

Begin clustering by writing your topic in the center of a sheet of paper. After circling the topic, surround it with the words and phrases that identify the major points you intend to discuss. (You can get ideas from your brainstorming notes, from your journal, or from your freewriting.) Circle these words and phrases and connect them to the topic in the center. Next, construct other clusters of ideas relating to each major point and draw lines connecting them to the appropriate point. By dividing and subdividing your points, you get more specific as you move outward from the center of the page. In the process, you identify the facts, details, examples, and opinions that illustrate and expand your main points.

▶ A STUDENT WRITER: CLUSTERING

Because Laura Bobnak was not particularly visually oriented, she chose not to use this method of grouping her ideas. If she had, however, her cluster diagram might have looked like this:

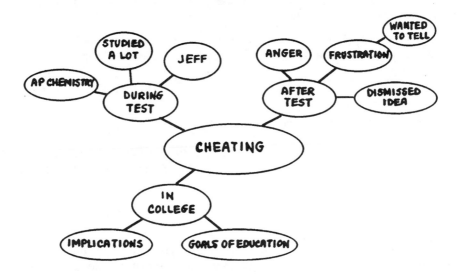

Making an Informal Outline

As an alternative or follow-up to clustering, you can organize your notes from brainstorming or other invention techniques into an *informal outline*. Quite often an informal outline is just a list of your major points, perhaps presented in some tentative order. Sometimes, however, an informal outline will include supporting details or suggest a pattern of development. Informal outlines do not specify all the major divisions and subdivisions of your paper or indicate the relative importance of your

---

⌨ **COMPUTER STRATEGY**

If you use a computer, you can easily arrange the notes generated from your prewriting activities into an informal outline. You can make an informal outline by typing words or phrases from your prewriting notes and rearranging them until the order makes sense. Later, you can use the categories from this informal outline when you construct a more formal outline.

---

ideas the way formal outlines do; they simply suggest the shape of your emerging essay.

▶ A STUDENT WRITER: MAKING AN INFORMAL OUTLINE

The following outline shows how Laura Bobnak grouped her ideas.

During test
    Found test hard
    Saw Jeff cheating

After test
    Got angry
    Wanted to tell
    Dismissed idea

In college
    Implications of cheating
    Goals of education

EXERCISE 7

Using the invention strategies discussed in this chapter, prepare to write an essay about one topic you selected in Exercise 5 on page 24. First, apply the questions for probing. Next, do five minutes of freewriting, and then brainstorm about the topic. Finally, select the ideas you plan to write about in your essay, and use either clustering or an informal outline to help you group ideas.

UNDERSTANDING THESIS AND SUPPORT

Once you have grouped your ideas and begun to see connections among them, you need to consider your essay's thesis.

A **thesis** is the main idea of your essay, its central point. The concept of *thesis and support* — stating your thesis and developing ideas that explain and expand it — is central to college writing. The essays you write will consist of several paragraphs: an *introduction* that presents your thesis statement, several *body paragraphs* that develop and support your thesis, and a *conclusion* that reinforces your thesis and provides closure. Your thesis holds this structure together; it is the center around which the rest of your essay develops.

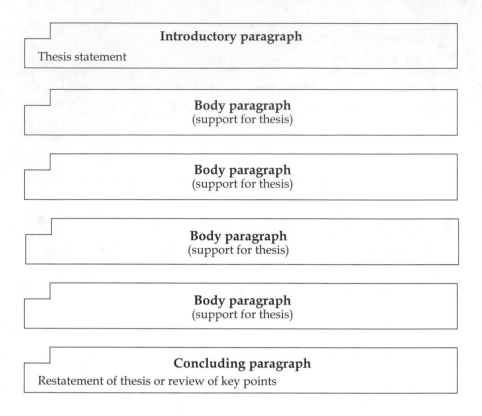

Introductory paragraph

Thesis statement

Body paragraph
(support for thesis)

Body paragraph
(support for thesis)

Body paragraph
(support for thesis)

Body paragraph
(support for thesis)

Concluding paragraph
Restatement of thesis or review of key points

FORMULATING A THESIS

Defining the Thesis Statement

A thesis statement is always more than a title, an announcement of your intent, or a statement of fact. Although a descriptive title orients your readers, it is seldom detailed enough to reveal your essay's purpose or direction. An announcement of your intent can reveal more, but it is stylistically distracting. Finally, a statement of fact — such as a historical fact or a statistic — is typically a dead end and therefore cannot be developed into an essay. A statement like "Alaska became a state in 1959" or "Tuberculosis is highly contagious" or "The population of Greece is about ten million" provides your essay with no direction. However, a judgment or opinion in response to a fact *can* be an effective thesis — for instance, "The continuing threat of tuberculosis, particularly in the inner cities, suggests it is necessary to administer more frequent diagnostic tests among high-risk populations."

To gain an appreciation of the differences among titles, announcements, statements of fact, and thesis statements, compare the statements in each of the following groups:

Title:	The Fifty-Five-Mile-per-Hour Speed Limit: Pro and Con
Announcement:	I will examine the pros and cons of doing away with the fifty-five-mile-per-hour speed limit on major highways.
Statement of fact:	There has been a sharp increase in highway deaths in those states that have abandoned the fifty-five-mile-per-hour speed limit.
Thesis statement:	The federal government should withhold highway funds from all states that have increased the speed limit from fifty-five to sixty-five miles per hour.
Title:	Orwell's "A Hanging"
Announcement:	This paper will discuss George Orwell's attitude toward the death penalty in his essay "A Hanging."
Statement of fact:	In his essay, Orwell describes a hanging that he witnessed in Burma.
Thesis statement:	In "A Hanging," George Orwell shows that capital punishment is not only unpleasant but immoral.
Title:	Speaking Out
Announcement:	This essay will discuss a time when I could have spoken out but did not.
Statement of fact:	Once I saw someone cheating and did not speak out.
Thesis statement:	As I look back on the situation, I wonder why I kept silent and what would have happened had I acted.

Deciding on a Thesis

No fixed rules determine when you formulate your thesis; the decision depends on such variables as the scope and difficulty of your assignment, your knowledge of the subject, and your method of writing. Sometimes, when you know a lot about a subject, you may be able to come up with a thesis before doing any invention activities (freewriting or brainstorming, for example). At other times, you may have to review all your material and then combine it into a single statement that communicates your position on the topic. Occasionally, your assignment may specify a thesis by telling you to take a particular position on a topic. Whatever the case, you should have a tentative thesis before you begin to write your first draft.

As you write, you will continue to discover new ideas, and you will probably move in directions that you did not anticipate. Still, because a tentative thesis gives you guidance and purpose, it is essential at the initial stages of writing. As you draft your essay, review the points you make in light of how they relate to your thesis, and revise the thesis statement or your support as necessary.

Stating Your Thesis

It is generally a good idea to include a one-sentence statement of your thesis in your essay. An effective thesis statement has three characteristics.

1. *An effective thesis statement clearly expresses your essay's main idea.* It does more than just state your topic; it indicates what you will say about your topic, and it signals how you will approach your material. The following thesis statement, from the essay "Grant and Lee: A Study in Contrasts" by Bruce Catton (page 340), clearly communicates the writer's main idea:

> They [Grant and Lee] were two strong men, these oddly different generals, and they represented the strengths of two conflicting currents that, through them, had come into final collision.

This statement indicates that the essay will compare and contrast Grant and Lee; more specifically, it reveals that Catton will present the two Civil War generals as symbols of two historical currents that were also in opposition. If the statement had been less fully developed — for example, had Catton written, "Grant and Lee were quite different from each other"— it would have just echoed the essay's title.

2. *An effective thesis statement reflects your essay's purpose.* Whether your purpose is to evaluate or analyze or simply to describe or recount, your thesis statement communicates that purpose to your readers. In general terms, your purpose may be to express personal feelings, to present information in a straightforward manner, or to persuade. Accordingly, your thesis can be *expressive,* conveying a mood or impression; it can be *informative,* perhaps listing the major points you will discuss or presenting an objective overview of the essay; or it can be *persuasive,* taking a strong stand or outlining the position you will argue.

Each of the following thesis statements expresses a different **purpose:**

To express feelings: The city's homeless families live in heartbreaking surroundings.

To inform: The plight of the homeless has become so serious that it is a major priority for many city governments.

To persuade: The only responsible reaction to the crisis at hand is to renovate abandoned city housing to provide suitable shelter for homeless families.

3. *An effective thesis statement is clearly worded.* To communicate your essay's main idea, an effective thesis statement — usually a single sentence — should be clearly and specifically worded. (It should also speak for itself. It is not necessary to write, "My thesis is that . . ." or "The thesis of this paper is. . . .") The thesis statement should give an accurate indication of what follows and not mislead readers about the essay's direction, emphasis, content, or point of view. Vague language, confusing abstrac-

tions, irrelevant details, and complex terminology have no place in a thesis statement. Keep in mind, too, that your thesis statement should not make promises that your essay is not going to keep. For example, if you are going to discuss just the effects of a new immigration law, your thesis statement should not emphasize the sequence of events that led to the law's passage.

Your thesis statement cannot, of course, include every point you will discuss in your paper. Still, it should be specific enough to indicate the direction and scope of your essay. The statement "The new immigration law has failed to stem the tide of illegal immigrants" does not give your essay much focus. Which immigration law will you be examining? Which illegal immigrants? The following sentence, however, *is* an effective thesis statement. It clearly indicates what the writer is going to discuss, and it establishes a specific direction and purpose for the essay.

> Because it fails to take into account the economic causes of illegal immigration, the 1996 immigration law does not solve the problem of illegal immigration from Mexico into the United States.

Implying a Thesis

Like an explicitly stated thesis, an *implied* thesis conveys an essay's purpose, but it does not do so directly. Instead, the purpose is suggested by the selection and arrangement of the essay's points. Many professional writers prefer this option because an implied thesis is subtler than a stated thesis. (An implied thesis is especially useful in narratives, descriptions, and some arguments, where an explicit thesis would seem heavy-handed or arbitrary.) In most college writing, however, you should state your thesis explicitly to avoid any risk of being misunderstood or of allowing the organization of your essay to go astray.

▶ A STUDENT WRITER: FORMULATING A THESIS

After experimenting with different ways of arranging her ideas for her essay, Laura Bobnak was eventually able to sum them up in a tentative thesis statement: "As I look back on the situation, I wonder why I kept silent and what would have happened had I acted."

EXERCISE 8

Assess the strengths and weaknesses of the following as thesis statements; ask yourself which statements would most effectively establish the direction of an essay, and why.

1. Myths and society.

2. Myths serve an important function in society.

3. Contrary to popular assumptions, myths are more than fairy tales; they express the underlying attitudes a society has toward important issues.

4. Today, almost two marriages in four will end in divorce.

5. Skiing, a popular sport for millions, is a major cause of winter injuries.

6. If certain reforms are not instituted immediately, our company will be bankrupt within two years.

7. Early childhood is an important period.

8. By using the proper techniques, parents can significantly improve the learning capabilities of their preschool children.

9. Fiction can be used to criticize society.

10. Fiction, in the hands of an able writer, can be a powerful tool for social reform.

EXERCISE 9

Rewrite the following factual statements to make them effective thesis statements. Make sure each thesis statement is a clearly and specifically worded sentence.

1. A number of hospitals have refused to admit patients without health insurance because they fear that such patients do not have the resources to pay their bills.

2. Several recent Supreme Court decisions say that art containing a sexual theme is not necessarily pornographic.

3. Many women earn less money than men do, in part because they drop out of the workforce during their child-rearing years.

4. People who watch more than five hours of television a day tend to think the world is more violent than do people who watch less than two hours of television daily.

5. In recent years the rate of suicide among teenagers — especially middle- and upper-middle-class teenagers — has risen dramatically.

EXERCISE 10

Read the following sentences from *Broca's Brain* by Carl Sagan. Then, formulate a one-sentence thesis statement that draws together the points Sagan makes about robots.

- "Robots, especially robots in space, have received derogatory notices in the press."
- "Each human being is a superbly constructed, astonishingly compact, self-ambulatory computer — capable on occasion of independent decision making and real control of his or her environment."
- "If we do send human beings to exotic environments, we must also send along food, air, water, waste recycling, amenities for entertainment, and companions."

- "By comparison, machines require no elaborate life-support systems, no entertainment, and no companionship, and we do not feel any strong ethical prohibitions against sending machines on one-way, or suicide, missions."
- "Even exceptionally simple computers — those that can be wired by a bright ten-year-old — can be wired to play perfect tic-tac-toe."
- "With this . . . set of examples of the state of development of machine intelligence, I think it is clear that a major effort over the next decade could produce much more sophisticated examples."
- "We appear to be on the verge of developing a wide variety of intelligent machines capable of performing tasks too dangerous, too expensive, too onerous, or too boring for human beings."
- "The main obstacle seems to be a very human problem, the quiet feeling that there is something threatening or 'inhuman' about machines."
- "But in many respects our survival as a species depends on our transcending such primitive chauvinisms."
- "There is nothing inhuman about an intelligent machine; it is indeed an expression of all those superb intellectual capabilities that only human beings . . . now possess."

EXERCISE 11

Go through as many steps as you need to formulate an effective thesis statement for an essay on the topic you developed in Exercise 7 (p. 29).

2

ARRANGEMENT

Each of the tasks discussed in Chapter 1 represents a series of choices you have to make about your topic and your material. Now, before you actually begin to write, you have another choice to make: how to arrange your material into an essay. This extremely important choice helps to determine how clear and convincing your essay will be and how your audience will react to it.

RECOGNIZING A PATTERN

Sometimes deciding how to arrange your ideas will be easy because your assignment specifies a particular pattern of development. This may often be the case in a composition class, where the instructor may assign, for example, a descriptive or a narrative essay. Also, certain assignments or exam questions suggest how your material should be structured. Probably no one except an English composition instructor will say to you "Write a narrative," but you will have assignments that begin "Give an account" or "Tell about." Likewise, few teachers will explicitly assign a process essay, but they will ask you to explain how something works. Similarly, an examination question might ask you to trace the circumstances leading up to an event. If you are perceptive, you will realize that this question calls for either a narrative or a cause-and-effect answer. The important thing is to recognize the clues such assignments give, or those you find in your topic or thesis statement, and to structure your essay accordingly.

One clue to the emerging structure of your essay may be found in the questions that proved most helpful when you probed your subject (see page 21). For example, if questions like "What happened?" and "When did it happen?" suggested the most useful material, you might consider structuring your paper as a narrative. The chart on page 38 links various questions to the patterns of development they suggest. Notice that the terms in the right-hand column — narration, description, and so on —

☑ **CHECKLIST: RECOGNIZING A PATTERN**

What happened? When did it happen? Where did it happen? Who did it?	Narration
What does it look like? What are its characteristics? What impression does it make?	Description
What are some typical cases or examples of it?	Exemplification
How did it happen? What makes it work? How is it made?	Process
Why did it happen? What caused it? What does it cause? What are its effects?	Cause and effect
How is it like other things? How is it different from other things?	Comparison and contrast

What are its parts or types?
How can its parts or types be
  separated or grouped?
Do its parts or types fit into a
  logical order?
Into what categories can its parts
  or types be arranged?
On what basis can it be
  categorized?
	Classification and division

What is it?
How does it resemble other
  members of its class?
How does it differ from other
  members of its class?
What are its limits?
	Definition

identify patterns of development that can help order your ideas. Chapters 4 through 11 explain and illustrate each of these patterns.

UNDERSTANDING THE PARTS OF THE ESSAY

No matter what pattern of development you use, an essay should have a beginning, a middle, and an end — that is, an *introduction,* a *body,* and a *conclusion.*

The Introduction

The introduction of your essay, usually one paragraph and rarely more than two, introduces your subject, engages your readers' interest, and often states your thesis.

You can introduce an essay and engage your readers' interest in a number of ways.

1. You can give some *background information* and then move directly to your thesis statement. This approach works well when you know that the audience is already interested in your topic and that you can therefore come directly to the point. This strategy is especially useful for exams, where there is no need (or time) for subtlety.

> With inflation slowing down, many companies have understandably lowered prices, and the oil industry should be no exception. Consequently, homeowners have begun wondering whether the relatively high price of home heating oil is justified given the economic climate. It makes sense, therefore, for us to start examining the pricing policies of the major American oil companies.   (economics essay)

2. You can introduce an essay with a *definition* of a relevant term or concept. (Keep in mind, however, that the "According to *Webster's Dictionary* . . ." formula is overused and trite.) This technique is especially useful for research papers or exams, where the meaning of a specific term is crucial.

> Democracy is a form of government in which the ultimate authority is given to and exercised by the people. This may be so in theory, but some recent local elections have raised concerns about the future of democracy. Extensive voting-machine irregularities and ghost voting have seriously jeopardized people's faith in the democratic process.
>   (political science exam)

3. You can begin your essay with an *anecdote* or *story* that leads readers to your thesis.

> Upon meeting the famous author James Joyce, a young student stammered, "May I kiss the hand that wrote *Ulysses?*" "No!" said Joyce. "It did a lot of other things, too." As this exchange shows, Joyce was a person who valued humor. His sense of humor is also present in his final work, *Finnegans Wake,* in which he uses humor to comment on the human condition.   (English literature paper)

4. You can begin with a *question.*

> What was it like to live through the Holocaust? Elie Wiesel, in *One Generation After,* answers this question by presenting a series of accounts about ordinary people who found themselves imprisoned in Nazi death camps. As he does so, he challenges some of the assumptions we hold in our smug, materialistic society.   (sociology book report)

5. You can begin with a *quotation*. If it arouses interest, it can encourage your audience to read further.

> "The rich are different," said F. Scott Fitzgerald more than fifty years ago. Apparently, they still are. As any examination of the tax laws shows, the wealthy receive many more benefits than the middle class or the poor do.
> (business law paper)

No matter which strategy you select, your introduction should be consistent in tone with the rest of your essay. If it is not, it can misrepresent your intentions and even destroy your credibility. (For this reason, it is a good idea to write your introduction after you have finished the rest of your rough draft.) A technical report, for instance, should have an introduction that reflects the formality and objectivity required by the occasion. The introduction to an autobiographical essay or a personal letter, however, may have a more informal, subjective tone.

EXERCISE 1

Look through magazine articles or the essays in this book and find one example of each kind of introduction. Why do you think each introductory strategy was chosen? What other strategies might have worked?

The Body Paragraphs

The middle section, or body, of your essay develops your thesis. The **body paragraphs** present the details that convince your audience that your thesis is reasonable. To do so, each body paragraph should be *unified, coherent,* and *well developed.* It should also follow a particular pattern of development and should clearly support your thesis.

* *Each body paragraph should be unified.* A paragraph has **unity** when every sentence relates directly to the main idea of the paragraph. Sometimes the main idea of a paragraph is stated in a **topic sentence.** Like a thesis statement, a topic sentence acts as a guidepost, making it easy for readers to follow the paragraph's discussion. Although the placement of a topic sentence depends on a writer's purpose and subject, beginning writers often make it the first sentence of a paragraph.

Sometimes the main idea of a paragraph is *implied* by the sentences in the paragraph. Professional writers frequently use this technique because they believe that in some situations — especially narratives and descriptions — a topic sentence can seem forced or awkward. As a beginning writer, however, you will usually find it helpful to use topic sentences to keep your paragraphs focused.

Whether or not you include an explicitly stated topic sentence, remember that each sentence in a paragraph should develop the paragraph's main idea. If the sentences in a paragraph do not support the main idea, the paragraph will lack unity.

In the following excerpt from a student essay, notice how the topic sentence unifies the paragraph by summarizing its main idea:

> <u>Built on the Acropolis overlooking the city of Athens in the fifth century B.C., the Parthenon illustrates the limitations of Greek architecture.</u> As a temple of the gods, it was supposed to represent heavenly or divine perfection. However, although at first glance its structure seems to be perfect, on closer examination it becomes clear that it is a static, two-dimensional object. As long as you stand in the center of any of its four sides to look at it, its form appears to be perfect. The strong Doric columns seem to be equally spaced, one next to another, along all four of its sides. But if you take a step to the right or left, the Parthenon's symmetry is destroyed.

The explicit topic sentence, located at the beginning of the paragraph, enables readers to grasp the writer's point immediately. The examples that follow all relate to that point, making the paragraph focused and unified.

• *Each body paragraph should be coherent.* A paragraph is coherent if its sentences are smoothly and logically connected to one another. **Coherence** can be achieved through three techniques. First, you can repeat key words to carry concepts from one sentence to another and to echo important terms. Second, you can use pronouns to refer to key nouns in previous sentences. Finally, you can use **transitions,** words or expressions that show chronological sequence, cause and effect, and so on (see the list of transitions on page 42). These strategies for connecting sentences — which you can also use to connect paragraphs within an essay — spell out for your readers the exact relationships among your ideas.

The following paragraph, from George Orwell's "Shooting an Elephant" (page 104), uses repeated key words, pronouns, and transitions to achieve coherence:

> I got up. The Burmans were already racing past me across the mud. It was obvious that the elephant would never rise again, but he was not dead. He was breathing very rhythmically with long rattling gasps, his great mound of a side painfully rising and falling. His mouth was wide open — I could see far down into the caverns of pale pink throat. I waited a long time for him to die, but his breathing did not weaken. Finally I fired my two remaining shots into the spot where I thought his heart must be. The thick blood welled out of him like red velvet, but still he did not die. His body did not even jerk when the shots hit him, the tortured breathing continued without a pause. He was dying, very slowly and in great agony, but in some world remote from me where not even a bullet could damage him further. I felt that I had got to put an end to that dreadful noise. It seemed dreadful to see the great beast lying there, powerless to move and yet powerless to die, and not even be able to finish him. I sent back for my small rifle and poured shot after shot into his heart and down his throat. They seemed to make no impression. The tortured gasps continued as steadily as the ticking of a clock.

TRANSITIONS

SEQUENCE OR ADDITION

again	first, . . . second, . . .third	next
also	furthermore	one . . . another
and	in addition	still
besides	last	too
finally	moreover	

TIME

afterward	finally	simultaneously
as soon as	immediately	since
at first	in the meantime	soon
at the same time	later	subsequently
before	meanwhile	then
earlier	next	until
eventually	now	

COMPARISON

also	in the same way
likewise	similarly
in comparison	

CONTRAST

although	in contrast	on the one hand . . .
but	instead	on the other hand . . .
conversely	nevertheless	still
despite	nonetheless	whereas
even though	on the contrary	yet
however		

EXAMPLES

for example	specifically
for instance	that is
in fact	thus
namely	

CONCLUSIONS OR SUMMARIES

as a result	in summary
in conclusion	therefore
in short	thus

CAUSES OR EFFECTS

as a result	so
because	then
consequently	therefore
since	

In the paragraph on page 41, Orwell keeps his narrative coherent by using transitional expressions *(already, finally, when the shots hit him)* to signal the passing of time. He uses pronouns *(he, his)* in nearly every sentence to refer back to the elephant, the topic of his paragraph. Finally, he repeats key words like *shot* and *die* (and its variants *dead* and *dying*) to link the whole paragraph's sentences together. The result is a coherent, cohesive whole.

• *Each body paragraph should be well developed.* A paragraph is well developed if it contains the examples, facts, and explanations readers need to understand its main idea. If a paragraph is not adequately developed, readers will feel they have been given only a partial picture of the subject. Just how much information you need depends on your audience, your purpose, and the claims you make in your topic sentence.

If you decide you need more information in a paragraph, you can look back at your brainstorming notes. If this doesn't help, you can freewrite or brainstorm again, talk with friends and instructors, read more about your topic, or (with your instructor's permission) even do some research. Your assignment and your topic will determine the kind and amount of information you need.

The following student paragraph develops two examples to support its topic sentence:

> Just look at how males have been taught that extravagance is a positive characteristic. Scrooge, the main character of Dickens's *A Christmas Carol,* is portrayed as an evil man until he is rehabilitated — meaning that he gives up his miserly ways and freely distributes gifts and money on Christmas day. This behavior, of course, is rewarded when people change their opinions about him and decide that perhaps he isn't such a bad person after all. Diamond Jim Brady is another interesting example. This individual was a financier who was known for his extravagant taste in women and food. On any given night, he would consume enough food to feed at least ten of the numerous poor who roamed the streets of late-nineteenth-century New York. Yet, despite his selfishness and infantile self-gratification, Diamond Jim Brady's name has become synonymous with the good life.

• *Each body paragraph should follow a particular pattern of development.* In addition to making sure that your body paragraphs are unified, coherent, and well developed, you need to organize each paragraph according to a specific pattern of development. (Chapters 4 through 11 each begin with a paragraph-length example of the pattern discussed in the chapter.)

• *Each body paragraph should clearly support the thesis statement.* No matter how many body paragraphs your essay has — three, four, five, or even more — each paragraph should introduce and develop an idea that supports the essay's thesis. Each paragraph's topic sentence should express one of these supporting points. The following diagram illustrates this thesis-and-support structure.

```
                      Introductory paragraph
  Thesis statement: Despite the emphasis by journalists on objective reporting,
  there are three reasons why television news is anything but objective.
```

```
                        Body paragraph
  Topic sentence: Television news is not objective because the people who gather
  and report the news are biased.
```

```
                        Body paragraph
  Topic sentence: In addition, television news is not objective because networks
  must cater to the likes and dislikes of sponsors.
```

```
                        Body paragraph
  Topic sentence: Finally, television news is not objective because networks
  focus on ratings rather than content.
```

```
                      Concluding paragraph
  Restatement of thesis: Even though television journalists give much lip service
  to objective reporting, the truth is that this ideal has been impossible to
  achieve.
```

EXERCISE 2

Choose one body paragraph from an essay in this text. Using the criteria discussed on pages 41–43, decide whether or not the paragraph is unified, coherent, and well developed.

EXERCISE 3

Choose one essay in this text, and underline its thesis statement. Then, determine how each of its body paragraphs supports the thesis statement. (Note that in a long essay, several body paragraphs may develop a single point, and some paragraphs may serve as transitions from one point to another.)

The Conclusion

Since readers remember best what they read last, your **conclusion** is extremely important. Always end your essay in a way that reinforces your thesis and your purpose.

Like your introduction, your conclusion should be brief. In a short essay, it is rarely longer than a paragraph. Regardless of its length, however, your conclusion should be consistent with the content of your essay. It should not introduce supporting material that you have not discussed earlier. Frequently, a conclusion will restate the thesis, summarizing your essay's main idea in different words, or review your key points. Like thesis statements, effective conclusions need no announcement, and you should avoid beginning your conclusion with the artificial phrase *In conclusion.*

Conclusions can be as challenging to construct as introductions. Here are several ways to conclude an essay:

1. You can conclude your essay by *reviewing your key points* or *restating your thesis.*

> Rotation of crops provided several benefits. It enriched soil by giving it a rest; it enabled farmers to vary their production; and it ended the cycle of "boom or bust" that had characterized the prewar South's economy when cotton was the primary crop. Of course, this innovation did not solve all the economic problems of the postwar South, but it did lay the groundwork for the healthy economy this region enjoys today.
>
> (history exam)

2. You can end a discussion of a problem with a *recommendation of a course of action.*

> While there is still time, American engineering has to reassess its priorities. We no longer have the luxury of exotic and wasteful experiments in design for purely aesthetic reasons. Instead, we need technology grounded in common sense and economic feasibility. That the proposed space station seems to have few practical applications illustrates how far we have strayed from old-fashioned common sense and ingenuity.
>
> (engineering ethics report)

3. You can conclude with a *prediction.* Be sure, however, that your prediction follows logically from the points you have made in the essay. Your conclusion is no place to make new points or change direction.

> It is too late to save parts of the great swamps in northern Florida, but it is not too late to preserve the Everglades in the southern part of the state. With intelligent planning and an end to the dam building program by the Army Corps of Engineers, we will be able to halt the destruction of what Native Americans called the "Timeless Swamp."
>
> (environmental science essay)

4. You can end with a relevant *quotation.*

> In *Walden,* Henry David Thoreau says, "The mass of men lead lives of quiet desperation." This sentiment is reinforced by a drive through the Hill District of our city. Perhaps the work of the men and women who run the clinic on Jefferson Street cannot totally change this situation, but it can give us hope to know that some people, at least, are working for the betterment of us all.   (public health essay)

EXERCISE 4

Look through magazine articles or the essays in this book and find one example of each kind of conclusion. Why do you think each concluding strategy was chosen? What other strategies might have worked?

CONSTRUCTING A FORMAL OUTLINE

At this point, you may want to construct a *formal outline* to guide you as you write your essay. Whereas informal outlines are preliminary lists that simply remind the writer which points to make, formal outlines are detailed, multilevel constructions that indicate the exact order in which you will present your points. The complexity of your assignment determines how complete an outline you need. For a short paper an informal outline like the one on page 29 is usually sufficient. For a longer, more complex essay, however, you may need to prepare a formal outline.

Begin by reviewing your thesis statement and all the ideas you compiled during prewriting. As you examine this material, you will see that some ideas seem more important than others. One way to construct a formal outline is to copy down the main headings from your informal outline. Then, arrange ideas from your brainstorming notes or cluster diagram as subheadings under the appropriate headings. As you work on your outline, make sure that each idea you include supports your thesis. Ideas that don't seem to fit should be reworded or discarded. As you revise your essay, continue to refer to your outline to make sure thesis and support are logically related. The following guidelines will help you prepare a formal outline (an example appears below).

☑ CHECKLIST: CONSTRUCTING A FORMAL OUTLINE

- Write your thesis statement at the top of the page.
- Group main headings under roman numerals (I, II, III, IV, and so forth), and place them flush with the left-hand margin.
- Indent each subheading under the first word of the heading above it. Use capital letters before major points and numbers before subtopics.
- Capitalize the first letter of the first word of each heading.
- Make your outline as simple as possible, avoiding overly complex divisions of ideas. (Try not to go beyond third-level headings — 1, 2, 3, and so on.)
- Your outline should be either a *topic outline,* with headings expressed as short phrases or single words ("Advantages and disadvantages") or a *sentence outline,* with headings expressed as complete sentences ("The advantages of advanced placement chemistry outweigh the disadvantages"). *Never use both phrases and complete sentences in the same outline.*
- Express all headings at the same level in parallel terms. (If roman numeral I is a noun, II, III, and IV should also be nouns.)
- Make sure each heading contains at least two subdivisions. You cannot have a *1* without a *2,* or an *a* without a *b.*
- Make sure your headings don't overlap.

▶ A STUDENT WRITER: CONSTRUCTING A FORMAL OUTLINE

The topic outline Laura Bobnak constructed follows the guidelines discussed above. Notice that her outline focuses on the body of her paper and does not include the introduction or conclusion — these are usually developed after the body has been drafted. (Compare this formal outline with the informal outline on page 29 in which Laura simply grouped her brainstorming notes under three general headings.)

SPEAKING OUT

Thesis statement: As I look back on the situation, I wonder why I kept silent and what would have happened had I acted.

I. The incident
  A. Taking test
  B. Witnessing cheating
  C. Reacting
    1. Anger
    2. Dismissal

II. Reasons for keeping silent
  A. Other students' attitudes
  B. My fears

III. Current opinion of cheating
  A. Effects of cheating on education
    1. Undercuts the process
    2. Is unfair to teachers
  B. Effects of cheating on students

This outline enabled Laura to arrange her points so that they supported her thesis. As she went on to draft her essay, the outline reminded her to emphasize the contrast between her present and former attitudes toward cheating.

EXERCISE 5

Read the thesis you developed in Chapter 1, Exercise 11 on page 35 as well as all the notes you made for the paper you are planning. Then, make a topic outline that lists the points you will discuss in your essay. When you are finished, check to make sure that your outline conforms to the guidelines in the checklist in page 46.

💻 COMPUTER STRATEGY

If you use a computer to construct a formal outline, you can easily arrange and rearrange your headings until your outline is logical and complete. If you saved your prewriting notes in computer files, you can refer to them while working on your outline and perhaps add or modify headings to reflect what you find.

3

DRAFTING
AND REVISING

After you decide on a tentative thesis and an arrangement for your ideas, you can begin to draft and revise your essay. Keep in mind that even as you carry out these activities, you may have to generate more material or revise your thesis statement or outline.

WRITING YOUR FIRST DRAFT

The purpose of your first draft is to get your ideas down on paper so you can react to them. Experienced writers know that the first draft is nothing more than a work in progress; it exists to be revised. With this in mind, you should be prepared to cross out and extensively rearrange material. In addition, don't be surprised if you think of new ideas as you write. If a new idea comes to you, follow it to its conclusion. Some of the best writing results from unexpected turns or accidents. The following guidelines will help you prepare your first draft.

☑ **CHECKLIST: DRAFTING**

- *Begin with the body paragraphs.* Because your essay will probably be revised extensively, don't take the time at this stage to write an introduction or conclusion. Let your thesis statement guide you as you draft the body paragraphs of your essay. When you have finished, you can write an appropriate introduction and conclusion.

- *Get your ideas down quickly.* Don't worry about correctness or word choice, and try not to interrupt the flow of your writing with concerns about style.

- *Take regular breaks as you write.* Don't continue writing until you are so exhausted you can't think straight. To avoid this problem, many writers divide their writing into stages, perhaps completing one or two body

(continued on next page).

(continued from previous page).

paragraphs and then taking a short break. This strategy reduces fatigue and in the long run is more efficient than trying to write without stopping.

- *Write with revision in mind.* Triple-space so you will have room to make changes by hand on hard copy.
- *Leave yourself time to revise.* Remember, your first draft is called a *rough draft* for a good reason. All writing profits from revision, so try to allow enough time to write two or more drafts.

▶ A STUDENT WRITER: WRITING A FIRST DRAFT

Here is the first draft of Laura Bobnak's essay.

When I was in high school, I had an experience like the one Henry Louis Gates talks about in his essay. It was then that I saw a close friend of mine cheat in chemistry class. As I look back on the situation, I wonder why I kept silent and what would have happened had I acted. [1]

The incident I am going to describe took place during the final examination for my advanced placement chemistry class. I had studied hard for it, but even so, I found the test difficult. As I struggled to balance a particularly difficult equation, I noticed that my friend Jeff Servin, who was sitting across from me, was acting strangely. I noticed that he was copying material from a paper. After watching him for a while, I dismissed the incident and got back to my test. [2]

After the test was over, I began to think about what I had seen. The more I thought about it the angrier I got. It seemed unfair that I had struggled for weeks to memorize formulas and equations while all Jeff had done was to copy them onto a cheat sheet. For a moment I considered going to the teacher, but I quickly dismissed this idea. After all, cheating was something everybody did. Besides, I was afraid if I told on Jeff, my friends would stop talking to me. [3]

Now that I am in college I see the situation differently. I find it hard to believe that I could ever have been so calm about cheating. Cheating is certainly something that students should not take for granted. It undercuts the education process and is unfair to teachers and to the majority of students who spend their time studying. [4]

```
         If I could go back to high school and relive the experi-   5
ence, I now know that I would have gone to the teacher. Natu-
rally Jeff would have been angry at me, but at least I would
have known I had the courage to do the right thing.
```

EXERCISE 1

Write a draft of the essay you have been working on in Chapters 1 and 2. Be sure to look back at the notes you made during prewriting as well as at your outline.

REVISING YOUR ESSAY

Remember that revision is not something you do after your paper is finished. It is a continuing process during which you consider the logic and clarity of your ideas as well as how effectively they are presented. Revision is not simply a matter of proofreading or editing, of crossing out one word and substituting another or correcting errors in spelling and punctuation; revision means reexamining and rethinking what you have written. In fact, you may even find yourself adding and deleting extensively, reordering whole sentences or paragraphs as you reconsider what you want to communicate to your audience. Revision can take a lot of time, so don't be discouraged if you have to go through three or four drafts of your essay before you think it is ready to hand in. The following pointers can help you when you revise your essay.

• *Give yourself a cooling-off period.* After you have written your first draft, put it aside for several hours, or even a day or two if you can. This cooling-off period lets you distance yourself from your essay so that you can read it more objectively when you return to it. When you read it again, you will see things you missed the first time.

• *Try to work from a typed draft.* Because a typed or printed draft is neat and easy to read, you will be able to see connections and gaps more easily than you will if you work with a handwritten draft. In addition, type enables you to distance yourself from your work and evaluate it objectively.

• *Read your draft aloud.* Before you revise, read your draft aloud to help you spot chopping sentences, missing words, or phrases that do not sound right.

💻 COMPUTER STRATEGY

Typing your first draft has several advantages. First, it enables you to generate a clean, easy-to-read first draft of your essay. In addition, the computer makes it easy for you to move ideas from one part of your essay to another, to reformat text, and to add new ideas easily as you write.

• *Take advantage of opportunities to get feedback.* Your instructor may organize peer critique sessions, hand out a revision checklist, refer students to a writing center, or schedule one-on-one conferences. Make use of as many of these opportunities for feedback as you can; each offers you a different way of gaining information about what you have written.

• *Try not to get overwhelmed.* It is easy to become overwhelmed by all the feedback you get about your draft. To avoid this, approach revision as a systematic process. Don't just automatically make all the changes that people suggest; consider the impact and the validity of each change. Also ask yourself whether comments suggest larger issues that are not being addressed. For example, does a comment about choppy sentences in a paragraph simply suggest a need for you to add transitions, or does it require you to rethink your ideas?

• *Don't let your ego get in the way.* Everyone likes praise, and receiving negative criticism is never a pleasant experience. Experienced writers know, however, that they must get feedback if they are going to improve their work. Learn to see criticism — whether by an instructor or by your peers — as a necessary (if painful) part of the revision process.

• *Revise in stages.* Deal with the large elements (essay and paragraph structure) before moving on to the smaller elements (sentence structure and word choice).

How you revise — what specific strategies you decide to use — depends on your own preference, your instructor's directions, and the time available. Like the rest of the writing process, revision varies from student to student and from assignment to assignment. Three of the most useful revision strategies are *revising with a checklist, revising with an outline,* and *revising with a peer critique.*

Revising with a Checklist

If you have time, you can use the checklist on page 53, adapting it to your own writing process.

Revising with an Outline

If you do not have time to consult a detailed checklist, you can check your essay's structure by making a *review outline.* Either an informal outline or a formal one can show you whether you have omitted any important points. An outline can also show you whether your essay follows the pattern of development you have chosen. Finally, an outline can clarify the relationship between your thesis statement and your body paragraphs.

Revising with a Peer Critique

Another revision strategy you may find helpful is seeking a *peer critique* — asking a friend to read your essay and comment on it. Sometimes

☑ CHECKLIST: REVISION

- **Thesis statement.** Is it clear and specific? Does it indicate the direction your essay is taking? Is it consistent with the body of your essay? If you departed from your essay's original direction while you were writing, you may need to revise your thesis statement so that it accurately sums up the ideas and information now contained in the body. Or you may need to delete from the body any material that is unrelated to the thesis statement — or revise it so it *is* relevant.

- **Body.** Are the body paragraphs unified? Coherent? Well developed? If not, you might have to add more facts or examples or smoother transitions. Does each body paragraph follow a particular pattern of development? Do the points you make in these paragraphs support your thesis?

- **Introduction and conclusion.** Are they appropriate for your material, your audience, and your purpose? Are they interesting? Do they reinforce your thesis?

- **Sentences.** Are they effective? Interesting? Varied in length and structure? Should any sentences be deleted, combined, or moved?

- **Words.** Should you make any substitutions?

- **Title.** Because it creates readers' first impression of your essay, your title should spark their interest. Usually, single-word titles ("Love") and cute ones ("The Cheery Cheerleader") do little to draw readers into your essay. To be effective, a title should reflect your purpose and your tone.

The essays in this book illustrate the various kinds of titles you can use.

Statement of essay's focus: "Grant and Lee: A Study in Contrasts"

Question: "Who Killed Benny Paret?"

Unusual angle: "How the Lawyers Stole Winter"

Controversy: "A Peaceful Woman Explains Why She Carries a Gun"

Provocative wording: "One Internet, Two Nations"

Quotation: "Memo to John Grisham: What's Next — 'A Movie Made Me Do It'?"

a peer critique can be quite formal. An instructor may require students to exchange papers and evaluate their classmates' work according to certain standards, perhaps by completing a *peer-editing worksheet.* (See page 56 for an example. A peer editing worksheet for each pattern of development can be found on the *Patterns for College Writing* Web site at: <http://www.bedfordstmartins.com/patterns>.) Often, however, a peer critique is informal. Even if a friend is unfamiliar with your topic, he or she can still tell you honestly whether you are getting your point across — and maybe even advise you about how to communicate more effectively. (Remember, though, that your critic should be only your reader, not your ghostwriter.)

The use of peer critiques mirrors the way people in the real world actually write. In the business world, reports are circulated in order to get feedback. Scientists and academics routinely collaborate when they write. (And, as you may have realized, even this book is the result of a collaboration.)

Your classmates can be quite helpful during the early drafts of your essay, providing suggestions that can guide you through the revision process. In addition, they can respond to questions you may have about your essay — for example, whether your introduction works, or whether one of your supporting points needs more explanation or additional support. When friends ask *you* to critique their work, the following guidelines should help you.

☑ **CHECKLIST: GUIDELINES FOR PEER CRITIQUES**

- *Be positive.* Remember that your purpose is to help other students improve their essays.

- *Be tactful.* Be sure to emphasize the good points about the essay; mention one or two things the writer has done particularly well.

- *Be specific.* Offer concrete suggestions about what the writer could do better. Vague words like *good* or *bad* provide little guidance.

- *Be attentive.* If you are doing a critique orally, make sure you interact with the writer as you read. Ask questions, listen to responses, and explain your comments.

- *Be thorough.* Don't focus on the mechanics of the paper. Although spelling and punctuation matter, you shouldn't expect these elements to be perfect in a first draft. At this stage, the clarity of the thesis statement, the effectiveness of the support, and the organization of the writer's ideas are much more important.

- *Be helpful.* When possible, write down your comments — either on a form your instructor provides or in the margins of the paper.

⌨ **COMPUTER STRATEGY**

A computer enables you to add, delete, and move information quickly and effortlessly. Still, it is usually not a good idea to begin revising directly on the computer screen. Since most screens show only a portion of a page, the connections between ideas are hard to see and to keep track of. Even with the split-screen option that some word-processing programs offer, you cannot view several sections of a draft at once or easily compare one draft to another. For these reasons, it is a good idea to revise on a hard copy of your essay. Once you have made your handwritten corrections, you can type them into your paper.

▶ **A STUDENT WRITER: REVISING A FIRST DRAFT**

Here is Laura Bobnak's first draft again, followed by a discussion of her revision process.

When I was in high school, I had an experience like the   1
one Henry Louis Gates talks about in his essay. It was then
that I saw a close friend of mine cheat in chemistry class.
As I look back on the situation, I wonder why I kept silent
and what would have happened had I acted.

The incident I am going to describe took place during   2
the final examination for my advanced placement chemistry
class. I had studied hard for it, but even so, I found the
test difficult. As I struggled to balance a particularly
difficult equation, I noticed that my friend Jeff Servin,
who was sitting across from me, was acting strangely. I
noticed that he was copying material from a paper. After
watching him for a while, I dismissed the incident and got
back to my test.

After the test was over, I began to think about what   3
I had seen. The more I thought about it the angrier I got.
It seemed unfair that I had struggled for weeks to memorize
formulas and equations while all Jeff had done was to copy
them onto a cheat sheet. For a moment I considered going
to the teacher, but I quickly dismissed this idea. After
all, cheating was something everybody did. Besides, I was
afraid if I told on Jeff, my friends would stop talking
to me.

Now that I am in college I see the situation differ-   4
ently. I find it hard to believe that I could ever have been
so calm about cheating. Cheating is certainly something that
students should not take for granted. It undercuts the education process and is unfair to teachers and to the majority
of students who spend their time studying.

If I could go back to high school and relive the ex-   5
perience, I now know that I would have gone to the teacher.
Naturally Jeff would have been angry at me, but at least I
would have known I had the courage to do the right thing.

POINTS FOR SPECIAL ATTENTION: FIRST DRAFT

After writing this rough draft, Laura put it aside for a few hours and then reread it. Later, Laura's instructor divided the class into small groups and had them read and write critiques of each other's papers. As a result of her own reading and three written critiques (one of which is reproduced below), Laura was able to focus on a number of areas that needed revision.

PEER-EDITING WORKSHEET

What is the essay's thesis? Is it clearly worded? Does it provide a focus for the rest of the essay? Is it appropriate for the assignment?

Thesis statement: "As I look back on the situation, I wonder why I kept silent and what would have happened had I acted." I don't really think the thesis talks about the second part of the assignment — would she have done the same thing today?

How clearly are the body paragraphs related to the essay's thesis? Which topic sentences could be more focused?

The topic sentences seem OK — each one seems to tell what the paragraph is about.

How do the body paragraphs develop the essay's main idea? Where could the writer have used more detail?

Each of the body paragraphs tells a part of the narrative, but as I said before, the paragraph that deals with the second part of the assignment is missing. You could add more detail — really can't picture everything you're talking about.

Can you follow the writer's ideas? Does the essay need transitions?

I have no problem following your ideas. Maybe you could have added some more transitions, but I think the essay moves nicely.

Which points are especially clear? What questions do you have that are not answered in the essay?

I think the things you didn't like about Jeff's cheating were good. I'm not sure what AP chemistry is like, though. Do people cheat because it's hard?

If this were your essay, what would you change before you handed it in?

I'd change the thesis so it reflects the assignment. I'd add more detail and explain more about AP chemistry. Also, what were the other students doing while the cheating was going on?

Overall, do you think the paper is effective? Explain.

Good paper; cheating is an important issue, and I think your story really puts it in focus.

The Introduction

Laura knew that she would eventually have to present more detail in her introduction. (Because she was writing a first draft, she had spent little time on this section.) At this stage, though, she was more concerned with her thesis statement, and the students in her peer editing group said that they didn't think it addressed the second half of the assignment — to explain whether or not she would act differently today.

Keeping their comments in mind, Laura rewrote her introduction. First, she created a context for her discussion by more specifically linking her story to Gates's essay. Next, she decided to postpone mentioning her subject — cheating — until later in the paper, hoping that this strategy would stimulate the curiosity of her readers and make them want to read further. Finally, she revised her thesis statement to reflect the specific wording of the assignment.

The Body Paragraphs

The students in her peer editing group also said that Laura needed to expand her body paragraphs. Although she had expected that most of her readers would be familiar with courses like advanced placement chemistry, she discovered this was not the case. One student suggested she explain how challenging it was. In addition, some students in her group thought she should expand the paragraph in which she described her reaction to the cheating. They wondered what the other students had thought about the incident. Did they know? Did they care? Laura's classmates were curious, and they thought other readers would be, too.

Before revising the body paragraphs, Laura did some brainstorming to come up with additional ideas. She decided to describe the difficulty of advanced placement chemistry and the pressure that the students in the class had felt. She also decided to summarize discussions she had had with several of her classmates after the test. In addition, she wanted to explain in more detail her present views on cheating; she felt that the paragraph in which she presented these ideas did not contrast clearly enough with the paragraphs that dealt with her high school experiences.

To make sure that her sentences led smoothly into one another, Laura added transitions and rewrote entire sentences when necessary, signaling the progression of her thoughts by adding words and phrases like *therefore, for this reason, for example,* and *as a result.* In addition, she tried to repeat key words so that important concepts would be reinforced.

The Conclusion

Laura's biggest concern as she revised was to make sure her readers would see the connection between her essay and the assignment. To make this connection clear, she decided to mention in her conclusion a specific effect the incident had on her: its impact on her friendship with Jeff. She also decided to link her reactions to those of Henry Louis Gates Jr.: like him, she had been upset by the actions of someone she knew. By employing this strategy, she was able to bring her essay full circle and develop an idea she had alluded to in her introduction. Thus, rewriting her conclusion helped Laura to reinforce her thesis statement and provide closure to her essay.

▶ A STUDENT WRITER: REVISING A SECOND DRAFT

The following draft incorporates Laura's revisions as well as some preliminary editing of punctuation and grammar.

Speaking Out

In his essay "'What's in a Name?'" Henry Louis Gates Jr.   1
recalls an incident from his past in which his father did not
speak up. Perhaps he kept silent because he was afraid or
because he knew that nothing he said or did would change the
situation in Piedmont, West Virginia. Although I have never
encountered the kind of prejudice Gates describes, I did
have an experience in high school where, like Gates's
father, I could have spoken up but did not. As I now look
back on the situation, I know I would not make the same
decision today.

The incident I am going to describe took place during   2
the final examination in my advanced placement chemistry
class. The course was very demanding and required hours of
studying every night. Every day after school, I would meet
with other students to outline chapters and answer homework
questions. Sometimes we would even work on weekends. We
would often ask ourselves whether we had gotten in over our
heads. As the semester dragged on, it became clear to me, as
well as to the other students in the class, that passing the
course was not something we could take for granted. Test
after test came back with grades that were well below the
"As" and "Bs" I was used to getting in the regular chemistry
course I took in tenth grade. By the time we were ready to
take the final exam, most of us were worried that we would
fail the course--despite the teacher's assurances that she
would mark on a curve.

The final examination for advanced placement chemistry   3
was given on a Friday morning from nine to twelve o'clock.

As I struggled to balance a particularly complex equation, I noticed that the person sitting across from me was acting strangely. At first I thought I was imagining things, but as I stared I saw Jeff Servin, my friend and study partner, fumbling with his test booklet. About a minute passed before I realized that he was copying material from a paper he had taped inside the cuff of his shirt. After a short time, I dismissed the incident and finished my test.

Surprisingly, when I mentioned the incident to others   4
in the class, they all knew what Jeff had done. The more I thought about Jeff's actions, the angrier I got. It seemed unfair that I had struggled for weeks to memorize formulas and equations while all Jeff had done was to copy them onto a cheat sheet. For a moment I considered going to the teacher, but I quickly dismissed this idea. Cheating was nothing new to me or to others in my school. Many of my classmates cheated at one time or another. Most of us saw school as a war between us and the teachers, and cheating was just another weapon in our arsenal. The worst crime I could commit would be to turn Jeff in. As far as I was concerned, I had no choice. I fell in line with the values of my high school classmates and dismissed the incident as "no big deal."

I find it hard to believe that I could ever have been   5
so complacent about cheating. The issues that were simple in high school now seem complex. I now ask questions that never would have occurred to me in high school. Interestingly, Jeff and I are no longer very close. Whenever I see him I have the same reaction Henry Louis Gates Jr. had when he met Mr. Wilson after he had insulted his father--I have a hard time looking him in the eye.

POINTS FOR SPECIAL ATTENTION: SECOND DRAFT

Laura could see that her second draft was stronger than her first. But after reading and analyzing it, she discovered a number of ways to improve her draft further.

The Title

Laura's original title was only a working title, and now she wanted one that would create interest and draw readers into her essay. She knew, however, that a humorous, cute, or catchy title would undermine the seriousness of her essay. After rejecting a number of possibilities, she decided on "The Price of Silence." Not only was this title thought provoking, but it was also descriptive; it prepared readers for what was to follow in the essay.

The Introduction

Although Laura was basically satisfied with her introduction, she identified one problem. She had assumed that everyone reading her essay would be familiar with Gates's essay. By adding material that summarized the problems Gates's father had faced, she could accommodate readers who didn't know or remember Gates's comments.

The Body Paragraphs

After reading her first body paragraph, Laura thought she could sharpen its focus. She decided to delete the first sentence of the paragraph because it seemed too conversational. She also deleted several other sentences that she thought gave too much detail about how difficult advanced placement chemistry was — even though she had added this material at the suggestion of a classmate. After all, cheating, not advanced placement chemistry, was the subject of her paper. If she included this kind of detail, she ran the risk of distracting readers with an irrelevant discussion.

In her second body paragraph, Laura noticed that her first and second sentences did not seem to be linked together, and she realized that a short discussion of her own reaction to the test would connect these two ideas. She also decided to add transitional words and phrases to the last part of the paragraph to clarify the sequence of events she described. Phrases like *at first, about a minute passed,* and *after a short time* would help readers follow her discussion.

Laura thought that the third body paragraph was her best, but even so, she felt that she needed to add some material. After reading the paragraph several times, she decided to expand her discussion of the students' reactions to cheating. More information — perhaps some dialogue — would help her make the point that cheating was condoned by the students in her class.

The Conclusion

Laura realized her conclusion began by mentioning her present attitude toward cheating and then suddenly shifted to the effect cheating had on her relationship with Jeff. To remedy this situation, she decided to take her discussion about her current view of cheating out of her conclusion and put it in a separate paragraph. By doing this, she would be able to focus her conclusion on the effect cheating had on both Jeff and her. This strategy would enable Laura to present her views about cheating in more detail and also help her to end her essay forcefully.

▶ A STUDENT WRITER: PREPARING A FINAL DRAFT

Based on her analysis, Laura revised and edited her draft and handed in this final version of her essay.

The Price of Silence

Introduction (provides background)

    In his essay "'What's in a Name?'" Henry Louis Gates Jr. recalls an incident from his past in which his father encountered prejudice and did not speak up. Perhaps he kept silent because he was afraid or because he knew that nothing he said or did would change the racial situation in Piedmont, West Virginia. Although I have never encountered the kind of prejudice Gates describes, I did have an experience in high school where, like Gates's father, I could have spoken out but did not. As I think back on **Thesis statement** the situation, I realize that I have outgrown the immaturity and lack of confidence that made me keep silent.   1

Narrative begins

    In my senior year in high school I, along with fifteen other students, took advanced placement chemistry. The course was very demanding and required hours of studying every night. As the semester dragged on, it became clear to me, as well as to the other students in the class, that passing the course was not something we could take for granted. Test after test came back with grades that were well below the "As" and "Bs" I was used to getting in the regular chemistry course I had taken in tenth grade. By the time we were ready to take the final exam, most of us were worried that we would fail the course--despite the teacher's assurances that she would mark on a curve.   2

Key incident occurs

    The final examination for advanced place-   3
ment chemistry was given on a Friday morning
between nine o'clock and noon. I had studied
all that week, but even so, I found the test
difficult. I knew the material, but I had a
hard time answering the long questions that
were asked. As I struggled to balance a particularly complex equation, I noticed that the
person sitting across from me was acting
strangely. At first I thought I was imagining
things, but as I stared I saw Jeff Servin, my
friend and study partner, fumbling with his
test booklet. About a minute passed before I
realized that he was copying material from a
paper he had taped to the inside of his shirt
cuff. After a short time, I stopped watching
him and finished my test.

Narrative continues: reactions to the incident

    It was not until after the test that I   4
began thinking about what I had seen. Surprisingly, when I mentioned the incident to others
in the class, they all knew what Jeff had done.
Some even thought that Jeff's actions were justified. "After all," one student said, "the
test was hard." But the more I thought about
Jeff's actions, the angrier I got. It seemed
unfair that I had struggled for weeks to memorize formulas and equations while all Jeff had
done was copy them onto a cheat sheet. For a
moment I considered going to the teacher, but I
quickly dismissed this idea. Cheating was nothing new to me or to others in my school. Many of
my classmates cheated at one time or another.
Most of us saw school as a war between us and
the teachers, and cheating was just another
weapon in our arsenal. The worst crime I could

Narrative ends

commit would be to turn Jeff in. As far as I was
concerned, I had no choice. I fell in line with
the values of my high school classmates and
dismissed the incident as "no big deal."

Analysis of key incident

Now that I am in college, however, I see   5
the situation differently. I find it hard to
believe that I could ever have been so complacent about cheating. The issues that were simple in high school now seem complex--especially
in light of the honor code that I follow in
college. I now ask questions that never would
have occurred to me in high school. What, for
example, are the implications of cheating?
What would happen to the educational system if
cheating became the norm? What are my obligations to all those who are involved in education? Aren't teachers and students interested
in achieving a common goal? The answers to
these questions give me a sense of the far-
reaching effects of my failure to act. If confronted with the same situation today, I know
I would speak out regardless of the consequences.

Reinforcement of thesis

Jeff Servin is now a first-year student at   6
the state university and, like me, was given
credit for chemistry. I feel certain that not
only did I fail myself by not turning him in but
I also failed him. I gave in to peer pressure
instead of doing what I knew to be the right
thing. The worst that would have happened to
Jeff had I spoken up is that he would have had
to repeat chemistry in summer school. By doing
so, he would have proven to himself that he
could, like the rest of us in the class, pass on
his own. In the long run, this knowledge would
serve him better than the knowledge that he
could cheat whenever he faced a difficult situation.

Conclusion (aftermath of incident)

Interestingly, Jeff and I are no longer   7
very close. Whenever I see him I have the same
reaction Henry Louis Gates Jr. had when he met
Mr. Wilson after he had insulted his father--
I have a hard time looking him in the eye.

With each draft of her essay, Laura sharpened the focus of her discussion. In the process, she clarified her thoughts about her subject and reached some new and interesting conclusions. Although much of Laura's paper is a narrative, it also contains a contrast between her current ideas about cheating and the ideas she had in high school. Perhaps Laura could have explained the reasons behind her current ideas about cheating more fully. Even so, her paper gives a straightforward account of the incident and analyzes its significance without lapsing into clichés or simplistic moralizing. Especially effective is Laura's conclusion, in which she examines the effects of cheating. By placing this material at the end of her discussion, she makes sure that her readers will not lose sight of the implications of her experience.

EXERCISE 2

Use the checklist on pages 53 to revise your draft. If you prefer, outline your draft and use that outline to help you revise.

EXERCISE 3

Have another student read your second draft. Then, using the student's peer critique as your guide, revise your draft.

A NOTE ON EDITING

When you finish revising your essay, it is tempting to hand it in to your instructor and breathe a sigh of relief. This is one temptation you should resist. You still have to edit your paper to correct many of the small problems that remain even after you revise.

When you edit, you put the finishing touches on your essay. You correct misspellings, check punctuation, search for grammatical errors, look at your paper's format, and consider any other surface features that might weaken its message or undermine your credibility. Editing is your last chance to make sure your paper says what you want it to say.

💻 COMPUTER STRATEGY

Just as you do when you revise, you should edit on a hard copy of your essay. Seeing your work on the printed page makes it easy for you to spot surface-level errors in spelling, grammar, and punctuation. Before you print, however, you can run a grammar check to find problems such as sentence fragments and sexist usage. (Grammar checkers, however, are far from perfect. They often miss problems — such as faulty modification — and they frequently highlight areas of text — such as long sentences — that may not contain an error. Finally, you can run a spell check to find words that are misspelled. Keep in mind, however, that a spell checker will not help you with many proper nouns, nor will it highlight words that are spelled correctly but used incorrectly — *there* for *their*, for example. Even if you run a spell check, you must still proofread carefully.

Of course, you could spend literally hours checking your essay for every possible error, but this approach would be time-consuming and impractical. As you edit, keep in mind that certain errors occur more frequently than others. By concentrating on these errors, and by keeping a record of the specific errors that you make most often, you will be able to edit your essays quickly and efficiently.

The following checklist includes many of the most common errors. Consult a handbook of grammar and usage for detailed discussions of these errors.

EXERCISE 4

Edit your essay, and then write a final draft. Even if you have used a spell checker, proofread carefully before submitting your paper.

☑ **CHECKLIST: EDITING**

- **Subject-verb agreement.** Do all your verbs agree in number with their subjects? Remember that singular subjects take singular verbs and plural subjects take plural verbs.

- **Clear pronoun reference.** Do pronouns that refer back to specific nouns do so clearly? Be especially careful of unclear references involving *this*. To avoid this problem, always follow *this* with a word that clarifies the reference — *this problem, this event,* and so on.

- **Punctuation.** Are any commas misplaced, missing, or unnecessary? Remember to use commas before coordinating conjunctions (such as *and* or *but*) that join independent clauses in compound sentences.

- **Misspelled words and typos.** Proofread for spelling even if you have run a computer spell check. Also, be on the lookout for mistakes in capitalization as well as for improper spacing and omitted letters.

- **Commonly confused words.** Be alert for words that are often confused with each other. Remember, for example, that *it's* is a contraction meaning *it is,* and *its* is the possessive form of *it.*

- **Sentence fragments.** Does each group of words punctuated as a sentence have a subject and a verb? Does it make sense on its own, without being attached to another sentence?

- **Comma splices.** Is a comma used alone to connect two independent clauses? If so, correct this problem by adding the appropriate coordinating conjunction (*and* or *but,* for example), changing the comma to a semicolon, or making the clauses separate sentences.

- **Inconsistencies.** Are you consistent in expressing yourself throughout your paper? For example, do not shift from the present to the past tense unless your meaning requires you to do so.

- **Manuscript format.** Have you followed your instructor's guidelines? Is your essay neat and clearly printed?

Part Two

READINGS
FOR WRITERS

The relationship between reading and writing is a complex one. Sometimes you will write an essay based on your own experience; more often than not, especially in college, you will respond in writing to something that you have read. The essays in this book give you a chance to do both.

As you are probably aware, the fact that information appears in print or on the Internet does not mean you should take it at face value. Of course, most of the books and articles you read will be reliable, but some — especially material found on World Wide Web pages and in online discussion groups — will contain contradictions, biased ideas, or even inaccurate or misleading information. For this reason, your goal should not be simply to understand what you are reading, but to assess the credibility of the writer and, eventually, to judge the soundness of his or her ideas.

When you read the essays in Part Two, you should approach them critically. In other words, you should question (and sometimes challenge) the writer's ideas — and, in the process, try to create new interpretations that you can explore in your writing. Approaching a text in this way is not easy, for it requires you to develop your own analytical and critical skills. In addition, you must develop a set of standards that you can use to judge and interpret what you read. Only after you have read and critically evaluated a text can you begin to draw your ideas together and write about them.

Every reading selection in Chapters 4–11 is accompanied by a series of questions intended to guide you through the reading process. In many ways, these questions are a warm-up for the intellectual workout of writing a paper. The more time you devote to them, the more you will develop your analytical skills. In a real sense, then, these questions will help you develop the critical thinking skills that you will need as you write. In becoming a proficient reader, you will also gain confidence in yourself as a writer.

Each of the following reading selections is organized around one dominant pattern of development. In your outside reading, however, you will often find more than one pattern used in a single piece of writing (see Chapter 13, Combining the Patterns, page 625). When you write, then, do not feel you must follow these patterns blindly; instead, think of them as tools for making your writing more effective, and adapt them to your subject, your audience, and your writing purpose.

4

NARRATION

WHAT IS NARRATION?

Narration tells a story by presenting events in an orderly, logical sequence. In the following paragraph from her memoir *I Know Why the Caged Bird Sings,* Maya Angelou recalls her high school graduation:

Narrative presents events in orderly sequence

Topic sentence

The school band struck up a march and all classes filed in as had been rehearsed. We stood in front of our seats, as assigned, and on a signal from the choir director, we sat. No sooner had this been accomplished than the band started to play the national anthem. We rose again and sang the song, after which we recited the pledge of allegiance. We remained standing for a brief minute before the choir director and the principal signaled to us, rather desperately I thought, to take our seats. The command was so unusual that our carefully rehearsed and smooth-running machine was thrown off. For a full minute we fumbled for our chairs and bumped into each other awkwardly. Habits change or solidify under pressure, so in our state of nervous tension we had been ready to follow our usual assembly pattern: the American national anthem, then the pledge of allegiance, then the song every Black person I knew called the Negro National Anthem. All done in the same key, with the same passion, and most often standing on the same foot.

Narration can be the dominant pattern in many kinds of writing and speech. Histories, biographies, and autobiographies follow a narrative form, as do personal letters, diaries, and journals. Narration is the dominant pattern in many works of fiction and poetry, and it is an essential part of casual conversation. Narration also underlies folk and fairy tales and radio and television news reports. In short, any time you tell what happened, you are using narration.

USING NARRATION

Although a narrative's purpose may be simply to recount events or create a particular mood or impression, in college writing a narrative essay is more likely to present a sequence of events for the purpose of supporting a thesis. For instance, in a narrative about your first date, your purpose may be to show your readers that dating is a bizarre and often unpleasant ritual. Accordingly, you do not simply tell the story of your date. Rather, you select and arrange details to show your readers *why* dating is bizarre and unpleasant. As in any other kind of essay, you may state your thesis explicitly ("My experiences with dating have convinced me that this ritual should be abandoned entirely"), or you may imply your thesis through your selection and arrangement of events.

Narration can provide the structure for an entire essay, but narrative passages may also appear in essays that are not primarily narrative. In an *argumentative essay* supporting stricter gun-control legislation, for example, you might devote one or two paragraphs to the story of a child accidentally killed by a handgun. In this chapter, however, we focus on narration as the dominant pattern of a piece of writing. During your college career, many of your assignments will call for such writing. In an English composition class, for instance, you may be asked to write about an experience that was important to your development as an adult; on a European history exam, you may need to relate the events that led to Napoleon's defeat at the Battle of Waterloo; in a technical writing class, you may be asked to write a letter of complaint summarizing in detail a company's negligent actions. In each of these situations (as well as in many additional assignments), the piece of writing has a structure that is primarily narrative, and the narrative supports a particular thesis.

The skills you develop in narrative writing will also help you in other kinds of writing. A *process essay,* such as an explanation of a laboratory experiment, is like a narrative because it outlines a series of steps in chronological order; a *cause-and-effect essay,* such as your answer to an exam question that asks you to analyze the events that led to the Great Depression, also resembles a narrative in that it traces a sequence of events. A process essay, however, explains how to do something, and a cause-and-effect essay explains how items or events are related. Still, writing process and cause-and-effect essays will be easier after you master narration. (Process essays and cause-and-effect essays are dealt with in Chapters 7 and 8, respectively.)

PLANNING A NARRATIVE ESSAY

Including Enough Detail

Narratives, like other types of writing, need rich, specific details if they are to be convincing. Each detail should help to create a picture for the reader; even exact times, dates, and geographical locations can be helpful. Look, for example, at the following paragraph from the essay "My Mother Never Worked," which appears later in this chapter:

> In the winter she sewed night after night, endlessly, begging cast-off clothing from relatives, ripping apart coats, dresses, blouses, and trousers to remake them to fit her four daughters and son. Every morning and every evening she milked cows, fed pigs and calves, cared for chickens, picked eggs, cooked meals, washed dishes, scrubbed floors, and tended and loved her children. In the spring she planted a garden once more, dragging pails of water to nourish and sustain the vegetables for the family. In 1936 she lost a baby in her sixth month.

In the paragraph above, the list of details gives the narrative authenticity and makes it convincing. The central figure in the narrative is a busy, productive woman, and readers know this because they are presented with an exhaustive catalog of her activities.

Varying Sentence Structure

When narratives present a long series of events, all the sentences can begin to sound alike: "She sewed dresses. . . . She milked cows. . . . She fed pigs. . . . She fed calves. . . . She cared for chickens." Such a predictable string of sentences may become monotonous for your readers. You can eliminate this monotony by varying your sentence structure — for instance, by using a variety of sentence openings or by combining simple sentences: "In the winter she sewed night after night, endlessly. . . . Every morning and every evening she milked cows, fed pigs and calves, cared for chickens. . . ."

Maintaining Clear Narrative Order

Many narratives present events in the exact order in which they occurred, moving from first event to last. Whether or not you follow a strict **chronological order** depends on the purpose of your narrative. If you are writing a straightforward account of a historical event or summarizing a record of poor management practices, you will probably want to move from beginning to end. In a personal experience essay or a fictional narrative, however, you may engage your readers' interest by beginning with an event from the middle of your story, or even from the end, and then presenting the events that led up to it. You may also begin in the present and then use one or more *flashbacks* (shifts into the past) to tell your story.

USING ACCURATE VERB TENSES.   Verb tense is extremely important in writing that recounts events in a fixed order because tenses indicate temporal (time) relationships — *earlier, simultaneous, later.* When you write a narrative, you must be careful to keep verb tenses consistent and accurate so your readers can follow the sequence of events. Naturally, you must shift tenses to reflect an actual time shift in your narrative. For instance, convention requires that you use present tense when discussing works of literature ("When Hamlet's mother *marries* his uncle . . ."), but a flashback to an earlier point in the story calls for a shift from present to past tense ("Before their marriage, Hamlet *was* . . ."). Nevertheless, you should avoid unwarranted shifts in verb tense; they will make your narrative confusing.

USING TRANSITIONS.   **Transitions** — connecting words or phrases — help link events in time, enabling narratives to flow smoothly. Without them, narratives would lack coherence, and readers would be unsure of the correct sequence of events. Transitions can indicate the order in which events occur, and they also signal shifts in time. In narrative writing, the transitions commonly used for these purposes include *first, second, next, then, later, at the same time, meanwhile, immediately, soon, before, earlier, after, afterward, now,* and *finally.* In addition to these transitions, specific time markers — such as *three years later, in 1927, after two hours,* and *on January 3* — indicate how much time has passed between events. A more complete list of transitions appears on page 41.

STRUCTURING A NARRATIVE ESSAY

Like other essays, narratives have an introduction, a body, and a conclusion. If your essay's thesis is explicitly stated, it will, in most cases, appear in the *introduction*. The *body* of your essay will recount the events that make up your narrative, following a clear and orderly plan. Finally, the *conclusion* will give your readers the sense that your story is complete, perhaps by restating your thesis or summarizing key points or events.

Suppose you are assigned a short history paper about the Battle of Waterloo. You plan to support the thesis that if Napoleon had kept more troops in reserve, he might have defeated the British troops under Wellington. Based on this thesis, you decide that the best way to organize your paper is to present the five major phases of the battle in chronological order. An informal outline of your essay might look like this:

Introduction:	Thesis statement — Had Napoleon kept more troops in reserve, he might have broken Wellington's line with another infantry attack and thus won the Battle of Waterloo.
Phase 1 of the battle:	Napoleon attacked the Château of Hougoumont.
Phase 2 of the battle:	The French infantry attacked the British lines.
Phase 3 of the battle:	The French cavalry staged a series of charges against the British lines that had not been attacked before; Napoleon committed his reserves.
Phase 4 of the battle:	The French captured La Haye Sainte, their first success of the day but an advantage that Napoleon,

	having committed troops elsewhere, could not maintain without reserves.
Phase 5 of the battle:	The French infantry was decisively defeated by the combined thrust of the British infantry and the remaining British cavalry.
Conclusion:	Restatement of thesis or review of key points or events.

By discussing the five phases of the battle in chronological order, you clearly support your thesis. As you expand your informal outline into a historical narrative, exact details, dates, times, and geographical locations are extremely important, for without them, your statements are open to question. In addition, to keep your readers aware of the order in which the events of the battle took place, you must select appropriate transitional words and phrases and pay careful attention to verb tenses.

☑ **CHECKLIST: NARRATION**

- Does your assignment call for narration?
- Does your essay's thesis suggest the significance of the events you discuss?
- Have you included enough specific details?
- Have you varied your sentence structure?
- Is the order of events clear to readers?
- Do your verb tenses enable readers to follow the sequence of events?
- Do your transitions link events in time?

▶ A STUDENT WRITER: NARRATION

The following essay is typical of the informal narrative writing many students are asked to do in English composition classes. It was written by Tiffany Forte in response to the assignment "Write an essay about a goal or dream you had when you were a child."

My Field of Dreams

Introduction   When I was young, I was told that when I   1
grew up I could be anything I wanted to be, and
I always took for granted that this was true.
I knew exactly what I was going to be, and I
would spend hours dreaming about how wonderful
my life would be when I grew up. One day,
though, when I did grow up, I realized that
Thesis statement   things had not turned out the way I had always
expected they would.

Narrative begins

When I was little, I never played with baby dolls or Barbies. I wasn't like other little girls; I was a tomboy. I was the only girl in the neighborhood where I lived, so I always played with boys. We would play army or football or (my favorite) baseball.   2

Almost every summer afternoon, all the boys in my neighborhood and I would meet by the big oak tree to get a baseball game going. Surprisingly, I was always one of the first to be picked for a team. I was very fast, and (for my size) I could hit the ball far. I loved baseball more than anything, and I wouldn't miss a game for the world.   3

My dad played baseball too, and every Friday night I would go to the field with my mother to watch him play. It was just like the big leagues, with lots of people, a snack bar, and lights that shone so high and bright you could see them a mile away. I loved to go to my dad's games. When all the other kids would wander off and play, I would sit and cheer on my dad and his team. My attention was focused on the field, and my heart would jump with every pitch.   4

Even more exciting than my dad's games were the major league games. The Phillies were my favorite team, and I always looked forward to watching them on television. My dad would make popcorn, and we would sit and watch in anticipation of a Phillies victory. We would go wild, yelling and screaming at all the big plays. When the Phillies would win, I would be so excited I couldn't sleep; when they would lose, I would go to bed angry just like my dad.   5

Key experience introduced (¶s 6–7)

It was when my dad took me to my first major league baseball game that I decided I wanted to be a major league baseball player. The excitement began when we pulled into the parking lot of Veterans Stadium. There were thousands of cars. As we walked from the car to the stadium,   6

my dad told me to hold on to his hand and not to
let go no matter what. When we gave the man our
tickets and entered the stadium, I understood
why. There were mobs of people everywhere. They
were walking around the stadium and standing in
long lines for hot dogs, beer, and souvenirs.
It was the most wonderful thing I had ever
seen. When we got to our seats, I looked down at
the tiny baseball diamond below and felt as if
I were on top of the world.

The cheering of the crowd, the singing,   7
and the chants were almost more than I could
stand. I was bursting with enthusiasm. Then, in
the bottom of the eighth inning, with the score
tied and two outs, Mike Schmidt came up to bat
and hit the game-winning home run. The crowd
went crazy. Everyone in the whole stadium was
standing, and I found myself yelling and
screaming along with everyone else. When Mike
Schmidt came out of the dugout to receive his
standing ovation, I felt a lump in my throat
and butterflies in my stomach. He was everyone's hero that night, and I could only imagine
the pride he must have felt. I slept the whole
way home and dreamed of what it would be like to
be the hero of the game.

**Narrative
continues**

The next day, when I met with the boys at   8
the oak tree, I told them that when I grew up, I
was going to be a major league baseball player.
They all laughed at me and said I could never be
a baseball player because I was a girl. I told
them that they were all wrong, and that I would
show them.

**Analysis of
childhood
experiences**

In the years to follow I played girls'   9
softball in a competitive fast-pitch league,
and I was very good. I always wanted to play
baseball with the boys, but there were no mixed
leagues. After a few years, I realized that the
boys from the oak tree were right: I was never
going to be a major league baseball player. I

realized that what I had been told when I was
younger wasn't the whole truth. What no one had
bothered to tell me was that I could be anything I wanted to be--as long as it was something that was appropriate for a girl to do.

Conclusion   In time, I would get over the loss of my   10
dream. I found new dreams, acceptable for a
young woman, and I moved on to other things.
Still, every time I watch a baseball game and
someone hits a home run, I get those same butterflies in my stomach and think, for just a
minute, about what might have been.

Points for Special Attention

INTRODUCTION.   Tiffany's introduction is very straightforward, yet it
arouses reader interest by setting up a contrast between what she
expected and what actually happened. Her optimistic expectation — that
she could be anything she wanted to be — is contradicted by her thesis
statement, encouraging readers to read on to discover how things turned
out, and why.

THESIS STATEMENT.   Tiffany's assignment was to write about a goal
or dream she had when she was a child, but her instructor made it clear
that the essay should have an explicitly stated thesis that made a point
about the goal or dream. Tiffany knew she wanted to write about her passion for baseball, but she also knew that just listing a series of events
would not fulfill the assignment. Her thesis statement —"One day,
though, when I did grow up, I realized that things had not turned out the
way I had always expected they would"— puts her memories in context,
suggesting that she will use them to support a general conclusion about
the gap between dreams and reality.

STRUCTURE.   The body of Tiffany's essay traces the chronology of her
involvement with baseball: playing with the neighborhood boys, watching her father's games, watching baseball on television, and, finally, seeing her first major league game. Each body paragraph introduces a
different aspect of her experience with baseball, culminating in the vividly
described Phillies game. The balance of the essay (paragraphs 8–10) summarizes the aftermath of that game, gives a brief overview of Tiffany's
later years in baseball, and presents her conclusion.

DETAIL.   Personal narratives like Tiffany's need a lot of detail because the writers want readers to see and hear and feel what they did. To

present an accurate picture, Tiffany includes all the significant sights and sounds she can remember: the big oak tree, the lights on the field, the popcorn, the excited cheers, the food and souvenir stands, the crowds, and so on. She also names Mike Schmidt ("everyone's hero"), his team, and the stadium in which she saw him play. Despite all these details, though, she omits a few important ones — in particular, how old she was at each stage of her essay.

VERB TENSE.   Maintaining clear chronological order is very important in narrative writing, where unwarranted shifts in verb tenses can confuse readers. Knowing this, Tiffany avoids unnecessary tense shifts. In her conclusion, she shifts from past to present tense, but this shift is both necessary and clear. Elsewhere she uses *would* to identify events that recurred regularly. For example, in paragraph 5 she says, "My dad *would* make popcorn" rather than "My dad *made* popcorn," which would suggest that he did so only once.

TRANSITIONS.   Tiffany's skillful use of transitional words and expressions links her sentences and moves her readers smoothly through her essay. In addition to transitional words like *when* and *then*, she uses specific time markers —"When I was little," "Almost every summer afternoon," "every Friday night," "As we walked," "The next day," "In the years to follow," and "After a few years"— to advance the narrative and carry her readers along.

Focus on Revision

In their responses to an earlier draft of Tiffany's essay, several students in her peer editing group recommended that she revise one particularly monotonous paragraph. (As one student pointed out, all its sentences began with the subject, making the paragraph seem choppy and its ideas disconnected.) Here is the paragraph from her draft:

> My dad played baseball too. I went to the field with my mother every Friday night to watch him play. It was just like the big leagues. There were lots of people and a snack bar. The lights shone so high and bright you could see them a mile away. I loved to go to my dad's games. All the other kids would wander off and play. I would sit and cheer on my dad and his team. My attention was focused on the field. My heart would jump with every pitch.

In the revised version of the paragraph (now paragraph 4 of her essay), Tiffany varies sentence length and opening strategies:

> My dad played baseball too, and every Friday night I would go to the field with my mother to watch him play. It was just like the big leagues, with lots of people, a snack bar, and lights that shone so high and bright you could see them a mile away. I loved to go to my dad's games. When

all the other kids would wander off and play, I would sit and cheer on my dad and his team. My attention was focused on the field, and my heart would jump with every pitch.

After reading Tiffany's revised draft, another student suggested that she might still polish her essay a bit. For instance, she could add some dialogue, quoting the boys' taunts and her own reply in paragraph 8. She could also edit to eliminate **clichés** (overused expressions), substituting fresher, more original language for phrases like "I felt a lump in my throat and butterflies in my stomach" and "I felt as if I were on top of the world." In another draft of her essay, Tiffany followed up on these suggestions.

The selections that follow illustrate some of the many possibilities open to writers of narratives.

JANET WU

Janet Wu (1960–), a Boston-based television news reporter, published the following personal essay in the *New York Times Magazine* in 1999. The daughter of a Chinese immigrant father and an American-born mother, Wu reflects here on her Chinese grandmother, whom she first met when she was twelve.

During World War II, Japan occupied much of northern China. At the close of the war in 1947, the Japanese retreat sparked a full-scale revolution in China as the Chinese government battled Communist insurgents to take control of these territories. The ensuing chaos and ultimate Communist victory led Wu's father and many others to flee the country. The oppressive regime established by the Communists and its hostile relations with the United States caused those who left the country to lose virtually all contact with their families who stayed behind. Not until President Richard Nixon visited China in 1972 to work out a peace agreement and establish economic ties did many Chinese Americans have an opportunity to be reunited with family members there.

Homeward Bound

My grandmother has bound feet.* Cruelly tethered since her birth, 1 they are like bonsai trees, miniature versions of what should have been. She is a relic even in China, where foot binding was first banned more than 80 years ago when the country could no longer afford a population that had to be carried. Her slow, delicate hobble betrays her age and the status she held and lost.

My own size 5 feet are huge in comparison. The marks and callouses 2 they bear come from running and jumping, neither of which my grandmother has ever done. The difference between our feet reminds me of the incredible history we hold between us like living bookends. We stand like sentries on either side of a vast gulf.

For most of my childhood, I didn't even know she existed. My father 3 was a young man when he left his family's village in northern China, disappearing into the chaos of the Japanese invasion and the Communist revolution that followed. He fled to Taiwan and eventually made his way to America, alone. To me, his second child, it seemed he had no family or history other than his American-born wife and four children. I didn't know that he had been writing years of unanswered letters to China.

I was still a young girl when he finally got a response, and with it the 4 news that his father and six of his seven siblings had died in those years of

---

*Eds. NOTE — For thousands of years, the feet of elite Chinese women were broken when they were young girls and then tightly bound so that they never grew beyond three to four inches and developed a high arch. These "lotus feet," so named because they were meant to resemble a lotus bud, were a symbol of high status as well as feminine beauty.

war and revolution. But the letter also contained an unexpected blessing: somehow his mother had survived. So 30 years after he left home, and in the wake of President Nixon's visit, my father gathered us up and we rushed to China to find her.

I saw my grandmother for the very first time when I was 12. She was almost 80, surprisingly alien and shockingly small. I searched her wrinkled face for something familiar, some physical proof that we belonged to each other. She stared at me the same way. Did she feel cheated, I wondered, by the distance, by the time we had not spent together? I did. With too many lost years to reclaim, we had everything and nothing to say. She politely listened as I struggled with scraps of formal Chinese and smiled as I fell back on "Wo bu dong" ("I don't understand you"). And yet we communicated something strange and beautiful. I found it easy to love this person I had barely met.

The second time I saw her I was 23, arriving in China on an indulgent post-graduate-school adventure, with a Caucasian boyfriend in tow. My grandmother sat on my hotel bed, shrunken and wise, looking as if she belonged in a museum case. She stroked my asymmetrically cropped hair. I touched her feet, and her face contorted with the memory of her childhood pain. "You are lucky," she said. We both understood that she was thinking of far more than the bindings that long ago made her cry. I wanted to share even the smallest part of her life's journey, but I could not conceive of surviving a dynasty and a revolution, just as she could not imagine my life in a country she had never seen. In our mutual isolation of language and experience, we could only gaze in wonder, mystified that we had come to be sitting together.

I last saw her almost five years ago. At 95, she was even smaller, and her frailty frightened me. I was painfully aware that I probably would never see her again, that I would soon lose this person I never really had. So I mentally logged every second we spent together and jockeyed with my siblings for the chance to hold her hand or touch her shoulder. Our departure date loomed like some kind of sentence. And when it came, she broke down, her face bowed into her gnarled hands. I went home, and with resignation awaited the inevitable news that she was gone.

But two months after that trip, it was my father who died. For me, his loss was doubly cruel: his death deprived me of both my foundation and the bridge to my faraway grandmother. For her, it was the second time she had lost him. For the 30 years they were separated, she had feared her son was dead. This time, there was no ambiguity, no hope. When she heard the news, my uncle later wrote us, she wept quietly.

When I hear friends complain about having to visit their nearby relatives, I think of how far away my grandmother is and how untouched our relationship remains by the modern age. My brief handwritten notes are agonizingly slow to reach her. When they do arrive, she cannot read them. I cannot call her. I cannot see, hear or touch her.

But last month my mother called to tell me to brush up on my Chi-   10
nese. Refusing to let go of our tenuous connection to my father's family,
she has decided to take us all back to China in October for my grandmother's 100th birthday. And so every night, I sit at my desk and study,
thinking of her tiny doll-like feet, of the miles and differences that separate
us, of the moments we'll share when we meet one last time. And I beg her
to hold on until I get there.

· · ·

COMPREHENSION

1. What is the significance of bound feet in this essay?

2. What does Wu mean when she says that she and her grandmother "stand like sentries on either side of a vast gulf" (2)? What is this gulf?

3. How is Wu different from her grandmother? List all the differences Wu identifies in the essay. What other differences do you imagine exist between them?

4. Wu visits her grandmother only three times. How are the three visits different?

5. In the last paragraph, Wu says, "Every night, I sit at my desk and study." What is she studying? Why?

6. In what sense is the relationship between Wu and her grandmother "untouched . . . by the modern age" (9)?

7. Why do you think this essay is called "Homeward Bound"? Consider all of the title's possible meanings.

PURPOSE AND AUDIENCE

1. Wu opens her essay abruptly with the statement "My grandmother has bound feet." How do you think she expects her readers to react to this statement?

2. What purpose does paragraph 9 serve? Do you find this paragraph intrusive, or does it seem to be a logical part of the essay?

3. What is the essay's thesis? Where is it stated? Besides this thesis, what other points does Wu want to communicate to her audience?

STYLE AND STRUCTURE

1. Where does Wu's narrative actually begin?

2. List the transitions Wu uses to move readers through her narrative.

3. In paragraph 8, Wu quotes her grandmother. Where else could she have used dialogue? How might it have strengthened her essay?

VOCABULARY PROJECTS

1. Define each of the following words as it is used in this selection.

   tethered (1)   indulgent (6)   jockeyed (7)
   bonsai (1)   asymmetrically (6)   gnarled (7)
   sentries (2)   contorted (6)   tenuous (10)

2. To communicate her grandmother's smallness and fragility, Wu uses the word *delicate* (1). List the other words she uses to convey these impressions. What additional words could she have used?

JOURNAL ENTRY

Write an imaginary dialogue between Wu and her grandmother about a current news event or a technological advance that occurred in Wu's lifetime.

WRITING WORKSHOP

1. One of the themes Wu develops is the difficulty she has communicating with her grandmother. To bridge this gap, write a letter to Wu from her grandmother in which you recount the grandmother's impressions of the events Wu discusses in her essay.

2. Tell the story of a series of visits with an elderly relative of your own. Begin your essay with Wu's words "When I hear friends complain about having to visit their nearby relatives . . ." (9).

3. Write a newspaper article in which you tell about the events leading up to Wu's grandmother's 100th birthday party. Open with the party itself, and then move back in time to begin the narrative with her discovery of her long-lost granddaughter.

COMBINING THE PATTERNS

Although this essay is a narrative, it also develops a contrast between Wu and her grandmother. How could Wu have developed this contrast further? What kind of material would she have to add to turn "Homeward Bound" into a **comparison-and-contrast** essay?

THEMATIC CONNECTIONS

- "The Way to Rainy Mountain" (page 148)
- "Words Left Unspoken" (page 133)
- "My First Conk" (page 228)
- "Mother Tongue" (page 405)

SANDRA CISNEROS

Born into a working-class family in 1954, Sandra Cisneros, the daughter of a Mexican-American mother and a Mexican father, spent much of her childhood shuttling between Chicago and Mexico City. A lonely, bookish child, Cisneros began writing privately at a young age but only began to find her voice when she was a creative writing student at Loyola University and later at the University of Iowa Writer's Workshop. Her best-known works are *The House on Mango Street* (1983), a collection of interlocking stories set in Chicago's Mexican-American community; and another collection of stories, *Woman Hollering Creek* (1991), set in both Mexico and the United States.

Cisneros's fiction has focused on the lives of first- and second-generation Mexican Americans — more specifically, on the narrowly defined roles often assigned to women within this conservative culture. In her autobiographical essay "Only Daughter," which appeared in *Glamour* in 1990, she describes the difficulties of growing up the only daughter in a Mexican-American family of six sons.

Only Daughter

Once, several years ago, when I was just starting out my writing 1 career, I was asked to write my own contributor's note for an anthology I was part of. I wrote: "I am the only daughter in a family of six sons. *That* explains everything."

Well, I've thought about that ever since, and yes, it explains a lot to 2 me, but for the reader's sake I should have written: "I am the only daughter in a *Mexican* family of six sons." Or even: "I am the only daughter of a Mexican father and a Mexican-American mother." Or: "I am the only daughter of a working-class family of nine." All of these had everything to do with who I am today.

I was/am the only daughter and *only* a daughter. Being an only 3 daughter in a family of six sons forced me by circumstance to spend a lot of time by myself because my brothers felt it beneath them to play with a *girl* in public. But that aloneness, that loneliness, was good for a would-be writer — it allowed me time to think and think, to imagine, to read and prepare myself.

Being only a daughter for my father meant my destiny would lead me 4 to become someone's wife. That's what he believed. But when I was in the fifth grade and shared my plans for college with him, I was sure he understood. I remember my father saying, "*Que bueno, ni'ja,* that's good." That meant a lot to me, especially since my brothers thought the idea hilarious. What I didn't realize was that my father thought college was good for girls — good for finding a husband. After four years in college and two more in graduate school, and still no husband, my father shakes his head even now and says I wasted all that education.

In retrospect, I'm lucky my father believed daughters were meant for 5
husbands. It meant it didn't matter if I majored in something silly like English. After all, I'd find a nice professional eventually, right? This allowed me the liberty to putter about embroidering my little poems and stories without my father interrupting with so much as a "What's that you're writing?"

But the truth is, I wanted him to interrupt. I wanted my father to 6
understand what it was I was scribbling, to introduce me as "My only daughter, the writer." Not as "This is only my daughter. She teaches." *Es maestra* — teacher. Not even *profesora.*

In a sense, everything I have ever written has been for him, to win his 7
approval even though I know my father can't read English words, even though my father's only reading includes the brown-ink *Esto* sports magazines from Mexico City and the bloody *¡Alarma!* magazines that feature yet another sighting of *La Virgen de Guadalupe* on a tortilla or a wife's revenge on her philandering husband by bashing his skull in with a *molcajete* (a kitchen mortar made of volcanic rock). Or the *fotonovelas,* the little picture paperbacks with tragedy and trauma erupting from the characters' mouths in bubbles.

My father represents, then, the public majority. A public who is unin- 8
terested in reading, and yet one whom I am writing about and for, and privately trying to woo.

When we were growing up in Chicago, we moved a lot because of my 9
father. He suffered bouts of nostalgia. Then we'd have to let go of our flat, store the furniture with mother's relatives, load the station wagon with baggage and bologna sandwiches, and head south. To Mexico City.

We came back, of course. To yet another Chicago flat, another Chicago 10
neighborhood, another Catholic school. Each time, my father would seek out the parish priest in order to get a tuition break, and complain or boast: "I have seven sons."

He meant *siete hijos,* seven children, but he translated it as "sons." "I 11
have seven sons." To anyone who would listen. The Sears Roebuck employee who sold us the washing machine. The short-order cook where my father ate his ham-and-eggs breakfasts. "I have seven sons." As if he deserved a medal from the state.

My papa. He didn't mean anything by that mistranslation, I'm sure. 12
But somehow I could feel myself being erased. I'd tug my father's sleeve and whisper: "Not seven sons. Six! and *one daughter.*"

When my oldest brother graduated from medical school, he fulfilled 13
my father's dream that we study hard and use this — our heads, instead of this — our hands. Even now my father's hands are thick and yellow, stubbed by a history of hammer and nails and twine and coils and springs. "Use this," my father said, tapping his head, "and not this," showing us those hands. He always looked tired when he said it.

Wasn't college an investment? And hadn't I spent all those years in 14
college? And if I didn't marry, what was it all for? Why would anyone go

to college and then choose to be poor? Especially someone who had always been poor.

Last year, after ten years of writing professionally, the financial re-   15
wards started to trickle in. My second National Endowment for the Arts Fellowship. A guest professorship at the University of California, Berkeley. My book, which sold to a major New York publishing house.

At Christmas, I flew home to Chicago. The house was throbbing, same   16
as always; hot *tamales* and sweet *tamales* hissing in my mother's pressure cooker, and everybody — my mother, six brothers, wives, babies, aunts, cousins — talking too loud and at the same time, like in a Fellini film, because that's just how we are.

I went upstairs to my father's room. One of my stories had just been   17
translated into Spanish and published in an anthology of Chicano writing, and I wanted to show it to him. Ever since he recovered from a stroke two years ago, my father likes to spend his leisure hours horizontally. And that's how I found him, watching a Pedro Infante* movie on Galavisión** and eating rice pudding.

There was a glass filmed with milk on the bedside table. There were   18
several vials of pills and balled Kleenex. And on the floor, one black sock and a plastic urinal that I didn't want to look at but looked at anyway. Pedro Infante was about to burst into song, and my father was laughing.

I'm not sure if it was because my story was translated into Spanish, or   19
because it was published in Mexico, or perhaps because the story dealt with Tepeyac, the *colonia* my father was raised in and the house he grew up in, but at any rate, my father punched the mute button on his remote control and read my story.

I sat on the bed next to my father and waited. He read it very slowly.   20
As if he were reading each line over and over. He laughed at all the right places and read lines he liked out loud. He pointed and asked questions: "Is this So-and-so?" "Yes," I said. He kept reading.

When he was finally finished, after what seemed like hours, my father   21
looked up and asked: "Where can we get more copies of this for the relatives?"

Of all the wonderful things that happened to me last year, that was the   22
most wonderful.

• • •

COMPREHENSION

1. What does Cisneros mean when she writes that being an only daughter in a family of six sons "explains everything" (1)?

2. What distinction does Cisneros make in paragraphs 2 and 3 between being "the only daughter" and being "only a daughter"?

---

*EDS. NOTE — Mexican actor.
**EDS. NOTE — A Spanish-language cable channel.

3. What advantages does Cisneros see in being the only daughter? In being only a daughter?

4. Why does her father think she has wasted her education? What is her reaction to his opinion?

5. Why was her father's reaction to her story the most wonderful thing that happened to Cisneros that year?

PURPOSE AND AUDIENCE

1. Although Cisneros uses many Spanish words in her essay, in most cases she defines or explains these words. What does this decision tell you about her purpose and audience?

2. What is Cisneros's thesis? What incidents and details support her point?

3. Do you think Cisneros intends to convey a sympathetic or an unsympathetic impression of her father? Explain.

STYLE AND STRUCTURE

1. Where does Cisneros interrupt a narrative passage to comment on or analyze events? What does this strategy accomplish?

2. Are the episodes presented in chronological order? Explain.

3. What transitional expressions does Cisneros use to introduce new episodes?

4. Cisneros quotes her father several times. What do we learn about him from his words?

5. Why does Cisneros devote so much space to describing her father in paragraphs 17–21? How does this portrait compare to the one she presents in paragraphs 9–11?

VOCABULARY PROJECTS

1. Define each of the following words as it is used in this selection.
   embroidering (5)   stubbed (13)

2. What is the difference in connotation between *sons* and *children*? Between *teacher* and *professor*? Do you think these distinctions are as significant as Cisneros seems to think they are? Explain.

JOURNAL ENTRY

In what sense do the number and gender(s) of your siblings "explain everything" about who you are today?

WRITING WORKSHOP

1. Write a narrative essay consisting of a series of related episodes that show how you gradually gained the approval and respect of one of your parents, another relative, or a friend.

2. In "Only Daughter," Cisneros traces the development of her identity as an adult, a female, and a writer. Write a narrative essay in which you trace the development of your own personal or professional identity.

3. Are male and female children treated differently in your family? Have your parents had different expectations for their sons and daughters? Write a narrative essay recounting one or more incidents that illustrate these differences (or the lack of differences). If you and your siblings are all of the same gender, or if you are an only child, write about another family you know well.

COMBINING THE PATTERNS

Cisneros structures her essay as a narrative in which she is the main character and her brothers barely appear. To give her readers a clearer understanding of how her father's attitude toward her differs from his attitude toward her brothers, Cisneros could have added one or more paragraphs of **comparison and contrast,** focusing on the different ways she and her brothers are treated. What specific points of contrast would readers find most useful? Where might such paragraphs be added?

THEMATIC CONNECTIONS

- "My Field of Dreams" (page 73)
- "Words Left Unspoken" (page 133)
- "Suicide Note" (page 315)
- "The Men We Carry in Our Minds" (page 399)

MAYA ANGELOU

Maya Angelou was born Marguerita Johnson in 1928 in St. Louis and spent much of her childhood in Stamps, Arkansas, living with her grandmother. She began her varied career as an actress and singer, appearing in several television dramas and films; in 1998 she made her debut as a director with the film *Down in the Delta*. In the 1960s she served as northern coordinator for the Southern Christian Leadership Conference, the civil rights group organized by Martin Luther King Jr., and she also worked as a journalist in Egypt and Ghana. A well-known poet, Angelou composed and read "On the Pulse of Morning" for Bill Clinton's 1993 presidential inauguration. The published version of the poem was a best-seller, and her recording of it won a Grammy award. She is currently on the faculty at Wake Forest University.

It is likely, however, that Angelou will be best remembered for her series of autobiographical works. For years she had entertained literary friends with tales of her childhood, and they encouraged her to write her life story. The result, the critically acclaimed *I Know Why the Caged Bird Sings* (1969), appeared at a time when African-American literature was beginning to flower in the United States, and Angelou's voice was quickly recognized as one of its most powerful. In the following chapter from *I Know Why the Caged Bird Sings,* Angelou remembers a difficult incident from her childhood in racially segregated Stamps, during the Great Depression. The Depression hit African Americans particularly hard, and opportunities for them were extremely limited — especially in the South.

Finishing School

Recently a white woman from Texas, who would quickly describe   1
herself as a liberal, asked me about my hometown. When I told her that in Stamps my grandmother had owned the only Negro general merchandise store since the turn of the century, she exclaimed, "Why, you were a debutante." Ridiculous and even ludicrous. But Negro girls in small Southern towns, whether poverty-stricken or just munching along on a few of life's necessities, were given as extensive and irrelevant preparations for adulthood as rich white girls shown in magazines. Admittedly the training was not the same. While white girls learned to waltz and sit gracefully with a tea cup balanced on their knees, we were lagging behind, learning the mid-Victorian values with very little money to indulge them. . . .

We were required to embroider and I had trunkfuls of colorful dish-   2
towels, pillowcases, runners, and handkerchiefs to my credit. I mastered the art of crocheting and tatting, and there was a lifetime's supply of dainty doilies that would never be used in sacheted dresser drawers. It went without saying that all girls could iron and wash, but the finer touches around the home, like setting a table with real silver, baking roasts, and cooking vegetables without meat, had to be learned elsewhere. Usually at the source of those habits. During my tenth year, a white woman's kitchen became my finishing school.

Mrs. Viola Cullinan was a plump woman who lived in a three-bedroom   3
house somewhere behind the post office. She was singularly unattractive
until she smiled, and then the lines around her eyes and mouth which
made her look perpetually dirty disappeared, and her face looked like the
mask of an impish elf. She usually rested her smile until late afternoon
when her woman friends dropped in and Miss Glory, the cook, served
them cold drinks on the closed-in porch.

The exactness of her house was inhuman. This glass went here and   4
only here. That cup had its place and it was an act of impudent rebellion to
place it anywhere else. At twelve o'clock the table was set. At 12:15 Mrs.
Cullinan sat down to dinner (whether her husband had arrived or not). At
12:16 Miss Glory brought out the food.

It took me a week to learn the difference between a salad plate, a bread   5
plate, and a dessert plate.

Mrs. Cullinan kept up the tradition of her wealthy parents. She was   6
from Virginia. Miss Glory, who was a descendant of slaves that had worked
for the Cullinans, told me her history. She had married beneath her
(according to Miss Glory). Her husband's family hadn't had their money
very long and what they had "didn't 'mount to much."

As ugly as she was, I thought privately, she was lucky to get a hus-   7
band above or beneath her station. But Miss Glory wouldn't let me say
a thing against her mistress. She was very patient with me, however,
over the housework. She explained the dishware, silverware, and servants' bells. The large round bowl in which soup was served wasn't a
soup bowl, it was a tureen. There were goblets, sherbet glasses, ice-cream
glasses, wine glasses, green glass coffee cups with matching saucers,
and water glasses. I had a glass to drink from, and it sat with Miss Glory's
on a separate shelf from the others. Soup spoons, gravy boat, butter knives,
salad forks, and carving platter were additions to my vocabulary and in
fact almost represented a new language. I was fascinated with the novelty,
with the fluttering Mrs. Cullinan and her Alice-in-Wonderland house.

Her husband remains, in my memory, undefined. I lumped him with   8
all the other white men that I had ever seen and tried not to see.

On our way home one evening, Miss Glory told me that Mrs. Cullinan   9
couldn't have children. She said that she was too delicate-boned. It was
hard to imagine bones at all under those layers of fat. Miss Glory went on
to say that the doctor had taken out all her lady organs. I reasoned that a
pig's organs included the lungs, heart, and liver, so if Mrs. Cullinan was
walking around without those essentials, it explained why she drank alcohol out of unmarked bottles. She was keeping herself embalmed.

When I spoke to Bailey* about it, he agreed that I was right, but he also   10
informed me that Mr. Cullinan had two daughters by a colored lady and
that I knew them very well. He added that the girls were the spitting

---

*Eds. note — Angelou's brother.

image of their father. I was unable to remember what he looked like, although I had just left him a few hours before, but I thought of the Coleman girls. They were very light-skinned and certainly didn't look very much like their mother (no one ever mentioned Mr. Coleman).

My pity for Mrs. Cullinan preceded me the next morning like the 11
Cheshire cat's smile. Those girls, who could have been her daughters, were beautiful. They didn't have to straighten their hair. Even when they were caught in the rain, their braids still hung down straight like tamed snakes. Their mouths were pouty little cupid's bows. Mrs. Cullinan didn't know what she missed. Or maybe she did. Poor Mrs. Cullinan.

For weeks after, I arrived early, left late and tried very hard to make up 12
for her barrenness. If she had her own children, she wouldn't have had to ask me to run a thousand errands from her back door to the back doors of her friends. Poor old Mrs. Cullinan.

Then one evening Miss Glory told me to serve the ladies on the porch. 13
After I set the tray down and turned toward the kitchen, one of the women asked, "What's your name, girl?" It was the speckled-faced one. Mrs. Cullinan said, "She doesn't talk much. Her name's Margaret."

"Is she dumb?" 14

"No. As I understand it, she can talk when she wants to but she's usu- 15
ally quiet as a little mouse. Aren't you, Margaret?"

I smile at her. Poor thing. No organs and couldn't even pronounce my 16
name correctly.

"She's a sweet little thing, though." 17

"Well, that may be, but the name's too long. I'd never bother myself. 18
I'd call her Mary if I was you."

I fumed into the kitchen. That horrible woman would never have the 19
chance to call me Mary because if I was starving I'd never work for her. . . .

That evening I decided to write a poem on being white, fat, old, and 20
without children. It was going to be a tragic ballad. I would have to watch her carefully to capture the essence of her loneliness and pain.

The very next day, she called me by the wrong name. Miss Glory and I 21
were washing up the lunch dishes when Mrs. Cullinan came to the doorway. "Mary?"

Miss Glory asked, "Who?" 22

Mrs. Cullinan, sagging a little, knew and I knew. "I want Mary to go 23
down to Mrs. Randall's and take her some soup. She's not been feeling well for a few days."

Miss Glory's face was a wonder to see. "You mean Margaret, ma'am. 24
Her name's Margaret."

"That's too long. She's Mary from now on. Heat that soup from last 25
night and put it in the china tureen and, Mary, I want you to carry it carefully."

Every person I knew had a hellish horror of being "called out of his 26
name." It was a dangerous practice to call a Negro anything that could be loosely construed as insulting because of the centuries of their having been called niggers, jigs, dinges, blackbirds, crows, boots, and spooks.

Miss Glory had a fleeting second of feeling sorry for me. Then as she handed me the hot tureen she said, "Don't mind, don't pay that no mind. Sticks and stones may break your bones, but words . . . You know, I been working for her for twenty years." 27

She held the back door open for me. "Twenty years. I wasn't much older than you. My name used to be Hallelujah. That's what Ma named me, but my mistress give me 'Glory,' and it stuck. I likes it better too." 28

I was in the little path that ran behind the houses when Miss Glory shouted, "It's shorter too." 29

For a few seconds it was a tossup over whether I would laugh (imagine being named Hallelujah) or cry (imagine letting some white woman rename you for her convenience). My anger saved me from either outburst. I had to quit the job, but the problem was going to be how to do it. Momma wouldn't allow me to quit for just any reason. 30

"She's a peach. That woman is a real peach." Mrs. Randall's maid was talking as she took the soup from me, and I wondered what her name used to be and what she answered to now. 31

For a week I looked into Mrs. Cullinan's face as she called me Mary. She ignored my coming late and leaving early. Miss Glory was a little annoyed because I had begun to leave egg yolk on the dishes and wasn't putting much heart in polishing the silver. I hoped that she would complain to our boss, but she didn't. 32

Then Bailey solved my dilemma. He had me describe the contents of the cupboard and the particular plates she liked best. Her favorite piece was a casserole shaped like fish and the green glass coffee cups. I kept his instructions in mind, so on the next day when Miss Glory was hanging out clothes and I had again been told to serve the old biddies on the porch, I dropped the empty serving tray. When I heard Mrs. Cullinan scream "Mary!" I picked up the casserole and two of the green glass cups in readiness. As she rounded the kitchen door I let them fall on the tiled floor. 33

I could never absolutely describe to Bailey what happened next, because each time I got to the part where she fell on the floor and screwed up her ugly face to cry, we burst out laughing. She actually wobbled around on the floor and picked up shards of the cups and cried, "Oh, Momma. Oh, dear Gawd. It's Mamma's china from Virginia. Oh Momma, I'm sorry." 34

Miss Glory came running in from the yard and the women from the porch crowded around. Miss Glory was almost as broken up as her mistress. "You mean to say she broke our Virginia dishes? What we gone do?" 35

Mrs. Cullinan cried louder. "That clumsy nigger. Clumsy little black nigger." 36

Old speckled-face leaned down and asked, "Who did it, Viola? Was it Mary? Who did it?" 37

Everything was happening so fast I can't remember whether her action preceded her words, but I know that Mrs. Cullinan said, "Her name's Margaret, goddamn it, her name's Margaret." And she threw a 38 wedge of broken plate at me. It could have been the hysteria which put her aim off, but the flying crockery caught Miss Glory right over her ear and she started screaming.

I left the front door wide open so all the neighbors could hear.   39

Mrs. Cullinan was right about one thing. My name wasn't Mary.   40

•   •   •

COMPREHENSION

1. What was Angelou required to do in the white woman's kitchen? Why were these tasks so important to Mrs. Cullinan?

2. Why did Angelou feel sorry for Mrs. Cullinan at first? When did her attitude change? Why?

3. Why did Mrs. Cullinan's friend recommend that Angelou be called "Mary" (18)? Why did this upset Angelou so deeply?

4. When Angelou decided she wanted to quit, she realized she could not quit "for just any reason" (30). How did Bailey help her resolve her dilemma?

5. What did Angelou actually learn through her experience?

PURPOSE AND AUDIENCE

1. Is Angelou writing for southerners, blacks, whites, or a general audience? Identify specific details that support your answer.

2. Angelou begins her narrative by summarizing a discussion between herself and a white woman. What is her purpose in doing this?

3. What is Angelou's thesis?

STYLE AND STRUCTURE

1. What exactly is a *finishing school*? What image does it usually call to mind? How is the use of this phrase **ironic** in view of its meaning in this selection?

2. How does Angelou signal the passage of time in this narrative? Identify some transitional phrases that show the passage of time.

3. How does the use of dialogue highlight the contrast between the black and the white characters? In what way does this contrast strengthen the narrative?

4. What details does Angelou use to describe Mrs. Cullinan and her home to the reader? How does this detailed description help advance the narrative?

VOCABULARY PROJECTS

1. Define each of the following words as it is used in this selection.

tatting (2)	pouty (11)	dilemma (33)
sacheted (2)	barrenness (12)	shards (34)
impudent (4)	ballad (20)	
embalmed (9)	construed (26)	

2. According to your dictionary, what is the difference between *ridiculous* and *ludicrous* (1)? Between *soup bowl* and *tureen* (7)? Why do you think Angelou draws a distinction between the two words in each pair?

3. Try substituting an equivalent word for each of the following, paying careful attention to the context of each in the narrative.

perpetually (3)   station (7)   biddies (33)
exactness (4)   peach (31)

Does Angelou's original choice seem more effective in all cases? Explain.

JOURNAL ENTRY

Have you ever received any training or education that you considered at the time to be "extensive and irrelevant preparations for adulthood" (1)? Do you now see any value in the experience?

WRITING WORKSHOP

1. Think about a time in your life when an adult in a position of authority treated you unjustly. How did you react? Write a narrative essay in which you recount the situation and your responses to it.

2. Have you ever had an experience in which you were the victim of name calling — or in which you found yourself doing the name calling? Summarize the incident, including dialogue and description that will help your readers understand your motivations and reactions. Include a thesis statement that presents your attitude toward the incident.

3. Write a narrative essay that includes a brief summary of an incident from a work of fiction — specifically, an incident that serves as a character's initiation into adulthood. In your essay, focus on how the experience helps the character grow up.

COMBINING THE PATTERNS

Angelou's essay is a narrative, but it is rich with descriptive details. Identify specific passages of the essay that are structured as **descriptions** of people and places. Is the description primarily visual, or does it incorporate other senses (sound, smell, taste, and touch) as well? Do you think any person, setting, or object should be described in greater detail? Explain.

THEMATIC CONNECTIONS

- "Midnight" (page 177)
- "The 'Black Table' Is Still There" (page 294)
- "Revelation" (page 436)

DONNA SMITH-YACKEL

Although this narrative essay, which was first published in Women: A Journal of Liberation *in 1975, is based on personal experience, it makes an interesting statement about how society values "women's work."*

Social Security is a federal insurance program that requires workers to contribute a percentage of their wages to a fund from which they may draw benefits if they become unemployed due to disability. After retirement they can receive a monthly income from this fund, which also provides a modest death benefit to survivors. The contribution is generally deducted directly from one's paycheck, and employers must contribute a matching amount. According to federal law, a woman who is a homemaker, who has never been a wage earner, is eligible for Social Security benefits only through the earnings of her deceased husband. (The same would be true for a man if the roles were reversed.) Therefore, a homemaker's survivors would not be eligible for the death benefit. Although the law has been challenged in the courts, a home-maker who has never claimed income can still collect no Social Security bene-fits except through a spouse.

My Mother Never Worked

"Social Security Office." (The voice answering the telephone sounds very self-assured.) 1

"I'm calling about . . . my mother just died . . . I was told to call you and see about a . . . death-benefit check, I think they call it. . . ." 2

"I see. Was your mother on Social Security? How old was she?" 3

"Yes . . . she was seventy-eight. . . ." 4

"Do you know her number?" 5

"No . . . I, ah . . . don't you have a record?" 6

"Certainly. I'll look it up. Her name?" 7

"Smith. Martha Smith. Or maybe she used Martha Ruth Smith? . . . Sometimes she used her maiden name . . . Martha Jerabek Smith?" 8

"If you'd care to hold on, I'll check our records — it'll be a few min-utes." 9

"Yes. . . ." 10

Her love letters — to and from Daddy — were in an old box, tied with ribbons and stiff, rigid-with-age leather thongs: 1918 through 1920; hers written on stationery from the general store she had worked in full-time and managed, single-handed, after her graduation from high school in 1913; and his, at first, on YMCA or Soldiers and Sailors Club stationery dispensed to the fighting men of World War I. He wooed her thoroughly and persistently by mail, and though she reciprocated all his feelings for her, she dreaded marriage. . . . 11

"It's so hard for me to decide when to have my wedding day — that's all. I've thought about these last two days. I have told you dozens of times that I won't be afraid of married life, but when it comes down to setting 12 the date and then picturing myself a married woman with half a dozen or more kids to look after, it just makes me sick. . . . I am weeping right now — I hope that some day I can look back and say how foolish I was to dread it all."

They married in February, 1921, and began farming. Their first baby, a   13
daughter, was born in January, 1922, when my mother was 26 years old. The second baby, a son, was born in March, 1923. They were renting farms; my father, besides working his own fields, also was a hired man for two other farmers. They had no capital initially, and had to gain it slowly, working from dawn until midnight every day. My town-bred mother learned to set hens and raise chickens, feed pigs, milk cows, plant and harvest a garden, and can every fruit and vegetable she could scrounge. She carried water nearly a quarter of a mile from the well to fill her wash boilers in order to do her laundry on a scrub board. She learned to shuck grain, feed threshers, shock and husk corn, feed corn pickers. In September, 1925, the third baby came, and in June, 1927, the fourth child — both daughters. In 1930, my parents had enough money to buy their own farm, and that March they moved all their livestock and belongings themselves, 55 miles over rutted, muddy roads.

In the summer of 1930 my mother and her two eldest children   14
reclaimed a 40-acre field from Canadian thistles, by chopping them all out with a hoe. In the other fields, when the oats and flax began to head out, the green and blue of the crops were hidden by the bright yellow of wild mustard. My mother walked the fields day after day, pulling each mustard plant. She raised a new flock of baby chicks — 500 — and she spaded up, planted, hoed, and harvested a half-acre garden.

During the next spring their hogs caught cholera and died. No cash   15
that fall.

And in the next year the drought hit. My mother and father trudged   16
from the well to the chickens, the well to the calf pasture, the well to the barn, and from the well to the garden. The sun came out hot and bright, endlessly, day after day. The crops shriveled and died. They harvested half the corn, and ground the other half, stalks and all, and fed it to the cattle as fodder. With the price at four cents a bushel for the harvested crop, they couldn't afford to haul it into town. They burned it in the furnace for fuel that winter.

In 1934, in February, when the dust was still so thick in the Minnesota   17
air that my parents couldn't always see from the house to the barn, their fifth child — a fourth daughter — was born. My father hunted rabbits daily, and my mother stewed them, fried them, canned them, and wished out loud that she could taste hamburger once more. In the fall the shotgun brought prairie chickens, ducks, pheasant, and grouse. My mother plucked each bird, carefully reserving the breast feathers for pillows.

In the winter she sewed night after night, endlessly, begging cast-off   18
clothing from relatives, ripping apart coats, dresses, blouses, and trousers to remake them to fit her four daughters and son. Every morning and

every evening she milked cows, fed pigs and calves, cared for chickens, picked eggs, cooked meals, washed dishes, scrubbed floors, and tended and loved her children. In the spring she planted a garden once more, dragging pails of water to nourish and sustain the vegetables for the family. In 1936 she lost a baby in her sixth month.

In 1937 her fifth daughter was born. She was 42 years old. In 1939 a second son, and in 1941 her eighth child — and third son.   19

But the war had come, and prosperity of a sort. The herd of cattle had grown to 30 head; she still milked morning and evening. Her garden was more than a half acre — the rains had come, and by now the Rural Electricity Administration and indoor plumbing. Still she sewed — dresses and jackets for the children, housedresses and aprons for herself, weekly patching of jeans, overalls, and denim shirts. She still made pillows, using feathers she had plucked, and quilts every year — intricate patterns as well as patchwork, stitched as well as tied — all necessary bedding for her family. Every scrap of cloth too small to be used in quilts was carefully saved and painstakingly sewed together in strips to make rugs. She still went out in the fields to help with the haying whenever there was a threat of rain.   20

In 1959 my mother's last child graduated from high school. A year later the cows were sold. She still raised chickens and ducks, plucked feathers, made pillows, baked her own bread, and every year made a new quilt — now for a married child or for a grandchild. And her garden, that huge, undying symbol of sustenance, was as large and cared for as in all the years before. The canning, and now freezing, continued.   21

In 1969, on a June afternoon, mother and father started out for town so that she could buy sugar to make rhubarb jam for a daughter who lived in Texas. The car crashed into a ditch. She was paralyzed from the waist down.   22

In 1970 her husband, my father, died. My mother struggled to regain some competence and dignity and order in her life. At the rehabilitation institute, where they gave her physical therapy and trained her to live usefully in a wheelchair, the therapist told me: "She did fifteen pushups today — fifteen! She's almost seventy-five years old! I've never known a woman so strong!"   23

From her wheelchair she canned pickles, baked bread, ironed clothes, wrote dozens of letters weekly to her friends and her "half dozen or more kids," and made three patchwork housecoats and one quilt. She made balls and balls of carpet rags — enough for five rugs. And kept all her love letters.   24

"I think I've found your mother's records — Martha Ruth Smith; married to Ben F. Smith?"   25

"Yes, that's right."   26

"Well, I see that she was getting a widow's pension. . . ."   27

"Yes, that's right."   28

"Well, your mother isn't entitled to our $255 death benefit."   29

"Not entitled! But why?"   30

The voice on the telephone explains patiently: 31

"Well, you see — your mother never worked."   32

• • •

COMPREHENSION

1. What kind of work did Martha Smith do while her children were growing up? List some of the chores she performed.

2. Why isn't Martha Smith eligible for a death benefit?

3. How does the government define *work*?

PURPOSE AND AUDIENCE

1. What point is the writer trying to make? Why do you suppose her thesis is never explicitly stated?

2. This essay appeared in *Ms.* magazine and other publications whose audiences are sympathetic to feminist goals. Could it just as easily have appeared in a magazine whose audience was not? Explain.

3. Smith-Yackel mentions relatively little about her father in this essay. How can you account for this?

4. This essay was first published in 1975. Is it dated?

STYLE AND STRUCTURE

1. Is the title effective? If so, why? If not, what alternate title can you suggest?

2. Smith-Yackel could have outlined her mother's life without framing it with the telephone conversation. Why do you think she includes this frame?

3. What strategies does Smith-Yackel use to indicate the passing of time in her narrative?

4. This narrative piles details one on top of another almost like a list. Why does the writer list so many details?

5. In paragraphs 20 and 21, what is accomplished by the repetition of the word *still*?

VOCABULARY PROJECTS

1. Define each of the following words as it is used in this selection.

scrounge (13)	rutted (13)	intricate (20)
shuck (13)	reclaimed (14)	sustenance (21)
shock (13)	flax (14)	
husk (13)	fodder (16)	

2. Try substituting equivalent words for those italicized in this sentence:

   He *wooed* her *thoroughly* and *persistently* by mail, and though she *reciprocated* all his feeling for her, she *dreaded* marriage . . . (11).

   How do your substitutions change the sentence's meaning?

3. Throughout her narrative, Smith-Yackel uses concrete, specific verbs. Review her choice of verbs, particularly in paragraphs 13–24, and comment on how such verbs serve the essay's purpose.

JOURNAL ENTRY

Do you believe homemakers should be entitled to Social Security death benefits? Explain your reasoning.

WRITING WORKSHOP

1. If you can, interview one of your parents or grandparents (or another person you know who might remind you of Donna Smith-Yackel's mother) about his or her work, and write a chronological narrative based on what you learn. Include a thesis statement that your narrative can support.

2. Write Martha Smith's obituary as it might have appeared in her hometown newspaper. If you are not familiar with the form of an obituary, read a few in your local paper.

3. Write a narrative account of a typical day at the worst job you ever had. Include a thesis statement that expresses your negative feelings.

COMBINING THE PATTERNS

Because of the repetitive nature of the farm chores Smith-Yackel describes in her narrative, some passages come very close to explaining a **process**, a series of repeated steps that always occur in a predictable order. Identify several such passages. If Smith-Yackel's essay were written entirely as a process explanation, what material would have to be left out? How would these omissions change the essay?

THEMATIC CONNECTIONS

- "Midnight" (page 177)
- "On Fire" (page 243)
- "I Want a Wife" (page 474)
- "The Company Man" (page 478)

MARTIN GANSBERG

Martin Gansberg (1920–1995), a native of Brooklyn, New York, was a reporter and editor for the *New York Times* for forty-three years. The following article, written for the *Times* two weeks after the murder it recounts, earned Gansberg an award for excellence from the Newspaper Reporters Association of New York. Gansberg's thesis, though not explicitly stated, still retains its power.

The events reported here took place on March 14, 1964, as contemporary American culture was undergoing a complex transition. The relatively placid years of the 1950s were giving way to edgier times: the Civil Rights movement had led to social unrest in the South and in northern inner cities; the escalating war in Vietnam had created angry political divisions; President John F. Kennedy had been assassinated the previous fall; violent imagery was on the rise in television and film; a growing drug culture was becoming apparent. The brutal, senseless murder of Kitty Genovese — and, more important, her neighbors' failure to respond immediately to her cries for help — became a nationwide symbol for what was perceived as an evolving culture of violence and indifference. Even today, social scientists debate the causes of "the Genovese syndrome."

Thirty-Eight Who Saw Murder Didn't Call the Police

For more than half an hour 38 respectable, law-abiding citizens in Queens watched a killer stalk and stab a woman in three separate attacks in Kew Gardens.

Twice their chatter and the sudden glow of their bedroom lights interrupted him and frightened him off. Each time he returned, sought her out, and stabbed her again. Not one person telephoned the police during the assault; one witness called after the woman was dead.

That was two weeks ago today.

Still shocked is Assistant Chief Inspector Frederick M. Lussen, in charge of the borough's detectives and a veteran of 25 years of homicide investigations. He can give a matter-of-fact recitation on many murders. But the Kew Gardens slaying baffles him — not because it is a murder, but because the "good people" failed to call the police.

"As we have reconstructed the crime," he said, "the assailant had three chances to kill this woman during a 35-minute period. He returned twice to complete the job. If we had been called when he first attacked, the woman might not be dead now."

This is what the police say happened beginning at 3:20 A.M. in the staid, middle-class, tree-lined Austin Street area:

Twenty-eight-year-old Catherine Genovese, who was called Kitty by almost everyone in the neighborhood, was returning home from her job as manager of a bar in Hollis. She parked her red Fiat in a lot adjacent to the

Kew Gardens Long Island Rail Road Station, facing Mowbray Place. Like many residents of the neighborhood, she had parked there day after day since her arrival from Connecticut a year ago, although the railroad frowns on the practice.

She turned off the lights of her car, locked the door, and started to   8
walk the 100 feet to the entrance of her apartment at 82–70 Austin Street, which is in a Tudor building, with stores in the first floor and apartments on the second.

The entrance to the apartment is in the rear of the building because the   9
front is rented to retail stores. At night the quiet neighborhood is shrouded in the slumbering darkness that marks most residential areas.

Miss Genovese noticed a man at the far end of the lot, near a seven-   10
story apartment house at 82–40 Austin Street. She halted. Then, nervously, she headed up Austin Street toward Lefferts Boulevard, where there is a call box to the 102nd Police Precinct in nearby Richmond Hill.

She got as far as a street light in front of a bookstore before the man   11
grabbed her. She screamed. Lights went on in the 10-story apartment house at 82–67 Austin Street, which faces the bookstore. Windows slid open and voices punctuated the early-morning stillness.

Miss Genovese screamed: "Oh, my God, he stabbed me! Please help   12
me! Please help me!"

From one of the upper windows in the apartment house, a man called   13
down: "Let that girl alone!"

The assailant looked up at him, shrugged, and walked down Austin   14
Street toward a white sedan parked a short distance away. Miss Genovese struggled to her feet.

Lights went out. The killer returned to Miss Genovese, now trying to   15
make her way around the side of the building by the parking lot to get to her apartment. The assailant stabbed her again.

"I'm dying!" she shrieked. "I'm dying!"   16

Windows were opened again, and lights went on in many apartments.   17
The assailant got into his car and drove away. Miss Genovese staggered to her feet. A city bus, 0–10, the Lefferts Boulevard line to Kennedy International Airport, passed. It was 3:35 A.M.

The assailant returned. By then, Miss Genovese had crawled to the   18
back of the building, where the freshly painted brown doors to the apartment house held out hope for safety. The killer tried the first door; she wasn't there. At the second door, 82–62 Austin Street, he saw her slumped on the floor at the foot of the stairs. He stabbed her a third time — fatally.

It was 3:50 by the time the police received their first call, from a man   19
who was a neighbor of Miss Genovese. In two minutes they were at the scene. The neighbor, a 70-year-old woman, and another woman were the only persons on the street. Nobody else came forward.

The man explained that he had called the police after much delibera-   20
tion. He had phoned a friend in Nassau County for advice and then he had crossed the roof of the building to the apartment of the elderly woman to get her to make the call.

"I didn't want to get involved," he sheepishly told police.   21

Six days later, the police arrested Winston Moseley, a 29-year-old busi-   22
ness machine operator, and charged him with homicide. Moseley had no
previous record. He is married, has two children and owns a home at
133–19 Sutter Avenue, South Ozone Park, Queens. On Wednesday, a court
committed him to Kings County Hospital for psychiatric observation.

When questioned by the police, Moseley also said that he had slain   23
Mrs. Annie May Johnson, 24, of 146–12 133d Avenue, Jamaica, on Feb. 29
and Barbara Kralik, 15, of 174–17 140th Avenue, Springfield Gardens, last
July. In the Kralik case, the police are holding Alvin L. Mitchell, who is
said to have confessed to that slaying.

The police stressed how simple it would have been to have gotten in   24
touch with them. "A phone call," said one of the detectives, "would have
done it." The police may be reached by dialing "0" for operator or SPring
7–3100.

Today witnesses from the neighborhood, which is made up of one-   25
family homes in the $35,000 to $60,000 range with the exception of the two
apartment houses near the railroad station, find it difficult to explain why
they didn't call the police.

A housewife, knowingly if quite casually, said, "We thought it was a   26
lovers' quarrel." A husband and wife both said, "Frankly, we were afraid."
They seemed aware of the fact that events might have been different. A
distraught woman, wiping her hands in her apron, said, "I didn't want my
husband to get involved."

One couple, now willing to talk about that night, said they heard the   27
first screams. The husband looked thoughtfully at the bookstore where the
killer first grabbed Miss Genovese.

"We went to the window to see what was happening," he said, "but   28
the light from our bedroom made it difficult to see the street." The wife, still
apprehensive, added: "I put out the light and we were able to see better."

Asked why they hadn't called the police, she shrugged and replied: 29
"I don't know."

A man peeked out from a slight opening in the doorway to his apart-   30
ment and rattled off an account of the killer's second attack. Why hadn't
he called the police at the time? "I was tired," he said without emotion. "I
went back to bed."

It was 4:25 A.M. when the ambulance arrived to take the body of Miss   31
Genovese. It drove off. "Then," a solemn police detective said, "the people
came out."

•   •   •

COMPREHENSION

1. How much time elapsed between the first stabbing of Kitty Genovese and
   the time when the people finally came out?

2. What excuses did the neighbors make for not coming to Kitty Genovese's
   aid?

PURPOSE AND AUDIENCE

1. This article appeared in 1964. What effect was it intended to have on its audience? Do you think it has the same impact today, or has its impact changed or diminished?

2. What is the article's main point? Why does Gansberg imply his thesis rather than stating it explicitly?

3. What is Gansberg's purpose in describing the Austin Street area as "staid, middle-class, tree-lined" (6)?

4. Why do you suppose Gansberg provides the police department's phone number in his article? (Note that New York City did not have 911 emergency service in 1964.)

STYLE AND STRUCTURE

1. Gansberg is very precise in this article, especially in his references to time, addresses, and ages. Why?

2. The objective newspaper style is dominant in this article, but the writer's anger shows through. Point to words and phrases that reveal his attitude toward his material.

3. Because it was originally set in the narrow columns of a newspaper, the article has many short paragraphs. Would it be more effective if some of these brief paragraphs were combined? If so, why? If not, why not? Give examples to support your answer.

4. Review the dialogue. Does it strengthen Gansberg's presentation? Would the article be more compelling without dialogue? Explain.

5. This article does not have a formal conclusion; nevertheless, the last paragraph sums up the writer's attitude. How?

VOCABULARY PROJECTS

1. Define each of the following words as it is used in this section.

stalk (1)	adjacent (7)	distraught (26)
baffles (4)	punctuated (11)	apprehensive (28)
staid (6)	sheepishly (21)	

2. The word *assailant* appears frequently in this article. Why is it used so often? What impact is this repetition likely to have on readers? What other words could have been used?

JOURNAL ENTRY

In a similar situation, would you have called the police? Would you have gone outside to help? What factors do you think might have influenced your decision?

WRITING WORKSHOP

1. In your own words, write a ten-sentence summary of the article. Try to reflect Gansberg's order and emphasis as well as his ideas.

2. Rewrite the article as if it were a diary entry of one of the thirty-eight people who watched the murder. Summarize what you saw, and explain why you decided not to call for help. (You may invent details that Gansberg does not include.)

3. If you have ever been involved in or witnessed a situation in which someone was in trouble, write a narrative essay about the incident. If people failed to help the person in trouble, explain why you think no one acted. If people did act, tell how. Be sure to account for your own actions.

COMBINING THE PATTERNS

Because the purpose of this newspaper article is to inform, it has no extended descriptions of the victim, the witnesses, or the crime scene. It also does not explain why those who watched did not act. Where might passages of **description** or **cause and effect** be added? How might such additions change the essay's impact on readers? Do you think they would strengthen the essay?

THEMATIC CONNECTIONS

- "Samuel" (page 212)
- "Who Killed Benny Paret?" (page 279)
- "It's Just Too Late" (page 304)

♪♪♪♪♪♪♪♪

GEORGE ORWELL

George Orwell (1903–1950) was born Eric Blair in Bengal, India, where his father was a British civil servant. Rather than attend university, Orwell joined the Imperial Police in neighboring Burma (now renamed Myanmar), where he served from 1922 to 1927. Finding himself increasingly opposed to British colonial rule, Orwell left Burma to live and write in Paris and London. A political liberal and fierce moralist, Orwell is best known today for his novels *Animal Farm* (1945) and *1984* (1949), which portray the dangers of totalitarianism. In "Shooting an Elephant," written in 1936, he recalls an incident from his days in Burma that clarified his thinking about British colonial rule.

The British had gradually taken over Burma through a succession of wars beginning in 1824; by 1885, the domination was complete. Like a number of other European countries, Britain had forcibly established colonial rule in countries throughout the world during the eighteenth and nineteenth centuries, primarily to exploit local resources. This empire building, known as *imperialism*, was justified on the grounds that European culture was superior to those of the indigenous peoples, particularly in Asia and Africa. Thus, it was "the white man's burden" to bring civilization to these "heathen" lands. In most cases, such control could only be achieved through forcible oppression. Anti-imperialist sentiment began to grow in the early twentieth century, but colonial rule continued in much of the less developed world. Not until the late 1940s did many European colonies begin to achieve independence. The British ceded home rule to Burma in 1947.

Shooting an Elephant

In Moulmein, in Lower Burma, I was hated by large numbers of 1 people — the only time in my life that I have been important enough for this to happen to me. I was sub-divisional police officer of the town, and in an aimless, petty kind of way anti-European feeling was very bitter. No one had the guts to raise a riot, but if a European woman went through the bazaars alone somebody would probably spit betel juice over her dress. As a police officer I was an obvious target and was baited whenever it seemed safe to do so. When a nimble Burman tripped me up on the football field and the referee (another Burman) looked the other way, the crowd yelled with hideous laughter. This happened more than once. In the end the sneering yellow faces of young men that met me everywhere, the insults hooted after me when I was at a safe distance, got badly on my nerves. The young Buddhist priests were the worst of all. There were several thousands of them in the town and none of them seemed to have anything to do except stand on street corners and jeer at Europeans.

All this was perplexing and upsetting. For at that time I had already 2 made up my mind that imperialism was an evil thing and the sooner I chucked up my job and got out of it the better. Theoretically — and secretly, of course — I was all for the Burmese and all against their oppressors, the British. As for the job I was doing, I hated it more bitterly than I can perhaps make clear. In a job like that you see the dirty work of Empire at close quarters. The wretched prisoners huddling in the stinking cages of the lockups, the grey, cowed faces of the long-term convicts, the scarred buttocks of the men who had been flogged with bamboos — all these oppressed me with an intolerable sense of guilt. But I could get nothing into perspective. I was young and ill-educated and I had had to think out my problems in the utter silence that is imposed on every Englishman in the East. I did not even know that the British Empire is dying, still less did I know that it is a great deal better than the younger empires that are going to supplant it.* All I knew was that I was stuck between my hatred of the empire I served and my rage against the evil-spirited little beasts who tried to make my job impossible. With one part of my mind I thought of the British Raj** as an unbreakable tyranny, as something clamped down, in *saecula saeculorum,**** upon the will of prostrate peoples; with another part I thought that the greatest joy in the world would be to drive a bayonet into a Buddhist priest's guts. Feelings like these are the normal by-products of imperialism; ask any Anglo-Indian official, if you can catch him off duty.

One day something happened which in a roundabout way was en-   3
lightening. It was a tiny incident in itself, but it gave me a better glimpse than I had had before of the real nature of imperialism — the real motives for which despotic governments act. Early one morning the sub-inspector at a police station the other end of the town rang me up on the phone and said that an elephant was ravaging the bazaar. Would I please come and do something about it? I did not know what I could do, but I wanted to see what was happening and I got on to a pony and started out. I took my rifle, an old .44 Winchester and much too small to kill an elephant, but I thought the noise might be useful *in terrorem.*† Various Burmans stopped me on the way and told me about the elephant's doings. It was not, of course, a wild elephant, but a tame one which had gone "must."‡ It had been chained up, as tame elephants always are when their attack of "must" is due, but on the previous night it had broken its chain and escaped. Its mahout,¶ the only person who could manage it when it was in that state, had set out in pursuit, but had taken the wrong direction and was now twelve hours' journey away, and in the morning the elephant had suddenly reappeared in the town. The Burmese population had no weapons and were quite helpless against it. It had already destroyed

---

*Eds. note — Orwell was writing in 1936, when Hitler and Stalin were in power and World War II was only three years away.

**Eds. note — *Raj:* sovereignty.

***Eds. note — From time immemorial.

†Eds. note — *In terrorem:* to frighten [it].

‡Eds. note — That is, gone into an uncontrollable frenzy.

¶Eds. note — A keeper and driver of an elephant.

somebody's bamboo hut, killed a cow, and raided some fruit-stalls and devoured the stock; also it had met the municipal rubbish van and, when the driver jumped out and took to his heels, had turned the van over and inflicted violences upon it.

The Burmese sub-inspector and some Indian constables were waiting   4 for me in the quarter where the elephant had been seen. It was a very poor quarter, a labyrinth of squalid bamboo huts, thatched with palm-leaf, winding all over a steep hillside. I remember that it was a cloudy, stuffy morning at the beginning of the rains. We began questioning people as to where the elephant had gone, and, as usual, failed to get any definite information. That is invariably the case in the East; a story always sounds clear enough at a distance, but the nearer you get to the scene of events the vaguer it becomes. Some of the people said that the elephant had gone in one direction, some said that he had gone in another, some professed not even to have heard of an elephant. I had almost made up my mind that the whole story was a pack of lies, when we heard yells a little distance away. There was a loud, scandalized cry of "Go away, child! Go away this instant!" and an old woman with a switch in her hand came round the cor-ner of a hut, violently shooing away a crowd of naked children. Some more women followed, clicking their tongues and exclaiming; evidently there was something that the children ought not to have seen. I rounded the hut and saw a man's dead body sprawling in the mud. He was an Indian, a black Dravidian coolie,* almost naked, and he could not have been dead many minutes. The people said that the elephant had come suddenly upon him round the corner of the hut, caught him with its trunk, put its foot on his back, and ground him into the earth. This was the rainy season and the ground was soft, and his face had scored a trench a foot deep and a couple of yards long. He was lying on his belly with arms cru-cified and head sharply twisted to one side. His face was coated with mud, the eyes wide open, the teeth bared and grinning with an expression of unendurable agony. (Never tell me, by the way, that the dead look peaceful. Most of the corpses I have seen looked devilish.) The friction of the great beast's foot had stripped the skin from his back as neatly as one skins a rabbit. As soon as I saw the dead man I sent an orderly to a friend's house nearby to borrow an elephant rifle. I had already sent back the pony, not wanting it to go mad with fright and throw me if it smelled the elephant.

The orderly came back in a few minutes with a rifle and five car-   5 tridges, and meanwhile some Burmans had arrived and told us that the elephant was in the paddy** fields below, only a few hundred yards away. As I started forward practically the whole population of the quarter flocked out of the houses and followed me. They had seen the rifle and were all shouting excitedly that I was going to shoot the elephant. They had not shown much interest in the elephant when he was merely rav-

*Eds. note — An unskilled laborer.
**Eds. note — Wet land in which rice grows.

aging their homes, but it was different now that he was going to be shot. It was a bit of fun to them, as it would be to an English crowd; besides they wanted the meat. It made me vaguely uneasy. I had no intention of shooting the elephant — I had merely sent for the rifle to defend myself if necessary — and it is always unnerving to have a crowd following you. I marched down the hill, looking and feeling a fool, with the rifle over my shoulder and an ever-growing army of people jostling at my heels. At the bottom, when you got away from the huts, there was a metalled road and beyond that a miry waste of paddy fields a thousand yards across, not yet ploughed but soggy from the first rains and dotted with coarse grass. The elephant was standing eight yards from the road, his left side towards us. He took not the slightest notice of the crowd's approach. He was tearing up bunches of grass, beating them against his knees to clean them and stuffing them into his mouth.

I had halted on the road. As soon as I saw the elephant I knew with   6
perfect certainty that I ought not to shoot him. It is a serious matter to shoot a working elephant — it is comparable to destroying a huge and costly piece of machinery — and obviously one ought not to do it if it can possibly be avoided. And at that distance, peacefully eating, the elephant looked no more dangerous than a cow. I thought then and I think now that his attack of "must" was already passing off; in which case he would merely wander harmlessly about until the mahout came back and caught him. Moreover, I did not in the least want to shoot him. I decided that I would watch him for a little while to make sure that he did not turn savage again, and then go home.

But at that moment I glanced round at the crowd that had followed   7
me. It was an immense crowd, two thousand at the least and growing every minute. It blocked the road for a long distance on either side. I looked at the sea of yellow faces above the garish clothes — faces all happy and excited over this bit of fun, all certain that the elephant was going to be shot. They were watching me as they would watch a conjurer about to perform a trick. They did not like me, but with the magical rifle in my hands I was momentarily worth watching. And suddenly I realized that I should have to shoot the elephant after all. The people expected it of me and I had got to do it; I could feel their two thousand wills pressing me forward, irresistibly. And it was at this moment, as I stood there with the rifle in my hands, that I first grasped the hollowness, the futility of the white man's dominion in the East. Here was I, the white man with his gun, standing in front of the unarmed native crowd — seemingly the leading actor of the piece; but in reality I was only an absurd puppet pushed to and fro by the will of those yellow faces behind. I perceived in this moment that when the white man turns tyrant it is his own freedom that he destroys. He becomes a sort of hollow, posing dummy, the conventionalized figure of a sahib.* For it is the condition of his rule that he shall

*EDS. NOTE — Term used among Hindus and Muslims in Colonial India when speaking of an official.

spend his life in trying to impress the "natives," and so in every crisis he has got to do what the "natives" expect of him. He wears a mask, and his face grows to fit it. I had got to shoot the elephant. I had committed myself to doing it when I sent for the rifle. A sahib has got to act like a sahib; he has got to appear resolute, to know his own mind and do definite things. To come all that way, rifle in hand, with two thousand people marching at my heels, and then to trail feebly away, having done nothing — no, that was impossible. The crowd would laugh at me. And my whole life, every white man's life in the East, was one long struggle not to be laughed at.

But I did not want to shoot the elephant. I watched him beating his bunch of grass against his knees, with the preoccupied grandmotherly air that elephants have. It seemed to me that it would be murder to shoot him. At that age I was not squeamish about killing animals, but I had never shot an elephant and never wanted to. (Somehow it always seems worse to kill a *large* animal.) Besides, there was the beast's owner to be considered. Alive, the elephant was worth at least a hundred pounds; dead, he would only be worth the value of his tusks, five pounds, possibly. But I had got to act quickly. I turned to some experienced-looking Burmans who had been there when we arrived, and asked them how the elephant had been behaving. They all said the same thing: he took no notice of you if you left him alone, but he might charge if you went too close to him.   8

It was perfectly clear to me what I ought to do. I ought to walk up to within, say, twenty-five yards of the elephant and test his behavior. If he charged I could shoot, if he took no notice of me it would be safe to leave him until the mahout came back. But also I knew that I was going to do no such thing. I was a poor shot with a rifle and the ground was soft mud into which one would sink at every step. If the elephant charged and I missed him, I should have about as much chance as a toad under a steamroller. But even then I was not thinking particularly of my own skin, only of the watchful yellow faces behind. For at that moment, with the crowd watching me, I was not afraid in the ordinary sense, as I would have been if I had been alone. A white man mustn't be frightened in front of "natives"; and so, in general, he isn't frightened. The sole thought in my mind was that if anything went wrong those two thousand Burmans would see me pursued, caught, trampled on, and reduced to a grinning corpse like that Indian up the hill. And if that happened it was quite probable that some of them would laugh. That would never do. There was only one alternative. I shoved the cartridges into the magazine and lay down on the road to get a better aim.   9

The crowd grew very still, and a deep, low, happy sigh, as of people who see the theatre curtain go up at last, breathed from innumerable throats. They were going to have their bit of fun after all. The rifle was a beautiful German thing with cross-hair sights. I did not then know that in shooting an elephant one would shoot to cut an imaginary bar running from ear-hole to ear-hole. I ought, therefore, as the elephant was sideways   10 on, to have aimed straight at his ear-hole; actually I aimed several inches in front of this, thinking the brain would be further forward.

When I pulled the trigger I did not hear the bang or feel the kick —   11 one never does when a shot goes home — but I heard the devilish roar of glee that went up from the crowd. In that instant, in too short a time, one would have thought, even for the bullet to get there, a mysterious, terrible change had come over the elephant. He neither stirred nor fell, but every line on his body had altered. He looked suddenly stricken, shrunken, immensely old, as though the frightful impact of the bullet had paralyzed him without knocking him down. At last, after what seemed a long time — it might have been five seconds, I dare say — he sagged flabbily to his knees. His mouth slobbered. An enormous senility seemed to have settled upon him. One could have imagined him thousands of years old. I fired again into the same spot. At the second shot he did not collapse but climbed with desperate slowness to his feet and stood weakly upright, with legs sagging and head drooping. I fired a third time. That was the shot that did for him. You could see the agony of it jolt his whole body and knock the last remnant of strength from his legs. But in falling he seemed for a moment to rise, for as his hind legs collapsed beneath him he seemed to tower upwards like a huge rock toppling, his trunk reaching skywards like a tree. He trumpeted, for the first and only time. And then down he came, his belly towards me, with a crash that seemed to shake the ground even where I lay.

I got up. The Burmans were already racing past me across the mud. It   12 was obvious that the elephant would never rise again, but he was not dead. He was breathing very rhythmically with long rattling gasps, his great mound of a side painfully rising and falling. His mouth was wide open — I could see far down into the caverns of pale pink throat. I waited a long time for him to die, but his breathing did not weaken. Finally, I fired my two remaining shots into the spot where I thought his heart must be. The thick blood welled out of him like red velvet, but still he did not die. His body did not even jerk when the shots hit him, the tortured breathing continued without a pause. He was dying, very slowly and in great agony, but in some world remote from me where not even a bullet could damage him further. I felt that I had got to put an end to that dreadful noise. It seemed dreadful to see the great beast lying there, powerless to move and yet powerless to die, and not even to be able to finish him. I sent back for my small rifle and poured shot after shot into his heart and down his throat. They seemed to make no impression. The tortured gasps continued as steadily as the ticking of a clock.

In the end I could not stand it any longer and went away. I heard later   13 that it took him half an hour to die. Burmans were bringing dahs* and baskets even before I left, and I was told they had stripped his body almost to the bones by the afternoon.

---

*EDS. NOTE — Heavy knives.

Afterwards, of course, there were endless discussions about the shoot-   14
ing of the elephant. The owner was furious, but he was only an Indian and
could do nothing. Besides, legally I had done the right thing, for a mad
elephant has to be killed, like a mad dog, if its owner fails to control it.
Among the Europeans opinion was divided. The older men said I was
right, the younger men said it was a damn shame to shoot an elephant for
killing a coolie, because an elephant was worth more than any damn Cor-
inghee coolie. And afterwards I was very glad that the coolie had been
killed; it put me legally in the right and it gave me a sufficient pretext for
shooting the elephant. I often wondered whether any of the others
grasped that I had done it solely to avoid looking a fool.

• • •

COMPREHENSION

1. Why was Orwell "hated by large numbers of people" (1) in Burma? Why
   did he have mixed feelings toward the Burmese people?

2. Why did the local officials want something done about the elephant? Why
   did the crowd want Orwell to shoot the elephant?

3. Why did Orwell finally decide to kill the elephant? What made him hesi-
   tate at first?

4. Why does Orwell say at the end that he was glad the coolie had been killed?

PURPOSE AND AUDIENCE

1. One of Orwell's purposes in telling his story is to show how it gave him a
   glimpse of "the real nature of imperialism" (3). What does he mean? How
   does the story illustrate this purpose?

2. Do you think Orwell wrote this essay to inform or to persuade his audience? How did Orwell expect his audience to react to his ideas? How can
   you tell?

3. What is the essay's thesis?

STYLE AND STRUCTURE

1. What does Orwell's first paragraph accomplish? Where does the introduction end and the narrative itself begin?

2. The essay includes almost no dialogue. Why do you think Orwell's voice
   as narrator is the only one readers hear? Is the absence of dialogue a
   strength or a weakness? Explain.

3. Why do you think Orwell devotes so much attention to the elephant's
   misery (11–12)?

4. Orwell's essay includes a number of editorial comments, which appear
   within parentheses or dashes. How would you characterize these comments? Why are they set off from the text?

5. Consider the following passages: "Some of the people said that the elephant had gone in one direction, some said that he had gone in another. . . ." (4); "Among the Europeans opinion was divided. The older men said I was right, the younger men said it was a damn shame to shoot an elephant. . . ." (14). How do these comments reinforce the theme expressed in paragraph 2 ("All I knew was that I was stuck between my hatred of the empire I served and my rage against the evil-spirited little beasts. . . .")? What other examples reinforce this theme?

VOCABULARY PROJECTS

1. Define each of the following words as it is used in this selection.

baited (1)	despotic (3)	conjurer (7)
perplexing (2)	labyrinth (4)	dominion (7)
oppressors (2)	squalid (4)	magazine (9)
lockups (2)	professed (4)	cross-hair (10)
flogged (2)	ravaging (5)	remnant (11)
supplant (2)	miry (5)	trumpeted (11)
prostrate (2)	garish (7)	pretext (14)

2. Because Orwell is British, he frequently uses words or expressions that an American writer would not be likely to use. Substitute a contemporary American word or phrase for each of the following, making sure it is appropriate in Orwell's context.

raise a riot (1)	rubbish van (3)	a bit of fun (5)
rang me up (3)	inflicted violences (3)	I dare say (11)

   What other expressions might need to be "translated" for a contemporary American audience?

JOURNAL ENTRY

Do you think Orwell is a coward? Do you think he is a racist? Explain your feelings.

WRITING WORKSHOP

1. Orwell says that even though he hated British imperialism and sympathized with the Burmese people, he found himself a puppet of the system. Write a narrative essay about a time when you had to do something that went against your beliefs or convictions.

2. Orwell's experience taught him something not only about himself but also about something beyond himself — the way British imperialism worked. Write a narrative essay that reveals how an incident in your life taught you something about some larger social or political force as well as about yourself.

3. Write an objective, factual newspaper article recounting the events Orwell describes.

COMBINING THE PATTERNS

Implicit in this narrative essay is an extended **comparison and contrast** that highlights the differences between Orwell and the Burmese people. Review the essay, and list the most obvious differences Orwell perceives between himself and them. Do you think his perceptions are accurate? If all of the differences were set forth in a single paragraph, how might such a paragraph change your perception of Orwell's dilemma? Of his character?

THEMATIC CONNECTIONS

- "Thirty-Eight Who Saw Murder Didn't Call the Police" (page 99)
- "Just Walk On By" (page 197)
- "The Untouchable" (page 461)

SAKI (H. H. MUNRO)

Hector Hugh Munro, who took the pen name Saki, was born in 1870 in Akyab, Burma (now known as Myanmar), the son of an officer in the British military police. Following his mother's death when Munro was not yet two years old, he was sent to England to be raised by his aunts. In 1893, Munro himself joined the military police in Burma, but he was forced to return to England after a year because of ill health. He then worked as a journalist, later serving as a foreign correspondent in the Balkans, Russia, and Paris. After his father's death, an inheritance allowed him to give up journalism and turn to writing fiction. He joined the British army during World War I and was killed by sniper fire in Germany in 1916.

Although Munro wrote a history of Russia, political satire, novels, and a play, he is best remembered for the playful, sometimes macabre short stories he published under the name of Saki. Set among England's leisured upper classes, these originally appeared in popular newspapers and periodicals; they were later collected in six separate volumes. "The Open Window," from *Beasts and Super-Beasts* (1914), displays the writer's much-noted knack for surprise endings.

The Open Window

"My aunt will be down presently, Mr. Nuttel," said a very self-possessed young lady of fifteen; "in the meantime you must try and put up with me." 1

Framton Nuttel endeavored to say the correct something which should duly flatter the niece of the moment without unduly discounting the aunt that was to come. Privately he doubted more than ever whether these formal visits on a succession of total strangers would do much towards helping the nerve cure which he was supposed to be undergoing. 2

"I know how it will be," his sister had said when he was preparing to migrate to this rural retreat; "you will bury yourself down there and not speak to a living soul, and your nerves will be worse than ever from moping. I shall just give you letters of introduction to all the people I know there. Some of them, as far as I can remember, were quite nice." 3

Framton wondered whether Mrs. Sappleton, the lady to whom he was presenting one of the letters of introduction, came into the nice division. 4

"Do you know many of the people round here?" asked the niece, when she judged that they had had sufficient silent communion. 5

"Hardly a soul," said Framton. "My sister was staying here, at the rectory, you know, some four years ago, and she gave me letters of introduction to some of the people here." 6

He made the last statement in a tone of distinct regret. 7

"Then you know practically nothing about my aunt?" pursued the self-possessed young lady. 8

"Only her name and address," admitted the caller. He was wonder- 9
ing whether Mrs. Sappleton was in the married or widowed state. An
undefinable something about the room seemed to suggest masculine habi-
tation.

"Her great tragedy happened just three years ago," said the child; 10
"that would be since your sister's time."

"Her tragedy?" asked Framton; somehow in this restful country spot 11
tragedies seemed out of place.

"You may wonder why we keep that window wide open on an Octo- 12
ber afternoon," said the niece, indicating a large French window that
opened on to a lawn.

"It is quite warm for the time of the year," said Framton; "but has that 13
window got anything to do with the tragedy?"

"Out through that window, three years ago to a day, her husband and 14
her two young brothers went off for their day's shooting. They never came
back. In crossing the moor to their favorite snipe-shooting ground they
were all three engulfed in a treacherous piece of bog. It had been that
dreadful wet summer, you know, and places that were safe in other years
gave way suddenly without warning. Their bodies were never recovered.
That was the dreadful part of it." Here the child's voice lost its self-
possessed note and became falteringly human. "Poor aunt always thinks
that they will come back, some day, they and the little brown spaniel that
was lost with them, and walk in at that window just as they used to do.
That is why the window is kept open every evening till it is quite dusk.
Poor dear aunt, she has often told me how they went out, her husband
with his white waterproof coat over his arm, and Ronnie, her youngest
brother, singing, 'Bertie, why do you bound?' as he always did to tease
her, because she said it got on her nerves. Do you know, sometimes on
still, quiet evenings like this, I almost get a creepy feeling that they will all
walk in through that window —"

She broke off with a little shudder. It was a relief to Framton when the 15
aunt bustled into the room with a whirl of apologies for being late in making her appearance.

"I hope Vera has been amusing you?" she said.   16

"She has been very interesting," said Framton.   17

"I hope you don't mind the open window," said Mrs. Sappleton 18
briskly; "my husband and brothers will be home directly from shooting,
and they always come in this way. They've been out for snipe in the
marshes today, so they'll make a fine mess over my poor carpets. So like
you men-folk, isn't it?"

She rattled on cheerfully about the shooting and the scarcity of birds, 19
and the prospects for duck in the winter. To Framton it was all purely horrible. He made a desperate but only partially successful effort to turn the
talk on to a less ghastly topic; he was conscious that his hostess was giving
him only a fragment of her attention, and her eyes were constantly stray-
ing past him to the open window and the lawn beyond. It was certainly an

unfortunate coincidence that he should have paid his visit on this tragic anniversary.

"The doctors agree in ordering me complete rest, an absence of mental 20 excitement, and avoidance of anything in the nature of violent physical exercise," announced Framton, who labored under the tolerably wide-spread delusion that total strangers and chance acquaintances are hungry for the least detail of one's ailments and infirmities, their cause and cure. "On the matter of diet they are not so much in agreement," he continued.

"No?" said Mrs. Sappleton, in a voice which only replaced a yawn at 21 the last moment. Then she suddenly brightened into alert attention — but not to what Framton was saying.

"Here they are at last!" she cried. "Just in time for tea, and don't they 22 look as if they were muddy up to the eyes!"

Framton shivered slightly and turned towards the niece with a look 23 intended to convey sympathetic comprehension. The child was staring out through the open window with dazed horror in her eyes. In a chill shock of nameless fear Framton swung round in his seat and looked in the same direction.

In the deepening twilight three figures were walking across the lawn 24 towards the window; they all carried guns under their arms, and one of them was additionally burdened with a white coat hung over his shoulders. A tired brown spaniel kept close at their heels. Noiselessly they neared the house, and then a hoarse young voice chanted out of the dusk: "I said, Bertie, why do you bound?"

Framton grabbed wildly at his stick and hat; the hall-door, the gravel- 25 drive, and the front gate were dimly noted stages in his headlong retreat. A cyclist coming along the road had to run into the hedge to avoid imminent collision.

"Here we are, my dear," said the bearer of the white mackintosh, com- 26 ing in through the window; "fairly muddy, but most of it's dry. Who was that who bolted out as we came up?"

"A most extraordinary man, a Mr. Nuttel," said Mrs. Sappleton; "could 27 only talk about his illness, and dashed off without a word of good-bye or apology when you arrived. One would think he had seen a ghost."

"I expect it was the spaniel," said the niece calmly; "he told me he had 28 a horror of dogs. He was once hunted into a cemetery somewhere on the banks of the Ganges by a pack of pariah dogs, and had to spend the night in a newly dug grave with the creatures snarling and grinning and foaming just above him. Enough to make any one lose their nerve."

Romance at short notice was her specialty. 29

• • •

THINKING ABOUT LITERATURE

1. Why is it essential that the story Vera tells Mr. Nuttel be extremely detailed?

2. How does the dialogue included in "The Open Window" characterize Mrs. Sappleton, Mr. Nuttel, and Vera? Give specific examples to support your answer.

3. Why is each of these details important to "The Open Window"?
   a. Mr. Nuttel is recovering from a nervous breakdown.
   b. Mr. Nuttel knows almost nothing about Mrs. Sappleton.
   c. Vera is "a very self-possessed young lady" (1).
   d. The window is open.

   How would the story be different without each of these details?

JOURNAL ENTRY

Explain the meaning of the story's last line (29). In what sense does it serve as a thesis statement for the story? How would the story be different if this "thesis statement" appeared earlier?

THEMATIC CONNECTIONS

- "Sex, Lies, and Conversation" (p. 367)
- "The Ways We Lie" (page 426)

WRITING ASSIGNMENTS FOR NARRATION

1. Trace the path you expect to follow to establish yourself in your chosen profession, considering possible obstacles you may face and how you expect to deal with them. Include a thesis statement that conveys the importance of your goals. If you like, you may consult some essays elsewhere in this book that focus on work — for example, "The Peter Principle" (page 181), "On Fire" (page 243), or "The Men We Carry in Our Minds" (page 399).

2. Write a personal narrative in which you look back from some point in the far future on your own life as you hope it will be seen by others. Use third person if you like, and write your own obituary; or use first person, assessing your life in the form of a letter to your great-grandchildren.

3. Write a news article recounting in objective terms the events described in an essay that appears elsewhere in this text — for example, "Who Killed Benny Paret?" (page 279) or "Grant and Lee: A Study in Contrasts" (page 340). Include a descriptive headline.

4. Write a historical narrative tracing the roots of your family or your hometown or community. Be sure to include specific details, dialogue, and descriptions of people and places.

5. Write an account of one of these "firsts": your first date; your first serious argument with your parents; your first experience with physical violence or danger; your first extended stay away from home; your first encounter with someone whose culture was very different from your own; your first experience with the serious illness or death of a close friend or relative. Make sure your essay includes a thesis statement that your narrative can support.

6. Both George Orwell and Martin Gansberg deal with the consequences of failing to act. Write an essay or story in which you recount what would have happened if Orwell had *not* shot the elephant or if one of the eyewitnesses *had* called the police right away.

7. Maya Angelou's "finishing school" was Mrs. Cullinan's kitchen. What institution served as your finishing school? What did you learn there, and how did this knowledge serve you later?

8. Write a short narrative telling what happened in a class, a short story, a television show, a conversation, a fable or fairy tale, or a narrative poem. Include as many details as you can.

9. Write a narrative about a time when you were an outsider, isolated because of social, intellectual, or ethnic differences between you and others. Did you resolve the problems your isolation created? Explain. If you like, you may refer to the Angelou or Orwell essays in this chapter or to "Just Walk On By" (page 197).

10. Imagine a meeting between any two people who appear in this chapter's reading selections. Using dialogue as well as narrative, write an account of this meeting.

COLLABORATIVE ACTIVITY FOR NARRATION

Working with a group of students of about your own age, write a history of your television-viewing habits. Start by working individually to list all your most-watched television shows in chronological order, beginning as far back as you can remember. Then compile a single list that reflects a consensus of the group's preferences, perhaps choosing one or two representative programs for each stage of your life (preschool, elementary school, and so on). Have a different student write a paragraph on each stage, describing the chosen programs in as much detail as possible. Finally, combine the individual paragraphs to create a narrative essay that traces the group's changing tastes in television shows. The essay's thesis statement should express what your group's television preferences reveal about your generation's development.

INTERNET ASSIGNMENT FOR NARRATION

Choose an important local or national event that you remember hearing about, and use the following World Wide Web sites to help you locate newspaper or magazine articles about the event to find out more. Then, imagining that you have witnessed the event firsthand, write a narrative of what you experienced. Referring to Martin Gansberg's "Thirty-Eight Who Saw Murder Didn't Call the Police," see how to use dialogue in your narrative.

Poynter Institute
<http://www.poynter.org/links/>
A list of links to journalistic sources including journalism organizations and libraries, research, newspapers, and radio and television channels.

The Len-Net Entertainment Web
<http://www.lni.net/cowabunga/>
This site offers links to media-related sites, including links to local newspapers across the United States.

Media Link
<http://www.kidon.com/media-link/index.shtml/>
This site offers links and in-depth information about news sources in virtually every nation in the world.

5

DESCRIPTION

WHAT IS DESCRIPTION?

You use **description** whenever you want to tell readers about the physical characteristics of a person, place, or thing. Description relies on the five senses — sight, hearing, taste, touch, and smell. In the following paragraph from "Knoxville: Summer 1915," James Agee uses sight, sound, and touch to recreate a scene for his audience:

Topic sentence	It is not of games children play in the evening that I want to speak now, it is of a contemporaneous atmosphere that has little to do with them; that of fathers and
Description using sight	families, each in his space of lawn, his shirt fishlike pale in the unnatural light and his face nearly anonymous, hosing their lawns. The hoses were attached to spigots that stood out of the brick foundations of the houses. The nozzles were variously set but usually so there was a long
Description using touch	sweet stream of spray, the nozzle wet in the hand, the water trickling the right forearm and the peeled-back cuff, and the water whishing out a long loose and low-curved
Description using sound	cone, and so gentle a sound. First an insane noise of violence in the nozzle, then the still irregular sound of adjustment, then the smoothing into steadiness and a pitch as accurately tuned to the size and style of stream as any violin. So many qualities of sound out of one hose: so many choral differences out of those several hoses that were in earshot. Out of any one hose, the almost dead silence of the release, and the short still arch of the separate big drops, silent as a held breath, and the only noise the flattering noise on leaves and the slapped grass at the fall of each big drop. That, and the intense hiss with the intense stream; that, and the same intensity not growing less but growing more quiet and delicate with the turn of the nozzle, up to that extreme tender whisper when the water was just a wide bell of film.

A descriptive essay tells what something looks like or what it feels like, sounds like, smells like, or tastes like. However, description often goes beyond personal sense impressions: novelists can create imaginary landscapes, historians can paint word pictures of historical figures, and scientists can describe physical phenomena they have never seen. When you write description, you use language to create a vivid impression for your readers.

Writers of descriptive essays often use an implied thesis when they describe a person, place, or thing. This technique allows them to convey an essay's **dominant impression** — the mood or quality that is emphasized in the piece of writing — subtly through the selection and arrangement of details. When they use description to support a particular point, however, many writers prefer to use an explicitly stated thesis. This strategy eliminates ambiguity by letting readers see immediately what point the writer is making — for example, "The sculptures that adorn Philadelphia's City Hall are a catalog of nineteenth-century artistic styles." Whether you state or imply your thesis, the details of your descriptive essay must work together to create a single dominant impression. In many cases your thesis may be just a statement of the dominant impression; sometimes, however, your thesis may go further and make a point about that dominant impression.

USING DESCRIPTION

Description is fundamental to many writing situations. Before we make judgments about the world, before we compare or contrast or classify our experiences, we describe. In your college writing, you use description in many different kinds of assignments. In a comparison-and-contrast essay, for example, you may describe the appearance of two cars to show that one is better engineered than the other. In an argumentative essay, you may describe a fish kill in a local river to show that industrial waste dumping is a problem. Through description, you communicate your view of the world to your readers. If your readers come to understand or share your view, they are more likely to accept your observations, your judgments, and your conclusions. Therefore, in almost every essay you write, knowing how to write effective description is important.

Understanding Objective and Subjective Description

Descriptions can be *objective* or *subjective.* In an **objective description,** you focus on the object itself rather than on your personal reactions to it. Your purpose is to present a precise, literal picture of your subject. Many writing situations require exact descriptions of apparatus or conditions, and in these cases your goal is to construct an accurate picture for your audience. A biologist describing what he sees through a microscope and a historian describing a Civil War battlefield would both write objectively. The biologist would not, for instance, say how exciting his observations were, nor would the historian say how disappointed she was at the outcome of the battle. Many newspaper reporters also try to achieve this impersonal objectivity, and so do writers of technical reports, scientific papers, and certain types of business correspondence. Still, objectivity is an ideal that writers strive for but never achieve. In fact, in selecting some details and leaving out others, writers are making subjective decisions.

In the following descriptive passage, Thomas Marc Parrott aims for objectivity by giving his readers all the factual information they need to visualize Shakespeare's theater:

> When James Burbage built the Theatre in 1576 he naturally designed it along the lines of inn-yards in which he had been accustomed to play. The building had two entrances — one in front for the audience; one in the rear for actors, musicians, and the personnel of the theatre. Inside the building a rectangular platform projected far out into what was called "the yard" — we know the stage of the Fortune ran halfway across the "yard," some twenty-seven and a half feet.

Note that Parrott is not interested in responding to or evaluating the theater he describes. Instead, he chooses words that convey sizes, shapes, and distances, such as *two* and *rectangular*. Only one word in the paragraph — *naturally* — suggests an opinion.

In contrast to objective description, **subjective description** conveys your personal response to your subject and tries to get your readers to share it. Your perspective is not necessarily expressed explicitly, in a direct statement. Often it is revealed indirectly, through your choice of words and phrasing. If an English composition assignment asks you to describe a place that has special meaning to you, you could give a subjective reaction to your topic by selecting and emphasizing details that show your feelings about the place. For example, you could write a subjective description of your room by focusing on particular objects — your desk, your window, and your bookshelves — and explaining the meanings these things have for you. Thus, your desk could be a "warm brown rectangle of wood whose surface contains the scratched impressions of a thousand school assignments."

A subjective description should convey not just a literal record of sights and sounds but also their significance. For example, if you objectively described a fire, you might include its temperature, duration, and scope. In addition, you might describe, as accurately as possible, the fire's color, movement, and intensity. If you subjectively described the fire, however, you would include more than these factual observations. Through your choice of words, you would try to recreate for your audience a sense of how the fire made you feel: your reactions to the crackling noise, to the dense smoke, to the sudden destruction.

In the following passage, notice how Mark Twain subjectively describes a sunset on the Mississippi River:

> I still kept in mind a certain wonderful sunset which I witnessed when steamboating was new to me. A broad expanse of the river was turned to blood; in the middle distance the red hue brightened into gold, through which a solitary log came floating, black and conspicuous; in one place a long, slanting mark lay sparkling upon the water; in another the surface was broken by boiling, tumbling rings, that were as many-tinted as an opal.

In this passage, Twain conveys his strong emotional reaction to the sunset by using vivid, powerful images such as the river "turned to blood," the "solitary log . . . black and conspicuous," and the "boiling, tumbling rings." He also chooses words that convey great value, such as *gold* and *opal.*

Neither objective nor subjective description exists independently. Objective descriptions usually contain some subjective elements, and subjective descriptions need some objective elements to convey a sense of reality. The skillful writer adjusts the balance between objectivity and subjectivity to suit the topic, thesis, audience, purpose, and occasion of an essay.

Using Objective and Subjective Language

As the passages by Parrott and Twain illustrate, both objective and subjective descriptions depend on specific and concrete words to appeal to readers' senses. But these two types of description use different kinds of language. Objective descriptions rely on precise, factual language that presents a writer's observations without conveying his or her attitude toward the subject. They use unambiguous words and phrases. Subjective descriptions, however, often use richer or more suggestive language. They are more likely to rely on the **connotations** of words, their emotional associations, than on their **denotations,** or more direct meanings. In addition, they may deliberately provoke the reader's imagination with striking phrases or vivid language, including **figures of speech** like *simile, metaphor,* and *personification.*

A **simile** uses *like* or *as* to compare two dissimilar things. These comparisons occur frequently in everyday speech — for example, when someone claims to be "happy as a clam," "free as a bird," or "hungry as a bear." As a rule, however, you should avoid overused expressions like these in your writing. Effective writers constantly strive to use original similes. In his short story "A & P," for instance, John Updike uses a striking simile when he likens people going through the checkout aisle of a supermarket to balls dropping down a slot in a pinball machine.

A **metaphor** compares two dissimilar things without using *like* or *as.* Instead of saying that something is like something else, a metaphor says it *is* something else. Twain uses a metaphor when he says "A broad expanse of river was turned to blood."

Personification speaks of concepts or objects as if they were endowed with life or human characteristics. If you say that the wind whispered or that an engine died, you are using personification.

In addition to these figures of speech, writers of subjective descriptions also use *allusions* to enrich their writing. An **allusion** is a reference to a person, place, event, or quotation that the writer assumes readers will recognize. In "Letter from Birmingham Jail" (page 000), for example, Martin Luther King Jr. enriches his argument by alluding to biblical passages and proverbs with which he expects his audience of clergy to be familiar.

Your purpose and audience determine whether you should use predominantly objective or subjective description. An assignment that specifically asks for reactions calls for a subjective description. Legal, medical, technical, business, and scientific writing assignments, however, frequently require objective descriptions because their primary purpose is to give the audience factual information. (Even in these areas, of course, figures of speech may be used. Scientists often use such language to describe an unfamiliar object or concept to an audience. In their pioneering article on the structure of DNA, for example, James Watson and Francis Crick use a simile when they describe a molecule of DNA as looking like two spiral staircases winding around each other.)

Selecting Details

Sometimes inexperienced writers pack their descriptions with empty words like *nice, great, terrific,* or *awful,* substituting their own reactions to an object for the qualities of the object itself. To produce an effective description, however, you must do more than just *say* something is wonderful — you must use details that evoke this response in your readers, as Twain does with the sunset. (Twain does in fact use the word *wonderful* at the beginning of his description, but he then goes on to supply many concrete details that make the scene he describes vivid and specific.)

All good descriptive writing, whether objective or subjective, relies on specific details. Your aim is not simply to *tell* readers what something looks like but to *show* them. Every person, place, or thing has its special characteristics, and you should use your powers of observation to detect them. Then, you need to select the concrete words that will convey your dominant impression, that will enable your readers to imagine what you describe. Don't be satisfied with "He looked angry" when you can say "His face flushed, and one corner of his mouth twitched as he tried to control his anger." What's the difference? In the first case, you simply identify the man's emotional state. In the second, you provide enough detail so that readers can tell not only that he was angry but also how he revealed the intensity of his anger.

Of course, you could have provided even more detail by describing the man's beard, or his wrinkles, or any number of other features. Keep in mind, however, that not all details are equally useful or desirable. You should take care to include only those that contribute to the dominant impression you wish to create. Thus, in describing a man's face to show how angry he was, you would probably not include the shape of his nose or the color of his hair. (After all, a person's hair color does not change when he or she gets angry.) In fact, the number of particulars you use is less important than their quality and appropriateness. You should select and use only those details relevant to your purpose.

Factors like the level, background, and knowledge of your audience also influence the kinds of details you include. For example, a description of a DNA molecule written for first-year college students would contain more basic details than a description written for junior biology majors. In addition, the more advanced description would contain details — the sequence of amino acid groups, for instance — that might be inappropriate for first-year students.

PLANNING A DESCRIPTIVE ESSAY

When you plan a descriptive essay, you usually begin by writing down details in no particular order. You then arrange these details in a way that supports your thesis and communicates your dominant impression. As you consider how to arrange your details, you have a number of options. For example, you can move from a specific description of an object to a general description of other things around it. Or you can reverse this order, beginning with the general and proceeding to the specific. You can also progress from the least important feature to the most important one, from the smallest to the largest item, from the least unusual to the most unusual detail, or from left to right, right to left, top to bottom, or bottom to top. Another option you have is to combine approaches, using different organizing schemes in different parts of the essay. The particular strategy you choose depends on the dominant impression you want to convey, your thesis, and your purpose and audience.

Be sure to include the transitional words and phrases readers will need to follow your description. Throughout your description, and especially in the topic sentences of your body paragraphs, include words or phrases that indicate the specific arrangement of details — for example, *at the top, in the middle,* and *at the bottom.*

STRUCTURING A DESCRIPTIVE ESSAY

Descriptive essays begin with an *introduction* that presents the thesis or establishes the dominant impression that the rest of the essay will develop. Each *body paragraph* includes details that support the thesis or convey the dominant impression. Your *conclusion* reinforces the thesis or dominant impression, perhaps echoing an idea that was stated in the introduction or using a particularly effective simile or metaphor.

Suppose your English composition instructor has asked you to write a short essay describing a person, place, or thing. After thinking about the assignment for a day or two, you decide to write an objective description of the Air and Space Museum in Washington, D.C., because you have visited it recently and many details are fresh in your mind. The museum is large and has many different exhibits, so you know you will not be able to describe them all. Therefore, you decide to concentrate on one, the heavier-than-air flight exhibit, and you choose as your topic the particular display that you remember most vividly: Charles Lindbergh's airplane, *The Spirit of St. Louis.* You begin by brainstorming to recall all the details you can. When you read over your notes, you realize that the organizing scheme of your essay could reflect your actual experience in the museum. You decide to present the details of the airplane in the order in which your eye took them in, from front to rear. The dominant impression you wish to create is how small and fragile *The Spirit of St. Louis* appears, and your thesis statement communicates this impression. An informal outline for your essay might look like this:

Introduction:	Thesis statement — It is startling that a plane as small as *The Spirit of St. Louis* could fly across the Atlantic.
Front of plane:	Single engine, tiny cockpit
Middle of plane:	Short wing span, extra gas tanks
Rear of plane:	Limited cargo space filled with more gas tanks
Conclusion:	Restatement of thesis or review of key points or details

---

☑ CHECKLIST: DESCRIPTION

- Does your assignment call for description?
- Does your descriptive essay clearly communicate its thesis or dominant impression?
- Is your description primarily objective or subjective?
- If your description is primarily objective, have you used precise, factual language?
- If your description is primarily subjective, have you used figures of speech?
- Have you included enough specific details?
- Have you arranged your details in a way that supports your thesis and communicates your dominant impression?
- Have you used the transitional words and phrases that readers need to follow your description?

▶ STUDENT WRITERS: DESCRIPTION

Each of the following student essays illustrates the principles of effective description. The first one, an objective description of the light microscope, by Joseph Tessari, was written for a scientific writing class. His assignment was to write a detailed, factual description of an instrument, mechanism, or piece of equipment used in his major field of study. The second essay, a subjective description of a place in Burma, was written by Mary Lim for her composition class. Her assignment was to write an essay about a place that has had a profound effect on her.

The Light Microscope

Introduction The simple light microscope is a basic   1
tool for biologists. The function of the microscope is to view objects or biological speci-
mens that would otherwise be invisible to the
naked eye. Light microscopes come in a variety
of shapes and sizes, with different degrees of
magnification and complexity. Most microscopes,
however, are made of metal or plastic (primarily
metal) and stand approximately ten to thirteen
Thesis statement inches tall. A description of the microscope's
design illustrates its function.

Description A simple light microscope consists of sev-   2
of stand eral integrated parts (see diagram). The largest
piece is the stand. The base of the stand, which
is wishbone-shaped, rests on the tabletop. A
vertical section approximately nine inches tall
extends out of the base and is shaped like a
question mark.

Description At the end of the vertical piece of the   3
of optic tube stand is the black metal optic tube, a vertical
cylinder approximately three to four inches
long. One entire side of this tube is attached
to the stand, so that the tube sits in front of
the stand when the microscope is viewed from
the front.

Description Directly on top of this tube is a cylindri-   4
of eyepiece cal eyepiece. The eyepiece, slightly smaller in
diameter than the optic tube, is approximately
two inches long. The top of the eyepiece is fitted
with a clear glass lens called the fixed lens.

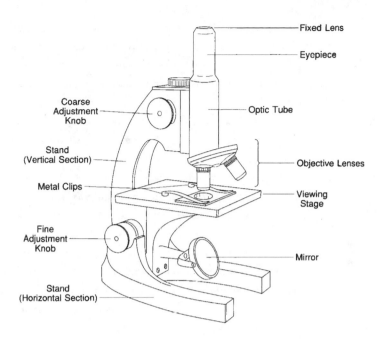

Fixed Lens

Eyepiece

Coarse Adjustment Knob

Optic Tube

Stand (Vertical Section)

Objective Lenses

Metal Clips

Viewing Stage

Fine Adjustment Knob

Mirror

Stand (Horizontal Section)

Description of coarse and fine adjustment knobs

On the stand, adjacent to the point where   5
it meets the optic tube, are two circular coarse
adjustment knobs--one on each side of the microscope. When rotated, these knobs raise and lower
the optic tube, focusing the image being viewed.
Two fine adjustment knobs at the bottom of the
stand permit finer adjustments in focus. These
knobs are especially useful at high magnifica-
tions, where smaller adjustments are needed.

Description of objective lenses

Attached to the bottom of the optic tube   6
is a rotating disk that contains two small
silver objective lenses spaced one hundred
eighty degrees apart. These lenses have different magnification powers. When an objective
lens is locked into place, the eyepiece, optic
tube, and objective lens fall in a vertical
line.

Description of viewing stage

Directly below the objective lens,   7
attached to the bend in the question mark of
the vertical stand, is the viewing stage, a
square horizontal plate with a small circular
hole in the center. This circular hole is

approximately the same diameter as the objective lens and falls along the same vertical
line. On either side of the hole are metal
clips that hold a glass slide or a specimen
plate in place.

**Description
of mirror**

A few inches below the viewing stage is a   8
small circular mirror that can pivot around a
horizontal axis. It is attached to the stand by
a Y-shaped clamp. When the mirror is adjusted,
light is reflected up through the hole in the
viewing stage and into the objective lens,
optic tube, and eyepiece.

Conclusion

The simple light microscope has been an   9
extremely useful biological tool for many years.
It has helped scientists learn more about human
anatomy and physiology as well as a number of
diseases. With modern technology, new and more
complex instruments, such as the electron
microscope, have been developed. Still, the
light microscope remains an important tool for
both students and serious researchers.

Points for Special Attention

OBJECTIVE DESCRIPTION.   Joseph Tessari, a toxicology major, wrote this paper as an exercise for a class in scientific writing. Because he is writing an objective description, he does not make subjective comments or point out the microscope's strengths and weaknesses; instead, he describes its physical features. Joseph's thesis statement emphasizes his purpose and conveys his intention to his readers.

OBJECTIVE LANGUAGE.   Because his essay is written for a class in scientific writing, Joseph keeps his description technical. His factual, concrete language concentrates on the size, shape, and construction of each part of the microscope and on the physical relationship of each part to other parts and to the whole. Although he does not use subjective language, he does use several figures of speech to help his readers visualize what he is describing (the "wishbone-shaped base," for example).

STRUCTURE.   Joseph describes the microscope piece by piece. He starts at the bottom of the microscope with its largest part — the stand. He next directs the reader's attention upward from the optic tube to the eye-piece and then downward past the coarse adjustment knobs to the bottom of the optic tube (where the objective lens is located) and down to the viewing stage and the mirror. In his introduction, Joseph comments on the microscope's purpose and general appearance; in his conclusion, he summarizes the microscope's historical significance and briefly considers its future.

SELECTION OF DETAIL.   Joseph's instructor defined his audience as a group of nonscientists. Joseph was told he could assume that his readers would know generally what a microscope looked like, but that he would have to describe the individual components in some detail.

DIAGRAM.   Joseph knew that describing the relationship among the parts of the microscope would not be easy. In fact, his initial attempts to do so produced sentences like "When viewed from the side, the objective lens makes a forty-five degree angle with the front of the optic tube and is higher in front of the microscope than in the back." In order to avoid complicated and tedious passages of description such as this one, Joseph included a diagram. Not only does the diagram present the parts of the microscope in relationship to one another, but it also depicts certain parts — like the objective lenses — that are difficult to visualize. Notice that the diagram is clearly labeled.

Focus on Revision

The peer critics of Joseph's paper identified two areas that they thought needed work. One student said that some of Joseph's sentences were wordy. Another suggested that he delete some of the details he had included because his diagram made them unnecessary. As a result of these criticisms, Joseph decided to edit for wordiness and to eliminate phrases such as "Y-shaped clamp" and "a small circular mirror." Since readers can see these structures on the diagram, he doesn't need to describe them in precise detail.

Unlike "The Light Microscope," Mary Lim's essay uses subjective description so that readers can share, as well as understand, her experience.

The Valley of Windmills

Introduction   In my native country of Burma, strange   1

happenings and exotic scenery are not unusual.

For Burma is a mysterious land that in some

areas seems to have been ignored by time. Moun-

tains stand jutting their rocky peaks into the

clouds as they have for thousands of years.

Jungles are so dense with exotic vegetation that human beings or large animals cannot even enter. But one of the most fascinating areas in Burma is the Valley of Windmills, nestled between the tall mountains near the fertile and beautiful city of Taungaleik. In this valley there is beautiful and breathtaking scenery, but there are also old, massive, and gloomy structures that can disturb a person deeply.

Description (identifying the scene)

The road to Taungaleik twists out of the coastal flatlands into those heaps of slag, shale, and limestone that are the Tennesserim Mountains in the southern part of Burma. The air grows rarer and cooler, and stones become grayer, the highway a little more precarious at its edges, until, ahead, standing in ghostly sentinel across the lip of a pass, is a line of squat forms. They straddle the road and stand at intervals up hillsides on either side. Are they boulders? Are they fortifications? Are they broken wooden crosses on graves in an abandoned cemetery?

Description (moving toward the valley)

Description (immediate view)

2

These dark figures are windmills standing in the misty atmosphere. They are immensely old and distinctly evil, some merely turrets, some with remnants of arms hanging derelict from their snouts, and most of them covered with dark green moss. Their decayed but still massive forms seem to turn and sneer at visitors. Down the pass on the other side is a circular green plateau that lies like an arena below, where there are still more windmills. Massed in the plain behind them, as far as the eye can see, in every field, above every hut, stand ten thousand iron windmills, silent and sailless. They seem to await only a call from a watchman to clank, whirr, flap, and groan into action. Visitors suddenly feel cold. Perhaps it is a sense of loneliness, the cool air, the desola-

Description (more distant view)

3

tion, or the weirdness of the arcane windmills--
but something chills them.

As you stand at the lip of the valley,   4
contrasts rush as if to overwhelm you. Beyond,

Conclusion

**Description
(windmills
contrasted
with city)**

glittering on the mountainside like a solitary
jewel, is Taungaleik in the territory once
occupied by the Portuguese. Below, on rolling
hillsides, are the dark windmills, still
enveloped in morning mist. These ancient windmills can remind you of the impermanence of

Thesis statement

life and the mystery that still surrounds these
hills. In a strange way, the scene in the valley can disturb you, but it also can give you an
insight into the contrasts that seem to define
our lives here in my country.

Points for Special Attention

SUBJECTIVE DESCRIPTION.   One of the first things her classmates
noticed when they read Mary's essay was her use of vivid details. The
road to Taungaleik is described in specific terms: it twists "out of the
coastal flatlands" into the mountains, which are "heaps of slag, shale, and
limestone." The iron windmills are decayed and stand "silent and sailless"
on a green plateau that "lies like an arena." Through her use of detail,
Mary creates her dominant impression of the Valley of Windmills as dark,
mysterious, and disquieting. The point of her essay — the thesis — is
stated in the last paragraph: the Valley of Windmills embodies the contrasts that characterize life in Burma.

SUBJECTIVE LANGUAGE.   By describing the windmills, Mary conveys
the sense of foreboding she felt. When she first introduces them, she
questions whether these "squat forms" are "boulders," "fortifications," or
"broken wooden crosses," each of which has a menacing connotation.
After telling readers what they are, she uses personification, describing
the windmills as dark, evil, sneering figures with "arms hanging derelict."
She sees them as ghostly sentinels awaiting "a call from a watchman" to
spring into action. Through this figure of speech, Mary skillfully recreates
the unearthly quality of the scene.

STRUCTURE.   Mary's purpose in writing this paper was to give her
readers the experience of actually being in the Valley of Windmills. She
uses an organizing scheme that takes readers along the road to

Taungaleik, up into the Tennesserim Mountains, and finally to the pass where the windmills wait. From her perspective on the lip of the valley, she describes the details closest to her and then those farther away, as if following the movement of her eyes. She ends by bringing her readers back to the lip of the valley, contrasting Taungaleik "glittering on the mountainside" with the windmills "enveloped in morning mist." Through her description, she builds up to her thesis about the nature of life in her country. She withholds the explicit statement of her main point until her last paragraph, when readers have been fully prepared for it.

Focus on Revision

One of Mary's peer critics thought that the essay's thesis about life in Burma needed additional support. The student pointed out that although Mary's description is quite powerful, it does not really convey the contrasts she alludes to in her conclusion. Mary decided that adding another paragraph in which she discussed something about her life, perhaps her reasons for visiting the windmills, could help supply this missing information. She could, for example, tell her reader that right after her return from the valley, she found out that a friend had been accidentally shot by border guards, and that it was this event that caused her to characterize the windmills as she did. Such information would help to explain the somber mood of the passage and underscore the ideas presented in the conclusion.

The following selections illustrate various ways in which description can shape an essay. As you read them, pay particular attention to the differences between objective and subjective description.

LEAH HAGER COHEN

Although she herself is not deaf, Leah Hager Cohen (1967–) lived for much of her childhood at the Lexington School for the Deaf in Queens, New York, where her mother was a teacher and her father was an administrator. (Both her paternal grandparents were deaf.) A graduate of the Columbia University School of Journalism, Cohen has been a writing instructor at Emerson College in Boston and an interpreter for deaf students in mainstream classes. Her books include *Glass, Paper, Beans: Revelations on the Nature and Value of Ordinary Things* (1997) and a novel, *Heat Lightning* (1998).

Cohen's strong identification with the deaf students at the Lexington School was the basis for her 1994 book about deaf culture; its title, *Train Go Sorry,* is a translation of the American Sign Language symbols meaning "to miss the boat" or "to be left behind." One of her goals in that book was to convince readers that deafness is "not a pathology but a cultural identity." In the following selection from *Train Go Sorry,* Cohen remembers her grandfather, Sam Cohen, whose parents had to hide their son's deafness from immigration officials when they passed through Ellis Island in the early 1900s.

Words Left Unspoken

My earliest memories of Sam Cohen are of his chin, which I remember   1
as fiercely hard and pointy. Not pointy, my mother says, jutting; Grandpa had a strong, jutting chin. But against my very young face it felt like a chunk of honed granite swathed in stiff white bristles. Whenever we visited, he would lift us grandchildren up, most frequently by the elbows, and nuzzle our cheeks vigorously. This abrasive ritual greeting was our primary means of communication. In all my life, I never heard him speak a word I could understand.

Sometimes he used his voice to get our attention. It made a shapeless,   2
gusty sound, like a pair of bellows sending up sparks and soot in a blacksmith shop. And he made sounds when he was eating, sounds that, originating from other quarters, would have drawn chiding or expulsion from the table. He smacked his lips and sucked his teeth; his chewing was moist and percussive; he released deep, hushed moans from the back of his throat, like a dreaming dog. And he burped out loud. Sometimes it was all Reba, Andy, and I could do not to catch one another's eyes and fall into giggles.

Our grandfather played games with us, the more physical the better.   3
He loved that hand game: he would extend his, palms up, and we would hover ours, palms down, above his, and lower them, lower, lower, until they were just nesting, and *slap!* he'd have sandwiched one of our hands, trapping it between his. When we reversed, I could never even graze his, so fast would he snatch them away, like a big white fish.

He played three-card monte* with us, arranging the cards neatly   4
between his long fingers, showing us once the jack of diamonds smirking,
red and gold, underneath. And then, with motions as swift and implausible as a Saturday morning cartoon chase, his hands darted and faked and
blurred and the cards lay still, face down and impassive. When we
guessed the jack's position correctly, it was only luck. When we guessed
wrong, he would laugh — a fond, gravelly sound — and pick up the cards
and begin again.

He mimicked the way I ate. He compressed his mouth into dainty pro-   5
portions as he nibbled air and carefully licked his lips and chewed tiny,
precise bites, his teeth clicking, his eyelashes batting as he gazed shyly
from under them. He could walk exactly like Charlie Chaplin and make
nickels disappear, just vanish, from both his fists and up his sleeves; we
never found them, no matter how we crawled over him, searching. All of
this without any words.

He and my grandmother lived in the Bronx, in the same apartment   6
my father and Uncle Max had grown up in. It was on Knox Place, near
Mosholu Parkway, a three-room apartment below street level. The kitchen
was a tight squeeze of a place, especially with my grandmother bending
over the oven, blocking the passage as she checked baked apples or
stuffed cabbage, my grandfather sitting with splayed knees at the dinette.
It was easy to get each other's attention in there; a stamped foot sent vibrations clearly over the short distance, and an outstretched arm had a good
chance of connecting with the other party.

The living room was ampler and dimmer, with abundant floor and   7
table lamps to accommodate signed conversation. Little windows set up
high revealed the legs of passersby. And down below, burrowed in black
leather chairs in front of the television, we children learned to love physical comedy. Long before the days of closed captioning, we listened to our
grandfather laugh out loud at the snowy black-and-white antics of Abbott
and Costello, Laurel and Hardy, the Three Stooges.

During the time that I knew him, I saw his hairline shrink back and his   8
eyes grow remote behind pairs of progressively thicker glasses. His athlete's bones shed some of their grace and nimbleness; they began curving
in on themselves as he stood, arms folded across his sunken chest. Even
his long, thin smile seemed to recede deeper between his nose and his
prominent chin. But his hands remained lithe, vital. As he teased and
argued and chatted and joked, they were the instruments of his mind, the
conduits of his thoughts.

As far as anyone knows, Samuel Kolominsky was born deaf (accord-   9
ing to Lexington** records, his parents "failed to take note until child was

---

*EDS. NOTE — A sleight-of-hand card game often played on urban streets, in
which the dealer gets onlookers to place bets that they can pick the jack of diamonds.

**EDS. NOTE — The Lexington School for the Deaf, where Cohen's grandfather was
once a student.

about one and a half years old"). His birthplace was Russia, somewhere near Kiev. Lexington records say he was born in 1908; my grandmother says it was 1907. He was a child when his family fled the czarist pogroms. Lexington records have him immigrating in 1913, at age five; my grandmother says he came to this country when he was three. Officials at Ellis Island altered the family name, writing down Cohen, but they did not detect his deafness, so Sam sailed on across the last ribbon of water to America.

His name-sign at home: *Daddy*. His name-sign with friends: the thumb   10
and index finger, perched just above the temple, rub against each other like grasshopper legs. One old friend attributes this to Sam's hair, which was blond and thick and wavy. Another says it derived from his habit of twisting a lock between his fingers.

Lexington records have him living variously at Clara, Moore, Siegel,   11
Tehema, and Thirty-eighth streets in Brooklyn and on Avenue C in Manhattan. I knew him on Knox Place, and much later on Thieriot Avenue, in the Bronx. Wherever he lived, he loved to walk, the neighborhoods revolving silently like pictures in a Kinetoscope,* unfurling themselves in full color around him.

Shortly before he died, when I was thirteen, we found ourselves walk-   12
ing home from a coffee shop together on a warm night. My family had spent the day visiting my grandparents at their apartment. My grandmother and the rest of the family were walking half a block ahead; I hung back and made myself take my grandfather's hand. We didn't look at each other. His hand was warm and dry. His gait was uneven then, a long slow beat on the right, catch-up on the left. I measured my steps to his. It was dark except for the hazy pink cones of light cast by streetlamps. I found his rhythm, and breathed in it. That was the longest conversation we ever had.

He died before I was really able to converse in sign. I have never seen   13
his handwriting. I once saw his teeth, in a glass, on the bathroom windowsill. Now everything seems like a clue.

•   •   •

COMPREHENSION

1. Why was Cohen's grandfather unable to speak? How did Cohen communicate with him?

2. What kind of relationship did Cohen have with her grandfather? Warm? Distant?

3. What is the significance of the essay's title? What does Cohen mean when she says, "That was the longest conversation we ever had" (12)?

---

*EDS. NOTE — A device for viewing a sequence of moving pictures as it rotates over a light source, creating the illusion of motion.

4. In paragraph 13, Cohen says that now, after her grandfather's death, "everything seems like a clue." What does she mean?

5. What do you think the "words left unspoken" are? Is the speaker of these words Cohen, her grandfather, or both? Explain.

PURPOSE AND AUDIENCE

1. Does "Words Left Unspoken" have an explicitly stated thesis? Why or why not?

2. What dominant impression is Cohen trying to create in this essay? How successful is she?

3. How much do you think Cohen expects her readers to know about deaf culture? How can you tell?

STYLE AND STRUCTURE

1. Why do you think Cohen begins with a description of her grandfather's chin?

2. What is the organizing principle of this essay? Would another organizing principle be more effective? Explain.

3. Are you able to picture Cohen's grandfather after reading her description? Do you think she expects you to?

4. Does Cohen develop her description fully enough? At what points could she have provided more detail?

5. What figures of speech does Cohen use in this essay? Where might additional figures of speech be helpful?

VOCABULARY PROJECTS

1. Define each of the following words as they are used in this selection.
   honed (1)   abundant (7)
   expulsion (2)   prominent (8)
   percussive (2)   lithe (8)
   smirking (4)   conduits (8)
   splayed (6)   gait (12)

2. Supply a synonym for each of the words listed above. In what way is each synonym different from the original word?

JOURNAL ENTRY

In what ways does Cohen's grandfather fit the traditional stereotype of a grandfather? In what ways does he not fit this stereotype?

WRITING WORKSHOP

1. Write a description of a person. Concentrate on one specific feature or quality that you associate with this person as Cohen does in her essay.

2. Choose three or four members of your family, and write a one-paragraph description of each. Combine these descriptions into a "family album" essay that has an introduction, a thesis statement, and a conclusion.

3. Write an essay in which you describe your earliest memories of a family member or close family friend. Before you write, decide on the dominant impression you want to convey.

COMBINING THE PATTERNS

Cohen uses **narration** to develop paragraph 9. Why does she include this narrative paragraph? Does it add to or detract from the dominant impression she is trying to convey? Explain.

THEMATIC CONNECTIONS

- "Only Daughter" (page 83)
- "The Way to Rainy Mountain" (page 148)
- "Mother Tongue" (page 405)

MARK TWAIN

Samuel L. Clemens (1835–1910), or Mark Twain, the pen name by which he is known, was born in Florida, Missouri, and raised in the river town of Hannibal, Missouri. He left school at the age of twelve and later traveled throughout the West. He was licensed as a Mississippi riverboat pilot in 1859 after two years of training and continued in this job until the Civil War stopped boat traffic on the river in 1861. After the war, he began a career as a humorist and writer, achieving great success as a lecturer as well. His novels *The Adventures of Tom Sawyer* (1876) and *The Adventures of Huck Finn* (1884) are American classics. He is also remembered for his tall tales and for his autobiographical volumes. One of these, *Life on the Mississippi* (1883), is about his experiences as a riverboat pilot.

The Mississippi is the United States' largest and most important river, flowing eighteen hundred miles from northern Minnesota to the Gulf of Mexico in southeastern Louisiana. It was a principal means of transporting goods and passengers from the advent of the steamboat in 1811 until the rise of railroads in the late 1800s. Because of its many narrows, bends, and shallows, the Mississippi can be treacherous to navigate. In Twain's time, as today, the role of the pilot was crucial in keeping the ship from getting snagged on debris or running aground. Pilots had to know what to expect under many conditions whether they were traveling in daylight or darkness. In this excerpt from *Life on the Mississippi,* Twain describes the river from the differing viewpoints of the average passenger and the experienced riverboat pilot.

Reading the River

The face of the water, in time, became a wonderful book — a book that 1 was a dead language to the uneducated passenger but which told its mind to me without reserve, delivering its most cherished secrets as clearly as if it uttered them with a voice. And it was not a book to be read once and thrown aside, for it had a new story to tell every day. Throughout the long twelve hundred miles there was never a page that was void of interest, never one that you could leave unread without loss, never one that you would want to skip, thinking you could find higher enjoyment in some other thing. There never was so wonderful a book written by man, never one whose interest was so absorbing, so unflagging, so sparklingly renewed with every reperusal. The passenger who could not read it was charmed with a peculiar sort of faint dimple on its surface (on the rare occasions when he did not overlook it altogether) but to the pilot that was an *italicized* passage; indeed it was more than that, it was a legend of the largest capitals with a string of shouting exclamation-points at the end of it, for it meant that a wreck or a rock was buried there that could tear the life out of the strongest vessel that ever floated. It is the faintest and simplest expression the water ever makes, and the most hideous to a pilot's eye. In truth, the passenger who could not read this book saw nothing but all manner of pretty pictures in it, painted by the sun and shaded by the clouds, whereas to the trained eye these were not pictures at all, but the grimmest and most dead-earnest of reading matter.

Now when I mastered the language of this water, and had come to 2 know every trifling feature that bordered the great river as familiarly as I knew the letters of the alphabet, I had made a valuable acquisition. But I had lost something, too. I had lost something which could never be restored to me while I lived. All the grace, the beauty, the poetry, had gone out of the majestic river! I still kept in mind a certain wonderful sunset which I witnessed when steamboating was new to me. A broad expanse of the river was turned to blood; in the middle distance the red hue brightened into gold, through which a solitary log came floating, black and conspicuous; in one place a long, slanting mark lay sparkling upon the water; in another the surface was broken by boiling, tumbling rings, that were as many-tinted as an opal; where the ruddy flush was faintest, was a smooth spot that was covered with graceful circles and radiating lines, ever so delicately traced; the shore on our left was densely wooded, and the somber shadow that fell from this forest was broken in one place by a long, ruffled trail that shone like silver; and high above the forest wall a clean-stemmed dead tree waved a single leafy bough that glowed like a flame in the unobstructed splendor that was flowing from the sun. There were graceful curves, reflected images, woody heights, soft distances; and over the whole scene, far and near, the dissolving lights drifted steadily, enriching it every passing moment with new marvels of coloring.

I stood like one bewitched. I drank it in, in a speechless rapture. The 3 world was new to me, and I had never seen anything like this at home. But as I have said, a day came when I began to cease from noting the glories and the charms which the moon and the sun and the twilight wrought upon the river's face; another day came when I ceased altogether to note them. Then, if that sunset scene had been repeated, I should have looked upon it without rapture, and should have commented upon it, inwardly, after this fashion: "This sun means that we are going to have wind tomorrow; that floating log means that the river is rising, small thanks to it; that slanting mark on the water refers to a bluff reef which is going to kill somebody's steamboat one of these nights, if it keeps on stretching out like that; those tumbling 'boils' show a dissolving bar and a changing channel there; the lines and circles in the slick water over yonder are a warning that that troublesome place is shoaling up dangerously; that silver streak in the shadow of the forest is the 'break' from a new snag, and he has located himself in the very best place he could have found to fish for steamboats; that tall dead tree, with a single living branch, is not going to last long, and then how is a body ever going to get through this blind place at night without the friendly old landmark?"

No, the romance and beauty were all gone from the river. All the value   4
any feature of it had for me now was the amount of usefulness it could
furnish toward compassing the safe piloting of a steamboat. Since those
days, I have pitied doctors from my heart. What does the lovely flush in a
beauty's cheek mean to a doctor but a "break" that ripples above some
deadly disease? Are not all her visible charms sown thick with what are to
him the signs and symbols of hidden decay? Does he ever see her beauty
at all, or doesn't he simply view her professionally and comment upon her
unwholesome condition all to himself? And doesn't he sometimes wonder
whether he has gained most or lost most by learning his trade?

• • •

COMPREHENSION

1. How is the Mississippi River like a book?

2. When a passenger sees a dimple in the water's surface, what does a riverboat pilot see?

3. What did Twain gain as he became a skilled pilot? What did he lose?

4. Why does Twain say, in his conclusion, that he feels sorry for doctors?
   What do doctors and riverboat pilots have in common?

PURPOSE AND AUDIENCE

1. State Twain's thesis in your own words.

2. Is Twain writing primarily for an audience of pilots or of passengers?
   Explain your conclusion.

3. What is Twain's attitude toward passengers? Toward pilots?

STYLE AND STRUCTURE

1. In the first lines of the selection, Twain compares the Mississippi River to
   a book. Trace this metaphor and the variations of it (other references to
   language, punctuation, or reading) throughout the selection. Are these
   comparisons between the river and the book effective? Explain.

2. How does Twain arrange the details in his description? What other organizational scheme could he have used? What are the advantages and disadvantages of this other scheme?

3. Why does Twain include the description of the sunset in paragraph 2?
   Would this description have the same effect if it were briefer? Why or
   why not?

4. Where does Twain restate his thesis? Do you think this restatement is necessary? Why or why not?

5. Why does Twain end his essay with observations about doctors? Why do
   you suppose he feels the need to include these comments?

VOCABULARY PROJECTS

1. Define each of the following words as it is used in this selection.

   unflagging (1)   conspicuous (2)   somber (2)
   reperusal (1)   opal (2)   rapture (3)
   italicized (1)   ruddy (2)   wrought (3)
   trifling (2)   radiating (2)

2. Make a list of the adjectives Twain uses to describe the river. What dominant impression do you think Twain seeks to convey with these adjectives? Is he successful? Explain.

3. What other adjectives could you substitute for the ones Twain uses? What are the advantages and disadvantages of your choices?

JOURNAL ENTRY

Do you agree with Twain's point that acquiring knowledge necessarily results in a loss of appreciation for beauty? What examples from your own experience illustrate the opposite point — that is, that knowledge increases the appreciation of beauty?

WRITING WORKSHOP

1. Write a subjective description of a scene you remember from your childhood. In your thesis statement and in your conclusion, explain how your adult impressions of the scene differ from those of your childhood.

2. Write an essay in which you show how increased knowledge of a subject actually increased your enthusiasm for it.

3. Think of a situation in which you were once a "passenger" but are now a "pilot." Write an essay in which you describe how becoming a pilot changed your perceptions of events. You may want to consult "How the Lawyers Stole Winter" (page 362) to get ideas for your essay.

COMBINING THE PATTERNS

In addition to containing a great deal of description, this essay also **compares and contrasts** two ways of reading the river. What points about each view of the river does Twain compare? What other points might he have included?

THEMATIC CONNECTIONS

- "Shooting an Elephant" (page 104)
- "Once More to the Lake" (page 154)
- "How the Lawyers Stole Winter" (page 362)

MARY GORDON

Mary Gordon was born in 1948 in Far Rockaway, New York, and grew up in a working-class Irish-Catholic neighborhood there. Her father died when she was seven, and she and her mother then moved in with her grandmother and aunt. Always interested in writing, Gordon began publishing short stories in the mid-1970s, and her first novel, *Final Payments,* appeared in 1978. It was an immediate critical and popular success. Since then Gordon has published a number of other works of fiction and nonfiction. She is currently on the faculty at Barnard College.

In much of her fiction, Gordon draws heavily on her own family heritage. In the following essay, first published in the *New York Times* in 1985, she describes a visit to Ellis Island in New York harbor, a primary processing center for European immigrants to the United States from 1892 to 1924. Disembarking from the cramped steerage decks of ocean liners, passengers were met by a series of officials testing immigrants' "fitness" to enter the country. Reminded of her immigrant grandparents (who both passed through Ellis Island), Gordon considers the humiliations such immigrants endured and the way in which their ghosts continue to color her sense of herself as an American.

More Than Just a Shrine: Paying Homage to the Ghosts of Ellis Island

I once sat in a hotel in Bloomsbury* trying to have breakfast alone. A 1 Russian with a habit of compulsively licking his lips asked if he could join me. I was afraid to say no; I thought it might be bad for détente. He explained to me that he was a linguist and that he always liked to talk to Americans to see if he could make any connection between their speech and their ethnic background. When I told him about my mixed ancestry — my mother is Irish and Italian, my father was a Lithuanian Jew — he began jumping up and down in his seat, rubbing his hands together and licking his lips even more frantically.

"Ah," he said, "so you are really somebody who comes from what is 2 called the boiling pot of America." Yes, I told him; yes, I was; but I quickly rose to leave. I thought it would be too hard to explain to him the relation of the boiling potters to the main course, and I wanted to get to the British Museum. I told him that the only thing I could think of that united people whose backgrounds, histories, and points of view were utterly diverse was that their people had landed at a place called Ellis Island.

I didn't tell him that Ellis Island was the only American landmark I'd 3 ever visited. How could I describe to him the estrangement I'd always felt

---

*EDS. NOTE — A neighborhood in London.

from the kind of traveler who visits shrines to America's past greatness, those rebuilt forts with muskets behind glass, sabers mounted on the walls and gift shops selling maple syrup candy in the shape of Indian headdresses, those reconstructed villages with tables set for fifty and the Paul Revere silver gleaming. All that Americana — Plymouth Rock, Gettysburg, Mount Vernon, Valley Forge — it all inhabits for me a zone of blurred abstraction with far less hold on my imagination than the Bastille or Hampton Court.* I suppose I've always known that my uninterest in it contains a large component of the willed: I am American, and those places purport to be my history. But they are not mine.

Ellis Island is, though; it's the one place I can be sure my people are   4
connected to. And so I made a journey there to find my history like any Rotarian** traveling in his Winnebago*** to Antietam† to find his. I had become part of that humbling democracy of people looking in some site for a past that has grown unreal. The monument I traveled to was not, however, a tribute to some old glory. The minute I set foot upon the island I could feel all that it stood for: insecurity, obedience, anxiety, dehumanization, the terrible and careful deference of the displaced. I hadn't traveled to the Battery‡ and boarded a ferry across from the Statue of Liberty to raise flags or breathe a richer, more triumphant air. I wanted to do homage to the ghosts.

I felt them everywhere, from the moment I disembarked I saw the   5
building with its high-minded brick, its hopeful little land, its ornamental cornices. The place was derelict when I arrived; it had not functioned for more than thirty years — almost as long as the time it had operated at full capacity as a major immigration center. I was surprised to learn what a small part of history Ellis Island had occupied. The main building was constructed in 1892, then rebuilt between 1898 and 1900 after a fire. Most of the immigrants who arrived during the latter half of the nineteenth century, mainly northern and western Europeans, landed not at Ellis Island but on the western tip of the Battery, at Castle Garden which had opened as a receiving center for immigrants in 1855.

By the 1880s, the facilities at Castle Garden had grown scandalously   6
inadequate. Officials looked for an island on which to build a new immigration center, because they thought that on an island immigrants could be more easily protected from swindlers and quickly transported to railroad terminals in New Jersey. Bedloe's Island was considered, but New Yorkers were aghast at the idea of a "Babel" ruining their beautiful new treasure, "Liberty Enlightening the World."¶ The statue's sculptor,

---

*EDS. NOTE — Landmarks in Paris and London.
**EDS. NOTE — A member of a Rotary club, a local branch of an international service organization.
***EDS. NOTE — A recreational vehicle (RV).
†EDS. NOTE — A U.S. Civil War battleground.
‡EDS. NOTE — The southern tip of Manhattan.
¶EDS. NOTE — More commonly known as the Statue of Liberty.

Frédéric-Auguste Bartholdi, reacted to the prospect of immigrants landing near his masterpiece in horror; he called it a "monstrous plan." So much for Emma Lazarus.*

Ellis Island was finally chosen because the citizens of New Jersey petitioned the federal government to remove from the island an old naval powder magazine that they thought dangerously close to the Jersey shore. The explosives were removed; no one wanted the island for anything. It was the perfect place to build an immigration center.   7

I thought about the island's history as I walked into the building and made my way to the room that was the center in my imagination of the Ellis Island experience: the Great Hall. It had been made real for me in the stark, accusing photographs of Louis Hine and others, who took those pictures to make a point. It was in the Great Hall that everyone had waited — waiting, always, the great vocation of the dispossessed. The room was empty, except for me and a handful of other visitors and the park ranger who showed us around. I felt myself grow insignificant in that room, with its huge semicircular windows, its air, even in dereliction, of solid and official probity.   8

I walked in the deathlike expansiveness of the room's disuse and tried to think of what it might have been like, filled and swarming. More than sixteen million immigrants came through that room; approximately 250,000 were rejected. Not really a large proportion, but the implications for the rejected were dreadful. For some, there was nothing to go back to, or there was certain death; for others, who left as adventurers, to return would be to adopt in local memory the fool's role, and the failure's. No wonder that the island's history includes reports of three thousand suicides.   9

Sometimes immigrants could pass through Ellis Island in mere hours, though for some the process took days. The particulars of the experience in the Great Hall were often influenced by the political events and attitudes on the mainland. In the 1890s and the first years of the new century, when cheap labor was needed, the newly built receiving center took in its immigrants with comparatively little question. But as the century progressed, the economy worsened, eugenics became both scientifically respectable and popular, and World War I made American xenophobia seem rooted in fact.   10

Immigration acts were passed; newcomers had to prove, besides moral correctness and financial solvency, their ability to read. Quota laws came into effect, limiting the number of immigrants from southern and eastern Europe to less than 14 percent of the total quota. Intelligence tests were biased against all non-English-speaking persons, and medical examinations became increasingly strict, until the machinery of immigration nearly collapsed under its own weight. The Second Quota Law of 1924 provided that all immigrants be inspected and issued visas at American consular offices in Europe, rendering the center almost obsolete.   11

---

*EDS. NOTE — Poet whose "The New Colossus" is engraved on the statue's pedestal ("Give me your tired, your poor / your huddled masses yearning to breathe free, . . .").

On the day of my visit, my mind fastened upon the medical inspec-   12
tions, which had always seemed to me most emblematic of the ignominy
and terror the immigrants endured. The medical inspectors, sometimes
dressed in uniforms like soldiers, were particularly obsessed with a disease of the eyes called trachoma, which they checked for by flipping back
the immigrants' top eyelids with a hook used for buttoning gloves —
a method that sometimes resulted in the transmission of the disease to
healthy people. Mothers feared that if their children cried too much, their
red eyes would be mistaken for a symptom of the disease and the whole
family would be sent home. Those immigrants suspected of some physical
disability had initials chalked on their coats. I remembered the photographs I'd seen of people standing, dumbstruck and innocent as cattle,
with their manifest numbers hung around their necks and initials marked
in chalk upon their coats: "E" for eye trouble, "K" for hernia, "L" for lame-
ness, "X" for mental defects, "H" for heart disease.

I thought of my grandparents as I stood in the room: my seventeen-   13
year-old grandmother, coming alone from Ireland in 1896, vouched for by
a stranger who had found her a place as a domestic servant to some Irish
who had done well. I tried to imagine the assault it all must have been for
her; I've been to her hometown, a collection of farms with a main street —
smaller than the athletic field of my local public school. She must have
watched the New York skyline as the first- and second-class passengers
were whisked off the gangplank with the most cursory of inspections
while she was made to board a ferry to the new immigration center.

What could she have made of it — this buff-painted wooden structure   14
with its towers and its blue slate roof, a place *Harper's Weekly* described as
"a latter-day watering place hotel"? It would have been the first time she
had heard people speaking something other than English. She would have
mingled with people carrying baskets on their heads and eating foods
unlike any she had ever seen — dark-eyed people, like the Sicilian she
would marry ten years later, who came over with his family at thirteen,
the man of the family, responsible even then for his mother and sister.
I don't know what they thought, my grandparents, for they were not ex-
pansive people, nor romantic; they didn't like to think of what they called
"the hard times," and their trip across the ocean was the single adventurous act of lives devoted after landing to security, respectability, and
fitting in.

What is the potency of Ellis Island for someone like me — an Amer-   15
ican, obviously, but one who has always felt that the country really
belonged to the early settlers, that, as J. F. Powers wrote in *Morte D'Urban*,
it had been "handed down to them by the Pilgrims, George Washington
and others, and that they were taking a risk in letting you live in it." I have
never been the victim of overt discrimination; nothing I have wanted has
been denied me because of the accidents of blood. But I suppose it is part
of being an American to be engaged in a somewhat tiresome but always
self-absorbing process of national definition. And in this process, I have
found in traveling to Ellis Island an important piece of evidence that could

remind me I was right to feel my differentness. Something had happened to my people on that island, a result of the eternal wrongheadedness of American protectionism and the predictabilities of simple greed. I came to the island, too, so I could tell the ghosts that I was one of them, and that I honored them — their stoicism, and their innocence, the fear that turned them inward, and their pride. I wanted to tell them that I liked them better than I did the Americans who made them pass through the Great Hall and stole their names and chalked their weaknesses in public on their clothing. And to tell the ghosts what I have always thought: that American history was a very classy party that was not much fun until they arrived, brought the good food, turned up the music, and taught everyone to dance.

●   ●   ●

COMPREHENSION

1. Why does Gordon visit Ellis Island? What does she hope to find there?

2. Why is Gordon unable to find meaning in the "shrines to America's past greatness" (2)?

3. Who are the "ghosts" of Ellis Island? Why does Gordon say that she wants to pay them homage?

4. What feelings did Ellis Island create in the immigrants? What feelings does it create in Gordon?

5. What insights about her ancestors and herself does Gordon achieve as a result of her visit to Ellis Island?

PURPOSE AND AUDIENCE

1. What dominant impression does Gordon try to convey? Is she successful? Explain.

2. In your own words, summarize the essay's thesis.

3. Is Gordon's essay an objective or a subjective description? What are the advantages and disadvantages of her choice?

4. What is Gordon's purpose in writing this essay? To instruct? To entertain? To persuade? Or does she have some other purpose?

STYLE AND STRUCTURE

1. What is the function of the anecdote in the first two paragraphs of the essay? Would the essay have been better without this anecdote? Could the essay have begun with the third paragraph?

2. In what order does Gordon arrange the details in her description? What does she gain with this arrangement? Would another order have been better?

3. At what point does Gordon state her thesis? Why does she state it where she does?

4. What strategy does Gordon use in her conclusion? What does she hope to accomplish by ending her essay in this way?

VOCABULARY PROJECTS

1. Define each of the following words as it is used in this selection.

compulsively (1)   dehumanization (4)   dumbstruck (12)
détente (1)   enlightening (6)   vouched (13)
linguist (1)   magazine (7)   cursory (13)
ethnic (1)   eugenics (10)   overt (15)
shrines (3)   xenophobia (10)   predictabilities (15)

2. Make a list of the adjectives that Gordon uses to describe Ellis Island. What conclusion can you draw about her attitude toward this place?

3. Find examples of similes, metaphors, and personification. In what way do these figures of speech help Gordon make her point?

JOURNAL ENTRY

Do you think that Gordon finds what she hopes to find on Ellis Island? Does she discover anything unexpected?

WRITING WORKSHOP

1. Write an essay in which you describe a place that has meaning to you and to your heritage — for example, a place of worship, a cultural center, or a museum. Be sure to describe the qualities that make this place special.

2. Find a picture of immigrants at Ellis Island, either in your school library or on the Internet. Then, write a description of the place from the point of view of one of the immigrants. As Gordon does in paragraph 13, try to convey the strangeness of the scene on Ellis Island for someone who has just arrived there.

3. Write a letter to a relative who is about to come to this country for the first time. Describe what this person will see when he or she comes to your hometown. Make sure you arrange your details in a way that conveys your dominant impression.

COMBINING THE PATTERNS

What purpose does **narration** serve in paragraphs 5–7? In what way do these paragraphs prepare readers for the description that follows?

THEMATIC CONNECTIONS

- "Only Daughter" (page 83)
- "Suicide Note" (page 315)
- "Two Ways to Belong to America" (page 357)
- The Declaration of Independence (page 516)

N. SCOTT MOMADAY

N. Scott Momaday was born in 1934 in Lawton, Oklahoma, of Kiowa ancestry. He holds degrees from the University of New Mexico and Stanford University and has taught English at a number of colleges; he is currently on the faculty at the University of Arizona. In 1969, Momaday won a Pulitzer Prize for his first novel, *House Made of Dawn* (1968). He followed this book with *The Way to Rainy Mountain* (1968), in which he retells Kiowa legends and folktales. Momaday has also published collections of poetry and stories, as well as a memoir, *The Names* (1976).

The following essay, excerpted from the introduction to *The Way to Rainy Mountain,* focuses both on the landscape of Momaday's childhood and on his grandmother. Momaday has said of the essay, "My grandmother, Aho, was the principal force in the homestead when I was a child. She was a beautiful and gracious woman, and she presided over family affairs with great generosity and goodwill. . . . The introduction to *The Way to Rainy Mountain* is in large measure an evocation of my grandmother's spirit, and for this reason among others that book is my favorite of my works." The book was written at a time when many groups outside of the white mainstream were beginning to assert the importance and legitimacy of their own cultures. Native Americans, in particular, had for years been discouraged by white educators, sometimes quite brutally, from using their own languages and following their ancient spiritual beliefs. Momaday was one of the first Native Americans to write about his culture for a popular audience.

The Way to Rainy Mountain

A single knoll rises out of the plain in Oklahoma, north and west of the Wichita Range. For my people, the Kiowas, it is an old landmark, and they gave it the name Rainy Mountain. The hardest weather in the world is there. Winter brings blizzards, hot tornadic winds arise in the spring, and in summer the prairie is an anvil's edge. The grass turns brittle and brown, and it cracks beneath your feet. There are green belts along the rivers and creeks, linear groves of hickory and pecan, willow and witch hazel. At a distance in July or August the steaming foliage seems almost to writhe in fire. Great green-and-yellow grasshoppers are everywhere in the tall grass, popping up like corn to sting the flesh, and tortoises crawl about on the red earth, going nowhere in the plenty of time. Loneliness is an aspect of the land. All things in the plain are isolate; there is no confusion of objects in the eye, but *one* hill or *one* tree or *one* man. To look upon that landscape in the early morning, with the sun at your back, is to lose the sense of proportion. Your imagination comes to life, and this, you think, is where Creation was begun. 1

I returned to Rainy Mountain in July. My grandmother had died in the spring, and I wanted to be at her grave. She had lived to be very old and at last infirm. Her only living daughter was with her when she died, and I was told that in death her face was that of a child. 2

I like to think of her as a child. When she was born, the Kiowas were   3
living that last great moment of their history. For more than a hundred
years they had controlled the open range from the Smoky Hill River to the
Red, from the headwaters of the Canadian to the fork of the Arkansas and
Cimarron. In alliance with the Comanches, they had ruled the whole of
the southern Plains. War was their sacred business, and they were among
the finest horsemen the world has ever known. But warfare for the
Kiowas was preeminently a matter of disposition rather than of survival,
and they never understood the grim, unrelenting advance of the U.S.
Cavalry. When at last, divided and ill-provisioned, they were driven onto
the Staked Plains in the cold rains of autumn, they fell into panic. In Palo
Duro Canyon they abandoned their crucial stores to pillage and had nothing then but their lives. In order to save themselves, they surrendered to
the soldiers at Fort Sill and were imprisoned in the old stone corral that
now stands as a military museum. My grandmother was spared the
humiliation of those high gray walls by eight or ten years, but she must
have known from birth the affliction of defeat, the dark brooding of old
warriors.

Her name was Aho, and she belonged to the last culture to evolve in   4
North America. Her forebears came down from the high country in western Montana nearly three centuries ago. They were a mountain people, a
mysterious tribe of hunters whose language has never been positively
classified in any major group. In the late seventeenth century they began a
long migration to the south and east. It was a long journey toward the
dawn, and it led to a golden age. Along the way the Kiowas were
befriended by the Crows, who gave them the culture and religion of the
Plains. They acquired horses, and their ancient nomadic spirit was suddenly free of the ground. They acquired Tai-me, the sacred Sun Dance
doll, from that moment the object and symbol of their worship, and so
shared in the divinity of the sun. Not least, they acquired the sense of destiny, therefore courage and pride. When they entered upon the southern
Plains, they had been transformed. No longer were they slaves to the simple necessity of survival; they were a lordly and dangerous society of
fighters and thieves, hunters and priests of the sun. According to their origin myth, they entered the world through a hollow log. From one point of
view, their migration was the fruit of an old prophecy, for indeed they
emerged from a sunless world.

Although my grandmother lived out her long life in the shadow of   5
Rainy Mountain, the immense landscape of the continental interior lay
like memory in her blood. She could tell of the Crows, whom she had
never seen, and of the Black Hills, where she had never been. I wanted to
see in reality what she had seen more perfectly in the mind's eye, and traveled fifteen hundred miles to begin my pilgrimage.

Yellowstone, it seemed to me, was the top of the world, a region of   6
deep lakes and dark timber, canyons and waterfalls. But, beautiful as
it is, one might have the sense of confinement there. The skyline in all

directions is close at hand, the high wall of the woods and deep cleavages of shade. There is a perfect freedom in the mountains, but it belongs to the eagle and the elk, the badger and the bear. The Kiowas reckoned their stature by the distance they could see, and they were bent and blind in the wilderness.

Descending eastward, the highland meadows are a stairway to the   7
plain. In July the inland slope of the Rockies is luxuriant with flax and buckwheat, stonecrop and larkspur. The earth unfolds and the limit of the land recedes. Clusters of trees and animals grazing far in the distance cause the vision to reach away and wonder to build upon the mind. The sun follows a longer course in the day, and the sky is immense beyond all comparison. The great billowing clouds that sail upon it are shadows that move upon the grain like water, dividing light. Farther down, in the land of the Crows and Blackfeet, the plain is yellow. Sweet clover takes hold of the hills and bends upon itself to cover and seal the soil. There the Kiowas paused on their way; they had come to the place where they must change their lives. The sun is at home in the plains. Precisely there does it have the certain character of a god. When the Kiowas came to the land of the Crows, they could see the dark lees of the hills at dawn across the Bighorn River, the profusion of light on the grain shelves, the oldest deity ranging after the solstices. Not yet would they veer southward to the caldron of the land that lay below; they must wean their blood from the northern winter and hold the mountains a while longer in their view. They bore Taime in procession to the east.

A dark mist lay over the Black Hills, and the land was like iron. At the   8
top of a ridge I caught sight of Devil's Tower upthrust against the gray sky as if in the birth of time the core of the earth had broken through its crust and the motion of the world was begun. There are things in nature that engender an awful quiet in the heart of man; Devil's Tower is one of them. Two centuries ago, because they could not do otherwise, the Kiowas made a legend at the base of the rock. My grandmother said:

> "Eight children were there at play, seven sisters and their brother. Suddenly the boy was struck dumb; he trembled and began to run upon his hands and feet. His fingers became claws, and his body was covered with fur. Directly there was a bear where the boy had been. The sisters were terrified; they ran, and the bear after them. They came to the stump of a great tree, and the tree spoke to them. It bade them climb upon it, and as they did so, it began to rise into the air. The bear came to kill them, but they were just beyond its reach. It reared against the tree and scored the bark all around with its claws. The seven sisters were borne into the sky, and they became the stars of the Big Dipper."

From that moment, and so long as the legend lives, the Kiowas have kinsmen in the night sky. Whatever they were in the mountains, they could be no more. However tenuous their well-being, however much they had suffered and would suffer again, they had found a way out of the wilderness.

My grandmother had a reverence for the sun, a holy regard that now   9
is all but gone out of mankind. There was a wariness in her, and an ancient

awe. She was a Christian in her later years, but she had come a long way about, and she never forgot her birthright. As a child she had been to the Sun Dances; she had taken part in those annual rites, and by them she had learned the restoration of her people in the presence of Tai-me. She was about seven when the last Kiowa Sun Dance was held in 1887 on the Washita River above Rainy Mountain Creek. The buffalo were gone. In order to consummate the ancient sacrifice — to impale the head of a buffalo bull upon the medicine tree — a delegation of old men journeyed into Texas, there to beg and barter for an animal from the Goodnight herd. She was ten when the Kiowas came together for the last time as a living Sun Dance culture. They could find no buffalo; they had to hang an old hide from the sacred tree. Before the dance could begin, a company of soldiers rode out from Fort Sill under orders to disperse the tribe. Forbidden without cause the essential act of their faith, having seen the wild herds slaughtered and left to rot upon the ground, the Kiowas backed away forever from the medicine tree. That was July 20, 1890, at the great bend of the Washita. My grandmother was there. Without bitterness, and for as long as she lived, she bore a vision of deicide.

Now that I can have her only in memory, I see my grandmother in the several postures that were peculiar to her: standing at the wood stove on a winter morning and turning meat in a great iron skillet; sitting at the south window, bent above her beadwork, and afterwards, when her vision had failed, looking down for a long time into the fold of her hands; going out upon a cane, very slowly as she did when the weight of age came upon her; praying. I remember her most often at prayer. She made long, rambling prayers out of suffering and hope, having seen many things. I was never sure that I had the right to hear, so exclusive were they of all mere custom and company. The last time I saw her she prayed standing by the side of her bed at night, naked to the waist, the light of a kerosene lamp moving upon her dark skin. Her long, black hair, always drawn and braided in the day, lay upon her shoulders and against her breasts like a shawl. I do not speak Kiowa, and I never understood her prayers, but there was something inherently sad in the sound, some merest hesitation upon the syllables of sorrow. She began in a high and descending pitch, exhausting her breath to silence; then again and again — and always the same intensity of effort, of something that is, and is not, like urgency in the human voice. Transported so in the dancing light among the shadows of her room, she seemed beyond the reach of time. But that was illusion; I think I knew that I should not see her again.

10

• • •

COMPREHENSION

1. What is the significance of the essay's title?

2. What does Momaday mean when he says that his grandmother was born when the Kiowas were living the "last great moment of their history" (3)?

3. How did meeting the Crows change the Kiowas (4)?

4. What effect did the soldiers have on the religion of the Kiowas?

5. What significance does Momaday's grandmother have for him?

PURPOSE AND AUDIENCE

1. Is Momaday writing only to express emotions, or does he have other purposes as well? Explain.

2. What assumptions does Momaday make about his audience? How do you know?

3. Why do you think Momaday includes the legend of Devil's Tower in his essay?

STYLE AND STRUCTURE

1. Why do you think Momaday begins his essay with a description of Rainy Mountain?

2. What determines the order in which Momaday arranges details in his description of his grandmother?

3. Why do you think Momaday ends his essay with a description of his grandmother praying?

4. Momaday includes many passages that describe landscapes. What do these descriptions add to readers' understanding of Momaday's grandmother?

VOCABULARY PROJECTS

1. Define each of the following words as it is used in this selection.

infirm (2)	billowing (7)	consummate (9)
preeminently (3)	profusion (7)	impale (9)
nomadic (4)	engender (8)	deicide (9)
luxuriant (7)	tenuous (8)	inherently (10)

2. Find three examples of figurative language in the essay. How do these examples help Momaday convey his impressions to his readers?

JOURNAL ENTRY

Which people in your family connect you to your ethnic or cultural heritage? How do they do so?

WRITING WORKSHOP

1. Write an essay describing a grandparent or any other older person who has had a great influence on you. Make sure that you include background information as well as a detailed physical description.

2. Describe a place that has played an important part in your life. Include a narrative passage that conveys the significance of the place to your readers.

3. Describe a ritual — such as a wedding or a confirmation — that you have witnessed or participated in.

COMBINING THE PATTERNS

Momaday weaves passages of **narration** throughout this descriptive essay. Bracket the narrative passages that Momaday uses in this essay, and explain how each one helps him describe his grandmother.

THEMATIC CONNECTIONS

- "Only Daughter" (page 83)
- "My Mother Never Worked" (page 94)
- "Words Left Unspoken" (page 133)

E. B. WHITE

Elwyn Brooks White (1899–1985) was born in Mount Vernon, New York, and graduated from Cornell University in 1921. He joined the newly founded *New Yorker* in 1925 and was associated with the magazine until his death. In 1937, White moved his family to a farm in Maine and began a monthly column for *Harper's* magazine entitled "One Man's Meat." A collection of some of these essays appeared under the same title in 1942. In addition to this and other essay collections, White published two popular children's books, *Stuart Little* (1945) and *Charlotte's Web* (1952). He also wrote a classic writer's handbook, *The Elements of Style* (1959), a revision of a text by one of his Cornell professors, William Strunk.

"Once More to the Lake," written for *Harper's* and later included in *One Man's Meat,* is based on White's personal experiences and observations. Having visited Maine's rustic Belgrade Lakes with his family from the time he was five until his teens, he returned there with his own son in July of 1941; this account of the visit appeared in October of that year. Of the essay, White wrote to a young reader that it was "about a man who feels a sense of identity with his son — a fairly common feeling. But the sense of identity is all mixed up with a feeling of being separated by the years." According to White, the final image of the wet bathing suit "is a truly chilling experience, because it suddenly seems to foreshadow death."

Once More to the Lake

One summer, along about 1904, my father rented a camp on a lake in Maine and took us all there for the month of August. We all got ringworm from some kittens and had to rub Pond's Extract on our arms and legs night and morning, and my father rolled over in a canoe with all his clothes on; but outside of that the vacation was a success and from then on none of us ever thought there was any place in the world like that lake in Maine. We returned summer after summer — always on August 1st for one month. I have since become a salt-water man, but sometimes in summer there are days when the restlessness of the tides and the fearful cold of the sea water and the incessant wind which blows across the afternoon and into the evening make me wish for the placidity of a lake in the woods. A few weeks ago this feeling got so strong I bought myself a couple of bass hooks and a spinner and returned to the lake where we used to go, for a week's fishing and to revisit old haunts. 1

I took along my son, who had never had any fresh water up his nose and who had seen lily pads only from train windows. On the journey over to the lake I began to wonder what it would be like. I wondered how time would have marred this unique, this holy spot — the coves and streams, the hills that the sun set behind, the camps and the paths behind the camps. I was sure that the tarred road would have found it out and I wondered in what other ways it would be desolated. It is strange how much 2 you can remember about places like that once you allow your mind to return into the grooves which lead back. You remember one thing, and that suddenly reminds you of another thing. I guess I remembered clearest of all the early mornings, when the lake was cool and motionless, remembered how the bedroom smelled of the lumber it was made of and the wet woods whose scent entered through the screen. The partitions in the camp were thin and did not extend clear to the top of the rooms, and as I was always the first up I would dress softly so as not to wake the others, and sneak out into the sweet outdoors and start out in the canoe, keeping close along the shore in the long shadows of the pines. I remembered being very careful never to rub my paddle against the gunwale for fear of disturbing the stillness of the cathedral.

The lake had never been what you would call a wild lake. There were   3
cottages sprinkled around the shores, and it was in farming country although the shores of the lake were quite heavily wooded. Some of the cottages were owned by nearby farmers, and you would live at the shore and eat your meals at the farmhouse. That's what our family did. But although it wasn't wild, it was a fairly large and undisturbed lake and there were places in it which, to a child at least, seemed infinitely remote and primeval.

I was right about the tar: it led to within half a mile of the shore. But   4
when I got back there, with my boy, and we settled into a camp near a farmhouse and into the kind of summertime I had known, I could tell that it was going to be pretty much the same as it had been before — I knew it, lying in bed the first morning, smelling the bedroom, and hearing the boy sneak quietly out and go off along the shore in a boat. I began to sustain the illusion that he was I, and therefore, by simple transposition, that I was my father. This sensation persisted, kept cropping up all the time we were there. It was not an entirely new feeling, but in this setting it grew much stronger. I seemed to be living a dual existence. I would be in the middle of some simple act, I would be picking up a bait box or laying down a table fork, or I would be saying something, and suddenly it would be not I but my father who was saying the words or making the gesture. It gave me a creepy sensation.

We went fishing the first morning. I felt the same damp moss covering   5
the worms in the bait can, and saw the dragonfly alight on the tip of my rod as it hovered a few inches from the surface of the water. It was the arrival of this fly that convinced me beyond any doubt that everything was as it always had been, that the years were a mirage and there had been no years. The small waves were the same, chucking the rowboat under the chin as we fished at anchor, and the boat was the same boat, the same color green and the ribs broken in the same places, and under the floor-boards the same freshwater leavings and débris — the dead helgramite,* the wisps of moss, the rusty discarded fishhook, the dried blood

---

*EDS. NOTE — An insect larva often used as bait.

from yesterday's catch. We stared silently at the tips of our rods, at the dragonflies that came and went. I lowered the tip of mine into the water, tentatively, pensively dislodging the fly, which darted two feet away, poised, darted two feet back, and came to rest again a little farther up the rod. There had been no years between the ducking of this dragonfly and the other one — the one that was part of memory. I looked at the boy, who was silently watching his fly, and it was my hands that held his rod, my eyes watching. I felt dizzy and didn't know which rod I was at the end of.

We caught two bass, hauling them in briskly as though they were   6
mackerel, pulling them over the side of the boat in a businesslike manner without any landing net, and stunning them with a blow on the back of the head. When we got back for a swim before lunch, the lake was exactly where we had left it, the same number of inches from the dock, and there was only the merest suggestion of a breeze. This seemed an utterly enchanted sea, this lake you could leave to its own devices for a few hours and come back to, and find that it had not stirred, this constant and trustworthy body of water. In the shallows, the dark, water-soaked sticks and twigs, smooth and old, were undulating in clusters on the bottom against the clean ribbed sand, and the track of the mussel was plain. A school of minnows swam by, each minnow with its small individual shadow, doubling the attendance, so clear and sharp in the sunlight. Some of the other campers were in swimming, along the shore, one of them with a cake of soap, and the water felt thin and clear and unsubstantial. Over the years there had been this person with the cake of soap, this cultist, and here he was. There had been no years.

Up to the farmhouse to dinner through the teeming, dusty field, the   7
road under our sneakers was only a two-track road. The middle track was missing, the one with the marks of the hooves and the splotches of dried, flaky manure. There had always been three tracks to choose from in choosing which track to walk in; now the choice was narrowed down to two. For a moment I missed terribly the middle alternative. But the way led past the tennis court, and something about the way it lay there in the sun reassured me; the tape had loosened along the backline, the alleys were green with plantains and other weeds, and the net (installed in June and removed in September) sagged in the dry noon, and the whole place steamed with midday heat and hunger and emptiness. There was a choice of pie for dessert, and one was blueberry and one was apple, and the waitresses were the same country girls, there having been no passage of time, only the illusion of it as in a dropped curtain — the waitresses were still fifteen; their hair had been washed, that was the only difference — they had been to the movies and seen the pretty girls with the clean hair.

Summertime, oh summertime, pattern of life indelible, the fade-proof   8
lake, the woods unshatterable, the pasture with the sweetfern and the juniper forever and ever, summer without end; this was the background, and the life along the shore was the design, the cottages with their innocent and tranquil design, their tiny docks with the flagpole and the American flag floating against the white clouds in the blue sky, the little

paths over the roots of the trees leading from camp to camp and the paths leading back to the outhouses and the can of lime for sprinkling, and at the souvenir counters at the store the miniature birch-bark canoes and the post cards that showed things looking a little better than they looked. This was the American family at play, escaping the city heat, wondering whether the newcomers in the camp at the head of the cove were "common" or "nice," wondering whether it was true that the people who drove up for Sunday dinner at the farmhouse were turned away because there wasn't enough chicken.

It seemed to me, as I kept remembering all this, that those times and   9
those summers had been infinitely precious and worth saving. There had been jollity and peace and goodness. The arriving (at the beginning of August) had been so big a business in itself, at the railway station the farm wagon drawn up, the first smell of the pineladen air, the first glimpse of the smiling farmer, and the great importance of the trunks and your father's enormous authority in such matters, and the feel of the wagon under you for the long ten-mile haul, and at the top of the last long hill catching the first view of the lake after eleven months of not seeing this cherished body of water. The shouts and cries of the other campers when they saw you, and the trunks to be unpacked, to give up their rich burden. (Arriving was less exciting nowadays, when you sneaked up in your car and parked it under a tree near the camp and took out the bags and in five minutes it was all over, no fuss, no loud wonderful fuss about trunks.)

Peace and goodness and jollity. The only thing that was wrong now,   10
really, was the sound of the place, an unfamiliar nervous sound of the outboard motors. This was the note that jarred, the one thing that would sometimes break the illusion and set the years moving. In those other summertimes all motors were inboard; and when they were at a little distance, the noise they made was a sedative, an ingredient of summer sleep. They were one-cylinder and two-cylinder engines, and some were make-and-break and some were jump-spark, but they all made a sleepy sound across the lake. The one-lungers throbbed and fluttered, and the twin-cylinder ones purred and purred, and that was a quiet sound too. But now the campers all had outboards. In the daytime, in the hot mornings, these motors made a petulant, irritable sound; at night, in the still evening when the afterglow lit the water, they whined about one's ears like mosquitoes. My boy loved our rented outboard, and his great desire was to achieve singlehanded mastery over it, and authority, and he soon learned the trick of choking it a little (but not too much), and the adjustment of the needle valve. Watching him I would remember the things you could do with the old one-cylinder engine with the heavy flywheel, how you could have it eating out of your hand if you got really close to it spiritually. Motor boats in those days didn't have clutches, and you would make a landing by shutting off the motor at the proper time and coasting in with a dead rudder. But there was a way of reversing them, if you learned the trick, by cutting the switch and putting it on again exactly on the final dying revolution of the flywheel, so that it would kick back against compression and

begin reversing. Approaching a dock in a strong following breeze, it was difficult to slow up sufficiently by the ordinary coasting method, and if a boy felt he had complete mastery over his motor, he was tempted to keep it running beyond its time and then reverse it a few feet from the dock. It took a cool nerve, because if you threw the switch a twentieth of a second too soon you could catch the flywheel when it still had speed enough to go up past center, and the boat would leap ahead, charging bull-fashion at the dock.

We had a good week at the camp. The bass were biting well and the   11
sun shone endlessly, day after day. We would be tired at night and lie down in the accumulated heat of the little bedrooms after the long hot day and the breeze would stir almost imperceptibly outside and the smell of the swamp drift in through the rusty screens. Sleep would come easily and in the morning the red squirrel would be on the roof, tapping out his gay routine. I kept remembering everything, lying in bed in the mornings — the small steamboat that had a long rounded stern like the lip of a Ubangi,* how quietly she ran on the moonlight sails, when the older boys played their mandolins and the girls sang and we ate doughnuts dipped in sugar, and how sweet the music was on the water in the shining night, and what it had felt like to think about girls then. After breakfast we would go up to the store and the things were in the same place — the minnows in a bottle, the plugs and spinners disarranged and pawed over by the youngsters from the boys' camp, the fig newtons and the Beeman's gum. Outside, the road was tarred and cars stood in front of the store. Inside, all was just as it had always been, except there was more Coca-Cola and not so much Moxie** and root beer and birch beer and sarsaparilla.*** We would walk out with a bottle of pop apiece and sometimes the pop would backfire up our noses and hurt. We explored the streams, quietly, where the turtles slid off the sunny logs and dug their way into the soft bottom; and we lay on the town wharf and fed worms to the tame bass. Everywhere we went I had trouble making out which was I, the one walking at my side, the one walking in my pants.

One afternoon while we were there at that lake a thunderstorm came   12
up. It was like the revival of an old melodrama that I had seen long ago with childish awe. The second-act climax of the drama of the electrical disturbance over a lake in America had not changed in any important respect. This was the big scene, still the big scene. The whole thing was so familiar, the first feeling of oppression and heat and a general air around camp of not wanting to go very far away. In midafternoon (it was all the same) a curious darkening of the sky, and a lull in everything that

---

*EDS. NOTE — An African tribe whose members wear mouth ornaments that stretch their lips into a saucerlike shape.

**EDS. NOTE — A soft drink that at one time was very popular.

***EDS. NOTE — A sweetened carbonated beverage flavored with birch oil and sassafras.

had made life tick; and then the way the boats suddenly swung the other way at their moorings with the coming of a breeze out of the new quarter, and the premonitory rumble. Then the kettle drum, then the snare, then the bass drum and cymbals, then crackling light against the dark, and the gods grinning and licking their chops in the hills. Afterward the calm, the rain steadily rustling in the calm lake, the return of light and hope and spirits, and the campers running out in joy and relief to go swimming in the rain, their bright cries perpetuating the deathless joke about how they were getting simply drenched, and the children screaming with delight at the new sensation of bathing in the rain, and the joke about getting drenched linking the generations in a strong indestructible chain. And the comedian who waded in carrying an umbrella.

When the others went swimming my son said he was going in too. He   13 pulled his dripping trunks from the line where they had hung all through the shower, and wrung them out. Languidly, and with no thought of going in, I watched him, his hard little body, skinny and bare, saw him wince slightly as he pulled up around his vitals the small, soggy, icy garment. As he buckled the swollen belt suddenly my groin felt the chill of death.

•   •   •

COMPREHENSION

1. In what ways are the writer and his son alike? In what ways are they different? What does White mean when he says, "I seemed to be living a dual existence" (4)?

2. In paragraph 5, White says there seem to be "no years" between past and present; elsewhere, he senses that things are different. How do you account for these conflicting feelings?

3. Why does White feel disconcerted when he discovers that the road to the farmhouse has two tracks, not three? What do you make of his comment that "now the choice was narrowed down to two" (7)?

4. In what way does sound "break the illusion and set the years moving" (10)?

5. To what is White referring in the last sentence?

PURPOSE AND AUDIENCE

1. What is the thesis of this essay? Is it stated or implied?

2. Do you think White expects the ending of his essay to be a surprise to his audience? Explain.

3. To what age group do you think this essay would appeal most? Why?

STYLE AND STRUCTURE

1. At what points in the essay does White describe the changes that have taken place on the lake? Does White emphasize these changes or play them down? Explain.

2. What ideas and images does White repeat throughout his essay? What is the purpose of this repetition?

3. White goes to great lengths to describe how things look, feel, smell, taste, and sound. How does this help him achieve his purpose in this essay?

4. In what way does White's conclusion refer to the first paragraph of the essay?

VOCABULARY PROJECTS

1. Define each of the following words as it is used in this selection.

placidity (1)	pensively (5)	melodrama (12)
gunwale (2)	jollity (9)	premonitory (12)
primeval (3)	petulant (10)	perpetuating (12)
transposition (4)	imperceptibly (11)	languidly (13)

2. Underline ten words in the essay that refer to one of the five senses. Make a list of synonyms you could use for these words. How close do your substitutions come to capturing White's meaning?

JOURNAL ENTRY

Do you identify more with the father or the son in this essay? Why?

WRITING WORKSHOP

1. Write a description of a scene you remember from your childhood. In your essay, discuss how your current view of the scene differs from the view you had when you were a child.

2. Assume you are a travel agent. Write a descriptive brochure designed to bring tourists to the lake. Be specific, and stress the benefits White mentions in his essay.

3. Write an essay in which you describe yourself from the perspective of one of your parents. Make sure your description conveys both the qualities your parent likes and the qualities he or she would want to change.

COMBINING THE PATTERNS

White opens his essay with a short narrative about his trip to the lake in 1904. How does this use of **narration** provide a context for the entire essay?

THEMATIC CONNECTIONS

- "Only Daughter" (page 83)
- "It's Just Too Late" (page 304)
- "How the Lawyers Stole Winter" (page 362)
- "The Men We Carry in Our Minds" (page 399)

KATHERINE ANNE PORTER

Katherine Anne Porter (1890–1980) was born in Indian Creek, Texas. After her mother's death when she was two, she lived with her paternal grandmother in the small farming town of Kyle. The Porters had been reasonably prosperous, but by the time Porter's grandmother died in 1901 their circumstances were greatly reduced. Always something of a rebel, Porter eloped at age fifteen, divorced nine years later, and headed to Chicago, an independent woman. There she found work as a journalist, after living for extended periods in New York, Europe, and Mexico. She began writing fiction in 1922 and had published three collections of highly regarded short stories by 1944 (her *Collected Stories* was published in 1965); her only novel, *Ship of Fools,* appeared in 1962.

Much of Porter's best fiction is drawn from her own family experiences during childhood and early adolescence. These stories focus on Miranda Gay — a stand-in for Porter herself — and often relate incidents very much as they actually happened. In "The Grave," first published in 1935, virtually everything in the story — from the grandfather's former grave site, to the childish hunting party, to the dead rabbit and its babies — had parallels in Porter's young life. Yet to these bare "facts" she adds ideas about death, womanhood, and the power of memory.

The Grave

The grandfather, dead more than thirty years, had been twice disturbed in his long repose by the constancy and possessiveness of his widow. She removed his bones first to Louisiana and then to Texas as if she had set out to find her own burial place, knowing well she would never return to the places she had left. In Texas she set up a small cemetery in a corner of her first farm, and as the family connection grew, the oddments of relations came over from Kentucky to settle, it contained at last about twenty graves. After the grandmother's death, part of her land was to be sold for the benefit of certain of her children, and the cemetery happened to lie in the part set aside for sale. It was necessary to take up the bodies and bury them again in the family plot in the big new public cemetery, where the grandmother had been buried. At last her husband was to lie beside her for eternity, as she had planned. 1

The family cemetery had been a pleasant small neglected garden of tangled rose bushes and ragged cedar trees and cypress, the simple flat stones rising out of uncropped sweet-smelling wild grass. The graves were lying open and empty one burning day when Miranda and her brother Paul, who often went together to hunt rabbits and doves, propped their twenty-two Winchester rifles carefully against the rail fence, climbed over and explored among the graves. She was nine years old and he was twelve. 2

They peered into the pits all shaped alike with such purposeful accu-   3
racy, and looking at each other with pleased adventurous eyes, they said
in solemn tones: "These were graves!" trying by words to shape a special,
suitable emotion in their minds, but they felt nothing except an agreeable
thrill of wonder: they were seeing a new sight, doing something they had
not done before. In them both there was also a small disappointment at the
entire commonplaceness of the actual spectacle. Even if it had once contained a coffin for years upon years, when the coffin was gone a grave was
just a hole in the ground. Miranda leaped into the pit that had held her
grandfather's bones. Scratching around aimlessly and pleasurably as any
young animal, she scooped up a lump of earth and weighed it in her palm.
It had a pleasantly sweet, corrupt smell, being mixed with cedar needles
and small leaves, and as the crumbs fell apart, she saw a silver dove
no larger than a hazel nut, with spread wings and a neat fan-shaped tail.
The breast had a deep round hollow in it. Turning it up to the fierce sunlight, she saw that the inside of the hollow was cut in little whorls. She
scrambled out, over the pile of loose earth that had fallen back into one
end of the grave, calling to Paul that she found something, he must guess
what. . . . His head appeared smiling over the rim of another grave. He
waved a closed hand at her. "I've got something too!" They ran to compare treasures, making a game of it, so many guesses each, all wrong, and
a final showdown with opened palms. Paul had found a thin wide gold
ring carved with intricate flowers and leaves. Miranda was smitten at
sight of the ring and wished to have it. Paul seemed more impressed by
the dove. They made a trade, with some little bickering. After he had the
dove in his hand, Paul said, "Don't you know what this is? This is a screw
head for a *coffin!* . . . I'll bet nobody else in the world has one like this!"

Miranda glanced at it without covetousness. She had the gold ring   4
on her thumb; it fitted perfectly. "Maybe we ought to go now," she said,
"maybe one of the niggers'll see us and tell somebody." They knew the
land had been sold, the cemetery was no longer theirs, and they felt like
trespassers. They climbed back over the fence, slung their rifles loosely
under their arms — they had been shooting at targets with various kinds
of firearms since they were seven years old — and set out to look for the
rabbits and doves or whatever small game might happen along. On these
expeditions Miranda always followed at Paul's heels along the path, obeying instructions about handling her gun when going through fences;
learning how to stand it up properly so it would not slip and fire unex-
pectedly; how to wait her time for a shot and not just bang away in the air
without looking, spoiling shots for Paul, who really could hit things if
given a chance. Now and then, in her excitement at seeing birds whizz up
suddenly before her face, or a rabbit leap across her very toes, she lost her
head, and almost without sighting she flung her rifle up and pulled the
trigger. She hardly ever hit any sort of mark. She had no proper sense
of hunting at all. Her brother would be often completely disgusted with
her. "You don't care whether you get your bird or not," he said. "That's no

way to hunt." Miranda could not understand his indignation. She had seen him smash his hat and yell with fury when he had missed his aim. "What I like about shooting," said Miranda, with exasperating inconsequence, "is pulling the trigger and hearing the noise."

"Then, by golly," said Paul, "whyn't you go back to the range and shoot at bulls-eyes?" 5

"I'd just as soon," said Miranda, "only like this, we walk around more." 6

"Well, you just stay behind and stop spoiling my shots," said Paul, who, when he made a kill, wanted to be certain he had made it. Miranda, who alone brought down a bird once in twenty rounds, always claimed as her own any game they got when they fired at the same moment. It was tiresome and unfair and her brother was sick of it. 7

"Now, the first dove we see, or the first rabbit, is mine," he told her. "And the next will be yours. Remember that and don't get smarty." 8

"What about snakes?" asked Miranda idly. "Can I have the first snake?" 9

Waving her thumb gently and watching her gold ring glitter, Miranda lost interest in shooting. She was wearing her summer roughing outfit: dark blue overalls, a light blue shirt, a hired-man's straw hat, and thick brown sandals. Her brother had the same outfit except his was a sober hickory-nut color. Ordinarily Miranda preferred her overalls to any other dress, though it was making rather a scandal in the countryside, for the year was 1903, and in the back country the law of female decorum had teeth in it. Her father had been criticized for letting his girls dress like boys and go careering around astride barebacked horses. Big sister Maria, the really independent and fearless one, in spite of her rather affected ways, rode at a dead run with only a rope knotted around her horse's nose. It was said the motherless family was running down, with the Grandmother no longer there to hold it together. It was known that she had discriminated against her son Harry in her will, and that he was in straits about money. Some of his old neighbors reflected with vicious satisfaction that now he would probably not be so stiff-necked, nor have any more high-stepping horses either. Miranda knew this, though she could not say how. She had met along the road old women of the kind who smoked corn-cob pipes, who had treated her grandmother with most sincere respect. They slanted their gummy old eyes side-ways at the granddaughter and said, "Ain't you ashamed of yoself, Missy? It's aginst the Scriptures to dress like that. Whut yo Pappy thinkin about?" Miranda, with her powerful social sense, which was like a fine set of antennae radiating from every pore of her skin, would feel shamed because she knew well it was rude and ill-bred to shock anybody, even bad-tempered old crones, though she had faith in her father's judgment and was perfectly comfortable in the clothes. Her father had said, "They're just what you need, and they'll save your dresses for school. . . ." This sounded quite simple and natural to her. She had been brought up in rigorous economy. Wastefulness was vulgar. It 10 was also a sin. These were truths; she had heard them repeated many times and never once disputed.

Now the ring, shining with the serene purity of fine gold on her rather 11 grubby thumb, turned her feelings against her overalls and sockless feet, toes sticking through the thick brown leather straps. She wanted to go back to the farmhouse, take a good cold bath, dust herself with plenty of Maria's violet talcum powder — provided Maria was not present to object, of course — put on the thinnest, most becoming dress she owned, with a big sash, and sit in a wicker chair under the trees. . . . These things were not all she wanted, of course; she had vague stirrings of desire for luxury and a grand way of living which could not take precise form in her imagination but were founded on family legend of past wealth and leisure. These immediate comforts were what she could have, and she wanted them at once. She lagged rather far behind Paul, and once she thought of just turning back without a word and going home. She stopped, thinking that Paul would never do that to her, and so she would have to tell him. When a rabbit leaped, she let Paul have it without dispute. He killed it with one shot.

When she came up with him, he was already kneeling, examining the 12 wound, the rabbit trailing from his hands. "Right through the head," he said complacently, as if he had aimed for it. He took out his sharp, competent bowie knife and started to skin the body. He did it very cleanly and quickly. Uncle Jimbilly knew how to prepare the skins so that Miranda always had fur coats for her dolls, for though she never cared much for her dolls she liked seeing them in fur coats. The children knelt facing each other over the dead animal. Miranda watched admiringly while her brother stripped the skin away as if he were taking off a glove. The flayed flesh emerged dark scarlet, sleek, firm; Miranda with thumb and finger felt the long fine muscles with the silvery flat strips binding them to the joints. Brother lifted the oddly bloated belly. "Look," he said, in a low amazed voice. "It was going to have young ones."

Very carefully he slit the thin flesh from the center ribs to the flanks, 13 and a scarlet bag appeared. He slit again and pulled the bag open, and there lay a bundle of tiny rabbits, each wrapped in a thin scarlet veil. The brother pulled these off and there they were, dark gray, their wet down lying in minute even ripples, like a baby's head just washed, their unbelievably small delicate ears folded close, their little blind faces almost featureless.

Miranda said, "Oh, I want to *see*," under her breath. She looked and 14 looked — excited but not frightened, for she was accustomed to the sight of animals killed in hunting — filled with pity and astonishment and a kind of shocked delight in the wonderful little creatures for their own sakes, they were so pretty. She touched one of them ever so carefully. "Ah, there's blood running over them," she said and began to tremble without knowing why. Yet she wanted most deeply to see and to know. Having seen, she felt at once as if she had known all along. The very memory of her former ignorance faded, she had always known just this. No one had ever told her anything outright, she had been rather unobservant of the animal life around her because she was so accustomed to animals. They seemed simply disorderly and unaccountably rude in their habits, but altogether natural and not very interesting. Her brother had spoken as if he had known about everything all along. He may have seen all this before. He had never said a word to her, but she knew now a part at least of what he knew. She understood a little of the secret, formless intuitions in her own mind and body, which had been clearing up, taking form, so gradually and so steadily she had not realized that she was learning what she had to know. Paul said cautiously, as if he were talking about something forbidden: "They were just about ready to be born." His voice dropped on the last word. "I know," said Miranda, "like kittens. I know, like babies." She was quietly and terribly agitated, standing again with her rifle under her arm, looking down at the bloody heap. "I don't want the skin," she said, "I won't have it." Paul buried the young rabbits again in their mother's body, wrapped the skin around her, carried her to a clump of sage bushes, and hid her away. He came out again at once and said to Miranda, with an eager friendliness, a confidential tone quite unusual in him, as if he were taking her into an important secret on equal terms: "Listen now. Now you listen to me, and don't ever forget. Don't you ever tell a living soul that you saw this. Don't tell a soul. Don't tell Dad because I'll get into trouble. He'll say I'm leading you into things you ought not to do. He's always saying that. So now don't you go and forget and blab out sometime the way you're always doing. . . . Now, that's a secret. Don't you tell."

Miranda never told, she did not even wish to tell anybody. She   15
thought about the whole worrisome affair with confused unhappiness for a few days. Then it sank quietly into her mind and was heaped over by accumulated thousands of impressions, for nearly twenty years. One day she was picking her path among the puddles and crushed refuse of a market street in a strange city of a strange country, when without warning, plain and clear in its true colors as if she looked through a frame upon a scene that had not stirred nor changed since the moment it happened, the episode of that far-off day leaped from its burial place before her mind's eye. She was so reasonlessly horrified she halted suddenly staring, the scene before her eyes dimmed by the vision back of them. An Indian vendor had held up before her a tray of dyed sugar sweets, in the shapes of all kinds of creatures: birds, baby chicks, baby rabbits, lambs, baby pigs. They were in gay colors and smelled of vanilla, maybe. . . . It was a very hot day and the smell in the market, with its piles of raw flesh and wilting flowers, was like the mingled sweetness and corruption she had smelled that other day in the empty cemetery at home: the day she had remembered always until now vaguely as the time she and her brother found treasure in the opened graves. Instantly upon this thought the dreadful vision faded, and she saw clearly her brother, whose childhood face she had forgotten, standing again in the blazing sunshine, again twelve years old, a pleased sober smile in his eyes, turning the silver dove over and over in his hands.

● ● ●

THINKING ABOUT LITERATURE

1. What is the significance of the dove? The ring? The rabbit?

2. What is so meaningful about the event described in the story that Miranda remembers it twenty years later?

3. In what way do specific, concrete details contribute to the effect of the story?

JOURNAL ENTRY

In "The Grave," Porter describes how a memory "leaped from its burial place" (15) years later. Write an entry about a childhood incident you remembered and understood only after having forgotten about it for some years.

THEMATIC CONNECTIONS

- "Shooting an Elephant" (page 104)
- "Once More to the Lake" (page 154)
- "Samuel" (page 212)

WRITING ASSIGNMENTS FOR DESCRIPTION

1. Choose a character from a work of fiction or film who you think is truly interesting. Write a descriptive essay that conveys what makes this character so special.

2. Describe a particularly memorable movie, concert, or sports event you have attended. Include both your own reactions and the reactions of other spectators.

3. Locate some photographs of your relatives. Describe three of these pictures, including details that provide insight into the lives of the people you discuss. Use your descriptive paragraphs to support a thesis about your family.

4. Visit an art museum, and select a painting that interests you. Study it carefully, and then write an essay-length description of it. Before you write, decide how you will organize your details and whether you will write a subjective or an objective description.

5. Select an object that you are familiar with, and write an objective description of it. Include a diagram.

6. Assume you are writing a letter to someone in another country who knows little about life in the United States. Describe to this person something that you consider to be typically American — a baseball stadium or a shopping mall, for example.

7. Visit your college library, and write an objective description of the reference area. Be specific, and select an organizing scheme before you begin your essay. Your goal is to acquaint students with some of the reference materials they will use.

8. Describe your neighborhood to a visitor who knows nothing about it. Include as much specific detail as you can.

9. After reconsidering "The Way to Rainy Mountain" (page 148), "Once More to the Lake" (page 154), or "Samuel" (page 212), write a description of a sight or scene that fascinated, surprised, or shocked you. Your description should explain why you were so deeply affected by what you saw.

10. Write an essay in which you describe an especially frightening horror film. What specific sights and sounds make this film so horrifying? Include a thesis statement that assesses the film's success as a horror film. (Be careful not to merely recount the plot of the film.)

COLLABORATIVE ACTIVITY FOR DESCRIPTION

Working in groups of three or four students, select a famous person — one you can reasonably expect your classmates to recognize. Then work as a group to write a physical description of that individual, including as much physical detail as possible. (Avoid any details that will be an instant giveaway.) Give your description a general title — *politician, movie* or *television star,* or *person in the news,* for example. Finally, have one person read the description aloud to the class, and see whether your classmates can guess the person's identity.

INTERNET ASSIGNMENT FOR DESCRIPTION

Visiting the following World Wide Web sites, find a painting or photograph that captures your interest. Imagine that you are inside the scene depicted in the artwork, and write a description of what you see and experience. If there is a person in the painting, evoke that person's experience. This exercise calls for imagination — going beyond what you see in the painting or photograph to think about the effects of what you see on other senses. Think about the details of the image — the mood, lighting, texture, color, brush-strokes, or shadows — to help you capture the overall impression of the artwork.

The Whitney Museum of American Art
<http://www.whitney.org>

The Museum of Modern Art
<http://www.moma.org>

International Center for Photography
<http://www.icp.org>

▰▰▰▰▰▰▰▰

6

EXEMPLIFICATION

WHAT IS EXEMPLIFICATION?

Exemplification uses one or more particular cases, or **examples,** to make a general point specific or an abstract concept concrete. In the following paragraph from *Sexism and Language,* Alleen Pace Nilsen uses a number of well-chosen examples to support her statement that the armed forces use words that have positive masculine connotations to encourage recruitment:

Topic sentence	The armed forces, particularly the Marines, use the <u>positive masculine connotation as part of their recruitment psychology.</u> They promote the idea that to join the Marines (or the Army, Navy, or Air Force) guarantees that you will become a man. But this brings up a problem, because much of the work that is necessary to keep a large organization running is what is traditionally thought of as *woman's work.* Now, how can the Marines ask someone who has signed up for a *man-sized job* to do *woman's work?* Since they can't, they euphemize and give the jobs titles that are more prestigious or, at least, don't make people
Series of related examples	think of females. Waitresses are called *orderlies,* secretaries are called *clerk-typists,* nurses are called *medics,* assistants are called *adjutants,* and cleaning up an area is called *policing* the area. The same kind of word glorification is used in civilian life to bolster a man's ego when he is doing such tasks as cooking and sewing. For example, a *chef* has higher prestige than a *cook* and a *tailor* has higher prestige than a *seamstress.*

USING EXEMPLIFICATION

You have probably noticed, when watching television talk shows or listening to classroom discussions, that the most interesting and persuasive exchanges take place when those involved support their points with specific examples. Sweeping generalizations and vague statements are not nearly as effective as specific observations, anecdotes, details, and opinions. It is one thing to say, "The mayor is corrupt and should not be reelected," and another to illustrate your point by saying, "The mayor should not be reelected because he has fired two city workers who refused to contribute to his campaign fund, has put his family and friends on the city payroll, and has used public employees to make improvements to his home." The same principle applies to writing: many of the most effective essays use examples extensively. Exemplification is used in every kind of writing situation to explain and clarify, to add interest, and to persuade.

Using Examples to Explain and Clarify

On a midterm exam in a film course, you might write, "Even though horror movies seem modern, they really aren't." You may think your statement is perfectly clear, but if this is all you say about horror movies, you should not be surprised if your exam comes back with a question mark in the margin next to this sentence. After all, you have only made a general statement or claim about your subject. It is not specific, nor does it anticipate readers' questions about the ways in which horror movies are not modern. To be certain your audience knows exactly what you mean, state your point precisely: "Despite the fact that horror movies seem modern, the two most memorable ones are adaptations of nineteenth-century Gothic novels." Then, use examples to ensure clarity and avoid ambiguity. For example, you could illustrate your point by discussing two films — *Frankenstein,* directed by James Whale, and *Dracula,* directed by Todd Browning — and linking them to the novels on which they are based. With the benefit of these specific examples, readers would know what you mean: that the literary roots of such movies are in the past, not that their cinematic techniques or production methods are dated. Moreover, readers would know which particular horror movies you are talking about.

Using Examples to Add Interest

Well-chosen examples add life to otherwise bland or straightforward statements. Laurence J. Peter and Raymond Hull use examples to add interest to their essay "The Peter Principle," which appears later in this chapter. Their claim that each employee in a system rises to a level of authority at which he or she is incompetent is not particularly intriguing. This statement becomes interesting, however, when it is supported by specific examples — the affable foreman who becomes the indecisive supervisor, the exacting mechanic who becomes the disorganized foreman, and the charismatic battlefield general who becomes the ineffective and self-destructive field marshal.

When you use exemplification, look for examples that are interesting as well as pertinent. Test the effectiveness of your examples by putting yourself in your readers' place. If you don't find your essay lively and absorbing, chances are your readers won't either. If this is the case, try to add more engaging, more spirited examples. After all, your goal is to communicate ideas to your readers, and imaginative examples can make the difference between an engrossing essay and one that is a chore to read.

Using Examples to Persuade

Although you may use examples to explain an idea or to entertain your readers, examples are also an effective way to demonstrate that what you are saying is reasonable and worth considering. A few well-chosen examples can eliminate pages of general, and often unconvincing, explanations. For instance, a statement that adequate health insurance is now too expensive for many Americans needs support. If you make such a statement on an exam, you need to back it up with appropriate examples — such as the fact that in one typical working-class neighborhood one out of every six primary wage earners is jobless and can no longer afford health insurance. Similarly, a statement in a biology paper that DDT should continue to be banned is unconvincing without persuasive examples such as these to support it:

- Although DDT has been banned since December 31, 1972, traces are still being found in the eggs of various fish and waterfowl.

- Certain lakes and streams still cannot be used for sport and recreation because DDT levels are dangerously high, presumably because of farm-land runoff.

- Because of its stability as a compound, DDT does not degrade quickly; therefore, existing residues will threaten the environment well into the twenty-first century.

Using Examples to Test Your Thesis

Examples can help you test your own ideas as well as the ideas of others. For instance, suppose you plan to write a paper for a composition class about students' writing skills. Your tentative thesis is that writing well is an inborn talent and that teachers can do little to help people write better. But is this really true? Has it been true in your own life? To test your point, you go back over your academic career and brainstorm about the various teachers who tried to help you improve your writing.

As you assemble your list, you remember Mrs. Colson, a teacher you had when you were a junior in high school. She was strict, required lots of writing, and seemed to accept nothing less than perfection. At the time neither you nor your classmates liked her; in fact, her nickname was Warden Colson. But looking back, you recall her one-on-one conferences, her organized lessons, and her pointed comments. You also remember her careful review of essay tests, and you realize that after being in her class, you felt much more comfortable taking such tests. After examining some papers that you saved, you are surprised to see how much your writing actually improved that year. These examples lead you to reevaluate your ideas and to revise your tentative thesis. Now, you conclude that even though some people seem to have a natural flair for writing, a good teacher can make a difference.

PLANNING AN EXEMPLIFICATION ESSAY

Providing Enough Examples

Unfortunately, no general rule exists to tell you how many examples you need to support your ideas. The number you use depends on your thesis statement. If, for instance, your thesis is that an educational institution, like a business, needs careful financial management, a detailed examination of one college or university could work well. In this case, a single example might provide all the information you need to make your point, and you wouldn't need to include examples from a number of schools. In fact, too many examples could be tedious and cause your readers to lose interest.

If, however, your thesis is that conflict between sons and fathers is a major theme in the writing of Franz Kafka, more than one example would be necessary. A single example would show only that the theme is present in *one* of Kafka's works. In this case, the more examples you include, the more effectively you prove your point. Of course, for some thesis statements, even several examples would not be enough. Examples alone, for instance, could not demonstrate convincingly that children from small families have more successful careers than children from large families. This thesis would have to be supported with a statistical study — that is, by collecting and interpreting numerical data representing a great many examples.

Selecting a sufficient *range* of examples is just as important as choosing an appropriate number. If you want to persuade readers that Colin Powell was an able general, you should choose examples from several stages of his career. Likewise, if you want to convince readers that outdoor advertising is ruining the scenic view from local highways, you should discuss an area larger than your immediate neighborhood. Your objective in each case is to select a cross section of examples appropriate for the boundaries of your topic.

Choosing Representative Examples

Just as professional pollsters take great pains to ensure that their samples reflect the makeup of the group they are polling, you should make sure that your examples fairly represent the group you are discussing. If you want to support a ban on smoking in all public buildings, you should not limit your examples to restaurants. To be convincing, you should include examples involving many public places, such as government office buildings, hospital lobbies, and sports stadiums. For the same reason, one person's experience is not enough to support a conclusion about many others unless you can establish that the experience is typical.

If you decide that you cannot cite enough representative examples to support your thesis, reexamine it. Rather than switching to a new topic, try to narrow your thesis. After all, the only way your paper will be convincing is if your readers believe that your examples and your claim about your topic correspond — that is, that your thesis is supported by your examples and that your examples fairly represent the scope of your topic.

Of course, to be convincing you must not only choose examples effectively but also *use* them effectively. One way to reinforce the connection between your examples and your thesis is by using transitional words and phrases ("*Another* example of successful programs for the homeless . . .") to introduce your examples. In addition, you should keep your thesis statement in mind as you write, taking care not to get so involved with one example that you digress from your main point. No matter how carefully developed, no matter how specific, lively, and appropriate, your examples accomplish nothing if they do not support your essay's main idea.

STRUCTURING AN EXEMPLIFICATION ESSAY

Exemplification essays usually begin with an *introduction* that includes the thesis statement, which is supported by examples in the body of the essay. Each *body paragraph* may develop a separate example, present a point illustrated by several brief examples, or explore one aspect of a single extended example that is developed throughout the essay. The *conclusion* reinforces the main idea of the essay, perhaps restating the thesis. At times, however, variations of this basic pattern are advisable and even necessary. For instance, beginning your paper with a striking example might stimulate your reader's interest and curiosity; ending with one might vividly reinforce your thesis.

Exemplification presents one special organizational problem. If you do not select your examples carefully and arrange them effectively, your paper can become a thesis statement followed by a list or by ten or fifteen very brief, choppy paragraphs. One way to avoid this problem is to select only your best examples, developing them fully in separate paragraphs and discarding the others. Another way is to group related examples in paragraphs. Within each paragraph, examples can then be arranged in order of increasing importance or persuasiveness, to allow your audience's interest to build. The following informal outline for a paper evaluating the nursing care at a hospital illustrates one way to arrange examples. Notice how the writer groups his examples under three general headings: *patient rooms, emergency room,* and *clinics.*

Introduction: Thesis statement — The quality of nursing care at Montgomery Hospital can serve as a model for nursing personnel at other medical facilities.

Patient Rooms

Example 1:   Responsiveness

Example 2:   Effective rapport

Example 3:   Good bedside care

Emergency Room

Example 4:   Adequate staffing

Example 5:   Nurses circulating among patients in the waiting room

Example 6:   Satisfactory working relationships between doctors and nursing staff

Clinics

Example 7:   Nurses preparing patients

Example 8:   Nurses assisting during treatment

Example 9:   Nurses instructing patients after treatment

Conclusion: Restatement of thesis or review of key points or examples

---

☑ **CHECKLIST: EXEMPLIFICATION**

- Does your assignment call for exemplification?
- Does your essay have a clear thesis statement that identifies the point or concept that you will illustrate?
- Do your examples explain and clarify your thesis statement?
- Have you provided enough examples?
- Have you chosen clear and representative examples?
- Are your examples persuasive?
- Do your examples add interest?
- Have you used transitional words and phrases that reinforce the connection between your examples and your thesis statement?

▶ **STUDENT WRITERS: EXEMPLIFICATION**

Exemplification is frequently used in nonacademic writing situations, such as fiscal reports, memos, progress reports, and proposals. One of the most important situations in which you will use exemplification is in a letter applying for a job. Elizabeth Bensley's letter of application to a prospective employer follows this pattern of development. (Grace Ku's essay on page 177 illustrates a more conventional academic use of the exemplification pattern.)

295 Main Street
Mount Kisco, NY 10549
October 3, 2000

Mr. Steven Seltzer
Wall Street Journal
420 Lexington Avenue
New York, NY 10017

Dear Mr. Seltzer:

Opening

Please consider my application for the position   1
of management trainee that you advertised in
the October 1, 2000, edition of the Wall Street
Journal. My advisor, Dr. David Sutton, an editorial consultant to the Journal, has inspired
much of my enthusiasm about my field and about
this opportunity to work in your business

Thesis statement

office. I am confident that my education and
experience qualify me to fulfill the responsibilities of this job.

**Series of brief
examples**

I am currently a senior in the College of Busi-   2
ness at Drexel University and will graduate in
June with a degree in management. I have completed courses in accounting, data processing,
economics, management, and communications. In
addition, I have taken a number of computer
courses and have a working knowledge of systems
programming. Throughout my college career, I
have maintained a 3.3 average and have been
secretary of the Management Society.

Major example

Drexel's five-year curriculum includes four work-   3
study periods, during which students gain practical experience in the business world. During

my most recent work-study period, I worked in the business office of the Philadelphia Inquirer, where I was responsible for accounts payable and worked closely with a number of people in the accounting department. During my six months in this position, I gained a working knowledge of both IBM and Macintosh computer systems and used them to record charges, payments, and work schedules. Eventually my supervisor, Ms. Nancy Viamonte, put me in charge of training and supervising two other work-study students. At the Inquirer, I also developed a computer program that verified charges and ensured the prompt disposition and payment of accounts.

Closing

I believe that my education and work experience   4
make me a good candidate for your position. I
have enclosed a résumé for your convenience
and will be available for an interview anytime
after October 15. I look forward to meeting
with you to discuss my qualifications.

Sincerely,

Elizabeth Bensley

Elizabeth Bensley

Points for Special Attention

ORGANIZATION.   Exemplification is ideally suited for letters of application. The only way Elizabeth Bensley can support her claims about her qualifications for the management trainee job is to set forth her experience and knowledge. The body of her letter is divided into two categories: her educational record and her work-study experience. Each of the body paragraphs has a clear purpose and function. Paragraph 2 contains a series of brief examples pertaining to Elizabeth's educational record. Paragraph 3 contains a more fully developed example that deals with her work-study experience. These examples tell the prospective employer what qualifies Elizabeth for the job. In her body paragraphs, she arranges her points and her examples in order of increasing importance. Although her academic record is relevant, in this case it is not as important to a potential employer as her experience. Because her work-study experience relates directly to the position she wants, Elizabeth considers this her strongest point and presents it last.

Elizabeth ends her letter on a strong note. She not only asserts her willingness to be interviewed but also gives the date after which she will be available. Because people remember best what they read last, a strong conclusion is as essential here as it is in other writing situations.

PERSUASIVE EXAMPLES.   To support a thesis convincingly, examples should convey specific information, not just generalizations. Saying "I am a good student who works hard at her studies" means very little. It is better to say, as Elizabeth does, "Throughout my college career, I have maintained a 3.3 average." A letter of application should specifically show a prospective employer how your strengths and background correspond to the employer's needs, and well-chosen, focused examples can help you accomplish this.

Focus on Revision

Elizabeth showed her letter to her work-study advisor, who thought it was effective but could be improved. She suggested that in addition to outlining her experience, Elizabeth could explain how her work at the *Philadelphia Inquirer* would make her an asset to the *Wall Street Journal*. She noted that Elizabeth could point out that her experience in the accounting department at the *Inquirer* would enable her to work either in the accounting department or in collections. Elizabeth could also explain why training and supervising two work-study students was important. Her advisor made the following recommendation as well: if Elizabeth's purpose is to show that she is able to assume responsibility, she should say so; if it is to illustrate that she has managerial ability, she should make this clear. Finally, Elizabeth's advisor suggested that she list the software programs with which she is familiar. This information would give the employer a clear idea of her extensive experience with computers.

The following essay by Grace Ku was written for a composition class, in response to the assignment "Write an essay about the worst job you (or someone you know) ever had."

Midnight

Introduction   It was eight o'clock, and like millions of   1
                            other Americans, I was staring at the televi-
                            sion set wondering what kind of lesson Mr.
                            Huxtable was going to teach his children next
                            on The Cosby Show. I was glued to the set like
                            an average eleven-year-old couch potato while
                            leisurely eating a can of cold Chef Boyardee

spaghetti in my empty living room. As I watched the show, I gradually fell asleep on the floor fully clothed in a pair of blue jeans and a T-shirt, wondering when my parents would come home. Around midnight I suddenly woke up to a rustling noise when my parents finally arrived from a long day at work. I could see in their tired faces the grief and the hardship of working at a dry cleaner.

Thesis statement

Transitional paragraph provides background

My parents worked in modern times, but in conditions like those of nineteenth-century factory workers. Because they were immigrants with little formal education and spoke broken English, they could get only hard, physically demanding jobs. Therefore, they worked at a dry cleaner that was as big as a factory, a place where smaller cleaners sent their clothes to be cleaned.

2

Series of brief examples: physical demands

My parents had to meet certain quotas: each day they had to clean and press several hundred garments--shirts, pants, and other clothing. By themselves, every day, they did the work of four laborers. The muscles of my mother's shoulders and arms became as hard as iron from working with the press, a difficult job even for a man. In addition to pressing, my father washed the clothes in the machines, which is the reason a strong odor of oil was permanently embedded in his work clothes.

3

Example: long hours

Not only were my parents' jobs physically demanding, but they also required long hours. My parents went to work at five o'clock in the morning and came home anytime between nine o'clock at night and midnight. They worked over twelve hours daily at the dry cleaner, where the eight-hour work day and labor unions did not exist. Their only rest was two ten- to twenty-minute breaks--one for lunch and one for dinner. They did not stop even when they were burned by the hot press or by the steam rising

4

Example:
frequent burns

from it. The scars on their arms made it obvious that they worked at a dry cleaner. Their
burned skin would blister and later peel off,
showing their raw flesh. In time they would
heal, but other burns would soon follow.

Example: low pay

Along with having to work overtime without   5
compensation and suffering injuries without
treatment, my parents were paid below the minimum wage. These two people (who did the work of
four) together received a paycheck equivalent
to that of a single worker. They then used this
money to feed and care for a household of five
people.

Conclusion

As my parents silently entered our home   6
around midnight, they did not have to complain
about their jobs. I could see their anguish in
the wrinkles on their foreheads and their
fatigue in the languid movements of their bod-

Restatement
of thesis

ies. Their eyes looked toward me, saying, "We
hate our jobs, but we work so our children will
have better lives than we do."

Points for Special Attention

ORGANIZATION.   Grace Ku begins her introduction by describing herself as an eleven-year-old sitting on the floor watching television. At first, her behavior seems typical of many American children, but two things suggest problems: first, she is eating her cold dinner out of a can, and second, even though it is quite late, she is waiting for her parents to return from work. This opening prepares readers for her thesis that her parents' jobs produce only grief and hardship.

In the body of her essay, Grace presents the examples that support her thesis statement. In the second paragraph she sets the stage for the discussion to follow, explaining that her parents' working conditions were similar to those of nineteenth-century factory workers, and in paragraph 3 she presents a series of examples that illustrate how physically demanding her parents' jobs were. In the remaining body paragraphs, she gives three other examples to show how unpleasant the jobs were: how long her parents worked, how often they were injured, and how little they were paid. Grace concludes her essay by returning to the scene in her introduction, using a quotation that is intended to stay with her readers after they have finished the essay.

ENOUGH EXAMPLES.   Certainly no single example, no matter how graphic, could adequately support the thesis of this essay. To establish the pain and difficulty of her parents' jobs, Grace uses several examples. Although more examples could add depth to the essay, the ones she uses are vivid and compelling enough to reinforce her thesis that her parents had to endure great hardship to make a living.

REPRESENTATIVE EXAMPLES.   Grace selects examples that illustrate the full range of her subject. She draws from the daily experience of her parents and does not include examples that are atypical. She also includes enough detail so that her readers, who she assumes do not know much about working in a dry cleaner, will understand her points. She does not, however, use so much detail that her readers will get bogged down and lose interest.

EFFECTIVE EXAMPLES.   All of Grace's examples support her thesis statement. While developing these examples, she never loses sight of her main idea; consequently, she does not get sidetracked in irrelevant digressions. She also avoids the temptation to preach to her readers about the injustice of her parents' situation. By allowing her examples to speak for themselves, Grace presents a powerful portrait of her parents and their hardships.

Focus on Revision

After reading this draft, a peer critic thought Grace could go into more detail about her parents' situation and could explain her examples in more depth — perhaps writing about the quotas her parents had to meet or the other physical dangers of their jobs. In addition, Grace thought she should expand the discussion in paragraph 5 about her parents' low wages, perhaps anticipating questions some of her readers might have about working conditions. For example, was it legal for her parents' employer to require them to work overtime without compensation or to pay them less than the minimum wage? If not, how was the employer able to get away with such practices? Grace also thought she should move the information about her parents' work-related injuries from paragraph 4 to paragraph 3, where she discusses the physical demands of their jobs. Finally, she decided to follow the advice of another student and include comments by her parents to make their experiences more immediate to readers.

The selections that appear in this chapter all depend on exemplification to explain and clarify, to add interest, or to persuade.

⟁⟁⟁⟁⟁⟁⟁⟁
LAURENCE J. PETER AND RAYMOND HULL

Laurence J. Peter (1919–1990), an academic and education specialist, and Raymond Hull (1919–1985), a humorist and playwright, collaborated on the 1969 best-seller *The Peter Principle: Why Things Always Go Wrong*. In the preface to the book, Hull explained that he had become increasingly appalled at the number of problems people experienced with businesses and organizations, from those of trifling significance (bills going to an old address despite numerous attempts to give the business a new one) to ones of catastrophic importance (bridges collapsing only a few years after construction). Dr. Peter, Hull discovered during an impromptu conversation, had the explanation for such widespread ineptitude: within any hierarchy, employees tend to be promoted to a level at which they are incompetent to perform the duties of the position. Within a short time of the publication of their book, the term *Peter Principle* had entered the language.

The Peter Principle struck such a chord because it appeared at a time when corporate and governmental bureaucracies were increasingly being viewed as unresponsive, inefficient, riddled with red tape, and mind-numbingly sterile. In addition, the acceptance of "management theory" as a legitimate academic discipline allowed Peter and Hull to have some fun spoofing the "experts." The following reading is the first chapter of *The Peter Principle*, which presents its thesis along with some quite striking examples.

The Peter Principle

When I was a boy I was taught that the men upstairs knew what they 1 were doing. I was told, "Peter, the more you know, the further you go." So I stayed in school until I graduated from college and then went forth into the world clutching firmly these ideas and my new teaching certificate. During the first year of teaching I was upset to find that a number of teachers, school principals, supervisors, and superintendents appeared to be unaware of their professional responsibilities and incompetent in executing their duties. For example my principal's main concerns were that all window shades be at the same level, that classrooms should be quiet, and that no one step on or near the rose beds. The superintendent's main concerns were that no minority group, no matter how fanatical, should ever be offended and that all official forms be submitted on time. The children's education appeared farthest from the administrator's mind.

At first I thought this was a special weakness of the school system in 2 which I taught so I applied for certification in another province. I filled out the special forms, enclosed the required documents, and complied willingly with all the red tape. Several weeks later, back came my application and all the documents!

No, there was nothing wrong with my credentials; the forms were 3 correctly filled out; an official departmental stamp showed that they had been received in good order. But an accompanying letter said, "The new

181

regulations require that such forms cannot be accepted by the Department of Education unless they have been registered at the Post Office to ensure safe delivery. Will you please remail the forms to the Department, making sure to register them this time?"

I began to suspect that the local school system did not have a monopoly on incompetence.   4

As I looked further afield, I saw that every organization contained a number of persons who could not do their jobs.   5

A UNIVERSAL PHENOMENON

Occupational incompetence is everywhere. Have you noticed it? Probably we have all noticed it.   6

We see indecisive politicians posing as resolute statesmen and the "authoritative source" who blames his misinformation on "situational imponderables." Limitless are the public servants who are indolent and insolent, military commanders whose behavioral timidity belies their dreadnought rhetoric, and governors whose innate servility prevents their actually governing. In our sophistication, we virtually shrug aside the immoral cleric, corrupt judge, incoherent attorney, author who cannot write, and English teacher who cannot spell. At universities we see proclamations authored by administrators whose own office communications are hopelessly muddled, and droning lectures from inaudible or incomprehensible instructors.   7

Seeing incompetence at all levels of every hierarchy — political, legal, educational, and industrial — I hypothesized that the cause was some inherent feature of the rules governing the placement of employees. Thus began my serious study of the ways in which employees move upward through a hierarchy, and of what happens to them after promotion.   8

For my scientific data hundreds of case histories were collected. Here are three typical examples.   9

Municipal Government File, Case No. 17

J. S. Minion[1] was a maintenance foreman in the public works department of Excelsior City. He was a favorite of the senior officials at City Hall. They all praised his unfailing affability.   10

"I like Minion," said the superintendent of works. "He has good judgment and is always pleasant and agreeable."   11

This behavior was appropriate for Minion's position: he was not supposed to make policy, so he had no need to disagree with his superiors.   12

The superintendent of works retired and Minion succeeded him. Minion continued to agree with everyone. He passed to his foreman every   13

---

[1]Some names have been changed, in order to protect the guilty.

suggestion that came from above. The resulting conflicts in policy, and the continual changing of plans, soon demoralized the department. Complaints poured in from the Mayor and other officials, from taxpayers and from the maintenance-workers' union.

Minion still says "Yes" to everyone, and carries messages briskly back   14 and forth between his superiors and his subordinates. Nominally a superintendent, he actually does the work of a messenger. The maintenance department regularly exceeds its budget, yet fails to fulfill its program of work. In short, Minion, a competent foreman, became an incompetent superintendent.

Service Industries File, Case No. 3

E. Tinker was exceptionally zealous and intelligent as an apprentice at   15 G. Reece Auto Repair Inc., and soon rose to journeyman mechanic. In this job he showed outstanding ability in diagnosing obscure faults, and endless patience in correcting them. He was promoted to foreman of the repair shop.

But here his love of things mechanical and his perfectionism became   16 liabilities. He will undertake any job that he thinks looks interesting, no matter how busy the shop may be. "We'll work it in somehow," he says.

He will not let a job go until he is fully satisfied with it.   17

He meddles constantly. He is seldom to be found at his desk. He is   18 usually up to his elbows in a dismantled motor and while the man who should be doing the work stands watching, other workmen sit around waiting to be assigned new tasks. As a result the shop is always overcrowded with work, always in a muddle, and delivery times are often missed.

Tinker cannot understand that the average customer cares little about   19 perfection — he wants his car back on time! He cannot understand that most of his men are less interested in motors than in their pay checks. So Tinker cannot get on with his customers or with his subordinates. He was a competent mechanic, but is now an incompetent foreman.

Military File, Case No. 8

Consider the case of the late renowned General A. Goodwin. His   20 hearty, informal manner, his racy style of speech, his scorn for petty regulations, and his undoubted personal bravery made him the idol of his men. He led them to many well-deserved victories.

When Goodwin was promoted to field marshal he had to deal, not   21 with ordinary soldiers, but with politicians and allied generalissimos.

He would not conform to the necessary protocol. He could not turn   22 his tongue to the conventional courtesies and flatteries. He quarreled with all the dignitaries and took to lying for days at a time, drunk and sulking, in his trailer. The conduct of the war slipped out of his hands into those of his subordinates. He had been promoted to a position that he was incompetent to fill.

AN IMPORTANT CLUE

In time I saw that all such cases had a common feature. The employee   23
had been promoted from a position of competence to a position of incompetence. I saw that, sooner or later, this could happen to every employee in
every hierarchy.

Hypothetical Case File, Case No. 1

Suppose you own a pill-rolling factory, Perfect Pill Incorporated. Your   24
foreman pill roller dies of a perforated ulcer. You need a replacement. You
naturally look among your rank-and-file pill rollers.

Miss Oval, Mrs. Cylinder, Mr. Ellipse, and Mr. Cube all show various   25
degrees of incompetence. They will naturally be ineligible for promotion.
You will choose — other things being equal — your most competent pill
roller, Mr. Sphere, and promote him to foreman.

Now suppose Mr. Sphere proves competent as foreman. Later, when   26
your general foreman, Legree, moves up to Works Manager, Sphere will
be eligible to take his place.

If, on the other hand, Sphere is an incompetent foreman, he will get no   27
more promotion. He has reached what I call his "level of incompetence."
He will stay there till the end of his career.

Some employees, like Ellipse and Cube, reach a level of incompetence   28
in the lowest grade and are never promoted. Some, like Sphere (assuming
he is not a satisfactory foreman), reach it after one promotion.

E. Tinker, the automobile repair-shop foreman, reached his level of in-   29
competence on the third stage of the hierarchy. General Goodwin reached
his level of incompetence at the very top of the hierarchy.

So my analysis of hundreds of cases of occupational incompetence led   30
me on to formulate *The Peter Principle:*

In a Hierarchy Every Employee Tends to Rise to His Level of Incompetence

A NEW SCIENCE!

Having formulated the Principle, I discovered that I had inadver-   31
tently founded a new science, hierarchiology, the study of hierarchies.

The term "hierarchy" was originally used to describe the system of   32
church government by priests graded into ranks. The contemporary meaning includes any organization whose members or employees are arranged
in order of rank, grade, or class.

Hierarchiology, although a relatively recent discipline, appears to   33
have great applicability to the fields of public and private administration.

THIS MEANS YOU!

My Principle is the key to an understanding of all hierarchical sys-   34
tems, and therefore to an understanding of the whole structure of civilization. A few eccentrics try to avoid getting involved with hierarchies, but
everyone in business, industry, trade-unionism, politics, government, the
armed forces, religion, and education is so involved. All of them are controlled by the Peter Principle.

Many of them, to be sure, may win a promotion or two, moving from   35
one level of competence to a higher level of competence. But competence
in that new position qualifies them for still another promotion. For each
individual, for *you*, for *me*, the final promotion is from a level of competence to a level of incompetence.[2]

So, given enough time — and assuming the existence of enough ranks   36
in the hierarchy — each employee rises to, and remains at, his level of
incompetence. Peter's Corollary states:

> *In time, every post tends to be occupied by an employee who is incompetent to
> carry out its duties.*

WHO TURNS THE WHEELS?

You will rarely find, of course, a system in which *every* employee has   37
reached his level of incompetence. In most instances, something is being
done to further the ostensible purposes for which the hierarchy exists.

> *Work is accomplished by those employees who have not yet reached their level of
> incompetence.*

•   •   •

COMPREHENSION

1. What things disillusioned Peter during his first year of teaching? What
   did he find out about organizations?

2. What is the Peter Principle? What happens when employees reach their
   "level of incompetence"?

3. What do Peter and Hull mean by *hierarchiology* (31)? How did hierarchiology lead Peter to the Peter Principle?

---

[2]The phenomena of "percussive sublimation" (commonly referred to as "being
kicked upstairs") and of "the lateral arabesque" are not, as the casual observer might
think, exceptions to the Principle. They are only pseudo-promotions. . . .

4. If the Peter Principle operates in hierarchies such as corporations, who does the work?

PURPOSE AND AUDIENCE

1. Is this essay aimed at a general or an expert audience? What led you to your conclusion?

2. What is the essay's thesis? Why do you think Peter and Hull wait so long to state it?

3. How serious are Peter and Hull? What words or phrases indicate whether their purpose is to instruct or to entertain — or both?

STYLE AND STRUCTURE

1. Why do you think Peter and Hull begin the essay with an example? Why do they present a series of brief examples before introducing the typical case histories?

2. Why do Peter and Hull say they collected hundreds of case histories for data? How are the three case histories analyzed here typical?

3. Does the reliance on hypothetical examples strengthen or weaken the writers' case? Explain.

4. Do Peter and Hull use a sufficient range of examples? Explain.

VOCABULARY PROJECTS

1. Define each of the following words as it is used in this selection.

imponderables (7)	incomprehensible (7)	protocol (22)
indolent (7)	hypothesized (8)	subordinates (22)
insolent (7)	hierarchy (8)	eccentrics (34)
dreadnought (7)	minion (10)	ostensible (37)
inaudible (7)	dismantled (18)	

2. Do Peter and Hull use **figures of speech** in their discussion? Why do you think they do or do not?

JOURNAL ENTRY

What examples of the Peter Principle have you encountered in your life?

WRITING WORKSHOP

1. Do Peter and Hull overstate their case? Write a letter to them in the form of an exemplification essay pointing out the weaknesses of their position.

2. Study a school, business, or organization with which you are familiar. Write an exemplification essay showing how the Peter Principle applies (or does not apply).

3. Do you know someone who has progressed to the highest level of his or her incompetence? Supporting your thesis with a single extended example, write an exemplification essay showing how the Peter Principle applies.

COMBINING THE PATTERNS

Peter and Hull use a series of narrative examples. What are the advantages and disadvantages of using **narration** here? Would other kinds of examples — such as statistics — have been more effective? Explain.

THEMATIC CONNECTIONS

- "Shooting an Elephant" (page 104)
- "The Company Man" (page 478)

NATE STULMAN

Nate Stulman was born in Morristown, New Jersey, in 1979 and grew up in Findlay, Ohio. He was a sophomore at Swarthmore College in Pennsylvania when this essay was published on the Op-Ed page of the *New York Times* in 1999, but he wrote the essay on his own, not as part of a class assignment.

As Stulman points out, colleges increasingly offer students virtually unlimited access to personal computers and the Internet. (Today 98 percent of four-year-college students have such access.) This practice has obvious benefits: students can stay in touch with faculty, other students, and even family members and friends at home through e-mail; the Internet provides broad opportunities for research; computers are useful for much academic work, including writing papers and problem solving in the sciences. But critics argue that the easy availability of computers and Internet access has its drawbacks as well. In his essay, Stulman offers first-hand observations to suggest that computers can, in fact, be detrimental to students' overall learning environment. (Responses to Stulman's essay varied: many professors agreed with him; student responses were more mixed.)

The Great Campus Goof-Off Machine

Conventional wisdom says that computers are a necessary tool for higher education. Many colleges and universities these days require students to have personal computers, and some factor the cost of one into tuition. A number of colleges have put high-speed Internet connections in every dorm room. But there are good reasons to question the wisdom of this preoccupation with computers and the Internet. 1

Take a walk through the residence halls of any college in the country and you'll find students seated at their desks, eyes transfixed on their computer monitors. What are they doing with their top-of-the-line PC's and high-speed T-1 Internet connections? 2

They are playing Tomb Raider instead of going to chemistry class, tweaking the configurations of their machines instead of writing the paper due tomorrow, collecting mostly useless information from the World Wide Web instead of doing a math problem set — a host of other activity that has little or nothing to do with traditional academic work. 3

I have friends who have spent whole weekends doing nothing but playing Quake or Warcraft or other interactive computer games. One friend sometimes spends entire evenings — six to eight hours — scouring the Web for images and modifying them just to have a new background on his computer desktop. 4

And many others I know have amassed overwhelming collections of music on their computers. It's the searching and finding that they seem to enjoy: some of them have more music files on their computers than they could play in months. 5

Several people who live in my hall routinely stay awake all night chatting with dormmates on line. Why walk 10 feet down the hall to have a conversation when you can chat on the computer — even if it takes three times as long?   6

You might expect that personal computers in dorm rooms would be used for nonacademic purposes, but the problem is not confined to residence halls. The other day I walked into the library's reference department, and five or six students were grouped around a computer — not conducting research, but playing Tetris. Every time I walk past the library's so-called research computers, it seems that at least half are being used to play games, chat or surf the Internet aimlessly.   7

Colleges and universities should be wary of placing such an emphasis on the use of computers and the Internet. The Web may be useful for finding simple facts, but serious research still means a trip to the library.   8

For most students, having a computer in the dorm is more of a distraction than a learning tool. Other than computer science or mathematics majors, few students need more than a word processing program and access to E-mail in their rooms.   9

It is true, of course, that students have always procrastinated and wasted time. But when students spend four, five, even ten hours a day on computers and the Internet, a more troubling picture emerges — a picture all the more disturbing because colleges themselves have helped create the problem.   10

• • •

COMPREHENSION

1. What do most people believe about computers and school?
2. According to Stulman, to what use do most college students put computers?
3. For what academic purposes do most students actually need computers?
4. Why, according to the essay, should colleges and universities "be wary of placing such emphasis on the use of computers and the Internet" (8)?
5. What problems relating to computers have colleges and universities helped to create?

PURPOSE AND AUDIENCE

1. What is the thesis of this essay? At what point is the thesis stated?
2. What preconceptions does Stulman think that his readers have? In your opinion, is he correct?
3. Does Stulman seem to think his readers will be sympathetic, neutral, or hostile to his ideas about computers? How can you tell?
4. Many of the examples Stulman gives relate to students living in campus residence halls. Do his observations also apply to commuter students? To adult students with families?

STYLE AND STRUCTURE

1. Why does Stulman begin his essay by referring to "conventional wisdom"?

2. Most of the examples that Stulman includes are from his own experience as a student. Does this reliance on personal experience make his essay less convincing than it might otherwise be? Explain.

3. In paragraph 7, Stulman tries to expand his discussion beyond computer use in dorm rooms. Why does he do this? Is he successful?

4. Does Stulman make any statements for which he should have supplied examples but did not? (For example, examine paragraph 9.)

5. Do you think that Stulman is stereotyping college students? (A *stereotype* is an oversimplified conception or image.) Do the college students you know conform to the image that Stulman presents, or are they different? Explain.

6. What points does Stulman reinforce in his conclusion? Should he have mentioned any others?

VOCABULARY PROJECTS

1. Define each of the following words as it is used in this selection.
   conventional (1)   scouring (4)
   preoccupation (1)   procrastinated (10)

2. Judging from its vocabulary, is this essay intended for a technical or a nontechnical audience? Does Stulman use any technical terms that he should have defined?

JOURNAL ENTRY

Do you agree with the conclusions Stulman reaches about computers and education? Do you think most students waste time on computers or put them to good use?

WRITING WORKSHOP

1. Observe the way various students at your school use computers. Then, write a letter to Stulman in which you agree or disagree with his thesis. Use examples from your informal research to support your points.

2. Write an essay in which you agree or disagree with Stulman's statement "The Web may be useful for finding simple facts, but serious research still means a trip to the library" (8).

3. Write an essay in which you discuss whether your school should do more (or less) to encourage students to use computers and the Internet. Include a number of examples from your experience to support your points.

COMBINING THE PATTERNS

Choose four or five examples that Stulman uses in his essay. What patterns of development does he use for these examples? Does any single pattern predominate? If so, why?

THEMATIC CONNECTIONS

- "Television: The Plug-In Drug" (page 283)
- "Never Do That to a Book" (page 345)
- "College Pressures" (page 390)
- "How the Web Destroys the Quality of Student Research Papers" (page 610)

RICHARD LEDERER

Richard Lederer (1938–) was born in Philadelphia and attended Haverford College, Harvard University, and the University of New Hampshire. From 1962 to 1989 he taught English at St. Paul's School, a private preparatory academy in Concord, New Hampshire. Lederer retired from teaching at the age of fifty-one so that he could, in his words, "extend my mission as a user-friendly English teacher." According to critic Paul Dickinson, Lederer has succeeded in "transforming the use of English into an activity that rivals sex as a source of pleasure." His popular, lighthearted works on the wonders and oddities of the English language — and how it is fractured by politicians and bureaucrats, among others — include *Anguished English* (1987) and *Adventures of a Verbivore* (1995).

The following essay is the opening chapter of Lederer's best-selling *Crazy English* (1989), a book that humorously explores the randomness, inconsistencies, and illogical structures of English. Here he offers a wide array of amusing examples to support the striking thesis stated in his title. (You may want to use your dictionary to confirm some of his points.)

English Is a Crazy Language

English is the most widely spoken language in the history of our planet, used in some way by at least one out of every seven human beings around the globe. Half of the world's books are written in English, and the majority of international telephone calls are made in English. English is the language of over sixty percent of the world's radio programs, many of them beamed, ironically, by the Russians, who know that to win friends and influence nations, they're best off using English. More than seventy percent of international mail is written and addressed in English, and eighty percent of all computer text is stored in English. English has acquired the largest vocabulary of all the world's languages, perhaps as many as two million words, and has generated one of the noblest bodies of literature in the annals of the human race.

Nonetheless, it is now time to face the fact that English is a crazy language.

In the crazy English language, the blackbird hen is brown, blackboards can be blue or green, and blackberries are green and then red before they are ripe. Even if blackberries were really black and blueberries really blue, what are strawberries, cranberries, elderberries, huckleberries, raspberries, boysenberries, mulberries, and gooseberries supposed to look like?

To add to the insanity, there is no butter in buttermilk, no egg in eggplant, no grape in grapefruit, neither worms nor wood in wormwood, neither pine nor apple in pineapple, neither peas nor nuts in peanuts, and no ham in a hamburger. (In fact, if somebody invented a sandwich consisting of a ham patty in a bun, we would have a hard time finding a name for it.) To make matters worse, English muffins weren't invented in England, french fries in France, or danish pastries in Denmark. And we discover even more culinary madness in the revelations that sweetmeat is candy, while sweetbread, which isn't sweet, is made from meat.

In this unreliable English tongue, greyhounds aren't always grey (or gray); panda bears and koala bears aren't bears (they're marsupials); a woodchuck is a groundhog, which is not a hog; a horned toad is a lizard; glowworms are fireflies, but fireflies are not flies (they're beetles); ladybugs and lightning bugs are also beetles (and to propagate, a significant proportion of ladybugs must be male); a guinea pig is neither a pig nor from Guinea (it's a South American rodent); and a titmouse is neither mammal nor mammaried.

Language is like the air we breathe. It's invisible, inescapable, indispensable, and we take it for granted. But when we take the time, step back, and listen to the sounds that escape from the holes in people's faces and explore the paradoxes and vagaries of English, we find that hot dogs can be cold, darkrooms can be lit, homework can be done in school, nightmares can take place in broad daylight, while morning sickness and daydreaming can take place at night, tomboys are girls, midwives can be men, hours — especially happy hours and rush hours — can last longer than sixty minutes, quicksand works *very* slowly, boxing rings are square, silverware can be made of plastic and tablecloths of paper, most telephones are dialed by being punched (or pushed?), and most bathrooms don't have any baths in them. In fact, a dog can go to the bathroom under a tree — no bath, no room; it's still going to the bathroom. And doesn't it seem at least a little bizarre that we go to the bathroom in order to go to the bathroom?

Why is it that a woman can man a station but a man can't woman one, that a man can father a movement but a woman can't mother one, and that a king rules a kingdom but a queen doesn't rule a queendom? How did all those Renaissance men reproduce when there don't seem to have been any Renaissance women?

A writer is someone who writes, and a stinger is something that stings. But fingers don't fing, grocers don't groce, hammers don't ham, and humdingers don't humding. If the plural of *tooth* is *teeth,* shouldn't the plural of *booth* be *beeth?* One goose, two geese — so one moose, two meese? One index, two indices — one Kleenex, two Kleenices? If people ring a bell today and rang a bell yesterday, why don't we say that they flang a ball? If they wrote a letter, perhaps they also bote their tongue. If the teacher taught, why isn't it also true that the preacher praught? Why is it that the sun shone yesterday while I shined my shoes, that I treaded water and then trod on soil, and that I flew out to see a World Series game in which my favorite player flied out?

If we conceive a conception and receive at a reception, why don't we grieve a greption and believe a beleption? If a horsehair mat is made from the hair of horses and a camel's hair brush from the hair of camels, from what is a mohair coat made? If a vegetarian eats vegetables, what does a humanitarian eat? If a firefighter fights fire, what does a freedom fighter fight? If a weightlifter lifts weights, what does a shoplifter lift? If *pro* and *con* are opposites, is congress the opposite of progress?

Sometimes you have to believe that all English speakers should be   10
committed to an asylum for the verbally insane. In what other language do people drive in a parkway and park in a driveway? In what other language do people recite at a play and play at a recital? In what other language do privates eat in the general mess and generals eat in the private mess? In what other language do men get hernias and women get hysterectomies? In what other language do people ship by truck and send cargo by ship? In what other language can your nose run and your feet smell?

How can a slim chance and a fat chance be the same, "what's going   11
on?" and "what's coming off?" be the same, and a bad licking and a good licking be the same, while a wise man and a wise guy are opposites? How can sharp speech and blunt speech be the same and *quite a lot* and *quite a few* the same, while *overlook* and *oversee* are opposites? How can the weather be hot as hell one day and cold as hell the next?

If *button* and *unbutton* and *tie* and *untie* are opposites, why are *loosen*   12
and *unloosen* and *ravel* and *unravel* the same? If *bad* is the opposite of *good,* *hard* the opposite of *soft,* and *up* the opposite of *down,* why are *badly* and *goodly, hardly* and *softly,* and *upright* and *downright* not opposing pairs? If harmless actions are the opposite of harmful actions, why are shameless and shameful behavior the same and pricey objects less expensive than priceless ones? If appropriate and inappropriate remarks and passable and impassable mountain trails are opposites, why are flammable and inflammable materials, heritable and inheritable property, and passive and impassive people the same and valuable objects less treasured than invaluable ones? If *uplift* is the same as *lift up,* why are *upset* and *set up* opposite in meaning? Why are *pertinent* and *impertinent, canny* and *uncanny,* and *famous* and *infamous* neither opposites nor the same? How can *raise* and *raze* and *reckless* and *wreckless* be opposites when each pair contains the same sound?

Why is it that when the sun or the moon or the stars are out, they are   13
visible, but when the lights are out, they are invisible, and that when I wind up my watch, I start it, but when I wind up this essay, I shall end it?

English is a crazy language.   14

• • •

COMPREHENSION

1. According to Lederer, in what sense is English a crazy language?

2. Why is English such an important language?

3. What does Lederer mean when he says that language is "like the air we breathe" (6)? Why does he believe this?

4. According to Lederer, what are "the paradoxes and vagaries of English" (6)?

PURPOSE AND AUDIENCE

1. What is the thesis of this essay? Where is this thesis stated?

2. What is Lederer's purpose in writing this essay? To instruct? To entertain? To persuade? Do you think he is serious or playful? Explain.

3. At whom are Lederer's comments aimed? Students of the English language? Those who know little about the language? Both? Explain.

STYLE AND STRUCTURE

1. What information does Lederer provide in his introduction? Why do you think he provides this background material?

2. What point does Lederer make in each of his body paragraphs? How do the examples in these paragraphs help to support each point?

3. Do you think Lederer uses too many examples? Should he have used fewer examples and discussed them in more depth? Should he have devoted one paragraph to a single example? Explain your position.

4. Lederer uses a one-sentence paragraph to end his essay. How appropriate is this conclusion? Is it too brief? Why or why not?

VOCABULARY PROJECTS

1. Define each of the following words as it is used in this selection.

annals (1)	mammaried (5)	canny (12)
culinary (4)	passive (12)	uncanny (12)
sweetbread (4)	pertinent (12)	infamous (12)
marsupials (5)	impertinent (12)	reckless (12)

2. At several points in the essay, Lederer says that English is a crazy language. What connotations does the word *crazy* have? Can you think of another word with a more precise meaning that he could have used? What might he have gained or lost by substituting this word for *crazy?*

JOURNAL ENTRY

Assume that you are learning to speak English. What expressions give you the most trouble? Do you, like Lederer, believe that English is a crazy language?

WRITING WORKSHOP

1. Write an essay in which you use your own list of words to support the idea that English is a crazy language. Use numerous short examples to support your thesis.

2. Make a list of the words you use at work, at home, or with your friends that have special associations for you. (These may be **slang, jargon,** or technical terms.) Then write an essay in which you make the point that your different uses of English reflect the different roles you play.

3. Make a list of occupational terms that indicate gender. Then, list their neutral equivalents — for example, *mailman* and *letter carrier; policeman* and *police officer; waiter, waitress,* and *waitstaff.* Write an essay in which you discuss whether or not English is a sexist language. (You may want to read, or reread, "Sexism in English: Embodiment and Language," page 413.)

COMBINING THE PATTERNS

This essay's primary pattern of development is **exemplification.** Does Lederer use any other patterns? How would a paragraph of **comparison and contrast,** comparing English to another language, help support Lederer's thesis? Do you think he should have included such a paragraph? Why or why not?

THEMATIC CONNECTIONS

- "The Human Cost of an Illiterate Society" (page 203)
- "Sexism in English: Embodiment and Language" (page 413)
- "Burdens" (page 466)

BRENT STAPLES

Born in Chester, Pennsylvania, in 1951, Brent Staples received his bachelor's degree from Widener University in 1973 and his doctorate in psychology from the University of Chicago in 1982. Staples joined the staff of the *New York Times* in 1985, writing on culture and politics, and he became a member of its editorial board in 1990. His columns appear regularly on the paper's Op-Ed pages. Staples has also written a memoir, *Parallel Time: Growing Up in Black and White* (1994), about his escape from the poverty and violence of his childhood.

"Just Walk On By" originally appeared in *Ms.* magazine in 1986 as part of a regular guest column titled "Can Men Have It All?" In an edited version titled "Black Men and Public Space," which later appeared in *Harper's*, Staples reflects on the many times people have reacted to him as a potential threat solely because of his gender and the color of his skin. His essay can be read in light of current controversies surrounding racial profiling, in particular the alleged practice by police of stopping black male drivers more often than others for minor infractions because they are suspected of drug possession or other crimes. Such stops are commonly referred to by their victims as "DWB" (driving while black).

Just Walk On By: A Black Man Ponders His Power to Alter Public Space

My first victim was a woman — white, well dressed, probably in her early twenties. I came upon her late one evening on a deserted street in Hyde Park, a relatively affluent neighborhood in an otherwise mean, impoverished section of Chicago. As I swung onto the avenue behind her, there seemed to be a discreet, uninflammatory distance between us. Not so. She cast back a worried glance. To her, the youngish black man — a broad six feet two inches with a beard and billowing hair, both hands shoved into the pockets of a bulky military jacket — seemed menacingly close. After a few more quick glimpses, she picked up her pace and was soon running in earnest. Within seconds she disappeared into a cross street.

That was more than a decade ago. I was 22 years old, a graduate student newly arrived at the University of Chicago. It was in the echo of that terrified woman's footfalls that I first began to know the unwieldy inheritance I'd come into — the ability to alter public space in ugly ways. It was clear that she thought herself the quarry of a mugger, rapist, or worse. Suffering a bout of insomnia, however, I was stalking sleep, not defenseless wayfarers. As a softy who is scarcely able to take a knife to a raw chicken — let alone hold it to a person's throat — I was surprised, embarrassed, and dismayed all at once. Her flight made me feel like an accomplice in tyranny. It also made it clear that I was indistinguishable from the muggers who occasionally seeped into the area from the surrounding ghetto. That first encounter, and those that followed, signified that a vast, unnerving gulf lay between nighttime pedestrians — particularly women — and me. And I soon gathered that being perceived as dangerous is a hazard in itself. I only needed to turn a corner into a dicey situation, or crowd some frightened, armed person in a foyer somewhere, or make an errant move after being pulled over by a policeman. Where fear and weapons meet — and they often do in urban America — there is always the possibility of death.

In that first year, my first away from my hometown, I was to become 3 thoroughly familiar with the language of fear. At dark, shadowy intersections in Chicago, I could cross in front of a car stopped at a traffic light and elicit the *thunk, thunk, thunk, thunk* of the driver — black, white, male, or female — hammering down the door locks. On less traveled streets after dark, I grew accustomed to but never comfortable with people who crossed to the other side of the street rather than pass me. Then there were the standard unpleasantries with police, doormen, bouncers, cab drivers, and others whose business it is to screen out troublesome individuals *before* there is any nastiness.

I moved to New York nearly two years ago and I have remained an 4 avid night walker. In central Manhattan, the near-constant crowd cover minimizes tense one-on-one street encounters. Elsewhere — visiting friends in SoHo, where sidewalks are narrow and tightly spaced buildings shut out the sky — things can get very taut indeed.

Black men have a firm place in New York mugging literature. Norman 5 Podhoretz in his famed (or infamous) 1963 essay, "My Negro Problem — and Ours," recalls growing up in terror of black males; they "were tougher than we were, more ruthless," he writes — and as an adult on the Upper West Side of Manhattan, he continues, he cannot constrain his nervousness when he meets black men on certain streets. Similarly, a decade later, the essayist and novelist Edward Hoagland extols a New York where once "Negro bitterness bore down mainly on other Negroes." Where some see mere panhandlers, Hoagland sees "a mugger who is clearly screwing up his nerve to do more than just *ask* for money." But Hoagland has "the New Yorker's quick-hunch posture for broken-field maneuvering," and the bad guy swerves away.

I often witness that "hunch posture," from women after dark on the 6 warrenlike streets of Brooklyn where I live. They seem to set their faces on neutral and, with their purse straps strung across their chests bandolier style, they forge ahead as though bracing themselves against being tackled. I understand, of course, that the danger they perceive is not a hallucination. Women are particularly vulnerable to street violence, and young black males are drastically overrepresented among the perpetrators of that violence. Yet these truths are no solace against the kind of alienation that comes of being ever the suspect, against being set apart, a fearsome entity with whom pedestrians avoid making eye contact.

It is not altogether clear to me how I reached the ripe old age of 22   7
without being conscious of the lethality nighttime pedestrians attributed
to me. Perhaps it was because in Chester, Pennsylvania, the small, angry
industrial town where I came of age in the 1960s, I was scarcely noticeable
against a backdrop of gang warfare, street knifings, and murders. I grew
up one of the good boys, had perhaps a half-dozen fist fights. In retrospect, my shyness of combat has clear sources.

Many things go into the making of a young thug. One of those things   8
is the consummation of the male romance with the power to intimidate.
An infant discovers that random flailings send the baby bottle flying out
of the crib and crashing to the floor. Delighted, the joyful babe repeats
those motions again and again, seeking to duplicate the feat. Just so, I
recall the points at which some of my boyhood friends were finally
seduced by the perception of themselves as tough guys. When a mark
cowered and surrendered his money without resistance, myth and reality
merged — and paid off. It is, after all, only manly to embrace the power to
frighten and intimidate. We, as men, are not supposed to give an inch of
our lane on the highway; we are to seize the fighter's edge in work and in
play and even in love; we are to be valiant in the face of hostile forces.

Unfortunately, poor and powerless young men seem to take all this   9
nonsense literally. As a boy, I saw countless tough guys locked away;
I have since buried several, too. They were babies, really — a teenage
cousin, a brother of 22, a childhood friend in his mid-twenties — all gone
down in episodes of bravado played out in the streets. I came to doubt the
virtues of intimidation early on. I chose, perhaps even unconsciously, to
remain a shadow — timid, but a survivor.

The fearsomeness mistakenly attributed to me in public places often   10
has a perilous flavor. The most frightening of these confusions occurred in
the late 1970s and early 1980s when I worked as a journalist in Chicago.
One day, rushing into the office of a magazine I was writing for with a
deadline story in hand, I was mistaken for a burglar. The office manager
called security and, with an ad hoc posse, pursued me through the
labyrinthine halls, nearly to my editor's door. I had no way of proving
who I was. I could only move briskly toward the company of someone
who knew me.

Another time I was on assignment for a local paper and killing time   11
before an interview. I entered a jewelry store on the city's affluent Near
North Side. The proprietor excused herself and returned with an enormous red Doberman pinscher straining at the end of a leash. She stood,
the dog extended toward me, silent to my questions, her eyes bulging
nearly out of her head. I took a cursory look around, nodded, and bade her
good night. Relatively speaking, however, I never fared as badly as
another black male journalist. He went to nearby Waukegan, Illinois, a
couple of summers ago to work on a story about a murderer who was
born there. Mistaking the reporter for the killer, police hauled him from
his car at gunpoint and but for his press credentials would probably have

tried to book him. Such episodes are not uncommon. Black men trade tales like this all the time.

In "My Negro Problem — and Ours," Podhoretz writes that the 12 hatred he feels for blacks makes itself known to him through a variety of avenues — one being his discomfort with that "special brand of paranoid touchiness" to which he says blacks are prone. No doubt he is speaking here of black men. In time, I learned to smother the rage I felt at so often being taken for a criminal. Not to do so would surely have led to madness — via that special "paranoid touchiness" that so annoyed Podhoretz at the time he wrote the essay.

I began to take precautions to make myself less threatening. I move 13 about with care, particularly late in the evening. I give a wide berth to nervous people on subway platforms during the wee hours, particularly when I have exchanged business clothes for jeans. If I happen to be entering a building behind some people who appear skittish, I may walk by, letting them clear the lobby before I return, so as not to seem to be following them. I have been calm and extremely congenial on those rare occasions when I've been pulled over by the police.

And on late-evening constitutionals along streets less traveled by, I 14 employ what has proved to be an excellent tension-reducing measure: I whistle melodies from Beethoven and Vivaldi and the more popular classical composers. Even steely New Yorkers hunching toward nighttime destinations seem to relax, and occasionally they even join in the tune. Virtually everybody seems to sense that a mugger wouldn't be warbling bright, sunny selections from Vivaldi's *Four Seasons*. It is my equivalent of the cowbell that hikers wear when they know they are in bear country.

• • •

COMPREHENSION

1. Why does Staples characterize the woman he encounters in paragraph 1 as a "victim"?

2. What does Staples mean when he says he has the power to "alter public space" (2)?

3. Why does Staples walk the streets at night?

4. What things does Staples say go "into the making of a young thug" (8)? According to Staples, why are young, poor, and powerless men especially likely to become thugs?

5. In what ways does Staples attempt to make himself less threatening?

PURPOSE AND AUDIENCE

1. What is Staples's thesis? Does he state it or imply it?

2. Does Staples use logic, emotion, or a combination of the two to appeal to his readers? How appropriate is his strategy?

3. What preconceptions does Staples assume his audience has? In what ways does he challenge these preconceptions?

4. What is Staples trying to accomplish with his first sentence? Do you think he succeeds? Why or why not?

STYLE AND STRUCTURE

1. Why does Staples mention Norman Podhoretz? Could he make the same points without referring to Podhoretz's essay?

2. Staples begins his essay with an anecdote. How effective is this strategy? Do you think another opening strategy would be more effective? Explain.

3. Does Staples present enough examples to support his thesis? Are they representative? Would other types of examples be more convincing? Explain.

4. In what order does Staples present his examples? Would another order be more effective? Explain.

VOCABULARY PROJECTS

1. Define each of the following words as it is used in this selection.
   discreet (1)   quarry (2)   constrain (5)
   uninflammatory (1)   insomnia (2)   bravado (9)
   billowing (1)   wayfarers (2)   constitutionals (14)

2. In his essay, Staples uses the word *thug*. List as many synonyms as you can for this word. Do these words convey the same idea, or are there differences in connotation? Explain.

JOURNAL ENTRY

Have you ever been in a situation such as the ones Staples describes, where you perceived someone as threatening? How did you react? After reading Staples's essay, do you think you would react the same way now? Discuss.

WRITING WORKSHOP

1. Use your journal entry to help you write an essay in which you use an extended example to support this statement: "When walking alone at night, you can (or cannot) be too careful."

2. Relying on examples from your own experience, write an essay in which you discuss what part you think race plays in people's reactions to Staples. Do you think his perceptions are accurate?

3. How accurate is Staples's observation concerning the "male romance with the power to intimidate" (8)? What does he mean by this statement? What examples from your own experience illustrate that this "romance" is an element of male upbringing in our society?

COMBINING THE PATTERNS

In paragraph 8, Staples uses **cause and effect** to demonstrate what goes "into the making of a young thug." Would a **narrative** example have better illustrated how a youth becomes a thug?

THEMATIC CONNECTIONS

- "The 'Black Table' Is Still There" (page 294)
- "Brains versus Brawn" (page 328)
- "The Ways We Lie" (page 426)

JONATHAN KOZOL

Jonathan Kozol was born in Boston in 1936 and graduated from Harvard University in 1958. After studying in England, he began teaching in public schools in Boston's inner city. His experiences there provided the source material for his first book, *Death at an Early Age* (1967), a startling indictment of the system's failure to provide an adequate education to poor, mostly minority children. In the years since, Kozol — himself a child of privilege — has continued to use first-hand experience to write about the poorest in our society, sometimes angrily, sometimes movingly, but always with respect and sympathy. His books have focused on homelessness, on the inequities between schools in poor neighborhoods and those in affluent ones, and, most recently, on the lives of children in a South Bronx housing project.

Kozol's *Illiterate America* (1985) examines the human and financial costs of illiteracy in the United States. The book offers the estimate that more than thirty-five million Americans read below the level needed to function in society. A comprehensive survey published in 1993 found that, in fact, more than forty million adults — as much as 23 percent of the population — are functionally illiterate and that another 28 percent read at only the lowest levels. (Illiteracy rates are much higher in the poorest communities.) This is a situation that Kozol argues "a sane society would not ignore." The following essay, a chapter from *Illiterate America*, uses examples to convey what it really means to be unable to read.

The Human Cost of an Illiterate Society

PRECAUTIONS. READ BEFORE USING.
Poison: Contains sodium hydroxide (caustic soda-lye).
Corrosive: Causes severe eye and skin damage, may cause
blindness.
Harmful or fatal if swallowed.
If swallowed, give large quantities of milk or water.
Do not induce vomiting.
Important: Keep water out of can at all times to prevent contents from violently erupting. . . .
— *warning on a can of Drano*

Questions of literacy, in Socrates' belief, must at length be judged as   1
matters of morality. Socrates could not have had in mind the moral compromise peculiar to a nation like our own. Some of our Founding Fathers did, however, have this question in their minds. One of the wisest of those Founding Fathers (one who may not have been most compassionate but surely was more prescient than some of his peers) recognized the special dangers that illiteracy would pose to basic equity in the political construction that he helped to shape.

"A people who mean to be their own governors," James Madison   2
wrote, "must arm themselves with the power knowledge gives. A popular

government without popular information or the means of acquiring it, is but a prologue to a farce or a tragedy, or perhaps both."

Tragedy looms larger than farce in the United States today. Illiterate citizens seldom vote. Those who do are forced to cast a vote of questionable worth. They cannot make informed decisions based on serious print information. Sometimes they can be alerted to their interests by aggressive voter education. More frequently, they vote for a face, a smile, or a style, not for a mind or character or body of beliefs.

The number of illiterate adults exceeds by 16 million the entire vote cast for the winner in the 1980 presidential contest. If even one third of all illiterates could vote, and read enough and do sufficient math to vote in their self-interest, Ronald Reagan would not likely have been chosen president. There is, of course, no way to know for sure. We do know this: Democracy is a mendacious term when used by those who are prepared to countenance the forced exclusion of one third of our electorate. So long as 60 million people are denied significant participation, the government is neither of, nor for, nor by, the people. It is a government, at best, of those two-thirds whose wealth, skin color, or parental privilege allows them opportunity to profit from the provocation and instruction of the written word.

The undermining of democracy in the United States is one "expense" that sensitive Americans can easily deplore because it represents a contradiction that endangers citizens of all political positions. The human price is not so obvious at first.

Since I first immersed myself within this work I have often had the following dream: I find that I am in a railroad station or a large department store within a city that is utterly unknown to me and where I cannot understand the printed words. None of the signs or symbols is familiar. Everything looks strange: like mirror writing of some kind. Gradually I understand that I am in the Soviet Union. All the letters on the walls around me are Cyrillic. I look for my pocket dictionary but I find that it has been mislaid. Where have I left it? Then I recall that I forgot to bring it with me when I packed my bags in Boston. I struggle to remember the name of my hotel. I try to ask somebody for directions. One person stops and looks at me in a peculiar way. I lose the nerve to ask. At last I reach into my wallet for an ID card. The card is missing. Have I lost it? Then I remember that my card was confiscated for some reason, many years before. Around this point, I wake up in a panic.

This panic is not so different from the misery that millions of adult illiterates experience each day within the course of their routine existence in the U.S.A.

Illiterates cannot read the menu in a restaurant.

They cannot read the cost of items on the menu in the *window* of the restaurant before they enter.

Illiterates cannot read the letters that their children bring home from their teachers. They cannot study school department circulars that tell them of the courses that their children must be taking if they hope to pass the SAT exams. They cannot help with homework. They cannot write a letter to the teacher. They are afraid to visit in the classroom. They do not want to humiliate their child or themselves.

Illiterates cannot read instructions on a bottle of prescription medi-   11 cine. They cannot find out when a medicine is past the year of safe consumption; nor can they read of allergenic risks, warnings to diabetics, or the potential sedative effect of certain kinds of nonprescription pills. They cannot observe preventive health care admonitions. They cannot read about "the seven warning signs of cancer" or the indications of blood-sugar fluctuations or the risks of eating certain foods that aggravate the likelihood of cardiac arrest.

Illiterates live, in more than literal ways, an uninsured existence. They   12 cannot understand the written details on a health insurance form. They cannot read the waivers that they sign preceding surgical procedures. Several women I have known in Boston have entered a slum hospital with the intention of obtaining a tubal ligation and have emerged a few days later after having been subjected to a hysterectomy. Unaware of their rights, incognizant of jargon, intimidated by the unfamiliar air of fear and atmosphere of ether that so many of us find oppressive in the confines even of the most attractive and expensive medical facilities, they have signed their names to documents they could not read and which nobody, in the hectic situation that prevails so often in those overcrowded hospitals that serve the urban poor, had even bothered to explain.

Childbirth might seem to be the last inalienable right of any female   13 citizen within a civilized society. Illiterate mothers, as we shall see, already have been cheated of the power to protect their progeny against the likelihood of demolition in deficient public schools and, as a result, against the verbal servitude within which they themselves exist. Surgical denial of the right to bear that child in the first place represents an ultimate denial, an unspeakable metaphor, a final darkness that denies even the twilight gleamings of our own humanity. What greater violation of our biological, our biblical, our spiritual humanity could possibly exist than that which takes place nightly, perhaps hourly these days, within such overburdened and benighted institutions as the Boston City Hospital? Illiteracy has many costs; few are so irreversible as this.

Even the roof above one's head, the gas or other fuel for heating that   14 protects the residents of northern city slums against the threat of illness in the winter months become uncertain guarantees. Illiterates cannot read the lease that they must sign to live in an apartment which, too often, they cannot afford. They cannot manage check accounts and therefore seldom pay for anything by mail. Hours and entire days of difficult travel (and the cost of bus or other public transit) must be added to the real cost of whatever they consume. Loss of interest on the check accounts they do not have, and could not manage if they did, must be regarded as another of the excess costs paid by the citizen who is excluded from the common instruments of commerce in a numerate society.

"I couldn't understand the bills," a woman in Washington, D.C., re- 15 ports, "and then I couldn't write the checks to pay them. We signed things we didn't know what they were."

Illiterates cannot read the notices that they receive from welfare offices 16 or from the IRS. They must depend on word-of-mouth instruction from the welfare worker — or from other persons whom they have good reason to mistrust. They do not know what rights they have, what deadlines and requirements they face, what options they might choose to exercise. They are half-citizens. Their rights exist in print but not in fact.

Illiterates cannot look up numbers in a telephone directory. Even if 17 they can find the names of friends, few possess the sorting skills to make use of the yellow pages; categories are bewildering and trade names are beyond decoding capabilities for millions of nonreaders. Even the emergency numbers listed on the first page of the phone book —"Ambulance," "Police," and "Fire"— are too frequently beyond the recognition of nonreaders.

Many illiterates cannot read the admonition on a pack of cigarettes. 18 Neither the Surgeon General's warning nor its reproduction on the package can alert them to the risks. Although most people learn by word of mouth that smoking is related to a number of grave physical disorders, they do not get the chance to read the detailed stories which can document this danger with the vividness that turns concern into determination to resist. They can see the handsome cowboy or the slim Virginia lady lighting up a filter cigarette; they cannot heed the words that tell them that this product is (not "may be") dangerous to their health. Sixty million men and women are condemned to be the unalerted, high-risk candidates for cancer.

Illiterates do not buy "no-name" products in the supermarkets. They 19 must depend on photographs or the familiar logos that are printed on the packages of brand-name groceries. The poorest people, therefore, are denied the benefits of the least costly products.

Illiterates depend almost entirely upon label recognition. Many labels, 20 however, are not easy to distinguish. Dozens of different kinds of Campbell's soup appear identical to the nonreader. The purchaser who cannot read and does not dare to ask for help, out of the fear of being stigmatized (a fear which is unfortunately realistic), frequently comes home with something which she never wanted and her family never tasted.

Illiterates cannot read instructions on a pack of frozen food. Packages 21 sometimes provide an illustration to explain the cooking preparations; but illustrations are of little help to someone who must "boil water, drop the food — *within* its plastic wrapper — in the boiling water, wait for it to simmer, instantly remove."

Even when labels are seemingly clear, they may be easily mistaken. A 22 woman in Detroit brought home a gallon of Crisco for her children's dinner. She thought that she had bought the chicken that was pictured on the label. She had enough Crisco now to last a year — but no more money to go back and buy the food for dinner.

Recipes provided on the packages of certain staples sometimes tempt 23 a semiliterate person to prepare a meal her children have not tasted. The longing to vary the uniform and often starchy content of low-budget meals provided to the family that relies on food stamps commonly leads to ruinous results. Scarce funds have been wasted and the food must be thrown out. The same applies to distribution of food-surplus produce in emergency conditions. Government inducements to poor people to "explore the ways" by which to make a tasty meal from tasteless noodles, surplus cheese, and powdered milk are useless to nonreaders. Intended as benevolent advice, such recommendations mock reality and foster deeper feelings of resentment and of inability to cope. (Those, on the other hand, who cautiously refrain from "innovative" recipes in preparation of their children's meals must suffer the opprobrium of "laziness," "lack of imagination. . . .")

Illiterates cannot travel freely. When they attempt to do so, they en-   24 counter risks that few of us can dream of. They cannot read traffic signs and, while they often learn to recognize and to decipher symbols, they cannot manage street names which they haven't seen before. The same is true for bus and subway stops. While ingenuity can sometimes help a man or woman to discern directions from familiar landmarks, buildings, cemeteries, churches, and the like, most illiterates are virtually immobilized. They seldom wander past the streets and neighborhoods they know. Geographical paralysis becomes a bitter metaphor for their entire existence. They are immobilized in almost every sense we can imagine. They can't move up. They can't move out. They cannot see beyond. Illiterates may take an oral test for drivers' permits in most sections of America. It is a questionable concession. Where will they go? How will they get there? How will they get home? Could it be that some of us might like it better if they stayed where they belong?

Travel is only one of many instances of circumscribed existence.   25 Choice, in almost all of its facets, is diminished in the life of an illiterate adult. Even the printed TV schedule, which provides most people with the luxury of preselection, does not belong within the arsenal of options in illiterate existence. One consequence is that the viewer watches only what appears at moments when he happens to have time to turn the switch. Another consequence, a lot more common, is that the TV set remains in operation night and day. Whatever the program offered at the hour when he walks into the room will be the nutriment that he accepts and swallows. Thus, to passivity, is added frequency — indeed, almost uninterrupted continuity. Freedom to select is no more possible here than in the choice of home or surgery or food.

"You don't choose," said one illiterate woman. "You take your wishes   26 from somebody else." Whether in perusal of a menu, selection of highways, purchase of groceries, or determination of affordable enjoyment, illiterate Americans must trust somebody else: a friend, a relative, a stranger on the street, a grocery clerk, a TV copywriter.

"All of our mail we get, it's hard for her to read. Settin' down and writ-   27 ing a letter, she can't do it. Like if we get a bill . . . we take it over to my sister-in-law. . . . My sister-in-law reads it."

Billing agencies harass poor people for the payment of the bills for   28
purchases that might have taken place six months before. Utility companies offer an agreement for a staggered payment schedule on a bill past
due. "You have to trust them," one man said. Precisely for this reason, you
end up by trusting no one and suspecting everyone of possible deceit. A
submerged sense of distrust becomes the corollary to a constant need to
trust. "They are cheating me. . . . I have been tricked. . . . I do not know. . . ."

Not knowing: This is a familiar theme. Not knowing the right word for   29
the right thing at the right time is one form of subjugation. Not knowing
the world that lies concealed behind those words is a more terrifying feeling. The longitude and latitude of one's existence are beyond all easy
apprehension. Even the hard, cold stars within the firmament above one's
head begin to mock the possibilities for self-location. Where am I? Where
did I come from? Where will I go?

"I've lost a lot of jobs," one man explains. "Today, even if you're a jan-   30
itor, there's still reading and writing. . . . They leave a note saying 'Go to
room so-and-so. . . .' You can't do it. You can't read it. You don't know."

"The hardest thing about it is that I've been places where I didn't   31
know where I was. You don't know where you are. . . . You're lost."

"Like I said: I have two kids. What do I do if one of my kids starts   32
choking? I go running to the phone. . . . I can't look up the hospital phone
number. That's if we're at home. Out on the street, I can't read the sign. I
get to a pay phone. 'Okay, tell us where you are. We'll send an ambulance.'
I look at the street sign. Right there, I can't tell you what it says. I'd have to
spell it out, letter for letter. By that time, one of my kids would be dead. . . .
These are the kinds of fears you go with, every single day. . . ."

"Reading directions, I suffer with. I work with chemicals. . . . That's   33
scary to begin with. . . ."

"You sit down. They throw the menu in front of you. Where do you go   34
from there? Nine times out of ten you say, 'Go ahead. Pick out something
for the both of us.' I've eaten some weird things, let me tell you!"

Menus. Chemicals. A child choking while his mother searches for a   35
word she does not know to find assistance that will come too late. Another
mother speaks about the inability to help her kids to read: "I can't read to
them. Of course that's leaving them out of something they should have.
Oh, it matters. You *believe* it matters! I ordered all these books. The kids
belong to a book club. Donny wanted me to read a book to him. I told
Donny: 'I can't read.' He said: 'Mommy, you sit down. I'll read it to you.' I
tried it one day, reading from the pictures. Donny looked at me. He said,
'Mommy, that's not right.' He's only five. He knew I couldn't read. . . ."

A landlord tells a woman that her lease allows him to evict her if her   36
baby cries and causes inconvenience to her neighbors. The consequence of
challenging his words conveys a danger which appears, unlikely as it
seems, even more alarming than the danger of eviction. Once she admits
that she can't read, in the desire to maneuver for the time in which to call
a friend, she will have defined herself in terms of an explicit impo-
tence that she cannot endure. Capitulation in this case is preferable to self-

humiliation. Resisting the definition of oneself in terms of what one cannot do, what others take for granted, represents a need so great that other imperatives (even one so urgent as the need to keep one's home in winter's cold) evaporate and fall away in face of fear. Even the loss of home and shelter, in this case, is not so terrifying as the loss of self.

"I come out of school. I was sixteen. They had their meetings. The 37 directors meet. They said that I was wasting their school paper. I was wasting pencils. . . ."

Another illiterate, looking back, believes she was not worthy of her 38 teacher's time. She believes that it was wrong of her to take up space within her school. She believes that it was right to leave in order that somebody more deserving could receive her place.

Children choke. Their mother chokes another way: on more than 39 chicken bones.

People eat what others order, know what others tell them, struggle not 40 to see themselves as they believe the world perceives them. A man in California speaks about his own loss of identity, of self-location, definition:

"I stood at the bottom of the ramp. My car had broke down on the 41 freeway. There was a phone. I asked for the police. They was nice. They said to tell them where I was. I looked up at the signs. There was one that I had seen before. I read it to them: ONE WAY STREET. They thought it was a joke. I told them I couldn't read. There was other signs above the ramp. They told me to try. I looked around for somebody to help. All the cars was going by real fast. I couldn't make them understand that I was lost. The cop was nice. He told me: 'Try once more.' I did my best. I couldn't read. I only knew the sign above my head. The cop was trying to be nice. He knew that I was trapped. 'I can't send out a car to you if you can't tell me where you are.' I felt afraid. I nearly cried. I'm forty-eight years old. I only said: 'I'm on a one-way street. . . .'"

The legal problems and the courtroom complications that confront 42 illiterate adults have been discussed above. The anguish that may underlie such matters was brought home to me this year while I was working on this book. I have spoken [in an earlier part of the book] of a sudden phone call from one of my former students, now in prison for a criminal offense. Stephen is not a boy today. He is twenty-eight years old. He called to ask me to assist him in his trial, which comes up next fall. He will be on trial for murder. He has just knifed and killed a man who first enticed him to his home, then cheated him, and then insulted him — as "an illiterate subhuman."

Stephen now faces twenty years to life. Stephen's mother was illiter- 43 ate. His grandparents were illiterate as well. What parental curse did not destroy was killed off finally by the schools. Silent violence is repaid with interest. It will cost us $25,000 yearly to maintain this broken soul in prison. But what is the price that has been paid by Stephen's victim? What is the price that will be paid by Stephen?

Perhaps we might slow down a moment here and look at the realities 44 described above. This is the nation that we live in. This is a society that most of us did not create but which our President and other leaders have been willing to sustain by virtue of malign neglect. Do we possess the character and courage to address a problem which so many nations, poorer than our own, have found it natural to correct?

The answers to these questions represent a reasonable test of our   45
belief in the democracy to which we have been asked in public school to swear allegiance.

• • •

COMPREHENSION

1. Why is illiteracy a danger to a democratic society?

2. According to Kozol, why do our reactions to the problem of illiteracy in America test our belief in democracy?

3. What does Kozol mean when he says that an illiterate person leads a "circumscribed existence" (25)? How does being illiterate limit a person's choices?

4. What legal problems and courtroom complications confront illiterate adults?

5. According to Kozol, what is being done to solve the problem of illiteracy in the United States?

PURPOSE AND AUDIENCE

1. What is Kozol's thesis? Where does he state it?

2. Kozol aims his essay at a wide general audience. How does he address the needs of this audience? In what ways would his discussion differ if it were intended for an audience of reading specialists? Of politicians?

3. Is Kozol's purpose to inform, to persuade, to express emotions, or some combination of these three? Does he have additional, more specific purposes as well? Explain.

STYLE AND STRUCTURE

1. Why does Kozol introduce his essay with references to Socrates and James Madison? How does this strategy help him support his thesis?

2. In paragraph 6 Kozol recounts a dream that he often has. Why does he include this anecdote? How does it help him move from his introduction to the body of his essay?

3. Kozol uses many short examples to make his point. Do you think fewer examples developed in more depth would be more effective? Why or why not?

4. How effective is Kozol's use of statistics? Do the statistics complement or undercut his illustrations of the personal cost of illiteracy?

VOCABULARY PROJECTS

1. Define each of the following words as it is used in this selection.

   prescient (1)   sedative (11)   opprobrium (23)
   farce (2)   admonitions (11)   concession (24)
   mendacious (4)   incognizant (12)   firmament (29)
   countenance (4)   jargon (12)   capitulation (36)
   Cyrillic (6)   numerate (14)

2. Reread paragraphs 24 and 25 and determine which words or phrases convey Kozol's feelings toward his subject. Rewrite these two paragraphs, eliminating as much subjective language as you can. Do you think your changes make the paragraphs more appealing or less so to a general audience? To a group of sociologists? To a group of reading teachers?

JOURNAL ENTRY

Keep a journal for a day, noting the difficulty you would have carrying out each activity in your daily routine if you were illiterate.

WRITING WORKSHOP

1. Using your journal entry as a starting point, write an essay in which you describe the tasks you would have difficulty accomplishing if you could not read. Include an explicit thesis statement, and use examples to illustrate your points.

2. People have not always had to read to function in society. Six hundred years ago, in fact, most people could not read. Similarly, the majority of people today are not computer literate. Write an essay giving examples of the kinds of jobs a person cannot hold today if he or she cannot use a computer.

3. Using Kozol's essay as source material, write an essay in which your thesis is Madison's statement, "A people who mean to be their own governors must arm themselves with the power knowledge gives" (2). Be sure to document any information you borrow from Kozol.

COMBINING THE PATTERNS WITH EXEMPLIFICATION

Why does Kozol choose to end his essay with a **narrative** about Stephen, one of his former students, who is in jail awaiting trial for murder? How does this anecdote help Kozol set up his concluding remarks in paragraphs 44 and 45?

THEMATIC CONNECTIONS

- "Words Left Unspoken" (page 133)
- "Mother Tongue" (page 405)
- "The Untouchable" (page 461)

GRACE PALEY

Grace Paley (1922–) grew up in New York City and attended Hunter College there. Initially interested in poetry, she began writing short fiction in the 1950s, at the same time raising a family and participating in a number of political causes. Her stories have been published in the collections *Little Disturbances of Man* (1959), *Enormous Changes at the Last Minute* (1974), and *Later the Same Day* (1985). Her *Collected Stories* appeared in 1994 and was nominated for a National Book Award.

Paley's stories are noted for their spare, deceptively simple style and lack of conventional plotting. She often relies on voice alone to carry the narrative forward. Her stories are generally peopled with husbands and wives, friends and neighbors in New York's middle class and focus on the shifting dynamics of personal relationships. "Samuel," originally published in *The Atlantic Monthly* and collected in 1974, represents something of a departure from this pattern. Here Paley explores the thoughts of a group of strangers, passengers riding in an elevated train. Although simply told, the story touches on complex emotions and raises difficult questions about responsibility and loss.

Samuel

Some boys are very tough. They're afraid of nothing. They are the ones who climb a wall and take a bow at the top. Not only are they brave on the roof, but they make a lot of noise in the darkest part of the cellar where even the super hates to go. They also jiggle and hop on the platform between the locked doors of the subway cars.   1

Four boys are jiggling on the swaying platform. Their names are Alfred, Calvin, Samuel, and Tom. The men and women in the cars on either side watch them. They don't like them to jiggle or jump but don't want to interfere. Of course some of the men in the cars were once brave boys like these. One of them had ridden the tail of a speeding truck from New York to Rockaway Beach without getting off, without his sore fingers losing hold. Nothing happened to him then or later. He had made a compact with other boys who preferred to watch: starting at Eighth Avenue and Fifteenth Street, he would get to some specified place, maybe Twenty-third and the river, by hopping the tops of the moving trucks. This was hard to do when one truck turned a corner in the wrong direction and the nearest truck was a couple of feet too high. He made three or four starts before succeeding. He had gotten this idea from a film at school called *The Romance of Logging.* He had finished high school, married a good friend, was in a responsible job, and going to night school.   2

These two men and others looked at the four boys jumping and jiggling on the platform and thought, It must be fun to ride that way, especially now the weather is nice and we're out of the tunnel and way high over the Bronx. Then they thought, These kids do seem to be acting sort of   3 stupid. They *are* little. Then they thought of some of the brave things they had done when they were boys and jiggling didn't seem so risky.

The ladies in the car became very angry when they looked at the four 4
boys. Most of them brought their brows together and hoped the boys could see their extreme disapproval. One of the ladies wanted to get up and say, be careful you dumb kids, get off that platform or I'll call a cop. But three of the boys were Negroes and the fourth was something else she couldn't tell for sure. She was afraid they'd be fresh and laugh at her and embarrass her. She wasn't afraid they'd hit her, but she was afraid of embarrassment. Another lady thought, their mothers never know where they are. It wasn't true in this particular case. Their mothers all knew that they had gone to see the missile exhibit on Fourteenth Street.

Out on the platform, whenever the train accelerated, the boys would 5
raise their hands and point them up to the sky to act like rockets going off, then they rat-tat-tatted the shatterproof glass pane like machine guns, although no machine guns had been exhibited.

For some reason known only to the motorman, the train began a sud- 6
den slowdown. The lady who was afraid of embarrassment saw the boys jerk forward and backward and grab the swinging guard chains. She had her own boy at home. She stood up with determination and went to the door. She slid it open and said, "You boys will be hurt. You'll be killed. I'm going to call the conductor if you don't just go into the next car and sit down and be quiet."

Two of the boys said, "Yes'm," and acted as though they were about to 7
go. Two of them blinked their eyes a couple of times and pressed their lips together. The train resumed its speed. The door slid shut, parting the lady and the boys. She leaned against the side door because she had to get off at the next stop.

The boys opened their eyes wide at each other and laughed. The lady 8
blushed. The boys looked at her and laughed harder. They began to pound each other's back. Samuel laughed the hardest and pounded Alfred's back until Alfred coughed and the tears came. Alfred held tight to the chain hook. Samuel pounded him even harder when he saw the tears. He said, "Why you bawling? You a baby, huh?" and laughed. One of the men whose boyhood had been more watchful than brave became angry. He stood up straight and looked at the boys for a couple of seconds. Then he walked in a citizenly way to the end of the car, where he pulled the emergency cord. Almost at once, with a terrible hiss, the pressure of air abandoned the brakes and the wheels were caught and held.

People standing in the most secure places fell forward, then back- 9
ward. Samuel had let go of his hold on the chain so he could pound Tom as well as Alfred. All the passengers in the cars whipped back and forth, but he pitched only forward and fell head first to be crushed and killed between the cars.

The train had stopped hard, halfway into the station, and the conduc- 10
tor called at once for the trainmen who knew about this kind of death and

how to take the body from the wheels and brakes. There was silence except for passengers from the other cars who asked, What happened! What happened! The ladies waited around wondering if he might be an only child. The men recalled other afternoons with very bad endings. The little boys stayed close to each other, leaning and touching shoulders and arms and legs.

When the policeman knocked at the door and told her about it, Samuel's mother began to scream. She screamed all day and moaned all night, though the doctors tried to quiet her with pills. 11

Oh, oh, she hopelessly cried. She did not know how she could ever find another boy like that one. However, she was a young woman and she became pregnant. Then for a few months she was hopeful. The child born to her was a boy. They brought him to be seen and nursed. She smiled. But immediately she saw that this baby wasn't Samuel. She and her husband together have had other children, but never again will a boy exactly like Samuel be known. 12

• • •

THINKING ABOUT LITERATURE

1. Paley supports the main point of the story with a single example. What is the example?

2. The story begins with the observation, "Some boys are very tough." Is Samuel really tough? What do you think Paley wants her readers to realize about Samuel?

3. What point do you think the story makes about bravery? Which of the characters do you consider brave? Why?

4. What effect does the incident have on the other characters? What do their reactions reveal about them?

JOURNAL ENTRY

Do you consider Samuel a hero? Is it true, as the narrator asserts, that "never again will a boy exactly like Samuel be known" (12)?

THEMATIC CONNECTIONS

- "Thirty-Eight Who Saw Murder Didn't Call the Police" (page 99)
- "It's Just Too Late" (page 304)
- "The Men We Carry in Our Minds" (page 399)

WRITING ASSIGNMENTS FOR EXEMPLIFICATION

1. Interview several businesspeople in your community. Begin by explaining the Peter Principle to them if they are unfamiliar with it. Then ask them to express their feelings about this concept, and take notes on their responses. Finally, write an essay about your findings that includes quotations from your notes.

2. Write a humorous essay about a ritual you experienced and the types of people who participated in it. Make a point about the ritual, and use the participants as examples to support your point.

3. Write an essay in which you establish that you are an optimistic or a pessimistic person. Use two or three examples to support your case.

4. If you could change three or four things at your school, what would they be? Use examples from your own experience to support your claims, and tie the three examples together with a single thesis statement.

5. Write an essay in which you discuss two or three of the greatest challenges facing the United States today. If you like, you may refer to essays in this chapter, such as "Just Walk On By" (page 197) or "The Human Cost of an Illiterate Society" (page 203), or to essays elsewhere in this book, such as "Two Ways to Belong in America" (page 357) or "On Dumpster Diving" (page 632).

6. Using your family and friends as examples, write an essay in which you suggest some of the positive or negative characteristics of Americans.

7. Write an essay in which you present your formula for achieving success in college. You may, if you wish, talk about things like scheduling time, maintaining a high energy level, and learning how to relax. Use examples from your own experience to make your point. You may wish to refer to "College Pressures" (page 390).

8. Write an exemplification essay in which you discuss how cooperation has helped you achieve some important goal. Support your thesis with a single well-developed example.

9. Choose an event that you believe illustrates a less-than-admirable moment in your life. Write an essay explaining your feelings.

10. Write an essay in which you identify and discuss what you believe is the most pressing personal problem you have faced and overcome.

COLLABORATIVE ACTIVITY FOR EXEMPLIFICATION

The following passage appeared in a handbook given to parents of entering students at a midwestern university:

> The freshman experience is like no other — at once challenging, exhilarating, and fun. Students face academic challenges as they are exposed to many new ideas. They also face personal challenges as they meet many new people from diverse backgrounds. It is a time to mature and grow. It is an opportunity to explore new subjects and familiar ones. There may be

no more challenging and exciting time of personal growth than the first year of university study.

Working in groups of four, brainstorm to identify examples that support or refute the idea that there "may be no more challenging and exciting time of personal growth" than the first year of college. Then, choose one person from each group to tell the class what position the group took and explain the examples you collected. Finally, work together to write an essay that presents your group's position. Have one student write the first draft, two others revise this draft, and the last student edit and proofread the revised draft.

INTERNET ASSIGNMENT FOR EXEMPLIFICATION

Using examples from your own experience and from the Internet, write an exemplification essay in which you explain the importance of protecting the privacy rights of individuals. Use the following World Wide Web sites to help you gain an understanding about current privacy issues and policies.

Federal Trade Commission
<http://www.ftc.gov/privacy/index.html>
The FTC's site is designed to educate consumers and businesses about the importance of protecting the privacy of personal information.

Electronic Privacy Information Center
<http://www.epic.org>
This site has news articles and other information about privacy and civil liberties issues in the information age.

Privacy Times
<http://www.privacytimes.com>
Privacy Times is a newsletter that covers information law and policy.

7

PROCESS

WHAT IS PROCESS?

A **process** essay explains how to do something or how something occurs. It presents a sequence of steps and shows how those steps lead to a particular result. In the following paragraph from *Language in Thought and Action,* the semanticist S. I. Hayakawa uses process to explain how an editor of a dictionary decides on a word's definition:

<table>
<tr>
<td>Process presents series of steps in chronological order</td>
<td>To define a word, then, the dictionary-editor places before him the stack of cards illustrating that word; each of the cards represents an actual use of the word by a writer of some literacy or historical importance. He reads the cards carefully, discards some, rereads the rest, and divides up the stack according to what he thinks are the several senses of the word. Finally, he writes his definitions, following the hard-and-fast rule that each definition *must* be based on what the quotations in front of him reveal about the meaning of the word. The editor cannot be influenced by what *he* thinks a given word *ought* to</td>
</tr>
<tr>
<td>Topic sentence</td>
<td>mean. He must work according to the cards or not at all.</td>
</tr>
</table>

Process, like narrative, presents events in chronological order. Unlike a narrative, however, a process essay explains a particular series of events that produces the same outcome whenever it is duplicated. Because these events form a sequence that has a fixed order, clarity is extremely important. Whether your readers are actually going to perform the process or are simply trying to understand how it occurs, your essay must make clear the exact order of the individual steps as well as their relationships to one another and to the process as a whole. You need to provide clear, logical transitions between the steps in a process, and you also need to present the steps in *strict* chronological order — that is, in the order in which they occur or are to be performed.

Depending on its purpose, a process essay can be either a set of *instructions* or a *process explanation.*

Understanding Instructions

Instructions enable readers to perform a process. Instructions have many practical uses. A recipe, a handout about using your library's online databases, and the operating manual for your VCR are all written as instructions. So are directions for locating an office building in Washington, D.C., or driving from Houston to Pensacola. Instructions use the present tense and, like commands, the imperative mood, speaking directly to readers: "*Disconnect* the system and *check* the electrical source."

Understanding Process Explanations

The purpose of a **process explanation** is not to enable readers to perform a process but rather to help them understand how it is carried out. Such essays may examine anything from how silkworms spin their cocoons to how Michelangelo and Leonardo da Vinci painted their masterpieces on plaster walls and ceilings. A process explanation may employ the first person (*I, we*) or the third (*he, she, it, they*), the past tense or the present. (Because its readers need to understand, not perform, the process, process explanation does not use the second person or the imperative mood.) The style of a process explanation varies, depending on whether a writer is explaining a process that takes place regularly or one that occurred in the past, and on whether the writer or someone else carries out the steps. The chart that follows suggests some of the options available to writers of process explanations.

	First person	*Third person*
Present tense	"After I place the chemicals in the tray, I turn out the lights in the darkroom." (*habitual process performed by the writer*)	"After photographers place the chemicals in the tray, they turn out the lights in the darkroom." (*habitual process performed by person other than the writer*)
Past tense	"After I placed the chemicals in the tray, I turned out the lights in the darkroom." (*process performed in the past by the writer*)	"After the photographer placed the chemicals in the tray, she turned out the lights in the darkroom." (*process performed in the past by someone other than the writer*)

USING PROCESS

College writing frequently calls for instructions or process explanations. In a biology term paper on some aspect of genetic engineering, you might devote a paragraph to an explanation of the process of amniocentesis; in an editorial about the negative side of fraternity life, you might decide to include a brief outline of the process of pledging. Or, you can organize an entire paper around a process pattern: in a literature essay, you might trace the steps through which a fictional character reaches some new insight; on a finance midterm, you might explain the procedure for approving a commercial loan.

You can use process writing to persuade or simply to present information. If its purpose is persuasive, a process paper may take a strong stand like "Applying for food stamps is a needlessly complex process that discourages many qualified recipients" or "The process of slaughtering baby seals is inhumane and sadistic." Many process essays, however, communicate nothing more debatable than the procedure for blood typing. Even in such a case, though, a process should have a clear thesis statement that identifies the process and perhaps tells why it is performed: "Typing their own blood can familiarize students with some fundamental laboratory procedures."

PLANNING A PROCESS ESSAY

As you plan a process essay, remember that your primary goal is to depict the process accurately. This means that you should distinguish between what usually or always happens and what occasionally or rarely happens, between necessary steps and optional ones. You should also mentally test all the steps in sequence to be sure that the process really works as you say it does, checking carefully for omitted steps or incorrect information. If you are writing about a process you witnessed, try to test your written explanation by observing the process again.

As you write, remember to keep your readers' needs in mind. When necessary, explain the reasons for performing the steps, describe unfamiliar materials or equipment, define unfamiliar terms, and warn readers about possible problems that may occur during the process. (Sometimes you may even need to include illustrations.) Besides complete information, your readers need a clear and consistent discussion without ambiguities or surprises. For this reason, you should avoid unnecessary shifts in tense, person, voice, and mood. You should also include appropriate articles (*a, an,* and *the*) so that your discussion moves smoothly, like an essay — not abruptly, like a cookbook.

Throughout your essay, be sure to use transitional words and phrases to ensure that each step, each stage, and each paragraph leads logically to the next. Transitions like *first, second, meanwhile, after this, next, then, when you have finished,* and *finally* help to establish sequential and chronological relationships so that readers can follow the process.

STRUCTURING A PROCESS ESSAY

Like other essays, a process essay generally consists of three sections. The *introduction* identifies the process and indicates why and under what circumstances it is performed. This section may include information about materials or preliminary preparations, or it may present an overview of the process, perhaps even listing its major stages. The paper's thesis is also usually stated in the introduction.

Each paragraph in the *body* of the essay typically treats one major stage of the procedure. Each stage may group several steps, depending on the nature and complexity of the process. These steps are presented in chronological order, interrupted only for essential definitions, explanations, or cautions. Every step must be included and must appear in its proper place.

A short process essay may not need a formal *conclusion*. If an essay does have a conclusion, however, it will often briefly review the procedure's major stages. Such an ending is especially useful if the paper has outlined a particularly technical procedure that may seem complicated to general readers. The conclusion may also reinforce the thesis by summarizing the results of the process or explaining its significance.

Suppose you are taking a midterm examination in a course in childhood and adolescent behavior. One essay question calls for a process explanation: "Trace the stages that children go through in acquiring language." After thinking about the question, you formulate the following thesis statement: "Although individual cases may differ, most children acquire language in a predictable series of stages." You then plan your essay and develop an informal outline, which might look like this:

Introduction:	Thesis statement — Although individual cases may differ, most children acquire language in a predictable series of stages.
First stage (two to twelve months):	Prelinguistic behavior, including "babbling" and appropriate responses to nonverbal cues.
Second stage (end of first year):	Single words as commands or requests; infant catalogs his or her environment.
Third stage (beginning of second year):	Expressive jargon (flow of sounds that imitates adult speech); real words along with jargon.
Fourth and final stage (middle of second year to beginning of third year):	Two-word phrases; longer strings; missing parts of speech.
Conclusion:	Restatement of thesis or review of major stages of process.

This essay, when completed, will show not only what the stages of the process are but also how they relate to one another. In addition, it will support the thesis that children learn language through a well-defined process.

☑ **CHECKLIST: PROCESS**

- Does your assignment call for a process explanation or a set of instructions?
- Does your writing style clearly and consistently indicate whether you are writing a process explanation or a set of instructions?
- Does your essay have a clearly stated thesis that identifies the process and perhaps tells why it is (or was) performed?
- Have you included all necessary reminders and cautions?
- Have you included all necessary steps?
- Are the steps presented in strict chronological order?
- Do transitions clearly indicate where one step ends and the next begins?

▶ **STUDENT WRITERS: PROCESS**

The following student essays, Joseph Miksitz's set of instructions and Melany Hunt's explanation of how a process was conducted, were both written in response to the same assignment: "Write an essay in which you give instructions for a process that can change a person's appearance — or explain a process that changed your own appearance in some way."

Pumping Iron

Introduction

Students of high school and college age   1
are often dissatisfied with their appearance.
They see actors and models on television and
in magazines, and they want to be thinner,
stronger, or better looking. Sometimes this
quest for perfection gets young adults into
trouble, leading them to eating disorders or
drug use. A healthier way for young adults to

Thesis statement

improve their appearance is through a weight-
training program, which can increase not only
their strength but also their self-esteem.

Overview of
the process;
getting started

If you want to avoid injury, you should   2
begin gradually. In the first week, you might
lift weights only two days, concentrating on
thigh and calf muscles in the lower body and on
triceps, biceps, chest, back, and shoulders in
the upper body. For the next three or four

weeks, lift three days a week, adding more
exercises each week. By the fourth week, you
will probably start to feel stronger. At this
point, you can begin a four-day lifting program, which many experts believe is the most
productive and shows the best results.

Steps in process of upper-body workout

On Monday and Thursday, concentrate on   3
your upper body. Begin with the bench press
(to work chest muscles) and then move on to
the military press (for the shoulders). After
that, work your back muscles with the lat pull-
down exercise on the Universal machine or
with some heavy and light dead lifts. Finally,
concentrate on your arms, doing bicep curls,
tricep extensions, and wrist curls (for the
forearms). To cool down, do a few sets of
sit-ups.

Steps in process of lower-body workout

On Tuesday and Friday, focus on your lower   4
body with a leg workout. Start with the leg
press. (Always begin your workout with your
most strenuous exercise, which is usually the
exercise that works the largest muscles.) Next,
do some leg extensions to build the thigh
muscles in the front of your leg, and then move
on to leg curls to strengthen your hamstring
muscle. After that, do calf raises to work your
calf muscles. When you are finished, be sure
to stretch all the major muscles to prevent
tightness and injuries.

Warnings and reminders

Of course, a balanced weight-training pro-   5
gram involves more than just lifting weights.
During your weight training, you should eat
four high-protein/high-carbohydrate meals a
day, limiting fat and eating four or five serv-
ings of fruit and vegetables daily. You should
also monitor your progress carefully, paying
attention to your body's aches and pains and
consulting a professional trainer when neces-
sary--especially if you think you may have
injured yourself.

Conclusion   Above all, don't let your weight-training   6
                          regimen take over your life. If you integrate
                          it into the rest of your life, balancing exer-
                          cise with school, work, and social activities,
                          a weight-training program can make you look and
                          feel terrific.

Points for Special Attention

INTRODUCTION.   The first paragraph of Joseph Miksitz's essay includes a thesis statement that presents the advantages of embarking on a weight-training program. Joseph begins with an overview of the image problems faced by young adults and then narrows his focus to present weight training as a possible solution to those problems.

STRUCTURE.   After his introduction, Joseph includes a paragraph that presents guidelines for getting started. The third and fourth paragraphs enumerate the steps in each of the two processes he describes: upper- and lower-body workouts. In his fifth paragraph, Joseph includes reminders and cautions so that his readers will get the most out of their exercise program while avoiding overexertion or injury. (The parenthetical sentence in paragraph 4 offers another helpful tip.) In his conclusion, Joseph advises readers to keep their exercise program in perspective and (echoing his thesis statement) reminds them of its benefits.

PURPOSE AND STYLE.   Because Joseph's readers should be able to perform the process themselves, he wrote it as a set of instructions. Therefore, he uses the second person ("*you* will probably start to feel stronger") and present-tense verbs in the form of commands ("*Begin* with the bench press").

TRANSITIONS.   To make his essay clear and easy to follow, Joseph includes transitions that indicate the order in which each step is to be performed ("After that," "Next," "Finally") as well as specific time markers ("On Monday and Thursday," "On Tuesday and Friday") to distinguish the two related processes on which his essay focuses.

Focus on Revision

Joseph is careful to name various parts of the body and to identify different exercises as well as the general objective of each. He has, however, omitted many other key details, as several students noted in their peer critiques of his essay. For example, how much time should be spent on each exercise? What exactly is a bench press? A bicep curl? How are "light" and "heavy" defined? How many is "some" leg extensions or "a few sets" of sit-ups? How many repetitions of each exercise are necessary? What specific danger signs should alert readers to possible overexertion or injury? Is the routine Joseph describes appropriate for females as well as males? When revising his essay, Joseph needs to remember that most members of his audience are not familiar with the processes he describes and therefore will need much more detailed explanations.

In contrast to "Pumping Iron," Melany Hunt's essay is a process explanation.

Medium Ash Brown

Introduction

    The beautiful chestnut-haired woman pictured on the box seemed to beckon to me. I reached for the box of Medium Ash Brown hair dye just as my friend Veronica grabbed the box labeled Sparkling Sherry. I can't remember our reasons for wanting to change our hair color, but they seemed to make sense at the time. Maybe we were just bored. I do remember that the idea of transforming our appearance came up unexpectedly. Impulsively, we decided to change our hair color--and, we hoped, ourselves--that

Thesis statement

very evening. Now I know that some impulses should definitely be resisted.

Materials assembled

    We decided to use my bathroom to dye our hair. Inside each box of hair color, we found two little bottles and a small tube wrapped in a page of instructions. Attached to the instruction page itself were two very large, one-size-fits-all plastic gloves, which looked and felt like plastic sandwich bags. The directions recommended having some old towels around to soak up any spills or drips that might occur. Under the sink we found some old, frayed towels that I figured my mom had forgotten about, and we spread them around the bathtub. After we

First stage of process: preparing the dye

put our gloves on, we began the actual dyeing process. First we poured the first bottle into the second, which was half-full of some odd-smelling liquid. The smell was not much better after we combined the two bottles. The directions advised us to cut off a small section of

1

2

hair to use as a sample. For some reason, we
decided to skip this step.

Second stage of process: applying the dye

At this point, Veronica and I took turns   3
leaning over the tub to wet our hair for the
dye. The directions said to leave the dye on
the hair for fifteen to twenty minutes, so we
found a little timer and set it for fifteen
minutes. Next, we applied the dye to our hair.
Again, we took turns squeezing the bottle in
order to cover all our hair. We then wrapped
the old towels around our sour-smelling hair
and went outside to get some fresh air.

Third stage of process: rinsing

After the fifteen minutes were up, we   4
rinsed our hair. According to the directions,
we were to add a little water and scrub as if
we were shampooing our hair. The dye lathered
up, and we rinsed our hair until the water ran
clear. So far, so good.

Last stage of process: applying conditioner

The last part of the process involved   5
applying the small tube of conditioner to our
hair (because dyed hair becomes brittle and
easily damaged). We used the conditioner as
directed, and then we dried our hair so that
we could see the actual color. Even before I

Outcome of process

looked in the mirror, I heard Veronica's gasp.

"Nice try," I said, assuming she was just   6
trying to make me nervous, "But you're not funny."

"Mel," she said, "look in the mirror."   7
Slowly, I turned around. My stomach turned into
a lead ball when I saw my reflection. My hair
was the putrid greenish-brown color of a winter
lawn, dying in patches yet still a nice green
in the shade.

The next day in school, I wore my hair   8
tied back under a baseball cap. I told only my
close friends what I had done. After they were
finished laughing, they offered their deepest,
most heartfelt condolences. They also offered
many suggestions--none very helpful--on what to
do to get my old hair color back.

Conclusion   It is now three months later, and I still   9
                    have no idea what prompted me to dye my hair. My
                    only consolation is that I resisted my first
                    impulse--to dye my hair a wild color, like blue
                    or fuchsia. Still, as I wait for my hair to grow
                    out, and as I assemble a larger and larger col-
                    lection of baseball caps, it is small consola-
                    tion indeed.

Points for Special Attention

STRUCTURE.   In her opening paragraph, Melany's thesis statement makes it very clear that the experience she describes is not one she would recommend to others. The temptation she describes in her introduction's first few sentences lures readers into her essay just as the picture on the box lured her. Her second paragraph lists the contents of the box of hair dye and explains how she and her friend assembled the other necessary materials. Then, she explains the first stage in the process, preparing the dye. Paragraphs 3–5 describe the other stages in the process in chronological order, and paragraphs 6–8 record Melany's and Veronica's reactions to their experiment. In paragraph 9, Melany sums up the impact of her experience and once again expresses her annoyance with herself for her impulsive act.

PURPOSE AND FORMAT.   Melany's purpose is *not* to enable others to duplicate the process she explains; on the contrary, she is trying to discourage readers from doing what she did. Consequently, she presents her process not as a set of instructions but as a process explanation, using first person and past tense to explain the actions of herself and her friend. She also largely eliminates cautions and reminders that her readers, who are not likely to undertake the process, will not need to know.

DETAIL.   Melany's essay includes vivid descriptive detail that gives readers a clear sense of the process and its outcome. Throughout, her emphasis is on the negative aspects of the process — the "odd-smelling liquid" and the "putrid greenish-brown color" of her hair, for instance — and this emphasis is consistent with her essay's purpose.

TRANSITIONS.   To move readers smoothly through the process, Melany includes clear transitions ("First," "At this point," "Next," "then") and clearly identifies the beginning of the process ("After we put our gloves on, we began the actual dyeing process") and the end ("The last part of the process").

Focus on Revision

Students who read Melany's essay thought that it was clearly written and structured and that its ironic, self-mocking tone was well suited to her audience and purpose. They felt, however, that some minor revisions would make her essay even more effective. Paragraph 2, for example, still needs a bit of work. For one thing, this paragraph begins quite abruptly: paragraph 1 records the purchase of the hair dye, and paragraph 2 opens with the sentence "We decided to use my bathroom to dye our hair," leaving readers wondering how much time has passed between purchase and application. Since the thesis rests on the idea of the foolishness of an impulsive gesture, it is important for readers to understand that the girls presumably went immediately from the store to Melany's house. After thinking about this criticism, Melany decided to write a clearer opening for paragraph 2: "As soon as we paid for the dye, we returned to my house, where, eager to begin our transformation, we locked ourselves in my bathroom. Inside each box. . . ." She also decided to divide paragraph 2 into two paragraphs, one describing the materials and another beginning with "After we put our gloves on," which introduces the first step in the process.

Another possible revision Melany considered was to develop Veronica's character further. Although both girls purchase and apply hair color, readers never learn what happens to Veronica. Melany knew she could easily add a brief paragraph after paragraph 7, describing Veronica's "Sparkling Sherry" hair in humorous terms, and she planned to do so in her paper's final draft.

The following selections illustrate how varied the purposes of process writing can be. Each essay, however, provides orderly and clear explanations so that readers can follow the process easily.

MALCOLM X

Malcolm X was born Malcolm Little in Omaha, Nebraska, in 1925. As a young man, he had a number of run-ins with the law, and he wound up in prison on burglary charges before he was twenty-one. There, he pursued his education and was influenced by the writings of Elijah Muhammed, the founder of the Black Muslims (now known as the Nation of Islam), a radical black separatist organization. On his release from prison, Malcolm X became a highly visible member of this group and a disciple of its leader. He left the movement in 1963, later converting to orthodox Islam and founding a rival African-American political organization. He was assassinated in 1965.

In 1964, he published *The Autobiography of Malcolm X* (written with Alex Haley). The following incident from that book took place in 1941, when the author was sixteen. He had recently moved to Boston to live with an older sister. A self-described "hick," he got his "baptism in fast living" from a street-savvy friend, Shorty, who was more than willing to serve as his guide to urban life. Part of this initiation into sophistication was the hair-straightening procedure described here. It would go out of favor in the 1960s, when the more natural Afro style became popular and straightening one's hair represented for many an attempt to imitate whites.

My First Conk

Shorty soon decided that my hair was finally long enough to be conked. He had promised to school me in how to beat the barber shops' three- and four-dollar price by making up congolene, and then conking ourselves.

I took the little list of ingredients he had printed out for me, and went to a grocery store, where I got a can of Red Devil lye, two eggs, and two medium-sized white potatoes. Then at a drugstore near the poolroom, I asked for a large jar of vaseline, a large bar of soap, a large-toothed comb and a fine-toothed comb, one of those rubber hoses with a metal spray-head, a rubber apron, and a pair of gloves.

"Going to lay on that first conk?" the drugstore man asked me. I proudly told him, grinning, "Right!"

Shorty paid six dollars a week for a room in his cousin's shabby apartment. His cousin wasn't at home. "It's like the pad's mine, he spends so much time with his woman," Shorty said. "Now, you watch me —"

He peeled the potatoes and thin-sliced them into a quart-sized Mason fruit jar, then started stirring them with a wooden spoon as he gradually poured in a little over half the can of lye. "Never use a metal spoon; the lye will turn it black," he told me.

A jelly-like, starchy-looking glop resulted from the lye and potatoes, and Shorty broke in the two eggs, stirring real fast — his own conk and dark face bent down close. The congolene turned pale-yellowish. "Feel the jar," Shorty said. I cupped my hand against the outside, and snatched it away. "Damn right, it's hot, that's the lye," he said. "So you know it's going to burn when I comb it in — it burns bad. But the longer you can stand it, the straighter the hair."

He made me sit down, and he tied the string of the new rubber apron   7
tightly around my neck, and combed up my bush of hair. Then, from the big vaseline jar, he took a handful and massaged it hard all through my hair and into the scalp. He also thickly vaselined my neck, ears and forehead. "When I get to washing out your head, be sure to tell me anywhere you feel any little stinging," Shorty warned me, washing his hands, then pulling on the rubber gloves, and tying on his own rubber apron. "You always got to remember that any congolene left in burns a sore into your head."

The congolene just felt warm when Shorty started combing it in. But   8
then my head caught fire.

I gritted my teeth and tried to pull the sides of the kitchen table   9
together. The comb felt as if it was raking my skin off.

My eyes watered, my nose was running. I couldn't stand it any   10
longer; I bolted to the washbasin. I was cursing Shorty with every name I could think of when he got the spray going and started soap lathering my head.

He lathered and spray-rinsed, lathered and spray-rinsed, maybe ten   11
or twelve times, each time gradually closing the hot-water faucet, until the rinse was cold, and that helped some.

"You feel any stinging spots?"   12

"No," I managed to say. My knees were trembling.   13

"Sit back down, then. I think we got it all out okay."   14

The flame came back as Shorty, with a thick towel, started drying my   15
head, rubbing hard. *"Easy, man, easy!"* I kept shouting.

"The first time's always worst. You get used to it better before long.   16
You took it real good, homeboy. You got a good conk."

When Shorty let me stand up and see in the mirror, my hair hung   17
down in limp, damp strings. My scalp still flamed, but not as badly; I could bear it. He draped the towel around my shoulders, over my rubber apron, and began again vaselining my hair.

I could feel him combing, straight back, first the big comb, then the   18
fine-tooth one.

Then, he was using a razor, very delicately, on the back of my neck.   19
Then, finally, shaping the sideburns.

My first view in the mirror blotted out the hurting. I'd seen some   20
pretty conks, but when it's the first time, on your *own* head, the transformation, after the lifetime of kinks, is staggering.

The mirror reflected Shorty behind me. We both were grinning and   21
sweating. And on top of my head was this thick, smooth sheen of shining red hair — real red — as straight as any white man's.

How ridiculous I was! Stupid enough to stand there simply lost in 22
admiration of my hair now looking "white," reflected in the mirror in
Shorty's room. I vowed that I'd never again be without a conk, and I never
was for many years.

This was my first really big step toward self-degradation: when I 23
endured all of that pain, literally burning my flesh to have it look like a
white man's hair. I had joined that multitude of Negro men and women in
America who are brainwashed into believing that the black people are
"inferior"—and white people "superior"—that they will even violate
and mutilate their God-created bodies to try to look "pretty" by white
standards.

Look around today, in every small town and big city, from two-bit 24
catfish and soda-pop joints into the "integrated" lobby of the Waldorf-
Astoria, and you'll see conks on black men. And you'll see black women
wearing these green and pink and purple and red and platinum-blonde
wigs. They're all more ridiculous than a slapstick comedy. It makes you
wonder if the Negro has completely lost his sense of identity, lost touch
with himself.

You'll see the conk worn by many, many so-called "upper class" 25
Negroes, and, as much as I hate to say it about them, on all too many
Negro entertainers. One of the reasons that I've especially admired some
of them, like Lionel Hampton and Sidney Poitier, among others, is that
they have kept their natural hair and fought to the top. I admire any Negro
man who has never had himself conked, or who has had the sense to get
rid of it — as I finally did.

I don't know which kind of self-defacing conk is the greater shame — 26
the one you'll see on the heads of the black so-called "middle class" and
"upper class," who ought to know better, or the one you'll see on the heads
of the poorest, most downtrodden, ignorant black men. I mean the legal-
minimum-wage ghetto-dwelling kind of Negro, as I was when I got my
first one. It's generally among these poor fools that you'll see a black ker-
chief over the man's head, like Aunt Jemima; he's trying to make his conk
last longer, between trips to the barbershop. Only for special occasions is
this kerchief-protected conk exposed — to show off how "sharp" and "hip"
its owner is. The ironic thing is that I have never heard any woman, white
or black, express any admiration for a conk. Of course, any white woman
with a black man isn't thinking about his hair. But I don't see how on earth
a black woman with any race pride could walk down the street with any
black man wearing a conk — the emblem of his shame that he is black.

To my own shame, when I say all of this, I'm talking first of all about 27
myself — because you can't show me any Negro who ever conked more
faithfully than I did. I'm speaking from personal experience when I say of
any black man who conks today, or any white-wigged black woman, that
if they gave the brains in their heads just half as much attention as they do
their hair, they would be a thousand times better off.

•   •   •

COMPREHENSION

1. What exactly is a conk? Why did Malcolm X want to get his hair conked? What did the conk symbolize to him at the time he got it? What does it symbolize at the time he writes about it?

2. List the materials Shorty asked Malcolm X to buy. Is the purpose of each explained? If so, where?

3. Outline the major stages in the procedure Malcolm X describes. Are they presented in chronological order? Which, if any, of the major stages are out of place?

PURPOSE AND AUDIENCE

1. Why does Malcolm X write this selection as a process explanation instead of as a set of instructions?

2. This process explanation has an explicitly stated thesis that makes its purpose clear. What is this thesis?

3. *The Autobiography of Malcolm X* was published in 1964, when many African Americans got their hair straightened regularly. Is the thesis of this selection still relevant today?

4. Why do you think Malcolm X includes so many references to the pain and discomfort he endures as part of the process?

5. What is the relationship between Malcolm X's personal experience and the universal statement he is making about conking?

STYLE AND STRUCTURE

1. Identify some of the transitional words Malcolm X uses to move from step to step.

2. Only about half of this piece of writing is devoted to the process explanation. Where does the process begin? Where does it end?

3. In paragraphs 22–26, Malcolm X encloses several words in quotation marks, occasionally prefacing them with the phrase *so-called*. What is the effect of these quotation marks?

VOCABULARY PROJECTS

1. Define each of the following words as it is used in this selection.

vowed (22)	mutilate (23)	downtrodden (26)
self-degradation (23)	slapstick (24)	emblem (26)
multitude (23)	self-defacing (26)	

2. Because this is an informal piece of writing, Malcolm X uses many **colloquialisms** and **slang** terms. Substitute a more formal word for each of the following.

beat (1)	glop (6)	"sharp" (26)
pad (4)	real (6)	"hip" (26)

Evaluate the possible impact of your substitutions. Do they improve the essay or weaken it?

JOURNAL ENTRY

Did you ever engage in behavior that you later came to view as unacceptable as your beliefs changed or as your social consciousness developed? What made you change your attitude toward this behavior?

WRITING WORKSHOP

1. Write a process explanation of an unpleasant experience you or someone you know has often gone through in order to conform to others' standards of physical beauty (for instance, dieting or undertaking strenuous exercise). Include a thesis statement that conveys your disapproval of the process.

2. Rewrite Malcolm X's process explanation as he might have written it when he still considered conking a desirable process, worth all the trouble. Include all his steps, but change his thesis and choose words that make conking sound painless and worthwhile.

3. Rewrite this essay as a set of instructions that Shorty might have written for a friend who is about to help someone conk his hair. Begin by telling the friend what materials to purchase.

COMBINING THE PATTERNS

Although "My First Conk" is very detailed, it does not include an extended **definition** of a conk. Do you think a definition paragraph should be added? If so, where could it be inserted? What patterns could be used to develop such a definition?

THEMATIC CONNECTIONS

- "Finishing School" (page 88)
- "Medium Ash Brown" (page 224)
- "The Secretary Chant" (page 488)

GARRY TRUDEAU

Garry Trudeau was born in 1948 in New York City and attended Yale University and Yale's School of Art and Architecture. He is the creator of the nationally syndicated comic strip *Doonesbury,* which was one of the first strips in the country to focus on social and political satire (in many papers, it runs on the editorial page). The strips have been collected in numerous books, most recently in *Virtual Doonesbury* (1996) and *Planet Doonesbury* (1997). Trudeau won a Pulitzer Prize for editorial cartooning in 1975 and was nominated for an Academy Award in 1977 for the animated film *A Doonesbury Special.*

"Anatomy of a Joke" appeared on the Op-Ed page of the *New York Times* in 1993. As the opening paragraph suggests, it was written in the wake of a spate of publicity surrounding some shakeups in late-night television programming. David Letterman was shifting networks and going head-to-head against Jay Leno in the 11:30 P.M. spot, Chevy Chase was gearing up to host a competing show (quickly canceled), and Conan O'Brian was taking over Letterman's post. Following so much interest in late-night comics, Trudeau took the opportunity to subtly skewer their abilities by outlining a detailed procedure for developing a single *Tonight Show* joke, from the initial idea to the comic's delivery. Professional joke writers have been around since comics came to prominence early in the twentieth century, but, as Trudeau suggests, today the process has been turned over to teams of writers.

Anatomy of a Joke

In the wake of last week's press "availabilities" of funnymen Dave Letterman, Jay Leno, Chevy Chase et al., there was much rim-shot critiquing, all of it missing the point. 1

The real jokes, the ones that count, occur not at press events but during those extraordinary little pieces called [late-night] monologues. Despite the popular conception of the monologue as edgy and unpredictable, it is actually as formal and structured as anything found in traditional kabuki. The stakes are too high for it to be otherwise. Even the ad-libs, rejoinders, and recoveries are carefully scripted. While it may suit Leno's image to portray *The Tonight Show* monologue as something that's banged out over late-night pizza with a few cronies, in fact each joke requires the concerted effort of a crack team of six highly disciplined comedy professionals. To illustrate how it works, let's follow an actual topical joke, told the night of Monday, July 26, as it makes its way through the pipeline. 2

The inspiration for a topical joke is literally torn from the headlines by a professional comedy news "clipper." Comedy news reading is sometimes contracted out to consultants, but the big-budget *Tonight Show* has 12 of its own in-house clippers who peruse some 300 newspapers every day. Clippers know that the idea for the joke must be contained in the headline or, at worst, the subhead. If the idea is in the body text, then the 3 general public has probably missed it and won't grasp the reference the joke is built around. In this case, the clipper has spied an item about flood relief.

A20 FRIDAY, JULY 23, 1993

House Delays Final Flood Aid Vote
$3 Billion Package Stalls in Dispute Over Budget Limits

The Washington Post

The news clip is then passed on to a comedy "engineer," whose job is   4
to decide what shape the joke should take. After analyzing the headline, the engineer decides how many parts the joke should have, the velocity of its build, whether it contains any red herrings (rare on *The Tonight Show*), and the dynamics of the payoff and underlaughing. With Monday's joke, the engineer chose a simple interrogatory setup, which telegraphs to the often sleepy audience that the next line contains a payoff. The finished sequencing is then sent on to the "stylist."

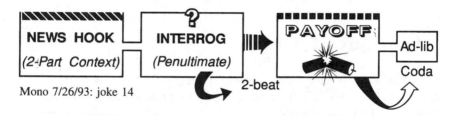

Mono 7/26/93: joke 14

The comedy stylist is the writer who actually fashions the raw joke.   5
The stylist is the prima donna of the team, the best paid, the worst dressed — and never in the office. The stylist, who is typically a per diem session player, is faxed the original headline, the structural scheme, and a gross time count, and from those elements creates the rough draft for the joke. It's up to him to find the joke's "spring," that tiny component of universal truth that acts as the joke's fulcrum. In this case, the joke hinges on the public's resentment of Congress, a hoary but proven truism. The stylist then faxes his finished rough to the "polish man."

1./It looks like the House of Representatives is having trouble voting flood relief because they're worried about where to appropriate the money from./
2. /Here's my question./
3./ How come when the House votes itself a pay raise, they never worry about <u>that</u> appropriation?

The polish man, usually a woman, is the joke's editor, charged with burnishing the joke until it gleams. Obscure references, awkward phrasing, and puns are all removed, and any potentially offensive material is run by an outside anti-defamation consultant. Unlike the stylist, who usually works at his beach house, the polish man is always on the premises, available in the event of emergency rewrites. For Monday's joke, the polish man adds a "fall from the sky" coda that will allow Leno some physical business. The decision to use it, however, ultimately rests with the "timing coach." 6

Ⓧ too long   ⎰Senate⎱

It looks like the ~~House of Representatives~~ is

         ⎰passing, Ⓧ where?⎱ ⎯for the midwest⎱

having trouble ~~voting~~ flood│relief │because ~~they're~~

⎰some Senators are⎱   ↑ is going to come,

Ⓘworried about where ~~to appropriate~~ the money │from.

⎰Now,⎱

ⒾHere's my question: How come when the ~~House~~ votes ⎰Senate⎱

         big⎱   ⎰wonder where⎱

itself a│pay raise, they never ~~worry~~ ~~about~~ that

money's coming from?
~~appropriation?~~   ad-libs: Ever notice that?

It just seems to fall from the sky.

The timing coach is responsible for timing out the phrasing and pauses, and bringing the 21-joke routine in under its seven-minute limit. Running over is a major no-no. During the Carson era, a timing coach, who asked not to be identified, signed off on a monologue that ran 13.5 seconds long, a deficit that came out of Barbra Streisand's guest segment. The coach was summarily sacked. Such errors are rare today, however, as the monologues are now digitalized on disk. A timer can modulate the phrasing pattern to within 0.01 of a second, well beyond the performance sensitivity of any comic but Robin Williams. 7

(6.3 sec. to pause) IT LOOKS LIKE...FLOOD RELIEF...WORRIED...MONEY IS GOING TO COME FROM. (.95 sec. beat) NOW, HERE'S MY QUESTION: (.6 second beat; 3.45 sec. to ad-lib) HOW COME...BIG PAY RAISE...WHERE THAT MONEY'S COMING FROM? (ad-lib under laugh; see menu).

The final joke is then e-mailed to the "talent," in this case Jay Leno.   8
Leno dry-runs the joke in his office, adding spin and body movement, and
locks in his ad-libs, including recovery lines in case the joke bombs. (Carson had such good recovery material that he used to commission intentionally bad jokes, but Leno has not yet reached that pinnacle of
impeccability.) Once Leno approves the joke, it is transferred to a hard
disk and laser-printed on cue cards with a special font to make it look
hand-lettered. Finally, at exactly 5:30 P.M., California taping time, Leno
walks on stage and reads it to 15 million people.

•   •   •

COMPREHENSION

1. Identify each of the six people involved in writing a typical joke, and
   explain what each contributes to the process.

2. What is the inspiration for most of the jokes that are told in late-night talk-
   show monologues? Why do you suppose this is so?

PURPOSE AND AUDIENCE

1. Trudeau, the creator of the *Doonesbury* comic strip, is known primarily as
   a cartoonist, yet this essay originally appeared as a column in the *New
   York Times*. What, if anything, does this information, along with Trudeau's
   comments in paragraphs 1 and 2, suggest about his purpose for explaining how a joke is created?

2. Does Trudeau assume his audience is familiar with late-night comedy
   programs? How can you tell?

3. Where does Trudeau state his essay's thesis? Restate it in your own
   words. Do you think such a restatement of the thesis should appear in the
   essay's conclusion? Explain.

STYLE AND STRUCTURE

1. Identify each stage in the process Trudeau describes.

2. What transitional expressions does Trudeau use to move his readers
   through each stage of the process? How does he connect one stage to the
   next? Would additional transitions improve the essay's clarity? Explain.

3. Do you think Trudeau is being serious when he refers to the joke writers
   as a "crack team of six highly disciplined comedy professionals" (2)?
   Explain your reasoning.

4. What elements typically included in a process explanation are absent
   here? Why?

5. Do you think the illustrations are necessary? Do they add to or detract
   from the essay's effectiveness? Explain.

VOCABULARY PROJECTS

1. Define each of the following words as it is used in this selection.

anatomy (title)	fulcrum (5)	summarily (7)
kabuki (2)	hoary (5)	spin (8)
rejoinders (2)	truism (5)	pinnacle (8)
velocity (4)	burnishing (6)	impeccability (8)
red herrings (4)	coda (6)	
per diem (5)	business (6)	

2. Trudeau's essay includes many examples of **colloquialisms**, such as paragraph 2's *cronies* and *banged out*. Choose one paragraph and identify additional examples of colloquialisms. What other features help to make this essay's style informal?

3. The essay also includes a good deal of **jargon**, such as paragraph 4's *underlaughing* and *sequencing*. Do you think Trudeau should define these terms? Why or why not?

JOURNAL ENTRY

Does Trudeau's essay change the way you view your favorite late-night television talk-show host or stand-up comedian? If so, how?

WRITING WORKSHOP

1. Write an essay (serious or humorous) in which you explain your process of writing and revision. Include a thesis statement that assesses the effectiveness of your writing process.

2. Write a set of instructions in which your goal is to convince a beginning writer of the importance of revision. Include an illustration like the one that follows paragraph 6 in Trudeau's essay.

3. Record the process of writing your own topical joke. Begin with an idea "literally torn from the headlines," and include a thesis statement that comments on how difficult the process is.

COMBINING THE PATTERNS

Although Trudeau's essay is structured as a process, he uses **exemplification** throughout his discussion. Why are examples so important to this essay?

THEMATIC CONNECTIONS

- "The Open Window" (page 113)
- "Television: The Plug-In Drug" (page 283)
- "The Ways We Lie" (page 426)

ALAN LIGHTMAN

Alan Lightman, born in Memphis, Tennessee, in 1948, received his under-graduate degree from Princeton University and earned a Ph.D. in theoretical physics from the California Institute of Technology. He has taught astronomy at Harvard and was a research scientist at the Harvard-Smithsonian Center for Astrophysics. However, Lightman has always been interested in the humanities as well as in science. (As a child, he built rockets but also wrote poetry.) Having written several textbooks, Lightman branched out in the early 1980s to reach a more popular audience, publishing articles in *Smithsonian* magazine. Since then, his essays and short fiction have appeared in numerous general-interest periodicals. In addition to three collections of essays and several books on scientific subjects, he has published two novels, including the widely acclaimed *Einstein's Dreams* (1993). In 1989, he joined the faculty of the Massachusetts Institute of Technology as a professor of science and writing and as a senior lecturer in physics.

In "Smile," which was most recently collected in his *Dance for Two: Essays* (1996), Lightman relies on his scientific expertise to explain the sensory processes of seeing and hearing. By focusing on a chance meeting between a man and a woman, however, he takes the physics of these processes a step further to hint at larger human mysteries.

Smile

It is a Saturday in March. The man wakes up slowly, reaches over and feels the windowpane, and decides it is warm enough to skip his thermal underwear. He yawns and dresses and goes out for his morning jog. When he comes back, he showers, cooks himself a scrambled egg, and settles down on the sofa with *The Essays of E. B. White*. Around noon, he rides his bike to the bookstore. He spends a couple of hours there, just poking around the books. Then he pedals back through the little town, past his house, and to the lake.

When the woman woke up this morning, she got out of bed and went immediately to her easel, where she picked up her pastels and set to work on her painting. After an hour, she is satisfied with the light effect and quits to have breakfast. She dresses quickly and walks to a nearby store to buy shutters for her bathroom. At the store, she meets friends and has lunch with them. Afterward, she wants to be alone and drives to the lake.

Now, the man and the woman stand on the wooden dock, gazing at the lake and the waves on the water. They haven't noticed each other.

The man turns. And so begins the sequence of events informing him of her. Light reflected from her body instantly enters the pupils of his eyes, at the rate of ten trillion particles of light per second. Once through the pupil of each eye, the light travels through an oval-shaped lens, then through a transparent, jellylike substance filling up the eyeball, and lands on the retina. Here it is gathered by one hundred million rod and cone cells.

Cells in the path of reflected highlights receive a great deal of light;   5
cells falling in the shadows of the reflected scene receive very little. The woman's lips, for example, are just now glistening in the sunlight, reflecting light of high intensity onto a tiny patch of cells slightly northeast of back center of the man's retina. The edges around her mouth, on the other hand, are rather dark, so that cells neighboring the northeast patch receive much less light.

Each particle of light ends its journey in the eye upon meeting a   6
retinene molecule, consisting of 20 carbon atoms, 28 hydrogen atoms, and 1 oxygen atom. In its dormant condition, each retinene molecule is attached to a protein molecule and has a twist between the eleventh and fifteenth carbon atoms. But when light strikes it, as is now happening in about 30,000 trillion retinene molecules every second, the molecule straightens out and separates from its protein. After several intermediate steps, it wraps into a twist again, awaiting arrival of a new particle of light. Far less than a thousandth of a second has elapsed since the man saw the woman.

Triggered by the dance of the retinene molecules, the nerve cells, or   7
neurons, respond. First in the eye and then in the brain. One neuron, for instance, has just gone into action. Protein molecules on its surface suddenly change their shape, blocking the flow of positively charged sodium atoms from the surrounding body fluid. This change in flow of electrically charged atoms produces a change in voltage that shudders through the cell. After a distance of a fraction of an inch, the electrical signal reaches the end of the neuron, altering the release of specific molecules, which migrate a distance of a hundred-thousandths of an inch until they reach the next neuron, passing along the news.

The woman, in fact, holds her hands by her sides and tilts her head at   8
an angle of five and a half degrees. Her hair falls just to her shoulders. This information and much, much more is exactingly encoded by the electrical pulses in the various neurons of the man's eyes.

In another few thousandths of a second, the electrical signals reach the   9
ganglion neurons, which bunch together in the optic nerve at the back of the eye and carry their data to the brain. Here, the impulses race to the primary visual cortex, a highly folded layer of tissue about a tenth of an inch thick and two square inches in area, containing one hundred million neurons in half a dozen layers. The fourth layer receives the input first, does a preliminary analysis, and transfers the information to neurons in other layers. At every stage, each neuron may receive signals from a thousand other neurons, combine the signals — some of which cancel each other out — and dispatch the computed result to a thousand-odd other neurons.

After about thirty seconds — after several hundred trillion particles   10
of reflected light have entered the man's eyes and been processed — the woman says hello. Immediately, molecules of air are pushed together,

then apart, then together, beginning in her vocal cords and traveling in a springlike motion to the man's ears. The sound makes the trip from her to him (twenty feet) in a fiftieth of a second.

Within each of his ears, the vibrating air quickly covers the distance to   11
the eardrum. The eardrum, an oval membrane about .3 inch in diameter and tilted fifty-five degrees from the floor of the auditory canal, itself begins trembling and transmits its motion to three tiny bones. From there, the vibrations shake the fluid in the cochlea, which spirals snail-like two and a half turns around.

Inside the cochlea the tones are deciphered. Here, a very thin mem-   12
brane undulates in step with the sloshing fluid, and through this basilar membrane run tiny filaments of varying thicknesses, like strings on a harp. The woman's voice, from afar, is playing this harp. Her hello begins in the low registers and rises in pitch toward the end. In precise response, the thick filaments in the basilar membrane vibrate first, followed by the thinner ones. Finally, tens of thousands of rod-shaped bodies perched on the basilar membrane convey their particular quiverings to the auditory nerve.

News of the woman's hello, in electrical form, races along the neurons   13
of the auditory nerve and enters the man's brain, through the thalamus, to a specialized region of the cerebral cortex for further processing. Eventually, a large fraction of the trillion neurons in the man's brain become involved with computing the visual and auditory data just acquired. Sodium and potassium gates open and close. Electrical currents speed along neuron fibers. Molecules flow from one nerve ending to the next.

All of this is known. What is not known is why, after about a minute,   14
the man walks over to the woman and smiles.

•   •   •

COMPREHENSION

1. What process does Lightman describe?

2. What are the most important stages of the process?

3. What is the outcome of the process? Do you think the outcome could have been different? Explain.

PURPOSE AND AUDIENCE

1. This essay describes a scientific process, but it is directed at a popular audience. What concessions does Lightman make to this audience?

2. This essay's general purpose is to provide information. Do you think Lightman had another purpose in mind as well? Explain.

3. Does this essay include an explicitly stated thesis? If so, where? If not, why not?

STYLE AND STRUCTURE

1. Where does the actual discussion of the process begin? How does Lightman signal the start of the process to his readers?

2. What function is served by paragraph 3? By paragraphs 1 and 2?

3. What transitional words and phrases help readers move through the process? Do you think more transitions should be added? If so, where?

4. Is "Smile" a misleading title for this essay, or is it appropriate? Explain.

5. What verb tense does Lightman use in his explanation of the process? Why does he use this tense?

6. List the major stages in the process Lightman describes. Notice that he does *not* use phrases like "the next step" to introduce these stages. Should he have done so? What signals does he use instead?

VOCABULARY PROJECTS

1. Define each of the following words as it is used in this selection.

   retinene (6)   auditory (11)   filaments (12)
   ganglion (9)   cochlea (11)   registers (12)
   cortex (9)   undulates (12)

2. In paragraph 4, Lightman uses a distinctly unscientific term — *jellylike* — to characterize a substance. Where else does he use such informal language in a scientific context?

JOURNAL ENTRY

What do you suppose happens when the process Lightman describes is complete? What new process (or processes) might now begin?

WRITING WORKSHOP

1. Write a process explanation that traces the steps presented in "Smile" from the point of view of the man or the woman. Use the first person ("I") and the past tense to describe the stages of the encounter. Omit all scientific terminology.

2. Beginning with Lightman's paragraph 3, retell this process, focusing on psychological rather than biological reactions. Try to supply what is missing —"what is not known" (paragraph 14) — from Lightman's process.

3. Continue the process. Building on your response to the Journal Entry question, trace the steps in a process that might follow the one Lightman describes. Focus on the psychological interaction between the man and the woman, naming and describing them in your introductory paragraphs.

COMBINING THE PATTERNS

Although this essay is structured as a process, Lightman uses a good deal of **description** as well. Is this description primarily *subjective* or *objective*? Do you think this kind of description is appropriate for Lightman's audience?

THEMATIC CONNECTIONS

- "Words Left Unspoken" (page 133)
- "Just Walk On By" (page 197)
- "Sex, Lies, and Conversation" (page 367)

LARRY BROWN

Larry Brown (1951–) was born into a farming family in Oxford, Mississippi. After serving as a marine during the Vietnam War, he attended the University of Mississippi and held a variety of odd jobs until he joined the Oxford Fire Department in 1973. Promoted to captain in 1986, Brown retired from fire-fighting in 1990 in order to pursue full time a writing career that had begun in 1986 with the publication of a collection of short stories, *Facing the Music*. This book was followed by the novel *Dirty Work* (1989), as well as *Joe* (1991) and *Father and Son* (1996), both of which won the Southern Book Critics' Award for fiction. Brown is noted for his sharply realistic stories of the rural South, which focus on working-class characters struggling with dead-end jobs, alcoholism, and family conflict.

On *Fire: A Personal Account of Life and Death and Choices* (1994), Brown's only work of nonfiction to date, is a series of diary-like entries about his life as a firefighter in a small town. The following selection from that book provides an unusual example of process writing. Rather than describing the stages of a single activity, Brown offers an impressionistic account of the many facets of a firefighter's job. Note that he writes in the second person throughout, a rarely used device that is nonetheless suitable in this context.

On Fire

You learn early to go in low, that heat and smoke rise into the ceiling, that cooler air is near the floor. You learn to button your collar tightly around your neck, to pull the gauntlets of your gloves up over the cuffs of your coat, that embers can go anywhere skin is exposed. You learn that you are only human flesh, not Superman, and that you can burn like a candle.

You try to go easy on the air that's inside the tank on your back, try to be calm and not overly exert yourself, try and save some of your strength. You learn about exhaustion and giving it all you've got, then having to reach back and pull up some more. Suck it up and go.

You learn eventually not to let your legs tremble when you're pressing hard on the gas or the diesel pedal, when you're driving into something that is unknown.

One day if you make rank you will be promoted to driver or pump operator or lieutenant and you will discover what it feels like to roll up to a burning structure, a house that somebody lives in, or a university dormitory where hundreds of people live, or a business upon whose commerce somebody's livelihood depends. You will change in that moment, stop being a nozzleman and become instead the operator of the apparatus the nozzlemen are pulling lines from, and you will know then that the knowledge pushed into your head at dry training sessions in the fire station must now be applied to practical use, quickly, with no mistakes, because there are men you know whose lives are going to depend on a steady supply of water, at the right pressure, for as long as it takes to put the fire out.

And on that first time you'll probably be like I was, scared shitless. But 5 you can't let that stop you from doing your job.

You learn the difficulty of raising a ladder and pulling the rope and 6 raising the extensions up to a second-floor window, and the difficulty of climbing that ladder with a charged inch-and-a-half line and then opening it and staying on the ladder without falling.

You learn of ropes and safety belts, insulated gloves to move downed 7 high-voltage lines, nozzle pressure and friction loss and the rule of thumb for a two-and-a-half-inch nozzle. You learn to check the flow pressure on a fire hydrant and what burning plastic tastes like, the way it will make you gag and cough and puke when those fumes get into your lungs and you know that something very bad has come inside your body. You see death and hear the sounds of the injured. Some days you look at the fire phone and have a bad feeling, smoke more cigarettes, glance at the phone, and sometimes it rings. Sometimes you're wrong and the night passes without trouble.

You learn to love a job that is not like sacking groceries or working in a 8 factory or painting houses, because everybody watches you when you come down the street. You wear a blue uniform with silver or brass or gold, and you get free day-old doughnuts from the bakery shop down the street. At Christmas people bring in pies, cakes, cookies, ham, smoked sausage, cheese, half-pints of whiskey. They thank you for your work in a season of good cheer. One freezing December night the whole department gathers with eighty steaks and Wally parks his wheeled cooker and dumps in sixty or seventy pounds of charcoal to cook them and you have drinks and play Bingo for prizes that businesses in your town have donated, a rechargeable flashlight from the auto supply, a hot-air popcorn popper from a department store, a case of beer from the grocery down the street.

You lay out hose in the deadly summer heat on a street with no shade, 9 hook it all up, hundreds and hundreds of feet of it, put closed nozzles on the end of the hose, and run the pressure up to three hundred psi* and hold it for five minutes. If a piece bursts and creates a waterstorm on the street, you remove that section from the line and throw it away. Then you shut it down and drain it and write down the identification number of every piece of hose that survived the test and put it all back on the truck, thirteen hundred feet of it, and you make new bends and turns so the rubber coating inside it won't kink and start to dry-rot.

You learn the major arteries of the body and the names of the bones 10 and how to splint a leg or an arm, how to tie off and cut an umbilical cord. You learn to read blood pressure, administer oxygen. You see amounts of blood that are unbelievable, not realizing until it's actually spilled how

---

*Eds. note — Pounds per square inch.

much the human body holds. You crawl up under taxpayers' houses for their dogs, go inside culverts where snakes may be hiding for their cats. You learn to do whatever is called for.

No two days are ever the same and you're thankful for that. You dread   11
the winter and the advent of ice. On an August day you pray that the city will behave and let you lie under the air conditioner and read a good book, draw easy money.

You learn that your muscles and bones and tendons get older and that   12
you cannot remain young forever. You test the pump on the truck every day when you come on duty, make sure it's full of fuel, clean, full of water, that the extinguishers are up. You check that your turnouts* are all together, hanging on the hook that has your name written above it, and that both your gloves are in your coat pocket. You make sure your flashlight works. You test the siren and the lights because everything has to be in readiness. You shut it all down and stand back and look at the deep red Imron paint, the gold leafing and lettering, the chrome valves and caps, the shiny chains and levers, the fluid-filled pressure gauges, the beds filled with woven nylon, the nozzles folded back into layers of hose, the hydrant wrenches snug in their holders, everything on this magnificent machine. You learn every inch of your truck and you know which compartments hold the forcible entry tools, the exhaust fans for removing smoke from a house, the power saws, the portable generator, the pike poles, the scoops, the salvage covers, the boltcutters, the axes, the ropes, the rappelling gear. You look at all of it over and over again and then you go inside the fire station and get a cup of coffee, sit down with a magazine or a newspaper, and once more, you wait for whatever comes your way.

• • •

COMPREHENSION

1. What process does Brown describe?

2. Into what general stages can you group the individual steps in the process?

3. Does Brown seem to consider some steps more important than others? If so, how does he indicate this?

4. What does Brown see as the good and bad points of his job?

PURPOSE AND AUDIENCE

1. For whom is this essay intended? Firefighters? A general audience? How can you tell?

2. What impressions of firefighting does Brown wish to convey? Do you think he achieves his purpose?

---

*Eds. note — Firefighter's apparel.

3. Does this essay have an explicitly stated thesis? If so, where is it? Do you think an explicit thesis statement is necessary here?

STYLE AND STRUCTURE

1. What words and phrases are repeated in this essay? Do these repetitions strengthen or weaken the essay? Explain your reasoning.

2. In paragraph 1, Brown uses a **simile** when he says that one of the things firefighters learn is that they "can burn like a candle." Where else does he use similes or other **figures of speech?** How does such language enhance the essay?

3. Brown uses a variety of stylistic devices in his essay. Comment on the effectiveness of each of these devices: sentence fragments; contractions; long, rhythmic sentences; juxtaposition of long and short paragraphs; repeated phrases.

4. How do you interpret the essay's title? Do you think Brown intends it to have more than one meaning?

5. Throughout his essay, Brown repeatedly uses the pronoun *you*. Some readers might find this usage too general or too informal for a discussion of such a serious subject. Why do you suppose Brown chooses this pronoun instead of the more usual *I* or *he*? Does *you* refer to his readers? Explain.

6. How is this essay like and unlike the typical process explanation? For example, does it include steps presented in chronological order? A list of materials and equipment? Warnings and cautions? How do you account for any departures from the typical process explanation?

7. Is paragraph 8 a digression, or is it part of the process? Explain.

VOCABULARY PROJECTS

1. Define each of the following words as it is used in this selection.
   gauntlets (1)   advent (11)
   culverts (10)   rappelling (12)

2. Brown uses **slang,** professional **jargon,** and impolite language in this essay. Identify one or two examples of each, and explain why it is used instead of a more formal, neutral, or polite term.

JOURNAL ENTRY

Brown clearly has mixed feelings about his job. What conflicting emotions do you see in his essay?

WRITING WORKSHOP

1. Recast "On Fire" as a letter of application for a position with a different fire department or as an application for promotion. Use process to struc-

ture the body of the essay, and write in the first person and the present tense. Try to be somewhat less emotional and subjective than Brown, but be sure to stress how valuable an employee you have been.

2. Write a process essay about a difficult job you have (or have had). As you explain your day-to-day routine, try to convey the challenges of your job to readers.

3. Use the material in Brown's essay to help you write a set of instructions directed at firefighter trainees. Be honest about the tasks required, and try to balance the positive and negative aspects of the job.

COMBINING THE PATTERNS

In paragraph 8, Brown comments that firefighting is "a job that is not like sacking groceries or working in a factory or painting houses, because everybody watches you when you come down the street," but he does not go beyond this comment to compare firefighting to other occupations. Do you think this essay would be strengthened if it began or ended with a **comparison-and-contrast** paragraph that explained exactly how different firefighting is from other jobs? How would the addition of such an opening or closing paragraph change the essay?

THEMATIC CONNECTIONS

- "Reading the River" (page 138)
- "Midnight" (page 177)
- "The Men We Carry in Our Minds" (page 399)

JESSICA MITFORD

Jessica Mitford (1917–1996) was born in Batsford Mansion, England, to a wealthy, aristocratic family. She rebelled against her sheltered upbringing, became involved in left-wing politics, and eventually immigrated to the United States. Mitford wrote two volumes of autobiography, *Daughters and Rebels* (1960), about her eccentric family, and *A Fine Old Conflict* (1976). In the 1950s, she began a career in investigative journalism, which produced the books *The American Way of Death* (1963), about abuses in the funeral business; *Kind and Unusual Punishment* (1973), on the U.S. prison system; and *The American Way of Birth* (1992), about the crisis in American obstetrical care.

"The Embalming of Mr. Jones" is excerpted from *The American Way of Death*. This scathing critique of the funeral industry was prompted, Mitford said, by her realization that her lawyer-husband's poorer clients had almost nothing left in their estates after funeral costs were paid. The book provoked angry responses from morticians but also led to greater government oversight of the industry. In fact, an inexpensive coffin manufactured in response to the controversy was — perhaps sarcastically — dubbed the "Jessica Mitford casket" by its maker. In this selection, Mitford painstakingly (and ironically) describes the dual processes of embalming and restoring a cadaver. (Mitford's own funeral plans called for a $475 cremation.)

The Embalming of Mr. Jones

Embalming is indeed a most extraordinary procedure, and one must wonder at the docility of Americans who each year pay hundreds of millions of dollars for its perpetuation, blissfully ignorant of what it is all about, what is done, how it is done. Not one in ten thousand has any idea of what actually takes place. Books on the subject are extremely hard to come by. They are not to be found in most libraries or bookshops. 1

In an era when huge television audiences watch surgical operations in the comfort of their living rooms, when, thanks to the animated cartoon, the geography of the digestive system has become familiar territory even to the nursery school set, in a land where the satisfaction of curiosity about almost all matters is a national pastime, the secrecy surrounding embalming can, surely, hardly be attributed to the inherent gruesomeness of the subject. Custom in this regard has within this century suffered a complete reversal. In the early days of American embalming, when it was performed in the home of the deceased, it was almost mandatory for some relative to stay by the embalmer's side and witness the procedure. Today, family members who might wish to be in attendance would certainly be dissuaded by the funeral director. All others, except apprentices, are excluded by law from the preparation room. 2

A close look at what does actually take place may explain in large measure the undertaker's intractable reticence concerning a procedure 3 that has become his major *raison d'être.** Is it possible he fears that public information about embalming might lead patrons to wonder if they really want this service? If the funeral men are loath to discuss the subject outside the trade, the reader may, understandably, be equally loath to go on reading at this point. For those who have the stomach for it, let us part the formaldehyde curtain. . . .

The body is first laid out in the undertaker's morgue — or rather, Mr. Jones is reposing in the preparation room — to be readied to bid the world farewell.   4

The preparation room in any of the better funeral establishments has the tiled and sterile look of a surgery, and indeed the embalmer-restorative artist who does his chores there is beginning to adopt the term "dermasurgeon" (appropriately corrupted by some mortician-writers as "demisurgeon") to describe his calling. His equipment, consisting of scalpels, scissors, augers, forceps, clamps, needles, pumps, tubes, bowls, and basin, is crudely imitative of the surgeon's as is his technique, acquired in a nine- or twelve-month post-high-school course in an embalming school. He is supplied by an advanced chemical industry with a bewildering array of fluids, sprays, pastes, oils, powders, creams, to fix or soften tissue, shrink or distend it as needed, dry it here, restore the moisture there. There are cosmetics, waxes, and paints to fill and cover features, even plaster of Paris to replace entire limbs. There are ingenious aids to prop and stabilize the cadaver: a Vari-Pose Head Rest, the Edwards Arm and Hand Positioner, the Repose Block (to support the shoulders during the embalming), and the Throop Foot Positioner, which resembles an old-fashioned stocks.   5

Mr. John H. Eckels, president of the Eckels College of Mortuary Science, thus describes the first part of the embalming procedure: "In the hands of a skilled practitioner, this work may be done in a comparatively short time and without mutilating the body other than by slight incision — so slight that it scarcely would cause serious inconvenience if made upon a living person. It is necessary to remove all the blood, and doing this not only helps in the disinfecting, but removes the principal cause of disfigurements due to discoloration."   6

Another textbook discusses the all-important time element: "The earlier this is done, the better, for every hour that elapses between death and embalming will add to the problems and complications encountered. . . ." Just how soon should one get going on the embalming? The author tells us, "On the basis of such scanty information made available to this profession through its rudimentary and haphazard system of technical research, we must conclude that the best results are to be obtained if the subject is embalmed before life is completely extinct — that is, before cellular death has occurred. In the average case, this would mean within an hour after somatic death." For those who feel that there is something a little   7

*EDS. NOTE — French expression meaning "reason for being."

rudimentary, not to say haphazard, about this advice, a comforting thought is offered by another writer. Speaking of fears entertained in early days of premature burial, he points out, "One of the effects of embalming by chemical injection, however, has been to dispel fears of live burial." How true; once the blood is removed, chances of live burial are indeed remote.

To return to Mr. Jones, the blood is drained out through the veins and   8 replaced by embalming fluid pumped in through the arteries. As noted in *The Principles and Practices of Embalming,* "every operator has a favorite injection and drainage point — a fact which becomes a handicap only if he fails or refuses to forsake his favorites when conditions demand it." Typical favorites are the carotid artery, femoral artery, jugular vein, subclavian vein. There are various choices of embalming fluid. If Flextone is used, it will produce a "mild, flexible rigidity. The skin retains a velvety softness, the tissues are rubbery and pliable. Ideal for women and children." It may be blended with B. and G. Products Company's Lyf-Lyk tint, which is guaranteed to reproduce "nature's own skin texture . . . the velvety appearance of living tissue." Suntone comes in three separate tints: Suntan; Special Cosmetic Tint, a pink shade "especially indicated for young female subjects"; and Regular Cosmetic Tint, moderately pink.

About three to six gallons of a dyed and perfumed solution of for-   9 maldehyde, glycerin, borax, phenol, alcohol, and water is soon circulating through Mr. Jones, whose mouth has been sewn together with a "needle directed upward between the upper lip and gum and brought out through the left nostril," with the corners raised slightly "for a more pleasant expression." If he should be buck-toothed, his teeth are cleaned with Bon Ami and coated with colorless nail polish. His eyes, meanwhile, are closed with flesh-tinted eye caps and eye cement.

The next step is to have at Mr. Jones with a thing called a trocar. This is   10 a long, hollow needle attached to a tube. It is jabbed into the abdomen, poked around the entrails and chest cavity, the contents of which are pumped out and replaced with "cavity fluid." This done, and the hole in the abdomen sewed up, Mr. Jones's face is heavily creamed (to protect the skin from burns which may be caused by leakage of the chemicals), and he is covered with a sheet and left unmolested for a while. But not for long — there is more, much more, in store for him. He has been embalmed, but not yet restored, and the best time to start restorative work is eight to ten hours after embalming, when the tissues have become firm and dry.

The object of all this attention to the corpse, it must be remembered, is   11 to make it presentable for viewing in an attitude of healthy repose. "Our customs require the presentation of our dead in the semblance of normality . . . unmarred by the ravages of illness, disease or mutilation," says Mr. J. Sheridan Mayer in his *Restorative Art.* This is rather a large order since few people die in the full bloom of health, unravaged by illness and unmarked by some disfigurement. The funeral industry is equal to the challenge: "In some cases the gruesome appearance of a mutilated or disease-ridden subject may be quite discouraging. The task of restoration may seem impossible and shake the confidence of the embalmer. This is the time for intestinal fortitude and determination. Once the formative work is begun and affected tissues are cleaned or removed, all doubts of success vanish. It is surprising and gratifying to discover the results which may be obtained."

The embalmer, having allowed an appropriate interval to elapse, 12 returns to the attack, but now he brings into play the skill and equipment of sculptor and cosmetician. Is a hand missing? Casting one in plaster of Paris is a simple matter. "For replacement purposes, only a cast of the back of the hand is necessary; this is within the ability of the average operator and is quite adequate." If a lip or two, a nose or an ear should be missing, the embalmer has at hand a variety of restorative waxes with which to model replacements. Pores and skin texture are simulated by stippling with a little brush, and over this cosmetics are laid on. Head off? Decapitation cases are rather routinely handled. Ragged edges are trimmed, and head joined to torso with a series of splints, wires, and sutures. It is a good idea to have a little something at the neck — a scarf or high collar — when time for viewing comes. Swollen mouth? Cut out tissue as needed from inside the lips. If too much is removed, the surface contour can easily be restored by padding with cotton. Swollen necks and cheeks are reduced by removing tissue through vertical incisions made down each side of the neck. "When the deceased is casketed, the pillow will hide the suture incisions. . . . as an extra precaution against leakage, the suture may be painted with liquid sealer."

The opposite condition is more likely to be present itself — that of 13 emaciation. His hypodermic syringe now loaded with massage cream, the embalmer seeks out and fills the hollowed and sunken areas by injection. In this procedure the backs of the hands and fingers and the underchin area should not be neglected.

Positioning the lips is a problem that recurrently challenges the inge- 14 nuity of the embalmer. Closed too tightly, they tend to give a stern, even disapproving expression. Ideally, embalmers feel, the lips should give the impression of being ever so slightly parted, the upper lip protruding slightly for a more youthful appearance. This takes some engineering, however, as the lips tend to drift apart. Lip drift can sometimes be remedied by pushing one or two straight pins through the inner margin of the lower lip and then inserting them between the two front upper teeth. If Mr. Jones happens to have no teeth, the pins can just as easily be anchored in his Armstrong Face Former and Denture Replacer. Another method to maintain lip closure is to dislocate the lower jaw, which is then held in its new position by a wire run through holes which have been drilled through the upper jaws at the midline. As the French are fond of saying, *il faut souffrir pour être belle.**

---

*Eds. note — It is necessary to suffer in order to be beautiful.

If Mr. Jones has died of jaundice, the embalming fluid will very likely   15
turn him green. Does this deter the embalmer? Not if he has intestinal fortitude. Masking pastes and cosmetics are heavily laid on, burial garments
and casket interiors are color-correlated with particular care, and Jones
is displayed beneath rose-colored lights. Friends will say, "How *well* he
looks." Death by carbon monoxide, on the other hand, can be rather a
good thing from an embalmer's viewpoint: "One advantage is the fact
that this type of discoloration is an exaggerated form of a natural pink
coloration." This is nice because the healthy glow is already present and
needs but little attention.

The patching and filling completed, Mr. Jones is now shaved, washed,   16
and dressed. Cream-based cosmetic, available in pink, flesh, suntan,
brunette, and blonde, is applied to his hands and face, his hair is sham-
pooed and combed (and, in the case of Mrs. Jones, set), his hands manicured. For the horny-handed son of toil special care must be taken; cream
should be applied to remove ingrained grime, and the nails cleaned. "If he
were not in the habit of having them manicured in life, trimming and
shaping is advised for better appearance — never questioned by kin."

Jones is now ready for casketing (this is the present participle of the   17
verb "to casket"). In this operation his right shoulder should be depressed
slightly "to turn the body a bit to the right and soften the appearance of
lying flat on the back." Positioning the hands is a matter of importance,
and special rubber positioning blocks may be used. The hands should be
cupped slightly for a more lifelike, relaxed appearance. Proper placement
of the body requires a delicate sense of balance. It should lie as high as
possible in the casket, yet not so high that the lid, when lowered, will hit
the nose. On the other hand, we are cautioned, placing the body too low
"creates the impression that the body is in a box."

Jones is next wheeled into the appointed slumber room where a few   18
last touches may be added — his favorite pipe placed in his hand or, if he
was a great reader, a book propped into position. (In the case of little Master Jones a Teddy bear may be clutched.) Here he will hold open house for
a few days, visiting hours 10 A.M. to 9 P.M.

• • •

COMPREHENSION

1. How, according to Mitford, has the public's knowledge of embalming
   changed? How does she explain this change?

2. To what other professionals does Mitford liken the embalmer? Are these
   analogies flattering or critical? Explain.

3. What are the major stages in the process of embalming and restoration?

PURPOSE AND AUDIENCE

1. Mitford's purpose in this essay is to convince her audience of something.
   What is her thesis?

2. Do you think Mitford expects her audience to agree with her thesis? How can you tell?

3. In one of her books, Mitford refers to herself as a *muckraker,* one who informs the public of misconduct. Does she achieve this status here? Cite specific examples.

4. Mitford's tone in this essay is very subjective, even judgmental. What effect does her tone have on you? Does it encourage you to trust her? Should she present her facts in a more objective way? Explain.

STYLE AND STRUCTURE

1. Identify the stylistic features that distinguish this process explanation from a set of instructions.

2. In this selection, as in many process essays, a list of necessary materials comes before the procedure. What additional details does Mitford include in her list in paragraph 5? How do these additions affect you?

3. Go through the essay and locate Mitford's remarks about the language of embalming. How do her comments about euphemisms, newly coined words, and other aspects of language help to support her thesis?

4. Throughout the essay, Mitford quotes various experts. How does she use their remarks to support her thesis?

5. What phrases serve as transitions between the various stages of Mitford's process?

6. Mitford uses a good deal of sarcasm and loaded language in this essay. Identify some examples. Does this kind of language strengthen or weaken her essay?

VOCABULARY PROJECTS

1. Define each of the following words as it is used in this selection.

perpetuation (1)	rudimentary (7)	stippling (12)
inherent (2)	haphazard (7)	emaciation (13)
mandatory (2)	entertained (7)	recurrently (14)
dissuaded (2)	pliable (8)	jaundice (15)
intractable (3)	repose (11)	toil (16)
reticence (3)	unravaged (11)	
loath (3)	fortitude (11)	

2. Substitute another word for each of the following.

territory (2)	ingenious (5)	presentable (11)
gruesomeness (2)	jabbed (10)	

What effect does each of your changes have on Mitford's meaning?

3. Reread paragraphs 5–9 very carefully. Then list all the words in this section of the essay that suggest surgical technique and all the words that suggest cosmetic artistry. What do your lists tell you about Mitford's intent in these paragraphs?

JOURNAL ENTRY

What are your thoughts about the way your religion or culture deals with death and dying? What practices, if any, make you uncomfortable? Why?

WRITING WORKSHOP

1. Rewrite this process explanation as a set of instructions for undertakers, condensing it so that your essay is about five hundred words long. Unlike Mitford, keep your essay objective.

2. In the role of a funeral director, write a letter to Mitford in which you take issue with her essay. Explain the practice of embalming as necessary and practical. Unlike Mitford, design your process explanation to defend the practice.

3. Write an explanation of a process that you personally find disgusting — or delightful. Make your attitude clear in your thesis statement and in your choice of words.

COMBINING THE PATTERNS

Although Mitford structures this essay as a process, many passages rely heavily on subjective **description.** Where is her focus on descriptive details most obvious? What is her purpose in describing particular individuals and objects as she does? How do these descriptive passages help to support her essay's thesis?

THEMATIC CONNECTIONS

- "English Is a Crazy Language" (page 192)
- "My First Conk" (page 228)
- "The Ways We Lie" (page 426)
- "The Secretary Chant" (page 488)

SHIRLEY JACKSON

Shirley Jackson (1919–1965) was born in California and graduated from Syracuse University in 1940. She is best known for her subtly macabre stories of horror and suspense, most notably her best-selling novel *The Haunting of Hill House* (1959), which Stephen King has called "one of the greatest horror stories of all time." She also published wryly humorous reflections on her experiences as a wife and mother of four children. Many of her finest stories and novels were anthologized after her death.

"The Lottery" first appeared in *The New Yorker* in 1948, three years after the end of World War II. Jackson, the wife of a professor interested in anthropology, was living somewhat uneasily in the New England college town of Bennington, Vermont, a village very similar to the setting of "The Lottery." She felt herself an outsider there in many ways: a sophisticated intellectual in an isolated, closely knit community suspicious of strangers. Here, Jackson, whose husband was Jewish, experienced frequent encounters with anti-Semitism; moreover, the full atrocity of Germany's wartime program to exterminate Jews, now called the Holocaust, had led many social critics to contemplate humanity's terrible capacity for evil. Most Americans of the time, however, wished to put the horrors of the war behind them, and many readers reacted with outrage to Jackson's tale of an annual small-town ritual, calling it "nasty," "nauseating," even "perverted." Others immediately recognized its genius, its power, and its many layers of meaning. This classic is now one of the most widely anthologized of twentieth-century short stories.

The Lottery

The morning of June 27th was clear and sunny, with the fresh warmth of a full-summer day; the flowers were blossoming profusely and the grass was richly green. The people of the village began to gather in the square, between the post office and the bank, around ten o'clock; in some towns there were so many people that the lottery took two days and had to be started on June 26th, but in this village, where there were only about three hundred people, the whole lottery took less than two hours, so it could begin at ten o'clock in the morning and still be through in time to allow the villagers to get home for noon dinner.

The children assembled first, of course. School was recently over for the summer, and the feeling of liberty sat uneasily on most of them; they tended to gather together quietly for a while before they broke into boisterous play, and their talk was still of the classroom and the teacher, of books and reprimands. Bobby Martin had already stuffed his pockets full of stones, and the other boys soon followed his example, selecting the smoothest and roundest stones; Bobby and Harry Jones and Dickie Delacroix — the villagers pronounced his name "Dellacroy"— eventually made a great pile of stones in one corner of the square and guarded it against the raids of the other boys. The girls stood aside, talking among themselves, looking over their shoulders at the boys, and the very small children rolled in the dust or clung to the hands of their older brothers or sisters.

Soon the men began to gather, surveying their own children, speaking   3 of planting and rain, tractors and taxes. They stood together, away from the pile of stones in the corner, and their jokes were quiet and they smiled rather than laughed. The women, wearing faded house dresses and sweaters, came shortly after their menfolk. They greeted one another and exchanged bits of gossip as they went to join their husbands. Soon the women, standing by their husbands, began to call to their children, and the children came reluctantly, having to be called four or five times. Bobby Martin ducked under his mother's grasping hand and ran, laughing, back to the pile of stones. His father spoke up sharply, and Bobby came quickly and took his place between his father and his oldest brother.

The lottery was conducted — as were the square dances, the teenage   4 club, the Halloween program — by Mr. Summers, who had time and energy to devote to civic activities. He was a round-faced, jovial man and he ran the coal business, and people were sorry for him, because he had no children and his wife was a scold. When he arrived in the square, carrying the black wooden box, there was a murmur of conversation among the villagers, and he waved and called "Little late today, folks." The postmaster, Mr. Graves, followed him, carrying a three-legged stool, and the stool was put in the center of the square and Mr. Summers set the black box down on it. The villagers kept their distance, leaving a space between themselves and the stool, and when Mr. Summers said, "Some of you fellows want to give me a hand?" there was a hesitation before two men, Mr. Martin and his oldest son, Baxter, came forward to hold the box steady on the stool while Mr. Summers stirred up the papers inside it.

The original paraphernalia for the lottery had been lost long ago, and   5 the black box now resting on the stool had been put into use even before Old Man Warner, the oldest man in town, was born. Mr. Summers spoke frequently to the villagers about making a new box, but no one liked to upset even as much tradition as was represented by the black box. There was a story that the present box had been made with some pieces of the box that had preceded it, the one that had been constructed when the first people settled down to make a village here. Every year, after the lottery, Mr. Summers began talking about a new box, but every year the subject was allowed to fade off without anything's being done. The black box grew shabbier each year; by now it was no longer completely black but splintered badly along one side to show the original wood color, and in some places faded and stained.

Mr. Martin and his oldest son, Baxter, held the black box securely on   6 the stool until Mr. Summers had stirred the papers thoroughly with his hand. Because so much of the ritual had been forgotten or discarded, Mr. Summers had been successful in having slips of paper substituted for the chips of wood that had been used for generations. Chips of wood, Mr.

Summers had argued, had been all very well when the village was tiny, but now that the population was more than three hundred and likely to keep on growing, it was necessary to use something that would fit more easily into the black box. The night before the lottery, Mr. Summers and Mr. Graves made up the slips of paper and put them in the box, and it was then taken to the safe of Mr. Summers' coal company and locked up until Mr. Summers was ready to take it to the square the next morning. The rest of the year, the box was put away, sometimes one place, sometimes another; it had spent one year in Mr. Graves' barn and another year under-foot in the post office, and sometimes it was set on a shelf in the Martin grocery and left there.

There was a great deal of fussing to be done before Mr. Summers   7 declared the lottery open. There were the lists to make up — of heads of families, heads of households in each family, members of each household in each family. There was the proper swearing-in of Mr. Summers by the postmaster, as the official of the lottery; at one time, some people remembered, there had been a recital of some sort, performed by the official of the lottery, a perfunctory, tuneless chant that had been rattled off duly each year; some people believed that the official of the lottery used to stand just so when he said or sang it, others believed that he was supposed to walk among the people, but years and years ago this part of the ritual had been allowed to lapse. There had been, also, a ritual salute, which the official of the lottery had had to use in addressing each person who came up to draw from the box, but this also had changed with time, until now it was felt necessary only for the official to speak to each person approach-ing. Mr. Summers was very good at all this; in his clean white shirt and blue jeans, with one hand resting carelessly on the black box, he seemed very proper and important as he talked interminably to Mr. Graves and the Martins.

Just as Mr. Summers finally left off talking and turned to the assem-   8 bled villagers, Mrs. Hutchinson came hurriedly along the path to the square, her sweater thrown over her shoulders, and slid into place in the back of the crowd. "Clean forgot what day it was," she said to Mrs. Delacroix, who stood next to her, and they both laughed softly. "Thought my old man was out back stacking wood," Mrs. Hutchinson went on, "and then I looked out the window and the kids were gone, and then I remembered it was the twenty-seventh and came a-running." She dried her hands on her apron, and Mrs. Delacroix said, "You're in time, though. They're still talking away up there."

Mrs. Hutchinson craned her neck to see through the crowd and found   9 her husband and children standing near the front. She tapped Mrs. Delacroix on the arm as a farewell and began to make her way through the crowd. The people separated good-humoredly to let her through; two or three people said, in voices just loud enough to be heard across the crowd, "Here comes your Missus, Hutchinson," and "Bill, she made it after all." Mrs. Hutchinson reached her husband, and Mr. Summers, who had been waiting, said cheerfully, "Thought we were going to have to get on without you, Tessie." Mrs. Hutchinson said, grinning, "Wouldn't have me leave m'dishes in the sink, now, would you, Joe?" and soft laughter ran through the crowd as the people stirred back into position after Mrs. Hutchinson's arrival.

"Well, now," Mr. Summers said soberly, "guess we better get started, get this over with, so's we can go back to work. Anybody ain't here?"   10

"Dunbar," several people said. "Dunbar, Dunbar."   11

Mr. Summers consulted his list. "Clyde Dunbar," he said. "That's right. He's broke his leg, hasn't he? Who's drawing for him?"   12

"Me, I guess," a woman said, and Mr. Summers turned to look at her. "Wife draws for her husband," Mr. Summers said. "Don't you have a grown boy to do it for you, Janey?" Although Mr. Summers and everyone else in the village knew the answer perfectly well, it was the business of the official of the lottery to ask such questions formally. Mr. Summers waited with an expression of polite interest while Mrs. Dunbar answered.   13

"Horace's not but sixteen yet," Mrs. Dunbar said regretfully. "Guess I gotta fill in for the old man this year."   14

"Right," Mr. Summers said. He made a note on the list he was holding. Then he asked, "Watson boy drawing this year?"   15

A tall boy in the crowd raised his hand. "Here," he said. "I'm drawing for m'mother and me." He blinked his eyes nervously and ducked his head as several voices in the crowd said things like "Good fellow, Jack," and "Glad to see your mother's got a man to do it."   16

"Well," Mr. Summers said, "guess that's everyone. Old Man Warner make it?"   17

"Here," a voice said, and Mr. Summers nodded.   18

A sudden hush fell on the crowd as Mr. Summers cleared his throat and looked at the list. "All ready?" he called. "Now, I'll read the names — heads of families first — and the men come up and take a paper out of the box. Keep the paper folded in your hand without looking at it until everyone has had a turn. Everything clear?"   19

The people had done it so many times that they only half listened to the directions; most of them were quiet, wetting their lips, not looking around. Then Mr. Summers raised one hand high and said, "Adams." A man disengaged himself from the crowd and came forward. "Hi, Steve," Mr. Summers said, and Mr. Adams said, "Hi, Joe." They grinned at one another humorlessly and nervously. Then Mr. Adams reached into the black box and took out a folded paper. He held it firmly by one corner as he turned and went hastily back to his place in the crowd, where he stood a little apart from his family, not looking down at his hand.   20

"Allen." Mr. Summers said. "Anderson. . . . Betham."   21

"Seems like there's no time at all between lotteries any more," Mrs. Delacroix said to Mrs. Graves in the back row. "Seems like we got through the last one only last week."   22

"Time sure goes fast," Mrs. Graves said. 23

"Clark. . . . Delacroix." 24

"There goes my old man," Mrs. Delacroix said. She held her breath 25
while her husband went forward.

"Dunbar," Mr. Summers said, and Mrs. Dunbar went steadily to the 26
box while one of the women said, "Go on, Janey," and another said,
"There she goes."

"We're next," Mrs. Graves said. She watched while Mr. Graves came 27
around from the side of the box, greeted Mr. Summers gravely, and
selected a slip of paper from the box. By now, all through the crowd there
were men holding the small folded papers in their large hands, turning
them over and over nervously. Mrs. Dunbar and her two sons stood
together, Mrs. Dunbar holding the slip of paper.

"Harburt. . . . Hutchinson." 28

"Get up there, Bill," Mrs. Hutchinson said, and the people near her 29
laughed.

"Jones." 30

"They do say," Mr. Adams said to Old Man Warner, who stood next to 31
him, "that over in the north village they're talking of giving up the lottery."

Old Man Warner snorted. "Pack of crazy fools," he said. "Listening to 32
the young folks, nothing's good enough for *them*. Next thing you know,
they'll be wanting to go back to living in caves, nobody work any more,
live *that* way for a while. Used to be a saying about 'Lottery in June, corn
be heavy soon.' First thing you know, we'd all be eating stewed chickweed
and acorns. There's *always* been a lottery," he added petulantly. "Bad
enough to see young Joe Summers up there joking with everybody."

"Some places have already quit lotteries," Mrs. Adams said. 33

"Nothing but trouble in *that*," Old Man Warner said stoutly. "Pack of 34
young fools."

"Martin." And Bobby Martin watched his father go forward. 35
"Overdyke. . . . Percy."

"I wish they'd hurry," Mrs. Dunbar said to her older son. "I wish 36
they'd hurry."

"They're almost through," her son said. 37

"You get ready to run tell Dad," Mrs. Dunbar said. 38

Mr. Summers called his own name and then stepped forward pre- 39
cisely and selected a slip from the box. Then he called, "Warner."

"Seventy-seventh year I been in the lottery," Old Man Warner said as 40
he went through the crowd. "Seventy-seventh time."

"Watson." The tall boy came awkwardly through the crowd. Some- 41
one said, "Don't be nervous, Jack," and Mr. Summers said, "Take your
time, son."

"Zanini." 42

After that, there was a long pause, a breathless pause, until Mr. Sum- 43
mers, holding his slip of paper in the air, said, "All right fellows." For a

minute, no one moved, and then all the slips of paper were opened. Suddenly, all the women began to speak at once, saying, "Who is it," "Who's got it?," "Is it the Dunbars?," "Is it the Watsons?" Then the voices began to say, "It's Hutchinson. It's Bill," "Bill Hutchinson's got it."

"Go tell your father," Mrs. Dunbar said to her older son.   44

People began to look around to see the Hutchinsons. Bill Hutchinson   45
was standing quiet, staring down at the paper in his hand. Suddenly, Tessie Hutchinson shouted to Mr. Summers, "You didn't give him time enough to take any paper he wanted. I saw you. It wasn't fair!"

"Be a good sport, Tessie," Mrs. Delacroix called, and Mrs. Graves said,   46
"All of us took the same chance."

"Shut up, Tessie," Bill Hutchinson said.   47

"Well, everyone," Mr. Summers said, "That was done pretty fast, and   48
now we've got to be hurrying a little more to get it done in time." He consulted his next list. "Bill," he said, "you draw for the Hutchinson family. You got any other households in the Hutchinsons?"

"There's Don and Eva," Mrs. Hutchinson yelled. "Make *them* take   49
their chance!"

"Daughters draw with their husbands' families, Tessie," Mr. Summers   50
said gently. "You know that as well as anyone else."

"It wasn't *fair*," Tessie said.   51

"I guess not, Joe," Bill Hutchinson said regretfully. "My daughter   52
draws with her husband's family, that's only fair. And I've got no other family except the kids."

"Then, as far as drawing for families is concerned, it's you," Mr. Sum-   53
mers said in explanation, "and as far as drawing for households is concerned, that's you, too. Right?"

"Right," Bill Hutchinson said.   54

"How many kids, Bill?" Mr. Summers asked formally.   55

"Three," Bill Hutchinson said. "There's Bill, Jr., and Nancy, and little   56
Dave. And Tessie and me."

"All right, then," Mr. Summers said. "Harry, you got their tickets back?"   57

Mr. Graves nodded and held up the slips of paper. "Put them in the   58
box, then," Mr. Summers directed. "Take Bill's and put it in."

"I think we ought to start over," Mrs. Hutchinson said, as quietly as   59
she could. "I tell you it wasn't *fair*. You didn't give him time enough to choose. *Every*body saw that."

Mr. Graves had selected the five slips and put them in the box, and he   60
dropped all the papers but those onto the ground, where the breeze caught them and lifted them off.

"Listen, everybody," Mrs. Hutchinson was saying to the people   61
around her.

"Ready, Bill?" Mr. Summers asked, and Bill Hutchinson, with one   62
quick glance around at his wife and children, nodded.

"Remember," Mr. Summers said, "take the slips and keep them folded   63
until each person has taken one. Harry, you help little Dave." Mr. Graves

took the hand of the little boy, who came willingly with him up to the box. "Take a paper out of the box, Davy," Mr. Summers said. Davy put his hand into the box and laughed. "Take just *one* paper," Mr. Summers said. "Harry, you hold it for him." Mr. Graves took the child's hand and removed the folded paper from the tight fist and held it while little Dave stood next to him and looked up at him wonderingly.

"Nancy next," Mr. Summers said. Nancy was twelve, and her school friends breathed heavily as she went forward, switching her skirt, and took a slip daintily from the box. "Bill, Jr.," Mr. Summers said, and Billy, his face red and his feet over-large, nearly knocked the box over as he got a paper out. "Tessie," Mr. Summers said. She hesitated for a minute, looking around defiantly, and then set her lips and went up to the box. She snatched a paper out and held it behind her.   64

"Bill," Mr. Summers said, and Bill Hutchinson reached into the box and felt around, bringing his hand out at last with the slip of paper in it.   65

The crowd was quiet. A girl whispered, "I hope it's not Nancy," and the sound of the whisper reached the edges of the crowd.   66

"It's not the way it used to be," Old Man Warner said clearly. "People ain't the way they used to be."   67

"All right," Mr. Summers said. "Open the papers. Harry, you open little Dave's."   68

Mr. Graves opened the slip of paper and there was a general sigh through the crowd as he held it up and everyone could see that it was blank. Nancy and Bill, Jr., opened theirs at the same time, and both beamed and laughed, turning around to the crowd and holding their slips of paper above their heads.   69

"Tessie," Mr. Summers said. There was a pause, and then Mr. Summers looked at Bill Hutchinson, and Bill unfolded his paper and showed it. It was blank.   70

"It's Tessie," Mr. Summers said, and his voice was hushed. "Show us her paper, Bill."   71

Bill Hutchinson went over to his wife and forced the slip of paper out of her hand. It had a black spot on it, the black spot Mr. Summers had made the night before with the heavy pencil in the coal-company office. Bill Hutchinson held it up, and there was a stir in the crowd.   72

"All right, folks," Mr. Summers said. "Let's finish quickly."   73

Although the villagers had forgotten the ritual and lost the original black box, they still remembered to use stones. The pile of stones the boys had made earlier was ready; there were stones on the ground with the blowing scraps of paper that had come out of the box. Mrs. Delacroix selected a stone so large she had to pick it up with both hands and turned to Mrs. Dunbar. "Come on," she said. "Hurry up."   74

Mrs. Dunbar had small stones in both hands, and she said, gasping for breath, "I can't run at all. You'll have to go ahead and I'll catch up with you."   75

The children had stones already, and someone gave little Davy Hutchinson a few pebbles.   76

Tessie Hutchinson was in the center of a cleared space by now, and she held her hands out desperately as the villagers moved in on her. "It isn't fair," she said. A stone hit her on the side of the head.   77

Old Man Warner was saying, "Come on, come on, everyone." Steve Adams was in the front of the crowd of villagers, with Mrs. Graves beside him.   78

"It isn't fair, it isn't right," Mrs. Hutchinson screamed, and then they were upon her.   79

•   •   •

THINKING ABOUT LITERATURE

1. List the stages in the process of the lottery. Then identify passages that explain the reasons behind each step. How logical are these explanations?

2. What is the significance of the fact that the process has continued essentially unchanged for so many years? What does this fact suggest about the people in the town?

3. Do you see this story as an explanation of a brutal process carried out in one particular town, or do you see it as a universal statement about dangerous tendencies in modern society — or in human nature? Explain your reasoning.

JOURNAL ENTRY

What do you think it would take to stop a process like the lottery? What could be done — and who would have to do it?

THEMATIC CONNECTIONS

- "Thirty-Eight Who Saw Murder Didn't Call the Police" (page 98)
- "Shooting an Elephant" (page 104)
- "Samuel" (page 212)

WRITING ASSIGNMENTS FOR PROCESS

1. Both Larry Brown and Jessica Mitford describe the process of doing a job. Write an essay in which you summarize the steps involved in applying for, performing, or quitting a particular job you have held.

2. Write a set of instructions explaining in very objective terms how the lottery Shirley Jackson describes should be conducted. Imagine you are setting these steps down in writing for generations of your fellow townspeople to follow.

3. Write a consumer-oriented article for your school newspaper in which you explain how to apply for financial aid, a work-study job, a student internship, or a permanent job in your field.

4. List the steps in the process you follow when you study for an important exam. Then, interview two friends about how they study, and take notes about their usual routine. Finally, combine the most helpful strategies into a set of instructions aimed at students entering your school.

5. Write a set of instructions explaining how to use a print reference work or an online database with which you are familiar. Assume your audience is not familiar with the research tool you are using.

6. Think of a series of steps in a bureaucratic process, a process you had to go through to accomplish something: getting a driver's license, becoming a U.S. citizen, or applying for financial aid, for instance. Write an essay in which you explain that process, and include a thesis statement that evaluates the efficiency of the process.

7. Imagine you have encountered a visitor from another country (or another planet) who is not familiar with a social ritual you take for granted. Try to outline the steps involved in one such ritual — for instance, choosing sides for a game or pledging a fraternity or sorority.

8. Write a process essay explaining how you went about putting together a collection, a scrapbook, a portfolio, or an album of some kind. Be sure your essay makes clear why you collected or compiled your materials.

9. Explain how a certain ritual or ceremony is conducted in your religion. Make sure someone of another faith will be able to understand the process, and include a thesis statement that explains why the ritual is important to you.

10. Think of a process you believe should be modified or discontinued. Formulate a persuasive thesis that presents your negative feelings, and then explain the process so that you make your objections to it clear to your readers.

COLLABORATIVE ACTIVITY FOR PROCESS

Working with three other students, create an illustrated instructional pamphlet to help new students survive four of your college's first "ordeals"— for example, registering for classes, purchasing textbooks, eating in the cafeteria, and moving into a dorm. Before beginning, decide as a group which processes to write about, whether you want your pamphlet to be practical and serious or humorous and irreverent, and what kind of illustrations it should include. Then decide which of you will write about which process — each student should do one — and who will be responsible for the illustrations. When all of you are ready, assemble your individual efforts into a single piece of writing.

INTERNET ASSIGNMENT FOR PROCESS

Write a letter to a friend giving him or her instructions for doing Internet research for a school project. Before you start to write, visit the following World Wide Web sites about the Internet to better understand the process your friend will need to go through when doing research on the Internet, and think carefully about what resources and steps will be most useful to him or her.

NetLearn: Internet Learning Resources Directory
<http://www.rgu.ac.uk/~sim/research/netlearn/callist.htm>
This site provides links to resources for learning and teaching Internet skills, including use of the Web, e-mail, and other Internet tools.

Life on the Internet
<http://www.screen.com/start>
This site includes a beginner's guide to the Internet, featured sites, and documentaries about the Internet.

Bedford/St. Martin's Interactive Research Tutorials
<http://www.bedfordstmartins.com/english_research/demos.htm>
This site offers tutorials on such skills as conducting Web searches and using online library catalogues.

8

CAUSE AND EFFECT

WHAT IS CAUSE AND EFFECT?

Process describes *how* something happens; **cause and effect** analyzes *why* something happens. Cause-and-effect essays examine causes, describe effects, or do both. In the following paragraph, journalist Tom Wicker considers the effects of a technological advance on a village in India:

Cause

Effects

Topic sentence

When a solar-powered water pump was provided for a well in India, the village headman took it over and sold the water, until stopped. The new liquid abundance attracted hordes of unwanted nomads. Village boys who had drawn water in buckets had nothing to do, and some became criminals. The gap between rich and poor widened, since the poor had no land to benefit from irrigation. Finally, village women broke the pump, so they could gather again around the well that had been the center of their social lives. Moral: technological advances have social, cultural, and economic consequences, often unanticipated.

Cause and effect, like narration, links situations and events together in time, with causes preceding effects. But causality involves more than sequence: cause-and-effect analysis explains why something happened — or is happening — and predicts what probably will happen.

Sometimes many different causes can be responsible for one effect. For example, as the following diagram illustrates, many elements may contribute to an individual's decision to leave his or her country of origin and come to the United States.

Causes

| Political repression
Desire to further education
Desire to join family members
Desire for economic opportunity
Desire for religious freedom |

Effect

| Immigrants come
to the United
States |

Similarly, many different effects can be produced by a single cause. Immigration, for instance, has had a variety of effects on the United States:

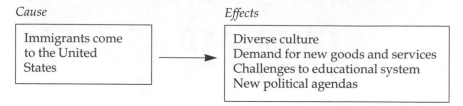

Cause

Immigrants come
to the United
States

Effects

Diverse culture
Demand for new goods and services
Challenges to educational system
New political agendas

USING CAUSE AND EFFECT

Of course, causal relationships are rarely as neat as these boxes suggest; in fact, such relationships are often subtle and complex. As you examine situations that seem suited to cause-and-effect analysis, you will discover that most complex situations involve numerous causes and many different effects.

Consider this example. For more than twenty years, from the 1960s to the 1980s, the college-board scores of high school seniors steadily declined. This decline began soon after television became popular, and therefore many people concluded that the two events were connected. The idea is plausible because children did seem to be reading less in order to watch television more, and because reading comprehension is one of the chief skills the tests evaluate.

But many other elements might have contributed to the decline of test scores. During the same period, for example, many schools reduced the number of required courses and deemphasized traditional subjects and skills, such as reading. Adults were reading less than they used to, and perhaps they were not encouraging their children to read. Furthermore, during the 1960s and 1970s, many colleges changed their policies and admitted students who previously would not have qualified. These new admission standards encouraged students who would not have taken college boards in earlier years to take the tests. Therefore, the scores may have been lower because they measured the top third of high school seniors rather than the top fifth. In any case, the reason for the lower scores is not clear. Perhaps television was the cause after all, but nobody knows for sure. In such a case, it is easy — too easy — to claim a cause-and-effect relationship without the evidence to support it.

Just as the drop in scores may have had many causes, television watching may have had many effects. For instance, it may have made those same students better observers and listeners, even if they did less well on standardized written tests. It may have encouraged them to have a national or even international outlook instead of a narrower local outlook. In other words, even if watching television did limit people in some ways, it may also have expanded their horizons.

To give a balanced analysis, try to consider all causes and effects, not just the most obvious ones or the first ones you think of. For example, suppose a professional basketball team, recently stocked with the best players money can buy, has had a mediocre season. Because the individual players are talented and were successful under other coaches, fans blame the current coach for the team's losing streak and want him fired. But is the coach alone responsible? Maybe the inability of the players to mesh well as a team is responsible for their poor performance. Perhaps some of the players are suffering from injuries, personal problems, or drug dependency. Or maybe the drop in attendance at games has affected the team's morale. Clearly, other elements besides the new coach could have caused the losing streak. Indeed, the suspected cause of the team's decline — the coach — may actually have saved the team from total collapse by keeping the players from quarreling with one another. When you write about such a situation, you need to be very careful to identify these complex causes and effects.

Understanding Main and Contributory Causes

Even when you have identified several causes of an effect, one — the *main cause* — is always more important than the others — the *contributory causes*. Understanding the distinction between the **main** (most important) cause and the **contributory** (less important) causes is vital for planning a cause-and-effect paper: once you identify the main cause, you can emphasize it in your paper and downplay the other causes. How, then, can you tell which cause is most important? Sometimes the main cause is obvious, but often it is not, as the following example shows.

During one winter a number of years ago, an abnormally large amount of snow accumulated on the roof of the Civic Center Auditorium in Hartford, Connecticut, and the roof fell in. Newspapers reported that the weight of the snow had caused the collapse, and they were partly right. Other buildings, however, had not been flattened by the snow, so the main cause seemed to lie elsewhere. Insurance investigators eventually decided that the design of the roof, not the weight of the snow (which was a contributory cause), was the main cause of the collapse. The cause-and-effect relationships summarized above are shown in this diagram:

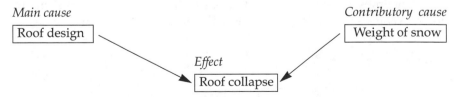

Because the main cause is not always obvious, you should be sure to consider the significance of each cause very carefully as you plan your essay — and to continue to evaluate the importance of each cause as you write and revise.

Understanding Immediate and Remote Causes

Another important distinction is the difference between an *immediate cause* and a *remote cause*. An **immediate cause** closely precedes an effect and is therefore relatively easy to recognize. A **remote cause** is less obvious, perhaps because it involves something in the past or far away. Assuming that the most obvious cause is always the most important can be dangerous as well as shortsighted.

For example, look again at the Hartford roof collapse. Most people agreed that the snow was the immediate, or most obvious, cause of the roof collapse. But further study by insurance investigators suggested remote causes that were not so apparent. The design of the roof was the most important remote cause of the collapse. In addition, perhaps the materials used in the roof's construction were partly to blame. Maybe maintenance crews had not done their jobs properly, or necessary repairs had not been made. If you were the insurance investigator analyzing the causes of this event, you would want to assess all possible contributing factors rather than just the most obvious. If you did not consider the remote as well as the immediate causes, you would reach an oversimplified and perhaps incorrect conclusion.

This diagram shows the cause-and-effect relationships summarized above:

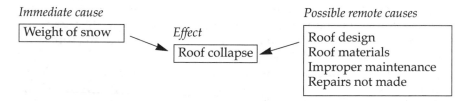

Remote causes can be extremely important. In the roof-collapse situation, as we have seen, a remote cause — the roof design — was the main cause of the accident.

Understanding Causal Chains

Sometimes an effect can also be a cause. This is true in a **causal chain**, where A causes B, B causes C, C causes D, and so on, as shown here:

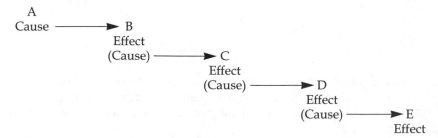

A simple example of a causal chain starts with the conclusion of World War II in 1945. Beginning in 1946, as thousands of American soldiers returned home, the U.S. birth rate began to rise dramatically. As the numbers of births increased, the creation of goods and services to meet the needs of this growing population also increased. As advertisers competed to attract this group's attention to various products, the so-called baby-boom generation became more and more visible. Consequently, baby boomers were perceived as more and more powerful — as voters as well as consumers. As a result, this group's emergence has been a major factor in shaping American political, social, cultural, and economic life.

Here is another example of a causal chain. In the last thirty years, the bicycle as a form of transportation for children, for example, has become increasingly rare, with fewer than 1 percent of children now riding bicycles to school. In addition, fewer and fewer children, for example, ride bicycles for recreation. Causes cited for this decline include the following: the absence of sidewalks in many suburban communities, parents' rising fears about crime and traffic accidents, the rise in the number of students who schedule back-to-back after-school activities (perhaps due in part to the increased number of households in which both parents work), the growing popularity of computer games, and the increased availability of after-school jobs for teenagers (who often need cars, not bikes, to get to work). The decreasing number of children who ride bikes has contributed to a corresponding steady decline, since the 1970s, in the sale of bicycles.

As a result of the decline in bicycle sales, bicycle thefts have decreased sharply, and bicycle deaths involving children under sixteen have also dropped dramatically (although this is due in part to increased use of helmets). At the same time, however, the number of American children who are obese has doubled since the mid-1980s. So, factors like fewer sidewalks and more working teenagers led to a decline in bicycle sales, which in turn has had a far-reaching impact.

In causal chains like these, the result of one action is the cause of another. Leaving out any link in the chain, or putting any link in improper order, destroys the logic and continuity of the chain.

If your analysis of a situation reveals a causal chain, this discovery can be useful in your writing. The very operation of a causal chain suggests an organizational pattern for a paper, and following the chain helps you to discuss items in their logical order. Be careful, however, to keep your emphasis on the causal connections and not to lapse into narration.

Avoiding *Post Hoc* Reasoning

When developing a cause-and-effect paper, you should not assume that just because event A *precedes* event B, event A has *caused* event B. This illogical assumption, called **post hoc reasoning,** equates a chronological sequence with causality. When you fall into this trap — assuming, for instance, that you failed an exam because a black cat crossed your path the day before — you are mistaking coincidence for causality.

Consider a classic example of *post hoc* reasoning. Until the late nineteenth century, many scientists accepted the notion of spontaneous generation — that is, they believed living things could arise directly from nonliving matter. To support their beliefs, they pointed to specific situations. For instance, they observed that maggots, the larvae of the housefly, seemed to arise directly from the decaying flesh of dead animals.

These scientists were confusing sequence with causality, assuming that just because the presence of decaying meat preceded the appearance of maggots, the two were connected in a causal relationship. In fact, because the dead animals were exposed to the air, flies were free to lay eggs in the animals' bodies, and these eggs hatched into maggots. Therefore, the living maggots were not a direct result of the presence of nonliving matter. Although these scientists were applying the best technology and scientific theory of their time, hindsight reveals that their conclusions were not valid.

A more recent example of *post hoc* reasoning occurred after medical researchers published findings reporting that female centenarians — women who reached the age of one hundred — were four times as likely to have given birth when they were past forty as were women in a control group who died at the age of seventy-three. Researchers saw no causal connection between childbirth after forty and long life, suggesting only that the centenarians might have been predisposed to live longer because they reached menopause later than the other women. Local television newscasts and tabloid newspapers, however, misinterpreted the implications of the study, presenting the relationship between late childbearing and long life as a causal one. In a vivid example of *post hoc* reasoning, one promotional spot for a local television newscast proclaimed, "Having kids late in life can help you live longer."

In your writing as well as in your observations, it is neither logical nor fair to assume that a causal relationship exists unless clear, strong evidence supports the connection. When you revise a cause-and-effect paper, make sure you have not confused words like *because, therefore,* and *consequently* — words that indicate a causal relationship — with words like *subsequently, later,* and *afterward* — words that indicate a chronological relationship. When you use a word like *because,* you are signaling to readers that you are telling *why* something happened; when you use a word like *later,* you are only showing *when* it happened.

Being able to identify and analyze cause-and-effect relationships; to distinguish causes from effects and recognize causal chains; and to distinguish immediate from remote, main from contributory, and logical from illogical causes are all skills that will improve your writing. Understanding the nature of the cause-and-effect relationship will help you decide when to use this pattern in a paper.

PLANNING A CAUSE-AND-EFFECT ESSAY

After you have sorted out the cause-and-effect relationships you will write about, you are ready to plan your paper. You have three basic options: to discuss causes, to discuss effects, or to discuss both causes and effects. Often your assignment will suggest which of these options to use. Here are a few likely topics for cause-and-effect treatment:

Focus on finding causes	Identify some possible causes of collective obsessional behavior. (psychology exam)
	Discuss the factors that have contributed to the declining population of state mental hospitals. (social work paper)
Focus on describing or predicting effects	Evaluate the probable effects of moving elementary school children from a highly structured classroom to a relatively open classroom. (education paper)
	Discuss the impact of World War I on two of Ernest Hemingway's characters. (literature exam)
Focus on both causes and effects	The 1840s were very volatile years in Europe. Choose one social, political, or economic event that occurred during those years, analyze its causes, and briefly note how the event influenced later developments in European history. (history exam)

Of course, a cause-and-effect essay usually does more than just enumerate causes or effects. For example, an economics paper treating the major effects of the Vietnam War on the U.S. economy could be a straightforward presentation of factual information — an attempt to inform readers of the war's economic impact. It is more likely, however, that the paper would indicate the significance of the war's effects, not just list them. In fact, cause-and-effect analysis often requires you to judge various factors so that you can assess their relative significance.

When you formulate a thesis statement, be sure that it identifies the relationships among the specific causes or effects you will discuss. This thesis statement should tell your readers three things: the points you plan to consider, the position you will take, and whether your emphasis is on causes, effects, or both. Your thesis statement may also indicate explicitly or implicitly the cause or effect you consider most important and the order in which you will treat your points.

When deciding on the sequence in which you will present causes or effects, you have several options. One option, of course, is chronological order — you can present causes or effects in the order in which they occurred. Another option is to introduce the main cause first and then the contributory causes — or to do just the opposite. If you want to stress positive consequences, begin by briefly discussing the negative ones; if you plan to emphasize negative results, summarize the less important positive effects first. Still another possibility is to begin by dismissing any events that were *not* causes and then explain what the real causes were. This method is especially effective if you think your readers are likely to jump to *post hoc* conclusions. Finally, you can begin with the most obvious causes or effects and move on to more subtle factors — and then to your analysis and conclusion.

STRUCTURING A CAUSE-AND-EFFECT ESSAY

Finding Causes

Suppose you are planning the social work paper mentioned earlier: "Discuss the factors that have contributed to the declining population of state mental hospitals." Your assignment specifies an effect — the declining population of state hospitals — and asks you to discuss possible causes, which might include the following:

- An increasing acceptance of mental illness in our society
- Prohibitive costs of in-patient care
- Increasing numbers of mental-health professionals, facilitating treatment outside of hospitals

Many health professionals, however, believe that the most important cause is the development and use of psychotropic drugs, such as chlorpromazine (Thorazine), which can alter behavior. To emphasize this cause in your paper, you could formulate the following thesis statement:

Less important causes	Although society's increasing acceptance of the mentally ill, the high cost of in-patient care, and the rise in the number of health professionals have all been influential in
Effect	reducing the population of state mental hospitals, the
Most important cause	most important cause of this reduction is the development and use of psychotropic drugs.

This thesis statement fully prepares your readers for your essay. It identifies the points you will consider, and it reveals your position — your assessment of the relative significance of the causes you identify. It states the less important causes first and indicates their secondary importance with *although*. In the body of your essay, the less important causes would come first so that the essay could gradually build up to the most convincing material. An informal outline for your paper might look like this:

Introduction:	Thesis statement — Although society's increasing acceptance of the mentally ill, the high cost of in-patient care, and the rise in the number of health professionals have all been influential in reducing the population of state mental hospitals, the most important cause of this reduction is the development and use of psychotropic drugs.
First cause:	Increasing acceptance of the mentally ill
Second cause:	High cost of in-patient care
Third cause:	Rise in the number of health professionals
Fourth (and most important) cause:	Development and use of psychotropic drugs
Conclusion:	Restatement of thesis or summary of key points

Describing or Predicting Effects

Suppose you were planning the education paper mentioned earlier: "Evaluate the probable effects of moving elementary school children from a highly structured classroom to a relatively open classroom." You would use a procedure similar to the preceding one, but you would focus on effects rather than on causes. After brainstorming and deciding which specific points to discuss, you might formulate this thesis statement:

Cause	Moving children from a highly structured classroom to a relatively open one is desirable because it is likely to en-
Effects	courage more independent play, more flexibility in forming friendship groups, and, ultimately, more creativity.

This thesis statement clearly tells readers the stand you will take and the main points your essay will consider; the thesis also clearly specifies that these points are *effects* of the open classroom. After introducing the cause, your essay would treat these three effects in the order in which they are presented in the thesis statement, building up to the most important point. An informal outline of your paper might look like this:

Introduction:	Thesis statement — Moving children from a highly structured classroom to a relatively open one is desirable because it is likely to encourage more independent play, more flexibility in forming friendship groups, and, ultimately, more creativity.
First effect:	More independent play
Second effect:	More flexible friendship groups
Third (and most important) effect:	More creativity
Conclusion:	Restatement of thesis or summary of key points

☑ **CHECKLIST: CAUSE AND EFFECT**

- Does your assignment call for a discussion of causes, of effects, or of both causes and effects?
- Does your essay have a clearly stated thesis that indicates your focus and the significance of the causes and/or effects you discuss?
- Have you considered all possible causes and all possible effects?
- Have you distinguished between the main (most important) cause and the contributory (less important) causes?
- Have you distinguished between immediate and remote causes?
- Have you identified a causal chain in your reasoning?
- Have you avoided *post hoc* reasoning?
- Have you used transitional words and phrases to show how the causes and/or effects you discuss are related?

▶ A STUDENT WRITER: CAUSE AND EFFECT

The following midterm exam, written for a history class, analyzes both the causes and effects of the Irish potato famine that occurred during the 1840s. Notice how the writer, Evelyn Pellicane, concentrates on causes but also discusses briefly the effects of this tragedy, just as the exam question directs.

Question: The 1840s were very volatile years in Europe. Choose one social, political, or economic event that occurred during those years, analyze its causes, and briefly note how the event influenced later developments in European history.

The Irish Famine, 1845–1849

Thesis statement	The Irish famine, which brought hardship and tragedy to Ireland during the 1840s, was caused and prolonged by four basic factors: the failure of the potato crop, the landlord-tenant system, errors in government policy, and the long-standing prejudice of the British toward Ireland.
First cause	The immediate cause of the famine was the failure of the potato crop. In 1845, potato disease struck the crop, and potatoes rotted in the ground. The 1846 crop also failed, and before long people were eating weeds. The 1847 crop was healthy, but there were not enough potatoes to go around, and in 1848 the blight

1

2

struck again, leading to more and more evic-
tions of tenants by landlords.

Second cause

The tenants' position on the land had   3
never been very secure. Most had no leases and
could be turned out by their landlords at any
time. If a tenant owed rent, he was evicted--
or, worse, put in prison, leaving his family to
starve. The threat of prison caused many tenants to leave their land; those who could leave
Ireland did so, sometimes with money provided
by their landlords. Some landlords did try to
take care of their tenants, but most did not.
Many were absentee landlords who spent their
rent money abroad.

Third cause

Government policy errors, although not an   4
immediate cause of the famine, played an important role in creating an unstable economy and
perpetuating starvation. In 1846, the government decided not to continue selling corn, as
it had during the first year of the famine,
claiming that low-cost purchases of corn by
Ireland had paralyzed British trade by inter-
fering with free enterprise. Therefore, 1846
saw a starving population, angry demonstrations, and panic; even those with money were
unable to buy food. Still, the government
insisted that if it sent food to Ireland,
prices would rise in the rest of the United
Kingdom and that this would be unfair to hard-
working English and Scots. As a result, no food
was sent. Throughout the years of the famine,
the British government aggravated an already
grave situation: they did nothing to improve
agricultural operations, to help people adjust
to another crop, to distribute seeds, or to
reorder the landlord-tenant system that made
the tenants' position so insecure.

Fourth cause

At the root of this poor government policy   5
was the long-standing British prejudice against
the Irish. Hostility between the two countries

went back some six hundred years, and the
British were simply not about to inconvenience
themselves to save the Irish. When the Irish so
desperately needed grain to replace the damaged
potatoes, it was clear that grain had to be
imported from England. This meant, however,
that the Corn Laws, which had been enacted to
keep the price of British corn high by taxing
imported grain, had to be repealed. The British
were unwilling to repeal the Corn Laws. Even
when they did supply cornmeal, they made no
attempt to explain to the Irish how to cook
this unfamiliar food. Moreover, the British
government was determined to make Ireland pay
for its own poor, and so it forced the collection of taxes. Since many landlords just did
not have the tax money, they were forced to
evict their tenants. The British government's
callous and indifferent treatment of the Irish
has been called genocide.

Effects

As a result of this devastating famine,   6
the population of Ireland was reduced from
about nine million to about six and one-half
million. During the famine years, men roamed
the streets looking for work, begging when they
found none. Epidemics of "famine fever" and
dysentery reduced the population drastically.
The most important historical result of the
famine, however, was the massive immigration to
the United States, Canada, and Great Britain of
poor, unskilled people who had to struggle to
fit into a skilled economy and who brought with
them a deep-seated hatred of the British. (This
same hatred remained strong in Ireland itself--
so strong that at the time of World War II,
Ireland, then independent, remained neutral
rather than coming to England's aid.) Irish
immigrants faced slums, fever epidemics, job-
lessness, and hostility--even anti-Catholic and

anti-Irish riots--in Boston, New York, London,
Glasgow, and Quebec. In Ireland itself, poverty
and discontent continued, and by 1848 those
emigrating from Ireland included a more highly
skilled class of farmer, the ones Ireland
needed to recover and to survive.

Conclusion (includes restatement of thesis)   The Irish famine, one of the great trage-   7
dies of the nineteenth century, was a natural
disaster compounded by the insensitivity of the
British government and the archaic agricultural
system of Ireland. Although the deaths that
resulted depleted Ireland's resources even
more, the men and women who immigrated to other
countries permanently enriched those nations.

Points for Special Attention

STRUCTURE.   This is a relatively long essay; if it were not so clearly organized, it would be difficult to follow. Because the essay was to focus primarily on causes, Evelyn first introduces the effect — the famine itself — and then considers its causes. After she examines the causes, she moves on to the results of the famine, treating the most important result last. In this essay, then, the famine is first treated as an effect and then, toward the end, as a cause. In fact, it is the central link in a causal chain. Evelyn devotes one paragraph to her introduction and one to each cause; she sums up the famine's results in a separate paragraph and devotes the final paragraph to her conclusion. (Depending on a particular paper's length and complexity, more — or less — than one paragraph may be devoted to each cause or effect.) An informal outline for her paper might look like this:

Introduction (including thesis statement)
First cause: Failure of the potato crop
Second cause: The landlord-tenant system
Third cause: Errors in government policy
Fourth cause: British prejudice
Results of the famine
Conclusion

Because Evelyn sees all the causes as important and interrelated, she does not present them in order of increasing importance. Instead, she begins with the immediate cause of the famine — the failure of the potato crop — and then digs more deeply until she arrives at the most remote cause, British prejudice. The immediate cause is also the main (most important) cause, for the other situations had existed before the famine began.

TRANSITIONS.   The cause-and-effect relationships in this essay are both subtle and complex; Evelyn considers a series of relationships as well as an intricate causal chain. Throughout the essay, many words suggest cause-and-effect connections: *so, therefore, because, as a result, since, led to, brought about, caused,* and the like. These are the most effective transitions for such an essay.

ANSWERING AN EXAMINATION QUESTION.   Before planning and writing her answer, Evelyn read the exam question very carefully. She noted that it asked for both causes and effects but that its wording directed her to spend more time on causes ("analyze") than on effects ("briefly note"). Consequently, she decided to organize her discussion to conform to these directions and is careful to indicate *explicitly* which are the causes ("government policy . . . played an important role") and which are the effects ("The most important historical result").

Evelyn's purpose is to convey factual information and, in doing so, to demonstrate her understanding of the course material. Rather than waste her limited time choosing a clever opening strategy or making elaborate attempts to engage her audience, Evelyn begins her essay with a direct statement of her thesis.

Evelyn has obviously been influenced by outside sources; the ideas in the essay are not completely her own. Because this is an exam, however, and because the instructor expected that students would base their essays on class notes and assigned readings, Evelyn does not have to document her sources.

Focus on Revision

Because this essay was written as an exam answer, Evelyn had no time — and no need — to revise it further. If she had been preparing this assignment outside of class, however, she might have done more. For example, she could have added a more arresting opening, such as a brief eyewitness account of the famine's effects. Her conclusion — appropriately brief and straightforward for an exam answer — could also have been strengthened, perhaps with the addition of information about the nation's eventual recovery. Finally, the addition of statistics, quotations by historians, or a brief summary of Irish history before the famine could have further enriched the essay.

All the selections that follow focus on cause-and-effect relationships. Some readings focus on causes, others on effects. As these essays illustrate, the cause-and-effect pattern is so versatile that it may be used to examine topics as dissimilar as boxing, television, racial segregation, gun ownership, and a young girl's life.

NORMAN COUSINS

Norman Cousins (1915–1990) was born in Union City, New Jersey, and graduated from Columbia University's Teachers College in 1933. He began his
career in journalism writing for the *New York Evening Post* and *Current History*
magazine. In 1940, Cousins joined the *Saturday Review,* where he served as
editor from 1942 to 1978. A noted social critic, Cousins lectured widely on
world affairs. An adjunct professor in the department of psychiatry at
U.C.L.A. Medical School from 1978 until his death, he is particularly remembered for his many books urging a positive outlook to combat illness, including *Anatomy of an Illness* (1979).

His 1962 essay "Who Killed Benny Paret?" written for the *Saturday
Review* focuses on a brutal boxing match at Madison Square Garden that
resulted in the death of one of the boxers. The event, witnessed by millions of
shocked television viewers, led to demands from many quarters that professional boxing be banned altogether. As a result, a number of rules for professional boxing were changed, but boxing remains an inherently dangerous
sport. There have been an estimated five hundred ring deaths in the last century; as recently as 1997, a professional boxer died following a knockout in
the ring. In addition, many boxers suffer from chronic latent brain damage,
known medically as *pugilistica dementia.* In answering the question posed by
his essay's title, Cousins takes a strong stand against violence in boxing.

Who Killed Benny Paret?

Sometime about 1935 or 1936 I had an interview with Mike Jacobs, the 1
prize-fight promoter. I was a fledgling reporter at that time; my beat was
education but during the vacation season I found myself on varied assignments, all the way from ship news to sports reporting. In this way I found
myself sitting opposite the most powerful figure in the boxing world.

There was nothing spectacular in Mr. Jacobs' manner or appearance; 2
but when he spoke about prize fights, he was no longer a bland little man
but a colossus who sounded the way Napoleon must have sounded when
he reviewed a battle. You knew you were listening to Number One. His
saying something made it true.

We discussed what to him was the only important element in success- 3
ful promoting — how to please the crowd. So far as he was concerned,
there was no mystery to it. You put killers in the ring and the people filled
your arena. You hire boxing artists — men who are adroit at feinting,
parrying, weaving, jabbing, and dancing, but who don't pack dynamite
in their fists — and you wind up counting your empty seats. So you
searched for the killers and sluggers and maulers — fellows who could hit
with the force of a baseball bat.

I asked Mr. Jacobs if he was speaking literally when he said people 4
came out to see the killer.

"They don't come out to see a tea party," he said evenly. "They come   5
out to see the knockout. They come out to see a man hurt. If they think
anything else, they're kidding themselves."

Recently, a young man by the name of Benny Paret was killed in the   6
ring. The killing was seen by millions; it was on television. In the twelfth
round, he was hit hard in the head several times, went down, was counted
out, and never came out of the coma.

The Paret fight produced a flurry of investigations. Governor Rocke-   7
feller was shocked by what happened and appointed a committee to
assess the responsibility. The New York State Boxing Commission decided
to find out what was wrong. The District Attorney's office expressed its
concern. One question that was solemnly studied in all three probes concerned the action of the referee. Did he act in time to stop the fight?
Another question had to do with the role of the examining doctors who
certified the physical fitness of the fighters before the bout. Still another
question involved Mr. Paret's manager; did he rush his boy into the fight
without adequate time to recuperate from the previous one?

In short, the investigators looked into every possible cause except the   8
real one. Benny Paret was killed because the human fist delivers enough
impact, when directed against the head, to produce a massive hemorrhage
in the brain. The human brain is the most delicate and complex mechanism in all creation. It has a lacework of millions of highly fragile nerve
connections. Nature attempts to protect this exquisitely intricate machinery by encasing it in a hard shell. Fortunately, the shell is thick enough to
withstand a great deal of pounding. Nature, however, can protect a man
against everything except man himself. Not every blow to the head will
kill a man — but there is always the risk of concussion and damage to the
brain. A prize fighter may be able to survive even repeated brain concus-
sions and go on fighting, but the damage to his brain may be permanent.

In any event, it is futile to investigate the referee's role and seek to   9
determine whether he should have intervened to stop the fight earlier.
That is not where the primary responsibility lies. The primary responsibility lies with the people who pay to see a man hurt. The referee who stops a
fight too soon from the crowd's viewpoint can expect to be booed. The
crowd wants the knockout; it wants to see a man stretched out on the canvas. This is the supreme moment in boxing. It is nonsense to talk about
prize fighting as a test of boxing skills. No crowd was ever brought to its
feet screaming and cheering at the sight of two men beautifully dodging
and weaving out of each other's jabs. The time the crowd comes alive is
when a man is hit hard over the heart or the head, when his mouthpiece
flies out, when the blood squirts out of his nose or eyes, when he wobbles
under the attack and his pursuer continues to smash at him with pole-axe
impact.

Don't blame it on the referee. Don't even blame it on the fight man-   10
agers. Put the blame where it belongs — on the prevailing mores that
regard prize fighting as a perfectly proper enterprise and vehicle of enter-

tainment. No one doubts that many people enjoy prize fighting and will miss it if it should be thrown out. And that is precisely the point.

• • •

COMPREHENSION

1. Why, according to Mike Jacobs, do people come to see a prizefight? Does Cousins agree with him?

2. What was the immediate cause of Paret's death? What remote causes did the investigators consider? What, according to Cousins, was the main cause? That is, where does the "primary responsibility" (9) lie?

3. Why does Cousins believe that "it is futile to investigate the referee's role" (9)?

4. Cousins ends his essay with "And that is precisely the point." What is the "point" to which he refers?

PURPOSE AND AUDIENCE

1. This persuasive essay has a strong thesis. What is it?

2. This essay appeared on May 5, 1962, a month after Paret died. What do you suppose its impact was on its audience? Is the impact the same today, or has it changed?

3. At whom is this essay aimed — boxing enthusiasts, sportswriters, or a general audience? On what do you base your conclusion?

4. Does Cousins expect his audience to agree with his thesis? How does he try to win sympathy for his position?

STYLE AND STRUCTURE

1. Does Cousins include enough detail to convince readers? Explain. Where, if anywhere, might more detail be helpful?

2. Sort out the complex cause-and-effect relationships discussed in paragraph 9.

3. What strategy does Cousins use in his conclusion? Is it effective? Explain your reasoning.

VOCABULARY PROJECTS

1. Define each of the following words as it is used in this selection.

promoter (1)	feinting (3)	lacework (8)
fledgling (1)	parrying (3)	encasing (8)
colossus (2)	maulers (3)	intervened (9)

2. The specialized vocabulary of boxing is prominent in this essay, but the facts Cousins presents would apply equally well to any sport in which violence is a potential problem.

a. Assume that you are writing a similar essay about football, hockey, rugby, or another sport; substitute an appropriate equivalent word for each of the following:

promoter (1)	feinting, parrying, weaving,	knockout (5)
prize fights (2)	jabbing, and dancing (3)	referee (7)
in the ring (3)	killers and sluggers	fighters/fight (7)
boxing artists (3)	and maulers (3)	

b. Rewrite this sentence so that it suits the sport you have chosen: "The crowd wants the knockout; it wants to see a man stretched out on the canvas. . . . It is nonsense to talk about prize fighting as a test of boxing skills. No crowd was ever brought to its feet screaming and cheering at the sight of two men beautifully dodging and weaving out of each other's jabs" (9).

JOURNAL ENTRY

Do Cousins's graphic descriptions convince you that boxing should be outlawed? Explain.

WRITING WORKSHOP

1. Write a cause-and-effect essay examining how the demands of the public affect a professional sport. (You might examine violence in hockey or football, for example, or the ways in which an individual player cultivates an image for the fans.)

2. Write a cause-and-effect essay about a time when, in response to peer pressure, you encouraged someone to do something you felt was dishonest or unwise. Be sure to identify the causes for your actions.

3. Why do you think a young person might turn to a career in boxing? Write a cause-and-effect essay in which you examine the possible motives.

COMBINING THE PATTERNS

This essay begins with five paragraphs of **narration** that summarize a meeting between Cousins and Mike Jacobs. What function does this narrative introduction serve in this essay? Once Paret's death is mentioned and the persuasive portion of the essay begins, Cousins never resumes the narrative. Do you think he should have returned to this narrative? If so, where might he have continued the story?

THEMATIC CONNECTIONS

- "Thirty-Eight Who Saw Murder Didn't Call the Police" (page 99)
- "Shooting an Elephant" (page 104)
- "Ex-Basketball Player" (page 374)

MARIE WINN

Marie Winn was born in 1936 in Prague, in what is now the Czech Republic, and came to the United States in 1939. She was educated at Radcliffe College and Columbia University. As a freelance writer, Winn has contributed articles to the *New York Times Magazine, Parade,* and *Smithsonian* magazine. She has written books for children and also for parents and teachers, including *The Plug-In Drug: Television, Children, and the Family* (1977, revised 1985), *Children without Childhood* (1983), and *Unplugging the Plug-In Drug* (1987). Her recent work has focused on urban wildlife; in 1998 she published *Red-Tails in Love: A Wildlife Drama in Central Park.*

Referred to as early as 1961 as a "vast wasteland" (by the then chairman of the Federal Communications Commission, no less), television has had its critics all along, particularly in relation to the effect of television watching on children. Some three thousand books and articles have been published on the subject, and current research suggests that the average young person watches twenty-eight hours of television a week (which, with the proliferation of cable channels devoted to children and the spread of videos, may be a low estimate). Studies show that children who spend four or more hours a day in front of the set do less schoolwork, have poorer reading and social skills, and are more likely to be overweight. In addition, much controversy surrounds the effects of television violence and advertising on young viewers. In this excerpt from *The Plug-In Drug* (updated by Winn for this edition), she considers the effects of television not only on children but on how family members relate to one another. (Winn's observations are even more relevant now than when she originally wrote her essay: today 66 percent of children live in a household with three or more television sets, and 54 percent have one in their own room.)

Television: The Plug-In Drug

Less than fifty years after the introduction of television into American 1 society, a period that has seen the medium become so deeply ingrained in American life that in at least one state the television set has attained the rank of a legal necessity, safe from repossession in case of debt along with clothes, cooking utensils, and the like, television viewing has become an inevitable and ordinary part of daily life. Only in the early years of television did writers and commentators have sufficient perspective to separate the activity of watching television from the actual content it offers the viewer. In those early days writers frequently discussed the effects of television on family life. However, a curious myopia afflicted those early observers: almost without exception they regarded television as a favorable, beneficial, indeed, wondrous influence upon the family.

"Television is going to be a real asset in every home where there are 2 children," predicts a writer in 1949.

"Television will take over your way of living and change your children's habits, but this change can be a wonderful improvement," claims another commentator.

"No survey's needed, of course, to establish that television has brought   4
the family together in one room," writes *The New York Times'* television
critic in 1949.

Each of the early articles about television is invariably accompanied   5
by a photograph or illustration showing a family cozily sitting together
before the television set, Sis on Mom's lap, Buddy perched on the arm of
Dad's chair, Dad with his arm around Mom's shoulder. Who could have
guessed that twenty or so years later Mom would be watching a drama in
the kitchen, the kids would be looking at cartoons in their room, while
Dad would be taking in the ball game in the living room?

Of course television sets were enormously expensive in those early   6
days. The idea that by 1982 more than half of all American families would
own two or more sets would have seemed preposterous back then. The
splintering of the multiple-set family was something the early writers
could not foresee. Nor did they anticipate the introduction of VCRs, video
games and other television-like home activities a few decades later. In
those days no one imagined the numbers of hours children would eventually devote to these activities, the changes they would effect upon
child-rearing methods, the increasing domination of family schedules by
children's viewing requirements — in short, the *power* of the little home
screen to dominate family life.

After the first years, as children's consumption of the new medium   7
increased, together with parental concern about the possible effects of so
much television viewing, a steady refrain helped to soothe and reassure
anxious parents. "Television always enters a pattern of influences that
already exist: the home, the peer group, the school, the church and culture
generally," wrote the authors of an early and influential study of television's effects on children. In other words, if the child's home life is
all right, parents need not worry about the effects of all that television
watching.

But television did not merely influence the child; it deeply influenced   8
that "pattern of influences" everyone hoped would ameliorate the new
medium's effects. Home and family life have changed in important ways
since the advent of television. The peer group has become television-
oriented, and much of the time children spend together is occupied by
viewing. Culture generally has been transformed by television. Therefore
it is improper to assign to television the subsidiary role its many apologists (too often members of the television industry) insist it plays. Television is not merely one of a number of important influences upon today's
child. Through the changes it has made in family life, television emerges
as *the* important influence in children's lives today.

THE QUALITY OF FAMILY LIFE

Television's contribution to family life has been an equivocal one. For   9
while it has, indeed, kept the members of the family from dispersing, it

has not served to bring them *together*. By its domination of the time families spend together, it destroys the special quality that distinguishes one family from another, a quality that depends to a great extent on what a family *does*, what special rituals, games, recurrent jokes, familiar songs, and shared activities it accumulates.

"Like the sorcerer of old," writes sociologist Urie Bronfenbrenner,   10
"the television set casts its magic spell, freezing speech and action, turning the living into silent statues so long as the enchantment lasts. The primary danger of the television screen lies not so much in the behavior it produces — although there is danger there — as in the behavior it prevents: the talks, the games, the family festivities and arguments through which much of the child's learning takes place and through which his character is formed. Turning on the television set can turn off the process that transforms children into people."

Yet parents have accepted a television-dominated family life so completely that they cannot see how the medium is involved in whatever problems they might be having. A first-grade teacher reports: 11

"I have one child in the group who's an only child. I wanted to find   12
out more about her family life because this little girl was quite isolated from the group, didn't make friends, so I talked to her mother. Well, they don't have time to do anything in the evening, the mother said. The parents come home after picking up the child at the baby-sitter's. Then the mother fixes dinner while the child watches TV. Then they have dinner and the child goes to bed. I said to this mother. 'Well, couldn't she help you fix dinner? That would be a nice time for the two of you to talk,' and the mother said, 'Oh, but I'd hate to have her miss "Zoom." It's such a good program!'"

Even when families make efforts to control television, too often its   13
very presence counterbalances the positive features of family life. Several decades ago a writer and mother of two boys aged 3 and 7 wrote about her family's television schedule in an article in *The New York Times*. Though programs have changed since then, television's tyrannical effect has remained the same:

> We were in the midst of a full-scale War. Every day was a new battle and every program was a major skirmish. We agreed it was a bad scene all around and were ready to enter diplomatic negotiations. . . . In principle we have agreed on 2½ hours of TV a day, "Sesame Street," "Electric Company" (with dinner gobbled up in between) and two half-hour shows between 7 and 8:30, which enables the grown-ups to eat in peace and prevents the two boys from destroying one another. Their pre-bedtime choice is dreadful, because, as Josh recently admitted, "There's nothing much on I really like." So . . . it's "What's My Line" or "To Tell the Truth.". . . Clearly there is a need for first-rate children's shows at this time. . . .

Consider the "family life" described here: Presumably the father   14
comes home from work during the "Sesame Street"–"Electric Company" stint. The children are either watching television, gobbling their dinner, or

both. While the parents eat their dinner in peaceful privacy, the children watch another hour of television. Then there is only a half-hour left before bedtime, just enough time for baths, getting pajamas on, brushing teeth, and so on. The children's evening is regimented with an almost military precision. They watch their favorite programs, and when there is "nothing much on I really like," they watch whatever else is on — because *watching* is the important thing. Their mother does not see anything amiss with watching programs just for the sake of watching; she only wishes there were some first-rate children's shows on at those times.

Without conjuring up memories of the Victorian era with family   15
games and long, leisurely meals, and large families, the question arises: isn't there a better family life available than this dismal, mechanized arrangement of children watching television for however long is allowed them, evening after evening?

Of course, families today still do *special* things together at times: go   16
camping in the summer, go to the zoo on a nice Sunday, take various trips and expeditions. But their *ordinary* daily life together is diminished — that sitting around at the dinner table, that spontaneous taking up of an activity, those little games invented by children on the spur of the moment when there is nothing else to do, the scribbling, the chatting, and even the quarreling, all the things that form the fabric of a family, that define a childhood. Instead, the children have their regular schedule of television programs and bedtime, and the parents have their peaceful dinner together.

The author of the article notes that "keeping a family sane means   17
mediating between the needs of both children and adults." But surely the needs of adults are being better met than the needs of the children, who are effectively shunted away and rendered untroublesome, while their parents enjoy a life as undemanding as that of any childless couple. In reality, it is those very demands that young children make upon a family that lead to growth, and it is the way parents accede to those demands that builds the relationships upon which the future of the family depends. If the family does not accumulate its backlog of shared experiences, shared *everyday* experiences that occur and recur and change and develop, then it is not likely to survive as anything other than a caretaking institution.

FAMILY RITUALS

Ritual is defined by sociologists as "that part of family life that the   18
family likes about itself, is proud of and wants formally to continue." Another text notes that "the development of a ritual by a family is an index of the common interest of its members in the family as a group."

What has happened to family rituals, those regular, dependable, re-   19
current happenings that gave members of a family a feeling of *belonging* to a home rather than living in it merely for the sake of convenience, those

experiences that act as the adhesive of family unity far more than any material advantages?

Mealtime rituals, going-to-bed rituals, illness rituals, holiday rituals —   20
how many of these have survived the inroads of the television set?

A young woman who grew up near Chicago reminisces about her   21
childhood and gives an idea of the effects of television upon family rituals:

"As a child I had millions of relatives around — my parents both   22
come from relatively large families. My father had nine brothers and sisters. And so every holiday there was this great swoop-down of aunts, uncles, and millions of cousins. I just remember how wonderful it used to be. These thousands of cousins would come and everyone would play and ultimately, after dinner, all the women would be in the front of the house, drinking coffee and talking, all the men would be in the back of the house, drinking and smoking, and all the kids would be all over the place, playing hide and seek. Christmas time was particularly nice because everyone always brought all their toys and games. Our house had a couple of rooms with go-through closets, so there were always kids running in a great circle route. I remember it was just wonderful.

"And then all of a sudden one year I remember becoming suddenly   23
aware of how different everything had become. The kids were no longer playing Monopoly or Clue or the other games we used to play together. It was because we had a television set which had been turned on for a football game. All of that socializing that had gone on previously had ended. Now everyone was sitting in front of the television set, on a holiday, at a family party! I remember being stunned by how awful that was. Somehow the television had become more attractive."

As families have come to spend more and more of their time together   24
engaged in video activities, those rituals and pastimes that once gave family life its special quality have become more and more uncommon. Not since prehistoric times, when cave families hunted, gathered, ate, and slept, with little time remaining to accumulate a culture of any significance, have families been reduced to such a sameness.

REAL PEOPLE

It is not only the activities that a family might engage in together that   25
are diminished by the powerful presence of television in the home. The relationships of the family members to each other are also affected, in both obvious and subtle ways. The hours that children spend in a one-way relationship with television people, an involvement that allows for no communication or interaction, surely affect their relationships with real-life people.

Studies show the importance of eye-to-eye contact, for instance, in   26
real-life relationships, and indicate that the nature of one's eye-contact patterns, whether one looks another squarely in the eye or looks to the

side or shifts one's gaze from side to side, may play a significant role in one's success or failure in human relationships. But no eye contact is possible in the child-television relationship, although in certain children's programs people purport to speak directly to the child and the camera fosters this illusion by focusing directly upon the person being filmed. How might such a distortion of real-life relationships affect a child's development of trust, of openness, of an ability to relate well to other *real* people?

Bruno Bettelheim writes: 27

> Children who have been taught, or conditioned, to listen passively most of the day to the warm verbal communications coming from the TV screen, to the deep emotional appeal of the so-called TV personality, are often unable to respond to real persons because they arouse so much less feeling than the skilled actor. Worse, they lose the ability to learn from reality because life experiences are much more complicated than the ones they see on the screen. . . .

A teacher makes a similar observation about her personal viewing experiences: 28

"I have trouble mobilizing myself and dealing with real people after watching a few hours of television. It's just hard to make that transition from watching television to a real relationship. I suppose it's because there was no effort necessary while I was watching, and dealing with real people always requires a bit of effort. Imagine, then, how much harder it might be to do the same thing for a small child, particularly one who watches a lot of television every day."   29

But more obviously damaging to family relationships is the elimination of opportunities to talk, and perhaps more important, to argue, to air grievances, between parents and children and brothers and sisters. Families frequently use television to avoid confronting their problems, problems that will not go away if they are ignored but will only fester and become less easily resolvable as time goes on.   30

A mother reports: 31

"I find myself, with three children, wanting to turn on the TV set when they're fighting. I really have to struggle not to do it because I feel that's telling them this is the solution to the quarrel — but it's so tempting that I often do it."   32

A family therapist discusses the use of television as an avoidance mechanism: 33

"In a family I know the father comes home from work and turns on the television set. The children come and watch with him and the wife serves them their meal in front of the set. He then goes and takes a shower, or works on the car or something. She then goes and has her own dinner in front of the television set. It's a symptom of a deeper-rooted problem, sure. But it would help them all to get rid of the set. It would be far easier to work on what the symptom really means without the television. The television simply encourages a double avoidance of each other. They'd find   34 out more quickly what was going on if they weren't able to hide behind the TV. Things wouldn't necessarily be better, of course, but they wouldn't be anesthetized."

The decreased opportunities for simple conversation between parents   35
and children in the television-centered home may help explain an observation made by an emergency room nurse at a Boston hospital. She reports that parents just seem to sit there these days when they come in with a sick or seriously injured child, although talking to the child would distract and comfort him. "They don't seem to know *how* to talk to their own children at any length," the nurse observes. Similarly, a television critic writes in *The New York Times:* "I had just a day ago taken my son to the emergency ward of a hospital for stitches above his left eye, and the occasion seemed no more real to me than real-life disasters seen on television. There was distance and numbness and an inability to turn off the total institution. I didn't behave at all; I just watched. . . ."

A number of research studies substantiate the assumption that televi-   36
sion interferes with family activities and the formation of family relationships. One survey shows that 78 percent of the respondents indicate no conversation taking place during viewing except at specified times such as commercials. The study notes: "The television atmosphere in most households is one of quiet absorption on the part of family members who are present. The nature of the family social life during a program could be described as 'parallel' rather than interactive, and the set does seem to dominate family life when it is on." Thirty-six percent of the respondents in another study indicated that television viewing was the only family activity participated in during the week.

In a summary of research findings on television's effect on family   37
interactions James Garbarino states: "The early findings suggest that television had a disruptive effect upon interaction and thus presumably human development. . . . It is not unreasonable to ask: 'Is the fact that the average American family during the 1950s came to include two parents, two children, and a television set somehow related to the psychosocial characteristics of the young adults of the 1970s?'"

UNDERMINING THE FAMILY

In its effect on family relationships, in its facilitation of parental with-   38
drawal from an active role in the socialization of their children, and in its replacement of family rituals and special events, television has played an important role in the disintegration of the American family. But of course it has not been the only contributing factor, perhaps not even the most important one. The steadily rising divorce rate, the increase in the number of working mothers, the decline of the extended family, the breakdown of neighborhoods and communities, the growing isolation of the nuclear family — all have seriously affected the family.

As Urie Bronfenbrenner suggests, the sources of family breakdown do   39
not come from the family itself, but from the circumstances in which the
family finds itself and the way of life imposed upon it by those circumstances. "When those circumstances and the way of life they generate
undermine relationships of trust and emotional security between family
members, when they make it difficult for parents to care for, educate, and
enjoy their children, when there is no support or recognition from the outside world for one's role as a parent, and when time spent with one's family means frustration of career, personal fulfillment, and peace of mind,
then the development of the child is adversely affected," he writes.

But while the roots of alienation go deep into the fabric of American   40
social history, television's presence in the home fertilizes them, encourages their wild and unchecked growth. Perhaps it is true that America's
commitment to the television experience masks a spiritual vacuum, an
empty and barren way of life, a desert of materialism. But it is television's
dominant role in the family that anesthetizes the family into accepting
its unhappy state and prevents it from struggling to better its condition,
to improve its relationships, and to regain some of the richness it once
possessed.

Others have noted the role of mass media in perpetuating an unsatis-   41
factory *status quo*. Leisure-time activity, writes Irving Howe, "must provide relief from work monotony without making the return to work too
unbearable; it must provide amusement without insight and pleasure
without disturbance — as distinct from art which gives pleasure through
disturbance. Mass culture is thus oriented towards a central aspect of
industrial society: the depersonalization of the individual." Similarly,
Jacques Ellul rejects the idea that television is a legitimate means of edu-
cating the citizen: "Education . . . takes place only incidentally. The cloud-
ing of his consciousness is paramount. . . ."

And so the American family muddles on, dimly aware that something   42
is amiss but distracted from an understanding of its plight by an endless
stream of video images. As family ties grow weaker and vaguer, as children's lives become more separate from their parents', as parents' educational role in their children's lives is taken over by television and schools,
family life becomes increasingly more unsatisfying for both parents and
children. All that seems to be left is love, an abstraction that family members *know* is necessary but find great difficulty giving each other because
the traditional opportunities for expressing love within the family have
been reduced or destroyed.

For contemporary parents, love toward each other has increasingly   43
come to mean successful sexual relations, as witnessed by the proliferation of sex manuals and sex therapists. The opportunities for manifesting
other forms of love through mutual support, understanding, nurturing,
even, to use an unpopular word, *serving* each other, are less and less available as mothers and fathers seek their independent destinies outside the
family.

As for love of children, this love is increasingly expressed through   44
supplying material comforts, amusements, and educational opportunities. Parents show their love for their children by sending them to good
schools and camps, by providing them with good food and good doctors,
by buying them toys, books, games, and a television set of their very own.
Parents will even go further and express their love by attending PTA meetings to improve their children's schools, or by joining groups that are acting to improve the quality of their children's television programs.

But this is love at a remove, and is rarely understood by children. The   45
more direct forms of parental love require time and patience, steady, dependable, ungrudgingly given time actually spent *with* children, reading to
them, comforting them, playing, joking, and working with them. But even
if parents were eager and willing to demonstrate that sort of direct love to
their children today, the opportunities are diminished. What with school
and Little League and piano lessons and, of course, the inevitable television programs, a day seems to offer just enough time for a good-night kiss.

• • •

COMPREHENSION

1. How did early observers view television? How, in general, does Winn's
   view differ from theirs?

2. How has the nature of family television viewing changed since its incep-
   tion? How does Winn account for this change?

3. How does television keep families apart? In what sense does Winn see
   television as a threat to the very nature of the family?

4. How does Winn define "family rituals" (19)? According to Winn, how has
   television affected these rituals?

5. What other factors besides television does Winn see as having a negative
   effect on the family?

6. Why does Winn believe today's families have such difficulty expressing
   love?

PURPOSE AND AUDIENCE

1. Winn states her thesis in paragraph 8. What is it?

2. In paragraphs 10 and 27, Winn quotes two noted psychologists. What
   effect do you think she expects their words to have on her audience?

3. What effect do you believe the young woman's testimony in paragraphs
   22–23 is calculated to have on Winn's readers?

4. Do you think Winn presents enough evidence to support her thesis?
   Explain your position.

5. In paragraph 24, Winn makes an **analogy** between modern families and
   cave families. What is her purpose in doing this? Is this a valid analogy?

STYLE AND STRUCTURE

1. Winn does not state her thesis until paragraph 8. What does she do in the paragraphs that precede this?

2. The length of Winn's paragraphs varies considerably. What effect do you think short paragraphs such as paragraphs 2, 3, 4, and 20 are likely to have on readers?

3. From what sources does Winn draw the many quotations she uses in this essay? How does the varied nature of these quotations help support her thesis?

4. This essay includes four headings: "The Quality of Family Life," "Family Rituals," "Real People," and "Undermining the Family." What functions do these headings serve? Could they be omitted? Should they be? Why or why not?

5. Winn's focus in this essay is on the effects of television on the American family. In the last four paragraphs, however, her focus widens, and she touches on television only incidentally. Does this concluding strategy strengthen or weaken her essay? Explain.

6. This is a fairly long essay. Is it *too* long? What, if anything, could Winn have cut?

VOCABULARY PROJECTS

1. Define each of the following words as it is used in this selection.

myopia (1)	counterbalances (13)	facilitation (38)
ameliorate (8)	regimented (14)	perpetuating (41)
advent (8)	mediating (17)	depersonalization (41)
subsidiary (8)	adhesive (19)	amiss (42)
apologists (8)	fosters (26)	abstraction (42)
equivocal (9)	substantiate (36)	remove (45)

2. One effect of television has been on our vocabulary: television has spawned new words (for example, *sitcom*) and suggested new uses for old words (for instance, *tube*). List as many television-inspired words as you can, and define each.

JOURNAL ENTRY

What effects — positive or negative — do you think television has had on your life? What would your life be like without it?

WRITING WORKSHOP

1. Write an essay in which you consider the effects (including any possible future effects) of one of these inventions on the American family: the cellular phone, the personal computer, the microwave, the calculator, the VCR, the Walkman, Nintendo, the answering machine, the pager.

2. Write a cause-and-effect essay in which you discuss the *positive* effects of television on American society.

3. Winn's essay, although recently updated for this book, is nearly thirty years old, and both television and viewers have changed considerably since she wrote "The Plug-In Drug." Write a cause-and-effect essay about television in which you consider developments that Winn does not take into account — for example, the availability of cable television, satellite dishes, and pay-per-view broadcasts.

COMBINING THE PATTERNS

Winn's essay relies on several patterns of development besides cause and effect. Where does she use **narration? Definition? Exemplification?** Why does she use each of these patterns?

THEMATIC CONNECTIONS

- "Once More to the Lake" (page 154)
- "The Great Campus Goof-Off Machine" (page 188)
- "The Human Cost of an Illiterate Society" (page 203)
- "It's Just Too Late" (page 304)

▰▰▰▰▰▰▰▰
LAWRENCE OTIS GRAHAM

Lawrence Otis Graham was born in 1962 into one of the few African-American families then living in an upper-middle-class community in Westchester County, near New York City. A graduate of Princeton University and Harvard Law School, Graham works as a corporate attorney in Manhattan and teaches at Fordham University. He is the author of some dozen books and has received considerable attention for "Invisible Man," an article recounting his experiences when he took a temporary leave from his job as an attorney to work as a busboy at a century-old country club in Greenwich, Connecticut ("the only way a black man like me could get in"). The article was included in the Best American Essays series. Graham's most recent book is *Our Kind of People: Inside the Black Upper Class* (1999).

The following essay was originally published in the *New York Times* in 1991 and was included in Graham's 1995 essay collection, *Member of the Club: Reflections on Life in a Racially Polarized Society*. In "The 'Black Table' Is Still There," Graham returns to his largely white junior high school and discovers to his dismay how little has changed since the 1970s. Although the federal government has strongly supported integration — for example, the Supreme Court found segregation of public schools unconstitutional in 1955, the Civil Rights Act of 1964 required school systems to initiate integration programs, and a 1971 Supreme Court decision upheld busing as a means to achieve integration — voluntary segregation still exists.

The "Black Table" Is Still There

During a recent visit to my old junior high school in Westchester County, I came upon something that I never expected to see again, something that was a source of fear and dread for three hours each school morning of my early adolescence: the all-black lunch table in the cafeteria of my predominantly white suburban junior high school.

As I look back on 27 years of often being the first and only black person integrating such activities and institutions as the college newspaper, the high school tennis team, summer music camps, our all-white suburban neighborhood, my eating club at Princeton, or my private social club at Harvard Law School, the one scenario that puzzled me the most then and now is the all-black lunch table.

Why was it there? Why did the black kids separate themselves? What did the table say about the integration that was supposedly going on in home rooms and gym classes? What did it say about the black kids? The white kids? What did it say about me when I refused to sit there, day after day, for three years?

Each afternoon, at 12:03 P.M., after the fourth period ended, I found myself among 600 12-, 13-, and 14-year-olds who marched into the brightly-lit cafeteria and dashed for a seat at one of the 27 blue formica lunch tables.

No matter who I walked in with — usually a white friend — no mat-   5
ter what mood I was in, there was one thing that was certain: I would not
sit at the black table.

I would never consider sitting at the black table.   6

What was wrong with me? What was I afraid of?   7

I would like to think that my decision was a heroic one, made in order   8
to express my solidarity with the theories of integration that my community was espousing. But I was just 12 at the time, and there was nothing
heroic in my actions.

I avoided the black table for a very simple reason: I was afraid that by   9
sitting at the black table I'd lose all my white friends. I thought that by sitting there I'd be making a racist, anti-white statement.

Is that what the all-black table means? Is it a rejection of white people?   10
I no longer think so.

At the time, I was angry that there was a black lunch table. I believed   11
that the black kids were the reason why other kids didn't mix more. I was
ready to believe that their self-segregation was the cause of white bigotry.

Ironically, I even believed this after my best friend (who was white)   12
told me I probably shouldn't come to his bar mitzvah because I'd be the
only black and people would feel uncomfortable. I even believed this after
my Saturday afternoon visit, at age 10, to a private country club pool
prompted incensed white parents to pull their kids from the pool in terror.

In the face of this blatantly racist (anti-black) behavior I still somehow   13
managed to blame only the black kids for being the barrier to integration
in my school and my little world. What was I thinking?

I realize now how wrong I was. During that same time, there were at   14
least two tables of athletes, an Italian table, a Jewish girls' table, a Jewish
boys' table (where I usually sat), a table of kids who were into heavy metal
music and smoking pot, a table of middle-class Irish kids. Weren't these
tables just as segregationist as the black table? At the time, no one thought
so. At the time, no one even acknowledged the segregated nature of these
other tables.

Maybe it's the color difference that makes all-black tables or all-black   15
groups attract the scrutiny and wrath of so many people. It scares and
angers people; it exasperates. It did those things to me, and I'm black.

As an integrating black person, I know that my decision *not* to join the   16
black lunch table attracted its own kinds of scrutiny and wrath from my
classmates. At the same time that I heard angry words like "Oreo" and
"white boy" being hurled at me from the black table, I was also dodging
impatient questions from white classmates: "Why do all those black kids
sit together?" or "Why don't you ever sit with the other blacks?"

The black lunch table, like those other segregated tables, is a comment   17
on the superficial inroads that integration has made in society. Perhaps I
should be happy that even this is a long way from where we started. Yet, I
can't get over the fact that the 27th table in my junior high school cafeteria
is still known as the "black table"— 14 years after my adolescence.

●　●　●

COMPREHENSION

1. What exactly is the "black table"?

2. In paragraph 1, Graham says that on a recent visit to his old junior high school he "came upon something that [he] never expected to see again." Why do you think the sight of the all-black lunch table was such a surprise to him?

3. In Graham's junior high school, what factors determined where students sat?

4. Why didn't Graham sit at the black table when he was in junior high?

5. When he was a junior high school student, whom did Graham blame for the existence of the exclusively black lunch table? Whom or what does he now see as the cause of the table's existence?

PURPOSE AND AUDIENCE

1. What is Graham's thesis?

2. Rather than introducing outside supporting information — such as statistics, interviews with educators, or sociological studies — Graham relies on his own opinions and on anecdotal evidence to support his thesis. Do you think this is enough? Explain.

3. What is Graham's purpose in giving background information about himself in this essay — for example, in paragraphs 2 and 12? How does this information affect your reaction to him as a person? To his essay? Do you think he needs to supply additional information about himself or his school? If so, what kind of information would be helpful?

4. Do you think Graham's primary purpose is to criticize a system he despises, to change his audience's views about segregated lunch tables, or to justify his own behavior? Explain your conclusion.

5. In paragraph 5, Graham tells readers that he usually entered the cafeteria with a white friend; in paragraph 12, he reveals that his best friend was white. Why do you suppose he wants his audience to know these facts?

STYLE AND STRUCTURE

1. Throughout his essay Graham asks **rhetorical questions.** Identify as many of these questions as you can. Are they necessary? Provocative? Distracting? Explain.

2. In paragraph 16, Graham quotes his long-ago classmates. What do these quotations reveal? Should he have included more of them?

3. Is Graham's focus on finding causes, describing effects, or both? Explain.

4. This essay uses first-person pronouns and contractions. Do you think Graham would have more credibility if he used a style that was less personal and more formal? Why or why not?

VOCABULARY PROJECTS

1. Define each of the following words as it is used in this selection.

   scenario (2)   incensed (12)   scrutiny (15)
   espousing (8)   blatantly (13)   inroads (17)

2. Does the phrase *black table* have a negative connotation for you? Do you think this is Graham's intention? What other names could he give to the table that might present it in a more neutral, even positive, light? What names could he give to the other tables he lists in paragraph 14?

JOURNAL ENTRY

Graham sees the continued presence of the black table as a serious problem. Do you agree?

WRITING WORKSHOP

1. In paragraph 14, Graham mentions other lunch tables that were limited to certain groups and asks, "Weren't these tables just as segregationist as the black table?" Answer his question in a cause-and-effect essay that explains why you believe "black tables" exist.

2. In addition to self-segregated lunch tables, many schools also have single-race social clubs, dormitories, fraternities, and even graduation ceremonies. Do you see such self-segregation as something that divides our society (that is, as a cause) or as something that reflects divisions that already exist (that is, as an effect)? Write an essay in which you discuss this issue, supporting your thesis with examples from your own experience.

3. Do the people in your school or workplace tend to segregate themselves according to race, gender, or some other principle? Do you see a problem in such behavior? Write a memo to your school's dean of students or to your employer explaining what you believe causes this pattern and what effects, positive or negative, you have observed.

COMBINING THE PATTERNS

In paragraph 14, Graham uses **classification and division.** What is he categorizing? What categories does he identify? What other categories might he include? Why is this pattern of development particularly appropriate for this essay?

THEMATIC CONNECTIONS

- "Just Walk On By" (page 197)
- "College Pressures" (page 390)
- "The Ways We Lie" (page 426)
- "Why Special Housing for Ethnic Students Makes Sense" (page 551)

◗◗◗◗◗◗◗◗

LINDA M. HASSELSTROM

Linda M. Hasselstrom (1943–) grew up in rural South Dakota, the daughter of a cattle ranching family. After receiving a master's degree in journalism from the University of Missouri, she returned to South Dakota to run her own ranch for a number of years, and now lives in Cheyenne, Wyoming. A highly respected poet, essayist, and writing teacher, she often focuses in her work on everyday life in the American West. Her publications include the poetry collections *Caught by One Wing* (1984), *Roadkill* (1987), and *Dakota Bones* (1991); the essay collection *Land Circle* (1991); and the nonfiction work *A Roadside History of South Dakota* (1994).

In this essay from *Land Circle,* Hasselstrom explains her reluctant decision to become licensed to carry a concealed handgun. Her gun ownership can certainly be considered in the context of the ongoing debate over how (and even whether) stricter gun control measures should be enacted in the United States. But equally important is the fact that her reason for carrying a gun is to protect herself from sexual assault. A study by the Bureau of Justice Statistics found that in 1997 some 115,000 women were raped in this country, with another 79,000 victims of rape attempts. Another study found that one in seven women interviewed had been raped at least once. Most experts agree that rape tends to be underreported, so there are probably more rapes than these figures indicate.

A Peaceful Woman Explains
Why She Carries a Gun

I am a peace-loving woman. But several events in the past 10 years   1
have convinced me I'm safer when I carry a pistol. This was a personal decision, but because handgun possession is a controversial subject, perhaps my reasoning will interest others.

I live in western South Dakota on a ranch 25 miles from the nearest   2
town: for several years I spent winters alone here. As a free-lance writer, I travel alone a lot — more than 100,000 miles by car in the last four years. With women freer than ever before to travel alone, the odds of our encountering trouble seem to have risen. Distances are great, roads are deserted, and the terrain is often too exposed to offer hiding places.

A woman who travels alone is advised, usually by men, to protect her-   3
self by avoiding bars and other "dangerous situations," by approaching her car like an Indian scout, by locking doors and windows. But these precautions aren't always enough. I spent years following them and still found myself in dangerous situations. I began to resent the idea that just because I am female, I have to be extra careful.

A few years ago, with another woman, I camped for several weeks in   4
the West. We discussed self-defense, but neither of us had taken a course in it. She was against firearms, and local police told us Mace was illegal. So

we armed ourselves with spray cans of deodorant tucked into our sleeping bags. We never used our improvised Mace because we were lucky enough to camp beside people who came to our aid when men harassed us. But on one occasion we visited a national park where our assigned space was less than 15 feet from other campers. When we returned from a walk, we found our closest neighbors were two young men. As we gathered our cooking gear, they drank beer and loudly discussed what they would do to us after dark. Nearby campers, even families, ignored them: rangers strolled past, unconcerned. When we asked the rangers point-blank if they would protect us, one of them patted my shoulder and said, "Don't worry, girls. They're just kidding." At dusk we drove out of the park and hid our camp in the woods a few miles away. The illegal spot was lovely, but our enjoyment of that park was ruined. I returned from the trip determined to reconsider the options available for protecting myself.

At that time, I lived alone on the ranch and taught night classes in   5 town. Along a city street I often traveled, a woman had a flat tire, called for help on her CB radio, and got a rapist who left her beaten. She was afraid to call for help again and stayed in her car until morning. For that reason, as well as because CBs work best along line-of-sight, which wouldn't help much in the rolling hills where I live, I ruled out a CB.

As I drove home one night, a car followed me. It passed me on a nar-   6 row bridge while a passenger flashed a blinding spotlight in my face. I braked sharply. The car stopped, angled across the bridge, and four men jumped out. I realized the locked doors were useless if they broke the windows of my pickup. I started forward, hoping to knock their car aside so I could pass. Just then another car appeared, and the men hastily got back in their car. They continued to follow me, passing and repassing. I dared not go home because no one else was there. I passed no lighted houses. Finally they pulled over to the roadside, and I decided to use their tactic: fear. Speeding, the pickup horn blaring, I swerved as close to them as I dared as I roared past. It worked: they turned off the highway. But I was frightened and angry. Even in my vehicle I was too vulnerable.

Other incidents occurred over the years. One day I glanced out at a   7 field below my house and saw a man with a shotgun walking toward a pond full of ducks. I drove down and explained that the land was posted. I politely asked him to leave. He stared at me, and the muzzle of the shotgun began to rise. In a moment of utter clarity I realized that I was alone on the ranch, and that he could shoot me and simply drive away. The moment passed: the man left.

One night, I returned home from teaching a class to find deep tire ruts   8 in the wet ground of my yard, garbage in the driveway, and a large gas tank empty. A light shone in the house: I couldn't remember leaving it on. I was too embarrassed to drive to a neighboring ranch and wake someone up. An hour of cautious exploration convinced me the house was safe, but once inside, with the doors locked, I was still afraid. I kept thinking of how vulnerable I felt, prowling around my own house in the dark.

My first positive step was to take a kung fu class, which teaches eva-   9
sive or protective action when someone enters your space without permission. I learned to move confidently, scanning for possible attackers.
I learned how to assess danger and techniques for avoiding it without
combat.

I also learned that one must practice several hours every day to be   10
good at kung fu. By that time I had married George: when I practiced with
him, I learned how *close* you must be to your attacker to use martial arts,
and decided a 120-pound woman dare not let a six-foot, 220-pound
attacker get that close unless she is very, very good at self-defense. I have
since read articles by several women who were extremely well trained in
the martial arts, but were raped and beaten anyway.

I thought back over the times in my life when I had been attacked or   11
threatened and tried to be realistic about my own behavior, searching for
anything that had allowed me to become a victim. Overall, I was convinced that I had not been at fault. I don't believe myself to be either paranoid or a risk-taker, but I wanted more protection.

With some reluctance I decided to try carrying a pistol. George had   12
always carried one, despite his size and his training in martial arts. I practiced shooting until I was sure I could hit an attacker who moved close
enough to endanger me. Then I bought a license from the county sheriff,
making it legal for me to carry the gun concealed.

But I was not yet ready to defend myself. George taught me that the   13
most important preparation was mental: convincing myself I could actually *shoot a person*. Few of us wish to hurt or kill another human being. But
there is no point in having a gun; in fact, gun possession might increase
your danger unless you know you can use it. I got in the habit of rehearsing, as I drove or walked, the precise conditions that would be required
before I would shoot someone.

People who have not grown up with the idea that they are capable of   14
protecting themselves — in other words, most women — might have to
work hard to convince themselves of their ability, and of the necessity.
Handgun ownership need not turn us into gunslingers, but it can be part
of believing in, and relying on, *ourselves* for protection.

To be useful, a pistol has to be available. In my car, it's within instant   15
reach. When I enter a deserted rest stop at night, it's in my purse, with my
hand on the grip. When I walk from a dark parking lot into a motel, it's in
my hand, under a coat. At home, it's on the headboard. In short, I take it
with me almost everywhere I go alone.

Just carrying a pistol is not protection; avoidance is still the best   16
approach to trouble. Subconsciously watching for signs of danger, I
believe I've become more alert. Handgun use, not unlike driving, becomes
instinctive. Each time I've drawn my gun — I have never fired it at
another human being — I've simply found it in my hand.

I was driving the half-mile to the highway mailbox one day when I   17
saw a vehicle parked about midway down the road. Several men were

standing in the ditch, relieving themselves. I have no objection to emergency urination, but I noticed they'd dumped several dozen beer cans in the road. Besides being ugly, cans can slash a cow's feet or stomach.

The men noticed me before they finished and made quite a perfor-   18
mance out of zipping their trousers while walking toward me. All four of them gathered around my small foreign car, and one of them demanded what the hell I wanted.

"This is private land. I'd appreciate it if you'd pick up the beer   19
cans."

"What beer cans?" said the belligerent one, putting both hands on the   20
car door and leaning in my window. His face was inches from mine, and the beer fumes were strong. The others laughed. One tried the passenger door, locked; another put his foot on the hood and rocked the car. They circled, lightly thumping the roof, discussing my good fortune in meeting them and the benefits they were likely to bestow upon me. I felt very small and very trapped and they knew it.

"The ones you just threw out," I said politely.   21

"I don't see no beer cans. Why don't you get out here and show them   22
to me, honey?" said the belligerent one, reaching for the handle inside my door.

"Right over there," I said, still being polite. "— there, and over there."   23
I pointed with the pistol, which I'd slipped under my thigh. Within one minute the cans and the men were back in the car and headed down the road.

I believe this incident illustrates several important principles. The   24
men were trespassing and knew it: their judgment may have been impaired by alcohol. Their response to the polite request of a woman alone was to use their size, numbers, and sex to inspire fear. The pistol was a response in the same language. Politeness didn't work: I couldn't match them in size or number. Out of the car, I'd have been more vulnerable. The pistol just changed the balance of power. It worked again recently when I was driving in a desolate part of Wyoming. A man played cat-and-mouse with me for 30 miles, ultimately trying to run me off the road. When his car passed mine with only two inches to spare, I showed him my pistol, and he disappeared.

When I got my pistol, I told my husband, revising the old Colt slogan,   25
"God made men *and women*, but Sam Colt made them equal." Recently I have seen a gunmaker's ad with a similar sentiment. Perhaps this is an idea whose time has come, though the pacifist inside me will be saddened if the only way women can achieve equality is by carrying weapons.

We must treat a firearm's power with caution. "Power tends to cor-   26
rupt, and absolute power corrupts absolutely," as a man (Lord Acton) once said. A pistol is not the only way to avoid being raped or murdered in today's world, but, intelligently wielded, it can shift the balance of power and provide a measure of safety.

•   •   •

COMPREHENSION

1. According to Hasselstrom, why does she carry a gun? In one sentence, summarize her rationale.

2. List the specific events that led Hasselstrom to her decision to carry a gun.

3. Other than carrying a gun, what means of protecting herself did Hasselstrom try? Why did she find them unsatisfactory? Can you think of other strategies she could have adopted instead of carrying a gun?

4. Where in the essay does Hasselstrom express her reluctance to carry a gun?

5. In paragraph 13, Hasselstrom says, "Gun possession might increase your danger unless you know you can use it." Where else does she touch on the possible pitfalls of carrying a gun?

6. What does Hasselstrom mean when she says, "The pistol just changed the balance of power" (paragraph 24)?

PURPOSE AND AUDIENCE

1. How does paragraph 1 establish Hasselstrom's purpose for writing this essay? What other purpose might she have?

2. What purpose does paragraph 5 serve? Is it necessary?

3. Do you think this essay is aimed at men, at women, or at both? Why?

4. Do you think Hasselstrom expects her readers to agree with her position? Where does she indicate that she expects them to challenge her? How does she address this challenge?

STYLE AND STRUCTURE

1. This essay is written in the first person, and it relies heavily on personal experience. Do you see this as a strength or a weakness? Explain.

2. What is the main cause in this cause-and-effect essay — that is, what is the most important reason Hasselstrom gives for carrying a gun? Can you identify any contributory causes?

3. Could you argue that simply being a woman is justification enough for carrying a gun? Do you think this is Hasselstrom's position? Explain.

4. Think of Hasselstrom's essay as the first step in a possible causal chain. What situations might result from her decision to carry a gun?

5. In paragraph 25, Hasselstrom says, "The pacifist inside me will be saddened if the only way women can achieve equality is by carrying weapons." In her title and elsewhere in the essay, Hasselstrom characterizes herself as a "peaceful woman." Do you think she is successful in using language like this to portray herself as a peace-loving woman who only reluctantly carries a gun? Why or why not?

VOCABULARY PROJECTS

1. Define each of the following words as it is used in this selection.

   posted (7)   belligerent (20)   wielded (26)
   muzzle (7)   bestow (20)

2. Some of the words and phrases Hasselstrom uses in this essay suggest that she sees her pistol as an equalizer, something that helps to compensate for her vulnerability. Identify the words and phrases she uses to characterize her gun in this way.

JOURNAL ENTRY

Do you agree that carrying a gun is Hasselstrom's only choice, or do you think there are other steps she could take to ensure her safety? Explain.

WRITING WORKSHOP

1. Hasselstrom lives in a rural area, and the scenarios she describes apply to rural life. Rewrite this essay as "A Peaceful Urban (or Suburban) Woman Explains Why She Carries a Gun."

2. What reasons might a "peace-loving" man have for carrying a gun? Write a cause-and-effect essay outlining such a man's motives, using any of Hasselstrom's reasons that might apply to him as well.

3. Write a cause-and-effect essay presenting reasons to support a position that opposes Hasselstrom's: "A Peaceful Woman (or Man) Explains Why She (or He) Will Not Carry a Gun."

COMBINING THE PATTERNS

Several times in her essay, Hasselstrom uses **narrative** to support her position. Identify these narrative passages. Are they absolutely essential to the essay? Could they be briefer? Could some be deleted? Explain.

THEMATIC CONNECTIONS

- "Shooting an Elephant" (page 104)
- "How the Lawyers Stole Winter" (page 362)
- "Unnatural Killers" (page 566)

CALVIN TRILLIN

Calvin Trillin was born in 1935 in St. Louis, Missouri, and graduated from Yale University in 1957. A writer of great versatility, he has published investigative pieces, humor columns, light verse, short stories, a novel, essays about American food and travel, and a memoir.

Between 1967 and 1982, Trillin contributed a regular column to the *New Yorker* called "U.S. Journal," reporting various human interest stories from around the country. "It's Just Too Late," which was part of this series, focuses on the events leading up to a fatal car crash and its aftermath in Knoxville, Tennessee, in 1979. In the introduction to *Killings* (1984), where this essay appears, Trillin notes that while he was researching the story, local reporters expressed surprise that readers of the *New Yorker* would be interested in a death that wouldn't have made the front pages of their own newspapers. After all, the dead girl, her family, and the person accused of causing her death were not "important," and the death did not even represent any sort of national "trend." For Trillin, however, this accident seemed "the central event in . . . a remarkable family drama," and in his hands the Cooper family's tragedy remains moving and powerfully revealing decades after it took place.

It's Just Too Late

— Knoxville, Tennessee
March 1979

Until she was sixteen, FaNee Cooper was what her parents sometimes   1
called an ideal child. "You'd never have to correct her," FaNee's mother has said. In sixth grade, FaNee won a spelling contest. She played the piano and the flute. She seemed to believe what she heard every Sunday at the Beaver Dam Baptist Church about good and evil and the hereafter. FaNee was not an outgoing child. Even as a baby, she was uncomfortable when she was held and cuddled. She found it easy to tell her parents she loved them but difficult to confide in them. Particularly compared to her sister, Kristy, a cheerful, open little girl two and a half years younger, she was reserved and introspective. The thoughts she kept to herself, though, were apparently happy thoughts. Her eighth-grade essay on Christmas — written in a remarkably neat hand — talked of the joys of helping put together toys for her little brother, Leo, Jr., and the importance of her parents' reminder that Christmas is the birthday of Jesus. Her parents were the sort of people who might have been expected to have an ideal child. As a boy, Leo Cooper had been called "one of the greatest high-school basketball players ever developed in Knox County." He went on to play basketball at East Tennessee State, and he married the homecoming queen, JoAnn Henson. After college, Cooper became a high-school basketball coach and teacher and, eventually, an administrator. By the time FaNee turned thirteen, in 1973, he was in his third year as the principal of Gresham

Junior High School, in Fountain City — a small Knox County town that had been swallowed up by Knoxville when the suburbs began to move north. A tall man with curly black hair going on gray, Leo Cooper has an elaborate way of talking ("Unless I'm very badly mistaken, he has never related to me totally the content of his conversation") and a manner that may come from years of trying to leave errant junior-high-school students with the impression that a responsible adult is magnanimous, even humble, about invariably being in the right. His wife, a high-school art teacher, paints and does batik, and created the name FaNee because she liked the way it looked and sounded — it sounds like "Fawnee" when the Coopers say it — but the impression she gives is not of artiness but of soft-spoken small-town gentility. When she found, in the course of cleaning up FaNee's room, that her ideal thirteen-year-old had been smoking cigarettes, she was, in her words, crushed. "FaNee was such a perfect child before that," JoAnn Cooper said some time later. "She was angry that we found out. She knew we knew that she had done something we didn't approve of, and then the rebellion started. I was hurt. I was very hurt. I guess it came through as disappointment."

Several months later, FaNee's grandmother died. FaNee had been   2
devoted to her grandmother. She wrote a poem in her memory — an almost joyous poem, filled with Christian faith in the afterlife ("Please don't grieve over my happiness/Rejoice with me in the presence of the Angels of Heaven"). She also took some keepsakes from her grandmother's house, and was apparently mortified when her parents found them and explained that they would have to be returned. By then, the Coopers were aware that FaNee was going to have a difficult time as a teenager. They thought she might be self-conscious about the double affliction of glasses and braces. They thought she might be uncomfortable in the role of the principal's daughter at Gresham. In ninth grade, she entered Halls High School, where JoAnn Cooper was teaching art. FaNee was a loner at first. Then she fell in with what could only be considered a bad crowd.

Halls, a few miles to the north of Fountain City, used to be known as   3
Halls Crossroads. It is what Knoxville people call "over the ridge"— on the side of Black Oak Ridge that has always been thought of as rural. When FaNee entered Halls High, the Coopers were already in the process of building a house on several acres of land they had bought in Halls, in a sparsely settled area along Brown Gap Road. Like two or three other houses along the road, it was to be constructed basically of huge logs taken from old buildings — a house that Leo Cooper describes as being, like the name FaNee, "just a little bit different." Ten years ago, Halls Crossroads was literally a crossroads. Then some of the Knoxville expansion that had swollen Fountain City spilled over the ridge, planting subdivisions here and there on roads that still went for long stretches with nothing but an occasional house with a cow or two next to it. The increase in population did not create a town. Halls has no center. Its commercial area

is a series of two or three shopping centers strung together on the Maynardville Highway, the four-lane that leads north into Union County — a
place almost synonymous in east Tennessee with mountain poverty. Its
restaurant is the Halls Freezo Drive-In. The gathering place for the group
FaNee Cooper eventually found herself in was the Maynardville Highway Exxon station.

At Halls High School, the social poles were represented by the Jocks   4
and the Freaks. FaNee found her friends among the Freaks. "I am truly
enlighted upon irregular trains of thought aimed at strange depots of
mental wards," she wrote when she was fifteen. "Yes! Crazed farms for
the mental off — Oh! I walked through the halls screams & loud laughter
fill my ears — Orderlys try to reason with me — but I am unreasonable!
The joys of being a FREAK in a circus of imagination." The little crowd of
eight or ten young people that FaNee joined has been referred to by her
mother as "the Union County group." A couple of the girls were from
backgrounds similar to FaNee's, but all the boys had the characteristics, if
not the precise addresses, that Knoxville people associate with the poor
whites of Union County. They were the sort of boys who didn't bother to
finish high school, or finished it in a special program for slow learners, or
get ejected from it for taking a swing at the principal.

"I guess you can say they more or less dragged us down to their level   5
with the drugs," a girl who was in the group — a girl who can be called
Marcia — said recently. "And somehow we settled for it. It seems like we
had to get ourselves in the pit before we could look out." People in the
group used marijuana and Valium and LSD. They sneered at the Jocks and
the "prim and proper little ladies" who went with Jocks. "We set ourselves
aside," Marcia now says. "We put ourselves above everyone. How we did
that I don't know." In a Knox County high school, teenagers who want to
get themselves in the pit need not mainline heroin. The Jocks they mean to
be compared to do not merely show up regularly for classes and practice
football and wear clean clothes; they watch their language and preach
temperance and go to prayer meetings on Wednesday nights and talk
about having a real good Christian witness. Around Knoxville, people
who speak of well-behaved high-school kids often seem to use words like
"perfect," or even "angels." For FaNee's group, the opposite was not difficult to figure out. "We were into wicked things, strange things," Marcia
says. "It was like we were on some kind of devil trip." FaNee wrote about
demons and vultures and rats. "Slithering serpents eat my sanity and bite
my ass," she wrote in an essay called "The Lovely Road of Life," just after
she turned sixteen, "while tornadoes derail and ever so swiftly destroy
every car in my train of thought." She wrote a lot about death.

FaNee's girl friends spoke of her as "super-intelligent." Her English   6
teacher found some of her writing profound — and disturbing. She was
thought to be not just super-intelligent but super-mysterious, and even, at
times, super-weird — an introverted girl who stared straight ahead with
deep-brown, nearly black eyes and seemed to have thoughts she couldn't

share. Nobody really knew why she had chosen to run with the Freaks —
whether it was loneliness or rebellion or simple boredom. Marcia thought
it might have had something to do with a feeling that her parents had
settled on Kristy as their perfect child. "I guess she figured she couldn't be
the best," Marcia said recently. "So she decided she might as well be the
worst."

Toward the spring of FaNee's junior year at Halls, her problems   7
seemed to deepen. Despite her intelligence, her grades were sliding. She
was what her mother called "a mental dropout." Leo Cooper had to visit
Halls twice because of minor suspensions. Once, FaNee had been caught
smoking. Once, having ducked out of a required assembly, she was spot-
ted by a favorite teacher, who turned her in. At home, she exchanged little
more than short, strained formalities with Kristy, who shared their parents' opinion of FaNee's choice of friends. The Coopers had finished their
house — a large house, its size accentuated by the huge old logs and a
great stone fireplace and outsize "Paul Bunyan"-style furniture — but
FaNee spent most of her time there in her own room, sleeping or listening
to rock music through earphones. One night, there was a terrible scene
when FaNee returned from a concert in a condition that Leo Cooper knew
had to be the result of marijuana. JoAnn Cooper, who ordinarily strikes
people as too gentle to raise her voice, found herself losing her temper regularly. Finally, Leo Cooper asked a counselor he knew, Jim Griffin, to stop
in at Halls High School and have a talk with FaNee — unofficially.

Griffin — a young man with a warm, informal manner — worked for   8
the Juvenile Court of Knox County. He had a reputation for being able to
reach teenagers who wouldn't talk to their parents or to school administrators. One Friday in March of 1977, he spent an hour and a half talking to
FaNee Cooper. As Griffin recalls the interview, FaNee didn't seem
alarmed by his presence. She seemed to him calm and controlled — Griffin thought it was something like talking to another adult — and, unlike
most teenagers he dealt with, she looked him in the eye the entire time.
Griffin, like some of FaNee's friends, found her eyes unsettling — "the
coldest, most distant, but, at the same time, the most knowing eyes I'd
ever seen." She expressed affection for her parents, but she didn't seem
interested in exploring ways of getting along better with them. The
impression she gave Griffin was that they were who they were, and she
was who she was, and there didn't happen to be any connection. Several
times, she made the same response to Griffin's suggestions: "It's too late."

That weekend, neither FaNee nor her parents brought up the subject   9
of Griffin's visit. Leo Cooper has spoken of the weekend as being particularly happy; a friend of FaNee's who stayed over remembers it as particularly strained. FaNee stayed home from school on Monday because of a
bad headache — she often had bad headaches — but felt well enough on
Monday evening to drive to the library. She was to be home at nine. When
she wasn't, Mrs. Cooper began to phone her friends. Finally, around ten,

Leo Cooper got into his other car and took a swing around Halls — past the teenage hangouts like the Exxon station and the Pizza Hut and the Smoky Mountain Market. Then he took a second swing. At eleven, FaNee was still not home.

She hadn't gone to the library. She had picked up two girl friends and   10 driven to the home of a third, where everyone took five Valium tablets. Then the four girls drove over to the Exxon station, where they met four boys from their crowd. After a while, the group bought some beer and some marijuana and reassembled at Charlie Stevens's trailer. Charlie Stevens was five or six years older than everyone else in the group — a skinny, slow-thinking young man with long black hair and a sparse beard. He was married and had a child, but he and his wife had separated; she was back in Union County with the baby. Stevens had remained in their trailer — parked in the yard near his mother's house, in a back-road area of Knox County dominated by decrepit, unpainted sheds and run-down trailers and rusted-out automobiles. Stevens had picked up FaNee at home once or twice — apparently, more as a driver for the group than as a date — and the Coopers, having learned that his unsuitability extended to being married, had asked her not to see him.

In Charlie's trailer, which had no heat or electricity, the group drank   11 beer and passed around joints, keeping warm with blankets. By eleven or so, FaNee was what one of her friends has called "super-messed-up." Her speech was slurred. She was having trouble keeping her balance. She had decided not to go home. She had apparently persuaded herself that her parents intended to send her away to some sort of home for incorrigibles. "It's too late," she said to one of her friends. "It's just too late." It was decided that one of the boys, David Munsey, who was more or less the leader of the group, would drive the Coopers' car to FaNee's house, where FaNee and Charlie Stevens would pick him up in Stevens's car — a worn Pinto with four bald tires, one light, and a dragging muffler. FaNee wrote a note to her parents, and then, perhaps because her handwriting was suffering the effects of beer and marijuana and Valium, asked Stevens to rewrite it on a large piece of paper, which would be left on the seat of the Coopers' car. The Stevens version was just about the same as FaNee's, except that Stevens left out a couple of sentences about trying to work things out ("I'm willing to try") and, not having won any spelling championship himself, he misspelled a few words, like "tomorrow." The note said, "Dear Mom and Dad. Sorry I'm late. Very late. I left your car because I thought you might need it tomorrow. I love you all, but this is something I just had to do. The man talked to me privately for one and a half hours and I was really scared, so this is something I just had to do, but don't worry. I'm with a very good friend. Love you all. FaNee. P.S. Please try to understand I love you all very much, really I do. Love me if you have a chance."

At eleven-thirty or so, Leo Cooper was sitting in his living room, look-   12 ing out the window at his driveway — a long gravel road that runs almost four hundred feet from the house to Brown Gap Road. He saw the car that FaNee had been driving pull into the driveway. "She's home," he called to his wife, who had just left the room. Cooper walked out on the deck over the garage. The car had stopped at the end of the driveway, and the lights had gone out. He got into his other car and drove to the end of the driveway. David Munsey had already joined Charlie Stevens and FaNee, and the Pinto was just leaving, travelling at a normal rate of speed. Leo Cooper pulled out on the road behind them.

Stevens turned left on Crippen Road, a road that has a field on one side and two or three small houses on the other, and there Cooper pulled his car in front of the Pinto and stopped, blocking the way. He got out and walked toward the Pinto. Suddenly, Stevens put the car in reverse, backed into a driveway a hundred yards behind him, and sped off. Cooper jumped in his car and gave chase. Stevens raced back to Brown Gap Road, ran a stop sign there, ran another stop sign at Maynardville Highway, turned north, veered off onto the old Andersonville Pike, a nearly abandoned road that runs parallel to the highway, and then crossed back over the highway to the narrow, dark country roads on the other side. Stevens sometimes drove with his lights out. He took some of the corners by suddenly applying his hand brake to make the car swerve around in a ninety-degree turn. He was in familiar territory — he actually passed his trailer — and Cooper had difficulty keeping up. Past the trailer, Stevens swept down a hill into a sharp left turn that took him onto Foust Hollow Road, a winding, hilly road not much wider than one car. 13

At a fork, Cooper thought he had lost the Pinto. He started to go right and then saw what seemed to be a spark from Stevens's dragging muffler off to the left, in the darkness. Cooper took the left fork, down Salem Church Road. He went down a hill and then up a long, curving hill to a crest, where he saw the Stevens car ahead. "I saw the car airborne. Up in the air," he later testified. "It was up in the air. And then it completely rolled over one more time. It started to make another flip forward, and just as it started to flip to the other side it flipped back this way, and my daughter's body came out." 14

Cooper slammed on his brakes and skidded to a stop up against the Pinto. "Book!" Stevens shouted — the group's equivalent of "Scram!" Stevens and Munsey disappeared into the darkness. "It was dark, no one around, and so I started yelling for FaNee," Cooper had testified. "I thought it was an eternity before I could find her body, wedged under the back end of that car. . . . I tried everything I could, and saw that I couldn't get her loose. So I ran to a trailer back up to the top of the hill back up there to try to get that lady to call to get me some help, and then apparently she didn't think that I was serious. . . . I took the jack out of my car and got under, and it was dark, still couldn't see too much what was going on . . . and started prying and got her loose, and I don't know how. And then I dragged her over to the side, and, of course, at the time I felt reasonably assured that she was gone, because her head was completely — on one 15 side just as if you had taken a sledgehammer and just hit it and bashed it in. And I did have the pleasure of one thing. I had the pleasure of listening to her breathe about the last three times she ever breathed in her life."

David Munsey did not return to the wreck that night, but Charlie   16
Stevens did. Leo Cooper was kneeling next to his daughter's body. Cooper insisted that Stevens come close enough to see FaNee. "He was kneeling down next to her," Stevens later testified. "And he said, 'Do you know what you've done? Do you really know what you've done?' Like that. And I just looked at her, and I said, 'Yes,' and just stood there. Because I couldn't say nothing." There was, of course, a legal decision to be made about who was responsible for FaNee Cooper's death. In a deposition, Stevens said he had been fleeing for his life. He testified that when Leo Cooper blocked Crippen Road, FaNee had said that her father had a gun and intended to hurt them. Stevens was bound over and eventually indicted for involuntary manslaughter. Leo Cooper testified that when he approached the Pinto on Crippen Road, FaNee had a strange expression that he had never seen before. "It wasn't like FaNee, and I knew something was wrong," he said. "My concern was to get FaNee out of the car." The district attorney's office asked that Cooper be bound over for reckless driving, but the judge declined to do so. "Any father would have done what he did," the judge said. "I can see no criminal act on the part of Mr. Cooper."

Almost two years passed before Charlie Stevens was brought to trial.   17
Part of the problem was assuring the presence of David Munsey, who had joined the Navy but seemed inclined to assign his own leaves. In the meantime, the Coopers went to court with a civil suit — they had "uninsured-motorist coverage," which requires their insurance company to cover any defendant who has no insurance of his own — and they won a judgment. There were ways of assigning responsibility, or course, which had nothing to do with the law, civil or criminal. A lot of people in Knoxville thought that Leo Cooper had, in the words of his lawyer, "done what any daddy worth his salt would have done." There were others who believed that FaNee Cooper had lost her life because Leo Cooper had lost his temper. Leo Cooper was not among those who expressed any doubts about his actions. Unlike his wife, whose eyes filled with tears at almost any mention of FaNee, Cooper seemed able, even eager to go over the details of the accident again and again. With the help of a school-board security man, he conducted his own investigation. He drove over the route dozens of times. "I've thought about it every day, and I guess I will the rest of my life," he said as he and his lawyer and the prosecuting attorney went over the route again the day before Charlie Stevens's trial finally began. "But I can't tell any alternative for a father. I simply wanted her out of that car. I'd have done the same thing again, even at the risk of losing her."

Tennessee law permits the family of a victim to hire a special prosecu-   18
tor to assist the district attorney. The lawyer who acted for the Coopers in

the civil case helped prosecute Charlie Stevens. Both he and the district attorney assured the jurors that the presence of a special prosecutor was not to be construed to mean that the Coopers were vindictive. Outside the courtroom, Leo Cooper said that the verdict was of no importance to him — that he felt sorry, in a way, for Charlie Stevens. But there were people in Knoxville who thought Cooper had a lot riding on the prosecution of Charlie Stevens. If Stevens was not guilty of FaNee Cooper's death — found so by twelve of his peers — who was?

At the trial, Cooper testified emotionally and remarkably graphically   19 about pulling FaNee out from under the car and watching her die in his arms. Charlie Stevens had shaved his beard and cut his hair, but the effort did not transform him into an impressive witness. His lawyer — trying to argue that it would have been impossible for Stevens to concoct the story about FaNee's having mentioned a gun, as the prosecution strongly implied — said, "His mind is such that if you ask him a question you can hear his mind go around, like an old mill creaking." Stevens did not deny the recklessness of his driving or the sorry condition of his car. It happened to be the only car he had available to flee in, he said, and he had fled in fear for his life.

The prosecution said that Stevens could have let FaNee out of the car   20 when her father stopped them, or could have gone to the commercial strip on the Maynardville Highway for protection. The prosecution said that Leo Cooper had done what he might have been expected to do under the circumstances — alone, late at night, his daughter in danger. The defense said precisely the same about Stevens: he had done what he might have been expected to do when being pursued by a man he had reason to be afraid of. "I don't fault Mr. Cooper for what he did, but I'm sorry he did it," the defense attorney said. "I'm sorry the girl said what she said." The jury deliberated for eighteen minutes. Charlie Stevens was found guilty. The jury recommended a sentence of from two to five years in the state penitentiary. At the announcement, Leo Cooper broke down and cried, JoAnn Cooper's eyes filled with tears; she blinked them back and continued to stare straight ahead.

In a way, the Coopers might still strike a casual visitor as an ideal fam-   21 ily — handsome parents, a bright and bubbly teenage daughter, a little boy learning the hook shot from his father, a warm house with some land around it. FaNee's presence is there, of course. A picture of her, with a small bouquet of flowers over it, hangs in the living room. One of her poems is displayed in a frame on a table. Even if Leo Cooper continues to think about that night for the rest of his life, there are questions he can never answer. Was there a way that Leo and JoAnn Cooper could have prevented FaNee from choosing the path she chose? Would she still be alive if Leo Cooper had not jumped into his car and driven to the end of the driveway to investigate? Did she in fact tell Charlie Stevens that her father would hurt them — or even that her father had a gun? Did she want to get away from her family even at the risk of tearing around dark country roads in Charlie Stevens's dismal Pinto? Or did she welcome the risk? The poem of FaNee's that the Coopers have displayed is one she wrote a week before her death:

I think I'm going to die
And I really don't know why.
But look in my eye
When I tell you good-bye.
I think I'm going to die.

• • •

COMPREHENSION

1. What early signs suggested that FaNee was not really an "ideal child" (1)?

2. During her high school years, what specific kinds of behavior caused FaNee's parents to worry about her?

3. In what ways, if at all, do FaNee's parents contribute to her problems? Consider their backgrounds, their personalities, and their positions in the town. What other factors might have caused her problems?

4. In what ways did the social structure of the town of Halls — and, in particular, of Halls High School — lead FaNee to become a "Freak" (4)?

5. Identify the immediate cause of FaNee's death. What other, more remote, causes do you see as significant?

6. In what sense might FaNee's decline be described as a causal chain?

7. What do you think Trillin means when he says, in paragraph 17, "There were ways of assigning responsibility . . . which had nothing to do with the law, civil or criminal"? Whom does he blame for the tragedy? Whom do *you* blame?

8. What do you think FaNee means by the statement "It's just too late" (8, 11)? What do you think Trillin means to suggest by using this statement as his essay's title?

PURPOSE AND AUDIENCE

1. Do you believe Trillin's primary purpose in this essay is to report information about FaNee and her family in a case study, or to suggest that her story has wider social or even moral implications for readers? Explain your conclusion.

2. In paragraph 5, Trillin says, "In a Knox County high school, teenagers who want to get themselves in the pit need not mainline heroin. The Jocks they mean to be compared to do not merely show up regularly for classes and practice football and wear clean clothes; they watch their language and preach temperance and go to prayer meetings on Wednesday nights and talk about having a real good Christian witness." Why do you think Trillin finds it necessary to include this explanation? What does it suggest about his view of his audience?

3. "It's Just Too Late" does not have an explicitly stated thesis. What do you think the essay's main idea is? State it in a single sentence. Why do you think Trillin chose not to include a thesis statement?

STYLE AND STRUCTURE

1. Trillin's essay might be divided into three parts: background (1–8); the events of the night FaNee dies (9–16); and the aftermath of that night, including the trial (17–21). How does Trillin signal movement from one part of the story to the next? Do you think he needs to make these signals more explicit? Would internal headings be useful, or would they be distracting? Explain.

2. What do you think Trillin hopes to accomplish by quoting FaNee's writing in paragraphs 2, 4, 5, 11, and 21? Is he successful? Explain.

3. What do the quotations from FaNee's parents, her friend Marcia, Jim Griffin, and others add to the essay? What other voices would you like to hear?

4. Trillin is a reporter, and his writing is both detailed and objective. Why is this level of detail and objectivity so important here? Where, if anywhere, does he reveal his own opinions?

5. In the last paragraph of his essay, Trillin asks (but does not answer) a series of questions. What do you think he hopes these **rhetorical questions** will suggest to readers?

VOCABULARY PROJECTS

1. Define each of the following words as it is used in this selection.

introspective (1)	affliction (2)	graphically (19)
errant (1)	temperance (5)	
magnanimous (1)	bald (11)	

2. "At Halls High School," Trillin explains, "the social poles were represented by the Jocks and the Freaks" (4). Write one-sentence definitions of *jock* and *freak.* Then, suggest a few alternate names for each group, being careful to choose words that convey the same meanings as the original terms.

JOURNAL ENTRY

Who, if anyone, do you think could have "saved" FaNee? Or do you believe it was really "just too late"? Discuss.

WRITING WORKSHOP

1. Write an essay in which you consider the possible effects of FaNee's death on those who knew her — her parents, her teachers, her friends.

2. Whom or what do you see as responsible for FaNee's death? Write an essay in which you consider both the main cause of her death and the contributory causes.

3. Taking the point of view of a school counselor, write a report in which you make specific recommendations for addressing FaNee's needs and problems. In your report, explain the beneficial results of the plan you propose.

COMBINING THE PATTERNS

Paragraphs 4 and 5 of "It's Just Too Late" develop a **comparison and contrast** between the Jocks and the Freaks. How do these two groups differ? Why is the sharp contrast revealed in these paragraphs so important in Trillin's profile of FaNee? Do you think Trillin should have expanded this discussion? Why or why not?

THEMATIC CONNECTIONS

- "Samuel" (page 212)
- "Television: The Plug-In Drug" (page 283)
- "Suicide Note" (page 315)
- "Unnatural Killers" (page 566)

JANICE MIRIKITANI

Janice Mirikitani, a third-generation Japanese American, was born in San Francisco in 1942 and graduated from the University of California at Los Angeles in 1962. In her poetry, Mirikitani often considers how racism in the United States affects Asian Americans, particularly the thousands of Japanese Americans held in internment camps during World War II. Her collections include *Awake in the River* (1978), *Shedding Silence* (1987), and *We Are the Dangerous: Selected Poems* (1995); She has also edited anthologies of Japanese-American and third world literature, as well as several volumes giving voice to children living in poverty. For many years she has been president of the Glide Foundation, which sponsors numerous outreach programs for the poor and homeless of San Francisco. Mirikitani is also a noted choreographer.

The following poem, which appears in *Shedding Silence,* takes the form of a suicide note written by a young Asian-American college student to her family and reveals the extreme pressure to excel placed on her by her parents and her culture. The theme, however, is one that has considerable relevance beyond the Asian-American community. Tragically, some five thousand teenagers and young adults commit suicide annually in the United States (there are thirty to fifty times as many attempts), and suicide is the third leading cause of death among fifteen- to twenty-four-year-olds.

Suicide Note

How many notes written . . .
ink smeared like birdprints in snow.

not good enough   not pretty enough   not smart enough

dear mother and father.
I apologize   5
for disappointing you.
I've worked very hard,

not good enough

harder, perhaps to please you.
If only I were a son, shoulders broad   10
as the sunset threading through pine,
I would see the light in my mother's
eyes, or the golden pride reflected
in my father's dream
of my wide, male hands worthy of work   15
and comfort.
I would swagger through life
muscled and bold and assured,
drawing praises to me
like currents in the bed of wind, virile   20
with confidence.

     not good enough   not strong enough   not good enough
I apologize.
Tasks do not come easily.
Each failure, a glacier.   25
Each disapproval, a bootprint.
Each disappointment,
ice above my river.
So I have worked hard.
                      not good enough   30
My sacrifice I will drop
bone by bone, perched
on the ledge of my womanhood,
fragile as wings.
                      not strong enough   35

It is snowing steadily
surely not good weather
for flying — this sparrow
sillied and dizzied by the wind
on the edge.   40
                      not smart enough
I make this ledge my altar
to offer penance.
This air will not hold me,
the snow burdens my crippled wings,   45
my tears drop like bitter cloth
softly into the gutter below.
     not good enough   not strong enough   not smart enough

                      Choices thin as shaved
                      ice. Notes shredded   50
                      drift like snow

on my broken body,
cover me like whispers
of sorries
sorries.   55
Perhaps when they find me
they will bury
my bird bones beneath
a sturdy pine
and scatter my feathers like   60
unspoken song
over this white and cold and silent
breast of earth.

                  •   •   •

THINKING ABOUT LITERATURE

1. An author's note that originally introduced this poem explained the main cause of the student's death:

   An Asian-American college student was reported to have jumped to her death from her dormitory window. Her body was found two days later under a deep cover of snow. Her suicide note contained an apology to her parents for having received less than a perfect four-point grade average. . . .

   What other causes might have contributed to her suicide?

2. Why does the speaker believe her life would be happier if she were male? Do you think she is correct?

3. What words, phrases, and images are repeated in this poem? What effect do these repetitions have on you?

JOURNAL ENTRY

Whom (or what) do you blame for teenage suicides such as the one the poem describes? How might the causes of such deaths be eliminated?

THEMATIC CONNECTIONS

- "Only Daughter" (page 83)
- "College Pressures" (page 390)
- "The Company Man" (page 478)

WRITING ASSIGNMENTS FOR CAUSE AND EFFECT

1. "Who Killed Benny Paret?" (page 279), "On Dumpster Diving" (page 632), and "Thirty-Eight Who Saw Murder Didn't Call the Police" (page 99) all encourage readers, either directly or indirectly, to take action rather than remaining uninvolved. Using information gleaned from these essays (or from others in the text) as support for your thesis, write an essay in which you explore the possible consequences of apathy.

2. Write an updated version of one of this chapter's essays. For example, you might reconsider Winn's points in light of the increasing influence of cable television in the twenty years since "Television: The Plug-In Drug" was written or explore the kinds of pressure that Lawrence Otis Graham ("The 'Black Table' Is Still There") might face as a middle school student today.

3. Various technological and social developments have contributed to the decline of formal letter writing. One of these is the telephone. Consider some other possible causes, and write an essay explaining why letter writing has become less popular. You may also consider the *effects* of this decline.

4. How do you account for the popularity of one of the following phenomena: shopping malls, MTV, fast food, e-mail, rap music, Pokémon, soap operas, sensationalist tabloids like the *Star?* Write an essay in which you consider remote as well as immediate causes for the success of the phenomenon you choose.

5. Between 1946 and 1964, the birth rate increased considerably. Some of the effects attributed to this baby boom include the 1960s antiwar movement, the increase in the crime rate, and the development of the women's movement. Write an essay in which you explore some possible effects of the baby-boom generation's growing older. What trends would you expect to find as most baby boomers reach middle age? When they reach retirement age?

6. Write an essay in which you trace a series of events in your life that constitutes a causal chain. Indicate clearly both the sequence of events and the causal connections among them, and be careful not to confuse coincidence with causality.

7. Consider the effects, or possible effects, of one of these scientific developments on your life and/or on the lives of your contemporaries: genetic engineering, space exploration, the Internet, human cloning. Consider negative as well as positive effects.

8. Almost half of American marriages now end in divorce. To what do you attribute this high divorce rate? Be as specific as possible, citing "case studies" of families with which you are familiar.

9. What do you see as the major cause of any *one* of these problems: acquaintance rape, binge drinking among college students, voter apathy, school violence, academic cheating? Based on your identification of its causes, formulate some specific solutions for the problem you select.

10. Write an essay in which you consider the likely effects of a severe, protracted shortage of one of the following commodities: food, rental

housing, medical care, computer hardware, reading matter. You may consider a community-, city-, or statewide shortage or a nation- or worldwide crisis.

COLLABORATIVE ACTIVITY FOR CAUSE AND EFFECT

Working in groups of four, discuss your thoughts about the increasing homeless population, and then list four *effects* the presence of homeless people is having on you, your community, and our nation. Assign each member of your group to write a paragraph explaining one of the effects the group identifies. Then, arrange the paragraphs in order of increasing importance, moving from the least to the most significant consequence. Finally, work together to turn your individual paragraphs into an essay: write an introduction, a conclusion, and transitions between paragraphs, and include a thesis statement in paragraph 1.

INTERNET ASSIGNMENT FOR CAUSE AND EFFECT

Write an essay in which you describe the effects of food irradiation, genetic engineering, or the use of pesticides on consumers' health. Visit the following World Wide Web sites to learn about the possible advantages and disadvantages of these food industry practices.

Center for Food Safety & Applied Nutrition
<http://vm.cfsan.fda.gov>
The site contains an overview and history of the Food and Drug Administration, as well as articles and information on specific programs and special topics such as biotechnology, food labeling, and nutrition.

Consumers International
<http://www.consumersinternational.org/campaigns/irradiation/irrad.html>
This report from Consumers International discusses the advantages and disadvantages of food irradiation.

Let's Keep Organic Organic Campaign
<http://www.saveorganic.org>
This campaign site provides an overview of the pro-organic position, key position statements on the U.S. Department of Agriculture's Proposed Rules, articles about current issues and debates, and links to other sites.

Foundation for Food Irradiation Education
<http://www.food-irradiation.com>
This site, which contains articles, links to other Web sites, and a students' corner, supports the adoption of food irradiation.

9

COMPARISON AND CONTRAST

WHAT IS COMPARISON AND CONTRAST?

In the narrowest sense, *comparison* shows how two or more things are similar, and *contrast* shows how they are different. In most writing situations, however, the two related processes of **comparison and contrast** are used together. In the following paragraph from *Disturbing the Universe*, scientist Freeman Dyson compares and contrasts two different styles of human endeavor, which he calls "the gray and the green":

Topic sentence (outlines elements of comparison)

Point-by-point comparison

> In everything we undertake, either on earth or in the sky, we have a choice of two styles, which I call the gray and the green. The distinction between the gray and green is not sharp. Only at the extremes of the spectrum can we say without qualification, this is green and that is gray. The difference between green and gray is better explained by examples than by definitions. Factories are gray, gardens are green. Physics is gray, biology is green. Plutonium is gray, horse manure is green. Bureaucracy is gray, pioneer communities are green. Self-reproducing machines are gray, trees and children are green. Human technology is gray, God's technology is green. Clones are gray, clades* are green. Army field manuals are gray, poems are green.

A special form of comparison, called **analogy,** looks for similarities between two essentially dissimilar things. An analogy explains one thing by comparing it to a second thing that is more familiar than the first. In the following paragraph from *The Shopping Mall High School*, Arthur G. Powell, Eleanor Farrar, and David K. Cohen use analogy to shed light on the nature of American high schools:

> If Americans want to understand their high schools at work, they should imagine them as shopping malls. Secondary education is another

---

*Eds. note — A group of organisms that evolved from a common ancestor.

consumption experience in an abundant society. Shopping malls attract a broad range of customers with different tastes and purposes. Some shop at Sears, others at Woolworth's or Bloomingdale's. In high schools a broad range of students also shop. They too can select from an astonishing variety of products and services conveniently assembled in one place with ample parking. Furthermore, in malls and schools many different kinds of transactions are possible. Both institutions bring hopeful purveyors and potential purchasers together. The former hope to maximize sales but can take nothing for granted. Shoppers have a wide discretion not only about what to buy but also about whether to buy.

USING COMPARISON AND CONTRAST

Throughout our lives we are bombarded with countless bits of information from newspapers, television, radio, the Internet, and personal experience: the police strike in Memphis; city workers walk out in Philadelphia; the Senate debates government spending; taxes are lowered in New Jersey. Somehow we must make sense of the jumbled facts and figures that surround us. One way we have of understanding information like this is to put it side by side with other data and then to compare and contrast. Do the police in Memphis have the same complaints as the city workers in Philadelphia? What are the differences between the two situations? Is the national debate on spending analogous to the New Jersey debate on taxes? How do they differ? We make similar distinctions every day about matters that directly affect us. When we make personal decisions, we consider alternatives, asking ourselves whether one option seems better than another. Should I buy a car with manual or automatic transmission? Should I major in history or business? What job opportunities will each major offer me? Should I register as a Democrat or a Republican, or should I join a third party? What are the positions of each on government spending, welfare, and taxes? To answer questions like these, we use comparison and contrast.

PLANNING A COMPARISON-AND-CONTRAST ESSAY

Because comparison and contrast is central to our understanding of the world, this way of thinking is often called for in papers and on essay examinations:

Compare and contrast the attitudes toward science and technology expressed in Fritz Lang's *Metropolis* and George Lucas's *Star Wars*. (film)

What are the similarities and differences between mitosis and meiosis? (biology)

Discuss the relative merits of establishing a partnership or a corporation. (business law)

Discuss the advantages and disadvantages of the heterogeneous grouping of pupils. (education)

Recognizing Comparison-and-Contrast Assignments

You are not likely to sit down and say to yourself, "I think I'll write a comparison-and-contrast essay today. Now what can I write about?" Instead, your assignment will suggest comparison and contrast, or you will decide it suits your purpose. In the preceding examples, for instance, the instructors have phrased their questions to tell students how to treat the material. When you read the questions, certain key words and phrases — *compare and contrast, similarities and differences, relative merits, advantages and disadvantages* — indicate that you should use a comparison-and-contrast pattern to organize your essay. Sometimes you may not even need a key phrase. Consider the question, "Which of the two Adamses, John or Samuel, had the greater influence on the timing and course of the American Revolution?" Here the word *greater* is enough to suggest a contrast.

Even when your assignment is not worded to suggest comparison and contrast, your purpose may point to this pattern of development. For instance, when you evaluate, you frequently use comparison and contrast. If, as a student in a management course, you are asked to evaluate two health-care systems, you can begin by researching the standards experts use in their evaluations. You can then compare each system's performance with those standards and contrast the systems with each other, concluding perhaps that both systems meet minimum standards but that one is more cost-efficient than the other. Or if you are evaluating two of this year's new cars for a consumer newsletter, you might establish some criteria — fuel economy, handling, comfort, safety features, style — and compare and contrast the cars with respect to each criterion. If each of the cars is better in different categories, your readers will have to decide which features matter most to them.

Establishing a Basis for Comparison

Before you can compare and contrast two things, you must be sure a **basis of comparison** exists — that is, that the things share some significant characteristics. For example, although cats and dogs are very different, they share several common elements: they are mammals, they make good pets, and so forth. Without at least one common element, there would be no basis for analysis, and no comparison would be possible.

A comparison should lead you beyond the obvious. For instance, at first the idea of a comparison-and-contrast essay based on an analogy between bees and people might seem absurd: after all, these two creatures differ in species, physical structure, and intelligence. In fact, their differences are so obvious that an essay based on them might seem pointless.

But after further analysis, you might decide that bees and people have quite a few similarities. Both are social animals that live in complex social structures, and both have tasks to perform and roles to fulfill in their respective societies. Therefore, you *could* write about them, but you would focus on the common elements that seem most provocative — social structures and roles — rather than on dissimilar elements. If you tried to draw an analogy between bees and Jeeps or humans and golf tees, however, you would run into trouble. Although some points of comparison could be found, they would be trivial. Why bother to point out that both bees and Jeeps travel great distances or that both people and tees are needed to play golf? Neither statement establishes a significant basis for comparison.

When two subjects are very similar, it is the contrast that may be worth writing about. And when two subjects are not very much alike, it is the similarities that you may find enlightening.

Selecting Points for Discussion

After you decide which subjects to compare and contrast, you need to select the points you want to discuss. You do this by determining your emphasis — on similarities, differences, or both — and the major focus of your paper. If your purpose for comparing two types of house plants is to explain that one is easier to grow than the other, you would contrast points having to do with plant care, not those having to do with plant biology.

When you compare and contrast, make sure you treat the same, or at least similar, elements for each subject you discuss. For instance, if you were going to compare and contrast two novels, you might consider the following elements in both works:

Novel A	*Novel B*
Major characters	Major characters
Minor characters	Minor characters
Themes	Themes

Try to avoid the common error of discussing entirely different elements for each subject. Such an approach obscures any basis of comparison that might exist. The two novels, for example, could not be meaningfully compared or contrasted if you discussed dissimilar elements:

Novel A	*Novel B*
Major characters	Plot
Minor characters	Author's life
Themes	Symbolism

Formulating a Thesis Statement

After selecting the points you want to discuss, you are ready to formulate your thesis statement. This thesis statement should tell your readers what to expect in your essay, identifying not only the subjects to be compared and contrasted but also the points you will make about them. Your thesis statement should also indicate whether you will concentrate on similarities or differences or whether you will balance the two. In addition, it may list the points of comparison and contrast in the order in which they will be discussed in the essay.

The structure of your thesis statement can indicate the focus of your essay. As the following sentences illustrate, a thesis statement can highlight the central concern of the essay by presenting it in the independent, rather than the dependent, clause of the sentence. The structure of the first thesis statement emphasizes similarities, and the structure of the second highlights differences:

> Despite the fact that television and radio are distinctly different media, they use similar strategies to appeal to their audiences.

> Although Melville's *Moby-Dick* and London's *The Sea Wolf* are both about the sea, minor characters, major characters, and themes of *Moby-Dick* establish its greater complexity.

STRUCTURING A COMPARISON-AND-CONTRAST ESSAY

Like every other type of essay in this book, a comparison-and-contrast essay has an introduction, several body paragraphs, and a conclusion. Within the body of your paper, you can use either of two basic comparison-and-contrast patterns — *subject by subject* or *point by point*. As you might expect, each organizational pattern has advantages and disadvantages. In general, you should use subject-by-subject comparison when your purpose is to emphasize overall similarities or differences, and you should use point-by-point comparison when your purpose is to emphasize individual points of similarity or difference.

Using Subject-by-Subject Comparison

In a **subject-by-subject comparison,** you essentially write a separate essay about each subject, but you discuss the same points for both subjects. In discussing each subject, you use the same basis of comparison to guide your selection of supporting points, and you arrange these points in some logical order, usually in order of their increasing significance. The following informal outline illustrates a subject-by-subject comparison:

Introduction:	Thesis statement — Despite the fact that television and radio are distinctly different media, they use similar strategies to appeal to their audiences.
Television audiences	
Point 1:	Men
Point 2:	Women
Point 3:	Children

Radio audiences
Point 1:	Men
Point 2:	Women
Point 3:	Children
Conclusion:	Restatement of thesis or review of key points

Subject-by-subject comparisons are most appropriate for short, uncomplicated papers. In longer papers, where many points are made about each subject, this organizational pattern puts too many demands on your readers, requiring them to keep track of all your points throughout your paper. In addition, because of the length of each section, your paper may seem like two separate essays weakly connected by a transitional phrase. For longer or more complex papers, then, it is usually best to use point-by-point comparison.

Using Point-by-Point Comparison

When you write a **point-by-point comparison,** you first make a point about one subject and then follow it with a comparable point about the other. This alternating pattern continues throughout the body of your essay until all your comparisons or contrasts have been made. The following informal outline illustrates a point-by-point comparison:

Introduction:	Thesis statement — Although Melville's *Moby-Dick* and London's *The Sea Wolf* are both about the sea, the minor characters, major characters, and themes of *Moby-Dick* establish its greater complexity.

Minor characters
Book 1:	*The Sea Wolf*
Book 2:	*Moby-Dick*

Major characters
Book 1:	*The Sea Wolf*
Book 2:	*Moby-Dick*

Themes
Book 1:	*The Sea Wolf*
Book 2:	*Moby-Dick*
Conclusion	Restatement of thesis or review of key points

Point-by-point comparisons are especially useful for longer, more complicated essays in which you discuss many different points. (If you treat only one or two points of comparison, you should consider a subject-by-subject organization.) In a point-by-point essay, readers can easily follow comparisons or contrasts and do not have to wait several paragraphs to find out, for example, the differences between minor characters in *Moby-Dick* and *The Sea Wolf* or to remember on page six what was said on page three. Nevertheless, it is easy to fall into a monotonous, back-and-forth movement between points when you write a point-by-point comparison. To avoid this problem, use clear transitions, and vary sentence structure as you move from point to point.

USEFUL TRANSITIONS FOR COMPARISON AND CONTRAST

COMPARISON

just as . . . so	in comparison
like	similarly
likewise	in the same way

CONTRAST

although	nevertheless
but	nonetheless
conversely	on the contrary
despite	on the one hand . . . on the other hand . . .
even though	still
however	unlike
in contrast	whereas
instead	yet

Supplying Clear Transitions

Transitions are especially important in comparison-and-contrast essays because you must supply readers with clear signals that indicate whether you are discussing similarities or differences. Without these cues, readers will have trouble following your train of thought and may lose track of the significance of the points you are making. (Some transitions indicating comparison and contrast are shown in the box above.)

Longer essays frequently contain *transitional paragraphs* that connect one part of an essay to another. A transitional paragraph can be a single sentence that signals a shift in focus or a longer paragraph that provides a concise summary of what was said before. In both cases, transitional

---

☑ **CHECKLIST: COMPARISON AND CONTRAST**

- Does your assignment call for comparison and contrast?
- What basis for comparison exists between the subjects you are comparing?
- Does your essay have a clear thesis statement that identifies both the subjects you are comparing and the points you are making about them?
- Do you discuss the same or similar points for both subjects?
- If you have written a subject-by-subject comparison, have you included a transitional paragraph that connects the two sections of the essay?
- Is the organizational pattern of your essay suited to your purpose?
- Have you included transitional words and phrases that indicate whether you are discussing similarities or differences?

paragraphs enable readers to pause and consider what has already been said before moving on to a new point.

▶ STUDENT WRITERS: COMPARISON AND CONTRAST

Both of the following essays illustrate comparison and contrast. The first, by Mark Cotharn, is a subject-by-subject comparison. The second, by Margaret Depner, is a point-by-point comparison. Both were written for a composition class in which the instructor asked students to write an essay comparing two experiences with education.

Brains versus Brawn

Introduction

When people think about discrimination, they usually associate it with prejudice and connect it with race or gender. But discrimination can take another form. For example, a person can gain an unfair advantage at a job interview by being attractive or knowing someone who works at the company or by being able to talk about something that has nothing to do with the job, like sports. Certainly, the people who do not get the job would claim that they were discriminated against, and to some extent they would be right. As a high school athlete, I experienced both types of discrimination. When I was a sophomore in high school, I benefited from discrimination. When I was a junior, however, I was penalized by it, treated as if there were no place for me in a classroom.

Thesis statement (emphasizing differences)

As a result, I learned that discrimination, whether it helps you or hinders you, is wrong.

First subject: Mark helped by discrimination

At my high school, football was everything, and the entire town supported the local team. In the summer, merchants would run special football promotions. Adults would wear shirts with the team's logo, students would collect money to buy equipment, and everyone would go to the games and cheer the team on. Coming out of junior high school, I was considered an exceptional athlete who was eventually going to start as the varsity quarterback. Because of my status, I was welcomed with open

Status of football

1

2

arms by the high school. Before I entered the
school, the varsity coach even visited my home,
and the principal called my parents and told
them how well I was going to do.

**Treatment by
teachers**

I knew that high school would be different   3
from junior high, but I wasn't prepared for the
treatment I received from teachers. Many of
them talked to me as if I were their friend, not
their student. My math teacher used to keep me
after class just to talk football; he would
even give me a note so I could be late for my
next class. My biology teacher told me I could
skip the afternoon labs so I would have some
time for myself before practice. Several of my
teachers told me that during football season I
didn't have to hand in homework because it might
distract me during practice. My Spanish teacher
even told me that if I didn't do well on a test,
I could take it over after the season. Everything I did seemed to be perfect.

**Mark's reaction to
treatment**

In spite of this favorable treatment, I   4
continued to study hard. I knew that if I wanted
to go to a good college, I would have to get
good grades, and I resented the implication
that the only way I could get good grades was by
getting special treatment. I had always been a
good student, and I had no intention of changing my study habits. Each night after practice,
I would stay up late outlining my notes and
completing my class assignments. Any studying
I couldn't do during the week, I would complete
on the weekends. Of course my social life suffered, but I didn't care. I took pride in the
fact that I never had to take advantage of the
special treatment my teachers were offering me.

**Transitional
paragraph: signals
shift from one
subject to another**

Then one day the unthinkable happened.   5
The township redrew the district lines, and I
suddenly found myself assigned to a new high
school--one that was academically more demanding than the one I attended, and, what was

worse, one that had a weak football team. When my parents appealed to the school board to let me stay at my current school, they were told that no exceptions could be made. If the board made a change for me, it would have to make changes for others, and that would lead to chaos. My principal and my coach also tried to get the board to change its decision, but they got the same response. So in my junior year, at the height of my career, I changed schools.

Second subject: Mark hurt by discrimination

Status of football

Unlike the people at my old school, no one   6 at my new school seemed to care much about high school football. Many of the students attended the games, but their primary focus was on getting into a good college. If they talked about football at all, they usually discussed the regional college teams. As a result, I didn't have the status I had when I attended my former school. When I met with the coach before school started, he told me the football team was weak. He also told me that his main goal was to make sure everyone on the team had a chance to play. So, even though I would start, I would have to share the quarterback position with two seniors whom he wanted to give a chance to play. Later that day I saw the principal, who told me that although sports were an important part of school, academic achievement was more important. He made it clear that I would play football only as long as my grades did not suffer.

Treatment by teachers

Unlike the teachers at my old school, the   7 teachers at my new school did not give any special treatment to athletes. When I entered my new school, I was ready for the challenge. What I was not ready for was the hostility of most of my new teachers. From the first day, in just about every class, my teachers made it obvious they had already made up their minds about what kind of student I was going to be. Some teachers told me I shouldn't expect any special con-

sideration just because I was the team's quarterback. One even said in front of the class
that I would have to study as hard as the other
students if I expected to pass. I was hurt and
embarrassed by these comments. I didn't expect
anyone to give me anything, and I was ready to
get the grades I deserved. After all, I had
gotten good grades up to this point, and I had
no reason to think that the situation would
Mark's reaction   change. Even so, my teachers' preconceived
to treatment   ideas upset me.

Just as I had in my old school, I studied   8
hard, but I didn't know how to deal with the
prejudice I faced. At first, it really bothered
me and even affected my performance on the
football field. However, after I thought about
it awhile, I realized that the best way to show
my teachers that I was not the stereotypical
jock was to prove to them what kind of student I
really was. In the long run, far from discouraging me, their treatment motivated me, and I
decided to work even harder in the classroom
than I did on the football field. I didn't care
if the football team lost every game as long as
I did my best in every class I had. By the end
of high school, not only had the team won half
of their games (a record season), but I had
proved to my teachers that I was a good student
as well as an athlete. (I still remember the
surprised look on the face of my chemistry
teacher when she handed my final exam back to
me and told me I had received the second highest grade in the class.)

Conclusion   Before I graduated, I talked to the teach-   9
ers about how they had treated me during my
junior year. Some admitted they had been harder
on me than on the rest of the students, but others denied they had ever discriminated against
me. After awhile, I realized they would never
understand what they had done. Even so, my

**Restatement
of thesis**

experience did have some positive effects. I
learned that you should judge people on their
merits, not by some preconceived standard. In
addition, I learned that although some people
are talented intellectually, others possess
special skills that should also be valued. And,
as I found out, discriminatory treatment,
whether it helps you or hinders you, is no substitute for fairness.

Points for Special Attention

BASIS OF COMPARISON.   Mark knew he could easily compare his two
experiences. Both involved high school, and both focused on the treatment he had received as a high school athlete. In one case, Mark was
treated better than other students because he was the team's quarterback;
in the other, he was stereotyped as a "dumb jock" because he was a football player. Mark also knew that his comparison would make an interesting point — that discrimination is unfair, even when it gives a person an
advantage.

SELECTING POINTS FOR COMPARISON.   Mark wanted to make certain
that he would discuss the same (or at least similar) points for the two
experiences he was going to compare. As he planned his essay, Mark consulted his brainstorming notes and made the following informal outline:

Experience 1 *(gained an advantage)*   **Experience 2** *(was put at a disadvantage)*

Status of football   Status of football

Treatment by teachers   Treatment by teachers

My reaction   My reaction

STRUCTURE.   Mark's essay makes three points about each of the two
experiences he compares. Because his purpose was to convey overall differences between the two experiences, he decided to use a subject-by-
subject strategy. In addition, Mark thought he could make his case more
convincingly if he discussed the first experience fully before moving on to
the next one, and he believed readers would have no trouble keeping his
individual points in mind as they read. Of course, Mark could have
decided to do a point-by-point comparison. He rejected this strategy,
though, because he thought that shifting back and forth between subjects
would distract readers from his main point.

In Mark's case, a subject-by-subject comparison made more sense than
a point-by-point comparison. Often, however, the choice is a matter of preference — a writer might simply like one strategy better than the other.

TRANSITIONS.   Without adequate transitions, a subject-by-subject comparison can read like two separate essays. Notice that in Mark's essay, paragraph 5 functions as a transitional paragraph that connects the two sections of the essay. In it, Mark sets up the comparison by telling how he suddenly found himself assigned to another high school.

In addition to connecting the sections of an essay, transitional words and phrases can identify similarities and differences for readers. Notice, for example, how the transitional word *however* emphasizes the contrast between the following sentences from paragraph 1:

Without transitions
When I was a sophomore in high school, I benefited from discrimination. When I was a junior, I was penalized by it. . . .

With transitions
When I was a sophomore in high school, I benefited from discrimination. When I was a junior, *however,* I was penalized by it. . . .

TOPIC SENTENCES.   Like transitional phrases, topic sentences help to guide readers through an essay. When reading a comparison-and-contrast essay, readers can easily forget the points that are being compared, especially if the paper is long or complex. Direct, clearly stated topic sentences act as guideposts, alerting readers to the comparisons and contrasts you are making. For example, Mark's straightforward topic sentence at the beginning of paragraph 5 dramatically signals the movement from one experience to the other ("Then one day the unthinkable happened"). In addition, as in any effective comparison-and-contrast essay, each point discussed in connection with one subject is also discussed in connection with the other. Mark's topic sentences reinforce this balance:

First subject
At my high school, football was everything.

Second subject
Unlike the people at my old school, no one at my new school seemed to care much about high school football.

Focus on Revision

Mark's peer critics thought he could have spent more time talking about what he did to counter the preconceptions about athletes that teachers in *both* his schools had. One student pointed out that the teachers at both schools seemed to think athletes were weak students. The only difference was that the teachers at Mark's first school were willing to make allowances for athletes, while the teachers at his second school were not. The student thought that although Mark alluded to this fact, he should have made his point more explicitly. After rereading his essay along with his classmates' comments, Mark decided to add information about how demanding football practice was. Without this information, readers would have a hard time understanding how difficult it was for him to keep up with his studies. He also thought Mark should concede that some student athletes do fit the teachers' stereotypes, although many do not. This information would reinforce his thesis and help him demonstrate how unfair his treatment was.

Unlike the preceding essay, Margaret Depner's paper is a point-by-point comparison.

The Big Move

Introduction

The adjustment began when I was a sopho-   1
more in high school. I was fifteen--a typical American teenager. I lived to talk on the telephone, hang out at the mall, watch lots of television, and go to the movies. Everything about my life seemed satisfying. I loved my neighborhood, my school, and my friends. But suddenly everything changed. One night my parents told me that my father had been transferred and that we were going to move to England. I felt as if everything I had grown to love was being torn away from me. I was going to have to start over, and I did not want to go. My parents ignored my pleas and told me in no uncertain terms that I had no choice in the matter. My fate was sealed. When we finally arrived in England I was so frightened that I felt sick.

Thesis statement (emphasizing differences)

Not only would I have to get used to a new neighborhood and a new school, but I would also have to get used to a new way of life.

First point: adjusting to a new neighborhood

The first thing I had to adjust to was   2
living in a new neighborhood. The Boston suburb we had left was a known quantity, and perhaps for this reason, I liked it. At home we lived in a new development that was just starting to get built up. There were houses everywhere with a few small trees scattered in between. Our house had a large lawn that my brother and I tried to

Neighborhood in U.S.

avoid cutting whenever we could. Moms carting children around in minivans was a common sight. My dad belonged to a neighborhood watch program and coached a girls' soccer team. My mom

had a part-time job and rushed around on weekends catching up on all the things she could
not do during the week. Every fall kids came
to the door selling Girl Scout cookies or raising money to fight heart disease. Every spring
and summer lawnmowers hummed away on Saturday
mornings, and everyone went to church on Sunday. Everything was familiar . . . almost predictable.

**Neighborhood
in England**

Our neighborhood outside of London, how-   3
ever, was far different from what I was used
to. The house we lived in was cozy but much
smaller than the house we had left in the
United States. It had a cute little lawn in
front--which my brother and I still argued
about cutting--and was exactly like the house
next door. Near our house was a forest in which
outlaws were said to have lived several hundred
years ago. Most of the women in this area
worked full time to supplement their husbands'
income, and my mother was no exception. She got
a job with my father's company and was very
busy most of the time. There was no need for a
neighborhood watch program because there was
almost no crime. (The only crimes I ever heard
about were a parked car that was sideswiped and
a cat that had allegedly been stolen.) Although
there was a soccer team, girls weren't allowed
to play on it. (In England soccer is considered
a boy's game, like tackle football.) Some
things were the same, however. Just as they did
at home, people cut their lawns on Saturday--
with a push mower, not a power mower--and went
to church every Sunday.

**Second point:
adjusting to a
new school**

The next thing I had to adjust to was   4
attending a new school. In the United States I
had attended a large suburban public high
school. It had been built in the 1970s and held
almost two thousand students. Sweatshirts and
jeans were the most common articles of clothing

for the students, and informality was a way of
life. Several of my teachers even encouraged
students to call them by their first names and
to talk whenever they had something to say. I
was able to choose from a long list of classes
and take almost any course I wanted to. Classes
had a relaxed atmosphere, to say the least.

School in U.S.   Some students had private conversations during
class and paid little attention to the teacher.
The only time they focused on the class was
when the teacher called on them or when they
made a funny comment or a sarcastic remark. We
frequently had no homework, and we didn't study
much, except for a test. Although most of us
wanted to go on to college, none of us seemed to
take learning seriously. If anyone did, he or
she was usually teased by the rest of us.

School in England   The school I attended in England was quite   5
different from the one I attended in the United
States. It was small even by English standards--
only four hundred students--and the building
was over three hundred years old. All the students wore uniforms--a black blazer, a freshly
ironed white shirt, and a pleated skirt if you
were female or black pants if you were male.
The teachers were the epitome of formality. You
called them "Sir" or "Ma'am" and always showed
respect. I never dreamed of using their first
names. The atmosphere in the classroom was also
quite formal. Students worked quietly and spoke
to the teachers only when they were called on.
When we were called on, our teachers expected
us to respond intelligently. No one joked or
made sarcastic remarks. All of us were serious
about our work. I spent hours studying each
night and wrote a thousand-word essay each
week. I always had papers to hand in or a tuto-
rial to prepare for. Eventually, I got used to
the workload and was able to budget my time so I
could go out on the weekends.

Third point: adjusting to a new way of life

My greatest challenge, however, was   6
adjusting to a new way of life. In the United
States my social life was predictable, if not
very interesting. Most of my friends lived in
my neighborhood within walking distance of my

Life in U.S.

house. I spent hours talking on the phone each
night. Every Friday my friends and I would hang
out at the local mall or go to the movies. On
Saturday we would get together at someone's
house and watch TV or rent a movie. Sometimes
we would go to a party or take a train into the
city and go to Quincy Market. During the summer
my friends and I would go to the beach or just
lie around the house complaining that we had
nothing to do. Although occasionally I would
volunteer to help a teacher, my friends and I
did not consider it acceptable to be too
involved with school. Once, when I tried out
for a school play, my friends teased me for
weeks.

Life in England

In England my social life was quite dif-   7
ferent. Most of my friends lived almost an hour
away. There were no malls to hang out in, we
never went to the movies, and I spent little
time on the phone. At first, my whole life
seemed upside down, but gradually I grew to
like it. I found new things to do. I got interested in sports and other school activities. I
became involved in community service, joined
the debating team, and was elected to student
council. Instead of hanging out at the mall, my
friends and I went to plays and concerts in
London. During the summer, I went on trips to
Spain and to the Isle of Wight. Perhaps the
most interesting thing I did was meet people
from all over the world and find out about
their customs. And I don't ever remember sitting around the house wondering what to do.

Conclusion

In my one year in England, I accomplished   8
more than I had dreamed I would before I left

```
the United States. It was hard to give up
everything that was familiar to me, but for the
first time I understood what my mother had
meant when she said, "Sometimes, you need to
lose something to gain something." By the end
of the year, when we returned home, I knew that
year had changed me and that I would never be
the same person I had been before.
```

Points for Special Attention

STRUCTURE.   Margaret's purpose in writing this essay was to highlight several specific differences between her two educational experiences. As a result, she chose to write a point-by-point comparison. She introduces three points of contrast between her two subjects, and she is careful to present these three points in the same order for both subjects. With this method of organization, she can be sure her readers will easily understand the specific differences between her life in the United States and her life in England. Had Margaret used a subject-by-subject comparison, her readers would have had to keep turning back to match points she made about the second subject to those she made about the first.

TOPIC SENTENCES.   Without clear transitions, Margaret's readers would have a difficult time determining where each discussion of life in the United States ended and one about life in England began. Margaret makes sure that her readers can follow her discussion by distinguishing the two subjects of her comparison with topic sentences that make the contrast between them clear:

> The Boston suburb we had left was a known quantity, and perhaps for this reason, I liked it.
> Our neighborhood outside of London, however, was far different from what I was used to.

> In the United States I had attended a large suburban public high school.
> The school I attended in England was quite different from the one I attended in the United States.

> In the United States, my social life was predictable, if not very interesting.
> In England my social life was quite different.

TRANSITIONS.   In addition to the clear and straightforward topic sentences, Margaret also includes transitional sentences that help readers move through the essay. Notice that by establishing a parallel structure, these sentences form a pattern that reinforces the essay's thesis:

> The first thing I had to adjust to was living in a new neighborhood.
> The next thing I had to adjust to was attending a new school.
> My greatest challenge, however, was adjusting to a new way of life.

Focus on Revision

Margaret's peer critics thought the biggest strength of her essay was its use of detail, which made the contrast between the United States and England clear. One student, however, thought that even more detail would improve her essay. For example, in paragraph 3 Margaret could describe her London suburb more precisely than she does. In paragraph 7 she could provide insight into how her English friends were different from her friends in the United States. Margaret agreed with these suggestions and also thought she could improve her conclusion. After rereading it, she decided it was little more than a loose collection of ideas that added little to the discussion. An anecdote that summed up her feelings about leaving England would be an improvement. So would a summary of how her experience changed her life once she returned to the United States.

The selections that follow illustrate both point-by-point and subject-by-subject comparison. Each uses transitional elements and topic sentences to enhance clarity and reinforce the comparisons and contrasts being made. Although the reading selections vary in their organization, length, and complexity, each is primarily concerned with the similarities and differences between its subjects.

BRUCE CATTON

Bruce Catton (1899–1978) was born in Petoskey, Michigan, and attended Oberlin College. His studies were interrupted by his service during World War I, after which he worked as a journalist and then for various government agencies. Catton edited *American Heritage* magazine from 1954 until his death. He was a notable authority on the American Civil War; among his many books on the subject are *Mr. Lincoln's Army* (1951); *A Stillness at Appomattox* (1953), which won both a Pulitzer Prize and a National Book Award; and *Gettysburg: The Final Fury* (1974). Catton also wrote a memoir, *Waiting for the Morning Train* (1972), in which he recalls listening as a young boy to the reminiscences of Union Army veterans.

"Grant and Lee: A Study in Contrasts," which first appeared in a collection of historical essays entitled *The American Story,* focuses on the two generals who headed the opposing armies during the Civil War. Robert E. Lee led the Army of Northern Virginia, the backbone of the Confederate forces, throughout much of the war. Ulysses S. Grant was commander in chief of the Union troops. By the spring of 1865, although it seemed almost inevitable that the Southern forces would be defeated, Lee made an attempt to lead his troops to join another Confederate army in North Carolina. Finding himself virtually surrounded by Grant's forces near the small town of Appomattox Court House, Lee chose to surrender to Grant. The following essay considers these two great generals in terms of both their differences and their important similarities.

Grant and Lee: A Study in Contrasts

When Ulysses S. Grant and Robert E. Lee met in the parlor of a modest house at Appomattox Court House, Virginia, on April 9, 1865, to work out the terms for the surrender of Lee's Army of Northern Virginia, a great chapter in American life came to a close, and a great new chapter began. 1

These men were bringing the Civil War to its virtual finish. To be sure, other armies had yet to surrender, and for a few days the fugitive Confederate government would struggle desperately and vainly, trying to find some way to go on living now that its chief support was gone. But in effect it was all over when Grant and Lee signed the papers. And the little room where they wrote out the terms was the scene of one of the poignant, dramatic contrasts in American history. 2

They were two strong men, these oddly different generals, and they represented the strengths of two conflicting currents that, through them, had come into final collision. 3

Back of Robert E. Lee was the notion that the old aristocratic concept might somehow survive and be dominant in American life. 4

Lee was tidewater Virginia, and in his background were family, culture, and tradition . . . the age of chivalry transplanted to a New World which was making its own legends and its own myths. He embodied a 5 way of life that had come down through the age of knighthood and the English country squire. America was a land that was beginning all over again, dedicated to nothing much more complicated than the rather hazy belief that all men had equal rights and should have an equal chance in the world. In such a land Lee stood for the feeling that it was somehow of advantage to human society to have pronounced inequality in the social structure. There should be a leisure class, backed by ownership of land; in turn, society itself should be keyed to the land as the chief source of wealth and influence. It would bring forth (according to this deal) a class of men with a strong sense of obligation to the community; men who lived not to gain advantage for themselves, but to meet the solemn obligations which had been laid on them by the very fact that they were privileged. From them the country would get its leadership; to them it could look for the higher values — of thought, of conduct, of personal deportment — to give it strength and virtue.

Lee embodied the noblest elements of this aristocratic ideal. Through   6
him, the landed nobility justified itself. For four years, the Southern states had fought a desperate war to uphold the ideals for which Lee stood. In the end, it almost seemed as if the Confederacy fought for Lee; as if he himself was the Confederacy . . . the best thing that the way of life for which the Confederacy stood could ever have to offer. He had passed into legend before Appomattox. Thousands of tired, underfed, poorly clothed Confederate soldiers, long since past the simple enthusiasm of the early days of the struggle, somehow considered Lee the symbol of everything for which they had been willing to die. But they could not quite put this feeling into words. If the Lost Cause, sanctified by so much heroism and so many deaths, had a living justification, its justification was General Lee.

Grant, the son of a tanner on the Western frontier, was everything Lee   7
was not. He had come up the hard way and embodied nothing in particular except the eternal toughness and sinewy fiber of the men who grew up beyond the mountains. He was one of a body of men who owed reverence and obeisance to no one, who were self-reliant to a fault, who cared hardly anything for the past but who had a sharp eye for the future.

These frontier men were the precise opposites of the tidewater aristo-   8
crats. Back of them, in the great surge that had taken people over the Alleghenies and into the opening Western country, there was a deep, implicit dissatisfaction with a past that had settled into grooves. They stood for democracy, not from any reasoned conclusion about the proper ordering of human society, but simply because they had grown up in the middle of democracy and knew how it worked. Their society might have privileges, but they would be privileges each man had won for himself. Forms and patterns meant nothing. No man was born to anything, except perhaps to a chance to show how far he could rise. Life was competition.

Yet along with this feeling had come a deep sense of belonging to a   9
national community. The Westerner who developed a farm, opened a shop, or set up in business as a trader, could hope to prosper only as his

own community prospered — and his community ran from the Atlantic to the Pacific and from Canada down to Mexico. If the land was settled, with towns and highways and accessible markets, he could better himself. He saw his fate in terms of the nation's own destiny. As its horizons expanded, so did his. He had, in other words, an acute dollars-and-cents stake in the continued growth and development of his country.

And that, perhaps, is where the contrast between Grant and Lee   10 becomes most striking. The Virginia aristocrat, inevitably, saw himself in relation to his own region. He lived in a static society which could endure almost anything except change. Instinctively, his first loyalty would go to the locality in which that society existed. He would fight to the limit of endurance to defend it, because in defending it he was defending everything that gave his own life its deepest meaning.

The Westerner, on the other hand, would fight with an equal tenacity   11 for the broader concept of society. He fought so because everything he lived by was tied to growth, expansion, and a constantly widening horizon. What he lived by would survive or fall with the nation itself. He could not possibly stand by unmoved in the face of an attempt to destroy the Union. He would combat it with everything he had, because he could only see it as an effort to cut the ground out from under his feet.

So Grant and Lee were in complete contrast, representing two diametrically opposed elements in American life. Grant was the modern man   12 emerging; beyond him, ready to come on the stage, was the great age of steel and machinery, of crowded cities and a restless burgeoning vitality. Lee might have ridden down from the old age of chivalry, lance in hand, silken banner fluttering over his head. Each man was the perfect champion of his cause, drawing both his strengths and his weaknesses from the people he led.

Yet it was not all contrast, after all. Different as they were — in back-   13 ground, in personality, in underlying aspiration — these two great soldiers had much in common. Under everything else, they were marvelous fighters. Furthermore, their fighting qualities were really very much alike.

Each man had, to begin with, the great virtue of utter tenacity and   14 fidelity. Grant fought his way down the Mississippi Valley in spite of acute personal discouragement and profound military handicaps. Lee hung on in the trenches at Petersburg after hope itself had died. In each man there was an indomitable quality . . . the born fighter's refusal to give up as long as he can still remain on his feet and lift his two fists.

Daring and resourcefulness they had, too; the ability to think faster   15 and move faster than the enemy. These were the qualities which gave Lee the dazzling campaigns of Second Manassas and Chancellorsville and won Vicksburg for Grant.

Lastly, and perhaps greatest of all, there was the ability, at the end, to   16 turn quickly from war to peace once the fighting was over. Out of the way these two men behaved at Appomattox came the possibility of a peace of reconciliation. It was a possibility not wholly realized, in the years to come, but which did, in the end, help the two sections to become one nation again . . . after a war whose bitterness might have seemed to make such a reunion wholly impossible. No part of either man's life became him more than the part he played in this brief meeting in the McLean house at Appomattox. Their behavior there put all succeeding generations of Americans in their debt. Two great Americans, Grant and Lee — very different, yet under everything very much alike. Their encounter at Appomattox was one of the great moments of American history.

• • •

COMPREHENSION

1. What took place at Appomattox Court House on April 9, 1865? Why did the meeting at Appomattox signal the closing of "a great chapter in American life" (1)?

2. How does Robert E. Lee represent aristocracy? How does Ulysses S. Grant represent Lee's opposite?

3. According to Catton, where is it that "the contrast between Grant and Lee becomes most striking" (10)?

4. What similarities does Catton see between the two men?

5. Why, according to Catton, are "succeeding generations of Americans" (16) in debt to Grant and Lee?

PURPOSE AND AUDIENCE

1. Catton's purpose in contrasting Grant and Lee is to make a general statement about the differences between two currents in American history. Summarize these differences. Do you think the differences still exist today? Explain.

2. Is Catton's purpose in comparing Grant and Lee the same as his purpose in contrasting them? That is, do their similarities also make a statement about U.S. history? Explain.

3. State the essay's thesis in your own words.

STYLE AND STRUCTURE

1. Does Catton use subject-by-subject or point-by-point comparison? Why do you think he chooses the structure he does?

2. In this essay, topic sentences are extremely helpful to the reader. Explain the functions of the following sentences: "Grant . . . was everything Lee was not" (7); "So Grant and Lee were in complete contrast . . ." (12); "Yet it was not all contrast, after all" (13); "Lastly, and perhaps greatest of all . . ." (16).

3. Catton uses transitions skillfully in his essay. Identify the transitional words or expressions that link each paragraph to the preceding one.

4. Why do you suppose Catton provides the background for the meeting at Appomattox but presents no information about the dramatic meeting itself?

VOCABULARY PROJECTS

1. Define each of the following words as it is used in this selection.

poignant (2)	obeisance (7)	tenacity (14)
chivalry (5)	implicit (8)	fidelity (14)
deportment (5)	inevitably (10)	indomitable (14)
sanctified (6)	diametrically (12)	reconciliation (16)
embodied (7)	burgeoning (12)	
sinewy (7)	aspiration (13)	

2. Look up **synonyms** for each of the following words and determine which synonyms would and would not be as effective as the word used in this essay. Explain your choices.

deportment (5)	obeisance (7)	indomitable (14)
sanctified (6)	diametrically (12)	

JOURNAL ENTRY

Compare your attitudes about the United States to those held by Grant and Lee. With which man do you agree?

WRITING WORKSHOP

1. Write a "study in contrasts" about two people you know well — two teachers, your parents, two relatives, two friends — or about two fictional characters with whom you are very familiar. Be sure to include a thesis statement.

2. Write a dialogue between two people you know that reveals their contrasting attitudes toward school, work, or any other subject.

3. Write an essay about two individuals from a period of American history other than the Civil War to make the same points Catton makes. Do some research if necessary.

COMBINING THE PATTERNS

In several places, Catton uses **exemplification** to structure a paragraph. For instance, in paragraph 7 he uses examples to support the topic sentence "Grant, the son of a tanner on the Western frontier, was everything Lee was not." Identify three paragraphs that use examples to support the topic sentence, and bracket the examples. In what ways do these examples in these paragraphs reinforce the similarities and differences between Grant and Lee?

THEMATIC CONNECTIONS

- "Does America Still Exist?" (page 482)
- "The Declaration of Independence" (page 516)
- "Letter from Birmingham Jail" (page 522)

ANNE FADIMAN

Anne Fadiman (1953–) was born in New York City into a highly literary family; her mother was a historian and her father was one of the country's most distinguished critics. She graduated from Harvard in 1975 and went on to become a staff writer at *Life* magazine. Later, as an editor for the Library of Congress's *Civilization*, she wrote a monthly column, "The Common Reader," which focused on her own experiences with family and friends. She is currently the editor of *The American Scholar*, a publication of the Phi Beta Kappa Society. In 1997, she published her first book, *The Spirit Catches You and You Fall Down*, about the clash between the medical community in a small California town and Hmong immigrants (people from the mountain region of Laos), who rely on spiritual healing practices.

Her second book, *Ex Libris: Confessions of a Common Reader* (1998), is a collection of her *Civilization* columns, all dealing with the subject of books and reading. In the following essay from that collection, Fadiman considers two different kinds of book lovers: courtly lovers and carnal lovers. (Courtly love is a medieval concept of love in which the lover must remain true and faithful to his lady, completely devoted to her, no matter what obstacles presented themselves.) In an age when a majority of people are more drawn to visual media and computers than to reading, Fadiman's view seems to be something of an anachronism.

Never Do That to a Book

When I was eleven and my brother was thirteen, our parents took us to Europe. At the Hôtel d'Angleterre in Copenhagen, as he had done virtually every night of his literate life, Kim left a book facedown on the bedside table. The next afternoon, he returned to find the book closed, a piece of paper inserted to mark the page, and the following note, signed by the chambermaid, resting on its cover:

SIR, YOU MUST NEVER DO THAT TO A BOOK.

My brother was stunned. How could it have come to pass that he — a reader so devoted that he'd sneaked a book and a flashlight under the covers at his boarding school every night after lights-out, a crime punishable by a swat with a wooden paddle — had been branded as *someone who didn't love books?* I shared his mortification. I could not imagine a more bibliolatrous* family than the Fadimans. Yet, with the exception of my mother, in the eyes of the young Danish maid we would all have been found guilty of rampant book abuse.

During the next thirty years I came to realize that just as there is more than one way to love a person, so is there more than one way to love a book. The chambermaid believed in courtly love. A book's physical self

---

*Eds. note — Book-worshiping.

was sacrosanct to her, its form inseparable from its content; her duty as a lover was Platonic adoration, a noble but doomed attempt to conserve forever the state of perfect chastity in which it had left the bookseller. The Fadiman family believed in carnal love. To us, a book's *words* were holy, but the paper, cloth, cardboard, glue, thread, and ink that contained them were a mere vessel, and it was no sacrilege to treat them as wantonly as desire and pragmatism dictated. Hard use was a sign not of disrespect but of intimacy.

Hilaire Belloc, a courtly lover, once wrote: 4

> Child! do not throw this book about;
> Refrain from the unholy pleasure
> Of cutting all the pictures out!
> Preserve it as your chiefest treasure.

What would Belloc have thought of my father, who, in order to reduce the weight of the paperbacks he read on airplanes, tore off the chapters he had completed and threw them in the trash? What would he have thought of my husband, who reads in the sauna, where heat-fissioned pages drop like petals in a storm? What would he have thought (here I am making a brazen attempt to upgrade my family by association) of Thomas Jefferson, who chopped up a priceless 1572 first edition of Plutarch's works in Greek in order to interleave its pages with an English translation? Or of my old editor Byron Dobell, who, when he was researching an article on the Grand Tour, once stayed up all night reading six volumes of Boswell's journals and, as he puts it, "sucked them like a giant mongoose"? Byron told me, "I didn't give a damn about the condition of those volumes. In order to get where I had to go, I underlined them, wrote in them, shredded them, dropped them, tore them to pieces, and did things to them that we can't discuss in public."

Byron loves books. Really, he does. So does my husband, an incorri-   5
gible book-splayer whose roommate once informed him, "George, if you ever break the spine of one of my books, I want you to know you might as well be breaking *my own spine*." So does Kim, who reports that despite his experience in Copenhagen, his bedside table currently supports three spreadeagled volumes. "They are ready in an instant to let me pick them up," he explains. "To use an electronics analogy, closing a book on a bookmark is like pressing the Stop button, whereas when you leave the book facedown, you've only pressed Pause." I confess to marking my place promiscuously, sometimes splaying, sometimes committing the even more grievous sin of dog-earing the page. (Here I manage to be simultaneously abusive and compulsive: I turn down the upper corner for page-marking and the lower corner to identify passages I want to xerox for my commonplace book.)

All courtly lovers press Stop. My Aunt Carol — who will probably   6
claim she's no relation once she finds out how I treat my books — places reproductions of Audubon paintings horizontally to mark the exact para-

graph where she left off. If the colored side is up, she was reading the left-hand page; if it's down, the right-hand page. A college classmate of mine, a lawyer, uses his business cards, spurning his wife's silver Tiffany book-marks because they are a few microns too thick and might leave vestigial stigmata. Another classmate, an art historian, favors Paris Métro tickets or "those inkjet-printed credit card receipts — but only in books of art criti-cism whose pretentiousness I wish to desecrate with something really crass and financial. I would never use those in fiction or poetry, which really *are* sacred."

Courtly lovers always remove their bookmarks when the assignation   7
is over; carnal lovers are likely to leave romantic mementos, often three-dimensional and messy. *Birds of Yosemite and the East Slope,* a volume belonging to a science writer friend, harbors an owl feather and the tip of a squirrel's tail, evidence of a crime scene near Tioga Pass. A book critic I know took *The Collected Stories and Poems of Edgar Allan Poe* on a backpack-ing trip through the Yucatán, and whenever an interesting bug landed in it, she clapped the covers shut. She amassed such a bulging insectarium that she feared Poe might not make it through customs. (He did.)

The most permanent, and thus to the courtly lover the most terrible,   8
thing one can leave in a book is one's own words. Even I would never write in an encyclopedia (except perhaps with a No. 3 pencil, which I'd later erase). But I've been annotating novels and poems — transforming monologues into dialogues — ever since I learned to read. Byron Dobell says that his most beloved books, such as *The Essays of Montaigne,* have been written on so many times, in so many different periods of his life, in so many colors of ink, that they have become palimpsests.* I would far rather read Byron's copy of Montaigne than a virginal one from the book-store, just as I would rather read John Adams's copy of Mary Woll-stonecraft's *French Revolution,* in whose margins he argued so vehemently with the dead author ("Heavenly times!" "A barbarous theory." "Did this lady think three months time enough to form a free constitution for twenty-five millions of Frenchmen?") that, two hundred years later, his handwriting still looks angry.

Just think what courtly lovers miss by believing that the only thing   9
they are permitted to do with books is *read* them! What do they use for shims, doorstops, glueing weights, and rug-flatteners? When my friend the art historian was a teenager, his cherished copy of *D'Aulaire's Book of Greek Myths* served as a drum pad on which he practiced percussion riffs from Led Zeppelin. A philosophy professor at my college, whose baby became enamored of the portrait of David Hume on a Penguin paperback, had the cover laminated in plastic so her daughter could cut her teeth on the great thinker. Menelik II, the emperor of Ethiopia at the turn of the century, liked to chew pages from his Bible. Unfortunately, he died after

---

*EDS. NOTE — Ancient manuscripts whose pages are "recycled"— written on more than once — with the erased writing still legible.

consuming the complete Book of Kings. I do not consider Menelik's fate an argument for keeping our hands and teeth off our books; the lesson to be drawn, clearly, is that he, too, should have laminated his pages in plastic.

"How beautiful to a genuine lover of reading are the sullied leaves, and worn-out appearance . . . of an old 'Circulating Library' Tom Jones, or Vicar of Wakefield!" wrote Charles Lamb. "How they speak of the thousand thumbs that have turned over their pages with delight! . . . Who would have them a whit less soiled? What better condition could we desire to see them in?" Absolutely none. Thus, a landscape architect I know savors the very smell of the dirt embedded in his botany texts; it is the alluvium of his life's work. Thus, my friend the science writer considers her *Mammals of the World* to have been enhanced by the excremental splotches left by Bertrand Russell, an orphaned band-tailed pigeon who perched on it when he was learning to fly. And thus, even though I own a clear plastic cookbook holder, I never use it. What a pleasure it will be, thirty years hence, to open *The Joy of Cooking* to page 581 and behold part of the *actual egg yolk* that my daughter glopped into her very first batch of blueberry muffins at age twenty-two months! The courtly mode simply doesn't work with small children. I hope I am not deluding myself when I imagine that even the Danish chambermaid, if she is now a mother, might be able to appreciate a really grungy copy of *Pat the Bunny* — a book that *invites* the reader to act like a Dobellian giant mongoose — in which Mummy's ring has been fractured and Daddy's scratchy face has been rubbed as smooth as the Blarney Stone.

The trouble with the carnal approach is that we love our books to pieces. My brother keeps his disintegrating *Golden Guide to Birds* in a Ziploc bag. "It consists of dozens of separate fascicles,"* says Kim, "and it's impossible to read. When I pick it up, the egrets fall out. But if I replaced it, the note I wrote when I saw my first trumpeter swan wouldn't be there. Also, I don't want to admit that so many species names have changed. If I bought a new edition, I'd feel I was being unfaithful to my old friend the yellow-bellied sapsucker, which has been split into three different species."

My friend Clark's eight thousand books, mostly works of philosophy, will never suffer the same fate as *The Golden Guide to Birds*. In fact, just *hearing* about Kim's book might trigger a nervous collapse. Clark, an investment analyst, won't let his wife raise the blinds until sundown, lest the bindings fade. He buys at least two copies of his favorite books, so that only one need be subjected to the stress of having its pages turned. When his visiting mother-in-law made the mistake of taking a book off the shelf, Clark shadowed her around the apartment to make sure she didn't do anything unspeakable to it — such as placing it facedown on a table.

---

*Eds. note — Bound sections of a book.

I know these facts about Clark because when George was over there   13
last week, he talked to Clark's wife and made some notes on the back fly-
leaf of Herman Wouk's *Don't Stop the Carnival,* which he happened to be
carrying in his backpack. He ripped out the page and gave it to me.

• • •

COMPREHENSION

1. Why does the Danish chambermaid leave Fadiman's brother a note? What reaction does he have to the note?

2. What are the characteristics of a courtly book lover? What are the characteristics of a carnal book lover?

3. What kind of book lover is Fadiman? At what point in the essay does she reveal herself?

4. Fadiman makes a distinction between a book's words and "the paper, cloth, cardboard, glue, thread, and ink that contained them . . ." (3). What does she mean? How does this distinction help her make her point?

5. What, according to Fadiman, is the main drawback of being a carnal book lover?

PURPOSE AND AUDIENCE

1. What preconceptions about books does Fadiman think her readers have? How can you tell?

2. What is Fadiman's purpose? Does she seek to instruct? To convince? To entertain? Or, does she have some other purpose? Explain.

3. What is the thesis of this essay? At what point does Fadiman state her thesis?

4. What kinds of examples does Fadiman use? What additional examples might she have included if she had wanted to appeal primarily to college students?

STYLE AND STRUCTURE

1. Why does Fadiman introduce her essay with the story of the Danish chambermaid? What does this story add to her essay?

2. Is this essay organized as a subject-by-subject or as a point-by-point comparison? Why do you think Fadiman made the choice she did?

3. What specific points does Fadiman discuss for both types of book lovers?

4. What transitions does Fadiman use to signal her movement from one subject to another?

5. Why does Fadiman conclude with a story about her friend Clark? What point is she trying to make?

VOCABULARY PROJECTS

1. Define each of the following words as it is used in this selection.

rampant (2)	fissioned (4)	pretentiousness (6)
sacrosanct (3)	brazen (4)	harbors (7)
Platonic (3)	spreadeagled (5)	virginal (8)
chastity (3)	promiscuously (5)	vehemently (8)
sacrilege (3)	grievous (5)	shims (9)
wantonly (3)	spurning (6)	alluvium (10)
pragmatism (3)	vestigial (6)	deluding (10)
dictated (3)	stigmata (6)	egrets (11)

2. This essay contains a number of rather difficult words. Choose a paragraph that contains several of these words (paragraph 3, for example), and rewrite it in more colloquial language. Then, evaluate what has been gained and lost as a result of your substitutions.

JOURNAL ENTRY

Do you feel intensely about some object — your computer, for example — the way that Fadiman feels about books? Are you a courtly or carnal lover? List some examples to support your contention.

WRITING WORKSHOP

1. Write an essay in which you compare and contrast two people you know who enjoy a particular activity — for example, watching sports on television, going to the movies, or surfing the Internet. How are their attitudes and actions different?

2. Write an essay in which you, like Fadiman, compare courtly and carnal book lovers. In your essay, support the thesis that one type of book lover is superior to the other when it comes to succeeding in college.

3. Compare the way you approach the reading you do for school or work and the reading you do for pleasure. How are your reading habits different in each case?

COMBINING THE PATTERNS

In paragraph 3, Fadiman presents **definitions** of the terms *courtly love* and *carnal love*. How clear are these definitions? Do you think Fadiman expects readers to be familiar with these terms before she defines them? How can you tell?

THEMATIC CONNECTIONS

TOM STANDAGE

Tom Standage is currently the science correspondent for the *Economist,* a weekly newsmagazine published in Great Britain. He is the former deputy editor of the "Connected" supplement of London's *Daily Telegraph,* a section that focuses on developments in new technology. He has also written for *Wired* and the electronic magazine *FEED* and has appeared as a commentator on technology and new media on British television.

In his 1998 book *The Victorian Internet: The Remarkable Story of the Telegraph and the Nineteenth Century's On-Line Pioneers,* Standage points out that the telegraph was one of the first mechanical systems of long-distance communication. Its prototype, invented by the Frenchman Claude Chappe in the late eighteenth century, was superseded in the nineteenth century by electrical systems and ultimately by wireless systems that send messages via electromagnetic waves. In each case, messages were transmitted in code. In the most common of these codes, developed by the American Samuel Morse, letters are represented by a series of dots and dashes, indicating short and long signals (for example, the letter *b* in Morse code is _ . . .). Highly skilled operators had to quickly translate written messages into code and vice versa. Depending on the distance traveled, messages might go through several stations before reaching their destination. In this section from *The Victorian Internet,* Standage compares the telegraph, now rarely used, with the Internet. His purpose, in part, is to convince readers that the sweeping claims made for new technologies should be regarded with some skepticism.

The Victorian Internet

Although it has now faded from view, the telegraph lives on within 1
the communications technologies that have subsequently built upon its foundations: the telephone, the fax machine, and, more recently, the Internet. And, ironically, it is the Internet — despite being regarded as a quintessentially modern means of communication — that has the most in common with its telegraphic ancestor.

Like the telegraph network, the Internet allows people to communi- 2
cate across great distances using interconnected networks. (Indeed, the generic term *internet* simply means a group of interconnected networks.) Common rules and protocols enable any sort of computer to exchange messages with any other — just as messages could easily be passed from one kind of telegraph apparatus (a Morse printer, say) to another (a pneumatic tube). The journey of an e-mail message, as it hops from mail server to mail server toward its destination, mirrors the passage of a telegram from one telegraph office to the next.

There are even echoes of the earliest, most primitive telegraphs — 3
such as the optical system invented by Chappe — in today's modems and network hardware. Every time two computers exchange an eight-digit binary number, or byte, they are going through the same motions as an

eight-panel shutter telegraph would have done two hundred years ago. Instead of using a codebook to relate each combination to a different word, today's computers use another agreed-upon protocol to transmit individual letters. This scheme, called ASCII (for American Standard Code for Information Interchange), says, for example, that a capital "A" should be represented by the pattern 01000001; but in essence the principles are unchanged since the late eighteenth century. Similarly, Chappe's system had special codes to increase or reduce the rate of transmission, or to request that garbled information be sent again — all of which are features of modems today. The protocols used by modems are decided on by the ITU, the organization founded in 1865 to regulate international telegraphy. The initials now stand for International Telecommunication Union, rather than International Telegraph Union.

More striking still are the parallels between the social impact of the telegraph and that of the Internet. Public reaction to the new technologies was, in both cases, a confused mixture of hype and skepticism. Just as many Victorians believed the telegraph would eliminate misunderstanding between nations and usher in a new era of world peace, an avalanche of media coverage has lauded the Internet as a powerful new medium that will transform and improve our lives.

Some of these claims sound oddly familiar. In his 1997 book *What Will Be: How the New World of Information Will Change Our Lives,* Michael Dertouzos of the Laboratory for Computer Science at the Massachusetts Institute of Technology wrote of the prospect of "computer-aided peace" made possible by digital networks like the Internet. "A common bond reached through electronic proximity may help stave off future flareups of ethnic hatred and national breakups," he suggested. In a conference speech in November 1997, Nicholas Negroponte, head of the MIT Media Laboratory, explicitly declared that the Internet would break down national borders and lead to world peace. In the future, he claimed, children "are not going to know what nationalism is."

The similarities do not end there. Scam artists found crooked ways to make money by manipulating the transmission of stock prices and the results of horse races using the telegraph; their twentieth-century counterparts have used the Internet to set up fake "shop fronts" purporting to be legitimate providers of financial services, before disappearing with the money handed over by would-be investors; hackers have broken into improperly secured computers and made off with lists of credit card numbers.

People who were worried about inadequate security on the telegraph network, and now on the Internet, turned to the same solution: secret codes. Today software to compress files and encrypt messages before sending them across the Internet is as widely used as the commercial codes that flourished on the telegraph network. And just as the ITU placed restrictions on the use of telegraphic ciphers, many governments today are trying to do the same with computer cryptography, by imposing limits on the complexity of the encryption available to Internet users. (The ITU, it should be noted, proved unable to enforce its rules restricting the types of code words that could be used in telegrams, and eventually abandoned them.)

On a simpler level, both the telegraph and the Internet have given rise   8
to their own jargon and abbreviations. Rather than plugs, boomers, or bonus men, Internet users are variously known as surfers, netheads, or netizens. Personal signatures, used by both telegraphers and Internet users, are known in both cases as sigs.

Another parallel is the eternal enmity between new, inexperienced   9
users and experienced old hands. Highly skilled telegraphers in city offices would lose their temper when forced to deal with hopelessly inept operators in remote villages; the same phenomenon was widespread on the Internet when the masses first surged on-line in the early 1990s, unaware of customs and traditions that had held sway on the Internet for years and capable of what, to experienced users, seemed unbelievable stupidity, gullibility, and impoliteness.

But while conflict and rivalry both seem to come with the on-line terri-   10
tory, so does romance. A general fascination with the romantic possibilities of the new technology has been a feature of both the nineteenth and twentieth centuries: On-line weddings have taken place over both the telegraph and the Internet. In 1996, Sue Helle and Lynn Bottoms were married on-line by a minister 10 miles away in Seattle, echoing the story of Philip Reade and Clara Choate, who were married by telegraph 120 years earlier by a minister 650 miles away. Both technologies have also been directly blamed for causing romantic problems. In 1996, a New Jersey man filed for divorce when he discovered that his wife had been exchanging explicit e-mail with another man, a case that was widely reported as the first example of "Internet divorce."

After a period of initial skepticism, businesses became the most   11
enthusiastic adopters of the telegraph in the nineteenth century and the Internet in the twentieth. Businesses have always been prepared to pay for premium services like private leased lines and value-added information — provided those services can provide a competitive advantage in the marketplace. Internet sites routinely offer stock prices and news headlines, both of which were available over a hundred years ago via stock tickers and news wires. And just as the telegraph led to a direct increase in the pace and stress of business life, today the complaint of information overload, blamed on the Internet, is commonplace.

The telegraph also made possible new business practices, facilitating   12
the rise of large companies centrally controlled from a head office. Today, the Internet once again promises to redefine the way people work, through emerging trends like teleworking (working from a distant location, with a network connection to one's office) and virtual corporations (where there is no central office, just a distributed group of employees who communicate over a network).

The similarities between the telegraph and the Internet — both in   13
their technical underpinnings and their social impact — are striking. But

the story of the telegraph contains a deeper lesson. Because of its ability to link distant peoples, the telegraph was the first technology to be seized upon as a panacea. Given its potential to change the world, the telegraph was soon being hailed as a means of solving the world's problems. It failed to do so, of course — but we have been pinning the same hope on other new technologies ever since.

In the 1890s, advocates of electricity claimed it would eliminate the   14
drudgery of manual work and create a world of abundance and peace. In the first decade of the twentieth century, aircraft inspired similar flights of fancy: Rapid intercontinental travel would, it was claimed, eliminate international differences and misunderstandings. (One commentator suggested that the age of aviation would be an "age of peace" because aircraft would make armies obsolete, since they would be vulnerable to attack from the air.) Similarly, television was expected to improve education, reduce social isolation, and enhance democracy. Nuclear power was supposed to usher in an age of plenty where electricity would be "too cheap to meter." The optimistic claims now being made about the Internet are merely the most recent examples in a tradition of technological utopianism that goes back to the first transatlantic telegraph cables, 150 years ago.

That the telegraph was so widely seen as a panacea is perhaps under-   15
standable. The fact that we are still making the same mistake today is less so. The irony is that even though it failed to live up to the utopian claims made about it, the telegraph really did transform the world. It also redefined forever our attitudes toward new technologies. In both respects, we are still living in the new world it inaugurated.

• • •

COMPREHENSION

1. According to Standage, what is ironic about the Internet's being like the telegraph?

2. What was the public's reaction to the telegraph? In what ways was this reaction similar to the public's reaction to the Internet?

3. How did business react to the telegraph? Was this reaction similar to or different from business's reaction to the Internet?

4. In paragraph 14, Standage discusses claims that advocates of various technological discoveries have made. How accurate were these claims? What do they suggest about claims now being made about the Internet?

5. How, according to Standage, has the telegraph changed our world?

PURPOSE AND AUDIENCE

1. Standage announces his thesis at the end of the first paragraph. Why do you think he uses this no-nonsense approach? Would a different approach have been more effective?

2. What do you think Standage hopes to accomplish by comparing the telegraph to the Internet?

3. Does the title of this essay accurately reflect its thesis? What other title(s) might Standage have used?

STYLE AND STRUCTURE

1. Is this essay actually an analogy? In other words, is Standage explaining one thing by comparing it to a second thing that is more familiar than the first?

2. What specific points does Standage make about both the telegraph and the Internet?

3. Is this essay organized as a subject-by-subject or as a point-by-point comparison? Why do you think Standage organized it the way he did?

4. What basis for comparison exists between the telegraph and the Internet? Do you think these two things share enough characteristics to justify a comparison?

5. In paragraph 15, Standage says, "The telegraph really did transform the world." Why doesn't he discuss the Internet in this context?

VOCABULARY PROJECTS

1. Define each of the following words as it is used in this selection.

subsequently (1)	garbled (3)	cryptography (7)
quintessentially (1)	digital (5)	enmity (9)
protocols (2)	proximity (5)	gullibility (9)
pneumatic (2)	purporting (6)	utopian (15)
binary (3)	encrypt (7)	

2. What words does Standage define in his essay? Why does he do this? What do these definitions tell you about the technical expertise Standage expects his readers to have?

JOURNAL ENTRY

Do you think that the Internet, like the telegraph, will transform the world? If so, how? In what ways has it already transformed your world?

WRITING WORKSHOP

1. Write an essay in which you compare an example of old technology with an example of contemporary technology — a regular telephone and a cell phone, for example. Make sure you discuss both negative and positive aspects of each.

2. Choose a type of contemporary technology that you have only recently begun to use frequently. Write a comparison-and-contrast essay in which

you discuss what your life was like before you began using this technology and what it is like now. Your essay can be serious or humorous.

3. Interview your parents or your grandparents, and ask them about their attitude toward the Internet. Then, write an essay in which you compare their attitudes toward the Internet to your own.

COMBINING THE PATTERNS

This essay contains a number of **cause-and-effect** paragraphs — for example, paragraphs 5 and 12. What do these paragraphs add to the essay?

THEMATIC CONNECTIONS

- "The Great Campus Goof-Off Machine" (page 188)
- "Television: The Plug-In Drug" (page 283)
- "The End of Serendipity" (page 604)

BHARATI MUKHERJEE

Born in 1940 in Calcutta, India, novelist Bharati Mukherjee attended the University of Calcutta before immigrating to the United States in 1961. After receiving an M.F.A. from the University of Iowa, she moved with her husband to Canada, where she taught at McGill University. Now a naturalized U.S. citizen, she teaches at Skidmore College. Mukherjee's novels include *Tiger's Daughter* (1972), *Jasmine* (1989), and *Leave It to Me* (1997); her story collections are *Darkness* (1975) and the prize-winning *The Middleman and Other Stories* (1988). Her fiction often explores the tensions between the traditional role of women in Indian society and their very different role in the United States as well as the racism often faced by immigrants.

The following essay, originally published in the *New York Times* in 1996, was written in response to proposals in Congress (eventually defeated) to enact legislation denying government benefits, such as Social Security, to resident aliens. (Not to be confused with illegal immigrants, resident aliens are immigrants who live in the United States legally, sometimes for their whole lives, but choose not to apply for citizenship. Most work and pay taxes like any citizen.) Mukherjee's larger subject in this essay is the differences between herself, who chose to become a U.S. citizen, and her sister, who remained a resident alien.

Two Ways to Belong in America

This is a tale of two sisters from Calcutta, Mira and Bharati, who have lived in the United States for some 35 years, but who find themselves on different sides in the current debate over the status of immigrants. I am an American citizen and she is not. I am moved that thousands of long-term residents are finally taking the oath of citizenship. She is not. 1

Mira arrived in Detroit in 1960 to study child psychology and pre-school education. I followed her a year later to study creative writing at the University of Iowa. When we left India, we were almost identical in appearance and attitude. We dressed alike, in saris; we expressed identical views on politics, social issues, love, and marriage in the same Calcutta convent-school accent. We would endure our two years in America, secure our degrees, then return to India to marry the grooms of our father's choosing. 2

Instead, Mira married an Indian student in 1962 who was getting his business administration degree at Wayne State University. They soon acquired the labor certifications necessary for the green card of hassle-free residence and employment. 3

Mira still lives in Detroit, works in the Southfield, Mich., school system, and has become nationally recognized for her contributions in the fields of pre-school education and parent-teacher relationships. After 36 years as a legal immigrant in this country, she clings passionately to her Indian citizenship and hopes to go home to India when she retires. 4

In Iowa City in 1963, I married a fellow student, an American of 5
Canadian parentage. Because of the accident of his North Dakota birth,
I bypassed labor-certification requirements and the race-related "quota"
system that favored the applicant's country of origin over his or her
merit. I was prepared for (and even welcomed) the emotional strain that
came with marrying outside my ethnic community. In 33 years of marriage, we have lived in every part of North America. By choosing a husband who was not my father's selection, I was opting for fluidity,
self-invention, blue jeans and T-shirts, and renouncing 3,000 years (at
least) of case-observant, "pure culture" marriage in the Mukherjee family.
My books have often been read as unapologetic (and in some quarters
overenthusiastic) texts for cultural and psychological "mongrelization."
It's a word I celebrate.

Mira and I have stayed sisterly close by phone. In our regular Sunday 6
morning conversations, we are unguardedly affectionate. I am her only
blood relative on this continent. We expect to see each other through the
looming crises of aging and ill health without being asked. Long before
Vice President Gore's "Citizenship U.S.A." drive, we'd had our polite
arguments over the ethics of retaining an overseas citizenship while
expecting the permanent protection and economic benefits that come with
living and working in America.

Like well-raised sisters, we never said what was really on our minds, 7
but we probably pitied one another. She, for the lack of structure in my
life, the erasure of Indianness, the absence of an unvarying daily core. I,
for the narrowness of her perspective, her uninvolvement with the mythic
depths or the superficial pop culture of this society. But, now, with the
scapegoatings of "aliens" (documented or illegal) on the increase, and the
targeting of long-term legal immigrants like Mira for new scrutiny and
new self-consciousness, she and I find ourselves unable to maintain the
same polite discretion. We were always unacknowledged adversaries, and
we are now, more than ever, sisters.

"I feel used," Mira raged on the phone the other night. "I feel manipu- 8
lated and discarded. This is such an unfair way to treat a person who was
invited to stay and work here because of her talent. My employer went to
the I.N.S. and petitioned for the labor certification. For over 30 years, I've
invested my creativity and professional skills into the improvement of *this*
country's pre-school system. I've obeyed all the rules, I've paid my taxes, I
love my work, I love my students, I love the friends I've made. How dare
America now change its rules in midstream? If America wants to make
new rules curtailing benefits of legal immigrants, they should apply only
to immigrants who arrive after those rules are already in place."

To my ears, it sounded like the description of a long-enduring, com- 9
fortable yet loveless marriage, without risk or recklessness. Have we the
right to demand, and to expect, that we be loved? (That, to me, is the sub-
text of the arguments by immigration advocates.) My sister is an expatri-

ate, professionally generous and creative, socially courteous and gracious, and that's as far as her Americanization can go. She is here to maintain an identity, not to transform it.

I asked her if she would follow the example of others who have   10 decided to become citizens because of the anti-immigration bills in Congress. And here, she surprised me. "If America wants to play the manipulative game, I'll play it, too," she snapped. "I'll become a U.S. citizen for now, then change back to India when I'm ready to go home. I feel some kind of irrational attachment to India that I don't to America. Until all this hysteria against legal immigrants, I was totally happy. Having my green card meant I could visit any place in the world I wanted to and then come back to a job that's satisfying and that I do very well."

In one family, from two sisters alike as peas in a pod, there could not   11 be a wider divergence of immigrant experience. America spoke to me — I married it — I embraced the demotion from expatriate aristocrat to immigrant nobody, surrendering those thousands of years of "pure culture," the saris, the delightfully accented English. She retained them all. Which of us is the freak?

Mira's voice, I realize, is the voice not just of the immigrant South   12 Asian community but of an immigrant community of the millions who have stayed rooted in one job, one city, one house, one ancestral culture, one cuisine, for the entirety of their productive years. She speaks for greater numbers than I possibly can. Only the fluency of her English and the anger, rather than fear, born of confidence from her education, differentiate her from the seamstresses, the domestics, the technicians, the shop owners, the millions of hard-working but effectively silenced documented immigrants as well as their less fortunate "illegal" brothers and sisters.

Nearly 20 years ago, when I was living in my husband's ancestral   13 homeland of Canada, I was always well-employed but never allowed to feel part of the local Quebec or larger Canadian society. Then, through a Green Paper that invited a national referendum on the unwanted side effects of "nontraditional" immigration, the Government officially turned against its immigrant communities, particularly those from South Asia.

I felt then the same sense of betrayal that Mira feels now. I will never   14 forget the pain of that sudden turning, and the casual racist outbursts the Green Paper elicited. That sense of betrayal had its desired effect and drove me, and thousands like me, from the country.

Mira and I differ, however, in the ways in which we hope to interact   15 with the country that we have chosen to live in. She is happier to live in America as expatriate Indian than as an immigrant American. I need to feel like a part of the community I have adopted (as I tried to feel in Canada as well). I need to put roots down, to vote and make the difference that I can. The price that the immigrant willingly pays, and that the exile avoids, is the trauma of self-transformation.

•   •   •

COMPREHENSION

1. At first, how long did Mukherjee and her sister intend to stay in America? Why did they change their plans?

2. What does Mukherjee mean when she says she welcomed the "emotional strain" of "marrying outside [her] ethnic community" (5)?

3. In what ways is Mukherjee different from her sister? What kind of relationship do they have?

4. Why does Mukherjee's sister feel used? Why does she think America has changed "its rules in midstream" (8)?

5. According to Mukherjee, how is her sister like all immigrants who "have stayed rooted in one job, one city, one house, one ancestral culture, one cuisine, for the entirety of their productive years" (12)?

PURPOSE AND AUDIENCE

1. What is Mukherjee's thesis? At what point does she state it?

2. At whom is Mukherjee aiming her remarks? Immigrants like herself? Immigrants like her sister? General readers? Explain.

3. What is Mukherjee's purpose? Is she trying to inform? To move readers to action? To accomplish something else? Explain.

STYLE AND STRUCTURE

1. What basis for comparison exists between Mukherjee and her sister? Where in the essay does Mukherjee establish this basis of comparison?

2. Is this essay a point-by-point or a subject-by-subject comparison? Why do you think Mukherjee chose the option she did?

3. What points does Mukherjee discuss for each subject? Should she have discussed any other points?

4. What transitional words and phrases does Mukherjee use to signal shifts from one point to another?

5. How effective is Mukherjee's conclusion? Does it summarize the major points of the essay? Would another strategy be more effective? Explain.

VOCABULARY PROJECTS

1. Define each of the following words as it is used in this selection.

certifications (3)	superficial (7)	divergence (11)
mongrelization (5)	scrutiny (7)	expatriate (11)
perspective (7)	discretion (7)	saris (11)
mythic (7)	curtailing (8)	trauma (15)

2. What, according to Mukherjee, is the difference between an *immigrant* and an *exile* (15)? What are the connotations of these two words? Do you think the distinction Mukherjee makes is valid?

JOURNAL ENTRY

Do you think Mukherjee respects her sister's decision? From your perspective, which sister has made the right decision?

COMBINING THE PATTERNS

Do you think Mukherjee should have used **cause and effect** to structure a section explaining why she and her sister are so different? Explain what such a section would add to or take away from the essay.

WRITING WORKSHOP

1. Assume that the sister, Mira, has just read Mukherjee's essay and wants to respond to it. Write a letter from Mira in which you compare her position about assimilation to that of Mukherjee. Make sure you explain Mira's position and address Mukherjee's points about assimilation.

2. Have you ever moved from one town or city to another? Write an essay in which you compare the two places. Your thesis statement should indicate whether you are emphasizing similarities or differences and convey your opinion of the new area to which you moved. (If you have never moved, write an essay comparing two places you are familiar with — college and your high school, for example.)

3. Assume you had to move to another country. Where would you move? Would you, like Mukherjee, assimilate into your new culture, or, like her sister, retain your own cultural values? Write an essay in which you compare life in your new country to life in the United States. Make sure your thesis reflects your attitude toward assimilation. If you have already moved from another country, compare your life in the United States with your life in your country of origin.

THEMATIC CONNECTIONS

- "Only Daughter" (page 83)
- "More Than Just a Shrine: Paying Homage to the Ghosts of Ellis Island" (page 142)
- "The Way to Rainy Mountain" (page 148)
- "The Big Move" (page 334)
- "The Untouchable" (page 461)

CHRISTOPHER B. DALY

Born in Boston, Christopher B. Daly (1954–) received a B.A. from Harvard and an M.A. in history from the University of North Carolina at Chapel Hill. A veteran journalist, Daly spent ten years working at the Associated Press and another seven years covering New England for the *Washington Post*. He has taught journalism and writing at Harvard and Brandeis; currently he is a visiting professor at Boston University as well as a freelance writer. His work has appeared in a variety of magazines and journals, and he is coauthor of *Like a Family* (1987), a prize-winning social history of the industrialization of the South.

In the following essay, which originally appeared in the *Atlantic* in 1995, Daly recalls the fun he and his boyhood friends had during the winter when they would go skating unsupervised on a local pond. Today, however, this activity would not be permitted in many communities because of the threat of lawsuits should someone drown. Lawsuits have been on the rise in the United States since the mid-1970s, sparked primarily by two events: the 1976 decision by the American Bar Association to allow its attorney members to advertise and a 1977 Supreme Court decision that made it easier for people to file lawsuits. As an example, New York City's payout for lawsuits jumped from 24 million dollars in 1977 to 114 million in 1985, and today an estimated 18 million lawsuits are filed nationally each year. Daly argues that children's lives today are much more sheltered, and consequently much narrower, than they were in less litigious times.

How the Lawyers Stole Winter

When I was a boy, my friends and I would come home from school each day, change our clothes (because we were not allowed to wear "play clothes" to school), and go outside until dinnertime. In the early 1960s in Medford, a city on the outskirts of Boston, that was pretty much what everybody did. Sometimes there might be flute lessons, or an organized Little League game, but usually not. Usually we kids went out and played.

In winter, on our way home from the Gleason School, we would go past Brooks Pond to check the ice. By throwing heavy stones on it, hammering it with downed branches, and, finally, jumping on it, we could figure out if the ice was ready for skating. If it was, we would hurry home to grab our skates, our sticks, and whatever other gear we had, and then return to play hockey for the rest of the day. When the streetlights came on, we knew it was time to jam our cold, stiff feet back into our green rubber snow boots and get home for dinner.

I had these memories in mind recently when I moved, with my wife and two young boys, into a house near a lake even closer to Boston, in the city of Newton. As soon as Crystal Lake froze over, I grabbed my skates and headed out. I was not the first one there, though: the lawyers had beaten me to the lake. They had warned the town recreation department to put it off limits. So I found a sign that said DANGER, THIN ICE. NO SKATING.

Knowing a thing or two about words myself, I put my own gloss on the sign. I took it to mean *When the ice is thin, there is danger and there should be no skating.* Fair enough, I thought, but I knew that the obverse was also true: *When the ice is thick, it is safe and there should be skating.* Finding the ice plenty thick, I laced up my skates and glided out onto the miraculous glassy surface of the frozen lake. My wife, a native of Manhattan, would not let me take our two boys with me. But for as long as I could, I enjoyed the free, open-air delight of skating as it should be. After a few days others joined me, and we became an outlaw band of skaters. 4

What we were doing was once the heart of winter in New England — and a lot of other places, too. It was clean, free exercise that needed no StairMasters, no health clubs, no appointments, and hardly any gear. Sadly, it is in danger of passing away. Nowadays it seems that every city and town and almost all property holders are so worried about liability and lawsuits that they simply throw up a sign or a fence and declare that henceforth there shall be no skating, and that's the end of it. 5

As a result, kids today live in a world of leagues, rinks, rules, uniforms, adults, and rides — rides here, rides there, rides everywhere. It is not clear that they are better off; in some ways they are clearly *not* better off. 6

When I was a boy skating on Brooks Pond, there were no grown-ups around. Once or twice a year, on a weekend day or a holiday, some parents might come by with a thermos of hot cocoa. Maybe they would build a fire (which we were forbidden to do), and we would gather round. 7

But for the most part the pond was the domain of children. In the absence of adults, we made and enforced our own rules. We had hardly any gear — just some borrowed hockey gloves, some hand-me-down skates, maybe an elbow pad or two — so we played a clean form of hockey, with no high-sticking, no punching, and almost no checking. A single fight could ruin the whole afternoon. Indeed, as I remember it, thirty years later, it was the purest form of hockey I ever saw — until I got to see the Russian national team play the game. 8

But before we could play, we had to check the ice. We became serious junior meteorologists, true connoisseurs of cold. We learned that the best weather for pond skating is plain, clear cold, with starry nights and no snow. (Snow not only mucks up the skating surface but also insulates the ice from the colder air above.) And we learned that moving water, even the gently flowing Mystic River, is a lot less likely to freeze than standing water. So we skated only on the pond. We learned all the weird whooping and cracking sounds that ice makes as it expands and contracts, and thus when to leave the ice. 9

Do kids learn these things today? I don't know. How would they? We don't let them. Instead we post signs. Ruled by lawyers, cities and towns 10 everywhere try to eliminate their legal liability. But try as they might, they cannot eliminate the underlying risk. Liability is a social construct; risk is a natural fact. When it is cold enough, ponds freeze. No sign or fence or ordinance can change that.

In fact, by focusing on liability and not teaching our kids how to take   11 risks, we are making their world more dangerous. When we were children, we had to learn to evaluate risks and handle them on our own. We had to learn, quite literally, to test the waters. As a result, we grew up to be savvier about ice and ponds than any kid could be who has skated only under adult supervision on a rink.

When I was a boy, despite the risks we took on the ice no one I knew   12 ever drowned. The only people I heard about who drowned were graduate students at Harvard or MIT who came from the tropics and were living through their first winters. Not knowing (after all, how could they?) about ice on moving water, they would innocently venture out onto the half-frozen Charles River, fall through, and die. They were literally out of their element.

Are we raising a generation of children who will be out of their ele-   13 ment? And if so, what can we do about it? We cannot just roll back the calendar. I cannot tell my six-year-old to head down to the lake by himself to play all afternoon — if for no other reason than that he would not find twenty or thirty other kids there, full of the collective wisdom about cold and ice that they had inherited, along with hockey equipment, from their older brothers and sisters. Somewhere along the line that link got broken.

The whole setting of childhood has changed. We cannot change it   14 again overnight. I cannot send my children out by themselves yet, but at least some of the time I can go out there with them. Maybe that is a start.

As for us, last winter was a very unusual one. We had ferocious cold   15 (near-zero temperatures on many nights) and tremendous snows (about a hundred inches in all). Eventually a strange thing happened. The town gave in — sort of. Sometime in January the recreation department "opened" a section of the lake, and even dispatched a snowplow truck to clear a good-sized patch of ice. The boys and I skated during the rest of winter. Ever vigilant, the town officials kept the THIN ICE signs up, even though their own truck could safely drive on the frozen surface. And they brought in "lifeguards" and all sorts of rules about the hours during which we could skate and where we had to stay.

But at least we were able to skate in the open air, on real ice.   16

And it was still free.   17

• • •

COMPREHENSION

1. What did Daly and his friends do when they came home from school in the 1960s?

2. According to Daly, why is winter "in danger of passing away" (5)?

3. During the 1960s, how did children make sure the ice was safe to skate on? Why don't children learn these things today?

4. According to Daly, in what ways has "the whole setting of childhood" (14) changed? What does he propose to do about this situation?

5. What does Daly mean when he says that "by focusing on liability and not teaching our kids how to take risks, we are making their world more dangerous" (11)?

PURPOSE AND AUDIENCE

1. At what point does Daly state his thesis? Why does he wait so long to state it? Should he have stated it sooner?

2. What is Daly's purpose in writing his essay? What does he hope to accomplish?

3. Does Daly think his readers will be sympathetic, neutral, or hostile to his ideas? How can you tell?

4. How would you expect an audience of Daly's contemporaries to react to his essay? Would an audience of Daly's children and their friends have a different reaction?

5. What is Daly's purpose in mentioning StairMasters and health clubs in paragraph 5? How might he expect his audience of fairly affluent, well-educated adults to react?

STYLE AND STRUCTURE

1. How does the introduction of this essay prepare readers for the discussion that follows?

2. Does Daly use a subject-by-subject or a point-by-point method of comparison, or a combination of the two? What is the advantage of the strategy he uses?

3. Daly refers to THIN ICE signs at the beginning and end of his essay. Why does he refer to the signs at these key points in his essay? Do the words *thin ice* suggest any meaning beyond the literal one? Explain.

4. What transitional words and phrases indicate that Daly is shifting from one subject to another? From one point to another? Does the essay need more transitions? If so, where?

5. Daly's essay has a one-sentence conclusion. Should it be expanded? If so, how? If not, why not?

VOCABULARY PROJECTS

1. Define each of the following words as it is used in this selection.

   gloss (4)   domain (8)
   liability (5)   connoisseurs (9)

2. Underline all the uses of the words *risk* and *liability* in Daly's essay. Do these words have the same meaning each time he uses them?

JOURNAL ENTRY

Do you agree with Daly's assertion that because of the threat of lawsuits and liability, children are being raised not to take risks? Are there other explanations for the rules and uniformity Daly observes?

WRITING WORKSHOP

1. Write an essay comparing how you performed a particular activity when you were a child with how you perform the same activity now. Make sure you focus on the differences and, like Daly, draw some conclusion about the present.

2. Write a letter to Daly in which you compare his memories of winter with your own. In your essay, address Daly's contention that children today are brought up not to take risks.

3. Write an essay in which you compare your own willingness to take risks with that of one of your friends or family members.

COMBINING THE PATTERNS

Daly ends his essay with a **narrative** about a particularly cold winter. Does the narrative contain enough detail? Would more detail make this paragraph more effective? Explain.

THEMATIC CONNECTIONS

- "Reading the River" (page 138)
- "The Way to Rainy Mountain" (page 148)
- "Once More to the Lake" (page 154)
- "Television: The Plug-In Drug" (page 283)
- "It's Just Too Late" (page 304)

DEBORAH TANNEN

Deborah Tannen was born in Brooklyn, New York, in 1945. She graduated from the State University of New York at Binghamton, was awarded a doctorate from the University of California at Berkeley, and currently teaches at Georgetown University. Tannen has written and edited several scholarly books on the problems of communicating across cultural, class, ethnic, and sexual divides. She has also presented her research to the general public in newspapers and magazines and in her best-selling books *That's Not What I Meant!* (1986), *You Just Don't Understand: Women and Men in Conversation* (1990), and *Talking from 9 to 5* (1994). Her latest book is *The Argument Culture* (1998).

"Sex, Lies, and Conversation" appeared in the *Washington Post* in 1990. It was written in conjunction with the publication of *You Just Don't Understand*, which Tannen wrote because the single chapter in *That's Not What I Meant!* on the difficulties men and women have communicating with one another had gotten such an overwhelming response. She realized the chapter might raise some controversy — that discussing their different communication styles might be used to malign men or to put women at a disadvantage — and indeed some critics have seen her work as reinforcing stereotypes. Still, her work on the subject, along with that of other writers (most notably John Gray in his *Men Are from Mars, Women Are from Venus* series), has proved enormously popular, and much research (and debate) is being carried on about male and female differences.

Sex, Lies, and Conversation

I was addressing a small gathering in a suburban Virginia living room — a women's group that had invited men to join them. Throughout the evening, one man had been particularly talkative, frequently offering ideas and anecdotes, while his wife sat silently beside him on the couch. Toward the end of the evening, I commented that women frequently complain that their husbands don't talk to them. This man quickly concurred. He gestured toward his wife and said, "She's the talker in our family." The room burst into laughter; the man looked puzzled and hurt. "It's true," he explained. "When I come home from work I have nothing to say. If she didn't keep the conversation going, we'd spend the whole evening in silence." 1

This episode crystallizes the irony that although American men tend to talk more than women in public situations, they often talk less at home. And this pattern is wreaking havoc with marriage. 2

The pattern was observed by political scientist Andrew Hacker in the late '70s. Sociologist Catherine Kohler Riessman reports in her new book *Divorce Talk* that most of the women she interviewed — but only a few of the men — gave lack of communication as the reason for their divorces. Given the current divorce rate of nearly 50 percent, that amounts 3 to millions of cases in the United States every year — a virtual epidemic of failed conversation.

In my own research, complaints from women about their husbands   4
most often focused not on tangible inequities such as having given up the chance for a career to accompany a husband to his, or doing far more than their share of daily life-support work like cleaning, cooking, social arrangements, and errands. Instead, they focused on communication: "He doesn't listen to me," "He doesn't talk to me." I found, as Hacker observed years before, that most wives want their husbands to be, first and foremost, conversational partners, but few husbands share this expectation of their wives.

In short, the image that best represents the current crisis is the stereo-   5
typical cartoon scene of a man sitting at the breakfast table with a newspaper held up in front of his face, while a woman glares at the back of it, wanting to talk.

LINGUISTIC BATTLE OF THE SEXES

How can women and men have such different impressions of commu-   6
nication in marriage? Why the widespread imbalance in their interests and expectations?

In the April issue of *American Psychologist,* Stanford University's   7
Eleanor Maccoby reports the results of her own and others' research showing that children's development is most influenced by the social structure of peer interactions. Boys and girls tend to play with children of their own gender, and their sex-separate groups have different organizational structures and interactive norms.

I believe these systematic differences in childhood socialization make   8
talk between women and men like cross-cultural communication, heir to all the attraction and pitfalls of that enticing but difficult enterprise. My research on men's and women's conversations uncovered patterns similar to those described for children's groups.

For women, as for girls, intimacy is the fabric of relationships, and talk   9
is the thread from which it is woven. Little girls create and maintain friendships by exchanging secrets; similarly, women regard conversation as the cornerstone of friendship. So a woman expects her husband to be a new and improved version of a best friend. What is important is not the individual subjects that are discussed but the sense of closeness, of a life shared, that emerges when people tell their thoughts, feelings, and impressions.

Bonds between boys can be as intense as girls', but they are based less   10
on talking, more on doing things together. Since they don't assume talk is the cement that binds a relationship, men don't know what kind of talk women want, and they don't miss it when it isn't there.

Boys' groups are larger, more inclusive, and more hierarchical, so boys   11
must struggle to avoid the subordinate position in the group. This may

play a role in women's complaints that men don't listen to them. Some men really don't like to listen, because being the listener makes them feel one-down, like a child listening to adults or an employee to a boss.

But often when women tell men, "You aren't listening," and the men protest, "I am," the men are right. The impression of not listening results   12
from misalignments in the mechanics of conversation. The misalignment begins as soon as a man and a woman take physical positions. This became clear when I studied videotapes made by psychologist Bruce Dorval of children and adults talking to their same-sex best friends. I found that at every age, the girls and women faced each other directly, their eyes anchored on each other's faces. At every age, the boys and men sat at angles to each other and looked elsewhere in the room, periodically glancing at each other. They were obviously attuned to each other, often mirroring each other's movements. But the tendency of men to face away can give women the impression they aren't listening even when they are. A young woman in college was frustrated: Whenever she told her boyfriend she wanted to talk to him, he would lie down on the floor, close his eyes, and put his arm over his face. This signaled to her, "He's taking a nap." But he insisted he was listening extra hard. Normally, he looks around the room, so he is easily distracted. Lying down and covering his eyes helped him concentrate on what she was saying.

Analogous to the physical alignment that women and men take in conversation is their topical alignment. The girls in my study tended to   13
talk at length about one topic, but the boys tended to jump from topic to topic. The second-grade girls exchanged stories about people they knew. The second-grade boys teased, told jokes, noticed things in the room, and talked about finding games to play. The sixth-grade girls talked about problems with a mutual friend. The sixth-grade boys talked about 55 different topics, none of which extended over more than a few turns.

LISTENING TO BODY LANGUAGE

Switching topics is another habit that gives women the impression men aren't listening, especially if they switch to a topic about themselves.   14
But the evidence of the 10th-grade boys in my study indicates otherwise. The 10th-grade boys sprawled across their chairs with bodies parallel and eyes straight ahead, rarely looking at each other. They looked as if they were riding in a car, staring out the windshield. But they were talking about their feelings. One boy was upset because a girl had told him he had a drinking problem, and the other was feeling alienated from all his friends.

Now, when a girl told a friend about a problem, the friend responded by asking probing questions and expressing agreement and understand-   15
ing. But the boys dismissed each other's problems. Todd assured Richard that his drinking was "no big problem" because "sometimes you're funny

when you're off your butt." And when Todd said he felt left out, Richard responded, "Why should you? You know more people than me."

Women perceive such responses as belittling and unsupportive. But the boys seemed satisfied with them. Whereas women reassure each other by implying, "You shouldn't feel bad because I've had similar experiences," men do so by implying, "You shouldn't feel bad because your problems aren't so bad." [16]

There are even simpler reasons for women's impression that men don't listen. Linguist Lynette Hirschman found that women make more listener-noise, such as "mhm," "uhuh," and "yeah," to show "I'm with you." Men, she found, more often give silent attention. Women who expect a stream of listener-noise interpret silent attention as no attention at all. [17]

Women's conversational habits are as frustrating to men as men's are to women. Men who expect silent attention interpret a stream of listener-noise as overreaction or impatience. Also, when women talk to each other in a close, comfortable setting, they often overlap, finish each other's sentences, and anticipate what the other is about to say. This practice, which I call "participatory listenership," is often perceived by men as interruption, intrusion, and lack of attention. [18]

A parallel difference caused a man to complain about his wife, "She just wants to talk about her own point of view. If I show her another view, she gets mad at me." When most women talk to each other, they assume a conversationalist's job is to express agreement and support. But many men see their conversational duty as pointing out the other side of an argument. This is heard as disloyalty by women, and refusal to offer the requisite support. It is not that women don't want to see other points of view, but that they prefer them phrased as suggestions and inquiries rather than as direct challenges. [19]

In his book *Fighting for Life,* Walter Ong points out that men use "agonistic," or warlike, oppositional formats to do almost anything; thus discussion becomes debate, and conversation a competitive sport. In contrast, women see conversation as a ritual means of establishing rapport. If Jane tells a problem and June says she has a similar one, they walk away feeling closer to each other. But this attempt at establishing rapport can backfire when used with men. Men take too literally women's ritual "troubles talk," just as women mistake men's ritual challenges for real attack. [20]

THE SOUNDS OF SILENCE

These differences begin to clarify why women and men have such different expectations about communication in marriage. For women, talk creates intimacy. Marriage is an orgy of closeness: you can tell your feelings and thoughts, and still be loved. Their greatest fear is being pushed [21] away. But men live in a hierarchical world, where talk maintains indepen- dence and status. They are on guard to protect themselves from being put down and pushed around.

This explains the paradox of the talkative man who said of his silent 22 wife, "She's the talker." In the public setting of a guest lecture, he felt chal- lenged to show his intelligence and display his understanding of the lecture. But at home, where he has nothing to prove and no one to de- fend against, he is free to remain silent. For his wife, being home means she is free from the worry that something she says might offend some- one, or spark disagreement, or appear to be showing off; at home she is free to talk.

The communication problems that endanger marriage can't be fixed 23 by mechanical engineering. They require a new conceptual framework about the role of talk in human relationships. Many of the psychological explanations that have become second nature may not be helpful, because they tend to blame either women (for not being assertive enough) or men (for not being in touch with their feelings). A sociolinguistic approach by which male-female conversation is seen as cross-cultural communication allows us to understand the problem and forge solutions without blaming either party.

Once the problem is understood, improvement comes naturally, as it 24 did to the young woman and her boyfriend who seemed to go to sleep when she wanted to talk. Previously, she had accused him of not listening, and he had refused to change his behavior, since that would be admitting fault. But then she learned about and explained to him the differences in women's and men's habitual ways of aligning themselves in conversation. The next time she told him she wanted to talk, he began, as usual, by lying down and covering his eyes. When the familiar negative reaction bubbled up, she reassured herself that he really was listening. But then he sat up and looked at her. Thrilled, she asked why. He said, "You like me to look at you when we talk, so I'll try to do it." Once he saw their differences as cross-cultural rather than right and wrong, he independently altered his behavior.

Women who feel abandoned and deprived when their husbands 25 won't listen to or report daily news may be happy to discover their hus- bands trying to adapt once they understand the place of small talk in women's relationships. But if their husbands don't adapt, the women may still be comforted that for men, this is not a failure of intimacy. Accepting the difference, the wives may look to their friends or family for that kind of talk. And husbands who can't provide it shouldn't feel their wives have made unreasonable demands. Some couples will still decide to divorce, but at least their decisions will be based on realistic expectations.

In these times of resurgent ethnic conflicts, the world desperately 26 needs cross-cultural understanding. Like charity, successful cross-cultural communication should begin at home.

•   •   •

COMPREHENSION

1. What pattern of communication does Tannen identify at the beginning of her essay?

2. According to Tannen, what do women complain about most in their marriages?

3. What gives women the impression that men do not listen?

4. What characteristics of women's speech do men find frustrating?

5. According to Tannen, what can men and women do to remedy the communication problems that exist in most marriages?

PURPOSE AND AUDIENCE

1. What is Tannen's thesis?

2. What is Tannen's purpose in writing this essay? Do you think she wants to inform or to persuade? On what do you base your conclusion?

3. Is Tannen writing to an expert audience or an audience of general readers? To men, women, or both? How can you tell?

STYLE AND STRUCTURE

1. What does Tannen gain by stating her thesis in paragraph 2 of the essay? Would there be any advantage in postponing the thesis statement until the end? Explain.

2. Is this essay a subject-by-subject or a point-by-point comparison? What does Tannen gain by organizing her essay the way she does?

3. Throughout her essay, Tannen cites scholarly studies and quotes statistics. How effectively does this information support her points? Could she have made a strong case without this material? Why or why not?

4. Would you say Tannen's tone is hopeful, despairing, sarcastic, angry, or something else? Explain.

5. Tannen concludes her essay with a far-reaching statement. What do you think she hopes to accomplish with this conclusion? Is she successful? Explain your reasoning.

VOCABULARY PROJECTS

1. Define each of the following words as it is used in this selection.

concurred (1)	pitfalls (8)	rapport (20)
crystallizes (2)	subordinate (11)	ritual (20)
inequities (4)	misalignment (12)	orgy (21)
imbalance (6)	analogous (13)	sociolinguistic (23)
peer (7)	alienated (14)	forge (23)
organizational (7)	intrusion (18)	

2. Where does Tannen use professional **jargon** in this essay? Would the essay be more or less effective without these words? Explain.

JOURNAL ENTRY

Based on your own observations of male-female communication, how accurate is Tannen's analysis? Can you relate an anecdote from your own life that illustrates (or contradicts) her thesis?

WRITING WORKSHOP

1. In another essay, Tannen contrasts the communication patterns of male and female students in classroom settings. After observing a few of your own classes, write an essay in which you, too, draw a comparison between the communication patterns of your male and female classmates.

2. Write an essay in which you compare the way male and female characters speak in films or on television. Use examples to support your points.

3. Write an essay in which you compare the vocabulary used in two different sports. Does one sport use more violent language than the other? For example, baseball uses the terms *bunt* and *sacrifice,* and football uses the terms *blitz* and *bomb.* Use as many examples as you can to support your points.

COMBINING THE PATTERNS

Tannen begins her essay with an anecdote. Why does she begin with a paragraph of **narration?** How does this story set the tone for the rest of the essay?

THEMATIC CONNECTIONS

- "The Grave" (page 161)
- "Sexism in English: A 1990s Update" (page 413)
- "I Want a Wife" (page 474)
- "It's a Jungle Out There" (page 538)

JOHN UPDIKE

John Updike was born in 1932 in Shillington, Pennsylvania. He graduated from Harvard in 1954 and then worked for several years as a staff writer for the *New Yorker* magazine. Updike is the author of numerous books of poetry, fiction, essays, and criticism. Among his recent works are *Collected Poems 1953–1993* (1993); *The Afterlife and Other Stories* (1994); the novels *Toward the End of Time* (1997) and *Bech at Bay* (1998); and *More Matters: Essays and Criticism* (1999). Updike received Pulitzer Prizes for the novels *Rabbit Is Rich* (1981) and *Rabbit at Rest* (1990). He is best known for his often bracing stories of average middle-class American lives.

"Ex–Basketball Player," published in *The Carpentered Hen and Other Tame Creatures* (1958), focuses on a phenomenon that is perhaps as common today as it was during the much simpler times at the middle of the twentieth century: the small-town high school athletic hero who never achieves his early promise. In recent decades, sports has come to be seen by many as a way out of poverty, yet for most student athletes, as for Updike's "ex–basketball player," dreams of great financial success are never realized.

Ex-Basketball Player

Pearl Avenue runs past the high-school lot,
Bends with the trolley tracks, and stops, cut off
Before it has a chance to go two blocks.
At Colonel McComsky Plaza, Berth's Garage
Is on the corner facing west, and there,   5
Most days, you'll find Flick Webb, who helps Berth out.

Flick stands tall among the idiot pumps —
Five on a side, the old bubble-head style,
Their rubber elbows hanging loose and low.
One's nostrils are two S's, and his eyes   10
An E and O.* And one is squat, without
A head at all — more of a football type.

Once Flick played for the high-school team, the Wizards.
He was good: in fact, the best. In '46
He bucketed three hundred ninety points,   15
A county record still. The ball loved Flick.
I saw him rack up thirty-eight or forty
In one home game. His hands were like wild birds.

He never learned a trade, he just sells gas,
Checks oil, and changes flats. Once in a while,   20
As a gag, he dribbles an inner tube,

---

*Eds. note — The letters spell *ESSO,* a popular brand of gas at the time the poem was written.

But most of us remember anyway.
His hands are fine and nervous on the lug wrench.
It makes no difference to the lug wrench, though.

Off work, he hangs around Mae's luncheonette.   25
Grease-gray and kind of coiled, he plays pinball,
Smokes those thin cigars, nurses lemon phosphates.*
Flick seldom says a word to Mae, just nods
Beyond her face toward bright applauding tiers
Of Necco Wafers, Nibs, and Juju Beads.**   30

• • •

THINKING ABOUT LITERATURE

1. What two things are being compared in the poem? What strategies does
   the speaker use to let readers know when he is shifting from one subject to
   another?

2. Do you know any people like Flick? How accurate do you think the
   speaker's characterization is? Do you think the speaker is stereotyping
   Flick? Explain.

3. What comment is the poem making about the role of sports in our society? About the relationship between education and sports?

JOURNAL ENTRY

What do you think went wrong with Flick's sports career? Why is Flick not a
success today?

THEMATIC CONNECTIONS

- "The Human Cost of an Illiterate Society" (page 203)
- "Who Killed Benny Paret?" (page 279)
- "Brains versus Brawn" (page 328)
- "The Men We Carry in Our Minds" (page 399)

---

*EDS. NOTE — Carbonated drinks.
**EDS. NOTE — Kinds of candy.

WRITING ASSIGNMENTS FOR COMPARISON AND CONTRAST

1. Find a description of the same event in two different magazines or newspapers. Write a comparison-and-contrast essay in which you discuss the similarities and differences between these two stories.

2. Go to the library and locate two children's books on the same subject, one written in the 1950s and one written today. Write an essay discussing which elements are the same and which are different. Include a thesis statement that makes a point about the significance of the differences between the two books.

3. Write a comparison-and-contrast essay in which you show how your knowledge of an academic subject has either increased or decreased your enthusiasm for it. If you like, you can refer to "Reading the River" (page 138).

4. Write an essay about a relative or friend you knew when you were a child. Consider in what respects your opinion of this person has changed and in what sense it has remained the same.

5. Are the academic standards for athletes different from the standards applied to other students at your school? Compare the academic requirements and other expectations for athletes and nonathletes. Include a thesis that states your opinion about any discrepancies you identify.

6. Since you started college, how have you changed, and how have you stayed the same? Write an essay that answers this question.

7. Taking careful notes, watch a local television news program and then a national news broadcast. Write an essay in which you compare the two programs, paying particular attention to the news content and to the broadcasting styles of the journalists.

8. Write an essay in which you compare your own early memories of school with those of a parent or an older relative.

9. Do students who work to finance their own education have different attitudes toward that education from students who do not? If so, why? Your thesis statement should explain why you believe a difference exists (or does not exist).

10. Write an essay in which you compare any two groups that have divergent values: vegetarians and meat eaters or smokers and nonsmokers, for example.

COLLABORATIVE ACTIVITY FOR COMPARISON AND CONTRAST

Form groups of four students. Assume you are consultants who have been asked by your college to suggest solutions for several problems students have been complaining about. Select the three areas — food, campus safety, and class scheduling for example — that you think are most in need of improvement. Then, as a group, write a short report to your college in which you describe the present conditions in these areas and compare them to the improvements you envision. (Be sure to organize your report as a comparison-and-contrast essay.) Finally, have one person from each group read the group's report to the class, and then decide as a class which group has the best suggestion.

INTERNET ASSIGNMENT FOR COMPARISON AND CONTRAST

Write an essay in which you compare and contrast the media coverage of men's and women's professional athletics. Use the following World Wide Web sites to familiarize yourself with how men's and women's sports are covered by the media.

CNN Sports Illustrated
<http://www.cnnsi.com>
This site offers up-to-the-minute sports coverage.

Stand-Up Sports
<http://www.standupsports.com/sucks/wnba>
This site is intended for humorous sports analysis and includes a link to the article "The WNBA 'Players' are the Female Firefighters of Pro Sports" by Debbie Schlussel.

Feminist Majority Foundation
<http://www.feminist.org/gateway/sp_exec2.html>
This site includes a spotlight on women's sports, links to sports magazines, information on grants and scholarships for athletes, and links to publications covering such topics as inequity and sex discrimination in sports.

10

CLASSIFICATION AND DIVISION

WHAT IS CLASSIFICATION AND DIVISION?

Division is the process of breaking a whole into parts; **classification** is the process of sorting individual items into categories. In the following paragraph from "Fans," Paul Gallico divides sports fans into categories based on the different sports they watch:

<table>
<tr>
<td>Parts: kinds of sports fans</td>
<td>The fight crowd is a beast that lurks in the darkness behind the fringe of white light shed over the first six rows by the incandescents atop the ring, and is not to be trusted with pop bottles or other hardware. The tennis crowd is the pansy of all the great sports mobs and is always preening and shushing itself. The golf crowd is the most unwieldy and most sympathetic, and is the only horde given to mass production of that absurd noise written generally as "tsk tsk tsk tsk," and made between tongue and teeth with head-waggings to denote extreme commiseration. The baseball crowd is the most hysterical, the football crowd the best-natured, and the polo crowd the most aristocratic. Racing crowds are the most restless, wrestling crowds the most tolerant, and soccer crowds</td>
</tr>
<tr>
<td>Topic sentence identifies whole (sports fans)</td>
<td>the most easily incitable to riot and disorder. Every sports crowd takes on the characteristics of the individuals who compose it. Each has its particular note of hysteria, its own little cruelties, mannerisms, and bad mannerisms, its own code of sportsmanship, and its own method of expressing its emotions.</td>
</tr>
</table>

Through **classification and division,** we can make sense of seemingly random ideas by putting scattered bits of information into useful, coherent order. By breaking a large group into smaller categories and assigning individual items to larger categories, we are able to identify relationships between a whole and its parts and among the parts themselves. (Remember, though, that classification involves more than simply comparing two items or enumerating examples; when you classify, you sort examples into a variety of different categories.)

In countless practical situations, classification and division brings order to chaos. Items in a Sunday newspaper are *classified* in clearly defined sections — international news, sports, travel, entertainment, comics, and so on — so that hockey scores, for example, are not mixed up with real estate listings. Similarly, department stores are *divided* into different departments so that managers can assign merchandise to particular areas and shoppers can know where to look for a particular item. Without such organization, an item might be anywhere in a store. Thus, order is brought to newspapers and department stores — and to supermarkets, biological hierarchies, and libraries — when a whole is divided into categories or sections and individual items are assigned to one or another of these subgroups.

Understanding Classification

Even though the interrelated processes of classification and division invariably occur together, they are two separate operations. When you *classify*, you begin with individual items and sort them into categories. Since most things have several different attributes, they can be classified in several different ways. Take as an example the students who attend your school. The most obvious way to classify these individuals might be according to their year in college. But you could also classify students according to their major, racial or ethnic background, home state, grade-point average, or any number of other principles. The **principle of classification** you choose — the quality your items have in common — would depend on how you wished to approach the members of this large and diverse group.

Understanding Division

Division is the opposite of classification. When you *divide*, you start with a whole (an entire class) and break it into its individual parts. For example, you might start with the large general class *television shows* and divide it into categories: *comedy, drama, action/adventure,* and so forth. You could then divide each of these still further. *Action/adventure programs,* for example, might include *Westerns, police shows,* and so on — and each of these categories could be divided as well. Eventually, you would need to identify a particular principle of classification to help you assign specific programs to one category or another — that is, to classify them. The guidelines on page 381 will help you understand the processes of classification and division.

USING CLASSIFICATION AND DIVISION

Whenever you write an essay, you use classification and division to bring order to the invention stage of the writing process. For example,

GUIDELINES FOR CLASSIFICATION AND DIVISION

- *All the categories should result from the same principle.* If you decide to divide *television shows* into *soap operas, police shows,* and the like, it is not logical to include *children's programs,* for this category results from one principle (target audience) while the others result from another principle (genre). Similarly, if you were classifying undergraduates at your school according to their year, you would not include *students receiving financial aid.*

- *All the categories should be at the same level.* In the series *comedy, drama, action/adventure,* and *Westerns,* the last item, *Westerns,* does not belong because it is at a lower level — that is, it is a subcategory of *action/adventure.* Likewise, *sophomores* (a subcategory of *undergraduates*) does not belong in the series *undergraduates, graduate students, continuing education students.*

- *You should treat all categories that are significant and relevant to your discussion.* Include enough categories to make your point, with no important omissions and no overlapping categories. In a review of a network's fall television lineup, the series *sitcoms, soap operas, police shows,* and *detective shows* is incomplete because it omits important categories like *news programs, game shows, talk shows,* and *documentaries;* moreover, *detective shows* may overlap with *police shows.* In the same way, the series *freshmen, sophomores, juniors,* and *transfers* is illogical: the important group *seniors* has been omitted, and *transfers* may include *freshmen, sophomores,* and *juniors.*

when you brainstorm, as Chapter 1 explains, you begin with your paper's topic and list all the related points you can think of. Next, you *divide* your topic into logical categories and *classify* the items in your brainstorming notes into one category or another, perhaps narrowing, expanding, or eliminating some categories — or some points — as you go along. This picking and choosing, sorting and grouping, enables you to condense and shape your material until it eventually suggests a thesis and the main points of your essay.

In addition, certain topics and questions, because of the way they are worded, immediately suggest a classification-and-division pattern. Suppose, for example, you are asked, "What kinds of policies can be used to direct and control the national economy?" Here the word *kinds* suggests classification and division. Other words — such as *types, varieties, aspects,* and *categories* — can also serve as clues.

PLANNING A CLASSIFICATION-AND-DIVISION ESSAY

Once you decide to use a classification-and-division pattern, you need to identify a principle of classification. Every group of people, things, or ideas can be categorized in many ways. When you are at your college bookstore with eighty dollars, the cost of different books may be the only principle of classification you use to decide what to buy. As you consider which books to carry across campus, however, weight may matter more. Finally, as you study and read, the usefulness of the books will determine which ones you concentrate on. Similarly, when you organize an essay, your principle of classification and division is determined by your writing situation — your assignment, your purpose, your audience, and your special knowledge and interests.

Selecting and Arranging Categories

After you define your principle of classification and apply it to your topic, you should select your categories by dividing a whole class into parts and grouping a number of different items together within each part. Next, you should decide how you will treat the categories in your essay. Just as a comparison-and-contrast essay makes comparable points about its subjects, so your classification-and-division essay should treat all categories similarly. When you discuss comparable points for each category, your readers are able to understand your distinctions among categories as well as your definition of each category.

Finally, you should arrange your categories in some logical order, so that readers can see how the categories are related and how significant each is. Whatever order you choose, it should be consistent with your purpose and support your thesis.

Formulating a Thesis Statement

Like other kinds of essays, a classification-and-division essay must have a thesis. Your thesis statement should identify your subject, present the categories you will discuss, and perhaps show readers the relationships of your categories to one another and to the subject as a whole. In addition, your thesis statement should tell your readers why your categories are significant or establish their relative value. For example, listing different kinds of investments would be pointless if you did not evaluate their strengths and weaknesses and then make recommendations based on your assessment. Similarly, a term paper about a writer's major works would accomplish little if it merely categorized his or her writings. Instead, your thesis statement should communicate your evaluation of these works, perhaps demonstrating that some deserve higher public regard than others.

STRUCTURING A CLASSIFICATION-AND-DIVISION ESSAY

Once you have formulated your essay's thesis and established your categories, you should plan your classification-and-division essay around the same three major sections that other essays have: introduction, body, and conclusion. Your *introduction* should orient your readers by mentioning your topic, the principle by which your material is classified, and the individual categories you plan to discuss; your thesis is also usually stated in the introduction. In the subsequent *body paragraphs,* you should treat the categories one by one in the order in which your introduction presents them. Finally, your *conclusion* should restate your thesis, summing up the points you have made and perhaps considering their implications.

Suppose you are preparing a term paper on Mark Twain's nonfiction works for an American literature course. You have read *Roughing It, Life on the Mississippi,* and *The Innocents Abroad.* Besides these travel narratives, you have read Twain's autobiography as well as some of his correspondence and essays. When you realize that the works you have studied can easily be classified as four different types of Twain's nonfiction — travel narratives, essays, letters, and autobiography — you decide to use classification and division to structure your essay. Therefore, you first divide the large class *Twain's nonfiction prose* into major categories — his travel narratives, essays, autobiography, and letters. Then you classify the individual works — that is, assign the works to these categories, which you plan to discuss one at a time. Your purpose is to persuade readers to reconsider the reputations of some of these works, and you formulate your thesis accordingly. You might then prepare a formal outline like this one for the body of your paper:

> *Thesis statement:* Most readers know Mark Twain as a writer of novels, such as *Huckleberry Finn,* but his nonfiction works — his travel narratives, essays, letters, and especially his autobiography — deserve more attention.

    I. Travel narratives
       A. *Roughing It*
       B. *The Innocents Abroad*
       C. *Life on the Mississippi*

    II. Essays
       A. "Fenimore Cooper's Literary Offenses"
       B. "How to Tell a Story"
       C. "The Awful German Language"

    III. Letters
       A. To W. D. Howells
       B. To his family

    IV. Autobiography

Because this will be a long term paper, each of the outline's divisions will have several subdivisions, and each subdivision might require several paragraphs.

This outline illustrates all the characteristics of an effective classification-and-division essay. To begin with, Twain's nonfiction works are classified according to a single principle of classification — literary genre. Depending on your purpose, of course, another principle — such as theme or subject matter — could work just as well. (If you were writing your term paper for a political science course, you might have decided to examine Twain as a social critic by classifying his works according to the kind of political commentary in each.) Literary genre, however, is an appropriate principle of classification for the writing situation at hand. In addition to illustrating a single principle of classification, the outline reveals that the paper's categories are on the same level (each is a different literary genre) and that all relevant categories are included. Had you left out *essays*, for example, you would have been unable to classify several significant works of nonfiction.

This outline also arranges the four categories so they will support your thesis most effectively. Because you believe Twain's travel narratives are somewhat overrated, you plan to discuss them early in your paper. Similarly, because you think the autobiography would make your best case for the merit of the nonfiction works as a whole, you decide it should be placed last. (Of course, you could arrange your categories in several other orders, such as shorter to longer works or least to most popular, depending on the thesis your paper will support.)

Finally, this outline helps you to treat all categories comparably in your paper. Now, you should identify each main point in your rough draft and cross-check the order of points from category to category. Your case would be weakened if, for example, you inadvertently skipped style in your discussion of Twain's letters while discussing style for every other category. This omission might lead your readers to suspect that you had not done enough research on the letters or that you had ignored them because the style of Twain's letters did not measure up to the style of his other works.

☑ CHECKLIST: CLASSIFICATION AND DIVISION

- Does your assignment call for classification and division?
- Have you identified a principle of classification for your material?
- Have you identified the categories you plan to discuss and decided how you will treat them?
- Have you arranged your categories in a logical order?
- Does your essay have a clearly stated thesis that identifies your subject and the categories you will discuss and indicates the significance of your classification?
- Have you used transitional words and phrases to show the relationships among categories, and among the examples illustrating each category?

▶ **A STUDENT WRITER: CLASSIFICATION AND DIVISION**

The following classification-and-division essay was written by Roger Bauer for a course in American literature. The essay *divides* a whole entity — fiction of the American West — into four parts, or elements, using a principle of division common in literary analysis. In addition, it *classifies* material — details about fiction of the American West — into categories.

The Western: More Than Just
"Popular" Literature

Introduction

Works of popular fiction--detective stories, Gothic novels, and Westerns, for example-- are usually not regarded very highly by literary critics. This evaluation is justified in many cases. All too often in popular fiction characters are familiar stereotypes, plot devices are predictable (and sometimes improbable), settings are overly familiar or only vaguely described, and themes are simplistic or undeveloped. To some extent, these characteristics apply to fiction of the American West--not only to contemporary Westerns, but also to those novels and stories that have

Thesis statement (identifies four elements to be discussed)

achieved status as classics. Still, although clichéd characters and trite plots dominate even classic Westerns, a strong sense of place and timeless themes give the Western the power to transcend the "popular fiction" category.

First element: characters

Readers encounter familiar characters in novels and short stories with western settings. The cast of characters is likely to include at least a few of the following: the cowboy, the dance hall girl, the sheriff, the deputy, the madam, the miner, the schoolmarm, the easterner, the gambler, the rancher, the hired hand, the merchant, the preacher, the traveling salesman, and assorted cavalry soldiers, cattle rustlers, Indians, and Mexicans. These people are seldom fully developed; rather, they are stock characters who play exactly the roles readers expect them to play. Some classic stories, such as "The Outcasts of Poker Flat" and "Stage to Lordsburg," gather an assortment of these characters together in an isolated setting, playing

1

2

them off against one another in a way that
emphasizes their status as types rather than as
individuals.

**Second element:
plot**

The plot elements are just as predictable.   3
Often, a gang terrorizes innocent settlers or
ranchers or townspeople, as in Shane; just as
often, a desperado is on the loose, as in "The
Bride Comes to Yellow Sky." Other common elements are a showdown on a dusty street, as in
"The Tin Star," or an ambush, as in "Stage to
Lordsburg." Scenes of chase and capture are
staples from James Fenimore Cooper to Louis
L'Amour, and standard boy-meets-girl plots can
be traced from The Virginian to current popular
novels.

**Third element:
setting**

But the Western has the potential to tran-   4
scend the limits of these familiar materials.
A particular strength is its geographical setting, which includes an unusually varied landscape and some magnificent scenery. The setting
in Western fiction is special for a variety
of reasons. First, the West is beautiful and
exotic. Second, the West is huge: towns are
widely separated, and characters travel great
distances. As a result, a sense of loneliness
and isolation pervades the Western. Third, the
West is frightening and unpredictable, characterized by untamed landscapes, wild animals,
and terrifying extremes of weather. The harsh-
ness and unpredictability of the climate are
especially frightening to newcomers to the West
(and to readers). Still, the very extreme conditions (tornadoes, blizzards, desert sun) and
unfamiliar topography (mesas, plains, canyons)
that are so disturbing are also fascinating.
Ultimately, the setting can be friend or enemy:
Zane Grey's Riders of the Purple Sage ends with
its lovers isolated in a canyon by a rock slide;
in Max Brand's "Wine on the Desert," a man dies
of thirst in the hostile sun. In these and

other Western stories, the setting is a powerful presence that is always strongly felt.

Fourth element: theme

Perhaps even more powerful than the setting are the themes of the Western--themes found in all great literature. Each of these themes adds interest to the Western, giving it substance and stature. One such theme is the classic conflict between East and West, civilization and the wilderness, illustrated in novels as diverse as Cooper's The Prairie and Wister's The Virginian. (In The Virginian, as in Crane's "The Bride Comes to Yellow Sky," it is the woman who is the symbol of civilization.) Typically, the East is portrayed as rigid, sterile, and limiting, while the West is natural and spontaneous, untamed and beautiful. Another classic theme frequently seen in Western literature is the initiation theme. Here a young man or a boy (or, occasionally, a girl) is initiated into the mysteries of adulthood through participation in a physical test of his courage--for example, a fistfight, a gun battle, or a feat of strength. This theme is developed in "The Tin Star" as well as in the 1952 film High Noon. A third theme frequently explored in Western fiction is the journey or search. The vast spaces and dangerous climate and topography of the West make it an ideal setting for this theme. In works as diverse as Charles Portis's True Grit, Louis L'Amour's Down the Long Hills, and the classic John Ford film The Searchers, the journey figures prominently. Whether the quest is for a long-lost relative, for land or gold or silver, or for knowledge or experience, the search theme dominates many works of Western literature, particularly longer works.

Conclusion (restates thesis)

Balancing the familiar plot elements and stereotypical characters of Western fiction are two other elements, setting and theme, that set

5

6

```
it apart from other kinds of popular fiction.
In addition to its vivid settings and universal
themes, the Western also boasts a strong sense
of history and an identity as a uniquely Ameri-
can genre. These two qualities should give it a
lasting importance consistent with its continu-
ing popularity.
```

Points for Special Attention

THESIS AND SUPPORT.   Roger Bauer's purpose in writing this essay was not just to describe the fiction of the American West but also to evaluate it. Consequently, his thesis statement presents his assessment of the genre's literary value, and his body paragraphs support his position with analysis and examples.

ORGANIZATION.   Roger planned his essay carefully, and his organization scheme keeps the four elements he discusses distinct; in addition, both the space he allots to each element and the order in which he presents them convey his emphasis to his readers. Thus, paragraphs 2 and 3 discuss the two elements Roger does not consider to be particularly noteworthy; in paragraphs 4 and 5, he goes on to give fuller treatment to his two main topics, setting and theme. Because he considers some elements to be more important than others, his treatment of the four categories is necessarily unequal. Still, Roger is careful to provide specific examples from various works of Western literature in all four cases.

TRANSITIONS BETWEEN CATEGORIES.   Roger uses clear transitional sentences to introduce each element of literature he discusses: "Readers encounter familiar characters in novels and short stories with Western settings"; "The plot elements are just as predictable"; "A particular strength is its geographical setting, which includes an unusually varied landscape and some magnificent scenery"; and "Perhaps even more powerful than the setting are the themes of the Western — themes found in all great literature." To indicate his shift from less important elements to more significant ones, Roger uses another strong transition: "But the Western has the potential to transcend the limits of these familiar materials." Each of these transitional sentences not only distinguishes the four elements from one another but also conveys Roger's direction and emphasis.

WRITING ABOUT LITERATURE.   Because he is writing for a course in American literature, Roger pays special attention to certain conventions that apply to writing about literature. For example, he uses the present tense when referring to literary works, and he places titles of short stories within quotation marks and underlines titles of novels and films to indicate italics. Also, he presents his interpretations and evaluations straight-forwardly, without using unnecessary phrases like *In my opinion* and *I think*.

Focus on Revision

One student who did a peer critique of this essay thought Roger could make a stronger case for the value of the fiction of the American West if he condensed paragraphs 2 and 3, which deal with the formulaic aspects of such fiction, and expanded the paragraphs about setting and theme. Another student suggested that quotations from a few of the works Roger mentions might add interest to his essay. Roger liked both of these suggestions and decided to follow up on them when he revised his paper. Of course, if he were writing a longer paper, Roger could provide brief plot summaries of the works he mentions in order to accommodate readers who might not be familiar with them. In a longer essay, additional examples — particularly from modern Westerns, which apply the conventions of the genre somewhat differently — would also be helpful.

Each of the following reading selections is developed by means of classification and division. In some cases, the pattern is used to explain ideas; in others, it is used to persuade the reader.

WILLIAM ZINSSER

Born in 1922 in New York City, William Zinsser graduated from Princeton University in 1944. He worked at the New York *Herald Tribune* as a feature and editorial writer, and he was a columnist for *Life* magazine and the *New York Times*. Zinsser has also taught English at Yale University and is the author of several books on writing, including six editions of *On Writing Well: An Informal Guide to Writing Nonfiction* (sixth edition, 1998). He has also written works on American culture, including *Spring Training* (1989), about the culture of baseball, and *American Places: A Writer's Pilgrimage to Fifteen of This Country's Most Visited and Cherished Sites* (1992).

In "College Pressures," written for *Country Journal* magazine in 1979, Zinsser analyzes the forces then contributing to the anxiety of Yale undergraduates. The late 1970s were a time of some economic uncertainty, with higher-than-normal rates of inflation and unemployment. Admission to Yale was, and still is, very competitive, and then, as now, tuition costs were steep. These factors, along with intense academic competition and parental pressure to succeed, created a good deal of stress for this select group of students.

College Pressures

Dear Carlos: I desperately need a dean's excuse for my chem midterm which will begin in about 1 hour. All I can say is that I totally blew it this week. I've fallen incredibly, inconceivably behind.

1

Carlos: Help! I'm anxious to hear from you. I'll be in my room and won't leave it until I hear from you. Tomorrow is the last day for. . . .

2

Carlos: I left town because I started bugging out again. I stayed up all night to finish a take home make-up exam and am typing it to hand in on the 10th. It was due on the 5th. P.S. I'm going to the dentist. Pain is pretty bad.

3

Carlos: Probably by Friday I'll be able to get back to my studies. Right now I'm going to take a long walk. This whole thing has taken a lot out of me.

4

Carlos: I'm really up the proverbial creek. The problem is I really *bombed* the history final. Since I need that course for my major. . . .

5

Carlos: Here follows a tale of woe. I went home this weekend, had to help my Mom, & caught a fever so didn't have much time to study. My professor. . . .

6

Carlos: Aargh! Nothing original but everything's piling up at once. To be brief, my job interview. . . .

7

Hey Carlos, good news! I've got mononucleosis.

8

Who are these wretched supplicants, scribbling notes so laden with   9
anxiety, seeking such miracles of postponement and balm? They are men
and women who belong to Bradford College, one of the twelve residential
colleges at Yale University, and the messages are just a few of the hundreds that they left for their dean, Carlos Hortas — often slipped under
his door at 4 A.M. — last year.

But students like the ones who wrote those notes can also be found on   10
campuses from coast to coast — especially in New England and at many
other private colleges across the country that have high academic standards and highly motivated students. Nobody could doubt that the notes
are real. In their urgency and their gallows humor they are authentic
voices of a generation that is panicky to succeed.

My own connection with the message writers is that I am master of   11
Bradford College. I live in its Gothic quadrangle and know the students
well. (We have 485 of them.) I am privy to their hopes and fears — and
also to their stereo music and their piercing cries in the dead of night
("Does anybody *ca-a-are?*"). If they went to Carlos to ask how to get
through tomorrow, they come to me to ask how to get through the rest of
their lives.

Mainly I try to remind them that the road ahead is a long one and   12
that it will have more unexpected turns than they think. There will be
plenty of time to change jobs, change careers, change whole attitudes and
approaches. They don't want to hear such liberating news. They want a
map — right now — that they can follow unswervingly to career security,
financial security, Social Security, and, presumably, a prepaid grave.

What I wish for all students is some release from the clammy grip of   13
the future. I wish them a chance to savor each segment of their education
as an experience in itself and not as a grim preparation for the next step. I
wish them the right to experiment, to trip and fall, to learn that defeat is as
instructive as victory and is not the end of the world.

My wish, of course, is naive. One of the few rights that America does   14
not proclaim is the right to fail. Achievement is the national god, venerated in our media — the million-dollar athlete, the wealthy executive —
and glorified in our praise of possessions. In the presence of such a potent
state religion, the young are growing up old.

I see four kinds of pressure working on college students today: eco-   15
nomic pressure, parental pressure, peer pressure, and self-induced pressure. It is easy to look around for villains — to blame the colleges for
charging too much money, the professors for assigning too much work,
the parents for pushing their children too far, the students for driving
themselves too hard. But there are no villains, only victims.

"In the late 1960s," one dean told me, "the typical question that I got   16
from students was 'Why is there so much suffering in the world?' or 'How
can I make a contribution?' Today it's 'Do you think it would look better
for getting into law school if I did a double major in history and political

science, or just majored in one of them?'" Many other deans confirmed this pattern. One said: "They're trying to find an edge — the intangible something that will look better on paper if two students are about equal."

Note the emphasis on looking better. The transcript has become a   17
sacred document, the passport to security. How one appears on paper is more important than how one appears in person. A is for Admirable and B is for Borderline, even though, in Yale's official system of grading, A means "excellent" and B means "very good." Today, looking very good is no longer good enough, especially for students who hope to go on to law school or medical school. They know that entrance into the better schools will be an entrance into the better law firms and better medical practices where they will make a lot of money. They also know that the odds are harsh. Yale Law School, for instance, matriculates 170 students from an applicant pool of 3,700; Harvard enrolls 550 from a pool of 7,000.

It's all very well for those of us who write letters of recommendation   18
for our students to stress the qualities of humanity that will make them good lawyers or doctors. And it's nice to think that admission officers are really reading our letters and looking for the extra dimension of commitment or concern. Still, it would be hard for a student not to visualize these officers shuffling so many transcripts studded with As that they regard a B as positively shameful.

The pressure is almost as heavy on students who just want to gradu-   19
ate and get a job. Long gone are the days of the "gentleman's C," when students journeyed through college with a certain relaxation, sampling a wide variety of courses — music, art, philosophy, classics, anthropology, poetry, religion — that would send them out as liberally educated men and women. If I were an employer I would rather employ graduates who have this range and curiosity than those who narrowly pursued safe subjects and high grades. I know countless students whose inquiring minds exhilarate me. I like to hear the play of their ideas. I don't know if they're getting As or Cs, and I don't care. I also like them as people. The country needs them, and they will find satisfying jobs. I tell them to relax. They can't.

Nor can I blame them. They live in a brutal economy. Tuition, room,   20
and board at most private colleges now comes to at least $7,000, not counting books and fees.* This might seem to suggest that the colleges are getting rich. But they are equally battered by inflation. Tuition covers only 60 percent of what it costs to educate a student, and ordinarily the remainder comes from what colleges receive in endowments, grants, and gifts. Now the remainder keeps being swallowed by cruel costs — higher every year — of just opening the doors. Heating oil is up. Insurance is up. Postage is up. Health-premium costs are up. Everything is up. Deficits are up.

---

*EDS. NOTE — Zinsser's essay was published in 1979; the figures quoted for tuition and other expenses would be much higher today.

We are witnessing in America the creation of a brotherhood of paupers — colleges, parents, and students, joined by the common bond of debt.

Today it is not unusual for a student, even if he works part time at col- 21
lege and full time during the summer, to accrue $5,000 in loans after four years — loans that he must start to repay within one year after gradua-tion. Exhorted at commencement to go forth into the world, he is already behind as he goes forth. How could he not feel under pressure throughout college to prepare for this day of reckoning? I have used "he" incidentally, only for brevity. Women at Yale are under no less pressure to justify their expensive education to themselves, their parents, and society. In fact, they are probably under more pressure. For although they leave college superbly equipped to bring fresh leadership to traditionally male jobs, society hasn't yet caught up with this fact.

Along with economic pressure goes parental pressure. Inevitably, the 22
two are deeply intertwined.

I see many students taking pre-medical courses with joyless tenacity. 23
They go off to their labs as if they were going to the dentist. It saddens me because I know them in other corners of their life as cheerful people.

"Do you want to go to medical school?" I ask them. 24

"I guess so," they say, without conviction, or "Not really." 25

"Then why are you going?" 26

"Well, my parents want me to be a doctor. They're paying all this 27
money and . . ."

Poor students, poor parents. They are caught in one of the oldest webs 28
of love and duty and guilt. The parents mean well; they are trying to steer their sons and daughters toward a secure future. But the sons and daugh-ters want to major in history or classics or philosophy — subjects with no "practical" value. Where's the payoff on the humanities? It's not easy to persuade such loving parents that the humanities do indeed pay off. The intellectual faculties developed by studying subjects like history and clas-sics — an ability to synthesize and relate, to weigh cause and effect, to see events in perspective — are just the faculties that make creative leaders in business or almost any general field. Still, many fathers would rather put their money on courses that point toward a specific profession — courses that are pre-law, pre-medical, pre-business, or, as I sometimes heard it put, "pre-rich."

But the pressure on students is severe. They are truly torn. One part of 29
them feels obliged to fulfill their parents' expectations; after all, their par-ents are older and presumably wiser. Another part tells them that the expectations that are right for their parents are not right for them.

I know a student who wants to be an artist. She is very obviously an 30
artist and will be a good one — she has already had several modest exhibits. Meanwhile she is growing as a well-rounded person and taking humanistic subjects that will enrich the inner resources out of which her art will grow. But her father is strongly opposed. He thinks that an artist is a "dumb" thing to be. The student vacillates and tries to please everybody.

She keeps up with her art somewhat furtively and takes some of the "dumb" courses her father wants her to take — at least they are dumb courses for her. She is a free spirit on a campus of tense students — no small achievement in itself — and she deserves to follow her muse.

Peer pressure and self-induced pressure are also intertwined, and they begin almost at the beginning of freshman year. 31

"I had a freshman student I'll call Linda," one dean told me, "who came in and said she was under terrible pressure because her roommate, Barbara, was much brighter and studied all the time. I couldn't tell her that Barbara had come in two hours earlier to say the same thing about Linda." 32

The story is almost funny — except that it's not. It's symptomatic of all the pressures put together. When every student thinks every other student is working harder and doing better, the only solution is to study harder still. I see students going off to the library every night after dinner and coming back when it closes at midnight. I wish they could sometimes forget about their peers and go to a movie. I hear the clacking of typewriters in the hours before dawn. I see the tension in their eyes when exams are approaching and papers are due: *"Will I get everything done?"* 33

Probably they won't. They will get sick. They will get "blocked." They will sleep. They will oversleep. They will bug out. *Hey Carlos, help!* 34

Part of the problem is that they do more than they are expected to do. A professor will assign five-page papers. Several students will start writing ten-page papers to impress him. Then more students will write ten-page papers, and a few will raise the ante to fifteen. Pity the poor student who is still just doing the assignment. 35

"Once you have twenty or thirty percent of the student population deliberating overexerting," one dean points out, "it's bad for everybody. When a teacher gets more and more effort from his class, the student who is doing normal work can be perceived as not doing well. The tactic works, psychologically." 36

Why can't the professor just cut back and not accept longer papers? He can, and he probably will. But by then the term will be half over and the damage done. Grade fever is highly contagious and not easily reversed. Besides, the professor's main concern is with his course. He knows his students only in relation to the course and doesn't know that they are also overexerting in their other courses. Nor is it really his business. He didn't sign up for dealing with the student as a whole person and with all the emotional baggage the student brought along from home. That's what deans, masters, chaplains, and psychiatrists are for. 37

To some extent this is nothing new: a certain number of professors have always been self-contained islands of scholarship and shyness, more comfortable with books than with people. But the new pauperism has widened the gap still further, for professors who actually like to spend time with students don't have as much time to spend. They also are overexerting. If they are young, they are busy trying to publish in order not to perish, hanging by their fingernails onto a shrinking profession. If 38

they are old and tenured, they are buried under the duties of adminis-
tering departments — as departmental chairmen or members of committees — that have been thinned out by the budgetary axe.

Ultimately it will be the students' own business to break the circles in   39
which they are trapped. They are too young to be prisoners of their parents' dreams and their classmates' fears. They must be jolted into believing in themselves as unique men and women who have the power to
shape their own future.

"Violence is being done to the undergraduate experience," says Car-   40
los Hortas. "College should be open-ended: at the end it should open
many, many roads. Instead, students are choosing their goal in advance,
and their choices narrow as they go along. It's almost as if they think that
the country has been codified in the type of jobs that exist — that they've
got to fit into certain slots. Therefore, fit into the best-paying slot.

"They ought to take chances. Not taking chances will lead to a life of   41
colorless mediocrity. They'll be comfortable. But something in the spirit
will be missing."

I have painted too drab a portrait of today's students, making them   42
seem a solemn lot. That is only half of their story; if they were so dreary I
wouldn't so thoroughly enjoy their company. The other half is that they
are easy to like. They are quick to laugh and to offer friendship. They are
not introverts. They are usually kind and are more considerate of one
another than any student generation I have known.

Nor are they so obsessed with their studies that they avoid sports and   43
extracurricular activities. On the contrary, they juggle their crowded hours
to play on a variety of teams, perform with musical and dramatic groups,
and write for campus publications. But this in turn is one more cause of
anxiety. There are too many choices. Academically, they have 1,300
courses to select from; outside class they have to decide how much spare
time they can spare and how to spend it.

This means that they engage in fewer extracurricular pursuits than   44
their predecessors did. If they want to row on the crew and play in the
symphony they will eliminate one; in the '60s they would have done both.
They also tend to choose activities that are self-limiting. Drama, for
instance, is flourishing in all twelve of Yale's residential colleges as it
never has before. Students hurl themselves into these productions — as
actors, directors, carpenters, and technicians — with a dedication to create
the best possible play, knowing that the day will come when the run will
end and they can get back to their studies.

They also can't afford to be the willing slave of organizations like the   45
Yale Daily News. Last spring at the one-hundredth anniversary banquet of
that paper — whose past chairmen include such once and future kings as
Potter Stewart, Kingman Brewster, and William F. Buckley, Jr.* — much
was made of the fact that the editorial staff used to be small and totally

---

*EDS. NOTE — Stewart is a former U.S. Supreme Court Justice; Brewster is a former
president of Yale; and Buckley is a conservative editor and columnist.

committed and that "newsies" routinely worked fifty hours a week. In effect they belonged to a club; Newsies is how they defined themselves at Yale. Today's student will write one or two articles a week, when he can, and he defines himself as a student. I've never heard the word Newsie except at the banquet.

If I have described the modern undergraduate primarily as a driven   46
creature who is largely ignoring the blithe spirit inside who keeps trying to come out and play, it's because that's where the crunch is, not only at Yale but throughout American education. It's why I think we should all be worried about the values that are nurturing a generation so fearful of risk and so goal-obsessed at such an early age.

I tell students that there is no one "right" way to get ahead — that   47
each of them is a different person, starting from a different point and bound for a different destination. I tell them that change is a tonic and that all the slots are not codified nor the frontiers closed. One of my ways of telling them is to invite men and women who have achieved success outside the academic world to come and talk informally with my students during the year. They are heads of companies or ad agencies, editors of magazines, politicians, public officials, television magnates, labor leaders, business executives, Broadway producers, artists, writers, economists, photographers, scientists, historians — a mixed bag of achievers.

I ask them to say a few words about how they got started. The stu-   48
dents assume that they started in their present profession and knew all along that it was what they wanted to do. Luckily for me, most of them got into their field by a circuitous route, to their surprise, after many detours. The students are startled. They can hardly conceive of a career that was not pre-planned. They can hardly imagine allowing the hand of God or chance to nudge them down some unforeseen trail.

•   •   •

COMPREHENSION

1. What advice does Zinsser give students when they bring their problems to him?

2. What does Zinsser wish for his students? Why does he believe his wish is naive?

3. What four kinds of pressure does Zinsser identify?

4. Whom does Zinsser blame for the existence of the pressures? Explain.

5. How, according to Zinsser, is his evaluation of students different from their own and from their potential employers' assessments?

6. Why does Zinsser believe that women are probably under even more pressure than men?

7. How does what Zinsser calls the "new pauperism" (38) affect professors?

8. Who, according to Zinsser, is ultimately responsible for eliminating college pressures? Explain.

9. In what sense are sports and other extracurricular activities another source of anxiety for students? How do they adapt to this pressure?

PURPOSE AND AUDIENCE

1. In your own words, state Zinsser's thesis. Is his intent in this essay simply to expose a difficult situation or to effect change? Explain.

2. On what kind of audience do you think this essay would have the most significant impact: students, teachers, parents, potential employers, graduate school admissions committees, or college administrators? Why?

3. What do you think Zinsser hopes to accomplish in paragraphs 42–46? How might the essay be different without this section?

4. What assumptions does Zinsser make about his audience? Do you think these assumptions are valid? Explain.

STYLE AND STRUCTURE

1. Evaluate the essay's introductory strategy. What impact do you think the notes to Carlos are likely to have on readers?

2. Identify the boundaries of Zinsser's actual classification. How does he introduce the first category? How does he indicate that his treatment of the final category is complete?

3. What function do paragraphs 22 and 31 serve in the essay?

4. Zinsser is careful to explain that when he refers to students as *he,* he includes female students as well. However, he also refers to professors as *he* (for example, in paragraphs 35–37). Assuming that not all professors at Yale are male, what other stylistic options does Zinsser have in this situation?

5. At various points in the essay, Zinsser quotes deans and students at Yale. What is the effect of these quotations?

6. Zinsser notes that his categories are "intertwined" (22, 31). In what ways do the categories overlap? Does this overlap weaken the essay? Explain.

7. What, if anything, seems to determine the order in which Zinsser introduces his categories? Is this order effective? Why or why not?

VOCABULARY PROJECTS

1. Define each of the following words as it is used in this selection.

   proverbial (5)   intangible (16)   blithe (46)
   supplicants (9)   accrue (21)   tonic (47)
   balm (9)   exhorted (21)   codified (47)
   privy (11)   tenacity (23)
   venerated (14)   faculties (28)

2. At times Zinsser uses religious language — *national god, sacred document* — to describe the students' quest for success. Identify other examples of such language, and explain why it is used.

JOURNAL ENTRY

Which of the pressures Zinsser identifies has the strongest impact on you? Why? Do you have any other pressures that Zinsser does not mention?

WRITING WORKSHOP

1. Zinsser describes problems faced by students at an elite private college in the late 1970s. Are the pressures you experience as a college student similar to or different from the ones Zinsser identifies? Classify your own college pressures, and write an essay with a thesis statement that takes a strong stand against the forces responsible for the pressures.

2. Write a classification essay in which you support a thesis about college students' drive for success. Categorize students you know either by the degree of their need to succeed or by the different ways in which they wish to succeed.

3. Zinsser takes a negative view of the college pressures he identifies. Using his four categories, write an essay that argues that in the long run, these pressures are not only necessary but valuable.

COMBINING THE PATTERNS

Exemplification is an important secondary pattern in this classification-and-division essay. Identify as many passages of exemplifications as you can. What do these examples add to Zinsser's essay? What other examples might be helpful to readers?

THEMATIC CONNECTIONS

- "The Great Campus Goof-off Machine" (page 188)
- "The 'Black Table' Is Still There" (page 294)
- "Suicide Note" (page 315)
- "The Company Man" (page 478)

▰▰▰▰▰▰▰▰

SCOTT RUSSELL SANDERS

Scott Russell Sanders was born in Memphis, Tennessee, in 1945 and graduated first in his class at Brown University. Now a professor of English at Indiana University, he has written science fiction, folktales, children's stories, essays, and novels. His many books include *Stone Country* (1985), about Indiana's limestone region; *The Invisible Company* (1989), a novel; a book for young adults, *Writing from the Inside* (1995); and his latest work, *Hunting for Hope* (1998).

In "The Men We Carry in Our Minds," from the essay collection *The Paradise of Bombs* (1987), Sanders writes from personal experience about class distinctions in the United States. A boy from a poor rural background, he saw the mostly uneducated men of his childhood community — small farmers, factory workers, miners — as essentially powerless. As a scholarship student at an elite college in the mid-1960s, however, he was confronted by female classmates who argued that society favored all males over females, that men had "cornered the world's pleasures." (Note, for example, that in 1970 only 2.5 percent of law degrees, 8.4 percent of medical degrees, and 3.6 percent of M.B.A.'s went to women; in 1996 those figures were 43.5 percent, 40.9 percent, and 37.6 percent respectively.) Twenty years later, Sanders still grapples with the vastly different images he and his wealthy female classmates had of what it means to be a man.

The Men We Carry in Our Minds

The first men, besides my father, I remember seeing were black convicts and white guards, in the cottonfield across the road from our farm on the outskirts of Memphis. I must have been three or four. The prisoners wore dingy gray-and-black zebra suits, heavy as canvas, sodden with sweat. Hatless, stooped, they chopped weeds in the fierce heat, row after row, breathing the acrid dust of boll-weevil poison. The overseers wore dazzling white shirts and broad shadowy hats. The oiled barrels of their shotguns flashed in the sunlight. Their faces in memory are utterly blank. Of course those men, white and black, have become for me an emblem of racial hatred. But they have also come to stand for the twin poles of my early vision of manhood — the brute toiling animal and the boss.

When I was a boy, the men I knew labored with their bodies. They were marginal farmers, just scraping by, or welders, steel workers, carpenters; they swept floors, dug ditches, mined coal, or drove trucks, their forearms ropy with muscle; they trained horses, stoked furnaces, built tires, stood on assembly lines wrestling parts onto cars and refrigerators. They got up before light, worked all day long whatever the weather, and when they came home at night they looked as though somebody had been whipping them. In the evenings and on weekends they worked on their own places, tilling gardens that were lumpy with clay, fixing broken-down cars, hammering on houses that were always too drafty, too leaky, too small.

1

2

The bodies of the men I knew were twisted and maimed in ways visible and invisible. The nails of their hands were black and split, the hands tattooed with scars. Some had lost fingers. Heavy lifting had given many of them finicky backs and guts weak from hernias. Racing against conveyor belts had given them ulcers. Their ankles and knees ached from years of standing on concrete. Anyone who had worked for long around machines was hard of hearing. They squinted, and the skin of their faces was creased like the leather of old work gloves. There were times, studying them, when I dreaded growing up. Most of them coughed, from dust or cigarettes, and most of them drank cheap wine or whiskey, so their eyes looked bloodshot and bruised. The fathers of my friends always seemed older than the mothers. Men wore out sooner. Only women lived into old age. 3

As a boy I also knew another sort of men, who did not sweat and break down like mules. They were soldiers, and so far as I could tell they scarcely worked at all. During my early school years we lived on a military base, an arsenal in Ohio, and every day I saw GIs in the guardshacks, on the stoops of barracks, at the wheels of olive drab Chevrolets. The chief fact of their lives was boredom. Long after I left the Arsenal I came to recognize the sour smell the soldiers gave off as that of souls in limbo. They were all waiting — for wars, for transfers, for leaves, for promotions, for the end of their hitch — like so many braves waiting for the hunt to begin. Unlike the warriors of older tribes, however, they would have no say about when the battle would start or how it would be waged. Their waiting was broken only when they practiced for war. They fired guns at targets, drove tanks across the churned-up fields of the military reservation, set off bombs in the wrecks of old fighter planes. I knew this was all play. But I also felt certain that when the hour for killing arrived, they would kill. When the real shooting started, many of them would die. This was what soldiers were *for*, just as a hammer was for driving nails. 4

Warriors and toilers: those seemed, in my boyhood vision, to be the chief destinies for men. They weren't the only destinies, as I learned from having a few male teachers, from reading books, and from watching television. But the men on television — the politicians, the astronauts, the generals, the savvy lawyers, the philosophical doctors, the bosses who gave orders to both soldiers and laborers — seemed as remote and unreal to me as the figures in tapestries. I could no more imagine growing up to become one of these cool, potent creatures than I could imagine becoming a prince. 5

A nearer and more hopeful example was that of my father, who had escaped from a red-dirt farm to a tire factory, and from the assembly line to the front office. Eventually he dressed in a white shirt and tie. He carried himself as if he had been born to work with his mind. But his body, remembering the earlier years of slogging work, began to give out on him in his fifties, and it quit on him entirely before he turned sixty-five. Even such a partial escape from man's fate as he had accomplished did not 6 seem possible for most of the boys I knew. They joined the Army, stood in line for jobs in the smoky plants, helped build highways. They were bound to work as their fathers had worked, killing themselves or preparing to kill others.

A scholarship enabled me not only to attend college, a rare enough   7
feat in my circle, but even to study in a university meant for the children of the rich. Here I met for the first time young men who had assumed from birth that they would lead lives of comfort and power. And for the first time I met women who told me that men were guilty of having kept all the joys and privileges of the earth for themselves. I was baffled. What privileges? What joys? I thought about the maimed, dismal lives of most of the men back home. What had they stolen from their wives and daughters? The right to go five days a week, twelve months a year, for thirty or forty years to a steel mill or a coal mine? The right to drop bombs and die in war? The right to feel every leak in the roof, every gap in the fence, every cough in the engine, as a wound they must mend? The right to feel, when the layoff comes or the plant shuts down, not only afraid but ashamed?

I was slow to understand the deep grievances of women. This was   8
because, as a boy, I had envied them. Before college, the only people I had ever known who were interested in art or music or literature, the only ones who read books, the only ones who ever seemed to enjoy a sense of ease and grace were the mothers and daughters. Like the menfolk, they fretted about money, they scrimped and made-do. But, when the pay stopped coming in, they were not the ones who had failed. Nor did they have to go to war, and that seemed to me a blessed fact. By comparison with the narrow, ironclad days of fathers, there was an expansiveness, I thought, in the days of mothers. They went to see neighbors, to shop in town, to run errands at school, at the library, at church. No doubt, had I looked harder at their lives, I would have envied them less. It was not my fate to become a woman, so it was easier for me to see the graces. Few of them held jobs outside the home, and those who did filled thankless roles as clerks and waitresses. I didn't see, then, what a prison a house could be, since houses seemed to me brighter, handsomer places than any factory. I didn't realize — because such things were never spoken of — how often women suffered from men's bullying. I did learn about the wretchedness of abandoned wives, single mothers, widows; but I also learned about the wretchedness of lone men. Even then I could see how exhausting it was for a mother to cater all day to the needs of young children. But if I had been asked, as a boy, to choose between tending a baby and tending a machine, I think I would have chosen the baby. (Having now tended both, I know I would choose the baby.)

So I was baffled when the women at college accused me and my sex of   9
having cornered the world's pleasures. I think something like my bafflement has been felt by other boys (and by girls as well) who grew up in dirt-poor farm country, in mining country, in black ghettos, in Hispanic barrios, in the shadows of factories, in Third World nations — any place

where the fate of men is as grim and bleak as the fate of women. Toilers and warriors. I realize now how ancient these identities are, how deep the tug they exert on men, the undertow of a thousand generations. The miseries I saw, as a boy, in the lives of nearly all men I continue to see in the lives of many — the body-breaking toil, the tedium, the call to be tough, the humiliating powerlessness, the battle for a living and for territory.

When the women I met at college thought about the joys and privileges of men, they did not carry in their minds the sort of men I had known in my childhood. They thought of their fathers, who were bankers, physicians, architects, stockbrokers, the big wheels of the big cities. These fathers rode the train to work or drove cars that cost more than any of my childhood houses. They were attended from morning to night by female helpers, wives and nurses and secretaries. They were never laid off, never short of cash at month's end, never lined up for welfare. These fathers made decisions that mattered. They ran the world.   10

The daughters of such men wanted to share in this power, this glory. So did I. They yearned for a say over their future, for jobs worthy of their abilities, for the right to live at peace, unmolested, whole. Yes, I thought, yes yes. The difference between me and these daughters was that they saw me, because of my sex, as destined from birth to become like their fathers, and therefore as an enemy to their desires. But I knew better. I wasn't an enemy, in fact or in feeling. I was an ally. If I had known, then, how to tell them so, would they have believed me? Would they now?   11

•   •   •

COMPREHENSION

1. What does Sanders mean in paragraph 1 when he characterizes the black convicts and white guards as "an emblem of racial hatred"? In what sense do they represent "the twin poles of [his] early vision of manhood"?

2. When he was a child, what did Sanders expect to become when he grew up? Why? How did he escape this destiny?

3. What advantages did Sanders initially attribute to women? Why? What challenged his assumptions?

4. What kind of men did the women Sanders met in college carry in their minds? Why did the women see Sanders as "an enemy to their desires" (11)? How did he defend himself against their charges?

PURPOSE AND AUDIENCE

1. What purpose do you think Sanders had in mind when he wrote this essay? Is his essay intended as a personal memoir, or does he have another agenda? Explain.

2. What is the essay's thesis?

3. Is this essay directed primarily at workers like the ones Sanders observed when he was growing up or at the "children of the rich" (7)? At men or at

women? On whom would you expect it to have the greatest impact? Explain.

STYLE AND STRUCTURE

1. What is Sanders categorizing in this essay? What categories does he name? What other, unnamed categories does he identify?

2. What principle of classification determines the categories Sanders discusses?

3. What, if anything, determines the order in which Sanders discusses his categories?

4. Is the treatment of the various categories in this essay balanced, or does Sanders give more attention to some than to others? If some categories are given more attention, does this weaken the essay? Explain.

VOCABULARY PROJECTS

1. Define each of the following words as it is used in this selection.

acrid (1)	finicky (3)	expansiveness (8)
boll weevil (1)	slogging (6)	undertow (9)
overseers (1)	fretted (8)	unmolested (11)
maimed (3)	ironclad (8)	

2. Invent descriptive titles for the categories Sanders does not name. Be sure to include categories that cover women's roles as well as men's, and be sure your categories do not overlap.

JOURNAL ENTRY

Do you agree with Sanders when he suggests that men have harder lives than women do? What is your reaction to his parenthetical comment at the end of paragraph 8?

WRITING WORKSHOP

1. Imagine the possible kinds of work available to you in the field you expect to study. Write a classification-and-division essay in which you discuss several categories of possible future employment, arranging them from least to most desirable.

2. Consider the adult workers you know best — your relatives, friends' parents, employers, teachers — and other workers with whom you come in contact on a regular basis (merchants, for example). Write a classification-and-division essay in which you devise categories that distinguish different types of workers. Then, discuss these categories of workers in terms of how fortunate (or unfortunate) they are. Consider income level, job security, working conditions, prestige, and job satisfaction in your discussion of each category. In your essay's introduction and conclusion, consider how the employment categories you have devised are like or unlike Sanders's.

3. What kinds of jobs do you see as "dream jobs"? Why? List as many of these ideal jobs as you can, and group them into logical categories according to a single principle of classification. Then, write an essay with a thesis statement that expresses the value you see in these jobs.

COMBINING THE PATTERNS

After he establishes his categories, Sanders uses **description** to characterize workers and distinguish them from one another. Identify and evaluate the passages that serve these two purposes. Is any category of worker identified but not described? Explain.

THEMATIC CONNECTIONS

- "Midnight" (page 177)
- "On Fire" (page 243)
- "Ex-Basketball Player" (page 374)
- "The Secretary Chant" (page 488)

AMY TAN

Amy Tan (1952–) was born in Oakland, California, the daughter of recent Chinese immigrants. She studied linguistics at San Francisco State University and began a career as a corporate communications specialist. In 1984, Tan began to write stories as a sort of do-it-yourself therapy. At the same time, she began thinking about the contradictions she faced as a highly American-ized Chinese American who was also the daughter of immigrant parents. Three years later, she published *The Joy Luck Club* (1987), a best-selling novel (made into a movie in 1993) about four immigrant Chinese women and their American-born daughters. Later works include *The Kitchen God's Wife* (1991) and *The Hundred Secret Senses* (1995) as well as two children's books.

In this 1990 essay, published in the literary journal *Threepenny Review,* Tan considers the heavily Chinese-influenced English her mother speaks. The children of Asian immigrants tend to be among the most assimilated of immigrant offspring in the United States. Yet, as Tan suggests, although they may speak English fluently, their parents' less certain grasp of the spoken language still influences the children's self-image. Not only do their parents face discrimination based on their English skills, but second-generation Asian-American students also face discrimination because they are assumed to be better in math and science than in English. To make her point in this essay, Tan explores the different "Englishes" she herself uses, particularly in relation to her mother.

Mother Tongue

I am not a scholar of English or literature. I cannot give you much more than personal opinions on the English language and its variations in this country or others.

I am a writer. And by that definition, I am someone who has always loved language. I am fascinated by language in daily life. I spend a great deal of my time thinking about the power of language — the way it can evoke an emotion, a visual image, a complex idea, or a simple truth. Language is the tool of my trade. And I use them all — all the Englishes I grew up with.

Recently, I was made keenly aware of the different Englishes I do use. I was giving a talk to a large group of people, the same talk I had already given to half a dozen other groups. The nature of the talk was about my writing, my life, and my book, *The Joy Luck Club.* The talk was going along well enough, until I remembered one major difference that made the whole talk sound wrong. My mother was in the room. And it was perhaps the first time she had heard me give a lengthy speech, using the kind of English I have never used with her. I was saying things like, "The inter-section of memory upon imagination" and "There is an aspect of my fiction that relates to thus-and-thus"— a speech filled with carefully wrought grammatical phrases, burdened, it suddenly seemed to me, with nominalized forms, past perfect tenses, conditional phrases, all the forms of standard English that I had learned in school and through books, the forms of English I did not use at home with my mother.

Just last week, I was walking down the street with my mother, and I again found myself conscious of the English I was using, and the English I do use with her. We were talking about the price of new and used furniture and I heard myself saying this: "Not waste money that way." My husband was with us as well, and he didn't notice any switch in my English. And then I realized why. It's because over the twenty years we've been together I've often used that same kind of English with him, and sometimes he even uses it with me. It has become our language of intimacy, a different sort of English that relates to family talk, the language I grew up with.

So you'll have some idea of what this family talk I heard sounds like, I'll quote what my mother said during a recent conversation which I videotaped and then transcribed. During this conversation my mother was talking about a political gangster in Shanghai who had the same last name as her family's, Du, and how the gangster in his early years wanted to be adopted by her family, which was rich by comparison. Later, the gangster became more powerful, far richer than my mother's family, and one day showed up at my mother's wedding to pay his respects. Here's what she said in part:

"Du Yusong having business like fruit stand. Like off the street kind. He is Du like Du Zong — but not Tsung-ming Island people. The local people call putong, the river east side, he belong to that side local people. The man want to ask Du Zong father take him in like become own family. Du Zong father wasn't looking down on him, but didn't take seriously, until that man big like become a mafia. Now important person very hard to inviting him. Chinese way, come only to show respect, don't stay for dinner. Respect for making big celebration, he shows up. Mean gives lots of respect. Chinese custom. Chinese social life that way. If too important won't have to stay too long. He come to my wedding. I didn't see. I heard it. I gone to boy's side, they have YMCA dinner. Chinese age I was nineteen."

You should know that my mother's expressive command of English belies how much she actually understands. She reads the *Forbes* report, listens to *Wall Street Week,* converses daily with her stockbroker, reads all of Shirley MacLaine's books with ease — all kinds of things I can't begin to understand. Yet some of my friends tell me they understand 50 percent of what my mother says. Some say they understand 80 to 90 percent. Some say they understand none of it, as if she were speaking pure Chinese. But to me, my mother's English is perfectly clear, perfectly natural. It's my mother's tongue. Her language, as I hear it, is vivid, direct, full of observation and imagery. This was the language that helped shape the way I saw things, expressed things, made sense of the world.

Lately, I've been giving more thought to the kind of English my mother speaks. Like others, I have described it to people as "broken" or "fractured" English. But I wince when I say that. It has always bothered me that I can think of no way to describe it other than "broken," as if it were damaged and needed to be fixed, as if it lacked a certain wholeness and soundness. I've heard other terms used, "limited English," for example. But they seem just as bad, as if everything is limited, including people's perceptions of the limited English speaker.

I know this for a fact, because when I was growing up, my mother's "limited" English limited *my* perception of her. I was ashamed of her English. I believed that her English reflected the quality of what she had to say. That is, because she expressed them imperfectly her thoughts were imperfect. And I had plenty of empirical evidence to support me: the fact that people in department stores, at banks, and at restaurants did not take her seriously, did not give her good service, pretended not to understand her, or even acted as if they did not hear her.

My mother has long realized the limitations of her English as well. When I was fifteen, she used to have me call people on the phone to pretend I was she. In this guise, I was forced to ask for information or even complain and yell at people who had been rude to her. One time it was a call to her stockbroker in New York. She had cashed out her small portfolio and it just so happened we were going to go to New York the next week, our very first trip outside California. I had to get on the phone and say in an adolescent voice that was not very convincing, "This is Mrs. Tan."

And my mother was standing in the back whispering loudly, "Why he don't send me check, already two weeks late. So mad he lie to me, losing me money."

And then I said in perfect English, "Yes, I'm getting rather concerned. You had agreed to send the check two weeks ago, but it hasn't arrived."

Then she began to talk more loudly. "What he want, I come to New York tell him front of his boss, you cheating me?" And I was trying to calm her down, make her be quiet, while telling the stockbroker, "I can't tolerate any more excuses. If I don't receive the check immediately I am going to have to speak to your manager when I'm in New York next week." And sure enough, the following week there we were in front of this astonished stockbroker, and I was sitting there red-faced and quiet, and my mother, the real Mrs. Tan, was shouting at his boss in her impeccable broken English.

We used a similar routine just five days ago, for a situation that was far less humorous. My mother had gone to the hospital for an appointment, to find out about a benign brain tumor a CAT scan had revealed a month ago. She said she had spoken very good English, her best English, no mistakes. Still, she said, the hospital did not apologize when they said they had lost the CAT scan and she had come for nothing. She said they did not seem to have any sympathy when she told them she was anxious to know the exact diagnosis, since her husband and son had both died of brain tumors. She said they would not give her any more information until the next time and she would have to make another appointment for that. So she said she would not leave until the doctor called her daughter. She wouldn't budge. And when the doctor finally called her daughter, me, who spoke in perfect English — lo and behold — we had assurances the CAT scan would be found, promises that a conference call on Monday would be held, and apologies for any suffering my mother had gone through for a most regrettable mistake.

I think my mother's English almost had an effect on limiting my pos-   15 sibilities in life as well. Sociologists and linguists probably will tell you that a person's developing language skills are more influenced by peers. But I do think that the language spoken in the family, especially in immigrant families which are more insular, plays a large role in shaping the language of the child. And I believe that it affected my results on achievement tests, IQ tests, and the SAT. While my English skills were never judged as poor, compared to math, English could not be considered my strong suit. In grade school I did moderately well, getting perhaps B's, sometimes B-pluses, in English and scoring perhaps in the sixtieth or seventieth percentile on achievement tests. But those scores were not good enough to override the opinion that my true abilities lay in math and science, because in those areas I achieved A's and scored in the ninetieth percentile or higher.

This was understandable. Math is precise; there is only one correct   16 answer. Whereas, for me at least, the answers on English tests were always a judgment call, a matter of opinion and personal experience. Those tests were constructed around items like fill-in-the-blank sentence completion, such as "Even though Tom was _____, Mary thought he was _____." And the correct answer always seemed to be the most bland combinations of thoughts, for example, "Even though Tom was shy, Mary thought he was charming," with the grammatical structure "even though" limiting the correct answer to some sort of semantic opposites, so you wouldn't get answers like, "Even though Tom was foolish, Mary thought he was ridiculous." Well, according to my mother, there were very few limitations as to what Tom could have been and what Mary might have thought of him. So I never did well on tests like that.

The same was true with word analogies, pairs of words in which you   17 were supposed to find some sort of logical, semantic relationship — for example, "*Sunset* is to *nightfall* as _____ is to _____." And here you would be presented with a list of four possible pairs, one of which showed the same kind of relationship: *red* is to *stoplight, bus* is to *arrival, chills* is to *fever, yawn* is to *boring*. Well, I could never think that way. I knew what the tests were asking, but I could not block out of my mind the images already created by the first pair, "*sunset* is to *nightfall*"— and I would see a burst of colors against a darkening sky, the moon rising, the lowering of a curtain of stars. And all the other pairs of words — red, bus, stoplight, boring — just threw up a mass of confusing images, making it impossible for me to sort out something as logical as saying: "A sunset precedes nightfall" is the same as "a chill precedes a fever." The only way I would have gotten that answer right would have been to imagine an associative situation, for example, my being disobedient and staying out past sunset, catching a chill at night, which turns into feverish pneumonia as punishment, which indeed did happen to me.

I have been thinking about all this lately, about my mother's English, about achievement tests. Because lately I've been asked, as a writer, why there are not more Asian Americans represented in American literature. Why are there few Asian Americans enrolled in creative writing programs? Why do so many Chinese students go into engineering? Well, these are broad sociological questions I can't begin to answer. But I have noticed in surveys — in fact, just last week — that Asian students, as a whole, always do significantly better on math achievement tests than in English. And this makes me think that there are other Asian-American students whose English spoken in the home might also be described as "broken" or "limited." And perhaps they also have teachers who are steering them away from writing and into math and science, which is what happened to me.

Fortunately, I happen to be rebellious in nature and enjoy the challenge of disproving assumptions made about me. I became an English major my first year in college, after being enrolled as pre-med. I started writing nonfiction as a freelancer the week after I was told by my former boss that writing was my worst skill and I should hone my talents toward account management.

But it wasn't until 1985 that I finally began to write fiction. And at first I wrote using what I thought to be wittily crafted sentences, sentences that would finally prove I had mastery over the English language. Here's an example from the first draft of a story that later made its way into *The Joy Luck Club*, but without this line: "That was my mental quandary in its nascent state." A terrible line, which I can barely pronounce.

Fortunately, for reasons I won't get into today, I later decided I should envision a reader for the stories I would write. And the reader I decided upon was my mother because these were stories about mothers. So with this reader in mind — and in fact she did read my early drafts — I began to write stories using all the Englishes I grew up with: the English I spoke to my mother, which for lack of a better term might be described as "simple"; the English she used with me, which for lack of a better term might be described as "broken"; my translation of her Chinese, which could certainly be described as "watered down"; and what I imagined to be her translation of her Chinese if she could speak in perfect English, her internal language, and for that I sought to preserve the essence, but neither an English nor a Chinese structure. I wanted to capture what language ability tests can never reveal: her intent, her passion, her imagery, the rhythms of her speech and the nature of her thoughts.

Apart from what any critic had to say about my writing, I knew I had   22
succeeded where it counted when my mother finished reading my book
and gave me her verdict: "So easy to read."

• • •

COMPREHENSION

1. What is Tan classifying in this essay? What individual categories does she identify?

2. Where does Tan identify the different categories she discusses in "Mother Tongue"? Should she have identified these categories earlier? Why or why not?

3. Does Tan illustrate each category she identifies? Does she treat all categories equally? If she does not, do you see this as a problem? Explain.

4. In what specific situations does Tan say her mother's "limited English" was a handicap? In what other situations might Mrs. Tan face difficulties?

5. How did her mother's English affect Tan's life?

6. How does Tan account for the difficulty she had in answering questions on achievement tests, particularly word analogies? Do you think her problems in this area can be explained by the level of her family's language skills, or might other factors have contributed to the problem? Explain.

7. In paragraph 18, Tan considers the possible reasons for the lack of Asian Americans in the fields of language and literature. What explanations does she offer? What other explanations can you think of?

PURPOSE AND AUDIENCE

1. Why do you suppose Tan opens her essay by explaining her qualifications? Why, for example, does she tell her readers that she is "not a scholar of English or literature" (1) but rather a writer who is "fascinated by language in daily life" (2)?

2. Do you think Tan expects most of her readers to be Asian American? To be familiar with Asian-American languages and culture? Explain your reasoning.

3. Is Tan's primary focus in this essay on language or on her mother? Explain your conclusion.

STYLE AND STRUCTURE

1. This essay's style is relatively informal. For example, Tan uses *I* to refer to herself and addresses her readers as *you*. Identify other features that characterize her style as informal. Do you think Tan would strengthen her credibility if she were to use a more formal style? Explain your reasoning.

2. In paragraph 6, Tan quotes a passage of her mother's speech. What purpose does Tan say is served by this quotation? What impression does it give of her mother? Do you think this effect is what Tan intended? Explain.

3. In paragraphs 10 through 13, Tan juxtaposes her mother's English with her own. What point do these quoted passages make?

4. The expression used in Tan's title, "Mother Tongue," is also used in paragraph 7. What does this expression generally mean? What does it seem to mean in this essay?

5. In paragraph 20, Tan quotes a "terrible line" from an early draft of part of her novel *The Joy Luck Club*. Why do you suppose she quotes this line? How is it different from the style she uses in "Mother Tongue"?

VOCABULARY PROJECTS

1. Define each of the following words as it is used in this selection.

nominalized (3)	guise (10)	semantic (16)
belies (7)	impeccable (13)	quandary (20)
empirical (9)	insular (15)	nascent (20)

2. In paragraph 8, Tan discusses the different words that might be used to describe her mother's spoken English. Which term seems most accurate? Do you agree with Tan that these words are unsatisfactory? What other term for her mother's English would be both neutral and accurate?

JOURNAL ENTRY

In paragraph 9, Tan says that when she was growing up she was sometimes ashamed of her mother because of her limited English proficiency. Have you ever felt ashamed of a parent (or a friend) because of his or her inability to "fit in" in some way? How do you feel now about your earlier reaction?

WRITING WORKSHOP

1. What different "Englishes" (or other languages) do you use in your day-to-day life as a student, employee, friend, and family member? Write a classification-and-division essay in which you identify, describe, and illustrate each kind of language and explain the purpose it serves.

2. What kinds of problems are faced today by a person whose English is as limited as that of Mrs. Tan? Write a classification-and-division essay that identifies and explains the kinds of problems you might encounter if the level of your spoken English were comparable to hers.

3. Tan's essay focuses on spoken language, but people also use different kinds of *written* language in different situations. Write a classification-and-division essay that identifies three different kinds of written English: one appropriate for your parents, one for a teacher or employer, and one for a friend. Illustrate each kind of language with an extended example in

which you write about your plans for your future. Then analyze the language used in each piece of writing. In your thesis statement, explain why you need all three kinds of language.

COMBINING THE PATTERNS

Tan develops her essay with a series of anecdotes about her mother and about herself. How does this use of **narration** strengthen her essay? Could she have made her point about the use of different "Englishes" without these anecdotes? What other strategy could she have used?

THEMATIC CONNECTIONS

- "Only Daughter" (page 83)
- "Words Left Unspoken" (page 133)
- "English Is a Crazy Language" (page 192)
- "The Human Cost of an Illiterate Society" (page 203)

ALLEEN PACE NILSEN

Alleen Pace Nilsen was born in 1936 in Phoenix, Arizona, and graduated from Brigham Young University in 1958. She received her doctorate from the University of Iowa in 1973, writing her dissertation on the effect of sexist language in children's literature. In 1975 Nilsen began teaching at Arizona State University, where she is currently professor of English-Education. She has also written, co-authored, and edited several books, including *Sexism and Language* (1977), a collection of scholarly essays; *Literature for Today's Young Adults* (sixth edition, 2000); *Living Language* (1999), a freshman composition text; and the *Encyclopedia of Twentieth Century American Humor* (2000).

The original version of the following essay, titled "Sexism in English: A Feminist View," appeared in the journal *Female Studies* in 1972. That year represented perhaps the height of the feminist movement in the United States. The National Organization for Women (NOW), established in 1966, had hundreds of chapters all over the country. The Equal Rights Amendment, barring discrimination against women, passed in Congress (although it was never ratified by the states). Congress also passed Title IX of the Education Amendments Act, which required equal opportunities (in sports as well as academics) for all students in any school that received federal funding. *Ms.* magazine, the icon of feminist publishing, also premiered in 1972. The issue of sexist language had been explored before, but rarely with the breadth of examples noted by Nilsen. In this version of her essay, revised in 1999, Nilsen updates her examination of how language, in particular the terms used for women and men, reveals much about social attitudes and assumptions.

Sexism in English: Embodiment and Language

During the late 1960s, I lived with my husband and three young children in Kabul, Afghanistan. This was before the Russian invasion, the Afghan civil war, and the eventual taking over of the country by the Taleban Islamic movement and its resolve to return the country to a strict Islamic dynasty, in which females are not allowed to attend school or work outside their homes.   1

But even when we were there and the country was considered moderate rather than extremist, I was shocked to observe how different were the roles assigned to males and females. The Afghan version of the *chaderi** prescribed for Moslem women was particularly confining. Women in religious families were required to wear it whenever they were outside their family home, with the result being that most of them didn't venture outside.   2

The household help we hired were made up of men, because women could not be employed by foreigners. Afghan folk stories and jokes were   3

---

*EDS. NOTE — Full-length outer garment traditionally worn by Muslim women in public.

blatantly sexist, as in this proverb: "If you see an old man, sit down and take a lesson; if you see an old woman, throw a stone."

But it wasn't only the native culture that made me question women's   4
roles, it was also the American community within Afghanistan.

Most of the American women were like myself — wives and mothers   5
whose husbands were either career diplomats, employees of USAID, or college professors who had been recruited to work on various contract teams. We were suddenly bereft of our traditional roles: The local economy provided few jobs for women and certainly none for foreigners; we were isolated from former friends and the social goals we had grown up with. Some of us became alcoholics, others got very good at bridge, while still others searched desperately for ways to contribute either to our families or to the Afghans.

When we returned in the fall of 1969 to the University of Michigan in   6
Ann Arbor, I was surprised to find that many other women were also questioning the expectations they had grown up with. Since I had been an English major when I was in college, I decided that for my part in the feminist movement I would study the English language and see what it could tell me about sexism. I started reading a desk dictionary and making note cards on every entry that seemed to tell something different about male and female. I soon had a dog-eared dictionary, along with a collection of note cards filling two shoe boxes.

The first thing I learned was that I couldn't study the language with-   7
out getting involved in social issues. Language and society are as intertwined as a chicken and an egg. The language a culture uses is telltale evidence of the values and beliefs of that culture. And because there is a lag in how fast a language changes — new words can easily be introduced, but it takes a long time for old words and usages to disappear — a careful look at English will reveal the attitudes that our ancestors held and that we as a culture are therefore predisposed to hold. My note cards revealed three main points. While friends have offered the opinion that I didn't need to read a dictionary to learn such obvious facts, the linguistic evidence lends credibility to the sociological observations.

WOMEN ARE SEXY; MEN ARE SUCCESSFUL

First, in American culture a woman is valued for the attractiveness   8
and sexiness of her body, while a man is valued for his physical strength and accomplishments. A woman is sexy. A man is successful.

A persuasive piece of evidence supporting this view are the   9
eponyms — words that have come from someone's name — found in English. I had a two-and-a-half-inch stack of cards taken from men's names but less than a half-inch stack from women's names, and most of those came from Greek mythology. In the words that came into American English since we separated from Britain, there are many eponyms based on

the names of famous American men: Bartlett pear, boysenberry, Franklin stove, Ferris wheel, Gatling gun, mason jar, sideburns, sousaphone, Schick test, and Winchester rifle. The only common eponyms that I found taken from American women's names are Alice blue (after Alice Roosevelt Longworth), bloomers (after Amelia Jenks Bloomer), and Mae West jacket (after the buxom actress). Two out of the three feminine eponyms relate closely to a woman's physical anatomy, while the masculine eponyms (except for "sideburns" after General Burnsides) have nothing to do with the namesake's body, but, instead, honor the man for an accomplishment of some kind.

In Greek mythology women played a bigger role than they did in the   10
biblical stories of the Judeo-Christian cultures, and so the names of goddesses are accepted parts of the language in such place names as Pomona, from the goddess of fruit, and Athens, from Athena, and in such common words as *cereal* from Ceres, *psychology* from Psyche, and *arachnoid* from Arachne. However, there is the same tendency to think of women in relation to sexuality as shown through the eponyms *aphrodisiac* from Aphrodite, the Greek name for the goddess of love and beauty, and *venereal disease* from Venus, the Roman name for Aphrodite.

Another interesting word from Greek mythology is *Amazon*. Accord-   11
ing to Greek folk etymology, the *a-* means "without," as in *atypical* or *amoral,* while *-mazon* comes from *mazos,* meaning "breast," as still seen in *mastectomy.* In the Greek legend, Amazon women cut off their right breasts so they could better shoot their bows. Apparently, the storytellers had a feeling that for women to play the active, "masculine" role the Amazons adopted for themselves, they had to trade in part of their femininity.

This preoccupation with women's breasts is not limited to the Greeks;   12
it's what inspired the definition and the name for "mammals" (from Indo-European *mammae* for "breasts"). As a volunteer for the University of Wisconsin's *Dictionary of American Regional English (DARE),* I read a western trapper's diary from the 1830s. I was to make notes of any unusual usages or language patterns. My most interesting finding was that the trapper referred to a range of mountains as "The Teats," a metaphor based on the similarity between the shapes of the mountains and women's breasts. Because today we use the French wording "The Grand Tetons," the metaphor isn't as obvious, but I wrote to mapmakers and found the following listings: Nipple Top and Little Nipple Top near Mount Marcy in the Adirondacks; Nipple Mountain in Archuleta County, Colorado; Nipple Peak in Coke County, Texas; Nipple Butte in Pennington, South Dakota; Squaw Peak in Placer County, California (and many other locations); Maiden's Peak and Squaw Tit (they're the same mountain) in the Cascade Range in Oregon; Mary's Nipple near Salt Lake City, Utah; and Jane Russell Peaks near Stark, New Hampshire.

Except for the movie star Jane Russell, the women being referred to   13
are anonymous — it's only a sexual part of their body that is mentioned. When topographical features are named after men, it's probably not going

to be to draw attention to a sexual part of their bodies but instead to honor individuals for an accomplishment.

Going back to what I learned from my dictionary cards, I was sur- 14
prised to realize how many pairs of words we have in which the feminine word has acquired sexual connotations while the masculine word retains a serious businesslike aura. For example, a callboy is the person who calls actors when it is time for them to go on stage, but a callgirl is a prostitute. Compare sir and madam. *Sir* is a term of respect, while *madam* has acquired the specialized meaning of a brothel manager. Something similar has happened to master and mistress. Would you rather have a painting "by an old master" or "by an old mistress"?

It's because the word *woman* had sexual connotations, as in "She's his 15
woman," that people began avoiding its use, hence such terminology as ladies' room, lady of the house, and girl's school or school for young ladies. Those of us who in the 1970s began asking that speakers use the term *woman* rather than *girl* or *lady* were rejecting the idea that *woman* is primarily a sexual term.

I found two-hundred pairs of words with masculine and feminine 16
forms; for example, *heir-heiress, hero-heroine, steward/stewardess, usher/ush-erette.* In nearly all such pairs, the masculine word is considered the base, with some kind of a feminine suffix being added. The masculine form is the one from which compounds are made; for example, from king/queen comes kingdom but not queendom, from sportsman/sportslady comes sportsmanship but not sportsladyship. There is one — and only one — semantic area in which the masculine word is not the base or more power-ful word. This is in the area dealing with sex, marriage, and motherhood. When someone refers to a virgin, a listener will probably think of a female unless the speaker specifies male or uses a masculine pronoun. The same is true for prostitute.

In relation to marriage, linguistic evidence shows that weddings are 17
more important to women than to men. A woman cherishes the wedding and is considered a bride for a whole year, but a man is referred to as a groom only on the day of the wedding. The word *bride* appears in *bridal attendant, bridal gown, bridesmaid, bridal shower,* and even *bridegroom. Groom* comes from the Middle English *grom,* meaning "man," and in that sense is seldom used outside of the wedding. With most pairs of male/female words, people habitually put the masculine word first: *Mr. and Mrs., his and hers, boys and girls, men and women, kings and queens, brothers and sisters, guys and dolls,* and *host and hostess.* But it is the bride and groom who are talked about, not the groom and bride.

The importance of marriage to a woman is also shown by the fact that 18
when a marriage ends in death, the woman gets the title of widow. A man gets the derived title of widower. This term is not used in other phrases or contexts, but widow is seen in widowhood, widow's peak, and widow's walk. A widow in a card game is an extra hand of cards, while in typeset-ting it is a leftover line of type.

Changing cultural ideas bring changes to language, and since I did   19
my dictionary study three decades ago the word *singles* has largely
replaced such gender-specific and value-laden terms as *bachelor, old maid,
spinster, divorcee, widow,* and *widower.* In 1970 I wrote that when people
hear a man called "a professional," they usually think of him as a doctor or
a lawyer, but when people hear a woman referred to as "a professional,"
they are likely to think of her as a prostitute. That's not as true today
because so many women have become doctors and lawyers, it's no longer
incongruous to think of women in those professional roles.

Another change that has taken place is in wedding announcements.   20
They used to be sent out from the bride's parents and did not even give
the name of the groom's parents. Today, most couples choose to list either
all or none of the parents' names. Also it is now much more likely that
both the bride and groom's picture will be in the newspaper, while twenty
years ago only the bride's picture was published on the "Women's" or the
"Society" page. In the weddings I have recently attended, the official has
pronounced the couple "husband and wife" instead of the traditional
"man and wife," and the bride has been asked if she promises to "love,
honor, and cherish," instead of to "love, honor, and obey."

WOMEN ARE PASSIVE; MEN ARE ACTIVE

However, other wording in the wedding ceremony relates to a second   21
point that my cards showed, which is that women are expected to play a
passive or weak role while men play an active or strong role. In the traditional ceremony, the official asks, "Who gives the bride away?" and the
father answers, "I do." Some fathers answer, "Her mother and I do," but
that doesn't solve the problem inherent in the question. The idea that a
bride is something to be handed over from one man to another bothers
people because it goes back to the days when a man's servants, his children, and his wife were all considered to be his property. They were
known by his name because they belonged to him, and he was responsible
for their actions and their debts.

The grammar used in talking or writing about weddings as well as   22
other sexual relationships shows the expectation of men playing the active
role. Men *wed* women while women *become* brides of men. A man *possesses*
a woman; he *deflowers* her; he *performs*; he *scores*; he *takes away* her virginity.
Although a woman can *seduce* a man, she cannot offer him her virginity.
When talking about virginity, the only way to make the woman the actor
in the sentence is to say that "she lost her virginity," but people lose things
by accident rather than by purposeful actions, and so she's only the grammatical, not the real-life, actor.

The reason that women brought the term *Ms.* into the language to   23
replace *Miss* and *Mrs.* relates to this point. Many married women resent
being identified in the "Mrs. Husband" form. The dictionary cards showed

what appeared to be an attitude on the part of the editors that it was almost indecent to let a respectable woman's name march unaccompanied across the pages of a dictionary. Women were listed with male names whether or not the male contributed to the woman's reason for being in the dictionary or whether or not in his own right he was as famous as the woman. For example:

Charlotte Brontë = Mrs. Arthur B. Nicholls

Amelia Earhart = Mrs. George Palmer Putnam

Helen Hayes = Mrs. Charles MacArthur

Jenny Lind = Mme. Otto Goldschmit

Cornelia Otis Skinner = daughter of Otis

Harriet Beecher Stowe = sister of Henry Ward Beecher

Dame Edith Sitwell = sister of Osbert and Sacheverell*

Only a small number of rebels and crusaders got into the dictionary without the benefit of a masculine escort: temperance leaders Frances Elizabeth Caroline Willard and Carry Nation, women's rights leaders Carrie Chapman Catt and Elizabeth Cady Stanton, birth control educator Margaret Sanger, religious leader Mary Baker Eddy, and slaves Harriet Tubman and Phillis Wheatley.

Etiquette books used to teach that if a woman had Mrs. in front of her   24 name, then the husband's name should follow because Mrs. is an abbreviated form of Mistress and a woman couldn't be a mistress of herself. As with many arguments about "correct" language usage, this isn't very logical because Miss is also an abbreviation of Mistress. Feminists hoped to simplify matters by introducing Ms. as an alternative to both Mrs. and Miss, but what happened is that Ms. largely replaced Miss to become a catch-all business title for women. Many married women still prefer the title Mrs., and some even resent being addressed with the term Ms. As one frustrated newspaper reporter complained, "Before I can write about a woman I have to know not only her marital status but also her political philosophy." The result of such complications may contribute to the demise of titles, which are already being ignored by many writers who find it more efficient to simply use names; for example, in a business letter: "Dear Joan Garcia," instead of "Dear Mrs. Joan Garcia," "Dear Ms. Garcia," or "Dear Mrs. Louis Garcia."

Titles given to royalty show how males can be disadvantaged by the   25 assumption that they always play the more powerful role. In British roy-

---

*EDS. NOTE — Charlotte Brontë (1816–1855), author of *Jane Eyre;* Amelia Earhart (1898–1937), first woman to fly over the Atlantic; Helen Hayes (1900–1993), actress; Jenny Lind (1820–1887), Swedish soprano known as the "Swedish nightingale"; Cornelia Otis Skinner (1901–1979), actress and writer; Harriet Beecher Stowe (1811–1896), author of *Uncle Tom's Cabin;* and Edith Sitwell (1877–1964), English poet and critic.

alty, when a male holds a title, his wife is automatically given the feminine equivalent. But the reverse is not true. For example, a count is a high political officer with a countess being his wife. The same pattern holds true for a duke and a duchess and a king and a queen. But when a female holds the royal title, the man she marries does not automatically acquire the matching title. For example, Queen Elizabeth's husband has the title of prince rather than king, but when Prince Charles married Diana, she became Princess Diana. If they had stayed married and he had ascended to the throne, then she would have become Queen Diana. The reasoning appears to be that since masculine words are stronger, they are reserved for true heirs and withheld from males coming into the royal family by marriage. If Prince Phillip were called "King Phillip," British subjects might forget who had inherited the right to rule.

The names that people give their children show the hopes and dreams   26
they have for them, and when we look at the differences between male and female names in a culture, we can see the cumulative expectations of that culture. In our culture girls often have names taken from small, aesthetically pleasing items; for example, Ruby, Jewel, and Pearl. Esther and Stella mean "star," and Ada means "ornament." One of the few women's names that refers to strength is Mildred, and it means "mild strength." Boys often have names with meanings of power and strength; for example, Neil means "champion"; Martin is from Mars, the God of war; Raymond means "wise protection"; Harold means "chief of the army"; Ira means "vigilant"; Rex means "king"; and Richard means "strong king."

We see similar differences in food metaphors. Food is a passive sub-   27
stance just sitting there waiting to be eaten. Many people have recognized this and so no longer feel comfortable describing women as "delectable morsels." However, when I was a teenager, it was considered a compliment to refer to a girl (we didn't call anyone a "woman" until she was middle-aged) as a cute tomato, a peach, a dish, a cookie, honey, sugar, or sweetie-pie. When being affectionate, women will occasionally call a man honey or sweetie, but in general, food metaphors are used much less often with men than with women. If a man is called "a fruit," his masculinity is being questioned. But it's perfectly acceptable to use a food metaphor if the food is heavier and more substantive than that used for women. For example, pin-up pictures of women have long been known as "cheesecake," but when Burt Reynolds posed for a nude centerfold the picture was immediately dubbed "beefcake," that is, a hunk of meat. That such sexual references to men have come into the language is another reflection of how society is beginning to lessen the differences between their attitudes toward men and women.

Something similar to the fruit metaphor happens with references to   28
plants. We insult a man by calling him a "pansy," but it wasn't considered particularly insulting to talk about a girl being a wallflower, a clinging vine, or a shrinking violet, or to give girls such names as Ivy, Rose, Lily, Iris, Daisy, Camelia, Heather, and Flora. A positive plant metaphor can be

used with a man only if the plant is big and strong; for example, Andrew Jackson's nickname of Old Hickory. Also, the phrases *blooming idiots* and *budding geniuses* can be used with either sex, but notice how they are based on the most active thing a plant can do, which is to bloom or bud.

Animal metaphors also illustrate the different expectations for males 29
and females. Men are referred to as studs, bucks, and wolves, while women are referred to with such metaphors as kitten, bunny, beaver, bird, chick, and lamb. In the 1950s we said that boys went "tom catting," but today it's just "catting around," and both boys and girls do it. When the term foxy, meaning that someone was sexy, first became popular it was used only for females, but now someone of either sex can be described as a fox. Some animal metaphors that are used predominantly with men have negative connotations based on the size and/or strength of the animals; for example, beast, bullheaded, jackass, rat, loanshark, and vulture. Negative metaphors used with women are based on smaller animals; for example, social butterfly, mousey, catty, and vixen. The feminine terms connote action, but not the same kind of large scale action as with the masculine terms.

WOMEN ARE CONNECTED WITH NEGATIVE CONNOTATIONS; MEN WITH POSITIVE CONNOTATIONS

The final point that my note cards illustrated was how many positive 30
connotations are associated with the concept of masculinity, while there are either trivial or negative connotations connected with the corresponding feminine concept. An example from the animal metaphors makes a good illustration. The word *shrew* taken from the name of a small but especially vicious animal was defined in my dictionary as "an ill-tempered scolding woman," but the word *shrewd* taken from the same root was defined as "marked by clever, discerning awareness" and was illustrated with the phrase "a shrewd businessman."

Early in life, children are conditioned to the superiority of the mascu- 31
line role. As child psychologists point out, little girls have much more freedom to experiment with sex roles than do little boys. If a little girl acts like a tomboy, most parents have mixed feelings, being at least partially proud. But if their little boy acts like a sissy (derived from *sister*), they call a psychologist. It's perfectly acceptable for a little girl to sleep in the crib that was purchased for her brother, to wear his hand-me-down jeans and shirts, and to ride the bicycle that he has outgrown. But few parents would put a boy baby in a white-and-gold crib decorated with frills and lace, and virtually no parents would have their little boy wear his sister's hand-me-down dresses, nor would they have their son ride a girl's pink bicycle with a flower-bedecked basket. The proper names given to girls and boys show this same attitude. Girls can have "boy" names — Cris, Craig, Jo, Kelly, Shawn, Teri, Toni, and Sam — but it doesn't work the other way around. A

couple of generations ago, Beverly, Frances, Hazel, Marion, and Shirley were common boys' names. As parents gave these names to more and more girls, they fell into disuse for males, and some older men who have these names prefer to go by their initials or by such abbreviated forms as Haze or Shirl.

When a little girl is told to be a lady, she is being told to sit with her 32 knees together and to be quiet and dainty. But when a little boy is told to be a man, he is being told to be noble, strong, and virtuous — to have all the qualities that the speaker looks on as desirable. The concept of manliness has such positive connotations that it used to be a compliment to call someone a he-man, to say that he was doubly a man. Today many people are more ambivalent about this term and respond to it much as they do to the word *macho*. But calling someone a manly man or a virile man is nearly always meant as a compliment. Virile comes from the Indo-European *vir*, meaning "man," which is also the basis of *virtuous*. Consider the positive connotations of both virile and virtuous with the negative connotations of *hysterical*. The Greeks took this latter word from their name for uterus (as still seen in *hysterectomy*). They thought that women were the only ones who experienced uncontrolled emotional outbursts, and so the condition must have something to do with a part of the body that only women have. But how word meanings change is regularly shown at athletic events where thousands of *virtuous* women sit quietly beside their *hysterical* husbands.

Differences in the connotations between positive male and negative 33 female connotations can be seen in several pairs of words that differ denotatively only in the matter of sex. Bachelor as compared to spinster or old maid has such positive connotations that women try to adopt it by using the term *bachelor-girl* or *bachelorette*. Old maid is so negative that it's the basis for metaphors: pretentious and fussy old men are called "old maids," as are the leftover kernels of unpopped popcorn and the last card in a popular children's card game.

Patron and *matron* (Middle English for "father" and "mother") have 34 such different levels of prestige that women try to borrow the more positive masculine connotations with the word *patroness*, literally "female father." Such a peculiar term came about because of the high prestige attached to patron in such phrases as a *patron of the arts* or a *patron saint*. Matron is more apt to be used in talking about a woman in charge of a jail or a public restroom.

When men are doing jobs that women often do, we apparently try to 35 pay the men extra by giving them fancy titles. For example, a male cook is more likely to be called a "chef" while a male seamstress will get the title of "tailor." The armed forces have a special problem in that they recruit under such slogans as "The Marine Corps builds men!" and "Join the Army! Become a Man." Once the recruits are enlisted, they find themselves doing much of the work that has been traditionally thought of as "women's work." The solution to getting the work done and not insulting anyone's masculinity was to change the titles as shown below:

waitress = orderly

nurse = medic or corpsman

secretary = clerk-typist

assistant = adjutant

dishwasher = KP (kitchen police) or kitchen helper

Compare *brave* and *squaw*. Early settlers in America truly admired   36
Indian men and hence named them with a word that carried connotations
of youth, vigor, and courage. But for Indian women they used an Algon-
quin slang term with negative sexual connotations that are almost opposite to those of brave. Wizard and witch contrast almost as much. The
masculine *wizard* implies skill and wisdom combined with magic, while
the feminine *witch* implies evil intentions combined with magic. When
witch is used for men, as in witch-doctor, many mainstream speakers feel
some carry-over of the negative connotations.

Part of the unattractiveness of both witch and squaw is that they have   37
been used so often to refer to old women, something with which our culture is particularly uncomfortable, just as the Afghans were. Imagine my
surprise when I ran across the phrases *grandfatherly advice* and *old wives'
tales* and realized that the underlying implication is the same as the
Afghan proverb about old men being worth listening to while old women
talk only foolishness.

Other terms that show how negatively we view old women as com-   38
pared to young women are *old nag* as compared to *filly, old crow* or *old bat*
as compared to *bird,* and being *catty* as compared to being *kittenish.* There
is no matching set of metaphors for men. The chicken metaphor tells the
whole story of a woman's life. In her youth she is a chick. Then she marries and begins feathering her nest. Soon she begins feeling cooped up, so
she goes to hen parties where she cackles with her friends. Then she has
her brood, begins to henpeck her husband, and finally turns into an old
biddy.

I embarked on my study of the dictionary not with the intention of   39
prescribing language change but simply to see what the language would
tell me about sexism. Nevertheless, I have been both surprised and
pleased as I've watched the changes that have occurred over the past three
decades. I'm one of those linguists who believes that new language customs will cause a new generation of speakers to grow up with different
expectations. This is why I'm happy about people's efforts to use inclusive
languages, to say "he or she" or "they" when speaking about individuals
whose names they do not know. I'm glad that leading publishers have
developed guidelines to help writers use language that is fair to both
sexes. I'm glad that most newspapers and magazines list women by their
own names instead of only by their husbands' names. And I'm so glad
that educated and thoughtful people no longer begin their business letters

with "Dear Sir" or "Gentlemen," but instead use a memo form or begin with such salutations as "Dear Colleagues," "Dear Reader," or "Dear Committee Members." I'm also glad that such words as *poetess, authoress, conductress,* and *aviatrix* now sound quaint and old-fashioned and that *chairman* is giving way to *chair* or *head, mailman* to *mail carrier, clergyman* to *clergy,* and *stewardess* to *flight attendant.* I was also pleased when the National Oceanic and Atmospheric Administration bowed to feminist complaints and in the late 1970s began to alternate men's and women's names for hurricanes. However, I wasn't so pleased to discover that the change did not immediately erase sexist thoughts from everyone's mind, as shown by a headline about Hurricane David in a 1979 New York tabloid, "David Rapes Virgin Islands." More recently a similar metaphor appeared in a headline in the *Arizona Republic* about Hurricane Charlie, "Charlie Quits Carolinas, Flirts with Virginia."

What these incidents show is that sexism is not something existing   40
independently in American English or in the particular dictionary that I happened to read. Rather, it exists in people's minds. Language is like an X-ray in providing visible evidence of invisible thoughts. The best thing about people being interested in and discussing sexist language is that as they make conscious decisions about what pronouns they will use, what jokes they will tell or laugh at, how they will write their names, or how they will begin their letters, they are forced to think about the underlying issue of sexism. This is good because as a problem that begins in people's assumptions and expectations, it's a problem that will be solved only when a great many people have given it a great deal of thought.

● ● ●

COMPREHENSION

1. Why did Nilsen first decide to study the English language?

2. What are some of the examples Nilsen uses to support the idea that language portrays women as sexy and men as successful?

3. How, according to Nilsen, does language suggest "weddings are more important to women than to men" (17)?

4. According to Nilsen, how have marriage customs changed since she wrote her original essay?

5. What are some of the examples Nilsen uses to support the idea that language casts women as weak and passive?

6. Why was the term *Ms.* introduced into the language? Does Nilsen believe it has solved the problems feminists hoped it would? Explain.

7. What are some of the examples Nilsen uses to support the idea that men are associated with positive connotations while women are associated with negative connotations?

8. Does Nilsen still see the English language as sexist, or does she believe that changes in language customs have largely eliminated such bias?

PURPOSE AND AUDIENCE

1. Is the primary purpose of this essay to inform or to persuade? Does Nilsen achieve this purpose?

2. What is Nilsen's thesis? Do you think the thesis should take a more argumentative stance — for example, suggesting the dangers of sexist language? Explain your conclusion.

3. This essay updates a piece Nilsen published nearly thirty years ago. Would you expect audience reaction in the 1970s to be different from audience reaction today? If so, how? If not, why not?

STYLE AND STRUCTURE

1. Into what three categories does Nilsen divide sexist language?

2. Where, if anywhere, do Nilsen's three categories overlap? Is this overlap to be expected, or does it reveal a flaw in Nilsen's classification system? Explain.

3. Nilsen uses headings to identify her categories. Are these headings helpful? Necessary? Misleading? Distracting? Does she need additional headings? Subheadings? Explain.

4. What function does the essay's introduction (1–7) serve? Do you think it could be condensed? How much of it do you consider essential to your understanding and appreciation of the essay that follows?

5. Which paragraph or paragraphs constitute Nilsen's conclusion? Should the conclusion be expanded? If so, what could be added?

6. Does Nilsen include enough examples to convince readers that sexism exists in English? Explain.

7. Nilsen's use of contractions and first-person pronouns in her essay gives it an informal, even conversational, style. Is this style appropriate for her subject matter? Explain.

8. Are paragraphs 17–20 a digression, or do they illustrate the statement "Women are sexy; men are successful"? Do any other paragraphs strike you as digressions? Explain.

VOCABULARY PROJECTS

1. Define each of the following words as it is used in this selection.

blatantly (3)	semantic (16)
bereft (5)	connote (29)
buxom (9)	ambivalent (32)

2. List as many additional examples of your own as you can of words that illustrate each of Nilsen's three points.

3. Even though Nilsen has updated her essay since she first wrote it in 1972, some of the usages she describes may no longer be current. Identify any words that you believe are no longer used as Nilsen says they are.

JOURNAL ENTRY

In paragraph 7, Nilsen writes, "Language and society are as intertwined as a chicken and an egg." Do you think language simply reflects society's values, or do you think it can actually influence (or even change) them?

WRITING WORKSHOP

1. What special kinds of language are used in sports — for example, by players, fans, and sportswriters? How do various sports differ in their idioms? Answer these questions in a classification-and-division essay about the language of sports. (How you organize your essay will depend on whether you write about one particular sport or several different ones.)

2. How does today's advertising portray women? Using Nilsen's general categories (and her headings if you like), collect examples to support the thesis that advertising, like language, has a sexist bias.

3. Many people believe that the English language reflects not only the sexism in people's minds but also the racism. Write an essay called "Racism in English." Begin by listing individual words and usage patterns you consider racist. Then divide your list into categories determined by a single principle of classification — for example, kinds of racist language, kinds of language applied to different racial groups, or different motives for using racist language. Your thesis can simply sum up current practices or take a stand against them. Reading (or rereading) some of the essays on this topic that appear in other chapters, such as "'What's in a Name?'" "The 'Black Table' Is Still There," and "Finishing School," might help you plan your paper.

COMBINING THE PATTERNS

Many of the paragraphs in this essay are developed by means of **exemplification.** Identify several of these paragraphs. How does Nilsen use topic sentences to unify the examples in each paragraph? What transitional words and expressions does she use to link the individual examples within each of these paragraphs?

THEMATIC CONNECTIONS

- "My Field of Dreams" (page 73)
- "Only Daughter" (page 83)
- "English Is a Crazy Language" (page 192)
- "Sex, Lies, and Conversation" (page 367)

STEPHANIE ERICSSON

Stephanie Ericsson (1953–) grew up in San Francisco and began writing as a teenager. She has worked as a screenwriter and an advertising copywriter and has published several books based on her own life. *Shamefaced: The Road to Recovery* and *Women of AA: Recovering Together* (both 1985) focus on her experiences with addiction; *Companion through the Darkness: Inner Dialogues on Grief* (1993) deals with the sudden death of her husband; and *Companion into the Dawn: Inner Dialogues on Loving* (1994), is a collection of essays.

The following piece originally appeared in the *Utne Reader* in January 1993. The *Utne Reader* is a bimonthly magazine that covers a wide range of social and lifestyle topics, with each issue including several articles focusing on a common theme. Ericsson's essay was the cover article of an issue devoted to lies and lying. The subject had particular relevance after a year in which the honesty of candidate Bill Clinton — newly elected president — had been questioned. Also, a furor had raged over allegations by attorney Anita Hill of sexual harassment by Supreme Court Justice nominee Clarence Thomas, allegations that Thomas denied. Thomas's confirmation hearings focused on who was telling the truth.

The Ways We Lie

The bank called today and I told them my deposit was in the mail, even though I hadn't written a check yet. It'd been a rough day. The baby I'm pregnant with decided to do aerobics on my lungs for two hours, our three-year-old daughter painted the living-room couch with lipstick, the IRS put me on hold for an hour, and I was late to a business meeting because I was tired.

I told my client the traffic had been bad. When my partner came home, his haggard face told me his day hadn't gone any better than mine, so when he asked, "How was your day?" I said, "Oh, fine," knowing that one more straw might break his back. A friend called and wanted to take me to lunch. I said I was busy. Four lies in the course of a day, none of which I felt the least bit guilty about.

We lie. We all do. We exaggerate, we minimize, we avoid confrontation, we spare people's feelings, we conveniently forget, we keep secrets, we justify lying to the big-guy institutions. Like most people, I indulge in small falsehoods and still think of myself as an honest person. Sure I lie, but it doesn't hurt anything. Or does it?

I once tried going a whole week without telling a lie, and it was paralyzing. I discovered that telling the truth all the time is nearly impossible. It means living with some serious consequences: The bank charges me $60 in overdraft fees, my partner keels over when I tell him about my travails, my client fires me for telling her I didn't feel like being on time, and my friend takes it personally when I say I'm not hungry. There must be some merit to lying.

But if I justify lying, what makes me any different from slick politi- 5
cians or the corporate robbers who raided the S&L industry? Saying it's
okay to lie one way and not another is hedging. I cannot seem to escape
the voice deep inside me that tells me: When someone lies, someone loses.

What far-reaching consequences will I, or others, pay as a result of my 6
lie? Will someone's trust be destroyed? Will someone else pay *my* penance
because I ducked out? We must consider the *meaning of our actions.* Decep-
tion, lies, capital crimes, and misdemeanors all carry meanings. *Webster's*
definition of *lie* is specific:

1: a false statement or action especially made with the intent to deceive;
2: anything that gives or is meant to give a false impression.

A definition like this implies that there are many, many ways to tell a 7
lie. Here are just a few.

THE WHITE LIE

> A man who won't lie to a woman has very little consideration
> for her feelings.
> — BERGEN EVANS

The white lie assumes that the truth will cause more damage than a 8
simple, harmless untruth. Telling a friend he looks great when he looks
like hell can be based on a decision that the friend needs a compliment
more than a frank opinion. But, in effect, it is the liar deciding what is best
for the lied to. Ultimately, it is a vote of no confidence. It is an act of subtle
arrogance for anyone to decide what is best for someone else.

Yet not all circumstances are quite so cut-and-dried. Take, for instance, 9
the sergeant in Vietnam who knew one of his men was killed in action but
listed him as missing so that the man's family would receive indefinite
compensation instead of the lump-sum pittance the military gives widows and children. His intent was honorable. Yet for twenty years this family kept their hopes alive, unable to move on to a new life.

FACADES

> Et tu, Brute?
> — CAESAR*

We all put up facades to one degree or another. When I put on a suit to 10
go to see a client, I feel as though I am putting on another face, obeying the
expectation that serious businesspeople wear suits rather than sweatpants.

---

*EDS. NOTE —"And you, Brutus?" In Shakespeare's play *Julius Caesar,* Caesar asks
this question when he sees Brutus, whom he has believed to be his friend, among the
conspirators who are stabbing him.

But I'm a writer. Normally, I get up, get the kid off to school, and sit at my computer in my pajamas until four in the afternoon. When I answer the phone, the caller thinks I'm wearing a suit (though the UPS man knows better).

But facades can be destructive because they are used to seduce others 11
into an illusion. For instance, I recently realized that a former friend was a liar. He presented himself with all the right looks and the right words and offered lots of new consciousness theories, fabulous books to read, and fascinating insights. Then I did some business with him, and the time came for him to pay me. He turned out to be all talk and no walk. I heard a plethora of reasonable excuses, including in-depth descriptions of the big break around the corner. In six months of work, I saw less than a hundred bucks. When I confronted him, he raised both eyebrows and tried to convince me that I'd heard him wrong, that he'd made no commitment to me. A simple investigation into his past revealed a crowded graveyard of disenchanted former friends.

IGNORING THE PLAIN FACTS

> Well, you must understand that Father Porter is only
> human. . . .
> — A Massachusetts priest

In the '60s, the Catholic Church in Massachusetts began hearing com- 12
plaints that Father James Porter was sexually molesting children. Rather than relieving him of his duties, the ecclesiastical authorities simply moved him from one parish to another between 1960 and 1967, actually providing him with a fresh supply of unsuspecting families and innocent children to abuse. After treatment in 1967 for pedophilia, he went back to work, this time in Minnesota. The new diocese was aware of Father Porter's obsession with children, but they needed priests and recklessly believed treatment had cured him. More children were abused until he was relieved of his duties a year later. By his own admission, Porter may have abused as many as a hundred children.

Ignoring the facts may not in and of itself be a form of lying, but 13
consider the context of this situation. If a lie is *a false action done with the intent to deceive,* then the Catholic Church's conscious covering for Porter created irreparable consequences. The church became a co-perpetrator with Porter.

DEFLECTING

> When you have no basis for an argument, abuse the plaintiff.
> — Cicero

I've discovered that I can keep anyone from seeing the true me by 14
being selectively blatant. I set a precedent of being up-front about intimate

issues, but I never bring up the things I truly want to hide; I just let people assume I'm revealing everything. It's an effective way of hiding.

Any good liar knows that the way to perpetuate an untruth is to 15 deflect attention from it. When Clarence Thomas exploded with accusations that the Senate hearings were a "high-tech lynching," he simply switched the focus from a highly charged subject to a radioactive subject. Rather than defending himself, he took the offensive and accused the country of racism. It was a brilliant maneuver. Racism is now politically incorrect in official circles — unlike sexual harassment, which still rewards those who can get away with it.

Some of the most skillful deflectors are passive-aggressive people 16 who, when accused of inappropriate behavior, refuse to respond to the accusations. This you-don't-exist stance infuriates the accuser, who, understandably, screams something obscene out of frustration. The trap is sprung and the act of deflection successful, because now the passive-aggressive person can indignantly say, "Who can talk to someone as unreasonable as you?" The real issue is forgotten and the sins of the original victim become the focus. Feeling guilty of name-calling, the victim is fully tamed and crawls into a hole, ashamed. I have watched this fighting technique work thousands of times in disputes between men and women, and what I've learned is that the real culprit is not necessarily the one who swears the loudest.

OMISSION

The cruelest lies are often told in silence.
— R. L. STEVENSON

Omission involves telling most of the truth minus one or two key facts 17 whose absence changes the story completely. You break a pair of glasses that are guaranteed under normal use and get a new pair, without mentioning that the first pair broke during a rowdy game of basketball. Who hasn't tried something like that? But what about omission of information that could make a difference in how a person lives his or her life?

For instance, one day I found out that rabbinical legends tell of another 18 woman in the Garden of Eden before Eve. I was stunned. The omission of the Sumerian goddess Lilith from Genesis — as well as her demonization by ancient misogynists as an embodiment of female evil — felt like spiritual robbery. I felt like I'd just found out my mother was really my stepmother. To take seriously the tradition that Adam was created out of the same mud as his equal counterpart, Lilith, redefines all of Judeo-Christian history.

Some renegade Catholic feminists introduced me to a view of Lilith 19 that had been suppressed during the many centuries when this strong goddess was seen only as a spirit of evil. Lilith was a proud goddess who defied Adam's need to control her, attempted negotiations, and when this failed, said adios and left the Garden of Eden.

This omission of Lilith from the Bible was a patriarchal strategy to   20
keep women weak. Omitting the strong-woman archetype of Lilith from
Western religions and starting the story with Eve the Rib has helped keep
Christian and Jewish women believing they were the lesser sex for thousands of years.

STEREOTYPES AND CLICHÉS

> Where opinion does not exist, the status quo becomes stereo-
> typed and all originality is discouraged.
> — BERTRAND RUSSELL

Stereotype and cliché serve a purpose as a form of shorthand. Our   21
need for vast amounts of information in nanoseconds has made the stereotype vital to modern communication. Unfortunately, it often shuts down
original thinking, giving those hungry for the truth a candy bar of misinformation instead of a balanced meal. The stereotype explains a situation
with just enough truth to seem unquestionable.

All the "isms"— racism, sexism, ageism, et al. — are founded on and   22
fueled by the stereotype and the cliché, which are lies of exaggeration,
omission, and ignorance. They are always dangerous. They take a single
tree and make it a landscape. They destroy curiosity. They close minds
and separate people. The single mother on welfare is assumed to be cheating. Any black male could tell you how much of his identity is obliterated
daily by stereotypes. Fat people, ugly people, beautiful people, old
people, large-breasted women, short men, the mentally ill, and the homeless all could tell you how much more they are like us than we want to
think. I once admitted to a group of people that I had a mouth like a truck
driver. Much to my surprise, a man stood up and said, "I'm a truck driver,
and I never cuss." Needless to say, I was humbled.

GROUPTHINK

> Who is more foolish, the child afraid of the dark, or the man
> afraid of the light?
> — MAURICE FREEHILL

Irving Janis, in *Victims of GroupThink,* defines this sort of lie as a psy-   23
chological phenomenon within decision-making groups in which loyalty
to the group has become more important than any other value, with the
result that dissent and the appraisal of alternatives are suppressed. If
you've ever worked on a committee or in a corporation, you've encountered groupthink. It requires a combination of other forms of lying —
ignoring facts, selective memory, omission, and denial, to name a few.

The textbook example of groupthink came on December 7, 1941. From   24
as early as the fall of 1941, the warnings came in, one after another, that

Japan was preparing for a massive military operation. The Navy command in Hawaii assumed Pearl Harbor was invulnerable — the Japanese weren't stupid enough to attack the United States' most important base. On the other hand, racist stereotypes said the Japanese weren't smart enough to invent a torpedo effective in less than 60 feet of water (the fleet was docked in 30 feet); after all, U.S. technology hadn't been able to do it.

On Friday, December 5, normal weekend leave was granted to all the   25
commanders at Pearl Harbor, even though the Japanese consulate in Hawaii was busy burning papers. Within the tight, good-ole-boy cohesiveness of the U.S. command in Hawaii, the myth of invulnerability stayed well entrenched. No one in the group considered the alternatives. The rest is history.

OUT-AND-OUT LIES

> The only form of lying that is beyond reproach is lying for its own sake.
> — OSCAR WILDE

Of all the ways to lie, I like this one the best, probably because I get   26
tired of trying to figure out the real meanings behind things. At least I can trust the bald-faced lie. I once asked my five-year-old nephew, "Who broke the fence?" (I had seen him do it.) He answered, "The murderers." Who could argue?

At least when this sort of lie is told it can be easily confronted. As the   27
person who is lied to, I know where I stand. The bald-faced lie doesn't toy with my perceptions — it argues with them. It doesn't try to refashion reality, it tries to refute it. *Read my lips. . . .* No sleight of hand. No guessing. If this were the only form of lying, there would be no such thing as floating anxiety or the adult-children of alcoholics movement.

DISMISSAL

> Pay no attention to that man behind the curtain! I am the Great Oz!
> — THE WIZARD OF OZ

Dismissal is perhaps the slipperiest of all lies. Dismissing feelings,   28
perceptions, or even the raw facts of a situation ranks as a kind of lie that can do as much damage to a person as any other kind of lie.

The roots of many mental disorders can be traced back to the dis-   29
missal of reality. Imagine that a person is told from the time she is a tot that her perceptions are inaccurate. *"Mommy, I'm scared."* "No, you're not, darling." *"I don't like that man next door, he makes me feel icky."* "Johnny, that's a terrible thing to say, of course you like him. You go over there right now and be nice to him."

I've often mused over the idea that madness is actually a sane reaction 30 to an insane world. Psychologist R. D. Laing supports this hypothesis in *Sanity, Madness & the Family,* an account of his investigations into families of schizophrenics. The common thread that ran through all of the families he studied was a deliberate, staunch dismissal of the patient's perceptions from a very early age. Each of the patients started out with an accurate grasp of reality, which, through meticulous and methodical dismissal, was demolished until the only reality the patient could trust was catatonia.

Dismissal runs the gamut. Mild dismissal can be quite handy for for- 31 giving the foibles of others in our day-to-day lives. Toddlers who have just learned to manipulate their parents' attention sometimes are dismissed out of necessity. Absolute attention from the parents would require so much energy that no one would get to eat dinner. But we must be careful and attentive about how far we take our "necessary" dismissals. Dis- missal is a dangerous tool, because it's nothing less than a lie.

DELUSION

> We lie loudest when we lie to ourselves.
> — ERIC HOFFER

I could write the book on this one. Delusion, a cousin of dismissal, is 32 the tendency to see excuses as facts. It's a powerful lying tool because it fil- ters out information that contradicts what we want to believe. Alcoholics who believe that the problems in their lives are legitimate reasons for drinking rather than results of the drinking offer the classic example of deluded thinking. Delusion uses the mind's ability to see things in myriad ways to support what it wants to be the truth.

But delusion is also a survival mechanism we all use. If we were to 33 fully contemplate the consequences of our stockpiles of nuclear weapons or global warming, we could hardly function on a day-to-day level. We don't want to incorporate that much reality into our lives because to do so would be paralyzing.

Delusion acts as an adhesive to keep the status quo intact. It shame- 34 lessly employs dismissal, omission, and amnesia, among other sorts of lies. Its most cunning defense is that it cannot see itself.

> The liar's punishment . . . is that he cannot believe anyone else.
> — GEORGE BERNARD SHAW

These are only a few of the ways we lie. Or are lied to. As I said earlier, 35 it's not easy to entirely eliminate lies from our lives. No matter how pious we may try to be, we will still embellish, hedge, and omit to lubricate the daily machinery of living. But there is a world of difference between telling functional lies and living a lie. Martin Buber* once said, "The lie is

---

*EDS. NOTE — Austrian-born Judaic philosopher (1878–1965).

the spirit committing treason against itself." Our acceptance of lies becomes a cultural cancer that eventually shrouds and reorders reality until moral garbage becomes as invisible to us as water is to a fish.

How much do we tolerate before we become sick and tired of being 36 sick and tired? When will we stand up and declare our *right* to trust? When do we stop accepting that the real truth is in the fine print? Whose lips do we read this year when we vote for president? When will we stop being so reticent about making judgments? When do we stop turning over our personal power and responsibility to liars?

Maybe if I don't tell the bank the check's in the mail I'll be less tolerant 37 of the lies told me every day. A country song I once heard said it all for me: "You've got to stand for something or you'll fall for anything."

• • •

COMPREHENSION

1. List and define each of the ten kinds of lies Ericsson identifies.

2. Why, in Ericsson's view, is each kind of lie necessary?

3. According to Ericsson, what is the danger of each kind of lie?

4. Why does Ericsson like "out-and-out lies" (26–27) best?

5. Why is dismissal the "slipperiest of all lies" (28)?

PURPOSE AND AUDIENCE

1. Is Ericsson's thesis simply that "there are many, many ways to tell a lie" (7)? Or is she defending — or attacking — the process of lying? Try to state her thesis in a single sentence.

2. Do you think Ericsson's choice of examples reveals a political bias? If so, do you think she expects her intended audience to share this bias? Explain.

STYLE AND STRUCTURE

1. Despite the seriousness of her subject matter, Ericsson's essay is informal; her opening paragraphs are especially personal and breezy. Why do you think she uses this kind of opening? Do you think her decision makes sense? Why or why not?

2. Ericsson introduces each category of lie with a quotation. What function do these quotations serve? Would the essay be more or less effective without them? Explain your conclusion.

3. In addition to a heading and a quotation, what other elements does Ericsson include in her discussion of each kind of lie? Are all the discussions parallel — that is, does each include *all* the standard elements, and *only* those elements? If not, do you think this lack of balance is a problem? Explain.

4. What, if anything, determines the order in which Ericsson arranges her categories? Should any category be relocated? Explain.

5. Throughout her essay, Ericsson uses **rhetorical questions.** Why do you suppose she uses this stylistic device?

6. Ericsson occasionally cites the views of experts. Why does she do so? If she wished to cite additional experts, what professional backgrounds or fields of study do you think they should represent? Why?

7. In paragraph 29, Ericsson says, "Imagine that a person is told from the time she is a tot. . . ." Does she use *she* in similar contexts elsewhere in the essay? Do you find the feminine form of the personal pronoun appropriate or distracting? Explain.

8. Paragraphs 35–37 constitute Ericsson's conclusion. How does this conclusion parallel the essay's introduction in terms of style, structure, and content?

VOCABULARY PROJECTS

1. Define each of the following words as it is used in this selection.

travails (4)	deflectors (16)	staunch (30)
hedging (5)	passive-aggressive (16)	catatonia (30)
pittance (9)	misogynists (18)	gamut (31)
facades (10)	counterpart (18)	foibles (31)
plethora (11)	archetype (20)	reticent (36)
pedophilia (12)	nanoseconds (21)	
blatant (14)	obliterated (22)	

2. Ericsson uses many **colloquialisms** in this essay — for example, "I could write the book on this one" (32). Identify as many of these expressions as you can. Why do you think she uses colloquialisms instead of more formal expressions? Do they have a positive or negative effect on your reaction to her ideas? Explain.

JOURNAL ENTRY

In paragraph 3, Ericsson says, "We lie. We all do." Later in the paragraph she comments, "Sure I lie, but it doesn't hurt anything. Or does it?" Answer her question.

WRITING WORKSHOP

1. Choose three or four of Ericsson's categories, and write a classification-and-division essay called "The Ways I Lie." Base your essay on personal experience, and include an explicit thesis statement that defends these lies — or is sharply critical of their use.

2. In paragraph 22, Ericsson condemns stereotypes. Write a classification-and-division essay with the following thesis statement: "Stereotypes are sometimes inaccurate, often negative, and always dangerous." In your

essay, consider the stereotypes applied to four of the following groups: the disabled, the overweight, the elderly, teenagers, welfare recipients, housewives, immigrants.

3. Using the thesis suggested in question 2, write a classification-and-division essay that considers the stereotype applied to four of the following occupations: police officers, librarians, used-car dealers, flight attendants, lawyers, construction workers, rock musicians.

COMBINING THE PATTERNS

A dictionary **definition** is a familiar — even tired — strategy for an essay's introduction. Would you advise Ericsson to delete the definition in paragraph 6 for this reason, or do you believe it is necessary? Explain.

THEMATIC CONNECTIONS

- "'What's in a Name?'" (page 5)
- "Thirty-Eight Who Saw Murder Didn't Call the Police" (page 99)
- "The Lottery" (page 255)

FLANNERY O'CONNOR

Flannery O'Connor (1925–1964) was born in Savannah and lived with her mother in the small town of Milledgeville, Georgia, for most of her life. She graduated from Georgia State College for Women in 1945 and received an M.F.A. in writing from the University of Iowa in 1947. In spite of suffering from the debilitating effects of lupus, a degenerative disease, O'Connor was able to write, travel, and lecture until shortly before her death at the age of thirty-nine. She wrote two novels, *Wise Blood* (1952) and *The Violent Bear It Away* (1960), and many short stories, which are collected in *A Good Man Is Hard to Find* (1955) and *Everything That Rises Must Converge* (1965), as well as her *Complete Stories* (1971).

"Revelation," one of her final works, was written as O'Connor's health was quickly declining. Set mostly in a doctor's waiting room, the story was, O'Connor wrote to a friend, her "reward" for all the time she had spent in such a setting herself. The story occurs at a time when the Civil Rights movement had begun to make significant gains in the equal treatment of African Americans, who had endured a century of discrimination since the abolition of slavery. But as the characters here suggest, a deeply entrenched racism still marked the attitudes of many whites, particularly rural southerners. In interpreting the story, keep in mind that O'Connor was a deeply religious Catholic who considered profoundly the Christian concept of grace, which awakens the soul to God's true call.

Revelation

The doctor's waiting room, which was very small, was almost full when the Turpins entered and Mrs. Turpin, who was very large, made it look even smaller by her presence. She stood looming at the head of the magazine table set in the center of it, a living demonstration that the room was inadequate and ridiculous. Her little bright black eyes took in all the patients as she sized up the seating situation. There was one vacant chair and a place on the sofa occupied by a blond child in a dirty blue romper who should have been told to move over and make room for the lady. He was five or six, but Mrs. Turpin saw at once that no one was going to tell him to move over. He was slumped down in the seat, his arms idle at his sides and his eyes idle in his head; his nose ran unchecked.

Mrs. Turpin put a firm hand on Claud's shoulder and said in a voice that included everyone that wanted to listen, "Claud, you sit in that chair there," and gave him a push down into the vacant one. Claud was florid and bald and sturdy, somewhat shorter than Mrs. Turpin, but he sat down as if he were accustomed to doing what she told him to.

Mrs. Turpin remained standing. The only man in the room besides Claud was a lean stringy old fellow with a rusty hand spread out on each knee, whose eyes were closed as if he were asleep or dead or pretending to be so as not to get up and offer her his seat. Her gaze settled agreeably on a well-dressed grey-haired lady whose eyes met hers and whose expression said: if that child belonged to me, he would have some manners and move over — there's plenty of room there for you and him too.

Claud looked up with a sigh and made as if to rise.   4

"Sit down," Mrs. Turpin said. "You know you're not supposed to stand on that leg. He has an ulcer on his leg." she explained.   5

Claud lifted his foot onto the magazine table and rolled his trouser leg up to reveal a purple swelling on a plump marble-white calf.   6

"My!" the pleasant lady said. "How did you do that?"   7

"A cow kicked him," Mrs. Turpin said.   8

"Goodness!" said the lady.   9

Claud rolled his trouser leg down.   10

"Maybe the little boy would move over," the lady suggested, but the child did not stir.   11

"Somebody will be leaving in a minute," Mrs. Turpin said. She could not understand why a doctor — with as much money as they made charging five dollars a day just to stick their head in the hospital door and look at you — couldn't afford a decent-sized waiting room. This one was hardly bigger than a garage. The table was cluttered with limp-looking magazines and at one end of it there was a big green glass ash tray full of cigaret butts and cotton wads with little blood spots on them. If she had anything to do with the running of the place, that would have been emptied every so often. There were no chairs against the wall at the head of the room. It had a rectangular-shaped panel in it that permitted a view of the office where the nurse came and went and the secretary listened to the radio. A plastic fern in a gold pot sat in the opening and trailed its fronds down almost to the floor. The radio was softly playing gospel music.   12

Just then the inner door opened and a nurse with the highest stack of yellow hair Mrs. Turpin had ever seen put her face in the crack and called for the next patient. The woman sitting beside Claud grasped the two arms of her chair and hoisted herself up; she pulled her dress free from her legs and lumbered through the door where the nurse had disappeared.   13

Mrs. Turpin eased into the vacant chair, which held her tight as a corset. "I wish I could reduce," she said, and rolled her eyes and gave a comic sigh.   14

"Oh, *you* aren't fat," the stylish lady said.   15

"Ooooo I am too," Mrs. Turpin said. "Claud he eats all he wants to and never weighs over one hundred and seventy-five pounds, but me I just look at something good to eat and I gain weight," and her stomach and shoulders shook with laughter. "You can eat all you want to, can't you, Claud?" she asked turning to him.   16

Claud only grinned.   17

"Well, as long as you have such a good disposition," the stylish lady said, "I don't think it makes a bit of difference what size you are. You just can't beat a good disposition."   18

Next to her was a fat girl of eighteen or nineteen, scowling into a thick   19
blue book which Mrs. Turpin saw was titled *Human Development*. The girl
raised her head and directed her scowl at Mrs. Turpin as if she did not like
her looks. She appeared annoyed that anyone should speak while she
tried to read. The poor girl's face was blue with acne and Mrs. Turpin
thought how pitiful it was to have a face like that at that age. She gave the
girl a friendly smile but the girl only scowled the harder. Mrs. Turpin herself was fat but she had always had good skin, and, though she was forty-
seven years old, there was not a wrinkle in her face except around her eyes
from laughing too much.

Next to the ugly girl was the child, still in exactly the same position,   20
and next to him was a thin leathery old woman in a cotton print dress. She
and Claud had three sacks of chicken feed in their pump house that were
in the same print. She had seen from the first that the child belonged with
the old woman. She could tell by the way they sat — kind of vacant and
white-trashy, as if they would sit there until Doomsday if nobody called
and told them to get up. And at right angles but next to the well-dressed
pleasant lady was a lank-faced woman who was certainly the child's
mother. She had on a yellow sweat shirt and wine-colored slacks, both
gritty-looking, and the rims of her lips were stained with snuff. Her dirty
yellow hair was tied behind with a piece of red paper ribbon. Worse than
niggers any day, Mrs. Turpin thought.

The gospel hymn playing was, "When I looked up and He looked   21
down," and Mrs. Turpin, who knew it, supplied the last line mentally,
"And wona these days I know I'll we-eara crown."

Without appearing to, Mrs. Turpin always noticed people's feet. The   22
well-dressed lady had on red and grey suede shoes to match her dress.
Mrs. Turpin had on her good black patent leather pumps. The ugly girl
had on Girl Scout shoes and heavy socks. The old woman had on tennis
shoes and the white-trashy mother had on what appeared to be bedroom
slippers, black straw with gold braid threaded through them — exactly
what you would have expected her to have on.

Sometimes at night when she couldn't go to sleep, Mrs. Turpin would   23
occupy herself with the question of who she would have chosen to be if
she couldn't have been herself. If Jesus had said to her before he made
her, "There's only two places available for you. You can either be a nigger
or white-trash," what would she have said? "Please, Jesus, please," she
would have said, "just let me wait until there's another place available,"
and he would have said, "No, you have to go right now and I have only
those two places so make up your mind." She would have wiggled and
squirmed and begged and pleaded but it would have been no use and
finally she would have said, "All right, make me a nigger then — but that
don't mean a trashy one." And he would have made her a neat clean
respectable Negro woman, herself but black.

Next to the child's mother was a red-headed youngish woman, read-   24
ing one of the magazines and working a piece of chewing gum, hell for

leather, as Claud would say. Mrs. Turpin could not see the woman's feet. She was not white-trash, just common. Sometimes Mrs. Turpin occupied herself at night naming the classes of people. On the bottom of the heap were most colored people, not the kind she would have been if she had been one, but most of them; then next to them — not above, just away from — were the white-trash; then above them were the home-owners, and above them the home-and-land owners, to which she and Claud belonged. Above she and Claud were people with a lot of money and much bigger houses and much more land. But here the complexity of it would begin to bear in on her, for some of the people with a lot of money were common and ought to be below she and Claud and some of the people who had good blood had lost their money and had to rent and then there were colored people who owned their homes and land as well. There was a colored dentist in town who had two red Lincolns and a swimming pool and a farm with registered white-face cattle on it. Usually by the time she had fallen asleep all the classes of people were moiling and roiling around in her head, and she would dream they were all crammed in together in a box car, being ridden off to be put in a gas oven.

"That's a beautiful clock," she said and nodded to her right. It was a   25
big wall clock, the face encased in a brass sunburst.

"Yes, it's very pretty," the stylish lady said agreeably. "And right on   26
the dot too," she added, glancing at her watch.

The ugly girl beside her cast an eye upward at the clock, smirked, then   27
looked directly at Mrs. Turpin and smirked again. Then she returned her eyes to her book. She was obviously the lady's daughter because, although they didn't look anything alike as to disposition, they both had the same shape of face and same blue eyes. On the lady they sparkled pleasantly but in the girl's seared face they appeared alternately to smolder and to blaze.

What if Jesus had said, "All right, you can be white-trash or a nigger or   28
ugly!"

Mrs. Turpin felt an awful pity for the girl, though she thought it was   29
one thing to be ugly and another to act ugly.

The woman with the snuff-stained lips turned around in her chair and   30
looked up at the clock. Then she turned back and appeared to look a little to the side of Mrs. Turpin. There was a cast in one of her eyes. "You want to know wher you can get one of themther clocks?" she asked in a loud voice.

"No, I already have a nice clock," Mrs. Turpin said. Once somebody   31
like her got a leg in the conversation, she would be all over it.

"You can get you one with green stamps," the woman said. "That's   32
most likely wher he got hisn. Save you up enough, you can get you most anythang. I got me some joo'ry."

Ought to have got you a wash rag and some soap, Mrs. Turpin   33
thought.

"I get contour sheets with mine," the pleasant lady said.   34

The daughter slammed her book shut. She looked straight in front of   35
her, directly through Mrs. Turpin and on through the yellow curtain and
the plate glass window which made the wall behind her. The girl's eyes
seemed lit all of a sudden with a peculiar light, an unnatural light like
night road signs give. Mrs. Turpin turned her head to see if there was anything going on outside that she should see, but she could not see anything.
Figures passing cast only a pale shadow through the curtain. There was no
reason the girl should single her out for her ugly looks.

"Miss Finley," the nurse said, cracking the door. The gum-chewing   36
woman got up and passed in front of her and Claud and went into the
office. She had on red high-heeled shoes.

Directly across the table, the ugly girl's eyes were fixed on Mrs. Turpin   37
as if she had some very special reason for disliking her.

"This is wonderful weather, isn't it?" the girl's mother said.   38

"It's good weather for cotton if you can get the niggers to pick it," Mrs. 39
Turpin said, "but niggers don't want to pick cotton any more. You can't
get the white folks to pick it and now you can't get the niggers — because
they got to be right up there with the white folks."

"They gonna *try* anyways," the white-trash woman said, leaning for-   40
ward.

"Do you have one of those cotton-picking machines?" the pleasant   41
lady asked.

"No," Mrs. Turpin said, "they leave half the cotton in the field. We   42
don't have much cotton anyway. If you want to make it farming now, you
have to have a little of everything. We got a couple of acres of cotton and a
few hogs and chickens and just enough white-face that Claud can look
after them himself."

"One thang I don't want," the white-trash woman said, wiping her   43
mouth with the back of her hand. "Hogs. Nasty stinking things, a-gruntin
and a-rootin all over the place."

Mrs. Turpin gave her the merest edge of her attention. "Our hogs are   44
not dirty and they don't stink," she said. "They're cleaner than some children I've seen. Their feet never touch the ground. We have a pig parlor —
that's where you raise them on concrete," she explained to the pleasant
lady, "and Claud scoots them down with the hose every afternoon and
washes off the floor." Cleaner by far than that child right there, she
thought. Poor nasty little thing. He had not moved except to put the
thumb of his dirty hand into his mouth.

The woman turned her face away from Mrs. Turpin. "I know I   45
wouldn't scoot down no hog with no hose," she said to the wall.

You wouldn't have no hog to scoot down, Mrs. Turpin said to herself.   46

"A-gruntin and a-rootin and a-groanin," the woman muttered.   47

"We got a little of everything," Mrs. Turpin said to the pleasant lady.   48
"It's no use in having more than you can handle yourself with help like it
is. We found enough niggers to pick our cotton last year but Claud he has
to go after them and take them home again in the evening. They can't

walk that half a mile. No they can't. I tell you," she said and laughed merrily, "I sure am tired of buttering up niggers, but you got to love em if you want em to work for you. When they come in the morning, I run out and I say, 'Hi, yawl this morning?' and when Claud drives them off to the field I just wave to beat the band and they just wave back." And she waved her hand rapidly to illustrate.

"Like you read out of the same book," the lady said, showing she   49
understood perfectly.

"Child, yes," Mrs. Turpin said. "And when they come in from the   50
field, I run out with a bucket of icewater. That's the way it's going to be from now on," she said. "You may as well face it."

"One thang I know," the white-trash woman said. "Two thangs I ain't   51
going to do: love no niggers or scoot down no hog with no hose." And she let out a bark of contempt.

The look that Mrs. Turpin and the pleasant lady exchanged indicated   52
they both understood that you had to *have* certain things before you could *know* certain things. But every time Mrs. Turpin exchanged a look with the lady, she was aware that the ugly girl's peculiar eyes were still on her, and she had trouble bringing her attention back to the conversation.

"When you got something," she said, "you got to look after it." And   53
when you ain't got a thing but breath and britches, she added to herself, you can afford to come to town every morning and just sit on the Court House coping and spit.

A grotesque revolving shadow passed across the curtain behind her   54
and was thrown palely on the opposite wall. Then a bicycle clattered down against the outside of the building. The door opened and a colored boy glided in with a tray from the drug store. It had two large red and white paper cups on it with tops on them. He was a tall, very black boy in discolored white pants and a green nylon shirt. He was chewing gum slowly, as if to music. He set the tray down in the office opening next to the fern and stuck his head through to look for the secretary. She was not in there. He rested his arms on the ledge and waited, his narrow bottom stuck out, swaying slowing to the left and right. He raised a hand over his head and scratched the base of his skull.

"You see that button there, boy?" Mrs. Turpin said. "You can punch   55
that and she'll come. She's probably in the back somewhere."

"Is that right?" the boy said agreeably, as if he had never seen the but-   56
ton before. He leaned to the right and put his finger on it. "She sometime out," he said and twisted around to face his audience, his elbows behind him on the counter. The nurse appeared and he twisted back again. She handed him a dollar and he rooted in his pocket and made the change and counted it out to her. She gave him fifteen cents for a tip and he went out with the empty tray. The heavy door swung to slowly and closed at length with the sound of suction. For a moment no one spoke.

"They ought to send all them niggers back to Africa," the white-trash   57
woman said. "That's wher they come from in the first place."

"Oh, I couldn't do without my good colored friends," the pleasant   58
lady said.

"There's a heap of things worse than a nigger," Mrs. Turpin agreed.   59
"It's all kinds of them just like it's all kinds of us."

"Yes, and it takes all kinds to make the world go round," the lady said   60
in her musical voice.

As she said it, the raw-complexioned girl snapped her teeth together.   61
Her lower lip turned downwards and inside out, revealing the pale pink
inside of her mouth. After a second it rolled back up. It was the ugliest face
Mrs. Turpin had ever seen anyone make and for a moment she was certain
that the girl had made it at her. She was looking at her as if she had known
and disliked her all her life — all of Mrs. Turpin's life, it seemed too, not
just all the girl's life. Why, girl, I don't even know you, Mrs. Turpin said
silently.

She forced her attention back to the discussion. "It wouldn't be practi-   62
cal to send them back to Africa," she said. "They wouldn't want to go.
They got it too good here."

"Wouldn't be what they wanted — if I had anythang to do with it,"   63
the woman said.

"It wouldn't be a way in the world you could get all the niggers back   64
over there," Mrs. Turpin said. "They'd be hiding out and lying down and
turning sick on you and wailing and hollering and raring and pitching. It
wouldn't be a way in the world to get them over there."

"They got over here," the trashy woman said. "Get back like they got   65
over."

"It wasn't so many of them then," Mrs. Turpin explained.   66

The woman looked at Mrs. Turpin as if here was an idiot indeed   67
but Mrs. Turpin was not bothered by the look, considering where it came
from.

"Nooo," she said, "they're going to stay here where they can go to   68
New York and marry white folks and improve their color. That's what
they all want to do, every one of them, improve their color."

"You know what comes of that, don't you?" Claud asked.   69

"No, Claud, what?" Mrs. Turpin said.   70

Claud's eyes twinkled. "White-faced niggers," he said with never a   71
smile.

Everybody in the office laughed except the white-trash and the ugly   72
girl. The girl gripped the book in her lap with white fingers. The trashy
woman looked around her from face to face as if she thought they were all
idiots. The old woman in the feed sack dress continued to gaze expres-
sionless across the floor at the high-top shoes of the man opposite her, the
one who had been pretending to be asleep when the Turpins came in. He
was laughing heartily, his hands still spread out on his knees. The child
had fallen to the side and was lying now almost face down in the old
woman's lap.

While they recovered from their laughter, the nasal chorus on the   73
radio kept the room from silence.

You go to blank blank
And I'll go to mine
But we'll all blank along
To-geth-ther,
And all along the blank
We'll hep each other out
Smile-ling in any kind of
Weath-ther!

Mrs. Turpin didn't catch every word but she caught enough to agree with the spirit of the song and it turned her thoughts sober. To help anybody out that needed it was her philosophy of life. She never spared herself when she found somebody in need, whether they were white or black, trash or decent. And of all she had to be thankful for, she was most thankful that this was so. If Jesus had said, "You can be high society and have all the money you want and be thin and svelte-like, but you can't be a good woman with it," she would have had to say, "Well don't make me that then. Make me a good woman and it don't matter what else, how fat or how ugly or how poor!" Her heart rose. He had not made her a nigger or white-trash or ugly! He had made her herself and given her a little of everything. Jesus, thank you! she said. Thank you thank you thank you! Whenever she counted her blessings she felt as buoyant as if she weighed one hundred and twenty-five pounds instead of one hundred and eighty.

"What's wrong with your little boy?" the pleasant lady asked the white-trashy woman. 74

"He has an ulcer," the woman said proudly. "He ain't give me a minute's peace since he was born. Him and her are just alike," she said, nodding at the old woman, who was running her leathery fingers through the child's pale hair. "Look like I can't get nothing down them two but Co' Cola and candy." 75

That's all you try to get down em, Mrs. Turpin said to herself. Too lazy to light the fire. There was nothing you could tell her about people like them that she didn't know already. And it was not just that they didn't have anything. Because if you gave them everything, in two weeks it would all be broken or filthy or they would have chopped it up for lightwood. She knew all this from her own experience. Help them you must, but help them you couldn't. 76

All at once the ugly girl turned her lips inside out again. Her eyes were fixed like two drills on Mrs. Turpin. This time there was no mistaking that there was something urgent behind them. 77

Girl, Mrs. Turpin explained silently, I haven't done a thing to you! The girl might be confusing her with somebody else. There was no need to sit by and let herself be intimidated. "You must be in college," she said boldly, looking directly at the girl. "I see you reading a book there." 78

The girl continued to stare and pointedly did not answer. 79

Her mother blushed at this rudeness. "The lady asked you a question, Mary Grace," she said under her breath. 80

"I have ears," Mary Grace said.   81

The poor mother blushed again. "Mary Grace goes to Wellesley   82
College," she explained. She twisted one of the buttons on her dress. "In
Massachusetts," she added with a grimace. "And in the summer she just
keeps right on studying. Just reads all the time, a real book worm. She's
done real well at Wellesley; she's taking English and Math and History
and Psychology and Social Studies," she rattled on, "and I think it's too
much. I think she ought to get out and have fun."

The girl looked as if she would like to hurl them all through the plate   83
glass window.

"Way up north," Mrs. Turpin murmured and thought, well, it hasn't   84
done much for her manners.

"I'd almost rather to have him sick," the white-trash woman said,   85
wrenching the attention back to herself. "He's so mean when he ain't.
Look like some children just take natural to meanness. It's some gets bad
when they get sick but he was the opposite. Took sick and turned good.
He don't give me no trouble now. It's me waitin to see the doctor," she said.

If I was going to send anybody back to Africa, Mrs. Turpin thought, it   86
would be your kind, woman. "Yes, indeed," she said aloud, but looking
up at the ceiling, "it's a heap of things worse than a nigger." And dirtier
than a hog, she added to herself.

"I think people with bad dispositions are more to be pitied than any-   87
one on earth," the pleasant lady said in a voice that was decidedly thin.

"I thank the Lord he has blessed me with a good one," Mrs. Turpin   88
said. "The day has never dawned that I couldn't find something to laugh at."

"Not since she married me anyways," Claud said with a comical   89
straight face.

Everybody laughed except the girl and the white-trash.   90

Mrs. Turpin's stomach shook. "He's such a caution," she said, "that I   91
can't help but laugh at him."

The girl made a loud ugly noise through her teeth.   92

Her mother's mouth grew thin and tight. "I think the worst thing in   93
the world," she said, "is an ungrateful person. To have everything and not
appreciate it. I know a girl," she said, "who has parents who would give
her anything, a little brother who loves her dearly, who is getting a good
education, who wears the best clothes, but who can never say a kind word
to anyone, who never smiles, who just criticizes and complains all day
long."

"Is she too old to paddle?" Claud asked.   94

The girl's face was almost purple.   95

"Yes," the lady said, "I'm afraid there's nothing to do but leave her to   96
her folly. Some day she'll wake up and it'll be too late."

"It never hurt anyone to smile," Mrs. Turpin said. "It just makes you   97
feel better all over."

"Of course," the lady said sadly, "but there are just some people you   98
can't tell anything to. They can't take criticism."

"If it's one thing I am," Mrs. Turpin said with feeling, "it's grateful.   99
When I think who all I could have been besides myself and what all I got, a
little of everything, and a good disposition besides, I just feel like shouting, 'Thank you, Jesus, for making everything the way it is!' It could have
been different!" For one thing, somebody else could have got Claud. At
the thought of this, she was flooded with gratitude and a terrible pang of
joy ran through her. "Oh thank you, Jesus, Jesus, thank you!" she cried
aloud.

The book struck her directly over her left eye. It struck almost at   100
the same instant that she realized the girl was about to hurl it. Before
she could utter a sound, the raw face came crashing across the table
toward her, howling. The girl's fingers sank like claws into the soft flesh of
her neck. She heard the mother cry out and Claud shout, "Whoa!" There
was an instant when she was certain that she was about to be in an earth-
quake.

All at once her vision narrowed and she saw everything as if it were   101
happening in a small room far away, or as if she were looking at it through
the wrong end of a telescope. Claud's face crumpled and fell out of sight.
The nurse ran in, then out, then in again. Then the gangling figure of the
doctor rushed out of the inner door. Magazines flew this way and that as
the table turned over. The girl fell with a thud and Mrs. Turpin's vision
suddenly reversed itself and she saw everything large instead of small.
The eyes of the white-trashy woman were staring hugely at the floor.
There the girl, held down on one side by the nurse and on the other by her
mother, was wrenching and turning in their gasp. The doctor was kneeling astride her, trying to hold her arm down. He managed after a second
to sink a long needle into it.

Mrs. Turpin felt entirely hollow except for her heart which swung   102
from side to side as if it were agitated in a great empty drum of flesh.

"Somebody that's not busy call for the ambulance," the doctor said in   103
the off-hand voice young doctors adopt for terrible occasions.

Mrs. Turpin could not have moved a finger. The old man who had   104
been sitting next to her skipped nimbly into the office and made the call,
for the secretary still seemed to be gone.

"Claud!" Mrs. Turpin called.   105

He was not in his chair. She knew she must jump up and find him but   106
she felt like someone trying to catch a train in a dream, when everything
moves in slow motion and the faster you try to run the slower you go.

"Here I am," a suffocated voice, very unlike Claud's, said.   107

He was doubled up in the corner on the floor, pale as paper, holding   108
his leg. She wanted to get up and go to him she could not move.
Instead, her gaze was drawn slowly downward to the churning face on
the floor, which she could see over the doctor's shoulder.

The girl's eyes stopped rolling and focused on her. They seemed a   109
much lighter blue than before, as if a door that had been tightly closed
behind them was now open to admit light and air.

Mrs. Turpin's head cleared and her power of motion returned. She   110
leaned forward until she was looking directly into the fierce brilliant eyes.
There was no doubt in her mind that the girl did know her, knew her in
some intense and personal way, beyond time and place and condition.
"What you got to say to me?" she asked hoarsely and held her breath,
waiting, as for a revelation.

The girl raised her head. Her gaze locked with Mrs. Turpin's. "Go   111
back to hell where you came from, you old wart hog," she whispered. Her
voice was low but clear. Her eyes burned for a moment as if she saw with
pleasure that her message had struck its target.

Mrs. Turpin sank back into her chair.   112

After a moment the girl's eyes closed and she turned her head wearily   113
to the side.

The doctor rose and handed the nurse the empty syringe. He leaned   114
over and put both hands for a moment on the mother's shoulders, which
were shaking. She was sitting on the floor, her lips pressed together, holding Mary Grace's hand in her lap. The girl's fingers were gripped like a
baby's around her thumb. "Go on to the hospital," he said. "I'll call and
make the arrangements."

"Now, let's see that neck," he said in a jovial voice to Mrs. Turpin. He   115
began to inspect her neck with his two fingers. Two little moonshaped
lines like pink fish bones were indented over her windpipe. There was the
beginning of an angry red swelling above her eye. His fingers passed over
this also.

"Let me be," she said thickly and shook him off. "See about Claud.   116
She kicked him."

"I'll see about him in a minute," he said and felt her pulse. He was a   117
thin grey-haired man, given to pleasantries. "Go home and have yourself
a vacation the rest of the day," he said and patted her on the shoulder.

Quit your pattin me, Mrs. Turpin growled to herself.   118

"And put an ice pack over that eye," he said. Then he went and squat-   119
ted down beside Claud and looked at his leg. After a moment he pulled
him up and Claud limped after him into the office.

Until the ambulance came, the only sounds in the room were the   120
tremulous moans of the girl's mother, who continued to sit on the floor.
The white-trash woman did not take her eyes off the girl. Mrs. Turpin
looked straight ahead at nothing. Presently the ambulance drew up, a
long dark shadow, behind the curtain. The attendants came in and set the
stretcher down beside the girl and lifted her expertly onto it and carried
her out. The nurse helped the mother gather up her things. The shadow of
the ambulance moved silently away and the nurse came back in the office.

"That ther girl is going to be a lunatic, ain't she?" the white-trash   121
woman asked the nurse, but the nurse kept on to the back and never
answered her.

"Yes, she's going to be a lunatic," the white-trash woman said to the   122
rest of them.

"Po' critter," the old woman murmured. The child's face was still in 123
her lap. His eyes looked idly over her knees. He had not moved during the
disturbance except to draw one leg up under him.

"I thank Gawd," the white-trash woman said fervently, "I ain't a 124
lunatic."

Claud came limping out and the Turpins went home. 125

As their pick-up truck turned into their own dirt road and made the 126
crest of the hill, Mrs. Turpin gripped the window ledge and looked out
suspiciously. The land sloped gracefully down through a field dotted with
lavender weeds and at the start of the rise their small yellow frame house,
with its little flower beds spread out around it like a fancy apron, sat
primly in its accustomed place between two giant hickory trees. She
would not have been startled to see a burnt wound between two black-
ened chimneys.

Neither of them felt like eating so they put on their house clothes and 127
lowered the shade in the bedroom and lay down, Claud with his leg on a
pillow and herself with a damp washcloth over her eye. The instant she
was flat on her back, the image of a razor-backed hog with warts on its
face and horns coming out behind its ears snorted into her head. She
moaned, a low quiet moan.

"I am not," she said tearfully, "a wart hog. From hell." But the denial 128
had no force. The girl's eyes and her words, even the tone of her voice, low
but clear, directed only to her, brooked no repudiation. She had been singled out for the message, though there was trash in the room to whom it
might justly have been applied. The full force of this fact struck her only
now. There was a woman there who was neglecting her own child but
she had been overlooked. The message had been given to Ruby Turpin,
a respectable, hard-working, church-going woman. The tears dried. Her
eyes began to burn instead with wrath.

She rose on her elbow and the washcloth fell into her hand. Claud was 129
lying on his back, snoring. She wanted to tell him what the girl had said.
At the same time, she did not wish to put the imaging of herself as a wart
hog from hell into his mind.

"Hey, Claud," she muttered and pushed his shoulder. 130

Claud opened one pale baby blue eye. 131

She looked into it warily. He did not think about anything. He just 132
went his way.

"Wha, whasit?" he said and closed the eye again. 133

"Nothing," she said. "Does your leg pain you?" 134

"Hurts like hell," Claud said. 135

"It'll quit terreckly," she said and lay back down. In a moment Claud 136
was snoring again. For the rest of the afternoon they lay there. Claud slept.
She scowled at the ceiling. Occasionally she raised her fist and made a
small stabbing motion over her chest as if she was defending her innocence to invisible guests who were like the comforters of Job, reasonable-
seeming but wrong.

About five-thirty Claud stirred. "Got to go after those niggers," he   137
sighed, not moving.

She was looking straight up as if there were unintelligible handwrit-   138
ing on the ceiling. The protuberance over her eye had turned a greenish-
blue. "Listen here," she said.

"What?"   139

"Kiss me."   140

Claud leaned over and kissed her loudly on the mouth. He pinched   141
her side and their hands interlocked. Her expression of ferocious concentration did not change. Claud got up, groaning and growling, and limped
off. She continued to study the ceiling.

She did not get up until she heard the pick-up truck coming back with   142
the Negroes. Then she rose and thrust her feet in her brown oxfords,
which she did not bother to lace, and stumped out onto the back porch
and got her red plastic bucket. She emptied a tray of ice cubes into it and
filled it half full of water and went out into the back yard. Every afternoon
after Claud brought the hands in, one of the boys helped him put out hay
and the rest waited in the back of the truck until he was ready to take them
home. The truck was parked in the shade under one of the hickory trees.

"Hi yawl this evening?" Mrs. Turpin asked grimly, appearing with the   143
bucket and the dipper. There were three women and a boy in the truck.

"Us doin nicely," the oldest woman said. "Hi you doin?" and her gaze   144
struck immediately on the dark lump on Mrs. Turpin's forehead. "You
done fell down, ain't you?" she asked in a solicitous voice. The old woman
was dark and almost toothless. She had on an old felt hat of Claud's set
back of her head. The other two women were younger and lighter and
they both had new bright green sun hats. One of them had hers on her
head; the other had taken hers off and the boy was grinning beneath it.

Mrs. Turpin set the bucket down on the floor of the truck. "Yawl hep   145
yourselves," she said. She looked around to make sure Claud had gone.
"No. I didn't fall down." she said, folding her arms. "It was something
worse than that."

"Ain't nothing bad happen to you!" the old woman said. She said it as   146
if they all knew that Mrs. Turpin was protected in some special way by
Divine Providence. "You just had you a little fall."

"We were in town at the doctor's office for where the cow kicked Mr.   147
Turpin," Mrs. Turpin said in a flat tone that indicated they could leave off
their foolishness. "And there was a girl there. A big fat girl with her face all
broke out. I could look at that girl and tell she was peculiar but I couldn't
tell how. And me and her mama were just talking and going along and all
of a sudden WHAM! She throws this big book she was reading at me
and...."

"Naw!" the old woman cried out.   148

"And then she jumps over the table and commences to choke me."   149

"Naw!" they all exclaimed, "naw!"   150

"Hi come she do that?" the old woman asked. "What ail her?"   151

Mrs. Turpin only glared in front of her.   152

"Somethin ail her," the old woman said.   153

"They carried her off in an ambulance." Mrs. Turpin continued, "but   154
before she went she was rolling on the floor and they were trying to hold
her down to give her a shot and she said something to me." She paused.
"You know what she said to me?"

"What she say?" they asked.   155

"She said," Mrs. Turpin began, and stopped, her face very dark and   156
heavy. The sun was getting whiter and whiter, blanching the sky overhead
so that the leaves of the hickory tree were black in the face of it. She could
not bring forth the words. "Something real ugly," she muttered.

"She sho shouldn't said nothin ugly to you." the old woman said.   157
"You so sweet. You the sweetest lady I know."

"She pretty too," the one with the hat on said.   158

"And stout," the other one said. "I never known no sweeter white   159
lady."

"That's the truth befo' Jesus," the old woman said. "Amen! You jes as   160
sweet and pretty as you can be."

Mrs. Turpin knew just exactly how much Negro flattery was worth   161
and it added to her rage. "She said," she began again and finished this
time with a fierce rush of breath, "that I was an old wart hog from hell."

There was an astounded silence.   162

"Where she at?" the youngest woman cried in a piercing voice.   163

"Lemme see her. I'll kill her!"   164

"I'll kill her with you!" the other one cried.   165

"She b'long in the sylum," the old woman said emphatically. "You the   166
sweetest white lady I know."

"She pretty too," the other two said. "Stout as she can be and sweet.   167
Jesus satisfied with her!"

"Deed he is," the old woman declared.   168

Idiots! Mrs. Turpin growled to herself. You could never say anything   169
intelligent to a nigger. You could talk at them but not with them. "Yawl
ain't drunk your water," she said shortly. "Leave the bucket in the truck
when you're finished with it. I got more to do than just stand around and
pass the time of day," and she moved off and into the house.

She stood for a moment in the middle of the kitchen. The dark pro-   170
tuberance over her eye looked like a miniature tornado cloud which
might any moment sweep across the horizon of her brow. Her lower lip
protruded dangerously. She squared her massive shoulders. Then she
marched into the front of the house and out the side door and started down
the road to the pig parlor. She had the look of a woman going single-
handed, weaponless, into battle.

The sun was a very deep yellow now like a harvest moon and was ris-   171
ing westward very fast over the far tree line as if it meant to reach the hogs
before she did. The road was rutted and she kicked several good-sized
stones out of her path as she strode along. The pig parlor was on a little

knoll at the end of a lane that ran off from the side of the barn. It was a square of concrete as large as a small room, with a board fence about four feet high around it. The concrete floor sloped slightly so that the hog wash could drain off into a trench where it was carried to the field for fertilizer. Claud was standing on the outside, on the edge of the concrete, hanging onto the top board, hosing down the floor inside. The hose was connected to the faucet of a water trough nearby.

Mrs. Turpin climbed up beside him and glowered down at the hogs   172
inside. There were seven long-snouted bristly shoats in it — tan with liver-colored spots — and an old sow a few weeks off from farrowing. She was laying on her side grunting. The shoats were running about shaking themselves like idiot children, their little slit pig eyes searching the floor for anything left. She had read pigs were the most intelligent animal. She doubted it. They were supposed to be smarter than dogs. There had even been a pig astronaut. He had performed his assignment perfectly but died of a heart attack afterward because they left him in his electric suit, sitting upright throughout his examination when naturally a hog should be on all fours.

A-gruntin and a-rooting and a-groanin.   173

"Gimme that hose," she said, yanking it away from Claud. "Go on   174
and carry them niggers home and then get off that leg."

"You look like you might have swallowed a mad dog," Claud   175
observed, but he got down and limped off. He paid no attention to her humors.

Until he was out of earshot, Mrs. Turpin stood on the side of the pen,   176
holding the hose and pointing the stream of water at the hind quarters of any shoat that looked as if it might try to lie down. When he had had time to get over the hill, she turned her head slightly and her wrathful eyes scanned the path. He was nowhere in sight. She turned back again and seemed to gather herself up. Her shoulders rose and she drew in her breath.

"What do you send me a message like that for?" she said in a low   177
fierce voice, barely above a whisper but with the force of a shout in its concentrated fury. "How am I a hog and me both? How am I saved and from hell too?" Her free fist was knotted and with the other she gripped the hose, blindly pointing the stream of water in and out of the eye of the old sow whose outraged squeal she did not hear.

The pig parlor commanded a view of the back pasture where their   178
twenty beef cows were gathered around the hay-bales Claud and the boy had put out. The freshly cut pasture sloped down to the highway. Across it was their cotton field. The sun was behind the wood, very red, looking over the paling of trees like a farmer inspecting his own hogs.

"Why me?" she rumbled. "It's no trash around here, black or white,   179
that I haven't given to. And break my back to the bone every day working. And do for the church."

She appeared to be the right size woman to command the arena before   180
her. "How am I a hog?" she demanded. "Exactly how am I like them?"

and she jabbed the stream of water at the shoats. "There was plenty of trash there. It didn't have to be me."

"If you like trash better, go get yourself some trash then," she railed. 181 "You could have made me trash. Or a nigger. If trash is what you wanted why didn't you make me trash?" She shook her fist with the hose in it and a water snake appeared momentarily in the air. "I could quit working and take it easy and be filthy," she growled. "Lounge about the sidewalks all day drinking root beer. Dip snuff and spit in every puddle and have it all over my face. I could be nasty."

"Or you could have made me a nigger. It's too late for me to be a nig- 182 ger," she said with deep sarcasm, "but I could act like one. Lay down in the middle of the road and stop traffic. Roll on the ground."

In the deepening light everything was taking on a mysterious hue. 183 The pasture was growing a peculiar grassy green and the streak of highway had turned lavender. She braced herself for a final assault and this time her voice rolled out over the pasture. "Go on," she yelled, "call me a hog! Call me a hog again. From hell. Call me a wart hog from hell. Put that bottom rail on top. There'll still be a top and bottom!"

A garbled echo returned to her. 184

A final surge of fury shook her and she roared, "Who do you think 185 you are?"

The color of everything, field and crimson sky, burned for a moment 186 with a transparent intensity. The question carried over the pasture and across the highway and the cotton field and returned to her clearly like an answer from beyond the wood.

She opened her mouth but no sound came out of it. 187

A tiny truck, Claud's, appeared on the highway, heading rapidly out 188 of sight. Its gears scraped thinly. It looked like a child's toy. At any moment a bigger truck might smash into it and scatter Claud's and the niggers' brains all over the road.

Mrs. Turpin stood there, her gaze fixed on the highway, all her mus- 189 cles rigid, until in five or six minutes the truck reappeared, returning. She waited until it had had time to turn into their own road. Then like a monumental statue coming to life, she bent her head slowly and gazed, as if through the very heart of mystery, down into the pig parlor at the hogs. They had settled all in one corner around the old sow who was grunting softly. A red glow suffused them. They appeared to pant with a secret life.

Until the sun slipped finally behind the tree line, Mrs. Turpin re- 190 mained there with her gaze bent to them as if she were absorbing some abysmal life-giving knowledge. At last she lifted her head. There was only a purple streak in the sky, cutting through a field of crimson and leading, like an extension of the highway, into the descending dusk. She raised her hands from the side of the pen in a gesture hieratic and profound. A visionary light settled in her eyes. She saw the streak as a vast swinging bridge extending upward from the earth through a field of living fire. Upon it a vast horde of souls were rumbling toward heaven. There were whole companies of white-trash, clean for the first time in their lives, and bands of black niggers in white robes, and battalions of freaks and lunatics shouting and clapping and leaping like frogs. And bringing up the end of the procession was a tribe of people whom she recognized at once as those who, like herself and Claud, had always had a little of everything and the God-given wit to use it right. She leaned forward to observe them closer. They were marching behind the others with great dignity, accountable as they had always been for good order and common sense and respectable behavior. They alone were on key. Yet she could see by their shocked and altered faces that even their virtues were being burned away. She lowered her hands and gripped the rail of the hog pen, her eyes small but fixed unblinkingly on what lay ahead. In a moment the vision faded but she remained where she was, immobile.

At length she got down and turned off the faucet and made her slow way on the darkening path to the house. In the woods around her the invisible cricket choruses had struck up, but what she heard were the voices of the souls climbing upward into the starry field and shouting hallelujah.

191

•   •   •

THINKING ABOUT LITERATURE

1. What is Mrs. Turpin's revelation? What causes it? What, if anything, does it teach her about herself?

2. On what basis does Mrs. Turpin classify people? What categories does she identify? How do hogs fit into her system of classification?

3. How would you classify Mrs. Turpin, the "white-trash woman," and the "pleasant lady" in terms of their attitudes toward blacks? Whose attitudes do you find most — and least — offensive?

JOURNAL ENTRY

What dangers do you see in classification systems like Mrs. Turpin's? Who — or what — is most at risk? Why?

THEMATIC CONNECTIONS

*   "'What's in a Name?'" (page 5)
*   "Just Walk On By" (page 197)
*   "The Untouchable" (page 461)

WRITING ASSIGNMENTS FOR CLASSIFICATION AND DIVISION

1. Choose a film you have seen recently, and list all the elements that you consider significant — plot, direction, acting, special effects, and so on. Then further subdivide each category (for instance, listing each of the special effects). Using this list as an organizational guide, write a review of the film.

2. Write an essay in which you classify the teachers or bosses you have had into several distinct categories and make a judgment about the relative effectiveness of the individuals in each group. Give each category a name, and be sure your essay has a thesis statement.

3. What styles of dress do you observe on your college campus? Establish four or five distinct categories, and write an essay in which you classify students on the basis of how they dress. Give each group a descriptive title.

4. Do some research to help you identify the subclasses of a large class of animals or plants. Write an essay in which you enumerate and describe the subclasses in each class for an audience of elementary school students.

5. Violence in sports is considered by many to be a serious problem. Write an essay in which you express your views on this problem. Use a classification-and-division structure, categorizing information according to sources of violence (such as the players, the nature of the game, and the fans).

6. Classify television shows according to type (action, drama, and so forth), audience (preschoolers, school-age children, adults, and so forth), or any other logical principle. Write an essay based on your system of classification, making sure to include a thesis statement. For instance, you might assert that the relative popularity of one kind of program over others reveals something about television watchers, or that one kind of program shows signs of becoming obsolete.

7. Write a lighthearted essay discussing kinds of snack foods, cartoons, pets, status symbols, toys, shoppers, vacations, weight-loss diets, hairstyles, or drivers.

8. Write an essay in which you assess the relative merits of several different politicians, news broadcasts, or academic majors.

9. What kinds of survival skills does a student need to get through college successfully? Write a classification-and-division essay in which you identify and discuss several kinds of skills, indicating why each category is important. If you like, you may write your essay in the form of a letter to a beginning college student.

10. After attending a party, lecture, or concert, write an essay in which you divide the people you observe there into categories according to some logical principle. Include a thesis statement that indicates how different the various groups are.

COLLABORATIVE ACTIVITY FOR CLASSIFICATION AND DIVISION

Working in groups, devise a classification system that encompasses all the different kinds of popular music favored by the members of your group. You may begin with general categories like country, pop, and rhythm and blues, but you should also include more specific categories, such as rap and heavy metal, in your classification system. After you decide on categories and sub-categories that represent the tastes of all members of your group, fill in examples for each category. Then, devise several different options for arranging your categories into an essay.

INTERNET ASSIGNMENT FOR CLASSIFICATION AND DIVISION

Imagine that you are a writer for *Beat* magazine and have been asked to write a feature article titled "American Music of the New Millennium." Referring to the following World Wide Web sites, use a classification-and-division structure to discuss the types of music you think represent the future of the music industry. Be sure to give each type of music a name and describe its characteristics so as to give your audience a sense of the differences between the categories.

Spin Magazine
<http://www.spin.com>
Along with articles on bands and "pop life," this site contains audio and video clips of new music.

New Music Box
<http://www.newmusicbox.org>
This magazine from the American Music Center includes articles, interviews, a calendar, news sections, and sound and audio files.

NewMusicNow.org
<http://www.newmusicnow.org>
This site features contemporary works for orchestra by American composers. Visitors can listen to pieces of music, explore their background, and learn about composers.

Muse: The Journal of Women in Music
<http://www.val.net/muse>
This site offers feature articles, interviews, and CD and concert reviews.

11

DEFINITION

WHAT IS DEFINITION?

A **definition** tells what a term means and how it is different from other terms in its class. In the following paragraph from *Nothing to Declare*, Mary Morris defines *traveler*:

Topic sentence	How do you know if you are a traveler? What are the tell-tale signs? As with most compulsions, such as being a gambler, a kleptomaniac, or a writer, the obvious proof is that you can't stop. If you are hooked, you are hooked. One sure sign of travelers is their relationship to maps. I cannot say how much of my life I have spent looking at maps, but there is no map I won't stare at and study. I love to measure each detail with my thumb, to see how far I have come, how far I've yet to go. I love maps the way stamp collectors love stamps. Not for their usefulness, but
Extended definition defines term by means of analogy, exemplification, and description	rather for the sheer beauty of the object itself. I love to look at a map, even if it is a map of Mars, and figure out where I am going and how I am going to get there, what route I will take. I imagine what adventures might await me even though I know that the journey is never what we plan for; it's what happens between the lines.

Most people think of definition in terms of dictionaries, which give brief, succinct explanations — called **formal definitions** — of what words mean. But definition also includes explaining what something, or even someone, *is* — that is, its essential nature. Sometimes a definition requires a paragraph, an essay, or even a whole book. These longer, more complex definitions are called **extended definitions.**

Understanding Formal Definitions

Look at any dictionary, and you will notice that all definitions have a standard three-part structure. First, they present the *term* to be defined,

455

then the general *class* it is a part of, and finally the *qualities that differentiate it* from the other terms in the same class.

Term	*Class*	*Differentiation*
Behaviorism	is a theory	that regards the objective facts of a subject's actions as the only valid basis for psychological study.
A cell	is a unit of protoplasm	with a nucleus, cytoplasm, and an enclosing membrane.
Naturalism	is a literary movement	whose original adherents believed that writers should treat life with scientific objectivity.
Mitosis	is the process	of nuclear division of cells, consisting of prophase, metaphase, anaphase, and telophase.
Authority	is the power	to command and require obedience.

Understanding Extended Definitions

An extended definition includes the three basic parts of a formal definition — the term, its class, and its distinguishing characteristics. Beyond these essentials, an extended definition does not follow a set pattern of development. Instead, it uses whatever strategies best suit the term being defined and the writing situation. In fact, any one (or more than one) of the essay patterns illustrated in this book can be used to structure a definition essay.

USING DEFINITION

Supplying a formal definition of each term you use is seldom necessary or desirable. Readers will often know what a word means or be able to look it up. Sometimes, however, defining your terms is essential — for example, when a word has several meanings, each of which might fit your context, or when you want to use a word in a special way.

When taking an exam, of course, you are likely to encounter questions that require extended definitions. You might, for example, be asked to define *behaviorism;* tell what a *cell* is; explain the meaning of the literary term *naturalism;* include a comprehensive definition of *mitosis* in your answer; or define *authority.* Such exam questions cannot always be answered in one or two sentences. In fact, the definitions they call for often require several paragraphs.

Extended definitions are useful for many academic assignments besides exams. A thoughtful definition can clarify a precise term or a general concept. Definitions can explain abstractions like *freedom* or controversial terms like *right to life* or **slang** terms, informal expressions whose meanings may vary from locale to locale or change as time passes. In a particular writing situation, a definition may be essential because a term has more than one meaning, because you are using it in an unusual way, or because you believe the term is unfamiliar to your readers.

Many extended-definition essays include shorter formal definitions like those in dictionaries. In such an essay, a brief formal definition can introduce readers to the extended definition, or it can help to support the essay's thesis. In addition, essays in which other patterns of development are dominant often incorporate brief definitions to clarify points or explain basic information for the reader. Whether it appears in another kind of essay or acts as a focus for an extended definition, the brief formal definition establishes the basic meaning of a term.

PLANNING A DEFINITION ESSAY

You can organize a definition essay according to one or more of the patterns of development described in this book, or you can use other strategies. This section gives advice for both approaches.

Using Patterns of Development

As you plan your essay and jot down your ideas about the term or subject you will define, you will see which patterns are most useful. The formal definitions of the five terms discussed previously, for example, could be expanded with five different patterns of development.

• *Exemplification* To explain *behaviorism,* you could give examples. Carefully chosen cases could show how this theory of psychology applies in different situations. These examples could help readers see exactly how behaviorism works and what it can and cannot account for. Often, examples are the clearest way to explain something unusual, especially when it is unfamiliar to your readers. Defining dreams as "the symbolic representation of mental states" might convey little to readers who do not know much about psychology. But a few examples would help you make your point. Many students have dreams about taking exams — perhaps dreaming that they are late for the test, that they remember nothing about the course, or that they are writing their answers in disappearing ink. You might explain the nature of dreams by interpreting these particular dreams, which may reflect anxiety about a course or about school in general.

• *Description*   You can explain the nature of something by describing it. For example, the concept of a *cell* is difficult to grasp from just a formal definition, but your readers would understand the concept more clearly if you were to explain what a cell looks like, possibly with the aid of a diagram or two. Concentrating on the cell membrane, cytoplasm, and nucleus, you could detail each structure's appearance and function. These descriptions would enable readers to visualize the whole cell and understand its workings. Of course, description involves more than the visual: a definition of Italian cooking might describe the taste and smell, as well as the appearance, of ravioli, and a definition of Parkinson's disease might include a description of how its symptoms feel to a patient.

• *Comparison and contrast*   An extended definition of *naturalism* could employ a comparison-and-contrast structure. Naturalism is one of several major movements in American literature, and its literary aims could be contrasted with those of other literary movements, such as romanticism or realism. Or you might compare and contrast the plots and characters of several naturalistic works with those of romantic or realistic works. If you needed to define something unfamiliar, you could compare it to something familiar to your readers. For example, your readers may never have heard of the Chinese dish called sweet-and-sour cabbage, but you can help them imagine it by saying it tastes something like cole slaw. You can also define a thing by contrasting it with something unlike it, especially if the two have some qualities in common. One way to explain the British sport of rugby is by contrasting it with American football, which is not as violent.

• *Process*   An extended definition of *mitosis* should be organized as a process analysis because mitosis is a process. You could explain the stages of mitosis, pointing out the transitions from one phase to another. By tracing the process from stage to stage, you would be able to clearly define this type of cell division for your readers. Similarly, some objects must be defined in terms of what they do. For example, because a computer carries out certain processes, an extended definition of a computer would probably include a process analysis.

• *Classification and division*   Finally, you could define *authority* by using classification and division. Basing your extended definition on the model developed by the German sociologist Max Weber, you could divide the class *authority* into the subclasses *traditional authority, charismatic authority,* and *legal-bureaucratic authority.* Then, by explaining each type of authority, you could clarify this very broad term for your readers. In both extended and formal definitions, classification and division can be very useful. By saying what class something belongs to, you are explaining what kind of thing it is. For instance, *monetarism* is an economic theory; *The Adventures of Huckleberry Finn* is a novel; *emphysema* is a disease. And by dividing a class into subclasses, you are defining something more specifically. Emphysema, for instance, is a disease of the lungs, and can therefore be classified with tuberculosis but not with appendicitis.

Using Other Strategies

In addition to using various patterns of development, you can expand a definition by using other strategies:

- You can define a term by using **synonyms** (words with similar meanings).
- You can define a term by using *negation* (telling what it is *not*).
- You can define a term by using *enumeration* (listing its characteristics).
- You can define a term by using **analogies** (comparisons that identify similarities between the term and something dissimilar).
- You can define a term by discussing its *origin and development* (the word's derivation, original meaning, and usages).

Whatever form your definitions take, make certain that they are clear and that they actually define. Be sure to provide a true definition, not just a descriptive statement such as "Happiness is a four-day weekend." Also, remember that repetition is not definition, so don't include the term you are defining in your definition. For instance, the statement "abstract art is a school of artists whose works are abstract" clarifies nothing for your readers. Finally, define as precisely as possible. Name the class of the term you are defining — for example, state "mitosis is *a process in which* a cell divides" rather than "mitosis is *when* a cell divides"— and define this class as narrowly and as accurately as you can. Be specific when you differentiate your term from other members of its class. Careful attention to the language and structure of your definition will help readers understand your meaning.

STRUCTURING A DEFINITION ESSAY

A definition essay should have an *introduction*, a *body*, and a *conclusion*. Although a formal definition strives for objectivity, an extended definition may not. Instead, it may define a term in a way that reflects your attitude toward the subject or your reason for defining it. For example, your extended-definition paper about literary *naturalism* might argue that the significance of this movement's major works has been underestimated by literary scholars. Or your definition of *authority* might criticize its abuses. In such cases, the thesis statement provides a focus for a definition essay, telling readers *your* approach to the definition.

Suppose you are assigned a short paper in your introductory psychology course. You decide to examine *behaviorism*. First, you have to determine whether your topic is appropriate for a definition essay. If the topic suggests a response such as "The true nature of A is B" or "A means B," then it is a definition. Of course, you can define the word in one sentence, or possibly two. But to explain the *concept* of behaviorism and its position in the field of psychology, you must go beyond the dictionary.

Second, you have to decide what kinds of explanations are most suitable for your topic and for your intended audience. If you are trying to define *behaviorism* for readers who know very little about psychology, you might use comparisons that relate behaviorism to your readers' experiences, such as how they were raised or how they train their pets. You might also use examples, but the examples would relate not to psychological experiments or clinical treatment but to experiences in everyday life. If, however, you direct your paper to your psychology instructor, who obviously already knows what behaviorism is, your purpose is to show that you know, too. One way to do this is to compare behaviorism to other psychological theories. Another way is to give examples of how behaviorism works in practice. You could also briefly summarize the background and history of the theory. (In a term paper, you might use all of these strategies.)

After considering your paper's scope and audience, you might decide that because behaviorism is somewhat controversial, your best strategy is to supplement a formal definition with examples showing how behaviorist assumptions and methods are applied in specific situations. These examples, drawn from your class notes and textbook, will support your thesis that behaviorism is a valid approach for treating certain psychological dysfunctions. Together, your examples will define *behaviorism* as it is understood today.

An informal outline for your essay might look like this:

Introduction	Thesis statement — Contrary to its critics' assertions, behaviorism is a valid approach for treating a wide variety of psychological dysfunctions.
Background:	Definition of behaviorism, including its origins and evolution
First example:	The use of behaviorism to help psychotics function in an institutional setting

---

☑ **CHECKLIST: DEFINITION**

- Does your assignment call for definition?
- Does your essay include a clearly stated thesis that identifies the term you will define and communicates your approach to the definition?
- Have you included a formal definition of your subject? Of any additional terms?
- Have you identified a pattern or patterns of development that you can use to expand your definition?
- Have you used other strategies — such as synonyms, negation, enumeration, or analogies — to expand your definition?
- Have you discussed the origin and development of the term you are defining?

Second example:	The use of behaviorism to treat neurotic behavior, such as chronic anxiety, a phobia, or a pattern of destructive acts
Third example:	The use of behaviorism to treat normal but anti-social or undesirable behavior, such as heavy smoking or overeating
Conclusion:	Restatement of thesis or review of key points

Notice how the three examples in this paper define behaviorism with the complexity, detail, and breadth that a formal definition could not duplicate. It is more like a textbook explanation — and, in fact, textbook explanations are often written as extended definitions.

▶ A STUDENT WRITER: DEFINITION

The following student essay, written by Ajoy Mahtab for a composition course, defines the untouchables, a caste whose members are shunned in India. In his essay Ajoy, who grew up in Calcutta, presents a thesis that is sharply critical of the practice of ostracizing untouchables.

The Untouchable

Introduction: background
A word that is extremely common in India yet uncommon to the point of incomprehension in the West is the word <u>untouchable</u>. It is a word that has had extremely sinister connotations throughout India's history. A rigorously worked-out caste system existed in traditional Indian society. At the top of the social ladder sat the Brahmins, the clan of the priesthood. These people had renounced the material world for a spiritual one. Below them came the Kshatriyas, or the warrior caste. This caste included the kings and all their nobles along with their armies. Third on the social ladder were the Vaishyas, who were the merchants of the land. Trade was their only form of livelihood. Last came the Shudras--the menials. Shudras were employed by the prosperous as sweepers and laborers. Originally a person's caste was determined only by his profession. Thus, if the son of a merchant joined the army, he automatically converted from a Vaishya to a Kshatriya. However, the system soon became hereditary and rigid. Whatever one's occupa-

1

tion, one's caste was determined from birth according to the caste of one's father.

Outside of this structure were a group of people, human beings treated worse than dogs and shunned far more than lepers, people who were not considered even human, people who defiled with their very touch. These were the Achhoots: the untouchables. The word untouchable is commonly defined as "that which cannot or should not be touched." In India, however, it was taken to a far greater extreme. The untouchables of a village lived in a separate community downwind of the borders of the village. They had a separate water supply, for they would make the village water impure if they were to drink from it. When they walked, they were made to bang two sticks together continuously so that passersby could avoid an untouchable's shadow. Tied to their waists, trailing behind them, was a broom that would clean the ground they had walked on. The penalty for not following these or any other rules was death for the untouchable and, in many instances, for the entire untouchable community.

2

One of the pioneers of the fight against untouchability was Mahatma Gandhi. Thanks to his efforts and those of many others, untouchability no longer presents anything like the horrific picture painted earlier. In India today, in fact, recognition of untouchability is punishable by law. Theoretically, there is no such thing as untouchability anymore. But old traditions linger on, and such a deep-rooted fear passed down from generation to generation cannot disappear overnight. Even today, caste is an important factor in most marriages. Most Indian surnames reveal a person's caste immediately, and so it is a difficult thing to hide. The shunning of the untouchable is more

3

Formal definition

Historical background

Present situation

prevalent in South India, where the general
public is much more devout, than in the North.
Some people would rather starve than share food
and water with an untouchable. This concept is
very difficult to accept in the West, but it is
true all the same.

Example

I remember an incident from my childhood.   4
I could not have been more than eight or nine
at the time. I was on a holiday staying at my
family's house on the river Ganges. There was a
festival going on and, as is customary, we were
giving the servants small presents. I was hand-
ing them out when an old lady, bent with age,
slowly hobbled into the room. She stood in the
far corner of the room all alone, and no one so
much as looked at her. When the entire line
ended, she stepped hesitantly forward and stood
in front of me, looking down at the ground.
She then held a cloth stretched out in front
of her. I was a little confused about how I was
supposed to hand her her present, since both
her hands were holding the cloth. Then, with
the help of prompting from someone behind me,
I learned that I was supposed to drop the gift
into the cloth without touching the cloth
itself. It was only later that I found out that
she was an untouchable. This was the first time
I had actually come face to face with prejudice, and it felt like a slap in the face. That
incident was burned into my memory, and I do
not think I will ever forget it.

Conclusion begins

The word <u>untouchable</u> is not often used in   5
the West, and when it is, it is generally used
as a complimentary term. For example, an avid
fan might say of an athlete, "He was absolutely
untouchable. Nobody could even begin to compare
with him." It seems rather ironic that a word
could be so favorable in one culture and so
derogatory in another. Why does a word that
gives happiness in one part of the world cause

pain in another? Why does the same word have
different meanings to different people around
the globe? Why do certain words cause rifts and
others forge bonds? I do not think anyone can
tell me the answer.

**Conclusion
continues**

No actual parallel can be found today that   6
compares to the horrors of untouchability. For
an untouchable, life itself was a crime. The
day was spent just trying to stay alive. From

Thesis statement

the misery of the untouchables, the world
should learn a lesson: isolating and punishing
any group of people is dehumanizing and
immoral.

Points for Special Attention

THESIS STATEMENT.   Ajoy Mahtab's assignment was to write an
extended definition of a term he assumed would be unfamiliar to his audience. Because he had definite ideas about the unjust treatment of the
untouchables, Ajoy wanted his essay to have a strong thesis that communicated his disapproval. Still, because he knew his American classmates
would need a good deal of background information before they would
accept such a thesis, he decided not to present it in his introduction.
Instead, he decided to lead up to his thesis gradually and state it at the end
of his essay. When other students in the class reviewed his draft, this subtlety was one of the points they reacted to most favorably.

STRUCTURE.   Ajoy's introduction establishes the direction of his
essay by introducing the word he will define; he then places this word in
context by explaining India's rigid caste system. In paragraph 2, he gives
the formal definition of the word *untouchable* and goes on to sketch the
term's historical background. Paragraph 3 explains the status of the
untouchables in present-day India, and paragraph 4 gives a vivid example
of Ajoy's first encounter with an untouchable. As he begins his conclusion
in paragraph 5, Ajoy brings his readers back to the word his essay defines.
Here he uses two strategies to add interest: he contrasts one contemporary
American usage of *untouchable* with its derogatory meaning in India, and
he asks a series of **rhetorical questions** (questions asked for effect and not
meant to be answered). In paragraph 6, Ajoy presents a summary of his
position to lead into his thesis statement.

PATTERNS OF DEVELOPMENT.   This essay uses a number of strategies
commonly encountered in extended definitions: it includes a formal definition, explains the term's origin, and explores some of the term's connota-

tions. In addition, the essay incorporates several familiar patterns of development. For instance, paragraph 1 uses classification and division to explain India's caste system; paragraphs 2 and 3 use brief examples to illustrate the plight of the untouchable; and paragraph 4 presents a narrative. Each of these patterns enriches the definition.

Focus on Revision

Because the term Ajoy defined was so unfamiliar to his classmates, many of the peer-editing worksheets asked for more information. One suggestion in particular — that he draw an **analogy** between the unfamiliar term *untouchable* and a more familiar concept — appealed to Ajoy as he planned his revision. Another student suggested that Ajoy could compare untouchables to other groups who are shunned — for example, people with AIDS. Although Ajoy states in his conclusion that no parallel exists, an attempt to find common ground between untouchables and other groups could make his essay more meaningful to his readers — and bring home to them an idea that is distinctly foreign. Such a connection could also make his conclusion especially powerful.

The readings that follow use exemplification, description, narration, and other methods of developing extended definitions. As you can see, no one pattern is more appropriate than another for a definition paper. (In fact, combining several patterns is often the most effective way to define the significant aspects of a term.) Your choice of pattern or patterns should evolve naturally from your knowledge of the material, your purpose, and the needs of your audience.

◣◣◣◣◣◣◣◣
JOHN KENNETH GALBRAITH

One of the twentieth century's most influential economists, John Kenneth Galbraith (1908–) was born in Ontario, Canada, the son of a farmer. He studied agriculture at the University of Toronto and received advanced degrees in economics at the University of California at Berkeley. He became a U.S. citizen in 1937. Galbraith has taught economics at Harvard and Princeton and has held a number of important government positions, most notably as economic advisor to Democratic presidents John F. Kennedy and Lyndon B. Johnson in the 1960s. He is the author of more than thirty books for general readers, including *The Affluent Society* (1958), *The Age of Uncertainty* (1977), and *The Good Society* (1996).

A staunch liberal in an economic climate that has grown increasingly conservative, Galbraith has consistently advocated greater distribution of wealth in the United States. At its most basic, this approach involves taxing wealthy citizens and corporations at higher rates so the government can provide greater services — adequate housing, food subsidies, fairer educational opportunities — for those less well off. Critical of those who argue for absolute free markets, Galbraith has always been concerned with the effects of economic policy on minorities and the poor. The following essay originally appeared on the *New York Times* Op-Ed page in 1995, at a time when the debate in Congress over reducing welfare and other benefits to the unemployed was at its peak. (Note that much of this "burden" on the government was eliminated by the 1998 Welfare Reform Act.)

Burdens

In these last years, and notably in these past months, we have heard   1
much of the burden imposed by government on the citizen. Nothing has been more emphasized in speech and possibly also in thought. This comment is not meant to regret this concern, as some might suppose: rather, it is to clarify the way the word *burden* is now employed. It has a very special connotation, of which all who cherish good or anyhow accepted English usage should be aware.

As now used, *burden* applies only to a very specific range of govern-   2
ment activities. Many are not a burden and are not to be so described. Defense expenditure is definitely not a burden; indeed, increases therein are now being proposed. That there is now no wholly plausible enemy does not affect the situation. Similarly, in recent years large sums, in a range upward from $50 billion, have been appropriated to bail out failed financial institutions, specifically the savings and loan associations. This was not a burden. A clear distinction must be made between a burden and an admittedly unfortunate and costly financial misadventure.

Social Security is not a burden; in no politically acceptable discourse is   3
it so described. Nor are farm price and income supports, although recipients regularly command incomes of a hundred grand or more. Medicare is

basically not a burden and is not to be so described. There are many lesser items of expenditure that are not a burden, including health care for members of the Congress.

On the other hand, some functions of government are a heavy burden. 4 Notable are welfare payments, especially those to unmarried mothers and their children. Likewise expenditures for food stamps and child nutrition. While Medicare is not a burden, Medicaid is a real burden.*

Education is a somewhat special case. While private education is not a 5 burden, public education, especially in our cities, can be a very heavy load. Here, as elsewhere, burden bears no necessary relation to cost.

And here one sees the rule by which students of contemporary English usage should be guided. Whether a public function or service or regulation is or is not a burden depends on the income of the individual so helped or favored.

As with all linguistic rules there can be exceptions. The National 7 Endowment for the Arts, support to public broadcasting, a few other items not specifically designed for the poor, are a burden. The exceptions, as ever, make the rule.

It is the generally accepted purpose of language to convey meaning. 8 All who use or hear the word *burden* should know the precise and subtle meaning that it conveys. Basically something is a burden when it is not for the rich, not for the merely affluent, but for the poor.

• • •

COMPREHENSION

1. How does Galbraith define *burden*? Where does he give his formal definition of the word? Why do you think he presents this definition where he does?

2. In paragraph 1, when Galbraith speaks of "all who cherish good or anyhow accepted English usage," what distinction do you think he means to make between *good* and *accepted* English? Why is this distinction important?

3. What distinction does Galbraith draw between a burden and "an admittedly unfortunate and costly financial misadventure" (2)?

4. What examples does Galbraith give of programs that are burdens? Of those that are not burdens? What do the programs in each group have in common?

5. Why, according to Galbraith, is education a "special case" (5)?

6. Why do the National Endowment for the Arts and public broadcasting qualify as burdens even though they are not designed for the poor? Does Galbraith state the reason or merely imply it? Why?

---

*EDS. NOTE — Medicare is government-supported health insurance for retired people; Medicaid is government-supported health-care benefits for the poor and disabled.

PURPOSE AND AUDIENCE

1. The original title of this essay was "Our Forked Tongue." A person who speaks with a forked tongue is someone who is taking two different positions at the same time — in other words, a liar. What effect do you think Galbraith might have expected the title "Our Forked Tongue" to have on his readers? Do you think this title was a good choice? Why or why not?

2. Is Galbraith's purpose in this essay to criticize social priorities or to criticize the use of language to justify those priorities? Do you think his primary target is government or individuals? Explain your reasoning.

STYLE AND STRUCTURE

1. Where does Galbraith define by enumeration? By negation? Why is negation a particularly effective strategy for this essay?

2. How could Galbraith use additional strategies to strengthen his definition? For example, could he discuss the origin and development of the word *burden*? Could he use **synonyms** or **analogies**? If so, where?

3. How would you characterize Galbraith's tone in this essay? Does he seem to be angry or bitter, or does he seem disheartened by what he observes?

4. Where does Galbraith use sarcasm? Do you think the sarcasm is appropriate? Necessary? Do you think Galbraith could reach more readers by adopting a more neutral tone? Explain your reasoning.

5. Do you think the essay would be more convincing if Galbraith had provided historical background for the social and political situation he describes — for example, discussions of other programs that were (or were not) perceived as burdens? Why or why not?

6. In paragraph 3, Galbraith sets down a rule: "Medicare is basically not a burden and is not to be so described." Where else does he use this kind of language? Who does he imply has established these rules? What is his attitude toward these rule makers?

VOCABULARY PROJECTS

1. Define each of the following words as it is used in this selection.

   therein (2)   plausible (2)   discourse (3)

2. Look up the word *burden* in a dictionary. How does the dictionary's primary definition differ from Galbraith's? How do you account for this difference?

JOURNAL ENTRY

Contrary to what Galbraith says in paragraph 3, some people today *do* see Social Security and Medicare as burdens. Do you? Why or why not?

WRITING WORKSHOP

1. Write an essay in which you define *burden* at a personal level, by giving examples of the kinds of things you consider burdens. You might want to develop your definition essay with comparison and contrast, exploring the differences between a *burden* and a *responsibility.*

2. What state, local, or national government program do you consider to be the biggest burden on citizens? Why? Write a definition essay in which you support your thesis with a single extended example.

3. Sometimes a person can be a burden. Define *burden* by explaining in what sense you find a particular friend or family member to be a burden to you — or in what respects you believe you are or have been a burden to someone else.

COMBINING THE PATTERNS

What pattern does Galbraith use most often to develop his definition? Where does he use this pattern? Could he have used **narration** to support his thesis? Where? Do you think he *should* have expanded his essay with a paragraph or two of narrative? Why or why not?

THEMATIC CONNECTIONS

- "The Human Cost of an Illiterate Society" (page 203)
- "The Ways We Lie" (page 426)
- "On Dumpster Diving" (page 632)
- "A Modest Proposal" (page 648)

JOSÉ ANTONIO BURCIAGA

José Antonio Burciaga (1940–1996) was born in El Chuco, Texas, and served in the U.S. Air Force from 1960 to 1964. He graduated from the University of Texas at El Paso in 1968 and attended the Corcoran School of Art and the San Francisco Art Institute. Burciaga was the founder of *Disseños Literarios,* a publishing company in California, as well as the comedy troupe Culture Clash. He contributed fiction, poetry, and articles to many anthologies as well as to journals and newspapers. He also published several books of poems, drawings, and essays, including the poetry collection *Undocumented Love* (1992) and the essay collection *Drink Cultura* (1993).

"Tortillas," originally titled "I Remember Masa," was first published in *Weedee Peepo* (1988), a collection of essays in Spanish and English. Tortillas have been a staple of Mexican cooking for thousands of years. These thin, round griddlecakes made of cornmeal *(masa)* are often eaten with every meal, and the art of making them is still passed from generation to generation (although they now are widely available commercially as well). The earliest Mexican immigrants introduced them to the United States, and in the last twenty years tortillas, along with many popular items of Mexican cuisine, have entered the country's culinary landscape (as, over the decades, has a wide variety of other "ethnic" foods like pizza, egg rolls, bagels, and gyros). Still, tortillas have special meaning for Mexican Americans, and in this essay Burciaga discusses the role of the tortilla within his family's culture.

Tortillas

My earliest memory of *tortillas* is my *Mamá* telling me not to play with 1
them. I had bitten eyeholes in one and was wearing it as a mask at the dinner table.

As a child, I also used *tortillas* as hand warmers on cold days, and my 2
family claims that I owe my career as an artist to my early experiments with *tortillas*. According to them, my clowning around helped me develop a strong artistic foundation. I'm not so sure, though. Sometimes I wore a *tortilla* on my head, like a *yarmulke,* and yet I never had any great urge to convert from Catholicism to Judaism. But who knows? They may be right.

For Mexicans over the centuries, the *tortilla* has served as the spoon 3
and the fork, the plate and the napkin. *Tortillas* originated before the Mayan civilizations, perhaps predating Europe's wheat bread. According to Mayan mythology, the great god Quetzalcoatl, realizing that the red ants knew the secret of using maize as food, transformed himself into a black ant, infiltrated the colony of red ants, and absconded with a grain of corn. (Is it any wonder that to this day, black ants and red ants do not get along?) Quetzalcoatl then put maize on the lips of the first man and woman, Oxomoco and Cipactonal, so that they would become strong. Maize festivals are still celebrated by many Indian cultures of the Americas.

When I was growing up in El Paso, *tortillas* were part of my daily life. 4
I used to visit a *tortilla* factory in an ancient adobe building near the
open *mercado* in Ciudad Juárez. As I approached, I could hear the rhythmic
slapping of the *masa* as the skilled vendors outside the factory formed
it into balls and patted them into perfectly round corn cakes between
the palms of their hands. The wonderful aroma and the speed with which
the women counted so many dozens of *tortillas* out of warm wicker baskets still linger in my mind. Watching them at work convinced me that the
most handsome and *deliciosas tortillas* are handmade. Although machines
are faster, they can never adequately replace generation-to-generation
experience. There's no place in the factory assembly line for the tender
slaps that give each *tortilla* character. The best thing that can be said about
mass-producing *tortillas* is that it makes possible for many people to enjoy
them.

In the *mercado* where my mother shopped, we frequently bought 5
taquitos de nopalitos, small tacos filled with diced cactus, onions, tomatoes,
and *jalapeños.* Our friend Don Toribio showed us how to make delicious,
crunchy *taquitos* with dried, salted pumpkin seeds. When you had no
money for the filling, a poor man's *taco* could be made by placing a warm
tortilla on the left palm, applying a sprinkle of salt, then rolling the *tortilla*
up quickly with the fingertips of the right hand. My own kids put peanut
butter and jelly on *tortillas,* which I think is truly bicultural. And speaking
of fast foods for kids, nothing beats a *quesadilla,* a *tortilla* grilled-cheese
sandwich.

Depending on what you intend to use them for, *tortillas* may be made 6
in various ways. Even a run-of-the-mill *tortilla* is more than a flat corn
cake. A skillfully cooked homemade *tortilla* has a bottom and a top; the top
skin forms a pocket in which you put the filling that folds your *tortilla* into
a taco. Paper-thin *tortillas* are used specifically for *flautas,* a type of taco
that is filled, rolled, and then fried until crisp. The name *flauta* means *flute,*
which probably refers to the Mayan bamboo flute; however, the only
sound that comes from an edible *flauta* is a delicious crunch that is music
to the palate. In México *flautas* are sometimes made as long as two feet and
then cut into manageable segments. The opposite of *flautas* is *gorditas,*
meaning *little fat ones.* These are very thick small *tortillas.*

The versatility of *tortillas* and corn does not end here. Besides being 7
tasty and nourishing, they have spiritual and artistic qualities as well. The
Tarahumara Indians of Chihuahua, for example, concocted a corn-based
beer called *tesgüino,* which their descendants still make today. And everyone has read about the woman in New Mexico who was cooking her husband a *tortilla* one morning when the image of Jesus Christ miraculously
appeared on it. Before they knew what was happening, the man's breakfast had become a local shrine.

Then there is *tortilla* art. Various Chicano artists throughout the South- 8
west have, when short of materials or just in a whimsical mood, used a

dry *tortilla* as a small, round canvas. And a few years back, at the height of the Chicano movement, a priest in Arizona got into trouble with the Church after he was discovered celebrating mass using a *tortilla* as the host. All of which only goes to show that while the *tortilla* may be a lowly corn cake, when the necessity arises, it can reach unexpected distinction.

• • •

COMPREHENSION

1. What exactly is a tortilla?

2. List the functions — both practical and whimsical — tortillas serve.

3. In paragraph 7, Burciaga cites the "spiritual and artistic qualities" of tortillas. Do you think he is being serious? Explain your reasoning.

PURPOSE AND AUDIENCE

1. Burciaga states his thesis explicitly in his essay's final sentence. Paraphrase this thesis. Why do you think he does not state it sooner?

2. Do you think Burciaga expects most of his readers to be of Hispanic descent? To be familiar with tortillas? How can you tell?

3. Why do you think Burciaga uses humor in this essay? Is it consistent with his essay's purpose? Could the humor have a negative effect on his audience? Explain.

4. Why are tortillas so important to Burciaga? Is it just their versatility he admires, or do they represent something more to him?

STYLE AND STRUCTURE

1. Where does Burciaga provide a formal definition of *tortilla*? Why does he locate this formal definition at this point in his essay?

2. Burciaga uses many Spanish words, but he defines only some of them — for example, *taquitos de nopalitos* and *quesadilla* in paragraph 5 and *flautas* and *gorditas* in paragraph 6. Why do you think he defines some terms but not others?

3. Does Burciaga use **synonyms** or negation to define *tortilla*? Does he discuss the word's origin? If so, where? If not, do you think any of these strategies would improve his essay? Explain.

VOCABULARY PROJECTS

1. Define each of the following words as it is used in this selection.
   yarmulke (2)   absconded (3)   concocted (7)
   maize (3)   adobe (4)

2. Look up each of the following words in a Spanish-English dictionary and (if possible) supply its English equivalent.

mercado (4)   *masa* (4)
deliciosas (4)   *jalapeños* (5)

JOURNAL ENTRY

Explore some additional uses — practical or frivolous — for tortillas that Burciaga does not discuss.

WRITING WORKSHOP

1. Write an essay in which you define a food that is important to your family, ethnic group, or circle of friends. Use several patterns of development, as Burciaga does. Assume that your audience is not very familiar with the food you define.

2. Relying primarily on description and exemplification, define a food that is sure to be familiar to all your readers. Don't name the food until your essay's last sentence.

3. Write an essay defining a food — but include a thesis statement that paints a very favorable portrait of a much-maligned food (for example, Spam or brussels sprouts) or a very negative picture of a popular food (for example, chocolate or ice cream).

COMBINING THE PATTERNS

Burciaga uses several patterns of development in his extended definition. Where, for example, does he use **description, narration, process,** and **exemplification?** Does he use any other patterns? Explain.

THEMATIC CONNECTIONS

- "Once More to the Lake" (page 154)
- "Does America Still Exist?" (page 482)
- "The Park" (page 626)

JUDY BRADY

Judy Brady was born in San Francisco in 1937 and earned a B.F.A. in painting from the University of Iowa in 1962. She has raised two daughters, worked as a secretary, and published articles on many social issues. Diagnosed with breast cancer in 1980, she became active in the politics of cancer and has edited *Women and Cancer* (1990) and *One in Three: Women with Cancer Confront an Epidemic* (1991). She also helped found the Toxic Links Coalition, an organization devoted to lobbying for cancer and environmental issues.

Brady has been active in the women's movement since 1969, and "I Want a Wife" first appeared in the premiere issue of *Ms.* magazine in 1972. As the headnote for "Sexism in English" (page 413) suggests, this was a year when the feminist movement had reached its full flowering, and nothing perhaps represented this as much as the start-up of *Ms.* The first periodical to focus on women's issues from a distinctly feminist perspective, *Ms.* led the way in challenging established gender roles in the popular press. Brady's essay is just the sort of provocative essay that epitomized much of what appeared in *Ms.* in its early years. Since its original publication, "I Want a Wife" has been one of the most widely anthologized essays in first-year composition texts. Even a quarter-century after it was written, it continues to spark controversy and debate.

I Want a Wife

I belong to that classification of people known as wives. I am A Wife. 1 And, not altogether incidentally, I am a mother.

Not too long ago a male friend of mine appeared on the scene fresh 2 from a recent divorce. He had one child, who is, of course, with his ex-wife. He is looking for another wife. As I thought about him while I was ironing one evening, it suddenly occurred to me that I, too, would like to have a wife. Why do I want a wife?

I would like to go back to school so that I can become economically 3 independent, support myself, and, if need be, support those dependent upon me. I want a wife who will work and send me to school. And while I am going to school I want a wife to take care of my children. I want a wife to keep track of the children's doctor and dentist appointments. And to keep track of mine, too. I want a wife to make sure my children eat properly and are kept clean. I want a wife who will wash the children's clothes and keep them mended. I want a wife who is a good nurturant attendant to my children, who arranges for their schooling, makes sure that they have an adequate social life with their peers, takes them to the park, the zoo, etc. I want a wife who takes care of the children when they are sick, a wife who arranges to be around when the children need special care, because, of course, I cannot miss classes at school. My wife must arrange to lose time at work and not lose the job. It may mean a small cut in my wife's income from time to time, but I guess I can tolerate that. Needless to say, my wife will arrange and pay for the care of the children while my wife is working.

I want a wife who will take care of *my* physical needs. I want a wife 4 who will keep my house clean. A wife who will pick up after my children, a wife who will pick up after me. I want a wife who will keep my clothes clean, ironed, mended, replaced when need be, and who will see to it that my personal things are kept in their proper place so that I can find what I need the minute I need it. I want a wife who cooks the meals, a wife who is a *good* cook. I want a wife who will plan the menus, do the necessary grocery shopping, prepare the meals, serve them pleasantly, and then do the cleaning up while I do my studying. I want a wife who will care for me when I am sick and sympathize with my pain and loss of time from school. I want a wife to go along when our family takes a vacation so that someone can continue to care for me and my children when I need a rest and change of scene.

I want a wife who will not bother me with rambling complaints about 5 a wife's duties. But I want a wife who will listen to me when I feel the need to explain a rather difficult point I have come across in my course of studies. And I want a wife who will type my papers for me when I have written them.

I want a wife who will take care of the details of my social life. When 6 my wife and I are invited out by my friends, I want a wife who will take care of the babysitting arrangements. When I meet people at school that I like and want to entertain, I want a wife who will have the house clean, will prepare a special meal, serve it to me and my friends, and not interrupt when I talk about things that interest me and my friends. I want a wife who will have arranged that the children are fed and ready for bed before my guests arrive so that the children do not bother us. I want a wife who takes care of the needs of my guests so that they feel comfortable, who makes sure that they have an ashtray, that they are passed the hors d'oeuvres, that they are offered a second helping of the food, that their wine glasses are replenished when necessary, that their coffee is served to them as they like it. And I want a wife who knows that sometimes I need a night out by myself.

I want a wife who is sensitive to my sexual needs, a wife who makes 7 love passionately and eagerly when I feel like it, a wife who makes sure that I am satisfied. And, of course, I want a wife who will not demand sexual attention when I am not in the mood for it. I want a wife who assumes the complete responsibility for birth control, because I do not want more children. I want a wife who will remain sexually faithful to me so that I do not have to clutter up my intellectual life with jealousies. And I want a wife who understands that *my* sexual needs may entail more than strict adherence to monogamy. I must, after all, be able to relate to people as fully as possible.

If, by chance, I find another person more suitable as a wife than the 8 wife I already have, I want the liberty to replace my present wife with another one. Naturally, I will expect a fresh new life; my wife will take the children and be solely responsible for them so that I am left free.

When I am through with school and have a job, I want my wife to quit   9
working and remain at home so that my wife can more fully and completely take care of a wife's duties.

My God, who *wouldn't* want a wife?   10

• • •

COMPREHENSION

1. In one sentence, define what Brady means by *wife*. Does this ideal wife actually exist? Explain.

2. List some of the specific duties of the wife Brady describes. Into what five general categories does Brady arrange these duties?

3. What complaints does Brady apparently have about the life she actually leads? To what does she seem to attribute her problems?

4. Under what circumstances does Brady say she would consider leaving her wife? What would happen to the children if she left?

PURPOSE AND AUDIENCE

1. This essay was first published in *Ms.* magazine. In what sense is it appropriate for the audience of this feminist publication? Where else can you imagine it appearing?

2. Does this essay have an explicitly stated thesis? If so, where is it? If the thesis is implied, paraphrase it.

3. Do you think Brady *really* wants the kind of wife she describes? Explain.

STYLE AND STRUCTURE

1. Throughout the essay, Brady repeats the words "I want a wife." What is the effect of this repetition?

2. The first and last paragraphs of this essay are quite brief. Does this weaken the essay? Why or why not?

3. In enumerating a wife's duties, Brady frequently uses the verb *arrange*. What other verbs does she use repeatedly? How do these verbs help her make her point?

4. Brady never uses the personal pronouns *he* or *she* to refer to the wife she defines. Why not?

5. Comment on Brady's use of phrases like *of course* (2, 3, and 7), *needless to say* (3), *after all* (7), *by chance* (8), and *naturally* (8). What do these expressions contribute to the sentences in which they appear? To the essay as a whole?

VOCABULARY PROJECTS

1. Define each of the following words as it is used in this selection.

   nurturant (3)   adherence (7)
   replenished (6)   monogamy (7)

2. Going beyond the dictionary definitions, decide what Brady means to suggest by the following words. Is she using any of these words sarcastically? Explain.

   proper (4)   necessary (6)   suitable (8)
   pleasantly (4)   demand (7)   free (8)
   bother (6)   clutter up (7)

JOURNAL ENTRY

Do you think Brady's 1972 characterization of a wife is still accurate today? Which of the characteristics she describes have remained the same? Which have changed? Why?

WRITING WORKSHOP

1. Write an essay in which you define your ideal spouse.

2. Write an essay entitled "I Want a Husband." Taking an **ironic** stance, use society's notions of the ideal husband to help you shape your definition.

3. Read "The Company Man" (page 478). Using ideas gleaned from that essay and "I Want a Wife," as well as your own ideas, write a definition essay called "The Ideal Couple." Your essay can be serious or humorous. Develop your definition with examples.

COMBINING THE PATTERNS

Like most **definition** essays, "I Want a Wife" uses several patterns of development. Which ones does it use? Which of these do you consider most important for supporting Brady's thesis? Why?

THEMATIC CONNECTIONS

- "My Mother Never Worked" (page 94)
- "Sex, Lies, and Conversation" (page 367)
- "The Men We Carry in Our Minds" (page 399)
- "The Company Man" (page 478)

ELLEN GOODMAN

Ellen Goodman was born in 1941 in Newton, Massachusetts, and graduated from Radcliffe College in 1963. She joined the *Boston Globe* in 1967 and is now a columnist and associate editor at the newspaper. Her regular column, "At Large," has been syndicated since 1976 and now appears in more than four hundred newspapers nationwide. She has published several volumes of her columns, including *Close to Home* (1975) and, most recently, *Value Judgments* (1993). Goodman received a Pulitzer Prize for commentary in 1980.

The concept of the "company man" dates from the 1950s when employees — almost exclusively male and particularly in large corporations — were expected to virtually give over their lives to their jobs if they expected to climb the corporate ladder. Any questioning of company policy or procedures, any sort of nonconformity, was implicitly discouraged. By the early 1970s, when Goodman's column appeared, however, the countercultural movements of the 1960s had led some, particularly younger people, to challenge such values and to view large corporations with distrust. It is within this context that Goodman defines a particularly grim vision of the "company man." More recently, some companies have modified their corporate culture to allow for more original thinking. Nevertheless, the company man — now, of course, just as likely to be a woman — still exists.

The Company Man

He worked himself to death, finally and precisely, at 3:00 A.M. Sunday morning. 1

The obituary didn't say that, of course. It said that he died of a coronary thrombosis — I think that was it — but everyone among his friends and acquaintances knew it instantly. He was a perfect Type A, a workaholic, a classic, they said to each other and shook their heads — and thought for five or ten minutes about the way they lived. 2

This man who worked himself to death finally and precisely at 3:00 A.M. Sunday morning — on his day off — was fifty-one years old and a vice-president. He was, however, one of six vice-presidents, and one of three who might conceivably — if the president died or retired soon enough — have moved to the top spot. Phil knew that. 3

He worked six days a week, five of them until eight or nine at night, during a time when his own company had begun the four-day week for everyone but the executives. He worked like the Important People. He had no outside "extracurricular interests," unless, of course, you think about a monthly golf game that way. To Phil, it was work. He always ate egg salad sandwiches at his desk. He was, of course, overweight, by 20 or 25 pounds. He thought it was okay, though, because he didn't smoke. 4

On Saturdays, Phil wore a sports jacket to the office instead of a suit, because it was the weekend. 5

He had a lot of people working for him, maybe sixty, and most of   6
them liked him most of the time. Three of them will be seriously considered for his job. The obituary didn't mention that.

But it did list his "survivors" quite accurately. He is survived by his   7
wife, Helen, forty-eight years old, a good woman of no particular mar-
ketable skills, who worked in an office before marrying and mothering.
She had, according to her daughter, given up trying to compete with his
work years ago, when the children were small. A company friend said, "I
know how much you will miss him." And she answered, "I already have."

"Missing him all these years," she must have given up part of herself   8
which had cared too much for the man. She would be "well taken care of."

His "dearly beloved" eldest of the "dearly beloved" children is a hard-   9
working executive in a manufacturing firm down South. In the day and a
half before the funeral, he went around the neighborhood researching his
father, asking the neighbors what he was like. They were embarrassed.

His second child is a girl, who is twenty-four and newly married. She   10
lives near her mother and they are close, but whenever she was alone with
her father, in a car driving somewhere, they had nothing to say to each other.

The youngest is twenty, a boy, a high-school graduate who has spent   11
the last couple of years, like a lot of his friends, doing enough odd jobs
to stay in grass and food. He was the one who tried to grab at his father,
and tried to mean enough to him to keep the man at home. He was his
father's favorite. Over the last two years, Phil stayed up nights worrying
about the boy.

The boy once said, "My father and I only board here."   12

At the funeral, the sixty-year-old company president told the forty-   13
eight-year-old widow that the fifty-one-year-old deceased had meant
much to the company and would be missed and would be hard to replace.
The widow didn't look him in the eye. She was afraid he would read her
bitterness and, after all, she would need him to straighten out the
finances — the stock options and all that.

Phil was overweight and nervous and worked too hard. If he wasn't   14
at the office, he was worried about it. Phil was a Type A, a heart-attack natural. You could have picked him out in a minute from a lineup.

So when he finally worked himself to death, at precisely 3:00 A.M. Sun-   15
day morning, no one was really surprised.

By 5:00 P.M. the afternoon of the funeral, the company president had   16
begun, discreetly of course, with care and taste, to make inquiries about
his replacement. One of three men. He asked around: "Who's been working the hardest?"

• • •

COMPREHENSION

1. In one sentence, define *the company man*. What does Goodman's extended
   definition convey that your one-sentence definition lacks?

2. When Phil's widow is told by a friend, "I know how much you will miss him," she answers, "I already have" (7). What does she mean?

3. Why does Phil's oldest son go around the neighborhood researching his father?

4. Why doesn't Phil's widow look the company president in the eye?

5. What kind of man will the company president seek for Phil's replacement?

PURPOSE AND AUDIENCE

1. What point is Goodman trying to make in this essay? Does she succeed? Explain.

2. What assumptions does Goodman make about her readers? What effect do you think she hopes the essay will have on her audience?

3. Why does Goodman imply her thesis and not state it?

STYLE AND STRUCTURE

1. Why does Goodman state the time of Phil's death at both the beginning and the end of her essay?

2. Is there a reason why Goodman waits until the end of paragraph 3 before she refers to the company man by name? Explain.

3. What is the effect of the bits of dialogue Goodman includes?

4. Goodman tells Phil's story in a flat, impersonal way. How does this tone help her achieve her purpose?

5. Why does Goodman put quotation marks around the phrases *extracurricular interests* (4), *survivors* (7), *missing him all these years, well taken care of* (8), and *dearly beloved* (9)?

VOCABULARY PROJECTS

1. Define each of the following words as it is used in this selection.

coronary thrombosis (2)   classic (2)   stock options (13)
workaholic (2)   conceivably (3)

2. This essay's style and vocabulary are quite informal. Substitute a more formal word or phrase for each of these expressions:

top spot (3)   odd jobs (11)   all that (13)
okay (4)   grab at (11)   a heart-attack natural (14)

How does each substitution change the sentence in which it appears?

JOURNAL ENTRY

Do you know anyone like Phil? What do you think really motivates people like him? Do you believe such forces drive women as well as men?

WRITING WORKSHOP

1. Write an essay defining the workaholic student (or the procrastinating student). As Goodman does, use an extended example to support your thesis.

2. Write a definition essay in which you define the company man (or the company woman), but use comparison and contrast to organize your definition.

3. Write a brief obituary for Phil, one that might appear in his company's newsletter. Using the title "A Valued Employee," develop the obituary as a definition essay. Your aim is to show readers what traits such an employee must have — and to present those traits as desirable ones.

COMBINING THE PATTERNS

Goodman relies on **narration** to develop her definition. Is this a good choice? Why? What other patterns of development would be helpful?

THEMATIC CONNECTIONS

- "Midnight" (page 177)
- "The Peter Principle" (page 181)
- "Suicide Note" (page 314)

RICHARD RODRIGUEZ

Born in 1944 to Mexican immigrant parents, Richard Rodriguez grew up in Sacramento, California. He graduated from Stanford University in 1967, and received a master's degree from Columbia University and a doctorate from the University of California at Berkeley, where he taught for a time before devoting himself to writing. He is now an editor with the Pacific News Service and has created film essays for PBS's *NewsHour With Jim Lehrer. Hunger of Memory: The Education of Richard Rodriguez,* his 1982 collection of autobiographical essays about assimilating into mainstream U.S. culture, is considered a classic. His second collection, *Days of Obligation: An Argument with My Mexican Father,* was published in 1992.

Rodriguez wrote the following essay in the early 1980s at a time when Americans were beginning to struggle with notions of ethnic identity and cultural heritage. Immigration patterns had shifted over the previous two decades, with a greater percentage of immigrants coming from Central and South America and Asia than from Europe. In previous waves of immigration, strict assimilation had been assumed; these immigrants wanted to be part of the "melting pot." Many newer immigrants, however, feel an obligation to maintain a culture and a language of their own. In the face of this call for greater cultural diversity, some Americans within the mainstream wonder, as Rodriguez's title suggests, whether America as it has traditionally been defined can still exist.

Does America Still Exist?

For the children of immigrant parents the knowledge comes easier. America exists everywhere in the city — on billboards, frankly in the smell of French fries and popcorn. It exists in the pace: traffic lights, the assertions of neon, the mysterious bong-bong through atriums of department stores. America exists as the voice of the crowd, a menacing sound — the high nasal accent of American English.

When I was a boy in Sacramento (California, the fifties), people would ask me, "Where you from?" I was born in this country, but I knew the question meant to decipher my darkness, my looks.

My mother once instructed me to say, "I am an American of Mexican descent." By the time I was nine or ten, I wanted to say, but dared not reply, "I am an American."

Immigrants come to America and, against hostility or mere loneliness, they recreate a homeland in the parlor, tacking up postcards or calendars of some impossible blue — lake or sea or sky. Children of immigrant parents are supposed to perch on a hyphen between two countries. Relatives assume the achievement as much as anyone. Relatives are, in any case, surprised when the child begins losing old ways. One day at the family picnic the boy wanders away from their spiced food and faceless stories to watch other boys play baseball in the distance.

There is sorrow in the American memory, guilty sorrow for having left   5
something behind — Portugal, China, Norway. The American story is the
story of immigrant children and of their children — children no longer
able to speak to grandparents. The memory of exile becomes inarticulate
as it passes from generation to generation, along with wedding rings and
pocket watches — like some mute stone in a wad of old lace. Europe. Asia.
Eden.

But, it needs to be said, if this is a country where one stops being Viet-   6
namese or Italian, this is a country where one begins to be an American.
America exists as a culture and a grin, a faith and a shrug. It is clasped in a
handshake, called by a first name.

As much as the country is joined in a common culture, however,   7
Americans are reluctant to celebrate the process of assimilation. We
pledge allegiance to diversity. America was born Protestant and bred Puritan, and the notion of community we share is derived from a seventeenth-
century faith. Presidents and the pages of ninth-grade civics readers yet
proclaim the orthodoxy: We are gathered together — but as individuals,
with separate pasts, distinct destinies. Our society is as paradoxical as a
Puritan congregation: We stand together, alone.

Americans have traditionally defined themselves by what they   8
refused to include. As often, however, Americans have struggled, turned
in good conscience at last to assert the great Protestant virtue of tolerance.
Despite outbreaks of nativist frenzy, America has remained an immigrant
country, open and true to itself.

Against pious emblems of rural America — soda fountain, Elks hall,   9
Protestant church, and now shopping mall — stands the cold-hearted city,
crowded with races and ambitions, curious laughter, much that is odd.
Nevertheless, it is the city that has most truly represented America. In the
city, however, the millions of singular lives have had no richer notion of
wholeness to describe them than the idea of pluralism.

"Where you from?" the American asks the immigrant child. "Mexico," the   10
boy learns to say.

Mexico, the country of my blood ancestors, offers formal contrast to   11
the American achievement. If the United States was formed by Protestant
individualism, Mexico was helped by a medieval Catholic dream of one
world. The Spanish journeyed to Mexico to plunder, and they may have
gone, in God's name, with an arrogance peculiar to those who intend to
convert. But through the conversion, the Indian converted the Spaniard. A
new race was born, the *mestizo,* wedding European to Indian. José Vason-
celos, the Mexican philosopher, has celebrated this New World creation,
proclaiming it the "cosmic race."

Centuries later, in a San Francisco restaurant, a Mexican-American   12
lawyer of my acquaintance says, in English, over *salade niçoise,* that he
does not intend to assimilate into gringo society. His claim is echoed by a
chorus of others (Italian-Americans, Greeks, Asians) in this era of ethnic
pride. The melting pot has been retired, clanking, into the museum of

quaint disgrace, alongside Aunt Jemima and the Katzenjammer Kids. But resistance to assimilation is characteristically American. It only makes clear how inevitable the process of assimilation actually is.

For generations, this has been the pattern. Immigrant parents have 13 sent their children to school (simply, they thought) to acquire the "skills" to survive in the city. The child returned home with a voice his parents barely recognized or understood, couldn't trust, and didn't like.

In Eastern cities — Philadelphia, New York, Boston, Baltimore — class 14 after class gathered immigrant children to women (usually women) who stood in front of rooms full of children, changing children. So also for me in the 1950s. Irish-Catholic nuns. California. The old story. The hyphen tipped to the right, away from Mexico and toward a confusing but true American identity.

I speak now in the chromium American accent of my grammar 15 school classmates — Billy Reckers, Mike Bradley, Carol Schmidt, Kathy O'Grady. . . . I believe I became like my classmates, became German, Polish, and (like my teachers) Irish. And because assimilation is always reciprocal, my classmates got something of me. (I mean sad eyes; belief in the Indian Virgin; a taste for sugar skulls on the Feast of the Dead.) In the blending, we became what our parents could never have been, and we carried America one revolution further.

"Does America still exist?" Americans have been asking the question 16 for so long that to ask it again only proves our continuous link. But perhaps the question deserves to be asked with urgency — now. Since the black civil rights movement of the 1960s, our tenuous notion of a shared public life has deteriorated notably.

The struggle of black men and women did not eradicate racism, but it 17 became the great moment in the life of America's conscience. Water hoses, bulldogs, blood — the images, rendered black, white, rectangular, passed into living rooms.

It is hard to look at a photograph of a crowd taken, say, in 1890 or in 18 1930 and not notice the absence of blacks. (It becomes an impertinence to wonder if America *still* exists.)

In the sixties, other groups of Americans learned to champion their 19 rights by analogy to the black civil rights movement. But the heroic vision faded. Dr. Martin Luther King Jr. had spoken with Pauline eloquence of a nation that would unite Christian and Jew, old and young, rich and poor. Within a decade, the struggles of the 1960s were reduced to a bureaucratic competition for little more than pieces of a representational pie. The quest for a portion of power became an end in itself. The metaphor for the American city of the 1970s was a committee: one black, one woman, one person under thirty.

If the small town had sinned against America by too neatly defining 20 who could be an American, the city's sin was a romantic secession. One noticed the romanticism in the antiwar movement — certain demonstrators who demonstrated a lack of tact or desire to persuade and seemed content to play secular protestants. One noticed the romanticism in the competition among members of "minority groups" to claim the status of Primary Victim. To Americans unconfident of their common identity, minority standing became a way of asserting individuality. Middle-class Americans — men and women clearly not the primary victims of social oppression — brandished their suffering with exuberance.

The dream of a single society probably died with *The Ed Sullivan Show.* 21 The reality of America persists. Teenagers pass through big-city high schools banded in racial groups, their collars turned up to a uniform shrug. But then they graduate to jobs at the phone company or in banks, where they end up working alongside people unlike themselves. Typists and tellers walk out together at lunchtime.

It is easier for us as Americans to believe the obvious fact of our sepa- 22 rateness — easier to imagine the black and white Americas prophesied by the Kerner report (broken glass, street fires) — than to recognize the reality of a city street at lunchtime. Americans are wedded by proximity to a common culture. The panhandler at one corner is related to the pamphleteer at the next who is related to the banker who is kin to the Chinese old man wearing an MIT sweatshirt. In any true national history, Thomas Jefferson begets Martin Luther King, Jr. who begets the Gray Panthers. It is because we lack a vision of ourselves entire — the city street is crowded and we are each preoccupied with finding our own way home — that we lack an appropriate hymn.

Under my window now passes a little white girl softly rehearsing to 23 herself a Motown obbligato.

• • •

COMPREHENSION

1. As a child, why didn't Rodriguez dare to call himself American?

2. What does Rodriguez mean by the statement "Children of immigrant parents are supposed to perch on a hyphen between two countries" (4)? What does he mean when he writes in paragraph 14 that the hyphen "tipped to the right"?

3. Why, according to Rodriguez, is there "sorrow in the American memory" (5)?

4. In Rodriguez's opinion, *does* America still exist?

5. Rodriguez sees assimilation as inevitable. Does he see it as a positive or a negative trend? Explain. Do you agree with him?

PURPOSE AND AUDIENCE

1. Whom do you see as Rodriguez's primary audience? Why? Does he seem to expect his readers to share his views? How can you tell?

2. Rodriguez's essay includes many references to his own childhood experiences as the American-born child of Mexican immigrant parents. What is

his purpose in recounting his personal experiences? Do these personal references make you more or less receptive to his argument?

3. In one sentence, paraphrase Rodriguez's thesis.

STYLE AND STRUCTURE

1. Rodriguez uses exemplification, narration, and comparison and contrast to develop his definition. Where does he use each of these patterns of development? Does he use others? Explain.

2. Rodriguez's essay begins somewhat abruptly. What strategy might he have used to develop his introduction further?

3. Do you think Rodriguez's essay could have been strengthened by the addition of a paragraph of *enumeration* (listing America's characteristics) and/or a paragraph of *negation* (telling what America is *not*)? Where might such paragraphs be added?

4. Reread Rodriguez's last paragraph. What do you think he means? Do you think this paragraph should be developed further? If so, how?

VOCABULARY PROJECTS

1. Define each of the following words as it is used in this selection.

orthodoxy (7)	gringo (12)	secular (20)
paradoxical (7)	reciprocal (15)	brandished (20)
nativist (8)	tenuous (16)	proximity (22)
pious (9)	eradicate (17)	obbligato (23)
emblems (9)	rendered (17)	
pluralism (9)	secession (20)	

2. Identify each use of the words *America* and *American* in Rodriguez's essay. Are the connotations of these words always positive? In general, do you see these words as essentially positive, negative, or neutral?

JOURNAL ENTRY

In paragraph 12, Rodriguez writes that "the melting pot has been retired . . . into the museum of quaint disgrace. . . ." What does he mean? Does your own experience support his view?

WRITING WORKSHOP

1. What does the word *American* mean to you? Define this word by means of exemplification, enumerating the characteristics that you associate with being American.

2. Write a definition essay in which you define *America* by comparing the United States with another nation. (Or, define another nation by comparing it with the United States.)

3. At what point does one stop being Vietnamese or Dominican or Italian and start being "American"? Develop a definition of *American* by explaining the process of assimilating into American culture. Be sure to include a thesis statement that indicates whether you see the process of assimilation as a positive or negative thing.

COMBINING THE PATTERNS

In paragraph 11, Rodriguez uses **comparison and contrast** to contrast Mexico and the United States. How are they different? Why is this difference significant? Does Rodriguez use comparison and contrast elsewhere in his essay? Do you see additional opportunities for him to do so? If so, where?

THEMATIC CONNECTIONS

- "More Than Just a Shrine: Paying Homage to the Ghosts of Ellis Island" (page 142)
- "The 'Black Table' Is Still There" (page 294)
- "Two Ways to Belong in America" (page 357)
- "Mother Tongue" (page 405)

MARGE PIERCY

Poet and novelist Marge Piercy was born in Detroit in 1934. She attended the University of Michigan on scholarship and later received her master's degree from Northwestern. Her work, which includes more than a dozen novels and a similar number of poetry collections, often reflects her intense involvement in many liberal and feminist causes. Her most recent works are two novels, *Three Women* (1999) and *Storm Tide* (1998), written with her husband, Ira Wood. She has said of her work that she imagines she speaks "for a constituency, living and dead, and that I give utterance to energy, experience, insights, words flowing from many lives."

The following poem was published in the collection *To Be of Use* in 1973 — a time when fewer women than today were in the workplace, and when those who were rarely held executive positions. (Women made up only about 17 percent of managers and executives in 1970; in 1998, that figure was just over 44 percent. Full-time working women in 1970 made 594 dollars to working men's 1,000 dollars; today they make 742 dollars.) Female office workers, the so-called pink-collar workers, in most cases had very little power or stature. Although Piercy's poem obviously conveys women's lack of power, it also suggests the dehumanization of work in big corporations generally, another theme of 1960s and 1970s counterculture.

The Secretary Chant

My hips are a desk.
From my ears hang
chains of paper clips.
Rubber bands form my hair.
My breasts are wells of mimeograph ink.   5
My feet bear casters.
Buzz. Click.
My head is a badly organized file.
My head is a switchboard
where crossed lines crackle.   10
Press my fingers
and in my eyes appear
credit and debit.
Zing. Tinkle.
My navel is a reject button.   15
From my mouth issue canceled reams.
Swollen, heavy, rectangular
I am about to be delivered
of a baby
Xerox machine.   20
File me under W

because I wonce
was
a woman.

• • •

THINKING ABOUT LITERATURE

1. According to this poem, what is a secretary? Develop a one-sentence defi-
    nition that conveys the speaker's viewpoint.

2. What pattern of development dominates this poem? Are other patterns
    used to develop the definition?

3. Who is speaking? What other voices could the poet have used to present
    the definition of *secretary*? Is the perspective Piercy chose more effective
    than these alternatives would be? Explain.

JOURNAL ENTRY

Write a brief objective definition of *secretary*. How is your definition different
from Piercy's?

THEMATIC CONNECTIONS

*   "Finishing School" (page 88)
*   "The Untouchable" (page 461)
*   "I Want a Wife" (page 474)

WRITING ASSIGNMENTS FOR DEFINITION

1. Choose a document or ritual that is a significant part of your religious or cultural heritage. Define it, using any pattern or combination of patterns you choose but making sure to include a formal definition somewhere in your essay. Assume your readers are not familiar with the term you are defining.

2. Define an abstract term — for example, stubbornness, security, courage, or fear — by making it concrete. You can develop your definition with a series of brief examples or with an extended narrative that illustrates the characteristic you are defining.

3. The readings in this chapter define (among other things) a food, a family role, and two occupational roles. Write an essay in which you define one of these topics — for instance, spaghetti (food), a stepmother (family role), or the modern baseball player (occupational role).

4. Do some research to learn the meaning of one of these medical conditions: angina, migraine, Down syndrome, attention deficit disorder, schizophrenia, autism, osteoporosis, Alzheimer's disease. Then write an extended definition essay explaining the condition to an audience of high school students.

5. Use an extended example to support a thesis in an essay that defines *racism, sexism,* or another type of bigoted behavior.

6. Choose a term that is central to one of your courses — for instance, *naturalism, behaviorism,* or *authority* — and write an essay in which you define the term. Assume that your audience is made up of students who have not yet taken the course. You may begin with an overview of the term's origin if you believe this is appropriate. Then develop your essay with examples and **analogies** that will facilitate your audience's understanding of the term.

7. Assume your audience is from a culture that is not familiar with modern American pastimes. Write a definition essay for this audience in which you describe the form and function of a Frisbee, a Barbie doll, an action figure, a skateboard, or a video game.

8. Review any one of the following narrative essays from Chapter 4, and use it to help you develop an extended definition of one of the following terms.

   "Homeward Bound"— family

   "Finishing School"— prejudice

   "My Mother Never Worked"— work

   "Thirty-Eight Who Saw Murder Didn't Call the Police"— apathy

   "Shooting an Elephant"— power

9. What constitutes an education? Define the term *education* by identifying several different sources of knowledge, formal or informal, and explaining what each contributes. You might read — or reread —"Finishing School" (page 88), "Reading the River" (page 138), or "The Human Cost of an Illiterate Society" (page 203).

10. What qualifies someone to be a hero? Developing your essay with a single extended example or a series of examples, define the word *hero*. Include a formal definition, and try to incorporate at least one paragraph in which you define the term by explaining and illustrating what a hero is *not*.

COLLABORATIVE ACTIVITY FOR DEFINITION

Working as a group, choose one of the following words to define: *pride, hope, sacrifice, courage, justice.* Then, define the term with a series of extended examples drawn from films that members of your group have seen, with each of you developing an illustrative paragraph based on a different film. (Before beginning, your group may decide to focus on one particular genre of film.) When each paragraph has been read by everyone in the group, work together to formulate a thesis that asserts the vital importance of the quality your examples have defined. Finally, write suitable opening and closing paragraphs for the essay, and arrange the body paragraphs in a logical order, adding transitions where necessary.

INTERNET ASSIGNMENT FOR DEFINITION

After visiting the following World Wide Web sites, write an essay in which you define the term *Industrial Revolution.* In order to give your readers a better understanding of the effects of industrialization, develop your definition by considering changes that occurred in the areas of art, science, technology, medicine, working conditions, and/or transportation.

IRWeb: The Industrial Revolution
<http://tqjunior.advanced.org/4132/index.htm>
This educational site about the Industrial Revolution contains information, links to other sites, and games, including an Industrial Revolution quiz.

Internet Modern History Sourcebook: The Industrial Revolution
<http://www.fordham.edu/halsall/mod/modsbook14.html>
This site offers original texts written during the Industrial Revolution, including lectures and discussions about the process of industrialization and the social and political effects of the revolution. It also features literary responses to the revolution.

The Industrial Revolution: A Trip to the Past
<http://members.aol.com/mhirotsu/kevin/trip2.html>
This site discusses advances in art, science, medicine, and transportation.

12

ARGUMENTATION

WHAT IS ARGUMENTATION?

Argumentation is a reasoned, logical way of asserting the soundness of a position, belief, or conclusion. Argumentation takes a stand — supported by evidence — and urges people to share the writer's perspective and insights. In the following paragraph from "Test-Tube Babies: Solution or Problem?" Ruth Hubbard argues that before we endorse further development of the technology that allows for the creation of test-tube babies, we should consider the consequences:

Issue identified	In vitro fertilization of human eggs and the implantation of early embryos into women's wombs are biotechnologies that may enable some women to bear children
Background presents both sides of issue	who have hitherto been unable to do so. In that sense, it may solve their particular infertility problems. On the other hand, this technology poses unpredictable hazards since it intervenes in the process of fertilization, in the first cell divisions of the fertilized egg, and in the implantation of the embryo into the uterus. At present we have no way to assess in what ways and to what extent these interventions may affect the women or the babies they acquire by this procedure. Since the use of the technology is only beginning, the financial and technical investments
Topic sentence (takes a stand)	it represents are still modest. It is therefore important that we, as a society, seriously consider the wisdom of implementing and developing it further.

Argumentation can have any of several purposes: to convince other people to accept — or at least acknowledge the validity of — your position; to defend your position, even if others cannot be convinced to agree; or to question or refute a position you believe to be misguided, untrue, dangerous, or evil, without necessarily offering an alternative.

UNDERSTANDING ARGUMENTATION AND PERSUASION

Although the terms *persuasion* and *argumentation* are frequently used interchangeably, they do not mean the same thing. **Persuasion** is a general term that refers to the method by which a writer moves an audience to adopt a belief or follow a course of action. To persuade an audience, a writer relies on various appeals — to the emotions, to reason, or to ethics.

Argumentation is the appeal to reason. In an argument, a writer connects a series of statements so that they lead logically to a conclusion. Argumentation is different from persuasion in that it does not try to move an audience to action; its primary purpose is simply to demonstrate that certain ideas are valid and others are not. And, unlike persuasion, argumentation has a formal structure: an argument makes points, supplies evidence, establishes a logical chain of reasoning, refutes opposing arguments, and accommodates the views of an audience.

As the readings in this chapter demonstrate, however, most effective arguments combine several appeals: even though their primary appeal is to reason, they may also appeal to emotions. For example, you could use a combination of logical and emotional appeals to argue against lowering the drinking age in your state from twenty-one to eighteen. You could appeal to *reason* by constructing an argument leading to the conclusion that the state should not condone policies that have a high probability of injuring or killing citizens. You could support your conclusion by presenting statistics showing that alcohol-related traffic accidents kill more teenagers than disease does. You could also cite a study showing that when the drinking age was raised from eighteen to twenty-one, fatal accidents declined. In addition, you could include an appeal to the *emotions* by telling a particularly sad story about an eighteen-year-old alcoholic or by pointing out how an increased number of accidents involving drunk drivers would cost taxpayers more money and could even cost some of them their lives. These appeals to your audience's emotions could strengthen your argument by widening its appeal. Keep in mind, however, that in an effective argument emotion does not take the place of logic; it supports and reinforces it.

The appeals you choose and how you balance them depend in part on your purpose and your sense of your audience. As you consider what strategies to use, remember that some extremely effective appeals are unfair. Although most people would agree that lies, threats, and appeals to greed and prejudice are unacceptable ways of reaching an audience, such appeals are used in political campaigns, international diplomacy, and daily conversation. Nevertheless, in your college writing you should use only those appeals that most people would consider fair.

PLANNING AN ARGUMENTATIVE ESSAY

Choosing a Topic

In an argumentative essay, as in all writing, choosing the right topic is important. Ideally, your topic should be one in which you have an intellectual or emotional stake. Still, you should still be open-minded and willing to consider all sides of a question. If the evidence goes against your position, you should be willing to change your thesis. And you should be able, from the outset, to consider your topic from other people's viewpoints; this will help you determine how much they know about your topic, what their beliefs are, and how they are likely to react. You can then use this knowledge to build your case. If you cannot be open-minded, then you should choose another topic that you can deal with more objectively.

Other factors should also influence your selection of a topic. You should be well informed about your topic. In addition, you should choose an issue narrow enough to be treated effectively in the space available to you, or be willing to confine your discussion to one aspect of a broad issue. It is also important to consider your purpose — what you expect your argument to accomplish and how you wish your audience to respond. If your topic is so far-reaching that you cannot identify what you want to convince readers to think, or if your purpose is so idealistic that your expectations of their response are impossible or unreasonable, your essay will suffer.

Taking a Stand

After you have chosen your topic, you are ready to take your stand — to state the position you will argue in the form of a thesis. Consider the following thesis statement:

> Education is the best way to address the problem of increased drug use among teenagers.

This thesis statement says that increased drug use is a problem among teenagers, that there is more than one possible solution to this problem, and that education is a better solution than any other. In your argument, you will have to support each of these three points logically and persuasively.

After stating your thesis, you should examine it to make sure it is *debatable.* There is no point in arguing a statement of fact or a point that most people accept as self-evident. A good argumentative thesis contains a proposition that at least some people would object to. A good way to test the suitability of your thesis for an argumentative essay is to formulate an **antithesis,** a statement that asserts the opposite position. If you know that some people would support the antithesis, you can be certain that your thesis is indeed debatable.

| Thesis: | Because immigrants have contributed much to the development of the United States, immigration quotas should be relaxed. |
| Antithesis: | Even though immigrants have contributed much to the development of the United States, immigration quotas should not be relaxed. |

Analyzing Your Audience

Before writing any essay, you should analyze the characteristics, values, and interests of your audience. In argumentation it is especially important to consider what beliefs or opinions your readers are likely to have and whether your audience is likely to be friendly, neutral, or hostile to your thesis. It is probably best to assume that some, if not most, of your readers are at least skeptically neutral — that they are open to your ideas but need to be convinced. This assumption will keep you from making claims you cannot support. If your position is controversial, you should assume that an informed and determined opposition is looking for holes in your argument.

In an argumentative essay, you face a dual challenge. You must appeal to readers who are neutral or even hostile to your position, and you must influence those readers so that they are more receptive to your viewpoint. For example, it would be relatively easy to convince college students that tuition should be lowered or instructors that faculty salaries should be raised. You could be reasonably sure, in advance, that each group would be friendly and would agree with your position. But argument requires more than telling people what they already believe. It would be much harder to convince college students that tuition should be raised to pay for an increase in instructors' salaries or to persuade instructors to forgo raises so that tuition can remain the same. Remember, your audience will not just take your word for the claims you make. You must provide evidence that will support your thesis and reasoning that will lead logically to your conclusion.

Gathering and Documenting Evidence

All the points you make in your paper must be supported. If they are not, your audience will dismiss them as unfounded, irrelevant, or unclear. Sometimes you can support a statement with appeals to emotion, but most of the time you support the points of your argument by appealing to reason — by providing **evidence,** facts and opinions in support of your position.

As you gather evidence and assess its effectiveness, keep in mind that evidence in an argumentative essay never proves anything conclusively. If it did, there would be no debate and hence no point in arguing. The best evidence can do is convince your audience that an assertion is reasonable and worth considering.

KINDS OF EVIDENCE.   Evidence can be fact or opinion. *Facts* are statements that most people agree are true and that can be verified independently. Facts — including statistics — are the most commonly used type of evidence. It is a fact, for example, that fewer people per year were killed in automobile accidents in the 1990s than in the 1970s. Facts may be drawn from your own experience as well as from reading and observation. It may, for instance, be a fact that you yourself may have had a serious automobile accident. Quite often, facts are more convincing when they are supplemented by *opinions,* or interpretations of facts. To connect your facts about automobile accidents to the assertion that the installation of side-impact airbags in all trucks as well as cars could reduce deaths still further, you could cite the opinions of an expert — consumer advocate Ralph Nader, for example. His statements, along with the facts and statistics you have assembled and your own interpretations of those facts and statistics, could convince readers that your solution to the problem of highway deaths is reasonable.

Keep in mind that not all opinions are equally convincing. The opinions of experts are more convincing than are those of individuals who have less knowledge of an issue. Your personal opinions can be excellent evidence (provided you are knowledgeable about your subject), but they are usually less convincing to your audience than expert opinions or facts. In the final analysis, what is important is not just the quality of the evidence but also the credibility of the person offering it.

What kind of evidence might change readers' minds? That depends on the readers, the issue, and the facts at hand. Put yourself in the place of your readers, and ask what would make them receptive to your thesis. Why should a student agree to pay higher tuition? You might concede that tuition is high but point out that it has not been raised for three years, while the college's costs have kept going up. The cost of heating and maintaining the buildings has increased, and professors' salaries have not, with the result that several excellent teachers have recently left the college for higher-paying jobs. Furthermore, cuts in federal and state funding have already caused a reduction in the number of courses offered. Similarly, how could you convince a professor to agree to accept no raise at all, especially in light of the fact that faculty salaries have not kept up with inflation? You could say that because cuts in government funding have already reduced course offerings and because the government has also reduced funds for student loans, any further rise in tuition to pay faculty salaries will cause some students to drop out — and that in turn would cost some instructors their jobs. As you can see, the evidence and reasoning you use in an argument depend to a great extent on whom you want to persuade and what you know about them.

CRITERIA FOR EVIDENCE.   As you select and review material, choose your evidence with three criteria in mind:

Your evidence should be *relevant*. It should support your thesis and be pertinent to the argument you are making. As you present evidence, be careful not to concentrate so much on a specific example that you lose sight of the point you are supporting. Such digressions may confuse your readers. For example, in arguing for mandatory HIV testing for all health-care workers, one student made the point that AIDS is at epidemic proportions. To illustrate this point, he offered a discussion of the bubonic plague in fourteenth-century Europe. Although interesting, this example was not really relevant. To show its relevance, the student would have to link his discussion to his assertions about AIDS, possibly by comparing the spread of the bubonic plague in the fourteenth century to the spread of AIDS today.

Your evidence should be *representative*. It should represent the *full range* of opinions about your subject, not just one side or another. For example, in an essay in which you argued against the use of animals in medical experimentation, you would not just use information provided by animal rights activists. You would also use information supplied by medical researchers, pharmaceutical companies, and possibly medical ethicists. In addition, the examples and expert opinions you include should be typical, not aberrant. Suppose you are writing an essay in support of building a trash-to-steam plant in your city. To support your thesis, you present the example of Baltimore, which has a successful trash-to-steam program. As you consider your evidence, ask yourself if Baltimore's experience with trash-to-steam is typical. Did other cities have less success? Take a close look at the opinions that disagree with the position you plan to take. If you understand your opposition, you will be able to refute it effectively when you write your paper.

Your evidence should be *sufficient*. Include enough evidence to support your claims. The amount of evidence you need depends on the length of your paper, your audience, and your thesis. It stands to reason that you would use fewer examples in a two-page paper than in a ten-page research assignment. Similarly, an audience that is favorably disposed to your thesis might need only one or two examples to be convinced, whereas a skeptical audience would need many more. As you develop your thesis, think about the amount of support you will need to write your paper. You may decide that a narrower, more limited thesis will be easier to support than one that is more inclusive.

DOCUMENTATION OF EVIDENCE.   As soon as you decide on a topic, you should begin to gather your evidence. Sometimes you will be able to use your own ideas and observations to support your claims. Most of the time, however, you will have to go to the library and search reference books, print indexes, and computer databases to locate the facts and expert opinions you need. Whenever you use such evidence in your paper, you have to *document* it by providing the source of the evidence. You can do this by following a format such as the one recommended by the Modern Language Association (MLA) and explained in the Appendix of this book. If you don't document your sources, your readers are likely to dismiss your evidence, thinking it is inaccurate, unreliable, or simply false. **Documentation** gives readers the ability to evaluate the sources you cite and to consult them if they wish. When you document sources, you are telling your readers that you are honest and have nothing to hide. Documentation also helps you avoid **plagiarism** — presenting the ideas or words of others as if they were your own. Certainly you don't have to document every idea you use in your paper. (**Common knowledge** — information you could easily find in several reference sources, for example — can be presented without documentation.) You must, however, document any use of a direct quotation and any ideas that are the original conclusions of your source.

Dealing with the Opposition

When gathering evidence, keep in mind that you cannot ignore arguments against your position. In fact, you should specifically address the most obvious — and sometimes the not-so-obvious — objections to your case. Try to anticipate the objections that a reasonable person would have to your thesis. By directly addressing these objections in your essay, you will help convince readers that your arguments are sound. This part of an argument, called **refutation,** is essential to making the strongest case possible.

You can *refute* opposing arguments by showing that they are unsound, unfair, or weak. Frequently, you will present contrasting evidence to show the weakness of your opponent's points and to reinforce your own case. Careful use of definition and cause-and-effect analysis may also prove effective. In the following passage from the classic essay "Politics and the English Language," George Orwell refutes an opponent's argument:

> I said earlier that the decadence of our language is probably curable. Those who deny this would argue, if they produced an argument at all, that language merely reflects existing social conditions, and that we cannot influence its development by any direct tinkering with words and constructions. So far as the general tone or spirit of a language goes, this may be true, but it is not true in detail. Silly words and expressions have often disappeared, though not through any evolutionary process but owing to the conscious actions of a minority.

Orwell begins by stating the point he wants to make, goes on to define the argument against his position, and then identifies its weakness. Later in the essay, Orwell bolsters his argument by presenting two examples that support his point.

When an opponent's argument is so compelling that it cannot be easily dismissed, you should concede its strength. By acknowledging that a point is well taken, you reinforce the impression that you are a fair-minded person. If possible, identify the limitations of the opposing position and then move your argument to more solid ground. Often an opponent's strong point addresses only *one* facet of a multifaceted problem.

When planning an argumentative essay, write down all possible arguments against your thesis that you can identify. Then, as you marshal your evidence, decide which points you will refute, keeping in mind that careful readers will expect you to refute the most compelling of your opponent's arguments. Take care, though, not to distort an opponent's argument by making it seem weaker than it actually is. This technique, called creating a *straw man,* can backfire and actually turn fair-minded readers against you.

Understanding Rogerian Argument

Psychologist Carl Rogers has written about how to argue without assuming an adversarial relationship. According to Rogers, traditional strategies of argument rely on confrontation — proving that an opponent's position is wrong. With this method of arguing, one person is "wrong" and one is "right." By attacking an opponent and repeatedly hammering home the message that his or her arguments are incorrect or misguided, a writer forces the opponent into a defensive position. The result is conflict, disagreement, and frequently ill will and hostility.

Rogers recommends that you think of the members of your audience as colleagues, not adversaries. With this approach, now known as **Rogerian argument,** you enter into a cooperative relationship with readers. Instead of refuting opposing arguments, you negotiate to determine points of agreement. The result is that you collaborate to find solutions

---

GUIDELINES FOR USING ROGERIAN ARGUMENT

- Begin by summarizing opposing viewpoints.
- Carefully consider the position of those who disagree with you. What are their legitimate concerns? If you were in their place, how would you react?
- Present opposing points of view accurately and fairly. Demonstrate your respect for the ideas of those who disagree with you.
- Concede the strength of a compelling opposing argument.
- Think of the concerns that you and your opposition share.
- Demonstrate to readers how they will benefit from the position you are defining.

that are mutually satisfying. By adopting a conciliatory attitude, you demonstrate your respect for opposing points of view and your willingness to compromise and work toward a position that both you and those who disagree with you will find acceptable. To use a Rogerian strategy in your writing, follow the guidelines on the previous page.

USING DEDUCTIVE AND INDUCTIVE ARGUMENTS

In an argument, you may move from evidence to conclusion in two basic ways. One method, called **deductive reasoning,** proceeds from a general premise or assumption to a specific conclusion. Deduction is what most people mean when they speak of logic. Using strict logical form, deduction holds that if all the statements in the argument are true, the conclusion must also be true. The other method of moving from evidence to conclusion is called **inductive reasoning.** Induction proceeds from individual observations to a more general conclusion and uses no strict form. It requires only that all the relevant evidence be stated and that the conclusion fit the evidence better than any other conclusion would. Most written arguments use a combination of deductive and inductive reasoning, but it is simpler to discuss and illustrate them separately.

Using Deductive Arguments

The basic form of a deductive argument is a **syllogism.** A syllogism consists of a *major premise,* which is a general statement; a *minor premise,* which is a related but more specific statement; and a *conclusion,* which has to be drawn from those premises. Consider the following example:

Major premise:	All Olympic runners are fast.
Minor premise:	Jesse Owens was an Olympic runner.
Conclusion:	Therefore, Jesse Owens was fast.

As you can see, if you grant each of the premises, then you must also grant the conclusion — and it is the only conclusion you can properly draw. You cannot conclude that Jesse Owens was slow, because that conclusion contradicts the premises. Nor can you conclude (even if it is true) that Jesse Owens was tall, because that conclusion goes beyond the premises.

Of course this argument seems obvious, and it is much simpler than an argumentative essay would be. But a deductive argument's premises can be fairly elaborate. The Declaration of Independence, which appears later in this chapter, has at its core a deductive argument that might be summarized in this way:

Major premise:	Tyrannical rulers deserve no loyalty.
Minor premise:	King George III is a tyrannical ruler.
Conclusion:	Therefore, King George III deserves no loyalty.

The major premise is a truth that the Declaration claims is self-evident. Much of the Declaration consists of evidence to support the minor premise that King George is a tyrannical ruler. And the conclusion, because it is drawn from those premises, has the force of irrefutable logic: the king deserves no loyalty from his American subjects, who are therefore entitled to revolt against him.

When a conclusion follows logically from the major and minor premises, then the argument is said to be *valid*. But if the syllogism is not logical, the argument is not valid and the conclusion is not sound. For example, the following syllogism is not logical:

Major premise:	All dogs are animals.
Minor premise:	All cats are animals.
Conclusion:	Therefore, all dogs are cats.

Of course the conclusion is absurd. But how did we wind up with such a ridiculous conclusion when both premises are obviously true? The answer is that although both cats and dogs are animals, cats are not included in the major premise of the syllogism, which deals only with dogs. Therefore, the form of the syllogism is defective, and the argument is invalid. Here is another example of an invalid argument:

Major premise:	All dogs are animals.
Minor premise:	Ralph is an animal.
Conclusion:	Therefore, Ralph is a dog.

This error in logic occurs when the minor premise refers to a term in the major premise that is *undistributed* — that is, it covers only some of the items in the class it denotes. In the major premise, *dogs* is the distributed term; it designates *all dogs*. The minor premise, however, refers not to *dogs* but to *animals*, which is undistributed because it refers only to animals that are dogs. As the minor premise establishes, Ralph is an animal, but it does not follow that he is also a dog. He could be a cat, a horse, or even a human being.

Even if a syllogism is valid — that is, correct in its form — its conclusion will not necessarily be *true*. The following syllogism draws a false conclusion:

Major premise:	All dogs are brown.
Minor premise:	My poodle Toby is a dog.
Conclusion:	Therefore, Toby is brown.

As it happens, Toby is black. The conclusion is false because the major premise is false: many dogs are *not* brown. If Toby were actually brown, the conclusion would be correct, but only by chance, not by logic. To be *sound*, a syllogism must be both logical and true.

The advantage of a deductive argument is that if you convince your audience to accept your major and minor premises, the force of logic should bring them to accept your conclusion. Therefore, you should try to select premises that you know your audience accepts or that are *self-evident* — that is, premises that most people believe to be true. Don't assume, however, that "most people" refers only to your friends and acquaintances. Consider, too, those who may hold different views. If you think that your premises are too controversial or difficult to establish firmly, you should use inductive reasoning.

Using Inductive Arguments

Inductive arguments move from specific examples or facts to a general conclusion. Unlike deduction, induction has no distinctive form, and its conclusions are less definitive than those of syllogisms whose forms are valid and whose premises are clearly true. Still, much inductive thinking (and writing based on that thinking) tends to follow a certain process. First, you usually decide on a question to be answered — or, especially in scientific work, you identify a tentative answer to such a question, called a *hypothesis*. Then, you gather all the evidence you can find that is relevant to the question and that may be important to finding the answer. Finally, you move from your evidence to your conclusion by making an *inference* that answers the question and takes the evidence into account. Here is a very simple example of the inductive process:

Question:	How did that living-room window get broken?
Evidence:	There is a baseball on the living-room floor.
	The baseball was not there this morning.
	Some children were playing baseball this afternoon.
	They were playing in the vacant lot across from the window.
	They stopped playing a little while ago.
	They aren't in the vacant lot now.
Conclusion:	One of the children hit or threw the ball through the window. Then they all ran away.

The conclusion, because it takes all of the evidence into account, seems obvious. But if it turned out that the children had been playing softball, not baseball, that one additional piece of evidence would make the conclusion doubtful — and the true answer could not be inferred. Even if the conclusion is believable, you cannot necessarily assume it is true: after all, the window could have been broken in some other way. For example, perhaps a bird flew against it, and perhaps the baseball in the living room had gone unnoticed all day, making the second piece of "evidence" on the list above not true.

Because inductive arguments tend to be more complicated than the preceding example, it is not always easy to move from the evidence you have collected to a sound conclusion. Of course, the more information you gather, the smaller the gap between your evidence and your conclusion.

Still, the crucial step from evidence to conclusion can be a big one, sometimes requiring what is called an *inductive leap*. With induction, conclusions are never certain, only highly probable. Although induction does not point to any particular type of conclusion the way deduction does, making sure that your evidence is *relevant, representative,* and *sufficient* (see page 498) can increase the probability that your conclusion will be sound.

Considering possible conclusions is a good way to avoid reaching an unjustified or false conclusion. In the preceding example, a hypothesis like this one might follow the question:

Hypothesis: One of those children playing baseball broke the living-room window.

Many people stop reasoning at this point, without considering the evidence. But when the gap between your evidence and your conclusion is too great, you may reach a hasty conclusion or one that is not borne out by the facts. This well-named error is called *jumping to a conclusion* because it amounts to a premature inductive leap. In induction, the hypothesis is merely the starting point. The rest of the inductive process continues as if the question were still to be answered — as in fact it is until all the evidence has been taken into account.

Using Toulmin Logic

Another method for structuring arguments has been advanced by philosopher Stephen Toulmin. Known as **Toulmin logic,** this method is an effort to describe argumentation as it actually occurs in everyday life. Toulmin puts forth a model that divides arguments into three parts: the *claim,* the *grounds,* and the *warrant.* The **claim** is the main point of the essay. Usually the claim is stated directly as the thesis, but in some arguments it may be implied. The **grounds** — the material a writer uses to support the claim — can be evidence (facts or expert opinion) or appeals to the emotions or values of the audience. The **warrant** is the inference that connects the claim to the grounds. It can be a belief that is taken for granted or an assumption that underlies the argument.

In its simplest form, an argument following Toulmin logic would look like this:

Claim: Carol should be elected class president.

Grounds: Carol is an honor student.

Warrant: A person who is an honor student would make a good class president.

When you formulate an argument using Toulmin logic, you can still use inductive and deductive reasoning. You derive your claim inductively from facts and examples, and you connect the grounds and warrant to your claim deductively. For example, the deductive argument in the Declaration of Independence that was summarized on page 516 can be represented this way:

Claim:	King George III deserves no loyalty.
Grounds:	King George III is a tyrannical ruler. (supported by facts and examples)
Warrant:	Tyrannical rulers deserve no loyalty.

As Toulmin points out, the clearer your warrant, the more likely readers will be to agree with it. Notice that in the two preceding examples, the warrants are very explicit.

Recognizing Fallacies

Fallacies are statements that may sound reasonable or true but are deceptive and dishonest. When your readers detect them, such statements can backfire and turn even a sympathetic audience against your position. Here are some of the more common fallacies that you should avoid:

BEGGING THE QUESTION.   Begging the question is a logical fallacy that assumes in the premise what the arguer should be trying to prove in the conclusion. This tactic asks readers to agree that certain points are self-evident when they are not.

> The unfair and shortsighted legislation that limits free trade is clearly a threat to the American economy.

Restrictions against free trade may or may not be unfair and shortsighted, but emotionally loaded language does not constitute proof. The statement begs the question because it assumes what it should be proving — that restrictive legislation is dangerous.

ARGUMENT FROM ANALOGY.   An **analogy** is a form of comparison that explains an unfamiliar element by comparing it to a more familiar one. Although analogies can explain abstract or unclear ideas, they do not constitute proof. An argument based on an analogy frequently ignores important dissimilarities between the two things being compared. When this occurs, the argument is fallacious.

> The overcrowded conditions in some parts of our city have forced people together like rats in a cage. Like rats, they will eventually turn on one another, fighting and killing until a balance is restored. It is therefore necessary that we vote to appropriate funds to build low-cost housing.

No evidence is offered that people behave like rats under these or any other conditions. Just because two things have some characteristics in common, you should not assume they are alike in other respects.

PERSONAL ATTACK (ARGUMENT *AD HOMINEM*). This fallacy tries to divert attention from the facts of an argument by attacking the motives or character of the person making the argument.

> The public should not take seriously Dr. Mason's plan for upgrading county health services. He is a recovering alcoholic whose second wife recently divorced him.

This attack on Dr. Mason's character says nothing about the quality of his plan. Sometimes a connection exists between a person's private and public lives — for example, a case of conflict of interest. But no evidence of such a connection is presented here.

HASTY OR SWEEPING GENERALIZATION. Sometimes called *jumping to a conclusion,* this fallacy occurs when a conclusion is reached on the basis of too little evidence.

> Our son Marc really benefited socially from going to nursery school; I think every child should go.

Perhaps other children would benefit from nursery school, and perhaps not, but no conclusion about children in general can be reached on the basis of one child's experience.

FALSE DILEMMA (*EITHER/OR FALLACY*). This fallacy occurs when you suggest that only two alternatives exist even though there may be others.

> We must choose between life and death, between intervention and genocide. There can be no neutral position on this issue.

An argument like this oversimplifies issues and forces people to choose between extremes instead of exploring more moderate positions.

EQUIVOCATION. This fallacy occurs when the meaning of a key term changes at some point in an argument. Equivocation makes it seem as if a conclusion follows from premises when it actually does not.

> As a human endeavor, computers are a praiseworthy and even remarkable accomplishment. But how human can we hope to be if we rely on computers to make our decisions?

The use of *human* in the first sentence refers to the entire human race. In the second sentence *human* means "merciful" or "civilized." By subtly shifting this term to refer to qualities characteristic of people as opposed to machines, the writer makes the argument seem more sound than it is.

RED HERRING. This fallacy occurs when the focus of an argument is changed to divert the audience from the actual issue.

> The mayor has proposed building a new baseball-only sports stadium. How can he even consider allocating millions of dollars to this irrespon-

sible scheme when so many professional baseball players have drug problems?

The focus of this argument should be the merits of the sports stadium. Instead, the writer shifts to the irrelevant issue of athletes' drug use.

You Also (*Tu Quoque*). This fallacy asserts that an opponent's argument has no value because the opponent does not follow his or her own advice.

How can that judge favor stronger penalties for convicted drug dealers? During his confirmation hearings, he admitted he had smoked marijuana as a student.

Appeal to Doubtful Authority. Often people will attempt to bolster an argument with references to experts or famous people. These appeals are valid when the person quoted or referred to is an expert in the area being discussed. They are not valid, however, when the individuals cited have no expertise on the issue.

According to Ted Koppel, interest rates will remain low during the next fiscal year.

Although Ted Koppel is a respected journalist, he is not an expert in business or finance. Therefore, his pronouncements about interest rates are no more than a personal opinion or, at best, an educated guess.

Misleading Statistics. Although statistics are a powerful form of factual evidence, they can be misrepresented or distorted in an attempt to influence an audience.

Women will never be competent firefighters; after all, 50 percent of the women in the city's training program failed the exam.

Here the writer has neglected to mention that there were only two women in the program. Because this statistic is not based on a large enough sample, it cannot be used as evidence to support the argument.

***Post Hoc, Ergo Propter Hoc* (After This, Therefore Because of This).** This fallacy, known as *post hoc reasoning,* assumes that because two events occur close together in time, the first must be the cause of the second.

Every time a Republican is elected president a recession follows. If we want to avoid another recession, we should elect a Democrat as our next president.

Even if it were true that recessions always occur during the tenure of Republican presidents, no causal connection has been established. (See pages 268–69.)

NON SEQUITUR (**IT DOES NOT FOLLOW**).   This fallacy occurs when a statement does not logically follow from a previous statement.

> Disarmament weakened the United States after World War I. Disarmament also weakened the United States after the Vietnam War. For this reason, efforts to control guns will weaken the United States.

The historical effects of disarmament have nothing to do with current efforts to control the sale of guns. Therefore, the conclusion is a *non sequitur*.

STRUCTURING AN ARGUMENTATIVE ESSAY

An argumentative essay, like other kinds of essays, has an *introduction*, a *body*, and a *conclusion*. But an argumentative essay has its own special structure, one that ensures that ideas are presented logically and convincingly. The Declaration of Independence follows the classic design typical of many arguments:

Introduction:	Introduces the issue
	States the thesis
Body:	Induction — offers evidence to support the thesis
	Deduction — uses syllogisms to support the thesis
	States the arguments against the thesis and refutes them
Conclusion:	Sums up the argument if it is long and complex
	Restates the thesis in different words
	Makes a forceful closing statement

Jefferson begins the Declaration by presenting the issue that the document addresses: the obligation of the people of the American colonies to tell the world why they must separate from Great Britain. Next, Jefferson states his thesis that because of the tyranny of the British king, the colonies must replace his rule with another form of government. In the body of the Declaration, he offers as evidence twenty-eight examples of injustice endured by the colonies. Following the evidence, Jefferson refutes counterarguments by explaining how time and time again the colonists have appealed to the British for redress, but without result. In his concluding paragraph, he restates the thesis and reinforces it one final time. He ends with a flourish: speaking for the representatives of the United States, he explicitly dissolves all political connections between England and America.

Not all arguments, however, follow this pattern. Your material, your thesis, your purpose, your audience, the type of argument you are writing, and the limitations of your assignment all help you determine the strategies you use. If your thesis is especially novel or controversial, for example, the refutation of opposing arguments may come first. In this instance, opposing positions might even be mentioned in the introduction — provided they are discussed more fully later in the argument.

Suppose your journalism instructor gives you the following assignment:

> Select a controversial topic that interests you, and write a brief editorial about it. Direct your editorial to readers who do not share your views, and try to convince them that your position is reasonable. Be sure to acknowledge the view your audience holds and to refute possible criticisms of your argument.

You are well informed about one local issue because you have just read a series of articles on it. A citizen group is lobbying for a local ordinance that would authorize government funding for parochial schools in your community. Since you have also recently studied the constitutional doctrine of separation of church and state in your American government class, you know you could argue fairly and strongly against the position taken by this group.

An informal outline of your essay might look like this:

Issue introduced:	Should public tax revenues be spent on aid to parochial schools?
Thesis statement:	Despite the pleas of citizen groups like Parochial School Parents United, using tax dollars to support church-affiliated schools directly violates the U.S. Constitution.
Evidence (deduction):	Explain general principle of separation of church and state in the Constitution.
Evidence (induction):	Present recent examples of court cases interpreting and applying this principle.
Evidence (deduction):	Explain how the Constitution and the court cases apply to your community's situation.
Opposition refuted:	Identify and respond to arguments used by Parochial School Parents United. Concede the point that parochial schools educate many children who would otherwise have to be educated in public schools at taxpayers' expense.
Conclusion:	Sum up the argument, restate the thesis, and end with a strong closing statement.

☑ CHECKLIST: ARGUMENTATION

- Does your assignment call for argumentation?
- Have you chosen a topic about which you can argue effectively?
- Do you have a debatable thesis?
- Have you considered the beliefs and opinions of your audience?
- Is your evidence relevant, representative, and sufficient?
- Have you documented evidence that you have gathered from sources?

(continued on next page).

(continued from previous page).

- Have you made an effort to address your audience's possible objections to your position?
- Have you refuted opposing arguments?
- Have you used inductive or deductive reasoning (or a combination of both) to move from your evidence to your conclusion?
- Have you avoided logical fallacies?
- Have you used appropriate transitional words and phrases?

▶ **A STUDENT WRITER: ARGUMENTATION**

The following editorial, written by Matt Daniels for his college newspaper, illustrates a number of the techniques discussed earlier in the chapter.

An Argument against the Anna Todd Jennings
Scholarship

Introduction

Summary of controversy

Thesis statement

Recently, a dispute has arisen over the "Caucasian-restricted" Anna Todd Jennings scholarship.* Anna Jennings died in 1955, and her will established a trust that granted a scholarship of up to $15,000 for a deserving student. Unfortunately, Jennings, who had certain racist views, limited her scholarship to "Caucasian students." After much debate with family and friends, I, a white, well-qualified, and definitely deserving student, have decided not to apply for the scholarship. It is my view that despite arguments to the contrary, applying for the Anna Todd Jennings scholarship furthers the racist ideas that were held by its founder.

Argument (deductive)

Most people would agree that racism in any form is an evil that should be opposed. The Anna Todd Jennings scholarship is a subtle but nonetheless dangerous expression of racism. It explicitly discriminates against African Americans, Asians, Latinos, Native Americans,

1

2

---

*EDS. NOTE — This essay discusses an actual situation, but the name of the scholarship has been changed here.

and others. By providing a scholarship for whites only, Anna Jennings frustrates the aspirations of groups who until recently had been virtually kept out of the educational mainstream. On this basis alone, students should refuse to apply and should actively work to encourage the school to challenge the racist provisions of Anna Todd Jennings's will. Such challenges have been upheld by the courts: the striking down of a similar clause in the will of the eighteenth-century financier Stephen Girard is just one example.

Argument (inductive)

The school itself must share some blame   3 in this case. Students who applied for the Anna Todd Jennings scholarship were unaware of its restrictions. The director of the financial aid office has acknowledged that he knew about the racial restrictions of the scholarship but

Evidence

thought that students should have the right to apply anyway. In addition, the materials distributed by the financial aid office gave no indication that the award was limited to Caucasians. Students were required to fill out forms, submit financial statements, and forward transcripts. In addition to this material, all students were told to attach a recent photograph to their application. Little did the applicants know that the sole purpose of this innocuous little picture was to distinguish whites from nonwhites. By keeping secret the restrictions of the scholarship, the school has put students, most of whom are not racists, in the position of unwittingly endorsing Anna Jen-

Conclusion (based on evidence)

nings's racism. Thus, both the school and the unsuspecting students have been in collusion with the administrators of the Anna Todd Jennings trust.

Refutation of opposing argument

The problem facing students is how best to   4 deal with the generosity of a racist. A recent edition of the school paper contained several

letters saying that students should accept Anna
Jennings's scholarship money. One student said,
"If we do not take that money and use our education to topple the barriers of prejudice, we
are giving the money to those who will use the
money in the opposite fashion." This argument,
although attractive, is flawed. If an individual accepts a scholarship with racial restrictions, then he or she is actually endorsing the
principles behind it. If a student does not
want to appear to endorse racism, then he or
she should reject the scholarship, even if this
action causes hardship or gives adversaries a
momentary advantage. To do otherwise is to
further the cause of the individual who set up
the scholarship. The best way to register a
protest is to work to change the requirement
for the scholarship and to encourage others not
to apply as long as the racial restrictions
exist.

Refutation of opposing argument   Another student letter made the point that   5
a number of other restricted scholarships are
available at the school and no one seems to
question them. For example, one is for the
children of veterans, another is for women, and
yet another is earmarked for African Americans.
Even though these scholarships have restrictions, to say that all restrictions are the
same is to make a hasty generalization. Women,
African Americans, and the children of veterans
are groups who deserve special treatment. Both
women and African Americans have been discriminated against for years, and many educational
opportunities have been denied them. Earmarking
scholarships for them is simply a means of
restoring some measure of equality. The children of veterans have been singled out because
their parents have rendered an extraordinary
service to their country. Whites, however, do
not fall into either of these categories. Spe-

cial treatment for them is based solely on race
and has nothing to do with any objective standard of need or merit.

Conclusion

    I hope that by refusing to apply for the   6
Anna Todd Jennings scholarship, I have encouraged other students to think about the issues

Restatement of thesis

involved in their own decisions. All of us have
a responsibility to ourselves and to society.
If we truly believe that racism in all its
forms is evil, then we have to make a choice

Concluding statement

between sacrifice and hypocrisy. Faced with
these options, our decision should be clear:
accept the loss of funds as an opportunity to
explore your values and fight for principles in
which you believe; if you do, this opportunity
is worth far more than any scholarship.

Points for Special Attention

GATHERING EVIDENCE.   Because of his involvement with his subject, Matt Daniels was able to provide examples from his own experience to support his points and did not have to do much research. Still, Matt did have to spend a lot of time thinking about ideas and selecting evidence. He had to review the requirements for the scholarship and decide on the arguments he would make. In addition, he reviewed an article that appeared in the school newspaper and the letters students wrote in response to the article. He then chose material that would create interest and add authority to his arguments.

Certainly statistics, studies, and expert testimony, if they exist, would strengthen Matt's argument. But even without such evidence, an argument such as this one, based on strong logic and personal experience, can be quite compelling.

REFUTING OPPOSING ARGUMENTS.   Matt devotes two paragraphs to presenting and refuting arguments made by those who believe qualified students should apply for the scholarship despite its racial restrictions. He begins this section by asking a **rhetorical question** — a question asked not to elicit an answer but to further the argument. He goes on to present what he considers the two best arguments against his thesis — that students should take the money and work to fight racism and that other scholarships at the school have restrictions. Matt refutes these arguments by identifying a flaw in the logic of the first argument and by pointing to a fallacy, a hasty generalization, in the second.

AUDIENCE.   Because his essay was written as an editorial for his college newspaper, Matt assumed his audience would be familiar with the issue he was discussing. Letters to the editor of the paper convinced him that his position was unusual, and he decided that his readers, mostly students and instructors, would have to be persuaded that his points were valid. To achieve this end, he was careful to present himself as a reasonable person, to explain issues that he believes are central to his case, and to avoid *ad hominem* attacks. In addition, he made sure to avoid sweeping generalizations and name-calling and to include many details to support his assertions and convince readers that his points are worth considering.

ORGANIZATION.   Matt uses several strategies discussed earlier in the chapter. He begins his essay by introducing the issue he is going to discuss and then states his thesis: "Applying for the Anna Todd Jennings scholarship furthers the racist ideas that were held by its founder."

Because Matt had given a good deal of thought to his subject, he was able to construct two fairly strong arguments to support his position. His first argument is deductive. He begins by stating a premise that he believes is self-evident — that most people think racism should be opposed. The rest of this argument follows a straightforward deductive pattern:

Major premise: Racism is an evil that should be opposed.

Minor premise: The Anna Todd Jennings scholarship is racist.

Conclusion: Therefore, the Anna Todd Jennings scholarship should be opposed.

Matt ends his first argument with a piece of factual evidence that reinforces his conclusion: the successful challenge to the will of financier Stephen Girard, which limited admittance to Girard College in Philadelphia to white male orphans.

Matt's second argument is inductive, asserting that the school has put students in the position of unknowingly supporting racism. The argument begins with Matt's hypothesis and presents the fact that even though the school is aware of the racist restrictions of the scholarship, it has done nothing to make students aware of them. According to Matt, the school's knowledge (and tacit approval) of the situation leads to the conclusion that the school is in collusion with those who manage the scholarship.

In his fourth and fifth paragraphs, Matt refutes two criticisms of his argument. Although his conclusion is rather brief, it does effectively reinforce and support his main idea. Matt ends his essay by recommending a course of action to his fellow students.

Focus on Revision

Matt constructed a solid argument that addresses the central issue very effectively. However, some students on the newspaper's editorial board thought he should add a section giving more information about

Anna Todd Jennings and her bequest. These students believed that such information would help them understand the implications of accepting her money. As it now stands, the essay dismisses Anna Todd Jennings as a racist, but biographical material and excerpts from the will — both of which appeared in the school paper — would enable readers to grasp the extent of her prejudice. Matt decided to follow up on this advice and to strengthen his conclusion as well. He thought that including the exact words of Anna Todd Jennings's will would help him to reinforce his points forcefully and memorably.

The essays that follow represent a wide variety of topics, and the purpose of each essay is to support a controversial thesis. In two cases, two essays that take opposing stands on the same issue are paired in debates. In two additional debates, several essays on a single topic are presented to offer a greater variety of viewpoints. As you read each essay, try to identify the strategies the writer uses to convince readers.

▟▟▟▟▟▟▟

THOMAS JEFFERSON

Thomas Jefferson was born in 1743 in what is now Albemarle County, Virginia, and attended the College of William and Mary. A lawyer, he was elected to Virginia's colonial legislature in 1769 and began a distinguished political career that strongly influenced the early development of the United States. In addition to his participation in the Second Continental Congress of 1775–1776, which ratified the Declaration of Independence, he served as governor of Virginia; as minister to France; as secretary of state under President George Washington; as vice president under John Adams; and finally as president from 1801 to 1809. After his retirement, he founded the University of Virginia. He died on July 4, 1826.

By the early 1770s, many residents of the original thirteen American colonies had come to believe that King George III and his ministers, both in England and the New World, wielded too much power over the colonists. In particular, they objected to a series of taxes imposed on them by the British Parliament, and, being without political representation, they asserted that "taxation without representation" amounted to tyranny. In response to a series of laws passed by Parliament in 1774 to limit the political and geographic freedom of the colonists, representatives of each colony met at the Continental Congress of 1774 to draft a plan of reconciliation, but it was rejected. As cries for independence increased, British soldiers and state militias began to engage in armed conflict, which by 1776 had become a full-fledged civil war. On June 11, 1776, the Second Continental Congress chose Jefferson, Benjamin Franklin, and several other delegates to draft a declaration of independence. The draft was written entirely by Jefferson, with suggestions and revisions contributed by other commission members. Jefferson's Declaration of Independence challenges a basic assumption of its time — that the royal monarch rules by divine right — and in so doing became one of the most important political documents in world history.

The Declaration of Independence

When in the course of human events, it becomes necessary for one people to dissolve the political bonds which have connected them with another, and to assume among the powers of the earth, the separate and equal station to which the Laws of Nature and of Nature's God entitle them, a decent respect to the opinions of mankind requires that they should declare the causes which impel them to the separation.   1

We hold these truths to be self-evident, that all men are created equal, that they are endowed by their Creator with certain unalienable rights, that among these are life, liberty and the pursuit of happiness. That to secure these rights, governments are instituted among men, deriving their just powers from the consent of the governed. That whenever any form of government becomes destructive to these ends, it is the right of the people to alter or to abolish it, and to institute new government, laying its foun-   2 dation on such principles and organizing its powers in such form, as to them shall seem most likely to effect their safety and happiness. Prudence, indeed, will dictate that governments long established should not be changed for light and transient causes; and accordingly all experience hath shown, that mankind are more disposed to suffer, while evils are sufferable, than to right themselves by abolishing the forms to which they are accustomed. But when a long rain of abuses and usurpations, pursuing invariably the same object, evinces a design to reduce them under absolute despotism, it is their right, it is their duty, to throw off such government, and to provide new guards for their future security. Such has been the patient sufferance of these Colonies; and such is now the necessity which constrains them to alter their former systems of government. This history of the present king of Great Britain is a history of repeated injuries and usurpations, all having in direct object the establishment of an absolute tyranny over these States. To prove this, let facts be submitted to a candid world.

He has refused his assent to laws, the most wholesome and necessary   3
for the public good.

He has forbidden his Governors to pass laws of immediate and press-   4
ing importance, unless suspended in their operation till his assent should be obtained; and when so suspended, he has utterly neglected to attend to them.

He has refused to pass other laws for the accommodation of large dis-   5
tricts of people, unless those people would relinquish the right of representation in the legislature, a right inestimable to them and formidable to tyrants only.

He has called together legislative bodies at places unusual, uncom-   6
fortable, and distant from the depository of their public records, for the sole purpose of fatiguing them into compliance with his measure.

He has dissolved representative houses repeatedly, for opposing with   7
manly firmness his invasions on the rights of people.

He has refused for a long time, after such dissolutions, to cause others   8
to be elected; whereby the legislative powers, incapable of annihilation, have returned to the people at large for their exercise; the State remaining in the meantime exposed to all the dangers of invasion from without and convulsions within.

He has endeavoured to prevent the population of these states; for that   9
purpose obstructing the laws for naturalization of foreigners; refusing to pass others to encourage their migration hither, and raising the conditions of new appropriations of lands.

He has obstructed the administration of justice, by refusing his assent   10
to laws for establishing judiciary powers.

He has made judges dependent on his will alone, for the tenure of   11
their offices, and the amount and payment of their salaries.

He has erected a multitude of new offices, and sent hither swarms of   12
officers to harass our people, and eat out their substance.

He has kept among us, in times of peace, standing armies without the consent of our legislatures. 13

He has affected to render the military independent of and superior to the civil power. 14

He has combined with others to subject us to a jurisdiction foreign to our constitution, and unacknowledged by our laws; giving his assent to their acts of pretended legislation: 15

For quartering large bodies of troops among us: 16

For protecting them, by a mock trial, from punishment for any murders which they should commit on the inhabitants of these States: 17

For cutting off our trade with all parts of the world: 18

For imposing taxes on us without our consent: 19

For depriving us in many cases of the benefits of trial by jury: 20

For transporting us beyond seas to be tried for pretended offences: 21

For abolishing the free system of English laws in a neighbouring Province, establishing therein an arbitrary government, and enlarging its boundaries so as to render it at once an example and fit instrument for introducing the same absolute rule into these Colonies: 22

For taking away our Charters, abolishing our most valuable laws, and altering fundamentally the forms of our governments: 23

For suspending our own legislatures, and declaring themselves invested with power to legislate for us in all cases whatsoever. 24

He had abdicated government here, by declaring us out of his protection and waging war against us. 25

He has plundered our seas, ravaged our coasts, burnt our towns, and destroyed the lives of our people. 26

He is at this time transporting large armies of foreign mercenaries to complete the works of death, desolation and tyranny, already begun with circumstances of cruelty and perfidy scarcely paralleled in the most barbarous ages, and totally unworthy the head of a civilized nation. 27

He has constrained our fellow citizens taken captive on the high seas to bear arms against their country, to become the executioners of their friends and brethren, or to fall themselves by their hands. 28

He has excited domestic insurrections amongst us, and has endeavoured to bring on the inhabitants of our frontiers, the merciless Indian savages, whose known rule of warfare, is an undistinguished destruction of all ages, sexes, and conditions. 29

In every stage of these oppressions we have petitioned for redress in the most humble terms: our repeated petitions have been answered only by repeated injury. A prince whose character is thus marked by every act which may define a tyrant is unfit to be the ruler of a free people. 30

Nor have we been wanting in attention to our British brethren. We have warned them from time to time of attempts by their legislature to extend an unwarrantable jurisdiction over us. We have reminded them of the circumstances of our emigration and settlement here. We have appealed to their native justice and magnanimity, and we have conjured them by 31 the ties of our common kindred to disavow these usurpations, which would inevitably interrupt our connections and correspondence. They too have been deaf to the voice of justice and of consanguinity. We must, therefore, acquiesce in the necessity, which denounces our separation, and hold them, as we hold the rest of mankind, enemies in war, in peace friends.

We, therefore, the Representatives of the United States of America, in   32 General Congress assembled, appealing to the Supreme Judge of the world for the rectitude of our intentions, do, in the name, and by authority of the good people of these Colonies, solemnly publish and declare, That these United Colonies are, and of right ought to be, Free and Independent States; that they are absolved from all allegiance to the British Crown, and that all political connection between them and the state of Great Britain, is and ought to be totally dissolved; and that as Free and Independent States, they have full power to levy war, conclude peace, contract alliances, establish commerce, and to do all other acts and things which Independent States may of right do. And for the support of this declaration, with a firm reliance on the protection of Divine Providence, we mutually pledge to each other our lives, our fortunes, and our sacred honor.

• • •

COMPREHENSION

1. What "truths" does Jefferson assert are "self-evident"?

2. What does Jefferson say is the source from which governments derive their powers?

3. What reasons does Jefferson give to support his premise that the United States should break away from Great Britain?

4. What conclusions about the British crown does Jefferson draw from the evidence he presents?

PURPOSE AND AUDIENCE

1. What is the major premise of Jefferson's argument? Should Jefferson have done more to establish the truth of this premise?

2. The Declaration of Independence was written during a period now referred to as the Age of Reason. In what ways has Jefferson tried to make his document appear reasonable?

3. For what audience (or audiences) is the document intended? Which groups of readers would have been most likely to accept it? Explain.

4. How effectively does Jefferson anticipate and refute the opposition?

5. In paragraph 31, following the list of grievances, why does Jefferson address his "British brethren"?

6. At what point does Jefferson state his thesis? Why does he state it where he does?

STYLE AND STRUCTURE

1. Does the Declaration of Independence rely primarily on inductive or deductive reasoning? Identify examples of each.

2. What techniques does Jefferson use to create smooth and logical transitions from one paragraph to another?

3. Why does Jefferson list all of his twenty-eight grievances? Why doesn't he just summarize them or mention a few representative grievances?

4. Jefferson begins the last paragraph of the Declaration of Independence with "We, therefore." How effective is this conclusion? Explain.

VOCABULARY PROJECTS

1. Define each of the following words as it is used in this selection.

station (1)	evinces (2)	tenure (11)
impel (1)	despotism (2)	jurisdiction (15)
self-evident (2)	sufferance (2)	arbitrary (22)
endowed (2)	candid (2)	insurrections (29)
deriving (2)	depository (6)	disavow (31)
prudence (2)	dissolutions (8)	consanguinity (31)
transient (2)	annihilation (8)	rectitude (32)
usurpations (2)	appropriations (9)	levy (32)

2. Underline ten words that have negative connotations. How does Jefferson use these words to help him make his point? Do you think words with more neutral connotations would strengthen or weaken his case? Why?

3. What words does Jefferson use that are rarely used today? Would the Declaration of Independence be more meaningful to today's readers if it were updated, with more familiar words substituted? To help you formulate your response, try rewriting a paragraph or two, and assess your updated version.

JOURNAL ENTRY

Do you think Jefferson is being fair to the king? Do you think he should be?

WRITING WORKSHOP

1. Following Jefferson's example, write a declaration of independence from your school, job, family, or any other institution with which you are associated.

2. Write an essay in which you state a grievance you share with other members of some group, and then argue for the best way to eliminate the grievance.

3. In an argumentative essay written from the point of view of King George III, try to convince the colonists that they should not break away from Great Britain. If you can, refute some of the points Jefferson lists in the Declaration.

COMBINING THE PATTERNS

The middle section of the Declaration of Independence is developed by means of **exemplification**; it presents a series of examples to support Jefferson's assertion that the colonists have experienced "repeated injuries and usurpations" (2). Are these examples relevant? Representative? Sufficient? Effective? What other pattern of development could Jefferson have used to support his assertion?

THEMATIC CONNECTIONS

- "The 'Black Table' Is Still There" (page 294)
- "Grant and Lee: A Study in Contrasts" (page 340)
- "Does America Still Exist?" (page 482)
- "Letter from Birmingham Jail" (page 522)

♪♪♪♪♪♪♪♪
MARTIN LUTHER KING JR.

Martin Luther King Jr. was born in Atlanta, Georgia, in 1929. He attended Morehouse College and Crozer Theological Seminary, and after receiving his doctorate in theology from Boston University in 1955, he became pastor of the Dexter Avenue Baptist Church in Montgomery, Alabama. There, he organized a 382-day bus boycott that led to the 1956 Supreme Court decision outlawing segregation on Alabama's buses. As leader of the Southern Christian Leadership Conference, he was instrumental in securing the civil rights of black Americans, using methods based on a philosophy of nonviolent protest. His books include *Stride Towards Freedom* (1958) and *Why We Can't Wait* (1964). In 1964 he was awarded the Nobel Peace Prize. He was assassinated in 1968 in Memphis, Tennessee.

In the mid-1950s, long-standing state support for segregation of the races and discrimination against blacks had begun to be challenged from a variety of quarters. Supreme Court decisions in 1954 and 1955 declared segregation in public schools and other publicly financed venues unconstitutional, while calls for an end to discrimination were being made by blacks and whites alike. Their actions took the form of marches, boycotts, and sit-ins (organized protests in which participants refuse to move from a public area). Many whites, however, particularly in the South, vehemently resisted any change in race relations. By 1963, when King organized a campaign against segregation in Birmingham, Alabama, tensions ran deep. He and his followers met fierce opposition from the police as well as from white moderates, who considered him an "outside agitator." During the demonstrations, King was arrested and jailed for eight days. He wrote his "Letter from Birmingham Jail" to white clergymen to explain his actions and answer those who urged him to call off the demonstrations.

Letter from Birmingham Jail

April 16, 1963

My Dear Fellow Clergymen:

While confined here in the Birmingham city jail, I came across your 1 recent statement calling my present activities "unwise and untimely." Seldom do I pause to answer criticism of my work and ideas. If I sought to answer all the criticisms that cross my desk, my secretaries would have little time for anything other than such correspondence in the course of the day, and I would have no time for constructive work. But since I feel that you are men of genuine good will and that your criticisms are sincerely set forth, I want to try to answer your statement in what I hope will be patient and reasonable terms.

I think I should indicate why I am here in Birmingham, since you have 2 been influenced by the view which argues against "outsiders coming in." I have the honor of serving as president of the Southern Christian Leadership Conference, an organization operating in every southern state, with headquarters in Atlanta, Georgia. We have some eighty-five affiliated organizations across the South, and one of them is the Alabama Christian Movement for Human Rights. Frequently we share staff, educational, and financial resources with our affiliates. Several months ago the affiliate here in Birmingham asked us to be on call to engage in a nonviolent direct-action program if such were deemed necessary. We readily consented, and when the hour came we lived up to our promise. So I, along with several members of my staff, am here because I was invited here. I am here because I have organizational ties here.

But more basically, I am in Birmingham because injustice is here. Just   3
as the prophets of the eighth century B.C. left their villages and carried their "thus saith the Lord" far beyond the boundaries of their home towns, and just as the Apostle Paul left his village of Tarsus and carried the gospel of Jesus Christ to the far corners of the Greco-Roman world, so am I compelled to carry the gospel of freedom beyond my own home town. Like Paul, I must constantly respond to the Macedonian call for aid.

Moreover, I am cognizant of the interrelatedness of all communities   4
and states. I cannot sit idly by in Atlanta and not be concerned about what happens in Birmingham. Injustice anywhere is a threat to justice everywhere. We are caught in an inescapable network of mutuality, tied in a single garment of destiny. Whatever affects one directly, affects all indirectly. Never again can we afford to live with the narrow, provincial, "outside agitator" idea. Anyone who lives inside the United States can never be considered an outsider anywhere within its bounds.

You deplore the demonstrations taking place in Birmingham. But   5
your statement, I am sorry to say, fails to express a similar concern for the conditions that brought about the demonstrations. I am sure that none of you would want to rest content with the superficial kind of social analysis that deals merely with effects and does not grapple with underlying causes. It is unfortunate that demonstrations are taking place in Birmingham, but it is even more unfortunate that the city's white power structure left the Negro community with no alternative.

In any nonviolent campaign there are four basic steps: collection of the   6
facts to determine whether injustices exist; negotiation; self-purification; and direct action. We have gone through all these steps in Birmingham. There can be no gainsaying the fact that racial injustice engulfs this community. Birmingham is probably the most thoroughly segregated city in the United States. Its ugly record of brutality is widely known. Negroes have experienced grossly unjust treatment in courts. There have been more unsolved bombings of Negro homes and churches in Birmingham than in any other city in the nation. These are the hard, brutal facts of the case. On the basis of these conditions, Negro leaders sought to negotiate with the city fathers. But the latter consistently refused to engage in good-faith negotiation.

Then, last September, came the opportunity to talk with leaders of   7
Birmingham's economic community. In the course of the negotiations,

certain promises were made by the merchants — for example, to remove the stores' humiliating racial signs. On the basis of these promises, the Reverend Fred Shuttlesworth and the leaders of the Alabama Christian Movement for Human Rights agreed to a moratorium on all demonstrations. As the weeks and months went by, we realized that we were the victims of a broken promise. A few signs, briefly removed, returned; the others remained.

As in so many past experiences, our hopes had been blasted, and the shadow of deep disappointment settled upon us. We had no alternative except to prepare for direct action, whereby we would present our very bodies as means of laying our case before the conscience of the local and the national community. Mindful of the difficulties involved, we decided to undertake a process of self-purification. We began a series of workshops on nonviolence, and we repeatedly asked ourselves: "Are you able to accept blows without retaliating?" "Are you able to endure the ordeal of jail?" We decided to schedule our direct-action program for the Easter season, realizing that except for Christmas, this is the main shopping period of the year. Knowing that a strong economic-withdrawal program would be the by-product of direct action, we felt that this would be the best time to bring pressure to bear on the merchants for the needed change.   8

Then it occurred to us that Birmingham's mayoral election was coming up in March, and we speedily decided to postpone action until after election day. When we discovered that the Commissioner of Public Safety, Eugene "Bull" Connor, had piled up enough votes to be in the run-off, we decided again to postpone action until the day after the run-off so that the demonstrations could not be used to cloud the issues. Like many others, we waited to see Mr. Connor defeated, and to this end we endured postponement after postponement. Having aided in this community need, we felt that our direct-action program could be delayed no longer.   9

You may well ask, "Why direct action? Why sit-ins, marches, and so forth? Isn't negotiation a better path?" You are quite right in calling for negotiation. Indeed, this is the very purpose of direct action. Nonviolent direct action seeks to create such a crisis and foster such a tension that a community which has constantly refused to negotiate is forced to confront the issue. It seeks so to dramatize the issue that it can no longer be ignored. My citing the creation of tension as part of the work of the nonviolent-resistor may sound rather shocking. But I must confess that I am not afraid of the word "tension." I have earnestly opposed violent tension, but there is a type of constructive, nonviolent tension which is necessary for growth. Just as Socrates felt that it was necessary to create a tension in the mind so that individuals could rise from the bondage of myths and half-truths to the unfettered realm of creative analysis and objective appraisal, so must we see the need for nonviolent gadflies to create the kind of tension in society that will help men rise from the dark depths of prejudice and racism to the majestic heights of understanding and brotherhood.   10

The purpose of our direct-action program is to create a situation so   11
crisis-packed that it will inevitably open the door to negotiation. I therefore concur with you in your call for negotiation. Too long has our beloved
Southland been bogged down in a tragic effort to live in monologue rather
than dialogue.

One of the basic points in your statement is that the action that I and   12
my associates have taken in Birmingham is untimely. Some have asked:
"Why didn't you give the new city administration time to act?" The only
answer that I can give to this query is that the new Birmingham administration must be prodded about as much as the outgoing one, before it will
act. We are sadly mistaken if we feel that the election of Albert Boutwell as
mayor will bring the millennium to Birmingham. While Mr. Boutwell is a
much more gentle person than Mr. Connor, they are both segregationists,
dedicated to maintenance of the status quo. I have hoped that Mr. Boutwell will be reasonable enough to see the futility of massive resistance to
desegregation. But he will not see this without pressure from devotees of
civil rights. My friends, I must say to you that we have not made a single
gain in civil rights without determined legal and nonviolent pressure.
Lamentably, it is an historical fact that privileged groups seldom give up
their privileges voluntarily. Individuals may see the moral light and voluntarily give up their unjust posture; but, as Reinhold Niebuhr* has
reminded us, groups tend to be more immoral than individuals.

We know through painful experience that freedom is never voluntar-   13
ily given by the oppressor; it must be demanded by the oppressed.
Frankly, I have yet to engage in a direct-action campaign that was "well
timed" in the view of those who have not suffered unduly from the disease of segregation. For years now I have heard the word "Wait!" It rings
in the ear of every Negro with piercing familiarity. This "Wait" has almost
always meant "Never." We must come to see, with one of our distinguished jurists, that "justice too long delayed is justice denied."

We have waited for more than 340 years for our constitutional and   14
God-given rights. The nations of Asia and Africa are moving with jetlike
speed toward gaining political independence, but we still creep at horse-
and-buggy pace toward gaining a cup of coffee at a lunch counter. Perhaps
it is easy for those who have never felt the stinging darts of segregation to
say, "Wait." But when you have seen vicious mobs lynch your mothers
and fathers at will and drown your sisters and brothers at whim; when
you have seen hate-filled policemen curse, kick, and even kill your black
brothers and sisters; when you see the vast majority of your twenty million Negro brothers smothering in an airtight cage of poverty in the midst
of an affluent society; when you suddenly find your tongue twisted and
your speech stammering as you seek to explain to your six-year-old
daughter why she can't go to the public amusement park that has just
been advertised on television, and see tears welling up in her eyes when

---

*EDS. NOTE — American religious and social thinker (1892–1971).

she is told that Funtown is closed to colored children, and see ominous clouds of inferiority beginning to form in her little mental sky, and see her beginning to distort her personality by developing an unconscious bitterness toward white people; when you have to concoct an answer for a five-year-old son who is asking, "Daddy, why do white people treat colored people so mean?"; when you take a cross-country drive and find it necessary to sleep night after night in the uncomfortable corners of your automobile because no motel will accept you; when you are humiliated day in and day out by nagging signs reading "white" and "colored"' when your first name becomes "nigger," your middle name becomes "boy" (however old you are) and your last name becomes "John," and your wife and mother are never given the respected title "Mrs."; when you are harried by day and haunted at night by the fact that you are a Negro, living constantly at tiptoe stance, never quite knowing what to expect next, and are plagued with inner fears and outer resentments; when you are forever fighting a degenerating sense of "nobodiness"— then you will understand why we find it difficult to wait. There comes a time when the cup of endurance runs over, and men are no longer willing to be plunged into the abyss of despair. I hope, sirs, you can understand our legitimate and unavoidable impatience.

You express a great deal of anxiety over our willingness to break laws. 15 This is certainly a legitimate concern. Since we so diligently urge people to obey the Supreme Court's decision of 1954 outlawing segregation in the public schools, at first glance it may seem rather paradoxical for us consciously to break laws. One may well ask: "How can you advocate breaking some laws and obeying others?" The answer lies in the fact that there are two types of laws: just and unjust. I would be the first to advocate obeying just laws. One has not only a legal but a moral responsibility to obey just laws. Conversely, one has a moral responsibility to disobey unjust laws. I would agree with St. Augustine* that "an unjust law is no law at all."

Now, what is the difference between the two? How does one determine whether a law is just or unjust? A just law is a man-made code that squares with the moral law or the law of God. An unjust law is a code that is out of harmony with the moral law. To put it in the terms of St. Thomas Aquinas:** An unjust law is a human law that is not rooted in eternal law and natural law. Any law that uplifts human personality is just. Any law that degrades human personality is unjust. All segregation statutes are unjust because segregation distorts the soul and damages the personality. It gives the segregator a false sense of superiority and the segregated a false sense of inferiority. Segregation, to use the terminology of the Jewish philosopher Martin Buber, substitutes an "I-it" relationship for an "I-thou" relationship and ends up relegating persons to the status of

*EDS. NOTE — Early church father and philosopher (354–430).
**EDS. NOTE — Italian philosopher and theologian (1225–1274).

things. Hence segregation is not only politically, economically, and sociologically unsound, it is morally wrong and sinful. Paul Tillich* has said that sin is separation. Is not segregation an existential expression of man's tragic separation, his awful estrangement, his terrible sinfulness? Thus it is that I can urge men to obey the 1954 decision of the Supreme Court, for it is morally right; and I can urge them to disobey segregation ordinances, for they are morally wrong.

Let us consider a more concrete example of just and unjust laws. An 17 unjust law is a code that a numerical or power majority group compels a minority group to obey but does not make binding on itself. This is *difference* made legal. By the same token, a just law is a code that a majority compels a minority to follow and that it is willing to follow itself. This is *sameness* made legal.

Let me give another explanation. A law is unjust if it is inflicted on a 18 minority that, as a result of being denied the right to vote, had no part in enacting or devising the law. Who can say that the legislature of Alabama which set up that state's segregation laws was democratically elected? Throughout Alabama all sorts of devious methods are used to prevent Negroes from becoming registered voters, and there are some counties in which, even though Negroes constitute a majority of the population, not a single Negro is registered. Can any law enacted under such circumstances be considered democratically structured?

Sometimes a law is just on its face and unjust in its application. For 19 instance, I have been arrested on a charge of parading without a permit. Now, there is nothing wrong in having an ordinance which requires a permit for a parade. But such an ordinance becomes unjust when it is used to maintain segregation and to deny citizens the First-Amendment privilege of peaceful assembly and protest.

I hope you are able to see the distinction I am trying to point out. In no 20 sense do I advocate evading or defying the law, as would the rabid segregationist. That would lead to anarchy. One who breaks an unjust law must do so openly, lovingly, and with a willingness to accept the penalty. I submit that an individual who breaks a law that conscience tells him is unjust, and who willingly accepts the penalty of imprisonment in order to arouse the conscience of the community over its injustice, is in reality expressing the highest respect for law.

Of course, there is nothing new about this kind of civil disobedience. 21 It was evidenced sublimely in the refusal of Shadrach, Meshach, and Abednego** to obey the laws of Nebuchadnezzar, on the ground that a higher moral law was at stake. It was practiced superbly by the early Christians, who were willing to face hungry lions and the excruciating pain of chopping blocks rather than submit to certain unjust laws of the

---

*Eds. note — American philosopher and theologian (1886–1965).

**Eds. note — In the book of Daniel, three men who were thrown into a blazing fire for refusing to worship a golden statue.

Roman Empire. To a degree, academic freedom is a reality today because Socrates practiced civil disobedience. In our own nation, the Boston Tea Party represented a massive act of civil disobedience.

We should never forget that everything Adolph Hitler did in Ger- 22 many was "legal" and everything the Hungarian freedom fighters did in Hungary was "illegal." It was "illegal" to aid and comfort a Jew in Hitler's Germany. Even so, I am sure that, had I lived in Germany at the time, I would have aided and comforted my Jewish brothers. If today I lived in a Communist country where certain principles dear to the Christian faith are suppressed, I would openly advocate disobeying that country's anti-religious laws.

I must make two honest confessions to you, my Christian and Jewish 23 brothers. First, I must confess that over the past few years I have been gravely disappointed with the white moderate. I have almost reached the regrettable conclusion that the Negro's great stumbling block in his stride toward freedom is not the White Citizens Counciler or the Ku Klux Klan-ner, but the white moderate, who is more devoted to "order" than to jus-tice; who prefers a negative peace which is the absence of tension to a positive peace which is the presence of justice; who constantly says, "I agree with you in the goal you seek, but I cannot agree with your methods of direct action"; who paternalistically believes he can set the timetable for another man's freedom; who lives by a mythical concept of time and who constantly advised the Negro to wait for a "more convenient season." Shallow understanding from people of good will is more frustrating than absolute misunderstanding from people of ill will. Lukewarm acceptance is much more bewildering than outright rejection.

I had hoped that the white moderate would understand that law and 24 order exist for the purpose of establishing justice and that when they fail in this purpose they become the dangerously structured dams that block the flow of social progress. I had hoped that the white moderate would understand that the present tension in the South is a necessary phase of the transition from an obnoxious negative peace, in which the Negro pas-sively accepted his unjust plight, to a substantive and positive peace, in which all men will respect the dignity and worth of human personality. Actually, we who engage in nonviolent direct action are not the creators of tension. We merely bring to the surface the hidden tension that is already alive. We bring it out in the open, where it can be seen and dealt with. Like a boil that can never be cured so long as it is covered up but must be opened with all its ugliness to the natural medicines of air and light, in-justice must be exposed, with all the tension its exposure creates, to the light of human conscience and the air of national opinion, before it can be cured.

In your statement you assert that our actions, even though peaceful, 25 must be condemned because they precipitate violence. But is this a logical assertion? Isn't this like condemning a robbed man because his possession of money precipitated the evil act of robbery? Isn't this like condemning

Socrates because his unswerving commitment to truth and his philosophical inquiries precipitated the act by the misguided populace in which they made him drink hemlock? Isn't this like condemning Jesus because his unique God-consciousness and never-ceasing devotion to God's will precipitated the evil act of crucifixion? We must come to see that, as the federal courts have consistently affirmed, it is wrong to urge an individual to cease his efforts to gain his basic constitutional rights because the quest may precipitate violence. Society must protect the robbed and punish the robber.

I had also hoped that the white moderate would reject the myth concerning time in relation to the struggle for freedom. I have just received a letter from a white brother in Texas. He writes: "All Christians know that the colored people will receive equal rights eventually, but it is possible that you are in too great a religious hurry. It has taken Christianity almost two thousand years to accomplish what it has. The teachings of Christ take time to come to earth." Such an attitude stems from a tragic misconception of time, from the strangely irrational notion that there is something in the very flow of time that will inevitably cure all ills. Actually, time itself is neutral; it can be used either destructively or constructively. More and more I feel that the people of ill will have used time much more effectively than have the people of good will. We will have to repent in this generation not merely for the hateful words and actions of the bad people, but for the appalling silence of the good people. Human progress never rolls in on wheels of inevitability; it comes through the tireless efforts of men willing to be co-workers with God, and without his hard work, time itself becomes an ally of the forces of social stagnation. We must use time creatively, in the knowledge that the time is always ripe to do right. Now is the time to make real the promise of democracy and transform our pending national elegy into a creative psalm of brotherhood. Now is the time to lift our national policy from the quicksand of racial injustice to the solid rock of human dignity.

You speak of our activity in Birmingham as extreme. At first I was rather disappointed that fellow clergymen would see my nonviolent efforts as those of an extremist. I began thinking about the fact that I stand in the middle of two opposing forces in the Negro community. One is a force of complacency, made up in part of Negroes who, as a result of long years of oppression, are so drained of self-respect and a sense of "somebodiness" that they have adjusted to segregation; and in part of a few middle-class Negroes who, because of a degree of academic and economic security and because in some ways they profit by segregation, have become insensitive to the problems of the masses. The other force is one of bitterness and hatred, and it comes perilously close to advocating violence. It is expressed in the various black nationalist groups that are springing up across the nation, the largest and best-known being Elijah Muhammad's Muslim movement. Nourished by the Negro's frustration over the continued existence of racial discrimination, this movement is made up of people who have lost faith in America, who have absolutely repudiated Christianity, and who have concluded that the white man is an incorrigible "devil."

I have tried to stand between these two forces, saying that we need emulate neither the "do-nothingism" of the complacent nor the hatred and despair of the black nationalist. For there is the more excellent way of love and nonviolent protest. I am grateful to God that, through the influence of the Negro church, the way of nonviolence became an integral part of our struggle.   28

If this philosophy had not emerged, by now many streets of the South would, I am convinced, be flowing with blood. And I am further convinced that if our white brothers dismiss as "rabble-rousers" and "outside agitators" those of us who employ nonviolent direct action, and if they refuse to support our nonviolent efforts, millions of Negroes will, out of frustration and despair, seek solace and security in black-nationalist ideologies — a development that would inevitably lead to a frightening racial nightmare.   29

Oppressed people cannot remain oppressed forever. The yearning for freedom eventually manifests itself, and that is what has happened to the American Negro. Something within has reminded him of his birthright of freedom, and something without has reminded him that it can be gained. Consciously or unconsciously, he has been caught up by the *Zeitgeist,* and with his black brothers of Africa and his brown and yellow brothers of Asia, South America, and the Caribbean, the United States Negro is moving with a sense of great urgency toward the promised land of racial justice. If one recognizes this vital urge that has engulfed the Negro community, one should readily understand why public demonstrations are taking place. The Negro has many pent-up resentments and latent frustrations, and he must release them. So let him march; let him make prayer pilgrimages to the city hall; let him go on freedom rides — and try to understand why he must do so. If his repressed emotions are not released in nonviolent ways, they will seek expression through violence; this is not a threat but a fact of history. So I have not said to my people, "Get rid of your discontent." Rather, I have tried to say that this normal and healthy discontent can be channeled into the creative outlet of nonviolent direct action. And now this approach is being termed extremist.   30

But though I was initially disappointed at being categorized as an extremist, as I continued to think about the matter I gradually gained a measure of satisfaction from the label. Was not Jesus an extremist for love: "Love your enemies, bless them that curse you, do good to them that hate you, and pray for them which despitefully use you, and persecute you." Was not Amos an extremist for justice: "let justice roll down like waters and righteousness like an everflowing stream." Was not Paul an extremist for the Christian gospel: "I bear in my body the marks of the Lord Jesus." Was not Martin Luther an extremist: "Here I stand; I cannot do otherwise, so help me God." And John Bunyan: "I will stay in jail to the end of my days before I make a butchery of my conscience." And Abraham Lincoln: 31

"This nation cannot survive half slave and half free." And Thomas Jefferson: "We hold these truths to be self-evident, that all men are created equal. . . ." So the question is not whether we will be extremists, but what kind of extremists we will be. Will we be extremists for hate or for love? Will we be extremists for the preservation of injustice or for the extension of justice? In that dramatic scene of Calvary's hill three men were crucified. We must never forget that all three were crucified for the same crime — the crime of extremism. Two were extremists for immorality, and thus fell below their environment. The other, Jesus Christ, was an extremist for love, truth, and goodness, and thereby rose above his environment. Perhaps the South, the nation, and the world are in dire need of creative extremists.

I hoped that the white moderate would see this need. Perhaps I was 32 too optimistic; perhaps I expected too much. I suppose I should have realized that few members of the oppressor race can understand the deep groans and passionate yearnings of the oppressed race, and still fewer have the vision to see that injustice must be rooted out by strong, persistent, and determined action. I am thankful, however, that some of our white brothers in the South have grasped the meaning of this social revolution and committed themselves to it. They are still all too few in quantity, but they are big in quality. Some — such as Ralph McGill, Lillian Smith, Harry Golden, James McBride Dabbs, Ann Braden, and Sarah Patton Boyle — have written about our struggle in eloquent and prophetic terms. Others have marched with us down nameless streets of the South. They have languished in filthy, roach-infested jails, suffering the abuse and brutality of policemen who view them as "dirty nigger-lovers." Unlike so many of their moderate brothers and sisters, they have recognized the urgency of the movement and sensed the need for powerful "action" antidotes to combat the disease of segregation.

Let me take note of my other major disappointment. I have been so 33 greatly disappointed with the white church and its leadership. Of course, there are some notable exceptions. I am not unmindful of the fact that each of you has taken some significant stands on this issue. I commend you, Reverend Stallings, for your Christian stand on this past Sunday, in welcoming Negroes to your worship service on a nonsegregated basis. I commend the Catholic leaders of this state for integrating Spring Hill College several years ago.

But despite these notable exceptions, I must honestly reiterate that I 34 have been disappointed with the church. I do not say this as one of those negative critics who can always find something wrong with the church. I say this as a minister of the gospel, who loves the church; who was nurtured in its bosom; who has been sustained by its spiritual blessings and who will remain true to it as long as the cord of life shall lengthen.

When I was suddenly catapulted into the leadership of the bus protest 35 in Montgomery, Alabama, a few years ago, I felt we would be supported by the white church. I felt that the white ministers, priests, and rabbis of the South would be among our strongest allies. Instead, some have been outright opponents, refusing to understand the freedom movement and misrepresenting its leaders; all too many others have been more cautious than courageous and have remained silent behind the anesthetizing security of stained-glass windows.

In spite of my shattered dreams, I came to Birmingham with the hope 36 that the white religious leadership of this community would see the justice of our cause and, with deep moral concern, would serve as the channel through which our just grievances could reach the power structure. I had hoped that each of you would understand. But again I have been disappointed.

There was a time when the church was very powerful — in the time 37 when the early Christians rejoiced at being deemed worthy to suffer for what they believed. In those days the church was not merely a thermometer that recorded the ideas and principles of popular opinion; it was a thermostat that transformed the mores of society. Whenever the early Christians entered a town, the people in power became disturbed and immediately sought to convict the Christians for being "disturbers of the peace" and "outside agitators." But the Christians pressed on, in the conviction that they were "a colony of heaven," called to obey God rather than man. Small in number, they were big in commitment. They were too God-intoxicated to be "astronomically intimidated." By their effort and example they brought an end to such ancient evils as infanticide and gladiatorial contests.

Things are different now. So often the contemporary church is a weak, 38 ineffectual voice with an uncertain sound. So often it is an archdefender of the status quo. Far from being disturbed by the presence of the church, the power structure of the average community is consoled by the church's silent — and often even vocal — sanction of things as they are.

But the judgment of God is upon the church as never before. If today's 39 church does not recapture the sacrificial spirit of the early church, it will lose its authenticity, forfeit the loyalty of millions, and be dismissed as an irrelevant social club with no meaning for the twentieth century. Every day I meet young people whose disappointment with the church has turned into outright disgust.

Perhaps I have once again been too optimistic. Is organized religion 40 too inextricably bound to the status quo to save our nation and the world? Perhaps I must turn my faith to the inner spiritual church, the church within the church, as the true *ekklesia** and the hope of the world. But again I am thankful to God that some noble souls from the ranks of organized religion have broken loose from the paralyzing chains of conformity and joined us as active partners in the struggle for freedom. They have left their secure congregations and walked the streets of Albany, Georgia, with us. They have gone down the highways of the South on torturous rides for freedom. Yes, they have gone to jail with us. Some have been dismissed

---

*EDS. NOTE — Greek word for the early Christian church.

from their churches, have lost the support of their bishops and fellow ministers. But they have acted in the faith that right defeated is stronger than evil triumphant. Their witness has been the spiritual salt that has preserved the true meaning of the gospel in these troubled times. They have carved a tunnel of hope through the dark mountain of disappointment.

I hope the church as a whole will meet the challenge of this decisive 41 hour. But even if the church does not come to the aid of justice, I have no despair about the future. I have no fear about the outcome of our struggle in Birmingham, even if our motives are at present misunderstood. We will reach the goal of freedom in Birmingham and all over the nation, because the goal of America is freedom. Abused and scorned though we may be, our destiny is tied up with America's destiny. Before the pilgrims landed at Plymouth, we were here. Before the pen of Jefferson etched the majestic words of the Declaration of Independence across the pages of history, we were here. For more than two centuries our forebears labored in this country without wages; they made cotton king; they built the homes of their masters while suffering gross injustice and shameful humiliation — and yet out of a bottomless vitality they continued to thrive and develop. If the inexpressible cruelties of slavery could not stop us, the opposition we now face will surely fail. We will win our freedom because the sacred heritage of our nation and the eternal will of God are embodied in our echoing demands.

Before closing I feel impelled to mention one other point in your state- 42 ment that has troubled me profoundly. You warmly commended the Birmingham police for keeping "order" and "preventing violence." I doubt that you would have so warmly commended the police force if you had seen its dogs sinking their teeth into unarmed, nonviolent Negroes. I doubt that you would so quickly commend the policemen if you were to observe their ugly and inhumane treatment of Negroes here in the city jail; if you were to watch them push and curse old Negro women and young Negro girls; if you were to see them slap and kick old Negro men and young boys; if you were to observe them, as they did on two occasions, refuse to give us food because we wanted to sing our grace together. I cannot join you in your praise of the Birmingham police department.

It is true that the police have exercised a degree of discipline in han- 43 dling the demonstrators. In this sense they have conducted themselves rather "nonviolently" in public. But for what purpose? To preserve the vile system of segregation. Over the past few years I have consistently preached that nonviolence demands that the means we use must be as pure as the ends we seek. I have tried to make clear that it is wrong to use immoral means to attain moral ends. But now I must affirm that it is just as wrong, or perhaps even more so, to use moral means to preserve immoral ends. Perhaps Mr. Connor and his policemen have been rather nonviolent in public, as was Chief Pritchett in Albany, Georgia, but they have used the moral means of nonviolence to maintain the immoral end of racial injustice. As T. S. Eliot has said, "The last temptation is the greatest treason: To do the right deed for the wrong reason."

I wish you had commended the Negro sit-inners and demonstrators   44
of Birmingham for their sublime courage, their willingness to suffer, and
their amazing discipline in the midst of great provocation. One day the
South will recognize its real heroes. They will be the James Merediths,*
with the noble sense of purpose that enables them to face jeering and hostile mobs, and with the agonizing loneliness that characterizes the life of
the pioneer. They will be old, oppressed, battered Negro women, symbolized in a seventy-two-year old woman in Montgomery, Alabama, who
rose up with a sense of dignity and with her people decided not to ride
segregated buses, and who responded with ungrammatical profundity to
one who inquired about her weariness: "My feets is tired, but my soul is at
rest." They will be the young high school and college students, the young
ministers of the gospel and a host of their elders, courageously and nonviolently sitting in at lunch counters and willingly going to jail for conscience' sake. One day the South will know that when these disinherited
children of God sat down at lunch counters, they were in reality standing
up for what is best in the American dream and for the most sacred values
in our Judaeo-Christian heritage, thereby bringing our nation back to
those great wells of democracy which were dug deeply by the founding
fathers in their formulation of the Constitution and the Declaration of
Independence.

Never before have I written so long a letter. I'm afraid it is much too   45
long to take your precious time. I can assure that it would have been much
shorter if I had been writing from a comfortable desk, but what else can
one do when he is alone in a narrow jail cell, other than write long letters,
think long thoughts, and pray long prayers?

If I have said anything in this letter that overstates the truth and indi-   46
cates an unreasonable impatience, I beg you to forgive me. If I have said
anything that understates the truth and indicates my having a patience
that allows me to settle for anything less than brotherhood, I beg God to
forgive me.

I hope this letter finds you strong in the faith. I also hope that circum-   47
stances will soon make it possible for me to meet each of you, not as an
integrationist or a civil-rights leader but as a fellow clergyman and a
Christian brother. Let us all hope that the dark clouds of racial prejudice
will soon pass away and the deep fog of misunderstanding will be lifted
from our fear-drenched communities, and in some not too distant tomorrow the radiant stars of love and brotherhood will shine over our great
nation with all their scintillating beauty.

Yours for the cause of Peace and Brotherhood,
Martin Luther King Jr.

•   •   •

---

*EDS. NOTE — James Meredith was the first African American to enroll at the Uni-
versity of Mississippi.

COMPREHENSION

1. King says he seldom answers criticism. Why, then, does he decide to do so in this instance?

2. Why do the other clergymen consider King's activities to be "unwise and untimely" (1)?

3. What reasons does King give for the demonstrations? Why does he think it is too late for negotiations?

4. What does King say *wait* means to black people?

5. What are the two types of laws King defines? What is the difference between the two?

6. What does King find illogical about the claim that the actions of his followers precipitate violence?

7. Why is King disappointed in the white church?

PURPOSE AND AUDIENCE

1. Why, in the first paragraph, does King establish his setting (the Birmingham city jail) and define his intended audience?

2. Why does King begin his letter with a reference to his audience as "men of genuine good will" (1)? Is this phrase ironic in light of his later criticism of them? Explain.

3. What indication is there that King is writing his letter to an audience other than his fellow clergymen?

4. What is the thesis of this letter? Is it stated or implied?

STYLE AND STRUCTURE

1. Where does King seek to establish that he is a reasonable person?

2. Where does King address the objections of his audience?

3. As in the Declaration of Independence, transitions are important in King's letter. Identify the transitional words and phrases that connect the different parts of his argument.

4. Why does King cite Jewish, Catholic, and Protestant philosophers to support his position?

5. King relies heavily on appeals to authority (Augustine, Aquinas, Buber, Tillich, and so forth). Why do you think he uses this strategy?

6. King uses both induction and deduction in his letter. Find an example of each, and explain how they function in the argument.

7. Throughout the body of his letter, King criticizes his audience of white moderates. In his conclusion, however, he seeks to reestablish a harmonious relationship with them. How does he do this? Is he successful?

VOCABULARY PROJECTS

1. Define each of the following words as it is used in this selection.

   affiliate (2)   devotee (12)   reiterate (34)
   cognizant (4)   estrangement (16)   intimidate (37)
   mutuality (4)   ordinances (16)   infanticide (37)
   provincial (4)   anarchy (20)   inextricably (40)
   gainsay (6)   elegy (26)   scintillating (47)
   unfettered (10)   incorrigible (27)
   millennium (12)   emulate (28)

2. Locate five **allusions** to the Bible in this essay. How do these allusions help King express his ideas?

3. In paragraph 14, King refers to his "cup of endurance." To what is this a reference? How is the original phrase worded?

JOURNAL ENTRY

Do you believe King's remarks go too far? Do you believe they do not go far enough? Explain.

WRITING WORKSHOP

1. Write an argumentative essay in which you support a deeply held belief of your own. Assume that your audience, like King's, is not openly hostile to your position.

2. Assume that you are a militant political leader writing a letter to Martin Luther King Jr. Argue that King's methods do not go far enough. Be sure to address potential objections to your position. You might want to go to the library and read some newspapers and magazines from the 1960s to help you prepare your argument. (Be sure to document all material you borrow from your sources. See the Appendix.)

3. Read your local newspaper for several days, collecting articles about a controversial subject that interests you. Using information from the articles, take a position on the issue, and write an essay supporting it. (Be sure to document all material you borrow from your sources. See the Appendix.)

COMBINING THE PATTERNS

In "Letter from Birmingham Jail," King includes several passages of **narration.** Find two of these passages, and discuss what use King makes of narration. Why do you think narration plays such an important part in King's argument?

THEMATIC CONNECTION

- "Finishing School" (page 88)
- "The 'Black Table' Is Still There" (page 294)
- "Two Ways to Belong in America" (page 357)
- "Burdens" (page 466)

◢◢◢◢◢◢◢◢
DEBATE:
Is Date Rape Really Rape?

The phenomenon known as date rape has existed for a long time, but in recent years it has become an important issue on many college campuses. The rise of feminism has called attention to the problem and has led to campus programs to help both male and female students avoid situations that could lead to date rape. Some colleges have even published behavior codes in an attempt to sensitize students to this issue. (Antioch College, for example, instituted a widely publicized code requiring students to ask a partner's permission to proceed at each stage of intimacy.)

Given the lack of controversy about the seriousness of rape, one might ask, "What is there to debate about date rape? Isn't rape always rape?" But for many people the issue is not this simple. Some argue that many incidents characterized as date rape are not rape at all. What actually occurs in these situations, they say, is a miscommunication that results in sex, which the woman may not really want or may later regret but which cannot be fairly characterized as rape. Others say drugs and alcohol frequently play a part in what are labeled date rapes. How can a woman cry "rape," they ask, when she has contributed to the situation? Finally, some say that by applying the term *rape* to situations like these, date-rape activists diminish the seriousness of "real" rape resulting from physical force or threats of violence. In response to these arguments, activists say such excuses continue a long tradition of women's subjugation. The vast majority of men, they argue, bestow their affections only on willing recipients, and the charge that large numbers of them are being falsely accused of rape by fickle or vindictive women not only ignores the facts but itself trivializes the severity of the crime.

The two writers in this section express opposite opinions about date rape. In "It's a Jungle Out There," Camille Paglia asserts that the only way to eliminate date rape is for women to take responsibility for their own actions. In "Common Decency," Susan Jacoby argues that there should be no distinction between rape and date rape because men should be expected to understand when "no" means "no."

CAMILLE PAGLIA

Camille Paglia was born in 1947 in Endicott, New York, graduated from the State University of New York at Binghamton in 1968, and received her doctorate from Yale University in 1974. She has taught at Bennington College, Wesleyan University, Yale, and, since 1984, the University of the Arts in Philadelphia. Paglia has published three books: *Sexual Personae: Art and Decadence from Nefertiti to Emily Dickinson* (1990), a best-selling scholarly work that examines pornographic elements in art and literature beginning in ancient Egypt and Greece; *Sex, Art, and American Culture* (1992), a collection of provocative articles, interviews, book reviews, and lectures on popular culture, in which the following piece appears; and the essay collection *Vamps and Tramps* (1994).

Dubbed by one interviewer "Hurricane Camille," the outspoken Paglia has provoked considerable controversy with her iconoclastic critique of the feminist movement. Largely a feminist herself in terms of her political views, she argues that feminist leaders have gotten locked into a social and cultural mindset that is out of step with mainstream reality. In "It's a Jungle Out There," which first appeared in *New York Newsday* in 1991, Paglia claims that feminism misleads women by offering them a fantasy of sexual empowerment instead of warning them of the inevitability of male sexual aggression.

It's a Jungle Out There

Rape is an outrage that cannot be tolerated in civilized society. Yet feminism, which has waged a crusade for rape to be taken more seriously, has put young women in danger by hiding the truth about sex from them.

In dramatizing the pervasiveness of rape, feminists have told young women that before they have sex with a man, they must give consent as explicit as a legal contract's. In this way, young women have been convinced that they have been the victims of rape. On elite campuses in the Northeast and on the West Coast, they have held consciousness-raising sessions, petitioned administrations, demanded inquests. At Brown University, outraged, panicky "victims" have scrawled the names of alleged attackers on the walls of women's rest rooms. What marital rape was to the '70s, "date rape" is to the '90s.

The incidence and seriousness of rape do not require this kind of exaggeration. Real acquaintance rape is nothing new. It has been a horrible problem for women for all of recorded history. Once fathers and brothers protected women from rape. Once the penalty for rape was death. I come from a fierce Italian tradition where, not so long ago in the motherland, a rapist would end up knifed, castrated, and hung out to dry.

But the old clans and small rural communities have broken down. In our cities, on our campuses far from home, young women are vulnerable and defenseless. Feminism has not prepared them for this. Feminism keeps saying the sexes are the same. It keeps telling women they can do anything, go anywhere, say anything, wear anything. No, they can't. Women will always be in sexual danger.

One of my male students recently slept overnight with a friend in a   5
passageway of the Great Pyramid in Egypt. He described the moon and sand, the ancient silence and eerie echoes. I will never experience that. I am a woman. I am not stupid enough to believe I could ever be safe there. There is a world of solitary adventure I will never have. Women have always known these somber truths. But feminism, with its pie-in-the-sky fantasies about the perfect world, keeps young women from seeing life as it is.

We must remedy social injustice whenever we can. But there are some   6
things we cannot change. There are sexual differences that are based in biology. Academic feminism is lost in a fog of social constructionism. It believes we are totally the product of our environment. This idea was invented by Rousseau.* He was wrong. Emboldened by dumb French language theory, academic feminists repeat the same hollow slogans over and over to each other. Their view of sex is naive and prudish. Leaving sex to the feminists is like letting your dog vacation at the taxidermist's.

The sexes are at war. Men must struggle for identity against the over-   7
whelming power of their mothers. Women have menstruation to tell them they are women. Men must do or risk something to be men. Men become masculine only when other men say they are. Having sex with a woman is one way a boy becomes a man.

College men are at their hormonal peak. They have just left their   8
mothers and are questing for their male identity. In groups, they are dangerous. A woman going to a fraternity party is walking into Testosterone Flats, full of prickly cacti and blazing guns. If she goes, she should be armed with resolute alertness. She should arrive with girlfriends and leave with them. A girl who lets herself get dead drunk at a fraternity party is a fool. A girl who goes upstairs alone with a brother at a fraternity party is an idiot. Feminists call this "blaming the victim." I call it common sense.

For a decade, feminists have drilled their disciples to say, "Rape is a   9
crime of violence but not of sex." This sugar-coated Shirley Temple nonsense has exposed young women to disaster. Misled by feminism, they do not expect rape from the nice boys from good homes who sit next to them in class.

Aggression and eroticism are deeply intertwined. Hunt, pursuit, and   10
capture are biologically programmed into male sexuality. Generation after generation, men must be educated, refined, and ethically persuaded away from their tendency toward anarchy and brutishness. Society is not the enemy, as feminism ignorantly claims. Society is woman's protection

---

*EDS. NOTE — Jean-Jacques Rousseau (1712–1778), a French philosopher and political theorist.

against rape. Feminism, with its solemn Carry Nation* repressiveness, does not see what is for men the eroticism or fun element in rape, especially the wild, infectious delirium of gang rape. Women who do not understand rape cannot defend themselves against it.

The date-rape controversy shows feminism hitting the wall of its own   11
broken promises. The women of my '60s generation were the first respectable girls in history to swear like sailors, get drunk, stay out all night — in short, to act like men. We sought total sexual freedom and equality. But as time passed, we woke up to cold reality. The old double standard protected women. When anything goes, it's women who lose.

Today's young women don't know what they want. They see that   12
feminism has not brought sexual happiness. The theatrics of public rage over date rape are their way of restoring the old sexual rules that were shattered by my generation. Because nothing about the sexes has really changed. The comic film *Where the Boys Are* (1960), the ultimate expression of '50s man-chasing, still speaks directly to our time. It shows smart, lively women skillfully anticipating and fending off the dozens of strategies with which horny men try to get them into bed. The agonizing date-rape subplot and climax are brilliantly done. The victim, Yvette Mimieux, makes mistake after mistake, obvious to the other girls. She allows herself to be lured away from her girlfriends and into isolation with boys whose character and intentions she misreads. *Where the Boys Are* tells the truth. It shows courtship as a dangerous game in which the signals are not verbal but subliminal.

Neither militant feminism, which is obsessed with politically correct   13
language, nor academic feminism, which believes that knowledge and experience are "constituted by" language, can understand pre-verbal or non-verbal communication. Feminism, focusing on sexual politics, cannot see that sex exists in and through the body. Sexual desire and arousal cannot be fully translated into verbal terms. This is why men and women misunderstand each other.

Trying to remake the future, feminism cut itself off from sexual his-   14
tory. It discarded and suppressed the sexual myths of literature, art, and religion. Those myths show us the turbulence, the mysteries and passions of sex. In mythology we see men's sexual anxiety, their fear of women's dominance. Much sexual violence is rooted in men's sense of psychological weakness toward women. It takes many men to deal with one woman. Woman's voracity is a persistent motif. Clara Bow,** it was rumored, took on the USC football team on weekends. Marilyn Monroe, singing "Dia-

---

*Eds. note — An American temperance leader and advocate of women's suffrage (1846–1911) who became legendary for her use of a hatchet to destroy liquor and other contents of saloons.

**Eds. note — An American actress in silent movies (1905–1965).

monds Are a Girl's Best Friend," rules a conga line of men in tuxes. Half-clad Cher, in the video for "If I Could Turn Back Time," deranges a battleship of screaming sailors and straddles a pink-lit cannon. Feminism, coveting social power, is blind to woman's cosmic sexual power.

To understand rape, you must study the past. There never was and never will be sexual harmony. Every woman must take personal responsibility for her sexuality, which is nature's red flame. She must be prudent and cautious about where she goes and with whom. When she makes a mistake, she must accept the consequences and, through self-criticism, resolve never to make that mistake again. Running to Mommy and Daddy or the campus grievance committee is unworthy of strong women. Posting lists of guilty men in the toilet is cowardly, infantile stuff.   15

The Italian philosophy of life espouses high-energy confrontation. A male student makes a vulgar remark about your breasts? Don't slink off to whimper and simper with the campus shrinking violets. Deal with it. On the spot. Say, "Shut up, you jerk! And crawl back to the barnyard where you belong!" In general, women who project this take-charge attitude toward life get harassed less often. I see too many dopey, immature, self-pitying women walking around like melting sticks of butter. It's the Yvette Mimieux syndrome: Make me happy. And listen to me weep when I'm not.   16

The date-rape debate is already smothering in propaganda churned out by the expensive Northeastern colleges and universities, with their overconcentration of boring, uptight academic feminists and spoiled, affluent students. Beware of the deep manipulativeness of rich students who were neglected by their parents. They love to turn the campus into hysterical psychodramas of sexual transgression, followed by assertions of parental authority and concern. And don't look for sexual enlightenment from academe, which spews out mountains of books but never looks at life directly.   17

As a fan of football and rock music, I see in the simple, swaggering masculinity of the jock and in the noisy posturing of the heavy-metal guitarist certain fundamental, unchanging truths about sex. Masculinity is aggressive, unstable, combustible. It is also the most creative cultural force in history. Women must reorient themselves toward the elemental powers of sex, which can strengthen or destroy.   18

The only solution to date rape is female self-awareness and self-control. A woman's number one line of defense is herself. When a real rape occurs, she should report it to the police. Complaining to college committees because the courts "take too long" is ridiculous. College administrations are not a branch of the judiciary. They are not equipped or trained for legal inquiry. Colleges must alert incoming students to the problems and dangers of adulthood. Then colleges must stand back and get out of the sex game.   19

• • •

COMPREHENSION

1. According to Paglia, how does feminism mislead women?

2. How does Paglia explain the prevalence of date rape in our society?

3. According to Paglia, "Women who do not understand rape cannot defend themselves against it" (10). What does she say women must understand?

4. Why, according to Paglia, do men and women misunderstand each other?

5. What is Paglia's solution to the problem of rape?

PURPOSE AND AUDIENCE

1. Does Paglia assume her readers are hostile, friendly, or neutral? How can you tell?

2. Is Paglia primarily addressing men, women, or both? How do you know?

3. Is Paglia's purpose to change people's ideas or to change their behavior? Explain.

STYLE AND STRUCTURE

1. Paglia makes no effort to hide her feelings toward those who disagree with her ideas. Underline the words that show her opinion of her opposition. How would you describe her tone? Reasonable? Angry? Sarcastic? Frustrated? Impatient?

2. Throughout her essay Paglia makes personal attacks against what she calls "academic feminists" and "militant feminists." Do you think these attacks strengthen or undercut her argument? Explain your reasoning.

3. Is Paglia's argument primarily inductive or deductive? Explain.

4. How effectively does Paglia refute the arguments against her position?

5. What strategy does Paglia use to conclude her essay? Is this a wise choice?

VOCABULARY PROJECTS

1. Define each of the following words as it is used in this selection.

pervasiveness (2)	eroticism (10)	motif (14)
incidence (3)	delirium (10)	conga line (14)
solitary (5)	subliminal (12)	transgression (17)
taxidermist (6)	turbulence (14)	spews (17)
testosterone (8)	voracity (14)	combustible (18)

2. Find several examples of **colloquialisms** Paglia uses in her essay. Do they help her make her point more clearly, or do they undermine her credibility?

JOURNAL ENTRY

Some of Paglia's critics have charged that she is more interested in shining the spotlight on herself than in addressing issues. After reading her essay, do you think this criticism is justified?

WRITING WORKSHOP

1. What do you think should be done to prevent date rape? Do you, like Paglia, think the solution is up to women? Or do you think the responsibility lies elsewhere?

2. Write an essay in which you take two of Paglia's points and refute them either by questioning their accuracy or by identifying flaws in their logic.

3. Find out what your college's policy is concerning date rape. Write an editorial for your school newspaper or a memo to the dean of students in which you argue that the policy is sound — or that it should be modified.

COMBINING THE PATTERNS

Paragraph 12 is developed by means of **exemplification.** What point is Paglia making? How does her example help her make it? Should she have used a series of brief examples instead of a single extended example? Why or why not?

THEMATIC CONNECTIONS

- "Just Walk On By" (page 197)
- "Sexism in English: Embodiment and Language" (page 413)
- "I Want a Wife" (page 474)

SUSAN JACOBY

Susan Jacoby is a freelance writer. Fluent in Russian, she lived in the Soviet Union from 1969 to 1971 and wrote two books, *Moscow Conversations* (1972) and *Inside Soviet Schools* (1974), on her experiences and research there. Jacoby also collaborated with Yelena Khanga on a biography of Khanga's family, *Soul to Soul: The Story of a Black Russian American Family 1865–1992* (1992). Jacoby has worked as an education reporter for the *Washington Post* and is a regular contributor to *Cosmopolitan, Glamour, McCall's,* and the *New York Times.* She is the author of *The Possible She* (1979), a collection of essays from her research and magazine writings; *Wild Justice: The Evolution of Revenge* (1983); and the forthcoming *Half Jew: A Daughter's Search for Her Family's Buried Past* (2000).

As may be suggested by the publications she regularly contributes to — *Cosmopolitan* and *Glamour,* in particular — Jacoby is not the kind of out-of-the-mainstream feminist Paglia criticizes. As a reporter, Jacoby closely examines and writes about the everyday world around her. Nevertheless, she refuses to accept Paglia's contention that men are, by nature, uncontrolled sexual predators. In "Common Decency," published in 1991 in the *New York Times Magazine,* Jacoby argues that excusing date rape on the grounds of "mixed signals" demeans men as well as women.

Common Decency

She was deeply in love with a man who was treating her badly. To assuage her wounded ego (and to prove to herself that she could get along nicely without him), she invited another man, an old boyfriend, to a dinner *à deux** in her apartment. They were on their way to the bedroom when, having realized that she wanted only the man who wasn't there, she changed her mind. Her ex-boyfriend was understandably angry. He left her apartment with a not-so-politely phrased request that she leave him out of any future plans. 1

And that is the end of the story — except for the fact that he was eventually kind enough to accept her apology for what was surely a classic case of "mixed signals." 2

I often recall this incident, in which I was the embarrassed female participant, as the controversy over "date rape". . . heats up across the nation. What seems clear to me is that those who place acquaintance rape in a different category from "stranger rape"— those who excuse friendly social rapists on grounds that they are too dumb to understand when "no" means no — are being even more insulting to men than to women. 3

These apologists for date rape — and some of them are women — are really saying that the average man cannot be trusted to exercise any impulse control. Men are nasty and men are brutes — and a woman must 4

---

*EDS. NOTE — French expression meaning "between two people" or "private."

be constantly on her guard to avoid giving a man any excuse to give way to his baser instincts.

If this view were accurate, few women would manage to get through 5
life without being raped, and few men would fail to commit rape. For the reality is that all of us, men as well as women, send and receive innumerable mixed signals in the course of our sexual lives — and that is as true in marital beds at age 50 as in the back seats of cars at age 15.

Most men somehow manage to decode these signals without using 6
superior physical strength to force themselves on their partners. And most women manage to handle conflicting male signals without, say, picking up carving knives to demonstrate their displeasure at sexual rejection. This is called civilization.

Civilized is exactly what my old boyfriend was being when he didn't 7
use my muddleheaded emotional distress as an excuse to rape me. But I don't owe him excessive gratitude for his decent behavior — any more than he would have owed me special thanks for not stabbing him through the heart if our situations had been reversed. Most date rapes do not happen because a man honestly mistakes a woman's "no" for a "yes" or a "maybe." They occur because a minority of men — an ugly minority, to be sure — can't stand to take "no" for an answer.

This minority behavior — and a culture that excuses it on grounds 8
that boys will be boys — is the target of the movement against date rape that has surfaced on many campuses during the past year.

It's not surprising that date rape is an issue of particular importance to 9
college-age women. The campus concentration of large numbers of young people, in a unsupervised environment that encourages drinking and partying, tends to promote sexual aggression and discourage inhibition. Drunken young men who rape a woman at a party can always claim they didn't know what they were doing — and a great many people will blame the victim for having been there in the first place.

That is the line adopted by antifeminists like Camille Paglia, author of 10
the controversial *Sexual Personae: Art and Decadence from Nefertiti to Emily Dickinson.* Paglia, whose views strongly resemble those expounded 20 years ago by Norman Mailer in *The Prisoner of Sex,* argues that feminists have deluded women by telling them they can go anywhere and do anything without fear of rape. Feminism, in this view, is both naïve and antisexual because it ignores the power of women to incite uncontrollable male passions.

Just to make sure there is no doubt about a woman's place, Paglia also 11
links the male sexual aggression that leads to rape with the creative energy of art. "There is no female Mozart," she has declared, "because there is no female Jack the Ripper." According to this "logic," one might expect to discover the next generation of composers in fraternity houses and dorms that have been singled out as sites of brutal gang rapes.

This type of unsubtle analysis makes no distinction between sex as an 12
expression of the will to power and sex as a source of pleasure. When

domination is seen as an inevitable component of sex, the act of rape is defined not by a man's actions but by a woman's signals.

It is true, of course, that some women (especially the young) initially   13
resist sex not out of real conviction but as part of the elaborate persuasion and seduction rituals accompanying what was once called courtship. And it is true that many men (again, especially the young) take pride in the ability to coax a woman a step further than she intended to go.

But these mating rituals do not justify or even explain date rape. Even   14
the most callow youth is capable of understanding the difference between resistance and genuine fear; between a halfhearted "no, we shouldn't" and tears or screams; between a woman who is physically free to leave a room and one who is being physically restrained.

The immorality and absurdity of using mixed signals as an excuse   15
for rape is cast in high relief when the assault involves one woman and a group of men. In cases of gang rape in a social setting (usually during or after a party), the defendants and their lawyers frequently claim that group sex took place but no force was involved. These upright young men, so the defense invariably contends, were confused because the girl had voluntarily gone to a party with them. Why, she may have even displayed sexual interest in *one* of them. How could they have been expected to understand that she didn't wish to have sex with the whole group?

The very existence of the term "date rape" attests to a slow change in   16
women's consciousness that began with the feminist movement of the late 1960's. Implicit in this consciousness is the conviction that a woman has the right to say no at any point in the process leading to sexual intercourse — and that a man who fails to respect her wishes should incur serious legal and social consequences.

The other, equally important half of the equation is respect for men. If   17
mixed signals are the real cause of sexual assault, it behooves every woman to regard every man as a potential rapist.

In such a benighted universe, it would be impossible for a woman   18
(and, let us not forget, for a man) to engage in the tentative emotional and physical exploration that eventually produces a mature erotic life. She would have to make up her mind right from the start in order to prevent a rampaging male from misreading her intentions.

Fortunately for everyone, neither the character of men nor the general   19
quality of relations between the sexes is that crude. By censuring the minority of men who use ordinary socializing as an excuse for rape, feminists insist on sex as a source of pure pleasure rather than as a means of social control. Real men want an eager sexual partner — not a woman who is quaking with fear or even one who is ambivalent. Real men don't rape.

•   •   •

COMPREHENSION

1. Why does Jacoby believe those who excuse "friendly social rapists" (3) are being more insulting to men than to women?

2. According to Jacoby, why do most date rapes occur?

3. Why is date rape a particularly important issue for college-age women?

4. According to Jacoby, why does using mixed signals as an excuse for rape show a lack of respect for men?

5. What does Jacoby mean in paragraph 16 when she says, "the very existence of the term *date rape* attests to a slow change in women's consciousness that began with the feminist movement of the late 1960's"?

PURPOSE AND AUDIENCE

1. Does Jacoby seem to be addressing her remarks primarily to men, to women, or to both? Explain.

2. How does Jacoby establish her credentials in the area of date rape? Should she have done more in this regard?

3. What preconceptions does she seem to think her readers have about her subject? Explain.

STYLE AND STRUCTURE

1. Jacoby begins her essay with a personal anecdote. How effective is this strategy? Would another strategy have been more effective?

2. How accurate is Jacoby's summary of Camille Paglia's position? How effectively does she refute Paglia's points?

3. What other arguments does Jacoby refute? How effective are these refutations?

4. What evidence does Jacoby use to support her points? Would other kinds of evidence strengthen her argument? Explain.

5. How well does Jacoby summarize her argument in her final paragraph? What new point does she introduce? Is this a wise strategy? Explain.

VOCABULARY PROJECTS

1. Define each of the following words as it is used in this selection.

   assuage (1)   elaborate (13)   rampaging (18)
   innumerable (5)   rituals (13)   ambivalent (19)

2. What does Jacoby mean by the phrase *common decency*? What connotations does it have?

3. *Date rape* is also referred to as *acquaintance rape*. What does each term suggest? How do the connotations of these terms differ? Which do you believe is more accurate?

JOURNAL ENTRY

Do you agree with Jacoby when she says apologists for date rape are even more insulting to men than they are to women?

WRITING WORKSHOP

1. Who makes a better argument, Paglia or Jacoby? Write an essay in which you summarize the positions of both writers and then support one or the other. Include the reasons why you prefer one argument over the other, and use material from both essays to support your points.

2. What do you think Camille Paglia would say about Jacoby's argument? Assuming you are Paglia, write a letter to Jacoby responding to the specific points she makes in her essay.

3. Write an essay in which you support Jacoby's point that "mating rituals do not justify or even explain date rape" (14). Use examples from personal experience (your own or someone else's) to support your thesis.

COMBINING THE PATTERNS

Paragraph 14 relies on **comparison and contrast.** What two things are being contrasted? Should Jacoby have developed her series of contrasts in more depth? For instance, should she have used narrative examples? What would be the advantages and disadvantages of such a strategy?

THEMATIC CONNECTIONS

- "Thirty-Eight Who Saw Murder Didn't Call the Police" (page 99)
- "The Lottery" (page 255)
- "Sex, Lies, and Conversation" (page 367)

▰▰▰▰▰▰▰▰
DEBATE:
Should We Live Together or Apart?

In his essay "The 'Black Table' Is Still There" (page 294), Lawrence Otis Graham wonders why, years after he graduated, the "black-only" lunch table is still present in his junior high school.

> Why was it there? Why did the black kids separate themselves? What did the table say about the integration that was supposed to be going on in homerooms and gym classes? What did it say about the black kids? The white kids? What did it say about me when I refused to sit there, day after day, for three years?

By the end of his essay, Graham is no closer to answering his questions than he was at the beginning. "Perhaps I should be happy," he says, "that even this is a long way from where we started." But, after fourteen years, he cannot get over the fact that the "black table" is still there. Graham's essay, like the two in this debate, contemplates a question that is fundamental to our multiracial and multiethnic society: should we live together or apart?

This question is central to many of the Supreme Court decisions and much of the civil rights legislation of the last fifty years. In 1954, the Supreme Court's decision in *Brown v. Board of Education of Topeka* said that separate educational facilities for blacks and whites were unconstitutional. The Civil Rights Act of 1964 and the Voting Rights Act of 1965 further integrated African Americans (and, by extension, other victims of discrimination) into the American mainstream. Today, however, some colleges seem to be moving toward voluntary segregation by creating ethnic-theme housing for students who want to live with others like themselves. This housing, supporters say, is necessary to ensure that minority students feel at home when they attend a primarily white institution. They liken ethnic-theme housing to honors dorms and say that it is just another way for students to explore their individuality.

Critics of such housing argue that this self-imposed segregation undermines the diversity that many colleges seek to promote. According to these critics, colleges should reject all efforts to segregate students and should randomly assign students to housing just as they randomly assign them to classes. Only in this way will people with different backgrounds learn to live together. Critics further assert that to avoid being hypocritical, educators should stop reinforcing values that they would reject in the larger society. In other words, how can educators endorse ethnic-theme housing when they would condemn segregated neighborhoods, "separate-but-equal" school systems, and black-only lunch tables?

The two essays that follow take different positions on the issue of voluntary segregated housing for students. In "Why Special Housing for Ethnic Students Makes Sense," Rebecca Lee Parker argues passionately for ethnic-theme housing. She makes the point that without special housing, colleges will have great difficulty recruiting and retaining minority students, who will feel isolated in a predominantly white environment.

In "College Housing Policies Should Avoid Ethnic and Religious Balkanization," Dena S. Davis takes the opposite position, arguing that four Orthodox Jewish students should not be exempt from Yale University's requirement that all unmarried first- and second-year undergraduates live on campus. According to Davis, although Yale should attempt to make these students welcome, it should not permit them to segregate themselves and thereby reject an important component of the Yale educational experience.

♪♪♪♪♪♪♪♪
REBECCA LEE PARKER

Rebecca Lee Parker (1956–) was born in Cincinnati, Ohio. She received her B.A. from Capital University in Columbus, Ohio, and both her M.A. and Ph.D. from Ohio State University. She is currently director of the Ohio Union, the student activities center at Ohio State.

For the first half of this century, a large majority of those attending college in the United States were white males. Over the past fifty years, these demographics have changed considerably. By 1996, for example, more than 55 percent of bachelor's degrees were awarded to women. But the college experience still remains predominantly white. According to the College Board, which administers the SAT test for college admissions, 67 percent of those taking the test in 1998 identified themselves as white, 11 percent as African American, 9 percent as Asian, and 8 percent as Hispanic. As a consequence, most four-year colleges, excluding those that are traditionally African American or whose location attracts larger numbers of minorities, have relatively small numbers of minority students. In this essay, which appeared in the *Chronicle of Higher Education* (a periodical for college faculty and administrators), Parker argues that colleges have a vested interest in trying to find ways to accommodate minority students on their campuses.

Why Special Housing for Ethnic Students Makes Sense

More than 20 years ago I had many debates with friends and classmates about where I should go to college. The issue was whether I, a young black woman, should attend a predominately white institution or one of the historically black colleges. I reasoned that, because I would probably always live in a world where whites were in the majority, it was only logical that I prepare myself by going to a predominately white institution.

Because I was already attending a majority-white high school, my decision wasn't difficult. But it should have been. I should have been told about more than tuition fees, academic programs, and the power of my standardized-test scores. *Someone* should have engaged me in a serious discussion about the quality of life that I might experience during the years that would take me from adolescence to young adulthood. No one initiated that conversation with me — not my mother or my sister (who had attended a historically black college), nor any teacher, counselor, or other trusted adult in my life. With the forms completed, the loan papers signed, and the scholarships awarded, I left the familiarity of high-school life to attend a small, private, predominately white, liberal-arts college in another city.

Within hours of arriving there, I experienced culture shock. Walking around the lush, green campus, I saw almost no other students from minority groups. I felt very alone. Although many of my feelings were part of the normal anxiety of going off to college, some of them were born of a sudden realization that fitting in was no longer just a daytime endeavor.

I had gone to high school several hours a day in an environment full   4
of people who were different from me — racially, religiously, culturally, or in other ways. But every afternoon and weekend I was home, where I was supported and encouraged for the next day's challenges.

College, on the other hand, would engage me 24 hours a day, seven   5
days a week. The isolation that I felt as I walked around the campus did not lessen once I returned to my room.

I did survive. I met and made good friends — all of them black. We   6
were drawn to one another by the natural human tendency to seek out people in similar circumstances. I also got along very well with my room-mate, a white woman from another state who spent most of her weekends at her grandparents' farm. But as friendly as she was, I never felt com-pletely at home in our room.

Thus when I was invited at the end of my freshman year to serve as a   7
resident adviser on a special floor for black women, I accepted, though with some trepidation: Living on an all-black hall would be another new experience for me. The floor was located in a dormitory for upper class-men and housed approximately 20 black women. For the next two years I served as the resident adviser of this special unit and as an officer of an organization of African-American students.

While living on this floor, I did more than survive. I flourished. I   8
learned about the history, variety, and complexity of my own culture. For the first time, I learned about black life in urban and rural areas different from the suburbs where I had grown up. Occasionally, I encountered ideas about black culture and history in a classroom, but I always processed them with my hall mates "on the floor." More typically, I learned through the casual observations, new relationships, formal and informal discus-sions, and heated debates that I engaged in with this new support group of neighbors. I also participated in other campus activities — both aca-demic and extracurricular — but every afternoon I "went home."

Twenty years later, I found myself once again participating in an   9
ethnic-theme program, as part of my research for a Ph.D. in education. I moved into an African-American living-learning center for an academic year to study the structure, culture, and impact of that environment on the students' college experience. I noticed that these students faced different challenges. Compared with my college hall mates, far fewer of them had been exposed to black history during high school. Just as often, though, I was struck by the many things that had *not* changed for ethnic students on a mostly white campus. They experienced similar feelings of isolation and were interested in the same issues of identity that had attracted black stu-dents to the theme hall at my undergraduate college.

As a result of my personal experience and research, I support special   10
housing for various types of college students. I see multi-cultural and eth-

nic housing serving the same purpose as that served by fraternities and sororities, honors dorms, women's halls, and housing for students majoring in specific academic subjects. Each experience is designed to provide students with shared interests the opportunity for greater immersion in those interests.

But in addition to providing environments for education and intellectual growth, special-housing programs of all kinds also provide cultural-comfort zones. Research shows that students who participate in these programs feel that they become familiar with the college or university and the variety of resources available to them more quickly. They get to know other students more easily, and receive more attention from associated faculty and staff members. Their intellectual growth and social development are accelerated.   11

Over the years, a lot of time and resources have gone into studying and developing these special-interest environments. Professional organizations, conferences, and journals have emerged to meet the growing need for information and discussion about them. Yet even such special-interest environments as honors dorms and international houses have come under fire.   12

Critics of honors dorms suggest that students of varying intellectual ability should be randomly assigned so that outstanding students can be academic role models for their peers. Opponents of international houses say that if foreign students are in the United States to learn about American culture, they should live with Americans. But if some students want to live and interact with other students who share a similar approach to the intellectual endeavor, shouldn't they have the opportunity? The honors students will serve as positive role models to others (and vice versa) in the classroom, during extracurricular activities, and as they work at on-campus jobs. Similarly, what is wrong with having a place where someone else speaks your language — literally? The same is true for ethnic-theme houses. They serve as both academic settings and cultural-comfort zones.   13

Among special-interest housing programs, however, clearly the most controversial is housing that focuses on race or ethnicity (though housing for gay and lesbian students is emerging as a rival). College administrators — and faculty members, parents, students, and the public — are less comfortable with ethnic-theme houses than with grouping students together based on other similar traits.   14

At the root of this is our own discomfort with race. Americans are obsessed with it. We are also eager, however, to prove that we are not. In a bid to demonstrate openness to and desire for diversity, opponents of race-based housing pose misguided questions and challenges to a concept that has already been demonstrated to be successful. One such challenge is the concern that ethnic-theme houses encourage segregation rather than integration. Critics argue that students must all live together — that minority students should be present in dorms in numbers representative   15 of their presence on campus. It's a very quantitative approach to a very qualitative issue.

And quite frankly, it is an illogical argument, one that puts the burden 16 of integration on minority students without addressing other ways to increase their overall numbers on campus or the quality of their experience. We are a society made rich (in spite of our best efforts) by our cultural enclaves, and we have been for years. Most cities have racial and ethnic communities that are sought after and enjoyed by their residents. We are not minimized by the existence of these communities or by the strong desire that some of us have to live in them.

Not all minority-group students want to live in theme houses focused 17 on their culture. These students have other interests, opportunities, and priorities in their college lives. Some students, however, are concerned about the day-to-day reality — often different from that suggested by admissions brochures — of life on a predominately white campus. These students know, either intuitively or because they received better information than I did at that age, that they are entering a different world. And they have the wisdom to know that they should prepare themselves for it. Different support structures should be available to them, including ethnic-theme houses.

The controversy about ethnic-theme houses becomes especially heated 18 if membership is restricted. Should these environments be limited to members of the ethnic group, as in the Cornell University experiment a few years ago, or should they be open to anyone? It depends. Philosophically, I am not a proponent of restricting membership, because special-interest housing serves intellectual needs as well as cultural ones, and I believe that no student should be denied the opportunity to pursue specific intellectual interests. Furthermore, just as academically average students have benefited from living in honors houses and American students have grown tremendously in international houses, the perspectives of white students have been enhanced by their participation in ethnic houses.

But some ethnic-theme houses operate quite well with homogenous 19 membership. I can conceive of some situations — depending on the campus environment, the history of the program, and the student body — in which program planners would be justified in restricting membership. As a colleague of mine is fond of saying, "Every flower doesn't bloom in the spring." It is up to administrators, after open-minded dialogue with their students, to decide which challenges various programs are ready for, and when.

We can choose, of course, to eliminate these opportunities from our 20 campuses. We can define for our students which of their needs we will and will not respond to. It is, after all, the prerogative of each university or college to define its culture. We are being extremely naïve, however, if we don't realize that the potential pool of students has a few prerogatives of its own. If students do not believe a particular campus is interested in their comfort, welfare, and growth, they will elect to go to places that are interested. One might argue that a case in point is the recent drop in minority applications and admissions to both the University of Texas and the University of California systems, after court rulings and decisions by regents, respectively, barred institutions from considering race in admissions decisions.

Even if we are lucky enough to recruit minority students to our campuses, there is no guarantee that we will retain them. Although some academics hate to think of students as customers, the fact is, they are just that. And the reality is that there are many places to shop. The question of whether ethnic housing is an appropriate environment for some students will be moot if interested students do not apply or remain enrolled.   21

All too often, I'm afraid, students survive not because of us, but in spite of us. This doesn't have to be the case. I propose that we look beyond our theoretical frameworks and ask students who they are and what they need to succeed. We should listen seriously, then respond accordingly. We don't all need to make the same choices. Intellectual freedom and debate are hallmarks of the academy, aren't they?   22

• • •

COMPREHENSION

1. Why did Parker decide to attend a predominantly white college? What information does she wish she had been given before she made her decision?

2. What culture shocks did Parker experience at the college she attended? How did she respond to these experiences?

3. What caused Parker to flourish during the time she spent as a resident advisor on a special floor for African-American women?

4. What reasons does Parker give for supporting special housing for various types of college students? What advantages does she think this type of housing offers students? Does she concede any disadvantages?

5. According to Parker, what would be the result of eliminating special housing for ethnic students?

PURPOSE AND AUDIENCE

1. Does Parker consider her audience to be friendly, hostile, or neutral? How can you tell?

2. Is Parker addressing college students? Parents? Educators? What in the essay leads you to your conclusion?

3. What is Parker's thesis? Why does she state it where she does?

STYLE AND STRUCTURE

1. Beginning in paragraph 13, Parker presents the arguments against her thesis. Are there any arguments that she neglects to mention? How significant are these omissions?

2. In paragraph 11, Parker uses research to support her point about special-housing programs. How compelling is her discussion of this research? Is the fact that she identifies neither the research nor the researcher significant?

3. This essay contains a number of unsupported generalizations — for example, "Americans are obsessed with [race]" (15). Underline several of these generalizations, and determine if each is a "self-evident truth" or a statement in need of support.

4. Parker likens restricted ethnic housing to other special-interest housing such as sorority houses and honors dorms. Is she justified in doing so?

5. In paragraph 16, Parker refutes an argument against her position by calling it illogical. According to Parker, what is the flaw in this argument? How effective is her refutation?

6. Parker ends her essay with a question. What other strategy could she have used?

VOCABULARY PROJECTS

1. Define each of the following words as it is used in this selection.

predominantly (1)	quantitative (15)	intuitively (17)
endeavor (3)	qualitative (15)	prerogative (20)
peers (13)	enclaves (16)	hallmarks (22)

2. What do you think Parker means by the word *special* in her title? What other connotations does this word have?

JOURNAL ENTRY

Do Parker's arguments also apply to the way we live in society? In other words, are segregated neighborhoods acceptable if the segregation is voluntary?

WRITING WORKSHOP

1. Write an essay in which you agree or disagree with Parker's thesis.

2. Expand your journal entry into an essay. Make sure that you include a thesis statement and that you specifically refute arguments against your position.

3. Read "The 'Black Table' Is Still There" by Lawrence Otis Graham, (page 294). Then, write a letter from Graham to Parker in which you argue against her support for restricted housing for ethnic groups. If you wish, you can also use material from Dena S. Davis's essay, which follows.

COMBINING THE PATTERNS

Paragraphs 1 through 9 are developed by **comparison and contrast**. What two things are being compared? In what way does this comparison help Parker introduce her essay?

THEMATIC CONNECTIONS

- "Finishing School" (page 88)
- "The 'Black Table' Is Still There" (page 294)
- "The Big Move" (page 334)
- "Two Ways to Belong in America" (page 357)

DENA S. DAVIS

Dena S. Davis has a doctorate in religion from the University of Iowa and a law degree from the University of Virginia. An associate professor at the Cleveland-Marshall College of Law, she has written numerous scholarly articles, many focusing on bioethical issues such as genetic testing, cloning, HIV testing, and organ transplants. She has also been a visiting scholar at the National Human Genome Research Institute.

In the following essay, which, like the preceding one, appeared in 1997 in the *Chronicle of Higher Education*, Davis considers the question of whether a college administration has the right to require students to live in dormitories. Many four-year colleges and universities have such requirements, excepting only married students and those twenty-one or older. She focuses specifically here on a suit brought by a group of Orthodox Jewish students against Yale, one of the country's most prestigious universities. Unlike most Jews in the United States, Orthodox Jews adhere to a strict code of religious ritual that defines virtually every aspect of their daily lives, including dietary restrictions and observation of the Sabbath that forbids work of any kind. Moreover, they strongly limit premarital contact between males and females. It was to the prevailing secular atmosphere in Yale's dormitories that the students who brought the suit objected. Although a judge later dismissed the suit, for Davis this case raises larger issues about "balkanization" on college campuses — that is, the fragmenting of students into groups based on race, ethnicity, or religion.

College Housing Policies Should Avoid Ethnic and Religious Balkanization[*]

Four Orthodox Jewish students have sued Yale University because it will not exempt them from a requirement that all unmarried freshmen and sophomores under the age of 21 live on the campus. According to a recent op-ed piece in *The New York Times* by one of the students, Elisha Dov Hack, living in Yale's dormitories "is contrary to the fundamental principles" of Orthodox Judaism, by which these students live their lives. The students object to dormitories that, while nominally segregated by sex, have no parietal rules, and in which men and women can visit each other — or stay the night — as they please. They also object to the "safe sex" messages and easily available condoms on campus, all of which make it "hard for students like us to maintain our moral standards through difficult college years."

1

---

[*]EDS. NOTE — In political terms, *balkanization* is the breaking up of an area into smaller, often hostile countries. The word originally referred to the nations of the Balkan Peninsula in Eastern Europe, such as Serbia and Bosnia, which have long been in territorial conflict.

Does Yale have a legal obligation to accede to these students' de-   2
mands? And if not, should Yale nonetheless grant the students the exemptions they seek, for reasons of good pedagogy or religious tolerance?

First, Yale probably does not have a legal obligation to give the stu-   3
dents an exemption from its housing requirements. Even if Yale were a
public institution, the students would face great difficulties in arguing
that the university is placing an impermissible burden on their right to the
free exercise of their religion. The relevant Supreme Court case is *Employment Division of Oregon v. Smith* (1990). In *Smith,* Justice Antonin Scalia
took the legal world by surprise when he persuaded a majority of the
Court to agree that people have no right to exemptions on religious
grounds from "neutral laws of general applicability." In other words, as
long as Yale's rule applies to all freshmen and sophomores and wasn't
cooked up to harass students of particular religious persuasions, Yale is
not obliged to grant the students an exemption.

Smith was a shock because it overturned three decades of Court deci-   4
sions holding that, when a government policy or statute restricts someone's free exercise of religion, the government must show that the policy is
the least burdensome way of fulfilling a compelling state purpose. In 1993,
as a result of public outcry against the *Smith* decision, a diverse coalition
of groups, including the American Civil Liberties Union and the National
Association of Evangelicals, lobbied Congress to pass the Religious Freedom Restoration Act, which basically reversed the effects of *Smith.* But last
spring, in *City of Boerne v. Flores,* the Supreme Court declared the act unconstitutional, on the grounds that Congress has the power only to enforce
and implement constitutional rights, not to determine their scope and substance. Thus, even if Yale were a public university, or even if the students
could successfully argue that Yale's acceptance of public funds requires it
to behave as if it were public, the students don't appear to have a case.

Assuming that the courts rule in Yale's favor, should the university   5
nonetheless voluntarily comply with the students' request to live off campus? With my own experience as a teacher and a student, I think that Yale
has taken the right position.

Arguments do exist in favor of granting the exemption. The strongest   6
argument is that, as one of the most prestigious universities in the country,
Yale has its pick of students; its decision to admit the undergraduates now
suing the university was based on much more than their grades and SAT
scores. Each of these students was chosen because of something unique
that she or he could bring to the Yale student body, and Yale will be
impoverished if they leave. In fact, it is their very obduracy, their radically
pre-modern view of sexual relations, their refusal to laugh at the jokes and
to appear to go along with the prevailing sexual mores, that make them
such a valuable (if annoying) piece of the Yale mosaic. My son has just
begun his freshman year (not at Yale), and I hope that he gets to know
some students like these, that he learns to respect their adherence to an
unpopular set of beliefs, that he has the benefit of their different views.

But I believe that the arguments in favor of Yale's position are   7
stronger. First, Yale has decided that living on the campus is an important
component of what it deems to be a Yale education. Although one can certainly get a great education at a non-residential college, that is a different
sort of experience, and not the one Yale offers. Yale has declined to allow
students to deconstruct the Yale experience by choosing to participate in
only one facet of it, just as it declines to allow undergraduates to enroll as
part-time students.

Second, Yale has good reason to resist the ethnic and religious balka-   8
nization of its student body, possibly learning from what has happened at
Cornell* and elsewhere, where students segregate themselves in racial
and ethnic "affinity housing" beginning in their freshman year. If these
Orthodox Jewish students are granted an exemption, it is likely that some
other Orthodox Jewish students, who have made their peace with the Yale
dormitory experience, will be tempted (or pressured) to follow suit. Evangelical Protestants and Mormons might then argue, successfully, for their
own exemptions. Dormitories based on race or sexual preference will not
be far behind. It makes good sense for Yale to hold its ground now.

Each of the hundreds of colleges and universities in the United States   9
presents a unique package of academic, residential, social, and extracurricular elements. At some colleges, the package includes fraternities and
sororities; at others, an emphasis on athletics. Some institutions require
everyone to take a foreign language; at others, one has to pass a swimming
test to graduate. Some colleges are known for a permissive sexual atmosphere, while others have strict parietal hours and single-sex dorms. Every
college that I am familiar with encourages prospective students to visit the
campus and to spend a night in the dorms, so that students have a chance
to see how comfortable they would feel there before they enroll.

Yale attempts to make Orthodox Jewish students comfortable on its   10
campus by, for example, making kosher food available and giving these
students metal, rather than electronic, room keys (so that they don't generate electricity on the Sabbath). But Yale does not wish to — nor should it
have to — change the package it offers in more-significant ways.

The four students who are suing the university want the cachet of a   11
Yale diploma without the complete experience that Yale has decided is a
necessary part of what that diploma represents. One of the four, Jeremy
Hershman, has even said that what he wants is to flee the "entire atmosphere" at Yale. If Yale were the only possible institution in which the students could get an education — if it were, for example, a public university
offering a unique opportunity for local students to receive a low-cost
degree — these students would have a stronger case. However, other fine

---

*Eds. note — Cornell University, which provides a variety of ethnic theme hous-
ing, attempted to require all freshmen to live in regular dormitories, sparking considerable protest.

institutions exist whose dormitories are less permissive. I hope these students decide to stay at Yale, but if they do not, they have many other options. Yale should stand its ground.

• • •

COMPREHENSION

1. What objections did the four Orthodox Jewish students have to living in Yale's dormitories?

2. According to Davis, why does Yale have no legal obligation to the four students? What Supreme Court cases support Davis's assertion?

3. What arguments support granting the students' request to live off campus?

4. What arguments support Yale's position? Why does Davis think these arguments are stronger?

5. What does Davis mean when she says, "Yale has good reason to resist the ethnic and religious balkanization of its student body . . ." (8)?

6. According to Davis, in what ways does Yale attempt to make Orthodox Jewish students more comfortable at Yale? Do you think these efforts are sufficient?

PURPOSE AND AUDIENCE

1. Does Davis assume her readers are familiar with the case she is discussing? How can you tell?

2. What efforts does Davis make to convince readers that she is being fair? Is she successful?

3. What is Davis's attitude toward the four students that she is discussing? Distant? Understanding? Condescending? Something else? Do you believe her when she says that she hopes her son will get to know students like these? Explain.

STYLE AND STRUCTURE

1. Davis devotes most of her argument to answering the questions that she asks in paragraph 2. What issues do these questions raise? Are there any other issues that Davis should have addressed but didn't?

2. In paragraphs 3 and 4, Davis makes the argument that Yale does not have a legal obligation to accommodate the four students. What type of evidence does she offer to support her points? Should she have offered a different type of evidence?

3. In paragraph 6, Davis presents the arguments against her position. Are these arguments strong, or is she setting up a *straw man* — introducing weak arguments that she can easily refute?

4. In paragraphs 7 and 8, Davis argues that no compelling pedagogical reason exists for granting the students' request. Is this argument primarily inductive or deductive? How convincing is it?

5. In paragraph 8, Davis says that if Yale grants Orthodox Jewish students an exemption, other students will probably request similar exemptions. Is this a reasonable assumption, or is Davis overstating her case?

6. Davis ends her essay with the simple statement "Yale should stand its ground" (11). Is this an effective final statement, or is it too abrupt? Can you think of another way to end the essay?

VOCABULARY PROJECTS

1. Define each of the following words as it is used in this selection.

Orthodox (1)   component (7)   evangelical (8)
parietal (1)   deconstruct (7)   kosher (10)
coalition (4)   facet (7)   cachet (11)
impoverished (6)   balkanization (8)
obduracy (6)   affinity (8)

2. What transitions does Davis use to move her argument from one point to another? How successfully do these transitions guide readers through the essay?

JOURNAL ENTRY

At the end of her essay, Davis says that if students don't like what Yale has to offer, they can go elsewhere. Do you think this response is fair? Do you think Davis is letting Yale off too easily?

WRITING WORKSHOP

1. Assume that you are the dean of students at Yale University. Write a letter to Elisha Dov Hack, one of the four students who does not want to live in student housing, telling him that you cannot grant his request. Assure him that despite your decision, you believe he is a valued member of the Yale community.

2. Write an essay in which you lay out a middle ground that might satisfy both Yale and the students who don't want to live in the dorm. Address the specific objections that Davis mentions in paragraphs 6 and 8 of her essay.

3. How would Rebecca Lee Parker respond to Davis's essay? Using Parker's essay as a resource, write a response to Davis.

COMBINING THE PATTERNS

Paragraph 6 is developed by **exemplification.** Does Davis provide enough examples? In what way do these examples help Davis set up her argument in paragraphs 7 and 8?

THEMATIC CONNECTIONS

🐦🐦🐦🐦🐦🐦🐦🐦

DEBATE CASEBOOK:
Does Media Violence Cause Societal Violence?

Violence is a disturbing and sometimes frightening undercurrent of life in the United States. In any given year, more murders occur in any one of our major cities than in all of the British Isles combined. This fact has not been lost on lawmakers, especially those running for reelection. Violent behavior (and how to curb it) has been a frequent issue in elections. Although the causes of violent crime are complex, some people look for a single cause that will point to a quick fix for the problem. In the 1950s, for example, parents and educators blamed graphically violent comic books for an increase in juvenile crime. In the 1970s, pressure from Congress caused Hollywood to institute a rating system so that parents could judge the suitability of movies. More recently, lawmakers mandated that a V-chip, enabling parents to block violent or sexually explicit programs, be built into all new television sets.

The debate about the connection between media violence and violent behavior heats up whenever a particularly horrible crime is linked to a movie. In one case, for example, two teenagers went on a murder spree and blamed their actions on Oliver Stone's movie *Natural Born Killers*. In another case, five young men seemingly imitated a scene from the movie *The Money Train* and killed a New York City subway toll clerk by setting him on fire. Movies, however, are not the only culprits. In 1996, Paladin Press, publisher of the how-to manual *Hit Man: A Technical Manual for Independent Contractors*, was sued by the family of a woman whose killer apparently followed a set of detailed instructions outlined in the book. The case was settled out of court, with Paladin agreeing to stop selling the book and to pay a multi-million dollar settlement to the family. In another case, two students who went on a shooting rampage that resulted in the deaths of twelve students and a teacher at Columbine High School in Littleton, Colorado, in 1997 were avid players of *DOOM*, a violent video game. The press was quick to establish a causal link between the excessive playing of *DOOM* (as well as the music of Marilyn Manson) and the mass murder.

The four essays in this casebook examine the issue of media violence. In "Unnatural Killers," lawyer and best-selling author John Grisham argues that filmmaker Oliver Stone should be held legally accountable for the aftereffects of his movie *Natural Born Killers*. A guilty verdict against Stone, says Grisham, will show Hollywood that it will have to rein itself in and take responsibility for its own actions. In "Memo to John Grisham" Stone replies, accusing Grisham of leading a witch hunt. According to Stone, Grisham has singled out his film for blame, ignoring the more direct causes of the crimes committed by those who saw his movie. In "Violent Films Cry 'Fire' in Crowded Theaters," attorney Michael Zimecki argues that legal precedents exist for finding filmmakers negligent when they make movies that glorify violence. Finally, in "Games as a Scapegoat," Steve Bauman argues that the link between violent video games and violent behavior has never been conclusively established. It is, he says, the media's need for a scapegoat and for easy answers that makes video games, movies, and music easy targets.

JOHN GRISHAM

One of the country's best-selling writers, John Grisham (1955–) almost failed English composition in high school. Born in Jonesboro, Arkansas, he graduated from Mississippi State University and received his law degree from the University of Mississippi. He practiced law for nine years until the publication of his first suspense novel, *A Time to Kill* (1989). His second book, *The Firm* (1991), remained on the *New York Times* best-seller list for almost a year. Other blockbusters followed in quick succession, most recently *The Brethren* (2000). Most of his books have also been made into successful films.

In 1995 (as Grisham relates in the following essay, which originally appeared in the *Oxford American*), a friend of his was killed by a pair of runaway teenagers on a crime spree, allegedly influenced by Oliver Stone's film *Natural Born Killers.* Grisham argues here that Hollywood has a responsibility to stop glamorizing and glorifying murder and mayhem, and he also urges that a wrongful-death lawsuit be brought against Stone and others involved in the making of the film. In 1996, a lawsuit was filed by Patsy Byers, another victim of the spree who survived though paralyzed, against Oliver Stone and Warner Brothers, who produced the film, as well as the two assailants and their families' insurance companies. A district court judge in Louisiana ruled that the movie-makers were protected by constitutional freedom of speech guarantees, but in 1998 a Louisiana appeals court overturned that ruling and sent the case back to trial.

Unnatural Killers

The town of Hernando, Mississippi has five thousand people, more or less, and is the seat of government for DeSoto County. It is peaceful and quiet, with an old courthouse in the center of the square. Memphis is only fifteen minutes away, to the north, straight up Interstate 55. To the west is Tunica County, now booming with casino fever and drawing thousands of tourists.

For ten years I was a lawyer in Southaven, a suburb to the north, and the Hernando courthouse was my hangout. I tried many cases in the main courtroom. I drank coffee with the courthouse regulars, ate in the small cafes around the square, visited my clients in the nearby jail.

It was in the courthouse that I first met Mr. Bill Savage. I didn't know much about him back then, just that he was soft-spoken, exceedingly polite, always ready with a smile and a warm greeting. In 1983, when I first announced my intentions to seek an office in the state legislature, Mr. Savage stopped me in the second-floor rotunda of the courthouse and offered me his encouragement and good wishes.

A few months later, on election night as the votes were tallied and the results announced to a rowdy throng camped on the courthouse lawn, it became apparent that *I* would win my race. Mr. Savage found me and expressed his congratulations. "The people have trusted you," he said. "Don't let them down."

He was active in local affairs, a devout Christian, and solid citizen   5
who believed in public service and was always ready to volunteer. For thirty years, he worked as the manager of a cotton gin two miles outside Hernando on a highway that is heavily used by gamblers anxious to get to the casinos in Tunica.

Around five P.M., on March 7, 1995, someone entered Bill Savage's   6
office next to the gin, shot him twice in the head at point-blank range, and took his wallet, which contained a few credit cards and two hundred dollars.

There were no witnesses. No one heard gunshots. His body was dis-   7
covered later by an insurance salesman making a routine call.

The crime scene yielded few clues. There were no signs of a struggle.   8
Other than the bullets found in the body, there was little physical evidence. And since Bill Savage was not the kind of person to create ill will or maintain enemies, investigators had nowhere to start. They formed the opinion that he was murdered by outsiders who'd stopped by for a fast score, then hit the road again, probably toward the casinos.

It had to be a simple robbery. Why else would anybody want to mur-   9
der Bill Savage?

The townspeople of Hernando were stunned. Life in the shadows of   10
Memphis had numbed many of them to the idea of random violence, but here was one of their own, a man known to all, a man who, as he went about his daily affairs, minding his own business, was killed in his office just two miles from the courthouse.

The next day, in Poncharoula, Louisiana, three hundred miles south,   11
and again just off Interstate 55, Patsy Byers was working the late shift at a convenience store. She was thirty-five years old, a happily married mother of three, including an eighteen-year-old who was about to graduate from high school. Patsy had never worked outside the home, but had taken the job to earn a few extra dollars to help with the bills.

Around midnight, a young woman entered the convenience store and   12
walked to a rack where she grabbed three chocolate bars. As she approached the checkout counter, Patsy Byers noticed the candy, but she didn't notice the .38. The young woman thrust it forward, pulled the trigger, and shot Patsy in the throat.

The bullet instantly severed Patsy's spinal cord, and she fell to the   13
floor bleeding. The young woman screamed and fled the store, leaving Patsy paralyzed under the cash register.

The girl returned. She'd forgotten the part about the robbery. When   14
she saw Patsy she said, "Oh, you're not dead yet."

Patsy began to plead. "Don't kill me," she kept saying to the girl who   15
stepped over her and tried in vain to open the cash register. She asked

Patsy how to open it. Patsy explained it as best she could. The girl fled with $105 in cash, leaving Patsy, once again, to die.

But Patsy did not die, though she will be a quadriplegic for the rest of   16
her life.

The shooting and robbery was captured on the store's surveillance   17
camera, and the video was soon broadcast on the local news. Several full facial shots of the girl were shown.

The girl, however, vanished. Weeks, and then months, passed without   18
the slightest hint to her identity making itself known.

Authorities in Louisiana had no knowledge of the murder of Bill Sav-   19
age, and authorities in Mississippi had no knowledge of the shooting of Patsy Byers, and neither state had reason to suspect the two shootings were committed by the same people.

The crimes, it was clear, were not committed by sophisticated crimi-   20
nals. Soon two youths began bragging about their exploits. And then an anonymous informant whispered to officials in Louisiana that a certain young woman in Oklahoma was involved in the shooting of Patsy Byers.

The young woman was Sarah Edmondson, age nineteen, the daughter   21
of a state court judge in Muskogee, Oklahoma. Her uncle is the Attorney General of Oklahoma. Her grandfather once served as Congressman, and her great uncle was Governor and then later a U.S. Senator. Sarah Edmond-son was arrested on June 2, 1995, at her parents' home, and suddenly the pieces fell into place.

Sarah and her boyfriend, Benjamin Darras, age eighteen, had drifted   22
south in early March. The reason for the journey has not been made clear. One version has them headed for Florida so that Ben could finally see the ocean. Another has them aiming at New Orleans and Mardi Gras. And a third is that they wanted to see the Grateful Dead concert in Memphis, but, not surprisingly, got the dates mixed-up.

At any rate, they stumbled through Hernando on March 7, and stayed   23
just long enough, Sarah says, to kill and rob Bill Savage. Then they raced deeper south until they ran out of money. They decided to pull another heist. This is when Patsy Byers met them.

Though Sarah and Ben have different socioeconomic backgrounds,   24
they made a suitable match. Sarah, a member of one of Oklahoma's most prominent political families, began using drugs and alcohol at the age of thirteen. At fourteen she was locked up for psychiatric treatment. She has admitted to a history of serious drug abuse. She managed to finish high school, with honors, but then dropped out of college.

Ben's family is far less prominent. His father was an alcoholic who   25
divorced Ben's mother twice, then later committed suicide. Ben too has a history of drug abuse and psychiatric treatment. He dropped out of high school. Somewhere along the way he met Sarah, and for awhile they lived that great American romance — the young, troubled, mindless drifters sur-viving on love.

Once they were arrested, lawyers got involved, and the love affair   26
came to a rapid end. Sarah blames Ben for the killing of Bill Savage. Ben
blames Sarah for the shooting of Patsy Byers, Sarah has better lawyers, and
it appears she will also attempt to blame Ben for somehow controlling her
in such a manner that she had no choice but to rob the store and shoot Patsy
Byers. Ben, evidently, will have none of this. It looks as if he will claim his
beloved Sarah went into the store only to rob it, that he had no idea whatsoever that she planned to shoot anyone, that, as he waited outside in the
getaway car, he was horrified when he heard a gunshot. And so on.

It should be noted here that neither Ben nor Sarah have yet been tried   27
for any of these crimes. They have not been found guilty of anything, yet.
But as the judicial wheels begin to turn, deals are being negotiated and
cut. Pacts are being made.

Sarah's lawyers managed to reach an immunity agreement with the   28
State of Mississippi in the Savage case. Evidently, she will testify against
Ben, and in return will not be prosecuted. Her troubles will be confined to
Louisiana, and if convicted for the attempted murder of Patsy Byers and
the robbing of the store, Sarah could face life in prison. If Ben is found
guilty of murdering and robbing Bill Savage, he will most likely face death
by lethal injection at the state penitentiary in Parchman, Mississippi.
Juries in Hernando are notorious for quick death verdicts.

On January 24, 1996, during a preliminary hearing in Louisiana, Sarah   29
testified, under oath, about the events leading up to both crimes. It is from
this reported testimony that the public first heard the appalling details of
both crimes.

According to Sarah, she and Ben decided to travel to Memphis to see   30
the Grateful Dead. They packed canned food and blankets, and left the
morning of March 6. Sarah also packed her father's .38, just in case Ben
happened to attack her for some reason. Shortly before leaving Oklahoma,
they watched the Oliver Stone movie *Natural Born Killers.*

For those fortunate enough to have missed *Natural Born Killers,* it is   31
the repulsive story of two mindless young lovers, Mickey (Woody Harrel-
son) and Mallory (Juliette Lewis), who blaze their way across the Southwest, killing everything in their path while becoming famous. According
to the script, they indiscriminately kill fifty-two people before they are
caught. It seems like many more. Then they manage to kill at least fifty
more as they escape from prison. They free themselves, have children, and
are last seen happily rambling down the highway in a Winnebego.

Ben loved *Natural Born Killers,* and as they drove to Memphis he spoke   32
openly of killing people, randomly, just like Mickey spoke to Mallory. He
mentioned the idea of seizing upon a remote farmhouse, murdering all its
occupants, then moving on to the next slaughter. Just like Mickey and
Mallory.

We do not know, as of yet, what role Sarah played in these discus-   33
sions. It is, of course, her testimony we're forced to rely upon, and she
claims to have been opposed to Ben's hallucinations.

They left Memphis after learning the concert was still a few days   34
away, and headed south. Between Memphis and Hernando, Ben again
talked of finding an isolated farmhouse and killing a bunch of people.
Sarah said it sounded like he was fantasizing from the movie. They left
Interstate 55, drove through Hernando and onto the highway leading to
the cotton gin where Bill Savage was working in his office.

Ben was quite anxious to kill someone, she says.   35

He professed a sudden hatred for farmers. This was the place where   36
they would kill, he said, and told Sarah to stop the car a short distance
away so he could test-fire the gun. It worked. They then drove to the gin,
parked next to Bill Savage's small office. Ben told her to act "angelic," and
then they went inside.

Ben asked Bill Savage for directions to Interstate 55. Sarah says that   37
Mr. Savage knew they were up to something. As he gave directions, he
walked around the desk toward Ben, at which point Ben removed the
.38 and shot Mr. Savage in the head. "He threw up his hands and made
a horrible sound," she testified. There was a brief struggle between the
two men, a struggle that ended when Ben shot Mr. Savage for the second
time.

Sarah claims to have been so shocked by Ben's actions that she started   38
to run outside, then, after a quick second thought, decided to stand by her
man. Together they rummaged through Mr. Savage's pockets and took his
wallet.

Back in the car, Ben removed the credit cards from the wallet, threw   39
the driver's license out the window, and found two one-hundred-dollar
bills. According to Sarah, "Ben mocked the noise the man made when Ben
shot him. Ben was laughing about what happened and said the feeling of
killing was powerful."

You see, the Mickey character in *Natural Born Killers* felt much the   40
same way. He sneered and laughed a lot when he killed people, and then
he sneered and laughed some more after he killed them. He felt powerful.
Murder for Mickey was the ultimate thrill. It was glorious. Murder was a
mystical experience, nothing to be ashamed of and certainly nothing to be
remorseful about. In fact, remorse was a sign of weakness. Mickey was,
after all, a self-described "natural born killer." And Mickey encouraged
Mallory to kill.

Ben encouraged Sarah.   41

After the murder of Mr. Savage, he and Sarah drove to New Orleans,   42
where they roamed the streets of the French Quarter. Ben repeatedly
assured Sarah that he felt no aftershocks from committing the murder. He
felt fine. Just like Mickey. He pressed her repeatedly to kill someone herself. "It's your turn," he kept saying. And, "We're partners."

Sarah, as might be expected, claims she was completely repulsed by   43
Ben's demands that she slay the next person. She claims that she considered killing herself as an alternative to surrendering to Ben's demands
that she shed blood.

But Sarah did not kill herself. Instead, she and Ben drove to Poncha-   44
toula for their ill-fated meeting with Patsy Byers.

According to Sarah, she did not want to rob the store, and she cer-   45
tainly didn't wish to shoot anyone. But they were out of money, and, just
like Mickey and Mallory, robbery was the most convenient way to survive. Ben selected the store, and, through some yet-to-be-determined variety of coercion, forced her out of the car and into the store, with the gun. It
was, after all, her turn to kill.

In *Natural Born Killers,* we are expected to believe that Mickey and   46
Mallory are tormented by demons, and that they are forced to commit
many of their heinous murders, not because they are brainless young
idiots, but because evil forces propel them. They both suffered through
horrible, dysfunctional childhoods, their parents were abusive, etc.
Demons have them in their clutches, and haunt them, and stalk them, and
make them slaughter fifty-two people.

This demonic theme, so as not to be missed by even the simplest   47
viewer, recurs, it seems, every five minutes in the movie.

Guess what Sarah Edmondson saw when she approached the check-   48
out stand and looked at Patsy Byers? She didn't see a thirty-five-year-old
woman next to the cash register. No.

She saw a "demon." And so she shot it.   49

Then she ran from the store. Ben, waiting in the car, asked where the   50
money was. Sarah said she forgot to take the money. Ben insisted she
return to the store and rob the cash register.

We can trust the judicial systems of both Mississippi and Louisiana to   51
effectively deal with the aftermath of the Sarah and Ben romance. Absent a
fluke, Sarah will spend the rest of her life behind bars in a miserable prison
and Ben will be sent to death row at Parchman, where he'll endure an
indescribable hell before facing execution. Their families will never be the
same. And their families deserve compassion.*

The wife and children and countless friends of Bill Savage have   52
already begun the healing process, though the loss is beyond measure.

Patsy Byers is a quadriplegic for life, confined to a wheelchair, faced   53
with enormous medical bills, unable to hug her children or do any one of a
million things she did before she met Sarah Edmondson. She's already
filed a civil suit against the Edmondson family, but her prospects of a
meaningful physical recovery are dim.

A question remains: Are there other players in this tragic episode?   54
Can fault be shared?

I think so.   55

Troubled as they were, Ben and Sarah had no history of violence. Their   56
crime spree was totally out of character. They were confused, disturbed,

---

*EDS. NOTE — Darras received a life sentence for the murder of Bill Savage;
Edmondson is serving a thirty-five-year sentence for the attempted murder of Patsy
Byers.

shiftless, mindless — the adjectives can be heaped on with shovels — but they had never hurt anyone before.

Before, that is, they saw a movie. A horrific movie that glamorized   57
casual mayhem and bloodlust. A movie made with the intent of glorifying random murder.

Oliver Stone has said that *Natural Born Killers* was meant to be a satire   58
on our culture's appetite for violence and the media's craving for it. But Oliver Stone always takes the high ground in defending his dreadful movies. A satire is supposed to make fun of whatever it is attacking. But there is no humor in *Natural Born Killers.* It is a relentlessly bloody story designed to shock us and to further numb us to the senselessness of reckless murder. The film wasn't made with the intent of stimulating morally depraved young people to commit similar crimes, but such a result can hardly be a surprise.

Oliver Stone is saying that murder is cool and fun, murder is a high, a   59
rush, murder is a drug to be used at will. The more you kill, the cooler you are. You can be famous and become a media darling with your face on magazine covers. You can get by with it. You will not be punished.

It is inconceivable to expect either Stone or the studio executives to   60
take responsibility for the aftereffects of their movie. Hollywood has never done so; instead, it hides behind its standard pious First Amendment arguments, and it pontificates about the necessities of artistic freedom of expression. Its apologists can go on, ad nauseam, about how meaningful even the most pathetic film is to social reform.

It's no surprise that *Natural Born Killers* has inspired several young   61
people to commit murder. Sadly, Ben and Sarah aren't the only kids now locked away and charged with murder in copycat crimes. Since the release of the movie, at least several cases have been reported in which random killings were executed by troubled young people who claim they were all under the influence, to some degree, of Mickey and Mallory.

Any word from Oliver Stone?   62

Of course not.   63

I'm sure he would disclaim all responsibility. And he'd preach a bit   64
about how important the film is as a commentary on the media's insatiable appetite for violence. If pressed, he'd probably say that there are a lot of crazies out there, and he can't be held responsible for what they might do. He's an *artist* and he can't be bothered with the effects of what he produces.

I can think of only two ways to curb the excessive violence of a film   65
like *Natural Born Killers.* Both involve large sums of money — the only medium understood by Hollywood.

The first way would be a general boycott of similar films. If people   66
refused to purchase tickets to watch such an orgy of violence as *Natural Born Killers,* then similar movies wouldn't be made. Hollywood is pious,

but only to a point. It will defend its crassest movies on the grounds that they are necessary for social introspection, or that they need to test the limits of artistic expression, or that they can ignore the bounds of decency as long as these movies label themselves as satire. This all works fine if the box office is busy. But let the red ink flow and Hollywood suddenly has a keen interest in rediscovering what's mainstream.

Unfortunately, boycotts don't seem to work. The viewing public is a large, eclectic body, and there are usually enough curious filmgoers to sustain a controversial work.   67

So, forget boycotts.   68

The second and last hope of imposing some sense of responsibility on Hollywood, will come through another great American tradition, the lawsuit. Think of a movie as a product, something created and brought to market, not too dissimilar from breast implants, Honda three-wheelers, and Ford Pintos. Though the law has yet to declare movies to be products, it is only one small step away. If something goes wrong with the product, whether by design or defect, and injury ensues, then its makers are held responsible.   69

A case can be made that there exists a direct causal link between the movie *Natural Born Killers* and the death of Bill Savage. Viewed another way, the question should be: Would Ben have shot innocent people *but for* the movie? Nothing in his troubled past indicates violent propensities. But once he saw the movie, he fantasized about killing, and his fantasies finally drove them to their crimes.   70

The notion of holding filmmakers and studios legally responsible for their products has always been met with guffaws from the industry.   71

But the laughing will soon stop. It will take only one large verdict against the likes of Oliver Stone, and his production company, and perhaps the screenwriter, and the studio itself, and then the party will be over. The verdict will come from the heartland, far away from Southern California, in some small courtroom with no cameras. A jury will finally say enough is enough; that the demons placed in Sarah Edmondson's mind were not solely of her making.   72

Once a precedent is set, the litigation will become contagious, and the money will become enormous. Hollywood will suddenly discover a desire to rein itself in.   73

The landscape of American jurisprudence is littered with the remains of large, powerful corporations which once thought themselves bulletproof and immune from responsibility for their actions. Sadly, Hollywood will have to be forced to shed some of its own blood before it learns to police itself.   74

Even sadder, the families of Bill Savage and Patsy Byers can only mourn and try to pick up the pieces, and wonder why such a wretched film was allowed to be made.   75

• • •

COMPREHENSION

1. What do Sarah Edmondson and Benjamin Darras have in common? How do they claim the movie *Natural Born Killers* influenced them?

2. Who does Grisham believe should share the responsibility for the two shootings Ben and Sarah committed?

3. According to Grisham, how does Oliver Stone defend the violent content of *Natural Born Killers*? How does Grisham respond to Stone's arguments?

4. In paragraph 60, Grisham says, "It is inconceivable to expect either Stone or the studio executives to take responsibility for the aftereffects of their movie." Why is it inconceivable?

5. What does Grisham think should be done to eliminate excessive violence from movies like *Natural Born Killers*?

PURPOSE AND AUDIENCE

1. What is the thesis of this essay? At what point does Grisham state it? Why does he wait as long as he does?

2. What do you think Grisham hopes to accomplish with his essay? Does he want to change attitudes? Call people to action? Accomplish something else? Explain.

3. This essay appeared in a magazine that Grisham publishes, the *Oxford American: A Magazine of the South.* Does Grisham seem to assume that his readers share his ideas about movie violence? Do you think he considers his readers hostile, friendly, or neutral? What makes you think so?

STYLE AND STRUCTURE

1. Is Grisham appealing mainly to logic or to his readers' emotions? On what do you base your conclusions?

2. What specific arguments does Grisham put forward to support his thesis? How effective do you think these arguments are?

3. At what point does Grisham refute the arguments against his thesis? Are there other arguments he should have addressed? If so, what are they?

4. What is Grisham's attitude toward Stone? Do Grisham's criticisms ever take the form of an *ad hominem* attack? Explain.

5. Grisham ends his essay with a one-sentence conclusion. How effective is this conclusion? Does it reinforce the main point of the essay? What other strategy could Grisham have used to conclude his essay?

VOCABULARY PROJECTS

1. Define each of the following words as it is used in this selection.

tallied (4)	depraved (58)
quadriplegic (16)	apologists (60)
socioeconomic (24)	guffaws (71)
heinous (46)	

2. Throughout this essay, Grisham uses words that contain built-in judgments. For example, in paragraph 23 Grisham says Sarah and Ben "*stumbled* through Hernando." Underline as many of these words as you can. How do they affect your response to this essay? Should Grisham have avoided using such words? Why or why not?

JOURNAL ENTRY

Does Grisham ever establish a strong link between *Natural Born Killers* and the crimes committed by Sarah Edmondson and Benjamin Darras? What other factors could have influenced their actions?

WRITING WORKSHOP

1. Write a letter from Grisham to Stone in which you argue why he shouldn't make films that glorify violence. Use material from Grisham's essay as well as from the next selection, Stone's "Memo to John Grisham: What's Next — 'A Movie Made Me Do It'?" to support your argument.

2. Assume you are a member of the jury in Benjamin Darras's trial. Would you accept or reject the defense's contention that *Natural Born Killers* compelled Darras to commit murder? Write an essay in which you explain your decision. Use facts from Grisham's essay to support your verdict.

3. Rent a copy of *Natural Born Killers* from a video store and view it. Then, write an editorial for your local paper in which you discuss the movie's violent content. Do you think the movie is, as Stone says, a satire of today's violent society? Or do you think, as Grisham says, that the movie glorifies senseless violence? Make sure your thesis statement clearly presents your assessment of the film.

COMBINING THE PATTERNS

This essay begins with a long **narrative** account of the crimes committed by Sarah Edmondson and Benjamin Darras. Why do you think Grisham begins his essay this way? Could he have made his point as effectively with **description?** Why or why not?

THEMATIC CONNECTIONS

- "Just Walk On By" (page 197)
- "Samuel" (page 212)
- "It's Just Too Late" (page 304)
- "It's a Jungle Out There" (page 438)

OLIVER STONE

Controversial filmmaker Oliver Stone (1946–) was born in New York City and educated at Yale. After serving in the Vietnam War, he studied film at New York University and in the following years wrote screenplays for violent but well-received films like *Midnight Express* (1978) and *Scarface* (1983). His directorial debut came with *Salvador* (1986), about the revolution then taking place in El Salvador; it was followed that same year by *Platoon,* a drama set during the Vietnam War, which won the Academy Award for best picture and earned Stone the award for best director. His films *JFK* (1991) and *Nixon* (1995) sparked considerable debate about the fictionalization of film biography.

Stone's most controversial film, however, is *Natural Born Killers* (1994), about a young couple who go on a crime spree, killing fifty-two people and becoming media stars in the process. Condemned for its apparent glorification of casual murder, the movie, according to Stone, is intended as a satire of the media's obsession with violence. While not a box-office hit, the film found a cult audience after it was released on videotape. In the following essay, commissioned by *LA Weekly* as a response to John Grisham's "Unnatural Killers" (page 566), Stone argues that his film had no influence on the couple who killed Grisham's friend and that Grisham's advocacy of "silencing artists" is only a small step from taking away freedom of speech altogether. A 1996 lawsuit brought against Stone and the film's producer by one of the victims, however, argues that because the moviemakers intended for *Natural Born Killers* to glorify violence, they should be held responsible for copycat crimes.

Memo to John Grisham: What's Next — "A Movie Made Me Do It"?

The hunt for witches to explain society's ills is ancient in our blood, but unholy for that nonetheless. The difference is that now we do not blame the village hag and her black cat, but the writer and the photographer and the filmmaker. Increasingly indicted by art and fearful of technology, our society scours them for scapegoats, in the process ignoring Shakespeare, who reminds us that artists do not invent nature but merely hold up to it a mirror. That the mirror now is electronic or widescreen or cyberspace is all the more intimidating to the unschooled, and the more tempting to the lawyers.

John Grisham predictably draws upon the superstition about the magical power of pictures to conjure up the undead specter of censorship. Too sophisticated to clamor for government intervention, he calls instead for civil action. Victims of crimes should, he declares, rise up against the purveyors of culture high and low and demand retribution, thereby "sending a message" about the mood of the popular mind. And so we arrive at yet another, more modern, more typically American superstition: that the lawsuit is the answer to everything. Fall victim to a crime acted out in the movies and all you have to do is haul the director into court. Has

1

2

your father been brutalized? Sue Oedipus and call Hamlet as a witness. Do you hate your mother? Blame Medea and Joan Crawford.* And has your lawyer-husband been unfaithful? Why, then slap a summons on John Grisham, since, after all, he wrote *The Firm*.

Grisham is at pains to insist that before seeing my film *Natural Born*   3
Killers, accused murderers Ben Darras (18) and Sarah Edmondson (19) had "never hurt anyone." But, even by his own admission, Ben and Sarah are deeply disturbed youths with histories of drug and/or alcohol abuse and psychiatric treatment. Ben's alcoholic father divorced his mother twice, then committed suicide. Grisham mentions as if it is insignificant that Sarah carried a gun because she feared that Ben would attack her. Far from never having hurt anyone, it seems Ben and Sarah had for years been hurting themselves and their families, and it was only a matter of time until they externalized their anger.

It is likely that, whether they had seen *Natural Born Killers* or *The Green*   4
Berets or a *Tom and Jerry* cartoon the night before their first crime, Ben and Sarah would have behaved in exactly the way they did. And it is equally clear that the specific identity of the victim was entirely irrelevant. "Ben was quite anxious to kill someone," Grisham states, and Sarah was ready to help. And at the crucial moment when the carefully twisted springs of their psyches finally uncoiled, as they were bound to do, not I nor Newt Gingrich nor Father Sullivan of Boys Town could or did influence them.**

Did *Natural Born Killers* have an impact on members of its audience?   5
Undoubtedly. Did it move some to a heightened sensitivity toward violence? It did, some. Does it reveal a truth about the media's obsession with the senseless sensational? Ask O.J. Simpson. But did it drive Ben and Sarah to commit two murders? No. If they are guilty, perhaps a negligent or abusive upbringing, combined with defects in their psyches, *did.* Parents, school, and peers shape children from their earliest days, not films. And, once grown and gone horribly wrong, those children must answer for their actions — not Hollywood directors. An elementary principle of our civilization is that people are responsible for their own actions. If Dan White, the killer of San Francisco Supervisor Harvey Milk and Mayor George Moscone, could claim that "Twinkies made me do it," what's next —"A movie made me do it"?

A recent study showed that the average teenager spends 1,500 hours   6
a year watching television, compared with 1,100 hours a year in school. According to the study, most programs contain violence, and fully half of these violent acts do not depict the victim's injuries or pain. Astonishingly,

---

*Eds. note — Oedipus, Hamlet, and Medea are tragic figures of classical drama. Former Hollywood star Joan Crawford was accused of child abuse by her adopted daughter in a best-selling memoir.

**Eds. note — Gingrich, former speaker of the U.S. House of Representatives, recommended homes like Boys Town as refuges for youths from troubled families.

only 16 percent of all programs show the long-term effects of violence, while three-quarters of the time, perpetrators of violence on television go unpunished. Is it just possible that these 15,000 hours of mostly violent TV programming might have had slightly more effect on these two youngsters than two hours of *Natural Born Killers*?

Grisham points to "at least several" anonymous youths who claim to   7
have committed crimes under the influence "to some degree" of my film. Leaving aside the self-serving vagueness of this statement, we might ask: How many thousands of murders have been committed under the influence of alcohol? Yet Grisham does not call for the breweries and distilleries to be shut down by lawsuits. How many homicidal lunatics have purchased guns? Yet he mounts no campaign to close the weapons factories. Even if we admit, for the sake of argument, that Ben and Sarah were influenced by a film, only a lawyer in search of a client could see in this an indictment of the entertainment industry and not of the teenage killers and those who reared them.

Grisham disparages the First Amendment (which also protects the   8
films that have sprung from Grisham's own brainless works of fiction) and those who believe in it. He has nothing to say, however, about the Second Amendment, which permits gun-toting crazies to litter the American landscape with bodies. To my mind, his priorities are severely distorted. But then, the First Amendment protects even the views of those who don't believe in it. In America, we call that freedom of speech.

It gives me a shiver of fear when an influential lawyer and writer   9
argues, as Grisham does, that a particular work of art *should never have been allowed to be made*. Strangle art in its infancy, he suggests, and society will be a better place. One might more persuasively argue that cold-blooded murderers should be strangled in their infancy. Yet as with human infants, we can never know the outcome of nascent art, and so both must be protected and nurtured, precisely for society's sake. For it is only a small step from silencing art to silencing artists, and then to silencing those who support them, and so on, until, while we may one day live in a lawyer's paradise, we will surely find ourselves in a human hell.

• • •

COMPREHENSION

1. In paragraph 1, Stone says that the function of an artist is to hold a mirror up to nature. What does he mean? How does this statement help explain why he made a movie as violent as *Natural Born Killers*?

2. In paragraphs 1 and 2, Stone calls Grisham's attack against *Natural Born Killers* a witch hunt. What does he mean? Do you agree?

3. In criticizing Grisham's article, Stone implies that Grisham is engaging in *post hoc* reasoning. At what point in his essay does Stone suggest this? Do you agree that Grisham's article is flawed by *post hoc* reasoning? Why or why not?

4. According to Stone, what impact does *Natural Born Killers* have on audiences? What impact does he say television has on viewers?

5. In paragraphs 7 and 8, Stone says that Grisham targets his movie while ignoring other possible causes of violence. What other causes can you identify? How persuasive is Stone's line of reasoning?

PURPOSE AND AUDIENCE

1. What preconceptions does Stone have about movie violence? Does he expect his readers to share his ideas? How do you know?

2. Do you think Stone respects his readers' intelligence, or does he talk down to his audience? Explain.

3. Why do you think Stone wrote this essay? What is his purpose?

4. Is Stone's argument likely to appeal to those who already think television and movies are too violent? Does he make any attempt to appeal to readers who are hostile to his position? If so, where?

STYLE AND STRUCTURE

1. Stone begins his essay by comparing Grisham's attack against *Natural Born Killers* to a witch hunt. Is this a good strategy? Is it likely to alienate some of his readers? Why or why not?

2. Where does Stone attempt to refute Grisham's major points? How successful is he in doing so?

3. In paragraph 5, Stone concedes some points to his opposition. Is this a good strategy, or should he have denied any connection between movie violence and societal violence?

4. In paragraph 8, Stone asks why those who want to censor him don't consider the implications of the Second Amendment, "which permits gun-toting crazies to litter the American landscape with bodies." What effect does the phrase *gun-toting crazies* have on you? Does Stone seem to overstate his case? Why or why not?

5. How effective is Stone's conclusion? Does it adequately restate his position? Is his point about lawyers valid or is it an *ad hominem* attack? Explain.

VOCABULARY PROJECTS

1. Define each of the following words as it is used in this selection.

scapegoats (1)	retribution (2)
cyberspace (1)	perpetrators (6)
specter (2)	nascent (9)

2. At times, Stone's feelings come through. Underline words and phrases in the essay that show his attitude toward Grisham. How would you describe his tone?

JOURNAL ENTRY

Do you believe there is a link between movie violence and societal violence? Do you think that seeing a movie such as *Natural Born Killers* can cause someone to do something he or she would not normally do?

WRITING WORKSHOP

1. Do you believe, as Stone does, that filmmakers should not be legally responsible for the consequences of their films? Or do you agree with Grisham when he says that filmmakers, like car manufacturers, are involved in a commercial enterprise and should be liable for damages caused by their products? Write an essay in which you argue for one side or the other.

2. Stone says that people like Grisham are creating a society in which people no longer have to take responsibility for their actions. Do you agree with Stone? Write an essay in which you argue for or against this position. Use your own experiences as well as examples from the news to support your points.

3. Assume you are either Ben Darras or Sarah Edmondson. Write a letter to Stone in which you argue that he is responsible for the crime you committed. Use the facts of the case as presented in Grisham's and Stone's essays to bolster your argument.

COMBINING THE PATTERNS

Stone includes several paragraphs organized according to a **cause-and-effect** pattern. Find two of these paragraphs, and determine how they help Stone support his thesis.

THEMATIC CONNECTIONS

- "Thirty-Eight Who Saw Murder Didn't Call the Police" (page 99)
- "Who Killed Benny Paret?" (page 279)
- "Burdens" (page 466)

MICHAEL ZIMECKI

Michael Zimecki (1950–) was born in Detroit and received degrees from the University of Pittsburgh and Carnegie Mellon. For many years he was a medical writer affiliated with the University of Pittsburgh Medical School. After receiving a law degree from Duquesne University, he established a private practice in Pittsburgh.

Zimecki contributed the following essay to the *National Law Journal* in 1996 in the aftermath of the torching of a New York City subway token booth attendant, a crime that was similar to a scene depicted in the movie *The Money Train*. (The following year, a Kentucky teenager killed three girls after firing on a prayer group; this crime was allegedly influenced by a dream sequence in *The Basketball Diaries* in which Leonardo DiCaprio played a student who gunned down his classmates.) Up through the 1960s, Hollywood adhered to a fairly strict production code that strictly limited onscreen violence. This code included the provision that "methods of crime shall not be explicitly presented." Its purpose was, in part, to ensure that movie violence would not lead viewers to copycat crimes. That code was extensively revised in 1966, however, opening the door to the graphic depictions of violence that prevail today. In this essay, Zimecki uses examples to argue that such violent images in the media undoubtedly contribute to real-life violence.

Violent Films Cry "Fire" in Crowded Theaters

The late Richard Weaver, professor of rhetoric at the University of Chi- 1
cago, was fond of reminding his students that "ideas have consequences."

Bad ideas can have abominable consequences. Nevertheless, U.S. 2
courts have permitted moviemakers, magazine publishers, and other members of the mass media to represent some of the most odious and repulsive scenes imaginable, "on the confidence," as Circuit Judge Alvin B. Run once said, "that the benefits society reaps from the free flow and exchange of ideas outweigh the costs society endures by receiving reprehensible or dangerous ideas." *Herceg v. Hustler Magazine Inc.*, 814 F.2d 1017 (1987).

In 1995, a few days after Thanksgiving, a group of five young men 3
torched a subway token booth in Brooklyn, N.Y., trapping the toll clerk inside. He died of his burns within the week. The act that caused his death bore an eerie resemblance to two scenes from the recently released Columbia Pictures movie *Money Train*. In the movie, a pyromaniac sets token booths on fire by squirting a flammable liquid through the token slots and throwing in a lighted match.

Senate Majority Leader Bob Dole, the *Wall Street Journal*, the head of 4
the New York Transit Authority and New York's police commissioners were quick to blame the movie for sparking a copycat crime. As it turned

out, the movie may not have been responsible. Shortly after his arrest, the youth accused of squirting the flammable liquid denied that the movie had any connection to the incident. In a letter to the *New York Times,* Jack Valenti, President and CEO of the Motion Picture Association of America, could scarcely contain his glee.

For its part, Columbia Pictures steadfastly maintained that it was merely holding a mirror up to life, noting that its film was based on a series of attacks in New York subway stations in 1988.   5

It may be premature to conclude that *Money Train* did or did not play a part in the 1995 Thanksgiving incident: As of this writing, police have declined to say whether any of the men in custody saw the movie. Moreover, two suspects remain at large, and the match-thrower, who could face a capital murder charge, has not been identified.   6

One thing is certain: Life and art exert a strong tug on each other.   7

Money Train was not the only such example. In 1993, a Pennsylvania youth died after he attempted to duplicate a scene from *The Program.* In a peculiar display of male bravado, he lay down on the center line of a highway and was run over by a car.   8

In an earlier era, the perpetrators of the 1974 Hi-Fi Murders in Ogden, Utah, forced their victims to drink liquid Drano after watching a similar scene in the Clint Eastwood picture *Magnum Force.*   9

That same year, a 9-year-old girl was raped with a bottle by a group of juveniles at a San Francisco beach — just days after the nationwide telecast of the film *Born Innocent,* which showed a young girl being sexually assaulted with a plunger. The parents of the San Francisco girl subsequently sued NBC for her physical and emotional injuries, alleging that they were attributable to the broadcaster's negligence and recklessness in airing the film. *Olivia N. v. National Broadcasting Co. Inc.,* 178 Cal. Rptr. 888, 126 Cal. App.3d 488 (1982). Although the suit proved to be unsuccessful, it was nonetheless a signal attempt to expand tort liability for speech outside the area of defamation.   10

COURTS SUPPORT FILMMAKERS

U.S. courts have routinely rejected attempts to hold filmmakers liable in tort for the harm they cause. Plaintiffs' attorneys seeking recovery on a theory of strict products liability have encountered some of the same difficulties that have impeded anti-gun and anti-tobacco litigation: Movies are meant to be seen, just as guns are meant to be fired and cigarettes to be smoked, and there is nothing defective about a product that accomplishes its purpose all too well. In fact, brutally violent films are especially popular box-office fare.   11

The biggest obstacle to plaintiff's attorneys, however, isn't the courts' rejection of claims based on negligence, nuisance or products liability. It's the courts' narrow interpretation of "incitement."   12

Speech that advocates violence but that does not incite imminent   13
harm is protected by the First Amendment under the U.S. Supreme
Court's holding in *Brandenburg v. Ohio,* 396 U.S. 444, 23 L.Ed.2d 430, 89
S.Ct. 1827 (1969).

In *Brandenburg,* the high court overturned the conviction of a Klans-   14
man under Ohio's criminal syndicalism statute for saying that "there
might have to be some revengence [sic] taken", if "our President, our Congress, our Supreme Court continues to suppress the white, Caucasian
race." The finding of the court was that the mere advocacy of violence is
not enough.

As Justice William O. Douglas wrote in his concurring opinion, the   15
line between what is permissible and what is not is "the line between
ideas and overt acts." The Klansman was on the constitutionally protected
side of the line because he was not advocating violent deeds now, in the
temporal present; his message had an abstract, rather than an urgent,
quality. By contrast, someone who falsely shouts "fire" in a crowded theater has impermissibly crossed the line because his speech is "brigaded
with action."

But what about a film that shouts "fire" in that same, proverbially   16
crowded theater? Film industry executives maintain that movies portray
violence but do not advocate it; to the contrary, industry spokespeople
claim, the perpetrators of movie violence typically get their comeuppance
by film's end.

Unfortunately, filmmakers say one thing while showing another. As   17
social psychologist Albert Bandura observed more than 20 years ago, the
message of most violent films is not that "crime does not pay," but rather
that the wages of violent sin are pretty good except for an occasional
mishap.

Indifferent to the anti-social repercussions of their cinematic special   18
effects, violent movies such as *Money Train* advocate violence implicitly, if
not explicitly. Violence is as much a product of external reinforcement as
internal pathology. By modeling, legitimizing, and sanctioning violence,
movies do not just loosen restraints on those who are already predisposed
to violence. Violent movies actively promote aggressive behavior as a
social norm.

LEGALLY FLAWED DEFINITION

By any definition other than the legal one, this would constitute "in-   19
citement." The rub, of course, is that harm delayed is no harm at all under
the *Brandenburg* standard, which distinguishes violence that takes to the
streets from violence that erupts in the theater. While fine in theory, the
Brandenburg concept of "speech brigaded with action" gets reduced in
practice to "Take it outside, boys!"— which is poor advice to a schoolchild
and hardly more sagacious as a constitutional principle.

The difference between a risk of eventual harm and immediate bodily   20
injury has been minimized of late in the toxic torts arena, where medical
monitoring awards embrace the principle that a polluter should not be
allowed to escape responsibility for his actions simply because environmen-
tally induced cancers are late-developing. Violence, too, can fester for years.

Unfortunately, constitutional law has been slow to appreciate the toxic   21
power of words, slow to recognize that exposure to cruel and degrading
images is like exposure to a carcinogen, slower still to understand that
speech and act occupy a continuum of cause and effect.

The premier of *Money Train* may not have been a substantial factor in   22
bringing about the death of subway token clerk Harry Kaufman. But
movies are a significant cause of the violence that has become so prevalent
in our society. Film-inspired violence may not be "imminent" in the constitutional sense, but the constitutional difference between "I will kill you
now" and "I will kill you later" is cold comfort to the victims of movie-
modeled murder.

The problem is that we, as a society, are becoming increasingly dead-   23
ened and desensitized to violence through repeated exposure to its display. Under *Brandenburg*, the onslaught continues. But film industry
executives should take heed: Violence is now so imminent in our society
that a wrong look can get you shot on many street corners. The hour has
come at last, and the rough beast that the poet William Butler Yeats
warned about is already born.* As we continue to split hairs, failing to
address the need for legislation, we can take comfort in the cliché, "Enjoy
yourself. It's later than you think."

• • •

COMPREHENSION

1. According to Zimecki, why have courts in the United States allowed
   moviemakers and magazine publishers "to represent some of the most
   odious and repulsive scenes imaginable" (2)?

2. In paragraph 7 Zimecki says, "Life and art exert a strong tug on each
   other." What does he mean? What examples does he offer to support this
   statement?

3. Why have courts routinely rejected attempts to hold filmmakers liable on
   the theory of product liability? How has the narrow interpretation of
   incitement created an obstacle for plaintiffs?

4. According to Zimecki, in what way do certain types of films shout "fire"
   in a crowded theater?

5. What does Zimecki mean when he says, "Unfortunately, constitutional
   law has been slow to appreciate the toxic power of words" (21)?

---

*EDS. NOTE — "And what rough beast, its hour come round at last, / Slouches
toward Bethlehem to be born?" (from "The Second Coming" by William Butler Yeats)

PURPOSE AND AUDIENCE

1. At what point does Zimecki state his thesis? Why does he wait as long as he does?

2. Is this essay aimed at an audience of lawyers or at a more general audience? How do you know?

3. What is Zimecki's purpose in writing this essay? Is it to change attitudes? To bring about legislation? To change policy? Explain.

STYLE AND STRUCTURE

1. Zimecki begins his essay with a quotation by Richard Weaver. Why do you think he chose this quotation? What other strategies could he have used to introduce his essay?

2. This essay appeared in the *National Law Journal.* If Zimecki were to rewrite the essay for *People* magazine, what kinds of changes would he need to make? What additional support would he need? Explain.

3. Do you think Zimecki undercuts his case by conceding the point that "*Money Train* may not have been a substantial factor in bringing about the death of subway token clerk Harry Kaufman" (22)? Why or why not?

4. What evidence does Zimecki use to support his assertions? Why do you think he chose this type of support?

5. Zimecki concludes his essay with a quotation that he admits is a cliché. How effective is this strategy? Would another quotation be more effective? Explain your reasoning.

VOCABULARY PROJECTS

1. Define each of the following words as it is used in this selection.

repulsive (2)	negligence (10)	brigaded (15)
reaps (2)	defamation (10)	repercussions (18)
endures (2)	tort (11)	pathology (18)
reprehensible (2)	liability (11)	norm (18)
pyromaniac (3)	incitement (12)	sagacious (19)
capital (6)	advocacy (14)	carcinogen (21)
attributable (10)	impermissibly (15)	

2. What is the dictionary definition of *incitement*? What additional meanings does Zimecki say the word has acquired?

JOURNAL ENTRY

Do you believe the courts should hold filmmakers responsible for the effects of their movies? What would be the possible effects on movies of such a change in policy?

WRITING WORKSHOP

1. Write an essay in which you argue that moviemakers should not be held responsible for the consequences of their films. Consider the effect on free expression of holding moviemakers liable years after their movies are released. Make sure you refute Zimecki's arguments against your position.

2. Using as evidence several violent movies you have seen, write an essay in which you argue that by glorifying violence, certain films encourage violent behavior.

3. How do you think Zimecki would respond to Stone's essay? Choose a section of Stone's essay, and refute it using any of Zimecki's points that are relevant to the issue.

COMBINING THE PATTERNS

In paragraph 15, Zimecki uses **comparison and contrast** to make his point. What point is he making? Would a paragraph of cause and effect be just as effective here? Why or why not?

THEMATIC CONNECTIONS

- "Thirty-Eight Who Saw Murder Didn't Call the Police" (page 99)
- "It's Just Too Late" (page 304)
- "How the Lawyers Stole Winter" (page 362)

STEVE BAUMAN

Steve Bauman was born in 1968 in Los Angeles and received his bachelor's degree from the University of California, Northridge, in 1992. Since 1994 he has been on the staff of *Computer Games* magazine, and he also contributes to *Games Business,* an industry trade publication. He is currently working on a collection of short stories.

"Games as a Scapegoat" appeared as an editorial in the July 1999 issue of *Computer Games* a few months after the widely reported shooting spree at Columbine High School in Littleton, Colorado. As Bauman notes, the two teenaged killers — who finally turned their guns on themselves — were avid players of the violent video game *DOOM.* (*DOOM* is one of the most popular interactive games of all time. It is estimated that some 15 million copies have been downloaded around the world since its appearance in 1993; *DOOM II,* which appeared in 1994, has sold more than 2 million copies.) Many commentators at the time speculated that the rampage at Columbine was directly influenced by the teenagers' immersion in the game. Despite the fact that he is writing to an audience of computer game players and developers, Bauman suggests that this possibility should not simply be dismissed.

Games as a Scapegoat

In our society of 24-hour news, soundbites that substitute for depth, and the eternal quest for bigger ratings, the pursuit of truth can be trampled by the pursuit of an easy scapegoat. In the case of the April 20 slaying of 12 students and a teacher in the Denver suburb of Littleton, Colorado, the media again exhibited its tendency to fall all over itself trying to place blame for the two killers' abhorrent behavior on various elements of our culture. In this case, the damning influence ranged from musicians Marilyn Manson and KMFDM to bi-sexuality and a predilection for Goth clothing. 1

But also receiving the lion's share of blame were the violent videogames suspects Eric Harris and Dylan Klebold enjoyed playing. id Software's *DOOM* was the game that was singled out by the media — the killers were allegedly avid players. The now five-year-old game was described (along with *Quake*) by the *New York Times* as "games in which players stalk their opponents through dungeonlike environments and try to kill them with high-powered weapons." The game even drew the attention of President Bill Clinton, who said "video games like *Mortal Kombat, Killer Instinct,* and *DOOM* — the very game played obsessively by the two young men who ended so many lives in Littleton — make our children more active participants in simulated violence." 2

On *20/20,* reporter Tom Jarriel called *DOOM* "one of the most violent computer games you can buy." He went on to say "the player gets to annihilate a nonstop stream of enemies" without placing the premise in any context. A reporter for NBC casually defined the students by two of their 3 activities, saying "they played violent videogames, they listened to the music of Marilyn Manson," as if we were all supposed to nod and somehow understand a causal relationship between those activities and mass murder.

The following Sunday, *60 Minutes* aired a segment where former Lieutenant Colonel and psychologist David Grossman called violent videogames "murder simulators." While *Quake* played on a monitor in the background, he went on to say that games teach young people to kill with all the precision of a military training program but with none of the character training that goes along with it.

While his choice of terminology can be dismissed as hyperbole, watching videotape of glassy-eyed teenagers playing Sega's *House of the Dead* in the arcade was a chilling experience. Seeing them hold a plastic toy gun in their hands, carefully aiming for the heads of rendered zombies, makes you wonder if a game like that is teaching children to be crack shots. If indeed it's true, as Grossman said, that Paducah killer Michael Carneal* had no prior experience with firearms, how do you explain the skill with which he wielded his weapon? (He said the 14-year-old Carneal was successful with 8–10 shots, the majority of which struck the victims in the head.)

Parents of the slain children in Paducah obviously agreed with Grossman. One week earlier, they filed a $130 million lawsuit against various entertainment companies (including id Software and Apogee), alleging that media influence turned Carneal into a murderer. "We intend to hurt Hollywood," said their lawyer. "We intend to hurt the video game industry." It's likely we'll see the same lawsuits brought against the same companies as a result of the Littleton tragedy.

However, as more details emerged about Harris and Klebold, it became clear that there were many things that may have set them off. Based on descriptions from classmates, they sounded a lot like average suburban teenagers, dabbling in subcultures that seemed exotic and forbidden to middle-class (or above) kids. They were trying to find a place where they felt comfortable, whether it was in the plastic cartoon nihilism of Marilyn Manson or the violent fantasy worlds of *DOOM* and *Quake*. The killers were ostracized from their peers, either by acting intentionally anti-social or because they were being singled out for being different.

But all of these issues raise the question that unfortunately has no answer to: why did the Littleton massacre happen? It's considerably easier to blame some nefarious outside influence than to face up to the true answer — there is none. It's unlikely that we'll ever really know what drove two children to brutally murder other children. It's a complex issue, too complex to be reduced to soundbites by newscasters or journalists.

---

*Eds. note — In 1997, Carneal fired on a prayer group in his hometown of Paducah, Kentucky, killing three people and wounding several others.

Looking back on the incident, there are more questions than answers. 9
By placing the blame for horrible acts primarily on cultural influences, are
we removing an individuals' ability to accept personal responsibility for
any act they commit? How does parental responsibility factor in to all of
this? Are we prepared for a society that predetermines what will be presented as entertainment based on what will not trigger abhorrent behavior
in an individual? And most relevant to gamers, are we in deep denial to
continue saying that the violence in videogames is not having a negative
affect on people?

Ultimately, videogames are an easy target, lacking the sort of high- 10
powered backing and artistic credibility movies and music receive from
the media-elite. While it's easy to dismiss attack on the hobby as being ill
informed or absurd, we need to evaluate the influence these games have
on the lives of those that play them. We should not overreact, but the game
industry needs to get its collective head out of the sand and not just say,
"It's not our fault."

• • •

COMPREHENSION

1. Why are the media in search of "an easy scapegoat" (1)? In what ways do
   violent video games satisfy this need?

2. Why did the parents in Paducah file a lawsuit against several entertainment companies?

3. What factors other than violent video games does Bauman suggest could
   have caused Harris and Klebold to murder their classmates?

4. Why does Bauman think that we will never know what caused Harris
   and Klebold to behave the way they did?

5. According to Bauman, what are the drawbacks of trying to blame the Littleton tragedy on violent videogames?

PURPOSE AND AUDIENCE

1. How would you describe Bauman's tone in this essay? Is he friendly? Sarcastic? Distant? Angry? Fed up? Something else?

2. At what point in the essay does Bauman state his thesis? What does he
   gain or lose by stating the thesis where he does?

3. What preconceptions does Bauman think his readers have? How can you
   tell?

4. In what way does the fact that Bauman is the editor of *Computer Games*
   magazine affect your response to his evidence?

STYLE AND STRUCTURE

1. Paragraphs 2 through 5 discuss specific violent video games. In what way
   do these paragraphs help Bauman construct his argument?

2. In paragraph 8, Bauman asks, "Why did the Littleton massacre happen?" Does he answer this question satisfactorily?

3. At what points does Bauman address arguments against his thesis? Does he refute these arguments effectively?

4. Bauman uses his own personal experience to support his argument. Is this type of support sufficient?

5. How convincing is the essay's conclusion? Should Bauman have been more decisive? What other strategy could he have used?

VOCABULARY PROJECTS

1. Define each of the following words as it is used in this selection.

   soundbites (1)   annihilate (3)
   scapegoat (1)   wielded (5)
   avid (2)   dabbling (7)
   simulated (2)   subcultures (7)

2. Look at the language Bauman uses to describe violent video games (paragraphs 2 through 5). In what way do the words convey value judgments? How would more neutral language affect the impact of these passages?

3. What transitions does Bauman use to move his argument from one point to another? How effectively do these transitions guide readers through the essay?

JOURNAL ENTRY

Go on the Internet and research the Littleton massacre. Then, write a journal entry in which you discuss what influences other than violent video games could have caused the two boys to commit murder.

WRITING WORKSHOP

1. In his conclusion, Bauman says, "ultimately, video games are an easy target." Do you agree? Write an essay in which you argue that other factors could have contributed to the Littleton massacre.

2. Go to a video arcade or a store that sells video games, and do your own survey of violent video games. Then, write an essay in which you present your findings. On the basis of your observations, do you think some of these games are so violent that they could trigger abhorrent behavior in individuals? Be specific.

3. Some recent studies have shown a link between violent video games and movies and aggressive behavior in children, but none of these studies has shown conclusively that excessive viewing of these games and movies actually cause children to go out and commit crimes. Even so, parents and educators struggle with the question of whether children should have access to this material. Write an essay in which you take a stand on the

issue. If you like, consult the other essays in this section for ideas — but be sure to document all words and ideas that you borrow from your sources.

COMBINING THE PATTERNS

Paragraph 5 is developed by **cause and effect.** What is the function of this paragraph? How effectively does it establish the causal link between *House of the Dead* and Paducah killer Michael Carneal?

THEMATIC CONNECTIONS

- "Thirty-Eight Who Saw Murder Didn't Call the Police" (page 99)
- "Television: The Plug-In Drug" (page 283)
- "A Peaceful Woman Explains Why She Carries a Gun" (page 298)
- "The End of Serendipity" (page 604)

◢◢◢◢◢◢◢◢
DEBATE CASEBOOK:
Is the Internet Good for Society?

In 1998, then–Vice President Al Gore delivered a speech in which he presented his vision of a future dominated by telecommunications and the Internet:

> My message to you is simple: today, on the eve of a new century and a new millennium, we have an unprecedented opportunity to use these powerful new forces of technology to advance our oldest and most cherished values. We have a chance to extend knowledge and prosperity to our most isolated inner cities, to the barrios, the favelas, the colonias, and our most remote rural villages; to bring twenty-first century learning and communication to places that don't even have phone service today; . . . to strengthen democracy and freedom by putting it online, where it is so much harder for it to be suppressed or denied.

This optimism is characteristic of those who are advocates of the digital revolution. To them, the Internet — which is changing the way we access and process information — heralds a new world, one in which human beings will be interconnected as never before. The result will be a political and social Renaissance where ideas flow freely across national borders and where the world's population will have economic opportunities they have never had before.

There are those, however, who do not share this confident declaration of digital interdependence. To them, there is a dark side to the information age. For example, what will happen to people who do not have access to the Internet? What about those who lack the skills required by our highly technological world? And finally, do we have the critical thinking skills to evaluate the millions of pages of information that the Internet brings to us? In other words, what are the implications of being in the midst of an ocean of information that we cannot easily navigate or control? Before our technological advances overtake our ability to assess their moral and social effects, we must try to find answers to these questions.

The five essays in this section examine the implications of the information age and the Internet. In "Bards of the Internet," Philip Elmer-DeWitt argues that even though much of the material accessible via the Internet is poorly written, e-mail, computer conferencing, and message boards are helping an entire generation learn about writing. To Elmer-DeWitt, the Internet has empowered thousands who would otherwise not have a voice. In "One Internet, Two Nations," Henry Louis Gates Jr. sees a "digital divide" that, according to him, threatens to turn the United States into two countries, one "white and plugged in and the other black and unplugged." In "The End of Serendipity," Ted Gup asserts that the Internet has redefined the way in which we access and perceive information. To him, the irony of this situation is that the Internet, which has been hailed as a technological advance that will bring us all together, may actually make us a world of isolationists. In "How the Web Destroys the Quality of Students' Research Papers," David Rothenberg discusses the implications of students' doing research on the Internet. According to Rothenberg, the Internet encourages students to cut and paste information together without bothering to understand or assimilate it. He suggests that instead of encouraging students to use the Internet, instructors should teach students to think on their own and to develop their own unique voices. Finally, in "An Age of Optimism," Nicholas Negroponte acknowledges the problems created by the Internet but goes on to praise its potential. According to Negroponte, the Internet will make it possible for young people to throw off national prejudices and live in a world of "friendship, collaboration, play, and neighborhood" (page 617).

♪♪♪♪♪♪♪♪
PHILIP ELMER-DEWITT

Philip Elmer-DeWitt, *Time*'s senior editor for technology, started out at the magazine as a secretary in 1979 and later worked as a science researcher. In 1982, when *Time* launched its new "Computers" section, Elmer-DeWitt was appointed its first writer, in part because he was one of the few writers on staff at the time who had much hands-on experience with computers. He has written on such issues as cyberpornography, human cloning, and genetics.

In the following *Time* essay from 1994, Elmer-DeWitt considers the extent to which the Internet is contributing to an increase in the amount of writing that is taking place through e-mail, bulletin boards, and discussion groups. It is estimated that in 1998 there were close to 81 million e-mail users in the United States and that a whopping 3.4 trillion e-mail messages were delivered (a figure expected to double in the year 2000). Although much of this electronic communication is business related, it is nevertheless, as Elmer-DeWitt suggests, bringing together people from all walks of life who might otherwise never "meet." It has been argued that in some colleges and businesses e-mail is replacing face-to-face communication, but at the same time it is helping people separated by great distances to stay connected.

Bards of the Internet

One of the unintended side effects of the invention of the telephone 1
was that writing went out of style. Oh, sure, there were still full-time scribblers — journalists, academics, professional wordsmiths. And the great centers of commerce still found it useful to keep on hand people who could draft a memo, a brief, a press release or a contract. But given a choice between picking up a pen or a phone, most folks took the easy route and gave their fingers — and sometimes their mind — a rest.

Which makes what's happening on the computer networks all the 2
more startling. Every night, when they should be watching television, millions of computer users sit down at their keyboards; dial into CompuServe, Prodigy, America Online or the Internet; and start typing — E-mail, bulletin-board postings, chat messages, rants, diatribes, even short stories and poems. Just when the media of McLuhan were supposed to render obsolete the medium of Shakespeare, the online world is experiencing the greatest boom in letter writing since the eighteenth century.

"It is my overwhelming belief that e-mail and computer conferencing 3
is teaching an entire generation about the flexibility and utility of prose," writes Jon Carroll, a columnist at the San Francisco *Chronicle*. Patrick Nielsen Hayden, an editor at Tor Books, compares electronic bulletin boards with the "scribblers' compacts" of the late eighteenth and early nineteenth centuries, in which members passed letters from hand to hand, adding a little more at each turn. David Sewell, an associate editor at the University of Arizona, likens netwriting to the literary scene Mark Twain discovered

in San Francisco in the 1860s, "when people were reinventing journalism by grafting it onto the tall-tale folk tradition." Others hark back to Tom Paine and the Revolutionary War pamphleteers, or even to the Elizabethan era, when, thanks to Gutenberg, a generation of English writers became intoxicated with language.

But such comparisons invite a question: If online writing today represents some sort of renaissance, why is so much of it so awful? For it can be very bad indeed: sloppy, meandering, puerile, ungrammatical, poorly spelled, badly structured and at times virtually content free. "HEY!!!!" reads an all-too typical message on the Internet, "I THINK METALLICA IZ REEL KOOL DOOD!!!!"   4

One reason, of course, is that E-mail is not like ordinary writing. "You need to think of this as 'written speech,'" says Gerard Van der Leun, literary agent based in Westport, Connecticut, who has emerged as one of the preeminent stylists on the Net. "These things are little more considered than coffeehouse talk and a lot less considered than a letter. They're not to have and hold; they're to fire and forget." Many online postings are composed "live" with the clock ticking, using rudimentary word processors on computer systems that charge by the minute and in some cases will shut down without warning when an hour runs out.   5

That is not to say that with more time every writer on the Internet would produce sparkling copy. Much of the fiction and poetry is second-rate or worse, which is not surprising given that the barriers to entry are so low. "In the real world," says Mary Anne Mohanraj, a Chicago-based poet, "it takes a hell of a lot of work to get published, which naturally weeds out a lot of the garbage. On the Net, just a few keystrokes sends your writing out to thousands of readers."   6

But even among the reams of bad poetry, gems are to be found. Mike Godwin, a Washington-based lawyer who posts under the pen name "mnemonic," tells the story of Joe Green, a technical writer at Cray Research who turned a moribund discussion group called rec.arts.poems into a real poetry workshop by mercilessly critiquing the pieces he found there. "Some people got angry and said if he was such a god of poetry, why didn't he publish his poems to the group?" recalls Godwin. "He did, and blew them all away." Green's *Well Met in Minnesota*, a mock-epic account of a face-to-face meeting with a fellow network scribbler, is now revered on the Internet as a classic. It begins, "The truth is that when I met Mart I was dressed as the *Canterbury Tales*. Rather difficult to do as you might suspect, but I wanted to make a certain impression."   7

The more prosaic technical and political discussion groups, meanwhile, have become so crowded with writers crying for attention that a Darwinian survival principle has started to prevail. "It's so competitive that you have to work on your style if you want to make any impact," says Jorn Barger, a software designer in Chicago. Good writing on the Net tends to be clear, vigorous, witty and above all brief. "The medium favors the terse," says Crawford Kilian, a writing teacher at Capilano College in   8

Vancouver, British Columbia. "Short paragraphs, bulleted lists, and one-liners are the units of thought here."

Some of the most successful netwriting is produced in computer con-   9
ferences, where writers compose in a kind of collaborative heat, knocking ideas against one another until they spark. Perhaps the best examples of this are found on the WELL, a Sausalito, California, bulletin board favored by journalists. The caliber of discussion is often so high that several publications — including the *New York Times* and the *Wall Street Journal* — have printed excerpts from the WELL.

Curiously, what works on the computer networks isn't necessarily   10
what works on paper. Netwriters freely lace their prose with strange acronyms and "smileys," the little faces constructed with punctuation marks and intended to convey the winks, grins and grimaces of ordinary conversations. Somehow it all flows together quite smoothly. On the other hand, polished prose copied onto bulletin boards from books and magazines often seems long-winded and phony. Unless they adjust to the new medium, professional writers can come across as self-important blowhards in debates with more nimble networkers. Says Brock Meeks, a Washington-based reporter who covers the online culture for *Communications Daily:* "There are a bunch of hacker kids out there who can string a sentence together better than their blue-blooded peers simply because they log on all the time and write, write, write."

There is something inherently democratizing — perhaps even revolu-   11
tionary — about the technology. Not only has it enfranchised thousands of would-be writers who otherwise might never have taken up the craft, but it has also thrown together classes of people who hadn't had much direct contact before: students, scientists, senior citizens, computer geeks, grassroots (and often blue-collar) bulletin-board enthusiasts and most recently the working press.

"It's easy to make this stuff look foolish and trivial," says Tor Books   12
Nielsen Hayden. "After all, a lot of everyone's daily life is foolish and trivial. I mean, really, smileys? Housewives in Des Moines who log on as VIXEN?"

But it would be a mistake to dismiss the computer-message boards or   13
to underestimate the effect a lifetime of dashing off E-mail will have on a generation of young writers. The computer networks may not be Brook Farm or the Globe Theatre, but they do represent, for millions of people, a living breathing life of letters. One suspects that the Bard himself, confronted with the Internet, might have dived right in and never logged off.

• • •

COMPREHENSION

1. According to Elmer-DeWitt, the invention of the telephone caused writing to go out of style. In what way is the effect of the Internet different?

2. Why is so much of the writing on the Internet "so awful" (4)?

3. In what ways has the Internet produced a kind of renaissance in writing?

4. How is writing online different from writing on paper?

5. What does Elmer-DeWitt mean when he says, "There is something inherently democratizing — perhaps even revolutionary — about the technology" [of the Internet] (11)?

PURPOSE AND AUDIENCE

1. Does Elmer-DeWitt assume that his readers are Internet users or people who don't know much about the Internet? Explain.

2. How does Elmer-DeWitt view his readers? Does he consider them hostile, skeptical, neutral, or friendly? How can you tell?

3. Where does Elmer-DeWitt state his thesis? Why does he place it where he does?

STYLE AND STRUCTURE

1. Why does Elmer-DeWitt begin his essay by talking about the telephone? Can you think of another way he could have prepared readers for his thesis?

2. At what point does Elmer-DeWitt address arguments against his position? Does he concede any points to his opposition?

3. What evidence does Elmer-DeWitt provide to support his points? How convincing is his evidence? What other kinds of evidence could he have presented?

4. Is Elmer-DeWitt's argument primarily inductive or deductive?

5. How effective is Elmer-DeWitt's conclusion? Do you, like him, believe that Shakespeare would have liked the Internet, or do you think Elmer-DeWitt overstates his position?

VOCABULARY PROJECTS

1. Define each of the following words as it is used in this selection.

bards (title)	preeminent (5)	collaborative (9)
wordsmiths (1)	rudimentary (5)	acronyms (10)
rants (2)	reams (7)	grimaces (10)
diatribes (2)	moribund (7)	enfranchised (11)
obsolete (2)	critiquing (7)	trivial (12)
renaissance (4)	prosaic (8)	

2. Identify all the computer terms that appear in this essay. Should any have been defined? Was Elmer-DeWitt correct in assuming that general readers would be familiar with these terms?

JOURNAL ENTRY

What effect do you think e-mail and computer message boards are having on young writers? Do you agree with Elmer-DeWitt that the effect is for the most part positive?

WRITING WORKSHOP

1. Do your own informal survey of writing on the Internet by assessing the quality of the writing on several Web pages and in two or three chat rooms. Write an essay in which you agree or disagree with Elmer-DeWitt's thesis.

2. In paragraph 11, Elmer-DeWitt says, "There is something inherently democratizing" about the Internet. Not only has it "enfranchised thousands of would-be writers," he points out, but it has also "thrown together classes of people who hadn't much direct contact before" (11). How would Ted Gup respond to Elmer-DeWitt's assessment of the Internet (see paragraphs 8 and 9 of Gup's essay)?

3. Write an essay in which you consider the effects of the Internet on your writing. Argue either that the Internet has caused a general "renaissance" in your writing, or that it has reinforced your worst writing habits. (You may, of course, take a middle position.) Be sure to refer to Elmer-DeWitt's ideas in your essay.

COMBINING THE PATTERNS

Paragraph 10 is developed by means of **comparison and contrast.** What point is Elmer-DeWitt making? How does comparison and contrast help him make this point?

THEMATIC CONNECTIONS

- "The Great Campus Goof-Off Machine" (page 188)
- "The Human Cost of an Illiterate Society" (page 203)
- "Never Do That to a Book" (page 345)

🍂🍂🍂🍂🍂🍂🍂🍂
HENRY LOUIS GATES JR.

Henry Louis Gates Jr. was born in 1950 in Keyser, West Virginia, and grew up in the small town of Piedmont. Currently W. E. B. Du Bois Professor of Humanities and chair of the Afro-American Studies Department at Harvard, he has edited many collections of works by African-American writers and published several volumes of literary criticism. However, he is probably best known as a social critic whose books and articles for a general audience explore a wide variety of issues and themes, often focusing on issues of race and culture.

In this essay, Gates examines the "digital divide" that exists in the United States today, where some groups (the poor, the elderly, and many in rural areas, for example) lack access to the Internet. In particular, he discusses the reluctance of many African Americans to take advantage of the digital revolution, and he considers the potentially devastating consequences of this situation.

One Internet, Two Nations

After the Stono Rebellion of 1739 in South Carolina — the largest up- 1
rising of slaves in the colonies before the American Revolution — legislators there responded by banishing two forms of communication among the slaves: the mastery of reading and writing, and the mastery of "talking drums," both of which had been crucial to the capacity to rebel.

For the next century and a half, access to literacy became for the slaves 2
a hallmark of their humanity and an instrument of liberation, spiritual as well as physical. The relation between freedom and literacy became the compelling theme of the slave narratives, the great body of printed books that ex-slaves generated to assert their common humanity with white Americans and to indict the system that had oppressed them.

In the years since the abolition of slavery, the possession of literacy 3
has been a cardinal value of the African-American tradition. It is no accident that the first great victory in the legal battle over segregation was fought on the grounds of education — of equal access to literacy.

Today, blacks are failing to gain access to the new tools of literacy: the 4
digital "knowledge economy." And while the dilemma that our ancestors confronted was imposed by others, this cybersegregation is, to a large degree, self-imposed.

The Government's latest attempt to understand why low-income 5
African-Americans and Hispanics are slower to embrace the Internet and the personal computer than whites — the Commerce Department study "Falling Through the Net"— suggests that income alone can't be blamed for the so-called digital divide. For example, among families earning $15,000 to $35,000 annually, more than 33 percent of whites own computers, compared with only 19 percent of African-Americans — a gap that has widened 64 percent over the past five years despite declining computer prices.

The implications go far beyond online trading and chat rooms. Net   6
promoters are concerned that the digital divide threatens to become a
twenty-first century poll tax that, in effect, disenfranchises a third of the
nation. Our children, especially, need access not only to the vast resources
that technology offers for education, but also to the rich cultural contexts
that define their place in the world.

Today we stand at the brink of becoming two societies, one largely   7
white and plugged in and the other black and unplugged.

One of the most tragic aspects of slavery was the way it destroyed   8
social connections. In a process that the sociologist Orlando Patterson calls
"social death," slavery sought to sever blacks from their history and culture, from family ties and a sense of community. And, of course, de jure
segregation after the Civil War was intended to disconnect blacks from
equal economic opportunity, from the network of social contacts that
enable upward mobility and, indeed, from the broader world of ideas.

Despite the dramatic growth of the black middle class since affirma-   9
tive action programs were started in the late 60's, new forms of discon-
nectedness have afflicted black America. Middle-class professionals often
feel socially and culturally isolated from their white peers at work and in
the neighborhood and from their black peers left behind in the underclass.
The children of the black underclass, in turn, often lack middle-class role
models to help them connect to a history of achievement and develop
their analytical skills.

It would be a sad irony if the most diverse and decentralized elec-   10
tronic medium yet invented should fail to achieve ethnic diversity among
its users. And yet the Commerce Department study suggests that the solution will require more than cheap PC's. It will involve content.

Until recently, the African-American presence on the Internet was   11
minimal, reflecting the chicken-and-egg nature of Internet economics.
Few investors have been willing to finance sites appealing to a PC-scarce
community. Few African-Americans have been compelled to sign on to a
medium that offers little to interest them. And educators interested in
diversity have repeatedly raised concerns about the lack of minority-
oriented educational software.

Consider the birth of the recording industry in the 1920's. Blacks   12
began to respond to this new medium only when mainstream companies
like Columbia Records introduced so-called race records, blues and jazz
discs aimed at a nascent African-American market. Blacks who would
never have dreamed of spending hard-earned funds for a record by Rudy
Vallee or Kate Smith would stand in lines several blocks long to purchase
the new Bessie Smith or Duke Ellington hit.

New content made the new medium attractive. And the growth of   13
Web sites dedicated to the interests and needs of black Americans can play
the same role for the Internet that race records did for the music industry.

But even making sites that will appeal to a black audience can only go   14
so far. The causes of poverty are both structural and behavioral. And it is

the behavioral aspect of this cybersegregation that blacks themselves are best able to address. Drawing on corporate and foundation support, we can transform the legion of churches, mosques, and community centers in our inner cities into after-school centers that focus on redressing the digital divide and teaching black history. We can draw on the many examples of black achievement in structured classes to re-establish a sense of social connection.

The Internet is the twenty-first century's talking drum, the very kind   15
of grass-roots communication tool that has been such a powerful source of education and culture for our people since slavery. But this talking drum we have not yet learned to play. Unless we master the new information technology to build and deepen the forms of social connection that a tragic history has eroded, African-Americans will face a form of cybersegregation in the next century as devastating to our aspirations as Jim Crow segregation was to those of our ancestors. But this time, the fault will be our own.

•   •   •

COMPREHENSION

1. Why did legislators pass laws after the Stono Rebellion in 1739 to ensure that slaves remained illiterate? In the years after this legislation, what status did literacy have in the African-American community?

2. What distinction does Gates draw between the segregation that existed in public schools before 1954 and the "cybersegregation" that presently exists on the Internet?

3. According to Gates, why don't African Americans take advantage of the Internet? What can be done to remedy this situation?

4. What does Gates mean in paragraph 14 when he says, "It is the behavioral aspect of this cybersegregation that blacks themselves are best able to address"?

5. According to Gates, what will happen if African Americans fail to gain access to the Internet?

PURPOSE AND AUDIENCE

1. Where does Gates state his thesis? How effective is this thesis? What other ideas could he have emphasized?

2. Who is Gates's intended audience? White readers? African Americans? All Americans? Explain.

3. What is the tone of this essay? Frustrated? Disappointed? Angry? Something else?

4. What was Gates's purpose in writing this essay? What do you think he hoped to accomplish?

STYLE AND STRUCTURE

1. Gates begins his essay by mentioning "talking drums," and he mentions them again at the end of his essay. Why does he do so? Does he achieve his purpose?

2. What specific arguments does Gates make to support his thesis? Can you think of any other arguments he might have made?

3. What evidence does Gates present to support his points? Does he offer enough evidence? What kind of additional evidence might have strengthened his case?

4. Paragraph 7 is only one sentence long. Why is it so short?

5. At what point does Gates refute arguments against his thesis? Do you think he should have addressed opposing arguments more forcefully than he does?

6. Gates ends his essay with the sentence "But this time, the fault will be our own" (15). What does he mean? How effective is this last line?

VOCABULARY PROJECTS

1. Define each of the following words as it is used in this selection.

banishing (1)	cardinal (3)	underclass (9)
literacy (2)	digital (5)	mainstream (12)
hallmark (2)	brink (7)	
abolition (3)	disconnectedness (9)	

2. In his essay, Gates coins the term *cybersegregation.* Try substituting another word or phrase for this term. What, if anything, does Gates gain by making up this new word?

JOURNAL ENTRY

Do you think that Gates gives an adequate explanation of why low-income African Americans do not use the Internet? Should he have provided more analysis of this problem?

WRITING WORKSHOP

1. Assume you are a volunteer at a community center where most of the young people are not interested in the Internet. Write a two- to three-page memo in which you propose a project to attract these young people to the Internet. Remember that the audience for your proposal is your supervisor, who must be persuaded that your proposal has merit before she will approve it.

2. According to Nicholas Negroponte, being digital is a natural force that draws "people into greater world harmony" (11). According to Gates, however, we are in danger of becoming two societies unless we address the needs of low-income African Americans and Hispanics. Write a letter

to Negroponte in which you argue that in light of this digital divide, his optimism seems unrealistic. (In addition to the Gates essay, you may refer to any other essay in this debate casebook.)

3. Gates says that unless African Americans master the Internet, they will face a form of segregation that is as bad as the segregation their ancestors faced during the Jim Crow era. Do you think Gates is making an accurate claim or overstating his case? Write a response to Gates in which you argue in support of or against his point.

COMBINING THE PATTERNS

Gates begins his essay with four paragraphs of **narration.** What does this narrative section add to the essay? What point is Gates attempting to make? Is he successful?

THEMATIC CONNECTIONS

- "The Human Cost of an Illiterate Society" (page 203)
- "The 'Black Table' Is Still There" (page 294)
- "Does America Still Exist?" (page 482)

TED GUP

Ted Gup (1950–) worked for ten years as a reporter for the *Washington Post* and then joined *Time* magazine as a correspondent. He now works as a free-lance writer, with articles appearing in such widely ranging publications as *National Geographic, Sports Illustrated, Gentlemen's Quarterly,* and *Mother Jones,* as well as several online publications. He is also a professor of journalism and media writing at Case Western Reserve University.

"The End of Serendipity" appeared in 1997 in the *Chronicle of Higher Education,* a journal aimed at academic faculty and administrators. Gup's subject here is readers' increasing use of electronic resources — CD-ROM references, online publications, Web browsers — for much of the information they seek. The benefits of such resources are clear: a CD-ROM encyclopedia, for example, can store up to twenty-eight volumes' worth of information, and CD-ROM sets are now outselling hardcover sets. In Gup's view, however, such modes of information gathering ensure that readers are less likely to discover information that might be irrelevant but might nonetheless enrich their understanding of the world.

The End of Serendipity

When I was a young boy, my parents bought me a set of *The World* 1 *Book Encyclopedia.* The 22 burgundy-and-gold volumes lined the shelves above my bed. On any given day or night I would reach for a book and lose myself for hours in its endless pages of maps, photographs, and text. Even when I had a purpose in mind — say, for instance, a homework assignment on salamanders — I would invariably find myself reading instead of Salem and its witch hunts or of Salamis, where the Greeks routed the Persians in the fifth century B.C. Like all encyclopedias of the day, it was arranged alphabetically, based on sound and without regard to subject. As a child, I saw it as a system wondrously whimsical and exquisitely inefficient. Perfect for exploration. The "S" volume alone could lead me down 10,000 unconnected highways.

The world my two young sons inherit is a very different place. That 2 same encyclopedia now comes on CD-ROM. Simply drop the platinum disk into the A-drive and type in a key word. In a flash the subject appears on the screen. The search is perfected in a single keystroke — no flipping of pages, no risk of distraction, no unintended consequences. And therein lies the loss.

My boys belong to an age vastly more efficient in its pursuit of infor- 3 mation but oblivious to the pleasures and rewards of serendipity. From Silicon Valley to M.I.T., the best minds are dedicated to refining our search for answers. Noble though their intentions may be, they are inadvertently smothering the opportunity to find what may well be the more important answers — the ones to questions that have not yet even occurred to us. I wish, then, to write on behalf of random epiphanies and the virtues of accidental discovery — before they, too, go the way of my old Remington manual.[1]

My boys are scarcely aware that they are part of a grand experiment in   4
which the computer, the Internet, and the World-Wide Web are redefining literacy and reshaping the architecture of how they learn. These innovations are ushering in a world that, at least to my tastes, is entirely too purposeful — as devoid of romance as an arranged marriage. Increasingly, we hone our capacity to target the information that we seek. More ominous still, we weed out that which we deem extraneous. In a world of information overload, this ability to filter what reaches us has been hailed as an unqualified good. I respectfully disagree.

Consider, for example, those of my sons' generation who are learning   5
to read the newspaper on a computer screen. They do not hold in their hands a cumbersome front page but instead see a neat menu that has sliced and diced the news into user-friendly categories. They need not read stories but merely scan topical headings — sports, finance, entertainment. The risk that they or any readers will inadvertently be drawn into a story afield from their peculiar interests, or succumb to some picture or headline, grows ever more remote. The users define their needs while the computer, like an overly eager waiter, stands ready to deliver, be it the latest basketball scores, updates of a personal stock portfolio, or tomorrow's weather. In my youth, information was a smorgasbord. Walking past so irresistible an array of dishes, I found it impossible not to fill my plate. Today, everything is à la carte.

There are moral consequences to being able to tailor the information   6
that reaches us. Like other journalists, I have spent much of my life writing stories that I knew, even as I worked on them, would not be welcomed by my readers. Accounts of war, of hardship or want seldom are. But those stories found their way first into readers' hands and then into their minds. They were read sometimes reluctantly, sometimes with resentment, and, most often, simply because they appeared on the printed page. Doubtless the photo of a starving child or a string of refugees stretching above the morning's shredded wheat and orange juice may be viewed as an unsightly intrusion, but it is hard to ignore.

In cyberspace, such intrusions will become less frequent. There will be   7
fewer and fewer uninvited guests. Nothing will come unless summoned. Unless the mouse clicks on the story, the account will not materialize. And who will click on the story headlined "Rwandans Flee," "Inner-City Children Struggle," or even "Endangered Butterflies Fight for Survival"? If the mouse is a key, it is also a padlock to keep the world out.

Those already on the margins of our consciousness — the homeless,   8
the weak, the disenfranchised — are being pushed right off the page, exiled into cyberspace and the ever-expanding domain of the irrelevant. Already the phrase "That's not on my screen" has found its way into common

---

[1]A manual — that is, non-electric — typewriter. [editor's note]

parlance. In the end, self-interest may be the most virulent form of censorship, inimical to compassion and our sense of community. It is the ultimate V-chip, this power to sanitize reality, to bar unpleasantries. "Technology," the Swiss playwright Max Frisch once observed, is "the knack of so arranging the world that we don't have to experience it."

It would be ironic if the computer, this great device of interconnectivity, should engender a world of isolationists. Yet increasingly we use its powers to read about ourselves and to feed our own parochial self-interests. Instead of a global village, we risk a race of cyber-hermits. And the World-Wide Web, the promised badge to that which is beyond ourselves, may be yet another moat to protect the self-absorbed.

A friend of mine recently joined Microsoft. He was struck by the 10 youthfulness of those around him and the absolute faith they had that every question had an answer, every problem a solution. It is the defining character of the Microsoft Culture, its celebration of answers. Within that church, there are few Luthers[2] to challenge its orthodoxy. So much energy is spent to produce the right answers that little time is left to ponder the correctness of the questions.

I find it amusing that Bill Gates, shrewd investor that he is, has 11 emerged as one of the world's premier art collectors, acquiring the notebooks of Leonardo da Vinci, the consummate figure of the Renaissance. I wonder: Does he identify with that genius, or, perhaps recognizing the peril in which that humanistic tradition is now placed, is he simply attempting to corner the market on its artifacts?

This is not a revolution but an evolution. In ancient caves can be found 12 flakes of flint left by early humans, evidence of the first impulse to put a point on our tools, to refine them. The computer, with its search engines, is simply an extension of that primal urge. From the Olduvai Gorge[3] to Silicon Valley, we have always been obsessed with bringing our tools to a perfect point. But where knowledge of the world is concerned, I suspect there is some virtue to possessing a blunter instrument. Sometimes a miss produces more than a hit.

Ironically, we continue to call entrées to cyberspace "Web browsers," 13 but increasingly they are used not to browse but to home in on a narrow slice of the universe. We invoke mystery with corporate names such as "Oracle," but we measure progress in purely quantitative terms — gigabits and megahertz, capacity and speed. Our search engines carry names such as "Yahoo" and "Excite," but what they deliver is ever more predictable. The parameters of the universe shrink, defined by key words and Boolean filters, sieves that — with each improvement in search engines — increasingly succeed in siphoning off anything less than responsive to our

9 (marginal paragraph number, appears beside paragraph beginning "It would be ironic")

---

[2]The reference is to Martin Luther (1483–1546), the religious reformer who broke with the Catholic Church. [editor's note]

[3]Site in Tanzania where the fossilized remains of many protohumans have been discovered. [editor's note]

inquiries. The more precise the response, the more the process is hailed as a success.

What has been billed as the information superhighway has, like all   14
superhighways, come with a price. We have shortened the time between departure and arrival but gone is all scenery in between, reduced to a Pentium blur. We settle for information at the expense of understanding and mistake retrieval for exploration. The vastness of the Internet's potential threatens to shrink into yet another utility. As the technology matures, the adolescent exuberance of surfing the Web yields to the drudgery of yet another commute.

One need not be a Luddite[4] or technophobe to sound a cautionary   15
word in the midst of euphoria over technology. I have a fantasy that one day I will produce a computer virus and introduce it into my own desktop, so that when my sons put in their key word — say, "salamander"— the screen will erupt in a brilliant but random array of maps and illustrations and text that will divert them from their task. This I will do so that they may know the sheer joy of finding what they have not sought. I might even wish for this virus to spread from computer to computer. And I would name this virus for that which ought not to be lost — serendipity.

•   •   •

COMPREHENSION

1. What "grand experiment" are Gup's sons a part of? According to Gup, what is wrong with this experiment?

2. What are the moral consequences of our being able to "tailor the information that reaches us" (6)?

3. In what way is the mouse "a padlock to keep the world out" (7)?

4. How, according to Gup, will "the homeless, the weak, the disenfranchised" be affected by our ability to control the information that comes to us (8)?

5. Why does Gup think it is ironic that we give our Web browsers names like *Oracle, Yahoo,* and *Excite*?

PURPOSE AND AUDIENCE

1. What is the meaning of the essay's title? In what way does this title express the essay's thesis?

2. At what point does Gup state his thesis? Why does he wait so long to state it?

3. Is Gup's essay too personal and subjective? Would a more objective essay have been more convincing?

---

[4]Name given to groups of laborers who rioted in 1811 and 1816 in parts of England, destroying knitting machines — a new technology — which they believed were responsible for unemployment; more generally, a term for one who opposes new technology. [editor's note]

STYLE AND STRUCTURE

1. Gup supports his points with examples from his own experience. What other kinds of evidence could he have used?

2. Is Gup's argument primarily inductive or deductive?

3. In paragraph 11, Gup discusses Bill Gates, founder of Microsoft Corporation. What function does this discussion serve? Would the essay have been more effective without this paragraph?

4. What points in his argument, if any, could Gup have developed in more detail? For example, what would have been the effect of expanding the discussion of the poor in paragraph 8?

5. Are there any places in the essay where Gup overstates his case? How do such overstatements affect you?

6. At what point does Gup refute arguments against his position? Should his refutations have been more direct and less subtle?

VOCABULARY PROJECTS

1. Define each of the following words as it is used in this selection.

invariably (1)	inadvertently (5)	consummate (11)
serendipity (3)	disenfranchised (8)	Renaissance (11)
epiphanies (3)	sanitize (8)	humanistic (11)
ominous (4)	isolationists (9)	quantitative (13)
cumbersome (5)	orthodoxy (10)	

2. In paragraph 14, Gup uses an extended metaphor. To what does he compare the Internet? What point does he make? How effective is this figure of speech?

JOURNAL ENTRY

In what ways do you think that the Internet has expanded your frame of reference? In what ways has it limited it?

WRITING WORKSHOP

1. Write an essay in which you argue against Gup's thesis that the computer's ability to filter information will have negative consequences for all of us. Be sure to directly refute several of his major points.

2. In paragraph 4, Gup says that the Internet is helping to create a world that is "as devoid of romance as an arranged marriage" (4). Write an essay in which you argue in favor of this sentiment.

3. Assume that you are either David Rothenberg or Philip Elmer-DeWitt. Write a letter to Gup in which you argue for or against his thesis. Use points from either Rothenberg's or Elmer-DeWitt's essay to support your points.

COMBINING THE PATTERNS

Paragraphs 1 through 4 depend on **comparison and contrast.** What two things are being compared? Why do you think Gup uses this strategy to introduce his thesis?

THEMATIC CONNECTIONS

- "Finishing School" (page 88)
- "Reading the River" (page 138)
- "The Victorian Internet" (page 351)

◢◢◢◢◢◢◢◢

DAVID ROTHENBERG

David Rothenberg is an associate professor of philosophy at the New Jersey
Institute of Technology and the editor of *Terra Nova: Nature and Culture,* a
scholarly journal published by the MIT Press. In addition to authoring several
books on philosophical topics, he also coproduced *Parliaments of Minds,* a 1999
public television series based on interviews with leading philosophers and
later adapted into book form.

College students have greater access to the World Wide Web than any
other segment of the population: fully 98 percent of the country's 8.8 million
four-year college students are able to go online, and they spend more time
surfing the Internet than any other group. The Web can obviously be a boon
for researchers, offering them a vast number of statistical abstracts, informational pages, newsletters, and even links to other resources. But in this article,
published in the *Chronicle of Higher Education* in 1997, Rothenberg argues that
such sources are all too often superficial, outdated, and even misleading. They
have resulted, he says, in a significant drop in the quality of his students'
work and in their ability to think carefully and critically.

How the Web Destroys the Quality of Students' Research Papers

Sometimes I look forward to the end-of-semester rush, when stu- 1
dents' final papers come streaming into my office and mailbox. I could
have hundreds of pages of original thought to read and evaluate. Once in
a while, it *is* truly exciting, and brilliant words are typed across a page in
response to a question I've asked the class to discuss.

But this past semester was different. I noticed a disturbing decline in 2
both the quality of the writing and the originality of the thoughts expressed.
What had happened since last fall? Did I ask worse questions? Were my
students unusually lazy? No. My class had fallen victim to the latest easy
way of writing a paper: doing their research on the World-Wide Web.

It's easy to spot a research paper that is based primarily on informa- 3
tion collected from the Web. First, the bibliography cites no books, just
articles or pointers to places in that virtual land somewhere off any map:
http:/www.etc. Then a strange preponderance of material in the bibliography is curiously out of date. A lot of stuff on the Web that is advertised
as timely is actually at least a few years old. (One student submitted a
research paper last semester in which all of his sources were articles published between September and December 1995; that was probably the time
span of the Web page on which he found them.)

Another clue is the beautiful pictures and graphs that are inserted 4
neatly into the body of the student's text. They look impressive, as though
they were the result of careful work and analysis, but actually they often
bear little relation to the precise subject of the paper. Cut and pasted from

the vast realm of what's out there for the taking, they masquerade as original work.

Accompanying them are unattributed quotes (in which one can't tell   5
who made the statement or in what context) and curiously detailed references to the kinds of things that are easy to find on the Web (pages and pages of federal documents, corporate propaganda, or snippets of commentary by people whose credibility is difficult to assess). Sadly, one finds few references to careful, in-depth commentaries on the subject of the paper, the kind of analysis that requires a book, rather than an article, for its full development.

Don't get me wrong, I'm no neo-Luddite.* I am as enchanted as any-   6
one else by the potential of this new technology to provide instant information. But too much of what passes for information these days is simply *advertising* for information. Screen after screen shows you where you can find out more, how you can connect to this place or that. The acts of linking and networking and randomly jumping from here to there become as exciting or rewarding as actually finding anything of intellectual value.

Search engines, with their half-baked algorithms, are closer to slot   7
machines than to library catalogues. You throw your query to the wind, and who knows what will come back to you? You may get 234,468 supposed references to whatever you want to know. Perhaps one in a thousand might actually help you. But it's easy to be sidetracked or frustrated as you try to go through those Web pages one by one. Unfortunately, they're not arranged in order of importance.

What I'm describing is the hunt-and-peck method of writing a paper.   8
We all know that word processing makes many first drafts look far more polished than they are. If the paper doesn't reach the assigned five pages, readjust the margin, change the font size, and . . . *voilà*! Of course, those machinations take up time that the student could have spent revising the paper. With programs to check one's spelling and grammar now standard features on most computers, one wonders why students make any mistakes at all. But errors are as prevalent as ever, no matter how crisp the typeface. Instead of becoming perfectionists, too many students have become slackers, preferring to let the machine do their work for them.

What the Web adds to the shortcuts made possible by word process-   9
ing is to make research look too easy. You toss a query to the machine, wait a few minutes, and suddenly a lot of possible sources of information appear on your screen. Instead of books that you have to check out of the library, read carefully, understand, synthesize, and then tactfully excerpt, these sources are quips, blips, pictures, and short summaries that may be

*Eds. note — One who opposes technological change. The Luddites were a group of British workers who in 1811 and 1816 destroyed textile machinery, which they thought threatened their jobs.

downloaded magically to the dorm-room computer screen. Fabulous! How simple! The only problem is that a paper consisting of summaries of summaries is bound to be fragmented and superficial, and to demonstrate more of a random montage than an ability to sustain an argument through 10 to 15 double-spaced pages.

Of course, you can't blame the students for ignoring books. When col-   10
lege libraries are diverting funds from books to computer technology that will be obsolete in two years at most, they send a clear message to students: Don't read, just connect. Surf. Download. Cut and paste. Originality becomes hard to separate from plagiarism if no author is cited on a Web page. Clearly, the words are up for grabs, and students much prefer the fabulous jumble to the hard work of stopping to think and make sense of what they've read.

Libraries used to be repositories of words and ideas. Now they are   11
seen as centers for the retrieval of information. Some of this information comes from other, bigger libraries, in the form of books that can take time to obtain through interlibrary loan. What happens to the many students (some things never change) who scramble to write a paper the night before it's due? The computer screen, the gateway to the world sitting right on their desks, promises instant access — but actually offers only a pale, two-dimensional version of a real library.

But it's also my fault. I take much of the blame for the decline in the   12
quality of student research in my classes. I need to teach students how to read, to take time with language and ideas, to work through arguments, to synthesize disparate sources to come up with original thought. I need to help my students understand how to assess sources to determine their credibility, as well as to trust their own ideas more than snippets of thought that materialize on a screen. The placelessness of the Web leads to an ethereal randomness of thought. Gone are the pathways of logic and passion, the sense of the progress of an argument. Chance holds sway, and it more often misses than hits. Judgment must be taught, as well as the methods of exploration.

I'm seeing my students' attention spans wane and their ability to rea-   13
son for themselves decline. I wish that the university's computer system would crash for a day, so that I could encourage them to go outside, sit under a tree, and read a really good book — from start to finish. I'd like them to sit for a while and ponder what it means to live in a world where some things get easier and easier so rapidly that we can hardly keep track of how easy they're getting, while other tasks remain as hard as ever — such as doing research and writing a good paper that teaches the writer something in the process. Knowledge does not emerge in a vacuum, but we do need silence and space for sustained thought. Next semester, I'm going to urge my students to turn off their glowing boxes and think, if only once in a while.

● ● ●

COMPREHENSION

1. According to Rothenberg, why is it easy to spot a paper in which the research has been done on the Web?

2. What does Rothenberg mean when he says, "Search engines, with their half-baked algorithms, are closer to slot machines than to library catalogues" (7)? Why is this situation a problem for student researchers?

3. How, according to Rothenberg, have spelling and grammar checkers caused students to become slackers?

4. How have colleges and college libraries contributed to the problems that Rothenberg discusses?

5. What does Rothenberg think instructors should do to improve the quality of student research?

PURPOSE AND AUDIENCE

1. How effective do you think Rothenberg's thesis statement is? What other ideas could he have emphasized in this thesis?

2. How can you tell Rothenberg is addressing teachers, not students?

3. What is the tone of this essay? Angry? Sad? Frustrated? Sarcastic? Something else?

4. What do you think Rothenberg's purpose was in writing this essay?

STYLE AND STRUCTURE

1. Rothenberg begins his essay by referring to his students and their research. Is this a good idea? If so, why? What other strategy could he have used?

2. What specific points does Rothenberg make in support of his thesis? How convincing are these points?

3. Rothenberg supports his points with observations and personal opinion. Is this kind of support enough? What other kinds of support might he have included?

4. Where does Rothenberg deal with opposing arguments? Can you think of any arguments that he should have refuted but did not?

5. In paragraphs 9 through 12, Rothenberg assigns blame for the situation he describes. Where does he think the blame lies? Do you agree with him?

VOCABULARY PROJECTS

1. Define each of the following words as it is used in this selection.

preponderance (3)	machinations (8)	obsolete (10)
unattributed (5)	perfectionists (8)	repositories (11)
snippets (5)	synthesize (9)	
query (7)	montage (9)	

2. Rothenberg uses contractions, such as *can't* and *it's,* throughout his essay. Find several places where he uses contractions. What is the effect of this usage? Do you think these contractions serve a useful purpose, or do they detract from the essay? Explain.

JOURNAL ENTRY

Do you agree with Rothenberg's explanation of why the quality of students' research is declining? Do you think that the problem is more complicated than he says it is? Explain.

WRITING WORKSHOP

1. Like Ted Gup in paragraph 15, Rothenberg says that he is not a *Luddite* — someone who opposes technology. After reading the two essays, decide for yourself whether Gup and Rothenberg could be considered Luddites. Then, write an argumentative essay in which you present your position.

2. Assess your own research process. Then, write a letter to Rothenberg in which you agree or disagree with his thesis.

3. Look at the sections of Rothenberg's essay in which he describes the shortcomings of the Internet (paragraphs 5 and 7, for example), and then write an essay in which you specifically refute these points. If you like, you may use information from Philip Elmer-DeWitt's "Bards of the Internet" to support your contentions.

COMBINING THE PATTERNS

Rothenberg begins his essay with two paragraphs of **narration.** What is the purpose of these paragraphs? In what way do they prepare readers for the discussion of research papers in paragraph 3?

THEMATIC CONNECTIONS

- "The Great Campus Goof-Off Machine" (page 188)
- "Television: The Plug-In Drug" (page 283)
- "College Pressures" (page 390)

NICHOLAS NEGROPONTE

As a graduate student in architecture at the Massachusetts Institute of Technology (MIT) in the mid-1960s, Nicholas Negroponte (1943–) specialized in the then-new field of computer design. He is now director of MIT's Media Laboratory, an interdisciplinary research center focusing on the study of future forms of communication. A founder of and senior columnist for *Wired* magazine (aimed at computer users), he is also the author of *Being Digital* (1995), an examination of the ways in which computer technologies are changing lives all over the world.

In the following essay, the conclusion to *Being Digital,* Negroponte considers some effects the digital revolution will have on national and international relations. It is astounding to realize how quickly computer technology has spread. As recently as 1990, only 15 percent of U.S. households owned a computer; by 1999, that figure had jumped to 50 percent and was continuing to climb. In 1989, 21 million personal computers were sold worldwide, 9 million of these in the United States; ten years later, in 1999, more than 93 million were sold worldwide, 36 million in the United States. In 1983, only 25 percent of jobs in the United States required computer skills; now that figure is approximately 60 percent. And it is estimated that since 1990 the computer industry has created one million new jobs. As Negroponte suggests, however, perhaps the greatest effect of the digital revolution has been on young people: 89 percent of U.S. teenagers now use computers at least several times a week, and 78 percent of U.S. schools are wired to the Internet.

An Age of Optimism

I am optimistic by nature. However, every technology or gift of science has a dark side. Being digital is no exception.   1

The next decade will see cases of intellectual-property abuse and invasion of our privacy. We will experience digital vandalism, software piracy, and data thievery. Worst of all, we will witness the loss of many jobs to wholly automated systems, which will soon change the white-collar workplace to the same degree that it has already transformed the factory floor. The notion of lifetime employment at one job has already started to disappear.   2

The radical transformation of the nature of our job markets, as we work less with atoms and more with bits, will happen at just about the same time the 2 billion-strong labor force of India and China starts to come on-line (literally). A self-employed software designer in Peoria will be competing with his or her counterpart in Pohang. A digital typographer in Madrid will do the same with one in Madras. American companies are already outsourcing hardware development and software production to Russia and India, not to find cheap manual labor but to secure a highly skilled intellectual force seemingly prepared to work harder, faster, and in a more disciplined fashion than those in our own country.   3

As the business world globalizes and the Internet grows, we will start 4
to see a seamless digital workplace. Long before political harmony and
long before the GATT* talks can reach agreement on the tariff and trade of
atoms (the right to sell Evian water in California), bits will be borderless,
stored and manipulated with absolutely no respect to geopolitical boundaries. In fact, time zones will probably play a bigger role in our digital
future than trade zones. I can imagine some software projects that literally
move around the world from east to west on a twenty-four-hour cycle,
from person to person or from group to group, one working as the other
sleeps. Microsoft will need to add London and Tokyo offices for software
development in order to produce on three shifts.

As we move more toward such a digital world, an entire sector of the 5
population will be or feel disenfranchised. When a fifty-year-old steel-
worker loses his job, unlike his twenty-five-year-old son, he may have no
digital resilience at all. When a modern-day secretary loses his job, at least
he may be conversant with the digital world and have transferable skills.

Bits are not edible; in that sense they cannot stop hunger. Computers 6
are not moral; they cannot resolve complex issues like the rights to life and
to death. But being digital, nevertheless, does give much cause for optimism. Like a force of nature, the digital age cannot be denied or stopped.
It has four very powerful qualities that will result in its ultimate triumph:
decentralizing, globalizing, harmonizing, and empowering.

The decentralizing effect of being digital can be felt no more strongly 7
than in commerce and in the computer industry itself. The so-called management information systems (MIS) czar, who used to reign over a glass-
enclosed and air-conditioned mausoleum, is an emperor with no clothes,
almost extinct. Those who survive are usually doing so because they out-
rank anybody able to fire them, and the company's board of directors is
out of touch or asleep or both.

Thinking Machines Corporation, a great and imaginative supercom- 8
puter company started by electrical engineering genius Danny Hillis, disappeared after ten years. In that short space of time it introduced the
world to massively parallel computer architectures. Its demise did not
occur because of mismanagement or sloppy engineering of their so-called
Connection Machine. It vanished because parallelism could be decentralized; the very same kind of massively parallel architectures have suddenly become possible by threading together low-cost, mass-produced
personal computers.

While this was not good news for Thinking Machines, it is an impor- 9
tant message to all of us, both literally and metaphorically. It means the
enterprise of the future can meet its computer needs in a new and scalable
way by populating its organization with personal computers that, when
needed, can work in unison to crunch on computationally intensive prob-

---

*EDS. NOTE — General *Agreement* on *Tariffs* and *Trade*, an international free trade
agreement.

lems. Computers will literally work both for individuals and for groups. I see the same decentralized mind-set growing in our society, driven by young citizenry in the digital world. The traditional centralist view of life will become a thing of the past.

The nation-state itself is subject to tremendous change and globaliza- 10 tion. Governments fifty years from now will be both larger and smaller. Europe finds itself dividing itself into smaller ethnic entities while trying to unite economically. The forces of nationalism make it too easy to be cynical and dismiss any broad-stroke attempt at world unification. But in the digital world, previously impossible solutions become viable.

Today, when 20 percent of the world consumes 80 percent of its 11 resources, when a quarter of us have an acceptable standard of living and three-quarters don't, how can this divide possibly come together? While the politicians struggle with the baggage of history, a new generation is emerging from the digital landscape free of many of the old prejudices. These kids are released from the limitation of geographic proximity as the sole basis of friendship, collaboration, play, and neighborhood. Digital technology can be a natural force drawing people into greater world harmony.

The harmonizing effect of being digital is already apparent as previ- 12 ously partitioned disciplines and enterprises find themselves collaborating, not competing. A previously missing common language emerges, allowing people to understand across boundaries. Kids at school today experience the opportunity to look at the same thing from many perspectives. A computer program, for example, can be seen simultaneously as a set of computer instructions or as concrete poetry formed by the indentations in the text of the program. What kids learn very quickly is that to know a program is to know it from many perspectives, not just one.

But more than anything, my optimism comes from the empowering 13 nature of being digital. The access, the mobility, and the ability to effect change are what will make the future so different from the present. The information superhighway may be mostly hype today, but it is an understatement about tomorrow. It will exist beyond people's wildest predictions. As children appropriate a global information resource, and as they discover that only adults need learner's permits, we are bound to find new hope and dignity in place where very little existed before.

My optimism is not fueled by an anticipated invention or discovery. 14 Finding a cure for cancer and AIDS, finding an acceptable way to control population, or inventing a machine that can breathe our air and drink our oceans and excrete unpolluted forms of each are dreams that may or may not come about. Being digital is different. We are not waiting on any invention. It is here. It is now. It is almost genetic in its nature, in that each generation will become more digital than the preceding one. The control bits of that digital future are more than ever before in the hands of the young. Nothing could make me happier.

●   ●   ●

COMPREHENSION

1. According to Negroponte, what are the main drawbacks of a digital world?

2. What is the advantage of working in "a seamless digital workplace" (4)?

3. What, according to Negroponte, are the four qualities that will result in the ultimate triumph of the digital age?

4. What does Negroponte mean when he says that being digital is "a natural force drawing people into greater world harmony" (11)?

5. According to Negroponte, what is "the empowering nature of being digital" (13)? Do you agree with his assertion that the Internet will enable the young to find "new hope and dignity" (13)?

PURPOSE AND AUDIENCE

1. At what point does Negroponte state his thesis? Should he have presented it sooner?

2. Does Negroponte assume that his readers share his optimism? At what points in this essay does he reveal his assessment of his readers?

3. Negroponte says that he is "optimistic by nature" (1). Would you describe his essay as optimistic, or does it have another tone?

STYLE AND STRUCTURE

1. Why does Negroponte begin his essay with a discussion of the dark side of the digital age?

2. Does Negroponte refute any of the arguments against his thesis? Should he have been more forceful in this respect?

3. As the headnote to this essay indicates, Negroponte is an expert in the area of technology and human communication. Does his status as an expert eliminate his need to provide factual support for his points? What other kinds of support could he have provided?

4. Does Negroponte structure his argument inductively or deductively? What are the advantages and disadvantages of the structure he uses?

5. In paragraph 8, Negroponte discusses the Thinking Machines Corporation. What does he hope to establish with this example? How successful is he?

VOCABULARY PROJECTS

1. Define each of the following words as it is used in this selection.

optimistic (1)	disenfranchised (5)	metaphorically (9)
vandalism (2)	empowering (6)	centrist (10)
typographer (3)	decentralizing (7)	viable (10)
tariff (4)	mausoleum (7)	genetic (14)
geopolitical (4)	literally (9)	

2. At points in this essay, Negroponte uses **jargon,** language that is appropriate for a particular discipline or industry —"global information resource," for example. Find several examples of this type of usage, and rewrite each phrase, using more colloquial diction. Which version works better in this essay? Explain.

JOURNAL ENTRY

Do you think that Negroponte's optimistic view of the digital age is realistic or idealistic? What leads you to your conclusion?

WRITING WORKSHOP

1. Write a letter to Negroponte in which you argue that he is too optimistic about the future. Make sure that you directly address the points he makes. Use material from any of the other essays in this casebook to support your arguments.

2. Write an essay in which you argue that the Internet has empowered you and your fellow students. Support your claims with examples from your own experience.

3. According to Negroponte, "in the digital world, previously impossible solutions become viable" (10). Write an essay in which you use Negroponte's statement as your thesis. In what ways do you think the Internet will change our lives for the better? Be sure to refute the obvious arguments against your position.

COMBINING THE PATTERNS

Negroponte begins his essay with several paragraphs (2 through 7) of **exemplification.** How convincing are these examples? Are there other negative consequences of a digital environment that he neglects to mention?

THEMATIC CONNECTIONS

- "The Peter Principle" (page 181)
- "The Human Cost of an Illiterate Society" (page 203)
- "The Victorian Internet" (page 351)

WRITING ASSIGNMENTS FOR ARGUMENTATION

1. Write an essay in which you discuss a teacher's right to strike. Address the major arguments against your position, and maintain an objective stance.

2. Assume that a library in your town has decided that certain books are objectionable and has removed them from the shelves. Write a letter to the local paper in which you argue for or against the library's actions. Make a list of the major arguments that might be advanced against your position, and try to refute some of them in your essay. Remember to respect the views of your audience and to address them in a respectful manner.

3. Write an essay in which you argue for or against the right of a woman to keep the baby after she has agreed to be a surrogate mother for another woman.

4. Write an essay in which you discuss under what circumstances, if any, animals should be used for scientific experimentation.

5. Write an essay in which you argue for or against the proposition that women soldiers should be able to serve in combat situations.

6. Research some criminal cases that resulted in the death penalty. Write an essay in which you use these accounts to support your arguments either for or against the death penalty. Don't forget to give credit to your sources. See the Appendix for information about documentation.

7. Write an argumentative essay in which you discuss whether there are any situations in which a nation has an obligation to go (or not to go) to war.

8. Write an essay in which you discuss whether health-care workers—doctors, nurses, and dentists, for example—should be required to be tested for the AIDS virus.

9. In the Declaration of Independence, Jefferson says that all individuals are entitled to "life, liberty, and the pursuit of happiness." Write an essay in which you argue that these rights are not absolute.

10. Write an argumentative essay on one of these topics: Should high school students be required to take sex-education courses? Should fraternities/ sororities be abolished? Should teachers be required to pass periodic competency tests? Should the legal drinking age be raised (or lowered)? Should any workers be required to submit to random drug testing?

COLLABORATIVE ACTIVITY FOR ARGUMENTATION

Working with three other students, select a controversial topic—one not covered in any of the debates in this chapter—that interests all of you. (You can review the Writing Assignments for Argumentation listed above to get ideas.) State your topic the way a topic is stated in a formal debate:

Resolved: The United States should suspend all immigration quotas.

Then divide into two two-member teams, and decide which team will take the pro position and which will take the con. Each team should list the arguments on its side of the issue and then write two or three paragraphs summarizing its position. Finally, each group should stage a ten-minute debate— five minutes for each side—in front of the class. (The pro side presents its argument first.) At the end of each debate, the class should discuss which side has presented the stronger arguments.

INTERNET ASSIGNMENT FOR ARGUMENTATION:
Is Date Rape Really Rape?

After visiting the following World Wide Web sites to read differing perspectives on date rape, write a letter to the editor of the *New York Times* in which you defend or refute the statement by journalist Katie Roiphe that "the so-called rape epidemic on campuses is more a way of interpreting, a way of seeing, than a physical phenomenon."

Date Rape's Other Victim
<http://www.vix.com/pub/men/books/roiphe.html>
This article by Katie Roiphe appeared in the June 13, 1993, issue of the *New York Times Magazine.*

The Marginalization of Sexual Violence against Black Women
<http://www.ncasa.org>
This article by Kimberle Williams Crenshaw appears on a site sponsored by the National Coalition against Sexual Assault, under "Articles and Information."

Andrea Dworkin's home page
<http://www.igc.org/Womensnet/dworkin.html>
"The Lie," by radical feminist Andrea Dworkin, was written as a speech and read at a rally on October 20, 1979, in Bryant Park in New York City.

Perspectives on Acquaintance Rape
<http://www.aaets.org/arts/art13.htm>
This article by David G. Curtis contains legal and social perspectives on date rape and summaries of date rape research. The site is sponsored by the American Academy of Experts in Traumatic Stress.

INTERNET ASSIGNMENT FOR ARGUMENTATION:
Does Media Violence Cause Societal Violence?

Write an essay in which you argue for or against holding the television and movie industries responsible for violence in our society. Use the following World Wide Web sites to explore the two viewpoints and their implications.

National Coalition on Television Violence
<http://www.nctvv.org>
The nonprofit organization sponsoring this site seeks to reduce the amount of gratuitous violence on television.

Culture Shock
<http://www.pbs.org/wgbh/cultureshock/index_1.html>
This companion site to the PBS series *Culture Shock* deals with art, cultural values, and freedom of expression in the arts.

Center for Educational Priorities
<http://www.cep.org/index.html>

This educational site "track[s] the powerful influences of television, media and telecommunications policy as they affect children and the learning process."

INTERNET ASSIGNMENT FOR ARGUMENTATION: Should We Live Together or Apart?

Does ethnic-theme housing undermine the efforts toward racial equality made by the struggle for integration? Or does it promote equality by allowing minority students to maintain their own ethnic and cultural identity within the larger culture of which they are a part? Write an essay in which you argue either that ethnic-theme housing promotes racial equality or that it prevents racial equality. Visit the following World Wide Web sites to learn about African-American identity and the struggle for integration.

Lessons of a Century: Struggles for Integration
<http://www.edweek.org/ew/vol-18/28intro.h18>
This article first appeared in the March 1999 issue of *Education Week*.

African-American History
<http://www.watson.org/~lisa/blackhistory/school-integration>
This site offers information about the history of school integration, as well as the Dred Scott Case, early civil rights struggles, and the Civil Rights movement of the 1950s and 1960s.

Beyond the Nationalism of Fools: Toward an Agenda for Black Intellectuals
<http://www-polisci.mit.edu/BostonReview/BR20.3/rivers.html>
This article by Eugene F. Rivers originally appeared in the *Boston Review*.

Philadelphia: Black Nationalism on Campus
<http://www.theatlantic.com/politics/race/lemann.htm>
In this article, which appeared in the *Atlantic Monthly* in 1993, author Nicholas Lemann cites conversations with students at the University of Pennsylvania and Temple University to show that the goals of black nationalism and assimilation are not inconsistent.

INTERNET ASSIGNMENT FOR ARGUMENTATION: Is the Internet Good for Society?

Assume that you are the president of a major corporation and have been asked to address the "digital divide" issue at a conference on the social responsibilities of business enterprises. You are aware of the federal government's initiatives to give more people Internet access, but you also realize that many observers believe access alone will not solve the problem. Your speech should address what you see as the underlying causes of the divide and what corporations can and should do to help. Visit the following World Wide Web sites to get more information about the digital divide and about how the business world could help narrow the gap.

The Digital Divide Network
<http://www.digitaldividenetwork.org/initiatives.adp>
This site contains digital divide news, research and data, and information about initiatives by corporations, nonprofit organizations, and government.

Digital Divide
<http://www.pbs.org/digitaldivide>
This is the site of a PBS television series that focuses on the effects of the digital divide — on education, employment, race, and gender.

The Civil Rights Forum
<http://www.civilrightsforum.org/home.htm>
The Civil Rights Forum contains articles and speeches, research, and information about community programs to educate community groups about the media.

13

COMBINING
THE PATTERNS

Few essays follow a single pattern of development; in fact, nearly every essay, including those in this text, combines a variety of patterns. Even though an essay may be organized primarily as, say, a comparison and contrast, it is still likely to include sentences, paragraphs, and even groups of paragraphs shaped by other patterns of development. In fact, combining various patterns in a single essay gives writers the flexibility to express their ideas most effectively. (For this reason, every essay in Chapters 4 through 12 of this text is followed by Combining the Patterns questions that focus on how the essay uses other patterns of development along with its dominant pattern.)

STRUCTURING AN ESSAY BY COMBINING THE PATTERNS

Essays that combine various patterns of development, like essays structured by a single pattern, include an introductory paragraph, several body paragraphs, and a concluding paragraph. The introduction typically ends with the thesis statement that gives the essay its focus, and the conclusion often restates that thesis or summarizes the essay's main points. Each body paragraph is structured according to the pattern of development that best suits the material it develops.

Suppose you are planning your answer to the following question on a take-home essay exam for a sociology of religion course:

What factors attract people to cults? For what reasons do they join? Support your answer with specific examples that illustrate how cults recruit and retain members.

The wording of this exam question clearly suggests both **cause and effect** ("for what reasons") and **exemplification** ("specific examples"); in addition, you may decide to develop your response with **definition** and **process.**

An informal outline for your essay might look like this:

Introduction:	Definition of *cult* (defined by negation and by comparison and contrast with *religion*). Thesis statement: Using aggressive recruitment tactics and isolating potential members from their families and past lives, cults appeal to new recruits by offering them a highly structured environment.
Cause and effect:	Why people join cults
Process:	How cults recruit new members
Exemplification:	Tactics cults use to retain members (series of brief examples)
Conclusion:	Restatement of thesis or review of key points

This essay will supply all the information the exam question asks for, with material organized and developed clearly and logically.

The essays in this chapter illustrate how different patterns of development work together in a single piece of writing. The first two essays — "The Park" by Michael Huu Truong, a student, and "On Dumpster Diving" by Lars Eighner — include annotations that identify the various patterns these writers use. Truong's essay relies primarily on narration, description, and exemplification to express his memories of childhood. Eighner's combines sections of definition, exemplification, classification and division, cause and effect, comparison and contrast, and process; at the same time, he tells the story (narration) and provides vivid details (description) of his life as a homeless person. Following these annotated essays are two additional selections that combine patterns: Jonathan Swift's classic satire "A Modest Proposal" and Alice Walker's contemporary essay "In Search of Our Mothers' Gardens." Each of the essays in this chapter is followed by the same types of questions that accompany the other reading selections in the text.

▶ A STUDENT WRITER: COMBINING THE PATTERNS

This essay was written by Michael Huu Truong for a first-year composition course in response to the assignment "Write an essay about the person and/or place that defined your childhood."

The Park

Background   My childhood did not really begin until   1
thirteen years ago, when I first came to this
country from the rural jungle of Vietnam. I
can't really remember much from this period,
and the things I do remember are vague images
that I have no desire or intention to discuss.
However, my childhood in the States was a lot

different, especially after I met my friend
James. While it lasted, it was paradise.

Thesis statement

Narrative begins

It was a cold wintry day in February after   2
a big snowstorm--the first I'd ever seen. My

Description: effects of cold

lips were chapped, my hands were frozen stiff,
and my cheeks were burning from the biting
wind, and yet I loved it. I especially loved

Comparison and contrast: U.S. vs. Vietnam

the snow. I had come from a country where the
closest things to snow were white paint and
cotton balls. But now, I was in America. On that
frosty afternoon, I was determined to build a
snowman. I had seen them in books, and I had
heard they could talk. I knew they could come
alive, and I couldn't wait.

"Eyryui roeow ierog," said a voice that   3

Description: James

came out of nowhere. I turned around, and right
in my face was a short, red-faced (probably
from the cold wind) Korean kid with a dirty,
runny nose. I responded, "Wtefkjkr ruyjft gsdfr"
in my own tongue. We understood each other perfectly, and we expressed our understanding with

Narration: the first day

a smile. Together, we built our first snowman.
We were disappointed that evening when the
snowman just stood there; however, I was happy
because I had made my first friend.

Analogies

Ever since then we've been a team like   4
Abbott and Costello (or, when my cousin joined
us, The Three Stooges). The two of us were inseparable. We could've made the greatest Krazy
Glue commercial ever.

Narration: what they did that summer

The summer that followed the big snow-   5
storm, from what I can recall, was awesome. We
were free like comets in the heavens, and we
did whatever our hearts wanted. For the most
part, our desires were fulfilled in a little
park across the street. This park was ours; it
was like our own planet guarded by our own
robot army (disguised as trees). Together we
fought against the bigger people who always

tried to invade and take over our world. The
enemy could never conquer our fortress because
they would have to destroy our robots, pene-
trate our force field, and then defeat us; this
last feat would be impossible.

Narrative
continues

    This park was our fantasy land where every-   6
thing we wished for came true and everything we
hated was banished forever. We banished vegeta-

Examples: what
they banished

bles, cheese, bigger people, and--of course--
girls. The land was enchanted, and we could be
whatever we felt like. We were super ninjas one
day and millionaires the next; we became the
heroes we idolized and lived the lives we

Examples: super-
hero fantasies

dreamed about. I had the strength of Bruce Lee
and Superman; James possessed the power of
Clint Eastwood and the Bionic Man. My weapons
were the skills of Bruce and a cape. James,
however, needed a real weapon for Clint, and
the weapon he made was awesome. The Death Ray
could destroy a building with one blast, and it
even had a shield so James was always protected.
Even with all his mighty weapons and gadgets,
though, he was still no match for Superman and
Bruce Lee. Every day, we fought until death (or
until our parents called us for dinner).

Narrative
continues

    When we became bored with our super pow-   7
ers, the park became a giant spaceship. We
traveled all over the Universe, conquering and
exploring strange new worlds and mysterious

Examples:
new worlds
and planets

planets. Our ship was a top secret, indestructible space warship called the X-007. We went
to Mars, Venus, Pluto, and other alien planets,
destroying all the monsters we could find. When
necessary, our spacecraft was transformed into
a submarine for deep-sea adventures. We found
lost cities, unearthed treasures, and saved
Earth by destroying all the sea monsters that
were plotting against us. We became heroes--
just like Superman, Bruce Lee, the Bionic Man,
and Clint Eastwood.

Cause and effect: prospect of school leads to problems

James and I had the time of our lives in the park that summer. It was great--until we heard about the horror of starting school. Shocked and terrified, we ran to our fortress to escape. For some reason, though, our magic kingdom had lost its powers. We fought hard that evening, trying to keep the bigger people out of our planet, but the battle was soon lost. Bruce Lee, Superman, the Bionic Man, and Clint Eastwood had all lost their special powers.   8

Narrative continues

School wasn't as bad as we'd thought it would be. The first day, James and I sat there with our hands folded. We didn't talk or move, and we didn't dare look at each other (we would've cracked up because we always made these goofy faces). Even though we had pens that could be transformed into weapons, we were still scared.   9

Description: school

Everyone was darker or lighter than we were, and the teacher was speaking a strange language (English). James and I giggled as she talked. We giggled softly when everyone else talked, and they laughed out loud when it was our turn to speak.   10

Narrative continues

The day dragged on, and all we wanted to do was go home and rebuild our fortress. Finally, after an eternity, it was almost three o'clock. James and I sat at the edge of our seats as we counted under our breath: "10, 9, 8, 7, 6, 5, 4, 3, 2, 1." At last the bell sounded. We dashed for the door and raced home and across the street--and then we stopped. We stood still in the middle of the street with our hearts pounding like the beats of a drum. The cool September wind began to pick up, and everything became silent. We stood there and   11

Description: the fence

watched the metal of the fence reflect the beautiful colors of the sun. It was beautiful, and yet we hated everything about it. The new

```
metal fence separated us from our fortress, our
planet, our spaceship, our submarine--and, most
important of all, our heroes and our dreams.
       We stood there for a long time. As the sun        12
slowly turned red and sank beneath the ground,
so did our dreams, heroes, and hearts. Darkness
soon devoured the park, and after a while we
walked home with only the memories of the sum-
mer that came after the big snowstorm.
```

Points for Special Attention

WRITING A PERSONAL EXPERIENCE ESSAY.   Michael's assignment specified that he was to write an essay about an experience that would help his readers — other students — understand what his childhood was like. Because it was a personal experience essay, Michael was free to use the first-person pronouns *I* and *we* as well as contractions, neither of which would be acceptable in a more formal essay.

THESIS STATEMENT.   Because Michael's primary purpose in this essay was to communicate personal feelings and impressions, an argumentative thesis statement (such as "If every television in the United States disappeared, more people would have childhoods like mine") would have been inappropriate. Still, Michael states his thesis explicitly in order to unify his essay around the dominant impression he wants to convey: "While it lasted, it was paradise."

COMBINING THE PATTERNS.   Michael also had more specific purposes, and these determined the patterns that shape his essay. His essay's dominant pattern is *narration,* but to help students visualize the person (James) and the place (the park) he discusses, he includes sections that *describe* and give concrete, specific *examples* as well as summarize his daily routine. These patterns work together to create an essay that *defines* the nature of his childhood.

TRANSITIONS.   The transitions between the individual sentences and paragraphs of Michael's essay — "now," "Ever since," "The summer that followed the big snowstorm" — serve primarily to move readers through time. This is appropriate because narration is the dominant pattern governing his essay's overall structure.

DETAIL.   Michael's essay is full of specific detail — for example, quoted bits of dialogue in paragraph 3 and names of his heroes and of particular games (and related equipment and weapons) elsewhere. The descriptive details that recreate the physical scenes — in particular, the snow, cold, frost, and wind of winter and the sun reflected in the fence — are vivid enough to help readers visualize the places Michael writes about.

FIGURATIVE LANGUAGE.   Michael's essay describes a time when his imagination wandered without the restraints of adulthood. Appropriately, he uses rich figurative language — "We were free like comets in the heavens"; "The park became a giant spaceship"; "We found lost cities, unearthed treasures, and saved Earth"; "darkness soon devoured the park" — to evoke the time and place he describes.

Focus on Revision

Michael's assignment asked him to write about his childhood, and he chose to focus on his early years in the United States. When his peer editing group discussed his essay, however, a number of students were curious about his life in Vietnam. Some of them thought he should add a paragraph summarizing the "vague images" he remembered of his earlier childhood, perhaps contrasting it with his life in the United States, as he does in passing in paragraph 2. An alternate suggestion, made by one classmate, was that Michael consider deleting the sentence that states he has "no desire or intention" to discuss this part of his life, since it raises issues his essay doesn't address. After thinking about these ideas, Michael decided to revise his essay by adding a brief paragraph about his life in Vietnam, contrasting the park and his friendship with James to some of his earlier memories.

Each of the following essays combines several patterns, blending strategies to achieve the writer's purpose.

LARS EIGHNER

Lars Eighner (1948–) dropped out of the University of Texas at Austin after his third year and took a job at a state mental hospital. After leaving his job over a policy dispute in 1988 and falling behind in his rent payments, Eighner became homeless. For three years he traveled between Austin and Los Angeles with his dog, Lizbeth, earning what money he could from writing stories for magazines. Eighner's memories of his experiences living on the street, *Travels with Lizbeth* (1993), was written on a personal computer he found in a Dumpster. The following chapter from that book details the practical dangers as well as the many possibilities he discovered in his "Dumpster diving." (Eighner now lives in Austin and operates an online writing course at <www.io.com/~eighner/wrtmain.html#ga>.)

Although the number of homeless is difficult to measure accurately, homelessness has become a highly visible issue over the last two decades. It is estimated, for example, that as many as ten million people experienced homelessness in this country in the late 1980s alone. There were a number of causes for this surge in homelessness. Perhaps most important, a booming real estate market led to a significant drop in affordable housing in many areas of the country. In a number of cities, single-room-occupancy hotels, which had long provided cheap lodging, were being demolished or converted into luxury apartments. At the same time, new technologies left many unskilled workers jobless. Government policies against detaining the nondangerous mentally ill against their will also played a significant role. (About a quarter of all homeless people are thought to be mentally ill.) Although Eighner seems almost perversely to have chosen his homelessness, many homeless people — particularly the 38 percent who are families with children — have no other options.

On Dumpster Diving

This chapter was composed while the author was homeless. The present tense has been preserved.

Definition:
Dumpster

Long before I began Dumpster diving I was impressed with Dumpsters, enough so that I wrote the Merriam-Webster research service to discover what I could about the word *Dumpster*. I learned from them that it is a proprietary word belonging to the Dempsey Dumpster company. Since then I have dutifully capitalized the word, although it was lowercased in almost all the citations Merriam-Webster photocopied for me. Dempsey's word is too apt. I have never heard these things called anything but Dumpsters. I do not know anyone who knows the generic name for these objects. From time to time I have heard a wino or hobo give some corrupted credit to the original and call them Dipsy Dumpsters.

1

Narration:
Eighner's story
begins

Definition: *diving*

I began Dumpster diving about a year before I 2
became homeless.

I prefer the word *scavenging* and use the word 3
scrounging when I mean to be obscure. I have heard
people, evidently meaning to be polite, use the word
foraging, but I prefer to reserve that word for gathering
nuts and berries and such, which I do also according to
the season and the opportunity. *Dumpster diving* seems
to me to be a little too cute and, in my case, inaccurate
because I lack the athletic ability to lower myself into
the Dumpsters as the true divers do, much to their
increased profit.

I like the frankness of the word *scavenging,* which I 4
can hardly think of without picturing a big black snail
on an aquarium wall. I live from the refuse of others. I
am a scavenger. I think it a sound and honorable niche,
although if I could I would naturally prefer to live the
comfortable consumer life, perhaps — and only perhaps — as a slightly less wasteful consumer, owing to
what I have learned as a scavenger.

Narration:
story continues

While Lizbeth and I were still living in the shack 5
on Avenue B as my savings ran out, I put almost all my
sporadic income into rent. The necessities of daily life I
began to extract from Dumpsters. Yes, we ate from
them. Except for jeans, all my clothes came from Dump-

Exemplification:
things found in
Dumpsters

sters. Boom boxes, candles, bedding, toilet paper, a
virgin male love doll, medicine, books, a typewriter,
dishes, furnishings, and change, sometimes amount-
ing to many dollars — I acquired many things from
Dumpsters.

Thesis statement

I have learned much as a scavenger. I mean to put 6
some of what I have learned down here, beginning
with the practical art of Dumpster diving and proceeding to the abstract.

What is safe to eat? 7

After all, the finding of objects is becoming some- 8
thing of an urban art. Even respectable employed
people will sometimes find something tempting sticking out of a Dumpster or standing beside one. Quite a
number of people, not all of them of the bohemian
type, are willing to brag that they found this or that
piece of trash. But eating from Dumpsters is what separates the dilettanti from the professionals. Eating
safely from the Dumpsters involves three principles:
using the senses and common sense to evaluate the

condition of the found materials, knowing the Dumpsters of a given area and checking them regularly, and seeking always to answer the question "Why was this discarded?"

Comparison and contrast: Dumpster divers vs. others

Perhaps everyone who has a kitchen and a regular supply of groceries has, at one time or another, made a sandwich and eaten half of it before discovering mold on the bread or got a mouthful of milk before realizing the milk had turned. Nothing of the sort is likely to happen to a Dumpster diver because he is constantly reminded that most food is discarded for a reason. Yet a lot of perfectly good food can be found in Dumpsters.   9

Classification and division: different kinds of food found in Dumpsters and their relative safety

Canned goods, for example, turn up fairly often in the Dumpsters I frequent. All except the most phobic people will be willing to eat from a can, even if it came from a Dumpster. Canned goods are among the safest foods to be found in Dumpsters but are not utterly foolproof.   10

Although very rare with modern canning methods, botulism is a possibility. Most other forms of food poisoning seldom do lasting harm to a healthy person, but botulism is almost certainly fatal and often the first symptom is death. Except for carbonated beverages, all canned goods should contain a slight vacuum and suck air when first punctured. Bulging, rusty, and dented cans and cans that spew when punctured should be avoided, especially when the contents are not very acidic or syrupy.   11

Heat can break down the botulin, but this requires much more cooking than most people do to canned goods. To the extent that botulism occurs at all, of course, it can occur in cans on pantry shelves as well as in cans from Dumpsters. Need I say that home-canned goods are simply too risky to be recommended.   12

From time to time one of my companions, aware of the source of my provisions, will ask, "Do you think these crackers are really safe to eat?" For some reason it is most often the crackers they ask about.   13

This question has always made me angry. Of course I would not offer my companion anything I had doubts about. But more than that, I wonder why he cannot evaluate the condition of the crackers for himself. I have no special knowledge and I have been wrong before. Since he knows where the food comes from, it seems to me he ought to assume some of the   14 responsibility for deciding what he will put in his mouth. For myself I have few qualms about dry foods such as crackers, cookies, cereal, chips, and pasta if they are free of visible contaminates and still dry and crisp. Most often such things are found in the original packaging, which is not so much a positive sign as it is the absence of a negative one.

Raw fruits and vegetables with intact skins seem   15
perfectly safe to me, excluding of course the obviously rotten. Many are discarded for minor imperfections that can be pared away. Leafy vegetables, grapes, cauliflower, broccoli, and similar things may be contaminated by liquids and may be impractical to wash.

Candy, especially hard candy, is usually safe if it   16
has not drawn ants. Chocolate is often discarded only because it has become discolored as the cocoa butter de-emulsified. Candying, after all, is one method of food preservation because pathogens do not like very sugary substances.

All of these foods might be found in any Dumpster   17
and can be evaluated with some confidence largely on the basis of appearance. Beyond these are foods that cannot be correctly evaluated without additional information.

I began scavenging by pulling pizzas out of the   18
Dumpster behind a pizza delivery shop. In general, prepared food requires caution, but in this case I knew when the shop closed and went to the Dumpster as soon as the last of the help left.

Such shops often get prank orders; both the orders   19
and the products made to fill them are called *bogus.* Because help seldom stays long at these places, pizzas are often made with the wrong topping, refused on delivery for being cold, or baked incorrectly. The products to be discarded are boxed up because inventory is kept by counting boxes: A boxed pizza can be written off; an unboxed pizza does not exist.

I never placed a bogus order to increase the supply   20
of pizzas and I believe no one else was scavenging in this Dumpster. But the people in the shop became suspicious and began to retain their garbage in the shop overnight. While it lasted I had a steady supply of fresh, sometimes warm pizza. Because I knew the Dumpster I knew the source of the pizza, and because I visited the Dumpster regularly I knew what was fresh and what was yesterday's.

Cause and effect:
why Eighner
visits certain
Dumpsters; why
students throw
out food

The area I frequent is inhabited by many affluent   21
college students. I am not here by chance; the Dumpsters in this area are very rich. Students throw out
many good things, including food. In particular they
tend to throw everything out when they move at the
end of a semester, before and after breaks, and around
midterm, when many of them despair of college. So I
find it advantageous to keep an eye on the academic
calendar.

Students throw food away around breaks because   22
they do not know whether it has spoiled or will spoil
before they return. A typical discard is a half jar of
peanut butter. In fact, nonorganic peanut butter does
not require refrigeration and is unlikely to spoil in
any reasonable time. The student does not know that,
and since it is Daddy's money, the student decides not
to take a chance. Opened containers require caution and some attention to the question "Why was this
discarded?" But in the case of discards from student
apartments, the answer may be that the item was
thrown out through carelessness, ignorance, or wastefulness. This can sometimes be deduced when the item
is found with many others, including some that are
obviously perfectly good.

Some students, and others, approach defrosting a   23
freezer by chucking out the whole lot. Not only do the
circumstances of such a find tell the story, but also the
mass of frozen goods stays cold for a long time and
items may be found still frozen or freshly thawed.

Yogurt, cheese, and sour cream are items that are   24
often thrown out while they are still good. Occasionally I find cheese with a spot of mold, which of course
I just pare off, and because it is obvious why such
a cheese was discarded, I treat it with less suspicion
than an apparently perfect cheese found in similar circumstances. Yogurt is often discarded, still sealed, only
because the expiration date on the carton had passed.
This is one of my favorite finds because yogurt will
keep for several days, even in warm weather.

Students throw out canned goods and staples at   25
the end of semesters and when they give up college at
midterm. Drugs, pornography, spirits, and the like are
often discarded when parents are expected — Dad's
Day, for example. And spirits also turn up after big
party weekends, presumably discarded by the newly
reformed. Wine and spirits, of course, keep perfectly

well even once opened, but the same cannot be said of beer.

My test for carbonated soft drinks is whether they 26
still fizz vigorously. Many juices or other beverages are too acidic or too syrupy to cause much concern, provided they are not visibly contaminated. I have discovered nasty molds in the vegetable juices, even when the product was found under its original seal; I recommend that such products be decanted slowly into a clear glass. Liquids always require some care. One hot day I found a large jug of Pat O'Brien's Hurricane mix. The jug had been opened but was still ice cold. I drank three large glasses before it became apparent to me that someone had added the rum to the mix, and not a little rum. I never tasted the rum, and by the time I began to feel the effects I had already ingested a very large quantity of the beverage. Some divers would have considered this a boon, but being suddenly intoxicated in a public place in the early afternoon is not my idea of a good time.

Example: a liquid that requires care

I have heard of people maliciously contaminating 27
discarded food and even handouts, but mostly I have heard of this from people with vivid imaginations who have had no experience with Dumpsters themselves. Just before the pizza shop stopped discarding its garbage at night, jalapeños began showing up on most of the thrown-out pizzas. If indeed this was meant to discourage me, it was a wasted effort because I am a native Texan.

For myself, I avoid game, poultry, pork, and egg- 28
based foods, whether I find them raw or cooked. I seldom have the means to cook what I find, but when I do I avail myself of plentiful supplies of beef, which is often in very good condition. I suppose fish becomes disagreeable before it becomes dangerous. Lizbeth is happy to have any such thing that is past its prime and, in fact, does not recognize fish as food until it is quite strong.

Home leftovers, as opposed to surpluses from 29
restaurants, are very often bad. Evidently, especially among students, there is a common type of personality that carefully wraps up even the smallest leftover and shoves it into the back of the refrigerator for six months or so before discarding it. Characteristic of this type are the reused jars and margarine tubs to which the remains are committed. I avoid ethnic foods I am

unfamiliar with. If I do not know what it is supposed to look like when it is good, I cannot be certain I will be able to tell if it is bad.

No matter how careful I am I still get dysentery at least once a month, oftener in warmer weather. I do not want to paint too romantic a picture. Dumpster diving has serious drawbacks as a way of life. 30

Process: how to scavenge

I learned to scavenge gradually, on my own. Since then I have initiated several companions into the trade. I have learned that there is a predictable series of stages a person goes through in learning to scavenge. 31

At first the new scavenger is filled with disgust and self-loathing. He is ashamed of being seen and may lurk around, trying to duck behind things, or he may try to dive at night. (In fact, most people instinctively look away from a scavenger. By skulking around, the novice calls attention to himself and arouses suspicion. Diving at night is ineffective and needlessly messy.) 32

Every grain of rice seems to be a maggot. Everything seems to stink. He can wipe the egg yolk off the found can, but he cannot erase from his mind the stigma of eating garbage. 33

That stage passes with experience. The scavenger finds a pair of running shoes that fit and look and smell brand-new. He finds a pocket calculator in perfect working order. He finds pristine ice cream, still frozen, more than he can eat or keep. He begins to understand: People throw away perfectly good stuff, a lot of perfectly good stuff. 34

At this stage, Dumpster shyness begins to dissipate. The diver, after all, has the last laugh. He is finding all manner of good things that are his for the taking. Those who disparage his profession are the fools, not he. 35

He may begin to hang on to some perfectly good things for which he has neither a use nor a market. Then he begins to take note of the things that are not perfectly good but are nearly so. He mates a Walkman with broken earphones and one that is missing a battery cover. He picks up things that he can repair. 36

At this stage he may become lost and never recover. Dumpsters are full of things of some potential value to someone and also of things that never have much intrinsic value but are interesting. All the Dump- 37 ster divers I have known come to the point of trying to acquire everything they touch. Why not take it, they reason, since it is all free? This is, of course, hopeless. Most divers come to realize that they must restrict themselves to items of relatively immediate utility. But in some cases the diver simply cannot control himself. I have met several of these pack-rat types. Their ideas of the values of various pieces of junk verge on the psychotic. Every bit of glass may be a diamond, they think, and all that glisters,* gold.

Cause and effect: why Eighner gains weight when he scavenges

I tend to gain weight when I am scavenging. Partly this is because I always find far more pizza and dough-nuts than water-packed tuna, nonfat yogurt, and fresh vegetables. Also I have not developed much faith in the reliability of Dumpsters as a food source, although it has been proven to me many times. I tend to eat as if I have no idea where my next meal is coming from. But mostly I just hate to see food go to waste and so I eat much more than I should. Something like this drives the obsession to collect junk.   38

Cause and effect: why Eighner collects junk

As for collecting objects, I usually restrict myself to collecting one kind of small object at a time, such as pocket calculators, sunglasses, or campaign buttons. To live on the street I must anticipate my needs to a cer-tain extent: I must pick up and save warm bedding I find in August because it will not be found in Dump-sters in November. As I have no access to health care, I often hoard essential drugs, such as antibiotics and antihistamines. (This course can be recommended only to those with some grounding in pharmacology. Anti-biotics, for example, even when indicated are worse than useless if taken in insufficient amounts.) But even if I had a home with extensive storage space, I could not save everything that might be valuable in some contingency.   39

Comparison and contrast: Dumpsters in rich and poorer areas

I have proprietary feelings about my Dumpsters. As I have mentioned, it is no accident that I scavenge from ones where good finds are common. But my lim-ited experience with Dumpsters in other areas sug-gests to me that even in poorer areas, Dumpsters, if attended with sufficient diligence, can be made to yield a livelihood. The rich students discard perfectly good kiwi fruit; poorer people discard perfectly good apples. Slacks and Polo shirts are found in one place;   40

*EDS. NOTE — Glitters.

jeans and T-shirts in the other. The population of competitors rather than the affluence of the dumpers most affects the feasibility of survival by scavenging. The large number of competitors is what puts me off the idea of trying to scavenge in places like Los Angeles.

Curiously, I do not mind my direct competition, other scavengers, so much as I hate the can scroungers.

Cause and effect: why people scrounge cans

People scrounge cans because they have to have a little cash. I have tried scrounging cans with an able-bodied companion. Afoot a can scrounger simply cannot make more than a few dollars in a day. One can extract the necessities of life from the Dumpsters directly with far less effort than would be required to accumulate the equivalent value in cans. (These observations may not hold in places with container redemption laws.)

Can scroungers, then, are people who must have small amounts of cash. These are drug addicts and winos, mostly the latter because the amounts of cash are so small. Spirits and drugs do, like all other commodities, turn up in Dumpsters and the scavenger will from time to time have a half bottle of a rather good wine with his dinner. But the wino cannot survive on these occasional finds; he must have his daily dose to stave off the DTs. All the cans he can carry will buy about three bottles of Wild Irish Rose.

I do not begrudge them the cans, but can scroungers tend to tear up the Dumpsters, mixing the contents and littering the area. They become so specialized that they can see only cans. They earn my contempt by passing up change, canned goods, and readily hockable items.

There are precious few courtesies among scavengers. But it is common practice to set aside surplus items: pairs of shoes, clothing, canned goods, and such.

Comparison and contrast: can scroungers vs. true scavengers

A true scavenger hates to see good stuff go to waste, and what he cannot use he leaves in good condition in plain sight.

Can scroungers lay waste to everything in their path and will stir one of a pair of good shoes to the bottom of a Dumpster, to be lost or ruined in the muck. Can scroungers will even go through individual garbage cans, something I have never seen a scavenger do.

Individual garbage cans are set out on the public easement only on garbage days. On the other days

41

42

43

44

45

46

47

Cause and effect: why scavengers do not go through individual garbage cans

going through them requires trespassing close to a dwelling. Going through individual garbage cans without scattering litter is almost impossible. Litter is likely to reduce the public's tolerance of scavenging. Individual cans are simply not as productive as Dumpsters; people in houses and duplexes do not move so often and for some reason do not tend to discard as much useful material. Moreover, the time required to go through one garbage can that serves one household is not much less than the time required to go through a Dumpster that contains the refuse of twenty apartments.

But my strongest reservation about going through 48 individual garbage cans is that this seems to me a very personal kind of invasion to which I would object if I were a householder. Although many things in Dumpsters are obviously meant never to come to light, a Dumpster is somehow less personal.

I avoid trying to draw conclusions about the 49 people who dump in the Dumpsters I frequent. I think it would be unethical to do so, although I know many people will find the idea of scavenger ethics too funny for words.

Examples: things found in Dumpsters

Dumpsters contain bank statements, correspon- 50 dence, and other documents, just as anyone might expect. But there are also less obvious sources of information. Pill bottles, for example. The labels bear the name of the patient, the name of the doctor, and the name of the drug. AIDS drugs and antipsychotic medicines, to name but two groups, are specific and are seldom prescribed for any other disorders. The plastic compacts for birth-control pills usually have complete label information.

Despite all of this sensitive information, I have 51 had only one apartment resident object to my going through the Dumpster. In that case it turned out the resident was a university athlete who was taking bets and who was afraid I would turn up his wager slips.

Occasionally a find tells a story. I once found a 52 small paper bag containing some unused condoms, several partial tubes of flavored sexual lubricants, a partially used compact of birth-control pills, and the torn pieces of a picture of a young man. Clearly she was through with him and planning to give up sex altogether.

Dumpster things are often sad — abandoned teddy 53
bears, shredded wedding books, despaired-of sales
kits. I find many pets lying in state in Dumpsters.
Although I hope to get off the streets so that Lizbeth
can have a long and comfortable old age, I know this
hope is not very realistic. So I suppose when her time
comes she too will go into a Dumpster. I will have no
better place for her. And after all, it is fitting, since for
most of her life her livelihood has come from the
Dumpster. When she finds something I think is safe
that has been spilled from a Dumpster, I let her have it.
She already knows the route around the best ones. I
like to think that if she survives me she will have a
chance of evading the dog catcher and of finding her
sustenance on the route.

Silly vanities also come to rest in the Dumpsters. I 54
am a rather accomplished needleworker. I get a lot of
material from the Dumpsters. Evidently sorority girls,
hoping to impress someone, perhaps themselves, with
their mastery of a womanly art, buy a lot of embroider-
by-number kits, work a few stitches horribly, and
eventually discard the whole mess. I pull out their
stitches, turn the canvas over, and work an original
design. Do not think I refrain from chuckling as I make
gifts from these kits.

I find diaries and journals. I have often thought of 55
compiling a book of literary found objects. And perhaps I will one day. But what I find is hopelessly commonplace and bad without being, even unconsciously,
camp. College students also discard their papers. I am
horrified to discover the kind of paper that now merits
an A in an undergraduate course. I am grateful, however, for the number of good books and magazines the
students throw out.

In the area I know best I have never discovered 56
vermin in the Dumpster, but there are two kinds of
kitty surprise. One is alley cats whom I meet as they
leap, claws first, out of Dumpsters. This is especially
thrilling when I have Lizbeth in tow. The other kind of
kitty surprise is a plastic garbage bag filled with some
ponderous, amorphous mass. This always proves to be
used cat litter.

City bees harvest doughnut glaze and this makes 57
the Dumpster at the doughnut shop more interesting.
My faith in the instinctive wisdom of animals is always
shaken whenever I see Lizbeth attempt to catch a bee

in her mouth, which she does whenever bees are present. Evidently some birds find Dumpsters profitable, for birdie surprise is almost as common as kitty surprise of the first kind. In hunting season all kinds of small game turn up in Dumpsters, some of it, sadly, not entirely dead. Curiously, summer and winter, maggots are uncommon.

The worst of the living and near-living hazards of   58
the Dumpsters are the fire ants. The food they claim is not much of a loss, but they are vicious and aggressive. It is very easy to brush against some surface of the Dumpster and pick up half a dozen or more fire ants, usually in some sensitive area such as the underarm. One advantage of bringing Lizbeth along as I make Dumpster rounds is that, for obvious reasons, she is very alert to ground-based fire ants. When Lizbeth recognizes a fire-ant infestation around our feet, she does the Dance of the Zillion Fire Ants. I have learned not to ignore this warning from Lizbeth, whether I perceive the tiny ants or not, but to remove ourselves at Lizbeth's first *pas de bourée*.* All the more so because the ants are the worst in the summer months when I wear flip-flops if I have them. (Perhaps someone will misunderstand this. Lizbeth does the Dance of the Zillion Fire Ants when she recognizes more fire ants than she cares to eat, not when she is being bitten. Since I have learned to react promptly, she does not get bitten at all. It is the isolated patrol of fire ants that falls in Lizbeth's range that deserves pity. She finds them quite tasty.)

Process: how
to go through
a Dumpster

By far the best way to go through a Dumpster is to   59
lower yourself into it. Most of the good stuff tends to settle at the bottom because it is usually weightier than the rubbish. My more athletic companions have often demonstrated to me that they can extract much good material from a Dumpster I have already been over.

To those psychologically or physically unprepared   60
to enter a Dumpster, I recommend a stout stick, preferably with some barb or hook at one end. The hook can be used to grab plastic garbage bags. When I find canned goods or other objects loose at the bottom of a Dumpster, I lower a bag into it, roll the desired object into the bag, and then hoist the bag out — a procedure more easily described than executed. Much Dumpster

---

*EDS. NOTE — A ballet step.

diving is a matter of experience for which nothing will do except practice.

61 Dumpster diving is outdoor work, often surprisingly pleasant. It is not entirely predictable; things of interest turn up every day and some days there are finds of great value. I am always very pleased when I can turn up exactly the thing I most wanted to find. Yet in spite of the element of chance, scavenging more than most other pursuits tends to yield returns in some proportion to the effort and intelligence brought to bear. It is very sweet to turn up a few dollars in change from a Dumpster that has just been gone over by a wino.

62 The land is now covered with cities. The cities are full of Dumpsters. If a member of the canine race is ever able to know what it is doing, then Lizbeth knows that when we go around to the Dumpsters, we are hunting. I think of scavenging as a modern form of self-reliance. In any event, after having survived nearly ten years of government service, where everything is geared to the lowest common denominator, I find it refreshing to have work that rewards initiative and effort. Certainly I would be happy to have a sinecure again, but I am no longer heartbroken that I left one.

Cause and effect: results of Eighner's experiences as a scavenger

63 I find from the experience of scavenging two rather deep lessons. The first is to take what you can use and let the rest go by. I have come to think that there is no value in the abstract. A thing I cannot use or make useful, perhaps by trading, has no value however rare or fine it may be. I mean useful in some broad sense — some art I would find useful and some otherwise.

64 I was shocked to realize that some things are not worth acquiring, but now I think it is so. Some material things are white elephants that eat up the possessor's substance. The second lesson is the transience of material being. This has not quite converted me to a dualist,* but it has made some headway in that direction. I do not suppose that ideas are immortal, but certainly mental things are longer lived than other material things.

65 Once I was the sort of person who invests objects with sentimental value. Now I no longer have those objects, but I have the sentiments yet.

*EDS. NOTE — Someone who believes the world consists of two opposing forces, such as mind and matter.

Many times in our travels I have lost everything 66
but the clothes I was wearing and Lizbeth. The things I
find in Dumpsters, the love letters and rag dolls of so
many lives, remind me of this lesson. Now I hardly
pick up a thing without envisioning the time I will cast
it aside. This I think is a healthy state of mind. Almost
everything I have now has already been cast out at
least once, proving that what I own is valueless to
someone.

Anyway, I find my desire to grab for the gaudy 67
bauble has been largely sated. I think this is an attitude
I share with the very wealthy — we both know there is
plenty more where what we have came from. Between
us are the rat-race millions who nightly scavenge the
cable channels looking for they know not what.

I am sorry for them. 68

• • •

COMPREHENSION

1. In your own words, give a formal definition of *Dumpster diving.*

2. List some of Eighner's answers to the question "Why was this discarded?" (8). What additional reasons can you think of?

3. What foods does Eighner take particular care to avoid? Why?

4. In paragraph 30, Eighner comments, "Dumpster diving has serious drawbacks as a way of life." What drawbacks does he cite in his essay? What additional drawbacks are implied?

5. Summarize the stages in the process of learning to scavenge.

6. In addition to food, what else does Eighner scavenge for? Into what general categories do these items fall?

7. Why does Eighner hate can scroungers?

8. What lessons has Eighner learned as a Dumpster diver?

PURPOSE AND AUDIENCE

1. In paragraph 6, Eighner states his purpose: to record what he has learned as a Dumpster diver. What additional purposes do you think he had in setting his ideas down on paper?

2. Do you think most readers are apt to respond to Eighner's essay with sympathy? Pity? Impatience? Contempt? Disgust? How do you react? Why?

3. Why do you think Eighner chose not to provide any background about his life — his upbringing, education, or work history — before he became homeless? Do you think this decision was a wise one? How might such

information (for example, any of the details in the headnote that precedes the essay) have changed readers' reactions to his discussion?

4. In paragraph 8, Eighner presents three principles one must follow to eat safely from a Dumpster; in paragraphs 59–60 he explains how to go through a Dumpster; and throughout the essay he includes many cautions and warnings. Clearly, he does not expect his audience to take up Dumpster diving. What, then, is his purpose in including such detailed explanations?

5. When Eighner begins paragraph 9 with "Perhaps everyone who has a kitchen, . . ." he encourages readers to identify with him. In what other ways does he help readers imagine themselves in his place? Are these efforts successful? Explain.

6. What effect do you think the essay's last line is calculated to have on readers? What effect does it have on you?

STYLE AND STRUCTURE

1. Eighner opens his essay with a very conventional strategy: an extended definition of *Dumpster diving*. What techniques does he use in paragraphs 1 through 3 to develop his definition? Is beginning with a definition the best strategy for this essay? Why or why not?

2. This long essay contains four one-sentence paragraphs. Why do you think Eighner isolates these sentences? Do you think any of them should be combined with an adjacent paragraph? Explain your reasoning.

3. As the introductory comment notes, Eighner retained the present tense even though he was no longer homeless when the essay was published. Why do you think he preserved the present tense? Was this a good decision?

4. Eighner's essay includes a number of lists that catalog items with which he came in contact (for example, in paragraphs 5 and 50). Identify as many of these lists as you can. Why do you think Eighner includes such extensive lists?

VOCABULARY PROJECTS

1. Define each of the following words as it is used in this selection.

proprietary (1)	decanted (26)	contingency (39)
niche (4)	ingested (26)	feasibility (40)
sporadic (5)	avail (28)	stave (43)
bohemian (8)	skulking (32)	commonplace (55)
dilettanti (8)	stigma (33)	vermin (56)
phobic (10)	pristine (34)	sinecure (62)
pared (15)	dissipate (35)	transience (64)
de-emulsified (16)	disparage (35)	gaudy (67)
pathogens (16)	intrinsic (37)	bauble (67)
staples (25)		

2. In paragraph 3, Eighner suggests several alternative words for *diving* as he uses it in his essay. Consult a dictionary to determine the connotations of each of his alternatives. What are the pros and cons of substituting one of these words for *diving* in Eighner's title and throughout the essay?

JOURNAL ENTRY

In paragraphs 21–25, Eighner discusses the discarding of food by college students. Does your own experience support his observations? Do you think he is being too hard on students, or does his characterization seem accurate?

WRITING WORKSHOP

1. Write an essay about a homeless person you have seen in your community. Use any patterns you like to structure your paper. When you have finished, annotate your essay to identify the patterns you have used.

2. Write a memo to your school's dean of students recommending steps that can be taken on your campus to redirect discarded (but edible) food to the homeless. Use process and exemplification to structure your memo.

3. Taking Eighner's point of view and using information from his essay, write an argumentative essay with a thesis statement that takes a strong stand against homelessness and recommends government and/or private measures to end it. If you like, you may write your essay in the form of a statement by Eighner to a congressional committee.

COMBINING THE PATTERNS

Review the annotations that identify each pattern of development used in this essay. Which patterns seem to be most effective in helping you understand and empathize with the life of a homeless person? Why?

THEMATIC CONNECTIONS

- "The Human Cost of an Illiterate Society" (page 203)
- "Burdens" (page 466)
- "The Untouchable" (page 461)
- The Declaration of Independence (page 516)

JONATHAN SWIFT

Jonathan Swift (1667–1745) was born in Dublin, Ireland, and spent much of his life journeying between his homeland, where he had a modest income as an Anglican priest, and England, where he wished to be part of the literary establishment. The author of many satires and political pamphlets, he is best known today for *Gulliver's Travels* (1726), a sharp satire that, except among academics, is now read primarily as a fantasy for children.

At the time that Swift wrote "A Modest Proposal," Ireland had been essentially under British rule since 1171, with the British often brutally suppressing rebellions by the Irish people. When Henry VIII of England declared a Protestant Church of Ireland, many of the Irish remained fiercely Roman Catholic, and this lead to even greater contention. By the early 1700s, the English-controlled Irish Parliament had passed laws that severely limited the rights of Irish Catholics, and British trade policies had begun to seriously depress the Irish economy. A fierce advocate for the Irish people in their struggle under British rule, Swift published several works supporting the Irish cause. The following sharply ironic essay was written during the height of a terrible famine in Ireland, at a time when the British were proposing a devastating tax on the impoverished Irish citizenry. Note that Swift does not write in his own voice here but adopts the persona of one who does not recognize the barbarity of his "solution."

A Modest Proposal

It is a melancholy object those who walk through this great town* or travel in the country, where they see the streets, the roads, and cabin doors, crowded with beggars of the female sex, followed by three, four, or six children, all in rags and importuning every passenger for an alms. These mothers, instead of being able to work for their honest livelihood, are forced to employ all their time in strolling to beg sustenance for their helpless infants, who, as they grow up, either turn thieves for want of work, or leave their dear native country to fight for the Pretender in Spain, or sell themselves to the Barbadoes.**

I think it is agreed by all parties that this prodigious number of children in the arms, or on the backs, or at the heels of their mothers, and frequently of their fathers, is in the present deplorable state of the kingdom a very great additional grievance; and therefore whoever could find out a fair, cheap, and easy method of making these children sound, useful members of the commonwealth would deserve so well of the public as to have his statue set up for a preserver of the nation.

But my intention is very far from being confined to provide only for the children of professed beggars; it is of a much greater extent, and shall

---

*Eds. note — Dublin.

**Eds. note — Many young Irishmen left their country to fight as mercenaries in Spain's civil war or to work as indentured servants in the West Indies.

take in the whole number of infants at a certain age who are born of parents in effect as little able to support them as those who demand our charity in the streets.

As to my own part, having turned my thoughts for many years upon   4
this important subject, and maturely weighed the several schemes of the other projectors, I have always found them grossly mistaken in their computation. It is true, a child just dropped from its dam may be supported by her milk for a solar year, with little other nourishment; at most not above the value of two shillings, which the mother may certainly get, or the value in scraps, by her lawful occupation of begging; and it is exactly at one year old that I propose to provide for them in such a manner as instead of being a charge upon their parents or the parish, or wanting food and raiment for the rest of their lives, they shall on the contrary contribute to the feeding, and partly to the clothing, of many thousands.

There is likewise another great advantage in my scheme, that it will   5
prevent those involuntary abortions, and that horrid practice of women murdering their bastard children, alas, too frequent among us, sacrificing the poor innocent babies, I doubt, more to avoid the expense than the shame, which would move tears and pity in the most savage and inhuman breast.

The number of souls in this kingdom being usually reckoned one mil-   6
lion and a half, of these I calculate there may be about two hundred thousand couples whose wives are breeders, from which number I subtract thirty thousand couples who are able to maintain their own children, although I apprehend there cannot be so many under the present distress of the kingdom; but this being granted, there will remain an hundred and seventy thousand breeders. I again subtract fifty thousand for those women who miscarry, or whose children die by accident or disease within the year. There only remain an hundred and twenty thousand children of poor parents annually born. The question therefore is, how this number shall be reared and provided for, which, as I have already said, under the present situation of affairs, is utterly impossible by all the methods hitherto proposed. For we can neither employ them in handicraft nor agriculture; we neither build houses (I mean in the country) nor cultivate land. They can very seldom pick up livelihood by stealing till they arrive at six years old, except where they are of towardly parts,* although I confess they learn the rudiments much earlier, during which time they can however be looked upon only as probationer, as I have been informed by a principal gentleman in the country of Cavan, who protested to me that he never knew above one or two instances under the age of six, even in a part of the kingdom so renowned for the quickest proficiency in that art.

I am assured by our merchants that a boy or a girl before twelve years   7
old is no salable commodity; and even when they come to this age, they

---

*Eds. note — Precocious.

will not yield above three pounds, or three pounds and half a crown at most on the Exchange; which cannot turn to account either to the parents or the kingdom, the charge of nutriment and rags having been at least four times that value.

I shall now therefore humbly propose my own thoughts, which I hope will not be liable to the least objection.   8

I have been assured by a very knowing American of my acquaintance in London, that a young healthy child well nursed is at a year old a most delicious, nourishing, and wholesome food, whether stewed, roasted, baked, or boiled; and I make no doubt that it will equally serve in fricasee or a ragout.   9

I do therefore humbly offer it to public consideration that of the hundred and twenty thousand children, already computed, twenty thousand may be reserved for breed, whereof only one fourth part to be males, which is more than we allow to sheep, black cattle, or swine; and my reason is that these children are seldom the fruits of marriage, a circumstance not much regarded by our savages, therefore one male will be sufficient to serve four females. That the remaining hundred thousand may at a year old be offered in sale to the persons of quality and fortune through the kingdom, always advising the mother to let them suck plentifully in the last month, so as to render them plump and fat for a good table. A child will make two dishes at an entertainment for friends; and when the family dines alone, the fore or hind quarter will make a reasonable dish, and seasoned with a little pepper or salt, will be very good boiled on the fourth day, especially in winter.   10

I have reckoned upon a medium that a child just born will weigh twelve pounds, and in a solar year if tolerably nursed increaseth to twenty-eight pounds.   11

I grant this food will be somewhat dear, and therefore very proper for landlords, who, as they have already devoured most of the parents, seem to have the best title to the children.   12

Infant's flesh will be in season throughout the year, but more plentiful in March, and a little before and after. For we are told by a grave author, an eminent French physician,* that fish being a prolific diet, there are more children born in Roman Catholic countries about nine months after Lent, than at any other season; therefore, reckoning year after Lent, the markets will be more glutted than usual, because the number of popish infants is at least three to one in this kingdom; and therefore it will have one other collateral advantage, by lessening the number of Papists** among us.   13

I have already computed the charge of nursing a beggar's child (in which list I reckon all cottages, laborers, and four fifths of the farmers) to be about two shillings per annum, rags included; and I believe no gentleman would repine to give ten shillings for the carcass of a good fat child,   14

---

*EDS. NOTE — François Rabelais, a sixteenth-century satirical writer.
**EDS. NOTE — Roman Catholics.

which, as I have said, will make four dishes of excellent nutritive meat, when he hath only some particular friend or his own family to dine with him. Thus the squire will learn to be a good landlord, and grow popular among the tenants; the mother will have eight shillings net profit, and be fit for work till she produces another child.

Those who are more thrifty (as I must confess the times require) may flay the carcass; the skin of which artificially* dressed will make admirable gloves for ladies, and summer boots for fine gentlemen. 15

As to our city of Dublin, shambles** may be appointed for this purpose in the most convenient parts of it, and butchers we may be assured will not be wanting; although I rather recommend buying the children alive, and dressing them hot from the knife as we do roasting pigs. 16

A very worthy person, a true lover of his country, and whose virtues I highly esteem, was lately pleased in discoursing on this matter to offer a refinement upon my scheme. He said that many gentlemen of his kingdom, having of late destroyed their deer, he conceived that the want of venison might be well supplied by the bodies of young lads and maidens, not exceeding fourteen years of age nor under twelve, so great a number of both sexes in every county being now ready to starve for want of work and service; and these to be disposed of by their parents, if alive, or otherwise by their nearest relations. But with due deference to so excellent a friend and so deserving a patriot I cannot be altogether in his sentiments; for as to the males, my American acquaintance assured me from frequent experience that their flesh was generally tough and lean, like that of our schoolboys, by continual exercise, and their taste disagreeable; and to fatten them would not answer the charge. Then as to the females, it would, I think with humble submission, be a loss to the public, because they soon would become breeders themselves; and besides, it is not improbable that some scrupulous people might be apt to censure such a practice (although indeed very unjustly) as a little bordering upon cruelty; which, I confess, hath always been with me the strongest objection against any project, how well soever intended. 17

But in order to justify my friend, he confessed that this expedient was put into his head by the famous Psalmanazar,*** a native of the island Formosa, who came from thence to London above twenty years ago, and in conversation told my friend that in his country when any young person happened to be put to death, the executioner sold the carcass to the persons of quality as a prime dainty; and that in his time the body of a plump girl of fifteen, who was crucified for an attempt to poison the emperor, was sold to the Imperial Majesty's prime minister of state, and other great mandarins of the court, in joints from the gibbet, at four hundred crowns. Neither indeed can I deny that if the same use were made of several 18

---

*EDS. NOTE — Skillfully.
**EDS. NOTE — A slaughterhouse or meat market.
***EDS. NOTE — Frenchman who passed himself off as a native of Formosa (present-day Taiwan).

plump young girls in this town, who without one single groat to their fortunes cannot stir abroad without a chair,* and appear at the playhouse and assemblies in foreign fineries which they never will pay for, the kingdom would not be the worse.

Some persons of a desponding spirit are in great concern about the vast number of poor people who are aged, diseased, or maimed, and I have been desired to employ my thoughts what course may be taken to ease the nation of so grievous an encumbrance. But I am not in the least pain upon that matter, because it is very well known that they are every day dying and rotting by cold and famine, and filth and vermin, as fast as can be reasonably expected. And as to the younger laborers, they are now in almost as hopeful a condition. They cannot get work, and consequently pine away for want of nourishment to a degree that if any time they are accidentally hired to common labor, they have not strength to perform it; and thus the country and themselves are happily delivered from the evils to come. 19

I have too long digressed, and therefore shall return to my subject. I think the advantages by the proposal which I have made are obvious and many, as well as of the highest importance. 20

For first, as I have already observed, it would greatly lessen the number of Papists, with whom we are yearly overrun, being the principal breeders of the nation as well as our most dangerous enemies; and who stay at home on purpose to deliver the kingdom to the Pretender, hoping to take their advantage by the absence of so many good Protestants, who have chosen rather to leave their country than to stay at home and pay tithes against their conscience to an Episcopal curate. 21

Secondly, the poorer tenants will have something valuable of their own, which by law may be made liable to distress,** and help to pay their landlord's rent, their corn and cattle being already seized and money a thing unknown. 22

Thirdly, whereas the maintenance of an hundred thousand children, from two years old and upwards, cannot be computed at less than ten shillings a piece per annum, the nation's stock will be thereby increased fifty thousand pounds per annum, besides the profit of a new dish introduced to the tables of all gentlemen of fortune in the kingdom who have any refinement in taste. And the money will circulate among ourselves, the goods being entirely of our own growth and manufacture. 23

Fourthly, the constant breeders, besides the gain of eight shillings sterling per annum by the sale of their children, will be rid of the charge for maintaining them after the first year. 24

Fifthly, this food would likewise bring great custom to taverns, where the vintners will certainly be so prudent as to procure the best receipts*** for dressing it to perfection, and consequently have their houses fre- 25

---

*EDS. NOTE — A sedan chair; that is, a portable, covered chair designed to seat one person and then to be carried by two men.

**EDS. NOTE — Property could be seized by creditors.

***EDS. NOTE — Recipes.

quented by all the fine gentlemen, who justly value themselves upon their knowledge in good eating; and a skillful cook, who understands how to oblige his guests, will contrive to make it as expensive as they please.

Sixthly, this would be a great inducement to marriage, after which all wise nations have either encouraged by rewards or enforced by laws and penalties. It would increase the care and tenderness of mothers toward their children, when they were sure of a settlement for life to the poor babes, provided in some sort by the public, to their annual profit instead of expense. We should see an honest emulation among the married women, which of them could bring the fattest child to the market. Men would become as fond of their wives during the time of pregnancy as they are now of their mares in foal, their cows in calf, or sows when they are ready to farrow; nor offer to beat or kick them (as is too frequent a practice) for fear of miscarriage. 26

Many other advantages might be enumerated. For instance, the addition of some thousand carcasses in our exportation of barreled beef, the propagation of swine's flesh, and improvements in the art of making good bacon, so much wanted among us by the great destruction of pigs, too frequent at our tables, which are no way comparable in taste or magnificence to a well-grown, fat, yearling child, which roasted whole will make a considerable figure at a lord mayor's feast or other public entertainment. But this and many others I omit, being studious of brevity. 27

Supposing that one thousand families in this city would be constant customers for infants' flesh, besides others who might have it at merry meetings, particularly weddings and christenings, I compute that Dublin would take off annually about twenty thousand carcasses, and the rest of the kingdom (where probably they will be sold somewhat cheaper) the remaining eighty thousand. 28

I can think of no one objection that will possibly be raised against this proposal, unless it should be urged that the number of people will be thereby much lessened in the kingdom. This I freely own, and it was indeed one principal design in offering it to the world. I desire the reader will observe; that I calculate my remedy for this one individual kingdom of Ireland and for no other than ever was, is, or I think ever can be upon earth. Therefore, let no man talk to me of other expedients: of taxing our absentees at five shillings a pound: of using neither clothes nor household furniture except what is of our own growth and manufacture: of utterly rejecting the materials and instruments that promote foreign luxury: of curing the expensiveness of pride, vanity, idleness, and gaming in our women: of introducing a vein of parsimony, prudence, and temperance: of learning to love our country, in the want of which we differ even from Lowlanders and the inhabitants of Topinamboo:* of quitting our animosities and factions, nor acting any longer like the Jews,** who were 29

---

*EDS. NOTE — A place in the Brazilian jungle.

**EDS. NOTE — In the first century B.C., the Roman general Pompey was able to conquer Jerusalem in part because the citizenry was divided among rival factions.

murdering one another at the very moment their city was taken: of being a little cautious not to sell our country and conscience for nothing: of teaching landlords to have at least one degree of mercy toward their tenants: lastly, of putting a spirit of honesty, industry, and skill into our shopkeepers; who, if a resolution could now be taken to buy only our native goods, would immediately unite to cheat and exact upon us in the price, the measure, and the goodness, nor could ever yet be brought to make one fair proposal of just dealing, though often and earnestly invited to it.

Therefore, I repeat, let no man talk to me of these and the like expedients, till he hath at least some glimpse of hope that there will ever be some hearty and sincere attempt to put them in practice.*   30

But as to myself, having been wearied out for many years with offering vain, idle, visionary thoughts, and the length utterly despairing of success, I fortunately fell upon this proposal, which, as it is wholly new, so it hath something solid and real, of no expense and little trouble, full in our own power, and whereby we can incur no danger in disobliging England. For this kind of commodity will not bear exploration, the flesh being of too tender a consistence to admit a long continuance in salt, although perhaps I could name a country which would be glad to eat up our whole nation without it.   31

After all, I am not so violently bent upon my own opinion as to reject any offer proposed by wise men, which shall be found equally innocent, cheap, easy, and effectual. But before something of that kind shall be advanced in contradiction to my scheme, and offering a better, I desire the author or authors will be pleased maturely to consider two points. First, as things now stand, how they will be able to find food and raiment for an hundred thousand useless mouths and backs. And secondly, there being a round million of creatures in human figure throughout this kingdom, whose sole subsistence put into a common stock would leave them in debt two million of pounds sterling, adding those who are beggars by profession to the bulk of farmers, cottagers, and laborers, with their wives and children who are beggars in effect; I desire those politicians who dislike my overture, and may perhaps be so bold to attempt an answer, that they will first ask the parents of these mortals whether they would not at this day think it a great happiness to have been sold for food at a year old in this manner I prescribe, and thereby have avoided such a perpetual scene of misfortunes as they have since gone through by the oppression of landlords, the impossibility of paying rent without money or trade, the want of common sustenance, with neither house nor clothes to cover them from the inclemencies of the weather, and the most inevitable prospect of entailing the like or greater miseries upon their breed forever.   32

I profess, in the sincerity of my heart, that I have not the least personal interest in endeavoring to promote this necessary work, having no other motive than the public good of my country, by advancing our trade, pro-   33

---

*EDS. NOTE — Note that these measures represent Swift's true proposal.

viding for infants, relieving the poor, and giving some pleasure to the rich. I have no children by which I can propose to get a single penny; the youngest being nine years old, and my wife past childbearing.

• • •

COMPREHENSION

1. What problem does Swift identify? What general solution does he recommend?

2. What advantages does Swift see in his plan?

3. What does he see as the alternative to his plan?

4. What clues indicate that Swift is not serious about his proposal?

5. In paragraph 29, Swift lists and rejects a number of "other expedients." What are they? Why do you think he presents and rejects these ideas?

PURPOSE AND AUDIENCE

1. Swift's target here is the British government, in particular its poor treatment of the Irish. How would you expect British government officials to respond to his proposal? How would you expect Irish readers to react?

2. What do you think Swift hoped to accomplish in this essay? Do you think his purpose was simply to amuse and shock, or do you think he wanted to change people's minds — or even inspire them to take some kind of action? Explain.

3. In paragraphs 6, 14, 23, and elsewhere, Swift presents a series of mathematical calculations. What effect do you think he expected these computations to have on his readers?

4. Explain why each of the following groups might have been offended by this essay: women, Catholics, butchers, poor people.

5. How do you think Swift expected the appeal in his conclusion to affect his audience?

STYLE AND STRUCTURE

1. In paragraph 6, Swift uses the word *breeders* to refer to fertile women. What connotations does this word have? Why does he use it rather than a more neutral alternative?

2. What purpose does paragraph 8 serve in the essay? Do the other short paragraphs have the same function? Explain.

3. Swift's remarks are presented as an argument. Where, if anywhere, does he anticipate and refute his readers' objections?

4. Swift applies to infants many words usually applied to animals who are slaughtered to be eaten — for example, *fore or hind quarter* (10) and *carcass* (15). List as many examples of this usage as you can. Why do you think Swift uses such words?

5. Throughout his essay, Swift cites the comments of others — "our merchants" (7), "a very knowing American of my acquaintance" (9), and "an eminent French physician" (13), for example. Cite additional examples. What, if anything, does he accomplish by referring to these people?

6. A **satire** is a piece of writing that uses wit, **irony,** and ridicule to attack foolishness, incompetence, or evil. How does "A Modest Proposal" fit this definition of satire?

7. Evaluate the strategy Swift uses to introduce each advantage he cites in paragraphs 21 through 26.

8. Swift uses a number of parenthetical comments in his essay — for example, in paragraphs 14, 17, and 26. Identify all of his parenthetical comments, and consider what they contribute to the essay.

9. Swift begins paragraph 20 with "I have too long digressed, and therefore shall return to my subject." Has he in fact been digressing? Explain.

VOCABULARY PROJECTS

1. Define each of the following words as it is used in this selection.

importuning (1)	rudiments (6)	encumbrance (19)
alms (1)	nutriment (7)	tithes (21)
prodigious (2)	repine (14)	vintners (25)
professed (3)	flay (15)	expedients (29)
dam (4)	scrupulous (17)	parsimony (29)
reckoned (6)	censure (17)	temperance (29)
apprehend (6)	desponding (19)	raiment (32)

2. The title states that Swift's proposal is a "modest" one; elsewhere he says that he proposes his ideas "humbly" (8). Why do you think he chooses these words? Does he really mean to present himself as modest and humble?

JOURNAL ENTRY

What is your emotional reaction to this essay? Do you find it amusing or offensive? Why?

WRITING WORKSHOP

1. Write a "modest proposal," either straightforward or satirical, for solving a problem in your school or community.

2. Write a "modest proposal" for achieving one of these national goals:
   • Making health care more affordable
   • Improving gun safety
   • Eliminating binge drinking on campus
   • Improving public education
   • Eliminating teenage pregnancy
   • Reducing the use of illegal drugs

3.   Write a letter to an executive of the tobacco industry, a television network, or an industry that threatens the environment. In your letter, set forth a "modest proposal" for making the industry more responsible.

COMBINING THE PATTERNS

What patterns of development does Swift use in his argument? Annotate the essay to identify each pattern. Use the annotations accompanying the preceding essay, "On Dumspter Diving," as a guide.

THEMATIC CONNECTIONS

- "The Embalming of Mr. Jones" (page 248)
- "The Irish Famine, 1845–1849" (page 274)
- "I Want a Wife" (page 474)
- The Declaration of Independence (page 516)

ALICE WALKER

Born in Eatontown, Georgia, one of eight children in a family of sharecroppers, Alice Walker (1944–) began her writing career in the late 1960s. She had published four volumes of well-received fiction when her novel *The Color Purple* (1982) first brought her to wide public attention. This best-seller won the Pulitzer Prize for fiction and served as the basis for a popular film directed by Steven Spielberg. Since then, Walker has published several novels, poetry collections, and volumes of memoirs. A writer who often explores feminist and antiracist themes, she has also published two highly influential collections of essays, including *In Search of Our Mothers' Gardens* (1983).

This title essay from Walker's 1983 collection was written in 1974, a time when the gains of the Civil Rights movement and the appearance of new African-American writers had resulted in a flowering of the black literary tradition in America. In particular, the writers of the Harlem Renaissance of some fifty years earlier — Langston Hughes, Jean Toomer, and Zora Neale Hurston, to name a few — were being reexamined after years of relative neglect. Their works were being introduced into college literature courses, and they themselves were becoming the subject of academic study. Even the work of less well-known figures — like the eighteenth-century slave poet Phillis Wheatley, who adopted a voice like that of her white owners — received increased interest. In this essay, Walker is particularly interested in examining the traditions of the black woman artist and considering how so many black women over the years had to suppress their creativity because of a racist and sexist culture that turned them into "mules."

In Search of Our Mothers' Gardens

> I described her own nature and temperament. Told how they
> needed a larger life for their expression. . . . I pointed out that
> in lieu of proper channels, her emotions had overflowed into
> paths that dissipated them. I talked, beautifully I thought,
> about an art that would be born, an art that would open the
> way for women the likes of her. I asked her to hope, and build
> up an inner life against the coming of that day. . . . I sang, with a
> strange quiver in my voice, a promise song.
>
> — JEAN TOOMER,
> *"Avey," Cane*

The poet speaking to a prostitute who falls asleep while he's talking — 1

When the poet Jean Toomer walked through the South in the early 2
twenties, he discovered a curious thing: black women whose spirituality
was so intense, so deep, so *unconscious*, that they were themselves
unaware of the richness they held. They stumbled blindly through their
lives: creatures so abused and mutilated in body, so dimmed and confused
by pain, that they considered themselves unworthy even of hope. In the
selfless abstractions their bodies became to the men who used them, they
became more than "sexual objects," even more than mere women: they

658

became "Saints." Instead of being perceived as whole persons, their bodies became shrines, what was thought to be their minds became temples suitable for worship. These crazy Saints stared out at the world, wildly, like lunatics — or quietly, like suicides; and the "God" that was in their gaze was as mute as a great stone.

Who were these Saints? These crazy, loony, pitiful women?   3

Some of them, without a doubt, were our mothers and grandmothers.   4

In the still heat of the post-Reconstruction South, this is how they   5
seemed to Jean Toomer: exquisite butterflies trapped in an evil honey, toiling away their lives in an era, a century, that did not acknowledge them, except as "the *mule* of the world." They dreamed dreams that no one knew — not even themselves, in any coherent fashion — and saw visions no one could understand. They wandered or sat about the countryside crooning lullabies to ghosts, and drawing the mother of Christ in charcoal on courthouse walls.

They forced their minds to desert their bodies and their striving spirits   6
sought to rise, like frail whirlwinds from the hard red clay. And when those frail whirlwinds fell, in scattered particles, upon the ground, no one mourned. Instead, men lit candles to celebrate the emptiness that remained, as people do who enter a beautiful but vacant space to resurrect a God.

Our mothers and grandmothers, some of them: moving to music not   7
yet written. And they waited.

They waited for a day when the unknown thing that was in them   8
would be made known; but guessed, somehow in their darkness, that on the day of their revelation they would be long dead. Therefore to Toomer they walked, and even ran, in slow motion. For they were going nowhere immediate, and the future was not yet within their grasp. And men took our mothers and grandmothers, "but got no pleasure from it." So complex was their passion and their calm.

To Toomer, they lay vacant and fallow as autumn fields, with harvest   9
time never in sight: and he saw them enter loveless marriages, without joy; and become prostitutes, without resistance, and become mothers of children, without fulfillment.

For these grandmothers and mothers of ours were not Saints, but   10
Artists; driven to a numb and bleeding madness by the springs of creativity in them for which there was no release. They were Creators, who lived lives of spiritual waste, because they were so rich in spirituality — which is the basis of Art — that the strain of enduring their unused and unwanted talent drove them insane. Throwing away this spirituality was their pathetic attempt to lighten the soul to a weight their work-worn, sexually abused bodies could bear.

What did it mean for a black woman to be an artist in our grandmoth-   11
ers' time? In our great-grandmothers' day? It is a question with an answer cruel enough to stop the blood.

Did you have a genius of a great-great-grandmother who died under   12
some ignorant and depraved white overseer's lash? Or was she required

to bake biscuits for a lazy backwater tramp, when she cried out in her soul to paint watercolors of sunsets, or the rain falling on the green and peaceful pasturelands? Or was her body broken and forced to bear children (who were more often than not sold away from her) — eight, ten, fifteen, twenty children — when her one joy was the thought of modeling heroic figures of rebellion, in stone or clay?

How was the creativity of the black woman kept alive, year after year   13
and century after century, when for most of the years black people have been in America, it was a punishable crime for a black person to read or write? And the freedom to paint, to sculpt, to expand the mind with an action did not exist. Consider, if you can bear to imagine it, what might have been the result if singing, too, had been forbidden by law. Listen to the voices of Bessie Smith, Billie Holiday, Nina Simone, Roberta Flack, and Aretha Franklin, among others, and imagine those voices muzzled for life. Then you may begin to comprehend the lives of our "crazy," "Sainted" mothers and grandmothers. The agony of the lives of women who might have been Poets, Novelists, Essayists, and Short Story Writers (over a period of centuries), who died with their real gifts stifled within them.

And, if this were the end of the story, we would have cause to cry out   14
in my paraphrase of Okot p'Bitek's* great poem:

O, my clanswomen
Let us all cry together!
Come,
Let us mourn the death of our mother,
The death of a Queen
The ash that was produced
By a great fire!
O, this homestead is utterly dead
Close the gates
With *lacari* thorns,
For our mother
The creator of the Stool is lost!
And all the young women
Have perished in the wilderness!

But this is not the end of the story, for all the young women — our   15
mothers and grandmothers, *ourselves* — have not perished in the wilderness. And if we ask ourselves why, and search for and find the answer, we will know beyond all efforts to erase it from our minds, just exactly who, and of what, we black American women are.

One example, perhaps the most pathetic, most misunderstood one,   16
can provide a backdrop for our mothers' work: Phillis Wheatley,** a slave in the 1700s.

---

*EDS. NOTE — (1931–1982) Ugandan writer and anthropologist.

**EDS. NOTE — Eventually achieving her freedom, Wheatley (1753?–1784) published several volumes of poetry and is considered the first important African-American writer in the United States.

Virginia Woolf,* in her book *A Room of One's Own,* wrote that in order 17
for a woman to write fiction she must have two things, certainly: a room of
her own (the key and lock) and enough money to support herself.

What then are we to make of Phillis Wheatley, a slave, who owned not 18
even herself? This sickly, frail black girl who required a servant of her own
at times — her health was so precarious — and who, had she been white,
would have been easily considered the intellectual superior of all women
and most of the men in the society of her day.

Virginia Woolf wrote further, speaking of course not of our Phillis, 19
that "any woman born with a great gift in the sixteenth century [insert
"eighteenth century," insert "black woman," insert "born or made a
slave"] would certainly have gone crazed, shot herself, or ended her days
in some lonely cottage outside the village, half witch, half wizard [insert
"Saint"], feared and mocked at. For it needs little skill and psychology to
be sure that a highly gifted girl who had tried to use her gift for poetry
would have been so thwarted and hindered by contrary instincts [add
"chains, guns, the lash, the ownership of one's body by someone else, submission to an alien religion"], that she must have lost her health and sanity
to a certainty."

The key words, as they relate to Phillis, are "contrary instincts." For 20
when we read the poetry of Phillis Wheatley — and when we read the
novels of Nella Larsen or the oddly false-sounding autobiography of that
freest of all black women writers, Zora Hurston** — evidence of "contrary
instincts" is everywhere. Her loyalties were completely divided, as was,
without question, her mind.

But how could this be otherwise? Captured at seven, a slave of 21
wealthy, doting whites who instilled in her the "savagery" of the Africa
they "rescued" her from . . . one wonders if she was even able to remember her homeland as she had known it, or as it really was.

Yet, because she did not try to use her gift for poetry in a world that 22
made her a slave, she was "so thwarted and hindered by . . . contrary
instincts, that she . . . lost her health. . . ." In the last years of brief life, burdened not only with the need to express her gift but also with a penniless,
friendless "freedom" and several small children for whom she was forced
to do strenuous work to feed, she lost her health, certainly. Suffering from
malnutrition and neglect and who knows what mental agonies, Phillis
Wheatley died.

So torn by "contrary instincts" was black, kidnapped, enslaved Phillis 23
that her description of "the Goddess" — as she poetically called the Liberty she did not have — is ironically, cruelly humorous. And, in fact, has
held Phillis up to ridicule for more than a century. It is usually read prior
to hanging Phillis's memory as that of a fool. She wrote:

---

*EDS. NOTE — Early-twentieth-century English essayist and novelist.
**EDS. NOTE — Larsen (1891–1964) wrote realistic novels about black and white
relations; Hurston (1903–1960) is noted for her folklore research and novels and stories
that reproduce southern black dialect.

> The Goddess comes, she moves divinely fair,
> Olive and laurel binds her *golden* hair.
> Wherever shines this native of the skies,
> Unnumber'd charms and recent graces rise. [My italics]

It is obvious that Phillis, the slave, combed the "Goddess's" hair every   24
morning; prior, perhaps, to bringing in the milk, or fixing her mistress's
lunch. She took her imagery from the one thing she saw elevated above all
others.

With the benefit of hindsight we ask, "How could she?"   25

But at last, Phillis, we understand. No more snickering when your   26
stiff, struggling, ambivalent lines are forced on us. We know now that you
were not an idiot or a traitor; only a sickly little black girl, snatched from
your home and country and made a slave; a woman who still struggled to
sing the song that was your gift, although in a land of barbarians who
praised you for your bewildered tongue. It is not so much what you sang,
as that you kept alive, in so many of our ancestors, *the notion of song.*

Black women are called, in the folklore that so aptly identifies one's   27
status in society, "the *mule* of the world," because we have been handed
the burdens that everyone else — *everyone* else — refused to carry. We
have also been called "Matriarchs," "Superwomen," and "Mean and Evil
Bitches." Not to mention "Castraters" and "Sapphire's Mama." When we
have pleaded for understanding, our character has been distorted; when
we have asked for simple caring, we have been handed empty inspira-
tional appellations, then stuck in the farthest corner. When we have asked
for love, we have been given children. In short, even our plainer gifts, our
labors of fidelity and love, have been knocked down our throats. To be an
artist and a black woman, even today, lowers our status in many respects,
rather than raises it: and yet, artists we will be.

Therefore we must fearlessly pull out of ourselves and look at and   28
identify with our lives the living creativity some of our great-grandmothers were not allowed to know. I stress *some* of them because it is well
known that the majority of our great-grandmothers knew, even without
"knowing" it, the reality of their spirituality, even if they didn't recognize
it beyond what happened in the singing at church — and they never had
any intention of giving it up.

How they did it — those millions of black women who were not   29
Phillis Wheatley, or Lucy Terry or Frances Harper or Zora Hurston or
Nella Larsen or Bessie Smith; or Elizabeth Catlett, or Katherine Dunham,*
either — brings me to the title of this essay, "In Search of Our Mothers'
Gardens," which is a personal account that is yet shared, in its theme and

---

*EDS. NOTE — Successful black female artists; the first five were writers, Smith was
a singer and songwriter, Catlett a sculptor, and Dunham a dancer and choreographer.

its meaning, by all of us. I found, while thinking about the far-reaching world of the creative black woman, that often the truest answer to a question that really matters can be found very close.

In the late 1920s my mother ran away from home to marry my father. 30 Marriage, if not running away, was expected of seventeen-year-old girls. By the time she was twenty, she had two children and was pregnant with a third. Five children later, I was born. And this is how I came to know my mother: she seemed a large, soft, loving-eyed woman who was rarely impatient in our home. Her quick, violent temper was on view only a few times a year, she battled with the white landlord who had the misfortune to suggest to her that her children did not need to go to school.

She made all the clothes we wore, even my brothers' overalls. She 31 made all the towels and sheets we used. She spent the summers canning vegetables and fruits. She spent the winter evenings making quilts enough to cover all our beds.

During the "working" day, she labored beside — not behind — my 32 father in the fields. Her day began before sunup, and did not end until late at night. There was never a moment for her to sit down, undisturbed, to unravel her own private thoughts; never a time free from interruption — by work or the noisy inquiries of her many children. And yet, it is to my mother — and all our mothers who were not famous — that I went in search of the secrets of what has fed that muzzled and often mutilated, but vibrant, creative spirit that the black woman has inherited, and that pops out in wild and unlikely places to this day.

But when, you will ask, did my overworked mother have time to 33 know or care about feeding the creative spirit?

The answer is so simple that many of us have spent years discovering 34 it. We have constantly looked high, when we should have looked high — and low.

For example: in the Smithsonian Institution in Washington, D.C., 35 there hangs a quilt unlike any other in the world. In fanciful, inspired, and yet simple and identifiable figures, it portrays the story of the Crucifixion. It is considered rare, beyond price. Though it follows no known pattern of quilt-making, and though it is made of bits and pieces of worthless rags, it is obviously the work of a person of powerful imagination and deep spiritual feeling. Below this quilt I saw a note that says it was made by "an anonymous Black woman in Alabama, a hundred years ago."

If we could locate this "anonymous" black woman from Alabama, she 36 would turn out to be one of our grandmothers — an artist who left her mark in the only materials she could afford, and in the only medium her position in society allowed her to use.

As Virginia Woolf wrote further, in *A Room of One's Own:* 37

Yet genius of a sort must have existed among women as it must have existed among the working class. [Change this to "slaves" and "the wives or the daughters of sharecroppers."] Now and again an Emily Brontë or a

Robert Burns [change this to "a Zora Hurston or a Richard Wright"] blazes out and proves its presence. But certainly it never got itself on to paper. When, however, one reads of a witch being ducked, of a woman possessed by devils [or "Sainthood"], of a wise woman selling herbs [our root workers], or even a very remarkable man who had a mother, then I think we are on the track of a lost novelist, a suppressed poet, of some mute and inglorious Jane Austen. . . . Indeed, I would venture to guess that Anon, who wrote so many poems without signing them, was often a woman. . . .

And so our mothers and grandmothers have, more often than not   38 anonymously, handed on the creative spark, the seed of the flower they themselves never hoped to see: or like a sealed letter they could not plainly read.

And so it is, certainly, with my own mother. Unlike "Ma" Rainey's*   39 songs, which retained their creator's name even while blasting forth from Bessie Smith's mouth, no song or poem will bear my mother's name. Yet so many of the stories that I write, that we all write, are my mother's stories. Only recently did I fully realize this: that through years of listening to my mother's stories of her life, I have absorbed not only the stories themselves, but something of the manner in which she spoke, something of the urgency that involves the knowledge that her stories — like her life — must be recorded. It is probably for this reason that so much of what I have written is about characters whose counterparts in real life are so much older than I am.

But the telling of these stories, which came from my mother's lips as   40 naturally as breathing, was not the only way my mother showed herself as an artist. For stories, too, were subject to being distracted, to dying without conclusion. Dinners must be started, and cotton must be gathered before the big rains. The artist that was and is my mother showed itself to me only after many years. This is what I finally noticed:

Like Mem, a character in *The Third Life of Grange Copeland,* my mother   41 adorned with flowers whatever shabby house we were forced to live in. And not just your typical straggly country stand of zinnias, either. She planted ambitious gardens — and still does — with over fifty different varieties of plants that bloom profusely from early March until late November. Before she left home for the fields, she watered her flowers, chopped up the grass, and laid out new beds. When she returned from the fields she might divide clumps of bulbs, dig a cold pit, uproot and replant roses, or prune branches from her taller bushes or trees — until night came and it was too dark to see.

Whatever she planted grew as if by magic, and her fame as a grower   42 of flowers spread over three counties. Because of her creativity with her flowers, even my memories of poverty are seen through a screen of blooms — sunflowers, petunias, roses, dahlias, forsythia, spirea, delphiniums, verbena . . . and on and on.

---

*EDS. NOTE — Famous blues singer and songwriter of the early twentieth century.

And I remember people coming to my mother's yard to be given cut-   43
tings from her flowers; I hear again the praise showered on her because
whatever rocky soil she landed on, she turned into a garden. A garden so
brilliant with colors, so original in its design, so magnificent with life and
creativity, that to this day people drive by our house in Georgia — perfect
strangers and imperfect strangers — and ask to stand or walk in my
mother's art.

I notice that it is not only when my mother is working in her flowers   44
that she is radiant, almost to the point of being invisible — except as Creator: hand and eye. She is involved in work her soul must have. Ordering
the universe in the image of her personal conception of Beauty.

Her face, as she prepares the Art that is her gift, is a legacy of respect   45
she leaves to me, for all that illuminates and cherishes life. She has handed
down respect for the possibilities — and the will to grasp them.

For her, so hindered and intruded upon in so many ways, being   46
an artist has still been a daily part of her life. This ability to hold on,
even in very simple ways, is work black women have done for a very long
time.

This poem is not enough, but it is something, for the woman who lit-   47
erally covered the holes in our walls with sunflowers:

They were women then
My mama's generation
Husky of voice — Stout of
Step
With fists as well as
Hands
How they battered down
Doors
And ironed
Starched white
Shirts
How they led
Armies
Headragged Generals
Across mined
Fields
Booby-trapped
Kitchens
To discovery books
Desks
A place for us
How they knew what we
Must know
Without knowing a page
Of it
Themselves.

Guided by my heritage of a love of beauty and a respect for   48
strength — in search of my mother's garden, I found my own.

And perhaps in Africa over two hundred years ago, there was just   49
such a mother; perhaps she painted vivid and daring decorations in
oranges and yellows and greens on the walls of her hut; perhaps she
sang — in a voice like Roberta Flack's — *sweetly* over the compounds of
her village; perhaps she wove the most stunning mats or told the most
ingenious stories of all the village storytellers. Perhaps she was herself
a poet — though only her daughter's name is signed to the poems that
we know.

Perhaps Phillis Wheatley's mother was also an artist.   50

Perhaps in more than Phillis Wheatley's biological life is her mother's   51
signature made clear.

●　●　●

COMPREHENSION

1. Why does Walker describe southern black women in the 1920s as "crazy, loony, pitiful women" (3)? What strengths did these women have?

2. In paragraph 5, Walker describes southern black women as "exquisite butterflies trapped in an evil honey." What is this "evil honey"? What does Walker believe poet Jean Toomer means when he characterizes these women as "the mule of the world"?

3. What is the "music not yet written" (7) to which Walker says these women moved? What, according to Walker, were they waiting for?

4. Walker sees the women not as saints but as something else. How does she characterize them? Why?

5. In paragraph 11, Walker asks, "What did it mean for a black woman to be an artist in our grandmothers' time?" In paragraph 13, she asks how their creativity was kept alive. Paraphrase her answers to these questions.

6. Why, according to Walker, is what she describes in paragraphs 1 through 14 "not the end of the story"? What is the rest of this story?

7. Paraphrase the story of Phillis Wheatley's life. What does her story contribute to Walker's essay?

8. What, specifically, does Walker believe black women should do? In what sense should they see their mothers and grandmothers as positive examples? As negative examples? Why does she call this essay "In Search of Our Mothers' Gardens"?

9. How does Walker link herself with her mother and grandmother? What legacy have they left her?

PURPOSE AND AUDIENCE

1. This essay was first published in *Ms.*, a feminist magazine. Do you think it is a feminist essay? Explain.

2. In this essay, Walker addresses African-American women. What does she advise her readers? Do you think her recommendations are relevant to women of other races? To men? Why or why not?

3. What is Walker's thesis? Do you think she expects her audience to be sympathetic to this position? Explain your reasoning.

STYLE AND STRUCTURE

1. The essay opens with a quotation from noted African-American novelist and poet Jean Toomer. Is this an effective opening strategy? Why do you think Walker begins her essay this way?

2. Throughout her essay Walker (sometimes quoting Toomer) uses elaborate figurative language to describe the women she is writing about. Give examples of some of the metaphors she uses, and evaluate their effectiveness. Do you think she uses enough figurative language? Too much? Explain.

3. In paragraphs 14, 23, and 37, Walker quotes three women writers; in paragraph 47, she presents a poem of her own. What do these excerpts have in common? Do you think they are distracting digressions or vital components of the essay? Explain.

4. Is Walker's tone sorrowful? Bitter? Regretful? Strident? On what do you base your conclusion?

5. Why does Walker summarize her own mother's life in paragraphs 30 through 32? What is the connection between the life of Walker's mother and the life of Phillis Wheatley? Do you think the biographical information Walker provides about these two women is necessary? Why or why not?

6. Walker introduces some of her key ideas with questions. For example, in paragraph 3 she asks, "Who were these Saints?" Where else does she ask questions? Does she answer them? Why do you suppose she uses this strategy instead of making direct statements?

VOCABULARY PROJECTS

1. Define each of the following words as it is used in this selection.

   overseer (12)   barbarians (26)   counterparts (39)
   lash (12)   matriarchs (27)

2. What images are usually associated with the word *garden?* Is *garden* simply a metaphor for art in this essay, or does it have other meanings as well?

JOURNAL ENTRY

In paragraph 27, Walker says "To be an artist and a black woman, even today, lowers our status in many respects, rather than raises it." Do you agree with Walker's statement? Do you think it is true for all women? For any artist?

WRITING WORKSHOP

1. In what sense might you see yourself as an artist? What kinds of creative expression do you believe constitute your own garden? Using a series of examples, develop an essay about these ideas.

2. Interview your mother or grandmother (or another female relative) on the subject of the creative outlets available to women of her generation — and the obstacles to those outlets. Use narration, exemplification, and cause and effect to shape an essay about their experiences and those of their peers.

3. Think about the various kinds of art Walker discusses in this essay — everything from poetry to quilting to singing to gardening. Do you consider all her examples legitimate kinds of art, or do you have different standards? Write a definition of *art* using classification and division as well as exemplification to develop your definition.

COMBINING THE PATTERNS

What patterns of development does Walker use in her essay? Annotate the essay to identify each pattern. Use the annotations accompanying "On Dumpster Diving" (which appears earlier in this chapter) as a guide.

THEMATIC CONNECTIONS

- "Homeward Bound" (page 79)
- "My Mother Never Worked" (page 94)
- "The Way to Rainy Mountain" (page 148)
- "The Men We Carry in Our Minds" (page 399)
- "Mother Tongue" (page 405)

WRITING ASSIGNMENTS FOR COMBINING THE PATTERNS

1. Reread Michael Huu Truong's essay at the beginning of this chapter. Responding to the same assignment he was given ("Write an essay about the person and/or place that defined your childhood"), use several different patterns to communicate to readers what your childhood was like.

2. Write an essay about the political, social, or economic events that you believe have dominated and defined your life, or a stage in your life. Use **cause and effect** and any other patterns you think are appropriate to explain and illustrate why these events were important to you and how they affected you.

3. Develop a thesis statement that draws a general conclusion about the nature, quality, or effectiveness of advertising in print media (in newspapers or magazines or on billboards). Write an essay that supports this thesis statement with a series of very specific paragraphs. Use the patterns of development that best help you to characterize particular advertisements.

4. Exactly what do you think it means to be an American? Write a **definition** essay that answers this question, developing your definition with whatever patterns best serve your purpose.

5. Many of the essays in this text recount the writers' personal experiences. Identify one essay in which a writer describes experiences that are either similar to your own or in sharp contrast to your own. Then, write a **comparison-and-contrast** essay in which you *either* compare *or* contrast your experiences with those of the writer. Use several different patterns to develop your essay.

COLLABORATIVE ACTIVITY FOR COMBINING THE PATTERNS

Working in pairs, choose two essays from Chapters 4 through 12 of this text. Then, working individually, identify the various patterns of development used in each essay. When you have finished, exchange ideas with the other student in your group. Have both of you identified the same patterns in each essay? If not, try to reach a consensus. Then, working together, choose one of the two essays, and write a paragraph summarizing why each pattern is used and explaining how the various patterns work together.

INTERNET ASSIGNMENT FOR COMBINING THE PATTERNS

Write an essay in which you consider the moral and ethical implications of new breakthroughs in cloning. Using several different patterns to support your thesis and to illustrate the potential benefits and/or dangers of cloning. Visit the following World Wide Web sites to learn more about the process of cloning and the future possibilities it suggests.

Slouching towards Creation: Peering into the Face of Cloning
<http://www.pathfinder.com/TIME/cloning/home.html>
This site sponsored by *Time* magazine offers information about the cloning process, futurist scenarios, and a discussion of the ethics of cloning.

Human Cloning Foundation
<http://www.humancloning.org>

This nonprofit group's site links to interviews, frequently asked questions, essays about the benefits of human cloning, and lists of books and movies that address human cloning issues.

World Book Encyclopedia: Cloning: Are Humans Next?
<http://www.worldbook.com/fun/bth/cloning/html/cloning.html>

This site discusses early attempts at cloning, recent cloning breakthroughs, uses of cloning, and ethical concerns.

Human Cloning and Re-Engineering
<http://cac.psu.edu/~gsg109/qs>

This site contains information on human embryo cloning and a discussion of its moral implications.

APPENDIX: WRITING A RESEARCH PAPER

When you write a research paper, you supplement your own ideas with material from books, articles, television programs, the Internet, and electronic databases. As you research and write, remember what you have learned about the writing process, and keep in mind that your main task is to present ideas clearly and convincingly. You will have an easier time writing a research paper if you follow an orderly process:

1. Choose a topic.
2. Look for sources.
3. Narrow your topic.
4. Do research.
5. Take notes.
6. Watch out for plagiarism.
7. Draft a thesis statement.
8. Make an outline.
9. Write your paper.
10. Document your sources.

STEP 1: CHOOSING A TOPIC

The first step in writing a research paper is finding a topic you can write about. Before you decide on a topic, ask yourself the following questions:

- What is my page limit?
- When is my paper due?
- How many sources am I expected to use?

The answers to these questions will help you make sure your topic is neither too broad nor too narrow.

When Allison Rogers, a student in a college composition course, was asked to write a three-to-five-page research paper due in five weeks, she knew she wanted to write about the violence she saw in society. She realized, however, that the general topic "violence" would be too broad for a short paper and that a topic like "one example of violence in the movie *Natural Born Killers*" would be too narrow. "The effect of the media on violent behavior," however, might work well because Allison could discuss this topic in the required number of pages and would be able to complete her paper within the time limit.

STEP 2: LOOKING FOR SOURCES

To get an overview of your topic and see if you can find enough to write about, quickly survey the resources of your library. (First, arrange a meeting with your college librarian, who can answer questions, give you suggestions, and point you toward helpful resources.)

Begin by looking at your library's *subject catalog* or its *online central information system* to see what books and articles about your topic are listed there. (Frequently, the online central information system contains the library's catalog as well as a number of databases such as *Readers' Guide to Periodical Literature* or *Humanities Index*.) For example, under the general topic "violence" Allison found the related headings "movie violence" and "media violence." Under these headings were a variety of books, numerous articles, and two government studies on her topic.

STEP 3: NARROWING YOUR TOPIC

As you survey the library's resources, the subject headings as well as the titles of the books and articles you find should help you narrow your topic further.

Allison discovered that several of the books and a number of articles she located focused on the effect of media violence on society. A few focused specifically on children and examined the effect of violent movies and television on their behavior. Because her major was early childhood education, Allison decided to concentrate on children. She knew from reading her instructor's guidelines that the purpose of her paper should be either to *present information* or *to make a point*. In other words, either she could simply present information about the relationship between violent media and violent behavior in children, or she could make the point that media violence can have a negative affect on the behavior of young children.

STEP 4: DOING RESEARCH

Once you have narrowed your topic, you need to gather information. Begin by going back to the library and checking out any books you think will be useful. Next, photocopy any magazine articles you need, and make copies of material on microfilm or microfiche. If you use a computer database such as InfoTrac, print out the text of any articles you plan to use or download them onto a diskette. Finally, browse the World Wide Web for possible sources. Remember, the quality and reliability of material found on the Web can vary, so use only information from reliable sources — a Web page sponsored by a well-known national publication or organization or by a university, for example.

When Allison searched the Web using the keywords *media violence,* she found the Web site produced by the ERIC Counseling and Student Services Clearinghouse. This site contained "Children and Television Violence," an article posted by the American Psychological Association, which her instructor told her was a nationally recognized professional organization.

STEP 5: TAKING NOTES

Once you have gathered the material you will need, read it carefully, writing down any information you think you can use in your paper. As you take notes, record relevant information on three-by-five-inch cards, on individual sheets of paper, or in a separate computer file.

When you use information from a source in your paper, you do not always *quote* the exact words of your source. In fact, most often you *paraphrase* or *summarize* a source, putting its ideas into your own words. For this reason, most of your notes should be in the form of paraphrase or summary.

When you **paraphrase,** you put the ideas of a source into your own words, following the order and emphasis of the original. You paraphrase when you want to make a discussion easier to understand while still conveying a clear sense of the original. Here is a passage from the article "Children and Television Violence" followed by Allison's paraphrase.

> ORIGINAL: Children often behave differently after they've been watching violent programs on television. In one study done at Pennsylvania State University, about 100 preschool children were observed both before and after watching television; some watched cartoons that had many aggressive and violent acts; others watched shows that didn't have any kind of violence. The researchers noticed real differences between the kids who watched the violent shows and those who watched nonviolent ones.

> PARAPHRASE: At Pennsylvania State University researchers did a study. They divided 100 young children into two groups: One group watched television programs that contained a lot of violence. The other group watched programs that contained very little violence. Researchers found that the two groups of children behaved very differently.

When you write a **summary,** you also put the ideas of a source into your own words. But unlike a paraphrase, a summary condenses a passage, giving only the general meaning of the original. Here is Allison's summary of the original passage quoted above.

SUMMARY: According to a study at Penn State University, young children who watched violent television shows behaved differently from those who watched nonviolent shows.

When you **quote,** you restate the exact words of a source, enclosing them in quotation marks. Because too many quotations can distract readers, quote only when an author's words are memorable or when you want to give readers the flavor of the original.

To show readers why you are using a source and to integrate source material smoothly into your paper, introduce paraphrases, summaries, and quotations with a phrase that identifies the source or its author. You can position this identifying phrase at various places in a sentence. You can also use different words to introduce source material — for example, *points out, observes, comments, notes, remarks,* and *concludes.*

IDENTIFYING PHRASE AT THE BEGINNING: *According to the article "Children and Television Violence,"* "Children often behave differently after they've been watching violent programs on television."

IDENTIFYING PHRASE AT THE END: "Children often behave differently after they've been watching violent programs on television," *observes one Pennsylvania State University study.*

IDENTIFYING PHRASE IN THE MIDDLE: "Children often behave differently," *claim researchers in a study reported by the American Psychological Association,* "after they've been watching violent programs on television."

STEP 6: WATCHING OUT FOR PLAGIARISM

As a rule, document any words or ideas from an outside source that are not **common knowledge** — information most readers will probably know or factual information widely available in reference works. When you present information from another source as if it were your own (whether intentionally or unintentionally), you are committing **plagiarism** — and plagiarism is theft. You can avoid plagiarism by understanding what you must document and what you do not have to document.

Whenever you consult a source to get ideas for your writing, be careful to avoid the errors that commonly lead to plagiarism. The following paragraph from Brian Siano's essay "Frankenstein Must Be Destroyed: Chasing the Monster of TV Violence" and the four rules outlined after it will help you understand and correct these common errors.

☑ GUIDELINES FOR AVOIDING PLAGIARISM

YOU SHOULD DOCUMENT

- Word-for-word quotations from a source
- Ideas from a source that you put in your own words
- Tables, charts, graphs, or statistics from a source

YOU DO NOT NEED TO DOCUMENT

- Your own ideas
- Common knowledge
- Familiar quotations

ORIGINAL: Of course, there are a few crazies out there who will be unfavorably influenced by what they see on TV. But even assuming that somehow the TV show (or movie or record) shares some of the blame, how does one predict what future crazies will take for inspiration? What guidelines would ensure that people write, act, or produce something that *will not upset a psychotic?* Not only is this a ridiculous demand, it's insulting to the public as well. We would all be treated as potential murderers in order to gain a hypothetical 5 percent reduction in violence.

1. DOCUMENT IDEAS FROM YOUR SOURCES

PLAGIARISM: Even if we were to control the programs that are shown on television, we would decrease violence in society by perhaps 5 percent.

Even though the writer does not quote Siano directly, she still must identify him as the source of the paraphrased material.

CORRECT: According to Brian Siano, even if we were to control the programs that are shown on television, we would decrease violence in society by perhaps 5 percent (24).

2. PLACE BORROWED WORDS IN QUOTATION MARKS

PLAGIARISM: According to Brian Siano, there will always be a few crazies out there who will be unfavorably influenced by what they see on TV (24).

Although the writer cites Siano as his source, the passage incorrectly uses Siano's exact words without quoting them. The writer must either quote the borrowed words or rephrase the material.

CORRECT (BORROWED WORDS IN QUOTATION MARKS):   According to Brian Siano, there will always be "a few crazies out there who will be unfavorably influenced by what they see on TV" (24).

CORRECT (BORROWED WORDS REPHRASED):   According to Brian Siano, some unstable people will commit crimes because of the violence they see in the media (24).

3. USE YOUR OWN WORDING

PLAGIARISM: Naturally, there will always be people who are affected by what they view on television. But even if we agree that television programs can influence people, how can we really know what will make people commit crimes? How can we be absolutely sure that a show will not disturb someone who is insane? The answer is that we can't. To pretend that we can is insulting to law-abiding citizens. We can't treat everyone as if they were criminals just to reduce violence by a small number of people (Siano 24).

Even though the writer acknowledgess Siano as her source, and even though she does not use Siano's exact words, her passage closely follows the order, emphasis, syntax, and phrasing of the original. In the following passage, the writer uses her own wording, quoting one distinctive phrase from her source.

CORRECT: According to Brian Siano, we should not censor a television program just because "a few crazies" may be incited to violence (24). Not only would such censorship deprive the majority of people of the right to watch what they want, but it would not significantly lessen the violence in society (24).

4. DISTINGUISH YOUR IDEAS FROM THE SOURCE'S IDEAS

PLAGIARISM: Any attempt to control television violence will quickly reach the point of diminishing returns. There is no way to make absolutely certain that a particular television program will not cause a disturbed person to commit a crime. It seems silly, then, to treat the majority of people as "potential murderers" just to control the behavior of a few (Siano 24).

In the preceding passage, it appears that only the quotation in the last sentence is borrowed from Siano's article. In fact, the ideas in the second sentence are also Siano's. The writer should use an identifying phrase (such as "According to Siano") to acknowledge the borrowed material in this sentence and to indicate where it begins.

CORRECT: Any attempt to control television violence will quickly reach the point of diminishing returns. According to Brian Siano, there is no way to make absolutely certain that a particular television program will not cause a disturbed person to commit a crime (24). It seems silly, then, to treat the majority of people as "potential murderers" just to control the behavior of a few (24).

STEP 7: DRAFTING A THESIS STATEMENT

After you have taken notes, review the information you have gathered and draft a **thesis statement** — a single sentence that states the main idea of your paper and tells readers what to expect.

After reviewing her notes, Allison Rogers came up with the following thesis statement for her paper on media violence.

Thesis Statement   Although the media can affect us in many ways, no amount of media violence can eliminate our responsibility for our actions.

STEP 8: MAKING AN OUTLINE

Once you have drafted a thesis statement, you are ready to make an outline. Your outline, which covers just the body paragraphs of your paper, can be either a *topic outline* (in which each idea is expressed in a word or short phrase) or a *sentence outline* (in which each idea is expressed in a complete sentence).

Allison Rogers constructed the following sentence outline for her paper.

```
  I. The teenagers claim the movie Natural Born
     Killers made them commit murder.
     A. According to John Grisham, the movie
        inspired the teenagers to commit their
        crimes.
     B. Grisham says that several murders have been
        committed by teenagers who say they were
        influenced by the movie.
 II. The idea that movie violence causes violent
     behavior is not supported.
     A. Other factors could have influenced the
        teenagers.
     B. No clear link between media violence and
        aggressive behavior has been discovered.
III. Anecdotal evidence supporting the link between
     "copycat crimes" and media violence has two
     problems.
     A. Movies are seldom definitively linked to
        crimes.
     B. Anecdotal evidence is not representative.
 IV. The right of the majority to watch television
     shows should not be limited because some
     unbalanced people may commit crimes.
```

> V. However, young children should be protected
>   from media violence.
>   A. Parents should protect young children.
>   1. Parents should monitor what children
>   watch.
>   2. Parents should watch with children and
>   discuss program content.
>   3. Parents should block violent shows.
>   B. The media should do more to protect young
>   children.
>   1. Movie theaters should enforce the rating
>   system.
>   2. Violent programs should not be shown on
>   stations whose audience is primarily
>   children.

Notice that Allison uses roman numerals for first-level headings, capital letters for second-level headings, and numbers for third-level headings. All her points are expressed in parallel terms.

STEP 9: WRITING YOUR PAPER

Once you have decided on a thesis and written an outline, you are ready to write a draft of your paper. Start by arranging your notes in the order in which you will use them. Follow your outline as you write, but don't be afraid to depart from it if new ideas occur to you.

Begin your paper with an **introduction** that includes your thesis statement. Usually your introduction will be a single paragraph, but sometimes it will be longer.

In the **body** of your paper, you support your thesis statement, with each body paragraph developing a single idea. Support your points with summaries, paraphrases, and quotations from your sources, as well as with your own ideas and opinions, Your body paragraphs should have clear topic sentences so that your readers will know exactly what points you are making, and you should use transitional words and phrases to help readers follow the progression of your ideas.

Finally, your **conclusion** should give readers a sense of completion. Like your introduction, your conclusion is usually a single paragraph, but it can be longer. It should reinforce your thesis statement and your paper's main ideas and should end with a sentence that will stay with readers.

Remember that you will probably write several drafts of your paper before you submit it. You can use the revision checklist on page 53 to help you revise and edit your paper.

Allison Rogers's completed paper on media violence appears on page 686.

STEP 10: DOCUMENTING YOUR SOURCES

When you **document** a source, you tell readers where you have found the information that you have used in your paper. The Modern Language Association (MLA) recommends the following documentation style for research papers.* This format consists of *parenthetical references* within a paper that refer to a *Works Cited* list at the end of the paper.

Parenthetical References in the Text

A parenthetical reference should include just enough information to guide readers to a specific entry in your Works Cited list. A typical parenthetical reference consists of the author's last name and the page number: (Grisham 2). If you use more than one work by the same author, include a shortened form of the title in the parenthetical reference: (Grisham, "Killers" 4). Notice that there is no *p.* or period before the page number.

Whenever possible, introduce information with a phrase that includes the author's name. (If you do this, include the page number in parentheses.)

▶   As John Grisham observes in "Unnatural Killers," Oliver

Stone celebrates gratuitous violence (4).

Place documentation so that it doesn't interrupt the flow of your ideas, preferably at the end of a sentence.

The format for parenthetical references departs from these guidelines in three special situations:

WHEN YOU ARE CITING A WORK BY TWO AUTHORS

▶   Film violence has been increasing during the past ten years

(Williams and Yorst 34).

WHEN YOU ARE CITING A WORK WITHOUT A LISTED AUTHOR

▶   Ever since cable television came on the scene, shows with

graphically violent content have become common ("Cable

Wars" 76).

WHEN YOU ARE CITING AN INDIRECT SOURCE

If you use a statement by one author that is quoted in the work of another author, show this by including the abbreviation *qtd. in* ("quoted in").

▶   When speaking of television drama, Leonard Eron, of the Uni-

versity of Illinois, says "perpetrators of violence should

not be rewarded for violent acts" (qtd. in Siano 23).

---

*For further information see the fifth edition of the *MLA Handbook for Writers of Research Papers* (New York: Mod. Lang. Assn., 1999) or the MLA Web site <http://mla.org>.

GUIDELINES FOR FORMATTING QUOTATIONS

Short quotations   Quotations of no more than four typed lines are run in with the text of your paper. End punctuation comes after the parenthetical reference (which follows the quotation marks).

According to Grisham, there are "only two ways to curb the excessive violence of a film like Natural Born Killers" (5).

Long quotations   Quotations of more than four lines are set off from the text of your paper. Indent a long quotation ten spaces (or one inch) from the left-hand margin, and do not enclose the passage in quotation marks. The first line of a long quotation is not indented even if it is the beginning of a paragraph. If a quoted passage has more than one paragraph, indent the first line of each paragraph after the first one three additional spaces (or one-quarter inch). Introduce a long quotation with a colon, and place the parenthetical reference one space *after* the end punctuation.

Grisham believes that eventually the courts will act to force studio executives to accept responsibility for the effects of their products:

> But the laughing will soon stop. It will take only one large verdict against the likes of Oliver Stone, and his production company, and perhaps the screenwriter, and the studio itself, and then the party will be over. The verdict will come from the heartland, far away from Southern California, in some small courtroom with no cameras. (5)

The Works Cited List

The Works Cited list includes all the works you cite (refer to) in your paper. Use the following guidelines to prepare your list.

The following sample works cited entries cover the situations you will encounter most often. Follow the formats exactly as they appear here.

Books

BOOK BY ONE AUTHOR

List the author, last name first. Underline the title. Include the city of publication and a shortened form of the publisher's name — for example, *Prentice* for *Prentice Hall* or *Random* for *Random House, Inc.* Use the abbreviation *UP* for *University Press,* as in *Princeton UP* and *U of Chicago P.* End with the date of publication.

> ## GUIDELINES FOR PREPARING THE WORKS CITED LIST
>
> - Begin the Works Cited list on a new page after the last page of your paper.
> - Number the Works Cited page as the next page of the paper.
> - Center the heading *Works Cited* one inch from the top of the page; don't underline the heading or put it in quotation marks.
> - Double-space the list.
> - List entries alphabetically according to the author's last name.
> - Alphabetize unsigned articles according to the first major word of the title.
> - Begin each entry flush with the left-hand margin.
> - Indent second and subsequent lines five spaces (or one-half inch).
> - Separate each division of the entry — author, title, and publication information — by a period and one space.

▶   Brown, Charles T. The Rock and Roll Story. Englewood Cliffs:
        Prentice, 1983.

BOOK BY TWO OR THREE AUTHORS

List second and subsequent authors, first name first, in the order in which they are listed on the book's title page.

▶   Coe, Sophie D., and Michael D. Coe. The True History of
        Chocolate. New York: Thames, 1996.

BOOK BY MORE THAN THREE AUTHORS

List only the first author, followed by the abbreviation *et al.* ("and others").

▶   Sklar, Robert E., et al. Movie-Made America: A Cultural
        History of American Movies. New York: Random, 1994.

TWO OR MORE BOOKS BY THE SAME AUTHOR

List two or more books by the same author in alphabetical order according to title. In each entry after the first, type three unspaced hyphens (followed by a period) instead of the author's name.

▶   Angelou, Maya. Getting Together in My Name. New York: Bantam,
        1980.
    ---. I Know Why the Caged Bird Sings. New York: Bantam, 1985.

EDITED BOOK

▶   Dickinson, Emily. The Complete Poems of Emily Dickinson. Ed.
        Thomas H. Johnson. New York: Little, 1990.

TRANSLATION

▶ García Márquez, Gabriel. <u>Love in the Time of Cholera</u>. Trans. Edith Grossman. New York: Knopf, 1988.

REVISED EDITION

▶ Gans, Herbert J. <u>The Urban Villagers</u>. 2nd ed. New York: Free, 1982.

ANTHOLOGY

▶ Kirszner, Laurie G., and Stephen R. Mandell, eds. <u>Patterns for College Writing</u>. 8th ed. New York: Bedford/St. Martin's, 2001.

ESSAY IN AN ANTHOLOGY

▶ Grisham, John. "Unnatural Killers." <u>Patterns for College Writing</u>. 8th ed. Ed. Laurie G. Kirszner and Stephen R. Mandell. New York: Bedford/St. Martin's, 2001. 000-00.

MORE THAN ONE ESSAY IN THE SAME ANTHOLOGY

List each essay separately with a cross-reference to the entire anthology.

▶ Grisham, John. "Unnatural Killers." Kirszner and Mandell 000-00.

▶ Kirszner, Laurie G., and Stephen R. Mandell, eds. <u>Patterns for College Writing</u>. 8th ed. New York: Bedford/St. Martin's, 2001.

▶ Stone, Oliver. "Memo to John Grisham: What's Next--'A Movie Made Me Do It'?" Kirszner and Mandell 000-00.

SECTION OR CHAPTER OF A BOOK

▶ Gordimer, Nadine. "Once upon a Time." <u>Jump and Other Stories</u>. New York: Farrar, 1991.

Periodicals

ARTICLE IN A JOURNAL WITH CONTINUOUS PAGINATION THROUGHOUT AN ANNUAL VOLUME

Some scholarly journals have continuous pagination; that is, one issue might end on page 234, and the next would then begin with page 235. In this case, the volume number is followed by the date of publication in parentheses.

▶ Allen, Dennis W. "Horror and Perverse Delight: Faulkner's 'A Rose for Emily.'" <u>Modern Fiction Studies</u> 30 (1984): 685-96.

ARTICLE IN A JOURNAL WITH SEPARATE PAGINATION IN EACH ISSUE

For a journal in which each issue begins with page 1, the volume number is followed by a period and the issue number and then by the date. Leave no space after the period.

▶   Lindemann, Erika. "Teaching as a Rhetorical Art." CEA Forum
         15.2 (1985): 9-12.

ARTICLE IN A MONTHLY MAGAZINE

If an article doesn't appear on consecutive pages — for example, if it begins on page 43, skips to page 47, and continues on page 49 — include only the first page, followed by a plus sign.

▶   O'Brien, Conor Cruise. "Thomas Jefferson: Radical and
         Racist." Atlantic Monthly Oct. 1996: 43+.

ARTICLE IN A WEEKLY MAGAZINE (SIGNED OR UNSIGNED)

▶   "The Dead Don't Tell Lies." Time 28 Oct. 1996: 37.

▶   Miller, Arthur. "Why I wrote The Crucible." New Yorker 21
         Oct. 1996: 158-63.

ARTICLE IN A NEWSPAPER

▶   Haberman, Clyde. "Is Graffiti 'Art'?" New York Times 22 Oct.
         1996, late ed.: B1.

EDITORIAL OR LETTER TO THE EDITOR

▶   "High Taxes Kill Cities." Editorial. Philadelphia Inquirer
         8 Aug. 1995, late ed., sec. 1: 17.

Internet Sources

When citing Internet sources appearing on the World Wide Web, include both the date of electronic publication (if available) and the date you accessed the source. In addition, include the URL (electronic address) in angle brackets. (*Note:* MLA style requires that you break URLs only after a slash.)

PROFESSIONAL SITE

▶   Words of the Year. American Dialect Society. 30 Dec. 1998.
         <http://www.americandialect.org/woty.shtml>.

PERSONAL SITE

▶   Lynch, Jack. Home page. 11 Nov. 1998 <http://dept.english.
         upenn.edu/~jlynch>.

ARTICLE IN A SCHOLARLY JOURNAL

▶   Condie, Kent C., and Jane Silverstone. "The Crust of the
        Colorado Plateau: New Views of an Old Arc." The Journal
        of Geology 107.4 (1999). 9 Aug. 1999 <http://www.
        journals.uchicago.edu/JG/journal/issues/v107n4/990034/
        990034.html>.

ARTICLE IN AN ONLINE REFERENCE BOOK OR ENCYCLOPEDIA

▶   "Croatia." The 1997 World Factbook. 30 Mar. 1998. Central
        Intelligence Agency. 30 Dec. 1998 <http://www.odci.gov/
        cia/publications/factbook/country-frame.html>.

ARTICLE IN A NEWSPAPER

▶   Lohr, Steve. "Microsoft Goes to Court." New York Times on the
        Web 19 Oct. 1998. 9 Apr. 1999 <http://archives.nytimes.
        com/archives/search/fastweb?search>.

EDITORIAL

▶   "Be Serious." Editorial. Washington Post 25 Mar. 1999. 9
        Apr. 1999 <http://newslibrary.Krmediastream.com/
        cgi-bin/search/wp>.

ARTICLE IN A MAGAZINE

▶   Webb, Michael. "Playing at Work." Metropolis Online. Nov.
        1997. 11 Nov. 1997 <http://www.metropolismag.com/nov97/
        eames/eames.html>.

POSTING TO A DISCUSSION LIST

Be sure to include the phrase "Online posting."

▶   Thune, W. Scott. "Emotion and Rationality in Argument." 23
        Mar. 1997. Online posting. CCCC/97 Online. 11 Nov. 1997
        <http://www.missouri.edu/HyperNews/get/cccc98/proplink/
        12.html>.

E-MAIL

▶   Laev, Talvi. E-mail to the author. 9 Aug. 2000.

MATERIAL ACCESSED THROUGH AN ONLINE SERVICE

Frequently, online services like America Online and Lexis-Nexis enable
you to access material without providing a URL. If you access such material by using a keyword, provide the keyword (following the date of
access) at the end of the entry.

▶ "Kafka, Franz." Compton's Encyclopedia Online. Vers. 2.0.

      1997. American Online. 8 June 1998. Keyword: Compton's.

If, instead of using a keyword, you follow a series of paths, list the paths separated by semicolons.

▶ "Elizabeth Adams." History Resources. 11 Nov. 1997. America

      Online. 28 June 1999. Path: Research: Biography; Women

      in Science; Biographies.

MATERIAL ACCESSED ON A CD-ROM

In addition to the publication information, include the medium (CD-ROM), the vendor (UMI-Proquest, for example), and the date you accessed the information.

▶ Braunmiller, A. R., ed. Macbeth. By William Shakespeare.

      CD-ROM. New York: Voyager, 1994.

Warning: Using information from an Internet source — especially a newsgroup or discussion list — is risky. Contributors are not necessarily experts on a topic, and they are frequently misinformed. Unless you can be certain that the information you are obtaining from these sources is reliable, don't use it. You can check the reliability of an Internet source by consulting the guidelines printed in many college handbooks or by asking your instructor or librarian for guidance.

Other Nonprint Sources

TELEVISION OR RADIO PROGRAM

▶ "Prime Suspect 3." Writ. Lynda La Plante. With Helen Mirren.

      Mystery! WNET, New York. 28 Apr. 1994.

VIDEOTAPE, MOVIE, RECORD, OR SLIDE PROGRAM

▶ Murray, Donald. Interview with John Updike. Dir. Bruce

      Schwartz. Videocassette. Harcourt, 1997.

PERSONAL INTERVIEW

▶ Garcetti, Gilbert. Personal interview. 7 May 1994.

SAMPLE STUDENT RESEARCH PAPER IN MLA STYLE

Here is Allison Rogers's final essay on the topic of media violence. The essay follows the conventions of MLA documentation style. It has been reproduced in a narrower format than you will have on a standard $(8\frac{1}{2}'' \times 11'')$ sheet of paper.

Allison Rogers

Professor Levitt

English 122-83

7 April 2000

Violence in the Media

Introduction

Mickey and Mallory, two characters in Oliver Stone's film <u>Natural Born Killers</u>, travel across the Southwest, killing a total of fifty-two people. After watching this movie, two teenagers went on a crime spree of their own and killed one person and wounded another, paralyzing her for the rest of her life. At their trial, their defense was that watching <u>Natural Born Killers</u> had made them commit their crimes and that Hollywood, along with the director of the movie, Oliver Stone, was to blame. As creative as this defense is, it is

Thesis statement

hard to accept. The power of the media to shape lives may be great, but no amount of violence on the screen can eliminate a person's responsibility for his or her actions, especially when it comes to murder.

Paragraph combines quotation and paraphrase from Grisham article with Allison's own observations.

According to John Grisham, Oliver Stone's <u>Natural Born Killers</u> "inspired" two teenagers "to commit murder" (5). Grisham goes on to say that since the movie was released, several murders have been committed by troubled young people who claimed they were "under the influence" of Mickey and Mallory (5). This type of defense keeps reappearing as the violence in our everyday lives increases: "I am not to blame," says the perpetrator. "That movie (or television show) made me do it."

The idea that violence in the media causes violent behavior is not supported by the facts. When we look at Ben and Sarah, the two teen-

Rogers 2

Paragraph combines clearly documented paraphrases of the Stone article with Allison's own conclusions.

agers who supposedly imitated Mickey and Mallory, it is clear that factors other than Natural Born Killers could have influenced their
decision to commit murder. Both young adults
had long histories of drug and alcohol abuse as
well as psychiatric treatment (Stone 39). In
addition, no clear experimental link between
violent movies and television shows and aggressive behavior has been discovered.

What, then, are we supposed to make of
crimes that seem to be inspired by the media?

Phrase "As Steve Bauman suggests," introduces Allison's summary of source's ideas.

As Steve Bauman suggests, many people believe
that there is a link between "copycat crimes"
and media violence (16). Two problems exist
with this type of anecdotal "evidence," however. The first problem is that in most cases,
the movie or television show is never definitely
linked to the crime. For example, after the
movie The Money Train was released, a clerk in
a New York City subway token booth was set on
fire in much the same way a subway token clerk

No documentation necessary for common knowledge.

was in the movie. Naturally, it appeared as if
the movie had inspired the crime. But at the
time of the crime, several newspapers reported
that the violent act depicted in the movie was
not unusual and had in fact occurred at least
twice in the year before the movie's release.
So the question remains: did the movie cause
the violence, or did it simply reflect a kind
of violent behavior that was already present in
society? The truth is that we cannot answer
this question conclusively.

The second problem with anecdotal evidence
is that it is not representative. Crimes that
are inspired by the media--killers imitating
Freddy Krueger, for example--are unusual. As

Bauman points out, most people who watch violent
movies do not go out and commit crimes (16).
Only a few people will have extreme reactions,
and because they are mentally unbalanced, we
cannot predict what will set them off. It could
be a movie like Natural Born Killers, but it
could also be a Bugs Bunny cartoon or a Three
Stooges movie. The point is that society should
not limit our right to watch the movies and
television shows we want to see just because a
few unbalanced individuals may go out and commit crimes.

**The two para-
graphs on this
page combine
paraphrases from
APA article with
Allison's own
observations.**

Even if the link between media violence
and violent behavior is not clear, most people
agree that young children are easily influenced
by what they see. One study has shown that young
children who watch violent television shows
behave differently from those who watch nonviolent television shows (American Psychological
Association). For this reason, young children
should be protected. First, parents need to
understand their responsibility for monitoring
what their children watch on television. This
monitoring needs to begin at home, where it is
the parents' job to give their children a sense
of what is real and what is not. Second, as the
American Psychological Association suggests,
parents should take the time to watch shows
along with their children and discuss the content with them. Finally, if parents cannot watch
television with their children, they can at
least buy devices that will prevent children
from watching violent programs.

The media have already taken steps to protect children. For example, rating systems now

Rogers 4

in place can help. These give parents the ability to judge the content of movies before children go to see them and to evaluate television
shows before they are turned on. Clearly, however, more needs to be done to protect young
children. For one thing, rating systems must be
enforced. If an R movie is being shown at a
theater, for example, the management must
require proof of age. In addition, any movie or
television show containing violence should not
be shown on stations whose audience is primarily children, such as Nickelodeon or the Disney
Channel, even at night. The time of day should
not matter. When you think of Nickelodeon or
Disney, The Brady Bunch and Mickey Mouse should
come to mind, not Dirty Harry (American Psychological Association).

Conclusion

There is no doubt that violence is learned
and that violent media images encourage violent
behavior. It is not clear, however, that violent movies and television shows will actually
cause a person to commit a crime. Placing the
blame on the media is just an easy way to side-

**This paragraph
needs no docu-
mentation
because it con-
tains Allison's
own ideas.**

step the hard questions, such as what is causing
so much violence in our society and what we can
do about it. If we prohibit violent programs,
we will only deprive many people of their right
to view the programs of their choice, and we
will prevent artists from expressing themselves
freely. In the process, these restrictions will
also deprive society of a good deal of worthwhile entertainment.

Rogers 5

Works Cited

American Psychological Association. "Children and
    Television Violence." School Violence Virtual
    Library 6 June 1997. 19 Oct. 1998 <http://
    www.uncg.edu/edu/ericcass/violence/index.htm>.

Bauman, Steve. "Games as a Scapegoat." Computer
    Games July 1999: 16.

Grisham, John. "Unnatural Killers." The Oxford Amer-
    ican Spring 1996: 2-5.

Stone, Oliver. "Memo to John Grisham: What's Next--
    'A Movie Made Me Do It'?" LA Weekly 29 Mar.-4
    Apr. 1996: 39.

GLOSSARY

Abstract/Concrete language   Abstract language names concepts or qualities that cannot be directly seen or touched: *love, emotion, evil, anguish.* Concrete language denotes objects or qualities that can be perceived by the senses: *fountain pen, leaky, shouting, rancid.* Abstract words are sometimes needed to express ideas, but they are very vague unless used with concrete supporting detail. The abstract phrase "The speaker was overcome with emotion" could mean almost anything, but the addition of concrete language clarifies the meaning: "He clenched his fist and shook it at the crowd" (anger).

Allusion   A brief reference to literature, history, the Bible, mythology, popular culture, and so on that readers are expected to recognize. An allusion evokes a vivid impression in very few words. "The gardener opened the gate, and suddenly we found ourselves in Eden" suggests in one word (*Eden*) the stunning beauty of the garden the writer visited.

Analogy   A form of comparison that explains an unfamiliar element by comparing it to another that is more familiar. Analogies also enable writers to put abstract or technical information in simpler, more concrete terms: "The effect of pollution on the environment is like that of cancer on the body."

Annotating   The technique of recording one's responses to a reading selection by writing notes in the margins of the text. Annotating a text might involve asking questions, suggesting possible parallels with other selections or with the reader's own experience, arguing with the writer's points, commenting on the writer's style, or defining unfamiliar terms or concepts.

Antithesis   A viewpoint opposite to one expressed in a *thesis.* In an argumentative essay, the thesis must be debatable. If no antithesis exists, the writer's thesis is not debatable. (See also **Thesis.**)

Antonym   A word opposite in meaning to another word. *Beautiful* is the antonym of *ugly. Synonym* is the antonym of *antonym.*

Argumentation   The form of writing that takes a stand on an issue and attempts to convince readers by presenting a logical sequence of points supported by evidence. Unlike *persuasion,* which uses a number of different appeals, argumentation is primarily an appeal to reason. (See Chapter 12.)

Audience   The people "listening" to a writer's words. Writers who are sensitive to their audience will carefully choose a tone, examples, and allusions that their readers will understand and respond to. For instance, an effective article attempting to persuade high school students not to drink alcohol would use examples and allusions pertinent to a teenager's life. Different examples would be chosen if the writer were addressing middle-aged members of Alcoholics Anonymous.

Basis for comparison   A fundamental similarity between two or more things that enables a writer to compare them. In a comparison of how two towns react to immigrants, the basis of comparison might be that both towns have a rapidly expanding immigrant population. (If one of the towns did not have any immigrants, this comparison would be illogical.)

Body paragraphs   The paragraphs that develop and support an essay's thesis.

Brainstorming   An invention technique that can be done individually or in a group. When writers brainstorm on their own, they jot down every fact or idea that relates to a particular topic. When they brainstorm in a group, they discuss a topic with others and write down the useful ideas that come up.

Causal chain   A sequence of events in which one event causes another event, which in turn causes yet another event.

Cause and effect   The pattern of development that discusses either the reasons for an occurrence or the observed or predicted consequence of an occurrence. Often both causes and effects are discussed in the same essay. (See Chapter 8.)

Causes   The reasons for an event, situation, or phenomenon. An *immediate cause* is an obvious one; a *remote cause* is less easily perceived. The *main cause* is the most important cause, whether it is immediate or remote. Other, less important causes that nevertheless encourage the effect in some way (for instance, by speeding it up or providing favorable circumstances for it) are called *contributory causes.*

Chronological order   The time sequence in which events occur. Chronological order is often used to organize a narrative; it is also used to structure a process essay.

Claim   In Toulmin logic, the thesis or main point of an essay. Usually the claim is stated directly, but sometimes it is implied. (See also **Toulmin logic.**)

Classification and division   The pattern of development that uses these two related methods of organizing information. *Classification* involves searching for common characteristics among various items and grouping them accordingly, thereby imposing orderly or randomly organized information. *Division* breaks up an entity into smaller groups or elements. Classification generalizes; division specifies. (See Chapter 10.)

Cliché   An overused expression, such as *beauty is in the eye of the beholder, the good die young,* or *a picture is worth a thousand words.*

Clustering   A method of invention whereby a writer groups ideas visually by listing the main topic in the center of a page, circling it, and surrounding it with words or phrases that identify the major points to be addressed. The writer then circles these words or phrases, creating new clusters or ideas for each of them.

Coherence   The tight relationship between all the parts of an effective piece of writing. Such a relationship ensures that the writing will make sense to readers. For a piece of writing to be coherent, it must be logical and orderly, with effective *transitions* making the movement between sentences and paragraphs clear. Within and between paragraphs, coherence may also be enhanced by the repetition of key words and ideas, by the use of pronouns to refer to nouns mentioned previously, and by the use of parallel sentence structure.

Colloquialisms   Expressions that are generally appropriate for conversation and informal writing but not usually acceptable for the writing you do in college, business, or professional settings. Examples of colloquial language include contractions; clipped forms (*dorm* for *dormitory, exam* for *examination*); vague expressions like *kind of* and *sort of;* conversation fillers like *you know;* and other informal words and expressions, such as *get across* for *communicate* and *kids* for *children.*

Common knowledge   Factual information that is widely available in reference sources. Writers do not need to document common knowledge.

Comparison and contrast   The pattern of development that focuses on similarities and/or differences between two or more subjects. In a general sense, *comparison* shows how two or more subjects are alike; *contrast* shows how they are different. (See Chapter 9.) (See also **Point-by-point comparison; Subject-by-subject comparison.**)

Conclusion   The group of sentences or paragraphs that brings an essay to a close. To *conclude* means not only "to end" but also "to resolve." Although a conclusion does not resolve all the issues in an essay, the conclusion is the place to show that they *have* been resolved. An effective conclusion indicates that the writer is committed to what has been expressed, and it is the writer's last chance to leave an impression of confidence with readers.

Concrete language   See **Abstract/Concrete language.**

Connotation   The associations, meanings, or feelings a word suggests beyond its literal meaning. Literally, the word *home* means one's place of residence, but *home* also connotes warmth and a sense of belonging. (See also **Denotation.**)

Contributory cause   See **Causes.**

Deductive reasoning   The method of reasoning that moves from a general premise to a specific conclusion. Deductive reasoning is the opposite of *inductive reasoning.* (See also **Syllogism.**)

Definition   An explanation of a word's meaning; the pattern of development in which a writer explains what something or someone is. See Chapter 11. (See also **Extended definition; Formal definition.**)

Denotation   The literal meaning of a word. The denotation of *home* is "one's place of residence." (See also **Connotation.**)

Description   The pattern of development that presents a word picture of a thing, a person, a situation, or a series of events. (See Chapter 5.) (See also **Objective description; Subjective description.**)

Digression   A remark or series of remarks that wanders from the main point of a discussion. In a personal narrative, a digression may be entertaining because of its very irrelevance, but in other kinds of writing it is likely to distract and confuse readers.

Division   See **Classification and division.**

Documentation   The formal way of giving credit to the sources from which a writer borrows words or ideas. Documentation allows readers to evaluate a writer's sources and to consult them if they wish. Papers written for classes in English and related disciplines use the documentation style recommended by the Modern Language Association (MLA).(See Appendix.)

Dominant impression   The mood or quality that is central to a piece of writing.

Essay   A short work of nonfiction writing on a single topic that usually expresses the author's impressions or opinions. An essay may be organized around one of the patterns of development presented in Chapters 4 through 12 of this book, or it may combine several of these patterns.

Euphemism   A polite term for an unpleasant concept. (*Passed on* is a euphemism for *died.*)

Evidence   Facts and opinions used to support a statement, position, or idea. *Facts,* which may include statistics, may be drawn from research or personal experience; *opinions* may represent the conclusions of experts or the writer's own ideas.

Example   A concrete, specific illustration of a general point.

Exemplification   The pattern of development that uses a single extended *example* or a series of shorter examples to support a thesis. (See Chapter 6.)

Extended definition   A paragraph-, essay-, or book-length definition developed by means of one or more of the rhetorical strategies discussed in this book.

Fallacy   A statement that resembles a logical argument but is not. Logical fallacies are often persuasive, but they unfairly manipulate readers to win agreement. Fallacies include begging the question; argument from analogy; personal (*ad hominem*) attacks; hasty or sweeping generalizations; false dilemmas (the either/or fallacy); equivocation; red herrings, you also (*tu quoque*); appeals to doubtful authority; distorting statistics; *post hoc* reasoning; and *non sequiturs.*

Figures of speech (also known as *figurative language*)   Imaginative language used to suggest a special meaning or create a special effect. Three of the most common figures of speech are *similes, metaphors,* and *personification.*

Formal definition   A brief explanation of a word's meaning as it appears in the dictionary.

Freewriting   A method of invention that involves writing without stopping for a fixed period — perhaps five or ten minutes — without paying attention to spelling, grammar, or punctuation. The goal of freewriting is to let ideas flow and get them down on paper.

Grounds   In Toulmin logic, the material that a writer uses to support a claim. Grounds may be evidence (facts or expert opinions) or appeals to the emotions or values of an audience. (See also **Toulmin logic.**)

Highlighting   A technique used by a reader to record responses to a reading selection by marking the text with symbols. Highlighting a text might involve underlining important ideas, boxing key terms, numbering a series of related points, circling unfamiliar words (or placing question marks next to them), drawing vertical lines alongside an interesting or important passage, drawing arrows to connect related points, or placing asterisks next to discussions of the selection's central issues or themes.

Hyperbole   Deliberate exaggeration for emphasis or humorous effect: "I froze to death out in the storm"; "She has hundreds of boyfriends"; "Senior year passed by in a second." The opposite of hyperbole is *understatement.*

Imagery   A set of verbal pictures of sensory experiences. These pictures, conveyed through concrete details, make a description vivid and immediate to the reader. Some images are literal ("The cows were so white they almost glowed in the dark"); others are more figurative ("The black and white cows looked like maps, with the continents in black and the seas in white"). A pattern of imagery (repeated images of, for example, shadows, forests, or fire) may run through a piece of writing.

Immediate cause   See **Causes.**

Inductive reasoning   The method of reasoning that moves from specific evidence to a general conclusion based on this evidence. Inductive reasoning is the opposite of *deductive reasoning.*

Instructions   A kind of process essay whose purpose is to enable readers to *perform* a process. Instructions use the present tense and speak directly to readers: "Walk at a moderate pace for twenty minutes."

Introduction   An essay's opening. Depending on the length of an essay, the introduction may be one paragraph, several paragraphs, or even a few pages long. In an introduction, a writer tries to encourage the audience to read the essay that follows. Therefore, the writer must choose tone and diction carefully, indicate what the paper is about, and suggest to readers what direction it will take.

Invention   (also known as *prewriting*) The stage of writing in which a writer explores the writing assignment, focuses ideas, and ultimately decides on a thesis for an essay. A writer might begin by thinking through the requirements of the assignment — the essay's purpose, length, and audience. Then, using one or more methods of invention — such as *freewriting, looping, questions for probing, brainstorming, clustering,* and *journal writing* — the writer can proceed to formulate a tentative thesis and begin to write the essay.

Irony   Language that points to a discrepancy between two different levels of meaning. *Verbal irony* is characterized by a gap between what is actually stated and what is really meant, which often has the opposite meaning — for instance, "his humble abode" (referring to a millionaire's estate). *Situational irony* points to a discrepancy between what actually happens and what readers expect will happen. This kind of irony is present, for instance, when a character, trying to frighten a rival, ends up being frightened himself. *Dramatic irony* occurs when the reader understands more about what is happening in a story than the character who is telling the story does. For example, a narrator might tell an anecdote that he intends to illustrate how clever he is, while it is obvious to the reader from the story's events that the narrator has made a fool of himself because of his gullibility. (See also **Sarcasm.**)

Jargon   The specialized vocabulary of a profession or academic field. Although the jargon of a particular profession is an efficient means of communication within that field, it may not be clear or meaningful to readers outside that profession.

Journal writing   A method of invention that involves recording ideas that emerge from reading or other experiences and then exploring them in writing.

Looping   A method of invention that involves isolating one idea from a piece of freewriting and using this idea as a focus for a new piece of freewriting.

Main cause   See **Causes.**

Metaphor   A comparison of two dissimilar things that does not use the words *like* or *as* ("Not yet would they veer southward to the caldron of the land that lay below" — N. Scott Momaday).

Narration   The pattern of development that tells a story. (See Chapter 4.)

Objective description   A detached, factual picture presented in as plain and direct a manner as possible. Although pure objectivity is difficult if not impossible to achieve, writers of science papers, technical reports, and news articles, among others, strive for precise language that is free of value judgments.

Paragraph   The basic unit of an essay. A paragraph is composed of related sentences that together express a single idea. This main idea is often stated in a single *topic sentence.* Paragraphs are also graphic symbols on the page, mapping the progress of the ideas in the essay and providing visual breaks for readers.

Parallelism   The use of similar grammatical elements within a sentence or sentences. "I like hiking, skiing, and to cook" is not parallel because *hiking* and *skiing* are gerund forms (*-ing*) while *to cook* is an infinitive form. Revised for parallelism, the sentence could read either "I like hiking, skiing, and cooking" or "I like to hike, to ski, and to cook." As a stylistic technique, parallelism can provide emphasis through repetition — for example, "Walk groundly, talk profoundly, drink roundly, sleep soundly" (William Hazlitt). Parallelism is also a powerful oratorical technique: "Until justice is blind to color, until education is unaware of race, until opportunity is unconcerned with the color of men's skins, emancipation will be a proclamation but not a fact" (Lyndon B. Johnson). Finally, parallelism can increase *coherence* within a paragraph or an essay.

Paraphrase   The restatement of another person's words in one's own words, following the order and emphasis of the original. Paraphrase is frequently used in source-based papers, where the purpose is to use information gathered during research to support the ideas in the paper. For example, Jonathan Kozol's "Illiterates cannot travel freely. When they attempt to do so, they encounter risks that few of us can dream of" (page 207) might be paraphrased like this: "According to Jonathan Kozol, people who cannot read find travel extremely risky."

Personification   Describing concepts or objects as if they were human ("the chair slouched"; "the wind sighed outside the window").

Persuasion   The method by which a writer moves an audience to adopt a belief or follow a course of action. To persuade an audience, a writer relies on the various appeals — to the emotions, to reason, or to ethics. Persuasion is different from *argumentation,* which appeals primarily to reason.

Plagiarism   Presenting the words or ideas of someone else as if they were one's own (whether intentionally or unintentionally). Plagiarism should always be avoided.

Point-by-point comparison   A comparison in which the writer first makes a point about one subject and then follows it with a comparable point about the other subject. (See also **Subject-by-subject comparison.**)

Post hoc **reasoning**   A logical fallacy that involves looking back at two events that occurred in chronological sequence and wrongly assuming that the first event caused the second. For example, just because a tree falls after a thunderstorm, one cannot automatically assume that the storm caused the tree to fall.

Prewriting   See **Invention.**

Principle of classification   In a classification-and-division essay, the quality the items have in common. For example, if a writer were classifying automobiles, one principle of classification might be "repair records."

Process   The pattern of development that presents a series of steps in a procedure in chronological order and shows how this sequence of steps leads to a particular result. (See Chapter 7.)

Process explanation   A kind of process essay whose purpose is to enable readers to understand a process rather than perform it.

Purpose   A writer's reason for writing. A writer's purpose may, for example, be to entertain readers with an amusing story, to inform them about a dangerous disease, to move them to action by enraging them with an example of injustice, or to change their perspective by revealing a hidden dimension of a person or situation.

Quotation   The exact words of a source, enclosed in quotation marks. A quotation should be used only for particularly memorable statements, or when a paraphrase would change the meaning of the original.

Refutation   The attempt to counter an opposing argument by revealing its weaknesses. Three of the most common weaknesses are logical flaws in the argument, inadequate evidence, and irrelevance. Refutation greatly strengthens an argument by showing that the writer is aware of the complexity of the issue and has considered opposing viewpoints.

Remote cause   See **Causes.**

Rhetorical question   A question asked for effect and not meant to be answered.

Rogerian argument   A strategy put forth by psychologist Carl Rogers that rejects the adversarial approach that characterizes many arguments. Rather than attacking the opposition, Rogers suggests acknowledging the validity of opposing positions. By finding areas of agreement, a Rogerian argument reduces conflict and increases the chance that the final position will satisfy all parties.

Running acknowledgment   The phrase that identifies the author of a paraphrase, summary, or quotation. "According to Judy Brady" and "As Amy Tan notes" are examples of running acknowledgments.

Sarcasm   Deliberately insincere and biting irony — for example, "That's okay — I love it when you borrow things and don't return them."

Satire   Writing that uses wit, irony, and ridicule to attack foolishness, incompetence, or evil in a person or idea. Satire has a different purpose from comedy, which usually intends simply to entertain. For a classic example of satire, see Jonathan Swift's "A Modest Proposal," page 648.

Sexist language   Language that stereotypes people according to gender. Writers often use plural constructions to avoid sexist language. For example, *the doctors . . . they* can be used instead of *the doctor . . . he.* Words such as *police officer* and *firefighter* can be used instead of *policeman* and *fireman.*

Simile   A comparison of two dissimilar things using the words *like* or *as* ("Hills Like White Elephants" — Ernest Hemingway).

Slang   Informal words whose meanings vary from locale to locale or change as time passes. Slang is frequently associated with a particular group of people — for example, bikers, musicians, or urban youth. Slang is inappropriate in college writing.

Subject-by-subject comparison   A comparison organized by subject rather than by the points on which the subjects are being compared. (See also **Point-by-point comparison.**)

Subjective description   A description that contains value judgments (*a saintly woman*, for example). Whereas objective language is distanced from an event or object, *subjective language* is involved. A subjective description focuses on the author's reaction to the event, conveying not just a factual record of details but also their significance. Subjective language may include poetic or colorful words that impart a judgment or an emotional response (*stride, limp, meander, hobble, stroll, plod*, or *shuffle* instead of *walk*). Subjective descriptions often include *figures of speech.*

Summary   The ideas of a source as presented in one's own words. Unlike a paraphrase, a summary conveys only a general sense of a passage, without following the order and emphasis of the original.

Syllogism   A basic form of deductive reasoning. Every syllogism includes three parts: a major premise that makes a general statement ("Confinement is physically and psychologically damaging"); a minor premise that makes a related but more specific statement ("Zoos confine animals"); and a conclusion drawn from these two premises ("Therefore, zoos are physically and psychologically damaging to animals").

Symbol   A person, event, or object that represents something more than its literal meaning.

Synonym   A word with the same basic meaning as another word. A synonym for *loud* is *noisy*. Most words in the English language have several synonyms, but each word has unique nuances or *connotations.*

Thesis   An essay's main idea; the idea that all the points in the body of the essay support. A thesis may be implied, but it is usually stated explicitly in the form of a *thesis statement.* In addition to conveying the essay's main idea, the thesis statement may indicate the writer's approach to the subject and the writer's purpose. It may also indicate the pattern of development that will structure the essay.

Topic sentence   A sentence stating the main idea of a paragraph. Often, but not always, the topic sentence opens the paragraph.

Toulmin logic   A method of structuring an argument according to the way arguments occur in everyday life. Developed by philosopher Stephen Toulmin, Toulmin logic divides an argument into three parts: the *claim*, the *grounds*, and the *warrant.*

Transitions   Words or expressions that link ideas in a piece of writing. Long essays frequently contain *transitional paragraphs* that connect one part of the essay to another. Writers use a variety of transitional expressions, such as *afterward, because, consequently, for instance, furthermore, however*, and *likewise*. See the list of transitions on page 42.

Understatement   Deliberate de-emphasis for effect: "The people who live near the Mississippi River are not exactly looking forward to more flooding"; "Emily was a little upset about flunking out of school." The opposite of understatement is *hyperbole*.

Unity The desirable attribute of a paragraph in which every sentence relates directly to the paragraph's main idea. This main idea is often stated in a *topic sentence*.

Warrant In Toulmin logic, the inference that connects the claim to the grounds. The warrant can be a belief that is taken for granted or an assumption that underlies the argument. (See also **Toulmin logic.**)

Writing process The sequence of tasks a writer undertakes when writing an essay. During *invention*, or *prewriting*, the writer gathers information and ideas and develops a thesis. During the *arrangement* stage, the writer organizes material into a logical sequence. During *drafting and revision*, the essay is actually written and then rewritten. Finally, during *editing*, the writer puts the finishing touches on the essay by correcting misspellings, checking punctuation, searching for grammatical inaccuracies, and so on. These stages occur in no fixed order; many effective writers move back and forth among them. (See Chapter 1.)

John Grisham, "Unnatural Killers." From *The Oxford American*, Spring 1996, pp. 2–5. Reprinted by permission.

Ted Gup, "The End of Serendipity" from *The Chronicle of Higher Education*, November 21, 1997. Copyright © 1997 by Ted Gup. Reprinted by permission of the author.

Linda M. Hasselstrom, "A Peaceful Woman Explains Why She Carries a Gun" from *Land Circle: Writings Collected From the Land* by Linda Hasselstrom. Copyright © 1991 by Linda Hasselstrom. Reprinted by permission of Fulcrum Publishing.

Shirley Jackson, "The Lottery." From *The Lottery* by Shirley Jackson. Copyright © 1948, 1949 by Shirley Jackson. Renewed © 1976, 1977 by Laurence Hyman, Barry Hyman, Ms. Sarah Webster, and Mrs. Joanne Schnurer. Reprinted by permission of Farrar, Straus & Giroux, Inc.

Susan Jacoby, "Common Decency." Originally published in the *New York Times Magazine*, May 9, 1991. Copyright © 1991 by Susan Jacoby. Reprinted by permission of Georges Borchardt, Inc.

Martin Luther King, Jr., "Letter from Birmingham Jail." Reprinted by arrangement with The Heirs to the Estate of Martin Luther King, Jr., c/o Writers House, Inc. as agent for the proprietor. Copyright © 1963 by Martin Luther King, Jr., copyright renewed 1991 by Coretta Scott King.

Jonathan Kozol, "The Human Cost of an Illiterate Society." From *Illiterate America* by Jonathan Kozol. Copyright © 1985 by Jonathan Kozol. Used by permission of Doubleday, a division of Bantam Doubleday Dell Publishing Group, Inc.

Richard Lederer, "English Is a Crazy Language." Reprinted with the permission of Pocket Books, a Division of Simon & Schuster, from *Crazy English* by Richard Lederer. Copyright © 1989 by Richard Lederer.

Alan Lightman, "Smile" from *Dance for Two: Selected Essays* by Alan Lightman. Copyright © 1996 by Alan Lightman. Reprinted by permission of Pantheon Books, a division of Random House, Inc.

Janice Mirikitani, "Suicide Note." From *Shedding Silence* by Janice Mirikitani. Copyright © 1987 by Janice Mirikitani. Reprinted by permission of the publisher, Ten Speed Press/Celestial Arts.

Jessica Mitford, "The Embalming of Mr. Jones." From *The American Way of Death* by Jessica Mitford. Reprinted by permission of Jessica Mitford. Copyright © 1963, 1978 by Jessica Mitford, all rights reserved.

N. Scott Momaday, "The Way to Rainy Mountain." From *The Reporter*, January 26, 1997. Copyright © 1967 by The University of New Mexico Press. Reprinted by permission.

Bharati Mukherjee, "Two Ways to Belong in America" from *The New York Times*, September 22, 1996. Copyright © 1996 by The New York Times Company. Reprinted by permission of the New York Times.

Nicholas Negroponte, "An Age of Optimism" from *Being Digital* by Nicholas Negroponte. Copyright © 1995 by Nicholas Negroponte. Reprinted by permission of Alfred A. Knopf, Inc., a division of Random House, Inc.

Alleen Pace Nielsen, "Sexism in English: Embodiment and Language" from *Living Language: Reading, Thinking and Writing*. Copyright © 1999 by Alleen Pace Nielsen. Reprinted by permission of Allyn & Bacon, Inc.

Flannery O'Connor, "Revelation." From *Everything That Rises Must Converge* by Flannery O'Connor. Copyright © 1964, 1965 by The Estate of Flannery O'Connor. Reprinted with the permission of Farrar, Straus & Giroux, Inc.

George Orwell, "Shooting an Elephant." From *Shooting an Elephant and Other Essays* by George Orwell. Copyright © 1950 by Sonia Brownell Orwell and renewed 1978 by Sonia Pitt-Rivers. Reprinted by permission of Harcourt Inc. Reproduced from *The Complete Orwell* by permission of A M Heath & Co. Ltd., on Behalf of Bill Hamilton as the Literary Executor of the estate of the Late Sonia Brownell Orwell and Secker and Warburg Ltd.

Camille Paglia, "It's a Jungle Out There." From *Sex, Art and American Culture*. Copyright © 1992 by Camille Paglia. Reprinted with the permission of Vintage Books, a Division of Random House, Inc.

Marie Winn, "Family Life," from *The Plug-In Drug, Revised Edition* by Marie Winn, Copyright © 1977, 1985 by Marie Winn Miller. Used by permission of Viking Penguin, a division of Penguin Putnam, Inc. and the author. Updated by the author.

Janet Wu, "Homeward Bound" from *The New York Times,* September 5, 1999. Copyright © 1999 by the author. Reprinted by permission of the author.

Malcolm X, "My First Conk." From *The Autobiography of Malcolm X* by Malcolm X, with the assistance of Alex Haley. Copyright © 1964 by Alex Haley and Malcolm X and Copyright © 1965 by Alex Haley and Betty Shabazz. Reprinted by permission of Random House, Inc.

Michael Zimecki, "Violent Films Cry 'Fire' in Crowded Theaters." From *The National Law Journal,* February 19, 1996. Michael Zimecki is an attorney in Pittsburgh, PA. Reprinted by permission of the author.

William Zinsser, "College Pressures" from *Blair & Ketchum's Country Journal,* Vol. vi, no. 4, April 1979. Copyright © 1979 by William K. Zinsser. Reprinted by permission of the author.

INDEX
OF TERMS,
AUTHORS,
AND TITLES

Resources for Instructors to Accompany

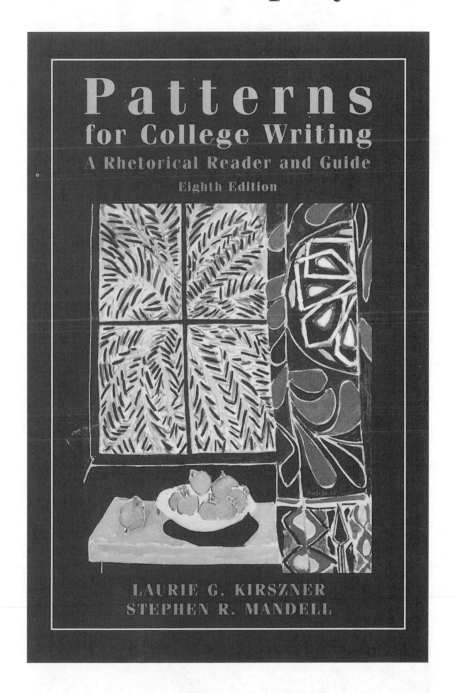

Patterns
for College Writing
A Rhetorical Reader and Guide
Eighth Edition

LAURIE G. KIRSZNER
STEPHEN R. MANDELL

Resources for Instructors
to Accompany

Patterns
for College
Writing

A RHETORICAL
READER
AND GUIDE

EIGHTH EDITION

LAURIE G. KIRSZNER
UNIVERSITY OF THE SCIENCES
IN PHILADELPHIA

STEPHEN R. MANDELL
DREXEL UNIVERSITY

with the assistance of
MARK GALLAHER

Bedford/St. Martin's
Boston ◆ New York

For *information,* write: Bedford/St. Martin's, 75 Arlington Street, Boston MA 02116 (617-399-4000)

ISBN: 0-312-25873-9

PREFACE

Our main purpose in this manual to accompany the eighth edition of *Patterns for College Writing* is to save the instructor time in choosing assignments and in working with the questions that follow each selection. For each reading in *Patterns*, we include a paragraph or two on the teaching opportunities it affords, and we sometimes add a personal comment on how we like to approach a favorite selection in our own classes. We also supply the answers that we had in mind as we constructed the questions. Most of the questions are open to a range of worthwhile answers, some of them perhaps more pointed and interesting than our own; not only do we encourage and applaud interpretations that differ from ours, but we would be grateful to hear about them from anyone willing to take the time to write to us. (Wherever appropriate, paragraph numbers are included in the answers so that instructors can easily refer to the text.)

The reading selections in *Patterns* range in subject across much of the college curriculum. They are meant to acquaint students with the rhetorical options open to them as they write for their college courses, and to show how the reading techniques presented in the Introduction and the writing strategies discussed and illustrated in Chapter 1 and throughout the book become crucial to the effectiveness of a finished piece. The selections are also meant to stimulate class discussion and serve as springboards for student writing assignments.

After each essay by a professional writer we ask four types of questions: Comprehension, Purpose and Audience, Style and Structure, and Vocabulary Projects. *Comprehension* questions help students test their understanding of basic content. The questions focus attention on facts, details, and references that are necessary for comprehension; underscore the major points of each essay; and lead students through the logical progression of a writer's ideas.

Purpose and Audience questions focus on how the writer's intent and sense of his or her readers establish boundaries for the essay and govern other decisions the writer must make—for example, how much detail, or what different kinds of detail, must be supplied for one audience as opposed to another. These questions ask students to imagine themselves in the author's place and to consider, from the evidence of the essay, how the audience was perceived.

Style and Structure questions focus on the stylistic and structural options the authors have exercised. Particular attention is paid to organization, sentence structure, and word choice.

Vocabulary Projects are designed to help students build their vocabularies and increase their sensitivity to the various connotations and denotations of key words. These questions also focus on using synonyms and antonyms and on identifying figurative language.

Following the questions about each essay is a *Writing Workshop* prompt, which asks students to use a particular rhetorical strategy and to write something in response (though not necessarily in reply) to the essay they have read. Some of the assignments require students to assume various roles and to address different audiences; others ask them to write in their own voices, drawing as necessary on the materials in the essay for examples, facts, or quotations.

Except for the chapter on argumentation, each of the chapters on a single rhetorical pattern includes a poem or a short story that illustrates the pattern. After each of these poems or stories we ask *Thinking about Literature* questions that focus students on many of the same concerns that they consider for the essays—

rhetorical organization, diction, imagery, and meaning. We want students to see that writers of various genres are involved in making many of the same choices.

After each selection by a professional writer, we include a *Journal Entry* prompt, a question that will stimulate students to examine and clarify their own value systems. We believes that regularly writing responses to these questions will assist students in developing good thinking, reading, and writing skills and, frequently, in generating paper topics. *Combining the Patterns* questions follow each professional essay. These encourage students to see other patterns at work within the dominant pattern of the essay.

Also included after each selection by a professional writer are *Thematic Connections*, which encourage students to perceive relationships between selections (including the student essays) they have read. The *Thematic Connections* can be used for classroom discussion or as topics for reading-based student essays.

At the end of each rhetorical chapter is a comprehensive list of *Writing Assignments*, some asking students to connect two or more selections. A suggested *Collaborative Activity* for writing follows this list. New to this edition is an *Internet Assignment* for each rhetorical pattern and each argument debate and casebook.

The final chapter, Combining the Patterns, presents one student essay and three professional essays, each of which demonstrates several different patterns within a single piece of writing. The student essay and the first professional essay have been annotated to identify these various patterns.

The Appendix, now includes a step-by-step discussion of writing a research paper as well as guidelines for citing and documenting sources. It gives advice about using quotation, paraphrase, and summary, as well as avoiding plagiarism, and it includes a sample student research paper. An updated Glossary defines terms important to good writers. We have cross-referenced them, whenever useful, to discussions within the text.

Peer-editing worksheets, to be used with writing assignments for Chapters 4–13, appear in this manual and are also available as part of the transparency master package.

A web site offering additional materials and access to the Toplinks database, with links on the most commonly chosen writing topics, can be accessed at <*http://www.bedfordstmartins.com/patterns*>.

Transparency masters, which include sample student essays from the textbook and peer-editing worksheets that students can use to evaluate each other's work, are available as a separate package.

In all cases we have tried to make the questions and writing assignments interesting, challenging, and accessible. We would be grateful for suggestions that might improve both this manual and *Patterns for College Writing*. Comments may be sent to us at our college addresses or c/o Bedford/St. Martin's, 33 Irving Place, New York, NY 10003.

Laurie G. Kirszner
Department of Humanities
University of the Sciences in Philadelphia
Philadelphia, Pennsylvania 19104

Stephen R. Mandell
Department of Humanities-Communications
Drexel University
Philadelphia, Pennsylvania 19104

CONTENTS

MODEL SYLLABI

We have included two sample syllabi that we hope will show you the flexibility you have with the eighth edition of *Patterns for College Writing*. The first uses the text's rhetorical approach for a 10-week term; the second uses both a thematic and a rhetorical approach for a 14-week term.*

SYLLABUS—RHETORICAL APPROACH:
10-week term, 3 meetings per week

Instructors can tailor readings to suit their own students' abilities and interests.

WEEK	ACTIVITIES
1	**Introduction**
	Introduction: Reading to Write
	Part 1: The Writing Process
	Diagnostic Essay
2	**Narration and Description, Chapters 4 and 5**
	Introduction
	Readings
	Narrative or Descriptive Essay
3	**Exemplification, Chapter 6**
	Introduction
	Readings
	Exemplification Essay
4	**Process Analysis, Chapter 7**
	Introduction
	Readings
	Process Analysis Essay
5	**Cause and Effect, Chapter 8**
	Introduction
	Readings
	Cause-and-Effect Essay
6	**Comparison and Contrast, Chapter 9**
	Introduction
	Readings
	Comparison-and-Contrast Essay
7	**Classification and Division, Chapter 10**
	Introduction
	Readings
	Classification-and-Division Essay

Suggestions for modifying these syllabi are discussed in this manual's introduction to Part I of text.

SYLLABUS—THEMATIC / RHETORICAL APPROACH:
14-week term, 3 meetings per week

This syllabus is organized primarily around a thematic approach; however, included with each theme is a rhetorical mode that the essays on the theme illustrate. Of course, instructors may modify the syllabus by deleting the rhetorical introductions and supplementing the units with additional selections (by professional or student writers) on the theme for each week.

WEEK	ACTIVITIES

WEEK

1   **The Writing Process**
Introduction: Reading to Write
Part 1: The Writing Process
Writing Activity: Diagnostic Essay

2   **Autobiography**
Using Description: Introduction to Chapter 5
Family Relationships:
     "Only Daughter," Sandra Cisneros
     "The Way to Rainy Mountain," N. Scott Momaday
     "Two Ways to Belong in America," Bharati Mukherjee
     "It's Just Too Late," Calvin Trillin
     "Suicide Note," Janice Mirikitani
Writing Assignment: Essay on a Family Relationship

3   **Autobiography**
Using Narration: Introduction to Chapter 4
Life Lessons:
     "Shooting an Elephant," George Orwell
     "Once More to the Lake," E. B. White
     "My First Conk," Malcolm X
     "The Grave," Katherine Anne Porter
     "Samuel," Grace Paley
Writing Assignment: Essay on an Epiphany
PEER EDITING WORKSHOP

4   **Education**
Using Exemplification: Introduction to Chapter 6
     "Reading the River," Mark Twain
     "The Great Campus Goof-Off Machine," Nate Stulman
     "The Human Cost of an Illiterate Society," Jonathan Kozol
     "Brains versus Brawn," Mark Cotharn
     "College Pressures," William Zinsser
Writing Assignment: Essay on Education

*Alternatively, the unit could focus on the Internet, with students reading using the essays in the casebook "Is the Internet Good for Society?"

USING THE END-OF-CHAPTER
COLLABORATIVE ACTIVITIES

Chapters 4–3 in this edition of *Patterns for College Writing* each conclude with a Collaborative Activity that allows students to work together to produce a paper or class presentation based on a particular rhetorical strategy. Although we don't expect that most instructors will assign a Collaborative Activity with every chapter for which they assign an individual paper, we do encourage you to give students at least one or two opportunities to complete an assignment collaboratively. A collaborative writing assignment allows students to witness a variety of writing styles and writing habits; it also provides a writing situation that students generally take seriously because they recognize that others' grades depend on their performance. Moreover, collaboration is a real-world activity; students should realize that much writing in business and professional setting is produced collaboratively, either with a different person taking on each different stage of the writing process (research, drafting, editing, and so forth) or with each person contributing a section to a larger report that is then refined and editing by the group. Finally, the assignments that call for class presentations give students practice in oral rhetoric, skills that have many academic and professional real-world applications.

Following are a few suggestions for setting up collaborative activities:

Make sure each group has a "leader." Although peer-editing groups can often be assigned randomly, collaborative groups generally work best if they are balanced in terms of individual members' abilities and the dynamics of the group. In assigning groups—particularly for the first few times—keep in mind that each should include at least one student you can depend on to motivate the others to keep the project moving forward. These "leaders" will not necessarily be the most adept writers but rather those students who are outgoing and responsible and who consistently make positive contributions to class discussion. For writing projects it can also be a good idea to see that each group has a good editor as well— a student whose command of grammar, mechanics, and spelling is strong.

Provide an explicit schedule. Most collaborative activities can be completed in one-and-a-half to two-and-a-half weeks (three to five class sessions); a few may require even less time. Generally, on the day you introduce the assignment, you should give students time in class to get started and provide a written schedule so they will know from the start what activities need to be divided up. Then, for each subsequent class session, students should come prepared to meet at least briefly with their group, bringing with them whatever materials are due for that session. It is up to you whether to require group meetings outside of class (although activities involving group drafting, like the one following Chapter 5, will almost have to involve some group work out of class, unless you're willing to devote several complete class sessions to the task.)

Here's a typical schedule for the most common kind of Collaborative Activity, which asks each group member to contribute a paragraph or section individually. (Note that the suggested activities for any of the four days could be extended into an outside meeting.)

Day 1:	Give the assignment and allow class time for the group discussion suggested by the assignment or for planning.
Day 2:	Have students bring drafts of their contributions for review and revision suggestions by other group members; have groups dis-

cuss possible strategies for the introduction and conclusion and determine who will draft each.

Day 3: Have students bring revised drafts of their contributions and the draft introduction and conclusion; have groups work to revise the individual parts into a whole essay and then determine which member will type the full draft.

Day 4: Have groups meet to discuss and revise the full draft and then determine who will edit and type the final version.

Day 5: Final version due; allow time for each group member to proofread quickly before collecting.

You might ask the groups to provide multiple copies of their final drafts to share in rotation with the other groups.

Allow for group self-evaluation. As groups are meeting in class, feel free to observe and even join each group for a few minutes to answer questions or make suggestions. If you observe a student behaving in a way seriously detrimental to the functioning of the group, you might want to talk to that student privately; but in general, try to give each group responsibility for "policing" lack of contribution or other inappropriate behavior. For example, if you grade a collaborative assignment, do so using points, and then require each group to determine collectively how many points each individual member will receive. Once the assignment is complete, you might also ask members to write a brief evaluation of the workings of their group to share—perhaps anonymously—with the rest of the group.

At several points during the semester, you may want to have students write briefly about their experience working with groups generally: what they've learned about group decision-making and group dynamics as well as their own usual function in groups.

USING THE END-OF-CHAPTER INTERNET ASSIGNMENTS

The Internet assignments at the ends of Chapters 4–13, new to this edition, give students an opportunity to access a wide variety of Internet sources. While these assignments will naturally interest students who are already experienced Internet users, they may be most useful for students who have little or no such experience. The sites Listed are all reliable, and well designed; they are also easy to navigate. As a group, they suggest the wide range of information available online. (Novice users could benefit enormously by accessing the three comprehensive online guides to using the Internet listed at the end of Chapter 7, "Process.")

Before assigning these activities, make sure all the students in your class have easy access to the Internet. Most campuses now offer students at least some access to the Internet. If you are not already familiar with what is available at your school, check with your library or with the office that oversees such services. Generally, workshops introducing the Internet and other electronic services are offered at regularly scheduled times. Many of your students, of course, may have access at home or in their work places. Additionally, students may be able to use computers linked to the Internet in local public libraries or in commercial "cybercafes."

(Alternatively, you could allow students to choose an Internet assignment for a paper in a particular mode but also allow them to complete the assignment by using the more traditional writing suggestions in the text. You might also allow the Internet assignments to be completed for extra credit.)

Each Internet assignment asks students to use information they find at suggested sites as support for an essay. (Complete URLs are provided for each site, along with a brief description of what the site has to offer.) By their nature, the assignments all involve at least some level of research, so before assigning them you might take the opportunity to have students practice documenting online sources; models are provided in the appendix, "Writing a Research Paper."

Although all the sites in these assignments are well regarded and reliable, you may want to warn students that not everything they find on the Internet can be trusted. Virtually anyone can create Internet sites and postings, and while most are harmless, they also provide a forum for biased arguments, crackpot theories, and even outright lies posing as fact. As with any research, students must view the sources of their information with a critical eye.

Resources for Instructors
to Accompany

Patterns
for College
Writing

A RHETORICAL
READER
AND GUIDE

INTRODUCTION: READING TO WRITE

The introductory discussion of reading as it relates to the writing process is extremely important because many students have not learned to read actively. Instead, they do little more than move their eyes across the lines of print—reading their textbooks as if they were reading a light novel. The Introduction prepares students to read critically, so the activities you use with it can prepare students to read—and to discuss—the materials in this (and any) text. The Introduction is especially important if you are using the text as the source of material for reading-based essays.

READING CRITICALLY

One way to help students read and respond critically is to conduct a simple exercise with class members. As you discuss the concept that reading is "a two-way street," ask where students grew up—near your school, in distant areas of your state, in other states, or even in other countries. You can then discuss what differences such diversity can make in the reading and writing process. Similar questions can be asked about students' ages and backgrounds—ethnic, economic, etc. Also, review Henry Louis Gates's essay "'What's in a Name?'" and ask your class how various students' backgrounds are likely to affect their reading of the essay. Such discussion not only suggests that different responses are likely as various people read, but it also gives students a sense of their own audience for the essays they will be writing.

As you discuss the Introduction, you will want to stress differences between subjective and objective responses—and the extent to which each is appropriate in the reading/writing process. Students will need reminders of the "rules" for validating an interpretation because many have not learned to do close readings of a text. Push your students beyond the recall level, and insist that they turn to the text to support their interpretations. When students distort, overlook details, or add irrelevant details, systematically ask them to point to evidence in the text. At first, many students will expect you to signal the right answer. Not telling them that they are wrong reinforces the concept that a text may lend itself to more than one interpretation. When you ask students to turn to the text, you may also discover another valid interpretation—one you had not anticipated. Saying as much enlivens discussions throughout the term as you and your students become a community of scholars. Students will quickly learn to question and respond in appropriate ways.

READING ACTIVELY

Do more than merely assign the Introduction. As you assign it, go over the signals given by the text's formatting—the items discussed in the section *Before You Read*. Show students that the headnotes and headings can be turned into questions for them to keep in mind as they read. Ask them to consider questions you might ask during the discussion—questions such as those listed in *As You Read*—which move students from making inferences (questions 1–4), to forming judgments (questions 5–8), and finally to making connections with their own experience and with other selections in the text—the sort of connections from which paper topics can grow (questions 9–10). Define both *highlighting* and *anno-*

tating and ask students to do both as they read the Introduction. When they come to class, you might ask them what questions would have been fair for you to have asked, had you quizzed them on their first reading assignment. Students will be happy to demonstrate that they read closely—and relieved that they are to receive reinforcement for good readings skills. Peer groups can also be used to reinforce the kinds for information students should have discovered in their first reading assignment.

READING THE SELECTION

As you discuss the Gates essay and the study questions that follow it, you will want to stress not only the ways the textbook can be used but also the kinds of questioning strategies that will make students better readers. You will also want to emphasize the questions that can lead to multiple answers—and consider reasons Gates might have had for leaving some details open to more than one interpretation. Explain that not every question has a single "right" answer, but explain as well that students need to be able to justify their responses from within an essay.

If your course calls for students to write reading-based (rather than personal) essays, you will want to focus very carefully on the discussions of *Thematic Connections*. Used throughout the text, these sections can be the source of subject matter for many essays. Using these in early discussions will illustrate for students the kinds of critical skills they will need in order to write effective essays based on selections from the text. (The student paper in the Appendix, Writing a Research Paper, is an example of an essay that draws on thematically linked readings in the text for its subject matter. Although this paper cites additional outside sources—to demonstrate documentation style for sources other than books—it can still show students how they may base their essays on readings linked by theme.)

You may also want to point out the questions under the Combining the Patterns section following the Gates essay. Questions about subsidiary patterns used within a dominant pattern follow every essay in the text. These questions can help students see that most writing mixes patterns at least to some degree, an idea that is reinforced in Chapter 13, Combining the Patterns, where we include three longer, more complex essays.

A final note about the questions following the readings. You may find, with the Gates essay as well as with the other essays throughout the book, that you do not want—or need—to deal with every question in class. For example, a class of fairly advanced readers might find the Comprehension questions a bit basic; or, you might want to stress style or audience rather than how patterns are combined. In fact, we have included more questions than we expect every instructor to use in order to provide the greatest degree of flexibility. You should certainly choose and assign questions for discussion according to your students' needs and the particular focus of your writing instruction.

PART ONE: THE WRITING PROCESS

Part One presents an overview of the entire writing process, from deciding on a topic through revising and editing the first draft. You may want to spend two or more weeks on these three chapters, having students work their way through the entire process as they complete their first paper for the class. You might even work through the three chapters in Part One in conjunction with the first pattern chapter you assign. For example, you might have your students read and discuss the essays in Chapter 4 and then have them draft and revise narrative essays of their own based on the guidelines in Part One. In any case, rather than assign students to read all of Part One at once, you will probably want to assign one chapter per class session.

Whatever your choice, you will want to link carefully the concepts discussed in Part One to those discussed in the Introduction: Reading to Write in order to make the reading/writing connection clear for students who see these activities as only loosely related. We have structured the introductions on reading and writing to assist you in making this connection: In Part One, Laura Bobnak's essay, with its multiple drafts, explicitly connects reading and writing since it responds to an assignment derived from the Gates essay—which is printed in the Introduction. As you work your way through other chapters in the text, remind students to read actively and to consider various ideas in their readings as potential paper topics. Encourage your students to read selections once for overall content and a second time to see the interplay between the writers' choices and their impact on readers. As you discuss various concepts in Part One, tell your students that throughout the term, you will ask them to identify the thesis statement in a selection; to point to major transitions; and to discuss stylistic and thematic subtleties that can only be understood by rereading difficult passages, looking up unfamiliar words, and considering them in context. Encourage students to continue using their highlighting and annotating skills. Ask them to use the questions after each selection to test their understanding before coming to class. Remind them that they will have to make many of the same choices the writers of the selections did; for this reason, developing greater awareness as readers will help them become better writers.

In class, closely focus your discussions on a writer's choices. Students will have a far clearer understanding of purpose, audience, occasion, and other concepts covered in Part One if you guide them both as they read and as they respond to your questions in class. Require students to keep journals with their responses to formal Journal Entries throughout the text as well as any other responses they may have to the text's selections. (You may wish to give a credit/no credit grade to encourage students to stretch and explore their own thinking.) Point out to students the value Laura Bobnak's journal entry (p. 50) had in the writing of her paper. Occasionally during the term, ask students to freewrite, brainstorm, or cluster using one or more of the Writing Workshop prompts at the end of reading selections so they see that what they read is vitally linked to what they write.

In Part One, by necessity, we discuss writing as a linear process, but as experienced writers know, it might more accurately be described as a series of spirals. We outline the steps of the writing process in succession but point out that they can also be performed simultaneously and recurrently. Whether or not you decide to stress this approach depends on the needs of your students. We prefer to give beginning writers a simple, concrete structure rather than overwhelm them with options they cannot fully understand or take advantage of.

Chapters 1 and 2 focus on the prewriting stage of the writing process. Most students entering college underrate prewriting. Thus the techniques we provide to narrow a topic, find something to say, develop a thesis, and arrange ideas will probably be new to them. You may find that, at first, students will resist using the techniques we present. Often a class or two devoted to illustrating prewriting can give students an understanding of how this preliminary work helps inform an entire essay. For example, you may want to tell students that using questions for probing closely parallels their normal thought processes. With these questions, students can construct a framework for the various topics they encounter. Your students should see these questions—and other techniques discussed in Chapters 1 and 2—as systematic ways both of exploring a topic's potential and of organizing the topic's presentation—whether the essay is personal or reading-based.

In Chapter 3 we focus on revision. Often students fail to understand that "finishing" a rough draft involves more than proofreading or correcting errors in grammar and spelling. They are unaware of the need to reconsider the quality of an essay's ideas and its organization into paragraphs and sentences. They do not realize that revision goes on throughout all the stages of their writing. To familiarize students with revision, we take them through three drafts of the sample essay; and, after each student essay in the chapter introductions, we include a Focus on Revision section, which suggests how an already effective essay could be made stronger. To guide your students as they revise, we include Revision and Editing Checklists for easy reference. Encourage students to use these aids.

We also include Guidelines for Peer Critiques and provide a sample peer critique following Laura Bobnak's first draft. (Model peer-editing worksheets for each chapter—like the one used to critique Bobnak's draft—appear on pages 56–57 of this manual and are also available as transparency masters.) Such critiques can be enormously useful in improving both a specific paper and students' overall sense of the connection between their writing and an audience's reading. As they critique their classmates' drafts, encourage students to be specific—to avoid simple "yes" or "no" answers, to refer to examples or passages within the draft, and to offer suggestions that might be incorporated into a subsequent draft. Also make it clear that, while they should take their peer readers' remarks seriously, writers need not follow every suggestion they receive. Ultimately, each writer must make his or her own decisions about how to go about revising a draft.

One possibility for peer critiquing in the classroom is to conduct class sessions as "writing workshops" on days when drafts are due. On these days you may require two or three students to photocopy their drafts and bring copies to class to distribute. After each of the students reads his or her paper aloud, a discussion (guided by the questions on the appropriate peer-editing worksheet) can follow. If possible, try to distribute drafts before the class in which they are to be discussed, so students can fill out peer-editing worksheets in advance. In any case, remind peer critics that their role is to make helpful suggestions, not to correct errors or impose their ideas on the draft they are critiquing. To reinforce this point, instruct them to write their comments on the worksheets, not directly on the photocopied draft.

If you want students to work in small groups, set up these groups well ahead of time so students know how many photocopies to make. (If you want to avoid the expense and possible confusion of making a number of photocopies, you can assign students to work in pairs; in this case they can simply exchange papers.)

Even if students are working in very small groups, with an "audience" of only one or two other students, it is still a good idea to require them to read their drafts aloud. Both student authors and their audiences will hear errors and inconsistencies that they may overlook when reading silently, and hearing students read aloud will sometimes alert you to reading difficulties they have.

Finally, be sure each student whose draft is the subject of a peer critique session knows to take careful notes about the other students' comments and suggestions and to ask for clarification when necessary.

As students revise their drafts—especially for your earlier assignments—you will want to make sure they recognize that an effective essay does not necessarily follow a five-paragraph formula. In fact, such a formula can impose restrictions on the development of a student's ideas. Students should see that, like Laura

Bobnak's essay, their own work should proceed organically, with the structure and organization growing out of the development of their ideas. As the semester progresses, you should also eventually encourage students to depart from the confining structure of the informal outlines presented in the text. For example, they can certainly move beyond a "there are three reasons" thesis statement and a simple restatement of their thesis in the conclusion.

As students write and revise, encourage them to use computers. Although *Patterns* does not require students to use computers, we have made suggestions in Computer Strategy boxes throughout Part One for those who do. Whether you teach a computer-assisted course or a traditional one, your students will probably have access to computers in a writing lab, library, or computer center. If so, you can use a variety of techniques to facilitate computer revision. For example, you can encourage students to put topic sentences in a draft in bold print—a form of review outlining—to help them analyze their papers' structure. You can also demonstrate (or have demonstrated) the ease with which they can rearrange whole sections of a paper by cutting and pasting, and the use of spell checkers and interactive software that raises such questions as the number of *be* verbs in a draft. If students have compatible hardware and software, you can even have them critique each other's disks, and you may want to react to students' disks yourself, placing your comments wherever they will be most helpful. Make sure your students understand that they should print out a hard copy of a draft sometime before they present a finished essay. Too few of them notice their mechanical errors on the screen. Also insist that your students keep backup disks of all their work.

To reinforce the various concepts of Part One, we suggest that you have students complete the exercises included throughout Chapters 1–3. You can have students work on these exercises individually or in small groups. You may want to assign all the exercises or just some of them. Later, as you assign and discuss selections in the text, you may wish to adapt some of the exercises in Part One to help students generate and organize ideas for reading-based essays by using one or more *Thematic Connections* included with a particular selection. Of course you may wish to reproduce essays your students have written and ask your class to discuss them.

Following are discussions of the exercises in Part One, each labeled with its appropriate topic heading.

1: INVENTION

Exercise 1—Setting Limits (pp. 15–18)

1. A history of animal testing in the cosmetics industry is too broad a topic for a two- to three-page paper. Without further narrowing, this topic could not be treated adequately in such a short essay.
2. This kind of topic is typical of an essay examination. Before writing an answer, a student should narrow the topic by deciding what points to discuss about the effectiveness of bilingual education programs. The number of points and the depth of the discussion are determined by the two hours allotted for the exam and the number of other questions.
3. An interpretation of Andy Warhol's soup cans is an unlikely in-class essay assignment for courses other than art history. This topic requires more knowl-

edge about art than most students ordinarily would have, and research would be impossible under the circumstances.

4. An examination of a school's policy on alcoholic beverages would be suitable for a letter to a college paper.

Exercise 2—Setting Limits (p. 19)

The purpose of this exercise is to make students aware of the different audiences they encounter daily. An even more important realization for students is that they accommodate themselves rhetorically to each of these audiences. Levels of diction, subjects, and strategies are adjusted to suit the various audiences.

Exercise 3—Questions for Probing (p. 22)

1. Limited topic
2. Limited topic
3. General subject
4. Limited topic
5. General subject
6. Limited topic
7. General subject
8. Limited topic
9. General subject
10. Limited topic
11. General subject

Exercise 4—Questions for Probing (p. 22)

Students should be encouraged to use the questions for probing. This exercise lets them practice generating limited topics from general subjects. Here, you can demonstrate to them that even the most mundane general subjects can yield several interesting and workable limited topics. This is the first step in breaking down many students' preconceptions that they have nothing to say.

Exercise 5—Freewriting (p. 50)

Your students may have difficulty at first and may begin several topics before they find one they can focus on. They may also wish to repeat Exercise 4, generating topics for different general subjects.

Exercise 6—Freewriting (p. 24)

Students who have narrowed their topics sufficiently Exercise 5 should be able to continue to freewrite from the summaries they generate. However, you may have to provide assistance for some students.

Exercise 7—Freewriting, Brainstorming, Clustering, and Making an Informal Outline (p. 24)

This exercise not only reinforces the concepts introduced in the previous section, but enables a student to progress from a general subject, to a limited topic, to a list of ideas that could be discussed in a paper, and to a rough outline of the first draft. Depending on their own learning styles, students will likely develop a preference for either clustering or informal outlining. This is a good time to tell students that some assignments, such as midterm and final examination questions, result from the narrowing of general subjects to limited topics. Knowing this can help students to prepare for such assignments and to complete them effectively by practicing the techniques described.

Exercise 8—Formulating a Thesis (p. 33)

1. This is a general subject, not a thesis statement. (Items a, b, and c need to be considered together. They illustrate the stages many students go through in writing a thesis.)
2. Many students' first thesis statements will resemble item b. Although this statement now expresses an opinion, it still lacks the clear limits of a good thesis.
3. This is an effective thesis statement; the paper that follows would discuss myths that express societal attitudes.
4. This is a statement of fact rather than opinion; therefore, it is not a thesis statement.
5. This is a thesis statement; the paper would discuss examples of skiing injuries.
6. This is a thesis statement; the paper would give examples of needed reforms.
7. This is a topic, not a thesis statement.
8. This is a thesis statement; the paper that follows would discuss techniques parents could use to help their preschool children learn.
9. You will want to compare this item to j. Although this statement expresses an opinion, it still lacks the clear limits of a good thesis.
10. This is a thesis statement; the paper that follows would demonstrate how fiction can encourage social reform.

Exercise 9—Formulating a Thesis (p. 34)

Students' thesis statements will vary. You may want to put several of them on a transparency for evaluation in class. Push your students beyond platitudes and stress clear wording.

Exercise 10—Formulating a Thesis (p. 34)

Even good statements of Sagan's thesis will vary somewhat. One possible statement might be the following: Because robots are becoming increasingly sophisticated and need no biological or safety provisions, we must overcome our "primitive chauvinisms" against using them in space.

Exercise 11—Formulating a Thesis (p. 35)

This exercise enables students to progress through the entire prewriting process. As students do this assignment, reinforce the importance of prewriting and tell them that this process should play a major part in all their writing assignments.

2: ARRANGEMENT

Exercise 1—The Introduction (p. 39)

Examples for each kind of introduction in the text include the following:

   Background information: "Television: The Plug-In Drug" (Ch. 8)
   Definition: "The Light Microscope" (Ch. 5)
   Anecdote or story: "Just Walk On By" (Ch. 6)
   Question: "In Search of Our Mothers' Gardens" (Ch. 13)
   Quotation: "Violent Films Cry 'Fire' in Crowded Theaters" (Ch. 12)

Exercise 2—Body Paragraphs (p. 44)

Any essay in the text could be used for this exercise, but you should probably limit students to paragraphs of five or more sentences.

Exercise 3—Body Paragraphs (p. 44)

Good choices for this exercise include "The Great Campus Goof-Off Machine" (Ch. 6) or "Sex, Lies, and Conversation" (Ch. 9).

Exercise 4—The Conclusion (p. 45)

Examples for each kind of conclusion in the text include the following:

   Review of key points: "The Victorian Internet" (Ch. 9)
   Recommendation: "Sexism in English: Embodiment and Language" (Ch. 10)
   Prediction: "An Age of Optimism" (Ch. 12)
   Quotation: "Violent Films Cry 'Fire' in Crowded Theaters" (Ch. 12)

Exercise 5—Formal Outlines (p. 47)

Some students find making formal topic outlines a difficult task. If you assign this exercise, you should carefully go over the sample outline in the text and also demonstrate how to construct an outline, using either the board or an overhead projector.

3: DRAFTING AND REVISING

Exercise 1—The First Draft (p. 51)

Remind students that first drafts do not have to be perfect. Encourage them to write as fluently as possible without stopping to make minor corrections or worrying too much about spelling and punctuation—particularly if doing so interrupts the flow of their writing.

Exercise 2 and Exercise 3—Revising the Draft (p. 64)

You may wish to combine these two exercises, having students revise their drafts after they have been read and commented on by another student or students. You might also choose to comment yourself on their first drafts before having students revise.

Exercise 4—Editing (p. 65)

Remind students how crucial editing process can be; call attention to mistakes in grammar, punctuation, and spelling that can seriously limit the effectiveness of a piece of writing, no matter how strong its content. This might be a good time to review with students their assigned handbook if you require one. If not, you might point out the importance of a good guide to grammar and punctuation, as well as a dictionary.

PART TWO: READINGS FOR WRITERS

The Introduction: Reading to Write, both in the text and in this manual, discusses how the readings in this part and their apparatus can be used.

Note that most of the headnotes in this edition have been revised or newly drafted to provide information not only about the author but also about the cultural or historical context crucial to understanding the reading. We have come to recognize that what we consider "common knowledge"—the extent of racial segregation prior to the 1960s, prevailing attitudes in the early days of the feminist movement, and how patterns of immigration have changed over the last hundred years, to cite a few examples—is not immediately available to many students in their teens and early twenties. In addition, some readings assume familiarity with certain historical facts or events that are *not* common knowledge today. In such cases, we have included in the headnote enough background information to help students read and understand the essay.

In other cases, we have used the headnotes to provide interesting background information—for example, statistics about homeless rates, the growth in the use of computers and the Internet, and so forth—to create a context for a reading.

We suggest that you review the headnotes with students—particularly the information provided in the second paragraphs—before discussing a reading selection. A good way to begin might be to summarize this information (perhaps by posing some version of a "Did you know before reading this . . . ?" question) and then apply the information to the reading itself.

4: NARRATION

Most first-year students seem to feel comfortable with narration because they have usually done a significant amount of first-person writing in high school. This does not necessarily mean, of course, that beginning students will already have mastered narrative writing. As the chapter moves through progressively more demanding narratives, you can gradually encourage your students to identify the techniques that can help them make their personal narratives more effective—dialogue, sentence variety, sharp detail. Eventually, you may ask your classes to experiment with other kinds of narrative writing, such as narrative journalism.

One way of handling the unit on narration is to assign the chapter's readings in the sequence in which they appear in the text, beginning with the paragraph by Maya Angelou on p. 88. The paragraph is useful because it allows you to illustrate the pattern quickly and helps you to teach the use of narrative examples as well.

The first two readings, Janet Wu's "Homeward Bound" and Sandra Cisneros's "Only Daughter," both tell about related events over a number of years. Wu recalls visits to her grandmother in China that began when she was a child, while Cisneros traces her relationship with her father from childhood onward. After pointing this out, you can then emphasize the thematic connection between "Only Daughter" and Maya Angelou's "Finishing School," both of which consider the effects of discrimination. First, "Only Daughter," by Sandra Cisneros, uses a series of short, related narratives to show the complexity and painfulness of gender discrimination when it is part of a family structure. Next, "Finishing School," by Maya Angelou, describes a pattern of events in a bigot's household and then focuses on a single dramatic event and its consequences to show the results of racial discrimination. From "Finishing School," you can move to "My Mother Never Worked," which remains relatively informal in style and simple in vocabulary but employs flashbacks and effective descriptive detail. After your students read Gansberg's "Thirty-Eight Who Saw Murder Didn't Call the Police," you can discuss the differences between personal and journalistic narrative. Next you can read Orwell's "Shooting an Elephant," which employs various narrative techniques to analyze political ideas as well as personal reactions. Finally, you can move your students from narrative essays into the realm of fiction with Saki's "The Open Window." Students will be able to see that effective narratives—whether factual or fictional—share a variety of techniques. Like "Finishing School" and "Shooting an Elephant," "The Open Window" builds to a dramatic climax, this climax, like that of "My Mother Never Worked," is ironic and also a bit surprising (like the climax of "Only Daughter"). With its simple sentence structure and time signals, "The Open Window" is also related stylistically to "Thirty-Eight Who Saw Murder Didn't Call the Police" while "Homeward Bound" is related by its attention to descriptive detail.

Thematic Connections at the end of each of these selections suggest other readings in the text that you may wish to assign during your narrative unit.

Janet Wu, *Homeward Bound*

Janet Wu's account of visits with her elderly grandmother in China over the years focuses on how her relationship with her grandmother has helped keep her connected with her cultural heritage. Although she emphasizes how different her very traditional grandmother is from her thoroughly Americanized self, she, nevertheless, highlights the strong emotional bond between them.

Beginning with the striking image of her grandmother's bound feet, Wu develops the physical contrast between herself and her grandmother in the second paragraph. Paragraph 3 offers background information, and the narrative proper begins with paragraph 4. Wu summarizes three visits with her grandmother, the first when she was twelve, a later visit when she was in her early twenties, and then a visit when she was in her late twenties. Each time she is struck by her grandmother's age and by how difficult it is for them to communicate across the barriers of language and experience, yet she comes away from each encounter with a sense of tender connectedness, tempered by the sadness of knowing they may never meet again. Wu ends with the anticipation of another visit in honor of her grandmother's 100th birthday.

You might begin discussion of this essay by asking why Wu feels so deeply for her grandmother even though their contact has been quite limited, in terms of both the time they have spent together and their ability to communicate verbally with one another.

COMPREHENSION (p. 81)

1. Foot-binding is an ancient Chinese custom. The feet of elite females were broken when they were young and then tightly bound so they never grew beyond three to four inches. Although bound beet were once a symbol of status and of beauty, foot-binding is rarely practiced today—and, indeed, is seen as barbarous. In the essay, Wu's grandmother's bound feet signify both her being from another era and the restrictions of her life compared with her American granddaughter's.
2. It is a gulf both in terms of time (almost seventy years separate them) and of culture. As Wu writes in paragraph 6, "I could not conceive of surviving a dynasty and a revolution, just as she could not imagine my life in a country she had never seen." *Sentries* is used metaphorically here.
3. Wu initially points out the difference between their feet, which for her represents the vast differences in the lives they have lived. She also notes her grandmother's "shockingly small" stature, presumably in comparison to her own. There are also, obviously, differences in language. Because Wu is not specific, students will probably need to speculate on how different their lives have been.
4. Each visit seems more intimate than the one before, each parting more difficult.
5. Wu is studying Chinese, the better to communicate with her grandmother.
6. Wu cannot communicate with her grandmother by telephone (let alone through other means of electronic media), but only through handwritten letters that take many weeks to reach China.
7. There is, of course, a play on the word *bound* in the title. "Homeward Bound" suggests a homecoming, the sense Wu feels of connecting with her grandmother when she visits her in China. In addition, *bound* also refers to her grandmother's feet, the symbol of their many differences. Finally *bound* reminds readers that the two are bound together by ties of familial affection.

PURPOSE AND AUDIENCE (p. 81)

1. The opening statement is quite bold. It may shock some readers and would certainly intrigue most of her intended audience.
2. Paragraph 9 describes how difficult it is for Wu to keep in touch with her grandmother, in comparison to her friends who complain about having to keep in touch with their own relatives nearby. It seems a logical part of the essay in that it emphasizes Wu's deep feelings for her grandmother.
3. Wu's thesis is suggested in the final two sentences of paragraph and more fully summed up in the next-to-last sentence of paragraph 6. Wu tries trying

to persuade her audience to appreciate their ability to relate more completely to family members than she can to her grandmother. And, she notes something larger about family ties generally ("I found it easy to love this person I had barely met" [5]).

STYLE AND STRUCTURE (p. 81)

1. The narrative begins with paragraph 4.
2. Students will note the time markers used as transitions throughout, often expressed in terms of Wu's age. It is quite clear when she is shifting to a later point in time.
3. More dialogue might allow readers a better sense of Wu's grandmother and their relationship. But Wu's point is that the language barrier made it difficult for them to communicate verbally, and the lack of dialogue contributes to this sense.

VOCABULARY PROJECTS (p. 82)

2. Other such words Wu uses include *shrunken and wise* (6), *frailty* (8), and *tiny, doll-like feet* (10). Other words suggesting such an impression are *dainty, infirm,* and *breakable.*

COMBINING THE PATTERNS (p. 82)

To make this a true comparison-and-contrast essay, Wu would need to include more description of their physical differences, as well as more specific information about their lives. These additions would emphasize the contrasts between them. Their primary similarity would seem to be their deep feelings of family loyalty.

THEMATIC CONNECTIONS (p. 82)

The Way to Rainy Mountain (p. 148): N. Scott Momaday's essay is also about his relationship with his grandmother and the ways in which she helped provide a connection to his cultural heritage. Momaday, however, had an ongoing relationship with his grandmother, and he emphasizes their closeness rather than their differences.

Words Left Unspoken (p. 133): In this essay, Leah Hager Cohen remembers her grandfather, who was congenitally deaf and died when she was thirteen ("before I was really able to converse in sign"). It is another poignant recollection of communication that must take place outside of language.

My First Conk (p. 228): Malcolm X's account of the first time he underwent the difficult process of straightening his hair may be compared to the practice of foot-binding. Both practices employ painful means to create an unnatural standard of "beauty."

Mother Tongue (p. 405): This is another interesting study of the difficulties of communicating across generational and cultural lines. Amy Tan writes about her Chinese-born mother, whose English most native speakers find difficult to understand. Tan explores the consequences of this for her mother and for their relationship.

Sandra Cisneros, *Only Daughter*

Sandra Cisneros's essay presents a thought-provoking look at how a particular culture may define gender identity. You will want to make certain that students respect other cultures—even while they may question some cultural practices. One way of doing this is to point out that Cisneros's father was able to appreciate her accomplishment as an author when it became accessible to him in Spanish and when it related to his realm of experience. Students need to recognize that, to a certain extent, we appreciate what we have the experience to appreciate. They also need to recognize Cisneros's father's many positive qualities—his love of family, his love of Mexico, and his hard work to provide for his family, including his children's educations.

You may also help students suspend their judgments about Cisneros's father by pointing out that other cultures—for example, the more conservative cultures of the Arab world—have similar views of women. You may want to make students aware of historical male dominance in the Anglo culture, and of some religious or ethnic groups' continuing male dominance—the debates, for instance, in some sects over the possibility of female clergy. Remind them of the continuing pay differential between men and women in this country and the debate in the military about women's value as soldiers.

You may want to discuss changes in the mainstream culture that have affected our perceptions of women's roles—such as the need for women to work in factories during World War II, or today's high cost of living, which forces many women to work—and therefore to address such issues as equal pay and opportunity.

COMPREHENSION (p. 85)

1. Cisneros means that her male-oriented household shaped her identity, even those elements of her personality that developed contrary to her father's expectations. Her father's pride in having six sons was so pronounced that she felt negated, especially when he, in a confusion of languages, mistakenly claimed he had seven sons rather than six sons and one daughter. As a result, Cisneros developed her talents to please her father. She says, "In a sense, everything I have ever written has been for him, to win his approval" (7).

2. The expression *the only daughter* is neutral—merely a description of gender in the family; however, the expression *only a daughter* suggests the family's belief that sons are worth more than daughters—a belief Cisneros tried to overcome through her achievements.

3. As "the only daughter," Cisneros was isolated from other family members—which ironically gave her time to read and develop the abilities of a good writer. As "only a daughter," Cisneros was sent to college to meet a suitable husband—which gave her a good education. Since her father saw college as a way for her to marry a man who would earn a good living with his mind, he did not monitor her choice of a major or question her writing—which allowed her to major in English and further develop her writing abilities.

4. Her father thought she had wasted her years of education because, even after two years of graduate school, she did not have a husband. As a result, she longed to have her father affirm her for being *profesora*, not just teacher, and for being a writer.

5. When Cisneros's father asked for additional copies of her story in Spanish translation, he affirmed her as a person, independent of her gender.

PURPOSE AND AUDIENCE (p. 86)

1. Choosing to define and explain Spanish words is a clear indication that Cisneros's primary audience is not Hispanic. She wishes to take an Anglo audience below the surface of her family's strong male orientation—to help them understand its negative effects on her but at the same time to see her father as a sympathetic person, as someone whose approval was worth seeking. She makes the Spanish words accessible to Anglo readers—as the translation of her story into Spanish made it accessible to her father.
2. Cisneros's thesis is that being the only daughter of a working-class Mexican father and Mexican-American mother "had everything to do with who I am today" (2). Many details support her point. Her father's pride in having six sons and her brothers' leaving her alone gave her "time to think and think, to imagine, to read and prepare myself" as a "would-be writer." Her father's belief that she would find herself a suitable husband while in college and his indifference to what she might be studying and writing further developed her abilities to teach and write. These abilities led her to two National Endowment for the Arts Fellowships, a guest professorship, and publications—including the one in Spanish translation that finally won her father's approval. Her teaching and publishing grew out of her need for her father's approval. He came to represent "a public who is uninterested in reading, and yet one whom I am writing about and for, and privately trying to woo" (8).
3. Cisneros felt diminished by her father's cultural attitudes toward gender, but she makes clear that his preference for sons was a result of his Mexican heritage, rather than a personal character flaw. Overall she presents him as sympathetic—as a hard-working man who loved his family and his homeland; as a father who wanted his children not to be poor; and, when able to read her story in Spanish, as a parent who was proud of her and wanted to share her accomplishment.

STYLE AND STRUCTURE (p. 86)

1. Each of Cisneros's episodes relates an experience or a cluster of experiences that helped to shape her, beginning with her writing of a contributor's note for an anthology, which caused her to recognize that being an only daughter of a Mexican father and Mexican-American mother has determined her identity. This awareness provides her with the thesis statement for "Only Daughter." Each of the short narratives that follows is accompanied by analysis, which explains how Cisneros felt herself "being erased" (12) but, at the same time, shaped as a writer. Consequently, when Cisneros tells about the Christmas her father affirmed her writing, readers fully understand the importance of that affirmation. The analysis following each episode helps readers understand Cisneros's thesis. Without it, readers would very likely not understand the development that grew out of her sense of diminishment and might also miss her father's positive qualities.
2. As the transitional expressions (question 3) show, episodes are generally presented in chronological order.
3. Transitional expressions indicating time introduce each new episode: *Once, several years ago* (1), *ever since* (2), *when I was in the fifth grade* (4), *After four years in college and two more in graduate school* (4), *Last year, after ten years of writing professionally* (15), and *At Christmas* (16).

4. When Cisneros quotes her father, she humanizes him by allowing him to reveal his pride in his sons, his hard physical work and desire for an easier life for his children, and his language limitations, which are partly responsible for Cisneros's feeling "erased." She also lets us see his doggedness in reading her story once it is presented to him in Spanish and lets us hear his desire to share it with relatives.

5. The details describing Cisneros's father in paragraphs 17–18 focus on evidence of his mortality. Although she says he recovered from a stroke he had two years earlier, the bland food, his horizontal position, the "vials of pills and balled Kleenex" and the "plastic urinal" undercut any sense of robustness that might come from her father's laughing at the movie he is watching. These details contrast strongly with details of her father's mobility in paragraphs 9–11.

VOCABULARY PROJECTS (p. 86)

1. *Embroidering,* in its context, ironically feminizes Cisneros's writing of poems and stories—activities that are not inherently gender-linked. Her father would no doubt see embroidering (needlework) as an appropriate—though insignificant—activity for women. Cisneros also conveys this irony when she calls the works she "embroiders" "little poems and stories." *Embroidering* may also suggest embellishing her "little poems and stories" beyond their inherent significance. Her father's early obliviousness to her writing makes his recognition at the end all the sweeter. *Stubbed* suggests that Mr. Cisneros's fingers are *worn down to stubs,* or *stumps,* by hard physical labor.

2. *Sons* suggests the continuation of a patriarchal lineage; *children* does not carry such associations. *Professor* may suggest greater status than *teacher.* Cisneros no doubt correctly interpreted the significance *sons* had for her father. One can argue that *professor* generally denotes an individual with advanced academic degrees, which *teacher* does not.

COMBINING THE PATTERNS (p. 87)

One difference that Cisneros mentions directly in paragraph 3 is that her brothers spent a lot of time together when they were growing up, while she was often alone. At this early point in the narrative, she might have offered other points of contrast between her brothers and herself in terms of family life during childhood and adolescence—for example, household responsibilities, restrictions on behavior (curfews and the like), methods of parental discipline. Later, after she mentions that her oldest brother graduated from medical school (13), she might have offered some more specific contrasts regarding her and her brothers' academic and career choices.

THEMATIC CONNECTIONS

My Field of Dreams (p. 73): Like Cisneros, Tiffany Forte must adjust to a culture that values male accomplishment more highly than it does female accomplishment. However, while Cisneros is ultimately able to achieve her dreams—and even to receive her father's approval for her work—Forte must abandon her childhood dream of becoming a major league baseball player because it is a role that is

15

simply not open to women. You might ask students why they think women—who have broken barriers in so many fields—remain less visible than men in both college and professional sports, except perhaps for tennis, golf, and figure skating.

Words Left Unspoken (p. 133): Leah Hager Cohen also paints a portrait of an older immigrant relative, in this case her grandfather. These two essays provide an interesting opportunity for discussion of differences in relationships across generations. Cohen, for example, sees her grandfather more objectively than Cisneros sees her father, and Cohen doesn't need her grandfather's approval in the way that Cisneros needs her father's. At the same time, the next-to-last paragraph of Cohen's essay suggests how strongly she wanted to find an emotional connection with her grandfather. Cohen's essay can also allow you to talk about the differences between a piece of writing that is primarily narrative and one that is primarily descriptive.

Suicide Note (p. 305): See *Thematic Connections*, "Suicide Note," p. 37 of this manual.

The Men We Carry in Our Minds (p. 399): Scott Russell Sanders considers the roles that are available for men and women in our society, focusing particularly on how class and economic level further limit what anyone—male or female—can dream for oneself. Like Cisneros, Sanders was born into the working class and viewed education as a way to make something better of himself. For him, the lot of men in the working class in which he grew up was harder than the lot of women, and in college he couldn't accept the judgment of upper-class female acquaintances that he was privileged because he was male. Sanders tries to move away from a simple view of sexism to suggest a broader notion of what constitutes power in society.

Maya Angelou, *Finishing School*

"Finishing School" is a personal, colloquial narrative of seemingly unremarkable events. By using dialogue effectively and recording her emotions carefully, Angelou brings her story to life and makes it important and memorable. When you teach this essay, you may need to explain its setting to your students—for instance, providing some background about the Great Depression and perhaps also about black/white relations in the South at the time. Besides stressing Angelou's strengths as a narrator, you might point to the theme of class consciousness in the story, examining the significance of Miss Glory's loyalty to her employer, of Mrs. Cullinan's having married beneath her, and of the narrator's unfamiliarity with the white woman's domestic rituals. The idea of ethnic pride should also be considered.

COMPREHENSION (p. 92)

1. Angelou was required to learn a variety of household rituals: a rigid time schedule for various tasks, the names and uses of a vast array of dishes and silverware, and the proper location of each item—including the separate shelf on which her own and Miss Glory's water glasses were to be placed (4–7). Mrs. Cullinan's rituals were an attempt to hold onto the old South. In the discussion of tasks Angelou performed, we learn that Mrs. Cullinan "kept up the tradition of her wealthy parents," that Miss Glory was "a descendant of slaves that had worked for the Cullinans," and that Mr. Cullinan's family "hadn't had their money very long and what they had 'didn't mount to much.'"

2. At first Angelou feels sorry for Mrs. Cullinan because she is ugly and cannot have children. Her attitude changed when Mrs. Cullinan insulted her by calling her "Mary." Angelou recognized that the impulse to rename her and to discuss her name as if she were not present was based on disrespect for her because she is black.
3. Mrs. Cullinan's friend felt "Margaret" was too long a name and therefore too much trouble to say. This upset Angelou because, as she notes in paragraph 26, every black person "had a hellish horror of being 'called out of his name.' "
4. Bailey advised his sister to get herself fired by breaking some of Mrs. Cullinan's favorite possessions, ones with symbolic value. Her "Mamma's china from Virginia," "the Virginia dishes," were part of Mrs. Cullinan's attempt to hold onto the traditions of the old South.
5. Angelou's experience prepared her for adulthood; it taught her that she had to stand up to "white folks" in order to retain her pride.

PURPOSE AND AUDIENCE (p. 92)

1. Angelou is clearly writing for a general audience. To help her audience understand circumstances with which they may be unfamiliar, she provides information in paragraph 2 about the activities of "Negro girls in small Southern towns" and explains in paragraph 26 why African Americans fear being called by names other than their own.
2. Angelou uses this exchange to show that the white woman, while ignorant of what Angelou's childhood was like, was no more "ridiculous" in her assumptions about Angelou's life than were the southern blacks themselves in their expectations for their daughters.
3. Angelou's thesis is that preparation for adulthood involves more than learning the social niceties; it involves learning what is important to you and how to get it.

STYLE AND STRUCTURE (p. 92)

1. A *finishing school* is a private academy for young women that focuses on social graces and accomplishments. The phrase usually evokes images of young ladies in Victorian dress learning to play the piano and speak French. Ironically, in this selection it is not the superficial social skills Angelou learns but the difficult realities of society.
2. Angelou signals the passage of time by using transitional phrases such as *During my tenth year* (2), *It took me a week* (5), *the next morning* (11), *For weeks after* (12), *Then one evening* (13), *That evening* (20), *The very next day* (21), and *For a week* (32).
3. The difference between the standard speech of Mrs. Cullinan and her friends and Miss Glory's nonstandard speech underscores the gap between blacks and whites. This strengthens the narrative by making even clearer the idea that Angelou has to make a choice between her employer's values and her own.
4. Angelou uses Mrs. Cullinan's wrinkles, the fat covering her fragile bones, and her drinking from unmarked bottles to highlight her unattractiveness and idleness. She uses Mrs. Cullinan's extensive collection of glasses, dishes, and silverware to contrast with what we assume to be the modest circumstances of Angelou's own house—and to suggest Mrs. Cullinan's rigid attempts to hold onto the rituals of the old South.

VOCABULARY PROJECTS (p. 92)

2. Essentially, the words have similar meanings. The difference lies in the degree—*ludicrous* means that it is even more laughable; a *tureen* is a larger, perhaps fancier soup bowl. The first distinction suggests Angelou's purpose is emphasis; the second that she means to point up Mrs. Cullinan's pretensions.
3. This exercise gives students an opportunity to see how important context is to word choice. Discuss some of their substitutions in class and have their classmates decide which word is more effective and why.

COMBINING THE PATTERNS (p. 93)

Descriptive passages include paragraphs 3 and 9 (Mrs. Cullinan), 11 (her husband's illegitimate daughters), and 34 (her reaction to Angelou's breaking of the casserole and cups). The descriptions are primarily visual. Students might suggest further descriptions of the setting (the Cullinan house) and of the objects that were broken.

THEMATIC CONNECTIONS

Midnight (p. 177): Grace Ku descries the abominable conditions under which her immigrant parents work in a large dry cleaning establishment, where they do dangerous, physically exhausting work that demands long hours at a substandard wage. Some students may be surprised that such conditions—only a few steps better than physical slavery—are allowed to exist in this country. In comparison with the days of Angelou's youth, few people today work as servants. But many, particularly immigrants with little English and even less knowledge of U.S. employment policies, labor in illegal sweatshops for considerably less than the minimum wage. Given the arguments for limiting immigration, do students think anyone else would take these jobs?

The "Black Table" Is Still There (p. 294): Lawrence Otis Graham's essay offers another African-American perspective on relations between blacks and whites. Graham focuses on the tendency of black students in the largely white junior high school he attended to segregate themselves from the white students—a practice he is sorry to see still exists some ten years after he was a student there. His essay and Angelou's provide an opportunity to compare what changes have occurred in race relations in the sixty years or so since Angelou attended Mrs. Cullinan's "finishing school"—and what hasn't changed.

Revelation (p. 436): Although Mrs. Cullinans' life is more idle than Ruby Turpin's and her marriage apparently more futile, students should be able to see that they are very much the same kind of snob and bigot—and will enjoy exploring many parallels. Like Ruby Turpin, Mrs. Cullinan sees money and race as determining human status. She sees Mr. Cullinan's family as inferior to her own because they "hadn't had their money very long and what they had 'didn't mount to much,'" and she certainly believes blacks are beneath her. The blacks who work for the Turpins are similar to Miss Glory in that they flatter Mrs. Turpin. However, they may well be more aware than Miss Glory and flatter Mrs. Turpin as a matter of expediency, whereas Miss Glory seems to have adopted Mrs. Cullinan's value system. In addition, Mrs. Cullinan quickly drops her pleasant social veneer when Angelou breaks the dishes—just as Mrs. Turpin drops her pleasant disposition when Mary Grace attacks her. Both Angelou and O'Connor emphasize their bigots' grotesqueness—as a way of emphasizing their prejudices.

Donna Smith-Yackel, *My Mother Never Worked*

A discussion of the rationale behind the injustices Smith-Yackel finds in our Social Security laws is bound to produce lively debate, as is the issue of whether Mrs. Smith really "worked." This narrative can be examined in light of its original appearance in *Women: A Journal of Liberation,* a small (now defunct) feminist publication, in the mid-1970s; its subsequent appearance in *Ms;* and its continued relevance today. Students may also want to talk about the differences between "men's work" and "women's work"; between the duties of farm wives and the duties of city wives who are not employed outside the home; and between the responsibilities of homemakers in Mrs. Smith's generation and in the present.

COMPREHENSION (p. 97)

1. Martha Smith worked very hard at raising her children, doing farm chores, and maintaining a household, but she did not work outside the home for pay—the only kind of work recognized by the government.
2. According to the government, Martha Smith is not eligible for a death benefit because she was never employed.
3. The government defines *work* as an activity performed for compensation.

PURPOSE AND AUDIENCE (p. 97)

1. The essay's thesis is that although Martha Smith did not work outside the home, the work she did should be considered valuable enough to entitle her to Social Security benefits. The thesis is never explicitly stated because the accumulation of concrete details argues the author's point more forcefully than would direct statement.
2. This essay might have found sympathetic audiences in other publications. For example, had it appeared in a magazine aimed at homemakers, many of these readers, regardless of their opinions about feminism, might have seen similarities between Martha Smith's story and their own (or their mothers') situations.
3. She mentions little about her father because the thesis of the essay does not concern him.
4. Students, depending on where they are from, may find the essay dated in that the rural way of life described is less common now. The issue the author raises, however, remains the same. A stay-at-home wife and mother is eligible for Social Security benefits only through her wage-earning husband.

STYLE AND STRUCTURE (p. 97)

1. Most students will find the title is effective because it introduces the irony that runs through the essay and is summed up in the conclusion.
2. The frame provides the bureaucratic definition of *work,* which is contrasted in the essay with the meaning of *work* for the individual. It also establishes the contrast between the impersonal efficiency of the present and the warm memories of the past. These contrasts produce the irony that makes the essay so effective.
3. She uses transitional words and phrases that mention the season or month and the year.

4. The many specific, concrete details make it clear that the writer, unlike the Social Security office, feels her mother *did* work.
5. This repetition adds to the enormity of Martha Smith's accomplishments by indicating that she continued to work even after illness and old age had set in.

VOCABULARY PROJECTS (p. 97)

2. Students will come up with a number of different examples, probably simpler and more modern in tone. Discuss how Smith-Yackel's choice of words fits the time in which the events occurred.
3. Smith-Yackel's use of concrete verbs clearly conveys the image of her mother that she wants to project: she shows Mrs. Smith constantly in motion.

COMBINING THE PATTERNS (p. 98)

Passages that suggest a process explanation include paragraphs 16–18 and 21; all relate the daily chores of a farm family. If Smith-Yackel had written her essay entirely as a process explanation, she would have had to eliminate most of the specifics regarding her mother's character and personality, particularly the passages about her parents' courtship (11–12), the births of their children (13, first sentence of 17, and 19), and the details about her mother's later years. The essay would no longer be about her mother.

THEMATIC CONNECTIONS

Midnight (p. 177): This student essay also focuses on hard-working parents, here Asian immigrants who labor in a dry cleaning sweatshop more than twelve hours a day for substantially less than the minimum wage. Although Grace Ku does not say so specifically, it is possible that her parents were working illegally; if so, no contributions were being made by their employer to Social Security. According to the bureaucracy that Smith-Yackel dealt with, Ku's parents may also have "never worked."

On Fire (p. 243): Larry Brown's essay focuses on a different, and certainly more dangerous, kind of labor: firefighting. One interesting question is whether Brown's job—dangerous (and sometimes tedious) though it may be—is more appealing than the backbreaking and precarious farm life Smith-Yackel describes. Note particularly paragraph 8 where Brown writes, "You learn to love a job that is not like sacking groceries or working in a factory or painting houses, because everybody watches you when you come down the street." Does Smith-Yackel's mother seem to have taken the same kind of satisfaction in her work?

I Want a Wife (p. 474): Judy Brady's highly ironic examination of "women's work" can provide an especially interesting pairing with "My Mother Never Worked." Both describe in detail what has traditionally been "expected" of a wife and mother, albeit in two different worlds—one rural and working class, the other urban and professional. Students might discuss the similarities and differences between these two images and what they suggest in terms of class and generational distinctions. They might also consider whether our ideas about the roles of wife and mother have changed in the twenty or so years since these pieces were written.

The Company Man (p. 476): Despite Martha Smith's fears of responsibility before her marriage, her total dedication to her family may be contrasted with Ellen Goodman's "company man," who feels responsibility only to his work—to the exclusion of his family. Students are sure to have strong feelings about the contrast and can discover paper ideas from discussion. Students can also be encouraged to see different ways in which we define *work* and to discuss the relative value of Phil's work and Mrs. Smith's.

Martin Gansberg, *Thirty-Eight Who Saw Murder Didn't Call the Police*

This is an essay that never fails to interest students. Some background about the 1964 incident and the public outcry it generated can open class discussion; the students will probably take it from there, volunteering information about similar incidents they have experienced or heard about. You might want to summarize for the class the psychological experiments described in the widely anthologized essay "Why People Don't Help in a Crisis" and try to examine the motives of those who watched but didn't act. You can also ask students to clip newspaper articles about similar situations—which are surprisingly easy to find. Finally, you can ask your students how they think they might react in such a situation.

COMPREHENSION (p. 101)

1. Kitty Genovese was first stabbed shortly after 3:20; the ambulance arrived at 4:25, but the people did not come out until after it drove away. Thus, over an hour elapsed.
2. The neighbors' excuses ranged from not wanting to get involved to assuming the attack was a lovers' quarrel to being tired or afraid. One woman replied, "I don't know."

PURPOSE AND AUDIENCE (p. 102)

1. The article was intended to make its audience aware of society's general apathy and of our responsibility to correct it. It probably has very much the same impact today as it did in 1964, leading readers to wonder whether they would have come to the victim's aid.
2. The article's main point is "If someone had called the police in time, Kitty Genovese might have been saved." Gansberg has Assistant Chief Inspector Lussen (who is accustomed to crime) express his being shocked by the "good people" who did not call the police. His responses are counterpointed by the weak excuses made by witnesses. An overt statement of the thesis would detract from the contrast.
3. Gansberg's description of Austin Street establishes the area as an ordinary American neighborhood. The idea that such a crime can happen anywhere, to anyone, increases the article's impact. In addition, many middle-class readers of the *New York Times,* Gansberg's original audience, could identify with the residents of such a neighborhood.
4. Gansberg prints the police department's telephone number both to inform his readers and to persuade them how simple it would have been to get help.

STYLE AND STRUCTURE (p. 102)

1. Gansberg's precision helps to establish him as an authority on his subject, someone who has investigated these events thoroughly. This precision makes the reader more likely to accept Gansberg's thesis.

2. The words and phrases that most clearly reveal the writer's anger include the ironic *respectable, law-abiding citizens* (1) and *good people* (4).
3. Many of the briefest paragraphs (3, for instance, or the concluding paragraph) are effective because their brevity makes them stand out. Others (16, for example) include a single line of dialogue and thus would stand as separate paragraphs in any essay. In general, then, the paragraphing probably is effective. Nevertheless, students may feel that the presentation of events is choppy and that combining paragraphs could eliminate this problem.
4. The dialogue makes the article more compelling by presenting the participants as real people with whom readers may identify.
5. The ironic comment by a police detective about the people finally coming out much too late expresses the writer's dismay.

VOCABULARY PROJECTS (p. 102)

2. The repetition of the word *assailant* matches the relentlessness of the attack. The word is also commonly used in reporting crimes. *Attacker* has the same meaning as *assailant*, although the latter is probably more commonly used in the media. *Murderer*, while it ultimately describes the crime, does not necessarily convey the sense of relentless attack since murders can seem relatively passive—in the case of a poisoning, for instance.

COMBINING THE PATTERNS (p. 103)

More descriptive detail about the neighborhood (6, 8–9, 18, and 25), about Kitty Genovese (7), and about her killer (22) would certainly add color and drama to the piece; the result would be something closer to a detailed magazine profile than to Gansberg's straightforward news story. The neighbors he interviewed do suggest some of their reasons for not getting involved, but if he were not reporting as a journalist, Gansberg might have concluded by offering his own analysis of causes. Students may be divided over the effectiveness of doing this because it would be difficult in such an analysis to go beyond simple moralizing about people's indifference. As it is, readers are left to struggle with their own conclusions and to consider what their own responses—and motivations—might be.

THEMATIC CONNECTIONS

Samuel (p. 212): Grace Paley's compact and thought-provoking short story offers an ironic contrast to the tragedy of Kitty Genovese. Here, it is a bystander's well-meaning attempt to intervene that results in the violent death of a boy recklessly fooling around on the platforms between two New York subway cars. In an interesting parallel to Gansberg's survey of Genovese's neighbors' reactions, Paley lets her readers inside the heads of the people in the subway car as they watch and judge the boys between the cars.

Who Killed Benny Paret? (p. 279): Norman Cousins's indictment of prizefighting focuses on another aspect of violence in the United States. Students may well want to broaden their discussion to include movies, cartoons, video games, contact sports, and other aspects of popular culture that suggest "prevailing mores" about violence in contemporary American society. Have we become so accustomed to violence that we are immune to shock when violence occurs in real life?

It's Just Too Late (p. 304): Calvin Trillin's *New Yorker* story about the death of a troubled, alienated Tennessee teenager offers another perspective on contemporary values. FaNee Cooper, while not an "innocent victim" in the sense that Genovese was, still suffered from a kind of indifference both at home and at school that led to her tragic end. She, of course, chose to become part of a rebellious group that her parents disapproved of. At the same time, however, that "choice" seems to have been based in part on a lack of other alternatives and on the absence of the support she needed to see her through a difficult adolescence. Just as with Kitty Genovese, had someone sympathetically intervened, FaNee Cooper might not have died. Students might consider the extent to which indifference has become a part of our culture.

George Orwell, *Shooting an Elephant*

Before discussing "Shooting an Elephant," you will probably need to provide students with some background about imperialism. This should include the extent of the British Empire, the purposes and methods of imperialism, and its effects on native populations or on the system's enforcers. Parallels could be drawn with American military forces stationed abroad or with the Vietnam War, with which students may be more familiar. A more helpful way of illustrating Orwell's predicament might be to ask students to put themselves in the position of a white police officer responding to an emergency in a black ghetto during times of unrest. While the situations are certainly quite different, the inner conflicts they produce may be similar.

Many students probably will have read either *Animal Farm* or *1984;* Orwell's views about political oppression in these novels can enlighten the discussion of "Shooting an Elephant."

COMPREHENSION (p. 110)

1. Orwell was hated because he was a European police officer and therefore a symbol to the Burmese of British imperialism. Despite his position, Orwell had mixed feelings. "Theoretically . . . [he] was all for the Burmese" because he was convinced that imperialism was evil. But he also considered the Burmese "evil-spirited little beasts who tried to make [his] job impossible" (2).
2. The local officials wanted something done about the elephant because it had been running loose and damaging property. The crowd, on the other hand, wanted to be entertained. Orwell notes that they wanted him to shoot just as an audience wants a magician to perform a trick; their faces were "happy and excited" (7) as they watched. Also, the crowd *expected* Orwell to shoot; they considered it his duty.
3. Orwell says he decided to kill the elephant "solely to avoid looking like a fool" (14). He realized that he really had no choice; by accepting his position as an imperialist, he had destroyed his own freedom. Thus, like other imperial rulers, "in every crisis he has got to do what the 'natives' expect of him" (7). He hesitated because he felt it would be murder to shoot the elephant, which appeared peaceful and harmless. He also felt that killing the elephant was "comparable to destroying a huge and costly piece of machinery" (6) and would cause a hardship for the beast's owner.
4. Orwell believed that the coolie's death justified his decision to shoot the elephant.

PURPOSE AND AUDIENCE (p. 110)

1. The narrative reveals the true nature of imperialism by showing how it oppresses the rulers as well as the ruled.
2. Orwell's essay is strongly persuasive; he hoped to convince his audience of the evils of imperialism, not just provide them with an informative account of his experiences in Burma. Orwell probably expected his audience to be surprised by his potentially controversial views on imperialism. As a consequence, he explains his mixed feelings, the incident, and his resulting recognitions in great detail so his audience can come to understand his perspective.
3. The essay's thesis is that imperialism is an evil practice that enslaves both the rulers and the ruled.

STYLE AND STRUCTURE (p. 110)

1. Orwell's first sentence attracts the reader's attention; the rest of the paragraph presents the story's setting and introduces the conflict between the Burmese and the Europeans. The actual narrative begins with paragraph 3, "One day something happened."
2. Orwell writes this narrative in order to show the effect the incident had on him; he is the story's dominant character. Therefore, his voice is logically the one heard above all others. Given Orwell's purpose, this narrative technique strengthens his essay.
3. Orwell devotes two paragraphs to the elephant's misery to show how much its death upset him. It is clear to the reader that the shooting is no casual event to Orwell.
4. The parenthetical comments in this essay may represent a sudden change in tone or subject, as in paragraph 4, or simply an explanatory aside to the reader, as in paragraphs 8 and 11. In both cases, the comments are isolated so they do not jar the reader with their abruptness.
5. The speaker feels he must choose between two worlds and that he is caught in a dichotomy. Paragraphs 4 and 14 reinforce this theme by showing sharply contrasted differences at all levels in the society.

VOCABULARY PROJECTS (p. 111)

2. Some equivalent expressions might be *cause trouble* or *raise a riot, called me* for *rang me up, garbage truck* for *rubbish van, damaged* for *inflicted violence, a little excitement* for *a bit of fun, I think* for *I daresay.* Your students will probably think of some equally acceptable examples. Other "Britishisms" include *chucked up my job* and *looking a fool* (14).

COMBINING THE PATTERNS (p. 112)

The contrasts Orwell implies between himself (along with others among the British ruling class in Burma) and the Burmese are primarily differences between those who rule and those who are ruled within an imperialist system. He is an intruder, and the Burmese are native to the country; he is comparatively well-off, and they are comparatively poor; he has power, and they are powerless (although he notes that, ironically, his "power" is basically a sham because, like other "tyrants," he "has got to do what the 'natives' expect of him . . . to appear resolute" even when he is uncertain). However, setting these contrasts in sharp opposition in a separate paragraph would tend to undercut Orwell's central point about the ambiguity inherent in the power relationships he describes.

THEMATIC CONNECTIONS

Thirty-Eight Who Saw Murder Didn't Call the Police **(p. 99):** The preceding piece by Martin Gansberg offers an interesting contrast to Orwell's story. Orwell was egged on to shoot the elephant by a crowd eager for a show, and Kitty Genovese's killer was abetted by thirty-eight neighbors who ignored her calls for help. Also, both stories raise issues of morality and personal responsibility. Orwell uses recalled experience to clarify his own failings; the episode is something of a turning point in his life. Is there any suggestion that Kitty Genovese's neighbors gained any similar insight?

Just Walk On By **(p. 197):** In this essay Brent Staples also considers issues of power and powerlessness and, in particular, the extent to which poor young black men may find themselves in a situation similar to the one Orwell describes: adopting a powerful persona—an intimidating mask of fearsomeness—that hides an essential powerlessness. The point Staples makes is that every day he must fight against such stereotypes that lead to suspicion and fear.

The Untouchable **(p. 461):** Orwell's essay can remind students that India had an additional "caste," one not described by Ajoy Mahtab in "The Untouchable"— British "sahibs." Students can quickly infer how Orwell, who was born in India, must have reacted to India's caste system and why. You can also remind your students of Mahatma Gandhi. Ask them to consider how Gandhi's passive resistance parallels the role of the Burmese natives in Orwell's shooting of the elephant and how his use of passive resistance further illustrates Orwell's thesis.

Saki (H. H. Munro), *The Open Window*

This is a clever little short story that many students will probably find amusing. You might begin discussion by asking whether they themselves believed the niece's story about the death of the husband and brothers—and, if so, how they responded to the first description of their reappearance. Were students fooled for a moment into believing that "The Open Window" was turning into a ghost story—just as Mr. Nuttel is fooled? In his characterization of the niece in the last line of the story ("Romance at short notice was her specialty"), is Saki perhaps suggesting something about the power of the storyteller? Does "romance," or fiction, make our lives more interesting? (Certainly, without the niece's fictions, there would be nothing to interest us in "The Open Window.")

THINKING ABOUT LITERATURE (p. 115)

1. Vera's story must be detailed so that it has an air of reality—so that Mr. Nuttel (and readers) will believe it. Further, the details of the spaniel and the white waterproof coat and the song the youngest brother sings appear again when the husband and brothers actually return; both Nuttel and readers "recognize" the "ghosts" through these details.
2. Saki's dialogue shows Mrs. Sappleton to be quite normal, despite Vera's characterization of her; she speaks "briskly" of the open window and her "men-

folk" in paragraph 18, "rattles on" in paragraph 19, and stifles a yawn when Nuttel goes on about his infirmities (21). Nuttel's dialogue suggests that he is quite a bore and a bit of a fool; he exhibits "distinct regret" at having to meet new people (6–7), and he talks of nothing but his health (20). Vera, the most fully realized character, also has the most dialogue: She is "self-possessed" (1), imaginative, and obviously intelligent as she tells her story with much flair, referring to her aunt's "great tragedy" (10) and acting out both a "falteringly human" note (14) and a shudder of fear that are quite believable to Nuttel. You might read Vera's dialogue aloud to give students a sense of how clearly it helps characterize her.

3. The detail of Nuttel's nervous breakdown is important because it explains his visit to the country and paves the way for his ultimate "scare." It is important that he knows nothing about Mrs. Sappleton so that he can be taken in by Vera's story. Vera's "self-possessed" quality is what gives her story such authority, and the story becomes all the more believable when she allows her self-possession to crack. The open window provides a focal point that contributes to the building of suspense. The tone and progress of the story would be quite different without these details.

THEMATIC CONNECTIONS

Sex, Lies, and Conversation (p. 367): Students might consider the extent to which "The Open Window" provides an example of the pitfalls of cross-cultural communication based on gender and/or age.

The Ways We Lie (p. 414): Ask students into which of Stephanie Ericsson's categories of lies Vera's story seems to fit best. Is it a "facade," an "out-and-out-lie," or a "delusion"? Do any students know people who fabricate stories as Vera does? In a hierarchy of lies, how bad are such fabrications?

5: DESCRIPTION

Many college students have previously written descriptions that involve painting verbal pictures of places or things, something the introductory paragraph by James Agee does with lush concreteness. Invoking the senses of sight, hearing, and touch, the paragraph is a good place to begin your descriptive unit. A subjective description, it offers colors, shapes, and movement, as well as a variety of tactile and auditory sensations, in both literal and figurative images. Although the language is a mixture of objective and subjective words and phrases, overall the paragraph focuses on the writer's impressions.

Having discussed the paragraph, students will need you to help them expand their ideas about the uses of description. The selections within this chapter were chosen to demonstrate stylistic diversity. Leah Hager Cohen describes her deaf grandfather's "strong, jutting chin" (1), the "shapeless, gusty sound" of his voice (2), and his "lithe, vital" hands (8) to paint a portrait that is both vivid and sympathetic. In "Reading the River" Mark Twain looks at the Mississippi from two perspectives: that of the passenger, who can see its romance and beauty, and that of the steamboat pilot, whose "trained eye" (1) sees only what is useful for purposes of navigation. Mary Gordon describes a visit to a specific place—Ellis Island—and imagines what it must have looked and felt like to her grandparents, who passed through as immigrants to the United States some hundred years ago. N. Scott Momaday uses recollections of his grandmother to describe a turning point in the history of his people. Perhaps the most difficult essay in this group is "Once More to the Lake" by E. B. White. White's vocabulary and intense imagery could be challenging for some students, and we recommend that you discuss several of the shorter essays before assigning his. If you include works of literature in your course, you will want to end your unit with Katherine Anne Porter's short story "The Grave" to show the ways in which a fiction writer makes superb use of description. With imagery as complex as White's, Porter describes a child's learning about the life cycle, including its culmination in death. The images help the reader to understand what the child understands mostly on an intuitive level. Classroom discussions can focus on the uses that both essay and fiction writers make of description and the techniques they use to convey ideas and impressions to their readers. Students should be encouraged to experiment and to open themselves up to the possibilities inherent in description.

Also, classroom discussions can concentrate on thematic threads that run though the selections, which also reflect a variety of cultures. Several of the selections deal with death as a means of understanding life.

Leah Hager Cohen, *Words Left Unspoken*

In this fond remembrance of her paternal grandfather, who died when she was thirteen, Cohen offers a number of details that relate specifically to his deafness: his ritual physical greeting, his wordless voice, the sound he made when eating "that, originating from other quarters, would have drawn chiding or expulsion from the table" (2), his delight in the visual antics of comics like Laurel and Hardy on television. But she also lets us see him as we might any grandfather: playing games, mimicking the way she ate, doing coin tricks, and ultimately aging. Students may want to begin by thinking about the final sentence of her first paragraph: "In all my life, I never heard him speak a word I could understand." How much does Cohen seem to regret this?

COMPREHENSION (p. 135)

1. Apparently deaf since birth, Cohen's grandfather communicated only in sign language. Cohen had not learned sign language before her grandfather died, so they could communicate only indirectly—through games, gestures, and shared physical jokes.
2. The relationship seems to have been as warm as it could be given the lack of verbal communication. Certainly, she seems to have found him a source of much fun.
3. Looking back, Cohen regrets not being able to know her grandfather better— as she might have if they had shared a language. During the walk with him she describes in paragraph 12, when she "found his rhythm, and breathed it in," she experienced a level of union that approached conversation.
4. Often when we lose a relative at an early age, we spend our lives trying to sort through the memories in order to reach a fuller understanding. In this sense "everything seems like a clue."
5. The "words left unspoken" represent conversations with her grandfather that Cohen didn't have. Her implied regret is that he died before she had a chance to learn to communicate with him. At another level, though, Cohen did communicate with her grandfather in ways that transcend speech.

PURPOSE AND AUDIENCE (p. 136)

1. The essay does not have an explicit thesis statement as is often the case with professional descriptive writing. The description stands for itself. You might have students create a thesis statement ("My grandfather was . . .") and discuss whether or not such a statement would contribute to the effectiveness of the essay.
2. Cohen seems to be trying to create a dominant impression of a funny, loving, good-natured grandfather who tried to close the emotional distance created by his deafness and her unfamiliarity with sign language.
3. Cohen neither explores deaf culture in much detail, nor expects her audience to be familiar with it. In some sense, she writes from the perspective of a child, which allows us to see her grandfather's world from an inexpert viewpoint.

STYLE AND STRUCTURE (p. 136)

1. As a child she found her grandfather's chin his most dominant feature. Moreover, he used his chin to nuzzle his grandchildren's cheeks as a means of silent, affectionate greeting.
2. The essay is organized for the most part chronologically, moving from the earliest to later memories. For Cohen's purposes, this probably creates the most effective organization.
3. Cohen gives relatively little physical description of her grandfather, except in paragraphs 1 and 8. She seems less interested in letting readers picture him than in giving a sense of his manner and personality.
4. Students will have different ideas about where Cohen could have provided more detail. Physical description is certainly one possibility.
5. Cohen uses similes in her early paragraphs: "like a chunk of honed granite" (1); "like a pair of bellows sending up sparks," "like a dreaming dog" (2); "like big white fish" (3); "motions as swift and implausible as a Saturday morning cartoon chase" (4). Paragraph 12 also includes strong images. Students may suggest that more figures of speech might have been included elsewhere as well.

VOCABULARY PROJECTS (p. 136)

2. Possible synonyms—honed: *sharpened;* expulsion: *banishment;* percussive: *staccato;* smirking: *smiling;* splayed: *spread;* abundant: *many;* prominent: *conspicuous;* lithe: *supple;* conduits: *channels;* gait: *stride.*

COMBINING THE PATTERNS (p. 137)

Paragraph 9 briefly recounts the bare facts of Sam Cohen's birth, his parents' emigration from Russia, and the discovery of his deafness. The narrative passage serves to create further sympathy for the man, whose childhood was obviously marked by poverty and hardship.

THEMATIC CONNECTIONS

Only Daughter (p. 83): Sandra Cisneros also writes about a complex relationship with a family member, her somewhat distant father who maintained old-fashioned expectations for the only daughter in the family. Both Cohen and Cisneros explore obstacles to communication, and both end their essays with a scene that shows the barriers to communication being breached.

The Way to Rainy Mountain (p. 148): N. Scott Momaday's remembrance of his grandmother as a keeper of tradition and an important connection to his Kiowa heritage provides an especially good companion piece to Cohen's remembrance of her deaf grandfather. Within very different contexts, both writers explore cross-generational relationships with great poignancy, suggesting a sense of intimacy but also the lost opportunities for communication. Momaday's inability to understand his grandmother's Kiowa prayers relates directly to Cohen's inability to use sign language with her grandfather.

Mother Tongue (p. 405): Amy Tan writes about communicating with her mother, a Chinese immigrant who speaks "broken" English. You might focus particularly on Tan's having to translate for her mother in dealing with authority figures. In what ways does lack of language put a person at a distinct disadvantage?

Mark Twain, *Reading the River*

Twain's brief but evocative description of the Mississippi is interesting in its two-part approach: looking at the river from the perspective of an "uneducated passenger," who sees "all manner of pretty pictures in it, painted by the sun and shaded by the clouds," (1), and looking at it from the perspective of an experienced steamboat pilot, for whom many of these "pretty pictures" were "the grimmest and most dead-earnest of reading matter" (1). Paragraphs 2 and 3 demonstrate the two perspectives with detailed, but contrasting descriptions of the same scene. Twain ends by lamenting that once he gained the eyes of a pilot, "romance and beauty were all gone from the river" (4) and by comparing his situation to that of a doctor who can only see a patient's symptoms—the "signs and symbols of hidden decay"—and not her beauty.

COMPREHENSION (p. 140)

1. Twain says the river is like a book because it must be read carefully for signs of danger to the boat and other matters of interest to the navigator.
2. When a passenger sees a dimple in the water's surface, a steamboat pilot sees a wreck or rock that may damage the boat.
3. As he became a skilled pilot, Twain learned what dangers ripples on the surface of the water indicated and how to predict currents, weather, and so forth. But he lost the ability to appreciate the river's scenic grandeur, to be awed by its beauty.
4. Like pilots, doctors have to learn to read their subjects for signs of danger—illness, disease—at the expense of being able to appreciate surface beauty.

PURPOSE AND AUDIENCE (p. 140)

1. Twain's thesis might be stated as "Where the uninitiated passenger sees beauty in the river, the experienced pilot can only read the river for signs of danger."
2. Twain writes primarily for an audience of passengers and explains how differently he saw the river once he became an experienced pilot.
3. Having seen through the eyes of a passenger, Twain appreciates the passenger's ability to regard the river's grandeur. But he also respects the ability of

the pilot to recognize the river's treachery, to navigate its water expertly. He understands all the pilot loses by gaining this expertise.

STYLE AND STRUCTURE (p. 140)

1. Throughout paragraphs 1 and 2, Twain refers to the metaphor of the river as a book "with a new story to tell every day": not a page can be unread without a loss; a ripple becomes an "*italicized* passage," a "legend of the largest capitals with a string of shouting exclamation-points at the end," revealing a possible danger to the boat; the river's language must be learned as completely as the letters of the alphabet. Most students will find this comparison effective.
2. The main descriptive passage in paragraph 2 is arranged spatially, beginning in the distance, then moving to closer objects, then expanding the view again to include the whole. Twain might have started in the distance and ended with the closest details, but he would have lost the sense of grandeur that open and close his description.
3. He includes this description to contrast it with how he would read the same scene as a pilot (3). All the detail is necessary to suggest the breathtaking beauty of the sunset.
4. The thesis is summarized in the final paragraph. Students may differ as to whether they think this is necessary.
5. Concluding by comparing his situation as a pilot to that of doctors, Twain gives readers an example they can easily understand. It also broadens his point, applying it to human beings as well as to the inanimate river.

VOCABULARY PROJECTS (p. 141)

2. Among the adjectives Twain uses are *majestic, broad, graceful, troublesome,* and *dangerous.* The dominant impression he creates is one that combines grandeur and treachery—the two ways of reading the river.
3. Students may have trouble thinking of additional effective adjectives. This illustrates how masterfully Twain uses language.

COMBINING THE PATTERNS (p. 141)

Twain presents his contrast in paragraph 1 and then again in paragraphs 2 and 3. The passenger sees beauty—Twain specifically describes a sunset on the river in detail—whereas the pilot sees potential dangers. Point by point, Twain contrasts his description of the scene as a passenger with what he would have seen after becoming an experienced pilot. His comparison seems sufficient to make his point.

THEMATIC CONNECTIONS

Shooting an Elephant (p. 104): Both Twain and Orwell focus on a process of maturing, of working through a life lesson that involves a loss of innocence—Orwell's in the moral and political realm, Twain's in the aesthetic and professional. Both writers realize that with knowledge comes disillusionment.

Once More to the Lake **(p. 154):** E. B. White's essay also focuses on natural beauty—in the case of "Once More to the Lake," a freshwater lake in rural Maine. White calls the lake "an utterly enchanted sea, this lake you could leave to its own devices for a few hours and come back to, and find that it had not stirred, this constant and trustworthy body of water" (6). Like Twain's passenger, White creates an aesthetic vision of the lake. Like Twain's pilot, White realizes how his view of the lake has changed now that he has grown older.

How the Lawyers Stole Winter **(p. 362):** Christopher Daly's two perspectives on the natural world are very similar to those described by Twain—although the context is very different. The natural skating ponds that were among the joys of Daly's childhood—and for years a hallmark of winter throughout New England's small towns and villages—are today being closed to skaters because municipalities fear lawsuits. Once sites of winter fun, such lakes have been turned by lawyers into treacherous spots to be avoided.

Mary Gordon, *More Than Just a Shrine: Paying Homage to the Ghosts of Ellis Island*

In this essay Mary Gordon reflects on her feelings evoked by a visit to New York's Ellis Island, a center for processing immigrants arriving from Europe during the late 19th and early 20th centuries. Gordon's own grandparents passed through Ellis Island, and it is this fact which brings her there—to honor their courage and to consider the suffering that they and other immigrants endured. Notice that a relatively small percentage of this essay is devoted to conventional description (paragraphs 5, 8–9, 12, 14); you might begin discussion by having students identify the places where description is most obvious. Then, ask students to consider how well Gordon evokes a sense of Ellis Island, both at the time of her visit and at the moment her grandparents would have passed through.

COMPREHENSION (p. 146)

1. Gordon says she visits Ellis Island "to find my history" because "it's the one place I can be sure my people are connected to" (4).
2. Gordon addresses this point in her final paragraph. The "shrines to America's past greatness" hold no meaning for her because she has "always felt that country really belonged to the early settlers," who, as she quotes J. F. Powers, "were taking a risk letting you live in it." As a second-generation American, she doesn't feel as connected to those who had the power to admit (or reject) immigrants as she does to those latecomers to the "party."
3. The "ghosts" are all those immigrants who passed through Ellis Island. Gordon wants to pay homage to their "stoicism, and their innocence, . . . and their pride" (15).
4. In Gordon's mind, Ellis Island, not only inspired fear and humiliation in the immigrants, but also a sense of awe. Ultimately, Gordon feels a sort of disgust with the way the immigrants were treated, but she is also inspired by their ability to endure.
5. Gordon gains a new understanding of her ancestors' need for "security, respectability, and fitting in" (14). Her visit also allows her to take pride in her sense of "differentness."

PURPOSE AND AUDIENCE (p. 146)

1. Gordon's dominant impression of Ellis Island describes an imposing place, cold, unwelcoming, even intimidating (4).
2. Gordon comes closest to summarizing a thesis in her final paragraph. You might have students read this passage and then condense it in their own words.
3. Gordon's description is essentially subjective, but as noted above, much of the essay is not overtly descriptive. In particular, Gordon offers a wealth of objective historical detail; however, students may notice that much of this factual information is chosen to reinforce her dominant impression. The result is to create a view of Ellis Island that expresses Gordon's feelings about the place. A disadvantage, if it may be called that, is that it remains hard to "see" Ellis Island based on Gordon's description.
4. Gordon's purpose seems, in part, to instruct and to provide insight into immigration as well as and, in part, to persuade and to create sympathy for the immigrant experience.

STYLE AND STRUCTURE (p. 146)

1. Although the essay would probably work just as effectively without the opening anecdote, it helps to establish Gordon as a flesh-and-blood person and it leads to her initial insight about Ellis Island.
2. Gordon moves from outside (5) to inside (8–9). Then, she imagines Ellis Island when it teamed with immigrants (12, 14). This order seems natural.
3. See question 2 under "Purpose and Audience." Concluding this way allows her to tie all the strands of her essay together.
4. In her final sentences, Gordon embraces the immigrants who passed through Ellis Island and introduces the image of "the very classy party that was not much fun until they arrived." This image suggests a very potent alternative to the idea of the "boiling pot" misnamed by the Russian in her introduction.

VOCABULARY PROJECTS (p. 147)

2. Students will want to look particularly at paragraphs 5 (*high-minded brick, hopeful little land, ornamental cornices*) and 8–9 (*stolid and official probity, death-like expansiveness*). Such adjectives help to create the dominant impression discussed under "Purpose and Audience." You might also have students consider the adjectives Gordon uses in her imaginative reconstruction of the place.
3. Similes include *like any Rotarian traveling in his Winnebago to Antietam* (4). The final image of American history as a *party* is an extended metaphor. And Ellis Island is personified in paragraph 4. These figures of speech suggest Gordon's sense of "differentness" and convey her central points about Ellis Island and the immigrant experience.

COMBINING THE PATTERNS (p. 147)

The historical narration in paragraphs 5–7 traces the beginnings of Ellis Island. It sets the stage for Gordon's entrance into the Great Hall, "the center . . . of the Ellis Island experience."

THEMATIC CONNECTIONS

Only Daughter (p. 83): The daughter of Mexican-American parents, Sandra Cisneros writes about growing up in a culture where females were often devalued. Although not directly related to Ellis Island, her essay suggests the desire to assimilate and to succeed in the United States that Gordon comes to see in her grandparents.

Suicide Note (p. 315): Janice Mirikatani's poem suggests some of the pressures children of immigrant parents may feel, particularly the need to succeed, to do better than their parents. Gordon would likely sympathize with the young speaker's anguish and sense of "differentness."

Two Ways to Belong in America (p. 357): Bharati Mukherjee writes about the immigrant experience from a very different perspective than Gordon's. An immigrant herself, Mukherjee embraces all things American, symbolized by her insistence on becoming a citizen. Her sister, on the other hand, remains a resident alien, an outsider as Gordon sometimes feels.

The Declaration of Independence (p. 516): Jefferson and the founding fathers are, in a sense, the very people Gordon refers to when she writes of feeling "that the country really belonged to the early settlers." Yet it is difficult to believe that Gordon would regard this document as one of the "shrines to America's past greatness" from which she always felt estranged. Students should have an opportunity to reflect on the ideals upon which the country was founded and the exclusion and dehumanization Ellis Island represents for Gordon.

N. Scott Momaday, *The Way to Rainy Mountain*

In this essay Momaday makes a pilgrimage to places his grandmother had described when telling him the history of the Kiowa people. Students should recognize Momaday's mythic sense of his people's past and his sense of loss at the passing of the old lifestyles and traditions. His calling the death of his people's religious rituals "deicide" (9), without railing against whites, clearly ascribes blame. He explains that the Kiowas were "forbidden without cause the essential act of their faith" (9), as herds of buffalo were slaughtered and left to rot and the Kiowas were scattered by soldiers from Fort Sill. Through his grandmother, Momaday learns about his heritage, but ironically he also participates in the loss of the past, since he does not speak Kiowa and could not understand his grandmother's prayers.

You might ask your students to interview their parents or grandparents to see if they can write a similar description of how their ancestors settled in the United States. You might also ask them to read other accounts of the settling of the American plains—selections from Willa Cather's *My Antonia*, for instance.

COMPREHENSION (p. 151)

1. The title describes both the journey of the Kiowas and his own journey.
2. He means that they were soon to leave their old lifestyles and traditions behind.
3. From the Crows they learned the Plains religion, obtained horses, and discovered courage and pride.
4. Because of the soldiers, they lost the opportunity to practice a sacred belief.
5. Momaday's grandmother gave him a connection to his Kiowa heritage and the land of his forebears.

PURPOSE AND AUDIENCE (p. 152)

1. His purpose is to describe his ancestry and give it meaning.
2. He assumes we have some knowledge of the history of Native Americans. We know this because he omits many details about their lives.
3. This legend gives further meaning to the life and struggle of the Kiowas.

STYLE AND STRUCTURE (p. 152)

1. This description sets the mood and tone of the essay.
2. Momaday begins at her death, goes back to her childhood, and presents a chronological account that again ends in her death. This allows him to present details from different times in her life.
3. This description adds a timeless spiritual note to the essay.
4. One point Momaday stresses is the close connection Native-American people feel to the natural landscape. He uses descriptions of landscapes to point up his grandmother's spiritual bond to the lands occupied by her forebears.

VOCABULARY PROJECTS (p. 152)

2. Three examples include *memory in her blood, cauldron of the land,* and *land was like iron.* They convey the hardships, the difficulty of survival, and the endurance of the Kiowas.

COMBINING THE PATTERNS (p. 153)

Narrative passages include paragraphs 3 and 4, which trace the history of the Kiowas, the legend Momaday quotes in paragraph 8, and the story he relates from his grandmother's childhood in paragraph 9. Each of these suggests something of his grandmother's Kiowa heritage, a heritage that became increasingly distant with the conquest of the West by white settlers.

THEMATIC CONNECTIONS

Only Daughter (p. 83): As Momaday does in "The Way to Rainy Mountain," Cisneros explores the role culture has played in her family. Although Momaday remembers the positive aspects of his grandmother and his Kiowa culture, Cisneros looks at a negative quality of her Hispanic culture—the higher value placed on a family's having sons rather than daughters. Interestingly, limits of language play a part in both essays. Momaday has not learned to speak Kiowa, which keeps him from understanding his grandmother's prayers—and no doubt some aspects of his heritage; Cisneros's father does not read English, a second language for him, which is at least partly responsible for his not affirming her as a writer—until he has a Spanish translation. Ask students to consider the importance that the language of someone's forebears has in transmitting his or her native culture and the importance that acquiring the mainstream culture's language has for someone living in a heterogeneous society. You might use these two essays as an opportunity to address the "English Only" movement. Also ask students to consider the delicate balance required to maintain one's cultural identity while rejecting a particular—perhaps even fundamental—cultural practice.

My Mother Never Worked (p. 94): Although of different cultures and genders, both Smith-Yackel and Momaday look to the lives of female family members to discover some meaning larger than themselves. After students discuss the social significance that each writer discovers in the life of a woman, you may want them to consider a family member who serves a similar function in each of their lives.

Words Left Unspoken p. 133): Leah Hager Cohen's remembrance of her grandfather provides an interesting counterpoint to Momaday's remembrance of his grandmother. This could provide a good comparison-and-contrast assignment.

E. B. White, *Once More to the Lake*

In "Once More to the Lake" White evokes a vivid sense of a lake in Maine. The essay flows effortlessly and seems to be connected without a seam. White uses words masterfully, and students should be encouraged to see how he chooses just the right word to express his thoughts. Sense impressions abound as White attempts to convey to readers the way the lake looked and felt. At points the essay becomes a lyrical poem extolling the beauty and mystery of nature. It is important to tell students that White's essay is not intended as a model, but as a *tour de force* of descriptive writing.

COMPREHENSION (p. 159)

1. The similarities and differences between White and his son concern their childhood experiences. The son relives some of White's experiences during his one trip to the lake, but White made regular childhood trips there and enjoyed a lake that had changed perceptibly by the time he returned as an adult. When he says, "I seemed to be living a dual existence," White means that, because he saw his son do the same things that he had done as a boy, he experienced the illusion that he was both father and son.
2. White keeps vacillating between the past and the present. In some ways the lake has remained the same as it was when he was a boy. But in other subtle ways the lake has changed and so has he.
3. White is disconcerted that he cannot sustain the impression that time has stood still at the lake. The change in the road shows that automobiles, not horses and wagons, now travel to the farmhouse. White seems to sense that, for him, life no longer holds the possibilities that it once did.
4. When White had visited the lake as a child, there were no outboard motors there. When he returned with his son, the sound of the roaring motors made the experience different than it had been years before.
5. White cannot maintain the illusion that he and his son are one. He realizes that like his father before him, he too, will die.

PURPOSE AND AUDIENCE (p. 159)

1. The thesis is complex and does not become apparent until the last line of the essay. Even though at the lake time seems to stand still, it really does not. White realizes that he, like his father, and even his son, are moving inevitably toward death.
2. The ending of this essay may come as no surprise to a careful reader. Throughout the essay White foreshadows his realization of the advance of time. The peacefulness of the lake, for example, is shattered by the harsh

sound of an outboard motor. White says that "this was the note that jarred, the one thing that would sometimes break the illusion and set the years moving" (10).

3. Although younger students will be able to grasp White's point, this essay appeals primarily to those in middle age. White's experience is not foreign to anyone who has watched his or her children growing up.

STYLE AND STRUCTURE (p. 159)

1. White mainly emphasizes similarities between his childhood visits and his visit with his son. The main difference he notes is in paragraph 10, where he describes the jarring noise of the outboard motors that hadn't been present when he was a child; he also mentions the two-track road (three-track before) and the waitresses having washed their hair (7).

2. White says over and over that he feels as if he were experiencing his own childhood. He also says that although at first the lake seems unchanged, he realizes there are differences. Finally, images of summer, such as swimming and bass fishing, occur repeatedly. These repetitions reinforce the main point of his essay.

3. White's use of precise sense imagery enables him to transport his readers to the lake and have them see what he saw and feel what he felt. Much of the effect of this essay would be lost if White's audience read with detachment.

4. In his conclusion White realizes his identity with his father. No longer identifying with his son, White understands that he has taken his father's place and, like him, will eventually die.

VOCABULARY PROJECTS (p. 160)

2. There are many words your students might list, as most of the essay relies on sensory description. Although many of these words refer to the same sense, each is used in a unique way, depending on the context. Students will discover that synonyms are easy to think of, but they do not convey White's meaning as completely.

COMBINING THE PATTERNS (p. 160)

By opening with a narration of his childhood visit to the lake, White sets the scene for his meditation on the inevitable advance of time that comes full circle in his concluding realization of his own mortality.

THEMATIC CONNECTIONS

Only Daughter (p. 83): White returns to the lake wondering how much his childhood spot will have changed. The site is mostly as it was when he was a child, which makes it difficult for him to distinguish the past from the present, but periodically he is jolted into acute awareness of the differences and therefore develops an awareness of his own mortality. Cisneros's father, on the other hand, assumes that past experiences for women will be exactly repeated for his daughter: her "destiny" is "to become someone's wife." He is so certain that old patterns will be repeated that he entirely misses the significance of Cisneros's plans for college. At least in his view of his daughter, he lacks White's sensitivity.

A father's mortality figures in both Cisneros's and White's accounts. White thinks of his dead father as his son pulls up his wet swimsuit. Cisneros does not mention her father's impending death, but her account of his sickroom with its "vials of pills and balled Kleenex" and her inability to ignore the "plastic urinal" are evidence that she is aware of his mortality. One can assume that both writers are aware of their own mortality, although only White discusses it explicitly.

It's Just Too Late (p. 304): Calvin Trillin's portrait of what might be called a dysfunctional contemporary family relationship provides a striking contrast to the sympathetic father-son relationship White describes. A comparison of the two fathers—White and Leo Cooper—could lead to interesting observations about styles of parenting.

How the Lawyers Stole Winter (p. 362): Like White, Christopher Daly looks back nostalgically to childhood pleasures—in Daly's case, the joy of skating in winter on local natural ponds. Also like White, Daly would like his sons to share his experience; but today many such ponds are declared off-limits by local governments fearful of lawsuits. Like the outboard motors that jar White back to the present, the lawyers represent for Daly the intrusive reality of modern life.

The Men We Carry in Our Minds (p. 399): Scott Russell Sanders's essay is also concerned with the relationships between fathers and sons, although the picture Sanders presents is a far cry from White's idyll by the lake. Writing from the perspective of a son, Sanders remembers the images of fatherhood he grew up with among the rural poor—men whose struggle to earn a living for their families left them little time for the sort of attention and love White can offer his son. Students might consider which of Sanders's categories a man like White comes closest to.

Katherine Anne Porter, *The Grave*

Assigning "The Grave" immediately after "Once More to the Lake" works well for a variety of reasons. Both selections deal with the mysteries of memory. Ask your students to consider why the Greeks would deify memory as Mnemosyne, mother of the Muses. The mystical way in which past experiences appear years later is something both White and Porter describe. You will want to point out the dual significance of Porter's title—as the former burial place of Miranda's grandfather and as her memory of an incident that lies buried until years later.

Both White and Porter also deal with an awareness of death at the end of the life cycle. Miranda is initiated at the gravesite into a new world. Although she has seen numerous dead animals, the rabbit Paul shoots has far greater significance than these because the rabbit is pregnant and Miranda sees the unborn baby rabbits. The experience focuses Miranda on life as well as death. While in the grave, she quickly trades the dove-shaped "screw head for a *coffin*" that she had found for the "thin wide gold ring" that Paul had found (3). No doubt a wedding band, "the ring, shining with the serene purity of fine gold on her rather grubby thumb" (11) makes Miranda want to shed her male garments for "the thinnest, most becoming dress she owned with a big sash" (11). The rabbit's pregnancy and the unborn fetuses also prepare Miranda to be a woman. The "blood running over them" causes her "to tremble without knowing why. The very memory of her former ignorance faded," and she understands "a little of the secret, formless intuitions in her own mind and body." She is "learning what she had to know" (14). The grave, the ring, and the rabbits reflect the life cycle. Her agitation over the dead fetuses, her sense of an "important secret," and her intuitive (rather than complete) understanding cause her to "bury" the memory until it emerges when she is a woman and sees the "dyed sugar sweets, in the shapes of all kinds of small creatures"—including "baby rabbits" (15). Discussing Porter's story will deepen your students' sense of the artistic ways in which description can be used.

THINKING ABOUT LITERATURE (p. 166)

1. The dove, often a religious image, is the screw head of a coffin—an image of death. The ring, an artifact of the grave, suggests marriage and fine things. The rabbit, though dead, suggests reproduction.
2. The event suggests to Miranda the whole life cycle—birth, marriage, and death. It teaches her "a little of the secret, formless intuitions in her own mind and body." Without a mother to teach her about being a woman, she learns from the experience "what she had to know" (14).
3. Animal images suggest life and death to Miranda, who is herself like "any young animal" (3). Images of precious metal (the silver coffin screw head and gold ring) suggest the value of the life cycle. The blood images associated with the dead doe and her fetuses are a sensuous mix of life and death—suggesting perhaps menstrual blood as well as birth, since Miranda is initiated into the adult female world. Images of smell suggest death and decay. The "mingled sweetness and corruption" of the marketplace (15) are like the "pleasantly sweet, corrupt smell" from the empty grave (3) and cause the resurrection of Miranda's memory.

THEMATIC CONNECTIONS

Shooting an Elephant (p. 104): In both Orwell's essay and Porter's story, animal deaths provide intense insight—insight that profoundly alters both Orwell and Miranda. As an adult, Orwell has the ability to understand immediately the significance of killing the elephant. As a child, Miranda understands on an intuitive level only and buries the incident until years later.

Once More to the Lake (p. 154): See the beginning of this entry for suggestions for discussing "Once More to the Lake" along with "The Grave."

Samuel (p. 212): Grace Paley's story also revolves around themes of maturity, memory, and mortality. Have your students imagine how the death of Samuel might be remembered by passengers in the subway car (the woman who chides the boys, for example, or the man who pulls the brake) and by Alfred or one of the other surviving boys. How does Paley's final line ("never again will a boy exactly like Samuel be known") tie in thematically with Porter's story of Miranda or White's "Once More to the Lake"?

6: EXEMPLIFICATION

Before writing exemplification essays, students should understand that exemplification is a way of supporting assertions, not a rhetorical pattern. As the essays in this section show, examples can be organized in a number of ways. Jonathan Kozol uses a number of descriptive examples, whereas Laurence J. Peter and

Raymond Hull rely on narrative examples, as does Nate Stulman. Regardless of their form, however, the main use of examples is to explain or persuade.

The biggest problem that students have when they write their first exemplification essays is knowing how many examples they need. Students should understand that the position they want to support determines how many examples they need. The Alleen Pace Nilsen paragraph in the chapter introduction begins this discussion. Although it is a topic sentence for a paragraph rather than a thesis for an essay, Nilsen's main idea presents general practice and therefore obligates her to provide a variety of examples. Of course, a general topic sentence can also be supported with one especially instructive example, and the same is true of essays. In most cases, though, essays will require more than a single example to fully support a thesis. For instance, Brent Staples is obliged to offer a variety of examples to support his statement that he can "alter public space in ugly ways" because of his black skin. His indication that his experience is not unique among black men requires him to offer—at the very least—one other black man's experience.

Students also should realize that a personal statement or observation might not be sufficient to support some assertions. If they say, for instance, "Women do not have to face the problems they once did being admitted to medical school," they cannot expect to overcome audience skepticism with examples telling how easy it was for friends or fellow students to be accepted. To support his statement they would need to report the findings of a study involving hundreds or thousands of female applicants.

Laurence J. Peter and Raymond Hull, *The Peter Principle*

Not all students will realize that this essay has a humorous edge to it. Peter and Hull present a number of examples to support their thesis, but a careful reading shows that there are not enough of them. To overcome this shortcoming the writers give the illusion of having carried out a systematic study and having more evidence by labeling their examples "Municipal Government File, Case No. 17" or "Military File, Case No. 8." Their purpose, however, is not to establish their case beyond a doubt or to engage in a statistical sampling. Indeed, their motivation seems to be to take a humorous poke at bureaucratic systems and, at the same time, to cause people to think.

COMPREHENSION (p. 185)

1. When he began teaching, Peter was disillusioned because many "teachers, school principals, supervisors, and superintendents appeared to be unaware of their professional responsibilities and incompetent in executing their duties" (1). He found out that "every organization contained a number of persons who could not do their jobs" (5).
2. The Peter Principle states that *"In a Hierarchy Every Employee Tends to Rise to His Level of Incompetence"* (30). When employees reach this level, they stay there. As Peter's Corollary observes, *"In time, every post tends to be occupied by an employee who is incompetent to carry out its duties"* (36).
3. By *hierarchiology* Peter and Hull mean "the study of hierarchies," organizations "whose members or employees are arranged in order of rank, grade, or class" (32). Observing how employees were promoted in such organizations and how they did their jobs led Peter to the Peter Principle.
4. In a hierarchy, work is done by the *"employees who have not yet reached their level of incompetence"* (37).

PURPOSE AND AUDIENCE (p. 186)

1. This essay is aimed at a general audience as its tone, its lack of technical vocabulary, and its humor indicate.
2. The statement of the Peter Principle is the thesis. Because the thesis is controversial, Peter and Hull do not present it until they have explained to their audience how Peter arrived at his conclusion. They assume that their readers will more readily accept his assertion if they first understand his reasoning.
3. The writers intend for Peter's "theory" to be instructive, but also entertaining. Their use of exaggerated claims, such as "I had inadvertently founded a new science" (31) and "My Principle is the key to . . . an understanding of the whole structure of civilization" (34), brings humor into the essay. The names the writers give to people promoted to incompetence bring additional humor into the essay. Unfortunately, many students entirely miss, for example, that *E. Tinker at the G. Reece Auto Repair, Inc.* can be read as *He tinkers at grease Auto Repair, Inc.* The humor in the essay probably lowers the audience's resistance to its thesis.

STYLE AND STRUCTURE (p. 186)

1. Before they present the thesis, Peter and Hull demonstrate, through examples, that the conditions they describe exist. They use the opening example to show how, as a new teacher, Peter became aware of occupational incompetence. They then use a series of brief examples to widen the essay's focus and show that this incompetence is everywhere. After establishing this point, they analyze their typical case histories.
2. Peter and Hull mention that they collected hundreds of case histories in order to establish that they are authorities on hierarchies and that their conclusions about hierarchies are valid and based on fact. The three case histories analyzed in the essay are typical because they all illustrate the Peter Principle in operation. Moreover, each represents a different type of hierarchical organization, thus showing the general applicability of the Peter Principle.
3. The hypothetical examples come late enough in the discussion to compensate for any inherent weakness in using them. Examples early in the selection are persuasive, intended to convince readers that promotional incompetence occurs. The hypothetical examples are expository: having demonstrated the problem's existence, the writers can clarify how it occurs. Students should be made aware, however, that hypothetical examples alone are not enough to convince an academic audience.
4. Yes, the range is sufficient. The examples come from many different kinds of hierarchies.

VOCABULARY PROJECTS (p. 187)

2. Yes. They personify the characteristics of the environment they are describing. The personification adds a humorous note to the essay and reinforces Peter and Hull's thesis.

COMBINING THE PATTERNS (p. 187)

The narrative examples give the essay its humorous edge, and they also illustrate clearly the central concept of rising to the level of one's incompetence. A possible disadvantage of this strategy is that the examples might not be taken seriously or considered representative. Statistical examples might be hard to come by, however, and including them—while possibly strengthening the writers' point—would not only make the reading dryer, but also more difficult for a general audience.

THEMATIC CONNECTIONS

Shooting an Elephant **(p. 104):** If your students have already read Orwell's essay, it will be interesting to return to it briefly to discuss whether his position as "subdivisional police officer" is an example of the Peter Principle at work. In what ways can he be seen as having been promoted to a position that he is incompetent to fill? Would a more "competent" police officer have performed differently? How often might incompetent workers act in a certain way "solely to avoid looking a fool"?

The Company Man **(p. 476):** Phil, the company man, when considered in light of "The Peter Principle," can be seen as someone who may have worked himself to death for a promotion to his level of incompetence. The two selections also suggest a flaw in the company's criterion for assessing competence among its executives: the president, in order to replace Phil, asks, "Who's been working the hardest?" rather than "Who does the best work?"

Nate Stulman, *The Great Campus Goof-Off Machine*

Stulman's thesis maintains that colleges that wire dorms for Internet access are doing students a disservice because the temptation to play on-line games, or to surf the Web, or simply to chat online is so great that it interferes with students' studies. If yours is not a "wired" residential campus, you might ask students about their use of computers elsewhere—in the library, at home, and so forth. Do they agree with Stulman that access to the Internet means they study less?

Particularly useful to point out about this essay is that a college sophomore wrote and published it as an unsolicited contribution to the Op-Ed page of the *New York Times*. It serves as an example of writing that is well within the reach of many students—not "professional" in terms of expertise, but clearly expressing an opinion supported by effective examples. Encourage students to think about writing opinion pieces of their own on some problem they see facing their community and to submit them to a local or campus newspaper.

COMPREHENSION (p. 189)

1. In his opening sentence Stulman states that "[c]onventional wisdom suggests that computers are a necessary tool for higher education."
2. Most students, Stulman claims, use computers more for playing games and "collecting mostly useless information from the World Wide Web," along with other activities that contribute little to their academic work.
3. Students not majoring in computer science or mathematics really only need computers, Stulman says, for word processing, e-mail, and, occasionally, legitimate research.
4. Stulman feels that such emphasis sends the mistaken signal that serious research no longer requires "a trip to the library."
5. By providing students with computer access, colleges and universities have encouraged procrastination and wasting time—already problems for many college students.

PURPOSE AND AUDIENCE (p. 189)

1. Stulman, states his thesis at the end of his opening paragraph.
2. Stulman expects most of his readers to accept "conventional wisdom": that "computers are a necessary tool for higher education." Student opinion will vary on whether or not he is correct.
3. Stulman seems to expect most readers to be neutral—accepting "conventional wisdom" but willing to hear the other side. Given the readership of the *Times,* he may expect an older audience less in touch with the computer habits of college students, and may even assume a certain sympathy once he begins to make his case. He is not writing to a "hostile audience," presumably of students who would not want to be disconnected from the Internet.
4. This raises a question similar to the discussion in the first paragraph of the introduction above. The more general question may be to ask students whether they consider themselves part of Stulman's intended audience.

STYLE AND STRUCTURE (p. 190)

1. He does so because he intends to refute this "conventional wisdom."
2. Students will probably differ here. His focus on personal observation is generally persuasive to the extent that it reflects behavior at a private, relatively elite school; but students could easily refute him by noting that their own experience does not bear his observations out.
3. This is probably Stulman's least arguable point. For students to monopolize library research computers to play games obviously is a problem, and his mentioning this is effective because most readers will concede that, at least here, he's right.
4. The greatest weakness of Stulman's argument is that he basically ignores any examples of legitimate computer/Internet use by college students. It could be argued that, for most students, the usefulness of computers far outweighs the temptation to misuse them.
5. Students may differ as to whether Stulman engages in stereotyping. He might argue that he is focusing on particularly "at-risk" students, and it is hard to disagree that a percentage of students are prone to procrastination and wasting time. Still, students may resist what they perceive as Stulman's sweeping generalization.
6. In his conclusion, Stulman sums his central point—that students are often distracted from their studies by computers and that colleges have created this problem by providing easy access. This seems a reasonable way to end.

VOCABULARY PROJECTS (p. 190)

2. The only technical language Stulman introduces is *tweaking the configurations of their machines* (3) and, for the truly uninitiated, *desktop* (4). This is clearly intended for a general readership.

COMBINING THE PATTERNS (p. 191)

Virtually all Stulman's examples are descriptive although a few might be interpreted as narrative (see, for example, paragraph 7).

THEMATIC CONNECTIONS

Television: The Plug-In Drug (p. 283): Marie Winn also writes about a technological innovation—initially seen as benign, if not beneficial—that has had negative consequences because it has been abused. Like Stulman, she questions conventional wisdom—in this case, that parents and children can spend quality time together watching television. These two readings might help students develop an essay of their own that questions conventional wisdom about other recent technological innovations.

Never Do That to a Book (p. 345): Ann Fadiman's essay embodies a premise that lies at the heart of Stulman's argument: books constitute our primary source of literacy and computer literacy is mostly for fun and games. It might be interesting to see how students respond to Fadiman's love of books.

College Pressures (p. 390): William Zinsser paints a very different picture of college students from that described by Stulman. Zinsser's Yale students are obsessed with their school work and with grades. Written years before computers became a standard feature of student life, the essay nevertheless provides an antidote to any stereotype Stulman may be presenting. There are a number of ways to focus a comparison-and-contrast essay based on these two pieces.

How the Web Destroys the Quality of Student Research Papers (p. 610): In this essay, which originally appeared in the *Chronicle of Higher Education,* a philosophy professor expands on one of Stulman's points: research on the Web may be fast and easy, but it can never replace library research and real critical thinking.

Richard Lederer, *English Is a Crazy Language*

Lederer's essay is an amusing look at the many inconsistencies of the English language, listing well over a hundred examples. You might caution students that although Lederer piles on the examples to excellent comic (even "crazy") effect, in most kinds of writing examples need to be expanded and explained rather than just listed one after another.

COMPREHENSION (p. 194)

1. English is a crazy language, according to Lederer, because of its many linguistic inconsistencies—its "paradoxes and vagaries" (6).
2. Lederer's first paragraph suggests the importance of English as a conduit of international communication and as the source of much great literature.
3. Like the air we breathe, language is something we take for granted. It is always around us, and we rarely stop to think about it in detail.
4. The "paradoxes and vagaries" of English refer to the ways that words can mean different things in different contexts, and to the fact that there's little logic to the formation of similar words and to spelling conventions that cannot be applied universally.

PURPOSE AND AUDIENCE (p. 195)

1. The thesis is stated in the title, in paragraph 2, and in the conclusion.
2. Lederer's intention is clearly to entertain—but secondarily to instruct, playfully getting readers to think about the craziness of English.

3. Lederer aims at a general, English-speaking audience, although many students learning English as a second language would likely find his examples amusing as well.

STYLE AND STRUCTURE (p. 195)

1. Lederer leads off by suggesting the importance of English as a world language, which leads effectively into his ironic claim for its craziness.
2. In paragraphs 3–5, Lederer presents examples of compound words that don't mean what they would seem to mean literally. Paragraph 6 presents paradoxes of vocabulary, often resulting in words that mean the opposite of what they appear to mean. Paragraph 7 focuses on inconsistencies in male/female designations. Paragraphs 8–9 offer examples of inconsistencies in word formation. Paragraphs 10–13 offer a series of inconsistent pairs of words and phrases, the meanings of which are related in potentially confusing ways.
3. It is certainly possible to complain that Lederer uses too many examples—some students may find the essay a bit overwhelming. But to have discussed any examples in more depth would not have served his purpose (which is to illustrate, not to explain, the reasons for the craziness of English). And, the sheer number of examples does add credibility to his thesis.
4. The next-to-last paragraph, with its quick rhythm and piling on of examples, leads nicely into the one-sentence conclusion, which is appropriate for Lederer's tone.

VOCABULARY PROJECTS (p. 195)

2. More precise substitutions for *crazy* in this context include *inconsistent, incoherent, insane,* and *absurd;* but none of these express Lederer's point quite so effectively as *crazy* with its more colloquial, lighthearted connotations.

COMBINING THE PATTERNS (p. 196)

Comparison and contrast is implicit in many of Lederer's paired examples, but he doesn't use it as a pattern of development. A paragraph comparing English to another language might be interesting, although such a brief comparison would probably add relatively little to his main point.

THEMATIC CONNECTIONS

The Human Cost of an Illiterate Society (p. 203): Jonathan Kozol's survey of the immense difficulties faced by the growing number of U.S. citizens who cannot read offers a much more serious look at language issues than does Lederer's lighthearted piece.

Sexism in English: Embodiment and Language (p. 413): Aleen Pace Nilsen's look at the way gender stereotypes are reinforced through language offers a particularly appropriate pairing with Lederer's essay. Like Lederer, she offers a wide variety of examples drawn from English and grouped into loosely related categories. But Nilsen explains and develops her examples in greater detail than Lederer does. You might productively discuss with students how the two writers' different purposes result in two very different essays with basically the same structure.

Burdens **(p. 466):** In this essay John Kenneth Galbraith looks at a single word—*burden*—to suggest that meanings change according to the political interests of the speaker. His is an ironic examination of the "rule by which contemporary English usage should be guided," the rule he defines as governed by economic interests, not linguistic accuracy.

Brent Staples, *Just Walk On By*

One way of approaching Staples's essay is to tell students about Lennel Geter, a black man in Texas who served jail time because of mistaken identity, which began when a woman saw him eating in a park each day and assumed his black skin was evidence that he was dangerous. She identified him as the man who had robbed a fast-food store. Students should also be aware of Yusuf Hawkins, a young black man who was killed in 1989 when he entered a white New York City neighborhood to inquire about a car that was for sale. You will want to ask students to consider the emotional effects of always being suspect. You will also want to stress Staples's fairness and ability to identify with his audience—a technique important for any writer of persuasion. Finally, you might ask students to identify Staples's clear topic sentences and to consider the number and kinds of examples he uses for each assertion.

COMPREHENSION (p. 200)

1. Calling the woman a "victim" has meaning on more than one level. Staples's description of the woman makes clear that she *feels* like a victim, which, in a sense, makes her one. Staples understands that her fear is genuine: "It was clear that she thought herself the quarry of a mugger, a rapist, or worse" (2). Primarily, however, the word *victim* is ironic. Since Staples was only "stalking sleep," *he* is the victim of her paranoia.
2. He has the power to "alter public space" because people, fearing him because he is black, react as if any public space were a danger zone. They flee from such zones or even become a hazard to Staples himself in an attempt to protect themselves from imaginary dangers.
3. Staples walks the streets at night because he is an insomniac (2). He also refers to his walks as "constitutionals" (14).
4. A "young thug" is created when he is "seduced" by the cultural idea that it is "only manly" to "frighten and intimidate." When he first robs someone who offers no resistance, he sees himself as a "tough guy," and "myth and reality merge" (8). Poor men are more likely to become thugs because they are powerless in a culture that values power "in work and in play and even in love." Their powerlessness causes them to see chivalric, romantic nonsense as literal. Men with power are less apt to romanticize it.
5. Staples uses a variety of tactics to appear less threatening: He stays away from nervous people on subway platforms, especially when he is casually dressed; he waits before entering building lobbies when he sees nervous people; he is extremely pleasant when stopped by police; and he whistles well-known classical melodies when walking on relatively deserted streets.

PURPOSE AND AUDIENCE (p. 200)

1. Staples states his thesis in paragraph 6. He acknowledges that some people may experience genuine fear of blacks, but he says that "is no solace against the kind of alienation that comes of being ever the suspect, against being set apart, a fearsome entity"—solely because of the color of one's skin.
2. Staples presents his appeal logically ("This is what happens to me and other black men: these are the facts; these are the consequences"), but students are likely to feel that it is because they sympathize with Staples emotionally that they best come to understand the point he is trying to make.
3. Staples seems to presume a white audience, in which case the preconceptions he must challenge are (1) that it is reasonable to fear all black male strangers, or (2) that white people don't really discriminate between black and white male strangers. He uses the example of himself as a way of challenging these preconceptions.
4. Staples's first sentence is intentionally misleading because the woman he describes was a "victim" only in her own mind. Staples's intention is ironic surprise, which works well in context.

STYLE AND STRUCTURE (p. 201)

1. Podhoretz provides evidence that "New York mugging literature" exists. In addition, he illustrates a they/we approach to race relations when he says blacks "were tougher than we were, more ruthless"—as if all members of an ethnic community were identical. His remarks are, as Staples suggests, "infamous" (5); they create alienation.
2. The opening anecdote, developed with irony, is highly effective. In concrete detail, it presents a "victim" "running in earnest" from Staples's "beard and billowing hair" and "bulky military jacket." An insensitive reader might make the same mistake that the "victim" did in thinking that Staples is a thug. However, in the second paragraph, Staples makes clear that his appearance did not make him dangerous—which is the point he tries to make in the essay. A sensitive reader will recognize his ironic use of "victim" from the "discreet, uninflammatory distance" he maintained from the woman. Had Staples begun with an angry statement of his thesis, the unconscious bigot might have seen reason to be suspicious.
3. Staples offers many examples, but his assertion that "standard unpleasantries" occur with police and "others whose business it is to screen out troublesome individuals *before* there is any nastiness" (3) needs to be illustrated. He could also strengthen the essay with more examples of other innocent blacks who have had experiences similar to his. Although he uses an example of one other reporter, his assertion that "such episodes are not uncommon" (11) is sweeping.
4. Staples presents his examples in essentially chronological order, beginning with the first time he realized as a young adult "the lethality nighttime pedestrians attributed to me," moving on to the late 1970s and early 1980s when he was working in Chicago, and ending in the present—although he breaks this order in paragraphs 4–6 when he jumps forward to the present. Some students might see a strictly chronological order as preferable.

VOCABULARY PROJECTS (p. 202)

2. Synonyms for *thug* include *hoodlum, gangster, mugger,* and *gunman.* The more general meaning of *thug* suits Staples's purpose. The connotations of the others are either too weak or too strong.

COMBINING THE PATTERNS (p. 202)

For the purposes of this essay, a narrative case study is probably more than is necessary—after all, Staples isn't writing about thugs, per se. You might direct students to another widely anthologized Staples's essay, "A Brother's Murder," in which he does trace his brother's evolution into a thug.

THEMATIC CONNECTIONS

The "Black Table" Is Still There (p. 294): Lawrence Otis Graham's essay offers a complementary perspective on black-white relationships and perceptions across racial lines.

Brains versus Brawn (p. 328): Student Mark Cotharn explores a different kind of stereotyping. As a student athlete at two different high schools, he found that teachers and administrators made unfounded assumptions about academic interest and capability.

The Ways We Lie (p. 426): Two of Stephanie Ericsson's categories of lying have particular pertinence to Staples's essay: facades (you might ask students the extent to which they think the actions Staples describes in his conclusion constitute a facade) and stereotypes/clichés.

Jonathan Kozol, *The Human Cost of an Illiterate Society*

This essay uses an appeal to emotion to argue for a commitment to literacy. Students may not, at first, believe that illiteracy exists to such an extent in our society. Some simple exercises in class may help them identify with the plight of the illiterate. You might, for example, use signs written in Russian, Chinese, or Hebrew to illustrate how English signs look to a nonreader.

COMPREHENSION (p. 210)

1. Illiteracy is a danger to democracy because governments will be elected by the small number of people who read well enough to vote.
2. If we believe in democracy, we will protect it by ensuring that citizens can make educated choices in elections.
3. Illiterates can participate in only a limited number of activities. They cannot buy, eat, or select from written choices such as menu items, product labels, or television listings.
4. They frequently do not pay bills, adhere to leases, meet insurance obligations, and the like because they cannot understand them.
5. According to Kozol's essay, virtually nothing is being done on a government level to solve the problem of illiteracy.

PURPOSE AND AUDIENCE (p. 210)

1. Kozol's thesis is that an illiterate society is in danger of becoming something other than a democracy. He discusses this point in paragraph 4 and states it specifically in paragraph 5.
2. Kozol writes of everyday experiences, familiar to a general audience. For an audience of reading experts or politicians, he might include a statistical analysis of the effects of illiteracy on a particular year's elections results.
3. His primary purpose is to persuade by giving numerous examples that create strong feelings in the reader, but he also means to inform and to express his own sense of anger and injustice. Additional purposes include identifying specific injustices inflicted upon the illiterate, such as their being denied the right to bear children.

STYLE AND STRUCTURE (p. 210)

1. Socrates and Madison were known as reasonable, responsible men. Their belief that knowledge is a moral imperative supports Kozol's thesis.
2. This anecdote puts the essay on a personal level. It introduces the reader to the emotional aspects of illiteracy and sets the tone for the examples that follow.
3. Kozol uses more than a dozen examples, the effect of which is to suggest the terrible extent of the problem. Fewer examples developed in more detail would not have this effect, although they might create greater sympathy for individual cases.
4. Kozol's use of statistics complements his personal illustrations because it presents the human cost in factual terms.

VOCABULARY PROJECTS (p. 211)

2. Students should select such words as *immobilized, paralysis, circumscribed.* The original version is more likely to appeal to a general audience and to reading teachers, the more objective version to sociologists.

COMBINING THE PATTERNS (p. 211)

Kozol wants the problems of illiteracy to be seen as personal rather than as statistical. Because of the persuasiveness of his narrative, readers must respond to the final paragraphs with a determination to do what they can to correct the situation.

THEMATIC CONNECTIONS

Words Left Unspoken (p. 133): Leah Hager Cohen's remembrance of her deaf grandfather who could communicate only in sign language presents a different kind of obstacle to being fully functional in society. Students might think about which of the two "disabilities"—being unable to hear and speak or being unable to read—poses the more serious problems. They might also do some research about the level of illiteracy support services offered in their communities as compared to the level of services offered for the deaf.

Mother Tongue (p. 405): Another aspect of reading and language is offered by Amy Tan in her description of her Chinese immigrant mother, who can read

English with little difficulty but has considerable difficulty communicating orally with native English speakers, particularly those in positions of power or authority. How different are Tan's mother's problems from those of native English speakers who cannot read? Are people who cannot read likely to have problems with oral communication as well?

The Untouchable (p. 461): This student essay focuses on the lowest caste of Indian society. Students might consider the extent to which those who cannot read occupy the lowest "caste" of American society. Indeed, the description of caste system in Indian society might provide a good starting point for discussion of class in American society and of the limitations on those who cannot read. Can students suggest any reforms to help the illiterate like those Ghandi instituted to help the untouchables?

Grace Paley, *Samuel*

Your students will likely find much to appreciate in this simply told but highly emphatic short story, most of which takes place on a moving subway train. The plot is quickly summarized. Four daredevil boys—three of them black—"jiggle and hop" on the platform between two cars. Adult passengers "don't like them to jiggle and jump but don't want to interfere" (2). The men think of "the brave things they had done when they were boys" (3). The women become angry ("their mothers never know where they are" [4]), and one opens the door to warn the boys that they should go into a car and sit down. The boys nod but don't move. When she returns to her seat, they begin laughing and pounding one another's backs. A man "whose boyhood had been more watchful than brave" (8) angrily pulls the emergency brake. The sudden stop causes one of the boys, Samuel, to fall, and he is killed instantly. His distraught mother eventually gives birth to another son but realizes that "never again will a boy exactly like Samuel be known" (12).

You might begin by asking which of the people in the story have the most clearly defined characters. We learn the most about the "tough" man who remembers riding the tail of a speeding truck as a boy, and we are given hints of the characters of several other passengers, particularly the two who contribute to the action. Samuel and the other boys, however, are hardly characterized at all—we know only that they are "tough," that they have been to the "missile exhibit," and that their mothers do in fact know where they are. They are much less differentiated than the passengers, yet each is given a name. Whom do students find most sympathetic?

THINKING ABOUT LITERATURE (p. 214)

1. The story's single example is Samuel. His death, like anyone's death, means the irretrievable loss of a unique individual.
2. Like the men on the subway, Samuel sees himself as tough. But like all our lives, his life is ultimately fragile, extinguishable.
3. Students will probably differ as to who in the story is brave. Some will say no one; others may see the woman who risks humiliation to warn the boys as the bravest. An interesting further question is whether it is possible for young people like Samuel, who see themselves as indestructible, ever to be truly brave.
4. Certainly, the man who pulls the emergency cord "in a citizenly way" strikes us as pompous, and even the woman who warns the boys comes off as foolish in her fears. Ultimately, it is their interference that causes Samuel's death.

THEMATIC CONNECTIONS

Thirty-Eight Who Saw Murder Didn't Call the Police (p. 99): See *Thematic Connections*, "Thirty-Eight Who Saw Murder Didn't Call the Police," p. 21 of this manual.

It's Just Too Late (p. 304): Calvin Trillin's report on the death of a rebellious teenage girl in Knoxville, Tennessee, in the late 1970s makes an interesting parallel with Paley's story. In discussing these two pieces, students will likely have stories of their own to tell about high school friends and acquaintances who were hurt or killed while participating in some dangerous or illegal activity, such as drunk driving. Ask students to try to explain why young people feel the need to rebel against authority or conventional wisdom. What are some ways—large and small—in which rebellion is exhibited? What do these rebellions say about the society we live in today?

The Men We Carry in Our Minds (p. 399): Scott Russell Sanders's essay considers the concept of manhood, particularly the idea of poor, disadvantaged boys growing into "tough" men. His essay connects closely to Paley's story of "tough" city boys—and their ultimate fragility. How close is Samuel to the boy Sanders describes himself as being? How much role-playing is involved in such youthful "toughness" as Samuel's, and to what extent does such role-playing result in an adult personality?

7: PROCESS

If your students have never written how-to essays, they are likely to assume that this pattern is useful only for recipes and scientific experiments. Even students who have written process essays will probably not have experimented much beyond "How to Play Monopoly." This, then, is your chance to introduce your classes to the possible uses and variations of process writing.

The paragraph in the chapter introduction from Hayakawa's *Language in Thought and Action* allows you to review the difference between instructions and process explanations and the differences in person and tense these forms require. Your students can easily see how Hayakawa would have altered the paragraph if he were giving instructions rather than explanations.

The first essay in the chapter, "My First Conk," draws on personal experience and uses process analysis as a vehicle for social criticism. Malcolm X uses his step-by-step account of how he got his hair conked for the first time to illustrate the degrading rituals African Americans were willing to go through to look like whites; his tone becomes increasingly angry. The next two essays detail processes more objectively. Garry Trudeau's "Anatomy of a Joke" is a humorist's analysis of the stages a joke goes through as it is scripted for Jay Leno's *Tonight Show*. Alan Lightman's "Smile" is a scientifically objective account of a chance meeting between a man and woman, focusing on the biological processes of seeing and hearing. In contrast, Larry Brown's "On Fire" is a personal, and often highly dramatic, account of the working life of a firefighter.

If you assign Jessica Mitford's "The Embalming of Mr. Jones," you will probably want to devote an entire class to the essay because the grisly subject matter and subtleties of tone and style will require a good deal of explanation. Shirley Jackson's "The Lottery" logically follows Mitford's essay since it also contains grisly subject matter used as a medium of social criticism.

By the end of the chapter, your students should have a dramatically altered sense of how flexible and significant process writing can be.

Malcolm X, *My First Conk*

If you have a class composed largely of white eighteen-year-olds, you may have to provide some background on Malcolm X for them, although they may be familiar with Spike Lee's movie version of his life. Some explanation of the methodology of *The Autobiography of Malcolm X* is also in order. Although students may be familiar with Alex Haley's work, particularly the book and television versions of *Roots*, they will probably not know that Haley first met Malcolm X in the course of interviewing him for *Playboy* and that Malcolm X, pleased with this interview, proposed that he dictate an account of his life to Haley. For further information on the working relationship between Malcolm X and Haley, consult the epilogue of *The Autobiography of Malcolm X*.

COMPREHENSION (p. 231)

1. A conk is a smooth, thick mane of chemically straightened hair. Malcolm X wanted to get his hair conked so that he would have hair "as straight as any white man's" (21). At the time the process was performed, the conk was a status symbol; at the time he writes about it, he considers it a symbol of degradation.
2. Shorty asked Malcolm X to buy lye, eggs, potatoes, Vaseline, soap, two combs, a rubber hose and apron, and a pair of gloves. The purpose of each is explained in the context of the process.
3. The major stages of the process include preparing the congolene, applying Vaseline, combing in the congolene, lathering and spray-rinsing, drying the hair, applying Vaseline, combing the hair, and trimming the conk with a razor. All the stages are presented in chronological sequence.

PURPOSE AND AUDIENCE (p. 231)

1. Malcolm X does not present the selection as a set of instructions because he does not intend his audience to perform the steps themselves; in fact, he advises against it. He merely explains an incident from his past.
2. The thesis is that trying to look like a white man is degrading and that blacks should concentrate on their brains, not their appearances, to get ahead.
3. Although conking is no longer a widespread practice, Malcolm X's general argument about black pride is still relevant. This thesis can be applied to many other instances of conformity (see Writing Workshop, p. 232, question 1) and to any race.
4. This emphasis on his discomfort supports his thesis by showing how much he was willing to endure for the dubious achievement of having straight hair.
5. Malcolm X's narrative is a personal illustration of his central point about the sacrifices people will make to conform.

STYLE AND STRUCTURE (p. 231)

1. Some of the transitional words Malcolm X uses to move from step to step are: *then, as, also, when, but, then, until,* and *finally.*
2. The process begins in paragraph 5; it ends in paragraph 19.
3. He uses the quotation marks to indicate sarcasm.

VOCABULARY PROJECTS (p. 231)

2. Suggested substitutions include *avoided* for *beat, room* for *pad, substance* for *glop, very* for *real, stylish* for *sharp, sophisticated* for *hip*. The substitutions weaken the essay because they are inconsistent with the overall tone.

COMBINING THE PATTERNS (p. 232)

A definition of a conk would certainly include description, showing in words what the result was intended to look like. (The result is briefly described in paragraph 21.) It might also include cause and effect, indicating more about how the chemical nature of the process worked, and perhaps set up a contrast with a natural style. Students may have different ideas about where such additions might be inserted.

THEMATIC CONNECTIONS

Finishing School **(p. 88):** Students can learn a lot about tone (as well as the mechanisms of discrimination) by comparing "My First Conk" to "Finishing School." Both Malcolm X and Maya Angelou describe situations in which parts of their African-American identities were challenged by white standards. Students should be able to explain at least some of the differences in tone by seeing that Malcolm X's anger was driven by self-contempt—by his having chosen to deny part of his identity—whereas Angelou refused the denial Mrs. Cullinan tried to force on her and even exacts revenge.

Medium Ash Brown **(p. 224):** This student essay in the introduction to this chapter seems in many ways patterned after "My First Conk." The process described by Melany Hunt is that of dyeing her hair using a commercial product. While not painful, as the process of conking was for Malcolm X, the dye job leaves Hunt's hair "the putrid greenish brown color of a winter lawn." As she concludes, "I still have no idea what prompted me to dye my hair." Students might want to consider why we want to change our appearances, and what happens when the attempt backfires.

The Secretary Chant **(p.488):** Writing in the early 1960s, Malcolm X protests against the then still-common practice among African Americans of straightening their hair. Marge Piercy's 1973 poem offers protest of another sort. Overtly feminist, it is an ironic depiction of the "dehumanization" of female secretaries. Both pieces are suggestive of the social and political upheavals that marked their era of composition, and students might consider the extent to which these issues continue to be relevant.

Garry Trudeau, *Anatomy of a Joke*

As Trudeau notes, the host's comic monologue at the beginning of most late-night talk shows is a carefully scripted set piece that is developed with the help of a number of different hands. His essay follows "an actual topical joke, told on the night of Monday, July 26 [in 1993 by Jay Leno on *The Tonight Show*], as it makes its way through the pipeline" (2) from headline clipper to delivery by Leno. Students may be particularly interested in the joke structure diagram that appears in paragraph 4 and in the concept of the "'spring,' that tiny component of universal truth that acts as the joke's fulcrum" (5). You might have students develop some jokes of their own based on this diagram and using a "spring." You'll also want to point out the collaborative nature of the process—typical of so much writing in the professional world—and the importance of revision, of which paragraph 6 offers a wonderfully illustrative example.

COMPREHENSION (p. 236)

1. The people involved in writing the joke are the headline "clipper" (3), who finds the topical subject for the joke; the "engineer" (4), who decides on the joke's shape; the "stylist" (5), who write the first draft; the "polish man" (6), who revises the joke and "improves" it; the "timing coach" (7), who puts the monologue together; and the "talent" (8), who ultimately "reads" the joke to an audience.
2. The news of the day provides the subject for most late-night talk-show monologues because the news offers subjects audience members have in common and fresh material every day. Moreover, using the news is easier than writing a joke from scratch.

PURPOSE AND AUDIENCE (p. 236)

1. Trudeau's purpose is apparently to point out that—despite their fame, fortune, and adoring audiences—talk-show hosts like Leno and Letterman do not write their own material. Trudeau is primarily a satirist, and this piece effectively suggests what a lot of time and money go into something so trivial.
2. Trudeau can fairly safely assume that most readers of the *New York Times* are familiar with late-night talk shows. He doesn't, for example, feel the need to explain what a monologue is.
3. Trudeau's thesis is the next-to-last sentence of the first paragraph. To restate it in this conclusion would mean simply providing an obvious—and unnecessary—summary of the essay.

STYLE AND STRUCTURE (p. 236)

1. The stages match the work of the professionals outlined in question 1 under Comprehension.
2. The second stage is introduced in paragraph 4 with the word *then,* as is the third stage at the end of that paragraph. *Then* also introduces the fourth stage at the end of paragraph 5. The fifth stage is introduced at the end of paragraph 6 with the word *however,* and the sixth at the beginning of paragraph 8, again with *then.* These transitions, while certainly not inspired, are serviceable and further transitions aren't really necessary.
3. It's likely, as suggested above, that Trudeau's tone is a bit satiric. He clearly doesn't have any special respect for the "crack professionals" who grind out the fairly lame joke he uses as his example.
4. The only thing missing that is common in a process explanation is a concluding summary. The absence of a summary allows Trudeau to end with the image of the "talent" with a cue card reading a joke he had no hand in creating.
5. With the possible exception of the firecracker, the illustrations are helpful (if not vital to readers' understanding). Students will probably feel that they make the essay more interesting to read.

VOCABULARY PROJECTS (p. 237)

2. Other examples of colloquialisms include *major no-no, signed off on,* and *sacked* in paragraph 7, and *dry-runs* and *locks in* in paragraph 8. In general, Trudeau's sentence structure and phrasing are fairly informal, almost conversational.
3. Some students may have a little trouble with the jargon, but they should still be able to understand the process. In an informal essay such as this one, too many definitions could be distracting.

COMBINING THE PATTERNS (p. 237)

The many examples contribute both to readers' understanding of the process and to the humor of the essay. Students may note that the entire process is presented as a single extended example of how a monologue joke is created.

THEMATIC CONNECTIONS

The Open Window (p. 113): The precocious niece in Saki's story is a truly creative storyteller, who is able to capture her audience's imagination and conjure up a believable (if romantic) fictional reality. You might have students consider the extent to which such creativity marks television programming today. Certainly, Trudeau's piece suggests the level of mediocrity and banality that results from most of the highly compensated committee writing for television sitcoms.

Television: The Plug-In Drug (p. 283): Marie Winn's indictment of television's influence on families—and, especially, on children—offers a different kind of critical perspective from Trudeau's. For one thing, Trudeau—whose wife is the television journalist Jane Pauley—writes very much as an insider, knowledgeable about the methods and motives of television production and its jargon. Winn maintains her distance as an outsider, concerned with the effects of television programming, not its sources. Trudeau treats television irreverently; Winn takes the problems it creates quite seriously. You might ask students which perspective provides the more effective critique.

The Ways We Lie p. (426): In Stepahanie Ericsson's system for classifying lies, the process described by Trudeau would most nearly fall under "omission." Talk show hosts recite their jokes as if they had composed them themselves, perhaps even spontaneously. Omitted is the fact that these hosts have very little to do with the creation of their jokes. (Most stand-up comedians, on the other hand, do write much—if not all—of their own material.) Students might consider whether they think any less of Leno, Letterman, and their fellow hosts now that they are aware of these facts.

Alan Lightman, *Smile*

The highly technical nature of this process explanation—and particularly the relatively sophisticated scientific terminology Lightman uses—may give students some problems. It is, however, a good essay to discuss in terms of audience, purpose, and level of detail. Students should realize that they don't have to grasp completely the processes Lightman is explaining. Indeed, it is the very complexity of these processes that he seems to be trying to communicate. He doesn't really expect his readers to remember everything here, as he would were he writing a textbook discussion of the same subject. Rather, he is making a larger point about what can be known scientifically about human beings and natural physics and what mysteries about human behavior remain. You might begin discussion by asking how a textbook presentation would differ from Lightman's explanation. For one thing, a textbook would almost certainly use illustrations. What difference would illustrations make? What does this difference suggest about the different purposes of Lightman's essay and a textbook discussion of the same processes?

COMPREHENSION (p. 240)

1. Lightman actually describes two processes: what happens as the man sees the woman (4–9) and what happens as he hears her say hello (10–13).
2. The most important stages of the visual process are the reflection of light off the woman's body, the light particles meeting the retinene molecules in the man's eyes, and the transmission of this sense data via neurons to the brain. The most important stages for the hearing process are the production of sound vibrations by the woman's vocal chords, the subsequent vibration of the man's eardrums, the deciphering of these vibrations by the cochlea, and the transmission of information via the audial nerve to the brain.
3. If students see the outcome of the process as the man seeing and hearing the woman, then the outcome could not have a different outcome. If, however, the outcome is seen as the man's smile, then it could have been different. Ask students to think about why the man smiles, and why he might not have done so.

PURPOSE AND AUDIENCE (p. 240)

1. Students may not feel that Lightman makes any real concessions to a popular audience. For example he offers few definitions of technical terms, few helpful analogies, and few summaries to give readers time to digest information. Still, the first three paragraphs and the last make it clear that a popular audience is intended. Lightman's purpose is less to "teach" than to suggest the complexity of these processes and to raise a fundamental question.
2. See question 1 in this section. Lightman's larger purpose highlights what we don't know—why the man smiles, why he is attracted to the woman, the emotional as opposed to the physical processes involved.
3. In a sense, the sentence "And so begins the sequence of events informing him of her" (4) serves as a kind of thesis. One can make the case that the final sentence also serves as a thesis.

STYLE AND STRUCTURE (p. 241)

1. The discussion of the process begins in paragraph 4, as suggested in question 3 under Purpose and Audience.
2. Paragraph 3 sets the scene for the encounter between the man and the woman, while the first two paragraphs suggest the ordinariness of this particular day for both of them. The final paragraph implies that the meeting is momentous for them.
3. Transitional words and phrases can be found throughout, generally focusing on the stages of the process ("Once through the pupil of the eye" [4], "After several intermediate steps" [6]) or on the passage of time ("In another few

thousandths of a second" [9]). While students may think more would be help-ful, it is really not a lack of transitions that makes this explanation difficult to read.
4. The title is misleading in that it is deceptively simple. Yet, given Lightman's larger purpose, it seems entirely appropriate.
5. Lightman uses the present tense throughout, which adds a sense of imme-diacy. This suggests that such processes are constantly ongoing, even though Lightman is ostensibly describing a unique encounter.
6. See question 2 under Comprehension and question 3 in this section. Again, students may feel Lightman could have been clearer if he had used more—or more obvious—transitions to mark the stages. In fact, however, more obvious transitions might have produced a more mechanical, less suggestive process.

VOCABULARY PROJECTS (p. 241)

2. Examples of such informal language—which are relatively few—include *dance* and *gone into action* (7), *bunch together* (9), and *sloshing* (12). Such ex-pressions suggest that Lightman has a popular audience in mind.

COMBINING THE PATTERNS (p. 242)

Lightman's description is quite objective (see, for example, in paragraph 8—"The woman . . . tilts her head at an angle of five and a half degrees. Her hair falls just to her shoulder. . . ."). Such objectivity suits Lightman's purpose and the sci-entific nature of the process he describes.

THEMATIC CONNECTIONS

Words Left Unspoken (p. 133) Having read about the process through which sound vibrations are received by the ear's biological structures, then converted into messages that are sent to the brain, students may wish to read about Leah Hager Cohen's deaf grandfather, whose disability prohibited this process. These two essays focus on a process students have probably taken for granted; both writers indicate that the process is anything but routine.

Just Walk On By (p. 197) Brent Staples considers perception from a very dif-ferent perspective. An African-American professional, he finds that when he is in public, white people often perceive him as a threat. This fact ties in interestingly with Lightman's final point: that while the "facts" of perception can be explained in terms of chemistry and biology, the "truth" of perception, why we respond as we habitually do, is far more difficult to understand. Are attraction and fear innate responses, conditioned responses, or something else?

Sex, Lies, and Conversation (p. 367) Linguist Deborah Tannen also focuses on perception—in her case, the different expectations men and women bring to rela-tionships and how these can lead to miscommunication and misunderstanding. A wife, for example, can perceive her husband as unsupportive because, when she tells him about a problem, he attempts to comfort her by minimizing the problem or offering a solution; she, however, expects him simply to express sympathy and understanding. As with Staples's scenarios, the "senses" are functioning normally, but "perception" is nonetheless faulty.

Larry Brown, *On Fire*

This essay is quite a bit more complex as a piece of process writing than the other essays in the chapter. Here, novelist Larry Brown, who served for many years as a firefighter in Oxford, Mississippi (four years as captain), evokes the full panoply of a firefighter's professional life in a style that is both intensely realistic and highly impressionistic. In fact, Brown presents a series of discrete processes, each making up a different facet of the job and all told in the second person. He begins dramatically by describing the action of entering a burning building (1–2), then jumps back to let us see the tension of the drive to the fire (3). Paragraphs 4 and 5 shift to the work of the pump operator, whose expertise the nozzlemen's lives depend on, and paragraph 6 describes the action of raising and climbing a ladder to the second floor of a burning building. Paragraph 7 focuses on some of the specific dangers firefighters face; then, paragraph 8 shifts to describe the way community members show their respect and gratitude. In paragraph 9 we see the crucial process of testing the fire hose. Paragraph 10 shows the firefighter helping human victims—as well as the more mundane tasks of retrieving lost pets. Finally, paragraphs 11–12 show the firefighter when no emergency looms, carefully checking equipment at the fire station and waiting "for whatever comes your way."

COMPREHENSION (p. 245)

1. This is a bit of a trick question. As noted above, Brown doesn't exactly describe steps in a single, discrete process but rather presents a number of different activities that add up to the firefighter's life. As he writes in paragraph 11, "no two days are ever the same"; his purpose is to suggest the many facets of the job.
2. There are two general stages in the firefighter's job: the actions involved in actually fighting fires and the preparations that take place at the firehouse.
3. Interestingly, Brown doesn't seem to suggest that any one part of the firefighter's job is of greater importance than the others. He gives as much weight to checking equipment and to waiting "for whatever comes your way" as he does to the more dangerous and dramatic activity of fighting a fire.
4. A firefighter lives with danger—even the threat of death—which is the job's main drawback. Also he or she also experiences much tedium in between being called to fight fires. The main benefits Brown describes are the feeling of helping others and the appreciation shown by the community.

PURPOSE AND AUDIENCE (p. 245)

1. The essay is intended for a general audience. The amount of detail provided suggests that Brown is not writing for experienced firefighters.
2. Brown is trying to convey both the danger and tension involved in the job as well as the quieter life at the firehouse. Students will probably think he is successful.
3. There is no explicitly stated thesis, but Brown does make his general point in several places ("You learn to do whatever is called for" (10); "you wait for whatever comes your way" (12), so no explicit thesis is necessary.

STYLE AND STRUCTURE (p. 246)

1. Throughout the essay, Brown repeats phrases at the beginnings of sentences: *you learn, you try, you see*. This repetition creates an overall coherence. Elsewhere, the repetition of words—for example, in paragraphs 6 (*difficulty*) and 7 (*sometimes*)—is used for emphasis.
2. Students may be surprised to discover that other than the simile in paragraph 1, Brown uses no other explicit figures of speech. His language is remarkably direct, which contributes to the simple frankness of his tone.
3. The different sentence structures add variety to the essay. The use of contractions contributes to an informal, straightforward tone. The juxtaposition of long and short paragraphs creates variety of rhythm.
4. One interpretation of the title is that it denotes an essay *about* fire. But Brown clearly intends his audience to read the title as a synonym for *burning* as well.
5. The use of the pronoun *you* (rather than *I* or *we*) throughout enables Brown to distance himself from his painful material. At the same time, paradoxically, it adds a sense of immediacy; although *you* does not refer to readers, it encourages readers to see through the firefighter's eyes, experiencing the job directly. (Note: You will need to remind students not to use *you* carelessly in their own essays, as it is nearly always too imprecise and informal for college writing.)
6. As noted in the introduction above, the essay is quite unlike a typical process explanation (except that it discusses materials and offers cautions). Brown's purpose is not to instruct readers so they can carry out a firefighter's duties, nor is it to explain just one function firefighters perform. Rather, his purpose is to create a sense of what it is like to be a firefighter by showing the variety of tasks a firefighter must fulfill.
7. Paragraph 8 is something of a digression because it is concerned not with the firefighter's duties but with the way the community responds. The details here are nevertheless effective because they suggest an everyday aspect of the firefighter's life.

VOCABULARY PROJECTS (p. 246)

2. Examples of slang include *puke* (7) and *dumps in* (8); examples of jargon include *charged inch-and-a-half line* (6), *friction loss* (7), and *three hundred psi* (9); students will quickly find an impolite expression in paragraph 5. This language contributes to the authenticity of Brown's voice. The jargon also establishes his credibility as an experienced professional firefighter.

COMBINING THE PATTERNS (p. 247)

The addition of an opening or concluding paragraph comparing firefighting to other occupations would not, in our view, strengthen the essay because it would dissipate the drama Brown establishes at these two crucial points in his essay. Also, it is quite obvious how firefighting differs from other jobs.

THEMATIC CONNECTIONS

Reading the River (p. 138): Mark Twain describes a very different occupation from firefighting—piloting a riverboat—but students will see that both Twain and

Brown are writing about the experience and expertise necessary to do a job well, as well as about how experience changes one's view of both work and the world.

Midnight (p. 177): Student Grace Ku's essay about the difficult life of her immigrant parents, who work long and grueling hours at a dry cleaning establishment, can be paired interestingly with "On Fire." If Ku's parents are at the bottom of the employment hierarchy, where does a firefighter fall?

The Men We Carry in Our Minds (p. 399): Scott Russell Sanders also looks at hierarchies within the workforce, dividing the world of work into "toilers," "warriors," and "bosses." Where might firefighters fit within this scheme?

Jessica Mitford, *The Embalming of Mr. Jones*

You should have no trouble getting students to participate in a discussion of this essay; your problem will more likely be getting them to move beyond the essay's content to focus on style and organization. You might open the discussion by asking why or why not students feel embalming is a necessary process. You might also ask students whether they think Mitford is being fair in her attack, and where her bias is most obvious. An interesting footnote on the book from which this piece is excerpted is Mitford's essay "My Way of Life Since *The American Way of Death*," reprinted in her 1979 book *Poison Penmanship* (Knopf).

COMPREHENSION (p. 252)

1. Mitford asserts that the public actually knows less about embalming than they used to because embalming is no longer done at home.
2. Mitford compares the embalmer unfavorably to the surgeon, describing the embalmer's technique as "crudely imitative of the surgeon's" (5). Later, in paragraph 12, she likens the embalmer to a sculptor and a cosmetician, again unfavorably since the techniques described are neither artistic nor skillful.
3. The major stages of the process of embalming and restoration are laying out the body; draining out the blood and pumping in embalming fluid; removing the contents of the chest cavity and replacing them with cavity fluid; creaming the face; replacing any missing parts of the body; reducing swelling or filling out hollow areas; positioning the lips; shaving, washing, dressing, and applying makeup to the body; and, finally, casketing.

PURPOSE AND AUDIENCE (p. 252)

1. Her thesis is that, if the public knew more about embalming, they might wonder whether they really wanted or needed to have it done.
2. Mitford seems prepared to have her audience disagree with her controversial thesis. Using such a critical, ironic tone for a sensitive topic reveals this.
3. Yes, she is muckraking in this essay. As her thesis indicates, she views her purpose as a kind of public service and expects her remarks to surprise, even shock, her readers. She suggests that undertakers are guilty of concealing information from the public that might threaten their business.
4. Mitford's judgmental tone helps to persuade readers that the process is in some ways ridiculous. Although her tone may not encourage readers to trust her entirely, they trust her enough to consider her thesis seriously. If she had presented the material more factually, she would probably diminish the interest of her readers.

STYLE AND STRUCTURE (p. 253)

1. The essay is written in present tense, but its sentences are statements, not commands, and it employs third, not second, person.
2. Mitford's list of materials includes quasi-surgical tools, chemical preparations, and "aids to prop and stabilize" the body. The tools are described as "crudely imitative of the surgeon's," the oils and creams are labeled *bewildering*, and one piece of equipment is given the negative connotation of *old-fashioned stocks*. In general, then, the effect on the reader is likely to be negative.
3. To reveal her negative feelings about the industry, Mitford stresses the way embalmers distort language. She points, for example, to corruptions like *demisurgeon* (5), understatements like *quite discouraging* (11), coinages like *casketing* (17), and euphemisms like *young female subjects* (8).
4. Mitford quotes experts out of context and then echoes their words in contexts of her own. Examples of this technique include *rudimentary, not to say haphazard* (7) and *intestinal fortitude* (11, 15). She thus presents her remarks in a negative light and supports her thesis that the consumer should beware.
5. Some of the transitions Mitford uses to move from one stage of the process to another are: *To return to Mr. Jones* (8), *The next step* (10), *This done* (10), *The embalmer . . . returns to the attack* (12), *The patching and filling completed* (16), and *Jones is now ready for casketing* (17).
6. Examples abound. See paragraphs 4, 7, 10, 11, 14, 15, 17, and 18. Mitford's many quotations from mortuary handbooks, even the brand names of the mortuary supplies, are also presented sarcastically throughout. The tone certainly serves Mitford's purpose, but it could put off some readers—particularly if they have recently lost a loved one.

VOCABULARY PROJECTS (p. 253)

2. Substitutions might include *landscape* for *territory; grisliness* for *gruesomeness; clever* for *ingenious; poked* for *jabbed; acceptable* for *presentable*. Many of the substitutions are less descriptive, which weakens the tone of the essay.
3. There are numerous examples of medical and cosmetic diction that your students might list. It should be apparent to them that the number of medical/surgical terms far exceeds the number of cosmetic terms, indicating that Mitford's intention is to ridicule that area of the embalming process more than the other.

COMBINING THE PATTERNS (p. 254)

Paragraph 8 describes the different colors of embalming fluid, and beginning with paragraph 11, every paragraph includes some description of the corpse before and after "restoration." Each of these descriptive details suggests the artificiality and gruesomeness of the process and supports Mitford's thesis that if people knew more about it, they might be less likely to subject deceased loved ones to the procedure.

THEMATIC CONNECTIONS

English Is a Crazy Language (p. 192): Richard Lederer looks at some of the absurdities we take for granted about the English language, while Mitford looks at another "absurdity" many take for granted.

My First Conk (p. 228): The process described by Malcolm X earlier in this chapter is, like embalming, a gruesome procedure, and the restorative part of the embalming process serves a similar function: artificially creating an image that conforms to a culturally determined standard of attractiveness or acceptability. (As Mitford ironically notes, *il faut souffrir pour être belle*.) While embalming may not be a debasing act, as Malcolm X suggests conking is, students may certainly want to question its necessity.

The Ways We Lie (p. 426): Obviously, embalming—and much of the ritual of funerals in the United States—can be seen as a certain kind of self-protective lie. Friends and family members want to see the deceased "one last time" so they can "say goodbye," but few would be willing to face a corpse *au naturel*. Stephanie Ericsson would probably classify our funeral practices in the category of *delusion*. Ask students to consider her final four paragraphs in particular. Is our avoidance of facing the reality of death a healthy aspect of our culture? If we began to treat death more honestly, would other aspects of our lives perhaps improve?

Secretary Chant (p. 488): The body of the secretary in Marge Piercy's poem is completely artificial—an amalgam of office supplies—and thus can be likened to the artificially "lifelike" corpses Mitford describes. Piercy's tone is also highly sarcastic, which may be related to question 6 under Style and Structure.

Shirley Jackson, *The Lottery*

Many of your students will have read Jackson's short story, but they will, in all likelihood, not have focused on it as detailing a process. Even more smoothly than Malcolm X's "My First Conk," it combines narration with process. Your discussion can help students differentiate between the two related forms of writing. Seeing the lottery that the villagers conduct each year as an inflexible process can also help students recognize that rituals are processes—although many evolve and change over time. Realizing that the villagers perform a traditional *scapegoating* will allow students to recognize other cruel traditions—traditions that continue to be observed for reasons similar to Mr. Warner's illogical justification that "there's *always* been a lottery" (32). You might point back, for example, to "Finishing School" and Mrs. Cullinan's trying to hold onto "the tradition of her wealthy parents"—that is, to the unjust traditions of the old South. Malcolm X also participated in a painful tradition when he conked his hair for many years without thinking about its significance. He later came to feel self-contempt precisely because he was unthinking in his observance of a harmful tradition. Discussing the conditions that make observing a particular tradition a valuable process and the conditions that make it harmful can help students become more thoughtful about themselves and about the world in which they live.

THINKING ABOUT LITERATURE (p. 262)

1. The first step of the process is preparation the night before the lottery is to be held. A slip of paper for each of the villagers—including the one with the black spot—is placed in the black box. The second step occurs the next day when the villagers gather in the square—first the children, with the boys piling up the stones; then the women; and finally the men. When everyone is gathered, the black box is brought to the square and placed on a three-legged stool. Mr. Summers, the lottery official, is then sworn in, and a roll call checks the attendance of the villagers. The next step is the first drawing of lots. After the family holding the paper with the black marks is identified, a "ballot" for

each individual in that family is placed back in the box. When the family member who draws the black spot is identified, the final step of the process—the stoning of that person—occurs.

Although the villagers still perform all of the steps in the process, they no longer understand the original significance of the steps. The only clue to the original meaning comes when Mr. Warner says, "Used to be a saying about 'Lottery in June, corn be heavy soon'"—which suggests that the lottery must have been a fertility ritual. Now, however, a lack of logic marks the way each step is performed. The black box is used because "no one liked to upset even as much tradition as was represented by the black box" (5). Slips of paper are used instead of the original wood chips "because so much of the ritual had been forgotten or discarded"—which allows Mr. Summers to successfully argue that wood chips for a growing village take up too much space (6). The swearing-in used to involve "a recital of some sort . . . a perfunctory tuneless chant" with the lottery official standing "just so," but "this part of the ritual had been allowed to lapse" (7). During the drawing itself, Mr. Summers merely speaks to each participant. The original "ritual salute" has been forgotten—further evidence that the lottery is not held because of its original meaning to the villagers (7). When the second drawing occurs, Mr. Summers asks the family members because "it was the business of the official of the lottery to ask such questions formally" (13). "Although the villagers had forgotten the ritual and lost the original black box, they still remembered to use the stones" (74). These explanations are not particularly logical.

2. Although the village has forgotten the lottery's original significance, the fact that the villagers still perform all of the steps of the process, especially the stoning, suggests a dark, cruel side to the villagers, and perhaps to humankind in general—cruelty for its own sake and a sinister need to scapegoat.

3. As a scapegoat story, "The Lottery" has universal implications. Cruel, unthinking traditions are maintained in many places in modern civilization. For example, novices are still forced to undergo hazing in order to be accepted into some military schools, fraternities, and sororities. Periodically someone dies from the cruelty of these traditions. Certainly, the Star of David pinned to the chests of Jews in Nazi Germany was the equivalent of the black spot—on an almost incomprehensible scale. Wherever and whenever someone is scapegoated—because of position, skin color, ethnic background—the equivalent of the lottery occurs, and the individual is sacrificed to fill some dark need of the group.

THEMATIC CONNECTIONS

Thirty-Eight Who Saw Murder Didn't Call the Police (p. 99): Martin Gansberg's newspaper report about a woman in New York City being murdered while her neighbors listened to her screams for help, refusing to get involved, is another kind of horror story about an almost banal evil at the heart of a community. Although Kitty Genovese was not a scapegoat, the actions of her neighbors suggest a lack of human feeling that parallels that of the townspeople who turn on Tessie Hutchinson. Students may well say that "The Lottery" is fiction and that nothing like its story would actually happen, but they have to admit the reality of stories such as Kitty Genovese's. You might expand the discussion to include other examples of members of our society "not getting involved" in the problems of others, from abused spouses or children to homeless people to functional illiterates. We would all probably say that, unlike Kitty Genovese's neighbors, we wouldn't ignore a person being attacked outside our window. Why, then, do we so easily ignore others with different kinds of troubles?

Shooting an Elephant (p. 104): Students should be able to see that Orwell becomes a scapegoat when he feels forced by the Burmese crowd to kill the elephant. He feels he has to act as a traditional "sahib": "A sahib has got to act like a sahib"— or be laughed at. He is, therefore, "an absurd puppet pushed to and fro by the will of those yellow faces behind." Tessie Hutchinson's protest at being scapegoated is more understandable than Orwell's lack of protest. She fears being stoned to death; he fears being laughed at. The Burmese natives show the same dark excitement that the villagers exhibit when they throw their stones at Tessie. The natives are a "sea of yellow faces . . . faces all happy and excited over this bit of fun." The natives' "devilish roar of glee," like the stonethrowing, comes from the dark side of humanity.

Samuel (p. 212): Grace Paley's is another kind of story about a community and the sometimes tragic roles people play in the functioning of that community and its mythology. There is an inevitability about Samuel's death that parallels in an interesting way the stoning of Tessie Hutchinson. The men on the subway car, recalling their own "tough" youths and "the brave things they had done as boys," tacitly egg Samuel and his friends on in their dangerous game between the cars. If one of these men had told the boys to get into one of the cars and sit down, they would perhaps have been intimidated into doing so. Unfortunately, action is left to others—who don't understand the boys—and the result is a horrible death. It is in death, however, that Samuel enters the realm of myth, a child the likes of whom will never be known again.

8: CAUSE AND EFFECT

Students are likely to find the concept of cause and effect intriguing but difficult; they may tend to oversimplify causal relationships or mistake chronology for causality. It is probably wise, then, to begin your discussion of cause and effect by illustrating terms such as main and contributory causes, and immediate and remote causes with concrete examples drawn from current news events or from your students' own experience.

When the class has a working knowledge of terms and can apply them accurately, you can proceed to the readings. Since so many students confuse cause and effect with narration, beginning with two shorter examples will be helpful—the paragraph by Tom Wicker, which emphasizes effects, and the student essay on the Irish famine, which emphasizes causes. Comparing the famine paper with "My Field of Dreams," "Finishing School," or "The Open Window" will also be helpful; cause and effect principles operate in these essays too, of course, but the emphasis is not on finding causes or predicting effects but rather on presenting the events in sequence—on telling the story. You might have students freewrite briefly about the causes and effects in one of these Chapter 4 selections, and then discuss in class what they have written. Another way of clarifying the difference between narration and cause and effect is to ask students to infer the causes for the speaker's suicide in "Suicide Note," a narrative poem at the end of the chapter. Together you might brainstorm for a cause-and-effect paper to show students that their causal analysis must take a form different from the original.

Consider assigning "Who Killed Benny Paret?" with "Television: The Plug-In Drug." Both are clearly organized, but Cousins offers very little detail to support his assertions. The two selections therefore allow you to discuss the amount of support necessary for proving cause-and-effect relationships. Other selections in this chapter explore significant social and economic issues through cause-and-effect analysis.

Norman Cousins, *Who Killed Benny Paret?*

Violence in sports—particularly in hockey, soccer, and boxing—remains a topic of great interest to students, who frequently have experienced it as players and as spectators. For this reason, class discussion of "Who Killed Benny Paret?" is usually lively. In this discussion you might consider whether sports have become more or less violent since this essay was written in 1962 and ask the class to try to account for the change. Has increased television coverage of sports, for instance, had any effect on violence in sports? Do the fans really want to see violent confrontations? You might also examine the *results* of this type of violence. For instance, does violence among the players lead to violence in the audience? Could frequent exposure to brutality in sports make people more tolerant of violence in other situations?

COMPREHENSION (p. 281)

1. Jacobs believes people come to see a prizefight because they want to see a man hurt. Cousins strongly agrees, as the rest of the essay demonstrates.
2. The immediate cause of Paret's death was the blow to the head he suffered during the fight. Remote causes considered by the investigators included the referee's failure to stop the fight, the doctors' willingness to certify Paret's physical fitness, and the manager's role in encouraging Paret to fight. Cousins feels the main cause of Paret's death was the crowd that wanted to see him hurt.
3. Cousins feels it is senseless to investigate the referee's role because the referee did not have "primary responsibility" (9) for the outcome of the fight; he only acted as the crowd expected him to.
4. "The point" is that people want prizefighting to continue just as it is.

PURPOSE AND AUDIENCE (p. 281)

1. The thesis of this essay is that Paret did not have to die; he died because the crowd wanted to see a man get hurt.
2. The case received a lot of publicity at the time of Paret's death. Even a month later, the essay would have moved readers to feel vaguely guilty about Paret's death. Because boxers continue to be killed during fights, the essay still forces readers to question their own motives as spectators.
3. This essay, which first appeared in *Saturday Review,* is aimed at a well-educated general audience. It is probably too strongly negative to impress either of the other groups; for those readers, Cousins would have presented a subtler argument.
4. Cousins writes as if he expects his audience to be receptive to this thesis but not necessarily to agree with it. He tries to win sympathy for his position by building sympathy for Paret and other fighters.

STYLE AND STRUCTURE (p. 281)

1. Cousins is eloquent and forceful, but the amount of detail is adequate only for an audience predisposed to accept his thesis. Many people, however, would find his argument to be slight. The fight promoter's testimony is one important piece of supporting evidence—but only one. Instead of accumulating other support, Cousins uses loaded language, saying "it is futile to investigate the referee's role . . . [and] it is nonsense to talk about prize fighting as a test of boxing skills" (9). He asserts that "no crowd was ever brought to its feet screaming and cheering" because of skill in a boxing match, but he fails to describe crowds at contests of skill instead of mayhem. He also neglects to interview referees and other participants.
2. Because the crowd pays to see a fighter hurt, if the referee stops the fight, the crowd boos; if the fighters dodge and weave skillfully, the crowd is quiet; if the referee does not halt the fight, thus allowing a fighter to be hit hard, the crowd comes alive.
3. In his conclusion, Cousin again refutes the two most obvious—but erroneous—explanations of Paret's death. The conclusion is effective because it firmly reiterates the cause on which the essay focuses and it forcefully sums up the essay's position.

VOCABULARY PROJECTS (p. 281)

2. a. For football, acceptable substitutions might include *general manager* for *promoter; football games* for *prize fights; on the field* for *in the ring; temperamental quarterbacks* for *boxing artists; dodging, weaving, grabbing, punching, and running* for *feinting, parrying, weaving, jabbing and dancing; killers and hitters and maulers* for *killers and sluggers and maulers; victory* for *knockout, players/play* for *fighters/fight*. (*Referee* would stay the same.)
   b. "The crowd wants the victory; it wants to see a man stretched out on the field. . . . It is nonsense to talk about football as a test of skills. No crowd was ever brought to its feet screaming and cheering at the sight of two teams beautifully running and breaking through each other's lines."

COMBINING THE PATTERNS (p. 282)

The narrative introduction establishes Jacobs as an authority on boxing, someone whose negative feelings about the crowd seem justified. Because of his authority, his opinions lend strong support to the thesis Cousins presents. Cousins might have returned to his meeting with Jacobs at the conclusion to offer a final quotation to clinch his argument.

THEMATIC CONNECTIONS

Thirty-Eight Who Saw Murder Didn't Call the Police (p. 99): Students can consider whether frequent exposure to prizefights (and to other forms of violence on television) can produce thirty-eight witnesses to murder who are not alarmed enough to call the police. (See also *Thematic Connections*, "Thirty-Eight Who Saw Murder Didn't Call the Police," p. 99 of this manual.)

Shooting an Elephant (p. 104): Both Cousins and Orwell discuss the power of public opinion. Looking at their essays together is one way of evaluating Cousins's use of evidence. Orwell recounts his own experience. Cousins, on the other hand, recounts no firsthand experience and fails to interview referees who, he says, continue fights because of pressure from spectators.

Ex-Basketball Player (p. 374): In discussing violence and other aspects of sports in contemporary culture, you might ask students to look at John Updike's poem about the decline of a high school basketball hero who "never learned a trade, he just sells gas, / Checks oil, and changes flats."

Marie Winn, *Television: The Plug-In Drug*

Winn's essay presents a historical account of the changes that television has wrought on the American family. She relates the positive early attitudes of educators and parents and then contrasts them with her own negative view of what the effects have actually been. Most of your students will have been raised with television as a dominant force in their lives. You may be startled to discover that some of your students have been raised in homes where several television sets play all day long. Winn makes a number of statements that will stimulate students to be more critical of their families' viewing patterns, but they may also see Winn's criticisms as a bit overstated. Discuss whether they believe television has been largely a positive or a negative influence—and how television and its influence have changed in the more than twenty years since Winn's essay was written.

COMPREHENSION (p. 291)

1. Early observers saw television as a boon to society and to the education of children; Winn feels it has had the opposite effect.
2. The amount of time spent watching television has increased. In addition, families have drifted into separate rooms to watch different programs.
3. Television keeps family members apart in a physical sense, as mentioned above, and in an emotional sense because they do not have to talk directly to one another.
4. Winn defines family rituals as those regular, dependable, recurrent happenings that give a family a feeling of belonging. She believes television has destroyed them.
5. According to Winn, a rising divorce rate, increasing numbers of working mothers, and loss of identification with neighborhoods and communities also have a negative impact.
6. Winn believes that families have difficulty expressing love because the opportunities for showing it are gone.

PURPOSE AND AUDIENCE (p. 291)

1. The thesis is that home and family life have deteriorated in important ways since the advent of television.
2. She expects the words of these experts to support her thesis.
3. These paragraphs present a concrete example of the changes that have occurred in social situations because of television. They also show how insidiously these changes occurred.

4. Much of Winn's evidence is anecdotal, based on reports by parents, a teacher, a therapist, and a nurse. She also quotes several authorities, including a sociologist and a psychiatrist who specializes in children (Bettelheim), and presents results from a survey of television viewing habits. Whether students feel she provides enough evidence to support her thesis will depend on how they respond to the essay in general and the extent to which they recognize the effects of television she describes in their own lives.
5. She wants to indicate that in some ways our advanced civilization is not advanced at all.

STYLE AND STRUCTURE (p. 292)

1. She establishes the opposite view through quotations and definitions taken from the early period of television.
2. These paragraphs are condensed, comprehensive statements that serve to hold together the material that follows.
3. She draws quotations from those who study the effects (educators, sociologists, psychologists) and from those who experience them (parents, children, teachers).
4. These headings divide the material into logical units and indicate a new direction in the development of the essay. Although they might be omitted without affecting Winn's point, they help guide the reader through her essay.
5. It tends to weaken the essay because it strays from the original design and consists mainly of unsupported generalizations.
6. Students may feel that some of Winn's more overt moralizing could have been cut. Again, this will depend on their overall response to the essay.

VOCABULARY PROJECTS (p. 292)

2. Some new words and usages might include *prime time, made-for-TV movie, cable-ready, game show, talk show, preview, lineup,* and *pilot.*

COMBINING THE PATTERNS (p. 293)

Winn uses narration in paragraphs 12–14, 22–23, and 34. She uses definition in paragraphs 16 and 18. She uses exemplification in paragraphs 2–4, 7, 22, and 34. Each of these patterns helps her to explain and clarify her point. For example, her definition of family rituals in paragraph 18 and her narrative example in paragraph 22 support her argument that television has replaced beneficial rituals with a ritual that diminishes personal involvement.

THEMATIC CONNECTIONS

Once More to the Lake (p. 154): An informal survey of your students can elicit important information about their opportunities in a television-dominated world to have parent-child experiences like E. B. White's—either as a child or as a parent. Or, you may wish to ask them to consider how White's vacation with his son would have been different if the camp had included a television set.

The Great Campus Goof-Off Machine (p. 188): Nate Stulman takes an equally critical look at college students' use of computers for everything but their studies. Like Winn, he questions some basic assumptions about the value of a new technology.

The Human Cost of an Illiterate Society (p. 203): Worth exploring is the possibility that television contributes to illiteracy by consuming enormous amounts of time that could be devoted to reading—and also the possibility that television, in addition to offering programs that overtly teach reading, may help nonreaders recognize important words when an announcer pronounces them as they appear printed on the screen. You might also survey your students about the time they spend reading in contrast to the time they spend watching television.

It's Just Too Late (p. 304): The family in Calvin Trillin's essay exhibits some of the emotional distance and lack of parent-child connection Winn describes as resulting from the replacement of family rituals with television watching. Do students see a causal connection here? That is, do they feel that alienated young people like FaNee may retreat because watching television has replaced close family relationships?

Lawrence Otis Graham, *The "Black Table" Is Still There*

Graham's essay about the "self-imposed" segregation of black students in his junior high school cafeteria—something he was saddened to see was still in effect when he returned to the school almost fifteen years after he had been a student there in the 1970s—is likely to spark interesting class discussion. For one thing, Graham describes himself as having had mostly white friends in junior high and so avoided the black table because he feared that if he sat there he would lose them. He also describes the "blatantly racist" behavior of some of his white friends—behavior he endured without protest, still blaming the black students, rather than "white bigotry," for their self-segregation. Finally he notes that his junior high school cafeteria in fact included a number of tables segregated by ethnicity, gender, and personal interests. Why, he asks, does a "black table" receive so much more criticism than these other forms of self-segregation? Opinion on these issues will vary, but it is likely that students can point to concrete examples of such self-segregation in their own lives—perhaps even on campus.

COMPREHENSION (p. 296)

1. The "black table" is the cafeteria table where the few black students in a largely white school choose to eat together, separate from other students.
2. He was surprised because he expected more integration after fourteen years.
3. See paragraph 14. Where students sat depended on race, religion, gender, ethnicity, and personal interests.
4. He was afraid he would lose all his white friends if he did.
5. As a student, he blamed the other black students for segregating themselves. Now he sees the causes as more complex: blacks wanting to associate with blacks as other groups tend to do and the lingering racism that continues to make blacks uncomfortable with whites.

PURPOSE AND AUDIENCE (p. 296)

1. Graham states his thesis in the first sentence of his final paragraph.
2. The opinions and anecdotal evidence Graham offers seems to be enough for his purpose of drawing a personal conclusion. But students may not think he succeeds in supporting a larger argumentative thesis.

3. Black and white students may respond differently to Graham's portrait of himself as a lone African-American man breaking color barriers in a largely white world. Some students may think that a bit more information about the racial/ethnic makeup of the school might be interesting.
4. Answers here will vary. To change his audience's view of "black tables" would seem to be his conscious purpose.
5. Throughout, Graham suggests that he was closer to white culture than to black culture as a youth.

STYLE AND STRUCTURE (p. 296)

1. Graham asks rhetorical questions in paragraphs 3, 7, and 10. These suggest his attempt to work through the issues both as a young student and as an adult.
2. These quotations suggest the dilemma he faced—scorned by blacks, yet a black "voice" for whites. Answers will vary as to the need for more quotations.
3. Graham focuses basically on finding causes.
4. Graham's personal, informal style is appropriate for the personal nature of his conclusions.

VOCABULARY PROJECTS (p. 297)

2. Again, black and white students may have different responses. You might ask if *African-American table* has different connotations. Students may offer some pejorative terms as they invent names for the other tables. If so, explore what this suggests about the nature of such labels.

COMBINING THE PATTERNS (p. 297)

Paragraph 14 classifies students according to where they sit in the lunch-room—and, by extension, according to how they identify themselves. Students will likely come up with other such categories. This strategy is appropriate because Graham's purpose is to get readers to think about the nature of such classifications.

THEMATIC CONNECTIONS

Just Walk On By (p. 197): Brent Staples offers another example of the dilemma facing an "integrating black person" who faces a certain level of stereo-typing by whites.

College Pressures (p. 390): William Zinsser's essay focuses on education in a different sense: the burnout college students can experience, particularly at highly competitive institutions like those Graham helped to integrate.

The Ways We Lie (p. 426): One of Stephanie Ericsson's categories of lying is stereotyping. Do students see any other types of lies in Graham's story? For example, in what sense does he reveal self-deception?

Why Special Housing for Ethnic Students Makes Sense (p. 551): In this essay reprinted from the *Chronicle of Higher Education*, Rebecca Lee Parker takes a more enthusiastically positive view of self-segregation than does Graham, arguing that ethnic students can benefit from college housing policies that allow, for example, for all-black dorms. Like Graham, she notes that other kinds of self-segregation—honors dorms, women's halls, housing for students majoring in specific academic subjects—do not draw the same sort of criticism that ethnic self-segregation does.

Linda M. Hasselstrom, *A Peaceful Woman Explains Why She Carries a Gun*

This essay is a good example of a personal causal explanation—Hasselstrom is not attempting to explain the causes of some social phenomenon, but only to explain what led her, a self-described pacifist, to begin carrying a gun. At the same time, she raises larger questions about equality between women and men and about the power their greater strength gives men over women. One way to begin discussion would be to ask if any of the women in your class would consider—or have considered—carrying a gun to protect themselves specifically from sexual assault (as opposed to, say, robbery). Another is to question students about their experiences with the kinds of threatening situations in which Hasselstrom finds herself in.

COMPREHENSION (p. 302)

1. Hasselstrom carries a gun for self-protection after having too often found herself in situations in which she felt threatened by men.
2. Students should easily be able to point the specific events that led to her decision.
3. She considered acquiring a CB radio, and she studied kung fu. The first she rejected because she realized that in calling for help she might in fact attract an assailant, and she came to see that her kung fu skills required expertise if she were to protect herself successfully from a large man. In one instance, she mentions the possibility of carrying mace, but says that she was warned by local police that mace is illegal; in fact, mace remains an alternative to a gun.
4. She mentions her reluctance in paragraphs 12 and 25.
5. She again refers to the dangers of carrying a gun in her final paragraph.
6. She means that before she drew her gun, the men considered her an easy mark and felt no compunction about giving her a hard time. Once they realized she had a gun, though, they did what she requested.

PURPOSE AND AUDIENCE (p. 302)

1. In her introduction, Hasselstrom suggests that she writes only because others might find her personal reasoning interesting. Students may recognize, however, that her larger purpose is to examine the physical balance of power between women and men.
2. Paragraph 5 serves to suggest the extent to which women are vulnerable. While Hasselstrom doesn't say whether she herself has been raped, the story about an actual rape victim graphically demonstrates the danger.
3. Students will probably see the essay speaks more acutely to women; however, we believe it has something to say to men as well. After all, Hasselstrom's central point is that if men behaved differently, she wouldn't need to carry a gun.
4. If not necessarily to agree, Hasselstrom clearly wants readers to at least understand her decision. She most clearly responds to readers' challenges with her final story of using the gun to achieve respect from the men trespassing on her property.

STYLE AND STRUCTURE (p. 302)

1. Students might see it as a weakness that Hasselstrom doesn't try to explain the extent to which women generally are in danger of assault. But because she is not really arguing that other women should carry guns—only explaining her personal reasons for doing so—relying only on her own experiences seems appropriate.
2. The main cause is clearly Hasselstrom's encounters with threatening men. Contributory causes include the fact that she doesn't feel she has viable alternatives and, perhaps, the fact that her husband at the time carried a gun.
3. Try to get students to see that it's not so much the fact that she is a woman that Hasselstrom uses to justify her decision; it is the fact that some men use their greater strength to intimidate women. If this didn't happen, a gun wouldn't be necessary.
4. Students might have fun coming up with possible situations that might result from Hasselstrom's virtually always carrying a gun. The larger question is whether they can imagine her actually killing someone—and when, if ever, this might be justified, especially for a pacifist. (See paragraph 13, where she describes "rehearsing . . . the precise conditions that would be required before I would shoot someone." Why isn't she more specific here?)
5. We find Hasselstrom successful at presenting herself as a peaceful woman who only reluctantly carries a gun. Students may suggest, however, that she seems to take a certain ironic delight in brandishing her weapon.

VOCABULARY PROJECTS (p. 303)

2. Examples include *changed the balance of power* (24 and, with a variation, 26) and the revised Colt slogan in paragraph 25.

COMBINING THE PATTERNS (p. 303)

Narrative passages include paragraphs 4, 6, 7, 8, and 17–23. They are clearly essential to Hasselstrom's purpose in the essay. Students probably won't feel that any should be briefer or deleted.

THEMATIC CONNECTIONS

Shooting an Elephant (p. 104): As a member of the Imperial Police in Burma in the 1920s, George Orwell carried a gun for very different reasons. But the dilemma he faces in this essay—whether or not to shoot an elephant that no longer seems to be posing a danger—applies to Hasselstrom as well: that is, how much of a threat must one perceive before shooting to kill is justified? It is far from unusual, for example, for police officers to kill unarmed people whom they erroneously perceive to be reaching for a gun. Tragically, there have been similar instances of civilians killing people whom they mistakenly perceive as a threat.

How the Lawyers Stole Winter (p. 362): Christopher Daly's focus on risks and liabilities ties this essay to the preceding discussion of "Shooting an Elephant."

Unnatural Killers (p. 566): John Grisham describes a killing spree carried out by a couple of disaffected teenagers on a rampage. Does the fact that such lawlessness exists in our society mean that more people—both men and women—should carry guns for self-protection? Note, of course, that Hasselstrom doesn't describe ever being threatened by someone with a gun, but she recognizes that if she is going to carry a gun, she has to be prepared to shoot it. If guns are in the hands of many potential criminals, should "peaceful' people also be encouraged to carry guns? Questions like these tie in nicely to the "Writing Workshop" suggestions for the Hasselstrom essay.

Calvin Trillin, *It's Just Too Late*

We mentioned in the introduction to this chapter of the manual the connection between narration and cause-and-effect analysis. Trillin's *New Yorker* magazine article is a good example of a cause-and-effect analysis that takes the form of a narrative. In order to reach some understanding of seventeen-year-old FaNee Cooper's death following a wild car chase in which she and her two drug-taking friends were apparently attempting to escape her pursuing father, Trillin traces the life of this "ideal child" from her birth to the circumstances of her tragic end and the trial that followed. He finds no simple explanation. In fact, you might point out that Trilllin's final paragraph poses a series of unanswered questions. How do your students—many of whom may well be acquainted with young women much like FaNee—answer these questions? Where do they assign responsibility for FaNee's death? Considering Trillin's concluding questions can be a good way to begin your class discussion.

COMPREHENSION (p. 312)

1. Trillin writes that FaNee "was not an outgoing child" and "as a baby, she was uncomfortable when she was held and cuddled." She found it difficult to confide in her parents and was "reserved and introspective" (1). The first real evidence that she was not an "ideal child" came when she was thirteen and her mother discovered cigarettes in her bedroom.

2. Most problematic for FaNee's parents was her association with the "Freaks," a group of self-consciously rebellious friends who set themselves up as the opposite of the clean-living "Jocks." Her grades began slipping, and she was twice suspended, once for smoking and once for skipping a required assembly. Her parents also believed that she was smoking marijuana.

3. FaNee's parents clearly could not understand their daughter. A former basketball star and junior high school principal, and a college homecoming queen and art teacher, respectively, Leo and JoAnn Cooper seem the soul of conventionality. In addition, as Trillin puts it, Leo Cooper seems "magnanimous, even humble, about invariably being in the right" (1), a personality trait that would not readily lead to confidences from a troubled daughter. Lack of communication in the family could certainly have contributed to FaNee's problems, as could the fact that her younger sister related more easily to her parents and was eventually cast in the role of the "perfect child." Her parents may also have been somewhat intimidated by FaNee's intelligence; this possibility is suggested by the impression Trillin gives that despite their dissatisfaction with her behavior, they don't seem to have done much to discipline her.

4. The town of Halls offered few recreational or cultural outlets, and many of its residents were poor rural people whose resistance to middle-class standards of education and propriety apparently attracted FaNee and some other girls of her background. Trillin suggests that she joined the Freaks out of "loneliness or rebellion or simple boredom" (6). Perhaps she saw herself as having no

choice, temperamentally unsuited as she was to what Trillin implies was her school's only other clearly identifiable social group, the Jocks.

5. The immediate cause of FaNee's death was the auto accident. Students will have different ideas about significant remote causes, but FaNee's relationship with her parents, the friends she chose, and her drug use are likely to be mentioned.

6. In a causal chain, one contributing cause leads to another. FaNee, naturally quiet and introspective, was unlike her parents. This fact probably contributed to her sense of alienation, which separated her emotionally from her parents even more. This sense of alienation led her to seek out friends who were different or rebellious and to act rebelliously herself, angering her parents. All of these factors led up to the situation that resulted in FaNee's death.

7. As the next few sentences make clear, Trillin is referring to the "court of public opinion." Trillin, as a reporter, presents the facts even-handedly; he doesn't seem to assign blame to any single party, but rather sees FaNee's death as the result of a complex interaction of events and personalities. Encourage students to discuss their own sense of who is most at fault.

8. FaNee believed that it was "just too late" to establish any kind of real relationship with her parents, to confide in them or seek their help or understanding. With this title Trillin seems to be suggesting the inevitability of her situation.

PURPOSE AND AUDIENCE (p. 312)

1. Although his primary purpose is that of any good reporter—to provide information accurately and objectively—Trillin certainly wants his audience to see in this story wider social and moral implications. Clearly, writing for the *New Yorker*, he saw FaNee's life and death as concerning more than just one Knoxville family.

2. Trillin is writing primarily for urban northeasterners, who may not be familiar with the behavior of small-town southern teenagers.

3. Reporters rarely state a thesis. Trillin's main point might be phrased as "FaNee Cooper died for a variety of complex reasons; the conviction of Charlie Stevens does not 'close the case.'"

STYLE AND STRUCTURE (p. 313)

1. Trillin separates each of these actions with a space. Some readers might appreciate more explicit signals, such as internal heads—and a magazine other than the *New Yorker* might well have added some.

2. In quoting FaNee's writing Trillin shows readers the changes she underwent as she entered adolescence, moving from the very conventional sentiments of the poem about her grandmother to the self-conscious weirdness of her high school journal entries. He also gives readers a sense of FaNee's emotional complexity, ranging from the violent imagery of "Slithery serpents eat my sanity and bite my ass" (5) to the pathetically childish plea for love in the letter to her parents (11).

3. By bringing different perspectives to bear, the quotations from various people who knew FaNee provide the reader with a more rounded picture of her.

4. As Trillin suggests, there is no simple interpretation of FaNee's story, so attention to detail and to an objective presentation remain essential if the reader

is to understand the complexity of the circumstances that contributed to her death. One way Trillin reveals his own opinions is in his presentation of Leo Cooper, whom he clearly sees as misguided in his self-righteous refusal to accept any blame for his daughter's death.

5. The series of unanswered questions leaves the reader with food for thought.

VOCABULARY PROJECTS (p. 313)

2. *Jocks* are athletes, cheerleaders, and other students who espouse traditional values, often with a Christian emphasis. *Freaks* are students who drop out, do drugs, and reject any traditional values. Alternate terms might be *goodies* and *druggies* or *straight arrows* and *rebels*.

COMBINING THE PATTERNS (p. 314)

The Jocks were the "good kids" who got to school on time, played sports, dressed neatly, avoided alcohol, and espoused Christian values. The Freaks did poorly academically, caused trouble in school, took drugs, and "were into wicked things" (5). It was FaNee's act of distancing herself from the Jocks and joining the Freaks that led to her tragic end. Trillin's discussion of the contrasts seem sufficient, particularly as the Jocks are not crucial to FaNee's story.

THEMATIC CONNECTIONS

Samuel (p. 212): Grace Paley's short story presents another reckless child whose actions adults disapprove of and who dies tragically because of his rebelliousness. You might have students consider whether FaNee and Samuel are equally sympathetic—or whether one seems more innocent.

Television: The Plug-In Drug (p. 283): The Coopers' relationship with FaNee resembles Marie Winn's description of one of the results of television, which "fertilizes" alienation and "anesthetizes the family into accepting its unhappy state and prevents it from struggling to better its condition, to improve its relationships, and to regain some of the richness it once possessed." Trillin doesn't mention the Coopers' television watching habits, but the family doesn't seem to have participated in other activities together. Ask students to consider whether other influences that, according to Winn, "undermine" the family are reflected in the Cooper family.

Suicide Note (p. 315): Although FaNee Cooper didn't actively commit suicide, it would appear from her obsession with death that she had definite thoughts of suicide. And in fact her reckless behavior may in some ways be attributed to a "death wish." You might have students compare FaNee's final note to her parents with Janice Mirikitani's poem, a suicide note from an Asian-American college student to her parents. Certainly, Mirikitani's refrain ("not good enough," "not strong enough," "not smart enough,") could have been written by FaNee, and certain lines ("Each failure, a glacier. / Each disapproval, a bootprint.") express what FaNee seems to have felt. Ask students to consider what can be done to help such troubled young people.

Unnatural Killers (p. 566): John Grisham's essay also focuses on disaffected teenagers, in this case a couple—apparently influenced by the film *Natural Born Killers*—who went on a violent crime spree. There are interesting comparisons to be made between FaNee Cooper's circle of friends and the two young people Grisham describes, but students should be reminded that FaNee died in the mid-1970s, while Benjamin Darras and Sarah Edmondson killed Bill Savage in the mid-1990s. The 1990s saw a startling rise in violent crime committed by teenagers, perhaps most notably symbolized by the Columbine High School killings. Students might wish to write a causal analysis exploring why teenagers might perceive themselves as "misfits."

Janice Mirikitani, *Suicide Note*

Suicide, more than most subjects, calls for causal analysis, and teenage suicides are all too frequent in this country. In one way or another, suicide may have personally touched the lives of many of your students. Some may have heard of situations in which one teen's suicide, reported widely in the press, led to a series of others. They may also be aware of despairing college students who have killed themselves. Discussing such suicides and trying to understand them can be vital to many of your students. You may want to make your students aware of your campus's mental health resources.

You will want to focus on the raw materials Mirikitani gives in narrative form, which suggest the complex chain that causes her speaker to commit suicide. In addition to discussing the cause-and-effect relationships in "Suicide Note," you will want to discuss Mirikitani's artistry. Her use of repetition and concrete image patterns will increase your students' sense of the ways in which language can be used.

THINKING ABOUT LITERATURE (p. 317)

1. Being a daughter in a family that values sons more than daughters is a less immediate but fundamental cause of the student's suicide. The speaker says,
   > If only I were a son . . .
   > I would see the light in my mother's
   > eyes, or the golden pride reflected
   > in my father's dream
   > of my wide, male hands worthy of work
   > and comfort. (ll. 10, 12–16)

   A causal chain operates from the fundamental cause. As a daughter, she is not praised as she believes a son would be. This, in turn, causes a lack of self-esteem: she feels "not good enough   not pretty enough   not smart enough." Her lack of self-esteem is explicitly tied to her gender: if she were a son, she asserts, "I would swagger through life / muscled and bold and assured, / drawing praises to me" (ll. 17–19). Feeling that she has disappointed her parents by being a daughter, she cannot live with feeling that she has further let them down by not getting a perfect 4.0 grade point average.

2. She believes she would be loved and praised more and would be "virile / with confidence" (ll. 20–21). Whether she would have been happier as a son is difficult to determine. If her parents really do value sons more than daughters, a son would have very likely developed a stronger sense of self-worth—which is fundamental to happiness. However, she may also mistakenly blame her parents' cultural biases for her unhappiness.

3. Mirikitani uses repetition as a means of communicating the extent of the speaker's unhappiness and desperation. The refrain "not good enough   not pretty enough   not smart enough" makes her unhappiness and desperation all-encompassing. She is obsessed with her sense of unworthiness. Other rep-

etitions—"I've worked very hard," "I apologize," and "sorries / sorries,"—suggest her driving need to live up to her parents' expectations and her sense of shame.

Mirikitani also effectively uses image patterns to communicate the speaker's despair. Bird imagery communicates her fragile self-image. She feels weak and inadequate—only a "sparrow / sillied and dizzied by the wind" (l. 38). "Perched / on the ledge of [her] womanhood," she is "fragile as wings / sillied and dizzied by the wind / on the edge" (ll. 32–40), and her wings are "crippled" (l. 45). Her suicide note, "like birdprints in snow" (l. 2), will leave no lasting imprint.

Repeated snow and ice imagery also communicates the speaker's despair. Snow and ice are frozen potential, not water in life-giving form. "Each failure [is] a glacier / . . . Each disappointment, / ice above my river" (ll. 25, 27–28). Her "Choices [are] thin as shaved / ice," and her "notes shredded / drift like snow" (ll. 49–51). She will fly from her ledge while "it is snowing," and "the snow burdens [her] crippled wings" (ll. 36, 45). Her "bird bones" will be buried beneath "this white and cold and silent / breast of earth." (ll. 58, 62–63). Ironically, her grave will be marked by an evergreen.

THEMATIC CONNECTIONS

Only Daughter (p. 83): Cisneros's sense that she was "only a daughter" in a Latino family can suggest to students that Asian cultures are not the only ones to historically devalue daughters. If they think carefully, students who have not been conscious of such partiality may remember subtle indications in their own lives that sons are "special." Cisneros also suggests to students a constructive way of handling being "only a daughter." She devoted herself to her own goals, and she turned the loneliness of being an only daughter into time to prepare herself to be a writer. Recognizing her father's goals for her college education, she took advantage of the opportunity to major in English. Ultimately, she was able to gain her father's affirmation for what she chose to be.

College Pressures (p. 390): The notes to Carlos at the beginning of "College Pressures" suggests the sense of desperation felt by many college students. Zinsser also analyzes the reasons many students become desperate—no doubt, in some cases, desperate enough to commit suicide. In a "brutal economy," they, their parents, and their peers feel they must major in "pre-rich" and compete without respite to find "an edge" over other students. Caught in "webs of love and duty and guilt," like Mirikitani's speaker, they fail to understand that they have "the right to fail" and to use their educations to discover who they are and enrich their lives. Zinsser is emphatic about the solution: "Ultimately it will be the students' own business to break the cycles in which they are trapped." (See also *Thematic Connections*, "College Pressures," p. 90.)

The Company Man (p. 476): Ellen Goodman describes another kind of death resulting from the pressure to succeed: an executive who works himself into a heart attack at the age of fifty-one. This essay can provide opportunities to discuss several different issues in relation to "Suicide Note." The most obvious is the debilitating influence in our society of the concept of "achievement" defined in terms of grades or income or status and divorced from any sense of personal satisfaction or individual worth. The second is the effect of the death of a loved one on those who survive. Look particularly at paragraphs 7–12 of Goodman's essay, and ask students to speculate about the reactions of the suicide note writer's survivors.

9: COMPARISON AND CONTRAST

Students have several problems with comparison and contrast. They often fail to appreciate the importance of prewriting when they write a comparison-and-contrast paper. The result can be a jumbled presentation that makes it difficult to understand the basis of comparison or, at times, exactly what elements are being compared. This situation occurs especially during examinations and in-class writings when time is short. In the chapter introduction we stress the necessity of planning when we discuss both point-by-point and subject-by-subject comparisons. Even so, we have found that you cannot repeat this advice enough to students.

Another problem students have is realizing that they have to compare the same or similar elements for each subject they discuss. Having your students outline one or two of the essays in this section can illustrate that writers do follow this strategy when they write. Make sure students understand that if they don't discuss the same or similar points for each subject, they are not actually comparing or contrasting anything.

Finally, students should understand that comparison-and-contrast essays need transitions to make them flow smoothly. Signals indicate movement from one point to another, highlight similarities and differences, and eliminate choppiness to help readers follow a discussion. Revision exercises concentrating on transitions can help students appreciate the importance of this concern.

We chose the two paragraphs in the introduction to illustrate the difference between comparison and analogy. You will need to explain both the value of a good analogy and its logical limits. Students should understand that analogies can be vivid, suggest important relationships, and draw readers into an essay by calling on whatever they already know, but they should also understand that analogies can be trivial or even faulty when similarities are assumed that do not exist.

We chose the selections in this chapter to illustrate the variety of subjects suitable for comparison and contrast. Bruce Catton's "Grant and Lee: A Study in Contrasts," Anne Fadiman's "Never Do That to a Book," and Tom Standage's "The Victorian Internet" are well-written point-by-point comparisons on very different subjects. Because they are straightforward in structure, they make excellent opening assignments. With them students can see professional writers applying many of the concepts they have read about. These are followed by three more point-by-point comparisons: Bharati Mukherjee's "Two Ways to Belong in America," Christopher Daly's "How the Lawyers Stole Winter," and Deborah Tannen's "Sex, Lies, and Conversation." Finally, John Updike's "Ex-Basketball Player" expands the use of comparison into the realm of literature and also suggests a subject-by-subject, "before-and-after" structure.

Bruce Catton, *Grant and Lee: A Study in Contrasts*

This essay is a classic point-by-point comparison. First Catton discusses Lee, the aristocratic representative of tidewater Virginia. Next he presents Grant, the son of a tanner, who was everything Lee was not. He moves from generalizations about each man to the ways they differed in character and orientation. You might point out to students how, beginning with paragraph 12, Catton sums up his discussion of Lee and Grant with a point-by-point comparison. This is a good opportunity to discuss strategy and to ask students why Catton uses both types of comparisons in his essay. In this essay, topic sentences and transitions are important. The questions in Style and Structure ask students to consider these elements, and you might want to go further, devoting an entire class to these issues.

COMPREHENSION (p. 377)

1. Grant and Lee met at Appomattox Court House to work out the terms for Lee's surrender, thus "bringing the Civil War to its virtual finish" (2).
2. Lee represented the aristocratic values of tidewater Virginia. He stood for a privileged class of landowners whose values and responsible leadership ideally were to repay the society that recognized their status. This regional ideal was embodied in Lee, "as if he himself was the Confederacy" (6). In contrast, Grant, who grew up on the western frontier, was independent, self-reliant, and democratic. He was committed to the nation as a whole and to its prosperity.
3. Grant and Lee contrast most strikingly in their attitudes about society. Lee saw himself in terms of his own locality: "He lived in a static society which could endure almost anything except change" (10). On the other hand, Grant believed in the nation as a whole, a "broader concept of society" defined by "growth, expansion, and a constantly widening horizon" (11).
4. Both men were "marvelous fighters" whose "fighting qualities were really very much alike" (13). Each had tenacity, fidelity, daring, and resourcefulness. And most importantly, each was able "to turn quickly from war to peace once the fighting was over" (16).
5. Catton suggests that "succeeding generations of Americans are in debt to Grant and Lee" because of the way they were able to "turn quickly from war to peace once the fighting was over."

PURPOSE AND AUDIENCE (p. 377)

1. The aristocratic current, represented by Lee, is based on a class structure ruled by the elite. The democratic current, represented by Grant, is based on individualism and a strong sense of national community. These differences have always defined two strong currents in America from Jefferson and Hamilton to Dole and Clinton, and they are still apparent in debates between conservative Republicans and liberal Democrats.
2. Catton uses Grant and Lee to represent "the strengths of two conflicting currents that, through them, had come into final collision" (3). Although their differences produced collision, their strengths made reconciliation possible. By comparing them, Catton makes a statement about the strengths of the American character and its ability to reconcile differences.
3. Catton's thesis is that Grant and Lee embodied two conflicting currents in America, the democratic and the aristocratic.

STYLE AND STRUCTURE (p. 343)

1. Catton uses point-by-point comparison since he includes too many points for an effective subject-by-subject comparison. An audience would have difficulty remembering all the details about the first subject once the essay moved to the second.

2. These topic sentences establish the comparison and contrast; moreover, they indicate whether Grant or Lee will be the focus of the paragraph. They also unify the essay by providing transitions from one paragraph to another.

3. Examples of transitions in this essay include *These men* (2), *They were two strong men* (3), *Grant . . . was everything Lee was not* (7), *Yet along with this feeling* (9), *And that, perhaps, is where the contrast . . . becomes most striking* (10), and so forth.

4. Catton uses the meeting at Appomattox as a frame for his essay. His major concern is Lee and Grant and the currents they represent, not the events during the meeting.

VOCABULARY PROJECTS (p. 344)

2. To do this exercise correctly, students will have to be sensitive to context. For example, although *manners* is a synonym for *deportment,* it does not convey the notion of *cultivated,* which is required by the context.

COMBINING THE PATTERNS (p. 344)

Paragraphs 9, 10, and 11 also use exemplification. Each suggests contrasting characteristics of the Westerner and the Virginia aristocrat.

THEMATIC CONNECTIONS

Does America Still Exist? **(p. 482):** Richard Rodriguez's essay focuses on issues of cultural diversity, assimilation, and, ultimately, the common culture that all Americans share, a "true national history" in which "Thomas Jefferson begets Martin Luther King, Jr., who begets the Gray Panthers." Students may examine the role the Civil War played in this national history—and, in light of recent controversies surrounding displays of the Confederate flag, the extent to which vestiges of the Civil War continue to define particular, sometimes opposing, subcultures. Catton's portraits of Grant and Lee further suggest that cultural differences are not simply ethnic or racial but regional and economic as well.

The Declaration of Independence **(p. 516):** The Declaration of Independence provides an underlying framework for discussing historical U.S. goals and values. Students might consider ways the Civil War tested the powers of this crucial document.

Letter from Birmingham Jail **(p. 522):** Catton asserts that Robert E. Lee fought for an ideal, but criticizes it by tying it to images from the Middle Ages—to the age of chivalry, knighthood, and English squires—dated images that depend on the existence of a subordinate class. Just as feudalism required the subjugation of peasants, so Lee's "feeling that it was somehow advantageous for human society to have a pronounced inequality in the social structure" required the subjugation of blacks. In his "Letter from Birmingham Jail," Martin Luther King Jr. shows that such inequalities continued to exist for blacks a century after the Civil War and calls on the ministers to whom he is writing—and by extension, all Americans—to stand up "for what is best in the American dream and for the most sacred values in our Judaeo-Christian heritage, thereby bringing our nation back to the great wells of democracy which were dug deeply by the founding fathers in the formulation of the Constitution and the Declaration of Independence."

Anne Fadiman, *Never Do That to a Book*

Although it contains some fairly sophisticated language and references students may find obscure, Fadiman's essay will still be accessible to most students because its subject is familiar and its comparison-contrast structure is easily identifiable. In discussing two different kinds of book lovers—those who wish to keep their books pristine and those who see "hard use" of books as "a sign not of disrespect but of intimacy"—Fadiman focuses almost exclusively on contrasts. You might begin discussion by asking students if they know people who fall into one or the other of Fadiman's categories—or if they themselves do. More realistically, you might ask whether they even know people they would call book lovers in this age increasingly dominated by electronic media. In addition, you may want to provide students with background on the conventions of courtly love.

COMPREHENSION (p. 349)

1. The Danish chambermaid left a note to Fadiman's thirteen-year-old brother admonishing him not to leave a book facedown and open. He was "stunned" because he considered himself a true lover of books.
2. The courtly book lover sees "a book's physical self" as "sancrosanct" and feels the need to "preserve forever the state of perfect chastity in which it had left the bookseller." For the carnal book lover, the physical book is "a mere vessel" of its "holy" words, and "hard use" is a sign of "intimacy."
3. Fadiman is a carnal book lover as she reveals directly in paragraph 3.
4. These physical aspects of a book are far less important to Fadiman than the ideas a book contains. A book that is worn, dog-eared, broken-spined, and scribbled in demonstrates that its owner has interacted with lovingly.
5. As she suggests in paragraph 11, the drawback of being a carnal book lover is that "we love our books to pieces."

PURPOSE AND AUDIENCE (p. 349)

1. Fadiman seems to expect her readers to share—or at least understand—a love of books, whether they be courtly or carnal lovers. She tries neither to encourage a love of books nor to explain how one comes to be a book lover.
2. Fadiman's purpose seems to be primarily to entertain—although it might be argued that she is trying subtly to convince the courtly readers out there that carnal readers love their books just as much.
3. Fadiman comes closest to a thesis statement in the first sentence of paragraph 3, but in fact the whole of paragraph 3 sets up her thesis in detail.
4. Fadiman primarily uses examples of friends and relatives who represent the two kinds of book lovers she describes. She also quotes Hilaire Belloc and Charles Lamb and mentions Thomas Jefferson and John Adams (all but Belloc, carnal lovers). To appeal more directly to college students, Fadiman could probably include examples of younger readers.

STYLE AND STRUCTURE (p. 349)

1. The opening story of her brother and the Danish chambermaid serves to introduce the two different types of book lovers. There's also irony in the fact that Fadiman's first example of a courtly book lover is a hotel maid.

2. This is a point-by-point comparison. Because such a comparison is more immediate and direct, it allows Fadiman to achieve her purpose of entertaining her audience better.
3. Her points of comparison involve tearing out the pages of books (4), marking one's place in books (5–7), writing in books (8), using books for things other than reading (9), and allowing book pages to become soiled (10).
4. In fact, Fadiman uses few transitional words and expressions. She simply segues from one kind of "hard use" into the next. She does use two page breaks that act as transitions.
5. Clark is an example of the courtly book lover *par excellence*. The concluding contrast with her husband couldn't be more striking.

VOCABULARY PROJECTS (p. 350)

2. You might even limit this "translation" to the third and fifth sentences of paragraph 3. This is an excellent dictionary exercise.

COMBINING THE PATTERNS (p. 350)

In defining *courtly love* and *carnal love*, Fadiman assumes a familiarity with these Medieval concepts on the part of her readers—but only to the extent that she expects them to see the irony of using these terms to apply to book lovers. Students' opinions may vary as to how clear they find the definitions, but Fadiman's vocabulary may be more problematic than the clarity of her definitions.

THEMATIC CONNECTIONS

Only Daughter (p. 83): Sandra Cisneros refers in her essay to "the public majority . . . who is uninterested in reading, and yet one whom I am writing about and for, and privately trying to woo." Her father represents for Cisneros this non-reading public, and it is a personal breakthrough for her when he reads one of her stories translated into Spanish and express his pride in her. Such non-readers stand in vivid contrast to the book lovers described by Fadiman. Students might use these two essays—and the Kozol essay on illiteracy—as the basis for a paper on reading in the United States today.

Reading the River (p. 138): Mark Twain in this essay describes two opposing ways of reading the "wonderful book" that the Mississippi River became for him over the course of career as a riverboat pilot. At first, like any passenger, he could simply be taken by the beauty of the scene of a sunset over rippling water. With experience, however, he came to see aspects of the river only in terms of their usefulness in helping him pilot the riverboat. How might these two different ways of reading be related to the two kinds of readers Fadiman describes?

The Human Cost of an Illiterate Society (p. 203): Jonathan Kozol offers a bleak picture of what it is like to be unable to read in contemporary society, along with some disturbing statistics regarding illiteracy rates. The examples he describes stand in stark contrast to the highly literate friends and relatives Fadiman discusses. Along with "Only Daughter," these two essays serve to suggest the varying levels of literacy in the United States today.

Mother Tongue (p. 405): Amy Tan writes about finding her voice as a writer by imagining a specific reader: her immigrant mother, whose grasp of English is somewhat "limited" (for lack of a better word, as Tan would say). She knew she had succeeded in reaching the audience she wanted when her mother pronounced her first novel "so easy to read." Again, the connection here is reading, accessibility, and levels of literacy.

Tom Standage, *The Victorian Internet*

In this essay, Tom Standage focuses on similarities between the telegraph, as it became a ubiquitous form of communication in the nineteenth century, and the Internet, as it plays a greater and greater role in our lives today. You might want to spend a little time familiarizing your students with the telegraph. (The headnote provides some background information, but you might also ask students if they recall the telegraph being used to send out messages in the film *Titanic*.) On the surface, the telegraph and the Internet seem to have little in common. Standage, however, provides an excellent example of using comparison of something relatively unfamiliar to help readers see something familiar in a new light. His larger point here is to suggest that some of the more grandiose claims for the Internet—like those that were made for the telegraph—have little likelihood of coming to pass. The clear structure of this essay makes it a particularly good model for students.

COMPREHENSION (p. 354)

1. The similarities between the telegraph and the Internet are ironic because the telegraph is now essentially obsolete—unlike telephones and fax machines—whereas the Internet is "regarded as a quintessentially modern means of communication."
2. See paragraph 4: "Public reaction to the new technologies was, in both cases, a confused mixture and hype and skepticism."
3. See paragraph 11: "After a period of initial skepticism, businesses became the most enthusiastic adopters of the telegraph in the nineteenth century and the Internet in the twentieth."
4. The claims that electricity would "create a world of abundance and peace," that television would "improve education, reduce social isolation, and enhance democracy," and so forth have not proved to be very accurate. Standage suggests that the same is true of many optimistic claims being made about the Internet.
5. The point is made in Standage's first and next to last sentences: The telegraph was the precursor of all subsequent communication technologies and "redefined forever our attitudes toward new technologies."

PURPOSE AND AUDIENCE (p. 354)

1. We find it one of the strengths of Standage's essay that he presents his thesis statement (and subsequent discussion) so straightforwardly. His thesis is a surprising one, and it seems effective for him to present it in a no-nonsense manner.
2. He probably hopes to suggest to those readers who are relatively unfamiliar with the telegraph what an important technological development it was. As suggested earlier, he also wants to debunk some of the more optimistic claims for the Internet.

3. You'll need to make sure that students know what *Victorian* refers to before asking them to evaluate the title. With this knowledge, the title is quite intriguing, although students might suggest alternative titles that include the word *telegraph*.

STYLE AND STRUCTURE (p. 355)

1. The essay could be read as an extended analogy, in that Standage does explain certain aspects of the telegraph by comparing it to the more familiar Internet. However, Standage also wants readers to recognize similarities the Internet has with the telegraph; in this sense the essay offers a true comparison.
2. Points of comparison involve the physical exchange of data across long distances (2–3), the claims made by proponents of both technologies (4–5), issues of fraudulent use and security (6–7), development of jargon and abbreviations (8), conflicts between experienced users and novices (9), romantic connections fostered by both technologies (10), their impact on business (11–12), and their image as a "panacea" (13).
3. Standage uses a point-by-point structure, which makes his discussion of the telegraph, in particular, easier to follow.
4. Students will probably agree that, in terms of his purpose, Standage does provide an effective basis of comparison between two things that clearly are dissimilar in many ways. You might point out that Standage does not even mention any differences because they are probably so obvious. (One pertinent difference he doesn't mention is that the telegraph couldn't be used by individuals from their homes; operating a telegraph required considerable skill, and those who wanted to send messages had to take them to commercial operators.)
5. He probably doesn't discuss the Internet in this context because most people take it as a given that the Internet is transforming our world.

VOCABULARY PROJECTS (p. 355)

2. Standage defines *byte* and *ASCII* (3), *sigs* (8), and *teleworking* and *virtual corporations* (12). He appears to assume that his readers will not have a considerable level of technical expertise.

COMBINING THE PATTERNS (p. 356)

Standage's major point compares the social and commercial effects of the telegraph and the Internet. Such paragraphs constitute the heart of his argument and enable us to think about future effects of the Internet by considering effects predicted for the telegraph.

THEMATIC CONNECTIONS

The Great Campus Goof-Off Machine (p. 188): In this essay, Nate Stulman argues that by providing students with almost unlimited access to computers and the Internet, college administrators have actually given students excuses not to study and learn. Like Standage, he might say that the optimistic claims for this new technology will always be thwarted by the baser aspects of human nature.

Television: The Plug-In Drug (p. 283): Marie Winn explores in detail a point Standage mentions in paragraph 14: that optimistic claims made in the 1950s and 1960s praising the future benefits of television have not proved true. An interesting essay of comparison and contrast might focus on television and the Internet, using "The Victorian Internet" as a model.

The End of Serendipity (p. 604): Ted Gup's essay also offers a word of caution for claims being made about new information technologies. He fears that researchers' faith in such technologies to guide their search for specific answers may be "inadvertently smothering the opportunity to find what may be the more important answers—the ones to questions that have not yet even occurred to us." Students could use this essay and Standage's as springboards toward an argument about future effects of the Internet.

Bharati Mukherjee, *Two Ways to Belong in America*

In the wake of congressional proposals to restrict the rights and government benefits allowed to resident aliens—that is, foreign-born people who live legally in the United States (and in many cases work and pay taxes) but who choose not to become U.S. citizens—Indian-born Mukherjee contrasts her sister, a resident alien, with herself, a naturalized citizen. With mixed feelings, Mukherjee sympathizes with her sister's anger over America's changing "its rules in midstream" (8) but at the same time characterizes her sister's relationship with America as a "comfortable yet loveless marriage, without risk or recklessness" (9). Mukherjee, however, embraces "the trauma of self-transformation" (15) that becoming a citizen has required. This essay provides a good opportunity to introduce current controversies about immigration policy, which are debated in depth in the argument chapter.

COMPREHENSION (p. 360)

1. They expected to stay only two years to attend school, but both married, found fulfilling jobs, and so decided to stay.
2. The strain results in part from differing expectations for the wives of Indian-born men and those who marry westerners. Mukherjee says she renounced "3,000 years (at least) of caste-observant, 'pure culture' marriage" in her family (5).
3. Mira "clings passionately to her Indian citizenship and hopes to go home to India when she retires" (4). Mukherjee feels the need to be "a part of the community . . . to put roots down, to vote and make the difference that I can" (15). Rather than "maintain an identity" as her sister did, Mukherjee chose to "transform" hers. The two seem to have an affectionate relationship, but the differences between them make them "pity" each other.
4. Mira's employer asked her to stay in the United States because of her talents. She has contributed a great deal to her community, paid her taxes, "obeyed all the rules" (8). Now, after thirty years, she is angry because she stands to be denied benefits she has come to expect.
5. Because she hasn't become a citizen but has chosen to maintain her status as an "outsider," Mira stands to lose almost as much as "the millions of hardworking but effectively silenced documented immigrants as well as their less fortunate 'illegal' brothers and sisters" (12).

PURPOSE AND AUDIENCE (p. 360)

1. Her thesis is stated in her final sentence.
2. Mukherjee seems to have an audience of general readers in mind, which might include educated immigrant readers like her sister and herself.
3. Mukherjee's primary purpose is to explore the different mindsets of immigrants who choose to become citizens and those who don't (informative). But her purpose is also to create in her readers some sympathy for her sister's situation—and so, perhaps, to have an effect on the kinds of laws that are eventually passed (persuasive).

STYLE AND STRUCTURE (p. 360)

1. The basis of comparison is the sisters' differing attitudes toward becoming U.S. citizens. Mukherjee establishes it in her opening paragraph.
2. The comparison is essentially point-by-point, which helps Mukherjee to keep the focus on both her sister and herself throughout.
3. She discusses their different marital and career paths, their different decisions about becoming U.S. citizens, and the different situations they face now that government policies toward resident aliens have changed. She also refers to finding herself in a situation similar to her sister's—and feeling a similar sense of betrayal—when she was living in Canada at a time when anti-immigration sentiments ran high. Discussing other points isn't really necessary.
4. Transitional words and phrases include *instead* (3), *nearly twenty years ago* (13), and *however* (15). Students may note that Mukherjee uses relatively few transitional words and phrases, and those she uses are set up as direct oppositions.
5. The conclusion is an effective summary of Mukherjee's points.

VOCABULARY PROJECTS (p. 360)

2. An *immigrant* adopts his or her new country, whereas an *exile* maintains the customs of the native country, feels a strong connection there, and hopes to return. The connotations of the first are fairly neutral, but those of the second are more charged, either negatively or positively depending on the particular context.

COMBINING THE PATTERNS (p. 361)

Some causal analysis of the reasons for the two sisters' differences would be interesting—and she might have included such an analysis in a longer essay. This was written with the length limitations of the *New York Times*'s Op-Ed page in mind.

THEMATIC CONNECTIONS

Only Daughter (p. 83): Sandra Cisneros also writes about the experience of being an immigrant and the difficulties involved in adjusting to the mores of a new culture.

More Than Just a Shrine: Paying Homage to the Ghosts of Ellis Island (p. 142): Second-generation American Mary Gordon also focuses on the experiences of immigrants, although her concern is with those like her grandparents who came from Europe early in this century. In cases such as theirs, there was often little question of becoming a citizen; a great many journeyed to the United States specifically to escape a life of poverty and lack of opportunity and citizenship became the key to prosperity. Students might use this essay and Mukherjee's to consider why American citizenship is attractive to so many who are nonetheless faced with prejudice and discrimination.

The Way to Rainy Mountain (p. 148): N. Scott Momaday's remembrances of his Kiowa grandmother suggest a different slant on maintaining traditional ways. Obviously not an immigrant, his grandmother nonetheless stood outside of mainstream U.S. culture and was in a sense denied full participation in the American system. But like Mira, she also chose not to assimilate.

The Big Move (p. 334): Student Margaret Depner's essay is about adjusting to life in England while living there for a year after her father was transferred. It provides a contrasting viewpoint—that of a U.S. citizen living abroad with the status of a resident alien. If your students found long-term careers in another country and married citizens there, how many of them would choose to give up their U.S. citizenship, as Mukherjee did, in order to participate more fully in their communities? How do their feelings about this color their views of Mukherjee and her sister?

The Untouchable (p. 461): Student Ajoy Mahtab's essay will provide students with some insight into the strict caste system of Indian life that Mukherjee refers to.

Christopher B. Daly, *How the Lawyers Stole Winter*

Daly contrasts the past with the present in this essay. Remembering with pleasure ice skating with friends on unsupervised natural ponds in rural Massachusetts, he laments the fact that today his sons are denied this activity because local governments (and their lawyers) have declared such ponds off-limits in order to avoid lawsuits. What his sons' generation loses, he says, is not only the freedom from adult intrusion that he and his childhood friends enjoyed playing hockey on the ice, but also the opportunity of learning to evaluate risks and handle them on one's own. By "not teaching our kids how to take risks," Daly says, "we are making the world more dangerous" (11). You might begin class discussion by raising this point: Are children today *too* protected? If so, to what extent does it make them more, rather than less, vulnerable? (See Comprehension question 5.)

COMPREHENSION (p. 364)

1. They put on play clothes and went outside to play until dinnertime—play that in winter often included ice skating and playing hockey.
2. Winter is "in danger of passing away" because towns, cities, and property holders are so afraid of lawsuits that they are declaring ponds off-limits for skating.
3. During his childhood, Daly and his friends tested the ice by "throwing heavy stones, hammering it with downed branches, and, finally, jumping on it" (2). (See also paragraph 9 for other ways they learned to gauge the ice.) Today, children are simply prohibited from skating on ponds, so they have no opportunity to learn these things.
4. As children, Daly and his friends learned to take risks judiciously; today children are encouraged not to take risks, and when they do anyway, Daly feels,

they are likely to do so without the "collective wisdom" necessary to evaluate the risks accurately. Daly implicitly proposes that children be given more freedom to play on their own, unsupervised.

5. As suggested in the introduction above, Daly means that children who are denied the experience of taking risks don't learn how to evaluate dangerous situations for themselves and so are more likely to get into trouble when they face risks.

PURPOSE AND AUDIENCE (p. 365)

1. Daly's thesis is stated in the first sentence of paragraph 11. Delaying his thesis allows him to set up his contrast clearly before getting into his main argument.
2. His purpose is to get readers to think about the situation he describes and perhaps to effect change.
3. Daly seems to think readers will be neutral or even sympathetic to his ideas. His opening evokes a sense of nostalgia that he expects his readers to share.
4. Answers will vary here. Probably many contemporary parents and children would find Daly's remarks persuasive.
5. By mentioning StairMasters and health clubs, Daly is contrasting the "clean, free exercise" (5) of his youth with the more structured exercise of contemporary life. He would expect his readers to see the irony.

STYLE AND STRUCTURE (p. 365)

1. The introduction establishes the "ideal" past which leads Daly into his discussion of the very different present.
2. The arrangement is basically point-by-point: Paragraphs 1–2 stand in contrast with paragraphs 3–4; paragraphs 5–6 contain another contrast; paragraphs 7–9 contrast with paragraphs 10–11; and paragraph 12 contrasts with paragraphs 13–14. Because of the length of these sections, students might see the essay as a combination of point-by-point and subject-by-subject.
3. The words *thin ice* are used both literally and figuratively. Literally, thin ice is the reason skating is prohibited. Figuratively, "skating on thin ice" is a metaphor for taking a risk.
4. Daly's transitions mostly deal with time: *recently* (3), *nowadays* (5), *when* (7), *today* (10). The transitions, while not prominent, seem sufficient to keep Daly's organization clear.
5. Answers will vary. Given the informality of Daly's essay, a one-sentence conclusion is acceptable, but it might be combined with the previous paragraph.

VOCABULARY PROJECTS (p. 365)

2. These words occur in paragraphs 5, 10, 11, and 12 and basically have the same meaning in each case. The repetition provides coherence.

COMBINING THE PATTERNS (p. 366)

The narrative is detailed enough to make Daly's ironic point that the "ever vigilant" (15) town officials overreact to the dangers of skating.

THEMATIC CONNECTIONS

Reading the River (p. 138): Mark Twain describes learning to read the Mississippi River as a riverboat pilot in ways that are surprisingly similar to the way Daly and his friends learned to read the thickness of the ice.

The Way to Rainy Mountain (p. 148): N. Scott Momaday's essay corresponds to Daly's in several ways, but particularly in terms of how different generations stand in relation to the natural world. Like Daly's sons, Momaday has not learned to "read" the landscape with the same kind of authority that his grandmother had. Momaday also senses that something is lost as later generations grow further from the land.

Once More to the Lake (p. 154): See the *Thematic Connections* entry for E. B. White's essay on p. 36 of this manual. With the Trillin essay below, these three could provide interesting topics for discussing or writing about parent-child relationships and generational differences. For a unit discussing how a person's perception of events changes as he or she matures, bring in Twain's "Reading the River" (p. 138).

Television: The Plug-In Drug (p. 283): Like Daly, Marie Winn considers how contemporary societal changes have affected children for the worse. You might have students expand Winn's discussion of rituals to include the kinds of childhood rituals Daly describes. How, in your students' view, have these changed over the last twenty years or so? Are children today, to use Daly's words, better off or not?

It's Just Too Late (p. 304): Calvin Trillin describes the tragic end of a Memphis teenager whose alienation from her family led fairly directly to her death in a car crash. FaNee Cooper provides a sad example of the lack of communication and the conflict between parents and children that characterize many families today. Students might also want to consider the extent to which FaNee was harmed because she hadn't been allowed to take the kinds of risks that would have allowed her to develop a stronger sense of self-reliance.

Deborah Tannen, *Sex, Lies, and Conversation*

Tannen contrasts male and female communication styles, suggesting that many misunderstandings between heterosexual couples are due less to real personal differences than to misread conversational signals. She looks first at differences between the way girls communicate with girls and the way boys communicate with boys and the resulting "misalignments in the mechanics of conversation" among men and women (6–13). She then describes differences in the way males and females read their conversational partners' responses (14–20) and differences in men's and women's reasons for talking (21–22). Her concluding paragraphs offer hope that by recognizing these differences as "cross-cultural," unhappy couples will be able to better understand one another. A good place to begin discussion is by asking students whether they think Tannen's examples are basically superficial stereotypes or whether they can see themselves in the men or the women she describes. Ask for specific exceptions to Tannen's generalizations. Do any such exceptions prove—or disprove—the rule?

COMPREHENSION (p. 372)

1. At the beginning of her article Tannen offers an example of a husband doing most of the talking in public and a wife doing most of the talking at home.

2. Women most often complain that their partners don't listen or talk to them.
3. Three basic behaviors give women the impression that men do not listen: men tend to face away from each other in conversation, they often switch topics instead of following up with questions, and they make less listener-noise than women.
4. Men often respond to listener-noise as overreaction or impatience. In addition, women are more likely to "finish each other's sentences, and anticipate what the other is about to say," which men interpret as "interruption, intrusion, and lack of attention" (18).
5. Understanding differences in communication style can lead couples to modify their conversational behavior in ways that the other will respond to more positively. Even without such modifications, women can recognize that a man's failure to participate in the kind of conversation she expects from her close female friends does not necessarily indicate a "failure of intimacy" (25) and simply accept the difference without taking offense.

PURPOSE AND AUDIENCE (p. 372)

1. Tannen's thesis is stated in two parts: in paragraph 2 and at the beginning of paragraph 8.
2. Tannen's purpose is basically to inform. She doesn't directly advocate any change in male and female communication styles, suggesting that understanding the differences can help couples avoid misunderstandings.
3. Tannen clearly intends an audience of general readers. both men and women. (The essay originally appeared in the *Washington Post*.) The terms she uses and the concepts she explains are accessible to virtually any educated person, and she doesn't limit her discussion to one gender.

STYLE AND STRUCTURE (p. 372)

1. Because she is writing to provide information most people are not aware of, it is best that she state her thesis early in order to orient readers so they can understand the specific points that follow.
2. This is a point-by-point comparison, which allows Tannen to enumerate clearly the differences in several specific conversational activities.
3. Tannen's use of scholarly studies and statistics helps her suggest that the differences she describes are not simply based on her own observations but that they are supported by the work of other experts and by objective research.
4. Tannen's tone is positive, generally hopeful that husbands and wives can reduce the frictions caused by problems of cross-cultural communication.
5. Tannen's concluding call for cross-cultural understanding in "these times of resurgent ethnic conflict" may strike some readers as a bit too far-reaching for her particular subject. Not everyone will agree that a resolution to racial and ethnic conflict might be more easily achieved if men and women in the United States learn to better understand their conversational differences.

VOCABULARY PROJECTS (p. 372)

2. Tannen doesn't use much professional jargon. Among the few examples are *organizational structures and interactive norms* (7), *physical alignment* and *topical*

alignment (13), and *listener-noise* and *participatory listenership* (18). Opinion will differ as to the effectiveness of such jargon in the essay. She generally defines her terms directly or though example, and the professional jargon tends to make her authority more credible.

COMBINING THE PATTERNS (p. 372)

The anecdote provides an example of the point Tannen makes throughout her essay—that women and men communicate in different ways but remain largely unaware of these differences, which leads to misunderstandings. The story is itself amusing and serves to establish Tannen's informal, friendly style.

THEMATIC CONNECTIONS

The Grave **(p. 161):** Porter's story depicts other sorts of differences between boys and girls. Miranda wants the gold ring—one assumes a wedding band—that her brother Paul finds, while he wants the silver dove because it is the screw head for a coffin. Also, their hunting styles are different: Paul's goal is to kill the game, while Miranda "hardly ever hit any sort of mark" and what she likes about shooting is "pulling the trigger and hearing the noise." You might ask students to consider Tannen's essay and Porter's story in terms of sexual stereotypes.

Sexism in English: Embodiment and Language **(p. 413):** In looking at issues of gender and language, you might also have students read Alleen Pace Nilsen's survey of sexist terminology. Our language is inherently sexist, she says, because our culture has been inherently sexist. Relating Nilsen to Tannen, you might ask whether men—and even women—tend to devalue female forms of communication, a topic that was a long-time staple of sitcoms and stand-up comedy routines. Or have societal changes over the last thirty years served to bring the values of men and women closer together in terms of personal relationships?

I Want a Wife **(p. 474):** Judy Brady's essay also looks at conflicts between wives and husbands, in this case based on stereotypical assumptions about the roles each should fulfill within a marriage. How might Tannen respond to Brady's portrait of a wife? Do the differences Tannen suggests between men and women in any way justify the popularly held stereotypes of male-female roles?

It's a Jungle Out There **(p. 538):** Camille Paglia (along with Susan Jacoby in her essay) considers date rape in terms of different expectations among men and women. See *Thematic Connections*, "It's a Jungle Out There," page 125 of this manual.

John Updike, *Ex-Basketball Player*

Updike's poem is a simple before-and-after comparison of a one-time high school basketball star, Flick Webb, who now works at a garage, his glory years quickly extinguished. You might start by asking students whether they find Flick as sympathetic as the speaker of the poem seems to. What accounts for the speaker's tone and point of view?

THINKING ABOUT LITERATURE (p. 375)

1. Flick's youthful days of basketball stardom (stanza 3) are compared with his far less heroic present (stanzas 1, 2, 4, and 5). The shift to the past in stanza 3

is signaled with the transitional word *once* and the shift from the present to the past tense. The shift back to the present in stanza 4 is also signaled by a shift in tense: "He never learned a trade, he just sells gas."

2. Students will have different responses to the accuracy of the speaker's depiction of Flick.

3. Whatever potential Flick had, he squandered it because he was blinded by the glory of being a local sports hero. Our society—particularly college athletics—tends to use young, talented male athletes at the expense of their education.

THEMATIC CONNECTIONS

The Human Cost of an Illiterate Society **(p. 203):** Flick Webb, while not illiterate, is a graphic example of how limited one's potential can be if one's education is deficient. You might also set up Flick in contrast to the people Jonathan Kozol describes. Why was Flick not able to take advantage of the opportunities that were probably presented him?

Who Killed Benny Paret? **(p. 279):** If you have students who wish to consider other aspects of American sports, this essay by Norman Cousins raises some fundamental questions about the appeal of violence in sporting contests and the extent to which athletes are sacrificed to the spectators' and promoters' craving for violence.

Brains versus Brawn **(p. 328):** Student Mark Cotharn writes about contrasting attitudes toward athletes. A hard-working student as well as a star football player, Cotharn found that in a school that put great emphasis on athletics, he was given preferential treatment by his teachers. But after he was forced to transfer to a school that put more emphasis on academics than it did on athletics, the fact that he was an athlete became a liability: teachers expected him to be an indifferent student and treated him accordingly. He had to prove that he was not a Flick Webb, that he did care about his education beyond the football field.

The Men We Carry in Our Minds **(p. 399):** Scott Russell Sanders's essay considers the dead-end lives of poor, uneducated men who "never learned a trade." Few of these men had the opportunities of a Flick Webb, so students might consider whether in light of these others Flick is a sympathetic character. Could he have done more with his life had he tried?

10: CLASSIFICATION AND DIVISION

A natural way to begin studying classification and division is to look closely at Paul Gallico's paragraph from "Fans." You might remind students of the destructive rioting of British soccer fans in Europe several years ago, which validates Gallico's discussion. You can also remind them of Norman Cousins's characterization of boxing fans ("Who Killed Benny Paret?"). Students will be able to see that Gallico perceives useful relationships when he divides fans on a clear basis into categories.

Remind students that as they write any essay they are classifying and dividing—classifying bits of information into categories that may become paragraphs, dividing a topic into parts, and so on. You might also review the many ways we use classification and division to simplify our lives—in everything from libraries to classified ads, from biological hierarchies to technical reports. You can easily devise an exercise to illustrate how we classify and divide: items on a list of twenty-five television shows, for instance, can be classified according to format (sitcom, detective story, etc.), degree of popularity, time of broadcast, or any of several other principles. Once students have practiced arranging the titles in various groupings, you can show them how they might use these categories as support for several different thesis statements concerning television programming.

The selections in this chapter use classification and division for a wide range of purposes. Students will readily relate to William Zinsser's "College Pressures," focusing on four kinds of pressures college students face. Next, Scott Russell Sanders uses classification to make a thoughtful point about class, gender, and power. In the following two essays, Amy Tan and Alleen Pace Nilsen apply classification to issues of language: Tan writes personally, classifying the different "Englishes" she uses when communicating with different audiences; Nilsen writes more objectively, classifying deeply rooted examples of sexism in the English language. Stephanie Ericsson's essay uses division to suggest the many kinds of lies we tell ourselves and others. Finally, Flannery O'Connor's short story "Revelation" reveals the muddled thinking of an individual bigot whose prejudices cause her to violate fundamental principles of classification and division.

William Zinsser, *College Pressures*

You will probably want to discuss this essay first in your classification unit because its subject matter is so close to students and because it so clearly demonstrates meaningful use of the pattern. From Zinsser's essay, you can raise any number of classification issues: the basis for the system, the logic behind the order in which categories are presented, questions about any overlapping categories, and the significance of the system.

As you assign the essay, you might ask students to consider causes of student suicide in this country. Of course, the causes are varied and complex, but they often include academic pressures. As you discuss the selection, you will want to emphasize Zinsser's belief that students "have the power to shape their own future" (39) and to discuss ways in which they can do so. You might also ask your students how closely Yale students parallel students elsewhere. Are the concerns of most Yale students trivial compared to pressures faced by students at state universities or community colleges, for instance? (Don't forget to remind students that Yale students, too, may have severe financial problems.)

COMPREHENSION (p. 396)

1. Zinsser advises students that their futures are unpredictable, with turns they will not expect, and that there is time to make changes of careers, jobs, attitudes, and approaches.
2. He wishes them "some release from the clammy grip of the future" (13) so that they will have the chance to enjoy each stage of their education, to experiment, and to learn that failure is not fatal and can even be valuable. He believes his wish is naive because America worships achievement and lauds the successful in the media.
3. Zinsser identifies economic, parental, peer, and self-induced pressures.
4. Zinsser blames no one. He sees only victims, not villains because the pressures to compete are all too real.

5. Zinsser evaluates students by the range of their learning, their curiosity, and their willingness to take risks. He cares little about their grades. In contrast, he sees employers evaluating them on the basis of their having taken a narrow spectrum of safe subjects and earned uniformly high grades.
6. Women are under even more pressure than men because society is so slow to recognize their leadership potential for jobs traditionally reserved for men.
7. The "new pauperism" causes professors to spend their time publishing to avoid "perishing" in a shrinking profession. Consequently, they do not spend as much time with students as many would like.
8. Ultimately students themselves must accept responsibility for eliminating college pressures. They are the ones who can find faith in themselves and refuse to be shaped by external pressures.
9. Because students have too many choices for the limited time they have available, sports and other extracurricular activities cause them further anxiety. Students adapt by selecting activities with a foreseeable end rather than choosing ongoing activities.

PURPOSE AND AUDIENCE (p. 397)

1. Zinsser's thesis is that students who are victims of enormous economic, parental, peer, and self-induced pressures must, nonetheless, free themselves—as only they can. Without discounting the difficulties, Zinsser intends to effect change, to make students aware that they can free themselves from "the clammy grip of the future" (13).
2. Very likely students would most feel the impact from Zinsser's ideas since they generally feel pressured without realizing that they can free themselves. Other potential audiences have more experience with academic and professional life.
3. In paragraphs 42 through 46, Zinsser hopes to make readers aware that anxiety even drives students' extracurricular pursuits: he sees students as "largely ignoring the blithe spirit inside who keeps trying to come out and play" (46) because of faulty American values.
4. Zinsser believes that his readers, for the most part, share the values that cause student anxiety and obsession without being aware of the impact these values have. However, he also believes that they can be enlightened. His assumption about the materialism of his audience is not entirely valid; many parents are already enlightened and do not insist that their students major in "pre-rich," and many employers look for qualities not shown on transcripts. Of course, Zinsser's assumptions are not without some foundation, although they need to be qualified. Certainly his assumption that Yale students are typical of students nationally could lead him to overgeneralize.

STYLE AND STRUCTURE (p. 397)

1. Zinsser effectively uses the introductory notes to Carlos to personalize students' struggling for success.
2. Zinsser signals his classification in paragraph 15 with his explicit statement of the four types of pressure. He begins his first category in paragraph 16 when he discusses the typical question of today's students—how can they find an "edge" for getting into the professional schools that almost guarantee their earning large incomes after graduation? He indicates the completion of

the final category when he asserts that the student, "as a driven creature who is largely ignoring the blithe spirit inside" (46), is the product of values that make him or her feel both driven and fearful.

3. Paragraphs 22 and 31 are transitional. Each introduces a new type of pressure by closely linking it to the one just discussed.

4. Zinsser has several options for referring to groups of mixed gender, including "he or she" and "he/she." The last obtrusive option is to make both antecedents and pronouns plural. Because it is unobtrusive, it is the preferred option. Certainly the most controversial option, at least in academic situations, is to use a plural pronoun to refer to a singular indefinite pronoun; however, this usage does sometimes appear in respected publications. Discuss your preferences and your logic with your students. The issue of gender usage creates an opportunity for you to discuss the notion of language as dynamic rather than fixed—a concept that will surprise some of your students.

5. Quotations from deans and students at Yale support Zinsser's thesis.

6. Economic pressures drive parents who, in turn, pressure students. Thus the two types of pressure overlap. Students feeling driven by economic and parental pressures are further pressured by seeing other students outclass them, and therefore they drive themselves even further. Zinsser's acknowledgment that the categories overlap strengthens the essay, making it clear that the pressures combine to trap students.

7. Zinsser discusses economic pressure first since it generates parental pressure. Both external pressures foster pressures inside the academic environment. Zinsser ends with self-induced pressure to emphasize the individual student who suffers.

VOCABULARY PROJECTS (p. 397)

2. Students who leave notes to Carlos are *supplicants* (9), and achievement is the *national god* that is venerated and glorified as the state religion (14). Colleges, students, and their parents, like religious ascetics, belong to a *brotherhood of paupers* (20). The language suggests that Zinsser believes American materialism has replaced (or even become) religion in American society.

COMBINING THE PATTERNS (p. 398)

In the opening paragraphs, Zinsser cites notes from students that exemplify the pressures they face, and he refers to specific students as examples in paragraphs 30 and 32. Other examples include the comments from deans in paragraph 16, the specifics about Yale and Harvard in paragraph 17, and the examples of the "brutal economy" in paragraphs 20–21. All the examples help make Zinsser's point more concrete. Additional examples of specific students might add to readers' understanding.

THEMATIC CONNECTIONS

The Great Campus Goof-Off Machine (p. 188): In this essay, a college student, Nate Stulman, paints a rather different picture of life at an elite eastern university. Today, Stulman suggests, many students spend more time surfing the Web, playing computer games, or chatting online than they do worrying about grades or academic excellence. When might it be a *good* thing for students to feel "pressured" by their college classes? Is a sense of pressure to achieve excellence always a negative thing? Might it be true that college students today feel less pressure than their counterparts in the 1970s?

The "Black Table" Is Still There (p. 294): See Thematic Connections, "The "Black Table" Is Still There," p. 69 of this manual. You might consider asking whether minority students like Graham face pressures in college that are different from those faced by the students Zinsser describes.

Suicide Note (p. 315): The suicide note written by Mirikitani's student and the accompanying note about an actual Asian-American student who leaped to her death from her dormitory suggest how intense parental pressures, real or assumed, can be on students. In her note, the girl apologizes to her parents "for disappointing you," repeatedly explaining, "I've worked very hard." She clearly suffers from being caught in what Zinsser calls "one of the oldest webs of love and duty and guilt" (28). Zinsser does not mention suicide, but news articles appear with some frequency about student suicides that can be traced to academic pressures. Your students can benefit from discussing this link—and from your informing them about your school's resources for troubled students. Be sure they understand that Zinsser does not blame anyone for the pressures but does suggest a solution (See also Thematic Connections, "Suicide Note," p. 76 of this manual.)

The Company Man (p. 476): Students tend not to see beyond today's academic pressures. When asked to consider a connection between Zinsser's discussion and Goodman's, they should see that Phil, the company man, dies in the service of achievement, "the state religion." Zinsser's belief that students can "break the circles in which they are trapped" (39) has much longer-range implications than he discusses. Phil's situation should show them good reasons for breaking the circle.

Scott Russell Sanders, *The Men We Carry in Our Minds*

Sanders uses classification as a way of making a larger point in this essay. He begins by suggesting that the images of manhood he knew growing up among the rural poor fell into two groups: "the brute toiling animal and the boss" (1). In paragraph 4 he adds a third group: the "warriors," local GIs who did not "toil" but were similarly at the mercy of a "boss." "Toiler" and "warrior" were the only roles he could imagine for his peers. In paragraph 7 he turns to his central point: ultimately a scholarship student at "a university meant for the children of the rich," he could not understand why the women he met there envied the "joys and privileges" of men, why they held such "deep grievances" (8), since his experience was that women seemed to have easier lives than men. Sanders says that in many parts of the world "the fate of men is as grim and bleak as the fate of women" (9), but that the women he met at college saw men only as their fathers were—power wielders, "bosses." He concludes that he himself was not that kind of man, not an "enemy to their desires" but rather an "ally" (11), even though he could not make the privileged young women he knew understand this.

You might begin discussion by asking why Sanders titled his essay "The Men We Carry in Our Minds." How do the images we absorb in childhood color our view of reality throughout our lives?

COMPREHENSION (p. 402)

1. The convicts represent the "toilers," and the guards represent the "bosses."
2. He saw no options other than to become a "toiler," but he escaped that fate as a scholarship student at a prestigious university.

3. As a boy he "envied" women because they had time to cultivate an interest in the arts, to "enjoy a sense of ease," and because most women worked in their houses, which seemed to him "brighter, handsomer places than any factory" (8). He only became aware of the "grievances" of women, of the narrowness of their choices and their potential for victimization, when confronted by feminists in college.

4. The women he met at college carried in their minds the images of their powerful fathers, similar to Sanders's "bosses." All men, they charged, are "destined from birth" (11) to oppress women. Sanders argues that the men he knew in his youth, those he carries in his mind, are just as much victims, so he was really an ally, not an enemy.

PURPOSE AND AUDIENCE (p. 402)

1. Sanders seems to have intended this essay as a way of exploring his own complicated feelings. Moreover, he wants readers to recognize that a concept like "masculine power" is far too sweeping; not all men have power. Power, he seems to suggest, is far more the prerogative of economic class.

2. Sanders's thesis is summarized in the introduction to this entry. Student summaries should bring together the ideas expressed in paragraphs 10 and 11.

3. Sanders seems to have in mind an educated audience rather than workers such as those he grew up with. Directed equally at men and women, the essay might well have a greater impact on the latter.

STYLE AND STRUCTURE (p. 403)

1. Sanders begins by considering the categories of "toiler" and "warrior" and their "bosses." In another sense the essay focuses on the categories *men of privilege* and *women of privilege, men of the working class* and *women of the working class.*

2. Sanders's principles of classification are class and gender.

3. Sanders begins with those categories with which he is most familiar and then moves to the categories of privilege.

4. Sanders gives more attention to the categories of working people than to the categories of privileged people, assuming perhaps that many of his readers will know little about the lives of poor working people.

VOCABULARY PROJECTS (p. 403)

2. See number 1 under Style and Structure. Students' titles may be somewhat different.

COMBINING THE PATTERNS (p. 404)

Sanders uses description to characterize his subjects in paragraphs 1 (convicts), 3 (working men), and 4 (his father). He doesn't describe the GIs in detail (4), but he does provide a lot of detail about their actions.

THEMATIC CONNECTIONS

Midnight (p. 177): This student essay described another kind of toiler: Asian immigrants working twelve hours and more a day in a dry cleaning sweatshop under uncomfortable, sometimes dangerous, conditions. Students should see an immediate connection between this essay and paragraph 9 of Sanders's essay, where he expands the category of toiler to include those "in mining country, in black ghettos, in Hispanic barrios, in the shadows of factories, in Third World nations—any place where the fate of men is as grim and bleak as the fate of women."

On Fire (p. 243): See *Thematic Connections*, "On Fire," p. 58 of this manual. Students might consider some of the similarities and differences between Larry Brown's job as a firefighter and the kinds of labor Sanders describes. In what sense does firefighting combine aspects of the "toiler" and the "warrior"? What are the greater advantages—and disadvantages—of the firefighter's job?

Ex-Basketball Player (p. 374): John Updike's poem presents readers with a toiler of a different sort. Once a widely admired high school basketball star, Flick Webb squandered his early promise and makes a living as a garage mechanic, offering only the occasional reminder of his early glory years. Do students think Webb fits Sanders's category of the toiler who is essentially trapped by "humiliating powerlessness"? Or is he representative of another category? If the latter, what might be a name for that category?

The Secretary Chant (p. 488): Marge Piercy's poem can be related to Sanders's essay in several ways. The women she gives voice to are, in many ways, the female version of Sanders's "toilers." They represent the sort of female powerlessness that the women Sanders met in college so resented. Finally, they provide a contrast to the rather romanticized version of "women's work" that Sanders remembers from his childhood.

Any Tan, *Mother Tongue*

The daughter of Chinese immigrant parents, Amy Tan describes the four "Englishes I grew up with" (2), focusing on their relation to her mother: the "simple" English she spoke to her mother, her mother's "broken" English, her "watered-down" translations of her mother's Chinese, and her imaginatively realized "perfect" translations of her mother's "internal language." Tan does not name these categories until her next-to-last paragraph, but she provides examples throughout: paragraphs 4–9 discuss her "simple" English and her mother's "broken" English, with Tan concluding ruefully that as a child she was embarrassed by her mother's English; paragraphs 10–14 give examples of her "watered-down" translations; and her final paragraphs describe her attempts to capture her mother's "internal language." In paragraphs 15–18, Tan suggests her purpose in considering these "Englishes": to explain the difficulties Asian-American students have with English, particularly English achievement tests, and the reason they end up pursuing degrees in math and science.

At some point you may want to ask students—even those whose families are native English speakers—how different their "home language" is from the language they encounter at school. What difficulties do they have adjusting to "academic English"?

COMPREHENSION (p. 410)

1. See the discussion of Tan's categories in the introduction above.
2. She identifies the categories in her next-to-last paragraph. Students might suggest that this identification could have come earlier to make the structure

of the essay clearer from the start. You might point out that this might have made the essay seem more formal.

3. Only the final category is not clearly illustrated. Tan might have provided an example from one of her books to do so, but her conclusion might then have had less force.

4. Her mother's English was a handicap when her mother needed to communicate about important matters with native English speakers in positions of authority—her stockbroker, for example, and hospital personnel. Other examples might include dealings with the police, the courts, government agencies, and the like.

5. Tan was embarrassed by her mother's English as a child, and she also believes that the language she heard at home contributed to her lowered scores on language achievement tests. But in adulthood the same language became an inspiration to her as a novelist.

6. Tan attributes her difficulty in answering questions on achievement tests to the fact that she could not easily limit the possibilities; her mind, she suggests, didn't process language in a simple either/or pattern. It is certainly possible that Tan's imagination—which would lead to her success as a writer—contributed as much to the problem as did the level of her family's language skills.

7. Because they score higher on math achievement tests than on language tests, Tan suggests that many Asian-American students are being steered to majors in math and science, effectively cutting them off from creative writing. Other explanations might include the possibility that such students simply feel more comfortable with more technical subjects.

PURPOSE AND AUDIENCE (p. 410)

1. Tan uses her opening to show that she is writing from personal experience, not from extensive study. She doesn't intend her ultimate claims about Asian-American students to be definitive.

2. The level of detail she offers about immigrant culture suggests that Tan expects her audience to be composed largely of native English speakers.

3. Tan focuses fairly equally on her mother and on the subject of language, but her larger purpose seems to make a point about language.

STYLE AND STRUCTURE (p. 410)

1. Both Tan's diction and her organizational structure are relatively informal. For an audience of nonexperts, such informality seems appropriate, but achieving credibility with a more expert audience would require a more formal style.

2. She includes the example to suggest what the "family talk" she grew up with sounds like. The impression it gives is that her mother's English is indeed "broken," which is the effect Tan intended.

3. These passages demonstrate the contrast between Tan's command of English and her mother's.

4. *Mother tongue* generally refers to one's native language. Here the phrase refers more exactly to Tan's mother's language, the language of home for the writer.

5. The "terrible" line shows Tan reaching to find an English suitable for formal expression—and in doing so, using diction that is artificial and stilted. The style she uses for the essay is more natural and fluid.

VOCABULARY PROJECTS (p. 411)

2. Students may have different opinions about this and, like Tan, will probably have difficulty coming up with a more neutral term. You might ask what this difficulty suggests about the way speakers like Tan's mother are viewed in American society.

COMBINING THE PATTERNS (p. 412)

The narration Tan uses adds color and vividness to the essay and is crucial to making her point concrete. No other strategy would be quite so appropriate, although the anecdotes do serve as examples.

THEMATIC CONNECTIONS

Only Daughter (p. 83): Sandra Cisneros also writes about growing up in an immigrant (Mexican-American) household. Although her focus isn't on language, her description of her relationship with her father—and the cultural assumptions against which she must struggle—have interesting parallels with Tan's experiences.

Words Left Unspoken (p. 133): In writing about her deaf grandfather, who could communicate only in sign, Leah Hager Cohen presents a different kind of language barrier, but one that can readily be compared to the barrier Tan's mother faces. If you have students who know sign language, they might want to explain for the class some differences between a spoken English sentence and its signed equivalent. How do these differences relate to Tan's translations of her mother's English into more formal prose?

English Is a Crazy Language (p. 192): Richard Lederer looks lightheartedly at the inconsistencies of English, which can make it especially difficult for a non-native speaker to master the language.

The Human Cost of an Illiterate Society (p. 203): Students can compare the problems of people who can't read with those of people who speak limited English. See *Thematic Connections*, "The Human Cost of an Illiterate Society," p. 48 of this manual.

Alleen Pace Nilsen,
Sexism in English: Embodiment and Language

Updating a project she began in 1970, Nilsen culls inherently sexist expressions from American dictionaries as a way of pointing out "the attitudes that our ancestors held and that we as a culture are therefore predisposed to hold" (5). These expressions fall into three categories: those that imply that "a woman is valued for the attractiveness of her body, while a man is valued for his physical strength and accomplishments" (6); those that imply that women are passive, while men are active; and those that connect women with negative connotations, while companion expressions connect men with positive connotations. Nilsen concludes by expressing her optimism over changes that have occurred since the early 1970s because she hopes "new language customs will cause a new generation of speakers to grow up with different expectations" (36).

Some of the expressions Nilsen mentions may not be familiar to younger students because they are not currently used very widely. You might ask students—

particularly those born after the political and cultural changes wrought by the feminist movement—if they are consciously aware that their English is probably much less sexist than was the English of the 1950s. For example, few students use *he* to refer to a singular antecedent that could be male or female—indeed, it is more natural for many students to use *they.* What other examples in their own English can they come up with that suggest the kinds of changes Nilsen mentions in her conclusion?

COMPREHENSION (p. 423)

1. In the late 1960s Nilsen lived with her husband in Afghanistan, where women's roles were particularly confining—even those in the American community. Returning to the United States in 1969, she discovered that a number of women were beginning to question gender expectations. A former English major, she decided to start her own movement of sorts by looking at the English language to see what it suggested about sexism.
2. Nilsen offers many examples of this category in paragraphs 9 through 15.
3. Most of the terminology of weddings revolves around the term *bride.* More intriguingly, the common pairing of the terms *bride and groom* stands in direct contrast to most such linguistic pairings in English, where the masculine term almost invariably comes first.
4. Changes in marriage customs include different conventions for wedding announcements, the inclusion of the groom in the newspaper picture, and the wording of the vows.
5. Examples of this category are found in paragraphs 21–22 and 25–29.
6. *Ms.* was introduced as an alternative to *Miss* and *Mrs.* that would avoid the issue of marital status. It has been less than successful, according to Nilsen, because it has essentially become just a business substitute for *Miss,* as many married women continue to prefer *Mrs.* The increasingly common solution is to avoid such titles—including *Mr.*—altogether.
7. These examples are presented in paragraphs 30 through 37.
8. Nilsen believes things are changing but that people should continue thinking deeply about "the underlying issue of sexism" (40) if such changes are to continue and become the norm.

PURPOSE AND AUDIENCE (p. 424)

1. While predominantly informative, Nilsen's purpose is persuasive as well. She is clearly advocating the use of alternatives to sexist language. While she succeeds in informing, student opinion on the success of her persuasive appeal may be divided.
2. She states her thesis in her final paragraph. A more argumentative stance might have been appropriate, but Nilsen assumes that her readers will agree that sexist language creates cultural images that affect women's lives negatively. Do most students agree with this?
3. Readers today probably would be more immediately sympathetic to Nilsen's views and even more aware of instances of sexist language; an audience in the early 1970s might have been more accustomed and conditioned to such language.

STYLE AND STRUCTURE (p. 424)

1. The three categories are named in the introduction to this entry.
2. Nilsen's categories do seem to overlap: several examples in the "sexy woman/successful man" category could also fit in the "passive woman/active man" category (see paragraph 16) and vice versa (see paragraph 27). This seems less a flaw in Nilsen's classification system than a problem of determining what a set of examples best represents.
3. The three headings seem helpful to most readers, as they introduce each category of Nilsen's discussion. You might ask students to try to come up with subheadings for each category. Are they helpful?
4. Most students will probably think the introduction could be condensed. The anecdote about living in Afghanistan doesn't seem entirely pertinent now. Suggest to students that it is probably a holdover from the original version of the essay, when Nilsen would have more reason to establish a rationale for studying sexist language in English.
5. The final two paragraphs present Nilsen's conclusion. Most readers find them a satisfying way to end, one that points to future development in American culture and language.
6. The examples are abundant and make it hard to deny that sexism exists in English.
7. Depending on her audience, Nilsen might have written more formally and academically. Since she is apparently writing to a general audience, however, her less formal style seems appropriate.
8. It is certainly possible to question paragraphs 17 through 20 as representative of the "sexy woman/successful man" category. They might better have been set off as a fourth category headed "Women want weddings; men don't care."

VOCABULARY PROJECTS (p. 424)

2. One example of the first category is the name of the restaurant chain Hooters; a masculine equivalent is unthinkable. One example of the second is the wide variety of negative terms applied to women who are aggressive competitors in business. An example of the third category is the common, recent use of *guys* to refer to a group that includes both men and women; a companion female term (*gals* or *girls*) would never be used to refer to a mixed group.
3. Younger students may point out that they've never heard of many of Nilsen's examples. Why do they think this is the case?

COMBINING THE PATTERNS (p. 425)

Paragraphs 27 and 28 are good examples to study in terms of transitions linking individual examples. They include *however, but, for example,* and *also*. Both paragraphs also have clear topic sentences that unify the examples.

THEMATIC CONNECTIONS

My Field of Dreams (p. 73): This student essay focuses on one particular aspect of our culture that remains blatantly sexist: athletics. As Tiffany Forte points out, regardless of a young woman's talent or ambition, she is ultimately prevented from aspiring to any kind of professional career in most sports. This provides a good opportunity to consider the extent to which sexism continues to mark our culture and limit possibilities for both men and women. Do students agree with Nilsen that things are moving in the direction of continuing expansion of equality for women? Or has a plateau been reached beyond which male and female roles are not likely to evolve much further?

Only Daughter **(p. 83):** Sandra Cisneros writes as the only daughter, along with six brothers, in a conservative Chicano household in the 1950s and 1960s—in fact, as she writes, both "the only daughter and *only* a daughter." Destined in her father's eyes for marriage and nothing else, Cisneros is a good example of the generation following Nilsen's, which benefited from the women's movement of the late 1960s and 1970s. Few fathers today would dismiss their daughters' futures as Cisneros's did.

English Is a Crazy Language **(p. 192):** Both Richard Lederer and Nilsen look at the English language by offering a wide variety of examples, but the essays also provide interesting contrasts. See *Thematic Connections,* "English Is a Crazy Language," p. 44 of this manual.

Sex, Lies, and Conversation **(p. 367):** Deborah Tannen's essay offers another way of discussing issues of gender and male-female relationships. Is it possible that Tannen is simply reinforcing the kinds of sexist stereotypes Nilsen points out when she identifies differences in the communication styles of men and women? Is she saying, for example, that "Women are needy; men are self-sufficient"? Is this a fair characterization?

Stephanie Ericsson, *The Ways We Lie*

Ericsson analyzes the effect of lying by dividing lies into ten different categories, moving from the most personal to those that affect our world in the most profound ways. Admitting that we can't really eliminate lies entirely from our lives, Ericsson nonetheless suggests that to create a sea change that will grant us as a public "our *right* to trust" the media, politicians, and others, we must begin on the smallest level: "Maybe if I don't tell the bank the check's in the mail I'll be less tolerant of the lies told me every day" (37).

One way to begin discussion is to have students provide some examples of their own for Ericsson's categories, particularly white lies, deflecting, omission, dismissal, and delusion. Ask whether there are any times when they feel justified in telling a lie (most will say "yes"); then ask if there are any times when they feel it is justified for someone else to lie to them (a much more difficult question).

COMPREHENSION (p. 433)

1. (1) *White lies* are generally "harmless untruths." (2) *Facades* are roles we play, often to impress others. (3) *Ignoring the plain facts* is a kind of lying to oneself. (4) *Deflecting* is distracting others from something negative about oneself or refusing to respond when accused of inappropriate behavior. (5) *Omission* is the leaving out of pertinent facts that don't correspond with the image one wants to present. (6) *Stereotypes and clichés* "shut down original thinking" and result in "all the 'isms.'" (7) *Groupthink* is a combination of other forms of lying in which a group's loyalty to itself outweighs any other value, including the truth. (8) *Out-and-out lies* are attempts to "refute reality" and can be "easily confronted." (9) *Dismissal* is ignoring "feelings, perceptions, or even

the raw facts of a situation," particularly as they relate to others. (10) *Delusion* is "the tendency to see excuses as facts," "the mind's ability . . . to support what it wants to be the truth."

2. Lies are often necessary to protect the feelings of others and to help us present the most positive images of ourselves. In addition, delusion is a "survival mechanism."

3. White lies can delude people into a false sense of security or hope. Facades can be used to "seduce others into an illusion" (11). Ignoring the plain facts can lead to all kinds of harm, particularly when criminal behavior is involved. Deflecting can let people hide what they don't want others to know by making it look as though they're being honest; it is also a way of resisting justified criticism. Omission on a historical level can keep people ignorant of their true past. Stereotypes "close minds and separate people" (22). Group-think leads to poor decision-making. Out-and-out lies can refute reality unless they are caught. Dismissal can result in mental illness. Delusion allows us to ignore our most serious problems.

4. Out-and-out lies are the most "honest" lies—that is, the liar knows he or she is lying and expects you to suspect the lie.

5. Dismissal often involves things that can't be "proved" unless we delve deeply. As long as we don't delve deeply, we can continue to believe that the problem doesn't exist.

PURPOSE AND AUDIENCE (p. 433)

1. Ultimately, Ericsson attacks lying. As she says in her conclusion, "Our acceptance of lies becomes a cultural cancer that eventually shrouds and reorders reality until moral garbage becomes as invisible to us as water is to a fish" (35). She ends by encouraging readers, at least implicitly, to think carefully before telling even little lies in order to become "less tolerant" (37) of the larger lies that surround us.

2. Ericsson's is a fairly liberal slant, most evident in the examples she offers in paragraphs 5, 12, 15, 18–20, 24–25, and 33. She seems to have imagined a fairly liberal audience, but it's clear that people of all political stripes are concerned about politicians' lying and lying in the media—although they might define those lies differently.

STYLE AND STRUCTURE (p. 433)

1. Ericsson's informal opening serves to draw readers in. She establishes common ground by telling about her own lies and noting that we all lie.

2. The quotations from a wide variety of time periods and sources serve to universalize the points she is making. Students, unfamiliar with many of these sources, may see them as interruptions.

3. Generally, each discussion includes an example or two, and Ericsson's evaluation of when that category of lie is beneficial and how it is harmful. Sometimes, however, she omits the discussion of benefits—one assumes because she sees no benefit in that category of lie. The discussions are not exactly balanced, however; some are more detailed than others. Students might feel that more balance would set up each category more clearly.

4. Ericsson basically moves from the least to the most problematic kinds of lies—although students will not necessarily agree with her ranking system.

Some, for example, might see ignoring the plain facts as more harmful than deflecting or omission.

5. Rhetorical questions help emphasize the point that lying is a double-edged sword, sometimes beneficial, sometimes harmful. Ericsson wants us as a society to find alternatives to lying, yet she has no simple answer as to how this might be accomplished.

6. Ericsson cites historians and psychologists, the very sorts of experts one would expect in a research paper on lying. Student opinion will vary regarding the need for other citations.

7. Ericsson also uses the feminine indefinite pronoun in paragraph 4, but she uses the male indefinite pronoun in paragraph 8. It is unlikely that students would find these few shifts distracting.

8. In both her conclusion and her introduction, Ericsson uses personal experience, quotation, and rhetorical questions. Her conclusion echoes much of the important language in the introduction as well.

VOCABULARY PROJECTS (p. 434)

2. Colloquialisms include *Sure I Lie . . .* (3); *ducked out* (6); *looks great . . . looks like hell* (8); *crawls into a hole* (16); *mouth like a truck driver* (22); and *good-ole-boy* (25). They lend a certain informality and accessibility to her prose, which most readers should view positively.

COMBINING THE PATTERNS (p. 435)

The dictionary definition is probably not necessary, but it does allow Ericsson to establish common terminology before discussing behaviors that readers might not have thought of as lying before.

THEMATIC CONNECTIONS

"What's in a Name?" (p. 5): Henry Louis Gates's essay offers the story of a childhood incident that revealed to him the extent to which African Americans were considered inferior by whites. Ericsson's discussion of stereotypes is pertinent here, as is her discussion of facades. Maya Angelou's "Finishing School," Brent Staples's "Just Walk On By," and student Mark Cotharn's "Brains versus Brawn" also deal with stereotypes.

Thirty-Eight Who Saw Murder Didn't Call the Police (p. 99): Have students decide, on the basis of the quotations in this newspaper article, what kind of lying the thirty-eight witnesses exhibited. The most likely categories are ignoring the plain facts and dismissal, with stereotypes playing a role in some instances.

The Lottery (p. 255): Students will easily see Shirley Jackson's short story as an example of groupthink. Tessie Hutchinson also uses deflection when she argues that the lottery drawing was unfair.

Flannery O'Connor, *Revelation*

O'Connor's brilliant story allows you to discuss a badly flawed classification system and its effects. Because Ruby Turpin classifies people on more than one basis, her thinking is confused and illogical. At the end of your classification unit, students should be fully prepared to understand the mechanisms of her thinking, for O'Connor's use of a limited omniscient narrator allows students to see inside the mind of this bigot. They should see a strong parallel to Mrs. Cullinan, for whom Maya Angelou worked (see "Finishing School," p. 88). Just as Mrs. Turpin drops her pleasant disposition when she is crossed, Mrs. Cullinan drops hers when she calls Angelou "That clumsy nigger" and growls, "Her name's Margaret, goddamn it, her name's Margaret."

In addition to exploring Mrs. Turpin's classifying, you will want to show students how effectively O'Connor uses imagery to develop meaning—the setting sun, Mary Grace's eyes, Mrs. Turpin's shadowy and distorted vision, pigs, even names. *Turpin* may suggest *turpitude* and *Mary Grace* certainly suggests the concept of *grace*—which Mrs. Turpin's vision, triggered by Mary Grace, could lead to. Ask students to explain why O'Connor would have Mary Grace hit Mrs. Turpin with a book entitled *Human Development,* and ask them, after carefully examining the details at the end of the story, to consider the extent to which her vision alters her. Students will enjoy your discussion of O'Connor's story and will have an increased understanding of classification. Do ask them to respond to the Journal Entry; considering the dangers of classification systems can be an extremely important result of reading the story.

THINKING ABOUT LITERATURE (p. 452)

1. In her revelation, Mrs. Turpin sees a procession of souls "rumbling toward heaven," with people like her marching behind the "white trash" and "niggers" whom she sees as her inferiors, and having "even their virtues . . . burned away" (190). In this, O'Connor, who was deeply religious, echoes the biblical edict, "But many that are first shall be last; and the last shall be first" (Matthew 19:30). However, Mrs. Turpin does not comprehend what she sees. In the revelation she still categorizes people as "trash" or "niggers" and believes that the people like herself "had always had a little of everything and the God-given wit to use it right." When the vision fades, Mrs. Turpin "remained where she was, immobile" (190). An argument can be made that her immobility is symbolic as well as literal. Furthermore, the vision comes as the sun sets, and when she does begin to move, she moves "on the darkening path" (191).

2. O'Connor demonstrates the terrible illogic of bigotry when she has Ruby Turpin "naming the classes of people" as she goes to bed. Mrs. Turpin makes the mistake of having more than one basis operating at the same time—both wealth and heredity (including race). "Trash" and "most colored people" are at the bottom of her system. People who own only their homes are next, then "home-and-land owners" including herself and Claud, and finally "people with a lot of money and much bigger houses and much more land" (24). Because of her flawed system, she struggles with overlapping categories— trying to place people "who had good blood" but "had lost their money" and "colored people" like the rich dentist who owns a farm, "two red Lincolns and a swimming pool" (24). She further muddles her classifying when she stereotypes rich people as unrighteous in order to rationalize her position in a category below the top. She thinks, "If Jesus had said, 'You can be high society and have all the money you want and be thin and svelte-like, but you can't be a good woman with it," she would have had to say, "Well don't make me that then'" (73). O'Connor's harsh assessment of bigots is clear: After struggling to classify people into her categories, Ruby Turpin would fall asleep with "the classes of people . . . moiling and roiling around in her head, and she would dream they were all crammed in together in a box car,

being ridden off to be put in a gas oven" (24)—a clear reference to Hitler's treatment of Jews.

Mrs. Turpin's classifying of pigs reflects her classifying of people. She believes that her pigs are not the "Nasty stinking things, a-gruntin and a-rootin all over the place" (43) that the "white-trash woman" detests because they are in a "pig parlor" (44) which she and Claud hose down periodically. She believes her pigs are superior—just as she believes she is superior.

3. Students should see that all three women are bigots—of differing degrees—but they may debate who is the worst. No doubt the pleasant lady is better than the other two, for her only offensive remark is to patronizingly say, "Oh, I couldn't do without my good colored friends" (58). She also exchanges a look with Mrs. Turpin, which Mrs. Turpin may or may not interpret correctly as an indication that "they both understood that you had to *have* certain things before you could *know* certain things" (52). Review with your students the use of characters as foils, and have them draw parallels between Mrs. Turpin and the white-trash woman. Encourage them to discuss whether bigotry in a pleasant guise is any better than open, unabashed bigotry.

THEMATIC CONNECTIONS

"What's in a Name?" (p. 5): Comparing "Revelation" and "'What's in a Name?'" will allow students to see that Ruby Turpin is not alone in her bigoted thinking. Gates's boyhood town operated on a classification system very much like Mrs. Turpin's—one based on race and money. Although his father's two jobs and their "financial security" put the Gates family in a special category, they were treated with "an odd mixture of resentment and respect" for not fitting neatly with other blacks. Mr. Wilson's calling Mr. Gates "George" was an insistence on categorizing him with other blacks.

Just Walk On By (p. 197): Staples's "first victim" was applying a classification not unlike Ruby Turpin's when she assumed that his black skin, "beard and billowing hair," and "bulky military jacket" identified him as a thug ready to attack her. Although Staples acknowledges the existence of some black thugs, he feels alienated by having the stereotype universally applied. No doubt students can infer from Staples's reaction how diminished African Americans feel because of this stereotyping done by people like Ruby Turpin. Because you may have some unconscious bigots in your classes, identifying the stereotypes is valuable.

The Untouchable (p. 461): Student Ajoy Mahtab's essay focuses on the Indian caste system and particularly on the members of the lowest caste, the untouchables. Students can consider whether this system of hierarchical classification is any more logical than Mrs. Turpin's. They might also think about parallels between the Indian untouchables and the "poor white trash" as viewed by Mrs. Turpin. Is any group in our society characterized as "untouchable"?

11: DEFINITION

Because definition encompasses all the patterns of arrangement, this chapter presents a good opportunity for review. A logical beginning model for your discussion is Mary Morris's paragraph defining a traveler, since it compactly illustrates a combination of techniques. As you read the essays in this chapter, you can show your students that these definition techniques and others can structure not only paragraphs but also sections of longer pieces and even whole essays, poems, or stories. You should also emphasize that any essay can include examples of several rhetorical patterns studied throughout the text. This might also be a good time to look back at earlier essays in which a definition is central—*work* in "My Mother Never Worked" and *sexist language* in "Sexism in English: Embodiment and Language," for instance.

John Kenneth Galbraith, *Burdens*

Galbraith's is a highly ironic use of definition; make sure students realize that the definition Galbraith offers is not one he agrees with. He defines the word *burden* specifically as it is used in the sense of "a burden imposed by government on the citizen" (1). (He doesn't say so directly, but his obvious reference is to taxes and to how tax dollars are distributed.) His point is that the term is used very selectively in this context. Expenditures for defense, for bailing out failed savings and loans, for Social Security, for farm supports, for Medicare, and for congressional health benefits are not seen as burdens, but expenditures for welfare programs, food stamps, Medicaid, and aid to inner-city schools are so defined. Galbraith's caustic conclusion is that government expenditures are not considered burdens when they benefit the rich, only when they benefit the poor. If there is a mix of political viewpoints in your classroom, this essay may spark some lively debate; some students will probably disagree strongly with Galbraith's implications about the role of government.

COMPREHENSION (p. 467)

1. Galbraith offers his formal definition in his final sentence. He does so as a way of clinching his implied argument.
2. By *good* he means language that is thoughtful and direct; *accepted,* however, implies that the language may be logically incorrect but widespread. The distinction is important because he wants to make the point that he disagrees with the accepted definition of *burden.*
3. Government spending to bail out the "costly financial misadventure" of the failed savings and loans—because it benefited well-off people—is not a burden.
4. See the introductory discussion above.
5. Education is a "special case" because it both *is* a burden (public education in inner-city schools) and is *not* a burden (private education, for which may are seeking tax relief).
6. Galbraith implies that funding for the arts and public broadcasting is a burden because these are seen as liberal interests.

PURPOSE AND AUDIENCE (p. 468)

1. The original title makes clear that Galbraith sees those who use *burden* in the way he describes as using language dishonestly, as serving their own interests at the expense of the poor. Students who disagree with him may see the title as overly provocative. (You might note the fact that the one source for title— "White man speaks with forked tongue"—suggests the kind of hypocritical exploitation Galbraith is criticizing. A "forked tongue" is also associated with snakes and poetically with Satan, as the serpent in the Garden of Eden.)
2. Galbraith's purpose is to criticize social priorities; he criticizes the use of the word *burden* in order to accomplish this larger goal. His primary targets are

those politicians and commentators—and average citizens—who seek budget cuts affecting the poor but who benefit from other government subsidies.

STYLE AND STRUCTURE (p. 468)

1. Galbraith defines by enumeration throughout. He defines by negation in paragraphs 2–3 and briefly in paragraph 5. The strategy is effective because his point ultimately is to suggest the hypocrisy of the selective use of the word *burden*; thus, what it is *not* becomes especially important.
2. Discussing the origin of *burden* would not strengthen Galbraith's definition in this context because he is focusing on its use in the present. He might have included some synonyms early on and then provided an analogy to strengthen the contrast between what is a burden and what is not.
3. Galbraith is clearly disheartened, but his tone is more caustic and ironic than angry.
4. Students will find sarcasm in virtually every paragraph. Their responses to the sarcasm may vary based on their own political beliefs.
5. Answers will vary here. In a longer essay, such additions might be instructive, but they would detract from Galbraith's pithiness.
6. Similar language occurs in paragraphs 6 and 7. Galbraith holds such rule makers—conservative politicians and their supporters—in disdain.

VOCABULARY PROJECTS (p. 468)

2. The dictionary defines *burden* as "something that is carried," a "load, duty, responsibility." Galbraith's purpose is not to define the word literally but rather as it is used in current political discourse.

COMBINING THE PATTERNS (p. 469)

Galbraith relies primarily on exemplification, providing examples of burdens and non-burdens. He might have recounted the events leading up to the savings-and-loan bailout or to the current situation in which "no wholly plausible enemy" (2) can justify defense spending, but we don't see that such narrative additions would improve his argument. Telling the story of a family losing welfare benefits might be effective, but it would not really be in keeping with his tone.

THEMATIC CONNECTIONS

The Human Cost of an Illiterate Society (p. 203): Jonathan Kozol is similarly concerned with the plight of society's disadvantaged and with the lack of concern on the part of those in power. His tone, however, is quite different from Galbraith's. Students might consider which approach they find more persuasive.

The Ways We Lie (p. 426): Students might explore what kind of lie (or lies) Galbraith would consider for the selective use of the word *burden*. Do they see it as deflecting, groupthink, or simply an out-and-out lie?

On Dumpster Diving (p. 632): Lars Eighner's experiences suggest a different aspect of poverty—homelessness—but Eighner does not seem representative of the poor in the United States. To what extent do students think that someone like Eighner— intelligent, able-bodied, and capable of work but apparently not quite able to adapt to conventional workplaces—deserves government aid? They might even do some research about the kind of aid a person like Eighner would be eligible for.

A Modest Proposal (p. 648): The specific situation is quite different, but Jonathan Swift's classic essay is also an ironic attack on attitudes and policies toward the poor. Although far less outrageous than Swift, Galbraith is writing in much the same vein.

José Antonio Burciaga, *Tortillas*

This lighthearted look at a staple of Mexican cuisine is an especially good example of definition. Not only is it interesting and immediately accessible, but it also shows the combination of rhetorical techniques that can go into making an extended definition: narration (1, 3), cause and effect (2), process (4), exemplification (5, 7–8), description (6), and comparison (6). You might begin discussion by asking what students remember first when they think of tortillas as described by Burciaga; then have them decide why the technique used to make that point is particularly effective.

COMPREHENSION (p. 472)

1. A tortilla is a flat, round corn cake that is fried or steamed.
2. Tortillas may be filled with a variety of fillings and rolled into tacos. They may be filled with cheese and grilled *(quesadillas)*. They may be deep-fried *(flautas* or *gorditas)*. More whimsically, they can be used as a mask or hat, as an artist's canvas, or even as the basis for a miraculous vision.
3. Burciaga is not entirely serious here, yet he does mean to suggest the fundamental role tortillas play in Mexican culture.
4. For Burciaga tortillas are a representation of his childhood and of his cultural heritage.

PURPOSE AND AUDIENCE (p. 472)

1. The thesis might be paraphrased as "Although we take tortillas for granted, they are in fact a special part of Mexico's cultural heritage." Burciaga doesn't state his thesis sooner because he wants to lead us to this understanding in his conclusion.
2. Students may have different opinions about Burciaga's intended audience. He certainly assumes that his audience is already familiar with tortillas because he spends very little time describing them, but this doesn't necessarily mean that he expects readers to be of Mexican descent. Given the level of detail and the tone, it would seem that Burciaga is writing for a general audience that includes both Chicanos and non-Chicanos.
3. Burciaga is trying in a lighthearted, humorous way to "elevate" the tortilla in his readers' minds, to show how versatile, even meaningful, it is. If he tried to be more serious, he would probably be less convincing because he might seem to be overstating his case.

STYLE AND STRUCTURE (p. 472)

1. The brief formal definition comes in paragraph 6. It is clear that Burciaga assumes an audience that already knows what a tortilla is and so does not feel

the need to provide an introductory definition. The definition in paragraph 6 serves to highlight the versatility of tortillas.

2. Burciaga doesn't define three Spanish words in paragraph 4: *mercado* (market), *masa* (the cornmeal dough from which tortillas are made), and *deliciosas* (delicious). He clearly assumes that readers will be familiar with these words or that their meanings will be clear in context. Note that he also doesn't define the Yiddish word *yarmulke* (skullcap) in paragraph 1.

3. Burciaga doesn't use synonyms, although he uses a helpful analogy at the beginning of paragraph 3; and he doesn't discuss the word's origin, although he traces its appearance in Mayan mythology. Neither does he use negation as part of his definition, probably because little would be gained by doing so.

VOCABULARY PROJECTS (p. 472)

2. See question 2 under Style and Structure. *Jalapeños* are hot green peppers used in much Mexican and southwestern cooking.

COMBINING THE PATTERNS (p. 473)

See the introduction to this entry for a survey of the rhetorical patterns Burciaga uses.

THEMATIC CONNECTIONS

Once More to the Lake (p. 154): Both Burciaga and E. B. White invoke childhood memories that represent their cultural heritage and that suggest deeply satisfying and meaningful rituals. In both cases the past seems to permeate the present, creating a warm feeling of nostalgia. Students might consider the differences in tone between the two essays.

Does America Still Exist? (p. 482): Richard Rodriguez's essay focuses on the broad issues of ethnic identity and assimilation within the United States. Burciaga's observations about his and his family's relationship to tortillas is a fairly lighthearted example of Rodriguez's more serious point about the inevitability of assimilation, even as some sense of ethnic heritage is maintained. The increasing popularity of tortillas and Mexican food generally also illustrate Rodriguez's point about the ways cultures in the United States meld.

The Park (p. 636): Student Michael Huu Truong's essay is also a reminiscence of childhood that focuses on culture and assimilation. Note that except for Bruce Lee, the heroes the two boys (one Vietnamese, the other Korean) imagine themselves to be are all American icons: Abbott and Costello, Superman, Clint Eastwood, the Bionic Man. Does assimilation mean losing one's heritage, or can assimilation result in something "truly bicultural," like Burciaga's children putting peanut butter and jelly on tortillas?

Judy Brady, *I Want a Wife*

This essay comments satirically on the demands placed on wives and mothers. You might begin by asking your students whether Brady overstates her case.

COMPREHENSION (p. 476)

1. She means a devoted "servant." This ideal wife exists in the pages of some women's magazines and in the minds of some men and women.
2. Some specific duties include washing clothes, cleaning, cooking, babysitting, and typing. The five categories are child care, household chores, cooking, managing social life, and providing for sexual needs.
3. She feels she must do the jobs of both husband and wife.
4. She might leave if she found a more suitable wife. In that case, her first wife would take care of the children.

PURPOSE AND AUDIENCE (p. 476)

1. It exaggerates the role of wife and mother to ridicule it. Most feminists would agree—perhaps in varying degrees—with her thesis. Students may not see this essay as likely to appear in any publication today.
2. The thesis, which is implied, is that too much is expected of wives.
3. No. She is merely using this to make her point.

STYLE AND STRUCTURE (p. 476)

1. This repetition reinforces her thesis and introduces a list of new reasons why she wants a wife.
2. No. In fact, the length of the paragraphs draws attention to the statements being made.
3. Students can find a number of verbs that are repeated, and they should be able to determine how they affect the tone of the essay.
4. She omits the pronouns because she means to suggest that her wife—or any wife—could just as easily be male as female.
5. These words help to convey the tone. There is to be no question that the wife described will be capable of easily and willingly performing all the tasks listed.

VOCABULARY PROJECTS (p. 477)

2. Students will readily see that many of these words are used sarcastically.

COMBINING THE PATTERNS (p. 477)

Brady uses exemplification and description as the major patterns in her definition—and contrasts between images of wives and husbands are implied. The implied contrasts might in fact be seen as the most important for Brady's purposes.

THEMATIC CONNECTIONS

My Mother Never Worked (p. 94): Even Brady's exhausting job description for a wife falls short of the work performed by Martha Smith. Students can discuss the extent to which a woman's life has improved since 1921, when Martha Smith became a wife, or make the necessary additions to turn Brady's essay into "I Want a Farm Wife."

Sex, Lies, and Conversation (p. 367): See *Thematic Connections*, "Sex, Lies, and Conversation," p. 90 of this manual. Deborah Tannen's essay provides a good opportunity to think about male-female stereotypes—and what actually governs gender roles.

The Men We Carry in Our Minds (p. 399): Scott Russell Sanders provides a different view of the roles of husbands and wives, focusing on the laboring classes. Here, he asserts, the lives of men are bound by everyday "toil" of factories and mines; as a child, he saw the lives of women as far easier than the lives of men. As a young adult, he adjusted his view to recognize that the division is not so much between men and women as between the "bosses"—traditionally, professional-class males much like the husband Brady describes— and those who serve them, either as wives or as paid "toilers." The women he met at college have the same "grievances" against men that Brady implies.

The Company Man (p. 476): Ellen Goodman paints a portrait of marital relationships and family life that provides an interesting companion piece to Brady's essay. The company man of the title literally works himself to death, devoting his entire life to his career while neglecting his wife and family. If your students think about the flip side of Brady's thesis ("I want a husband"), they might consider the extent to which Phil in Goodman's essay represents the kinds of sacrifices many husbands make.

Ellen Goodman, *The Company Man*

In her essay, Goodman uses a number of short examples to form a single extended definition. She suggests her thesis and then focuses on different aspects of Phil's life to support it. The result is a devastating portrait of a man who worked himself to death. Students should understand that Goodman is not trying to portray a specific individual. Phil is a corporate "everyman" who represents all people who give themselves to their jobs. Some students might miss the irony that Goodman uses throughout her presentation. For this reason, several of the questions in Style and Structure focus students' attention on this feature of the essay.

COMPREHENSION (p. 479)

1. The company man devotes all of his time, and literally his "life," to his job. A one-sentence definition fails to convey the tragedy Goodman reveals through her extended definition.
2. She means that working as he has been, he has actually been gone from the family for a long time.
3. He feels he never really knew his father and wants to get to know him now.
4. She's afraid her bitterness might show.
5. The president will seek someone just like Phil.

PURPOSE AND AUDIENCE (p. 480)

1. Goodman makes the point that Phil's compulsion cost him his happiness, his family, and ultimately his life. In a larger sense she suggests that people who live like Phil hurt not only themselves but also those who love and care for them.
2. Goodman assumes that her readers can identify in part with Phil. Her detached, unsentimental tone and her irony are designed to make her readers question their priorities.

3. To state her thesis directly could alienate her readers. By focusing on Phil and supplying her readers with details about his life, Goodman overcomes their skepticism and leads them to accept her point of view.

STYLE AND STRUCTURE (p. 480)

1. Goodman wants to assume the detached tone of a report or case study for her essay. The times at the beginning and end of her essay help her achieve this end.
2. The character Goodman creates is supposed to be representative of all workaholics. Therefore, before giving him a name she presents some general characteristics that all workaholics possess.
3. The dialogue adds an ironic dimension to the story and tells readers how Phil's family and employer feel about him. When a company friend says to Phil's widow that he knows she will miss her husband, she laconically replies, "I already have" (7). Phil's son makes the comment that both he and his father only board at home, and after the funeral, Phil's boss asks, "Who's been working the hardest?" (16). These comments indicate that Phil has sacrificed the love of his family for a job that another person can fill by 5:00, the afternoon of the funeral.
4. Goodman's tone is ironic and detached. She wants her readers to look at Phil without emotion. She is not trying to create a character for whom her audience will feel sympathy. Her tone enables her to keep her distance from Phil and to illustrate to her audience that Phil has foolishly wasted his life.
5. The quotation marks make the comments seem realistic and also draw attention to their irony.

VOCABULARY PROJECTS (p. 480)

2. Various substitutions are possible, but students should see that the more formal diction makes the tone less conversational and perhaps less ironic.

COMBINING THE PATTERNS (p. 481)

Narration is an effective choice because it allows Goodman to trace Phil's almost neurotic devotion to work—and his distance from family and friends. Goodman also uses exemplification and description.

THEMATIC CONNECTIONS

Midnight (p. 177): Student Grace Ku writes about the sacrifices her immigrant parents make to provide for their family's well-being. Working long hours in menial, physically demanding jobs—the only employment available because of their limited education and lack of English skills—the Kus provide an interesting contrast to Goodman's Phil: their "devotion" to work grows out of necessity, not choice. But students may also think about similarities between the two families. For example, in both cases family life suffers because of the demands of the workplace.

The Peter Principle (p. 181): See *Thematic Connections,* "The Peter Principle," p. 41 of this manual.

Suicide Note (p. 315): Janice Mirikitani's poem takes the form of a suicide note from a young Asian-American college student to her parents. It is an apology that reveals the intense pressure she feels to excel in order to meet her family's expectations. Students can relate the pressures they feel in college, and perhaps in their jobs as well, to those experienced by the author of the suicide note—and also by Phil. If Phil had been able to write a similar note to his family before his death, what might he have said?

Richard Rodriguez, *Does America Still Exist?*

This is by far the most complex essay in this chapter, and initially students may have trouble seeing exactly what it is that Rodriguez is trying to define. In fact, Rodriguez proposes a re-definition of the concept of "America" and what it means to be an "American." His definition occupies a place between what he offers as two extremes: the strictly assmilationist America, in which those whose skin is other than white or who speak with an accent are expected to adapt to the dominant European culture (and even then are accepted with a degree of suspicion); and the strictly ethnic culturalist America, in which "minority groups" cling to ethnic heritage and claim to reject assimilation (the friend Rodriguez describes in paragraph 12 is an example of this kind of American). For Rodriguez, both of these definitions are essentially false myths. In the real world where people live and interact, America embodies both assimilationist elements and a plethora of ethnic cultures. Admittedly, immigrants do assimilate while holding on to certain traditions. We may feel most comfortable with those most like ourselves, but we are nonetheless part of a larger society that influences us (and that we influence). Ultimately, for Rodriguez, it is America's celebration of the individual that allows us to tolerate difference within an essentially cohesive society.

COMPREHENSION (p. 485)

1. The young Rodriguez cannot call himself an American because the question "Where you from?" assumes he isn't an American because of his darker skin.
2. He's playing with the idea of terms such as *Mexican-American*. "[T]ipped to the right" means having moved closer to the American side of the hyphen.
3. The sorrow is for having left something behind in "the old country," for having lost a measure of one's traditions as each generation grows farther away.
4. Rodriguez would answer that, yes, America does still exist, but only in the sense that it is constantly evolving as each new wave of immigration and each renewed assertion of ethnic identity is incorporated into the fabric of society. Of course, America still exists, but it does not conform to some outdated paradigm of "white" culture.
5. For Rodriguez, assimilation is ultimately benign because it is never complete. As immigrants assimilate, the country changes to accommodate their special traditions.

PURPOSE AND AUDIENCE (p. 485)

1. Rodriguez is writing for a broad, though fairly sophisticated, audience. Rather than assuming agreement or disagreement, he tries to refocus the question for his audience in a new light.

2. References to his personal experience allow readers to see something of Rodriguez's own process of assimilation. They allow a greater understanding of the sources of his ideas.
3. See the introduction to this essay on p. 114 for a discussion of Rodriguez's thesis.

STYLE AND STRUCTURE (p. 486)

1. Examples of exemplification include paragraphs 9, 14–15, 19, and 21; of narration, paragraphs 4 and 15; of comparison and contrast, paragraphs 9, 11, 17–18, and 20. Rodriguez also uses description and much of his development throughout is based on cause and effect.
2. Students may feel Rodriguez could have clarified that his opening sentence answers the question posed in his title, perhaps by repeating the title as his first sentence.
3. Students should realize that Rodriguez is not writing a conventional definition in the "What America means to me" mold, wherein enumeration and negation would be more expected. Nevertheless, they may suggest that these more conventional tools of definition might be helpful to their understanding. You might have students themselves enumerate a list of those things Rodriguez would consider "American" or compose a paragraph exploring, what, according to Rodriguez, America is not.
4. In part, this brief final paragraph refers back to the notion of an "appropriate hymn" in the preceding paragraph. The image of the "white girl . . . rehearsing . . . a Motown obbligato" suggests the very blend that Rodriguez sees America to be. The paragraph might be developed further to indicate other ethnic influences, although for us it has a kind of sweetness that ends the essay effectively.

VOCABULARY PROJECTS (p. 486)

2. Rodriguez uses the words *America* and *American* mostly for their positive connotations. Only in his opening paragraph does he suggest that, to the immigrant child, the voice of the American crowd may seem "menacing."

COMBINING THE PATTERNS (p. 487)

The United States was founded on "Protestant individualism," while Mexico was shaped by "a medieval Catholic dream of one world." The Spaniards went to Mexico to plunder, not to settle, but they wound up mating with the native peoples and forming a "new race, . . . the *mestizo*." Other instances of comparison and contrast include paragraphs 9 (rural vs. urban America), 17–18 (early vs. later images of black people), and 20 (small town vs. city).

THEMATIC CONNECTIONS

More Than Just a Shrine: Paying Homage to the Ghosts of Ellis Island (p. 142): In her essay about immigrants from Europe early in the twentieth century, Mary Gordon touches on many of the same issues as Rodriguez does, in particular the idea that immigrants suffer from exclusion in an "America born Protestant and bred Puritan," but that assimilation occurs nonetheless. An interesting area of research for students would be the process immigrants today undergo before they are allowed to enter the U.S. (Some of your students, of course, may have first-hand knowledge of this process.) How is it different from the rather brutal and dehumanizing process Gordon describes taking place on Ellis Island?

The "Black Table" Is Still There (p. 294): Rodriguez notes in paragraph 13 and elsewhere in his essay that in our "era of ethnic pride" many Americans feel they can identify much more closely with a particular ethnic or racial group than with American society more generally. Lawrence Otis Graham's description of his high school's lunch room having a black table, an Italian table, a Jewish girls' table, a Jewish boys' table, a table of middle-class Irish kids, and so forth is a graphic representation of such ethnic identification. Students might consider this kind of self-segregation in light of Rodriguez's point that "Americans are wedded by proximity to a common culture." Do they agree that this is the case?

Two Ways of Belonging in America (p. 357): Bharati Mukherjee and her sister Mira provide contrasting examples of two immigrants: one who embraces assimilation (Mukherjee), and one who resists it (her sister). How might Mira respond to Rodriguez's assertion that the process of assimilation is "inevitable"? What difference does it make that she has chosen not to become an American citizen?

Mother Tongue (p. 405): Amy Tan focuses on an issue that Rodriguez doesn't deal with directly but that goes to the heart of the debate over assimilation: an immigrant's command of the English language. Elsewhere, Rodriguez has written about this subject in detail. Interested students might be directed to his *Hunger of Memory: The Education of Richard Rodriguez* and particularly to the essay "Aria: A Memoir of a Bilingual Childhood," where the relationship with his parents provides an interesting parallel to Tan's relationship with her mother, particularly in terms of language.

Marge Piercy, *The Secretary Chant*

Students should enjoy the outrageous imagery in Piercy's brief poem. One way to begin discussion would be to ask what is Piercy's intended point. Is that point as relevant today as it was in 1973 when the poem was first published? In particular, ask students to consider the significance of the final four lines. Why might Piercy have chosen to spell *once* as *wonce*? Is the effect of all her exaggeration more comic than serious? Do students sense any hint of anger?

THINKING ABOUT LITERATURE (p. 489)

1. A one-sentence definition would run along the lines of "A secretary is a thing, a tool, just one more office supply, not human at all."
2. The primary pattern of development is (ironic) description, with a suggestion of cause and effect in the conclusion.
3. The speaker is a clearly imaginary secretary. Piercy might have developed her definition in the voice of a more realistic secretary, perhaps maintaining elements of exaggeration as Judy Brady does in "I Want a Wife," or might have written in the third person. Students may disagree about to whether an alternative perspective would be more effective. However, the unusual imagery is part of the poem's appeal for most readers, and using a more realistic approach would eliminate this.

THEMATIC CONNECTIONS

Finishing School **(p. 88):** Like the secretary in Piercy's poem, blacks in the American South throughout much of history were dehumanized by their white employers (and, earlier, by their owners). Maya Angelou describes just such a situation from her childhood when she worked for a wealthy white woman who refused to address her by her rightful name because it was "too long." Unlike Piercy's beleaguered secretary, however, Angelou gets her sweet revenge.

The Untouchable **(p. 461):** Student writer Ajoy Mahtab, in his chapter introduction essay, defines the lowest members of India's caste system, "people who were not considered even human." This is dehumanization taken to its furthest extreme. Students might consider whether the kind of dehumanization Piercy suggests is at all comparable to that described by Mahtab or by Angelou.

I Want a Wife **(p. 474):** Written at roughly the same time as "The Secretary Chant," Judy Brady's essay also uses exaggeration to make a point about exploitation and gender roles. Using this essay as a model and Piercy's poem for inspiration, students might write their own piece titled "I Want a Secretary."

12: ARGUMENTATION

Argumentation is a difficult rhetorical form for students to understand. In the chapter introduction we take pains to describe it and relate it to the other types of writing we have discussed. Although our primary emphasis is the appeal to reason, we recognize the emotional dimension that most good arguments possess. At the risk of oversimplifying the issue, however, we do not discuss in any depth the other appeals acceptable for persuasive writing. We choose to focus on argumentation because it is the principal form of persuasion used in college and because many beginning student writers confuse appeals to emotion with the feeling that "because I feel it is right, it must be."

Our suggestion is that you spend a good deal of time emphasizing the rhetoric of argumentation. You can illustrate to students that a good argument usually relies on a number of patterns of development. In order to convince an audience, they should use all of the rhetorical tools at their disposal.

Another point you will want to make is that argumentative essays are flexible and develop out of a writer's concept of audience and purpose. Many students are all too willing to apply simple formulas to their writing and fail to appreciate how good writers adjust their material to a particular audience. The paragraph taken from Ruth Hubbard's "Test-Tube Babies: Solution or Problem?" provides an excellent beginning example of a writer who has a clear sense of audience. She begins by carefully acknowledging the chief argument of her opposition—that in vitro fertilization can enable some women to bear children who would otherwise be unable—before she makes her own argument against this biotechnology. Because many infertile women desperately feel a need to bear a child, Hubbard recognizes that she must acknowledge their argument at once rather than wait until the end of her own argument as she might otherwise have done.

Carefully illustrate for students how writers support their assertions. You can, for example, ask students to point out the information Thomas Jefferson uses to support his points. You can also ask students to judge the quality and effectiveness of the deductive argument he presents. Of course, other essays included in the unit can be examined for their uses of evidence. Pointing out inadequate evidence can also be an effective way to teach students. Some of the questions at the ends of selections will help your students make such judgments.

One of the more exciting and challenging aspects of argumentation is refutation, which requires students to develop a dynamic and subtle sense of audience. Earlier in the semester students were concerned with presenting information to an audience, but now they not only have to evaluate an audience, they also must anticipate and react to its probable responses to a subject. We suggest you begin your "Letter from Birmingham Jail." You will want to explore King's excellent uses of induction and deduction and then to consider his care in refuting his opposition. If students use a highlighter to mark each time King addresses his opponents' view, they will see that these refutations organize King's tightly logical argument.

To further sharpen students' awareness of the need to identify audience and refute arguments, we have grouped essays into four widely debated subject areas. In the first grouping, Camille Paglia and Susan Jacoby take opposite sides on the question of who bears responsibility in cases of date rape. The second grouping offers contrasting views from Rebecca Lee Parker and Dena S. Davis on the subject of special ethnic housing for college students. This is followed by a casebook in which writers debate issues of media violence: Does violence depicted in movies, on television, and in video games lead viewers to act violently? Should moviemakers bear responsibility for "copycat" crimes that seem related to their movies? How far should the law go in censoring violence in the entertainment media? A second casebook follows and focuses on the Internet; here, five writers consider issues such as whether the Internet brings people together or isolates individuals, and how the Internet affects the quality of students' research and learning. In these two casebooks, students are presented with multiple sides of each issue. As a result, they can more clearly see refutations at work. Before asking students to write a full argumentative essay, have them write a short essay in which they refute a specific argument. This assignment will help them build up to more demanding argumentation assignments.

The section on deductive and inductive reasoning is intended as an introduction to logic. Our purpose is to give an overview of the basic principles of logic and to provide a list of the problems in reasoning that plague many student writers. You can use this section as the subject for a class discussion, or you can refer students to it as the need arises. For more information on reasoning and logic we suggest you consult *With Good Reason: An Introduction to Informal Fallacies* by S. Morris Engel (St. Martin's Press).

Thomas Jefferson, *The Declaration of Independence*

The Declaration of Independence stands as a classic model of deductive argument. It begins with a major premise, progresses to a minor premise, and draws a logical conclusion. Often, students approach this document with a closed mind and see it as a musty, boring piece of history that has nothing to do with them. Many students have never read it and are surprised to see how clear and exciting it really is. You might point out to them how genuinely revolutionary it was and how it shocked the world when it first appeared. Once students realize this fact, they can have great fun analyzing the rhetorical strategy that Jefferson and the other writers employed. Especially interesting in this regard are the many grievances that the document lists. Not only do they make for an interesting class discussion, but they also show the lengths to which the writers felt they had to go to establish the reasonableness of their case.

COMPREHENSION (p. 519)

1. Paragraph 2 enumerates that self-evident truths that Jefferson asserts: "that all men are created equal, that they are endowed by their Creator with certain unalienable rights, that among these are life, liberty, and the pursuit of happiness. That to secure these rights, governments are instituted among men, deriving their just powers from the consent of the governed. That whenever any form of government becomes destructive of these ends, it is the right of the people to alter or abolish it, and to institute a new government, laying its foundation on such principles and organizing its powers in such form, as to them shall seem most likely to effect their safety and happiness."
2. Governments derive "their just powers from the consent of the governed" (2).
3. Paragraphs 3 through 31 list the reasons that justify the break with Great Britain.
4. Jefferson concludes that the British crown no longer deserves allegiance because it no longer protects the rights of the governed.

PURPOSE AND AUDIENCE (p. 519)

1. The major premise of Jefferson's argument is that all men are created equal. He could not have done more to establish that premise in this essay and still have accomplished his purpose.
2. Jefferson structures the Declaration like a formal argument in logic. In paragraph 2, he states the general premises upon which he bases his argument. In paragraphs 3 through 31, he states specific justifications for the actions of the colonies. Finally, in paragraph 32, he sums up his argument and states his conclusions.
3. Jefferson realized that he would have to address several very distinct audiences. The Declaration announced to Great Britain that the colonies no longer owed allegiance to the crown; to other European countries that the colonies were free states that would trade, wage war, and make alliances independent of Great Britain; and to the colonists themselves that some of their number were ready to fight for independence. Jefferson surely knew that some people would never accept his conclusions no matter how well reasoned they were—as evidenced by the strong and continued support of the king by many of the colonists.
4. In paragraphs 2, 30, and 31, Jefferson effectively anticipates the opposition and presents convincing evidence that all reasonable approaches have been attempted.
5. Jefferson speaks of his "British brethren" to emphasize the cultural bonds that connected the colonies with England. By doing this, he hopes to gain empathy from his audience. In part, this was also an effort to defuse the violent reaction that Jefferson expected from the British.
6. Jefferson states his thesis, so to speak, in the final paragraph. Because its claim is so decisively revolutionary, it is necessary that he present all pertinent evidence before stating it directly.

STYLE AND STRUCTURE (p. 520)

1. Jefferson primarily uses deductive reasoning. The Declaration of Independence resembles a syllogism. It begins with a major premise, progresses to a minor premise, and ends with a conclusion. Jefferson argues that his major premise is "self-evident." However, when he provides evidence that his minor premise is sound (3–29), he reasons inductively.

2. In addition to the syllogistic structure discussed above, Jefferson uses the language of formal logic to create transitions between sections. He introduces his premises by saying, "We hold these truths to be self-evident." He then prefaces the list of grievances by saying, "To prove this, let facts be submitted to a candid world" (2). Finally, he beings his conclusion by saying, "We, therefore, the Representatives of the United States of America" (32).

3. Jefferson includes all twenty-eight grievances to establish the reasonableness of the colonists' position. Summarizing them or stating only a few of them would materially weaken the Declaration, since anyone not already inclined to agree with the colonists would suspect they are being unfair to the king and his government.

4. Jefferson concludes with "We, therefore" to emphasize the deductive structure of the document and the reasonableness of his argument. He has effectively built to this conclusion with the long list of evidence that precedes it.

VOCABULARY PROJECTS (p. 520)

2. Your students will find numerous examples of words with negative connotations, including *abuses, usurpations, despotism, injuries, forbidden, invasions, obstructed, plundered, ravaged,* and *burnt.* These words portray the actions of the king in a strongly negative light, justifying the Declaration of Independence. Had Jefferson used more neutral words, the case against the king would not have seemed so strong nor the action of the colonists so justified.

3. Jefferson's text includes a number of words that may be unfamiliar to students: *usurpations, evinces, prudence, sufferance, tyrant, dissolutions, quartering, perfidy,* and *magnanimity.* Whether students prefer their updated versions will depend to some extent on their sophistication as writers. Certainly, they are bound to sound less formal and incantatory.

COMBINING THE PATTERNS (p. 521)

History suggests that Jefferson's examples are relevant, representative, sufficient, and effective. Implicit in the examples is a pattern of cause and effect (the effects of British policies on the colonists); students might consider whether making this pattern more explicit would add to the argument.

THEMATIC CONNECTIONS

The "Black Table" Is Still There (p. 294): Pairing the Declaration of Independence with Lawrence Otis Graham's essay about self-segregation in a suburban junior high school provides an opportunity to consider the extent to which the values embodied in the Declaration have been achieved in contemporary U.S. life. Is it possible for groups to be separate but equal?

Grant and Lee: A Study in Contrasts (p. 340): Consulting both the Declaration and Bruce Catton's essay, students should determine how the Confederate cause differed from Jefferson's cause. Both involved throwing off a government that participants deemed to be unjust.

Does America Still Exist? (p. 482): Richard Rodriguez's essay suggests a view of the United States today as a culture of diversity in which different groups still share a common sense of "Americanness." To what extent do historical documents such as "The Declaration of Independence" contribute to providing Americans with a common culture?

Letter from Birmingham Jail (p. 513): This country, founded on a belief that "all men are created equal," failed to extend that equality to blacks. Although slavery was discussed by the Founding Fathers, political differences led them to essentially ignore the problem. Students may not know that Jefferson himself was a slaveholder. Ask your students to read the Declaration of Independence a second time. As they reread the list of abuses the colonists believed justified their actions, ask them to keep in mind the injustices that Martin Luther King talks about. Many of Jefferson's complaints have parallels in slavery and, later, in segregation. Ask students to reread King's "Letter from Birmingham Jail" as well. Because of its length and complexity, they will need a second reading. As they reread, have them mark King's explicit and implicit references to Jefferson, the Declaration of Independence, and the Constitution. Doing so will help them appreciate and understand King's arguments and gain a stronger sense of their country's history.

Martin Luther King Jr., *Letter from Birmingham Jail*

King's letter is an excellent illustration of a complex argument. Many critics have pointed out the similarities between it and the Declaration of Independence. Both documents attack injustice and take pains to establish the reasonableness of their positions. Like Jefferson, King realizes that the specific audience he is addressing (the king and Parliament in Jefferson's case) is not the only audience to whom he must appeal. He is aware that people all over the world are watching the events in which he is involved. His carefully crafted argument aligns him with the three men to whom he feels as spiritual heir: Jefferson, Thoreau, and Gandhi. Many students will not be familiar with these men or the fact that they all sought to influence public opinion by acts of civil disobedience. A short summary of their lives and causes will enable students to perceive some of the subtleties of King's argument. This essay offers a good opportunity to introduce the term *allusion* and to show students how King makes conscious reference to the Declaration of Independence, the Bible, and "Civil Disobedience."

COMPREHENSION (p. 535)

1. King says he decided to answer criticism because he feels that his fellow clergymen are men of good will and that their criticisms were sincerely set forth (1).
2. Since the demonstrations occurred after an election in Birmingham, the clergymen think that King and his associates have not allowed the new administration enough time to act.
3. King says that "Birmingham is probably the most thoroughly segregated city in the United States" (6) and mentions brutality, unfair courts, and bombings. Because the city fathers "consistently refused to engage in good-faith negoti-

ation" (6) and because promises made by white merchants were broken (7), King says, "We had no alternative except to prepare for direct action" (8).

4. For African Americans, *wait* usually means never, as King observes in paragraph 13.

5. King defines two types of laws, *just* and *unjust*: "A just law is a man-made code that squares with the moral law or the law of God. An unjust law is a code that is out of harmony with the moral law" (16).

6. King says that condemning nonviolent protests because they precipitate violence is "like condemning a robbed man because his possession of money precipitated the evil act of robbery" (25). He goes on to say that "as the federal courts have consistently affirmed, it is wrong to urge an individual to cease his efforts to gain his basic constitutional rights because the quest may precipitate violence."

7. King is disappointed that the white churches did not support him. Some, he says, have been outright opponents.

PURPOSE AND AUDIENCE (p. 535)

1. King's purpose is to reach and inspire white clergymen in the South to support his cause. By establishing his setting as the Birmingham city jail, he hopes to make his audience sympathetic and to demonstrate his commitment to his cause. By defining his audience as "fellow clergymen," King can address them as "men of genuine good will," an assumption that is basic to his argument.

2. Throughout his letter, King scolds his fellow clergymen for being insensitive to the moral rightness of his cause. He does this in paragraphs 5, 12, 13, 15, 23, 24, 25, 26, 27, 32, 33, 34, 35, and 36. Although King says he believes his audience comprises men of good will, it is clear from his didactic tone throughout these passages that he has his doubts about their altruism.

3. King is aware that his letter will be picked up by the press and read by a wide general audience. His detailed description of the situation in Birmingham (already familiar to the clergymen) is one indication of this fact.

4. King's implied thesis is that men of good will should support the demonstrations in Birmingham by the Southern Christian Leadership Conference.

STYLE AND STRUCTURE (p. 535)

1. In the first paragraph, King says that since his audience of clergymen are men of good will, he will try to answer their statements patiently and reasonably.

2. King addresses the possible objections of his audience in paragraphs 5, 12, 15, 25, and 27.

3. King makes the transition from one section of his argument to another with rhetorical questions and statements that directly address his audience. For instance, when moving from his introduction (4) to his definition of the problem (5), he says, "You deplore the demonstrations taking place in Birmingham." When turning from the end of his definition of the problem (9) to a discussion of direct action (10), he says, "You may well ask, 'Why direct action?'" After this section ends with paragraph 14, King introduces his discussion of just and unjust laws with the statement, "You express a great deal of anxiety over our willingness to break laws" (15).

4. King is seeking support from all of the United States' major religions; therefore, he carefully reinforces his arguments with references to Jewish, Catholic, and Protestant philosophers. Also, he wants to establish that his conclusions are basic to Western philosophical thought.
5. King uses appeals to authority to indicate that his argument is supported by the writings and teachings of famous philosophers and theologians.
6. King's explanation of why he came to Birmingham is an example of inductive reasoning. His examination of just and unjust laws is an example of deductive reasoning.
7. King tries to reestablish a harmonious relationship with his audience by first asking their forgiveness if he has overstated the truth (46). He then reasserts his common bond with the other clergymen and ends with a remark that asserts his optimism about the future (47). Students are likely to find King's strategy successful.

VOCABULARY PROJECTS (p. 536)

2. Allusions to the Bible appear in paragraphs 3, 21, 25, 26, and 31. These allusions refer to events or teachings in scripture that support King's position of justice, equality, and love.
3. King is alluding to the phrase "my cup runneth over" in Psalm 23. With this allusion, King reinforces the point that he, too, is walking "through the valley of the shadow of death" and, because of his faith, "will fear no evil." Thus King effectively uses a biblical reference to express his impatience.

COMBINING THE PATTERNS (p. 536)

Passages of narration include paragraphs 7–9, 14, 32, and 35–36. Each of these narratives shows how King and his African-American followers have been disappointed by the policies of the white power elite.

THEMATIC CONNECTIONS

Finishing School (p. 88): The childhood incident described by Maya Angelou dramatically suggests the institutionalized bias and personal degradation faced daily by black people in the segregated South prior to the civil rights movement.

The "Black Table" Is Still There (p. 294): In writing about self-segregation in a suburban junior high school, Lawrence Otis Graham suggests the extent to which racial polarities continue to exist some thirty-five years after the height of the civil rights movement, when King's letter was written. You might ask students to consider how King would view the current state of race relations in the United States if he were alive today. Would he feel that most of his goals have been achieved? Or would he be disappointed at how little progress has been made?

Two Ways to Belong in America (p. 357) Bharati Mukherjee's essay focuses on the discrimination sometimes suffered by immigrants to the United States. Anti-immigrant sentiment has in the past been almost as virulent as racism, and in recent years there have been attempts by several states—and by the federal government—to limit the rights of immigrants who are not citizens. One issue students might consider is why the "silenced" immigrants Mukherjee describes in paragraph 12 are so much less likely to protest their condition than are African Americans.

Burdens **(p. 466):** John Kenneth Galbraith criticizes current government spending policies, which he sees as discriminating against the poor in the United States. Students might compare Galbraith's biting irony to King's reasonable, measured argument. Which approach do they think is more effective in changing an audience's mind?

DEBATE: Is Date Rape Really Rape?

You might begin by asking your students what they know about date rape and where they first heard the term. Does your institution have support groups for women or gender relation workshops for male and female students? Was the issue discussed in their high school health classes or counseling centers? You might ask older students specifically when they first encountered the concept. Was the issue given much attention ten or twenty years ago?

You might also note that arguments over the issue of date rape—or acquaintance rape—often revolve around a definition of the term and of what constitutes consent and coercion. Can your students pose a hypothetical situation that they all agree would constitute date rape? If not, what accounts for their differing opinions?

In the first argument, outspoken social critic Camille Paglia focuses on biology: "the sexes are at war," she says, men are natural sexual aggressors, and women must be "prudent and cautious" or "accept the consequences." In the essay that follows, Susan Jacoby takes the opposite position: "neither the character of men nor the general quality of relations between the sexes is that crude."

Camille Paglia, *It's a Jungle Out There*

Comprehension (p. 542)

1. According to Paglia, feminism misleads women by presenting "pie-in-the-sky fantasies about a perfect world" (5) where "the sexes are the same" and women "can do anything, go anywhere, say anything, wear anything." On the contrary, says Paglia, "Women will always be in sexual danger" (4).
2. The prevalence of date rape is due to the fact that "hunt, pursuit, and capture are biologically programmed into male sexuality" (10), and young men in particular will naturally be led by their raging hormones.
3. According to Paglia, women must understand that rape is instinctive in males, not some aberrant behavior.
4. Men and women misunderstand each other about sex because "sexual desire and arousal cannot be fully translated into verbal terms" (13).
5. Paglia's solution is for women to take "personal responsibility" (15) for their sexuality, to achieve "self-awareness and self-control" (19). If they are truly raped, they should go to the police. If they make a mistake, they must accept the consequences.

PURPOSE AND AUDIENCE (p. 542)

1. Paglia writes to a relatively hostile audience whom she is deliberately trying to shock or perhaps offend. Her purpose seems to be to jolt this audience into awareness with a strong dose of reality. How successful this strategy proves to be is open to debate.

2. Paglia's audience is primarily women.
3. Paglia is trying to change both ideas and behavior. She attempts to get young women influenced by feminism to see male and female sexuality in a different light and to act accordingly as a way of protecting themselves from sexual danger.

STYLE AND STRUCTURE (p. 542)

1. Paglia's sarcastic and dismissive characterization of opponents is evidenced by words like *consent as explicit as a legal contract* (2), *pie-in-the-sky-fantasies* (5), *fog of social constructionism, dumb French language theory, leaving sex to the feminists is like letting your dog vacation at the taxidermist's* (6), and *dopey, immature, self-pitying women* (16).
2. Whether Paglia's attacks on feminists strengthen or undercut her argument depends on the reader's stance toward feminism. It's certainly the case that some readers who might find Paglia's arguments worth considering will reject them because of her tone.
3. Paglia's argument is primarily deductive, based on her major premise that men are naturally sexual aggressors, although it is not easily stated as a syllogism.
4. The only argument that Paglia refutes is the "feminist" position that "sexes are the same" (4). This could be viewed as a straw man. Paglia basically dismisses opposing arguments as not worth her attention, a strategy that can be effective, depending on the reader.
5. Paglia concludes her essay by presenting "the only solution to date rape" (19). To many her solution—"female self-awareness and self-control"—will seem insensitive. By putting all the responsibility on women, she seems to be absolving men of all blame. Certainly the conclusion agrees in tone with the rest of the essay. But its glib generalizations and its tendency to blame the victims will alienate many readers who might otherwise be sympathetic to Paglia's arguments.

VOCABULARY PROJECTS (p. 542)

2. Some colloquialisms include *hung out to dry* (3), *stupid enough* (5), *Testosterone Flats* (8), *swear like sailors* (11), and *take-charge attitude* (16). These contribute to the feisty, scrappy tone of her essay, which many would see as one of its strengths.

COMBINING THE PATTERNS (p. 543)

The extended example of the film *Where the Boys Are* helps Paglia develop her point that courtship is "a dangerous game in which the signals are not verbal but subliminal." Students may think that further examples from real life might have helped her make the point more effectively.

THEMATIC CONNECTIONS

Just Walk On By (p. 197): Paglia bases her argument on some pretty drastic stereotypes of male behavior. How do such images contribute to the fearfulness exhibited by Staples's "victims," especially the women? How serious is most women's fear of rape by a stranger? Note that Staples says one of the things that goes into the making of a thug is "the male romance with the power to intimidate," with the image of men as having to "seize the fighter's edge in work and in play and even in love," an image that he calls "nonsense." How might Staples respond to Paglia's views?

Sexism in English: Embodiment and Language **(p. 413):** Alleen Pace Nilsen's essay categorizes language that implicitly objectifies women or suggests they are subordinate to men. Nilsen suggests that becoming more aware of this linguistic prejudice and, as far as possible, using language that is nonsexist will have the effect of changing attitudes about women as well. How do students think Paglia might respond to Nilsen's observation that "nothing about the sexes has really changed"?

I Want a Wife **(p. 474):** How do Judy Brady's images of *husband* and *wife* fit into Paglia's description of the sexes being at war? Does Paglia's vision of *male* and *female* logically lead to the unequal distribution of power described by Brady? How would you expect Paglia to define the ideal relationship between a man and woman?

Susan Jacoby, *Common Decency*

COMPREHENSION (p. 547)

1. To excuse men because "they are too dumb to understand when 'no' means no" (3) is to insult male intelligence in the most basic way. Jacoby, of course, is not entirely serious because it is clear that she believes excusing "friendly social rapists" is highly insulting to women.
2. According to Jacoby, most date rapes occur not because "a man mistakes a woman's 'no' for a 'yes' or a 'maybe'" but because "a minority of men . . . can't take "'no' for an answer" (7).
3. The unsupervised college environment plays a large role: "drinking and partying" tend to "promote sexual aggression and discourage inhibition" (9).
4. It is absurd to think that young men who participate in a gang rape actually believe that the woman—no matter how much she may have flirted with one of them—wanted to have sex with the whole group.
5. Jacoby means that prior to the women's movement a woman who was forced into having sex after saying "no" to a man she had been making out with would never have considered claiming rape. She would have had no legal recourse and probably would have garnered little sympathy from authorities or even friends.

PURPOSE AND AUDIENCE (p. 547)

1. Jacoby assumes a mixed audience. She suggests appropriate behaviors for both men and women.
2. Jacoby opens with a particularly pertinent anecdote from her own youth. If this does not exactly establish her credentials to write about date rape, it certainly strengthens her argument by example and elicits reader sympathy for her case.
3. Unlike Paglia, Jacoby seems to have a neutral audience in mind or one that has given little thought to date rape. It is also possible that she wishes to reach

an audience that has recently been exposed to the arguments of Paglia and other "apologists for date rape," since she sets out specifically to refute their views.

STYLE AND STRUCTURE (p. 547)

1. See number 2 under Purpose and Audience
2. Paragraph 4 is a reasonable summation of Paglia's argument, which is augmented by quotations in paragraph 10. Paragraph 11 quotes Paglia in another context, probably to cast doubt on the reasonableness of the previously quoted assertions. Most readers will probably find Jacoby's refutation in paragraphs 5–6 fairly effective, and the refutation in paragraphs 12–14 is equally strong. Note, however, that Jacoby doesn't respond to Paglia's assertion that women should avoid situations where an unwanted sexual advance would occur.
3. In paragraph 15 she also refutes the argument in defense of a group of young men who would have group sex with a drunken girl.
4. Jacoby uses what might be called the evidence of common sense, of everyday experience. Look around, she says; if Paglia is right, then "few women would manage to get through life without being raped, and few men would fail to commit rape" (5). This is obviously not the case.
5. Jacoby's conclusion is a brief but clear summary of her argument. Introducing the idea of "social control" is perhaps a bit distracting, but her final sentence is certainly striking.

VOCABULARY PROJECTS (p. 547)

2. *Common decency* refers to modes of social behavior that we as a society recognize as appropriate and fair. Its connotations are so positively ingrained in our culture that they are almost neutral.
3. Because many such rapes occur at parties or on other occasions unrelated to dating as a couple, *acquaintance rape* is often the more accurate term.

COMBINING THE PATTERNS (p. 548)

Jacoby is describing the difference between a woman being in control and a woman not being in control during a physical encounter with a man. Students will have varying responses regarding whether narrative examples would help make the point clearer.

THEMATIC CONNECTIONS

Thirty-Eight Who Saw Murder Didn't Call the Police (p. 99): The incident Martin Gansberg describes is certainly an instance of a man exercising control—the ultimate control—over a woman. Is this, as Jacoby says, an example of "minority behavior" (8), or is it sadly an event that is repeated all too often? Students should be made aware that some psychologists say it is no coincidence that the rise of feminism has been accompanied by an increase in violence against women. Does this fact undercut Jacoby's observation in paragraph 19 that "neither the character of men nor the general quality of relations between the sexes is that crude"?

The Lottery (p. 255): Shirley Jackson's story presents a barbaric custom that survives in a modern community. As civilized readers we find what the towns-people do appalling. Camille Paglia suggests that a similar carryover of barbaric behavior into civilized life—"male anarchy and brutishness"—is inevitable. Are we equally appalled? Who is closer to the truth—Paglia or Jacoby?

Sex, Lies, and Conversation (p. 367): Deborah Tannen writes about how different conversational styles based on gender result in miscommunication between men and women. Do her observations support the claims of either Jacoby or Paglia? Do students think a man could innocently misread a woman's signals and really not know that she didn't want to have sex? Or do they agree with Jacoby, who writes in paragraph 14 that "even the most callow youth is capable of understanding" when his advances are threatening?

DEBATE: Should We Live Together or Apart?

You will probably want to begin discussion of these two readings by asking students to talk about any special housing available on your campus, including ethnic dorms, honors dorms, international housing, even sororities and fraternities. You will also want students to consider organizations on campus that appeal to particular ethnic, religious, or other groups (and, of course, if your campus has no special housing, you will need to focus on such campus organizations). As the introduction to the debate suggests, you might also encourage students to think about the kind of self-segregation Lawrence Otis Graham writes about in "The 'Black Table' Is Still There" in Chapter 8.

Another question you might raise is how much access does one who is not a member of a particular group have to housing or other organizations catering to that group. That is, for example, could a white student choose to live in a black dorm?

Discussion of race is notoriously difficult for many Americans, so your students may be a bit reticent. If so, use this fact to prod your students' critical thinking about the issue. If we did more to assure that we "live together," as the title of this debate suggests, might this provoke the sort of open discussion that could lead to greater mutual understanding?

Rebecca Lee Parker, *Why Special Housing for Ethnic Students Makes Sense*

COMPREHENSION (p. 555)

1. Parker chose to attend a predominantly white school because she felt doing so would help prepare her to "live in a world where whites were in the majority." She wished she had been given more information about how isolated she would feel in such a setting, particularly in terms of not having a black "home" to return to, as she had had when she attended her predominantly white high school.
2. The culture shock she felt resulted from finding so few minority students on campus and the realization that "fitting in was no longer just a daytime endeavor."
3. She flourished on the special floor for African-American women because it allowed her to learn about black life in urban and rural environments and to

discuss in detail with "this new support group of neighbors" ideas about black history and culture.

4. Parker suggests that such housing offers students "environments for education and intellectual growth" and "cultural-comfort zones." Students benefit by becoming acclimated more quickly to their school's resources, by meeting people more easily, and by receiving more attention from faculty and staff associated with these facilities: "Their intellectual growth and social development are accelerated." She concedes no disadvantages.

5. Eliminating special housing for ethnic students, according to Parker, would make it more difficult for schools to recruit and retain such students.

PURPOSE AND AUDIENCE (p. 555)

1. Parker seems to consider her audience a bit more hostile than neutral, although able to be addressed reasonably. Implicitly, she is writing to white administrators who might question special housing for ethnic students. In all probability, she argues against such housing arrangements because she assumes her audience believes in some of them.

2. It is clear that she is writing to educators when in paragraph 20, for example, she says "We can choose, of course, to eliminate these opportunities from our campuses." She is a campus administrator herself.

3. She states her thesis in paragraph 10, after leading up to it by describing her own experience and research.

STYLE AND STRUCTURE (p. 554)

1. She doesn't directly address the argument that requiring students of all races and ethnic backgrounds to live together can promote greater respect and understanding among diverse communities. This doesn't necessarily hurt her argument unless a reader holds such an opinion strongly.

2. It's not really clear whether Parker is referring here only to her own research, mentioned in paragraphs 9 and 10, or to a broader body of research. If this information is not based on more than her own research, then her argument is weakened.

3. Students answers will vary here. Although some of Parker's generalities may seem a bit broad, none seem so sweeping or unfounded to negate her central point.

4. A student's response to this element of Parker's argument will likely determine his or her response to her argument as a whole. The analogy of ethnic housing to other special-interest housing is absolutely key to Parker's point.

5. She calls it illogical that ethnic students should be responsible for integrating dorms when the other challenges they face on predominantly white campuses haven't been addressed. As she notes, many of our neighborhoods remain ethnically and racially segregated, so why should college housing be artificially integrated by some sort of quota?

6. Again, student responses will vary. In fact, she could have dropped the tag question, and begun her concluding sentence with a phrase like "after all." Have students compare such a revised ending and Parker's original. The intended effect of the question is to elicit a "yes" from her readers.

2. The word is used in a context similar to that in "special needs" or "special rights"—that is, to suggest that a small group, potentially the subject of discrimination, benefits. For critics, the word *special* in this context implies negative connotations.

COMBINING THE PATTERNS (p. 556)

The main point of comparison in these paragraphs is Parker's experience in a predominantly white high school, when she still had the support of her family at home, and her experience at college, when "fitting in was no longer just a daytime endeavor." The comparison establishes how important it was for her to be able to have housing on campus to return to each day, where she felt the same kind of support she received at home.

THEMATIC CONNECTIONS

Finishing School (p. 88): Maya Angleou's story of experiencing a particularly demeaning form of racism in her childhood reflects the history of discrimination that often leads minority students to feel uncomfortable on predominantly white campuses—even though such overt racism is far less prevalent today than fifty years ago. Why does the legacy of racial injustice continue to exert such a strong hold on the attitudes of many African Americans?

The "Black Table" Is Still There (p. 334): Lawrence Otis Graham's essay addresses issues of self-segregation from a more ambiguous viewpoint. See the introduction to this debate in both the text and in this manual.

The Big Move (p. 334): Student Margaret Depner describes the challenges she faced in her encounter with a different culture when she lived and attended school in England for a year. Although difficult for her in some ways, the adjustment she describes was far easier than the adjustment Parker describes to life at her predominantly white college. What might account for these differences?

Two Ways to Belong in America (p. 357): Bharati Mukherjee's sister, as the writer describes her, seems to be an example of someone who regards her ethnic culture as paramount to her identity. Mukherjee herself takes a more assimilationist stance. These two perspectives suggest the fundamental underpinnings to the debate over special housing for ethnic or international students that Parker describes.

Dena S. Davis, *College Housing Policies Should Avoid Ethnic and Religious Balkanization*

COMPREHENSION (p. 561)

1. The Orthodox students' main complaints revolved around issues of sexual permissiveness. Davis mentions in particular their concern that even sexually segregated dormitories at Yale are not restricted sexually and that "safe sex" information and condoms are widely available on campus.
2. Davis says that Yale has no legal obligation to accommodate the students because their policies are neutral and apply to all students. They are not intended to "harass" students of a particular religion. The two Supreme Court

decision Davis cites, *Employment Division of Oregon v. Smith* and *City of Boerne v. Flores,* both hold that one has no right to exemption to "neutral laws of general applicability."

3. Davis offers only one argument in support of Yale's position that voluntarily allowed the students to remain but to live off-campus: their presence in classes and so forth would allow other Yale students to have at least some access to a culture strikingly different from their own.

4. Davis's main argument for Yale's position, in addition to the legal one, is that Yale has a right to set its own policies, such as its requirement that students live on-campus and thus benefit from this part of the Yale experience. Students who object to these policies have other options and thus should attend more congenial schools or accept Yale's rules.

5. When Davis refers to Yale resisting "ethnic and religious balkanization," she means that Yale should be discouraging students from self-segregating into ethnic and religious enclaves.

6. Davis mentions only a few accommodations that Yale makes for Orthodox Jewish students: making kosher food available and providing non-electric locks on dorm room doors so that such students need not violate Sabbath strictures. Students might suggest that the school could go further and create housing governed by stricter rules regarding the mixing of the sexes; students other than Orthodox Jews might be interested in such housing as well.

PURPOSE AND AUDIENCE (p. 561)

1. She doesn't seem to assume that readers are particularly familiar with the case. She provides enough background information that unfamiliar readers— as most of your students probably are—will understand the issues clearly.

2. Davis does present the Orthodox students' side of the case, in an apparent attempt suggest her fair-mindedness. Students may, however, detect a sense of bias in her treatment of these students.

3. Davis seems a bit dismissive of these students' concerns and not particularly sympathetic to their demands. Saying that she hopes her son will get to know students like these at college seems to be more than a rhetorical strategy, but it's hard to know how seriously to take this assertion.

STYLE AND STRUCTURE (p. 561)

1. The two questions raised in paragraph 2 focus, first, on the legal issue and, second, on the ethical: Does Yale have a legal obligation to accommodate these students, and, if not, should Yale do so anyway "for reasons of good pedagogy or religious toleration"? Another possible issue is whether Yale should try to find ways to accommodate these students to keep them on-campus.

2. She describes two separate Supreme Court rulings that support Yale's right to enforce policies that are neutral from a religious perspective. No further evidence is necessary to address the legal issue—as opposed to the ethical issue.

3. Her argument favoring Yale's accommodating the students is presented only in the context of how Yale might benefit. She doesn't really present the sort of opposing arguments the students' themselves might make—that they have a right to attend Yale without having their religious beliefs compromised. Hers is not exactly a straw man, but neither is it a truly opposing argument.

4. This argument is primarily deductive, based on the general principle that Yale, like any other school, has a right to establish and enforce its own policies. Opinions will vary as to how convincing this argument is.

5. Again, opinions will vary. There is no evidence that other students would demand such exemptions should Yale give in to these Orthodox students, but it is certainly within the realm of possibility.

VOCABULARY PROJECTS (p. 562)

2. Such transitions are found in paragraphs 3 (*First*) and 5 (*nonetheless*) to introduce her answers to the two questions she poses in paragraph 2. Similarly, in paragraph 7 (*but, first*) and 8 (*second*), transitions set up her two main arguments. Students will probably find these helpful.

COMBINING THE PATTERNS (p. 562)

The examples here help lead into Davis's opposing view that Yale's rights outweigh the benefits of having such students on campus.

THEMATIC CONNECTIONS

Just Walk On By (p. 197): Brent Staples describes how his mere presence as a black man can often provoke mistrust, concern, even fear in white strangers. Davis would probably argue that greater integration, in the college experience and elsewhere, would lead to a diminishing of the kind of stereotyping Staples writes about. How legitimate do students find this sort of argument?

Suicide Note (p. 315): Based on a true incident, Janice Mirikatani's poem is written in the voice of an Asian-American girl who suffers, in part, from the pressures she feels in her academic environment. Might a more supportive environment, such as Parker describes and Davis seems to find less important, have made a difference for this young woman? Students might want to consider what more colleges in general—or their particular school—could be doing to lessen the pressures of college life.

The Untouchable (p. 461): This student essay describes the strict class divisions of Indian society, focusing particularly on the lowest caste, which is literally seen as unclean and virtually shunned by everyone else. Here, the idea of difference is taken to its absolute extreme. What lessons can be learned from such a rigidly structured society to help understand and better deal with divisions in our own?

Does America Still Exist? (p. 482): Like Bharati Mukherjee's essay, this piece by Richard Rodriguez speaks to ideas of cultural "balkanization" vs. assimilation. Would Rodriguez be more likely to support Parker's view or Davis's? Or would he perhaps fall somewhere in the middle?

DEBATE CASEBOOK: Does Media Violence Cause Societal Violence?

This casebook presents four different perspectives on the issue of violence in the media and the possible effects of such violence on society. You might begin by asking students how they respond to media violence. Do they enjoy violent movies, television shows, and video games? What are some particular examples that have been especially popular? How do they account for this popularity? Do they see different levels or kinds of violence—that is, are some depictions of violence more graphic than others? More believable? More gruesome? What especially memorable images of movie or television, or video violence can they recall?

Then you might ask specifically about Oliver Stone's *Natural Born Killers,* the subject of the first two essays in the casebook. Encourage students who have seen the film to describe the plot and the level of violence depicted. (You might also consider screening some of the film for your class—it's available on video—but you will probably want to do so fairly selectively. Or you might suggest that students who are interested rent the film to view for themselves.)

Finally, ask students to talk about whether their experiences suggest a link between violence in the media and violence in life. Do they have friends or family members who have been influenced directly by media images? Have they ever noticed young children act out in ways that could reflect their television viewing? Have they read any news reports or other stories that suggest such linkages?

The four essays that follow are summarized in the text's introduction to the casebook, p. 564.

John Grisham, *Unnatural Killers*

COMPREHENSION (p. 574)

1. Grisham describes both Sarah and Ben as having a history of drug abuse and psychiatric treatment. Both had dropped out of school. Neither had a history of violence. They were "confused, disturbed, shiftless, mindless" (56). Apparently, both the thrill of killing depicted in the movie and the "demonic theme" (47) running through it influenced them to murder.
2. He believes the movie industry should share the responsibility.
3. Grisham suggests that Stone defends the movie as a "satire on our culture's appetite for violence and the media's craving for it" (58). Grisham counters that the movie is not a satire because there is no humor in it; it is designed "to shock us and further numb us" to violence.
4. Hollywood has consistently pointed to the guarantee of free speech and artistic freedom and has never taken any responsibility for the effects of film violence.
5. Grisham proposes boycotts of such films—which he concedes are unlikely to work—and lawsuits based on the claim that such films are products that result in injuries.

PURPOSE AND AUDIENCE (p. 574)

1. Grisham has a double thesis: that *Natural Born Killers* influenced the couple to murder (70) and that the only way to stop such films from being made is to slap Hollywood with major lawsuits (71). For readers who might not agree, Grisham builds his case carefully before stating his thesis.
2. Grisham wants to change attitudes toward movie violence and convince people that lawsuits are an appropriate means of decreasing such violence.
3. Grisham's natural tone and his sarcasm regarding Oliver Stone suggest he expects his readers to be sympathetic.

STYLE AND STRUCTURE (p. 574)

1. Grisham's appeal is basically to the emotions—creating sympathy for the victims, painting Hollywood as unconcerned, and so forth. But he also tries to draw a logical connection between Ben's and Sarah's crimes and *Natural Born Killers.*

2. His main argument is that Sarah and Ben, troubled as they were, had no history of violence and so would not have killed except that they were influenced by *Natural Born Killers.* He also argues that because movies are products, their makers should be held responsible for any damage they cause.

3. Grisham doesn't explicitly refute the arguments against his thesis, although he summarizes them in paragraphs 60 and 64. He seems to feel that the story of Sarah and Ben—along with his readers' common sense—is refutation enough. You might ask students if they think that stronger refutation is needed.

4. Grisham clearly has no respect for Stone. Although his attacks are not quite *ad hominem,* the words he puts in Stone's mouth in paragraph 60 verge on *ad hominem.*

5. Most students will find the conclusion effective, leaving as it does an image of the sad fates of the victims of this "wretched film." Another possible ending would be to take a final swipe at Oliver Stone.

VOCABULARY PROJECTS (p. 574)

2. If you want your students to focus on a short passage, paragraphs 57–60 provide a number of obvious examples of such loaded language. Students may differ about whether such overtly judgmental language is appropriate.

COMBINING THE PATTERNS (p. 574)

The narrative helps Grisham establish the connections between Sarah and Ben's viewing of *Natural Born Killers* and their eventual violent behavior. (Grisham similarly narrates the plot of the movie in order to establish the connections even more clearly.) He might have spent time explicitly describing the victims, the crime scenes, and so forth, but doing so would not have served his purpose as well as the narrative does.

THEMATIC CONNECTIONS

Just Walk On By (p. 197): Paragraphs 8–9 of Brent Staples's essay focus on "the making of a young thug" and the "male romance with the power to intimidate." To what extent do Ben—and Mickey in the movie—exhibit these tendencies? Do Staples's remarks in any way undercut Grisham's argument?

Samuel (p. 202): Grace Paley's short story offers a younger version of youthful recklessness culminating in tragic consequences.

It's Just Too Late (p. 212): Calvin Trillin writes about a troubled young woman who is very similar to Sarah Edmondson and who also comes to an unhappy end when she falls in with the wrong crowd. Students might consider whether Trillin makes FaNee Cooper more sympathetic than Grisham makes Sarah, and, if so, why.

It's a Jungle Out There (p. 538): According to Camille Paglia, "aggression and eroticism are deeply entwined" and "men must be persuaded away from their tendency toward anarchy and brutishness." How do thoughts such as these apply to the relationship between Sarah and Ben? Would Paglia suggest that theirs is a *natural* relationship?

Oliver Stone, *Memo to John Grisham: What's Next?—"A Movie Made Me Do It?"*

COMPREHENSION (p. 578)

1. He means that artists have historically reflected the concerns of human beings during the times in which they live. He sees *Natural Born Killers* as a reflection of the world in which we live today.
2. The participants in a witch hunt go after innocent victims, claiming that they are the cause of some evil in the world. Students may consider whether Stone goes too far here.
3. Stone suggests Grisham's *post hoc* reasoning in paragraphs 4–6, stating that many factors other than his film are responsible for the violent behavior of Sarah and Ben.
4. He says the film can move some audience members toward "a heightened sensitivity toward violence" (5). He also says that watching "15,000 hours of mostly violent television programming" (6) is more likely to have an effect than watching a single movie.
5. Stone's other causes include alcohol and the availability of firearms. He talks earlier about how damaged families can produce violent children. Students' opinions will differ as to the persuasiveness of Stone's reasoning.

PURPOSE AND AUDIENCE (p. 579)

1. Stone doesn't believe that movie violence is responsible for real-life violence. His scathing tone indicates he assumes that his audience will agree.
2. Students may differ about Stone's attitude toward his audience. He seems fairly dismissive of those who would disagree with him.
3. Stone's essay is a direct response to Grisham's, and his purpose is to prove Grisham wrong.
4. Stone's argument does not seem likely to win many converts. He concedes virtually nothing to the opposition and is openly hostile toward Grisham—and those who might agree with him.

STYLE AND STRUCTURE (p. 579)

1. Such an exaggerated claim always risks alienating some readers.
2. Stone refutes Grisham's major points in paragraphs 3–6. Students may or may not see his refutations as successful.
3. Actually, Stone only pretends to concede points to his opposition here. He admits his movie had an impact on audiences, but not the one his critics claim.
4. Stone's loaded language is not likely to appeal to those who strongly support the Second Amendment. He may not exactly be overstating his case by referring to "gun-toting crazies," but he is tarring with a broad brush.

5. Stone doesn't so much restate his position in the conclusion as make a strongly worded plea for artistic freedom. The attack on lawyers here isn't *ad hominem,* but one in paragraph 7 is ("only a lawyer in search of a client"). And in paragraph 8 he refers to Grisham's novels as "brainless"—a sterling example of *ad hominem* argument.

VOCABULARY PROJECTS (p. 579)

2. Stone's feelings come through especially strongly in paragraphs 2, 5, 8, and 9. Students might find his tone somewhat arrogant. Is Stone unwilling to see beyond his own feelings?

COMBINING THE PATTERNS (p. 580)

Cause-and-effect analysis is found in paragraphs 3, 5, 6, and 9. Cause and effect supports Stone's thesis by suggesting causes other than *Natural Born Killers* for the crimes committed by Sarah and Ben and by claiming that "silencing artists" will lead to a "human hell" (9).

THEMATIC CONNECTIONS

Thirty-Eight Who Saw Murder Didn't Call the Police **(p. 99):** In a sense, Martin Gansberg writes of a less violent time, more than thirty years ago, when none of Kitty Genovese's neighbors did anything to help as she was being brutally murdered outside on the street. Are we more or less callous toward violence today? In a more violent society, are people more or less likely to intercede when they encounter a crime in progress?

Who Killed Benny Paret? **(p. 279):** Norman Cousins suggests that boxing is violent because those who watch want it that way. Is the same true of movies and television?

Burdens **(p. 466):** The link here is less one of subject matter than of tone and intent. Both Stone and John Kenneth Galbraith use biting sarcasm to lambaste what they see as self-righteous, self-serving, and wrong-headed propaganda. Students might analyze both essays to consider how effective such a style of argumentation can be.

Michael Zimecki, *Violent Films Cry "Fire"* *in Crowded Theaters*

COMPREHENSION (p. 584)

1. The courts have held that freedom of expression outweighs the cost to society of receiving such "odious" images.
2. He means that there is a link between what goes on in life and what goes on in movies. He then points out several examples of movie-inspired violence: a boy who was killed attempting to duplicate a scene in the movie *The Program,* and a group of boys who raped a nine-year-old girl with a bottle after seeing a similar rape in a television film.
3. As products, movies are meant to be seen, so their producers can't be held responsible just because audiences go to see them. The concept of incitement is legally limited to speech that results—or could result—in immediate action;

action that takes place outside a theater after a movie is over is too far removed in time to be considered incited action.

4. Certain films glorify violence—and thus "advocate violence implicitly, if not explicitly" (18). This, for Zimecki, is tantamount to incitement.
5. He means that the courts have not recognized the effects of violence that "can fester for years" (20) and that they have not recognized the cause-and-effect relationship between media violence and real-life violence.

PURPOSE AND AUDIENCE (p. 585)

1. Zimecki states his thesis at the end of paragraph 22. One reason he waits so long is that he needs to introduce, clarify, and refine the concept of incitement.
2. The essay is aimed primarily at lawyers, as the many legal citations suggest. But Zimecki seems to be writing to his audience more as general readers, concerned about media violence, than as experts concerned with the fine points of the law.
3. His purpose is to contribute to the debate over how to curb violence in the media by redefining the concept of incitement so that it can apply to movies and television programs.

STYLE AND STRUCTURE (p. 585)

1. The quotation sets up the cause-and-effect relationship between images and actions that is the basis for his argument. He might have opened by dramatically recounting the torching of the New York City subway clerk, but this strategy would have been less appropriate for an audience of lawyers.
2. For a more general publication, Zimecki would need to get rid of—or simply summarize—most of the legal citations, revise his more specialized language, and explain more graphically why the courts should see that violent media images incite real-life violence.
3. This concession does seem to undercut his case, although he suggests that the relationship between the movie and the crime may still be established. But, particularly in writing for a legal publication, he has to admit contrary evidence.
4. His primary evidence is the examples in paragraphs 8–10, which suggest a direct link between depictions of violence in the media and violence in real life.
5. Students may differ over whether the concluding cliché is effective. Another possible conclusion would be to return to the idea of shouting "fire" in a crowded theater.

VOCABULARY PROJECTS (p. 585)

2. *Incitement* means "the act of spurring others to action." In legal parlance, it generally refers to "spurring others to violent action or action that will result in 'imminent harm'" but not to "abstract" action at some unspecified time in the future.

COMBINING THE PATTERNS (p. 586)

The analogy of shouting "fire" in a crowded theater has been legally established as an act of incitement. Zimecki wants to suggest that movies incite violent action in much the same way. He uses cause and effect elsewhere, so it is not necessary here.

THEMATIC CONNECTIONS

Thirty-Eight Who Saw Murder Didn't Call the Police (p. 99): See *Thematic Connections*, "Memo to John Grisham: What's Next?—'A Movie Made Me Do It?'" p. 136 of this manual.

It's Just Too Late (p. 304): Zimecki suggests that violence is now "so prevalent in our society" because of violent media images. Might media images have contributed in any way to the fate of FaNee Cooper, as Calvin Trillin describes her?

How the Lawyers Stole Winter (p. 362): Christopher Daly decries the fact that the threat of lawsuits has put even the simple pleasure of ice skating on public property off-limits in many communities. Oliver Stone's essay also suggests that lawyers like John Grisham and Michael Zimecki, who wish to "stifle artistic expression," pose a threat to personal freedom. Do students agree that threats of such lawsuits are ultimately not to society's benefit?

Steve Bauman, *Games as a Scapegoat*

COMPREHENSION (p. 589)

1. The media tend to go for easy answers that will fit into a quick soundbite. Video games, because of their often violent nature, offer one such easy scapegoat for the sources of violent behavior.
2. The lawsuit was filed because the parents believed that media influence had turned their son into a murderer.
3. He suggests that social ostracization might have been a contributing cause, but then says that there is no simple answer.
4. He feels that the roots of such an incident are too complex to ever be understood fully. Many influences, he feels, are at work.
5. Blaming any outside influences removes the notion of personal responsibility—and parental responsibility—from consideration, In addition, blaming media violence could lead to all entertainment being predetermined based on "what will not trigger abhorrent behavior in an individual."

PURPOSE AND AUDIENCE (p. 589)

1. Bauman is fairly sarcastic when he talks about the media latching onto video games as a scapegoat. In dealing the the issue of violence and its sources, though, he's more neutral, even sympathetic to the need to find answers.
2. Students may suggest that Bauman has two separate theses here. The first, that there is no easy answer to explain such shootings, he states in paragraph 8. The second, that the video industry needs to think more carefully about the potential influence of violent video games, he states in his final paragraph. Waiting until late in his essay to state these directly allows him lay the groundwork for his points.
3. Bauman writes to game enthusiasts and industry insiders and he assumes that they will agree that violent video games don't in themselves cause violent behavior. He does, however, make a point less acceptable to his audience—that they may in some way contribute to such violence.
4. Student opinion will vary. His credentials obviously suggest that he is a proponent of video games.

STYLE AND STRUCTURE (p. 589)

1. In these paragraphs, Bauman makes his point that media "experts" were much too glib in their assertions of a direct causal connection between violent video games and real-life violence. He also lays the groundwork for his secondary thesis when he refers to watching a tape of "glassy-eyed" arcade players as "chilling," because their use of plastic guns in playing games may amount to a kind of target practice.
2. Student opinion will vary, but most will probably agree video games, by themselves, are not a final answer to the question.
3. He doesn't directly address arguments against his thesis, but he creates a strategy within his own argument in such a way as to suggest that blaming video games for acts of real-life violence is so simplistic as to require no refutation.
4. Student opinion will vary. His main evidence consists of the television sound-bites he reports having observed.
5. Students should note that Bauman's conclusion represents a shift in strategy and in purpose. They may find it somewhat tacked on, but it also lends the argument a tone a reasonableness—that is, he acknowledges that video games may be a contributing factor and that the industry should do more to evaluate this possibility.

VOCABULARY PROJECTS (p. 590)

2. Students should note that these descriptions are not Bauman's. He quotes these to support his idea that media commentators used loaded language to describe the games in order to paint them as *nefarious*.
3. Students should see that Bauman begins almost every paragraph with a clear transition that points to a shift in subject, time, or intent.

COMBINING THE PATTERNS p. (591)

Bauman doesn't try to establish a strict causal link here. Rather, he suggests that Carneal's dexterity with a gun, assuming the claim that he had not used firearms before is true, could have been the result of playing games like *House of the Dead*.

THEMATIC CONNECTIONS

Thirty-Eight Who Saw Murder Didn't Call the Police (p. 99): Students may use this essay as a way of considering the extent to which the nature of violence and our attitudes toward it have changed in our society since the early 1960s. It is also an interesting way to compare media coverage of violent crime then and now. How does Martin Gansberg's style compare with the style reflected in the sound-bites Bauman quotes?

Television: The Plug-In Drug (p. 283): This essay provides another interesting basis of comparison over time. Updating an essay written some twenty-five years ago about the effects of television on children, Marie Winn doesn't focus on issues of violence at all. Her concerns pertain almost exclusively to the way television stifles children's imaginations and substitutes for close family relationships. Younger students might consider how different programming aimed at children today is from that described by Winn, while older students may reflect on changes in television programming over the course of their lives. What further effects have be wrought by video games?

A Peaceful Woman Explains Why She Carries a Gun (p. 298): Linda Hasselstrom paints a rather unsettling picture of brutish male behavior in the various examples she describes of being threatened by men who were strangers to her. It is well established that violent games such as *DOOM* appeal primarily to young males in our culture. Why are males so much more likely to be attracted to violence and to threaten or use violence to get their way? Is this primarily innate? Or does it have some connection with the images of men participating in violence that permeate our media?

The End of Serendipity (p. 604): Ted Gup offers a very different picture of young male computer users when he describes his sons doing research using a CD-ROM encyclopedia or reading an online newspaper. How might boys' attention be diverted from video games to more productive pursuits on their computers?

DEBATE CASEBOOK: Is the Internet Good for Society?

This final debate casebook presents five essays offering differing views of the Internet. The focus is on two basic issues: (1) Will the Internet have the effect of bringing people together in an equalizing way, or will it bring about greater isolation and inequality?; (2) Will this "information superhighway" provide us with better tools for learning and understanding, or will it serve to keep us too narrowly focused and only superficially informed? (The content of each essay is summarized in the text's introduction to the casebook.)

You might want to begin discussion by surveying your students' use of and attitudes toward the Internet. What percentage of the class logs onto the Internet on a regular basis? (You could break this down more specifically: daily, several times a week, once a week? Number of hours spent weekly on-line?) What do users most commonly do online? Exchange e-mail? Participate in chat rooms or discussion groups? Play games? Visit Web sites on topics of personal interest? Conduct research for school projects or on matters of practical concern? Read online magazines and other news sources? Create Web pages of their own? What else? Students who are regular users may surprise you with the breadth of their awareness of what the Internet has to offer.

Those students who are not regular users might be asked to explain why they are not. Is their lack of use primarily a matter of access, or is it more a matter of lack of interest? Are there students in your class who are simply intimidated by the complexity of the technology? Do any feel that there is little on the Internet that is pertinent to their lives?

Then, you might ask students to consider the various controversies involving the Internet. There are many others besides the ones we focus on in this casebook. Some of the most contentious are those involving minors, such as access to pornography and, through chat rooms, to strangers who may be masquerading their true identity. Moreover, the Internet provides a widespread forum for hate-mongering and for the dissemination of all sorts of potentially dangerous information, such as instructions for making bombs. People in many quarters worry about the "Big Brother" aspects of the Internet and the extent to which so much previously confidential information can be accessed by anyone who knows how to do so. In addition, each new study showing an increased use of the Internet raises alarm in some circles regarding how spending lots of time online serves to limit true human interaction.

Finally, introduce the controversies that the class will focus on in the debate casebook and link them to the previous discussion about you own students' access to the Internet, about the amount of time they spend on the Internet, and about the kinds of research they do on the Internet.

Philip Elmer-DeWitt, *Bards of the Internet*

COMPREHENSION (p. 596)

1. Unlike the telephone, the Internet has led to more and more people communicating in writing.
2. Most writing on the Internet is done quickly and is closer in style to speech than to writing for books or journals.
3. This renaissance in writing has been produced because the Internet makes it easy to be "published."
4. "Good writing on the Internet tends to be clear, vigorous, witty and above all brief," formatting is important, and Internet writers often use specialized acronyms and symbols. Elmer-DeWitt goes on to say that polished prose copied onto the Internet often seems "long-winded and phony."
5. This technology allows virtually anyone to air his or her views within a broad public forum, and it "has also thrown together classes of people who hadn't had much direct contact before."

PURPOSE AND AUDIENCE (p. 597)

1. He seems to assume his readers have some familiarity with the Internet. For example, he doesn't define many terms that unfamiliar readers wouldn't know.
2. His tone suggests that he sees his readers as neutral to friendly about the benefits of the Internet. He doesn't seem especially argumentative.
3. He states his thesis at the end of paragraph 2 and reiterates it in his next to last sentence. These are both places where readers expect to find a thesis.

STYLE AND STRUCTURE (p. 597)

1. He uses his discussion of the telephone to suggest that the increase in writing on the Internet is "startling." Students will probably find this effective, but they may come up with alternative openings.
2. He doesn't really address arguments against his position. As suggested earlier, he doesn't assume strong opposition from his readers.
3. Most of Elmer-DeWitt's evidence consists of quotations from other professional writers and editors familiar with the culture of writing online. Other pertinent evidence might have included quotations from non-professional writers who publish on the Internet; these, after all, are the true focus of his essay.
4. The argument is primarily inductive, based on gathering facts and coming to a conclusion.
5. Students will probably see that Elmer-DeWitt is exaggerating for humorous effect in his conclusion, whether they agree with him or not.

2. Such terms occur throughout, but especially in paragraph 2. Of course, these represent basic terms for most people with even a little online experience. Ask students whether definitions here would have seemed to "talk down" to them.

COMBINING THE PATTERNS (p. 598)

He uses comparison and contrast here to make the point that writing for the Internet is different from writing on paper. He is implicitly defending the legitimacy of the Internet style, even though he had suggested earlier much online writing is "awful."

THEMATIC CONNECTIONS

The Great Campus Goof-Off Machine (p. 188): College student Nate Stulman writes about other students who spend hours chatting on-line with dorm mates right down the hall. Why might chatting online be preferable to having a conversation face-to-face? Does such a habit have any downsides? Elmer-DeWitt doesn't suggest any negative consequences for the increasing obsession with communicating on-line. Should he have?

The Human Cost of an Illiterate Society (p. 203): Jonathan Kozol writes movingly about illiteracy, a problem that will only become more serious as peoples' lives increasingly move online, where the ability to read and write is fundamental. People who lack these basic skills will become doubly disenfranchised. This fact certainly calls into question some of Elmer-DeWitt's optimism about the bright future for communication afforded by the Internet. See also the *Thematic Connections* under the Henry Louis Gates essay that follows.

Never Do That to a Book (p. 345): Anne Fadiman writes here from the standpoint of a bibliophile, a lover of books, who cherishes the tactile act of reading, of marking up books with notes and underlining, of dog-earing favorite passages, and so forth. What would likely be her response to "literature online," so to speak? How does reading electronically differ from reading a physical book? More and more, written works are being published only in online formats. Is it possible that "literature online" could ever replace books altogether?

Henry Louis Gates Jr., *One Internet, Two Nations*

COMPREHENSION (p. 601)

1. Keeping slaves illiterate served to keep them from participating in the kind of communication that helped them to organize the Stono Rebellion; slave holders wanted to prevent any future rebellions. In the following century and a half, "access to literacy became for the slaves a hallmark of their humanity and an instrument of liberation, spiritual as well as physical."
2. African Americans actively fought against the segregation of public schools in an attempt to have equal access to education. Today, however, there has been very little effort on the part of middle-class African Americans to gain access the "new tools of literacy" provided by the Internet.

3. Gates suggests that African Americans are not attracted to the Internet because much of the content found there is of relatively little interest to them; parents seem less interested in providing their families with computers because of "the lack of minority-oriented educational software." Gates says that "providing more sites that appeal to black audiences" is only part of the solution, though. Black communities themselves must establish after-school programs to redress the digital divide, particularly among poor children.
4. She means that black communities must take responsibility for the stifling effects poverty has on the education of young blacks.
5. They will be further isolated from the opportunities of mainstream society.

PURPOSE AND AUDIENCE (p. 601)

1. Gates initially states his thesis in paragraph 4 reiterates it in paragraph 7, and in his conclusion. He waits to make his initial statement of his thesis in order to set up the contrast with how highly valued access to literacy has historically been for African Americans. Students may think his thesis might have more clearly indicated his thoughts on how profoundly negative the effects of suffering "cybersegregation" on African Americans.
2. Interestingly, Gates's primary audience seems to be African-American readers in the middle to upper classes. He uses *we*, for example, to refer specifically to African Americans, and paragraph 14 is a call to action for the black community. He probably wants to reach white readers as well, though; if they recognize the problem, then they may be more likely to create more appealing content and to help provide the "corporate and foundational support" required for the kinds of programs Gates advocates.
3. The tone is reasonable, tinged with a sort of sadness over the state of affairs.
4. His purpose was to highlight what he sees as a major problem and to gain support for remedies to that problem.

STYLE AND STRUCTURE (p. 602)

1. His reference to "talking drums" at the opening and closing serves two purposes. First, he neatly provides a sense of closure by returning in his conclusion to an image mentioned in his introduction. Second, the talking drums are a symbol both of black empowerment and, in his conclusion, of the new information technologies that he feels blacks must gain access to.
2. His specific arguments are that middle-class and poorer African Americans are falling far behind in computer literacy and in cyber-literacy and that, if this problem isn't addressed, they will suffer social and economic consequences in the future. He offers two solutions: more electronic content to attract African-American users and programs within the black community to foster access to the electronic community. Students may think he could have done more to elaborate on these potential solutions.
3. He uses the government study "Falling Through the Net" to support his assertion that Blacks—and Hispanics—"are slower to embrace the Internet and the personal computer than whites." He later uses the example of the recording industry as evidence that content makes a differences in attracting a black audience. He also refers to "the examples of black achievement in structured classes" to support his point that community based educational programs can be effective. Interestingly, he offers no real evidence that lack of access to

the electronic community will have dire effects, assuming that the point is obvious. Do students agree?

4. The shortness of the paragraph serves to make this central point especially emphatic.

5. In fact, Gates doesn't deal with any opposing arguments, seemingly assuming that there are no reasonable ones. (He doesn't even blame content providers for not catering more to African Americans, using the chicken and egg analogy.) Can students come up with any opposing arguments?

6. He is, of course, referring to his belief that African Americans must themselves see to it that their community is not left out out of the digital revolution; they will have no one else to blame if much of it ultimately is. The sentence serves as stirring wake-up call.

VOCABULARY PROJECTS (p. 636)

2. *Cybersegregation* seems an apt neologism in this context, technically accurate and suitably sober. A phrase such as "segregation from the electronic community" is a bit unwieldy.

COMBINING THE PATTERNS (p. 603)

As mentioned earlier, the narrative opening sets up the contrast between the value placed on literacy by African Americans throughout history and many current African Americans' lack of concern about computer literacy and cyber-literacy. It also suggests the connection between literacy and liberation. Gates wants to convince his readers that the new literacy is just as important as the old.

THEMATIC CONNECTIONS

The Human Cost of an Illiterate Society (p. 203): Encouraging computer literacy may seem almost a luxury in a society where so many people are functionally illiterate as readers and writers. Obviously, those who have only rudimentary reading and writing skills are shut off from cyberspace, but they are also shut off from a good deal more. Gates offers a proposal to increase computer literacy among African Americans. What proposals would students suggest to increase print literacy skills within our society as a whole? In terms of allocating resources, should one kind of literacy have priority over the other?

The "Black Table" Is Still There (p. 294): Lawrence Otis Graham's essay focuses on self-segregation, the tendency of those in integrated settings to "stick with their own kind." To what extent can this kind of self-segregation be related to Gates's point about cybersegregation? Other than online content, why might blacks and Hispanics choose not to participate in cyberspace? (An interesting point to consider in this regard is the facelessness of cyberspace. In online communications, race is never an issue unless it is revealed. Is there somehow an implicit assumption on the part of many users that all those anonymous screen names represent white users?)

Does America Still Exist? (p. 482): In this essay, Richard Rodriguez explores issues of maintaining cultural distinctiveness and assimilating into the mainstream. How is cultural distinctiveness asserted in cyberspace? For example, Gates suggests that African Americans find little content on the Internet relevant to their culture. What kinds of sites might enterprising people create to attract hits from more African Americans? How might current electronic service providers and businesses attract more black customers? Students might also conduct some research online to see what they can discover about culture-specific sites on the Internet.

Ted Gup, *The End of Serendipity*

COMPREHENSION (p. 607)

1. Gup refers to computers, the Internet, and the World Wide Web as a "grand experiment" that is "redefining literacy and reshaping the architecture of how [we] learn." The problem with this experiment, in Gup's view, is that these technologies allow users to narrow the field of information they seek and "weed out that which we deem extraneous."
2. Gup sees moral consequences in the fact that, when we can so tailor the information that reaches us, we are likely to ignore the serious social, political, and environmental problems the world faces. The already marginalized— "the homeless, the weak, the disenfranchised"—will become even more irrelevant to our lives.
3. A mouse allows a computer user to access only what he or she clicks on. It is a padlock in the sense that it give people the ability to shut out what they don't want to see or read about.
4. See question 2.
5. The names suggest connotations of mystery and excitement, but to Gup, "what they deliver is ever more predictable."

PURPOSE AND AUDIENCE (p. 607)

1. To answer this question, students will first need to define *serendipity* ("the faculty or phenomenon of finding valuable or agreeable things not sought for"). Gup sees our ever-increasing ability to narrow the search for information as an "end" to our ability to discover the answers "to questions that have not yet occurred to us." In this sense, the title sums up his thesis.
2. He states his thesis in paragraph 3. He leads up to it with his comparison of traditional encyclopedias and CD-ROM encyclopedias because this comparison summarizes his point.
3. Student opinion will vary. Gup clearly could have been more objective in his treatment of the value of more precise Web searches.

STYLE AND STRUCTURE (p. 608)

1. It would certainly have bolstered his argument if Gup had included testimony from computer experts who agree that, despite their obvious value, something is lost in terms of discovery as Web searches become narrower and more precise.
2. The argument is essentially deductive, starting with the premise that because there are many "virtues of accidental discovery," research should be conducted in such a way that it encourages at least some randomness.

3. Gup's point in bringing up Bill Gates is to introduce the figure of Leonardo Da Vinci, the consummate dabbler in many fields of inquiry. He fears that the humanistic tradition Leonardo represents is in peril because of the mindset at companies like Microsoft. The paragraph is really an aside, but we don't find that it limits the essay's effectiveness.
4. Students may feel that Gup could have expanded his discussion of the positive results produced by random discoveries, perhaps by offering more concrete examples. In terms of his discussion of the poor, he might have given more examples to support the idea that "they are being pushed right off the page."
5. It's possible to read paragraphs 8 and 9 as overstatement. Student opinion is likely to vary as to whether such overstatement diminishes Gup's argument.
6. Essentially, Gup's entire essay is a refutation of the argument that "[i]n a world of information overload, [the] ability to filter what reaches [is] an unqualified good" (4). Again, students may feel that Gup could have argued more directly for the benefits of serendipity in research.

VOCABULARY PROJECTS (p. 608)

2. He compares the information superhighway to physical superhighways and makes the point that efficiency in information gathering, like efficiency in travel, comes at a price: we miss all the "scenery," and using the Web can take on "the drudgery of yet another commute." Student opinion will vary as to the effectiveness of the analogy.

COMBINING THE PATTERNS (p. 609)

The comparison is between traditional encyclopedias and those on CD-ROM. For Gup, the differences between the two epitomize what is lost when we are able to narrowly define the information we wish to retrieve. The comparison offers a clearcut example of his thesis.

THEMATIC CONNECTIONS

Finishing School (p. 88): Maya Angelou's essay suggests that the elite classes have a long history of ignoring the disenfranchised, of pursuing "parochial self-interests," of being "self-absorbed" at the expense of those less fortunate. How might this pattern of self-interestedness be connected to Gup's argument? That is, are Gup's worries based simply on facts of human nature that have little to do with the Internet? Or could the Internet, in fact, reinforce such tendencies?

Reading the River (p. 138): As a riverboat pilot, Mark Twain learned to read the Mississippi River as an expert, seeing it only in terms of what was expedient, what he needed to know in order to navigate its hazards. Lost, he writes, was any ability to appreciate its beauty and poetry. Indeed, this was for him an "end of serendipity." In what sense does mastery of any subject limit one's ability to make unexpected discoveries?

The Victorian Internet (p. 351): Like Gup, Tom Standage questions some common assumptions about the Internet. Focusing on claims made for the telegraph a century and a half ago—that by enhancing people's ability to communicate across great distances, the telegraph would "eliminate misunderstanding between nations and usher in a new era of world peace"—Standage finds a parallel with claims currently being made for the Internet. Just as the telegraph failed as a panacea, so, says Standage, will the Internet.

David Rothenberg, *How the Web Destroys the Quality of Students' Research Papers*

COMPREHENSION (p. 648)

1. It is easy to spot such a paper because the bibliography doesn't cite any books, only articles and Web addresses; much of the material is out of date; impressive graphics are included that often have little relevance to the subject of the paper; and it contains unattributed quotations and detailed references to material readily available on the Web, such as government documents and corporate propaganda.
2. Search engines are like slot machines, according to Rothenberg, because what they turn up is so random. Student researchers, faced with thousands of hits, are unlikely to be able to retrieve useful information easily, so research takes on a "hunt-and-peck" quality.
3. Such word processing features have lulled students into thinking that the machine can do all their work for them.
4. Colleges and college libraries, by diverting resources from books to computer technology, have created the perception that access to the Internet is more important than books.
5. Rothenberg thinks instructors need to do more to teach their students how to read critically, "to work through arguments, to synthesize disparate sources to come up with original thought."

PURPOSE AND AUDIENCE (p. 613)

1. Rothenberg's thesis is implied in the answer to his questions at the end of paragraph 2. Students may feel he could have stated his thesis more explicitly by combining the ideas in the first and last sentences of the paragraph..
2. One clue is that the essay was originally published in the *Chronicle of Higher Education*. Also, Rothenberg's confession and advice in the final two paragraphs seem clearly directed at other instructors.
3. The tone seems one of serious concern, but Rothenberg is hopeful as well.
4. His purpose seems to be to alert other instructors to the kind of poor research he describes and to suggest remedies.

STYLE AND STRUCTURE (p. 613)

1. Rothenberg's opening offers the specific example of his students to provide a springboard for his discussion of the kind of research they are doing. This is an effective way to get his readers' interest—particularly if they too are teachers.
2. He argues that the process of Internet research can be as exciting as actually finding useful information; that search engines don't help sort information; that much of what one finds on the Internet is superficial and outdated; that papers consisting of such research are more a "random montage" than a true

argument; that colleges have contributed to the problem by emphasizing computer research; and, finally, that students need to be taught to think more critically and to recognize the value of books. These points seem convincing.

3. Student opinion will vary as to whether Rothenberg provides adequate support. He might have interviewed other instructors to see whether they also find Internet research a problem, or he could have included some of his students' opinions.

4. He deals with objections only briefly in paragraph 6. Students may feel he should have more directly refuted the argument that, when conducted thoughtfully, Internet research can be as rigorous as library research.

5. He takes much of the blame himself for not doing more to teach his students to research more critically and to trust their own ideas. Ask your students whether they think this extra effort would make a difference.

VOCABULARY PROJECTS (p. 613)

2. The use of contractions throughout lends the essay a less formal, more conversational tone, which seems suitable given its relatively personal nature.

COMBINING THE PATTERNS (p. 614)

See question 1 under Style and Structure.

THEMATIC CONNECTIONS

The Great Campus Goof-Off Machine (p. 188): College student Nate Stulman argues that on-campus computers serve primarily to distract students from their studies. He also points out the superficiality of much online research.

Television: The Plug-In Drug (p. 283): Like Rothenberg, Marie Winn questions the value of technology as an educational tool. Students might consider the extent to which young people's television watching habits have contributed to the popularity of using the Internet for research instead of books.

College Pressures (p. 390): Students might consider this essay and Rothenberg's in terms of whether college students' heavy workloads make the efficiency of Internet searching and downloading necessary. Researching in books and periodicals is far more time-consuming, so is it inevitable that students will rely on the Internet? How might Rothenberg respond?

Nicholas Negroponte, *An Age of Optimism*

COMPREHENSION (p. 318)

1. Negroponte mentions the following drawbacks: abuse of intellectual property, invasion of privacy, and other instances of online fraud. Most important, though, are "the loss of jobs to wholly automated systems" and the disenfranchisement of those who are not "digital."

2. The "seamless digital workplace" provides greater efficiency and easily connects business around the world.

3. They are decentralizing, globalizing, harmonizing, and empowering.
4. He means that because people, especially younger people, are no longer limited by geography in terms of those they may communicate with, they "are emerging from the digital landscape free of many of the old prejudices."
5. The digital world, according to Negroponte, is empowering because it provides access to information, mobility, and "the ability to effect change." The possibilities, he feels, are literally endless. You might ask students why his optimism is so vested in the young.

PURPOSE AND AUDIENCE (p. 618)

1. Negroponte states his thesis in paragraph 3. Students may feel that his strategy is misleading because he starts as though he is going to focus on the "dark side" of the digital world.
2. He doesn't seem to assume that his readers necessarily share his optimism although he doesn't seem to assume that they don't, either. In paragraphs 2–5 he concedes, for skeptical readers, some of the drawbacks of the digital world. In his conclusion, he seems to imply that this is the future whether you believe him or not.
3. Students will likely find the tone optimistic.

STYLE AND STRUCTURE (p. 618)

1. He apparently does so to clarify that his essential optimism is tempered by an awareness of reality so that critics have no reason to fault him for over-optimism.
2. He doesn't so much refute arguments against his thesis; rather, he responds to critics by admitting some of the drawbacks of the digital world and conceding that problems like pollution and disease won't necessarily be solved because of it. He might well have refuted critics of some of his larger claims—for example, that the digital world can lead to global harmony.
3. In this case, Negroponte's status as an expert perhaps requires that he do more to provide factual support. He's writing as a cheerleader here, making broad claims based on little evidence other than his own convictions. Students may note that it's rather difficult to provide factual support for the argument that the digital world can lead to global harmony.
4. The argument is primarily inductive. He surveys what is happening now to make postulations about the future. The only disadvantage is that predictions such as his must necessarily rest on assumptions not all readers might share.
5. The parallel computer architectures developed by Thinking Machines Corporation were made obsolete when new programs allowed personal computers to do the same thing. This new development served as a agent of decentralization, allowing linkage of computers around the globe.

VOCABULARY PROJECTS (p. 618)

2. "Global information resource" might be rewritten as "a resource for information available to anyone in the world." Students will probably feel that such jargon is appropriate in the context of the essay.

COMBINING THE PATTERNS (p. 619)

The examples effectively suggest some of the short-term negative consequences of a digital world. Students might consider some of the more long-term consequences Negroponte could have addressed.

THEMATIC CONNECTIONS

The Peter Principle (p. 181): How might the Peter Principle be applied to the digital revolution? Do greater decentralization and more flexible hierarchies mean that the Peter Principle will become less operable? Or, will it result in a different level of online incompetence?

The Human Cost of an Illiterate Society (p. 203): As the *Thematic Connections* with other readings in this casebook have suggested, Jonathan Kozol's essay brings to light a whole class of people who stand to benefit very little, if at all, from the digital revolution. In fact, it could be argued that those who lack reading and writing skills will be permanently disenfranchised in a digital world. Where do they fit into Negroponte's optimistic scheme? Henry Louis Gates's "One Internet, Two Nations" offers a similar cautionary note in terms of minorities.

The Victorian Internet (p. 351): Negroponte is quoted in Tom Standage's essay as one of those Internet experts whose optimism Standage questions. Standage's point is that similar utopian claims were made for the telegraph a century and a half ago and for any number of new technologies since then. Standage argues that we should be skeptical of the kind of grand claims Negroponte makes in this essay.

13: COMBINING THE PATTERNS

In this section are two essays—one student, one professional—that we have annotated to indicate each writer's use of multiple patterns, along with two further unannotated professional essays. You may not wish to wait until you have completed the chapter on argumentation to discuss these essays. In fact, a good time to have students look at the two annotated essays might be prior to Chapter 8 or Chapter 9. At that point it can be useful for students to recognize that although their papers may be structured primarily as cause-and-effect or comparison-and-contrast essays, for example, they may well include passages of narration, description, exemplification, and process.

Another approach would be to look at the student essay in conjunction with Chapter 4. Michael Huu Truong's "The Park" is primarily a narrative essay, and you might use it early in the course to point out the interplay in most writing of the various patterns to be practiced in subsequent chapters. Then, in conjunction with Chapter 11, you could repeat this point by having students look at Lars Eighner's "On Dumpster Diving"—an essay of definition that, like many extended definitions, uses virtually every technique in the writer's repertoire of development strategies. Similarly, Alice Walker's "In Search of Our Mothers' Gardens" could be read in conjunction with the other cause-and-effect essays in the text, and Jonathan Swift's "A Modest Proposal" could be read as a special form of argumentation. Alternatively, you might introduce these two essays independently at the end of the course, as examples of the complex purposes to which writing can be put.

Lars Eighner, *On Dumpster Diving*

Students are bound to find much to fascinate, appall, and stimulate discussion in Eighner's guide to living on the street out of garbage cans and Dumpsters. Writing with rueful good humor, an eye for telling detail, and an engagingly personal style, Eighner does more to suggest the day-to-day reality of homelessness than would any number of documentaries or clinical studies.

He begins with his situation and his terminology, which lead him to his thesis. Then he looks at the theory, technique, and dangers (mainly dysentery) of scavenging through garbage for food. (If your campus is a residential one, students might be especially interested in Eighner's description of why college students are among his best sources.) Then he turns to the "predictable series of stages a person goes through in learning to scavenge" (31). He next considers the collection of objects and why he hates people who scrounge for cans to turn in for cash. He explains why he has reservations about going through individual garbage cans, which leads him to think about the personal lives of those whose garbage he sifts through. He also explains the animal dangers—vermin, cats, fire ants—as well as why it is best to lower oneself into a Dumpster. He concludes by noting the two "rather deep lessons" (63) he has learned from scavenging.

It will probably be easy to get students talking about Eighner and his essay, but as part of your discussion, be sure to have students think about his intended purpose and audience. Does he really expect readers to follow his directions and advice? Or does he want to affect his audience in a different way?

COMPREHENSION (p. 645)

1. *Dumpster diving* might be defined as "a systematic method of scouring refuse containers for items useful for living on little or no money."
2. Fruits and vegetables may be discarded for minor imperfections; pizzas may end up in a pizzeria's Dumpster because they were ordered as a prank or incorrectly made: college students often throw away food when they are going on a break ("through carelessness, ignorance, or wastefulness" [22]).
3. He avoids "game, poultry, pork, and egg-based foods" (28) and "home leftovers" (29), as well as anything that looks or smells obviously bad.
4. Obvious drawbacks include the threat of dysentery, dealing with the fire ants, and the lack of medical care and storage space. Implied drawbacks include the nastiness of rooting through garbage and the hunger that could result from several days without a successful "dive."
5. The stages of learning to scavenge are (a) scavenging at first with a sense of disgust and loathing; (b) realizing that a lot of good, usable stuff is discarded and therefore taking pleasure in scavenging; (c) becoming obsessed with scavenging to the point of trying to acquire everything one finds.
6. He also scavenges for collectible items (pocket calculators and the like), personal needs (like warm bedding), and essential drugs (like antibiotics) because he has no access to health care.
7. Can scroungers, who are usually addicts and winos, "tend to tear up the Dumpsters, mixing the contents and littering the area" (44), and Eighner is contemptuous of them because they pass up many useful items.
8. He has learned "to take what you can use and let the rest go by" (63) and that material being is transient: "mental things are longer lived than other material things" (64).

PURPOSE AND AUDIENCE (p. 645)

1. He apparently also wants to encourage some compassion in his audience for those like himself, living on the fringe. And in his final paragraphs, he suggests an even larger purpose—to let his audience see that material things are transient.
2. Students may respond in a variety of ways to the essay—feeling everything from real sympathy to outright contempt. Try to get them to explore the reasons for their different responses.
3. There may be many reasons to explain why Eighner does not provide background information about himself. For one thing, not doing so makes him essentially anonymous—like the homeless people readers actually encounter on the streets. Also, the facts of his earlier life may not be particularly interesting—or flattering. Many students, however, are likely to think he could have explained in more detail why he ended up as he did.
4. His purpose in including such detail is probably twofold: he wants to provide an in-depth view of a subject most readers know nothing about, and he wants to suggest that homelessness is fraught with peril and difficulty.
5. His telling about the stages of scavenging is a way of helping readers imagine themselves in his place (everyone can imagine being "filled with disgust and self-loathing" [32]), and his scruples about going through individual cans is something readers can share. In addition, when he describes the process of going through a Dumpster, he does so in a way that puts his readers directly on the scene.
6. The last line is calculated to suggest that even in his distressed state he has reached a level of inner understanding through Dumpster diving that makes him better off than the "rat-race millions" (67).

STYLE AND STRUCTURE (p. 646)

1. He describes the source of the term *Dumpster* and offers alternatives to the phrase *Dumpster diving*. This opening definition seems appropriate to establish the subject and Eighner's tone of clarity and preciseness.
2. The one-sentence paragraphs are 2, 7, 41, and the final paragraph. The first and last are for dramatic effect; the middle two each introduce a new section of discussion and might be combined with the following paragraph.
3. The present tense adds a greater sense of immediacy than the past tense would allow.
4. Other paragraphs of lists include 14–16, 24–25, 28, 38, 40, 53, and 55. As mentioned earlier, Eighner's goal seems to be to establish a very precise, even fastidious, tone; the careful listing helps accomplish this goal.

VOCABULARY PROJECTS (p. 646)

2. *Scrounging* seems less purposeful than *scavenging* (hence, his use of the term when he's trying "to be obscure"), and *foraging,* as he suggests, has come to be associated with finding food in the wilderness. *Diving,* he says, is too cute and not quite accurate in his case. So he prefers *scavenging.*

COMBINING THE PATTERNS (p. 647)

Students will have different responses here, but certainly the passages of exemplification, cause and effect, and process are particularly instructive.

THEMATIC CONNECTIONS

The Human Cost of an Illiterate Society (p. 203): As Jonathan Kozol's essay suggests, illiteracy and poverty often go hand in hand. Eighner, however, is clearly highly literate. What do students make of this seeming contradiction in his life? Is it easier to sympathize with those in our society who can't read and write than with someone in Eighner's situation who has obviously mastered these skills? (Kozol, by the way, has also written extensively about homelessness. Students interested in this subject might look at some of the other books mentioned in the headnote to his essay.)

Burdens (p. 466): John Kenneth Galbraith writes about how governmental aid to the poor in the United States has come to be regarded as a "burden," while government spending that aids the middle-class and the wealthy is not seen in this way. Eighner's description of his down-and-out existence suggests how little aid is actually available to the poor. Should welfare be available to people like Eighner? Students might research current policies concerning welfare recipients in their community, particularly "welfare-to-work" programs.

The Untouchable (p. 461): In this essay student Ajoy Mahtab defines the lowest level of the Indian caste system, "human beings treated worse than dogs and shunned far more than lepers." To what extent are the homeless in the United States the "untouchables" of our society? Based on Eighner's essay, how fair do students find the attitudes toward the homeless?

The Declaration of Independence (p. 516): The United States is founded on the notion that "all men are created equal, that they are endowed by their Creator with certain unalienable rights, that among these are life, liberty and the pursuit of happiness." What does *equality* mean in this context? Using "On Dumpster Diving" and "Burdens" as a starting point, students might consider issues of class, privilege, and power in the United States in terms of the ideals on which the country is based.

Jonathan Swift, *A Modest Proposal*

Swift's brilliant, scathingly ironic attack on the devastating policies of the British ruling class toward an impoverished Irish peasantry is one of the classics of English prose. It will also be a challenging essay for most first-year students. Not only is the complex eighteenth-century rhetoric unfamiliar, but the essay also includes many historical references that will be difficult for students, even with footnotes. In addition, students often have trouble recognizing that Swift is adopting a persona and some may take his horrifying proposal at face value. Unless you already know the essay well and have an affinity for explaining its complexities in terms of both language and tone, you probably should reserve this essay for a course for advanced students. Even then, you should provide some historical background and make students aware that they don't need to understand every reference in order to appreciate Swift's irony and ultimate compassion. You might also point out that the main thrust of Swift's argument comes in paragraphs 3–16 and 20–30; the long digression in paragraphs 17–19 often bogs students down.

COMPREHENSION (p. 655)

1. Swift notes the problem of poverty in Ireland and satirically proposes that such poverty could be eliminated if the children of the poor were sold to be butchered and eaten.

2. The advantages of the plan are that it would lessen the number of Catholics, that poor tenants would have an income with which to pay the landlord, that poor parents wouldn't have to maintain their children after two years of age, that taverns would benefit by increased business, and that it would encourage marriage.
3. Paragraph 29 enumerates the "alternatives," which involve the wealthy giving up a squanderous lifestyle, the uniting of the Irish people, and an increased compassion for the poor. These are what Swift is actually proposing.
4. The very outrageousness of the proposal suggests that Swift is not serious. Other clues include the over-attention to detail and, of course, the seriousness of his true proposals outlined in paragraphs 29–33.
5. See question 3 above. He rejects them to suggest the callousness with which his audience has treated the poor.

PURPOSE AND AUDIENCE (p. 655)

1. Many British readers would likely dismiss the proposal as the rantings of a madman. Irish readers, however—at least those who realized the harm British control was doing to the country of Ireland—would understand Swift's point.
2. Swift seems to have wanted to inspire change; only by shocking the sensibilities of his audience so thoroughly could he make readers stop and consider real solutions.
3. Such computations establish the "proposer" as a meticulous, even finicky, man.
4. Only those who took the proposal seriously—or who disagreed with Swift's politics—would likely be offended.
5. He expected his conclusion to be viewed as comically ironic.

STYLE AND STRUCTURE (p. 655)

1. The term suggests livestock; Swift's proposer is dehumanizing poor women as Swift would suggest the ruling classes have already done.
2. Paragraph 8 is a transition. Paragraph 20 is another brief transitional paragraph. Paragraphs 12 and 30 are brief for emphasis.
3. The "objections" in paragraph 29 aren't really refuted because they represent Swift's real proposals. In paragraph 30 he simply writes that there is little hope they will be put into practice.
4. Other examples include *food* (9), *excellent nutritive meat* (14), and *yearling child* (27). Again, these words dehumanize the peasantry.
5. He refers to "a very worthy person" in paragraph 17 and to "some persons of a desponding spirit" in paragraph 19. Such references lend an air of authenticity to the proposal by suggesting the proposer has conducted research.
6. Swift's essay is sharply ironic, and he is ridiculing the callousness of the ruling classes toward the peasant by wittily attacking their attitude.
7. By enumerating each advantage he adds a level of formality to the proposal.
8. The parenthetical asides—generally amplifications or qualifications—serve to suggest a tone of fastidious regard for exactitude.
9. He has been digressing from the subject of slaughtering infants for meat—to take up the subject of substituting adolescents for deer as the prey in hunting!

2. Swift's proposal is hardly a modest one, and the use of the word *humbly* is a common rhetorical device even today. ("I humbly propose" often introduces a major proposal.)

COMBINING THE PATTERNS (p. 657)

The patterns Swift uses are description (1), cause and effect (2–3), process (4), cause and effect (5), exemplification (6–7), description (9), process (10), description (11–12), cause and effect (13), description (14–16), comparison (17), exemplification (18), description (19), cause and effect (21–28), and argumentation (29–33).

THEMATIC CONNECTIONS

The Embalming of Mr. Jones (p. 248): Jessica Mitford uses irony in a more straightforward way to describe the fairly horrifying process of embalming.

The Irish Famine, 1845–1849 (p. 274): Student Evelyn Pellicane's essay-exam response, though focusing on a period more than a hundred years after Swift wrote, provides useful historical detail for understanding conditions of Irish life and the relationship between Ireland and Britain.

I Want a Wife (p. 474): Judy Brady's ironic look at gender expectations has a goal similar to "A Modest Proposal": to present an exaggerated, even outrageous, view of the status quo in order to get readers to see the situation in a new light.

The Declaration of Independence (p. 516): This important document, written only fifty years after "A Modest Proposal," employs many rhetorical strategies common to eighteenth-century composition—although in a completely straightforward way. Reading the Declaration might help students recognize some of the conventions Swift was playing with.

Alice Walker, In Search of Our Mothers' Gardens

Walker writes of the way the creative voices of African-American women have been stifled over the centuries—as a result of slavery, the denial of access to education, other forms of discrimination, grim economic realities, and their subjugation to the needs of menfolk and families. Yet, she writes, their creative spirit blossomed nonetheless: in the singing of spirituals, in the making of quilts, in the cultivation of spectacular flower gardens, and in the passing down of oral stories. As an artist, Walker has come to see herself (and other black women artists) as part of this tradition of untutored artistic expression—extending from mother to grandmother and back to female forebears in Africa painting "vivid and daring decorations," singing sweetly, weaving "the most stunning mats," telling "the most ingenious stories," perhaps even creating poetry (49).

COMPREHENSION (p. 666)

1. Because they had no outlet for their intense spirituality, their deep wells of creativity, "the strain of enduring their unused and unwanted talent drove them insane" (10).

2. "Evil honey" refers to the lives of hard work that stifled their creativity. Black women have been referred to as "the mule of the world" because they occupied the lowest rung of the economic ladder, subject to the control even of black men—the metaphor implies a beast of burden.
3. This unwritten music represents the creative impulses stifled by their hard lives—"music" that would have to wait generations to emerge.
4. She sees these women as "Artists," as "Creators" forced to "throw away [their] spirituality. . .to lighten the soul to a weight their. . .abused bodies could bear" (10).
5. To "be an artist in our grandmothers' time" was to live in a kind of agony and to die "with their real gifts stifled within them" (13). Their creativity was kept alive in accepted venues, such as singing.
6. It is not the end of the story because the creativity of these thwarted souls lives on in the work of black female artists today.
7. Wheatley, a former slave, became a published poet despite the many odds against her. But her heritage made her a divided person, trying to please a white European audience that had once seen her as less than human. After she had children, the strain of not being able to find any outlet for her creativity led, according to Walker, to her early death. This woman, "who, had she been white, would have been easily considered the intellectual superior of all the women and most of the men in the society of her day" (18), was ultimately no more able to realize her true creativity than any other black woman.
8. Walker sees these mothers and grandmothers as positive examples in that they channeled their creativity in the ways that they could, but as negative examples in that they had so little freedom. The title suggests a search for these women's sources of creativity, which are the heritage of the contemporary black woman artist.
9. They have left the legacy of their own lives.

PURPOSE AND AUDIENCE (p. 666)

1. The sentiments of the essay are deeply feminist, locating a unique strain of female creativity.
2. She advises readers to tap into the roots of their mothers' and grandmothers' creativity, a creativity they may not immediately recognize. Women of other races will probably find the message relevant; men may also see roots of creativity from fathers, mothers, and other forebears.
3. Her thesis might be summed up most simply by a sentence in paragraph 46: "This ability to hold on, even in very simple ways, is work black women have done for a very long time." Walker's expectations for her audience seem fairly complex. Her tone suggests that she feels the need to convince her readers of the viability of the heritage she describes, but she also expects them to be sympathetic to her position.

STYLE AND STRUCTURE (p. 667)

1. The Toomer quotation is a way of introducing the concept of black women's deep inner spirituality being thwarted by societal and economic constraints. Students may have trouble seeing this.
2. Examples of figurative language can be found in paragraphs 5, 6, 9, 27, 44, and in the poem in paragraph 47. Students may find some of this imagery a little difficult.
3. Except for the stylistic similarities of the poem in paragraph 14 and Walker's poem, the excerpts don't have much in common. In fact, the Wheatley excerpt

in paragraph 23 is meant to contrast with the more authentic voices of the other two. The excerpt from Woolf's *A Room of One's Own* allows Walker to apply that famous essay about the difficulties facing women writers to her own complementary thoughts about black women. Each quote has an important place in the essay.

4. Walker's tone is both sorrowful, in a sense, and celebratory; she laments the stifling of black female creativity but also celebrates the fact that this creativity has been passed down.

5. Walker summarizes her mother's life to provide an example of the kinds of women she is writing about—and also to make the connection between her own artistic creativity and her mother's. Wheatley's creativity was stifled in different, more tragic ways.

6. Other questions can be found in paragraphs 11–13, 18, 21, 29, and 33. As Walker's title suggests, hers has been a search for answers to these questions.

VOCABULARY PROJECTS (p. 667)

2. Gardens are associated with images of growth, of cultivation and nurturance, of beauty and natural abundance. Gardens are also refuges, havens into which one can escape from the everyday toils of the world. In addition to art, the word *garden* in Walker's essay suggests all of these images, as well as the central idea of creative expression.

COMBINING THE PATTERNS (p. 668)

The patterns Walker uses are narration and description (1–8), cause and effect (9–10), contrast (12), exemplification (13), exemplification and cause and effect (14–25), definition and cause and effect (26), exemplification (27–28), narration (29), process (30–31), cause and effect (32–33), example and description (34–35), cause and effect (36–37), contrast and cause and effect (38), process (39–40), narration and description (41–43), cause and effect (44–45), and narration and description (46–48). She concludes with an example of cause and effect (49–50).

THEMATIC CONNECTIONS

Homeward Bound (p. 79): Like Walker, Chinese-American writer Janet Wu pays honor to a female forebear—in this case, her Chinese grandmother whom she has been able to visit only a few times in her life. While her grandmother was of the upper classes before the revolution in China, her bound feet are a symbol of the narrow range of activities she and other Chinese women were expected to pursue. "Homeward Bound," along with several other essays listed here, would be a good basis for considering the evolution of women's roles over the past century.

My Mother Never Worked (p. 94): Donna Smith-Yackel also writes to honor her hard-working mother, who—like Walker's mother—had little time for creative expression. Martha Smith exemplifies the way many women's lives have been constricted by the demands of work and family, resulting, in Virginia Woolf's phrase, in many a "lost novelist, a suppressed poet, . . . some mute and inglorious Jane Austen."

The Way to Rainy Mountain (p. 148): In this essay N. Scott Momaday honors the memory of his Kiowa grandmother. She is an artistic influence of a different kind, linking him to the traditions, legends, and religion of "the last culture to evolve in North America." Note that, interestingly, it is not to a male forebear that Momaday pays tribute. The relevance of Walker's essay to male readers might be considered here.

The Men We Carry in Our Minds **(p. 399):** Scott Russell Sanders mediates on the poor, working-class white men he grew up with, whose lives seem to have been just as stifled as those of the black women Walker writes about. For Sanders, it was women he envied because "they were the only people . . . who were interested in art or music or literature, the only ones who read books." You might ask students to consider why the working-class women Sanders remembers are so different, in this sense, from the poor black women of the same generation as described by Walker. Is race the operating factor?

Mother Tongue **(p. 405):** Amy Tan writes that her mother also provided artistic inspiration for her work. When she started writing stories, she says, she wrote artificially crafted sentences; not until she began writing with her mother in mind as her reader did she find an authentic voice using "all the Englishes" she grew up with. In her stories she wanted to capture her mother's "intent, her passion, her imagery, the rhythms of her speech and the nature of her thoughts." She argues that the artistic impulses of many Asian Americans are stifled because their language skills are wrongly seen as limited.

APPENDIX: WRITING A RESEARCH PAPER

This appendix provides an overview of the entire research process: choosing a topic, looking for sources, narrowing a topic, doing research, taking notes, avoiding plagiarism, drafting a thesis statement, making an outline, writing the paper, and documenting sources. Each section offers specific advice and includes examples from the research process of a student writer. The appendix concludes with the final draft of the student's paper, which is based on the media violence casebook in Chapter 12. (You might find this or another debate in Chapter 12 a good starting place for student research.)

For further resources on research, you might direct your students to the online English Research Room at <http://www.bedfordstmartins.com/english_research>. Here they will find interactive tutorials for conducting simple and advanced electronic searches; links to useful sites, including search engines, online writing centers, and reference works; and general advice on the research process and on evaluating and citing sources.

The appendix includes guidelines for citing sources using MLA documentation style and provides sample entries for a Works Cited page, including examples of citations for electronic sources. The sample research paper follows MLA guidelines and so has no separate cover page; if you require such a cover page, you should explain to students the format you prefer.

While you will want to use much of the material in the appendix in conjunction with a formal research paper if you have students write essays analyzing any of the readings in the book, you should probably cover the material on paraphrasing, summarizing, and using quotations early on. You might use the examples in the text and have students practice paraphrasing and summarizing in class—being careful to point out any inadvertent plagiarism.

PEER-EDITING WORKSHEETS

Following are models of peer-editing worksheets—one for each of the patterns discussed in Chapters 4 through 13 of the text. You may retype and duplicate these to distribute to students or adapt them to create versions of your own. The worksheets are also available as transparency masters. Advice about using the peer-editing worksheets appears on page 4 of the manual.

Peer-Editing Worksheet: Narration

1. What is the subject of this narrative essay?

2. What point is the writer making about the essay's subject? Is this point explicitly stated in a thesis statement? If so, where? If not, is the essay's thesis clearly implied? Would a stated thesis be more effective?

3. Does the writer include enough detail? Where could more detail be added? What kind of detail? Be specific.

4. Does the writer vary sentence structure and avoid monotonous strings of similar sentences? Should some sentences be combined? If so, which ones? Can you suggest different openings for any sentences?

5. Is the order in which events occur clear? Should any events be relocated? Should any transitions be added to clarify relationships between events?

6. Are verb tenses consistent? Identify any verb tenses that you believe are incorrect.

7. What could the writer *add* to this essay?

8. What could the writer *take out* of this essay?

9. What is the essay's greatest strength? Why?

10. What is the essay's greatest weakness? What steps should the writer take to correct this problem?

159

Peer-Editing Worksheet: Description

1. What is the essay's dominant impression or thesis?

2. What points does the writer emphasize in the introduction? Should any other points be included? If so, which ones?

3. Would you characterize the essay as primarily an objective or subjective description? What leads you to your conclusions?

4. Point out some examples of figures of speech. Could the writer use figures of speech in other places? If so, where?

5. What specific details does the writer use to help readers visualize what he or she is describing? Are there any places where the writer could use more details?

6. Are all the details necessary? Do any seem excessive or redundant? Are there enough details to support the thesis or reinforce the dominant impression?

7. How is the essay organized? Would another arrangement principle be clearer or more effective?

8. List some transitional words and phrases that the writer uses to help readers follow his or her discussion. Do any sentences need transitional words or phrases to link them to other sentences?

9. Copy down an example of a particularly clear sentence. Are any sentences wordy or choppy? If so, which ones?

10. How effective is the essay's conclusion? Does the conclusion reinforce the dominant impression?

Peer-Editing Worksheet: Exemplification

1. What strategy does the writer use in the essay's introduction? Would another strategy be more effective?

2. What is the essay's thesis? Is it specific enough? Does it prepare readers for the examples that follow?

3. What points do the body paragraphs make? Does each of these points develop one aspect of the thesis?

4. Does the writer use one example or many to illustrate his or her points? Should the writer use more examples? Fewer? Explain.

5. List the examples the writer uses. Is there a sufficient range of examples? Are the examples explained in enough depth?

6. Are the examples representative of the idea the writer is discussing?

7. How persuasive are the examples? List a few other examples that might be more persuasive.

8. What transitional words and phrases does the writer use to reinforce the connections between examples? At what other points should transitional words and phrases be used?

9. In what order are the examples presented? Would another order be more effective? Explain.

10. What strategy does the writer use in the conclusion? What other strategy could the writer use?

Peer-Editing Worksheet: Process

1. What process does this essay describe? How familiar were you with this process before you read the essay?

2. Does the writer include all the information the audience needs? Is any vital step or piece of information missing? Is any step or piece of information irrelevant? Is any necessary definition, explanation, or warning missing or incomplete?

3. Is the essay a set of instructions or a process explanation? How can you tell? Why do you think the writer chose this format rather than the alternative? Do you think this was the right choice?

4. Does the writer consistently follow the stylistic conventions for the format—instructions or process explanation—he or she has chosen? Identify any inconsistencies in mood, person, or tense.

5. Are the steps presented in clear, logical order? Are they grouped logically into paragraphs? Should any steps be combined or relocated? If so, which ones?

6. Does the writer use enough transitions to move readers through the process? Should any transitions be added? If so, where? Do the transitions clearly indicate the logical and sequential relationships between steps?

7. Is the essay interesting? What descriptive details would add interest to the essay?

8. How would you characterize the writer's opening strategy? Is it appropriate for his or her purpose and audience? What alternative strategy might be more effective?

9. How would you characterize the writer's closing strategy? Would a different conclusion be more effective? Explain.

10. Is anything unclear or confusing? What might the writer do to help you understand the process more fully?

Peer-Editing Worksheet: Cause and Effect

1. Paraphrase the essay's thesis. Is it explicitly stated? Should it be?

2. Does the essay focus on causes, effects, or both? Does the thesis statement clearly identify this focus? If not, how should the thesis statement be revised?

3. Does the writer consider *all* relevant causes and/or effects? Are any key causes or effects omitted? Are any irrelevant causes or effects included?

4. Make an informal outline of the essay in the space below.

   What determines the order in which the causes and/or effects are arranged? Is this the most effective order? If not, what revisions do you suggest?

5. What transitional words and phrases are used to indicate causal connections? List them below.

   Are any additional transitions needed? If so, where?

6. Does the writer avoid *post hoc* reasoning? Are all causal connections logical?

7. Does the writer explain each cause and/or effect clearly and convincingly? Are more examples or details needed to help readers understand causal connections? If so, where?

8. Do you agree with the writer's assessment of the cause-and-effect relationships examined in this essay? Do you agree with his or her conclusions? Why or why not?

9. Are any sentences worded in an imprecise, unclear, or awkward manner? If so, which ones?

10. Are any words used incorrectly? If so, suggest substitutes.

Peer-Editing Worksheet: Comparison and Contrast

1. Does the essay have a clearly stated thesis? What is it?

2. What two things are being compared? What basis for comparison exists between the two?

3. Does the essay treat the same or similar points for each of its two subjects? List the points discussed below.

First subject	Second subject
1.	1.
2.	2.
3.	3.
4.	4.

Are these points discussed in the same order for both subjects? Do any points need to be relocated? If so, which ones? Where should they go?

4. Does the essay use a point-by-point or subject-by-subject arrangement? Is this the best choice? Why?

5. Are transitional words and expressions used appropriately to make the points of comparison and contrast clear? List below some of the transitions that are used.

6. Are additional transitions needed? If so, where?

7. How could the introductory paragraph be improved?

8. How could the concluding paragraph be improved?

9. What could the writer add to this essay?

10. What could the writer take out of this essay?

Peer-Editing Worksheet: Classification and Division

Make an informal outline of the essay in the space below, and consult it as you answer the questions that follow.

1. What thesis does the body of the essay support? Is this thesis explicitly stated? Does it clearly indicate the purpose of the classification and division?

2. What whole is being divided into parts in this essay? Into what general categories is the whole divided?

3. Is each category clearly identified and defined? If not, what revisions can you suggest (for example, can you suggest a different title for a particular category?)

4. Are the categories arranged in a logical order, one that indicates their relationships to one another and their relative importance? If not, how might they be rearranged?

5. Do the individual items discussed in the essay seem to be classified logically in appropriate categories? Should any items be located elsewhere? Explain.

6. Does the writer treat all relevant categories and no irrelevant ones? Which categories, if any, should be added, deleted, or combined?

7. Does the writer include all necessary items, and no unnecessary ones, within each category? What additional items might be added?

8. Does the writer treat all categories similarly, discussing comparable points for each? What additional points should be discussed? Where?

9. Do topic sentences clearly signal the movement from one category to the next? Do they signal the writer's direction and emphasis? Should any topic sentences be strengthened to mark the boundaries between categories more clearly? If so, which ones?

10. Could the writer use another pattern of development to structure this essay, or is classification and division the best choice? Why?

Peer-Editing Worksheet: Definition

1. What term is the writer defining? Does the essay include a formal dictionary definition? If so, where? If not, should one be added?

2. Why is the writer defining the term? Does the essay include a thesis statement that makes this purpose clear?

3. What patterns does the writer use to develop the definition? What other patterns could be used?

4. Does the essay define the term appropriately for its audience? Does the definition help you understand the meaning of the term?

5. Does the writer use synonyms to develop the definition? If so, where? If not, where could synonyms be used to help communicate the term's meaning?

6. Does the writer use negation to develop the definition? If so, where? If not, could the writer strengthen the definition by stating what the term is not?

7. Does the writer use enumeration to develop the definition? If so, where? If not, where might the term's special characteristics be listed?

8. Does the writer use analogies to develop the definition? If so, where? Do you find these analogies helpful? What additional analogies might help readers understand the term more fully?

9. Does the writer explain the term's linguistic origin and development? If so, where? If not, do you believe this information should be added?

10. Reread the essay's introduction. If the writer uses a dictionary definition as an opening strategy, try to suggest an alternative opening.

Peer-Editing Worksheet: Argumentation

1. Does the essay take a stand? What is it? At what point does the writer state his or her thesis?

2. Does the writer consider the audience friendly, hostile, or neutral? How do you know?

3. What evidence does the writer include to support his or her position? What additional evidence could the writer supply?

4. Does the essay attempt to refute the opposition's arguments? List these arguments below.

5. How effective are the writer's refutations? What other arguments should the writer address?

6. Does the essay rely mainly on inductive or deductive reasoning, or both? Provide an example of each type of reasoning from the essay.

   Inductive reasoning:

   Deductive reasoning:

7. Does the essay contain any logical fallacies? List them below. How would you correct these fallacies?

8. How could the introduction be improved?

9. How could the conclusion be improved?

10. What would you add to make this essay more convincing?

Peer-Editing Worksheet: Combining the Patterns

1. Using the annotations for "The Park" (p. 626) or "On Dumpster Diving" (p. 632) as a guide, annotate the essay to identify the patterns of development it uses.

2. What is the essay's thesis? If it is not explicitly stated, write it in your own words. What pattern or patterns of development are suggested by the wording of the thesis statement?

3. What pattern of development determines the essay's overall structure? Could the writer use a different pattern for this purpose? Which one?

4. What patterns does the writer use to develop the body paragraphs of the essay? Explain why each pattern is used in a particular paragraph or group of paragraphs.

5. What patterns are not used? Where, if anywhere, might one of these absent patterns serve the writer's purpose?

6. Review the essay's topic sentences. Is the wording of each topic sentence consistent with the particular pattern it introduces? If not, suggest possible ways some of the topic sentences might be reworded.

BIBLIOGRAPHY

Rhetoric and Composition Theory

Bloom, Lynn Z., Donald A. Daiker, and Edward M White, *Composition in the Twenty-First Century: Crisis and Change*. Carbondale: Southern Illinois UP, 1995.

Graves, Richard, ed. *Rhetoric and Composition: A Sourcebook for Teachers and Writers*. 3rd ed. Portsmouth: Heinemann, Boynton/Cook, 1990.

Lindemann, Erika. *A Rhetoric for Writing Teachers*. 3rd ed. New York: Oxford UP, 1995.

Lindemann, Erika, and Gary Tate. *An Introduction to Composition Studies*. New York: Oxford UP, 1994.

Reynolds, Mark, ed. *Two-Year College English: Essays for a New Century*. Urbana: NCTE, 1994.

The Composing Process

Perl, Sondra, ed. *Landmark Essays on Writing Process*. Davis: Hermagoras, 1994.

Tobin, Lad, and Thomas Newkirk, eds. *Taking Stock: The Writing Process Movement in the '90s*. Portsmouth: Heinemann, Boynton/Cook, 1994.

Young, Richard and Yameng Liu, eds. *Landmark Essays on Rhetorical Invention in Writing*. Davis: Hermagoras, 1994.

Teaching Methods

Belanoff, Pat, and Marcia Dickson. *Portfolios: Process and Product*. Portsmouth: Heinemann, Boynton/Cook, 1991.

Brooke, Robert, Ruth Mirtz, and Rick Evans, *Small Groups in Writing Workshops*. Urbana: NCTE, 1994.

Handa, Carolyn. ed *Computers and Community: Teaching Composition in the Twenty-First Century*. Portsmouth: Boynton/Cook, 1990.

Harnack, Andrew, and Eugene Kleppinger. *Online! A Reference Guide to Using Internet Sources*. New York: Bedford, 2000.

Hunter, Susan, and Ray Wallace. eds. *The Place of Grammar in Writing Instruction: Past, Present, Future*. Portsmouth: Heinemann, Boynton/Cook, 1995.

Murray, Donald. *A Writer Teaches Writing*. 2nd ed. Boston Houghton, 1985.

———. *A Writer Teaches Writing*. 2nd ed. Boston: Houghton, 1985.

Tate, Gary, ed. *Teaching Composition: Twelve Biographical Essays*. Fort Worth: Texas Christian UP, 1987.

Tate, Gary, Edward P. J. Corbett, and Nancy Myers. *The Writing Teacher's Sourcebook*, 3rd ed. New York: Oxford UP, 1994.

Spear, Karen. *Sharing Writing: Peer Response Groups in English Classes*. Portsmouth: Heinemann, Boynton/Cook, 1988.

Walvoord, Barbara E. Fassler, *Helping Students Write Well: A Guide for Teachers in All Disciplines*. 2nd ed, New York: MLA, 1990.